Contract Law

Significantly streamlined and updated, the second edition of Andrews' *Contract Law* provides a clear and succinct examination of all of the topics in the contract law curriculum. Chapters direct students to the most important decisions in case law and employ a two-level structure to integrate short judicial excerpts into detailed discussion and analysis. Exploration of the law's 'loose ends' strengthens students' ability to analyse case law, and new end-of-chapter questions, which focus on both core aspects of the law and interesting legal loopholes, assist students in preparing for exams. Students are guided through chapter material by concise chapter overviews and a two-colour text design that highlights important chapter elements. Suggestions for further reading and a rich bibliography, which point readers to important pieces of contemporary literature and provide a springboard for deeper investigation of particular topics, lend further support for student learning.

Neil Andrews is a Fellow of Clare College, Cambridge. He is a highly experienced contract law teacher and scholar and has published widely.

Contract Law

NEIL ANDREWS

SECOND EDITION

CAMBRIDGE
UNIVERSITY PRESS

University Printing House, Cambridge CB2 8BS, United Kingdom

Cambridge University Press is part of the University of Cambridge.

It furthers the University's mission by disseminating knowledge in the pursuit of education, learning and research at the highest international levels of excellence.

www.cambridge.org
Information on this title: www.cambridge.org/9781107660649

© Neil Andrews 2015

First edition published 2011
Second edition published 2015
Reprinted 2016

Printed in the United Kingdom by Clays, St Ives plc

A catalogue record for this publication is available from the British Library

Library of Congress Cataloguing in Publication data
Andrews, Neil (Barrister)
Contract law / Neil Andrews. – Second edition.
    pages   cm
ISBN 978-1-107-06168-2 (hardback)
1. Contracts – Great Britain.   I. Title.
KD1554.A944   2015
346.4202'2–dc23
                                        2014042934

ISBN 978-1-107-06168-2 Hardback
ISBN 978-1-107-66064-9 Paperback

For
Liz, Samuel, Hannah and Ruby

Contents

Preface

I hope that the second edition of this book will be of use and interest to both students and lawyers in practice.

A new feature is a list of questions at the end of each chapter. These are intended to enable the reader to test whether the main points have been absorbed. The author has 'test-driven' these questions in class and found them to be useful.

At the beginning of each chapter there is an introductory summary, and at the end of each there is a list of selected reading. The opening footnotes of each chapter or topic contain copious references to further literature. At the end of the book there is a short bibliography of general works.

There are now three concluding chapters on good faith, case law technique versus codification, and soft law codes (Chapters 21, 22, and 23, respectively).

Despite the best endeavours of the legislature, the English courts, and fellow commentators, this edition is shorter by c.26,000 words than the previous edition.

The Consumer Rights Bill remained unenacted when this work went to print. The Bill's important changes are reflected in the work.

I am grateful to the following for assistance in various ways: Peter Zawada in the Squire Law Library; members of Cambridge University Press; Carsten Kern and Sophie Shaw.

But I am especially grateful for the support and distraction provided by my wife, Elizabeth Deyong, and our children (no longer minors), Samuel, Hannah, and Ruby.

Table of cases

Table of statutes

Table of statutory instruments

Introduction

Chapter contents

1

Main features of contract law

1. CHARACTERISTICS OF ENGLISH CONTRACT LAW

1.01 English contract law is organised into topics, as set out in the chapter headings of this work. These form the 'general part' of the subject.[1] The general principles and doctrinal structure of English contract law emerged during the nineteenth century, as many have noted,[2] as a result of both judicial and academic analysis. Hedley explains:[3]

> the Victorians ... were given a law of contracts, but turned it into a law of contract, with general principles applicable to all agreements. The responsibility for this development is largely that of Leake [1st edition, 1867], Pollock [1st edition, 1876] and Anson [1st edition, 1879], who each produced major textbooks expounding a law of contract and not merely collecting together rules on different types of contracts.

1.02 In modern times, Parliament[4] and judges[5] have consistently assumed the existence of a coherent body of general rules applicable to all types of contracts (in *Geys* v. *Société*

---

1 Cf Roman law, which comprises a system of particular contracts: B. Nicholas, *An Introduction to Roman Law* (Oxford, 1962), 165 ff.

2 P. S. Atiyah, *Essays on Contract* (Oxford, 1986), 16 ff: '[I]t was the nineteenth century which very largely saw the supersession of the importance of special kinds of contracts by the general principles of contract. It was, of course, an Age of Principles.' P. S. Atiyah, *The Rise and Fall of Freedom of Contract* (Oxford, 1979), 681 ff, notes the importance of the textbooks by Leake (1867), Pollock (1876) and Anson (1879), especially the last two; Atiyah's remarkable historical *magnum opus* surveys the entire intellectual and economic scene; S. Hedley, (1985) 5 OJLS 391, 402; D. Ibbetson, *A Historical Introduction to the Law of Obligations* (Oxford, 1999), chapters 5, 11, 12 and 13; M. Lobban, in W. Cornish, J. S. Anderson, R. Cocks, M. Lobban, P. Polden and K. Smith, *The Oxford History of the Laws of England*, vol. XII, *1820–1914: Private Law* (Oxford, 2010), 295 ff; A. W. B. Simpson, (1975) 91 LQR 247, at 250–7, notes especially the influence of textbook writers; W. Swain, 'The Classical Model of Contract: The Product of a Revolution in Legal Thought?' (2010) 30 LS 513; S. Waddams, *Principle and Policy in Contract Law: Competing or Complementary Concepts?* (Cambridge, 2011), chapter 1, notably at 17 ff.

3 S. Hedley, (1985) 5 OJLS 391, 402.

4 E.g., the Misrepresentation Act 1967 (9.20) applies to all contracts and to deeds; the Contracts (Rights of Third Parties) Act 1999 applies to all contracts and deeds, except five specific categories (7.23).

5 E.g., Roskill LJ's judgment in *'The Hansa Nord'* [1976] QB 44, 71, CA (general concept of 'innominate term' applicable to sale of goods transactions). But sometimes statute precludes mechanical application of general Common Law principles, e.g., *Hurst* v. *Bryk* [2002] 1 AC 185, HL: dissolution of partnership; contractual termination following acceptance of a repudiation rested on a concession; Lord Millett doubted, *ibid.* at 196–8, whether a partnership can be terminated in this way because the Partnership Act 1890 does not refer to this mode of termination; those doubts have been vindicated in *Golstein* v. *Bishop* [2014] EWCA

Générale, London Branch (2012) Lord Wilson said that all contracts are at anchor 'within the harbour which the Common Law has solidly constructed for the entire fleet of contracts').[6]

1.03 During the last twenty years, much collaborative energy has been spent identifying principles of contract acceptable to legal systems in general, whether Common Law, civilian or other. In fact, there are various 'soft law' codes (see 21.01 ff for details). None of these is binding, either in England and Wales or elsewhere. But, on many topics in this book, reference will be made to common features or differences between English law and these 'soft law' codes (for example, there are many references to UNIDROIT's *Principles of International Commercial Contracts* (2010)[7] in these pages).

1.04 The 'general part'[8] of English contract law is a combination of rules and principles. 'Rules' tend to be quite specific; 'principles' rather more general.[9] Principles (properly so-called) tend to be fundamental standards underpinning many rules. We will consider two such principles below: the principle of 'freedom of contract' (at 1.08) and 'the objective principle' (at 1.10).[10]

1.05 Rules can sometimes be subject to exceptions, and such exceptions can proliferate (for example, the cluster of exceptions to the rule in *Woodar's* case, 17.19 ff). The fact that the courts have recognised a network of exceptions often reveals that the major rule is itself unsatisfactory.

1.06 English contract law is predominantly a case law subject.[11] And so the main source of law in this field is precedent, namely decisions on points of law given by:[12] (i) the High Court

Civ 10; [2014] Ch 455 (affirming [2013] EWHC 881 (Ch); [2014] Ch 131, at [116] to [120] (Nugee QC), adopting Neuberger J in *Mullins* v. *Laughton* [2002] EWHC 2761 (Ch); [2003] Ch 250).
6   [2012] UKSC 63; [2013] 1 AC 523, at [97] (noted D. Cabrelli and R. Zahn, (2013) 76 MLR 1106–19).
7   3rd edition, 2010, text and comment, is available at: www.unidroit.org/english/principles/contracts/p rinciples2010/integralversionprinciples2010-e.pdf. M. J. Bonell has for many years been a leading force within the UNIDROIT organisation and has had a remarkable influence upon this influential work; see also M. J. Bonell, 'Do We Need a Global Commercial Code?' (2000–2003) vol. V, *Revue de droit uniforme (Uniform Law Review)* 469–81; M. J. Bonell (ed.), *The UNIDROIT Principles in Practice: Case Law and Bibliography on the UNIDROIT Principles of International Commercial Contracts* (2nd edn, New York, 2006); S. Vogenauer and J. Kleinheisterkamp (eds.), *Commentary on the UNIDROIT Principles of International Commercial Contracts* (Oxford, 2009) (antedating the third edition of the UNIDROIT principles, 2010). See also observations by M. Furmston, (2014) 31 JCL 61, 65–6.
8   On the 'general part', see S. A. Smith, 'The Limits of Contract', in J. W. Neyers, R. Bronaugh and S. G. A. Pitel (eds.), *Exploring Contract Law* (Oxford, 2009), 1–24; and, for a civilian perspective, see H. Dedek, 'Border Control: Some Comparative Remarks on the Cartography of Obligations', in J. W. Neyers, R. Bronaugh and S. G. A. Pitel (eds.), *Exploring Contract Law* (Oxford, 2009), 2 ff, especially at 36 ff.
9   For reflections on the nature of 'rules' and 'principles' in contract law, S. Waddams, *Principle and Policy in Contract Law: Competing or Complementary Concepts?* (Cambridge, 2011), 17–21.
10   For a summary of deeper values within contract law, see M. Hesselink, 'European Contract Law? A Matter of Consumer Protection, Citizenship, or Justice?', in *Liber Amicorum Guido Alpa: National Private Law Systems* (London, 2007), 500, 516–20.
11   Even in the nineteenth century casebooks had emerged, e.g., *Finch's Cases on Contract: A Selection of Cases on the English Law of Contract* (2nd edn, Cambridge, 1896) (R. T. Wright and W. W. Buckland, eds.).
12   For a convenient summary of the English precedent rules, J. Bell, in A. Burrows (ed.), *English Private Law* (3rd edn, Oxford, 2013), 1.61 to 1.100.

(sitting in London or other parts of England and Wales), (ii) the Court of Appeal (sitting in London), and (iii) the (former) House of Lords (sitting in Westminster, London), now the Supreme Court of the United Kingdom (sitting in Westminster, London). Decisions of these courts are binding sources of English law. Decisions at level (iii) are binding on all courts below; decisions at level (ii) are binding on the Court of Appeal and on all courts below; decisions at level (i) are binding on courts inferior to the High Court, and will tend to be followed by other High Court decisions, unless demonstrably erroneous in law.

Technically, decisions of the Privy Council (the Judicial Committee of the Privy Council) are not binding on the English courts, but the reality is that most of these decisions are treated as highly authoritative pronouncements of the Common Law and thus binding unless there is an unusual reason for not following the case.[13] Within contract law, the Privy Council has been highly influential, for example, decisions on formation,[14] trusts of promises,[15] third parties and exclusion clauses,[16] duress[17] and frustration.[18] It has been said that the Court of Appeal will follow Court of Appeal decisions even when there is a conflict with a Privy Council decision, unless it is a foregone conclusion that the Supreme Court of the United Kingdom would prefer the Privy Council decision and overturn the conflicting English Court of Appeal decision.[19]

There are few statutes governing the general part of contract law, although the topics of exclusion clauses and unfair terms in consumer contracts are now dominated by legislation.[20] The Law Reform (Frustrated Contracts) Act 1943; the Law Reform (Contributory Negligence) Act 1945; the Misrepresentation Act 1967; the Unfair Contract Terms Act 1977 (non-consumer contracts) (as amended by the Consumer Rights Bill, 'the Bill'); the Sale of Goods Act 1979 (as amended by the Bill); the Supply of Goods And Services Act 1982 (as amended by the Bill; the Contracts (Rights of Third Parties) Act 1999; the Bill[21] and the Consumer Contracts (Information, Cancellation and Additional Charges) Regulations (2013).[22] There is also the Limitation Act 1980. the limitation periods applicable to contractual actions are: six years for ordinary ('simple')[23]

13   Cf *Lord Strathcona Steamship Co Ltd* v. *Dominion Coal Co Ltd* [1926] AC 108; 42 TLR 86, PC, which was not followed, and indeed declared wrong, by Diplock J in *Port Line* v. *Ben Line Steamers Ltd* [1958] 2 QB 146, 165–8.
14   *Pratt Contractors Ltd* v. *Transit New Zealand* [2003] UKPC 83; [2004] BLR 143; 100 Con LR 29 (tenders) 3.49; *Hart* v. *O'Connor* [1985] 2 All ER 880, PC (insanity not known to other party), 3.59; *Pao On* v. *Lau Yiu Long* [1980] AC 614, 629, PC (pre-existing contractual duty, consideration; and duress) 5.17 and 11.13.
15   *Vandepitte* v. *Preferred Accident Insurance Corporation of New York* [1933] AC 70, 80, PC (restrictive approach to trusts of promises) 7.12.
16   *New Zealand Shipping Co. Ltd* v. *AM Satterthwaite & Co. Ltd* ('The Eurymedon') [1975] AC 154, PC, 7.50; distinguished 'The Mahkutai' [1996] AC 650, PC, 7.52.
17   *Barton* v. *Armstrong* [1976] AC 104, PC, 11.12.
18   *Maritime National Fish Ltd* v. *Ocean Trawlers Ltd* [1935] AC 524, PC, 16.18.
19   *Sinclair Investments (UK) Ltd* v. *Versailles Trade Finance Ltd* [2011] EWCA Civ 347; [2012] Ch 453, at [72] to [76], *per* Lord Neuberger MR.
20   Generally, A. Burrows, 'The Relationship between Common Law and Statute in the Law of Obligations' (2012) 128 LQR 232–59.
21   The Explanatory Notes are helpful (www.publications.parliament.uk/pa/bills/cbill/2013–2014/0161/en/1 4161en.htm); see also the summary available within the following document: www.parliament.uk/business/ publications/research/briefing-papers/LLN-2014–023/consumer-rights-bill-hl-bill-29-of-201415.
22   Consumer Contracts (Information, Cancellation and Additional Charges) Regulations 2013/3134.
23   Section 5 of the Limitation Act 1980.

contracts and twelve years for deeds; for the latter, see 5.03.[24] The possibility of codification of contract law is discussed at 22.01.[25]

1.07 English contract law has a reputation for precision[26] and stability (although it has been fairly stated that finding this 'precise' statement often involves expensive legal advice, in order that decades or centuries of case law can be combed).[27] Foreign businesses often choose English law to govern their transactions by use of 'choice of law' clauses: 12.07. Such 'cross-border' transactions occur when one or both parties are resident or situated outside England.

2. FREEDOM OF CONTRACT

1.08 This principle,[28] recognised both in English law and in other legal traditions,[29] permits parties to conclude agreements on a wide range of matters, and on such terms as they wish. As noted by Christopher Clarke J in the *BNP Paribas* case (2009), English law places great emphasis on the need for the courts to respect contractual autonomy when it is exercised by commercial parties, especially when the relevant transaction has been relied upon in international commerce.[30] The classic statement (made in response to an unsuccessful plea that a contract was contrary to public policy) is by Sir George Jessel in *Printing & Numerical Registering Co* v. *Sampson* (1875):[31]

> if there is one thing which more than another public policy requires it is that men of full age and competent understanding shall have the utmost liberty of contracting, and that their contracts when entered into freely and voluntarily shall be held sacred and shall be enforced by Courts of justice. Therefore, you have this paramount public policy to consider – that you are not lightly to interfere with this freedom of contract.

---

24 Section 8 of the Limitation Act 1980 refers to actions on 'specialties', for example, a deed.

25 Noting especially M. Arden, 'Time for an English Commercial Code?' [1997] CLJ 516; R. Goode, 'Removing the Obstacles to Commercial Law Reform' (2007) 123 LQR 602–17.

26 But on the problem of open-ended rules, which are subject to imprecisely formulated exceptions, R. Ahdar, 'Contract Doctrine, Predictability and the Nebulous Exception' [2014] CLJ 39–60.

27 R. Goode, 'Removing the Obstacles to Commercial Law Reform' (2007) 123 LQR 602–17.

28 *Chitty on Contracts* (31st edn, London, 2012), 1–028 ff; P. S. Atiyah, *The Rise and Fall of Freedom of Contract* (Oxford, 1979); *Atiyah's Introduction to the Law of Contract* (6th edn, Oxford, 2006); R. Brownsword, *Contract Law: Themes for the Twenty-First Century* (2nd edn, Oxford, 2006), chapter 2; H. G. Collins, *The Law of Contract* (4th edn, Cambridge, 2003); C. Fried, *Contract as Promise: A Theory of Contractual Obligation* (Cambridge, MA, 1981); J. Gordley, *The Philosophical Origins of Modern Contract Doctrine* (Oxford, 1991); D. Kimel, *From Promise to Contract* (Oxford, 2005), chapter 5; D. Ibbetson, *A Historical Introduction to the Law of Obligations* (Oxford, 1999), chapters 7, 11, 12 and 13; A. Ogus and W. H. van Boom (eds.), *Juxtaposing Autonomy and Paternalism in Private Law* (Oxford, 2011); S. A. Smith, *Contract Theory* (Oxford, 2004); and M. J. Trebilcock, *The Limits of Freedom of Contract* (Cambridge, MA, 1997).

29 M. J. Bonell (ed.), *The UNIDROIT Principles in Practice: Case Law and Bibliography on the UNIDROIT Principles of International Commercial Contracts* (2nd edn, New York, 2006), 69; S. Vogenauer and J. Kleinheisterkamp (eds.), *Commentary on the UNIDROIT Principles of International Commercial Contracts* (Oxford, 2009), 118.

30 *BNP Paribas* v. *Wockhardt EU Operations (Swiss) AG* [2009] EWHC 3116 (Comm), at [24], [42], *per* Christopher Clarke J, referring to 'a carefully drawn standard form intended for widespread commercial use' and quoting other judicial discussion.

31 (1875) LR 19 Eq 462, 465 (heard at first instance).

The principle of freedom of contract embraces the following liberties. First, parties have a general freedom to enter into transactions which are intended (explicitly or otherwise) to create legal obligations.[32] This freedom includes the power to formulate individual terms within such a transaction, or to acquiesce in 'default' terms 'implied' by statute or Common Law. Secondly, parties to a transaction can stipulate that it will not be legally binding, 6.05 ff. Thirdly, freedom to contract includes the liberty to compromise a legal dispute, or to waive legal liability. But a contract of compromise must be very clearly worded if it is to extend one party's prospective liability towards the other, that is, liability which has not yet arisen but which might arise in the future if there were to be a change in the law.[33]

1.09 Exercise of these interrelated freedoms is subject to the overarching limitations of (1) public policy (Chapter 20) (including the problem of sham transactions[34] and protection against use of the law as a punitive mechanism, 19.23); (2) the parties' inability to exclude liability for fraud at Common Law (15.04); (3) statutory regulation of adhesion clauses (15.07, 15.08, 15.28); and (4) personal capacity. As regards personal capacity, for persons under eighteen (so-called 'minors'), for reasons of space the law on this topic can only be sketched in this note;[35] as for mental capacity, it should be noted that if a party's insanity is not known to the other party, the Privy Council in *Hart* v. *O'Connor* (1985) held that a contract will arise (see 3.59);[36] as for 'legal persons', the company or other legal entity (such as a local authority)[37] must have capacity to enter into the relevant transaction.[38]

---

32 E.g. contractual estoppel, including estoppel by deed, enables the parties to establish agreed facts, even though they know them to be untrue, if this is not inconsistent with public policy: *Prime Sight Ltd* v. *Lavarello* [2013] UKPC 22; [2014] AC 436, at [47], *per* Lord Toulson (noted A. Trukhtanov, (2014) 130 LQR 3–8).

33 *BCCI* v. *Ali* [2001] UKHL 8; [2002] 1 AC 251, at [19], [21], [35] and [86]; cf the dissent at [73] by Lord Hoffmann; N. Andrews, *English Civil Procedure* (Oxford, 2003), 23.65 to 23.77; see also *Satyam Computer Services Ltd* v. *Upaid Systems Ltd* [2008] EWCA Civ 487; [2008] 2 All ER (Comm) 465, at [84].

34 E.g. the cases noted by K. R. Handley, (2011) 127 LQR 171–3.

35 *Chitty on Contracts* (31st edn, London, 2012), 8–002 ff (see also S. Hedley, [2004] CLJ 435, 440–2); (1) a minor is liable for 'necessaries' purchased: section 3 of the Sale of Goods Act 1979; *Nash* v. *Inman* [1908] 2 KB 1, CA; 'necessaries' can include certain services (*Chitty on Contracts* (31st edn, London, 2012), 8–013); (2) a minor is bound by a contract of employment or apprenticeship as long as it is on the whole beneficial to him; but this does not extend to a contract to promote the prospects of a talented footballer: *Proform Sports Management Ltd* v. *Proactive Sports Management Ltd* [2006] EWHC 2903 (Ch); [2007] 1 All ER 542 (the 'Wayne Rooney' case); (3) contracts for the sale or purchase of land, or the grant or acquisition of a lease, or for the onerous acquisition of shares, can be repudiated by a minor or, after he reaches eighteen, repudiated within a reasonable time (on the problematic grant of a lease to a minor, see *Hammersmith and Fulham London Borough Council* v. *Alexander-David* [2009] EWCA Civ 259; [2009] 3 All ER 1098); (4) all other types of contract (e.g. a contract of insurance or a trading contract, or a contract for a luxury item not within the scope of 'necessaries') are not binding on the minor unless he ratifies the transaction after reaching eighteen: *Chitty on Contracts* (31st edn, London, 2012), 8–043 ff); (5) section 3 of the Minors' Contracts Act 1987 permits the court to order restitution of 'any property acquired by the [minor] under the contract, or any property representing it', even if the minor had not lied about his age, and this provision applies to all contracts other than those at (1) and (2).

36 *Hart* v. *O'Connor* [1985] 2 All ER 880, PC (the 'rule in *Imperial Loan Co* v. *Stone* [1892] 1 QB 599', see *Blankley* v. *Central Manchester and Manchester Children's University Hospitals NHS Trust* [2014] EWHC 168; [2014] 1 WLR 2683, at [30], *per* Phillips J); however, where the incapax's property is subject to the control of the court, under sections 15 ff of the Mental Capacity Act 2005, transactions which would be inconsistent with the court's control of those assets will be void as against that party; *Chitty on Contracts* (31st edn, London, 2012), 8–074, and *Treitel* (13th edn, London, 2011), 12–056, 12–057.

37 *Hazell* v. *Hammersmith & Fulham LBC* [1992] 2 AC 1, HL, and the flood of 'swaps' litigation resulting from this decision (on which, conveniently, see *Haugesund Kommune* v. *Depfa ACS Bank (No. 1)* [2010] EWCA Civ 579; [2011] 1 All ER 190; [2010] 1 CLC 770).

38 *Haugesund* case, preceding note, decided in the context of restitution of a void loan, and with discussion of the difference between English and foreign notions of corporate incapacity.

3. THE OBJECTIVE PRINCIPLE

1.10   This principle is a fundamental and pervasive aspect of *contract law* (for further detail, 3.55 ff). A person's words or conduct must be interpreted in the manner in which the other party (or alleged party) might objectively and reasonably understand them.[39] As Lord Reid said in *McCutcheon* v. *David MacBrayne Ltd* (1964):[40] 'the judicial task is not to discover the actual intentions of each party; it is to decide what each was reasonably entitled to conclude from the attitude of the other.' Thus the objective principle concerns the following matters: is there an offer (3.02); has there been acceptance of that offer; if so on what terms (on these last two questions, see the 'snapping up' cases, examined at 3.63); how should the terms of a written contract be interpreted (14.02 ff); has the contract been varied or terminated by consensus; has a party repudiated the agreement (see discussion of '*The Pro Victor*' (2009)[41] at 17.07); has the other party accepted that repudiation (17.37 ff); has a voidable contract been 'affirmed' by a party (11.14); is there an intent to create legal relations (*per* Aikens LJ in *Barbudev* v. *Eurocom Cable Management Bulgaria Eood* (2012)[42] and *Attrill* v. *Dresdner Kleinwort Ltd* (2013) (6.04)).[43]

4. OVERVIEW OF CONTRACTUAL DOCTRINES

1.11   Contracts are legally enforceable agreements involving two or more parties. The agreement can involve one party assuming an obligation only if the other does something (or refrains from something): a so-called 'unilateral contract'. An example is an offer of reward payable only if the other party supplies desired information. But most contracts involve reciprocal obligations: a so-called 'bilateral contract'; for example, to sell and buy, to insure and pay the premium, to hire out and to pay the hire charge, to work and to pay a salary, etc.

1.12   Many contractual obligations are promises to do something, or to pay money, or to transfer property. Occasionally, a party might undertake to refrain from doing something, such as not to work for a rival employer for a specified period. In short, most promises are forward-looking commitments to do, pay, transfer or abstain. But there are two main variations.

---

39   McLauchlan has lucidly distinguished (although this distinction has a long lineage) (1) the 'promisee'-based form of objectivity from (2) the 'detached observer' or 'fly-on-the-wall' form of objectivity. The preferred form is (1). The passage from McLauchlan, too long to quote here, merits close attention: D. McLauchlan, 'Refining Rectification' (2014) 130 LQR 83, at 88–90. See also: D. Friedmann, (2003) 119 LQR 68; J. R. Spencer, [1974] CLJ 104; W. Howarth, (1984) 100 LQR 265; J. Vorster, (1987) 103 LQR 274; M. Chen-Wishart, in J. W. Neyers, R. Bronaugh and S. G. A. Pitel (eds.), *Exploring Contract Law* (Oxford, 2009), 341; T. Endicott, 'Objectivity, Subjectivity and Incomplete Agreements' in J. Horder (ed.), *Oxford Essays in Jurisprudence* (Fourth Series, Oxford, 2000), 159; see also, from an American perspective, L. DiMatteo, Q. Zhou, S. Saintier, K. Rowley (eds.), *Commercial Contract Law: Transatlantic Perspectives* (Cambridge, 2014), chapter 3 (by T. Joo).
40   [1964] 1 WLR 125, HL; see also *Shogun Finance Co. Ltd* v. *Hudson* [2003] UKHL 62; [2004] 1 AC 919, HL, at [183].
41   *SK Shipping (S) PTE Ltd* v. *Petroexport Ltd* ('*The Pro Victor*') [2009] EWHC 2974, Flaux J at at [89] to [98].
42   [2012] EWCA Civ 548; [2012] 2 All ER (Comm) 963, at [30]: 'On the issue of whether the parties intended to create legal relations . . . [the] court has to consider the objective conduct of the parties as a whole.'
43   [2013] EWCA Civ 394; [2013] 3 All ER 807 at [61], [62], [86], [87] *per* Elias LJ.

A contractual assurance need not involve a promise of *future* conduct (or abstention). Thus, a 'warranty' is an assurance that something is the case, or has been the case. Another variation is that a promise need not concern the promisor's own primary conduct. Thus, a guarantee (5.06) is a surety's undertaking (normally) to indemnify a creditor if a debtor fails to satisfy a debt owed, or becoming due, to that creditor.

1.13 Some elements of basic contract law will now be explained. Formation of contract requires analysis in terms of offer and acceptance (Chapter 3); certainty (Chapter 4); intent to create legal relations (Chapter 6); absence of a vitiating factor rendering the contract either void (Common Law mistake, Chapter 10) or voidable (misrepresentation, duress, undue influence or unconscionability, Chapter 11).

1.14 An agreement must either be supported by consideration (Chapter 5) or contained in a 'deed': a deed is a formal written contract, which is normally gratuitous (see also 5.03 ff). The requirements for a valid deed are:[44] (1) the statement must be in writing; (2) this document must be declared to be a deed; (3) the document must be signed by the promisor (the 'covenantor'); (4) the document must be witnessed by another; and (5) the document must be 'delivered' (this word is misleading because the covenantor need not physically transfer the deed to the covenantee: it is enough that there is conduct indicating that the covenantor intends to be bound by it).[45]

1.15 In general, contracts do not need to be in writing or comply with special formality (thus, an agreement for the purchase of a £10m ship or a £20m – inevitably over-priced – English footballer can be made without writing). The main exceptions, where a contract must be in writing or formalised, are agreements for the creation or transfer of interests in land (see also 5.07) and guarantees (5.06). Many contractual obligations are express, whether oral or written (for an overview, see 12.06). But implied terms (Chapter 13) are readily found as a result of statute or Common Law doctrine.

1.16 An agreement might be expressly 'subject to contract' (6.06), so that it does not create any legally binding duties. Or an agreement might be subject to so-called 'conditions precedent' (12.06). For example, the contract might be contingent upon a third party, such as a government minister or planning authority, giving permission which is vital to the relevant transaction. Sometimes one party might agree to exercise best or reasonable endeavours to apply for such permission (2.11).

1.17 A contracting party's unexcused failure to perform, or his defective performance, constitutes a breach (Chapter 17). The other party has a range of possible remedies in respect of breach (18.01 for an overview): orders to compel agreed performance (a claim in

---

44   Section 1(2) and (3) of the Law of Property (Miscellaneous Provisions) Act 1989; as amended by Article 7(3) of the Regulatory Reform (Execution of Deeds and Documents) Order 2005 (SI 2005 No. 1906); *Treitel* (13th edn, London, 2011), 3–170 ff; *Bolton Metropolitan Borough Council v. Torkington* [2004] Ch 66, CA; *Chitty on Contracts* (31st edn, London, 2012), 1–107.
45   *Treitel* (13th edn, London, 2011), 3–172.

debt, 18.02; or, exceptionally, recourse to equitable and coercive relief by injunction, 18.36; or specific performance, 18.33); claims for damages at Common Law (18.07); restitutionary claims in respect of the guilty party's unjust enrichment (18.26); declarations that the guilty party is in breach (18.32) (or the award of merely nominal damages, 18.07 at (1), that is, a token amount designed to register that there has been a breach of contract or commission of a tort); self-help measures (forfeiture of a deposit, 19.27); or a stipulated right to liquidated damages (19.02); or a possible right to repossess property (10.32) or to withhold reciprocal performance (17.46 ff).

1.18 A party's non-performance or defective performance might be excused by an exclusion clause (Chapter 15) or under the Common Law doctrine of frustration (Chapter 16). Frustration applies if the contractual situation has been drastically affected by a change of circumstances subsequent to the agreement's formation. It will not be enough that one party has experienced unforeseen price increases, even if they are very large. Nor is it enough that other changes have occurred which severely hamper his performance, or which render the transaction highly unattractive to him.

1.19 The agreement at Common Law does not confer rights of enforcement on a third party (for a summary, see 7.02). Nor does it impose obligations on a third party (for a summary, see 7.55). The main qualifications upon these fundamental propositions of 'privity of contract' are: a third party might acquire rights, including a right to require performance, by a trust of a promise (7.09); and the Contracts (Rights of Third Parties) Act 1999 (7.22) might enable the third party to take the benefit of the contract and sue the promisor for nonperformance, or the third party might be permitted under the same Act to take the benefit of an exclusion clause. Alternatively, the benefit of the contract might be assigned. If so, the assignee acquires a direct right of action against the promisor (Chapter 8).

1.20 An agreement can be reconstituted or varied in various ways:
(1) by waiver (5.37) or estoppel, at Common Law or in Equity (5.38), suspending or modifying the agreement;
(2) by a variation supported by consideration;
(3) by a variation formalised by deed;
(4) by the substitution of a new agreement between the same parties in one of two ways:
   (a) either by 'transaction' novation, in which the first contract is replaced by a second contract between the same parties; or
   (b) by 'new party' novation, in which one of the parties to the original contract is substituted by a new third party; thus a contract between A and B is replaced by a contract between A or B and C, a new party (8.12 at (1)).
On these two forms of novation, see the remarks in *Scarf* v. *Jardine* (1882) by Lord Selborne LC.[46]

---

46 (1882) LR 7 App Cas 345, 351, HL, *per* Lord Selborne LC.

1.21 An agreement can be discharged or terminated in various ways: first, by performance in full (unhappily for lawyers, the most common situation); secondly, a contract might be terminated without a breach by either side, if a party exercises a right to cancel the contract explicitly or implicitly contained in the agreement (on termination clauses,[47] see 16.29, 17.25 ff); thirdly, by the occurrence of an event covered by an *express* 'condition subsequent' clause contained in the contract (10.12); fourthly, by reason of supervening illegality or frustration which brings the contract to an end by operation of law (Chapter 16); fifthly, by consensual termination of the agreement[48] (The consideration – element of mutual bargain – supporting this agreement to cancel will be the release of each party from his unperformed obligations under the contract.); sixthly, by merger of outstanding obligations in a judgment;[49] seventhly, in the case of written instruments, including guarantees and deeds, the relevant contract is rendered void by the promisee's unauthorised, unilateral, deliberate and material[50] alteration (that is, a change occurring after the document's execution) of the document's contents.[51] The eighth way in which a contract might be terminated involves an innocent party choosing to end the contract because of the other's serious breach. This topic is complex (17.01 ff). The innocent party has the choice of ending the contract if: (1) the other party has repudiated the agreement, by unequivocally declaring or indicating that he does not intend to perform his obligations; or (2) the other party has committed a breach of a condition (a promissory term which is so labelled by the parties, or so classified by statute or judicial decision, or which must be construed as such, having regard to its importance); or (3) a clause which, when breached, is expressly classified by the agreement as equivalent to a condition; or (4) there is a really serious breach of an innominate term so as to deprive the innocent party of substantially the entire expected performance.

5. CONTRACT AND TORT LAW

1.22 Many contractual obligations[52] are strict in the sense that a party can be in breach of agreement even though he has exercised all reasonable care to try to satisfy his obligation (see also, on the relationship between implied terms and the tort of negligence, 13.20 to 13.22). However, some contractual obligations are less demanding and merely require the

---

47 S. Whittaker, 'Termination Clauses', in A. S. Burrows and E. Peel (eds.), *Contract Terms* (Oxford, 2007), chapter 13; J. Randall, 'Express Termination Clauses' [2014] CLJ 113–41.

48 *Paal Wilson & Co A/S* v. *Partenreederei Hannah Blumental, 'The Hannah Blumental'* [1983] 1 AC 854, notably 915–6 (*per* Lord Diplock); for observations on implicit mutual abandonment, 914 (*per* Lord Brandon), 924–5 (*per* Lord Brightman), HL; *Allied Marine Transport Ltd* v. *Vale do Rio Doce Navegacao SA, 'The Leonidas D'* [1985] 1 WLR 925, CA; J. W. Carter, *Breach of Contract* (2nd edn, Sydney, 1991), [1216].

49 *Director General of Fair Trading* v. *First National Bank plc* [2002] 1 AC 481, HL.

50 *Raiffeisen Zentralbank Österreich AG* v. *Crossseas Shipping Ltd* [2000] 1 WLR 1135, 1146, CA, *per* Potter LJ (this judgment is a lucid examination of the entire doctrine; and see the *Habibson* case, next note).

51 *Habibsons Bank Ltd* v. *Standard Chartered Bank (Hong Kong) Ltd* [2010] EWCA Civ 1335; [2011] QB 943, at [25], where Moore-Bick LJ explained this, 'the rule in *Pigot's* Case (1614) 11 Co Rep 26b', as follows: 'The principle is described in *Chitty on Contracts* ... as follows: "If a promisee, without the consent of the promisor, deliberately makes a material alteration in a specialty or other instrument containing words of contract, this will discharge the promisor from all liability thereon, even though the original words of the instrument are still legible."'

52 A. S. Burrows, *Understanding the Law of Obligations* (Oxford, 1998), chapters 1, 2 and 8.

exercise of reasonable care, or a similar standard (see 17.02 and 18.23). Normally in a contract for the performance of professional services, the performing party will owe merely an obligation to exercise due care, rather than to guarantee the success of the task: 17.02.

The distinction between 'a duty to achieve a specific result' and 'a duty of best efforts' is drawn within the (non-binding) UNIDROIT's *Principles of International Commercial Contracts* (2010),[53] Articles 5.1.4 and 5.1.5.

1.23 In some situations, the relationship underlying the agreement simultaneously involves a Common Law or extra-contractual duty to exercise reasonable care. There might then be overlapping rights and duties in contract and in tort. This is true of many professional relationships. The House of Lords affirmed in *Henderson* v. *Merrett Syndicates Ltd* (1995)[54] that when a contractual duty of care overlaps with an essentially similar duty of care imposed by the tort of negligence, a claimant can select whichever cause of action he prefers, or indeed plead both (so-called 'concurrence' of claims, 17.02; on remoteness of damage, see 18.17;[55] on contributory negligence, see 18.23). The main difference between these 'concurrent' sources of claim ('causes of action') is the commencement of the limitation period: 'in cases of breach of contract the cause of action arises at the date of the breach of contract'; but 'in tort the cause of action arises, not when the culpable conduct occurs, but when the plaintiff first sustains damage'.[56] The limitation periods for breach of contract are six years for ordinary ('simple')[57] contracts (oral, written, and partly written contracts, other than deeds or covenants) and twelve years for deeds (for the latter, see 5.03).[58] Tort also interrelates with the law of contract in the field of pre-contractual misrepresentations,[59] where the torts of negligent misstatement and deceit provide sources of damages for inaccurate statements (9.07, 9.23).

6. CONTRACT AND RESTITUTION OR UNJUST ENRICHMENT

1.24 Contract law often interacts with the law of restitution or unjust enrichment,[60] a category of obligations subsisting separately from contract and tort.[61] Overlap between restitution and

---

53   3rd edition, 2010, text and comment, is available at: www.unidroit.org/english/principles/contracts/principles2010/integralversionprinciples2010-e.pdf.
54   [1995] 2 AC 145, HL.
55   On aspects of the remoteness tests in contract and tort, see A. Kramer, in D. Saidov and R. Cunnington (eds.), *Contract Damages: Domestic and International Perspectives* (Oxford, 2008), chapter 12.
56   *Nykredit Mortgage Bank plc* v. *Edward Erdman Group (No. 2)* [1997] 1 WLR 1627, 1630, HL.
57   Section 5 of the Limitation Act 1980.
58   Section 8 of the Limitation Act 1980 refers to actions on 'specialties', for example, a deed.
59   J. Cartwright, 'Liability in Tort for Pre-Contractual Non-Disclosure', in A. S. Burrows and E. Peel (eds.), *Contract Formation and Parties* (Oxford, 2010).
60   Leading works include: T. Baloch, *Unjust Enrichment and Contract* (Oxford, 2009); A. Burrows, *The Law of Restitution* (3rd edn, 2011); A. S. Burrows, *A Restatement of the English Law of Unjust Enrichment* (Oxford, 2012); *Goff and Jones on the Law of Unjust Enrichment* (8th edn, London, 2011); G. Virgo, *The Principles of the Law of Restitution* (2nd edn, Oxford, 2006); A. Burrows, E. McKendrick, J. Edelman, *Cases and Materials on the Law of Restitution* (2nd edn, Oxford, 2007); for a provocative rejoinder, in the context of performance of services, D. Priel, 'In Defence of Quasi-Contract' (2012) 75 MLR 54; for a symposium on 'restitution and unjust enrichment' (2012) 92 *Boston Univ LR* 763–1080.
61   A. S. Burrows, *Understanding the Law of Obligations* (Oxford, 1998), chapters 1 and 3.

contract will be noted not just in the chapter on remedies (18.26 ff), but also in respect of contracts which 'fail to materialise' (2.03) and rescission following misrepresentation (9.26 ff). Restitutionary claims are based on the defendant's unjust enrichment. Most restitutionary remedies become available without the need to show a contractual breach. However, breach of contract is an essential element in one restitutionary remedy: the remedy of 'equitable account' (see *Attorney-General* v. *Blake*,[62] 18.30). A restitutionary claim is not made to remedy a claimant's loss. Instead, it is a claim in respect of the defendant's unjust enrichment at the claimant's expense (for example, if the claimant has mistakenly paid money to the defendant), or at any rate enrichment arising as a result of breach of duty or violation of the claimant's rights. The enrichment can constitute money or services or goods or the saving of necessary expense. The cause of action based on restitution or unjust enrichment can take various forms: it might be that the benefit was conferred as a result of the claimant's mistake of fact or law; or that there was a (total) failure of consideration, or duress, or undue influence, or abuse of fiduciary relationship[63] or an unjustified tax demand. There are three main forms of restitutionary relief relevant to contract law (18.26 ff): (1) money recovered for a total failure of consideration; (2) recovery in respect of goods or services; and (3) disgorgement of gains made in breach of contract.

7. COMMON LAW AND EQUITY

1.25 The English notion of 'Equity' is rooted in legal history.[64] Before 1875 there were separate judicial systems: Common Law courts and the Court of Chancery. In the latter, the Lord Chancellor had developed a complex body of doctrine which qualified and supplemented, sometimes indeed contradicted, the Common Law. Different remedies were historically available in these courts, the Common Law not having developed the injunction, whereas the Court in Equity (the Court of Chancery) had developed a rich set of remedies, including injunctions (for example, equitable remedies included rescission, rectification, account, declarations). The Supreme Court of Judicature Acts 1873 and 1875 (its provisions are now contained in the Senior Courts Act 1981, as amended) enabled the High Court and county courts to administer both Common Law and Equity in the same case. However, even today, the distinction between Common Law and Equity remains important for the exposition of contract law. It remains fundamental to distinguish between Common Law and equitable doctrines[65] and remedies. Some recent

---

62 [2001] 1 AC 268, HL; J. Edelman, *Gain-Based Damages* (Oxford, 2002), chapter 5; E. McKendrick, in A. S. Burrows and E. Peel (eds.), *Commercial Remedies: Current Issues and Problems* (Oxford, 2003), 93–119; A. S. Burrows, *Remedies for Torts and Breach of Contract* (3rd edn, Oxford, 2004), 395–407.

63 *Calvert* v. *William Hill Credit Ltd* [2008] EWCA Civ 1427; [2009] Ch 330, at [53]; J. Edelman, 'When Do Fiduciary Duties Arise?' (2010) 126 LQR 302.

64 *Snell's Principles of Equity* (32nd edn, London, 2010), chapter 1; on wider notions of Equity, L. DiMatteo, Q. Zhou, S. Saintier, K. Rowley (eds.), *Commercial Contract Law: Transatlantic Perspectives* (Cambridge, 2014), chapter 7 (by T. Arvind).

65 In the USA, the fact that the remedy of injunction is 'equitable' places a claim for such relief outside the constitutional guarantee of jury trial: see G. Hazard and M. Taruffo, *American Civil Procedure* (Connecticut, 1993), 130.

decisions have tended to diminish the Common Law/equitable distinction.[66] Even so, the distinction between Common Law and Equity remains 'bed-rock' within English private law, and in other Common Law jurisdictions. It will prove hard to eradicate. And although a debate has emerged on whether English law should 'move on' and jettison this historical baggage (in particular, Andrew Burrows from Oxford University has advocated abandonment of this distinction),[67] it is likely that this distinction will endure for many years. Indeed even a codification of contract law would merely probably echo the fundamental conceptual distinctions between Common Law and Equity. Examples of this classification are: the equitable doctrines of rectification (9.25), undue influence, unconscionability (on these see Chapter 7) and equitable bars upon rescission (9.28); and the Common Law doctrines of 'mistake' or duress (on these see Chapters 6 and 7). As for remedies for breach of contract (see 18.01 for an overview), the money claims for debt and damages are both Common Law remedies (for a claim in debt, see 18.02; for damages at Common Law, see 18.07), but injunctions (18.36), specific performance (18.33) and an account of profits (18.30) are 'equitable'.

1.26 There is scope for confusion because the expression 'Common Law rule' is sometimes used to denote the distinction between judge-made law (both Common Law and equitable doctrine) and legislation. An example of a judge-made rule observed at 'Common Law' and in 'Equity' is the doctrine of consideration. This rule prevents a person from suing a defendant for breach of contract (in the absence of a formal contract known as a 'deed') unless the claimant has provided some element of bargain at the defendant's request (on deeds, see 5.03; generally on the consideration doctrine, see Chapter 5). The consideration rule was observed both by the pre-Judicature Act (see 1.25 above) Common Law courts (Queen's Bench, Court of Common Pleas, Exchequer Court) and the Court of Chancery ('Court of Equity'). The modern courts continue to adhere to it. In short, 'Common Law' is sometimes the antithesis to 'Equity'. However, 'Common Law' doctrine is sometimes the antithesis to 'statutory' or 'legislative', and in this sense the expression 'Common Law' embraces both Common Law and equitable doctrines, because both are the product of judicial law-making.

8. GOOD FAITH

1.27 This topic has produced a vast literature,[68] and it is further examined in Chapter 21. This concept applies potentially both to performance of contracts and to the pre-contractual phase. Good faith in the performance of contracts is a prominent feature of civil law systems of contract law (for example, section 242 of the German Civil Code; Article 1134 of the French Civil Code; and Articles 1337, 1366 and 1375 of the Italian Civil Code); and the same concept has been adopted in the USA, both in the *Restatement of the*

---

66   E.g., no separate doctrine of shared 'equitable' mistake, *The Great Peace* [2003] QB 679, CA; no separate equitable principles of construction of contracts, *BCCI* v. *Ali* [2001] UKHL 8; [2002] 1 AC 251, at [17].
67   Inaugural Oxford lecture, A. S. Burrows, 'We do this at Common Law but that in Equity' (2002) 22 OJLS 1.
68   See the literature cited in nn. 1 and 2 in Chapter 21.

Law Second, Contracts (1981), section 205, and in the Uniform Commercial Code, section 1–203. Furthermore, UNIDROIT's *Principles of International Commercial Contracts* (2010), Article 1.7,[69] PECL, Article 2:201 and the *Common Frame of Reference*, Article III-1:103[70] all adopt this principle. But good faith is not an explicitly recognised general doctrine in English contract law.[71] As Bingham LJ said in *Interfoto Picture Library Ltd* v. *Stiletto Visual Programmes Ltd* (1989):[72] 'English law has, characteristically, committed itself to no such overriding principle but has developed piecemeal solutions in response to demonstrated problems of unfairness.' The author's contentions at 21.02 ff will be: (1) in England, the principle of good faith is not required in the context of pre-contractual negotiations (for current law, see Chapter 2) because of the highly developed and fertile array of existing doctrines; but (2) as for good faith as a general principle governing the validity, interpretation, performance and enforcement of contracts, the case is more evenly balanced. In the case of (2), there would be only a slight benefit in making such a change. The courts would be unlikely to use the concept dynamically. The inevitable anxiety and uncertainty experienced within the legal profession, when advising their clients, might outweigh the possible and marginal benefits of such a change.

9. EUROPEAN UNION LAW

1.28 English law is subject to various EU Directives and Regulations.[73] Examples are: the Consumer Protection from Unfair Trading Regulations (2008) (3.15 and 11.01),[74] the Consumer Contracts (Information, Cancellation and Additional Charges) Regulations (2013) (3.14),[75] and the Consumer Rights Bill[76] (notably see text at 15.08 and 15.28).

---

69 3rd edition, 2010, text and comment, is available at: www.unidroit.org/english/principles/contracts/prin ciples2010/integralversionprinciples2010-e.pdf.

70 *Principles, Definitions and Model Rules of European Private Law Draft Common Frame of Reference*, C. von Bar and E. Clive (eds.) (6 vols., Oxford, 2010).

71 E. McKendrick, *Contract Law: Text, Cases and Materials* (6th edn, Oxford, 2014), chapter 15 (examining R. Brownsword's sophisticated discussion in R. Brownsword, *Contract Law: Themes for the Twenty-First Century* (2nd edn, Oxford, 2006), chapter 5 (also in R. Brownsword, in M. Furmston (ed.), *The Law of Contract* (4th edn, London, 2010), chapter 1).

72 [1989] QB 433, 439, CA.

73 L. DiMatteo, Q. Zhou, S. Saintier, K. Rowley (eds.), *Commercial Contract Law: Transatlantic Perspectives* (Cambridge, 2014), chapters 20 and 21 (by Q. Zhou and H. MacQueen respectively); C. Twigg-Flesner, *The Europeanisation of Contract Law* (2nd edn, Abingdon, 2013); S. Weatherill, 'An Ever Tighter Grip: The European Court's Pro-Consumer Interpretation of the EC's Directives Affecting Consumer Law', in *Liber Amicorum Guido Alpa: National Private Law Systems* (London, 2007), 1037; S. Whittaker, 'A Framework of Principle for European Contract Law' (2009) 125 LQR 617; S. Whittaker, 'The Proposed "Common European Sales Law": Legal Framework and the Agreement of the Parties' (2012) 75 MLR 578; and see the EU consumer literature collected in P. Cartwright, 'Under Pressure: Regulating Aggressive Commercial Practices in the UK' [2011] LMCLQ 123 at beginning of the article.

74 The Consumer Protection from Unfair Trading Regulations 2008 (SI 2008 No. 1277; P. Cartwright, 'Under Pressure: Regulating Aggressive Commercial Practices in the UK' [2011] LMCLQ 123–41.

75 The Consumer Contracts (Information, Cancellation and Additional Charges) Regulations 2013 (SI 2013 No. 3134).

76 See n. 21 above.

10. TRANSNATIONAL CONTRACT LAW[77]

1.29 This topic is considered in detail in Chapters 21 to 23.

11. THE WIDER PICTURE: 'NETWORKS' AND 'RELATIONAL CONTRACTS'

1.30 These topics have in common that they require the discrete contract to be placed in a broader context, either as part of a chain or constellation of contracts ('networks') or as part of a wider, longer or deeper relationship between the parties. Such a broadening of the landscape of contract law and contractual activity has attracted attention in modern scholarship. As for 'networks',[78] in the discussion of protection of third parties by use of exclusion clauses (7.48 ff), we will encounter a good example of how relations between parties A and B require further attention of the relations between A and B and Z (or further parties in a chain, or in a contractual circle). As for 'relational contracts',[79] at 21.16 we will note Leggatt J's suggestion in *Yam Seng Pte Ltd* v. *International Trade Corp Ltd* (2013)[80] that 'relational' contracts require a more energetic use of an implied term of good faith, 'fair dealing', or mutual trust between parties.

12. BIBLIOGRAPHY

1.31 A bibliography is set out at the end of this book. At the end of each chapter there is a list of selected reading.

QUESTIONS

(1) Summarise (a) the principle of freedom of contract and (b) the objective principle of consensus.

---

77 See especially H. MacQueen and R. Zimmermann (eds.), *European Contract Law: Scots and South African Perspectives* (Edinburgh, 2006), chapter 1; R. Goode, *Commercial Law in the Next Millennium* (London, 1998) (Hamlyn Lecture Series, 1997), 88–105; A. Chong, 'Transnational Public Policy in Civil and Commercial Matters' (2012) 128 LQR 88–113; R. Goode, 'Usage and its Reception in Transnational Commercial Law' (1997) 46 ICLQ 1.

78 See reviews by R. Brownsword (2012) 75 MLR 455, Y. Marique [2012] CLJ 725–9, and J. Morgan (2012) 128 LQR 472–5 of G. Teubner, *Networks as Connected Contracts* (Oxford, 2011); L. DiMatteo, Q. Zhou, S. Saintier, K. Rowley (eds.), *Commercial Contract Law: Transatlantic Perspectives* (Cambridge, 2014), chapter 6 (by R. Brownsword).

79 See the essays in D. Campbell, L. Mulcahy and S. Wheeler (eds.), *Changing Concepts of Contract* (Basingstoke, 2013) (for example, H. Beale, chapter 6); D. Campbell, 'Good Faith and the Ubiquity of the "Relational" Contract' (2014) 77 MLR 475; L. DiMatteo, Q. Zhou, S. Saintier, K. Rowley (eds.), *Commercial Contract Law: Transatlantic Perspectives* (Cambridge, 2014), chapter 9 (by Z. Ollerenshaw).

80 [2013] EWHC 111 (QB); [2013] 1 All ER (Comm) 1321; [2013] 1 Lloyd's Rep 526; [2013] BLR 147 (notably at [141], [144], [147], and [154]); noted by S. Bogle, 'Disclosing Good Faith in English Contract Law' (2014) 18 *Edinburgh Law Review* 141–5; D. Campbell, 'Good Faith and the Ubiquity of the "Relational" Contract' (2014) 77 MLR 475–92; S. Whittaker, 'Good Faith, Implied Terms and Commercial Contracts' (2013) 129 LQR 463; E. Granger [2013] LMCLQ 418; more generally, H. Hoskins, 'Contractual obligations to negotiate in good faith: faithfulness to the agreed common purpose' (2014) 130 LQR 131–59.

(2) Summarise the nature of the following relationships:
  (a) Common Law and Equity
  (b) contract and tort
  (c) contract and restitution (or unjust enrichment).

Selected further reading

J. Adams and R. Brownsword, 'The Ideologies of Contract Law' (1987) 7 LS 205

R. Brownsword, *Contract Law: Themes for the Twenty First Century* (2nd edn, Oxford, 2006), chapter 5

A. S. Burrows, 'We do this at Common Law but that in Equity' (2002) 22 OJLS 1

E. McKendrick, 'English Contract Law: A Rich Past, an Uncertain Future' (1997) 50 CLP 25

A. W. B. Simpson, 'Innovation in Nineteenth Century Contract Law' (1975) 91 LQR 247

Formation

Chapter contents

2

The pre-contractual phase

1. INTRODUCTION

2.01 Summary of main points

(1) The principle of freedom of contract (1.08) permits negotiating parties to 'walk away' from a proposed deal, provided they have not already committed themselves in law to a binding agreement.

(2) In the absence of a binding contract, a person's requested performance, whether delivery of goods or performance of services, can give rise to a restitutionary obligation to pay the reasonable market value of the relevant performance (generally on this type of restitutionary claim see 2.04, 18.26).

(3) A supposed agreement to negotiate in good faith or reasonably the terms of the main contract is void for uncertainty; similarly, an agreement to use best or reasonable endeavours to settle the terms of the main agreement is also void.

(4) However, a so-called 'lock out' agreement for a fixed period is valid (known also in practice as an 'exclusivity agreement').

(5) Where *the main contract is valid, the courts will uphold an ancillary negotiation clause* requiring the parties in *good faith or reasonably* to negotiate aspects of the transaction, but only if there is an objective criterion to regulate those further dealings.

(6) An agreement to use best endeavours to obtain planning permission, or an export licence, is also valid.

(7) Furthermore, *when the main contract is valid*, the law will uphold an express ancillary clause imposing a duty of *performance in 'utmost good faith'* by the parties; the effect of such a clause is to require the parties, *during performance*, to take action consistent with the achievement of the contract's main purpose, or to desist from action which will stultify that purpose.

2.02 English law has fashioned an intricate set of rules governing the pre-contractual context.[1] Readers hoping to find a single formula, such as a pre-contractual duty to negotiate in good faith, will find English law lacking in such simplicity. The English courts have used a 'Swiss army knife' for this purpose, rather than a single blade. But to those willing to read between the lines of the judgments it will be apparent that English law is not allergic to notions of pre-contractual fair dealing or responsibility for culpable or bad faith rupture of negotiations. On the contrary, English law energetically intervenes to correct an injustice in this context. It will also be convenient here to examine the related topic of mediation clauses (4.22), even though such clauses normally arise from within an existing contract.

2. ABORTIVE PRE-CONTRACTUAL NEGOTIATIONS

2.03 Freedom of contract involves freedom not to contract (generally on the principle of freedom of contract, see 1.08). As Lord Ackner said in *Walford* v. *Miles* (1992):[2] 'Each party to [pre-contractual] negotiations is entitled to pursue his (or her) own interest, so long as he avoids making misrepresentations. To advance that interest he must be entitled, if he thinks it appropriate, to … withdraw [with impunity].'[3] However, the pre-contractual zone is not a lawless jungle. Some civil law jurisdictions police the pre-contractual zone on the basis of general principles of good faith or fair dealing, or a wide notion of *culpa in contrahendo* (fault during the process of bargaining). For example, Israeli law uses the principle of good faith, drawing upon German law.[4] But English courts do not recognise a general doctrine of fault in bargaining,[5] nor a general doctrine of good faith negotiation. Traditionally, English lawyers regard good faith as an unattractively vague concept (for 'soft law' codes on this, such as UNIDROIT's *Principles of International Commercial Contracts* (2010)[6] and the *Principles of European Contract Law*, see 21.01;[7] generally on (traditional) English antipathy to good faith as an implicit contractual norm,

---

1   E. McKendrick, 'Work Done in Anticipation of a Contract Which Does Not Materialise', in W. Cornish, R. Nolan, J. O'Sullivan and G. Virgo (eds.), *Restitution: Past, Present and Future* (Oxford, 1998), chapter 11; M. Spence, *Protecting Reliance: The Emergent Doctrine of Equitable Estoppel* (Oxford, 1999), 87–106; D. K. Allen, 'Pre-Contractual Liability', in J. Gardner (ed.), *UK Law in the 1990s* (London, 1990), 90 ff; J. Dietrich, 'Classifying Pre-Contractual Liability: A Comparative Analysis' (2001) LS 153; R. Zimmermann and S. Whittaker (eds.), *Good Faith in European Contract Law* (Cambridge, 2000), 236–57; P. Giliker, *Pre-Contractual Liability in English and French Law* (Nijmegen, 2002); P. Giliker, 'A Role for Tort in Pre-Contractual Negotiations? An Examination of English, French, and Canadian Law' (2003) 52 ICLQ 968.
2   [1992] 2 AC 128, HL.
3   See also Article 28 of the Contract Law of the Dubai International Financial Centre: www.difc.ae/laws-reg ulations/.
4   N. Cohen, in J. Beatson and D. Friedmann (eds.), *Good Faith and Fault in Contract Law* (Oxford, 1995), 32.
5   P. Giliker, 'A Role for Tort in Pre-Contractual Negotiations? An Examination of English, French, and Canadian Law' (2003) 52 ICLQ 968; J. Cartwright and M. Hesselink (eds.), *Precontractual Liability in European Private Law* (Cambridge, 2008); J. Cartwright, 'The English Law of Contract: Time for Review?' (2009) 17 *European Review of Private Law* 155, 156; as for French law, see J. Ghestin, 'La Responsabilité Délictuelle pour Rupture des Pourparlers … ', in *Liber Amicorum Guido Alpa: National Private Law Systems* (London, 2007), 436.
6   3rd edition, 2010, text and comment, is available at: www.unidroit.org/english/principles/contracts/princi ples2010/integralversionprinciples2010-e.pdf.
7   O. Lando and H. Beale (eds.), *Principles of European Contract Law* (The Hague, 2000).

see 21.01 ff). Instead, English law uses a mix of Common Law and equitable doctrines to protect a party to negotiations. Gathering together the threads of this topic, Aikens LJ in the *Barbudev* case (2012) made this helpful summary:[8]

> (1) it is for the parties to decide at what stage they wish to be contractually bound ... the parties are 'masters of their contractual fate'.[9] (2) They can agree to be bound contractually, even if there are further terms to be agreed between them.[10] (3) The question is whether the agreement is unworkable or fails for uncertainty. (4) However, where commercial men intend to enter into a binding commitment the courts are reluctant to conclude that such an agreement fails for uncertainty.[11] [numbering added]

2.04 *Unjust enrichment or restitutionary relief.* The main source of relief in English law for a person who has lost out because a deal has not been concluded is to seek protection within the law of unjust enrichment. On the facts of the *British Steel* case (1984; for further comment on the case, see 18.29), Robert Goff J held that there was no contract because there had been a failure of offer and acceptance[12] (this case was approved, and examined in detail, by the Supreme Court in the *RTS* case, 2010, see 4.17). In the *British Steel* case, the claimant had delivered a large number of special 'steel nodes' for use by the defendant construction company in erecting a building. Eventually all the nodes had been supplied. But the defendant alleged that the claimant had delivered them too slowly and in the wrong sequence and that, as a result, the defendant had suffered delay in completing its project. The dispute concerned both the main claim for payment (the market value of the goods was £229,832), and a counterclaim against the claimant for compensation in respect of the defendant's commercial loss caused by the alleged slow and haphazard delivery of these materials (£867,735). Goff J held that no contract had arisen, not only because the parties had yet to reach consensus on the price to be paid, but there remained an unresolved issue concerning the supplier's possible liability for consequential loss (for example, because of slow delivery).[13] Goff J also held that it made no difference that a letter of intent[14] had been issued (relatedly, see *Kleinwort Benson* v. *Malaysian Mining* (1989) at 6.14, concerning 'letters of comfort').[15] Instead Goff J awarded the claimant the market value of the goods

---

8   *Barbudev* v. *Eurocom Cable Management Bulgaria Eood* [2012] EWCA Civ 548; [2012] 2 All ER (Comm) 963, at [32].
9   *Pagnan Spa* v. *Feed Products Limited* [1987] 2 Lloyd's Rep 601, 611, *per* Bingham J.
10   *RTS Flexible Systems Ltd* v. *Molkerei Alois Müller GmbH* [2010] 1 WLR 753 at [48], per Lord Clarke: 'In the Pagnan case ... [the] parties agreed to bind themselves to agreed terms, leaving certain subsidiary and legally inessential terms to be decided later.'
11   *Hillas* v. *Arcos Ltd* (1932) 147 LT 503, 514 *per* Lord Wright.
12   *British Steel Corporation* v. *Cleveland Bridge and Engineering Company* [1984] 1 All ER 504; S. Ball, 'Work Carried Out in Pursuance of Letters of Intent – Contract or Restitution?' (1983) 99 LQR 572; E. McKendrick, 'The Battle of the Forms and the Law of Restitution' (1988) 8 OJLS 197, at 212, 215 and 217; J. Edelman, 'Liability in Unjust Enrichment Where a Contract Fails to Materialise', in A. Burrows and E. Peel (eds.), *Contract Formation and Parties* (Oxford, 2010).
13   [1984] 1 All ER 504, 509–11, *per* Goff J.
14   Even if the arrangements remain evidenced by a letter of intent, a valid construction contract might arise, provided the court can discern the four requirements of the parties' identities, the scope of the work, the price, and time for commencement and completion; *Glendalough Associated SA* v. *Harris Calnan Construction Co Ltd* [2013] EWHC 3142 (TCC); [2014] 1 WLR 1751, at [47] ff, *per* Edwards-Stuart J.
15   *Ibid.*, at 510.

(£229,832), on the basis of restitution, an extra-contractual cause of action (18.26). This was just because it was plain that the goods were not a present. They were requested on the understanding that they would be paid for. But Goff J could not uphold the counter-claim because that presupposed breach of a contractual duty and hence a valid contract. In any event, Goff J said[16] that even if there had been a contract on these facts, the supplier had delivered within a reasonable time. As for the allegation that there had been delivery out of sequence, he said that this claim would require an express term,[17] and he chose not to comment further on this allegation.

And so the *British Steel* case vividly illustrates that restitution can be a second-best solution for the recipient of materials or work, where both parties have a grievance: restitution might confer victory on the supplier, who gains the full market value of the goods supplied; but there can be no correlative victory for the defendant in respect of the alleged slow performance. There is an asymmetry here: the restitutionary award made in this case operates solely in favour of the performer. In response to the *British Steel* case, Ball (1993) contended that the courts should adopt a more flexible approach to finding a contract. He further suggested that businessmen would welcome such an approach as pragmatic and reasonable.[18] However, the objection to this is that it would involve imposing a contract in the teeth of the parties' failure to agree. That would offend the principle of freedom of contract (1.08): parties to negotiations should not be treated as having reached final agreement if it is clear that they have yet to finalise the agreement and have instead reserved to themselves the task of establishing final consensus. Consistent with this, Goff J decided (see the first passage quoted above) that the parties in the *British Steel* case had clearly not settled major difficulties in their negotiations. They had decided to proceed with performance but only in the hope that a final contract would take shape later.

Another possible approach would be to reduce the amount of the claimant's restitutionary claim to reflect the fact that performance was slow. But, perhaps regrettably, restitution law has yet to develop a method of making such a reduction for defective performance, including the present situation where goods have been delivered 'late' or 'out of sequence' (although Burrows, a leading commentator on the law of restitution, has attractively approved this possibility).[19] A more flexible restitutionary approach is needed. After all, the defence of contributory negligence (18.23) requires the courts to work out on a rough-and-ready basis the claimant's damages, allowing a discount for his own culpable conduct. And, in the context of frustrated contracts, the Law Reform (Frustrated Contracts) Act 1943 (16.21) creates a flexible scheme for awarding a 'just sum', taking into account factors on both the claimant's side and his opponent's. However, it must be admitted that even if this flexibility could be shown in the restitution context, the technique has its limits. On the facts of the *British Steel* case, this 'discount for defective performance' approach would have achieved an imperfect result: the value

---

16   [1984] 1 All ER 504, 512.
17   *Ibid.*
18   S. Ball, 'Work Carried Out in Pursuance of Letters of Intent – Contract or Restitution?' (1983) 99 LQR 572.
19   A. Burrows, *A Casebook on Contract* (4th edn, Oxford, 2013), 78.

of the counter-claim (approximately £868,000) greatly exceeded the reasonable value of the goods supplied (approximately £230,000).

As noted at 18.29, the Supreme Court in *Benedetti* v. *Sawiris* (2013) held that a *quantum meruit* is based on the normal 'market value' of the services and not on any higher figures bandied around during the parties' negotiations.[20] A figure lower than market rate was awarded in *Whittle Movers Ltd* v. *Hollywood Express Ltd* (2009)[21] (on which see 4.17) to reflect the fact that the contemplated agreement (which did not become operative) imposed a preliminary tranche of low prices, which would be augmented over time.

2.05 *Subject to Contract Clause overtaken by completion of all negotiations and substantial performance of contemplated contract.* It is sometimes possible to impose a contractual solution on the basis that the parties' dealings *have implicitly overridden the negotiation snag or implicitly waived a 'subject to contract' bar.* It was on this basis that the *British Steel* case was distinguished in *RTS Flexible Systems Ltd* v. *Molkerei Alois Müller GmbH* (2010).[22] In the latter case, the Supreme Court rationalised the *British Steel* case as an example of unresolved points of difference which precluded a finding of a contract, and where non-contractual performance was understood to have proceeded pending a final and completely agreed set of terms. By contrast, in the *RTS* case the parties had agreed on all the essential terms and had simply failed to sign the formal contract. They had contemplated that they would (as it were) seal the deal by joint signatures. The Supreme Court held that the parties' decision to carry out nearly three-quarters of the contemplated transaction could be objectively construed as a tacit joint waiver of the 'subject to contract' bar which the parties had earlier expressly imposed, but which they had now implicitly lifted (the *RTS* case is examined in detail at 4.17).

2.06 *Proprietary estoppel.* This doctrine can be used to achieve justice in the pre- or extra-contractual zone. To avoid repetition, the reader is referred to the discussion at 5.45.

3. NEGOTIATION AGREEMENTS AND RELATED ARRANGEMENTS

2.07 *Invalid: Agreement to negotiate the main contract in good faith or reasonably.*[23] The House of Lords in *Walford* v. *Miles* (1992) (see later in this paragraph for details of this case) decided that an agreement to negotiate in good faith or reasonably is uncertain and void.[24]

20 [2013] UKSC 50; [2013] 3 WLR 351 (noted M. McInnes (2014) 130 LQR 8–13; G. Virgo [2013] CLJ 508–11; C. Mitchell [2013] LMCLQ 436); see also *Littlewoods Retail Ltd* v. *Revenue and Customs Commissioners* [2014] EWHC 868 (Ch) and *Harrison* v. *Madejski* [2014] EWCA Civ 361.
21 *Whittle Movers Ltd* v. *Hollywood Express Ltd* [2009] EWCA Civ 1189; [2009] CLC 771 (Waller, Dyson and Lloyd LJJ); noted by P. S. Davies, (2010) 126 LQR 175–9.
22 [2010] UKSC 14; [2010] 1 WLR 753, at [55].
23 M. Furmston and G. J. Tolhurst, *Contract Formation: Law and Practice* (Oxford, 2010), 11.33 ff; E. Peel, 'The Status of Agreements to Negotiate in Good Faith', in A. Burrows and E. Peel (eds.), *Contract Formation and Parties* (Oxford, 2010).
24 [1992] 2 AC 128, HL.

Such a wide-ranging and nebulous obligation would embroil the courts in conducting complicated inquiries to determine why negotiations had broken down. It is submitted that a bare agreement to negotiate the main agreement in good faith or reasonably is rightly condemned as fatally void for uncertainty. Adjudication of such a 'commitment' would be drenched with subjectivity and commercial value-judgements.

In *Walford* v. *Miles* (1992),[25] the parties had entered into a preliminary agreement to regulate the conduct of their negotiations for the sale of a photographic business. The defendant vendor promised, for consideration, to negotiate only with the claimant and not to negotiate with any third party. The main agreement for sale was expressly made 'subject to contract' and so had no legal effect. The proposed contract price for this sale was £2m. Because the defendant vendor was ill, he did not want to have to assist in the business after it had been sold. For that reason, he sold the business to a third party for £2m. This third party would be able to take immediate control of the business (the defendant sensing that if he sold it instead to the claimant, the defendant would need to remain involved during a substantial period of transition). In fact the £2m figure involved a sale at an undervalue: the property was worth £3m. The claimant knew this, but had not told the defendant (nor was the claimant obliged to do so, according to established English doctrine, 3.65 ff).

The House of Lords held that an agreement to negotiate, whether in good faith or reasonably, in fact lacked sufficient certainty.

In the following seminal passage Lord Ackner said that an agreement to agree, or to negotiate in good faith, or reasonably, or for a reasonable period, is void for uncertainty because the court is faced with a vacuous obligation which lacks content; 'reasonably' or 'in good faith' are hopelessly vague criteria; and so the court or arbitral tribunal cannot adjudicate reliably upon an allegation that there has been a breach:[26]

> The reason why an agreement to negotiate, like an agreement to agree, is unenforceable, is simply because it lacks the necessary certainty . . . How can a court be expected to decide whether, *subjectively*, a proper reason existed for the termination of negotiations? . . . [How] is a vendor ever to know that he is entitled to withdraw from further negotiations? How is the court to police such an 'agreement?' . . . [While] negotiations are in existence either party is entitled to withdraw from those negotiations, at any time and for any reason. There can be thus no obligation to continue to negotiate until there is a 'proper reason' to withdraw. Accordingly a bare agreement to negotiate has no legal content.

There is no doubt that *Walford* v. *Miles* remains a cornerstone of the formation of contract in English law. For example, Aikens LJ in the *Barbudev* case (2012)[27] acknowledged that *Walford* v. *Miles* is binding authority for the proposition that an agreement to agree (the main contract's terms) is not binding, and it makes no difference that the negotiation agreement is couched as one to negotiate in good faith or reasonably.

---

25 *Ibid.*
26 [1992] 2 AC 128, 138, HL.
27 *Barbudev* v. *Eurocom Cable Management Bulgaria Eood* [2012] EWCA Civ 548; [2012] 2 All ER (Comm) 963, at [46].

The *Barbudev* case (2012)[28] concerned a written arrangement intended to allow a party to become an active investment participant in a company. This was a complex set of arrangements and not a simple purchase of a specified percentage of shares at an agreed price. The court concluded that this was an irredeemably half-baked investment agreement, including a commitment to negotiate all further terms in good faith (the latter was condemned as void on the authority of *Walford* v. *Miles*).

A qualification must be noted in the context of tenders. The Privy Council in *Pratt Contractors Ltd* v. *Transit New Zealand* (2003) acknowledged that there is an implied duty on the part of the invitor to conduct the tender process in good faith[29] (3.49).

However, the Court of Appeal in *MRI Trading AG* v. *Erdenet Mining Corp LLC* (2013)[30] distinguished the situation where an agreement to agree concerns matters around the rim of the core agreement and the latter is already valid, effective and operative. This is the context of an ancillary negotiation agreement, more precisely:

(i) the substance of the main agreement is established and clear; the 'agreement to agree' is thus ancillary to that main agreement and relates to matters not central to that transaction; and

(ii) the parties have demonstrated a clear intention to enter into a binding arrangement, notwithstanding this gap; and

(iii) there has either been extensive performance (as in the *Foley* case, 1934,[31] which is considered at length at 4.16); or

(iv) the transaction forms part of a wider set of arrangements so that it would be commercially inconvenient if this part of the jigsaw were to fail on grounds of uncertainty.

(v) It will also help (*although this is not necessary*) if the parties have specified machinery (on the present facts, arbitration) for filling the gap in the event that the parties fail to agree on the relevant matters.

In *MRI Trading AG* v. *Erdenet Mining Corp LLC* (2013) the court held that there should be an implied term that, if the parties fail to agree, an objective determination based on reasonableness will be imposed by the court or (as on the present facts) by an arbitral tribunal. The Court of Appeal in *MRI Trading AG* v. *Erdenet Mining Corp LLC* (2013) concluded therefore (agreeing with Eder J) that the arbitral tribunal had wrongly decided that the agreement to agree in this context rendered the relevant agreement void for incompleteness.

---

28   *Ibid.*
29   [2003] UKPC 83; [2004] BLR 143; 100 Con LR 29.
30   [2013] EWCA Civ 156; [2013] 1 CLC 423; [2013] 1 Lloyd's Rep 638 (considering *Mamidoil-Jetoil Greek Petroleum Co. Ltd* v. *Okta Crude Oil Refinery (No. 1)* [2001] EWCA Civ 406; [2001] 2 Lloyd's Rep 76, at [69]; and this passage from the *Mamidoil-Jetoil* case was analysed by Chadwick LJ in *BJ Aviation Ltd* v. *Pool Aviation Ltd* [2002] EWCA Civ 163; [2002] 2 P & CR 25, at [18] ff).
31   *Foley* v. *Classique Coaches* [1934] 2 KB 1, CA.

MRI Trading AG v. *Erdenet Mining Corp LLC* (2013) concerned a commercial settlement which envisaged three fresh contracts for the sale of copper concentrates. Only two were fully performed. A dispute arose as to the third. E claimed that the contract was unenforceable because various loose ends were left to be agreed (particular charges, but not the main price, and the shipping schedule). Tomlinson LJ said[32]

> [The third contract] was . . . an integral part of an overall deal pursuant to which both parties had derived benefits, a deal which they had worked through together for over a year without any suggestion that the final part thereof fell into a different and unenforceable category of obligation.

Tomlinson LJ added:[33]

> where the parties had agreed every other aspect of the contract, including quality, specification and price, and where they had stipulated for the arbitration of disputes by a market tribunal, it is almost perverse to attribute to them an intention not to conclude a binding agreement, a fortiori where the agreement was an integral part of a wider overall transaction compromising an earlier dispute.

By contrast, *BJ Aviation Ltd* v. *Pool Aviation Ltd* (2002) demonstrates that an agreement to agree will be invalid if the relevant issue is a condition precedent to the proposed contract, requiring agreement to have been achieved by a specified date (in that case an agreement to negotiate the rent for a new lease); and, if the parties fail to agree, the fixed timetable leaves no opportunity to invoke external machinery to establish such a term by reference to objective criteria.[34]

2.08 *Invalid: Agreement to use best or reasonable endeavours to negotiate the main contract.* As noted above (2.07), the House of Lords in *Walford* v. *Miles* (1992)[35] held that an agreement to negotiate *in good faith* is void for uncertainty. Similarly, English law will not give effect to an undertaking *to use best or reasonable endeavours to reach agreement on the main parts of the proposed deal*, for example, dealings designed to clarify the nature of the subject matter or to fix the price. In *Little* v. *Courage* (1995), Millett LJ explained this approach: 'an undertaking to use one's best endeavours to agree ... is no different from an undertaking to agree, to try to agree, or to negotiate with a view to reaching an agreement; all are equally uncertain and incapable of giving rise to an enforceable obligation.'[36] The Court of Appeal endorsed this statement in *London & Regional Investments Ltd* v. *TBI plc* (2002).[37] (Here English law differs from New York law, as the English Court of Appeal in *AT&T Corporation* v. *Saudi Cable Co.* (2000)[38] noted.)

---

32 [2013] EWCA Civ 156; [2013] 1 CLC 423; [2013] 1 Lloyd's Rep 638, at [18].
33 *Ibid.*, at [21].
34 [2002] EWCA Civ 163; [2002] 2 P & CR 25, at [27], [29], and [32], *per* Chadwick LJ.
35 [1992] 2 AC 128, HL.
36 (1995) 70 P & CR 469, 476, CA; similarly, *Dany Lions Ltd* v. *Bristol Cars Ltd* [2014] EWHC 817 (QB).
37 [2002] EWCA Civ 355, at [39] and [40].
38 [2000] 2 Lloyd's Rep 127, at [3] and [4].

2.09 *Criticism of the* Walford *case.* However, the decision in the *Walford* case has been criticised.[39]

Hoskins[40] contends that an agreement to negotiate in good faith might be legally binding if (a) the parties' agreement discloses an intent to create legal relations and (b)(i) either there are explicit criteria, of requisite certainty, regulating the agreement to negotiate, or (b)(ii) such criteria are implicit (that is, the agreement to negotiate, read in context, supplies such criteria). The courts are unlikely to find element (a) if there are no explicit criteria under (b)(i). The chances of implying criteria under (b)(ii) are slim if the main agreement has not arisen. But, as Hoskins explores at length, it will be much more likely that problems of certainty will be overcome where the negotiation agreement is ancillary to a main agreement which has already taken effect.

As for express agreements to negotiate in good faith, Berg, writing in the *Law Quarterly Review* (2003), has suggested a radically new approach:[41] even where the main contract has not yet been formed, an agreement to negotiate in good faith should validly impose various implied negotiation duties. Berg proposes as follows:

> An undertaking to negotiate 'in good faith' is to be construed as an agreement to renounce purely adversarial negotiation. Subject to the particular factual setting, such an undertaking can be taken to involve: (1) an obligation to commence negotiations and to have some minimum participation in them; compare *Cable & Wireless plc* v. *IBM United Kingdom Ltd* (2002),[42] where the contract required the parties to go through a clearly defined mediation procedure.

However, the objection to Berg's suggested obligation (1) is that this proposal is misleading and Berg has overstated the content of the 'contractual obligation to pursue mediation'. The current law satisfactorily distinguishes (a) a 'no show', that is, an absolute refusal to consider mediation and (b) alleged unreasonable conduct of the mediation process. Complaints of type (b) do not involve contractual wrongdoing, unlike a complaint concerning 'stonewalling' at stage (a), as the *Cable & Wireless* case (2002) (4.22) shows. In that case, Colman J accepted that parties should not proceed to formal litigation if they have agreed that they will first attempt to settle their dispute before a neutral mediator. He ordered a 'stay' of the premature court litigation (such suspension of court proceedings would permit the parties to resort to mediation, as they had agreed; if mediation did not work, the court proceedings would resume: the 'stay' would be lifted). It should be noted, however, that the *Cable & Wireless* case does not *legally require* negotiating parties to meet and to discuss a dispute or to participate in mediation. How

---

39 Lord Steyn, 'Contract Law: Fulfilling the Reasonable Expectations of Honest Men' (1997) 113 LQR 433, 439, educated in the Roman-Dutch system, has suggested that the House of Lords (or now, the Supreme Court) might one day reconsider this point; Lord Neill QC in (1992) 108 LQR 404, 410; H. Kötz, in P. Cane and J. Stapleton (eds.), *The Law of Obligations: Essays in Celebration of John Fleming* (Oxford, 1998), 244, 253 n. 30, cites other literature on this case; H. Hoskins, 'Contractual Obligations to Negotiate in Good Faith: Faithfulness to the Agreed Common Purpose' (2014) 130 LQR 131–59; L. DiMatteo, Q. Zhou, S. Saintier, K. Rowley (eds.), *Commercial Contract Law: Transatlantic Perspectives* (Cambridge, 2014), chapter 9 (by Z. Ollerenshaw).
40 H. Hoskins, cited previous note.
41 (2003) 110 LQR 357.
42 [2002] EWHC 2059; [2002] 2 All ER (Comm) 1041.

would damages be assessed? An injunction to compel such a duty is unthinkable. Furthermore, the English courts will not scrutinise the parties' conduct before a mediator (unless both parties waive the evidential privilege attaching to those negotiations; 4.23).

Berg further proposes that a promise to negotiate in good faith will also impose:

(2) an obligation to have an open mind [during negotiations] in the sense of: (i) a willingness to consider such options for the resolution of the dispute as may be proposed by the other party, and (ii) a willingness to give consideration to putting forward options for the resolution of the dispute;[43]

(3) an obligation not to take advantage, in the course of the negotiations, of the known ignorance of the other party; and

(4) (A) an obligation not to withdraw from the negotiations without first giving a reason and a reasonable opportunity for the other party to respond; (B) not to withdraw giving a reason which is untrue (e.g., 'I have received a higher offer', when none has been received); and (C) not to withdraw giving as the cause something which the withdrawing party knows is extremely unreasonable (in approximately the *Wednesbury* sense),[44] such as the other party's failure to agree to a request which the withdrawing party knows that the other party could not reasonably be expected to have accepted.

The objection to this is that obligation (2) is unacceptably vague; and it is doubtful whether an agreement to impose such an obligation would be commercially attractive. Obligations (3), and (4) (A) and (C), even if contained in an express clause, would unacceptably fetter the process of bargaining and would produce difficult and protracted disputes. Obligation (3) is clearly not English law (3.65 ff). Obligation (4) (B), a duty to refrain from giving a deliberately false reason for quitting a negotiation, is also troublesome. It is a pervasive and innocuous feature of business negotiation that one side will 'gently let down the other' by giving a pretext for not proceeding with the negotiations. To outlaw such 'white lies' and 'face-saving' untruths would be out of step with commercial practice and would commit the law to a naïve approach. Berg's suggestions seem unsuitable for use within the rough-and-tumble of commercial dealings. Nor should it matter that the parties have freely undertaken to 'negotiate in good faith', thus triggering Berg's cascade of obligations. There are practical limitations upon the principle of freedom of contract (1.08). Berg's criteria lie beyond the boundary of practical common sense and provide no satisfactory criteria for adjudication by the courts or arbitrators.

Mills and Loveridge (2011)[45] contend that the courts can and should determine whether the conduct of negotiations has been unreasonable, drawing on the analogy of Jack J's decision in *Carleton* v. *Strutt and Parker* (2008) (see also discussion at 4.23), where a party's position at a mediation was described as 'plainly unrealistic and unreasonable'.[46] In fact Jack J found that both parties had adopted unreasonable positions in the relevant

---

43 Berg adds this reference: *Aiton Australia Pty Ltd* v. *Transfield Pty Ltd* [1999] NSWSC 996, at [147] to [156].
44 Berg is alluding to the principles of judicial review of administrative decisions founded upon *Associated Provincial Picture Houses* v. *Wednesbury Corporation* [1948] 1 KB 223, CA, *per* Lord Greene MR.
45 A. Mills and R. Loveridge, 'The Uncertain Future of *Walford* v. *Miles*' [2011] LMCLQ 528, 541.
46 [2008] EWHC 424 (QB); 118 Con LR 68; [2008] 5 Costs LR 736, at [72] *per* Jack J; noted on this point by J. Sorabji (2008) 27 CJQ 288, 291–2.

mediation. This is an isolated case. It was the first occasion when an English court decided to make a costs adjustment to reflect its conclusion that a party had behaved unreasonably during the conduct of mediation (as distinct from refusal to engage in mediation).

But how usual will this be? Because mediation negotiations are jointly privileged,[47] it will be very unusual for both parties to waive privilege: if only one party wishes to waive privilege, the other party retains privilege. This makes the *Carleton* case a highly unusual instance of the court having the evidential opportunity to lift the lid on events which occurred during the conduct of the mediation. And so the mediation context hardly provides a store of judicial experience of 'unreasonable negotiation'. It is submitted, therefore, that the fact that this has been adjudicated in one first instance case and that the judge felt confident on this occasion to make a costs decision to indicate censure of *both parties* does not indicate that it would be safe and practicable in all pre-formation contexts to scrutinise the conduct of negotiations in order to determine which party was 'in the wrong', or 'dragging his feet', or 'merely going through the motions', etc. As the author has suggested elsewhere, the courts are unlikely to embrace an expansive 'duty to mediate'.[48]

2.10 *Valid: Fixed-term 'lock out' ('negotiation exclusivity')   agreements and negotiation agreements within dispute resolution clauses.* Lord Ackner in *Walford* v. *Miles* (1992) made clear that parties can validly agree for consideration (in other words, for a price or something in return) that one or both will not negotiate with third parties (nor solicit offers, etc.), provided this period of 'exclusivity' is fixed (such as 'for 21 days' as distinct from for a 'reasonable' or 'necessary' period).[49] On this basis, a 'lock out' agreement for two weeks was upheld by the Court of Appeal in *Pitt* v. *PHH Asset Management Ltd* (1994).[50] In *Walford* v. *Miles* (1992) the House of Lords explained that objection to a chronologically vague or open-ended 'exclusivity' commitment is that the courts would need to address whether the lock out or exclusivity agreement had been prematurely disapplied by a party. That would require the court to determine the 'impossible' issue whether a party had failed to negotiate reasonably or in good faith.[51]

In the *Pitt* case (1994)[52] the claimant and a third party were in a 'property race'. The 'lock out' agreement gave the claimant the benefit of a fourteen-day period of exclusive dealing with the defendant. But the defendant breached this commitment by selling the property to a third party because the claimant could not beat the third party's offer. This rival offer had been accepted by the defendant within the period of the 'lock out' agreement. Following *Walford* v. *Miles* (above), the Court of Appeal in the *Pitt* case recognised that a 'lock out' agreement is not uncertain, provided its duration is fixed. The court ordered damages to be assessed for breach of the 'lock

47   On mediation privilege, *Andrews on Civil Processes* (Cambridge, 2013), vol. 2, *Arbitration and Mediation*, 1.128 to 1.135.
48   N. Andrews, 'The Duty to Consider Mediation: Salvaging Value from the European Mediation Directive', in N. Trocker and A. De Luca (eds.), *La Mediazione Civile all Luce della Direttiva 2008/52/CE* (Florence, 2011), 13–34.
49   [1992] 2 AC 128, 139–40, HL.
50   [1994] 1 WLR 327, CA.
51   *Walford* v. *Miles* [1992] 2 AC 128, 140, HL.
52   [1994] 1 WLR 327, CA.

out' agreement.[53] In *Emirates Trading Agency LLC* v. *Prime Mineral Exports Private Ltd* (2014) Teare J upheld a negotiation clause, restricted to a fixed period of four weeks, requiring the parties to conduct 'friendly' negotiations as a prelude to commencing arbitration proceedings.[54]

2.11 *Valid: Agreement to use reasonable or best endeavours to obtain a vital (normally official) permission (planning permission or export licence or third party's consent).* The *Walford* case (1992)[55] and *Little* v. *Courage* (1995)[56] acknowledge as settled law[57] the validity of an agreement to use 'best endeavours', 'all reasonable endeavours' or 'reasonable endeavours' to obtain planning permission, or an export licence, or to procure a third party's consent. Such an undertaking is sufficiently clear and restricted. Its recognition does not fetter the parties' freedom to negotiate. It is an obligation to try to procure a specific external consent necessary for the achievement of the main transaction: in other words, to try to unlock the door controlled by a third party. It is not an absolute commitment, or guarantee of success.

A thesaurus of graduated obligations is emerging. Obligations to exercise '*best* endeavours' or '*all reasonable* endeavours' are more onerous than an undertaking to exercise '*reasonable* endeavours' (although 'all reasonable endeavours' might be similar to 'best endeavours'). As Judge Julian Flaux QC (as he then was) said in the *Rhodia* case (2007):[58] 'An obligation to use *reasonable* endeavours to achieve the aim probably only requires a party to take one reasonable course, not all of them, whereas an obligation to use *best* endeavours probably requires a party to take all the reasonable courses he can.'

Vos J in the 'Chelsea Barracks' case (2010) suggested, first, that 'the obligation to use "all reasonable endeavours" does not always require the obligor to sacrifice his commercial interests.' Secondly, he added: 'In this case, the matter is, however, clearer because the contract itself . . . contains other indications that [the defendant] was not to be required to sacrifice its commercial interests. Indeed the words of clause 7.1 itself make that clear by using the added words "but commercially prudent" in the phrase "all reasonable but commercial prudent endeavours".'[59] And Vos J confirmed that an obligation to use 'all reasonable but commercially prudent endeavours' is 'not equivalent to a "best endeavours" obligation'.[60]

---

53 *Sharma* v. *Simposh Ltd* [2011] EWCA Civ 1383; [2013] Ch 23 (as noted at 19.29) decides that even if an exclusivity agreement is legally invalid, a deposit made to secure such an undertaking will not be recoverable if the payee has honoured the terms of the (invalid) exclusivity agreement.
54 [2014] EWHC 2104 (Comm), notably at [59] to [64], distinguishing *Walford* v. *Miles* [1992] 2 AC 128, 140, HL on the basis that it was not concerned with a negotiation clause incorporated into a dispute resolution clause.
55 [1992] 2 AC 128, at 139–40, HL.
56 (1995) 70 P & CR 469, 476, CA.
57 Other authorities: *P&O Property Holdings Ltd* v. *Norwich Union Life Insurance Society* (1994) 68 P & CR 261, HL; *Phillips Petroleum Co. UK Ltd* v. *Enron Europe Ltd* [1997] CLC 329, CA; *Rae Lambert* v. *HTV Cymru (Wales) Ltd* [1998] FSR 874, CA; and see the cases cited in the next note.
58 *Rhodia International Holdings Ltd* v. *Huntsman International LLC* [2007] EWHC 292 (Comm); [2007] 2 Lloyd's Rep 325, at [33] ff (noted by B. Holland, (2007) 18 *International Company and Commercial Law Review* 349); also examining *Yewbelle Ltd* v. *London Green Developments Ltd* [2006] EWHC 3166 (Ch) (Lewison J), at [118] ff; Lewison J's analysis was considered in the *Yewbelle* case on appeal, [2007] EWCA Civ 475; [2008] 1 P & CR 17, at [29] ff by Lloyd LJ; and these remarks were applied by Vos J in *CPC Group Ltd* v. *Qatari Diar Real Estate Investment Company* [2010] EWHC 1535; [2010] NPC 74, at [249] ff (the 'Chelsea Barracks' case).
59 *CPC Group Ltd* v. *Qatari Diar Real Estate Investment Company* [2010] EWHC 1535; [2010] NPC 74, at [252].
60 *Ibid.*, at [253].

2.12 *Valid: Post-formation or 'ancillary' negotiation agreements.* As Longmore LJ has noted, in reasoned dicta in *Petromec Inc.* v. *Petroleo Brasiliero SA* (2005)[61] that the *Walford* case (1992)[62] is confined to negotiations concerning the main contract (that is, where the main contract has yet to be crystallised following successful agreement). The position is different when the negotiation clause[63] is bolted onto a subsisting main agreement (no such main agreement had arisen in the *Walford* case) and the parties have provided an *objective and clear criterion* to determine whether the obligation has been breached. The following cases make clear the need for an objective criterion, but also illustrate that the courts approach that issue pragmatically and that the whole context must be considered in order to determine whether a reliable criterion has been identified.

> The Court of Appeal in *Didymi Corporation* v. *Atlantic Lines* (1988)[64] upheld a hire variation clause designed to reflect the ship's speed and efficiency. Adjustment should be 'agreed' according to what was 'equitable'. The contract had already lasted for a significant period before the disputed issue arose. Although the *Didymi* decision upholds the word 'equitable' in that particular commercial context (efficiency of a chartered vessel's sailing performance), the same word might not possess sufficient certainty in all other contexts. The case was borderline.
>
> Another borderline case (discussed by Lord Neill QC observed in 1992)[65] is *Queensland Electricity Generating Board* v. *New Hope Collieries* (1989).[66] Here the Privy Council upheld a price variation clause. As Neill (in his journal article) explains:[67]
>
>> The case concerned a 15-year supply contract whereby the Colliery Company agreed to supply coal to the Generating Board. For the first five-year period the contract contained a scale of base prices and elaborate 'escalation' or 'price variation' provisions for adjusting the base prices for changes in the company's costs. For purchases after the first five years the general terms of the agreement were to continue. It was stipulated: 'The base price and provisions for variations in prices . . . shall be agreed by the parties.' There was a comprehensive arbitration clause. The Generating Board contended (*inter alia*) that for the period after the first five years the agreement was uncertain and constituted nothing more than an agreement to agree. The Privy Council rejected this plea.
>
> Three aspects of the *Queensland* case are noteworthy: (i) the negotiation clause applied to a renewal of a commercial contract, which had already run for five years; (ii) the judgment, given by Sir Robin Cooke, emphasises[68] that the arrangement was subject to a widely drafted arbitration

61   [2005] EWCA Civ 891; [2006] 1 Lloyd's Rep 121, at [115] (Longmore LJ acknowledging that these comments are *dicta*); E. McKendrick, 'The Meaning of Good Faith', in *Liber Amicorum Guido Alpa: National Private Law Systems* (London, 2007), 687.

62   [1992] 2 AC 128, at 139–40, HL.

63   *Chitty on Contracts* (31st edn, London, 2012), 2–140 suggests that a court might *imply a term* to negotiate minor details if the main parts of a contract are established and those parts are intended to be binding (citing *Donwin Productions Ltd* v. *EMI Films Ltd*, 9 March 1984 (Peter Pain J); decision not followed in the context of incomplete compromise in *Dalgety Foods Holland BV* v. *Deb-its Ltd* [1994] FSR 125, Nugee QC; and *Donwin* case not cited in *Walford* v. *Miles* [1992] 2 AC 128, HL).

64   [1988] 2 Lloyd's Rep 108, CA; noted F. M. B. Reynolds, (1988) 104 LQR 353.

65   (1992) 108 LQR 405, 407–8.

66   *Queensland Electricity Generating Board* v. *New Hope Collieries* [1989] 1 Lloyd's Rep 205, PC (the court's judgment was given by Sir Robin Cooke; the other judges were Lords Diplock, Fraser, Roskill, and Brightman).

67   *Ibid.*

68   [1989] 1 Lloyd's Rep 205, 210, PC.

clause, so that in default of agreement there was a safety-net; (iii) the Privy Council expressly distinguished between a 'subjective' determination of fairness by the arbitrator (something which would be unacceptably uncertain) and the arbitrator's capacity in this context to reach an 'objectively fair and reasonable' determination, based upon admittedly 'broad' factors.

The Court of Appeal in *Phillips Petroleum Co. (UK) Ltd* v. *Enron (Europe) Ltd* (1999)[69] approved (1) the *Didymi case* (1988) and (2) the *Queensland* case (1989) on the basis that both these decisions turned on the presence of objective criteria (see further 4.09). But on the facts of the *Phillips case*, the Court of Appeal held[70] that the relevant negotiation clause lacked objective criteria, and no criteria could be convincingly or reliably implied. This was a gas supply agreement. The Court of Appeal (reversing Colman J) held that there was not enough certainty to support an obligation to use reasonable endeavours to agree the date for supply of gas. Instead this was an open-ended agreement to agree lacking reliable criteria. The Court of Appeal held that Colman J's first instance decision to fetter this commercial bargaining discretion by prohibiting the purchaser from relying on its own commercial interests (the wholesale price had declined sharply) had involved reading in a restriction for which there was no sensible commercial support.

2.13 *Valid: Post-formation obligation to observe 'utmost good faith'.* In *Berkeley Community Villages Ltd* v. *Pullen* (2007), Morgan J held that *once a contract has been formed*, the law will recognise as valid a clause which *expressly imposes a duty of 'utmost good faith'* on the parties *during performance.*[71] The notion of good faith is not uncertain if it is linked to (1) a *performance* obligation, as distinct from (2) a *negotiation* obligation. If good faith is linked to (1), it will impose a positive duty to take action consistent with the achievement of the contract's main purpose; and it will impose a negative duty to refrain from conduct which will stultify that purpose (see the further discussion of the 'Chelsea Barracks' case (2010) below).

In the *Berkeley Community Villages* case (2007) landowner P and consultant B had agreed to develop P's property. B was to obtain planning permission. B would then gain a commission. B incurred considerable sums attempting to gain this planning permission (these were not steps taken at its own risk; the whole matter was *not* 'subject to contract'; compare the *Cobbe* case (2008), discussed at 5.46). Before this permission had been formally obtained, P proposed to sell part of the land to a third party. That would deprive B of his right to commission. One of the relevant clauses (cl 33) in this development contract stated: 'the parties will act with the utmost good faith towards one another and will act reasonably and prudently at all times.' Morgan J held that this clause validly imposed 'on the Defendants a contractual obligation to observe reasonable commercial standards of fair dealing and . . . faithfulness to the agreed common purpose'[72] and that the proposed sale would breach that duty.[73] He granted an injunction to

---

69 [1996] EWCA Civ 693; [1997] CLC 329, 343–4, *per* Potter LJ, on *Didymi* and at 330 on the *Queensland* case. Similarly, Toulson LJ in *BBC Worldwide Ltd* v. *Bee Load Ltd* [2007] EWHC 134 (Comm), at [93] and [95].
70 Kennedy and Potter LJJ; Sir John Balcombe dissenting.
71 [2007] EWHC 1330 (Ch); [2007] NPC 71, Morgan J.
72 *Ibid.*, at [97].
73 *Ibid.*, at [110].

prevent P from selling the land to a third party until B had gained the right to a commission (that is, after planning permission had been finalised in favour of P).

In the 'Chelsea Barracks' case (2010),[74] Vos J, after considering the *Berkeley Homes* case (2007) and related decisions, noted that the obligation in the present case was that the parties to a development agreement 'shall both act in the utmost good faith towards each other'. Vos J held[75] that this imposed a duty 'to adhere to the spirit of the contract, which was to seek to obtain planning consent for the maximum Developable Area in the shortest possible time, and to observe reasonable commercial standards of fair dealing, and to be faithful to the agreed common purpose, and to act consistently with the justified expectations of the parties'. And he added: 'I do not need, it seems to me, to decide whether this obligation could *only* be broken if [the parties] acted in bad faith, but it might be hard to understand . . . how, without bad faith, there can be a breach of a "duty of good faith, utmost or otherwise".'

QUESTIONS

(1) In the absence of a valid contract, what type of relief is available to a party who has performed work, or supplied goods, at the other's request? How is the relief quantified?

(2) When is a 'lock out' or 'exclusivity' agreement binding?

(3) Why is an agreement to negotiate in good faith or reasonably not binding (see also (6) below)?

(4) Should the law adopt the suggestions made by Berg concerning an agreement to bargain in good faith (A. Berg, 'Promises to Negotiate in Good Faith' (2003) 110 LQR 357–63)?

(5) An agreement to use 'best endeavours', 'all reasonable endeavours' or 'reasonable endeavours' to procure planning permission or an export licence is binding on the relevant party. Why is this? What do these obligations entail?

(6) If the main contract is valid and certain, might an ancillary provision create a binding obligation to negotiate variations of the contract (or extension or renewal of the contract) in good faith, or reasonably, etc.?

(7) For completeness, refer also to questions (1) to (5) at the end of Chapter 4, concerning general issues of uncertainty.

Selected further reading

S. Ball, 'Work Carried Out in Pursuance of Letters of Intent – Contract or Restitution?' (1983) 99 LQR 572, especially 576–9, 581–2

A. Berg, 'Promises to Negotiate in Good Faith' (2003) 110 LQR 357–63

H. Hoskins, 'Contractual Obligations to Negotiate in Good Faith: Faithfulness to the Agreed Common Purpose' (2014) 130 LQR 131

A. Mills and R. Loveridge, 'The Uncertain Future of *Walford v. Miles*' [2011] LMCLQ 528

---

74   *CPC Group Ltd* v. *Qatari Diar Real Estate Investment Company* [2010] EWHC 1535; [2010] NPC 74, at [237] ff.
75   *Ibid.*, at [246].

Chapter contents

3

Offer and acceptance

1. INTRODUCTION

3.01 Summary of main points

This chapter concerns the process of reaching a consensus.[1] Here the analysis is dominated by 'offer and acceptance'. The main points of discussion will be:

The process of offer and acceptance

(1) In many situations, especially when the parties are in correspondence, English law requires an agreement to result from acceptance of an offer; however, it is admitted that some situations produce a consensus without such a clear-cut form of dealing.

(2) Offers should be distinguished from a mere 'invitation to treat'; such an invitation is an opportunity for further dealings, but the invitor is not exposed to having his goods (or services etc.) immediately accepted.

(3) Goods on display in shops are not available to be immediately accepted; and most advertisements for goods or services are regarded as 'invitations to treat'.

(4) An offeree can make a counter-offer; if this is rejected, and the original offer is not reaffirmed, the offeree cannot accept the original offer.

(5) In the absence of a binding option, the offeree cannot validly accept an offer which he knows to have been revoked or which has lapsed.

(6) An offer can be directly revoked if the offeror successfully communicates cancellation of the offer; or the offer can be indirectly revoked if the offeree discovers that events make (objectively) clear that the offer is no longer open to acceptance by him. And an offer will lapse after a specified period or, in the absence of a specific deadline, after the effluxion of a reasonable period.

---

1 On the nineteenth-century history of this topic, see M. Lobban, in W. Cornish, J. S. Anderson, R. Cocks, M. Lobban, P. Polden and K. Smith, *The Oxford History of the Laws of England*, vol. XII, *1820–1914: Private Law* (Oxford, 2010), 329 ff.

(7) If it is reasonable to send an acceptance by post, and provided the offeror has not expressly required receipt of the acceptance, the English 'postal rule' fixes a valid agreement at the moment of posting; when the postal rule applies, acceptance is complete upon posting, even if the letter is delayed by the postal service (for reasons other than the offeree's fault) and even if the letter is lost in the post; however, it appears that the postal rule will not apply to circumstances where it would involve 'manifest inconvenience' or 'absurdity'; this restriction might be interpreted to apply whenever a deadline for response has been specified; for example, notification of the intention to exercise an option by a specified date.

(8) English law applies strictly the offer and acceptance analysis even if negotiations involve competing standard terms; the 'battle of forms' is won by the party whose offer is eventually accepted by the opponent; other approaches to this problem might be suggested, but these have not been adopted in England.

Particular contexts

(9) An 'invitor' requesting tenders does not normally commit himself to award a tender, but he must at least consider valid tenders, disregard invalid tenders, refrain from making a final decision before a specified deadline has passed and generally adhere to the specified terms of his tendering process.

(10) If there is no reserve price (or where the bid exceeds the reserve price), an auctioneer who refuses to 'knock down' in favour of the highest bidder is in breach of a collateral contract (even though there is no contract of sale between the owner and the bidder).

(11) An offeror can commit himself to accept the highest or best bid, for example, by issuing invitations for interested persons to send 'sealed bids' to purchase property; each bid must normally be for a fixed and free-standing amount; the law invalidates a 'referential bid' designed to top the other's (as yet unascertained) fixed bid by a specified sum (at any rate if a referential bid, subject to an overall financial 'cap', has not been expressly requested from each competitor).

Unilateral contracts

(12) In the case of a unilateral contract, it is normal to regard the offeror as having 'waived the need for express acceptance'; the promisor becomes fully obliged to honour his commitment if the requested act has been fully performed; however, in some situations (but not in all), protection of the offeree's reliance and expectations requires that the offeror should lose his power to revoke the offer pending complete performance by the offeree; the better view is that such protection, where it is appropriate, is based on the implication of a collateral contract.

The objective principle

(13) The parties' language and conduct must be assessed according to their apparent and reasonable meaning and appearance; this is the 'objective principle of consensus'.

(14) If party B knows that party A has made an apparent offer in error, or that A has presented the terms of the offer erroneously (for example, the price), B cannot take advantage of A's error; similarly, short of proof of actual knowledge, it might be enough that B ought reasonably to have realised that A has made such an error; however, where B knows that A is mistaken concerning the quality of the relevant subject matter, or its unwarranted value, the law does not

object to B taking advantage of A's error, even though this might be regarded as morally 'shabby'; however, in this last situation, it is different if B knows that A believes that there is a tacit warranty that the subject matter should possess the relevant quality or value (the rule in *Smith* v. *Hughes*, 1871); and it is possibly the law that A can then insist on enforcing the bargain on A's supposed terms.

2. NATURE OF AN OFFER

3.02 An offer[2] is a clear expression of an unequivocal willingness to be bound upon the offeree's acceptance. Whether a communication contains an offer is a matter for objective determination (on the objective principle, see 1.10 and 3.55), taking into account all the circumstances within which the alleged offeree receives the putative offer (on this, see discussion of the *Crest* case, 2010, Court of Appeal, in this paragraph, below). An offer can be made to an ascertained individual, to two or more persons, or even to the world at large. Offers must be contrasted with preliminary communications not intended to be open to acceptance, namely 'invitations to treat', on which see 3.03. Only an intended offeree can accept an offer, and not an unauthorised busybody.[3] Normally it will be safe to assume that the word 'offer' can be taken at face value. But sometimes the word 'offer' is used inaccurately in casual language, even in commercial contexts,[4] when in fact the relevant communication is merely a preliminary statement not intended to create the possibility of immediate acceptance.

> The Court of Appeal in *Crest Nicholson (Londinium) Limited* v. *Akaria Investments Ltd* (2010)[5] made clear that the supposed offeree (Y) must have objective and reasonable evidence that the other party (X) is making a sufficiently clear offer which expressly or impliedly invites acceptance. Y will fail if Y knows (or reasonably ought to have known) that X had become manifestly confused or mistaken, in ways inconsistent with the making of a true offer. Sir John Chadwick said: 'the correct approach is to ask whether a person in the position of B (having the knowledge of the relevant circumstances which B had), acting reasonably, would understand that A was making a proposal to which he intended to be bound in the event of an unequivocal acceptance.'[6]

---

2 M. Furmston and G. J. Tolhurst, *Contract Formation: Law and Practice* (Oxford, 2010), chapter 2; J. Cartwright, *Formation and Variation of Contracts; The Agreement, Formalities, Consideration and Promissory Estoppel* (London, 2014). On the test for ascertaining whether a communication discloses an offer, *Crest Nicholson* v. *Akaria* [2010] EWCA Civ 1331, at [25].

3 *Boulton* v. *Jones* (1857) 27 LJ Ex 117.

4 E.g., *Datec Electronics Holdings Ltd* v. *United Parcels Services Ltd* [2007] UKHL 23; [2007] 1 WLR 1325; *Chitty* (31st edn, London, 2012), 2–009.

5 [2010] EWCA Civ 1331, at [25], *per* Sir John Chadwick; also citing *Harvey* v. *Facey* [1893] AC 552, PC: and see the statement of principles in *Schuldenfrei* v. *Hilton (Inspector of Taxes)* [1999] STC 821; 72 TC 167; [1999] BTC 310; *Times*, August 12, 1999, CA, at [44], *per* Jonathan Parker LJ (amplified at [46], [48], and [49]) (approved by Mummery LJ in *Customs & Excise* v. *DFS Furniture* [2002] EWCA Civ 1708; [2003] STC 1, at [42]).

6 *Ibid.*

3.03 *Invitations to treat (1): advertisements.* The general rule is that an advertisement of goods or services is prima facie an 'invitation to treat' and *not an offer*. This is supported by various decisions, notably *Grainger & Sons* v. *Gough* (1896) and *Partridge* v. *Crittenden* (1968).[7] Therefore, the advertiser is not subject to immediate demands for acceptance. He can decide whether to accept the responding public's requests for delivery. The rationale for this presumption is that the advertiser might otherwise be exposed to a torrent of demands. As Lord Herschell said in the *Grainger* case (1896): 'the merchant might find himself involved in any number of contractual obligations to supply [goods] of a particular description which he would be quite unable to carry out, his stock … being necessarily limited.'[8] However, it would be easy to imply the qualification that the offer applies 'while stocks last'. Therefore, a better approach would be to treat *a clear-cut expression of willingness to be bound*, even if contained in an advertisement, as open to acceptance, either where there is only one item, on the implicit basis 'first come, first served', or where a series of sales is contemplated, on the implicit basis 'while stocks last'.

The restrictive approach of English law to this matter can be contrasted with a leading decision in the USA, *Lefkowitz* v. *Great Minneapolis Surplus Stores* (1957), where a *clear-cut* advertisement of (non-hazardous) goods at a store has been held to be capable of acceptance, the store-owner having left no further opportunity to quibble. A newspaper advertisement stated that the defendant store was willing to sell a fur stole 'worth $139.50 for $1.00, first come, first served'. It was held that this left nothing for further negotiation. The defendant's refusal to sell to the claimant was a breach of contract, and the store was liable for damages to compensate for the claimant's loss of bargain, $138.50. However, other items were not subject to the same analysis because their real value had not been clearly disclosed in the advertisement: '3 brand new coats worth up to $100'.[9]

Consumer protection law prohibits misleading statements or omissions within advertisements.[10] And the European Court of Justice in the *Trento Svilippo srl* case (2013) made clear that it would be a breach of European consumer protection law if a person responded to an advertised special deal by entering a shop but was denied the relevant product on those advertised terms.[11] An Italian supermarket was justifiably fined for such misleading advertising. Discounted laptops were not available to the consumer at the relevant shop during the specified discount period. It should be noted that this case is concerned with criminal sanctions for breach of European consumer protection. The case does not stand for the proposition that in English law an advertisement is other than an invitation to treat. As noted above, the general rule is that an advertisement concerning a product or service is not an offer.

---

7 *Grainger & Sons* v. *Gough* [1896] AC 325, HL; *Partridge* v. *Crittenden* [1968] 1 WLR 1204, Divisional Court.
8 *Grainger & Sons* v. *Gough* [1896] AC 325, 334, HL.
9 86 NW 2d 689 (1957) (Sup Court of Minnesota).
10 Consumer Protection from Unfair Trading Regulations 2008/1277, Part 2, prohibits misleading statements or omissions within advertisements directed at consumers.
11 *Trento Svilippo srl* v. *Autorita Garante della Concorrenza e del Mercato* (Case C-281/12) [2014] 1 WLR 890, ECJ.

Treitel also suggests that (in England) a supplier's list of goods sent *on request* to a possible customer might be treated as a definitive set of offers, because the supplier would be implying that he has adequate supplies.[12]

As for *unilateral contracts, Carlill* v. *Carbolic Smoke Ball Co.* (1893)[13] (3.43) shows that an advertisement containing an unequivocal offer of a reward can be construed as a true offer, not a mere invitation to treat, provided also that there is an intent to create legal relations (generally on that last topic, Chapter 6). The advertisement in that context is intended to spur readers into action. In law it is intended to create a unilateral contract. There can be only one, or at least a limited number of, successful offerees. No haggling is contemplated.

3.04 *Invitations to treat (2): goods on display.*[14] The rule is that goods displayed in a shop are not available for immediate acceptance. Such a display is regarded as an 'invitation to treat', that is, a preliminary stage without the possibility of immediate binding acceptance. The customer cannot immediately accept. An offer is made by the customer when she takes the goods to the cash desk. The proprietor and staff can refuse to accept that offer even for quite capricious or odd reasons, for example, membership of the wrong university (or college), or support for the wrong football team (but it would be legally unacceptable to do so on grounds of gender,[15] sexual orientation,[16] racial group[17] or disability[18]). Indeed, in some situations, it will be an offence for the proprietor to sell controlled or prohibited substances: persons under age wishing to purchase alcohol,[19] tobacco (and cigarette papers),[20] fireworks,[21] gunpowder,[22] knives and axes;[23] adults wishing to buy methylated spirits for consumption,[24] poisons (and various glues),[25] flick knives,[26] machine guns, and mortar-launchers and other missile-launchers.[27]

---

12 *Treitel* (13th edn, London, 2011), 2–011 n. 60.

13 [1893] 1 QB 256, CA.

14 *Pharmaceutical Society of Great Britain* v. *Boots etc. Ltd* [1953] 1 QB 401, CA; see also *Fisher* v. *Bell* [1961] 1 QB 394, Divisional Court (on which, R. Munday '*Fisher* v. *Bell* Revisited: Misjudging the Legislative Craft' [2013] CLJ 50).

15 Section 6(1)(c) of the Sex Discrimination Act 1975.

16 Cf (not decided in the context of shopping for goods), *Black* v. *Wilkinson* [2013] EWCA Civ 820; [2013] 1 WLR 2490, applying the Equality Act (Sexual Orientation) Regulations 2007(SI 2007/1263), Reg 4(2)(b) (bed and breakfast no discrimination by reference to sexual orientation of guests, notwithstanding religious convictions of proprietor of premises).

17 Sections 4(1)(c), 17, 20 and 21 of the Race Relations Act 1976; cf *Timothy* v. *Simpson* (1834) 6 C & P 499; 172 ER 1337; (1835) 1 CM & R 757; 149 ER 1285 (shopkeeper's anti-semitic refusal to serve a Jew at listed price; attempt to raise ticketed price on the spot; altercation; affray; arrest; allegation of false imprisonment).

18 Disability Discrimination Act 2005; Disability Discrimination Act (Amendment) Regulations 2003 (SI 2003 No. 1673).

19 Section 146 of the Licensing Act 2006.

20 Section 7 of the Children and Young Persons Act 1933.

21 Section 3 of the Fireworks Act 2003; and the Pyrotechnic Articles (Safety) Regulations 2010/1554.

22 Section 31 of the Explosives Act 1875.

23 Section 6 of the Offensive Weapons Act 1996 (sale to under-16-year-olds).

24 Section 80 of the Alcoholic Liquor Duties Act 1979.

25 Poisons Rules 1982 (SI 1982 No. 218); Poisons List (Amendment) Order 1992/2292.

26 Section 1 of the Restriction of Offensive Weapons Act 1959 (sale to anyone).

27 Section 5 of the Firearms Act 1968; for lesser guns, see the controls within section 3 of the Firearms Act 1968 (amended by section 31 of the Violent Crime Reduction Act 2006).

3. THE PROCESS OF OFFER AND ACCEPTANCE IN GENERAL

3.05 A contract is normally formed by the exchange of an offer and acceptance[28] and, usually, only between two parties. The House of Lords in *Gibson* v. *Manchester City Council* (1979) reaffirmed the need to apply the analysis of offer and acceptance in negotiations by sequential correspondence, notably regarding the sale of land[29] (rejecting the majority decision in the Court of Appeal, Lane LJ dissenting,[30] where Lord Denning MR had heretically suggested that offer and acceptance analysis was too rigid and out of date).

> On the facts of the *Gibson* case (1979), the council decided to resile from proposals to sell a council house to the appellant, because the incoming Labour administration had decided to stop selling off its 'housing stock'. This was despite the fact that the price for the proposed sale had been fixed and the council had earlier assumed that the sale would proceed. The House of Lords held that the parties had yet to achieve a final agreement on the proposed purchase by a tenant of the freehold of a council house.[31] Reaffirming the 'conventional analysis' of offer and acceptance in such a context, Lord Diplock said in the *Gibson* case (1979):[32]
>
>> [T]here may be certain types of contract, though I think they are exceptional, which do not fit easily into the normal analysis of a contract as being constituted by offer and acceptance; but a contract alleged to have been made by an exchange of correspondence between the parties in which the successive communications other than the first are in reply to one another, is not one of these.

3.06 However, there will not always be a readily identifiable exchange of articulated offer and acceptance.[33] Instead, occasionally the courts must find consensus more flexibly, having regard to the offeree's conduct, or even a combination of conduct by both parties.[34] (For a neat example of acceptance by conduct, see 3.19 below on *Nissan UK Ltd* v. *Nissan Motor Manufacturing (UK) Ltd*, 1994.[35]

---

28   M. Furmston and G. J. Tolhurst, *Contract Formation: Law and Practice* (Oxford, 2010), chapters 2 to 4.
29   [1979] 1 WLR 294, HL; objective scrutiny is required, e.g., *Liberty Mercian Ltd* v. *Cuddy Civil Engineering Ltd* [2013] EWHC 2688 (TCC); [2014] 1 All ER (Comm) 761, at [53] to [56], Ramsey J; *Glencore Energy Ltd* v. *Cirrus Oli Services Ltd* [2014] EWHC (Comm) 87, at [57] to [68], Cooke J; *Proton Energy Group SA* v. *Orlen Liuteva* [2013] EWHC 2872 (Comm); [2014] 1 All ER (Comm) 972; [2014] 1 Lloyd's Rep 100, at [39], Judge Mackie QC.
30   [1978] 1 WLR 520, CA (Geoffrey Lane LJ dissenting).
31   *Storer* v. *Manchester City Council* [1974] 1 WLR 1403, CA, the sister case, which went the other way.
32   [1979] 1 WLR 294, 296–7, HL; *Wilkie* v. *London Passenger Transport Board* [1947] 1 All ER 258, 259, CA, *per* Lord Greene MR: a contract between the bus owner and passenger would not arise until a passenger had stood fully on its platform (dictum).
33   *New Zealand Shipping Co. Ltd* v. *AM Satterthwaite & Co. Ltd* (*'The Eurymedon'*) [1975] AC 154, 167, PC; *Trentham (Percy) Ltd* v. *Archital Luxfer* [1993] 1 Lloyd's Rep 25, 27, CA; see Lord Clarke's summary of Steyn LJ's remarks in *RTS Flexible Systems Ltd* v. *Molkerei Alois Müller GmbH* [2010] UKSC 14; [2010] 1 WLR 753, at [47], notably the statement: 'Contracts may come into existence, not as a result of offer and acceptance, but during and as a result of performance'; *Maple Leaf Macro Volatility Master Fund* v. *Rouvroy* [2009] EWHC 257 (Comm); [2009] 1 Lloyd's Rep 475, at [242], *per* Andrew Smith J (affirmed on appeal, but without discussion of this point, [2009] EWCA Civ 1334) (see also *Clarke* v. *Dunraven* (*'The Satanita'*) [1897] AC 59, HL).
34   Also problematic is the context of multilateral contracts: *'The Satanita'* [1897] AC 59, 63, HL; *Re Recher* [1972] Ch 526, *per* Brightman J (unincorporated association; multi-party contractual matrix).
35   Court of Appeal December 1994, unreported (the case was contested by two leading counsel, Gordon Pollock QC and Lord Grabiner QC).

3.07 *Cross-offers. Tinn* v. *Hoffman & Co.* (1873) decides that cross-offers indicate a bare coincidence of minds, but not a binding contract. This is because a simultaneous expression of interest from both sides will not disclose a sequential offer *and acceptance*; that is, there will have been no exchange of proposal and acceptance.[36]

> In this case, Grove J observed that if X were to send Y an offer by letter, and coincidentally Y then sent an identical offer to X but X made a speedier communication cancelling his offer, it would become troublesome if the posting of the identical offers were regarded as having already created a contract.

3.08 *Acceptance: need for awareness of offer.* Three propositions arise here: (1) the offeree must have become aware of the offer (this is supported by *Gibbons* v. *Proctor*, 1891);[37] (2) and have remembered it (as illustrated by *R* v. *Clarke* (1927), a decision of the High Court of Australia);[38] but (3) he need not be motivated to act solely on the basis of this offer (as decided in *Williams* v. *Carwardine* (1833), for the ghoulish facts of which, see below).[39]

> Proposition (1) can have a bearing on a person's capacity to comply with the criminal law's requirement that a car should be validly insured when driven on the public highway. In *Taylor* v. *Allon* (1966), a person drove his car on the public highway between expiry of the old insurance cover and commencement of the proposed new cover. He had been offered temporary insurance cover, without having explicitly accepted this offer. The Divisional Court held that the driver was covered only if he 'knew of the temporary cover and he had taken out his car in reliance on it'.[40]
>
> As for point (3), in *Williams* v. *Carwardine* (1833)[41] a dying woman gave information entitling her to a reward – of which she was aware. She did so primarily to increase her chances 'of going to Heaven'. The offeror said that the offeree's motivation had been her sense that she owed a moral or spiritual duty to supply this information. But the court held that this did not matter. Even if she had been actuated by higher obligations, factually she had satisfied the offer by providing the information and she had been aware of the offer. And so her estate was entitled to the promised sum.

36 (1873) 29 LT 271 (Court of Exchequer Chamber: note Hoynman J's dissent).
37 (1891) 64 LT 594; 55 JP 616; *Treitel* (13th edn, London, 2011), 2–048; A. H. Hudson, 'Gibbons v. Proctor Revisited' (1968) 84 LQR 503; P. Mitchell and J. Phillips, 'The Contractual Nexus: Is Reliance Essential?' (2002) 22 OJLS 115; cf the *New Zealand Shipping* case, [1975] AC 154, PC, in the context of third parties and exclusion clauses, at 7.50.
38 (1927) 40 CLR 227 (High Court of Australia).
39 (1833) 4 B & Ad 621; 110 ER 590; 5 C & P 566; 172 ER 1104; 1 Nev & M (KB) 418; 2 LJKB 101; P. Mitchell and J. Phillips, 'The Contractual Nexus: Is Reliance Essential?' (2002) 22 OJLS 115.
40 [1966] 1 QB 304, 309, Divisional Court, *per* Lord Parker CJ.
41 (1833) 4 B & Ad 621; 110 ER 590; 5 C & P 566; 172 ER 1104; 1 Nev & M (KB) 418; 2 LJKB 101; P. Mitchell and J. Phillips, 'The Contractual Nexus: Is Reliance Essential?' (2002) 22 OJLS 115.

3.09 *Notification and prescribed modes of acceptance.* In this paragraph we will consider (1) the general requirement that acceptances should be successfully notified to the offeror and (2) stipulations prescribing that acceptance should be by a particular 'prescribed' method.

Notification. As for (1), normally, the acceptance must come to the offeror's attention. In the following passage in *Entores Ltd* v. *Miles Far East Corporation* (1955),[42] Denning LJ distinguished, on the one hand, communications by telex or telephone (and he would now be bound to add, by e-mail) which are (virtually) *instantaneous* modes of communicating acceptance and, on the other hand, slow-acting communication via the mail system ('the post', or 'Royal Mail').[43] He explained that contracts made orally, or by telephone, and nowadays by e-mail, involve communications which are ' virtually instantaneous', and that in such a context a 'contract is only complete when the acceptance is received by the offeror: and the contract is made at the place where the acceptance is received'. An offeror might realise that the offer has not been successfully accepted, or the offeree might realise that the attempted acceptance has not been successfully received or heard. Denning LJ illustrated this:

> Suppose, for instance, that I make an offer to a man by telephone and, in the middle of his reply, the line goes 'dead' so that I do not hear his words of acceptance. There is no contract at that moment. The other man may not know the precise moment when the line failed. But he will know that the telephone conversation was abruptly broken off: because people usually say something to signify the end of the conversation. If he wishes to make a contract, he must therefore get through again so as to make sure that I heard.

However, the general requirement that the offeror must receive notification of acceptance will not apply if the offeror has expressly or impliedly waived the need for actual communication.[44] Such waiver occurs: (i) where the postal acceptance is *appropriately employed* (3.26 to 3.27) but the letter is lost in the post without the acceptor's fault); or (ii) in respect of unilateral contracts, in situation (ii) the offeree need not first tell the offeror of the offeree's wish to 'accept' the terms of a unilateral contract, for example, the offer of a reward for information, because here the offeror is normally *deemed* to have waived the requirement of notice (3.43); and it is enough that a person satisfies the relevant condition (for example, the return of a lost object).

Prescribed method of acceptance. Where the offeror stipulates that acceptance must occur using a prescribed mode, the general rule is that the offeror is not bound (even if

---

42 [1955] 2 QB 327, 332–4, CA.
43 *Ibid.*
44 *Manchester Diocesan Council for Education* v. *Commercial & General Investments Ltd* [1970] 1 WLR 241, 245–6, *per* Buckley J: 'If an offeror stipulates by the terms of his offer that it may, or that it shall, be accepted in a particular manner a contract results as soon as the offeree does the stipulated act, whether it has come to the notice of the offeror or not. In such a case the offeror conditionally waives either expressly or by implication the normal requirement that acceptance must be communicated to the offeror to conclude a contract.'

that non-compliant communication reaches the offeree).[45] However, the offeree's non-compliance makes no difference (and instead a contract arises) if: (i) the non-compliant mode of acceptance is as good as, or even better than, the prescribed method (for example, where the offeror stated that acceptance must be 'by ordinary post' but the offeree takes the additional precaution of using registered post);[46] or (ii) the prescription was inserted for the offeree's benefit and hence the requirement is one which, in fairness, he can unilaterally waive.[47]

3.10 *Timing of acceptance: communications (other than by post) to places of work. Brinkibon* v. *Stahag Stahl* (1983) decides that a non-postal acceptance (telex, e-mail, fax, hand delivery, and perhaps voice mail or voice message) received in normal working hours is deemed to be received straightaway, even if the relevant communication is not immediately read (or played back).[48] Lord Fraser said in the *Brinkibon* case:[49] 'once the message has been received on the offeror's telex machine, it is not unreasonable to treat it as delivered to the principal offeror, because it is his responsibility to arrange for prompt handling of messages within his own office.'

If a non-postal acceptance (telex, e-mail, fax, hand delivery, and perhaps voice mail or voice message) reaches the offeror outside that party's business hours, acceptance occurs when business hours recommence on the next working day, at the location where the offeror is situated (probably 'normal' working days and 'normal' working hours): *Schelde Delta Shipping BV* v. *Astarte Shipping BV ('The Pamela')* (1995) (also known as *Mondial Shipping & Chartering BV* v. *Astarte Shipping Ltd*).[50]

The *Mondial* case itself concerned a ship-owner's contractual right to withdraw a vessel for non-payment by the charterer, and the issue was when the owner's notice of default, sent by telex, for non-payment had been received by the charterer. But the case illuminates the cognate issue of offer and acceptance. The owner's telex arrived Friday at 23.41 hours, that is, not during the charterer's business hours (of course, some businesses might be run on a 24-hour basis). The charterer's office did not open again until 09.00 hours on Monday. Gatehouse J held that the time when the recipient's office reopened for business was the moment of receipt of this notice:[51]

> If the telex is sent in ordinary business hours, the time of receipt is the same as the time of despatch because it is not open to the charterer to contend that it did not in fact then come to his attention (see '*The Brimnes*' [1975] QB 929, CA).

3.11 *Acceptance by fax*: As for faxes, Colman J said in *JSC Zestafoni G Nikoladze Ferroalloy Plant* v. *Ronly Holdings Ltd* (2004):[52]

45 *Ibid.*, at 246, *per* Buckley J.
46 *Ibid.*, and citing *Tinn* v. *Hoffman & Co* (1873) 29 LT 271, 274, *per* Honeyman J: where acceptance was requested by return of post, 'That does not mean exclusively a reply by letter by return of post, but you may reply by telegram or by verbal message or by any means not later than a letter written by return of post.'
47 246, *per* Buckley J.
48 [1983] 2 AC 34, HL.
49 [1983] 2 AC 34, 43, HL.
50 [1995] 2 Lloyd's Rep 249; [1995] CLC 1011, Gatehouse J.
51 [1995] 2 Lloyd's Rep 249, 252.
52 [2004] EWHC 245 (Comm); [2004] 2 Lloyd's Rep 335, at [75].

A fax is a form of instantaneous communication: if a message has not been received, the sender is informed by his machine. Most machines also indicate to the sender whether the message has been effectively as distinct from only partly received. Accordingly, by analogy with telegrams and telex messages (see *Entores Ltd* v. *Miles Far East Corporation* (1955),[53] as approved by the House of Lords in *Brinkibon Ltd* v. *Stahag Stahl und Stahlwarenhandelsgesellschaft mbh* (1982),[54] the agreement to appoint [X] as sole arbitrator was made when on 30 May the fax was received in England. That was the place where the contract was made.

3.12 *Acceptance by e-mail.*[55] E-mail is also classified as 'virtually instantaneous', as *Bernuth Lines Ltd* v. *High Seas Shipping Ltd ('The Eastern Navigator')* (2005) shows (the case concerned the effectiveness of e-mailed notice of an arbitration reference). In that case, Christopher Clarke J noted that technology will sometimes make clear that the e-mail has not found its target:[56]

> There is no reason why ... delivery of a document by e-mail ... should be regarded as essentially different from communication by post, fax or telex. That is not to say that clicking on the 'send' icon automatically amounts to good service. The e-mail must, of course, be despatched to what is, in fact, the e-mail address of the intended recipient. It must not be rejected by the system.

> In the *Bernuth* case, notice of commencement of arbitral proceedings was held to have been effective when it had been sent by e-mail, even though the recipient chose to ignore it, regarding the communications as 'junk' mail.[57] It was also held that the recipient's e-address had been held out to the world as an effective address and so it was not possible to contend that service of the relevant communication had to be sent to an address specifically nominated by the recipient for this purpose.[58]

When dealing with e-mailed offer and acceptance, it appears that the courts will apply the analogy of the rules established in *Brinkibon* v. *Stahag Stahl* (1983)[59] and *Schelde Delta Shipping BV* v. *Astarte Shipping BV ('The Pamela')* (1995) (also known as *Mondial Shipping & Chartering BV* v. *Astarte Shipping Ltd*)[60] (both of which were examined above, at 3.10). The following propositions will apply:

(a) non-postal communications received in normal working hours are deemed to be received straightaway, provided the communication is available to be read by the receiving party;

53 [1955] 2 QB 327, CA.
54 [1982] 1 Lloyd's Rep 217, HL.
55 S. Hill, 'Flogging a Dead Horse – The Postal Acceptance Rule and Email' (2001) 17 JCL 151.
56 [2005] EWHC 3020 (Comm); [2006] 1 All ER (Comm) 359; [2006] 1 Lloyd's Rep 537, at [28] to [35], *per* Christopher Clarke J.
57 [2006] 1 Lloyd's Rep 537, at [34].
58 *Ibid.*, at [35].
59 [1983] 2 AC 34, HL.
60 [1995] 2 Lloyd's Rep 249; [1995] CLC 1011, Gatehouse J.

(b) if a non-postal communication is received during non-business hours, the moment of receipt will be postponed until recommencement of the receiving party's normal working hours. And so notification of an e-mailed acceptance occurs at the moment of receipt if that falls within the recipient's normal office hours; otherwise when the recipient's office reopens for normal business.[61]

To make this clear, it will be prudent for the offeror to state that an e-mailed acceptance will only occur if the e-mail (1) reaches the offeror's inbox (2) during the offeror's normal working hours.

> Another position, presented by Donal Nolan, is that the e-mailed acceptance should take effect as soon as the e-mail becomes accessible to the offeror (on his server or capable of being downloaded), and this rule should apply on a '24/7' basis, regardless of the offeror's ordinary business hours.[62] This would create a commercial nightmare. Why should offerors be continuously subject to e-mailed acceptance, even outside normal working hours?

3.13 *Loose-end: Communications sent to non-business addresses.* Where the postal rule does not apply (see 3.21 ff), what should be the position if the (alleged) recipient (Y), who was not engaged in business, is said to have received the relevant communication (e-mail, fax, phone message) at home? The courts will need to develop practical guidelines. It is submitted that the following should apply:

(1) The burden of proof must be on X to prove that a fax, e-mail, or voice message was sent to, or a hand-delivered note left at, the relevant address.

(2) The court might then infer that the communication was received by Y unless: (a) Y can show that he or she was absent; or (b) Y excusably failed to notice the communication; or (c) Y had already nominated an alternative mode of communication (such as notification to a different address, or to a third party agent, including a company or lawyer) which X had chosen to bypass. There is little judicial guidance on this (see *Gisda Cyf* v. *Barratt* (2010), examined in text below).[63] However, it seems likely that the courts will lean in favour of Y in this type of context.

> On this point, although not necessary for its decision – since the point turned on statutory employment law – the Supreme Court in *Gisda Cyf* v. *Barratt* (2010)[64] (in a case which concerned letters in circumstances where the postal rule does not apply) noted the sensible remarks of Bean J in the Employment Appeal Tribunal:
>
>> There is no principle equivalent to *The Brimnes* [1975] QB 929, CA, that an individual is expected to be at home to receive and open the post when it arrives or in the evening when he or she gets home, or that some arrangement must be made for someone else to open what may well be confidential correspondence in the recipient's absence.

---

61   E. Haslam, (1996) NLJ 597, 562.
62   D. Nolan, 'Offer and Acceptance in the Electronic Age', in A. Burrows and E. Peel (eds.), *Contract Formation and Parties* (Oxford, 2010) (e-mail, and offer and acceptance).
63   [2010] UKSC 41; [2010] ICR 1475; [2010] 4 All ER 851, at [16]: quoting Bean J.
64   *Ibid.*

3.14 *Cooling-off periods: European consumer protection; rights to cancel certain contracts.* In 'distance and off-premises contracts between a trader and a consumer' for the supply of certain goods and services, the consumer enjoys rights of cancellation within a fourteen-day period.[65]

3.15 *Acceptance and the problem of silence.*[66] The general rule is that the offeree's silence does not constitute consent in bilateral contracts. Two policies support this general approach. First, it is necessary to protect offerees from having contracts thrust upon them by aggressive offerors, for example: 'Unless you respond and say "no" within [a specified period], we will infer that you have consented to my terms.' The policy of protecting against such forced dealing is enshrined in the Unsolicited Goods and Services Act 1971 and the Consumer Protection from Unfair Trading Regulations (2008).[67] The second problem is that silence is equivocal: mistaken inferences can be drawn from a person's failure to respond, as the House of Lords acknowledged in *Vitol SA* v. *Norelf Ltd ('The Santa Clara')* (1996),[68] although Lord Steyn suggested that in some situations silence might not be equivocal and the context might indicate clear acceptance[69] (giving the example, in respect of the termination of a contract, of a wrongly dismissed employee who is told to pack his things and leave, and who responds in complete silence by taking all his personal items away and does not return the next day).

> An illustration of the problem of equivocality is *Allied Marine Transport Ltd* v. *Vale do Rio Doce Navegacao SA ('The Leonidas D')* (1985),[70] where the Court of Appeal concluded that many years of inactivity by a party to an arbitration reference did not unequivocally indicate implied assent to the other party's (also implied) offer to abandon the arbitration. Robert Goff LJ said:[71] 'At most, there was simply an apparent coincidence of contentment that the *status quo* should continue indefinitely, but that is not . . . a binding agreement that it should do so.'

---

65 Consumer Contracts (Information, Cancellation and Additional Charges) Regulations 2013/3134, Part 3 (see *Wei* v. *Cambridge Power and Light Ltd* (2010) unreported HHJ Moloney), considering *Martin* v. *EDP Editores* [2010] 2 CMLR 27 (17 December 2009, ECJ, and applying an earlier version of these Regulations); *Robertson* v. *Swift* [2014] UKSC 50; [2014] 1 WLR 3438, applying Cancellation of Contracts made in a Consumer's Home or Place of Work, etc Regulations 2008 (SI 2008/1816).
66 M. Furmston and G. J. Tolhurst, *Contract Formation: Law and Practice* (Oxford, 2010), 4.62 ff.
67 Consumer Protection from Unfair Trading Regulations 2008 (SI 2008, No. 1277), Part 5 (as amended by the Consumer Contracts (Information, Cancellation and Additional Charges) Regulations 2013/3134).
68 [1996] AC 800, 811–12, HL, in the context of acceptance of repudiation: see 17.46 to 17.47.
69 *Ibid.*, at 812 (and citing *Rust* v. *Abbey Life Assurance Co. Ltd* [1979] 2 Lloyd's Rep 334 (on which see 3.20 at (3) below).
70 [1985] 1 WLR 925, CA.
71 *Ibid.*

3.16 As mentioned, the general proposition is that silence does not constitute consent. *Felthouse* v. *Bindley* (1862) is the decision normally cited in support of this.[72] However, the case is problematic on its facts.

In *Felthouse* v. *Bindley* (1862), there had been negotiations on the price between a nephew, the prospective seller, and his uncle, a prospective buyer, for the sale of a horse. The uncle wrote, offering a compromise price, adding that unless he heard to the contrary, he would assume that the nephew was prepared to sell at this figure. The nephew read the letter, decided he did want to sell at this price to the uncle, and so told the defendant, an auctioneer, not to sell the horse to any third party. But the defendant auctioneer became confused and sold the horse to a third party.

The uncle unsuccessfully sued the auctioneer in the tort of conversion, alleging that the horse had already become the uncle's property or at least that he had a right to possess the horse. The Court of Common Pleas (upheld by the Court of Exchequer Chamber) rejected this claim on the basis that no contract had arisen between the nephew and the uncle (the court considered that this meant that no proprietary or possessory rights had arisen in the uncle's favour).

A better analysis would have been that the buyer had acquired no immediate right to possession because, until the seller received payment, the seller retained a lien over the horse. That approach would have justified the same result (for the decision enabled the courts to avoid the injustice of rendering the auctioneer strictly liable on these facts – the tort of conversion not requiring fault or bad faith).

3.17 As mentioned above, the rule that silence does not constitute consent is primarily designed to protect offerees. It follows that the rule should not be invoked *by an offeror* if this will cause *injustice to an offeree*. This problem can arise if the offeree has reasonably relied on an offer stating: 'Unless I hear from you to the contrary, I will assume that you accept this proposal.' In this situation, the courts ought in principle to be less reluctant to find a contract.

3.18 Another possible qualification upon the 'general silence rule' is that the offeree might have undertaken to break his silence *if he wishes not to be* bound.

This situation was considered in a dictum in *Re Selectmove* (1995).[73] Peter Gibson LJ suggested that where an offer is made by X to Y, and Y tells X that, unless he hears from Y to the contrary by a specified time, X should assume that Y has accepted the offer, Y's undertaking to get in contact with X will be binding on Y if X elects to hold Y to the bargain. This seems sound because Y is not unfairly pressurised by X. Nor is Y's failure to contact X an equivocal example of inactivity. Instead, 'it speaks volumes' because Y had made clear that silence means assent.

---

72 (1862) 11 CB (NS) 869; 31 LJCP 204; 10 WR 423, Court of Common Pleas; affirmed, (1863) 1 New Rep 401; 11 WR 429; 7 LT 835, Court of Exchequer Chamber; Miller, (1972) 35 MLR 489; cf *Re Selectmove* [1995] 1 WLR 474, 478-9, CA.
73 [1995] 1 WLR 474, 478F, CA.

3.19 *Conduct by offeree.* The general rule that silence does not constitute consent can be displaced if a person's conduct clearly indicates that he has made an overt and free decision to accede to the proposed terms (see also 3.15).

> In *Nissan UK Ltd* v. *Nissan Motor Manufacturing (UK) Ltd* (1994), Nissan UK was the distributor of cars manufactured by Nissan Manufacturing. The parties exchanged many faxes concerning dates for the supply of cars by Nissan Manufacturing to Nissan UK, but had yet to achieve a crystal-clear agreement.[74] Then Nissan UK made a specific proposal for such a schedule of deliveries by Nissan Manufacturing. In response, Nissan Manufacturing started to deliver the cars at intervals coinciding with this schedule. This was an example of the offeree's conduct matching the offeror's proposed timings. The Court of Appeal held that the contract had been activated by Nissan Manufacturing's implied acceptance by conduct of Nissan UK's proposal concerning the timing of deliveries. Nourse LJ encapsulated this as follows:
>
> > [I]f one of two contracting parties are 'toing and froing' with offer and counter-offer and one maintains his proposals to the last, receiving no [verbal] comeback, it is natural to infer that subsequent conduct on the part of the other is referable to there being a contract between them and this denotes acceptance of that proposal.

3.20 There are other qualifications upon the general proposition that silence does not constitute acceptance:

(1) *Unilateral contract.* An offer of a unilateral contract (3.42) is generally taken to dispense with the need for the offeree to communicate acceptance: the offeree is not prejudiced since only the offeror in this situation will assume an obligation.

(2) *Course of dealing between the parties: repeat transactions.* Acceptance by silence can occur if there have been repeated dealings.[75]

(3) *Silence by party initiating solid proposal for a deal.* As discussed below, if X starts the negotiations, and receives an offer or counter-offer from Y on which X 'sits' for a significant period, X's silence might be treated as consent, because in this context X cannot complain that he has been taken by surprise.[76]

> In *Rust* v. *Abbey Life Assurance Co. Ltd* (1979),[77] the defendant had acted on the claimant's request to open an investment bond, and the claimant had earlier sent a cheque for this bond. But the claimant now sought the return of her money. The first ground of decision was that the claimant had made an offer to the defendant which the latter had accepted by conduct. But a second ground of decision emerged. Even if the offer in fact emanated from the defendant, who had sent the relevant policy to the claimant, the claimant's substantial delay in acquiescing in receipt of that policy, and not seeking to cancel the apparent deal, was enough to indicate assent.[78]

74 Court of Appeal December 1994, unreported (the case was contested by two leading counsel, Gordon Pollock QC and Lord Grabiner QC).
75 *Treitel* (13th edn, London, 2011), 2–044.
76 *Ibid.*, at 2–047, on *obiter* aspect of *Rust* v. *Abbey Life Assurance Co. Ltd* [1979] 2 Lloyd's Rep 334 (for comment, see Lord Steyn in *Vitol SA* v. *Norelf Ltd* ('*The Santa Clara*') [1996] AC 800, 812, HL).
77 [1979] 2 Lloyd's Rep 334, CA.
78 *Ibid.*, at 340.

4. POSTAL ACCEPTANCES

3.21 *The rule.* The so-called 'postal rule' has lasted for nearly two centuries.[79] The rule states that the offeree's acceptance occurs at the moment[80] of posting, using the Royal Mail (but does not apply to hand delivery, faxes or e-mail, etc.; see 3.09). The rule favours the offeree because he is immediately protected against the risk that the offeror had earlier attempted to revoke the offer. But the postal rule will not apply (or, in the case of (3), not apply the 'date of posting' facet of the rule) in any of these four situations:

(1) use of the post was expressly or impliedly ruled out by the offeror (3.29);

(2) the offeree should have realised that use of the post was inappropriate (for example, the post was not known to be affected during the relevant period by industrial disputes, 3.27, 3.28);

(3) the offeree had been at fault when using the post (for example, by failing to address the letter correctly, 3.28); and

(4) the offeree had become aware that the offer had been revoked (3.36) (or the offeree had reasonable access to information which would indicate revocation, 3.37).

As we shall see, this controversial and complex Victorian rule has proved troublesome in some contexts.

3.22 *Material scope of postal rule.* The postal rule applies to inland postal acceptance using the Royal Mail, but does *not* apply to acceptances by faxes (see below) or e-mail (see the quotation below) (nor by telex, now obsolete). The Court of Appeal in *Entores* v. *Miles Far East Corporation* (1955) regarded these non-postal forms of acceptance as 'virtually instantaneous'.[81] Nor does the postal rule apply to hand delivery, to delivery by private courier, to voice mail, or to voice machine messages. The main incidents of the postal rule will now be explained.

3.23 *Posting before discovering attempted revocation.* As soon as the acceptance is properly posted, the offeror can no longer revoke the offer. *Byrne* v. *Van Tienhoven* (1880) decides that the offeror's revocation of the offer must *be known to*, or at least it must have *reached*, the offeree before the latter posts a letter of acceptance.[82] If not, posted acceptance will be effective. There would probably be no contract if the offeror's revocation reached the acceptor before the latter posted his acceptance, *but* at the time of posting the acceptor had failed to open his mail or check his inbox. This last proposition is deducible from *The*

---

79 S. Gardner, 'Trashing with Trollope: A Deconstruction of the Postal Rules in Contract' (1992) 12 OJLS 170; D. McLauchlan, 'The Uncertain Basis of the Postal Acceptance Rule' (2013) 30 JCL 33.

80 By contrast, section 7 of the Interpretation Act 1978 provides that statutory service of various notices normally occur on a deemed day of delivery, unless a particular statute provides otherwise: *Freetown Ltd* v. *Assethold Ltd* [2012] EWHC 1351 (QB) [2013] 1 WLR 385, Slade J (held that section 15(1) of the Party Wall etc. Act 1996 rendered date of posting decisive).

81 [1955] 2 QB 327, 332, CA, *per* Denning LJ.

82 (1880) 5 CPD 344.

Brimnes (1975), concerning an unread telex,[83] in which the court held that the recipient of that telex had effective notice of its contents once the communication had appeared on his machine during normal office hours.

3.24 *Place of formation.* The contract is formed at the place where the acceptance letter is posted. The place of formation is important in establishing a 'connecting link' between the contract and the jurisdiction of the English courts. The Civil Procedure Rules 1998 (CPR) permit the English courts to give permission for a claim form to be served outside the UK and the EU where the relevant contract was formed within the English jurisdiction.[84] By contrast, in the case of a fax, the place of receipt fixes the location of the contract.[85]

3.25 *Lost postal acceptance*: The high-water mark of the postal rule is the Court of Appeal's majority decision in *Household Fire Insurance Co.* v. *Grant* (1879),[86] which decides that posting is enough even if the letter never reaches the offeror, provided it was properly stamped and addressed, and the delay was not otherwise attributable to the offeree's fault.

The defendant in *Household Fire Insurance Co.* v. *Grant* (1879) offered to buy a hundred shares in the claimant company. The claimant sent a letter accepting this offer. The letter never arrived. The Court of Appeal held that the defendant was liable to pay for the shares. Thesiger LJ, a member of the majority, said that this approach could be justified either because the Post Office was the common agent of the parties, so that posting would take immediate effect, irrespective of accidents within the postal system; or because, otherwise, it would be necessary to determine whether the acceptance had reached the offeror, and this might give rise to fraud and delay. A third suggestion (which is really no more than a restatement of the rule's effect) is that the risk of postal delay or complete postal failure is borne by the offeror. The offeror can avoid this risk by specifying that acceptance must actually reach him (which was the result in the *Holwell* case (1974),[87] see 3.29).

3.26 *Appropriateness of postal acceptance.* The offeree can invoke the postal rule if the offeror stipulated that acceptance should be by post (which will be rare), or if posting was objectively 'reasonable', having regard to the nature of the proposed transaction and the practicalities of effective communication by this rather slow mode. Offer

---

83 'The Brimnes' [1975] QB 929, CA (withdrawal of offer effective when telex received during ordinary business hours, even if not in fact read).
84 Practice Direction 6, para. 3.1(6)(a) in the Civil Procedure Rules 1998; perhaps indicating posting rule applicable to UK outward-bound posting.
85 *JSC Zestafoni G Nikoladze Ferroalloy Plant* v. *Ronly Holdings Ltd* [2004] EWHC 245 (Comm); [2004] 2 Lloyd's Rep 335, at [75].
86 *Household Fire Insurance Co.* v. *Grant* (1879) 4 Ex D 217, CA (note Bramwell LJ's dissent); Scots law is different: *Mason* v. *Benhar Coal Co.* (1882) 9 R 883.
87 [1974] 1 WLR 155, CA.

and acceptance need not involve matching modes of communication. There are two possibilities: (i) postal offer and non-postal acceptance or (ii) non-postal offer and postal acceptance. Permutation (ii) is illustrated by *Henthorn v. Fraser* (1892),[88] where the offeree received a written offer from the offeror when he visited the latter's Liverpool office. The offeree went home to Birkenhead, a distance of some miles, to think over the proposal. He then posted his acceptance from Birkenhead. The court regarded postal acceptance as reasonable because the offeree's home and the offeror's offices were separated by a significant distance.

Conversely, although posted acceptance has been requested, a non-postal acceptance might be effective: *Tinn v. Hoffman & Co.* (1873).[89]

Henthorn v. Fraser shows, as was already clear from *Tinn v. Hoffman & Co.* (1873),[90] that offer and acceptance need not be communicated by the same medium. For example, in the *Tinn* case (1873) the court had said that if A invites acceptance by post, giving a specified time for acceptance, B can legitimately accept by some other method, provided this is no less speedy than the post.

3.27 The courts will not expect instantaneously communicated responses to complicated and delicate proposals. The postal rule continues to operate in such circumstances. Of course, sometimes special and temporary difficulties, known by the offeree or the public, will render the post unsuitable: for example, normal service has been, or is about to be, disrupted by a strike or national petrol shortage. In such circumstances, it would not be prudent to use the post, at any rate when time is pressing because the deadline for acceptance is imminent, and instead acceptance by phone or e-mail might be reasonably expected. But, in other situations, where acceptance is not time-specific and there is adequate opportunity to use the post, the postal mode might be wholly appropriate: everything must depend on the circumstances.

3.28 *Delayed postal acceptance*: The moment of posting is normally decisive even if the letter is then delayed in transmission, without this being attributable to the acceptor's fault (for example, provided the latter had not carelessly omitted the postcode or used the wrong address). Toulson J in *LJ Korbetis v. Transgrain Shipping BV* (2005) acknowledged this point in a dictum (the case was not concerned with posted acceptance but with a fax sent negligently to the wrong telephone number), and he approved the following passage in *Chitty on Contracts* in which the operation of the postal rule, and its timing, are made to hinge on whether the delay or failure is due to the offeror or offeree's fault:[91]

---

88   [1892] 2 Ch 27, CA.
89   (1873) 29 LT 271 (Court of Exchequer Chamber) (offeror invites postal acceptance; acceptance could be effected by a no less speedy alternative route); see also fn 44 above: *Manchester Diocesan Council for Education v. Commercial & General Investments Ltd* [1970] 1 WLR 241, 246, *per* Buckley J.
90   (1873) 29 LT 271 (Court of Exchequer Chamber).
91   [2005] EWHC 1345 (QB), at [15], citing *Chitty on Contracts* (31st edn, London, 2010), at 2–058 (as the passage is now numbered).

A letter of acceptance may be lost or delayed because it bears a wrong or an incomplete address, or because it is not properly stamped. Normally such defects would be due to the carelessness of the offeree ... [The position is different] where the misdirection is due to the fault of the offeror, for example, where his own address is incompletely or illegibly given in the offer itself. In such a case, the offeror shall not be allowed to rely on the fact that the acceptance was misdirected, except perhaps where his error in stating his own address was obvious to the offeree, for in such a case the offeror's fault would not be the effective cause of the misdirection of the acceptance. It is submitted that a misdirected acceptance should take effect, if at all, at the time which is least favourable to the party responsible for the misdirection.

3.29 *Express or implied exclusion of the postal rule by the offeror.* The Court of Appeal in *Holwell Securities Ltd* v. *Hughes* (1974)[92] held that this rule can be 'disapplied' by clear or adequate (sufficiently indicative) language contained in the offer. But Lawton LJ added a dictum that the rule will also be 'disapplied' if, objectively, it would be absurd to treat the moment of posting as decisive, notably when the offeror has imposed a clear deadline for successful acceptance and especially when the offer creates a competition between offerees to make the most attractive response.

Holwell Securities Ltd v. *Hughes* (1974) concerned an attempted acceptance by an option-holder for the purchase of land. The option was granted on 19 October 1971 and had to be exercised within six months thereafter. The offeree posted acceptance on 14 April 1972 (with five days to spare), but the letter never arrived. The terms of the option required 'notice [of acceptance] ... to' the offeror.

The Court of Appeal held that this wording ('notice [of acceptance] ... to') was a sufficiently clear indication that the grantor required actual notice of acceptance to reach the offeror. This was the decision of both Russell and Lawton LJJ. Therefore, the date of posting was not the critical date.

But Lawton LJ went further. Even in the absence of a clear requirement, expressly made, he suggested that, in this context, posted acceptance would need to reach the offeror. He referred to the manifest good sense that an option grantor should actually become aware whether the option had been accepted (and similarly, perhaps, in other contexts).[93] This was a dictum not necessary for the decision (the case having already been decided on the basis that 'notice ... to' explicitly connotes the need for actual receipt of acceptance). Lawton LJ's dictum broadens the position: his *suggestion* is that the postal rule should not apply if, in a particular case, this rule 'would produce manifest inconvenience and absurdity'. He said:[94]

---

92 [1974] 1 WLR 155, CA. On the more general *procedural* issue of service at the date of sending or of deemed or actual receipt, see *Freetown Ltd* v. *Assethold Ltd* [2012] EWCA Civ 1657; [2013] 1 WLR 701 (and see comment at [42], *per* Rix LJ concerning *FP (Iran)* v. *Secretary of State for the Home Department* [2007] EWCA Civ 13; [2007] Imm AR 450 at [61] and [74]).
93 But assent to third party promise rights, section 2(2)(b) of the Contracts (Rights of Third Parties) Act 1999, requires notification of acceptance by third party, by letter or otherwise, *to reach the promisor*: 7.35.
94 [1974] 1 WLR 155, 161, CA.

First, [the rule that posting concludes the contract even if the letter is lost] does not apply when the express terms of the offer specify that the acceptance must reach the offeror. Secondly, it probably does not operate if its application would produce manifest inconvenience and absurdity.

Lawton LJ linked this suggestion to the search for the parties' *implicit intention* when he concluded: 'the factors of inconvenience and absurdity are but illustrations of a wider principle', namely, the objective determination that, in a particular context, 'the negotiating parties cannot have intended that there should be a binding agreement until the party accepting an offer . . . had in fact communicated the acceptance'.

It is submitted that Lawton LJ's dictum concerning 'manifest inconvenience and absurdity' should be rationalised as based on the offeror's implied disapplication of the postal rule; secondly, this should be inferred whenever the offeror has explicitly set a deadline for acceptance. In such situations, the offeror has sufficiently indicated his 'need to know by a specified date', and that is inconsistent with the acceptance letter being delayed beyond the relevant date or complete non-delivery of that posted acceptance (certainly, it would be impossible to apply the rule in *Household Fire Insurance Co.* v. *Grant* (1879: see above).[95] Consider these two contexts, in both of which a deadline is specified:

(1) The offer is made to rival bidders, the offeror requesting each to make a sealed fixed bid. In this context, the offeror needs to discover by a specified date whose purported acceptance has 'won' (illustrated by the *Harvela* case, discussed at 3.51 ff). Without receipt of hard information, the bidding process will be stultified or delayed unsatisfactorily.

(2) But, even when the offer is made to a designated *individual*, and the immediate problem of distinguishing rival bids does not arise, but the offeror has specified a deadline for a response, it is possible that posting prior to the deadline will not be enough and that the dictum concerning 'manifest inconvenience and absurdity' will govern, so as to require receipt of acceptance before the deadline. (A qualification arises where special legislation operates in favour of a party issuing a rent review notice, or other notices concerning real property, and where use of registered post or recorded delivery fixes the addressee with effective notice on a deemed date,[96] sometimes even if the registered posting or (attempted) recorded delivery never arrives.)[97]

3.30 *An unresolved issue: acceptor's second thoughts.* After dropping the letter into the post box, can the acceptor change his mind and validly send an SMS message (a 'text' message) or an e-mail to retract his acceptance, provided this arrives before the acceptance letter? Or is the acceptor bound upon posting? The point is moot in England.[98] (The present point is confined to the postal rule: and so the discussion summarised in the remainder of this paragraph is concerned with posted (Royal Mail) acceptances rather than e-mail or hand-delivered acceptances.) It is submitted that the best of the three theories is that an overtaking retraction of an acceptance by the acceptor should be effective.

95   *Household Fire Insurance Co.* v. *Grant* (1879) 4 Ex D 217, CA (note Bramwell LJ's dissent); Scots law is different: *Mason* v. *Benhar Coal Co.* (1882) 9 R 883.
96   *WX Investments Ltd* v. *Begg* [2002] EWHC 925 (Ch); [2002] 1 WLR 2849, Patten J, considering section 196 of the Law of Property Act 1925 (in *Holwell Securities* v. *Hughes* [1974] 1 WLR 155, CA, option notice was not sent by registered or recorded delivery, but *by ordinary post*, and so section 196 did not apply).
97   *WX Investments Ltd* v. *Begg* [2002] EWHC 925 (Ch); [2002] 1 WLR 2849, at [18], noting Neuberger J's statement in *Kinch* v. *Bullard* [1999] 1 WLR 423, 427.
98   A. H. Hudson, 'Retraction of Letters of Acceptance' (1966) 82 LQR 169–73.

There are three possible answers to this problem:

(1) *The acceptor cannot retract the posted acceptance.* South African[99] and New Zealand decisions[100] support this position. But Colin Turpin attractively opposes this solution. He argues: 'The offeror would in no way be prejudiced if the [retraction by the acceptor] were held effective . . . for [the offeror] would not have known of the posting of the acceptance and could not have acted in reliance upon it.'[101]

(2) *Acceptor's revocation of acceptance is effective.* The second possible solution is to allow the acceptor to retract by a speedier mode. This is favoured by Hudson,[102] Burrows,[103] a Scots decision, *Dunmore* v. *Alexander* (1830),[104] the Indian Contract Act 1872,[105] and by English dicta, notably Bramwell LJ, dissenting, in *Household Fire Insurance Co.* v. *Grant* (1879)[106] and by Neuberger J in *Kinch* v. *Bullard* (1999), whose dictum states that where a person has posted a letter, he can change his mind and, using phone or other speedy mode, validly cancel the effect of the posted letter in which he purported to sever a joint tenancy. This 'speedier' cancellation will be effective provided it is received before the letter is delivered.[107]

(3) *Acceptor should not abuse the capacity to retract.* A third approach is that although retraction will normally be permitted, it should be disallowed if the acceptor is behaving reprehensibly and cannily trying to 'play the market', that is, speculating at the offeror's expense by playing fast-and-loose with the postal rule in response to market fluctuations. Treitel has proposed this third solution.[108] For example, someone (with an excess of candour) posts a letter of acceptance at 11.00 am and then telephones at 11.05 am to say 'ignore my letter of acceptance, the market has just plummeted, and it has suddenly become a very bad deal. I'm out.' Treitel's idea is based on a notion of abuse of right or perhaps good faith. But it enjoys no case law support. It seems simply moralistic to say that the acceptor should be bound when he is 'guilty' of speculating. It is also arguable that the offeror can easily protect himself from such behaviour by expressly displacing the postal rule: ('acceptance to reach me by . . . ').

It is submitted that solution (2) should be preferred: an overtaking retraction of an acceptance by the acceptor is effective, once the retraction comes to the other party's notice. The postal rule should not mechanically bind the acceptor to his earlier posted acceptance.

3.31 *Posted rejection overtaken by speedier acceptance.*[109] What if, conversely, the offeree posts a letter of rejection and then changes his mind and wishes to accept after all? Can he validly 'accept' by, for example, sending an e-mail which arrives before the rejection

---

99   South Africa: *A to Z Bazaars (Pty) Ltd* v. *Minister of Agriculture* (1974) (4) SA 392 (c), noted C. Turpin, [1975] CLJ 25.
100   New Zealand: *Wenckheim* v. *Arndt* (1874) 1 JR 73.
101   [1975] CLJ 25, 26.
102   A. H. Hudson, 'Retraction of Letters of Acceptance' (1966) 82 LQR 169.
103   A. S. Burrows, *A Casebook on Contract* (4th edn, Oxford, 2013), 39 (approving Hudson article, previous note).
104   Indian Contract Act 1872, sections 4 and 5.
105   Scotland: *Dunmore* v. *Alexander* (1830) 9 S 190.
106   (1879) 4 Ex D 216, 235–6, CA.
107   [1999] 1 WLR 423, 429, *per* Neuberger J (letter posted and *delivered*, and then destroyed by sender before addressee could read it: held that the notice was properly served under a statutory rule).
108   Treitel, editing *Chitty on Contracts* (31st edn, London, 2012), 2–060; and (consistently) *Treitel* (13th edn, London, 2011), 2–038; *Anson's Law of Contract* (29th edn, Oxford, 2010), 52–3, uses this argument to justify adoption of position (1) ('acceptor cannot retract'), see above.
109   For the position concerning communicated rejections of offers see 3.39.

letter (the e-mail stating, 'I'm accepting: ignore the letter sent by Royal Mail in which I rejected the offer')? It is submitted that this is a straightforward situation. The acceptance arrived before the posted rejection. The postal rule applies only to acceptances and not to rejections. And so there has been a valid acceptance. It would be different if the rejection letter arrived before the acceptance communication: the offeror should then be entitled to assume that the deal is off.

5. COUNTER-OFFERS

3.32 A counter-offer is a clear presentation by the offeree of an alternative set of terms, or the alteration of a significant term. A counter-offer is to be distinguished from a tentative or exploratory request for further information; for example, 'can I just check you meant £1,000 and not £10,000?' Lush J made this distinction in *Stevenson, Jacques & Co.* v. *McLean* (1880)[110] (the Court of Appeal in *Grant* v. *Bragg* (2009)[111] has also acknowledged this distinction).

> In the *Stevenson, Jacques* case, the defendant offered to sell iron to the claimant at 40 shillings per ton, the offer to be open for a specified time. The claimant telegraphed to ask whether delivery at that price would be spread over two months or a longer period. Lush J said that this was a mere inquiry, and the defendant's original offer remained available to be accepted by the claimant within the specified time (unless in the meantime the claimant had heard, directly or indirectly, that this offer had been withdrawn).[112]

However, where the response is a clear counter-offer, the counter-offeree (that is, the original offeror) can respond in one of four ways: (1) accept the counter-offer (deal done); (2) reject the counter-offer without more; (3) reject the counter-offer but reaffirm the original offer; or (4) propose different terms, that is, make a counter-counter-offer.

3.33 If the response is of type (2), outright and unqualified rejection of the counter-offer, the original offer is no longer available for acceptance. The offeree has no second bite of the acceptance cherry. This was established in *Hyde* v. *Wrench* (1840):[113]

> The facts of *Hyde* v. *Wrench* (1840) involved the following stages: (i) A offered in writing to sell to B a farm for £1,000; (ii) B wrote and counter-offered £950; (iii) a few weeks later, A wrote and said he could not accept this; (iv) two days later, B wrote, purporting to accept A's original offer, that is, for £1,000; (v) A contested whether B had the right to revert to the original offer; (vi) and so B sued

---

110 (1880) 5 QBD 346.
111 [2009] EWCA Civ 1228; [2010] 1 All ER (Comm) 1166, at [22], *per* Lord Neuberger MR.
112 (1880) 5 QBD 346, 350 (approved in a dictum in *Gibson* v. *Manchester City Council* [1979] 1 WLR 294, 302, HL).
113 (1840) 3 Beav 334; 4 Jur 1106; 49 ER 132.

for specific performance of the alleged concluded agreement to buy for £1,000. The claim failed. Lord Langdale MR held that B could not revive A's original offer.

The merits of this rule are its clarity and its sound protection of the offeror. He knows that his rejection of the counter-offer leaves him unexposed to acceptance of the original offer. The rule thus offers *protection against haggling*: otherwise the offeree could offer (on the facts of *Hyde* v. *Wrench*) £900, £910, £920, etc., while reserving the right to accept the original offer.

A further possibility is that the recipient of the counter-offer might remain silent (assuming that silence does indicate consent, unlike in *Rust* v. *Abbey Life Assurance Co. Ltd* (1979), 3.20). Might the sender of the counter-offer, provided he acts with reasonable speed, return to the original offer? Or is the presentation of the counter-offer enough to destroy the original offer? It is arguable – although this point does not yet appear to be settled – that the communication by B of a counter-offer precludes B from reverting to the original offer even if A merely fails to respond (by contrast, an express rejection occurred in *Hyde* v. *Wrench*, as explained). B's counter-offer is equivalent to a rejection by B of the original offer (see 3.39 where it is noted that communicated rejection of an offer immediately terminates the original offer).

What of possibility (3) mentioned at 3.32, where the counter-offer is rejected but the original offeror reaffirms the original offer? This requires an objective and explicit indication that the offer was being replaced on the table by the original offeror. In a Canadian decision, *Livingstone* v. *Evans* (1925), the original offeror replied to the counter-offer 'cannot reduce price'. That was held to have kept the original offer alive.[114] In *Re Cowan & Boyd* (1921), another Canadian decision, an offer was also held to have been 'placed back on the table' when the offeror said that he would call on the counter-offeror to discuss the matter further.[115]

6. BATTLE OF THE FORMS

3.34 This is the problem of competing proposals contained within the parties' standard terms.[116] The law has to decide which set of terms, if any, wins the battle to govern the contract. English law has adopted the so-called 'last shot' analysis: victory goes to the party proposing its own terms as the final part of the sequence of terms, provided the other side acquiesces. This is the result of the Court of Appeal's decision in *Tekdata Intercommunications* v. *Amphenol Ltd* (2009)[117] which endorsed the authority of the

---

114   [1925] 3 WWR 454 (Alberta Supreme Court).
115   (1921) 61 DLR 497 (Ontario Supreme Court App Div).
116   M. Furmston and G. J. Tolhurst, *Contract Formation: Law and Practice* (Oxford, 2010), 4.122 ff; J. Adams, [1983] JBL 297; S. Ball, (1983) 99 LQR 572; E. McKendrick, (1988) 8 OJLS 197; R. Rawlings, (1979) 42 MLR 715; for the approach to the 'battle of forms' in other jurisdictions or transnational 'soft law', see the UN Vienna Convention on Contracts for the International Sale of Goods (Article 19(2) and (3)), the *Principles of European Contract Law* (Articles 2:208 and 2:209), the Uniform Commercial Code (USA) (Article 2.207) and UNIDROIT's *Principles of International Commercial Contracts* (Article 2.1.11).
117   [2009] EWCA Civ 1209; [2010] 1 Lloyd's Rep 357; followed by Coulson J in *Trebor Bassett Holdings Limited* v. *ADT Fire and Security plc* [2011] EWHC 1936 (TCC), at [157]; and see Coulson J's summary, *ibid.*, at [155] and [156], of the decision in the *Tekdata* case.

Court of Appeal's majority decision (Lawton and Bridge LJJ) in *Butler Machine Tool Co. Ltd v. Ex-Cell-O Corporation (England) Ltd* (1979)[118] (3.35) and earlier of the Court of Appeal in *British Road Services Ltd* v. *Arthur V. Crutchley & Co. Ltd* (1968).[119]

To illustrate the problem of the 'battle' between standard forms, suppose that A, the supplier, offers goods to B on A's standard payment terms: £1,000 per unit, payable by B without discount, payment to be made within thirty days. B's competing set of terms are that B, as prospective buyer, will order goods at £1,000 per unit with 10 per cent discount if B pays within ninety days. A then delivers the goods with an invoice which reasserts A's terms. B's warehouseman signs this. This signature is effective to incorporate A's terms. In this situation, the *possible* options (for the English approach, see the following discussion) are: (a) A's terms apply (£1,000); or (b) B's discount terms apply (£900); or (c) the court might 'split the difference' between the parties (£950); or (d) conclude that the parties have failed to reach any agreement and award A the reasonable market value of the goods at the time of delivery (say, £1,100). English law is clear: applying the 'last shot' approach (see (1) above), solution (a) governs this case. Thus, A's terms have prevailed because B has accepted A's terms. B must pay £1,000.

In *Tekdata Intercommunications* v. *Amphenol Ltd* (2009)[120] A supplied high specification materials to T, for eventual use in the construction of Rolls-Royce aero engines. A's written terms contained an exclusion clause in favour of A, but T's written terms did not. Applying the 'last shot' approach, the Court of Appeal (Longmore, Dyson and Pill LJJ) accepted that A had made the last presentation of terms, and T had acquiesced in these. Therefore, the exclusion clause contained in A's standard form had been incorporated. The judgments emphasise the benefit of commercial certainty in adhering to this established analysis. To displace this traditional analysis it would be necessary to show a clear course of dealing[121] between the parties which manifested a contrary arrangement (for example, if there had been ninety-nine deals on A's terms, B should not win the battle of the forms on the hundredth occasion). But no such course of dealing had been proved in the present case.

Emphasising the need for a 'bright-line' or sharp-edged rule, Dyson LJ said:[122]

> the general rule should be that the traditional offer and acceptance analysis is to be applied in battle of the forms cases. That has the great merit of providing a degree of certainty which is both desirable and necessary in order to promote effective commercial relationships.

The present appeal concerned merely a preliminary point of law. The decision, that the supplier's exclusion clause had been incorporated, does not extend to the question whether the seller's written standard term might be vulnerable as unreasonable under section 3 of the Unfair

---

118 [1979] 1 WLR 401, 405H, 406D, 407E, CA.

119 [1968] 1 All ER 811, CA (A had delivered whisky to B for storage on A's terms. B stamped this standard form with its own terms, and A's driver then handed over the goods; the Court of Appeal held that B's stamping the document rendered delivery subject to B's terms; Lord Pearson, sitting in the Court of Appeal, noted a course of dealing between A and B, and that B's terms were standard in the warehousing industry: *ibid.*, at 817).

120 [2009] EWCA Civ 1209; [2010] 1 Lloyd's Rep 357; followed by Coulson J in *Trebor Bassett Holdings Limited* v. *ADT Fire and Security plc* [2011] EWHC 1936 (TCC), at [157]; and see Coulson J's summary, *ibid.*, at [155] and [156], of the decision in the *Tekdata* case.

121 [2009] EWCA Civ 1209; [2010] 1 Lloyd's Rep 357, at [21]; on this legal approach, E. Macdonald, (1988) 8 LS 48.

122 *Ibid.*, at [25].

Contract Terms Act 1977 (non-consumer contracts) (modified by the Consumer Rights Bill)[123] (15.10 ff).

3.35 The rejected alternative analyses: In *Butler Machine Tool Co. Ltd* v. *Ex-Cell-O Corporation (England) Ltd* (1979),[124] the majority of the Court of Appeal, consisting of Lawton and Bridge LJJ, adopted the 'last shot' approach (confirmed in *Tekdata Intercommunications* v. *Amphenol Ltd* (2009), 3.34).[125] However, in the *Butler* case (1979), Lord Denning MR, in the minority, suggested three alternative analyses:[126]

(1) *The first shot.* 'In some cases the battle is won by the man who gets the blow in first. If he offers to sell at a named price on the terms and conditions stated on the back, and the buyer orders the goods purporting to accept the offer – on an order form with his own different terms and conditions on the back – then if the difference is so material that it would affect the price, the buyer ought not to be allowed to take advantage of the difference unless he draws it specifically to the attention of the seller.'

(2) *Both sets construed together.* 'There are yet other cases where the battle depends on the shots fired on both sides. There is a concluded contract but the forms vary. The terms and conditions of both parties are to be construed together. If they can be reconciled so as to give a harmonious result, all well and good.' In effect this is a plea for courts to create an amalgam of the parties' competing terms ('picking and choosing').

(3) *Default resort to 'reasonable implication'.* 'If differences are irreconcilable – so that they are mutually contradictory – then the conflicting terms may have to be scrapped and replaced by a reasonable implication.'

There is indeed a fourth possibility: (4) the court might declare that there is no contract, leaving the parties to restitutionary remedies for the value of goods or services supplied and used or enjoyed.

As for Lord Denning's suggested approaches (2) and (3) (see above), such flexible approaches are favoured both by US law and by the 'soft law' (non-binding) international codes.[127] In this respect, Lord Denning's minority approach has the advantage that broad Equity can be inserted into the discovery of the contractual terms. In short, this approach favours the finding of a contract on a compromise or customary basis.

---

123   In respect of *business to consumer contracts* the Unfair Contract Terms Act 1977's provisions are to be replaced by the Consumer Rights Bill; and the 1977 Act is amended so that it covers business to business and consumer to consumer contracts only.
124   [1979] 1 WLR 401, 405H, 406D, 407E, CA.
125   [2009] EWCA Civ 1209; [2010] 1 Lloyd's Rep 357; applied in *Trebor Bassett Holdings Ltd* v. *ADT Fire & Security plc* [2011] EWHC 1936 (TCC); [2011] BLR 661, Coulson J; for a Scottish example: supplier's last shot accepted by purchaser's conduct: *Specialist Insulation Ltd* v. *Pro-Duct (Fife)* [2012] CSOH 79 (Court of Session, Outer House).
126   [1979] 1 WLR 401; *ibid.*, at 404H–405D, suggesting that approaches (1), (2), (4) or even the 'last shot' approach might apply to other facts.
127   UN Vienna Convention on Contracts for the International Sale of Goods (Article 19(2) and (3)), *Principles of European Contract Law* (Article 2:208), Uniform Commercial Code (USA) (Article 2.207) and UNIDROIT's *Principles of International Commercial Contracts* (Article 2.1.11); however, the *Principles of European Contract Law*, Article 2:209 permits 'general conflicting terms' to produce a contract 'to the extent that they are common in substance'; some of these materials are collected in E. McKendrick, *Contract Law: Text, Cases and Materials* (4th edn, Oxford, 2010), 90–1; F. Vergne, 'The "Battle of the Forms" Under the 1980 United Nations Convention on Contracts for the International Sale of Goods' (1985) 33 *American Journal of Comparative Law* 233–58.

But the clear disadvantage of Lord Denning's approach is that it ignores the responsive analysis of the offer and acceptance process. And that orthodox approach (generally endorsed by the House of Lords in *Gibson* v. *Manchester City Council* (1979), 3.05) is rooted in freedom of contract (on this principle, see 1.08).

A second disadvantage of Lord Denning's minority approach is that it creates uncertainty by giving the court leeway to determine the eventual set of terms.

The anxiety concerning uncertainty should not be dismissed as some form of commercial rigidity or pedantry. The 'last shot' analysis is easy to apply because advisors are required only to consider whose terms were asserted last and acquiesced in by the opponent.

Admittedly, the 'last shot' approach might not provide 'perfect justice' because there is an element of gamesmanship in winning this contest. But it is clear that English law would not be improved by a frequent and uncertain quest (requiring resort to arbitration or judicial determination) for 'some middle ground' whenever the parties have produced non-matching versions of the proposed terms.

The parties' arbitration clause might cast this issue into a different light. Under the liberal rules governing choice of substantive norms in English arbitration practice, it is possible for parties *expressly* to agree that a dispute concerning the terms of a contract, or of a supposed contract, will be settled by reference to principles of Equity and fair dealing, or some similar extra-legal formula.[128]

For the position under the 'soft law' codes, see PECL, *Principles of European Contract Law*, Article 2:209, stating that 'general conditions form part of the contract to the extent that they are common in substance';[129] and UNIDROIT's *Principles of International Commercial Contracts* (2010), Article 2 (1.22),[130] stating that 'a contract is concluded on the basis of the agreed terms and of any standard terms which are common in substance unless one party clearly indicates in advance, or later and without undue delay informs the other party, that it does not intend to be bound by such a contract'.

---

7. REVOCATION AND TERMINATION OF OFFERS

3.36 *Revocation of offer*[131] *directly or indirectly: firm offers*. An offeree can safely and effectively accept the offer unless he knows of the offer's revocation (or its lapse through effluxion of time). Revocation by the offeror of the offer can be either direct, by telling the offeree to forget it, or indirect. Where the revocation is *direct*, the question is whether the offeree has in fact *discovered* or had the *reasonable opportunity to discover* that the offer is no longer open to acceptance by him. We have seen (see 3.23 on *'The Brimnes'*

---

128 See the reference in section 46(1)(b) of the Arbitration Act 1996 to 'such other considerations as are agreed by them or determined by the tribunal'; *Mustill & Boyd, Commercial Arbitration: Companion Volume* (London, 2001), 326–8 (and 124–7).

129 A. D. M. Forte, in H. MacQueen and R. Zimmermann (eds.), *European Contract Law: Scots and South African Perspectives* (Edinburgh, 2006), chapter 4.

130 3rd edition, 2010, text and comment, is available at: www.unidroit.org/english/principles/contracts/principles2010/integralversionprinciples2010-e.pdf.

131 M. Furmston and G. J. Tolhurst, *Contract Formation: Law and Practice* (Oxford, 2010), chapter 3.

(1975),[132] concerning an unread telex) that an e-mailed, posted or faxed revocation, arriving within normal working hours, will be effective to preclude valid acceptance once the offeree has had a reasonable opportunity (during normal working hours, if he is in business: for this qualification, see *Mondial Shipping & Chartering BV* v. *Astarte Shipping Ltd, 'The Pamela'* (1995)[133] at 3.10) to read the revocation. As for the *indirect* situation, a third party might tell the offeree that the offeror has acted in some way which clearly shows that the offer is no longer open to acceptance by that offeree (for a clear case of indirect revocation, see *Dickinson* v. *Dodds* (1876), 3.37). Treitel suggests this test: 'It is sufficient if the offeree knows from any reliable source that the offeror no longer intends to contract with him.'[134] Treitel notes that this rule imposes a burden upon the offeree of determining whether his source is 'reliable' and thus whether the offer is alive or dead. It is submitted that once a 'real and genuine doubt' has reached the offeree, the offer ceases to be open for acceptance. (Even if the indirectly received information is false or exaggerated, the offeree cannot be liable for not completing the transaction: a positive response from the offeree will be required before legal liability can arise.)

3.37　The leading case on *indirect* revocation is *Dickinson* v. *Dodds* (1876).[135] The case decides the following points: (1) Even if a period for acceptance has been stipulated, the offer cannot be validly accepted once the offeree discovers that the 'deal is off' (see (2)(a) and (b) below). It would be different, however, if the offeree holds a binding option, granted by deed (5.03) or supported by consideration. (2) However: (a) the offeror can revoke the offer by communicating this revocation directly to the other party; or (b) the offeror can escape liability by relying on the fact that the offeree has by some chance acquired knowledge of the offeror's decision or of conduct on the part of the offeror manifestly inconsistent with the offer remaining open for acceptance by the offeree.

> In *Dickinson* v. *Dodds* (1876), on Wednesday the defendant offered to sell a house to the claimant for £800 (in Croft-on-Tees, County Durham). The defendant said that the offer would be left open until 9.00 am on Friday. On Thursday, the defendant sold the house to a third party, but without letting the claimant know. The claimant quickly found out about the sale to the third party from a fourth party. The claimant was undeterred and handed over a letter of acceptance to the defendant before the Friday 9.00 am deadline.
>
> The Court of Appeal (reversing Bacon V-C) held that no contract had arisen because the claimant already knew from the fourth party of the defendant's revocation (or at least of conduct which made satisfaction of the contemplated deal between the claimant and the defendant manifestly impossible). The defendant's assurance that the offer was open for acceptance until 9.00 am on Friday was an empty promise, *nudum pactum*, a bare 'moral' undertaking. It would have been different if, when he made his acceptance, the claimant had been unaware of the defendant's sale to the third party.

132　'The Brimnes' [1975] QB 929, CA (withdrawal of offer effective when telex received during ordinary business hours, even if not in fact read).
133　[1995] 2 Lloyd's Rep 249; [1995] CLC 1011, Gatehouse J.
134　*Treitel* (13th edn, London, 2011), 2–059.
135　(1876) 2 Ch D 463, CA.

3.38 *Reform of the firm offer rule.* It might be objected that the offeree should enjoy protection even if he has not been granted by deed, nor – in the absence of a deed (5.03) – paid for, a binding option agreement (see the preceding paragraph). Some have posed the question: should it not be enough that the offeree has assumed that the promise to keep open the offer was binding?[136] But the response to this is that the offeree has not bought, nor earned the right to, legal protection: the offeror's promise was gratuitous; nor, in the absence of a deed, has the offeror solemnly bound himself to making a legally binding commitment.

> In 1975, the Law Commission, in a working paper, recommended that firm offers, whether in writing or oral, made 'in the course of business', should be binding. But this suggestion has not become law.[137]
>
> The Dubai International Financial Centre has a firm offer rule which permits an irrevocable offer to be made without consideration: there is no need for writing and no need for a specified period.[138] This is the Dubai system's modification of English contract law, based on the perception of this 'commercial hub' of what business people expect in the global marketplace.

3.39 *Communicated rejection of offer.* Any *communicated* rejection kills off the original offer, even if that response is not a counter-offer (3.32).[139] This proposition was characterised as 'trite law' by the Court of Appeal in *Grant* v. *Bragg* (2009).[140] This approach is sound because offerees should be expected to make their minds up and communicate their last thoughts (but, for the situation where a rejection letter, not yet received, is overtaken by a speedier acceptance, and the contract treated as valid, see 3.30). If instead the offeree were at liberty to blow cold and hot, rejecting and then accepting, this would be unfair, cause confusion and stir up litigation.

3.40 *Lapse of time: fixed deadline for acceptance.* Where an offeree is given a specified time within which to accept, but the deadline is missed, the offer will not have been validly accepted (as noted by the Court of Appeal in *Grant* v. *Bragg*, 2009).[141] Of course, a specified period for acceptance can be revoked by the offeror, unless the offeror has given the offeree a binding option, exercisable for a specified time: see above at 3.38.[142]

---

136 M. Spence, *Protecting Reliance* (Oxford, 1999), 116 ff; J. Gordley (ed.), *The Enforceability of Promises in European Law* (Cambridge, 2001), 279 ff (case 13, options given without a charge).

137 Law Commission, 'Firm Offers' (Working Paper No. 60, 1975), at [55] (but suggesting that proposed reform should apply only where the offer is expressed to be irrevocably open for a definite period, not exceeding six months).

138 Article 17(2)(a) of the Contract Law, www.difc.ae/laws-regulations/ (Dubai International Financial Centre).

139 J. Cartwright, *Contract Law: An Introduction to the English Contract Law for the Civil Lawyer* (2nd edn, Oxford, 2013), 110; *Chitty on Contracts* (31st edn, London, 2012), 2–090 (citing *Tinn* v. *Hoffman & Co* (1873) 29 LT 271, 278, Court of Exchequer Chamber).

140 [2009] EWCA Civ 1228; [2010] 1 All ER (Comm) 1166, at [17], *per* Lord Neuberger MR (less clearly, at [22]).

141 [2009] EWCA Civ 1228; [2010] 1 All ER (Comm) 1166, at [25], *per* Lord Neuberger MR (and the point was further accepted as basic Common Law doctrine in *Gibbon* v. *Manchester City Council* [2010] EWCA Civ 726; [2010] 1 WLR 2081, at [16], *per* Moore-Bick LJ).

142 (1876) 2 Ch D 463, CA.

3.41 *Lapse of time: no fixed deadline for acceptance.* In the absence of a specified period, an (unrevoked) offer is open for acceptance only for a reasonable time.[143] In *Manchester Diocesan Council for Education* v. *Commercial & General Investments Ltd* (1970) Buckley J suggested[144] that the better rationale for this is (i) that the offeree's silence or inactivity impliedly indicates rejection of the offer, rather than (ii) the offer at its inception was restricted to a reasonable period and that it will lapse thereafter, or (iii) that the offer has been impliedly withdrawn by the offeror. But, with respect, (ii) should ordinarily govern and be preferred to (i), although test (i) should be treated as potentially supplementing test (ii). Finally, approach (iii) is a 'general' feature of revocation, illustrated by *Dickinson* v. *Dodds* (1876),[145] on which see 3.37.

8. ACCEPTANCE IN THE CONTEXT OF UNILATERAL CONTRACTS

3.42 A unilateral contract is typified by the offer of a reward: 'If you find my lost cat, I will pay you £1,000.' This is an 'if' contract, one party alone being obliged to perform or pay, and that obligation being dependent on the offeree's (non-obligatory) response to the relevant offer. The concept has arisen in family, consumer and commercial contexts.[146] Three issues arise (but only the third is problematic):

(1) *acceptance by performance*: A unilateral contract is normally accepted by complete performance, for example, by the offeree supplying information under an offer of reward.

(2) *no need for explicit acceptance*: There is no need for the offeree(s) to say in advance: 'Yes, we accept your proposal and will do our best to find your cat.' This is because the offeror is deemed to have waived the need for such formal acceptance.

(3) *fixing the moment when the offeror cannot retract*: this is the vexed issue. The better view (see 3.44 below) is that if the offeree has started to perform, an ancillary duty will *sometimes* arise (but not invariably; this will be appropriate only if it would be unjust for the offeror to revoke the offer; and that must depend on various factors; see discussion of the *Luxor* case at 3.44).

3.43 *Waiver of need for explicit acceptance. Carlill* v. *Carbolic Smoke Ball Co.* (1893)[147] is an early example of zealous judicial protection of the 'consumer'.[148] Mrs Carlill seems to fit

---

143   Toulson J in *LJ Korbetis* v. *Transgrain Shipping BV* [2005] EWHC 1345 (QB), at [18]; *Ramsgate Victoria Hotel Co. Ltd* v. *Montefiore* (1866) LR 1 Ex 109; *Manchester Diocesan Council for Education* v. *Commercial & General Investments Ltd* [1970] 1 WLR 241, 247–9, *per* Buckley J (also considering *In re Bowron Bailey & Co* (1868) LR 3 Ch App 592 (obscure reasoning); *Meynell* v. *Surtees* (1855) 1 Jur NS 737, Lord Cranworth LC (emphasising the revocable nature of offers); *Williams* v. *Williams* (1853) 17 Beav 213, Sir John Romilly MR, a contrary dictum).
144   [1970] 1 WLR 241, 247–9, *per* Buckley J (but this point was a dictum).
145   (1876) 2 Ch D 463, CA.
146   *Shadwell* v. *Shadwell* (1860) 9 CB (NS) 159; *Carlill* v. *Carbolic Smoke Ball Co.* [1893] 1 QB 256, CA; *Luxor (Eastbourne) Ltd* v. *Cooper* [1941] AC 108, HL; *Errington* v. *Errington & Woods* [1952] 1 KB 290, CA; *New Zealand Shipping Co. Ltd* v. *AM Satterthwaite & Co. Ltd* ('The Eurymedon') [1975] AC 154, PC; similarly *Shadwell* v. *Shadwell* (1860) 9 CB (NS) 159; *Daulia* v. *Four Millbank Nominees* [1978] Ch 231, 239, CA; *Harvela* v. *Royal Trust Bank of Canada* [1986] AC 207, HL; *Soulsbury* v. *Soulsbury* [2007] EWCA Civ 969; [2008] Fam 1, at [49], [50]; *Attrill* v. *Dresdner Kleinwort Ltd* [2013] EWCA Civ 394; [2013] 3 All ER 807, at [98].
147   [1893] 1 QB 256, CA.
148   A. W. B. Simpson, 'Innovation in Nineteenth Century Contract Law' (1975) 91 LQR 247, at 263–5; and A. W. B. Simpson, 'Quackery and Contract Law: The Case of the Carbolic Smoke Ball' (1985) 14 JLS 345 (the

uncannily the description of Lord Simon of Glaisdale in *Esso Petroleum Ltd* v. *Commissioners of Customs & Excise* (1976): 'a suburban Hampden who was not prepared to forego what he conceived to be his rights or to allow a tradesman to go back on his word.'[149] In the *Carlill* case, the Court of Appeal said that when a contract is construed as 'unilateral', that is, one which imposes a (contingent) obligation only on the offeror, it is no objection that the offeree has not communicated acceptance. This is because the offeror has implicitly 'waived' the need for communication. Therefore, what counts is that the offeree has acted in response to, and in the manner stipulated by, the offer.

In the *Carlill* case (1893), the Carbolic Smoke Ball Company advertised in the *Pall Mall Gazette* that they would pay £100 to anyone who contracted influenza despite using their 'smoke ball'. They also stipulated that this device had to be used both for the period and in the manner specified. To induce custom, the company also said that £1,000 had been deposited in a bank, ready to be paid out. 'Use' of this product involved sniffing the powder several times daily for two weeks. Mrs Carlill bought the smoke ball and used it as stipulated. But she then contracted influenza. She sued successfully for the £100 promised by the company. The Court of Appeal held that an offer can be made to an indefinite class of people. Bowen LJ explained:[150] 'although the offer is made to the world, the contract is made with that limited portion of the public who come forward and perform the condition on the faith of the advertisement.'

The court also held that the company had implicitly waived the need for 'acceptance' before petitioning it for the promised £100. Bowen LJ explained:[151]

> if the person making the offer, expressly or impliedly intimates in his offer that it will be sufficient to act on the proposal without communicating acceptance of it to himself, performance of the condition is a sufficient acceptance without notification.

The court also held that there was 'consideration' supporting the company's promise, notably the detriment suffered in using this appliance;[152] or consideration might be found because the company would receive a benefit, each individual purchase tending to boost trade in the product[153] (on the consideration doctrine, see Chapter 5).

Similarly, the Court of Appeal in *Attrill* v. *Dresdner Kleinwort Ltd* (2013)[154] (see also on this case 3.44, 4.08, 5.12, 5.23 and 6.12) held that an investment bank's announcement to its workforce that the bank would be creating a guaranteed minimum €400m bonus chest, to be distributed on a discretionary basis, was an offer which did not require express acceptance because (a) the bonus scheme was beneficial and did not confer any hardship on the class of offerees, and (b) it would not make sense to confine the bonus scheme to those who had positively accepted.

---

latter is reprinted in A. W. B. Simpson, *Leading Cases in the Common Law* (Oxford, 1995), chapter 10); the *Carbolic Smoke Ball* case was applied in *Bowerman* v. *ABTA Ltd* [1996] CLC 451, noted by G. McMeel, (1997) 113 LQR 47–9.

149   [1976] 1 WLR 1, 6, HL.
150   [1893] 1 QB 256, 268, CA.
151   *Ibid.*, at 269–70.
152   *The Spectator* magazine calculated that Mrs Carlill must have sneezed over 1,000 times administering the ball to herself: A. W. B. Simpson, *Leading Cases in the Common Law* (Oxford, 1995), 274.
153   Similarly, *Edmonds* v. *Lawson* [2000] QB 501, CA (barristers' chambers gaining benefit from having pupil barristers competing for places in chambers as tenants).
154   [2013] EWCA Civ 394; [2013] 3 All ER 807, at [98] and [99].

3.44 *When can the offeror no longer retract the offer without liability to compensate?* The better view is that the offeror is not automatically bound by the offeree's 'commencement of performance' (a view adopted in *Errington* v. *Errington & Woods* (1952)[155] and *Soulsbury* v. *Soulsbury* (2007) (for details see below))[156] and instead the courts will occasionally impose an implied condition which prevents the offeror from revoking (which, if breached, will yield liability in damages, or perhaps produce other contractual relief). This rival and preferable analysis[157] was suggested by Reginald Goff LJ in a dictum in *Daulia* v. *Four Millbank Nominees* (1978),[158] who referred to a possible implied 'obligation on the part of the offeror not to prevent the condition being satisfied, which obligation ... must arise as soon as the offeree starts to perform'. It is submitted that the offeree should enjoy such protection only where the merits of the case manifestly require. Relevant factors should include: (1) the nature and intensity of the offeree's reliance; (2) whether the offeror might otherwise be unjustly enriched (as on the facts of the *Errington* case); (3) whether the offeree has a strong interest in completing performance or indeed any realistic alternative (again, note the facts of the *Errington* case); and (4) whether the offeree should stoically accept his wasted efforts and disappointment, taking it 'on the chin', as one of the hazards accompanying his activity in the relevant field (as in the *Luxor* case).[159] If, applying these criteria, it is decided that the offeree requires legal protection, the court must further decide: (a) whether the offeree should be permitted to perform and so satisfy the condition, giving him entitlement to the promised 'prize' or consideration, as on the facts of the *Errington* case (see above); or (b) whether it is enough to indemnify the offeree for the reliance loss incurred in attempting to satisfy that condition (money expended in preparation for, or partial performance of, the contemplated response).

The decision of the House of Lords in *Luxor (Eastbourne) Ltd* v. *Cooper* (1941) shows that not all offerees should receive such protection.[160] Here it was held that an estate agent was not entitled to payment of an agreed commission (or compensatory damages) even though he had 'found' a prospective buyer, who was ready and willing to proceed, and then the agent had introduced this potential buyer to the principal/owner. On these facts, therefore, the principal/owner was at liberty to change his mind, without triggering a liability to pay commission. It would have been different if the principal/owner failed to pay the commission to the agent after the principal had decided to enter into a binding contract of sale with the purchaser who had been found by the agent.[161] The

---

155 [1952] 1 KB 290, 295, CA.
156 [2007] EWCA Civ 969; [2008] Fam 1, at [49] and [50].
157 J. O'Sullivan and J. Hilliard, *The Law of Contract* (6th edn, Oxford, 2014), 2.73 to 2.75, attractively prefer the implied collateral contract analysis, citing Lord Cave in *Morrison Shipping Co. Ltd* v. *The Crown* (1924) 20 Lloyd's Rep 283, HL; C. Harpum and D. Lloyd-Jones, [1979] CLJ 31; cf *Treitel* (13th edn, London, 2011), 2–053, regards this 'ancillary obligation' analysis as 'artificial'; but why?
158 [1978] Ch 231, 239, CA.
159 *Luxor (Eastbourne) Ltd* v. *Cooper* [1941] AC 108, HL.
160 [1941] AC 108, HL.
161 Cf *Alpha Trading Ltd* v. *Dunnshaw-Patten Ltd* [1981] QB 290, 306, CA (principal has actually entered into a binding transaction with a third party, but the principal fails to honour that contract, choosing not to perform; the agent is entitled to compensation for loss of his commission); and see Lord Wright in the *Luxor* case, [1941] AC 108, 149–50; furthermore, selling agent must be the effective cause for securing a buyer if that agent's commission is to become payable, otherwise, where more than one agent is used, a seller would be exposed to the risk of having to pay commission more than once: *County Homesearch Co. (Thames & Chilterns) Ltd* v. *Cowham* [2008] EWCA Civ 26; [2008] 1 WLR 909, at [11] ff (the case itself concerned a purchaser's agent).

contract in the *Luxor* case is 'aleatory', that is, the estate agent runs the risk of no gain if the principal/owner, for whatever reason, decides not to seal the deal. In normal times, estate agents can make a good living (although, sadly, in times of deep recession, their working lives are devoted to sharpening pencils and tidying drawers).[162] As Lord Russell said:

> The agent takes the risk in the hope of a substantial remuneration for comparatively small exertion. In the case of the [agent] his [commission contract] was made on September 23, 1935; his client's offer [to buy the cinemas] was made on October 2, 1935. A sum of £10,000 (the equivalent of the remuneration of a year's work by a Lord Chancellor) for work done within a period of eight or nine days is no mean reward, and is one well worth a risk. There is no lack of business efficacy in such a contract, even though the principal is free to refuse to sell to the agent's client.[163]

By contrast, in *Errington* v. *Errington & Woods* (1952)[164] the merits of the offeree were strong and the transaction was not 'aleatory' and indeed not commercial. A father told his son and daughter-in-law: 'If you pay off the remaining mortgage instalments on this house, the property will be yours.' By saying this, the father furthermore impliedly promised that they would enjoy undisturbed possession of the property so long as they kept paying the mortgage. Acquisition of the full title, therefore, would require the couple to make all remaining mortgage payments. Denning LJ explained:[165]

> The father's promise was a unilateral contract – a promise of the house in return for their act of paying the instalments. It could not be revoked by him once the couple entered on performance of the act, but it would cease to bind him if they left it incomplete and unperformed, which they have not done . . . If the daughter-in-law continues to pay all the building society instalments, the couple will be entitled to have the property transferred to them as soon as the mortgage is paid off.

Soulsbury v. *Soulsbury* (2007)[166] followed the *Errington* case's analysis. Here an ex-husband promised to leave his ex-wife £100,000 in his will if she refrained from enforcing a maintenance order against him. She complied with that condition. Shortly before his death, the ex-husband remarried, and his will was revoked by operation of law, thus denying the first wife her promised sum. After his death, it was held that the first wife had a good claim to the sum against the husband's estate. Longmore LJ said of the *Carlill* and *Errington* cases:

> Once the promisee acts on the promise by inhaling the smoke ball, by starting the walk to York [a 'classroom' example] or (as here) by not suing for the maintenance to which she was entitled, the promisor cannot revoke or withdraw his offer.

But it is not clear how this approach would work where, as in *Soulsbury* v. *Soulsbury* (2007),[167] the offeree is not being asked to do anything positive, but is instead being asked to refrain from doing something; in such a case, 'commencement of abstention' is a difficult criterion.

---

162   P. S. Atiyah, *Essays on Contract* (Oxford, 1987), 203 ff; the problem is analogous to the question of a legitimate interest in performing, as developed in the *White & Carter* v. *McGregor* line of cases, see 18.03 ff.
163   [1941] AC 108, 125–6, HL.
164   [1952] 1 KB 290, CA; *Soulsbury* v. *Soulsbury* [2007] EWCA Civ 969; [2008] Fam 1, at [49] and [50].
165   [1952] 1 KB 290, 295, CA.
166   [2007] EWCA Civ 969; [2008] Fam 1.
167   *Ibid.*, at [49], [50].

9. AUCTIONS, TENDERS AND SEALED BID COMPETITIONS

3.45 *Auctions.*[168] The Court of Appeal in *Barry* v. *Davies* (2000)[169] awarded damages *against an auctioneer* when he refused to accept a bidder's acceptance of an item put up for auction without a reserve price (and perhaps the same analysis would apply when the unaccepted bid has exceeded the reserve price).

> In *Barry* v. *Davies* (2000) a third party's engine analysers were offered for sale by Customs & Excise at auction. Customs told the auctioneer (Cross) to sell them without reserve. The claimant saw the machines being delivered to the auction house five days before the auction. Cross told him that they would be sold without reserve. The claimant attended the auction house a few minutes before noon. The law report then states:
>
> > When it came to the lots in question Cross said that the machines were to be 'sold that day' on behalf of the VAT office, that each was worth £14,000, 'ready to plug in and away you go'. He tried to obtain a bid of £5,000 to start with; there was no bid; he tried £3,000; still no response. He then asked what bids there were for the machines, and the plaintiff bid £200 for each. No other bid was made. In fact Mr Cross had received a bid [before the auction had begun] from his son-in-law for £400 each; but he made no mention of this. Mr Cross then withdrew the machines from the sale.
>
> And so the claimant's bid had not been accepted, even though it was the highest bid. The court awarded damages against the auctioneer to compensate for the bidder's 'loss of bargain', that is, the difference between the amount of the claimant's bid and the market value of the goods. It was held that the auctioneer had impliedly committed himself to a collateral contract to accept the highest bid. The consideration (the element of bargain supplied by the bidder to support this collateral contract: see Chapter 5) was twofold: the bidder assumes the risk that his bid might be accepted; secondly, auctioneers receive the benefit that sales interest might be stimulated by the bidder's intervention.

The 'implied collateral' obligation is a juristic tool deployed to achieve a contractual solution in pre-contractual contexts, where the justice of the case demands. Indeed, a leitmotiv in the ensuing paragraphs will be the courts' willingness to construct an implied collateral obligation and, in support of this, the courts' strategic finding of 'consideration'.

3.46 *Tenders.* A tender is an invitation to bid for a specified project, such as construction of a building, or provision of other services. There is now statutory regulation of certain types of tender, as a result of EU law. As Treitel explains:[170]

> The Common Law position . . . is in some situations modified by legislation . . . [giving] effect to EC Council Directives, the object of which is to prevent discrimination in the award of major contracts for public works, supplies and services in one Member State against nationals of another Member State. These

---

168 M. Furmston and G. J. Tolhurst, *Contract Formation: Law and Practice* (Oxford, 2010), chapter 5.
169 [2000] 1 WLR 1962, CA.
170 *Treitel* (13th edn, London, 2011), 2–013.

Regulations[171] restrict the freedom of the body seeking tenders to decide which tender it will accept and provide a remedy in damages for a person who has made a tender and is prejudiced by breach of the rules.

3.47 At Common Law (for the statutory regulation of some types of tender, see 3.46) a person who invites tenders (the 'invitor') does not (unless he states otherwise) assume an obligation to accept any of these tenders. This was decided in *Spencer* v. *Harding* (1870)[172] (and acknowledged in *William Lacey (Hounslow) Ltd* v. *Davis* (1957)).[173] Thus there is no duty to accept the highest tender for the purchase of goods, nor is there any duty to accept the lowest tender price for the opportunity to construct a building, etc. This laissez-faire approach is sound; otherwise, the invitor would have no discretion to decide which, if any, tender to accept. For example, the invitor might lack confidence in the relevant entity's capacity to deliver on time, or might find reason to suspect that company of bad employment practices.

As for the problem of delay, consider, for example, the very late completion of the new Wembley Stadium in London. The building contract was won by an Australian company, which had presented a low tender. But there was a substantial delay in completing the stadium.[174] During the period of delay, the Millennium Stadium in Cardiff had to be used to host FA Cup finals and other important matches.

3.48 However, the Court of Appeal's decision in *Blackpool and Fylde Aero Club* v. *Blackpool Borough Council* (1990)[175] imposes three obligations upon the invitor:

(1) The invitor must 'consider' each valid tender.

(2) The invitor must ignore invalid tenders. (For example, in *Fairclough Building* v. *Port Talbot BC* (1992)[176] the Court of Appeal held that the invitor had not acted wrongly when it refused to consider a particular tender; that tender would have been invalid or at least highly problematic because a member of the tender committee was married to a director of the relevant tendering company.)

(3) The invitor must not 'jump the gun' and award the contract ahead of the deadline for submission of tenders. (Query: what if the invitor decided before the deadline to call the whole tender off? It would appear that the invitor can do so without incurring liability.) These are minimal standards of fair dealing. Their recognition shows that, in this context, the English courts explicitly (for example, in the *Pratt* case (2003), discussed at 3.49) recognise a principle of good faith bargaining (generally on good faith, see 21.01 ff).[177]

---

171 Public Contracts Regulations 2006 (SI 2006 No. 5) and Utilities Contracts Regulations 2006 (SI 2006 No. 6). On the first of these, *Natural World Products Ltd* v. *ARC 21* [2007] NIQB 19; *Croft House Care Ltd* v. *Durham CC* [2010] EWHC 909 (TCC); *Mears Ltd* v. *Leeds CC* [2011] EWHC 40 (QB).
172 (1870) LR 5 CP 561.
173 [1957] 1 WLR 932, 939, Barry J.
174 *Daily Telegraph*, 4 October 2007.
175 [1990] 1 WLR 1195, CA.
176 (1992) 62 BLR 82; 33 Con LR 24, CA.
177 On Commonwealth cases, see I. Duncan Wallace, (2001) 117 LQR 351–8, noting especially *Martel Building Ltd* v. *Canada* (2000) 193 DLR (4th) 1 (Supreme Court of Canada); and I. Duncan Wallace, (1999) 115 LQR 583–6, noting *MJB Enterprises Ltd* v. *Defence Construction (1951) Ltd* (1999) 170 DLR (4th) 577 (Supreme Court of Canada), prescribing implied contractual obligations binding upon an invitor towards tenderers.

The facts of the *Blackpool and Fylde Aero Club* v. *Blackpool Borough Council* (1990)[178] case were as follows. The defendant council invited seven organisations to tender to run a franchise at the council's airport. The deadline for submission of tenders was noon on 17 March 1983. The franchise was to fly pleasure trips over Blackpool for tourists. Three prospective franchisees responded. One of these was the claimant who had been running the franchise under the previous contract. The claimant submitted objectively the best tender for the new franchise. But, as noted at 3.47 above, the basic rule in *Spencer* v. *Harding* (1870) does not give the person making the best tender the contractual right to 'win'.

In the *Blackpool* case, the claimant delivered its tender by hand (not by Royal Mail) to the council's letter box, at 11.00 am on 17 March 1983, just one hour before the deadline. But the council's janitor failed to clear the letter box until the next day. In error, the council stamped the claimant's tender bid 'late'. And so the council decided it would be improper to consider it. Instead, they awarded the franchise to a third party who had undoubtedly met the deadline for his tender. The claimant sued the council, alleging that it had been unfairly excluded from the tender competition.

The Court of Appeal held that the council had breached an implied collateral contract regulating the fair and proper management of the tendering process.[179] On these facts, the breach was the failure to consider a valid tender made in good time.[180] The claimant was entitled to damages for loss of the chance to compete in the tender competition (although assessment of those damages was a matter remitted to the first instance court; in *Allied Maples Group* v. *Simmons & Simmons* (1995),[181] the leading modern contract case on this topic, the Court of Appeal held that there can be no recovery in respect of a lost chance if the likelihood of its occurrence cannot be regarded as 'realistic' or 'substantial': see 18.32).

In the *Blackpool* case, Bingham LJ said:[182]

> where, as here, tenders are solicited from selected parties all of them known to the invitor, and ... [the] invitation prescribes a clear, orderly and familiar procedure ... the invitee is ... protected at least to this extent: if he submits a conforming tender before the deadline he is entitled ... to be sure that his tender will after the deadline be opened and considered in conjunction with all other conforming tenders or at least that his tender will be considered if others are.

3.49   More broadly, there is an implied duty on the part of the invitor to conduct the tender process in good faith.[183] This proposition, which can now be safely said to represent English law, was approved by the Privy Council in *Pratt Contractors Ltd* v. *Transit New Zealand* (2003),[184] adopting an Australian decision, *Hughes Aircraft Systems International* v. *Air*

---

178   [1990] 1 WLR 1195, CA.
179   [1990] 1 WLR 1195, 1201–2, CA, *per* Bingham LJ.
180   Stocker LJ added as a dictum the obligation to consider the tender in good faith: [1990] 1 WLR 1195, 1204E; on this, see the Privy Council's decision in *Pratt Contractors Ltd* v. *Transit New Zealand* (2003), summarised at 3.49.
181   [1995] 1 WLR 1602, CA (noted by T. Church, [1996] CLJ 187); considered in *4 Eng Ltd* v. *Harper* [2008] EWHC 915 (Ch); [2009] Ch 91 (noted by P. Mitchell, (2009) 125 LQR 12–17).
182   [1990] 1 WLR 1195, 1201–2, CA.
183   [2003] UKPC 83; [2004] BLR 143; 100 Con LR 29.
184   *Ibid.*

Services Australia (1997)[185] (the same Australian decision has been adopted by a court in Northern Ireland in *Natural World Products Ltd* v. *ARC 21* (2007)).[186] In the *Hughes Aircraft* case (1997), Finn J (a distinguished judge and academic commentator)[187] declared that the invitor owes an obligation to adhere strictly to its *stipulated tender criteria*.[188] These must be applied objectively and fairly (no such stipulated tender criteria existed on the facts of the *Blackpool* case, 3.48).

The *Hughes Aircraft* case (1997)[189] concerned rival tenders within the aircraft industry. The defendant ('the invitor') was a public corporation. It was responsible for the air traffic system in Australia. In response, Hughes, a Californian company, and a second company, tendered. Hughes lost. The tender invitation had requested best and final offers, and it had specified various criteria, including use of an independent auditor. Furthermore, the successful tenderer had been allowed to make a substantial reduction in its price at the last stage of the bidding.

Finn J held that the defendant had breached an implied obligation to conduct the process fairly: (1) the tender contained various criteria but these had not been applied correctly; (2) there had been a breach of confidentiality so that one bidder had been told details of the other's bid; in light of this leaked information, a revised bid had been made; and this had been illegitimately accepted.

The Privy Council in *Pratt Contractors Ltd* v. *Transit New Zealand* (2003) held that although there is an implied duty on the part of the invitor to conduct the tender process in good faith, this does not preclude the tender committee from drawing on its members' specific knowledge of the competing parties' commercial performance and 'track record'.[190] The committee was entitled to make informed commercial decisions whether to select or reject particular tenders.

In *Pratt Contractors Ltd* v. *Transit New Zealand* (2003), P submitted two unsuccessful tenders to T for a contract to realign a state highway. T's tender committee included Y, who knew of P's business methods and engineering competence. P contended that T had breached its duty to act fairly as there was a real risk of bias due to Y's involvement in the evaluation process. The case looks to be an example of 'sour grapes' by the loser. Lord Hoffmann explained:[191]

> The duty to act fairly meant that all the tenderers had to be treated equally. One tenderer could not be given a higher mark than another if their attributes were the same. But [the tender committee] was not obliged to give tenderers the same mark if it honestly thought

---

185   (1997) 146 ALR 1, 35, 37, 40, 66–7, 228–9.
186   [2007] NIQB 19.
187   Arthur Goodhart Visiting Professor in Legal Science, University of Cambridge, 2010–11.
188   (1997) 146 ALR 1, 35, 37, 40, 66–7, 228–9 (referring to *Pratt Contractors Ltd* v. *Palmerston North City Council* [1995] 1 NZLR 469, 478–9).
189   [1990] 1 WLR 1195, CA.
190   [2003] UKPC 83; [2004] BLR 143; 100 Con LR 29.
191   *Ibid.*, at [47].

that their attributes were different. Nor did the duty of fairness mean that [the tender committee] were obliged to appoint people who came to the task without any views about the tenderers, whether favourable or adverse. It would have been impossible to have a [tender committee] competent to perform its function unless it consisted of people with enough experience to have already formed opinions about the merits and demerits of roading contractors.

3.50 *Sealed bids.* This is an arm's length competition over price, without the opportunity for revision of bids. Two or more prospective bidders are invited to submit their best bid by a sealed bidding process.

This is not an auction, because the latter requires sequential bidding – traditionally by presence of principals or agents in an auction room – although on-line auctions have now become common; by contrast, the respondent in a sealed bid context (i) makes a shot in the dark because the others' responses are confidential; and (ii) has only one chance to name a figure.

3.51 The leading case on sealed bids is *Harvela* v. *Royal Trust Company of Canada* (1986).[192] This case (examined more fully in the next two paragraphs) establishes two points.

(1) A person submitting the best sealed bid is entitled (in the absence of relevant formalities: see 5.03 ff) to receive the promised subject matter (in that case, shares in a private company); and that entitlement should be conceptualised as the bidder's successful completion of a unilateral contract: 'if you make the best sealed bid, you will be entitled to victory.'

(2) A bidder will infringe the implicit rules of the sealed bid contest if he makes a free-standing or supplementary (uninvited) 'referential bid': for example, 'I furthermore bid £1,000 more than the highest fixed sealed bid' (for the possibility that capped referential bids are valid, provided the invitation makes this clear, see 3.53 (at the end of that paragraph) and 3.54). The referential bid will then be invalid.

The defendant, Royal Trust, had asked Harvela and Sir Leonard Outerbridge to submit rival sealed bids for the purchase of shares in a private company. Royal Trust said it would accept the higher bid. Sir Len's bid comprised two elements: (1) C$2.1m (despite the Canadian currency, this was an English decision); or (2) '$101,000 (Canadian) in excess of any other offer'. Bid (1) is a fixed bid, and bid (2) is a referential bid. In the event, Harvela's fixed bid was higher than Sir Len's fixed bid. So Royal Trust accepted Sir Len's referential bid. It awarded victory to Sir Len at a sum C$101,000 higher than Harvela's fixed bid. The House of Lords declared that the referential bid was invalid (see further below). Harvela was the true winner. It was entitled to have the shares transferred and registered in its name, by the remedy of specific performance (18.33 ff; this equitable remedy is available to compel transfers of shares in a private company, but not in a public company).

192 [1986] AC 207, HL.

3.52 *Harvela: the unilateral contract analysis.* In his judgment in *Harvela*, Lord Diplock suggested that the sealed bidding process involved two stages. First, Royal Trust's invitation to accept the higher bid involved[193] a unilateral contract: if you prepare a valid higher bid, you will win, or perhaps be compensated for being denied the chance to win. The second stage is as follows: if it is clear that you are the outright winner, you are entitled to the private company shares, provided the winner pays for them; at this second stage, a contract of sale, a bilateral arrangement, has arisen.

3.53 *Harvela and the 'referential bid' issue.* In the *Harvela* case, Lord Templeman gave two main reasons for rejecting Sir Leonard's attempt to make a referential bid.[194] First, the reason why the other bidder, Harvela, had not made a referential bid was that the invitation to bid, on an objective view, did not indicate that such a 'sneaky' bid was permissible. This is the objection that the terms of the invitation expressly *or impliedly* prohibit a referential bid. Secondly, Lord Templeman noted that an impasse would emerge if more than one respondent made a referential bid (unless, where there are only two bidders, the referential bid is capped, that is, subject to a maximum figure). This is the objection based upon practicability. As for the first point, it appears that the correct analysis is that the referential bid is invalid, but the same party's fixed bid is valid (there is no sound reason to punish the maker of a referential bid by invalidating his fixed bid). And so, if X bids £1,000, and Y bids '£1,001, or £10 higher than another's bid, if the other's bid is greater than my fixed bid', Y should win by virtue of his fixed bid of £1,001.

However, in the following passage, Lord Templeman contemplated the possibility that referential bids might be expressly invited, provided each was capped. He said:[195]

> It would have been possible for the vendors to conduct an auction sale through the medium of confidential referential bids but only by making express provision in the invitation for the purpose. It would not have been sufficient for the invitation expressly to authorise 'referential bids' without more ... *It would have been necessary for the invitation to require each bidder who made a referential bid to specify a maximum sum he was prepared to bid. That requirement would ensure that the sale was not abortive and that both bidders had a genuine chance of winning* ... The sale would in effect be an auction sale and produce the consequences of an auction sale because the vendors would have made express provision for bids to be adjusted and finalised by reference to the maximum bid of the unsuccessful bidder. But without such express provisions the invitation is not consistent with an auction sale. [emphasis added]

Furthermore, unless all bidding parties make referential capped bids, one party might come badly unstuck. Consider this example: A asked X and Y to submit fixed bids and permitted them also to make a referential bid (A failed to specify that (i) the referential bids must be capped and (ii) each party must make a referential bid and a fixed bid); X asked Y if Y was going to make a referential bid. Y said 'yes'; whereupon X (maliciously) presented a

193   *Ibid.*, at 224.
194   [1986] AC 207, 231–2, HL.
195   *Ibid.*, at 232–3.

fixed bid of £1m, much higher than expected. Y's fixed bid was for £100,000, and Y's referential bid was for '£100 more than the X's fixed bid'. Y is not prepared to pay £1,000,100.

3.54 *Summary concerning 'referential bids'.* To sum up: (1) it is possible that future cases will permit a capped referential bid to be considered, *if the invitation expressly permits a referential bid*; (2) such a permission should be interpreted as requiring each referential bid to be capped; and so *a person who makes an uncapped referential bid should not count*; (3) parties presenting referential bids would need to make two bids: one fixed bid, and a second referential bid subject to a cap; (4) but it is not clear what would happen if X bid 1,000, and a referential bid of 10, subject to a cap of 2,000 and Y bid 3,000, with a referential bid of 20, but failed to specify a cap. Should Y be disqualified, so that his fixed bid of 3,000 (greater than X's cap of 2,000) is irrelevant? It is submitted that there is no sound reason to punish the maker of the uncapped referential bid by invalidating his fixed bid.

10. THE OBJECTIVE PRINCIPLE OF CONSENT

3.55 The English courts recognise the so-called 'objective principle' of agreement.[196] As Lord Reid said in *McCutcheon* v. *David MacBrayne Ltd* (1964):[197] '[T]he judicial task is not to discover the actual intentions of each party; it is to decide what each was reasonably entitled to conclude from the attitude of the other.' This principle requires a party's language or conduct to be interpreted in the manner in which objectively and reasonably it might be understood by the other party. The principle has a large application because it will determine the following issues: whether the relevant words or conduct should be regarded as an offer or as an invitation to treat; whether there has been an acceptance of an offer; whether a particular term is being proposed; whether a person is repudiating a contract; and whether the other party is accepting such a repudiation.

3.56 *Rationale of the objective principle.* This principle protects an addressee against the surprise and injustice which would result if the communicating party's true but non-apparent intentions or private meanings were to govern instead. The objective principle also promotes certainty and predictability. It promotes out-of-court settlement by the parties: guided by this objective criterion, the parties are more likely to be correct in predicting the manner in which the courts will interpret disputed conduct and words. Furthermore, it facilitates decision-making. It would be hopeless for the courts to seek to discover, many

---

196 D. Friedmann, (2003) 119 LQR 68; J. R. Spencer, [1974] CLJ 104; W. Howarth, (1984) 100 LQR 265; J. Vorster, (1987) 103 LQR 274; M. Chen-Wishart, in J. W. Neyers, R. Bronaugh and S. G. A. Pitel (eds.), *Exploring Contract Law* (Oxford, 2009), 341; T. Endicott, 'Objectivity, Subjectivity and Incomplete Agreements' in J. Horder (ed.), *Oxford Essays in Jurisprudence* (Oxford, 2000), 159. McLauchlan has lucidly distinguished (although this distinction has a long lineage) (1) the 'promisee'-based form of objectivity from (2) the 'detached observer' or 'fly-on-the-wall' form of objectivity. The preferred form is (1). The passage from McLauchlan, too long to quote here, merits close attention: D. McLauchlan, 'Refining Rectification' (2014) 130 LQR 83, at 88–90.
197 [1964] 1 WLR 125, HL; traced in *Shogun Finance Co. Ltd* v. *Hudson* [2004] 1 AC 919, at [183], to *Gloag on Contract* (2nd edn, Edinburgh, 1929), at 7 (Scots contract textbook); see also the clear statement by Lord Steyn, 'Contract Law: Fulfilling the Reasonable Expectations of Honest Men' (1997) 113 LQR 433–4.

months or years after the relevant facts occurred, whether a party's words or conduct had been intended by him in some sense different from their apparent meaning.[198]

Lord Diplock in 'The Hannah Blumenthal' (1983)[199] said that the objective principle should not be understood to require actual detrimental reliance upon the language used in order to activate this principle. It is enough that the addressee can be taken to have assumed (that is, to have relied cognitively) that the objective meaning of the words would operate. (Andrew Smith J in the *Maple Leaf* case (2009) suggested – the point did not directly arise for decision in the case – that the addressee, B, cannot rely on the objective appearance that A is intending to enter into contractual relations if A's words and conduct had neither led B to believe that A so intended, nor if B 'had simply formed no view one way or the other as to whether [A] so intended'; for, in this situation, B has not adopted the objective inference that A was intending to contract; but it will be incumbent on A to show that B did not entertain the objective meaning.)[200]

In *Shah* v. *Shah* (2001) (5.03), the Court of Appeal held that the covenantor's act of delivering an imperfect deed (imperfect because the deed was invalidly witnessed) to the covenantee created an estoppel by representation.[201] This estoppel rendered effective the technically invalid deed. The covenantee's 'reliance' on the representation was his assumption that the deed was legally valid.

3.57 *Situations where there is no objective consensus.* No objective consensus can be discerned if the parties have purported to agree terms but even their explicit versions are manifestly and irreconcilably in conflict. A subtler problem emerges if, as *Raffles* v. *Wichelhaus* (1864) decided, parties have used the same language but on closer examination of the surrounding facts it emerges that they have referred to two distinct subject matters, producing a *latent* conflict which the courts cannot resolve[202] (see 4.10 for details of that case).

3.58 *Illustrations of the objective principle producing the conclusion that a valid contract exists.* Several situations will be examined: one party's lack of awareness of the other's insanity (3.59); one party's genuine belief that the other party is proposing an offer to the first party (3.60); and one party's confusion concerning the terms of the proposal (the other party not having caused, nor having been aware of, that confusion) (3.61).

---

198   Cf St Germain, *Doctor and Student*, Book III, chapter VI, section V: 'of the intent inward of the heart man's law cannot judge'.
199   [1983] 1 AC 834, 915–16, HL.
200   *Maple Leaf Macro Volatility Master Fund* v. *Rouvroy* [2009] EWHC 257 (Comm); [2009] 2 All ER (Comm) 287; [2009] 1 Lloyd's Rep 476, at [228]; in fact, this point was *obiter* because the judge held, at [229], that the addressee did assume that the objective meaning would operate in his favour (affirmed on appeal, but without discussion of this point, at [2009] EWCA Civ 1334).
201   [2001] 4 All ER 138, CA, at [30] ff (witness not in room at time of covenantor's signature; non-compliance with section 1(3) of the Law of Property (Miscellaneous Provisions) Act 1989). For a restriction, see 5.03, n. 10.
202   (1864) 2 H & C 906, Court of Exchequer; G. Gilmore, *The Death of Contract* (Columbus, OH, 1974), 35 ff; A. W. B. Simpson, *Leading Cases in the Common Law* (Oxford, 1995), 135 ff; C. MacMillan, *Mistakes in Contract Law* (Oxford, 2010), 186 ff; G. Spark, *Vitiation of Contracts* (Cambridge, 2013), chapter 7; on this 1864 decision, see 'The Great Peace' [2003] QB 679, CA, at [28] and [29].

3.59 *One party's insanity not known to the other.*[203] At Common Law the objective principle protects a party who is unaware of the other's mental incapacity. The Privy Council in *Hart* v. *O'Connor* (1985)[204] made clear that a contract will arise in this situation. This is a strong application of the objective principle, because (against this decision) it might be argued that there should be no contract if one party suffers mental incapacity. This was in fact the original rule. But that approach was long ago rejected by the English courts, and this application of the objective principle was confirmed in *Hart* v. *O'Connor* (1985).[205]

By contrast, the Supreme Court in *Dunhill* v. *Burgin (No.'s 1 and 2)* (2014)[206] held that an agreement reached without awareness that a party is in fact suffering from a lack of mental capacity is invalid if the agreement is a compromise or settlement of pending or contemplated civil proceedings (whether the party under a disability is a claimant or defendant).[207] Such a settlement requires the court's approval,[208] including settlement before formal civil proceedings are begun[209] (here judicial approval will require an application under CPR Part 8 by a 'litigation friend').[210]

3.60 *One party is unaware that the offer is not aimed at him.* If X reasonably believes that the other is making a contractual offer to him, X should be entitled to accept that proposal.

In *Moran* v. *University College Salford (No. 2)* (1993),[211] the defendant university offered Moran a place to study physiotherapy for the forthcoming academic year, which he accepted in good faith. But the offer was a clerical error. The fact that this was an error was revealed to him only in early September. University central clearing had been completed by then, and so he missed an academic year because his Salford place had been denied him at the last minute. Relying on his assumption that he had a secure place, he had quit his job and accommodation in London.

The Court of Appeal held that a contract had arisen, in accordance with the objective principle. Moran was entitled to relief. But this took the form of compensation for his detrimental reliance on the offer, rather than an order compelling the university to take him that year or in the future.

---

203   G. Spark, *Vitiation of Contracts* (Cambridge, 2013), chapter 2, 53–61.

204   [1985] 2 All ER 880, PC (the 'rule in *Imperial Loan Co* v. *Stone* [1892] 1 QB 599', see *Blankley* v. *Central Manchester and Manchester Children's University Hospitals NHS Trust* [2014] EWHC 168; [2014] 1 WLR 2683, at [30], *per* Phillips J); however, where the *incapax's* property is subject to the control of the court, under sections 15 ff of the Mental Capacity Act 2005, transactions which would be inconsistent with the court's control of those assets will be void as against that party; *Chitty on Contracts* (31st edn, London, 2012), 8-074, and *Treitel* (13th edn, London, 2011), 12-056, 12-057.

205   *Molton* v. *Camroux* (1849) 4 Exch 17, 154 ER 1107 (Court of Exchequer Chamber), examined in *Hart* v. *O'Connor* [1985] 2 All ER 880, 888E; for citation of the opposite approach in Scotland, see *ibid.*, at 888A.

206   [2014] UKSC 18; [2014] 1 WLR 933.

207   CPR 21.10 (introduced in 2007); D. Foskett, *The Law and Practice of Compromise* (7th edn, London, 2010), chapter 27, and noting the impact of the Mental Capacity Act 2005, which took effect on 1 October 2007.

208   CPR 21.10.

209   CPR 21.10(2).

210   CPR 21.2.

211   *Moran* v. *University College Salford (No. 2)* [1993] 4 Educ LR 187; *Independent*, 26 November 1993, CA (cf the problematic reasoning in *Upton-on-Severn Rural District Council* v. *Powell* [1942] 1 All ER 220: contract found for hire of fire services, even where neither party contemplated a contractual arrangement: *Treitel* (13th edn, London, 2011), 2–048).

It should be noted that no contract would have arisen if Moran had known – or perhaps ought reasonably to have known – of the university's mistake.

3.61 *No 'snapping up' of obviously erroneous presentation of terms.* One party is unaware of the other party's mistaken presentation of the terms of the proposed deal. A contracting party cannot invoke his own mistake concerning a term if (1) the other was not aware of it; (2) nor can he be deemed to have been aware of it (on the latter permutation, see *OT Africa Lines* v. *Vickers plc* (1996) at 3.063, 10.20); (3) nor did he induce the other's error (on this see the Scriven Bros case at 3.62).

In *Centrovincial Estates plc* v. *Merchant Investors Assurance Co. Ltd* (1983),[212] the landlord proposed a renewal of a lease at rent of £ *x* (but it had intended a higher rent). The tenant accepted the offer of £ *x*. In an appeal concerning a summary judgment, the Court of Appeal held that the tenant was prima facie entitled to a lease at that rent, unless at trial it could be shown by the landlord that the error was apparent to the tenant. If the error were shown to be apparent, the tenant could not take advantage of it and the objective principle would then melt away.

3.62 *One party innocently misleads the other into mistakenly presenting or accepting terms.* X cannot take advantage of Y's error if the latter has been led into error by misleading conduct on X's part, even if that conduct was innocent. Conduct is enough: there is no need for a verbal misrepresentation (on misrepresentation, see Chapter 9).

In *Scriven Bros* v. *Hindley* (1913), a buyer had successfully bid for goods at auction.[213] He then tried to resile from the contract, contending that he had honestly believed he was bidding for hemp, whereas the relevant lot was 'tow', an inferior commodity. Normally, the buyer would be bound by the objective principle to pay for the tow because the other party would assume reasonably that this is what the buyer wanted. However, it appeared that the auction had been organised in a confusing manner and that this had misled the buyer. He had assumed that chalk marks on the auction floor indicated that the lot was hemp rather than tow. The judge directed the jury that the buyer could resist a claim for payment if the auctioneer, who was the seller's agent, had (even innocently) induced the buyer's understandable confusion in this way.

3.63 *One party's awareness of the other's mistaken presentation or acceptance of terms.* A line of cases demonstrates that errors concerning a term of the supposed transaction cannot be 'snapped up' in bad faith by the other party. In *Hartog* v. *Colin & Shields* (1939), Singleton J held that if the buyer knows of the seller's error concerning the price, the buyer cannot 'snap up' the mistaken offer.[214] In *OT Africa Lines* v. *Vickers plc* (1996), Mance J suggested that

212 [1983] Com LR 158.
213 [1913] 3 KB 564.
214 [1939] 3 All ER 566, Singleton J.

the 'knowledge' test is wider: whether one party knew *or should reasonably have known* of the other party's error concerning price[215] (although, on the facts of that case, there was no reason for the offeree to have realised that the other party had become flustered over the relevant term: see further 10.20).

See also 3.02 concerning *Crest Nicholson (Londinium) Limited v. Akaria Investments Ltd* (2010)[216] on the related but prior question whether party A has made an offer to party B, or whether B did realise, or should have realised, that there was no such offer made.

See the end of 3.64 for the suggestion that where an error as to terms is 'known to the other', the transaction, although provisionally void for unilateral error, can be ratified on the non-mistaken party's supposed terms.[217]

The Court of Appeal in Singapore in *Chwee Kin Keong v. Digilandmall.com Pte Ltd* (2005)[218] held that in the absence of A's knowledge of B's error as to terms, the Common Law is of no assistance to B, leaving only the possibility that Equity might provide relief for B. To attract such equitable assistance, B would need to show that A had sufficient suspicion of B's error that it was unconscionable for A to maintain the contract. The court would then rescind the contract, to protect B. On the facts of that case, the court would then be responding to the fact that A had taken advantage, in suspicious circumstances, of a glaring error in the price at which computer equipment had been offered for sale by B.

It is submitted that in England a more straightforward approach would be adopted: (1) Was A aware of B's mistake as to terms, or at least was A sufficiently alerted to the probability that B was mistaken in this way? (2) If so, the contract is void at Common Law. (3) There is no need to revert to Equity in order to render the contract voidable. This suggested unitary approach to the question gains support from a brief consideration of the Singaporean case, just cited, by an English Commercial Court judge, Aikens J, in the *Statoil* case (2008).[219] He said that the pricing error in the Singaporean case fell:

> squarely within the classic rule. There was a unilateral mistake by the seller about the price of the printers. The buyers knew that the mistake had been made, but went ahead and 'snapped up the offer'. Plainly, when the subjective evidence was examined, the parties were not agreed as to the most fundamental term of the contract: the price.

3.64 *One party's awareness of the other party's mistake as to unwarranted quality, value or nature of subject matter.* Now we come to a thorny topic. This concerns 'unilateral' errors relating to the 'quality', 'attributes' or the 'utility' of the proposed subject matter, for

---

215 [1996] 1 Lloyd's Rep 700.
216 [2010] EWCA Civ 1331, at [25]: 'In determining [whether there was] a proposal made by one party (A) which was capable of being accepted by the other (B) – the correct approach is to ask whether a person in the position of B (having the knowledge of the relevant circumstances which B had), acting reasonably, would understand that A was making a proposal to which he intended to be bound in the event of an unequivocal acceptance.'
217 R. Stevens, in A. Burrows and E. Peel (eds.), *Contract Terms* (Oxford, 2007), 101, 117.
218 [2005] 1 SLR 502, at [80] (Singapore Court of Appeal); noted by Kelvin F. K. Low, [2005] LMCLQ 423–8, and by T. M. Yeo, 'Great Peace: A Distant Disturbance' (2005) 121 LQR 393.
219 *Statoil ASA v. Louis Dreyfus Energy Services LP ('The Harriette N')* [2008] EWHC 2257 (Comm); [2009] 1 All ER (Comm) 1035; [2008] 2 Lloyd's Rep 685, at [95]; J. Cartwright, 'Unilateral Mistake in the English Courts: Reasserting the Traditional Approach' (2009) *Singapore Journal of Legal Studies* 226–34.

example, of the nature of goods to be supplied following a sample of the goods at the point of sale. The starting point is the proposition that where B knows that A is mistaken concerning the quality of the subject matter, B is under no duty to point out that error to A. It is different if (i) A's mistake concerns the supposed terms of the proposed contract, that is, A believes that there is a tacit warranty that the subject matter of the transaction, normally goods, will possess a particular characteristic or value, or that it will have a particular nature; and (ii) B knows of that type of error and stays silent; for, if (i) and (ii) are shown, the law favours A (as we shall see). It should also be noted (see further 10.20) that B will be treated as having knowledge if he ought reasonably to have known that A was mistaken in this special fashion. And so the core of the *Smith* v. *Hughes* doctrine is the rather subtle distinction between A's mistake as to 'quality' (old oats/new oats or pure silk/man-made fabric) and a mistake concerning the existence of an implied or express term concerning that quality (goods described as 'old oats' or 'pure silk', or goods implicitly traded as such). If A is to rebut the inference that he has objectively assented to a contract for the relevant subject matter, A needs to show (1) that he believed there was such an implied term (that the goods will have the relevant quality), and (2) that the other party, B, knew precisely that this was A's belief. In practice, this rather teasing double psychological inquiry – into A's belief and B's alleged knowledge of A's belief – will be resolved by taking an objective view.

The twofold question will be whether A had a reasonable basis for believing that there was an implicit warranty that goods should be of a certain type; and whether it can be inferred safely that B must have known (or perhaps ought to have known, 10.19) that this was A's precise belief. In the absence of such a reasonable and contractual belief, A's miscalculation concerning the nature or quality of the goods is at his own risk (and B's knowledge of A's 'non-warranty belief' will make no difference, as *Smith* v. *Hughes* (1871) states; see text below). Instead, A will be bound to the objective agreement, without the supposed implied term operating in his favour. The leading case is *Smith* v. *Hughes* (1871).[220]

Facts. Smith v. *Hughes* (1871) was a Common Law action by a seller of oats for non-payment of the price. It was an appeal from a jury direction (in the twentieth century jury trial was abolished for claims framed in contract). The seller allowed the purchaser (the manager of an Epsom stable) to sample the oats, and in fact the purchaser held on to this sample for two days. The purchaser wanted oats to feed to his racing horses.[221] It should be noted, therefore, that this was not a consumer purchase. New oats would be likely to induce 'colic' in horses, which can prove fatal. The purchaser bought a quantity of oats without stipulating that he wanted 'old' oats (and it appears that neither party used the word 'old').[222] The purchaser then refused to pay for the new oats and asserted that he was entitled to (i) reject the goods delivered and (ii) to refuse to accept a remaining quantity which he had ordered from the seller. So the seller sued for the price in respect of (i) and damages on the resale of (ii).

220   *Ibid.*; on the pre-contractual duty to disclose in contracts of insurance, see 9.44.
221   The word 'oats' appears in Samuel Johnson's 1755 dictionary: 'Oats: a grain which in England is generally given to horses but in Scotland supports the people.'
222   Cf *Scriven Bros* v. *Hindley* [1913] 3 KB 564.

In this case it was apparent, in accordance with the objective principle, that prima facie there was a valid contract for the new oats: the purchaser's own ('unilateral') mistake during the sampling process would not exonerate him from the duty to pay. However, it was necessary to consider the following twist: what if the seller knew that the other party believed the oats which he, as a prospective purchaser, had sampled were old, but the seller did nothing to disabuse him of this error? On this last point, the county court judge had wrongly directed the jury that the buyer would then have a good defence. On appeal, this direction was rejected as an error of law. Instead, the Court of Queen's Bench held that the seller's acquiescence in the buyer's error would count only if the buyer's (reasonable) belief had been that there was an implied warranty that the oats should be 'old'. If that were shown, the buyer would be entitled to reject the goods.

Sale of Goods Act. Smith v. *Hughes* was decided in 1871. Twenty-two years later, the Common Law sale of goods was codified by the Sale of Goods Act 1893, updated now in the 1979 Act. Section 15(2) Sale of Goods Act 1979, re-enacted from the earlier legislation without change (in the case of consumer purchases made by sampling, see now the Consumer Rights Bill), affirms that the seller is liable only if the goods supplied did not correspond to the sampled goods, or if there is some 'defect' in the goods which the buyer could not be expected to discover from sampling. But the oats in *Smith* v. *Hughes* were not defective. The real problem was that they were the wrong sort. They were new, and not old.

True analysis of acquiescence in another's belief as to the existence of a term. If a buyer did believe that the seller was impliedly warranting that, for example, oats available for immediate purchase are old, and the seller knew of this error, it should follow that the contract would be composed on the buyer's assumed terms. In that situation, the buyer could reject the goods, or, if he had kept them, he could go on the offensive and sue the seller for loss caused by the failure to supply goods as implicitly warranted. Lord Atkin in *Bell* v. *Lever Bros Ltd* (1932)[223] supported this analysis. Stevens has suggested that the result might be explained as a void contract which can be ratified, that is, activated, by the innocent party.[224]

3.65 *Commercial law and ethics.* The aspect of *Smith* v. *Hughes* (1871) (see above) which some find troubling, even distasteful, is the general proposition that one party can acquiesce in another's miscalculation of the subject matter's (unwarranted) nature, or 'error as to quality', or error as to value (as distinct from error as to terms, including terms containing the legally binding description of the goods). Is this not to countenance sharp practice? Cockburn CJ and Blackburn J in *Smith* v. *Hughes* (1871) admitted[225] that such behaviour is indeed morally reprehensible. But he suggested that one's sense of moral disapproval cannot be legally decisive. Legal standards should not be set too high. The courts should not be overly fastidious. The law of contract in England is administered by judges for businesses and wide-awake consumers and not by saints or philosophers intent on remedying every moral infringement in the marketplace.

223 [1932] AC 161, 222, HL.
224 R. Stevens, in A. Burrows and E. Peel (eds.), *Contract Terms* (Oxford, 2007), 101, 117.
225 (1871) LR 6 QB 597, 604 ('The question is not what a man of scrupulous morality or nice honour would do under such circumstances', *per* Cockburn J); *ibid.* at 607 ('whatever may be the case in a court of morals', *per* Blackburn J).

This robust approach is an example of the pragmatism which permeates English commercial law.

> In *Thames Trains Ltd* v. *Adams* (2006),[226] A, a victim of the Paddington train crash in October 1999, had sent, through his solicitor, a fax to the railway company, Thames Trains, in which A expressed willingness to accept a settlement sum paid into court (the court held that this was an offer made by A, and not an acceptance). That settlement sum was US$9.3m. A's fax was in response to Thames Trains' statement, made an hour before, that no more money could be found. Within an hour of A's fax, but unaware of A's offer, Thames Trains raised its settlement figure by US$500,000. A's solicitors realised that their fax had either not been received or, if received, not read. A accepted the increased settlement offer of US$9.8m. Nelson J held that the resulting settlement was binding, and he rejected the contention that this involved a unilateral error unconscionably acquiesced in by the other side:[227] 'a reasonable man would expect [A's solicitor to be] entitled to stay silent, act in her client's best interests and accept the increased offer.'

3.66 *Lord Atkin's support for a robust approach.* In *Bell* v. *Lever Bros Ltd* (1932), Lord Atkin confirmed that, in general, a contracting party is not obliged to speak up and correct the other's error as to the subject matter of the proposed deal:[228]

> A buys B's horse; he thinks the horse is sound and pays the price of a sound horse; he would certainly not have bought the horse if he had known as a fact that the horse was unsound. If B made no representation as to soundness and has not contracted that the horse is sound, A is bound and cannot recover the price ... A has no remedy, and the position is the same whether B knew the facts or not.

3.67 *Further support.* In the *BCCI* litigation (2002), Lord Hoffmann[229] attractively endorsed the *Smith* v. *Hughes* and *Bell* v. *Lever Bros Ltd* doctrine: 'there is obviously room in the dealings of the market for legitimately taking advantage of the known ignorance of the other party.' This is a succinct restatement of the (commercially) obvious: that a party to negotiation is not generally required to look out for his rival negotiating party's economic interests. To require otherwise would be naïve, even commercially injurious. Much economic activity involves one party enjoying superior knowledge of the proposed contract's value, characteristics or application. Finally, Aikens J in the *Statoil* case (2008),[230] noting the *Smith* v. *Hughes* doctrine, acknowledged that if X is aware of Y's error, but Y's error does not concern a supposed term, the contract is valid.[231] He further held that there is no equitable doctrine of unilateral error suffered by X as to subject matter known to Y.[232]

---

226 [2006] EWHC 3291 (QB).
227 *Ibid.*, at [56].
228 [1932] AC 161, 224, HL.
229 *BCCI* v. *Ali* [2002] 1 AC 251, HL, at [70].
230 *Statoil ASA* v. *Louis Dreyfus Energy Services LP ('The Harriette N')* [2008] EWHC 2257 (Comm); [2009] 1 All ER (Comm) 1035; [2008] 2 Lloyd's Rep 685.
231 *Ibid.*, at [96].
232 *Ibid.*, at [105].

Rix LJ in *ING Bank NV* v. *Ros Roca SA* (2011)[233] (also examined at 9.44) acknowledged the general absence of a duty to disclose. But estoppel (estoppel by convention according to Carnwath LJ, or estoppel by representation according to Rix LJ; on these species of estoppel see 5.38, 5.48, 5.49) created a qualification, enabling the Court of Appeal to conclude that a party was prevented from denying that the parties had already agreed the level of an additional fee. The estopped party knew, but had silently acquiesced in, the other party's understanding that this fee would not exceed £4m (the 2006 formula), whereas the written formula (the 2007 formula) was almost £8m. The Court of Appeal held that the 2006 formula should prevail.

3.68 *'Reasonableness': a qualification upon the objective principle.* The Court of Appeal's rejection of a *contractual action* in the 'unsuccessful vasectomy case', *Thake* v. *Maurice* (1986),[234] shows that the objective principle does not enable a person to rely unreasonably on the literal comments made by the opponent. 'Common sense' non-literal interpretation will prevail, where appropriate. This proposition is a corollary of the fact that the objective principle is rooted in the notion of *reasonable interpretation* of words, oral or written, and the outward appearance of conduct.

In *Thake* v. *Maurice* (1986),[235] the claimants, husband and wife, went to the defendant, a private medical consultant, to arrange a vasectomy for the husband. The doctor told them that the operation was bound to succeed. Although the operation was an initial success, the husband later became fertile (this was both unusual and contrary to the doctor's assurance).

Unaware of the husband's return to fertility, the couple were lured into an unwanted pregnancy. After the birth, they sued the doctor for the financial cost of bringing up the child. Unable to show negligence on these facts, the claimants based their action on an alleged breach of a contractual guarantee that the operation would be and remain successful. At first instance, they were awarded £10,000 damages.[236] But a majority of the Court of Appeal (Neill and Nourse LJJ, with Kerr LJ dissenting) reversed this, and found in favour of the consultant. The majority decision rests on the objective principle: in their opinion, the doctor's oral assurance was 'mere therapeutic comfort'. It was not reasonable that the claimants had been impressed by the doctor's sanguine assurance that the operation would be a success. Nourse LJ observed that 'medicine is not an exact science'.

233 [2011] EWCA Civ 353; [2012] 1 WLR 472, notably Rix LJ at [92].
234 [1986] QB 644, CA.
235 *Ibid.*; cf *Malcolm* v. *Chancellor, Masters and Scholars of the University of Oxford* [1994] EMLR 17, CA (publisher's oral assurance that it will publish author's work upheld: 4.13).
236 In this context in the *tort of negligence*, see now: *McFarlane* v. *Tayside* [2000] 2 AC 59, HL (and *Parkinson* v. *St James and Seacroft University Hospital NHS Trust* [2002] 2 QB 266, CA): financial cost of support of child not recoverable, unless child has special needs arising from congenital abnormality, provided not unforeseeable; but damages for pain of pregnancy, etc.

It would have been different if the claimants had had the wit to ask the consultant doctor at the relevant time: 'Do you really mean that, or are you just offering us well-intentioned reassurance?' If the consultant had responded, 'You can bank on my assurance,' or words to that effect, his statement would have lost its quality as 'mere therapeutic comfort'. (Compare the successful claim for strict liability for the accuracy of an express valuation certificate given by a property valuer in *Platform Funding Ltd* v. *Bank of Scotland plc*, 2009.)[237]

See also 3.02 concerning *Crest Nicholson (Londinium) Limited* v. *Akaria Investments Ltd* (2010)[238] on the question whether party A has made an offer to party B, or whether B did realise, or should have realised, that no such offer was made.

QUESTIONS

(1) What is an invitation to treat, and what is an offer?

(2) What must an offeree know in order to be able to accept an offer?

(3) What must the offeree do in order successfully to accept an offer?

(4) When will an offer be treated as (a) revoked or (b) lapsed?

(5) In what sense is the postal rule an exception to the general process of offer and acceptance?

(6) When will the postal rule not apply?

(7) When the offeree successfully sends a faxed or e-mailed acceptance which is received within the offeror's business premises, when does acceptance occur?

(8) When the offeree successfully sends a faxed or e-mailed acceptance which is received within the offeror's non-business or residential premises, when does acceptance occur?

(9) When does the offeror cease to be able to revoke an offer made under a unilateral contract?

(10) What is the result if a counter-offer is rejected or the original offer is not explicitly reaffirmed by the offeror?

(11) What is the English approach to the problem of the battle of the forms, and is this approach satisfactory?

(12) What are the Common Law obligations regulating the process of tendering?

(13) What is the position concerning responses by bidders to invitations to make sealed bids?

(14) Distinguish auctions from sealed bidding arrangements and from tenders. What is the position concerning auctions conducted 'without a reserve price'?

(15) What is the position if a negotiating party A fails to point out B's error before A purports to conclude a contract with B?

Selected further reading

J. Cartwright, *Formation and Variation of Contracts: The Agreement, Formalities, Consideration and Promissory Estoppel* (London, 2014) (practitioner work: for reference)

M. Furmston and G. J. Tolhurst, *Contract Formation: Law and Practice* (Oxford, 2010) (rich in Commonwealth and American discussion), notably chapters 2–4 (practitioner work: for reference)

237 [2008] EWCA Civ 930; [2009] QB 426.
238 [2010] EWCA Civ 1331, at [25].

S. Gardner, 'Trashing with Trollope: A Deconstruction of the Postal Rules in Contract' (1992) 12 OJLS 170, especially 192 to end

S. Hill, 'Flogging a Dead Horse – The Postal Acceptance Rule and Email' (2001) 17 JCL 151

A. H. Hudson, 'Retraction of Letters of Acceptance' (1966) 82 LQR 169–73

E. McKendrick, 'The Battle of the Forms and the Law of Restitution' (1988) 8 OJLS 197, especially 215–18, 220–1

D. McLauchlan, 'The Uncertain Basis of the Postal Acceptance Rule' (2013) 30 JCL 33

D. Nolan, 'Offer and Acceptance in the Electronic Age', in A. Burrows and E. Peel (eds.), *Contract Formation and Parties* (Oxford, 2010) (e-mail, and offer and acceptance)

Chapter contents

4

Certainty

1. INTRODUCTION

4.01 Summary of main points

Scope of the doctrine of uncertainty

(1) Problems of 'uncertainty'[1] involve either an initial failure to agree ('vagueness' and 'ambiguity') or a postponement of agreement and eventual failure to agree ('incompleteness').

(2) Lack of certainty can affect a contract in one of three ways:

    (a) by invalidating the whole contract;[2] or

    (b) by rendering inoperative only part of the contract;[3] or

    (c) by entitling the court to withhold specific performance (a remedy which requires a high degree of precision, because this remedy is ultimately sanctioned by quasi-criminal powers of fines, imprisonment or seizure of assets, under the contempt of court doctrine, 18.33).[4]

(3) However, uncertainty has no impact on a contract if:

    (a) the relevant uncertainty leaves a gap which can be filled easily by a statutory or judicial default rule;[5] or

    (b) the vague words can be simply ignored, leaving no gap at all.[6]

---

1   M. Furmston and G. J. Tolhurst, *Contract Formation: Law and Practice* (Oxford, 2010), chapter 11.

2   E.g. *May & Butcher* v. *R* (1929) [1934] 2 KB 17 n., HL; *Scammell* v. *Ouston* [1941] AC 251, HL; *British Steel* case, [1984] 1 All ER 504, *per* Goff J; *Baird Textile Holdings Ltd* v. *Marks and Spencer plc* [2001] EWCA Civ 274; [2002] 1 All ER (Comm) 737, at [59] to [70], *per* Mance LJ.

3   See *Didymi Corporation* v. *Atlantic Lines and Navigation Co. Inc.* [1988] 2 Lloyd's Rep 108, CA (discussed at 4.09).

4   *Co-operative Insurance Society Ltd* v. *Argyll Stores (Holdings) Ltd* [1998] AC 1, HL; G. H. Jones, [1997] CLJ 488–91; A. M. Tettenborn, [1998] Conv 23 (18.34).

5   E.g. section 8(2) of the Sale of Goods Act 1979, imposing reasonable price if a contract for the sale of goods does not specify a price (see 4.15).

6   *Nicolene Ltd* v. *Simonds* [1953] 1 QB 543, CA (uncertain language ignored; remainder upheld).

Judicial desire to uphold various types of bargain

(4) Agreement on essential terms normally suffices, because the courts or the relevant statutory framework can fill any gap.[7] For example, in a sale of goods, essential matters are confined to the subject matter of the sale, since the price can be implied by law (provided the parties are silent on the price). The price, if left open, *can* be implied by section 8 of the Sale of Goods Act 1979 (4.15 ff).

(5) The courts strive to resolve problems of uncertainty in favour of finding an agreement.

(6) The courts are especially keen to find an agreement when there has been significant performance under a purported agreement.

(7) The parties can stipulate that a third party (or set of third parties) can fill a blank (for example, fix the price). If so, the courts might regard this as inessential machinery. But it is a question of construction, assessed by reference to the commercial context, whether the third party resolution is essential to the parties' relations. If it is, the court cannot substitute its own objective determination (4.20).

Overlap with intent to create legal relations

(8) The less precise an agreement is, the greater the chance that the courts will conclude that the parties had no real intention to conclude a legally binding agreement (on intent to create legal relations, see Chapter 6).

Reserving the right to autonomous negotiation ('freedom of contract')

(9) The courts will not override the negotiating parties' clear reservation of the right to negotiate terms or a particular term. The principle of 'freedom of contract' (1.08) will then preclude the courts from imposing a contract (4.19). But restitutionary relief might be available if goods have been delivered or services performed.

(10) Finally, the law also upholds agreements to mediate disputes.

4.02 *Need for objective guidelines for adjudication.* The law of 'certainty' is largely the task of determining the practical limits of contractual adjudication over disputes concerning the breakdown of consensus (although largely a matter of practicality, the topic of uncertainty also involves a point of principle, namely, the reservation by the parties of a central issue for negotiation, 4.19). The need for adjudicative standards for dispute resolution explains why agreements to agree (and to negotiate reasonably or in good faith, etc.) (2.07 ff) are treated as too vague to receive legal force: there are not enough pointers to guide and regulate reliable decision-making by the courts (or by arbitrators).[8] *Walford* v. *Miles* (1992)[9] (which is fully treated at 2.07) shows that the courts have prudently avoided the high risk that adjudicators would become embroiled in the hopeless task of assessing the fairness or reasonableness of each party's bargaining steps. We have seen that an agreement to

---

7   *May & Butcher* v. *R* [1934] 2 KB 17, 22, HL, *per* Lord Warrington; *Scammell* v. *Dicker* [2005] 3 All ER 838, CA, at [40] (third sentence from end), *per* Rix LJ.
8   *Walford* v. *Miles* [1992] 2 AC 128, HL; and *Little* v. *Courage* (1995) 70 P & CR 469, CA.
9   [1992] 2 AC 128, HL.

negotiate in good faith or reasonably is void for uncertainty (2.07).[10] By contrast, when determining whether a party has taken adequate steps to procure the third party's permission, there are sufficient commercial and objective guidelines to enable the courts to reach a satisfactory answer to such a dispute. In this latter context, the relevant party is making a commitment to try to attain a specific goal (2.11). Whether he has failed to take adequate steps to achieve it is a commercial matter open to objective determination by the courts. The line is drawn, therefore, between open-ended declarations of intent to negotiate the terms of the proposed main contract and a more specific undertaking to obtain from a third party a 'green light' necessary for the main contract.

More generally, Sir Andrew Morritt V-C in *Baird Textile Holdings Ltd* v. *Marks and Spencer plc* (2001)[11] and Potter LJ in *Phillips* v. *Enron* (1997)[12] spelt out the need for objective standards. Potter LJ in *Phillips* v. *Enron* (1997) noted the difficulty of 'drawing the line between what is to be regarded as reasonable or unreasonable in an area where the parties may legitimately have differing views or interests, but have not provided for any criteria on the basis of which a third party can assess or adjudicate the matter in the event of dispute'.[13]

4.03   *Fledgling agreement insufficiently certain on central issues.* As noted at 2.07, Aikens LJ in the *Barbudev* case (2012)[14] concluded that the parties' investment agreement lacked sufficient certainty and crucial matters remained to be hammered out (the court added that the parties' commitment to negotiate these points in good faith was void for uncertainty – see discussion of *Walford* v. *Miles* at 2.07).

4.04   *Agreement already substantially settled.* Secondly, the courts recognise the practical need to facilitate an agreement once its terms have been substantially settled: see the instructive remarks – too long to cite here – of Neuberger J in *Liverpool City Council* v. *Walton* (2001).[15]

4.05   *Supposed agreement already partly performed.* This leads to another theme in this area of contract law, the question of part-performance: the courts are especially willing to overcome problems of suggested uncertainty if the parties have conducted themselves in a manner which suggests that they had assumed that a binding transaction has arisen. On this point, Lord Steyn, echoing several leading judicial statements,[16] has written:[17]

---

10   Acknowledged in *Walford* v. *Miles* [1992] 2 AC 128, HL.

11   [2001] EWCA Civ 274; [2002] 1 All ER (Comm) 737, at [26].

12   [1997] CLC 329, 343, CA.

13   *Ibid.*, 343, CA; also, at 339, explaining *Queensland Electricity Generating Board* v. *New Hope Collieries* [1989] 1 Lloyd's Rep 205, PC, on this basis: see 2.12.

14   *Barbudev* v. *Eurocom Cable Management Bulgaria Eood* [2012] EWCA Civ 548; [2012] 2 All ER (Comm) 963, at [50] and [51].

15   [2002] 1 EGLR 149; [2001] NPC 135, at [49] to [54] (the case was argued by two eminent QCs, Derek Wood and Kim Lewison); and for the four requirements for a valid construction contract (parties, scope, price, and time), *Glendalough Associated SA* v. *Harris Calnan Construction Co Ltd* [2013] EWHC 3142 (TCC); [2014] 1 WLR 1751, at [47] ff, *per* Edwards-Stuart J.

16   Proposition affirmed in *Scammell* v. *Dicker* [2005] EWCA Civ 405; [2005] 3 All ER 838, at [31]; and *per* Lord Tomlin in the *Hillas* case (1932) 147 LT 503, 512, HL; and *per* Steyn LJ in *Trentham Ltd* v. *Archital Luxfer Ltd* [1993] 1 Lloyd's Rep 25, 27, CA.

17   Lord Steyn, 'Contract Law: Fulfilling the Reasonable Expectations of Honest Men' (1997) 113 LQR 433, 435, echoing his decision in the *Trentham* case (see the previous note).

The reasonable expectations of the parties, albeit that they are still in disagreement about minor details of the transaction, often demand that the court must recognise that a contract has come into existence. The greater the evidence of reliance, and the further along the road towards implementation the transaction is, the greater the prospect that the court will find a contract made and do its best, in accordance with the reasonable expectations of the parties, to spell out the terms of the contract.

4.06 *Contracts of compromise.* In *Scammell* v. *Dicker* (2005),[18] Rix LJ emphasised the need for consent orders, resting on the parties' settlement of a dispute, to be generously upheld, especially when the order has already caused legal proceedings to be terminated and there has been a significant passage of time before the challenge to the order's validity.[19]

4.07 *Parties' reservation of right to determine the agreement.* The negotiating parties might postpone the legal operation of their proposed transaction until they have themselves (without outside interference or extraneous reference) settled its various aspects. The principle of 'freedom of contract' (1.08) requires the courts to respect this autonomous zone of private negotiation. For example, negotiating parties might have reserved exclusively to themselves the task of agreeing the price in a contract for the sale of goods. In default of agreement, they might have (expressly or impliedly) barred any form of outside determination of that price. Such a joint veto on contractual enforcement can only be lifted if both parties consent. However, as a matter of practical justice, this can be inconvenient: if the goods are in the meantime delivered, the courts cannot find a contract in order to justify imposing a reasonable price for the goods. All that can be done is to impose on the recipient a *non-contractual* duty to pay a reasonable sum for the goods (based on the law of restitution). But this is a one-sided solution: the recipient of the goods must pay, but he has no contractual rights to complain of bad delivery; for example, slow and muddled delivery of building materials (as in the *British Steel* case (1984),[20] 2.04).

2. OBJECTIVE CRITERIA FOR RECOGNITION OF CONTRACTUAL RIGHTS

4.08 The House of Lords found an objective yardstick in *Hillas & Co.* v. *Arcos Ltd* (1932) and so was able to uphold a 'repeat' contract.[21] The essence of the case was that the specification of timber delivered successfully in 1930 disclosed sufficient commercial guidance to regulate the repeat deal in 1931.

18   [2005] EWCA Civ 405; [2005] 3 All ER 838; generally, D. Foskett, *The Law and Practice of Compromise* (7th edn, London, 2010).
19   [2005] EWCA Civ 405; [2005] 3 All ER 838, at [39], [40] and [42].
20   [1984] 1 All ER 504, Goff J.
21   (1932) 147 LT 503; [1932] All ER 494, HL; Lord Thankerton's reference to an 'objective yardstick' was cited by Sir Andrew Morritt V-C in *Baird Textile Holdings Ltd* v. *Marks and Spencer plc* [2001] EWCA Civ 274; [2002] 1 All ER (Comm) 737, at [26] to [30] (generally on the latter case, see 6.15).

In *Hillas & Co.* v. *Arcos Ltd* (1932) the parties had contracted in 1930 that the defendants would sell to the claimant at an agreed price 22,000 'standards' of Russian 'softwood goods of fair specification'. An option (the subject of this dispute) allowed the claimant to purchase 100,000 timber standards for delivery during 1931. Although the option specified the price adequately, there was a dispute whether it also provided adequate certainty concerning its subject matter, notably the timber's size and quality. But the House of Lords held that these problems melted away if the 1931 option were construed by objective reference to the criterion of a 'fair specification' contained in the 1930 agreement. This was a clear enough yardstick. It would enable the court to control the vendor's delivery of timber during 1931, once the option was exercised by the purchaser. Lord Thankerton said:[22] '[T]he contract is a commercial one and . . . the parties undoubtedly thought that they had concluded a contract; and I have come to the conclusion . . . that [they did].'

The Court of Appeal in *Durham Tees Valley Airport Ltd* v. *bmibaby Ltd* (2010)[23] applied the *Hillas* case. In this case a low-cost airline attempted to pull out, having entered into an arrangement that it would run flights from the claimant's airport for a ten-year period. The problem was the extreme (but not fatal) brevity of the terms of that commitment.

The Court of Appeal in *Durham Tees Valley Airport Ltd* v. *bmibaby Ltd* (2010) held that the defendant's agreement to run a low-cost flight service at the claimant's airport for a period of ten years by 'establishing a 2 based aircraft operation' was not void for uncertainty. Admittedly those terms were extremely scanty, but they were enough to disclose a binding contract, which the defendant had clearly repudiated. Toulson LJ said:[24] 'The present contract may be unusual in . . . the degree of discretion given to the airline, but I do not see that the court would have an insuperable difficulty in deciding whether the airline had altogether ceased to conduct the operation.' And Patten LJ laid down guidelines for assessment of damages on these facts (summarised at 18.07 at (10)(c)).[25]

In *Jet2.com Ltd* v. *Blackpool Airport Ltd* (2012)[26] it was the turn of the airport to try (unsuccessfully) on the basis of uncertainty to escape a similar arrangement. But again the problems of uncertainty were not insurmountable once the context was taken flexibly into account.

In *Jet2.com Ltd* v. *Blackpool Airport Ltd* (2012) a dispute arose concerning an airport's obligation (Blackpool Airport, 'BAL') to use best endeavours to promote a low-cost airline (Jet2's) business in running a service at BAL's airport. But a majority of the Court of Appeal (Lewison LJ dissenting)

22 [1932] All ER 494, 502, HL.
23 [2010] EWCA Civ 485; [2011] 1 All ER (Comm) 731; [2011] 1 Lloyd's Rep 68.
24 *Ibid.*, at [91].
25 *Ibid.*, at [79], *per* Patten LJ (Toulson and Mummery LJJ agreed: *ibid.*, at [147] and [150]).
26 [2012] EWCA Civ 417; [2012] 2 All ER (Comm) 1053; [2012] 1 CLC 605; Moore-Bick and Longmore LJJ (Lewison LJ dissenting).

held that the contractual commitment was certain enough. The contract should be construed (a) to prevent BAL from restricting Jet2's aircraft movements to (that provincial airport's) normal opening hours; (b) BAL could not confine Jet2's flights to normal hours just because such latitude had proved more expensive to BAL than had expected; (c) but it would be different if it became clear that Jet2 could never expect to operate low-cost services from Blackpool profitably, since BAL would not be obliged to incur further losses in seeking to promote a failing business.

Similarly, Elias LJ in *Attrill* v. *Dresdner Kleinwort Ltd* (2013)[27] (see also on this case 3.44, 5.12, 5.23 and 6.12) held that the investment bank's assurance in the late summer of 2008 that in January 2009 traders would be entitled, on an individual discretionary basis, to a minimum bonus pool of €400m did not lack certainty. This offer was made against a background of regular usage: the criteria for allocation of the bonus had been used on numerous occasions. Elias LJ said '[the] fundamental principles of the scheme were entirely clear and the fact that there were some loose ends does not in my view begin to constitute a degree of uncertainty necessary to defeat the parties' intention that the agreement should be capable of enforcement.'[28]

4.09 *Hire rate to be 'equitably' adjusted under a charterparty.* The Court of Appeal's decision in *Didymi Corporation* v. *Atlantic Lines and Navigation Co. Inc.* (1988) shows that a clause will be upheld if there is an objective yardstick, even if not immediately transparent, against which the court can regulate the parties' entitlement and obligations.[29]

Didymi Corporation v. *Atlantic Lines and Navigation Co. Inc.* (1988) concerned a charterparty for five years. The basic rate of hire was agreed. But the contract further provided that this sum could be raised or reduced to reflect the ship's speed and efficiency. The relevant clause provided that adjustment should be 'mutually agreed' according to what was 'equitable'. The owners claimed such an increase. The hirer said that the variation clause was void. The Court of Appeal, somewhat optimistically, regarded the word 'equitable' as a clear enough criterion to permit objective assessment of the disputed hire payment. The other terms were unproblematic, and it was significant that the contract had already lasted for a substantial period before the dispute arose (for a similar point, see the *Foley* case at 4.16). Although the Court of Appeal in the *Didymi* case upheld 'equitable' in that particular commercial context (efficiency of a chartered vessel's sailing performance), that word might not possess sufficient certainty in other contexts. For example, an agreement for the 'equitable' award of a specified bonus fee to a lecturer to reflect students' appreciation of a particular course would not satisfy the requirement of contractual certainty.

---

27 [2013] EWCA Civ 394; [2013] 3 All ER 807.
28 *Ibid.*, at [60] (citing also *Hillas* v. *Arcos* (1932) LT 503, 512 & 514 *per* Lord Tomlin and Lord Wright).
29 [1988] 2 Lloyd's Rep 108, CA (noted by Reynolds, (1988) 104 LQR 353), considering *Sudbrook Trading Estate Ltd* v. *Eggleton* [1983] 1 AC 444, HL; *Brown* v. *Gould* [1972] Ch 53, Megarry J (both contracts certain); and *Courtney* v. *Tolaini* [1975] 1 WLR 297, CA and *Mallozzi* v. *Carapelli SpA* [1976] 1 Lloyd's Rep 407, CA (both contracts uncertain).

4.10 *Hopeless ambiguity in description of goods. Raffles* v. *Wichelhaus* (1864)[30] is the leading authority on a type of written contract where 'latent ambiguity' *might* render the apparent agreement void for uncertainty. In essence the contract for the purchase of a cargo of cotton was held probably to be void (following an appeal, the case was remitted to trial by jury) because there seemed to be no objective means of distinguishing between identical cargoes arriving from the same port and being delivered to Liverpool on ships which had the same name. The facts disclosed an impenetrable coincidence. Chitty notes that it would be unlikely that in modern conditions a contract would be as sparsely worded as this and thus fail to provide any objective clue as to its true subject matter.[31]

Raffles v. *Wichelhaus* (1864) concerned a supposed contract for the purchase of a cargo of 'cotton ex Peerless' from Bombay for delivery at Liverpool. The background revealed a bizarre coincidence. It turned out that there were two ships (ironically) called 'Peerless'. One was leaving Bombay in October, the other in December, in the same year. Both were to bring cotton to Liverpool from Bombay. The buyer refused to accept delivery of cotton from the December ship, and instead alleged that he had intended cotton from the October ship. The seller sued for non-payment of the price in respect of the December cargo. But to which ship and cargo did the contract refer? The appellate decision on this preliminary issue (the problem of 'latent ambiguity') was that the case must proceed to the jury (this form of adjudication was still common in the nineteenth century, but has ceased to apply in modern contract law) to determine whether the parties were truly at cross-purposes (if so, the contract would be void) or, conversely, that the seller should win (if so, the buyer would be liable to pay the price claimed). Perhaps it would prove impossible to resolve this impasse on the facts, since both versions were equally 'reasonable'. The result of the further proceedings is not recorded.

4.11 *Hire-purchase: subject matter.* In *Scammell* v. *Ouston* (1941),[32] the House of Lords held that it could not discern a clear enough transaction, only the shadowy beginnings of a real contract. In the early 1940s, when the case was decided, hire-purchase law was in its infancy and this factor influenced the result. The relevant clause stated that a lorry would be bought 'on the understanding that the balance of the purchase price can be had on hire-purchase terms over a period of two years'. The House of Lords held that the arrangement was void for uncertainty.

Scammell v. *Ouston* (1941) concerned a proposed sale of a lorry in part-exchange for an old one. The transaction was made 'on the understanding that the balance of the purchase price can be had on hire-purchase terms over a period of two years'. The vendor refused to deliver. The House of Lords held that this transaction was irredeemably vague and thus a nullity. In the early 1940s

---

30 (1864) 2 H & C 906; G. Gilmore, *The Death of Contract* (Columbus, Ohio, 1974), 35 ff; A. W. B. Simpson, *Leading Cases in the Common Law* (Oxford, 1995), 135 ff; C. MacMillan, *Mistakes in Contract Law* (Oxford, 2010), 186 ff; G. Spark, *Vitiation of Contracts* (Cambridge, 2013), chapter 7; on this 1864 decision, see 'The Great Peace' [2003] QB 679, CA, at [28] and [29].
31 *Chitty on Contracts* (31st edn, London, 2012), 5–072.
32 [1941] AC 251, HL.

hire-purchase agreements were novel and unfamiliar, and that there were different forms of hire-purchase, so that terms could not be securely implied. Viscount Maugham concluded that the House of Lords could not make out a clear enough contractual framework here:[33]

> [N]othing is said (except as to the two years period) as to the terms of the hire-purchase agreement, for instance, as to the interest payable, and as to the rights of the [owner] . . . in the event of default by the respondents in payment of the instalments at the due dates. [And] . . . there was no evidence to suggest that there are any well known 'usual terms' in such a contract.

3. INTERACTION OF THE 'INTENT TO CREATE LEGAL RELATIONS' AND 'CERTAINTY' DOCTRINES

4.12 *Vague publishing contract.* The vaguer the suggested agreement, especially in a context where precision and detail are normally to be expected, the less likely it is that the court will infer that the negotiating parties had reached an immediate agreement, intending to give it legal force (generally on the doctrine of 'intent to create legal relations', see Chapter 6). As for the problem of vagueness, Mustill LJ said in *Malcolm v. Chancellor, Masters and Scholars of the University of Oxford* (1994),[34] 'the first question must always be whether any legally binding contract has been made.' The court should not prejudge this question by first constructing an agreement from a set of implied terms and then declaring that the parties must have reached an agreement. However, as we shall see in the next paragraph, the majority's decision in that case (in which Mustill LJ dissented) is at the extreme limits of acceptable certainty. But even if the parties evinced a clear intent to create legal relations, this is not decisive, because the purported agreement might lack sufficient certainty (as in the *Sulamerica* (2012)[35] (4.22) and *Barbudev* (2012)[36] (2.07) cases).

4.13 A majority of the Court of Appeal in *Malcolm v. Chancellor, Masters and Scholars of the University of Oxford* (1994)[37] held that a telephone commitment to publish an academic study was sufficiently certain even though the parties had yet to agree in writing on the detailed provisions of the publishing agreement and even though it was clear in the relevant context that final decisions about publications would normally be made by the senior advisors to the university press (known as 'The Delegates'). The decision is a surprisingly generous and extreme example of the courts heroically filling in large gaps in an oral agreement to publish a book.

33   *Ibid.*, at 256–7.
34   [1994] EMLR 17, CA, citing *Aoterroa International Scancarriers* [1985] 1 NZLR 513, PC; for an excellent example, see 6.13 on *Baird* v. *Marks and Spencer plc* [2001] EWCA Civ 274; [2002] 1 All ER (Comm) 737.
35   *Sulamerica Cia Nacional de Seguros SA* v. *Enesa Engenharia SA* [2012] EWCA Civ 638; [2013] 1 WLR 102, at [35], *per* Moore-Bick LJ.
36   *Barbudev* v. *Eurocom Cable Management Bulgaria Eood* [2012] EWCA Civ 548; [2012] 2 All ER (Comm) 963, at [37], [38], *per* Aikens LJ.
37   [1994] EMLR 17, CA.

In the *Malcolm* case (1994), a telephone conversation occurred between Malcolm, author of a philosophical treatise, and a senior editor of Oxford University Press (OUP). It was found that the latter had indicated orally that the Press would definitely publish Malcolm's book: 'I am pleased that we are going to do your book,' he said, and added at 'a fair royalty'. The editor was later disciplined for these casual and fateful remarks. In due course, OUP's Delegates (the decision-making board for proposed new publications) decided that the book was unsuitable for OUP. This was a change of mind by the Press[38] (although this possibility is well known within the academic community which deals with such distinguished publishing houses). And so Malcolm sought specific performance of the oral undertaking. Nourse and Leggatt LJJ (Mustill LJ attractively dissented) held that this exiguous oral undertaking was sufficiently certain. Although Malcolm succeeded in establishing a contract on these facts, specific performance was denied. Instead, the Court of Appeal awarded damages, assessment of which would be made by the trial judge, to whom the case was remitted.[39]

In his convincing dissent, Mustill LJ suggested that a reasonable person would know that a signed publishing contract sanctioned at the highest level by a hierarchically structured publisher, such as OUP, would be the earliest point at which a solid agreement would arise. In short, oral assurances were impliedly 'subject to final confirmation by the Delegates (the publisher's board of control)'.[40]

4. ESTABLISHING THE PRICE IN CONTRACTS FOR THE SALE OF GOODS

4.14 The courts will often strain to find a contract if at least one of the parties has begun to perform a supposed transaction. This tendency is illustrated by cases concerning the ascertainment of the price in contracts for the sale of goods.

4.15 The Sale of Goods Act 1979 provides four rules governing ascertainment of the price:

(i) The Sale of Goods Act 1979 will impose a reasonable price if the parties have simply left the matter of price as a blank item. This default rule is contained in section 8, which states:
Section 8(1): The price in a contract of sale may be fixed by the contract, or may be *left to be fixed in a manner agreed by the contract*, or may be determined by the course of dealing between the parties.
Section 8(2): Where the price is not determined as mentioned in subsection (1) above the buyer must pay the reasonable price.[41]

---

38   *Malcolm* v. *University of Oxford* [2002] EWHC 10; [2002] EMLR 277, at [2], *per* Lightman J: 'Dr Alan Ryan, a Fellow of New College Oxford and an OUP Delegate, in two reports dated the 11th February 1985 and the 18th July 1985 made the recommendation to the OUP commissioning editor Mr Henry Hardy ("Mr Hardy") that the OUP publish it. But in February 1986, after the Work had been revised and improved, Dr Ryan changed his mind and recommended that the Work be rejected. The OUP acted on this recommendation.' Malcolm published an account of the saga: A. Malcolm, *The Remedy* (Brighton, 1997).
39   On the inquiry as to damages, [2002] EWHC 10; [2002] EMLR 277.
40   Cf consultant doctor's assurance not a contractual guarantee: *Thake* v. *Maurice* [1986] QB 644, CA: see 3.71.
41   M. Bridge, *The Sale of Goods* (Oxford, 2014), 1.43.

Section 8(3): What is a reasonable price is a question of fact dependent on the circumstances of each particular case.

(ii) If the price is fixed by reference to some ascertainable price register, the contract will be upheld by ascertaining the relevant figure. This follows from the wording of section 8(1) where it states that the price 'may be left to be fixed in a manner agreed by the contract'.

(iii) If the price is to be fixed by a panel of valuers, but one party fails to cooperate in the appointment of the valuers, section 9(2) of the Sale of Goods Act 1979 renders the party at fault liable for damages[42] (generally on the issue of third party resolution, see 4.20).

(iv) Where there has been no performance (a situation known as an 'executory' sale of goods), the contract might be void for incompleteness. Section 8 of the Sale of Goods Act 1979 will not supply the 'reasonable price' if the parties have expressly left the price open saying 'at a price to be agreed', and there is no default provision such as reference of the price to a third party valuer. The authority supporting proposition (4) is the House of Lords decision in *May & Butcher* v. *R* (1929).[43] This decision continues to apply where there has been no performance under the contemplated contract and instead the contract remains wholly 'executor' (for the converse situation, where goods have been delivered, at least for a significant period, see *Foley* v. *Classique Coaches* (1934),[44] at 4.16 below).

In *May & Butcher* v. *R* (1929)[45] the relevant clause referred to the purchase of old tentage, 'the price or prices to be paid . . . shall be agreed from time to time between [the parties].' The House of Lords (in a decision not reported until 1934) held that there was no contract on these facts. The contract was not simply silent on the question of price: instead, the matter had been left for determination by the parties, without specific recourse to a 'fall-back' if they should fail to agree.

Although the arrangement was subject to an arbitration clause, the House of Lords held that this did not alter the analysis. The arbitration clause clothed the arbitrator with power to determine matters 'with reference to or arising out of this agreement'. But that last phrase begged the question whether there was in fact a valid contract. On this last point, Lord Buckmaster said: 'The arbitration clause relates to the settlement of whatever may happen when the agreement has been completed and the parties are regularly bound. There is nothing in the arbitration clause to enable a contract to be made which in fact the original bargain has left quite open.'[46]

May & Butcher v. *R* (1929) has been criticised by the New Zealand Court of Appeal in *Electricity Corporation of New Zealand Ltd* v. *Fletcher Challenge Ltd* (2001), especially in light of the fact that there had been an arbitration clause:[47]

We find curious the notion that, in a commercial contract where price is left to be agreed, a reasonable price cannot be fixed and that, even where there is an arbitration clause, that clause cannot be used to determine the price because 'unless the price has been fixed, the

---

42   The 1979 Act uses the remedy of damages; cf *Sudbrook Trading Estate* v. *Eggleton* [1983] 1 AC 444, HL (4.20 below, party frustrating an agreement that each side should appoint valuers to determine the price concerning a proposed sale of land; specific performance to compel the grant of a lease at a fair valuation).
43   [1934] 2 KB 17 n., HL.
44   [1934] 2 KB 1, CA.
45   [1934] 2 KB 17 n., HL.
46   *Ibid.*, at 21.
47   [2001] NZCA 289; [2002] 2 NZLR 433, at [61] and [62].

agreement is not there'. [The better view is that] the court can step in and apply the formula or standard if the parties fail to agree or can substitute other machinery if the designated machinery breaks down.

If this point were to recur in England, one possible construction of an arbitration clause similar to that in the *May & Butcher* case would be that the parties had intended that the arbitrator should fix a (reasonable) price in the absence of the parties' agreement on that aspect. It is now clear that an arbitration clause can subsist even if the main contract is prima facie invalid. Such an approach would be consistent with section 8(1) of the Sale of Goods Act 1979, which states, inter alia: 'The price in a contract of sale . . . may be left to be fixed in a manner agreed by the contract.' The argument that the arbitration agreement cannot subsist unless and until the main agreement is activated melts away: section 7 of the Arbitration Act 1996 (England and Wales) renders the validity of the arbitration clause independent of the validity of (or currently inoperative status of) the main agreement.[48]

4.16 *Substantial dealings under a contract for regular supply of goods.* It appears that a contract of sale will not be regarded as void for incompleteness if the goods have been delivered and accepted. In *Foley* v. *Classique Coaches* (1934),[49] the Court of Appeal distinguished the House of Lords decision in *May & Butcher* v. *R* (1929) (4.15) as concerned with a contract where no delivery or deliveries had occurred.[50] In the *Foley* case, the court found an implied term that if the parties failed to agree the price, a reasonable sum should be imposed to be fixed by the arbitrator (the contract included an arbitration clause). The arrangement in the *Foley* case had already operated for three years. This was in contrast to the executory agreement in *May & Butcher*. Another factor supporting the result was that the petrol supply agreement contained an arbitration clause to cover disputes, including failure to agree on the price of petrol, although the arbitration agreement was perhaps not decisive. Yet another supporting factor was that the claimant had insisted on the supply contract being signed before selling some land to the defendant.

The *Foley* case concerned an agreement for the exclusive purchase of petrol by the defendant from the claimant 'at a price to be agreed by the parties in writing from time to time'. The defendant ran a coach business. The defendant bought petrol from the claimant for roughly three years at prices below the retail level. Then the defendant considered it could obtain 'better' petrol from elsewhere. So it contended that there was no real agreement, merely an agreement to agree, so that the supposed contract for exclusive purchase had all along been void for uncertainty. The Court of Appeal, affirming the trial judge (Lord Hewart CJ), rejected that argument. It held that there was an implied term that if the parties failed to agree the price, a reasonable sum should be imposed by the arbitrator.

In the *Foley* case Scrutton LJ explained:[51]

---

48   Section 7 of the Arbitration Act 1996, as explained in *Premium Nafta Products Ltd* v. *Fili Shipping Co. Ltd* (otherwise known as the *Fiona Trust* case) [2007] UKHL 40; [2007] 4 All ER 951, at [10] (noted by L. Flannery, (2007) NLJ 1756; A. Rushworth, (2008) 124 LQR 195; A. Briggs, [2008] LMCLQ 1).
49   [1934] 2 KB 1, CA.
50   The House of Lords approved the *Foley* case in *Scammell* v. *Ouston* [1941] AC 251.
51   [1934] 2 KB 1, 9–10, CA.

> [T]he parties (1) obviously believed they had a contract and (2) they acted for three years as if they had; they had an arbitration clause which relates to the subject matter of the agreement as to the supply of petrol, and (3) it seems to me that this arbitration clause[52] applies to any failure to agree as to the price . . . There is to be implied in this contract a term that the petrol shall be supplied at a reasonable price and shall be of reasonable quality. For these reasons . . . there was an effective and enforceable contract, although as to the future no definite price had been agreed with regard to the petrol. [numbering added]
>
> As for factor (3), in *Beer* v. *Bowden* (1981) (Reginald) Goff LJ held that the *Foley* case did not turn on the existence of an arbitration clause.[53] Instead, he interpreted its *ratio* as the implication *by the court (without the need for arbitration)* of a reasonable price, if the parties failed to agree upon a price (that is, based on factors (1) and (2)).

The *Foley* case can be interpreted as permitting the court to impose a reasonable price where there has been a supply and consumption of goods, even though the contract expressly left the price to be agreed. This analysis was endorsed by Rix LJ in the *Mamidoil-Jetoil* case (2001) (his comprehensive remarks, which should be studied in detail, are too lengthy to be quoted here).[54]

4.17 *Parties manifesting an intention to displace a 'subject to contract' provision.* The formula 'subject to contract' is used to denote, by agreement, that the parties have not yet created binding legal relations. The Supreme Court in *RTS Flexible Systems Ltd* v. *Molkerei Alois Müller GmbH* (2010)[55] held that, *exceptionally*, the 'subject to contract' bar can be disapplied if the parties have steamed ahead with performance (in that case, one party performed over two-thirds of the work), indicating a joint wish to give effect to the terms of the negotiated deal without formal signing. In this case, RTS agreed to install machinery in Müller's dairy products factory, but disputes arose over payments and liabilities during this work. RTS had not yet received 30 per cent of the payment (the total price being £1.3m), but the defendant's counter-claim for allegedly defective performance was for £3m. The question was whether there was a contract and, if so, on what terms. The parties had initially contemplated (as indicated by a 'subject to contract' formula) that they would only enter a contract by formally signing it, following satisfactory negotiations. But the Supreme Court held (1) that an implied contract had arisen, in the sense that the parties' informal agreement rested on their conduct, which manifested a joint wish to give effect to the terms of the negotiated deal without formal signing; and (2) that the parties had impliedly waived by conduct the 'subject to contract' bar (this important decision is now set out in great detail).

---

52 *Beer* v. *Bowden* [1981] 1 WLR 522, 526, CA, *per* Goff LJ: absence of an arbitration clause not conclusive.
53 *Ibid.*
54 *Mamidoil-Jetoil Greek Petroleum Co. Ltd* v. *Okta Crude Oil Refinery (No. 1)* [2001] EWCA Civ 406; [2001] 2 Lloyd's Rep 76, at [69]; and this passage was analysed by Chadwick LJ in *BJ Aviation Ltd* v. *Pool Aviation Ltd* [2002] EWCA Civ 163; [2002] 2 P & CR 25, at [18] ff, and *MRI Trading AG* v. *Erdenet Mining Corp LLC* [2013] EWCA Civ 156; [2013] 1 CLC 423; [2013] 1 Lloyd's Rep 638 (on which see 2.07).
55 [2010] UKSC 14; [2010] 1 WLR 753; this case's analysis of acceptance by conduct was adopted in *Mulcaire* v. *News Group Newspapers Ltd* [2011] EWHC 3469 (Ch); [2012] Ch 435, at [35], *per* Sir Andrew Morritt C; on the issue concerning the effect of 'subject to contract', M. Yip and Y. Goh, [2012] LMCLQ 289 297–8.

This decision comprises three elements.

(1) *Intent to form a contract.* The true analysis, based on objective evaluation of this substantially fulfilled project, was that the parties intended their dealings to be governed by a contractual framework, namely, the terms of the negotiated written agreement. And so an 'implied contract' (implied by reference to joint conduct) had arisen after the lapse of the letter of intent.

(2) *Explanation of the expiry of the 'subject to contract' phase.* There had been very substantial dealings: over two-thirds of the projected work had been accomplished. The parties, by their conduct, had objectively manifested an intention to waive the 'subject to contract' express formula on these facts.

(3) *Content of the agreement.* This implied contract should be held to mirror all the points (the overall price, liquidated damages and limitation of liability clauses) contained in the proposed written agreement, even though the parties had initially envisaged that such an agreement would require formal signing.

Lord Clarke identified the crucial features of this case in the following passages:[56]

> Whether in such a case the parties agreed to enter into a binding contract, waiving reliance on the 'subject to [written] contract' term or understanding, will again depend upon all the circumstances of the case, although the cases show that the court will not lightly so hold.
>
> [The *RTS* case is] not a case like the *British Steel* case [2.04] because here all the terms which the parties treated as essential were agreed and the parties were performing the contract without a formal contract being signed or exchanged, whereas [in the *British Steel* case] the parties were still negotiating terms which they regarded as essential ... [In the *RTS* case] neither party wanted the negotiations to get in the way of the project. The project was the only important thing. The only reasonable inference to draw is that by [the time all the loose ends had been resolved by the parties in the *RTS* case] the parties had in effect agreed to waive the 'subject to contract' provision [and so dispense with the need for joint signature].

Three further points arise from the *RTS* case:

(1) *Nature of the 'implied' contract.* The dangerous word 'implied' should be understood to refer to an agreement which was not written and which arose as an inference from the parties' conduct. This 'implied' agreement mirrored the express terms of the intended, but still unsigned, written agreement. Therefore, the Supreme Court gave effect to an *agreement evidenced by conduct but implicitly incorporating a complex set of express terms hammered out by the parties but never formally signed.* Only in that elaborate and qualified sense was it 'implied'.

(2) *Implied waiver of 'subject to contract'.* The formula 'subject to contract' can be waived, that is, overridden implicitly by the parties' dealings (or, of course, explicitly). But implicit waiver by conduct, which will be rare (see paragraph 56 of the judgment, cited later in this text), will occur if: (a) there has been significant performance; provided (b) all the essential loose ends, that is, the vital points of disagreement, have been settled during the negotiations, so that formalising the contract in writing, and perhaps by signature (as contemplated in the *RTS* case), has become an unnecessary ritual. Element (a) does not suffice: element (b) must also apply.

---

56   [2010] UKSC 14; [2010] 1 WLR 753, at [56] and [87].

(3) *Two-sided protection achieved by finding a bilateral contract.* The *RTS* decision attractively gives both parties contractual causes of action: the supplier for remuneration; and the recipient of performance might make a counter-claim for allegedly defective performance, and loss flowing from that. This can be contrasted with the one-sided result in the *British Steel* case (1984),[57] where only the restitutionary award succeeded. In the *British Steel* case, the recipient could not bring a counter-claim for consequential loss because such a claim would presuppose the existence of a contract: see 2.04 and the discussion below.

By contrast with the result in the *RTS* case (2010), analysed above, no contract was found in a similar case, *Whittle Movers Ltd* v. *Hollywood Express Ltd* (2009).[58] Instead, the Court of Appeal in the *Whittle* case preferred to make a restitutionary award, on principles of unjust enrichment, in respect of the value of goods supplied. The award was lower than market rate because the contemplated agreement, which did not become operative, imposed a preliminary tranche of low prices, which would be augmented over time. Conversely, in *Benedetti* v. *Sawiris* (2013) the Supreme Court held that a *quantum meruit* is based on the normal 'market value' of the services and not any higher figures bandied around during the parties' negotiations.[59]

The *Whittle* and *RTS* cases are not in fact in conflict because in the *Whittle* case the parties were still engaged in lively negotiations concerning key terms, whereas in the *RTS* case the negotiations had been completed successfully, although this fully agreed set of terms had not been formally signed off.

5. UPHOLDING COMPROMISE AGREEMENTS

4.18 Settlement or compromise agreements, whether reached in contemplation of civil proceedings or in conclusion of such litigation, are intended to bring finality to a dispute (see 5.12 at (3)). As the Court of Appeal emphasised in *Scammell* v. *Dicker* (2005), considerations of general efficiency and fairness between the parties require that such an agreement should not be readily invalidated.[60] This includes difficulties in construing or applying the terms of the compromise agreement.

6. NEGOTIATION EXCLUSIVELY RESERVED TO THE PARTIES

4.19 As mentioned above (4.07), the parties retain a trump card, based on the principle of freedom of contract (1.08), enabling them to retain autonomy of the settlement of the terms of their proposed dealings. A case which might be rationalised in this way is *Courtney & Fairbairn Ltd* v. *Tolaini Bros (Hotels) Ltd* (1975), where the Court of Appeal held that no building contract arose where a landowner and developer had left open for future

---

57 [1984] 1 All ER 504.
58 *Whittle Movers Ltd* v. *Hollywood Express Ltd* [2009] EWCA Civ 1189; [2009] CLC 771 (Waller, Dyson and Lloyd LJJ); noted by P. S. Davies, (2010) 126 LQR 175–9.
59 [2013] UKSC 50; [2014] AC 938 (noted M. McInnes (2014) 130 LQR 8–13; G. Virgo [2013] CLJ 508–11; C. Mitchell [2013] LMCLQ 436); see also *Littlewoods Retail Ltd* v. *Revenue and Customs Commissioners* [2014] EWHC 868 (Ch) and *Harrison* v. *Madejski* [2014] EWCA Civ 361.
60 [2005] EWCA Civ 405; [2005] 3 All ER 838.

negotiation the fixing of 'fair and reasonable' prices for building work to be done by the developer.[61] But where the construction contract refers to rates of payment which will be applied to the relevant job, this problem will not arise.[62]

7. THIRD PARTY RESOLUTION OF TERMS

4.20 The parties might agree that a blank term, normally the price, will be determined by a third party, or set of third parties. As mentioned in the context of the sale of goods (4.15), if the price is to be fixed by a panel of valuers, but one party fails to cooperate in the appointment of the valuers, section 9(2) of the Sale of Goods Act 1979 renders the party at fault liable for damages.[63] At Common Law, *Sudbrook Trading Estate Ltd* v. *Eggleton* (1983) (see below) decides that the court can determine the objective content of the relevant blank term, despite the fact that the relevant third party machinery was inoperative (whether as a result of a party's default, or otherwise), provided (1) there is an objective criterion enabling the court to make this assessment, and (2) the parties have not impliedly rendered that third party resolution crucial to their prospective relations.

The *Sudbrook* case concerned leases of industrial premises, each lease containing an option permitting the tenant to purchase the reversion at a price to be agreed by valuers appointed by both parties. The lessees exercised their options to purchase, but the lessors refused to appoint a valuer. Lord Fraser said:[64]

> The true distinction is between those cases where the mode of ascertaining the price is an essential term of the contract, and those cases where the mode of ascertainment, though indicated in the contract, is subsidiary and non-essential . . . [Where], as here, the machinery consists of valuers and an umpire, none of whom is named or identified, it is in my opinion unrealistic to regard it as an essential term. If it breaks down there is no reason why the court should not substitute other machinery to carry out the main purpose of ascertaining the price in order that the agreement may be carried out.

However, the fact that a third party is not named does not necessarily render the stipulation 'inessential' (and, conversely, the fact that he is named should not necessarily render his intervention essential – this too should be a question of construction, rather than a mechanical presumption). The true question is whether the parties have impliedly rendered the success of the stipulated third party resolution, the vital hinge upon which their transaction turns. If so, the court cannot come to the rescue and itself fill the relevant blank.

By contrast, in *Gillatt* v. *Sky Television Ltd* (2000), the Court of Appeal considered a stipulation for valuation 'of the open market value' of shares in a private company by 'an independent chartered accountant'.[65] The court held that this was 'essential' machinery which could not be

---

61 [1975] 1 WLR 297, CA.
62 *Glendalough Associated SA* v. *Harris Calnan Construction Co Ltd* [2013] EWHC 3142 (TCC); [2014] 1 WLR 1751, at [50], *per* Edwards-Stuart J.
63 See n. 42 at 4.15 above.
64 [1983] 1 AC 444, 483–4, HL (a majority decision, Lord Russell of Killowen dissenting).
65 [2000] 1 All ER (Comm) 461, CA.

bypassed by resort to the court. In this case, neither party had taken steps to appoint 'an independent chartered accountant', and so the relevant machinery had not 'broken down' for reasons outside the claimant's control.[66] In any event, the court further held that there was no objective means of determining which manner of valuation should be adopted. Private company shares are capable of being valued on various 'bases': asset value, earnings, discounted cash flow or a combination of these.

8. NO SPECIFIC PERFORMANCE OF VAGUE CLAUSES

4.21   *Co-operative Insurance Society Ltd* v. *Argyll Stores (Holdings) Ltd* (1998) [67] (see further on this case, 18.34) shows that a higher degree of precision is required for specific performance or an injunction, compared with a claim for damages or debt (for an overview of these remedies, see 18.01). The approach is sound because once specific performance is ordered, the defendant is in peril of suffering quasi-criminal sanctions for contempt of court (possible fines, seizure of property or even imprisonment).[68] It follows that the court must be able to determine clearly whether the order for specific performance has been breached; and fairness requires the defendant to receive guidance as to where the line is drawn between compliance and default.

9. MEDIATION AGREEMENTS

4.22   Mediation agreements[69] normally arise out of a pre-existing relationship, especially contractual relations. Mediation clauses (often part of a more complex multi-level dispute clause: see the next paragraph) are now inserted into many commercial contracts. As Colman J decided in *Cable & Wireless plc* v. *IBM United Kingdom Ltd* (2002),[70] the courts will 'stay' (that is, place in suspense) formal proceedings until the stipulated prior mediation process has been properly considered. The innocent party can validly complain that the other party should not have bypassed the contractually obligatory mediation phase (although exceptionally this might be excused: see the case discussed below). It is relevant that the English procedural rules (the CPR) emphasise generally the civil courts' responsibility to promote alternative dispute resolution.[71]

---

66   This facet of the *Gillatt* case was applied in *Infiniteland Ltd* v. *Artisan Contracting Ltd* [2005] EWCA Civ 758; [2006] 1 BCLC 632, at [58]; and by Aikens J in *Harper* v. *Interchange Group Ltd* [2007] EWHC 1834 (Comm), at [132].

67   [1998] AC 1, HL; noted by G. H. Jones, [1997] CLJ 488–91; A. M. Tettenborn, [1998] Conv 23.

68   On contempt of court, see 18.33.

69   *Andrews on Civil Processes* (Cambridge, 2013), vol. 2, *Arbitration and Mediation*, 3.14 ff; T. Allen, *Mediation Law and Civil Practice* (London, 2013).

70   *Cable & Wireless plc* v. *IBM United Kingdom Ltd* [2002] 2 All ER (Comm) 1041.

71   CPR 1998, Rule 1.4(2)(e).

In *Cable & Wireless plc* v. *IBM United Kingdom Ltd* (2002),[72] IBM had agreed to supply long-term IT services to Cable & Wireless. The contract contained a multi-level dispute-resolution clause. It provided that if a dispute arose concerning the adequacy of IBM's performance, the parties would first try to settle the matter in good faith among themselves. If the dispute remained unsettled, they agreed to take it to a higher level of management, again among themselves. If that did not work, they agreed to refer it to mediation before an external and named commercial mediator. If that failed, it was agreed that they would litigate. But Cable & Wireless skipped the mediation phase and went straight to the High Court. The substantive claim was for £45m damages. Colman J upheld IBM's complaint that Cable & Wireless' commencement of High Court litigation was premature and a breach of the dispute-resolution clause. Cable & Wireless should not have leapfrogged the mediation. To remedy this, Colman J ordered a 'stay' of the High Court proceedings. This was to enable the parties to pursue mediation. Only if that failed would the High Court proceedings be reactivated, whereupon the stay would be lifted. A stay, therefore, merely places proceedings 'on pause' or 'in suspense' and is not the same as termination or dismissal.

The Court of Appeal in *Sulamerica Cia Nacional de Seguros SA* v. *Enesa Engenharia SA* (2012)[73] established that a mediation agreement will be valid in English law only if (i) the mediation clause is final and thus does not require any further negotiation over its own terms; (ii) the clause nominates a mediation provider or indicates how one is to be appointed; and (iii) the mediation process should be either already finalised under the rules of the agreed mediation provider or the parties must themselves supply minimum details. (No problem of certainty will arise if the mediation clause refers to a well-established institutional 'model' set of mediation rules, as in *Cable & Wireless* v. *IBM United Kingdom Ltd* (2002) (noted above), where the mediation clause incorporated an institutional set of mediation rules,[74] containing a detailed process.)[75]

The mediation clause in the *Sulamerica* case (2012)[76] failed under all three of these heads. Clause 11 stated: 'the parties undertake that, prior to a reference to arbitration, they will seek to have the Dispute resolved amicably by mediation.' The Court of Appeal held that this was merely a 'gentlemen's agreement' that each party would invite the other to consider the possibility of an ad hoc mediation.[77]

---

72 *Cable & Wireless case* [2002] 2 All ER (Comm) 1041.
73 [2012] EWCA Civ 638; [2013] 1 WLR 102; for criticism, N. Andrews, 'Mediation Agreements: Time for a More Creative Approach by the English Courts' (2013) 18 *Revue de Droit Uniforme* 6–16 (also known as *Uniform Law Review*).
74 [2002] EWHC 2059 (Comm); [2002] 2 All ER (Comm) 1041; [2002] CLC 1319; [2003] BLR 89, at [21] *per* Colman J.
75 *Ibid.*
76 [2012] EWCA Civ 638; [2013] 1 WLR 102; for criticism, N. Andrews, 'Mediation Agreements: Time for a More Creative Approach by the English Courts' (2013) 18 *Revue de Droit Uniforme* 6–16 (also known as *Uniform Law Review*).
77 [2012] EWCA Civ 638; [2013] 1 WLR 102, at [36], *per* Moore-Bick LJ.

4.23 However, the English courts will not normally be able to scrutinise the parties' conduct during a mediation hearing. Not only would such a judicial examination be difficult (as the author has suggested elsewhere, the courts are unlikely to embrace an expansive 'duty to mediate'),[78] but mediation discussions are also confidential and privileged.[79] This means that no evidence can be adduced of what was said or written by the parties during the course of mediation discussions, unless both parties' permission is obtained to use such evidence. It is different if there has been a joint waiver of this evidential rule. And so Jack J in *Carleton* v. *Strutt & Parker* (2008) (see also discussion at 2.09) said that the courts will consider the 'unreasonableness' of positions taken in the mediation if *the parties have waived privilege in their mediation communications*, and the question concerns assessment of costs in litigation subsequent to an unsuccessful mediation.[80]

4.24 Sometimes the parties might insert a clause requiring 'expert determination', for example the valuation of shares by a neutral third party auditor. The expert's decision is binding on the parties, but the process takes place outside the Arbitration Act 1996. Clark J in *Thames Valley Power Ltd* v. *Total Gas & Power Ltd* (2005) held that the court might stay English court proceedings if they would involve a failure to adhere to an undertaking to refer the matter to 'expert determination'.[81] But on the facts of this case he exercised his discretion by deciding not to award a 'stay' because of the need for speed and also because he could see no substantive merit in the defaulting party's case.

QUESTIONS

(1) Explain the different results between group (a) (no valid contract) and group (b) (contract upheld):
   (a) *Raffles* v. *Wichelhaus* (1864), *Scammell* v. *Ouston* (1941), *Walford* v. *Miles* (1992), the *Barbudev* case (2012);
   (b) *Hillas & Co.* v. *Arcos Ltd* (1932), *Didymi Corporation* v. *Atlantic Lines and Navigation Co. Inc.* (1988), *Scammell* v. *Dicker* (2005), *Durham Tees Valley Airport Ltd* v. *bmibaby Ltd* (2010), *Jet2.com Ltd* v. *Blackpool Airport Ltd* (2012), *Attrill* v. *Dresdner Kleinwort Ltd* (2013).

(2) Was *Malcolm* v. *Chancellor, Masters and Scholars of the University of Oxford* (1994) convincingly decided?

(3) Discuss these propositions: (a) in a sale of goods context, the price will be determined by objective reference to market value unless the parties have 'agreed to agree', but then failed to agree, on the price (*May & Butcher* v. *R*, 1929); (b) but even the latter problem will be overcome

---

78   N. Andrews, 'The Duty to Consider Mediation: Salvaging Value from the European Mediation Directive', in N. Trocker and A. De Luca (eds.), *La Mediazione Civile all Luce della Direttiva 2008/52/CE* (Florence, 2011), 13–34.

79   On mediation privilege, *Andrews on Civil Processes* (Cambridge, 2013), vol. 2, *Arbitration and Mediation*, 1.128 to 1.135.

80   [2008] EWHC 424; 118 Con LR 68; [2008] 5 Costs LR 736; (2008) 105(15) LSG 24; (2008) 158 NLJ 480, at [72]; J. Sorabji, (2008) 27 *Civil Justice Quarterly* 288, 291–2.

81   [2005] EWHC 2208 (Comm); [2006] 1 Lloyd's Rep 441, at [6], for the terms of the relevant *force majeure* clause.

if there has been substantial performance of the contemplated agreement (*Foley* v. *Classique Coaches*, 1934).

(4) When will the courts decide that the parties have impliedly abandoned the protection of the 'subject to contract' formula?

(5) What are the minimal ingredients of a mediation agreement, and how is such an agreement enforced?

(6) For completeness, refer also to questions (2) to (6) at the end of Chapter 2, concerning negotiation agreements and related matters.

Selected further reading

A. Berg, 'Promises to Negotiate in Good Faith' (2003) 110 LQR 357–63 (these issues, concerning negotiation agreements, are examined in Chapter 2)

M. Furmston and G. J. Tolhurst, *Contract Formation: Law and Practice* (Oxford, 2010), ch 11

H. Hoskins, 'Contractual Obligations to Negotiate in Good Faith: Faithfulness to The Agreed Common Purpose' (2014) 130 LQR 131 (these issues, concerning negotiation agreements, are examined in Chapter 2)

III

Consideration and intent to create legal relations

Chapter contents

5

Consideration and estoppel

1. INTRODUCTION

5.01 Summary of main points

(1) *Nature of 'consideration'.*[1] Consideration to support B's promise to A can be found in any of the following four ways:

    (a) detriment suffered by A, the claimant (unless the promised act is illegal or contrary to public policy (see Chapter 20), or an undertaking to do something which you are already legally obliged to do (see (4) below)); or

    (b) A, the claimant, confers a benefit on B, the defendant/promisor, or even on a third party, for example, B's child; or

    (c) A suffers a detriment and B conversely receives a benefit (the usual case, as where A pays money to B at B's request); or

    (d) A and B exchange lawful promises, A agreeing to do one thing and B agreeing to do another thing, as an executory bargain.

In situations (a) to (c), the benefit or detriment 'moving from A, the promisee', must be requested by B, the defendant/promisor. In situation (d), the interdependence of A and B's promises will be obvious.

(2) *The courts do not assess the adequacy of consideration.* There is no general doctrine of a 'just price' (*iustum pretium*)[2] or a fair exchange. And so, bypassing the formalities of a deed, parties can convert gratuitous promises into binding agreements by resort to nominal consideration. The classic example is the grant of a lease at a so-called 'peppercorn' rent. Such use of nominal consideration creates a 'quasi-deed', a gratuitous promise specially earmarked for legal enforcement, without the bother of extensive formality. Nominal consideration thus signals the

---

1 On the nineteenth-century history of this topic, see M. Lobban, in W. Cornish, J. S. Anderson, R. Cocks, M. Lobban, P. Polden and K. Smith, *The Oxford History of the Laws of England*, vol. XII, *1820–1914: Private Law* (Oxford, 2010), 358 ff. For an attractive overview, S. Waddams, *Principle and Policy in Contract Law: Competing or Complementary Concepts?* (Cambridge, 2011), chapter 3.

2 Cf the French doctrine of *lésion*, on which see B. Nicholas, *French Law of Contract* (2nd edn, Oxford, 1992), 137 ff.

parties' understanding that a legally binding gratuitous promise is being created by a 'short-cut', that is, by dispensing with the formality of a deed (5.03).

(3) *Past consideration.* Y's promise to X, made in gratitude for a previous and unrequested service performed by X, is regarded as gratuitous. It lacks consideration because X's prior service and Y's later promise of gratitude or acknowledgment are sequential and not linked by an initial request by Y to X. However, X can enforce Y's promise in respect of X's earlier performance if: (a) X expected to be rewarded and so was not acting gratuitously; (b) Y had requested X's performance; (c) Y later promised to reward X; and (d) the context is not one where it is against public policy to enforce the promise.

(4) *Pre-existing statutory or public duty.* Consideration is not supplied by a person's promise or performance if the relevant act is already obligatory by virtue of a statutory or other public duty. This is because the making of that promise, or its performance, will not involve any fresh detriment.

(5) *Pre-existing duty owed to a third party.* If A contracts with X to do something and A later contracts with Y to do the very same thing, A's promise to perform, or A's actual performance, counts as consideration for Y's promise to pay A, even though A was already contractually obliged to X (in return for X's payment) to perform the very same act.

(6) *Consideration and variation of contracts.* Consideration's operation within the field of variation of contracts has produced controversy. The current law is conveniently stated in two decisions:

(a) *Williams* v. *Roffey & Nicholls (Contractors)* (1991)[3] decides that an increasing pact (a promise to increase payment for the same performance) is prima facie enforceable on the principle that A receives B's commitment not to abandon his duties; however, B will not be able to enforce A's 'increasing pact' if the variation was procured by B's fraud or duress (see further (7) below).

(b) *Collier* v. *P & MJ Wright (Holdings) Ltd* (2007).[4] This case decides that a decreasing pact (a promise to reduce a debt, even to extinguish it completely) is prima facie valid in Equity ('promissory estoppel') if the debtor acts on the creditor's assurance that part of the debt will be waived and the debtor makes a partial payment to the creditor, unless the debtor has been guilty of coercing the creditor into agreeing this favourable adjustment.

(7) 'Estoppel' is a general concept in private law (see also the more detailed discussion of *promissory* estoppel at 5.38 ff).[5] In general, estoppel by representation applies if: (i) D makes a statement (At Common Law this must be a statement of past or present fact; but in Equity the doctrine of 'promissory estoppel' encompasses promises.); (ii) the statement leads P to assume that X is indeed the case (or will be the case), and so P relies on that assumption; and (iii) D can be prevented by law ('estopped') from acting inconsistently with the statement; or, at least, D's legal rights might be diminished or adjusted to accommodate P's reliance. And the general notion of

3 [1991] 1 QB 1, CA.
4 [2007] EWCA Civ 1329; [2008] 1 WLR 643.
5 Specialist works: G. Spencer Bower and A. K. Turner, *Estoppel by Representation* (4th edn, London, 2003); K. R. Handley, *Estoppel by Conduct and Election* (2nd edn, London, 2014); E. Cooke, *The Modern Law of Estoppel* (Oxford, 2000); and S. Wilken and K. Ghalys, *The Law of Waiver, Variation and Estoppel* (3rd edn, Oxford, 2012).

estoppel is recognised in UNIDROIT's (non-binding) *Principles of International Commercial Contracts* (2010), Article 1.8 ('Inconsistent Behaviour') of which provides:[6] 'A party cannot act inconsistently with an understanding it has caused the other party to have and upon which that other party reasonably has acted in reliance to its detriment.'

5.02 There are three alternative reasons for enforcing a promise in English law:[7]
(1) formality, by use of a 'deed' (5.03 ff);
(2) 'consideration', that is, the element of bargain (requested detriment and/or benefit, of the exchange of promises); or
(3) induced but unrequested reliance (here a positive right of action requires resort to proprietary estoppel, 5.45).

As for (2), the doctrine of consideration encompasses not only the *formation* of contracts but their *variation and discharge by agreement*. The tradition has been to deal with both contexts in the same chapter, and this will be the approach here. Formalities, consideration, and promissory and proprietary estoppel will be discussed in that order.

As regards (3), the essence is that a representee acts in response to a statement. But the representee's reliance is *not requested*, merely induced by the relevant representation. *Promissory* estoppel (see 5.38 for a summary of the types of estoppel) might give the representee the benefit of a *defence* (more time to pay, or even release from the remainder of a debt: see the discussion below). However, an active right of action in this situation of 'induced but unrequested reliance' is confined to *proprietary* estoppel in English law; in other words, only proprietary estoppel gives rise to an independent 'cause of action'. This doctrine is confined to situations where the representee has been induced detrimentally to rely in the belief that *he has, or will shortly acquire, rights in, or in respect of, the representor's land*, or the representor has unconscionably acquiesced in that misunderstanding (see the discussion below).

2. FORMALITIES

5.03 In English law, the starting point is that a gratuitous promise is not enforceable. This is because the element of bargain, of 'consideration', is missing (5.10 ff). And so a promise to give money to a charity[8] is not binding even if made in writing and signed. It is different if a gratuitous promise is presented as a 'deed', that is: (1) signed by 'the covenantor' (the promisor); (2) this signature is witnessed by a third party ('attestation'); and (3) the document is then activated by 'delivery' (this normally, but not necessarily, involves the

6   3rd edition, 2010, text and comment, is available at: www.unidroit.org/english/principles/contracts/princi ples2010/integralversionprinciples2010-e.pdf.
7   For an overview of various theories of contractual obligation, see L. DiMatteo, Q. Zhou, S. Saintier, K. Rowley (eds.), *Commercial Contract Law: Transatlantic Perspectives* (Cambridge, 2014), chapter 2 (by M. Hogg).
8   Gratuitous promises to charity: *Re Hudson* (1885) 54 LJ Ch 811, Pearson J; *Re Cory* (1912) 29 TLR 18, Eve J.

document's physical transfer to the covenantee or his representative).[9] A deed, therefore, is exceptional because it creates a binding promise without 'consideration'. Elements (2) and (3), especially element (2), distinguish a deed from an ordinary contract in writing, even if signed (a so-called 'contract under hand').

> As noted, the witnessing of a covenantor's signature is crucial. So what happens if there has been a purported witnessing ('attestation') of the covenantor's signature, but the witness did not duly attest because he was in a different room at the crucial moment of signature?
>
> In *Shah* v. *Shah* (2001), the Court of Appeal held that such a purported deed (containing a promise to pay £1.5m), although technically a nullity, should be treated as binding.[10] This was achieved by invoking the doctrine of estoppel by representation (see 5.45 below for a summary of the types of estoppel). The court attractively decided that the covenantor's act of handing over the deed to the other party (the 'covenantee') involved an implied 'representation', indeed an obvious suggestion, that the deed had been validly executed. The covenantee had acted sufficiently in reliance on that representation because he had lost the opportunity to demand on the spot a fresh deed to be executed, containing a true attestation.

5.04 Finally, it should be noted that where the gift is not merely promised but actually 'executed', that is, completed, the transferee ('donee') becomes owner: as where the donor says 'I, Izaak, hereby hand you, Yehudi, as a gift this Stradivarius violin', and then hands the instrument to Yehudi. Also, an oral declaration of a trust of movable property (as distinct from land) is valid: 'I declare myself trustee of this Picasso painting for the benefit of Natasha, as sole beneficiary.'[11]

5.05 Most types of contract need not be made in writing (for exceptions, see the next paragraph). Sometimes, a proposed contract will require signature, not because this is a positive rule of law applicable to the transaction, but because the parties have rendered the agreement 'subject to contract' (on which generally, see 4.17). In other situations, however, parties might enter into a binding contract even though a signature has not been added to a 'signature box'. The Court of Appeal in the *Maple Leaf* case (2009) held that a company ('Lion Capital') had become party to

---

9   Section 1(2)(3) of the Law of Property (Miscellaneous Provisions) Act 1989 (as amended by the Regulatory Reform (Execution of Deeds and Documents) Order 2005 (SI 2005 No. 1906, Article 7(3)); *Treitel* (13th edn, London, 2011), 3–170 ff; *Bolton Metropolitan Borough Council* v. *Torkington* [2004] Ch 66, CA; *Chitty on Contracts* (31st edn, London, 2012), 1–115 ff, summarising the effect of the 2005 Order; J. Cartwright, *Formation and Variation of Contracts: The Agreement, Formalities, Consideration and Promissory Estoppel* (London, 2014).

10   [2001] EWCA Civ 527; [2002] QB 35, at [30] to [33]; but *Shah* case distinguished where purported deed lacks attestation of the covenantor's signature, *Re Gleeds, Briggs* v. *Gleeds* [2014] EWHC 1178 (Ch); [2014] 3 WLR 1469, Newey J, at [40], [43]; and cf *Actionstrength Ltd* v. *International Glass Engineering In.Gl.En SpA* [2003] 2 AC 541, HL (oral guarantee ineffective and does not give rise to an estoppel: see [8] to [9], [26] to [29], [34] to [35] and [51], explicitly distinguishing *Shah* v. *Shah*).

11   Express trusts concerning land must comply with the writing formality in section 53(1)(b) of the Law of Property Act 1925; a transfer ('disposition') of a 'subsisting' 'equitable interest' (whether concerning land or other property) must comply with the writing formality in section 53(1)(c); informal trusts ('resulting, implied or constructive trusts') can be created or operate under section 53(2) (see also *Yaxley* v. *Gotts* [2000] Ch 162, CA, examined at 5.07).

the relevant transaction even though it (unlike the other two parties) did not sign the relevant documentation. Instead, it had notified its assent by e-mail. Longmore LJ said:[12]

> There was no prescribed mode of acceptance in this case. The fact that the agreement envisages a signature and leaves a space for those signatures is not a 'prescription' that the agreement can only become binding on the appending of signatures. The signatures are evidence and no doubt the best evidence of what had been agreed, but they are not themselves conditions of the agreement.

5.06 The main exceptional situations, where the law requires a transaction to be in writing, are: (1) certain land transactions, in accordance with the Law of Property (Miscellaneous Provisions) Act 1989 (see the next paragraph for details); (2) guarantees of debts;[13] (3) cheques, bills of exchange and bills of sale;[14] (4) certain credit agreements.[15] Subject to those exceptions, therefore, an agreement can take legal effect even though it was concluded orally or merely evidenced in writing. Thus, a binding agreement to 'buy' a football player for £50m, or a ship for £20m, can be made without writing, on the telephone or during a face-to-face meeting. In the 1950s, Parliament abolished the requirement, contained in the Statute of Frauds 1677,[16] that contracts for the sale of goods of even a moderate, specified value had to be evidenced in writing.

5.07 *Formalities in land transactions.* Section 2 of the Law of Property (Miscellaneous Provisions) Act 1989 provides:[17]

(1) A contract for the sale or other disposition of an interest in land can only be made in writing and only by incorporating all the terms which the parties have expressly agreed in one document or, where contracts are exchanged, in each.

(2) The terms may be incorporated in a document either by being set out in it or by reference to some other document.

(3) The document incorporating the terms or, where contracts are exchanged, one of the documents incorporating them (but not necessarily the same one) must be signed by or on behalf of each party to the contract.

However, section 2(5) creates an exception with respect to 'the creation or operation of resulting, implied or constructive trusts'.

---

12   *Maple Leaf Macro Volatility Master Fund* v. *Rouvroy* [2009] EWCA Civ 1334, at [16].
13   *Actionstrength Ltd* v. *International Glass Engineering In.Gl.En SpA* [2003] 2 AC 541, HL, on section 4 of the Statute of Frauds 1677; *Treitel* (13th edn, London, 2011), 5–013 ff; unwritten guarantee invalid in *Pitts* v. *Jones* [2007] EWCA Civ 1301; [2008] QB 706.
14   For statutory references, see *Treitel* (13th edn, London, 2011), 5–006; on the Bills of Sale Act 1878 (as amended), *Online Catering Ltd* v. *Acton* [2010] EWCA Civ 58; [2011] QB 204 (applicable only to individuals and not to companies).
15   *Treitel* (13th edn, London, 2011), 5–007.
16   Law Reform (Enforcement of Contracts) Act 1954, following Law Revision Committee, 'Sixth Interim Report on The Statute of Frauds and the Doctrine of Consideration' (1937, Cmd 5449).
17   Leading cases on section 2 of the 1989 Act include: *North Eastern Properties Ltd* v. *Coleman & Quinn Conveyancing* [2010] EWCA Civ 277; [2010] 1 WLR 2715; *Yeates* v. *Line* [2012] EWHC 3085 (Ch); [2013] Ch 363, Kevin Prosser QC; *Keay* v. *Morris Homes (West Midlands) Ltd* [2012] EWCA Civ 900; [2012] 1 WLR 2855; *Sharma* v. *Simposh Ltd* [2011] EWCA Civ 1383; [2013] Ch 23. Over 200 reported cases have considered this provision.

For example, in *Yaxley* v. *Gotts* (2000), B, a friend of A, orally promised A that he would be entitled to ownership of the ground-floor portion of a property if he refurbished the whole property.[18] In fact, the property belonged to C, B's relative. C acquiesced in A's belief that B owned the property. The Court of Appeal held that A should be granted a ninety-nine-year lease of the ground floor because it would be 'unconscionable' for C to take advantage of the lack of formality in this context. This decision was an example of equitable relief, a 'constructive trust' awarded under section 2(5) of the 1989 Act.

5.08 *Formality Clauses.* Mediation agreements often prescribe that a binding settlement must be reduced to writing and signed by the parties or their authorised representatives.[19]

5.09 *Unilateral Alteration of Deeds or Guarantees.* A deed or guarantee or other written instrument which is unilaterally and 'materially' altered without the other party's permission is rendered void.[20]

3. BASIC ELEMENTS OF THE CONSIDERATION DOCTRINE

5.10 *Gratuitous promises are not enforceable unless made by deed.* Diabolo promises (orally or by e-mail or in writing, but without a deed) to pay Pius £100,000 on 1 May (a deed, also known as a covenant, is an undertaking which is written, signed, witnessed and delivered,[21] as distinct from an ordinary signed document or a mere memorandum of agreement: 5.03).[22] It is now 14 May and Pius is affronted by Diabolo's failure to pay. Pius exclaims: 'You broke your promise and I'm suing you.' Diabolo coolly responds: 'I made you a promise: so what? Did you promise me anything in return, or have you done anything which I asked you to do?' The Common Law supports Diabolo. Pius is a 'donee-promisee' and has no legal protection. A bare promise, a wholly voluntary undertaking, is not legally binding and is characterised as a *nudum pactum*: it has no legal effect, in the absence of a deed or facts disclosing proprietary estoppel (5.45). That is why charities want willing donors not merely to 'pledge' money (which is merely to enter into a moral commitment), but either to hand the money over straightaway or to enter into a deed or covenant to pay.

However, a bargain, that is, a promise supported by consideration, is binding, provided the agreement is also accompanied by an 'intent to create legal relations' (on which see Chapter 6) and there is sufficient 'certainty' and, furthermore, there are no problems of

18 [2000] Ch 162, CA.
19 *Brown* v. *Rice* [2007] EWHC 625 (Ch), Stuart Isaacs QC.
20 *Habibsons Bank Ltd* v. *Standard Chartered Bank (Hong Kong) Ltd* [2010] EWCA Civ 1335; [2011] QB 943, at [34], *per* Moore-Bick LJ.
21 See 5.03 on the requirements for a deed.
22 An English eighteenth-century attempt to render writing a substitute for consideration was rejected in *Rann* v. *Hughes* (1778) 7 Term Rep 350 n.; 4 Bro PC 27; 2 ER 18 (repudiating Lord Mansfield in *Pillans* v. *Van Mierop* (1765) 3 Burr 1663; 97 ER 1035); C. Mitchell and P. Mitchell (eds.), *Landmark Cases in the Law of Contract* (Oxford, 2008), 23 ff; S. Waddams, 'Principle in Contract Law: The Doctrine of Consideration', in J. W. Neyers, R. Bronaugh and S. G. A. Pitel (eds.), *Exploring Contract Law* (Oxford, 2009), 51, at 55 ff); *Anson's Law of Contract* (29th edn, Oxford, 2010), 93.

capacity (1.09, note 23) or illegality (Chapter 20). This emphasis on bargain reflects the general assumption that you get nothing (much) for free in the marketplace: if you want contractual rights, you should pay for them.

The upshot is that moral obligations and legal obligations do not always coincide. The courts need not apologise for drawing a line in this way; otherwise, if every promise produced legal rights, an unworkable and oppressive system of promise enforcement would result. Moreover, people do not expect all promises to be legally enforceable. Some matters are merely a matter of conscience, others involve the hazard of possible legal suit.

5.11 *Anatomy of a bargain, the requirement of consideration.* A's claim for breach of promise by B must rest on a cause of action which is supported by consideration. It is common to describe A's claim against B in respect of B's breach of promise as resting on consideration in the sense that A has 'bought' (in a metaphorical sense) the right to sue.

> The definition given by Pollock (an influential nineteenth-century legal writer) is as follows: '[Consideration is] an act or forbearance of one party [the promisee], or the promise thereof, is the price for which the promise of the other [the promisor] is bought, and the promise thus given is enforceable.'[23]
>
> This definition was adopted in *Dunlop* v. *Selfridge* (1915)[24] by Lord Dunedin.

More precisely, the consideration requirement can be analysed as follows:

(1) A must either (i) promise something in return (exchanges of promises are classic 'bargains')[25] (provided what is promised is a recognised detriment, not the subject of a pre-existing duty, to the promisee or a 'practical' benefit to the promisor or a third party), or (ii) do something which B asks A to do (or not do something which B asks A not to do). A's (i) counter-promise or (ii) requested conduct is the price or ticket which entitles A to sue B. It is called the consideration supporting B's promise.

(2) As for (1)(i) above, the exchange of promises generates consideration on both sides. This is known as an 'executory' contract.

(3) As for (1)(ii) above, there is a sub-division, according to whether the performance by A, requested by B, is (a) a detriment to A or (b) a benefit to B or perhaps to a third party whom B wishes to favour.

The benefit or detriment must be *requested* by the defendant/promisor. But, as Denning and Asquith LJJ said in *Combe* v. *Combe* (1951), the request can be 'express or implied', that is, the fact that the claimant's conduct was carried out or promised in exchange for the defendant's promise can be clear from the relevant context.[26]

---

23 *Pollock's Principles of Contract* (13th edn, London, 1950), 133.
24 [1915] AC 847, 855 HL, *per* Lord Dunedin; privately, Pollock thought little of the consideration doctrine: see N. Duxbury, *Sir Frederick Pollock and the English Juristic Tradition* (Oxford, 2004), 204.
25 'I promise to mow your lawn if you promise to feed my prize pig'; 'sure, it's a deal'; in this situation, each promise is the price given for the other's counter-promise; and there is no need to search for further detriment, or for immediate fulfilment of the promise.
26 *Combe* v. *Combe* [1951] 2 KB 215, 221, 226–7, CA: on the 'implied' category, *Re Casey's Patents* [1892] 1 Ch 104, CA: 5.17.

(4) Unrequested detriment is not consideration: at best it might give rise to a claim for proprietary estoppel, although that applies only with respect to dealings concerning land (5.45).

(5) But there is 'no testing of the adequacy of consideration'.[27] The classic example, which has passed into the vernacular, is the grant of a lease at a 'peppercorn' rent. And so, bypassing the formalities of a deed (5.03), parties can convert gratuitous promises into binding agreements through the manipulation of *nominal* consideration. Use of nominal consideration is a 'quasi-deed': it signals the parties' understanding that a legally binding gratuitous promise is being created by a 'short-cut' route, that is, by dispensing with the formality of a deed.[28]

> However, the 'no testing of adequacy' doctrine is tempered by specific rules governing compromises affecting minors or the mentally ill,[29] and anti-avoidance provisions in the insolvency legislation.[30] And the 'penalty' jurisdiction will invalidate an excessive stipulation for the payment of agreed damages (19.01 ff); and excessive deposits are almost capable of being invalidated (19.31 to 19.37). Subject to those exceptions and qualifications, there is no general doctrine of a 'just price' (*iustum pretium*)[31] or a fair exchange.

(6) The requirement of consideration operates in two contexts: formation and variation or discharge by agreement. Indeed, modern decisions have endeavoured to unpick much of its effect in the latter context (see the discussion of 'increasing pacts' and 'decreasing pacts' at 5.25 and 5.30 ff).

5.12 *Three illustrations of benefit/detriment analysis.* As mentioned, the essence of A's consideration is that A and B have swapped promises or A has done something at B's request. As for the notion of requested detriment, etc., in *Currie* v. *Misa* (1875) Lush J said: 'A valuable consideration, in the sense of the law, may consist either in some right, interest, profit, or benefit accruing to the [promisor], or some forbearance, detriment, loss, or responsibility, given, suffered, or undertaken by the [promisee].'[32] But the judge failed to emphasise the need for A's plea that he has provided consideration to disclose that A's

---

27 *Anson's Law of Contract* (29th edn, Oxford, 2010), 99–100 (discussing *Haigh* v. *Brooks* (1839) 10 Ad & El 309; 113 ER 119, affirmed (1840) 10 Ad & El 323; 113 ER 124; and *Chappell & Co. Ltd* v. *Nestle* [1960] AC 87, HL); *Hill* v. *Haines* [2007] EWCA Civ 1284; [2008] Ch 412, at [79].

28 Cf M. Arden, [1997] CLJ 516, 533: 'nominal consideration' is potentially the nail in the doctrine's coffin (citing Harvey McGregor QC, in the preface to his *Contract Code: Drawn up on Behalf of the English Law Commission* (Milan, 1993), 3).

29 The court supervises the settlement of claims affecting (either on behalf of or against) children (those under 18) and mental patients: CPR 1998, Rule 21.10.

30 Such legislation enables the courts to examine the substance and to discover whether the sale has been at a significant undervalue, for example, sections 238, 339 and 423 of the Insolvency Act 1986 (as amended), on which see *Re Kumar* [1993] 1 WLR 224, 240–1, Ferris J; *Hill* v. *Haines* [2007] EWCA Civ 1284; [2008] Ch 412, at [79].

31 Cf the French doctrine of *lésion*, on which see B. Nicholas, *French Law of Contract* (2nd edn, Oxford, 1992), 137 ff; such a doctrine also applies in Jersey: *Snell* v. *Beadle* [2001] UKPC 5; [2001] 2 AC 304, PC.

32 (1874–5) LR 10 Ex 153, 162.

detrimental conduct, etc., was requested by the promise, B. The following three illustrations will help to clarify these matters.

(1) *The benefit or detriment box must be ticked*: only one of these boxes needs to be ticked, but both were ticked in *Barry* v. *Davies* (2000). Here the Court of Appeal held that once a bid is made at auction, consideration is supplied by the bidder: 'in the form of detriment to the bidder, since his bid can be accepted unless and until it is withdrawn, and benefit to the auctioneer as the bidding is driven up.'[33]

(2) *Both the benefit and detriment boxes ticked in favour of high-earning traders employed by an investment bank*: in *Attrill* v. *Dresdner Kleinwort Ltd* (2013)[34] (see also on this case 3.44, 4.08 and 6.12) a bank promised to create a guaranteed minimum bonus pool of € 400m from which to pay bonuses to its investment traders, on a discretionary individual basis. The bank tried to resile from this, pleading (at first instance, but abandoning this hopeless argument on appeal) a lack of consideration. Owen J (the Court of Appeal did not disturb his reasoning) held that this was a bargain because the bank received something in return. The consideration was (i) the *general benefit* obtained by incentivising staff to work profitably (this was during the era when banks were not expected to make losses) during the uncertainty of the 2008 financial crisis;[35] (ii) a second analysis[36] was that, *more concretely*, individual employees might show that they had incurred *detriment* by refraining from resigning. Either (i) or (ii) would suffice to support the relevant promise. The facts also neatly demonstrate that the benefit or detriment can be impliedly requested. It was obvious that the defendant's promise was intended to motivate its investment-trading employees both to generate higher revenue and to remain loyal to the company and not seek work elsewhere. In this context, the promisor's quid pro quo went without saying.

(3) *Compromises*:[37] this topic demonstrates both the pliable and pragmatic application of 'detriment' and 'benefit' and the unwillingness to test the adequacy of consideration (5.11 at (6)). *Callisher* v. *Bischoffsheim* (1870)[38] and *Miles* v. *NZ Alford Estate* (1886)[39] establish that a compromise is supported by consideration provided (i) the claim is made in good faith[40] and (ii) the claim has some objective plausibility (that is, it was not manifestly hopeless, vexatious or frivolous,[41] 'fanciful' or 'unrealistic').[42] The 'compromise' rule applies not just to claims where formal proceedings are started but also where litigation is contemplated or a possibility. Below the surface of this analysis there are, of course, strong

---

33 [2000] 1 WLR 1962, 1967.
34 [2013] EWCA Civ 394; [2013] 3 All ER 807; [2013] ICR D30.
35 [2012] EWHC 1189 (QB) at [182], *per* Owen J; not challenged on appeal [2013] EWCA Civ 394; [2013] 3 All ER 807; [2013] ICR D30.
36 [2012] EWHC 1189 (QB) at [183], *per* Owen LJ (not challenged on appeal; but noted [2013] EWCA Civ 394; [2013] 3 All ER 807; [2013] ICR D30, at [95], *per* Elias LJ).
37 D. Foskett, *The Law and Practice of Compromise* (7th edn, London, 2010).
38 (1870) LR 5 QB 449, CA.
39 (1886) 32 Ch D 266, 291, CA.
40 *Callisher* v. *Bischoffsheim* (1870) LR 5 QB 449, 452, *per* Cockburn CJ; *Cook* v. *Wright* (1861) 1 B & S 559; the *Callisher* case and later authorities were noted in *LCP Holding Ltd* v. *Homburg Holdings BV* [2012] EWHC 3643 (QB), at [47] ff, *per* Judge Mackie QC, notably *Hill* v. *Haines* [2007] EWCA Civ 1284; [2008] Ch 412, at [79], *per* Rix LJ.
41 *Miles* v. *NZ Alford Estate* (1886) 32 Ch D 266, 291, *per* Bowen LJ.
42 For these last two epithets, *Birmingham City Council* v. *Forde* [2009] EWHC 12 (QB); [2010] 1 All ER 802, at [90], *per* Christopher Clarke J.

issues of policy: settlements are to be encouraged; formal proceedings should be avoided; and it would be contrary to 'finality' or 'closure' if such compromises were to be readily overturned (see also 4.06 on *Scammell* v. *Dicker* (2005)).[43]

4. CONSIDERATION'S FUNCTIONS

5.13 Admittedly, the doctrine of consideration ('a fundamental principle of the law of contract')[44] – or the bargain principle – is a peculiarity of Common Law systems.[45] The fact that the English Common Law system (and other Common Law systems which still employ consideration as a test of legal enforceability) is isolated in this respect from the civilian tradition prompts the question: what is the justification for the 'consideration' requirement?

5.14 Consideration is a sensible and efficient mechanism to prevent bare, non-formalised gratuitous promises from being legally enforceable. The criterion of an 'intent to create legal relations' (see Chapter 6) is insufficient. The additional requirement of 'consideration', the element of a bargain, is both (1) a protective or paternalistic rule and (2) a rule which avoids or simplifies disputes. As for (1), this doctrine shields promisors *and their estates* from ill-considered, informal and over-generous gratuitous undertakings.[46] As for (2), the consideration doctrine avoids the need to engage in meticulous factual inquiries to determine whether (i) a gratuitous promise was really made and, if so, (ii) whether the parties intended it to have legal force. These points will now be elaborated briefly.

5.15 The first function of the consideration doctrine is to protect a promisor from legal enforcement of informal gratuitous promises. (Even if such a promise is made in writing, it will be invalid unless made formally by deed; see 5.03.) Suppose X promises by telephone or letter that she will pay the appeal office of Thatcher College £1m, stipulating nothing in return. The office must wait for the deed or cheque to clear: 'pledges' do not count.[47] It is different if the money is handed over in cash, or gold bullion is delivered. These will be valid transfers, completed gifts (5.04) not requiring confirmation in writing. This protective or paternalistic policy also protects the promisor's estate, shareholders or liquidators from the depletion of assets by gratuitous promises. If the father drinks or gambles away his fortune,

---

43 On this last factor, *Scammell* v. *Dicker* [2005] EWCA Civ 405; [2005] 3 All ER 838, on which see 4.06.
44 *Prime Sight Ltd* v. *Lavarello* [2013] UKPC 22; [2014] AC 436, at [30], *per* Lord Toulson.
45 cf in the USA, an informal promise to subscribe to charity is enforceable even if the promisee has not relied upon it: *Restatement of the Law Second, Contracts*, section 90(2).
46 In *Pillans* v. *Van Mierop* (1765) 3 Burr 1663, 1670; 97 ER 1035, 1039, Wilmot J emphasised the 'deliberative' rationale, saying that the doctrine of consideration has been adopted 'in order to put people upon attention and reflection, and to prevent obscurity and uncertainty ... Therefore it was intended as a guard against rash inconsiderate declarations: but if an undertaking was entered into upon deliberation and reflection, it had activity' (The *Pillans* case sought to subvert consideration by substituting bare writing, not under seal, as a sufficient cause of action; and it was reversed by the House of Lords in *Rann* v. *Hughes* (1778) 7 Term Rep 350 n.; 4 Bro PC 27; 2 ER 18).
47 For gratuitous promises to charity: *Re Hudson* (1885) 54 LJ Ch 811, Pearson J; *Re Cory* (1912) 29 TLR 18, Eve J; cf, in the USA, an informal promise to subscribe to charity is enforceable once the promisee has relied upon it: *Restatement of the Law Second, Contracts*, section 90(2).

that is one thing. But if he enters into a series of gift promises and then dies before satisfying them, the doctrine of consideration ensures that the folly of his promised generosity is not visited upon his offspring. Similarly, during the promisor's lifetime, the same doctrine and the same policy ensure that his trustee in bankruptcy will have more assets to distribute to ordinary creditors who have supplied goods, etc.

5.16 Secondly, the consideration doctrine efficiently filters out potential contractual disputes. Otherwise, a gratuitous promise *might* be binding and the courts would need to test each set of facts to discover whether a legally binding promise was truly intended or understood to have been intended. The additional requirement of a bargain, the element of 'consideration', avoids in millions of situations each year a possible dispute over whether the promise should be legally enforceable. Instead, English law provides a clear rule: a gratuitous promise is manifestly unenforceable unless formalised as a deed.

> A reform body recommended its removal in 1937, and the Law Commission did not include it in its abortive 1960s general contract code (see 22.12 on this abortive code).[48] But the doctrine of consideration survives. It is also interesting that consideration has not been incorporated into the Dubai International Financial Centre's rules on contract law, which is substantially (although not exclusively) based on English law.[49]
>
> See also the observations by Phang JA in Singapore, where he concluded an impressively learned 'judicial essay' (extended dicta) as follows:[50]
>
>> maintenance of the status quo (*viz*, the availability of both (a somewhat dilute) doctrine of consideration *as well as* the alternative doctrines canvassed above) may well be the *most practical* solution inasmuch as it will afford the courts *a range of legal options* to achieve a just and fair result in the case concerned. However, problems of *theoretical* coherence may remain and are certainly intellectually challenging . . . Nevertheless, given the long pedigree of the doctrine, the fact that no single doctrine is wholly devoid of difficulties, and (more importantly) the need for a legal mechanism to ascertain which promises the courts will enforce, the 'theoretical untidiness' may well be acceptable in the light of the existing practical advantages . . . However, this is obviously a provisional view only as the issue of reform was not before the court in the present appeal.

5. PAST CONSIDERATION

5.17 A promise made in gratitude for a previous and *unrequested* service is regarded as gratuitous and lacking in consideration. It is, therefore, unenforceable. The rationale is

---

48 E.g., the remark of Harvey McGregor QC in the preface to his *Contract Code: Drawn up on Behalf of the English Law Commission* (Milan, 1993), 3; and Law Revision Committee, Sixth Interim Report on 'The Statute of Frauds and the Doctrine of Consideration' (1937, Cmd 5449).
49 Available at www.difc.ae/laws-regulations/ (Dubai International Financial Centre).
50 Phang JA's 'coda' in *Gay Choon Ing* v. *Loh Sze Ti Terence Peter* [2009] SGCA 3; [2009] 2 SLR 332, at [92] to [118] (the quotation is of [118]); for brief comment, E. McKendrick, *Contract Law* (10th edn, London, 2013), 5.29.

that the service was unrequested. Therefore the performer, even if he was not acting benevolently but in hope of payment, took the risk of non-payment. He jumped the gun. The promise to pay came too late. The element of bargain is missing. Such a promise savours of a gift. The leading decision is *Eastwood* v. *Kenyon* (1840).[51] The decision can be rationalised on the double basis that (i) it offers protection against people being 'guilt-tripped' into paying for unrequested benefits and (ii) the same decision also removes the incentive to create such an opportunity to 'guilt-trip'.

However, an earlier request entirely changes this legal equation. The past considera-tion rule does not apply if the promisor had earlier requested the benefit which he is now recognising. The element of request removes the double mischief of artful 'guilt-tripping' and over-generous promise-making. And so the Privy Council confirmed in *Pao On* v. *Lau Yiu Long* (1980),[52] adopting the English Court of Appeal's analysis in *Re Casey's Patents* (1892) that a valid promise made by Y will arise in favour of X in this situation:[53] X can enforce Y's promise in respect of X's earlier performance if: (1) X expected to be rewarded in some way; (2) Y requested X's performance; (3) Y later promised to reward X; and (4) if X had made an initial agreement to perform in return for reimbursement by Y, that exchange of promises would not have been contrary to public policy. The 'request' mentioned at (2) is crucial: this element was missing in *Eastwood* v. *Kenyon* (1840)[54] (above). If elements (1) and (2) are present, the parties have created an inchoate bargain. The amount of X's reward (of course, the reward need not be pecuniary) is then fixed at stage (3) or, if the sum is not specified at this stage, Y at least acknowledges a contractual obligation to pay.

> In *Re Casey's Patents* (1892), Bowen LJ said[55] that the promise at stage (3) 'may be treated either as an admission which evidences or as a positive bargain which fixes the amount of that reasonable remuneration on the faith of which the service was originally rendered'.

Element (4) is merely a public policy safety valve (for example, if X killed T at Y's request and Y later promised to pay X for this, this 'contract killing' would not give rise to a legally enforceable right).

51 (1840) 11 Ad & El 438; 113 ER 482; Court of Queen's Bench; rejecting Lord Mansfield's moral obligation theory for grounding liability for the promise made in recognition of past services in *Hawkes* v. *Saunders* (1782) 1 Cowp 289, 290; 98 ER 1091: 'Where a man is under a moral obligation, which no Court of Law or Equity can inforce, and promises, the honesty and rectitude of the thing is a consideration. As if a man promises to pay a just debt, the recovery of which is barred by the Statute of Limitations: or if a man, after he comes of age, promises to pay a meritorious debt contracted during his minority, but not for necessaries; or if a bankrupt, in affluent circumstances after his certificate, promises to pay the whole of his debts; or if a man promises to perform a secret trust, or a trust void for want of writing, by the Statute of Frauds ... [The] promise is only to do what an honest man ought to do, the ties of conscience upon an upright mind are a sufficient consideration.'
52 [1980] AC 614, 629, PC, *per* Lord Scarman.
53 [1892] 1 Ch 104, 115–16, CA.
54 (1840) 11 Ad & El 438, Court of Queen's Bench.
55 [1892] 1 Ch 104, 115–16, CA.

Eastwood v. *Kenyon* (1840) is an early Victorian cameo case. John Sutcliffe died (he left a will but it did not cover all the property and so he died partly intestate). His estate was administered by the claimant, P. P was also guardian of Sarah, the testator's daughter. At the time of her father's death, Sarah was under 21 and hence a minor (the age of majority is nowadays 18). The facts are thinly reported but it appears that P expended money on (i) improving some cottages forming part of the estate, for Sarah's benefit, and (ii) on Sarah's education, so that her marriage prospects would be improved. P borrowed £140 from Blackburn to finance (i) and (ii). Sarah then promised to reimburse P. She failed to do so. Then the defendant, Sarah's husband, made the same promise, but again failed to pay. The court held that the husband had a valid defence because his promise to reimburse P was not supported by consideration. Instead the promise involved 'past consideration', but this did not count.

Lord Denman gave two reasons to support his decision: (1) it would be bad policy to uphold promises made in a spirit of generosity in response to unsolicited benefits, for the function of consideration is to protect promisors against legal liability springing from spontaneous, often rash, expressions of generosity;[56] and (2) the recipients of gratuitous promises, 'donee-promisees', should not be preferred to those 'promisees' who have entered into transactions supported by clearly onerous consideration (for example, creditors who have sold goods, etc., and await payment); in other words, preference must be accorded to debts or other rights founded on true (non-gratuitous) bargains.

The case is a strong refusal to allow even the fact of substantial benefit to confuse the inquiry whether the claimant-promisee had acted in response to a request. Successive promises, first by Sarah and then by her husband, were insulated from enforcement by virtue of the 'past consideration' doctrine, for these promises were *ex post facto* acknowledgements of gratitude and hence gratuitous.

A strong undercurrent in the case is the fear of financial entanglement between executors and guardians and wards (under-age beneficiaries): 'The temptations of executors would be much increased . . . and the faithful discharge of their duty be rendered more difficult' (see the passage below).

Perhaps this fear was a general one and not the product of any wrongdoing by the plaintiff. The facts are presented starkly. It is not possible to discern whether the executor/guardian was perceived to have overstepped the mark in being so financially 'pro-active', or whether the promises made by Sarah and her husband had been suspiciously procured.

However, the clear upshot of the case is that someone in the position of the executor or guardian would be acting very foolishly if he financed such 'improvements' out of his own pocket, hoping for eventual reimbursement.

The judgment, although concise, is rather jumbled in places. Lord Denman CJ's reasons appear in the following passages:[57]

> The enforcement of such promises by law, however plausibly reconciled by the desire to effect all conscientious engagements, might be attended with mischievous consequences to society; one of which would be the frequent preference of voluntary undertakings to claims for just debts. Suits would thereby be multiplied, and voluntary undertakings would also be multiplied, to the prejudice of real creditors. The temptations of executors would be much increased by the prevalence of such a doctrine, and the faithful discharge of their duty be rendered more difficult.

---

56 (1840) 11 Ad & El 438, 450–2; 113 ER 482, 486–7.
57 *Ibid.*

Lord Denman continued:

> Taking then the promise of the defendant [to reimburse the plaintiff for £140] to have been an express promise, we find that the consideration for it was past and executed long before, and yet it is not laid to have been at the request of the defendant, nor even of his wife while [unmarried and adult] . . . [The claim] really discloses nothing but a benefit voluntarily conferred by the plaintiff and received by the defendant, with an express promise by the defendant to pay money.

He added:

> If the subsequent assent of the defendant could have amounted to [acknowledgment of receipt of a requested benefit, the claim] should have stated the money to have been expended at [the defendant's] request . . . but this was obviously impossible, because the defendant was in no way connected with the property or with the plaintiff, when the money was expended . . . In holding this [claim] bad because it states no consideration but a past benefit not conferred at the request of the defendant, we conceive that we are justified by the old common law of England.

The 'past consideration' rule was applied in *Roscorla* v. *Thomas* (1842), where it was held that a warranty given after sale had no legal effect.[58]

The rule was also applied in *Re McArdle* (1951).[59] This case concerned a mother's expenses incurred when improving a house. Her work was later acknowledged by written agreement of grown-up children. They promised her £488. The Court of Appeal held that the mother's expenses had not been requested by the children and so this promise was unenforceable.

In 1937, the Law Revision Committee unsuccessfully recommended abolition of the 'past consideration rule'.[60]

6. PRE-EXISTING STATUTORY OR OTHER PUBLIC DUTY

5.18 Consideration is absent if the relevant act (or promised act) is already obligatory by virtue of a statutory or other public duty. This is because satisfaction of that promise, or performance of the relevant act, will not involve any fresh detriment. Nor will the promisee receive any real legal benefit from the performance: such conduct, even if it happens to be *factually* beneficial to the promisee, was already required by either a statutory or Common Law rule, so that the promisee was entitled already to be benefited by the promisor's performance (where the duty is aimed at the public at large), or at least to receive the satisfaction of seeing that such performance took place (where the performance is aimed at someone other than the promisor, as in the duty to take care of a child born to the promisee and fathered by the promisor; see the discussion of the 'child maintenance' cases at 5.20).

---

58   (1842) 3 QB 234, Court of Queen's Bench.
59   [1951] Ch 669, CA.
60   Law Revision Committee, Sixth Interim Report on 'The Statute of Frauds and the Doctrine of Consideration' (1937, Cmd 5449), at [32]; similarly, Denning LJ in *Ward* v. *Byham* [1956] 1 WLR 496, 498, CA, and *Williams* v. *Williams* [1957] 1 WLR 148, 151, CA, on which see 5.20.

5.19 The preceding analysis remains English law, as the House of Lords decision in *Glasbrook Bros Ltd* v. *Glamorgan County Council* (1925) makes clear.[61] In that case a mine-owner promised to pay local police to protect his property from trade union pickets. The police formed a garrison and were billeted at the colliery. The House of Lords held that the promise to pay the police was enforceable if the level of policing provided exceeded that required in the ordinary course of performance of the police's duty.

> The Court of Appeal in the *Reading Festival* case (2006)[62] explained the *Glasbrook* decision as follows: '[T]he police are entitled to [payment for providing] special police services if requested to do so, "special police services"[63] being broadly defined as those over and above their general obligation to maintain law and order and keep the peace.' The emphasis, therefore, is upon some 'special' need for extra police support.

The line between private use (requested policing then requiring payment) and public policing (for which no payment is required) was delineated in *Leeds United FC* v. *Chief Constable of West Yorkshire Police* (2013)[64] where the Court of Appeal held that (i) requested policing inside a stadium or on land owned by the football club must be paid for; but (ii) the police could not charge for policing beyond the club's premises (even though requested by the football club); nor, *a fortiori*,[65] was payment due for policing two miles away at Leeds railway station, where the police were placed to greet, and later bid fond farewell to, travelling fans.

5.20 *The child maintenance cases.* The general proposition that satisfaction of a public or statutory duty cannot constitute consideration (5.18 and 5.19) underpins, as we have just seen, the law concerning agreements for payment for police services. The police must do something 'extra' to earn the right to enforce a promise to pay for their services, and those services must have been requested by the promisor. However, in the context of child or matrimonial maintenance agreements, Denning LJ twice attacked this proposition, first in *Ward* v. *Byham* (1956)[66] and then in *Williams* v. *Williams* (1957).[67] In his view, which was a minority approach in these cases, the law should find consideration on such facts unless public policy specifically justifies treating the relevant agreement as invalid and hence unenforceable. But Denning LJ's analysis in these two cases was a minority view, the majority adhering to the 'logic' of the traditional view that the claimant must have earned the right to sue by doing something more onerous or detrimental than simply satisfying the pre-existing statutory or public duty. For the moment, therefore, the

---

61 [1925] AC 270, 277–8, 281, HL; *Treitel* (13th edn, London, 2011), 3–046.
62 [2006] EWCA Civ 524; [2006] 1 WLR 2005 (containing a detailed examination of the *Glasbrook* and *Harris* cases).
63 The police's capacity to uphold promises to pay for 'special . . . services' is now governed by section 25(1) of the Police Act 1996 (adopting without change section 15(1) of the Police Act 1964).
64 [2013] EWCA Civ 115; [2014] QB 168, at [4] to [21].
65 *Ibid.*, at [40].
66 [1956] 1 WLR 496, 498, CA.
67 [1957] 1 WLR 148, CA.

authority of the *Glasbrook* case (1925) (5.19) governs and applies not just to the context of police services but to all other statutory and public duties. Consideration will be found only if the promised performance outstrips the demands of the public duty and (it must be added) there is no public policy objection to upholding the relevant agreement.

At the time of *Ward* v. *Byham* (1956),[68] a statutory provision[69] in a 1948 Act placed the burden of maintaining illegitimate children upon the mother alone. Nowadays, the child-support legislation has achieved symmetry between the sexes here by making genetic fathers liable also for the financial upkeep of children. In the *Ward* case, a father promised a mother, not his wife, to pay £1 a week if she would do two things: look after their child and make sure the child was 'happy'. The Court of Appeal unanimously held that the father's undertaking to pay was enforceable. The majority (Morris and Parker LJJ), applying the *Glasbrook* case (1925) (5.19), held that the mother's bare promise to care for the child added nothing to the statutory obligation placed upon mothers under the 1948 Act. But consideration was lurking in the (adventitious) fact that the second undertaking (the conferment of happiness) did supply something extra, beyond the bare statutory minimum. Making baby happy was a supererogatory act, and it made all the difference.

Morris LJ said:[70]

> [T]he father was saying, in effect: . . . what I am asking is that you shall prove that Carol will be well looked after and happy, and also that you must agree that Carol is to be allowed to decide for herself whether or not she wishes to come and live with you.

This search for an element of requested detriment is consistent with the reasoning in the *Glasbrook* case (1925). The reasoning is logical but stretches doctrinal reason to breaking point. (There was, of course, scope for another approach: did the father receive a 'practical benefit' as a result of the mother's promise? See the discussion of *Williams* v. *Roffey Bros* (1991) at 5.27 below; he received the reassurance that the child would be cared for; and the mother's efforts would save him the practical labour of finding some other means of providing for the child, or doing so directly himself.)

Denning LJ was in the minority in *Ward* v. *Byham* (1956), although he reached the same decision to uphold the father's promise. He boldly (and attractively) suggested that the law should eliminate the need to find detriment on the part of the mother. Denning LJ said:[71]

> I have always thought that a promise to perform an existing duty, or the performance of it, should be regarded as good consideration, because it is a benefit to the person to whom it is given. Take this very case. It is as much a benefit for the father to have the child looked after by the mother as by a neighbour. If he gets the benefit for which he stipulated, he ought to honour his promise; and he ought not to avoid it by saying that the mother was herself under a duty to maintain the child.

In Denning LJ's (minority) view, the three questions should be: (1) whether the contract was intended to create legal relations (generally on that requirement see Chapter 6); (2) was the mother promising to do something beneficial to the father; and (3) was that promised act contrary to public policy? As for this last point, enforcement of promises in some contexts might clearly subvert an important public value. For example, jurors and the press should not agree that

---

68 [1956] 1 WLR 496, 498, CA.
69 Section 42 of the National Assistance Act 1948.
70 [1956] 1 WLR 496, 498–9, CA; with which Parker LJ simply agreed.
71 [1956] 1 WLR 496, 498, CA.

jurors will receive payment 'for carrying out their jury duties'. But Denning LJ's approach in these cases has not changed the law. He was outnumbered in both. Instead, only the House of Lords can reverse its own decisions.

Denning LJ's minority approach to this question was repeated by him in *Williams* v. *Williams* (1957), where again his reasoning was not supported by the other two members of the Court of Appeal (see below).[72] That case concerned the objection that a promise to pay maintenance to a wife who had deserted the marriage was unsupported by consideration because she had placed herself in a situation where she had a duty – admittedly not a statutory or 'public' duty – to maintain herself. Hodson and Morris LJJ found (by a convoluted route) consideration in the wife's undertaking not to pledge the husband's credit or require him to indemnify her debts not only during the period of desertion but if she were to cease to be in desertion (analysis involving the giving up of future rights and hence the incurring of a detriment).[73] The minority approach, adopted by Denning LJ, dispensed with the need to find a detriment on the wife's part and focused instead on the factual benefit to the husband in being spared the inconvenience of a dispute concerning the question of maintenance:[74]

> By paying her 30s a week and taking this promise from her that she will maintain herself and will not pledge his credit, he has an added safeguard to protect himself from all this worry, trouble and expense. That is a benefit to him which is good consideration.

7. PRE-EXISTING CONTRACTUAL DUTY OWED TO A THIRD PARTY

5.21 This is the second aspect of the pre-existing duty doctrine (for the first, pre-existing statutory or public duties, see the preceding discussion at 5.18). If A contracts with X to do something, contract 1, and A later contracts with Y to do the same thing, contract 2, Y's objection will be that neither A's promise to perform nor A's actual performance should count as consideration because A was already contractually obliged to another to perform the very same act. But English law is now clearly against Y on this point.

For example, suppose Blackburn, a contract law scholar, agrees with the University of Fenbog for £10,000 to give a course of five lectures on the doctrine of consideration. Next he agrees with Aethetes' College (a college within the same university) to give the same lectures in the same auditorium at the same time, for £5,000. He gives the lectures, and pockets Fenbog's £10,000, but Aethetes' College refuses to pay the £5,000. The College argues that Blackburn was already obliged by his contract with Fenbog to do the very same thing; neither his promise to do that, nor his actual giving of the lectures, was beneficial to the College nor detrimental to him. The College, in effect, promised him a gift of £5,000. But the courts have pragmatically rejected the College's contention. Instead, it has held that consideration is supplied by Blackburn in this context.

72 *Williams* v. *Williams* [1957] 1 WLR 148, CA.
73 See also Glidewell LJ's summary in *Williams* v. *Roffey & Nicholls* [1991] 1 QB 1, 13, CA, of *Williams* v. *Williams* [1957] 1 WLR 148, CA.
74 [1957] 1 WLR 148, 151, CA.

In *New Zealand Shipping Co. Ltd* v. *AM Satterthwaite & Co. Ltd ('The Eurymedon')* (1975), the Privy Council affirmed[75] that Blackburn's (simultaneous) performance of the first and second promises will supply consideration for both contracts. Next, in *Pao On* v. *Lau Yiu Long* (1980), Lord Scarman in the Privy Council affirmed that, even before performance, the second promise (to the College) supplies consideration.[76] English law is now clear, therefore, on both aspects of this conundrum (no conflict with the *Glasbrook* decision (1925)[77] (5.19) is perceived to exist, that case remaining authority only as far as pre-existing statutory or public duties are concerned).

8. CONSIDERATION AND THE VARIATION OF CONTRACT: INTRODUCTION

5.22 This is the third aspect of the pre-existing duty problem (see 5.18 and 5.21 for the first two).[78] Here, the objection by B to A's assertion of a favourable variation by B is that A has not 'bought' that favourable variation. Once again, the logic of bargaining and of 'consideration' arises: for B can ask, 'Can you, A, show, over and above the original bargain, that you have earned the right to B's favourable variation?'

5.23 In this context of consensual modification or extinction of existing contractual promises, there is a sub-division: 'increasing pacts' (a promise by B to pay more for A's services or work, for example, building work) and 'decreasing pacts'[79] (B's promise to accept part-payment by A as full discharge of A's debt).

And it might be contended that there is a sub-division of each: 'interim pacts' (situations where the increasing or decreasing pact is given to a party whose obligations to work or to pay will continue to arise after the date of the relevant negotiation, as in the leading cases of *Williams* v. *Roffey & Nicholls* (5.27) and the *High Trees* case (5.40 to 5.41)) and 'final pacts' (situations where the pact is made after the obligation to work or to pay owed by the promisee has already arisen in full, as in *D & C Builders* v. *Rees* (5.35) and *Collier* v. *Wright* (5.41 and 5.42)).

It now appears that both *interim* and *final decreasing pacts* are enforceable in Equity, according to the doctrine of promissory estoppel, in that the creditor might find his right to unpaid sums extinguished by the debtor's reliance on his promise to forgo the relevant sum: *Collier* v. *Wright* (5.41).

In the case of an *interim increasing pact*, the liberal resort to 'practical benefit' as sufficient consideration (see the discussion of *Williams* v. *Roffey & Nicholls* at 5.27) has rendered such a pact enforceable at Common Law.

---

75 [1975] AC 154, 168, PC, citing *Scotson* v. *Pegg* (1861) 6 H & N 295; 159 ER 121.
76 [1980] AC 614, 632, PC.
77 [1925] AC 270, HL.
78 J. Cartwright, *Formation and Variation of Contracts: The Agreement, Formalities, Consideration and Promissory Estoppel* (London, 2014).
79 The upwards or downwards 'pact' terminology is adopted with gratitude from G. H. Treitel, *Some Landmarks of Twentieth Century Contract Law* (Oxford, 2002), 11.

A *final increasing pact* (a promise to pay more for a job already completed) would appear to lack consideration, and to fall within the scope of the 'past consideration' rule (5.17).

The following discussion assumes (1) that the parties have not entered into a new agreement, having consensually terminated the old, *both parties surrendering their rights under that old contract to unperformed duties.*[80] It is also assumed (2) that the parties have not varied the existing contract by *conferring mutual benefits or incurring mutual detriment.*[81] In both cases, 'consideration' will arise from the fact that there has been an exchange of rights or exchange of releases, that is, a (two-way) bargain has been struck. Finally, it is also assumed that the relevant contract does not include an express variation clause. The Court of Appeal in *Attrill v. Dresdner Kleinwort Ltd* (2013)[82] (see also on this case 3.44, 4.08 and 6.12) acknowledged that a clause might stipulate within a long-term contract that one party X can vary the terms operating vis-à-vis party Y. Such a clause has been upheld in the context of employment contracts. Such a variation, at least if favourable to Y, does not require Y to furnish independent consideration. And for the courts giving effect to a hire variation clause, see the *Didymi* case (4.09).

5.24 Consideration's operation within the field of variations of contracts has produced controversy. In the nineteenth century, Sir Frederick Pollock wrote on this aspect of consideration: 'the doctrine of consideration has been extended, with not very happy results, beyond its proper scope, which is to govern the formation of contracts, and has been made to regulate [also] their discharge.'[83] However, two modern Court of Appeal decisions, *Williams v. Roffey & Nicholls (Contractors)* (1991)[84] and *Collier v. P & MJ Wright (Holdings) Ltd* (2007),[85] have transformed the approach to both 'increasing' and 'decreasing' pacts. These respective decisions establish these propositions:

(1) Party A's agreement to pay more (or otherwise to increase A's contribution to the contract) for B's continuation of his contractual obligations becomes enforceable on the principle that A receives B's commitment not to abandon his duties. However, B will not be able to enforce A's 'increasing pact' if the variation was procured by B's fraud or duress.

(2) *Under principles of Equity and the doctrine of promissory estoppel,* a creditor's agreement to release his debtor from the remainder of a debt, or to forgo part of a debt, becomes binding on the creditor if the debtor acts on this assurance and makes a partial payment to the creditor (if not even part-payment is made, the position is unclear; nor is the position

---

80 *Argo Fund Ltd* v. *Essar Steel Ltd* [2005] EWHC 600, Aikens J; [2006] 1 All ER (Comm) 56; [2005] 2 Lloyd's Rep 203, at [51] (affirmed on other grounds at [2006] 2 All ER (Comm) 104, CA).
81 E.g. *South Caribbean Trading* v. *Trafigura Beheer BV* [2004] EWHC 2676 (Comm), Colman J; [2005] 1 Lloyd's Rep 128, at [105]; for adoption in the USA of such reasoning, *Watkin & Son Inc.* v. *Carrig* (1941) 21 A 2d 591 (Sup Ct of New Hampshire); such reasoning is regarded by Purchas LJ in *Williams* v. *Roffey & Nicholls* [1991] 1 QB 1, 20, CA, as 'attractive', but the court did not adopt it.
82 [2013] EWCA Civ 394; [2013] 3 All ER 807.
83 *Pollock's Principles of Contract* (13th edn, London, 1950), 150 (repeating his nineteenth-century observation); Sir Frederick Pollock was an influential textbook writer and, for many years, editor of the *Law Quarterly Review*. On the Commonwealth tendency to expunge consideration in the context of variation agreements, see B. Coote, 'Variations Sans Consideration' (2011) 27 JCL 307.
84 [1991] 1 QB 1, CA.
85 [2007] EWCA Civ 1329; [2008] 1 WLR 643.

clear if, contrary to the terms of the decreasing pact, the debtor only partially or perhaps dilatorily pays a part-payment of a part-payment, as where the part-payment is staggered in tranches, and the schedule of payments is not adhered to). However, the debtor will not receive the benefit of this 'decreasing pact' if he has been guilty of coercing the creditor into the agreement of this favourable adjustment.

The upshot of (1) and (2), therefore, is that the longhand of 'consideration' has been effectively removed from the context of post-formation agreements. The Supreme Court has yet to ratify either proposition. Whether it should do so, and if so whether the law might be presented in a simpler and more coherent fashion, are questions requiring a careful survey of the history of both topics.

9. VARIATIONS TO PAY MORE THAN THE ORIGINAL RATE ('INCREASING PACTS')

5.25 *Background.* Suppose A agrees to do work for B for £5,000. If B later agrees to pay A an extra sum for the very same job, is this 'increasing pact' a gift and so unenforceable, or should the law solemnly uphold such a promise of variation? There is a conceptual point: English lawyers regard a variation of a subsisting contract as itself a species of contract. Therefore, this agreed variation must be formalised by deed (5.03) or supported by fresh consideration; and, if the latter, A must promise or do something extra or different to earn the right to the promised increase.

From 1809 until 1990, the law had said that such an increasing pact is invalid because it is unsupported by consideration. Two arguments might be said to support that robust approach. First, there is the disciplinary need to hold A to the initial bargain. This is especially important if A has only won the job after a competition, formal (for example, during a competitive tender) or informal, over price. Secondly, there is the need to protect B against duress, that is, unfair pressure exerted mid-contract by A to renegotiate the terms. But there are two counter-arguments: first, freedom of contract (1.08) should permit the parties to revise the payment if circumstances change; and, secondly, the spectre of duress should be specifically addressed by an independent doctrine of duress rather than by a blunt and wholesale declaration that every 'increasing pact' must be invalid unless a more onerous set of obligations have been assumed by the intended payee. As for this second point, it should be noted that the English courts in the mid-1970s recognised that economic duress can invalidate the increasing pact if it results from illegitimate coercion, normally on one party to end his performance of the job forthwith, and so breach his contract (the breakthrough decision was Kerr J's alternative[86] *ratio* in *'The Siboen and the Sibotre'*, 1976, 11.16).[87] Before this development, the doctrine of duress had been confined to threats to the person or threats to damage or seize property (generally on economic duress, see 11.02).

---

86 Cleverly rendering the decision 'appeal-proof' by deciding the case also on the basis of misrepresentation, and thus on a secure legal basis.
87 [1976] 1 Lloyd's Rep 293, Kerr J; noted, J. Beatson, (1976) 92 LQR 496.

5.26 *Stilk* v. *Myrick and its reconsideration.* Until 1991, the consideration rule in *Stilk* v. *Myrick* (1809)[88] had prevailed: an 'increasing pact', a promise to pay more, needed to be supported by consideration. Until 1991 (see the next paragraph), this was interpreted to mean that a mere promise to carry on with one's contractual duties would not constitute consideration.

In *Stilk* v. *Myrick* (1809) for a fixed sum of £5 a month each, eleven sea-hands agreed to work on a sailing ship carrying a cargo between London and the Baltic and back. It was agreed that their wages would be paid on completion of the return voyage. While in Cronstadt, a port on the Baltic, two of the sailors absconded. The master of the ship agreed to pay the nine remaining loyal sailors the wages of the two deserters, if they helped to get the ship back to London. On arrival back in England, the master refused to pay the bonus. One of the loyal sailors sued for the extra sum. He failed.

There are two reports of the *Stilk* v. *Myrick* decision.[89] Espinasse's report[90] (he was one of the counsel) says that the decision was based on public policy: the need to protect ships' masters from coercion to pay more during the perilous stages of such voyages. A specific rule against mutiny and coercion within the merchant navy made sense. This was the very basis on which Lord Kenyon had decided *Harris* v. *Watson* (1791).[91] Espinasse might have had many fine qualities, but his capacity as an accurate law reporter was diminished by the fact that he was virtually deaf (and not, it seems, an accurate lip-reader).[92] The accuracy of his report of an *ex tempore* oral judgment (given immediately after conclusion of legal argument, without a full written text) is open to doubt.[93]

But what of the second report? Campbell's rival report introduces the language of consideration: because the loyal sailors had done nothing new or additionally burdensome, the master's promise was a gift. It was unsupported by consideration. According to Campbell,[94] Lord Ellenborough's judgment emphasised that before leaving London for the two-leg trip, the men had agreed impliedly 'to exert themselves to the utmost to bring the ship to her destined port'. This meant that the originally agreed rate of payment, recorded in writing,[95] covered all maritime hazards, including the extra strain created by the death or disability suffered by fellow members of the crew during the trip, or by their desertion.

Campbell's report[96] in *Stilk* v. *Myrick* (1809), based upon 'consideration', prevailed.[97] Indeed, this analysis became a general aspect of contract law: an 'increasing pact', a promise to pay more, needed to be supported by consideration. Until the *Roffey* case in 1991 (5.27), this was interpreted to mean that a mere promise to carry on with one's contractual duties would not

88 *Stilk* v. *Myrick* (1809) 2 Camp 317; 6 Esp 129; R. Halson, *Contract Law* (2nd edn, London, 2013), 329 ff; G. H. Treitel, *Some Landmarks of Twentieth Century Contract Law* (Oxford, 2002), 11–46; G. Gilmore, *The Death of Contract* (Columbus, OH, 1974), 22–8.
89 On the discrepancy between these reports, see P. Luther, (1999) LS 526.
90 *Stilk* v. *Myrick* (1809) 6 Esp 129.
91 (1791) Peake 102.
92 Glanville Williams records an incident involving Maule J when a report of Espinasse was cited before him. Maule J claimed that he did not care for Espinasse 'or any other ass': *Glanville Williams: Learning the Law*, A. T. H. Smith (ed.) (12th edn, London, 2002), 44.
93 R. E. Megarry, *A Second Miscellany-at-Law* (London, 1973), 118.
94 *Stilk* v. *Myrick* (1809) 2 Camp 317.
95 To satisfy a statute: 2 Geo. II, c. 36, section 1.
96 (1809) 2 Camp 317.
97 Thus, in *Williams* v. *Roffey & Nicholls* [1991] 1 QB 1, CA, this is the only report cited; note also Mocatta J's comments in *'The Atlantic Baron'* [1979] QB 705, 712.

provide consideration, so that the promisor could resile from his promise to pay more, without having to show that he had been the victim of fraud, exploitation or any other kind of misconduct. Indeed, the true events of the voyage in *Stilk* v. *Myrick* are not recorded. It is simply unknown whether the ship's hands had been guilty of any underhand dealing, duress or fraud, or whether there had been some conspiracy between the deserters and the loyal crew.

Stilk v. *Myrick* (1809) was distinguished in later cases concerning claims for maritime wages. A mid-voyage agreement to pay an extra sum would be enforceable if, as on the extreme facts of *Hartley* v. *Ponsonby* (1857), a large proportion of the men had deserted or perished and the remaining crew's task had become radically different;[98] or if, as in *Hanson* v. *Royden* (1867), the bonus was in recognition of the promotion of an ordinary seaman to a higher rank, such as to petty officer or ship's surgeon. This would be a 'new job' and additional payment would be appropriate.[99]

5.27 *'Practical benefits': the new analysis.* The Court of Appeal in *Williams* v. *Roffey & Nicholls (Contractors)* (1991)[100] circumvented *Stilk* v. *Myrick* (1809) (5.26) by overt manipulation of the consideration rule. In *Williams* v. *Roffey & Nicholls (Contractors)* (1991), the main contractor, sensing that he might run into trouble on the main contract, promised subcontractors more money if they would speed up their work. Although the strategy did not entirely work, the Court of Appeal held that in the absence of duress, the subcontractors could claim for the bonus payment. It is enough that the main contractor obtained some short-term practical benefit or commercial assurance that the project would be moving ahead smoothly.

The facts in greater detail:
  X owned a block of flats. X commissioned the defendant, the main contractor, to fit out these flats. The defendant, the main contractor, subcontracted the carpentry work to the claimant, who agreed to do the work for £20,000, a low sum. But the claimant's work was so slow that the defendant became concerned that he might become liable to pay X liquidated damages for late completion. To avoid this, the defendant, the main contractor, tried to 'incentivise' the claimant by agreeing to pay him an extra sum of £575 for each completed flat. The facts did not involve any suggestion that the claimant had coerced the defendant. On the contrary, as Purchas LJ said:[101] 'The initiative in coming to the [renegotiation] agreement . . . came from [the main contractors, the defendant] and not from the claimant.' In fact, the defendant's incentive had a feeble effect. The claimant finished eight more flats,

---

98 (1857) 7 E & B 872 (drastic percentage of desertion).
99 *Hanson* v. *Royden* (1867) LR 3 CP 47 (promotion).
100 [1991] 1 QB 1, CA; noted B. Coote, (1990) 3 JCL 23; B. Reiter, (1977) 27 *University of Toronto Law Journal* 439; M. Chen-Wishart, (1991) 14 NZULR 270; M. Chen-Wishart, in J. Beatson and D. Friedmann (eds.), *Good Faith and Fault in Contract Law* (Oxford, 1995), 130–2; M. Chen-Wishart, in A. Burrows and E. Peel (eds.), *Contract Formation and Parties* (Oxford, 2010), 89; M. Chen-Wishart, *Reciprocity in Contract* (Hong Kong, 2010).
101 [1991] 1 QB 1, 21, CA.

but then abandoned the remainder of the job. Perhaps not surprisingly, the defendant chose not to pay the claimant the £575 bonus for each of those eight flats.

The Court of Appeal held that there had been a valid renegotiation which was supported by consideration,[102] and so the claimant was entitled to the bonus payments.[103] This was so even though the court could not discern any 'detriment' incurred by that party's promise to carry on for more money (but see point (4) below for the author's suggestion that such a detriment might have existed on these facts). Instead, the court noted that consideration has two faces: detriment and benefit. Either face will do. It suffices that a benefit is conferred by the subcontractor on the main contractor at the latter's request. This will furnish consideration and so make the renegotiation binding.

In the *Roffey* case (1991), Russell LJ explained:[104]

> Where, as in this case, a party undertakes to make a payment because by so doing it will gain an advantage arising out of the continuing relationship with the promisee the new bargain will not fail for want of consideration.

Practical benefits: the defendant had received these 'practical benefits':[105]

(1) (a) the subcontractor went on with the job, and so (b) the main contractor avoided the hassle of seeking substitutes (in fact this benefit was short-lived because, ultimately, the subcontractor did cease work: but the Court of Appeal upheld the judge who had held that at that later point, work on the additional eight flats was substantially done, to justify pro rata payment. The job was eventually completed by substitutes);

(2) the main contractor was reassured that timely completion would avoid his having to pay liquidated damages for delay in completion of the site to X; in fact of course this reassurance was short-lived because the subcontractor did not complete all the work, and the main contractor became liable to the site owner for late completion;

(3) the parties agreed a new and clearer system of periodical payments for the work; but the report is vague on this suggested benefit;

(4) the subcontractor agreed to concentrate on finishing one flat at a time rather than manically trying to do every job at the same time; this would leave room for other trades to work efficiently on the site. [In fact factor (4) is two-edged: it is not entirely fanciful to regard this cooperative change of performance as a possible 'detriment', but this is not how the case was reasoned.] Glidewell LJ encapsulated the law as follows:[106]

> if . . . B has reason to doubt whether A will . . . complete his side of the bargain, and B thereupon promises A an additional payment in return for A's promise to perform his contractual obligations on time, and . . . B obtains in practice a benefit . . . [provided also that] B's promise is not given as a result of economic duress or fraud on the part of A, . . . the benefit to B is capable of being consideration for B's promise.

---

102   [1991] 1 QB 1, 10, CA.
103   Agreeing with Rupert Jackson QC, the county court trial judge.
104   [1991] 1 QB 1, 18–19, CA.
105   [1991] 1 QB 1, CA.
106   [1991] 1 QB 1, 15–16, CA; this statement was adopted by Christopher Clarke J in *Birmingham City Council* v. *Forde* [2009] EWHC 12 (QB); [2010] 1 All ER 802, at [86].

5.28 *Duress cases can now be handled without resort to consideration reasoning.* It is obvious that the Court of Appeal in the *Roffey* case (1991)[107] chose to abandon, without formally purporting to overrule, the rule in *Stilk* v. *Myrick* (5.26). By 1991, the old approach had ceased to be an attractive solution. It was too blunt (it was 'over-inclusive'). At the time of *Stilk* v. *Myrick*, 'duress' was confined to threats of personal violence or physical damage to property. It was not until the 1970s that English law extended duress to encompass threats to breach a contract, that is, to inflict purely economic harm (for that development, see 11.16). It is clear that this doctrinal development enabled the Court of Appeal in the *Roffey* case to bypass the blunt device of consideration and to confine a contracting party's protection against unfairness to the specific doctrines of duress and fraud. The concept of 'practical benefits' was the key chosen to unlock the door to that new approach. That door had seemed to be locked by the authority of *Stilk* v. *Myrick*.

In the *Roffey* case (1991)[108] Purchas LJ distinguished the old cases of *Stilk* v. *Myrick* (1809)[109] and *Harris* v. *Watson* (1791),[110] in both of which the courts rejected claims by merchant sailors to enforce mid-voyage promises to pay extra wages:[111]

> [These two old cases] involved . . . the extraordinary conditions existing at the turn of the 18th century [involving] seamen . . . There were strong public policy grounds at that time to protect the master and owners of a ship from being held to ransom by disaffected crews . . . The modern cases tend to depend more upon the defence of duress in a commercial context rather than lack of consideration for the second agreement. In the present case the question of duress does not arise.

5.29 *Taking stock of the increasing pact revolution: a single practical benefit is enough.* It appears that English law can now be stated as follows: any single 'practical benefit' will provide consideration, including factor (1) identified above, a bare promise to carry on with precisely the same job. If so, consideration has been effectively eliminated from the context of increasing pacts.

A leading specialist work states: 'a variation is supported by consideration in all cases where it is possible to find that the variation results in the accrual of a benefit to the parties to the contract . . . [And] the Court should not find that a variation of a contract is invalid even if the practical benefit is merely the due performance of existing obligations under the contract to be varied to the benefit of both parties.'[112]

---

107   [1991] 1 QB 1, CA.
108   [1991] 1 QB 1, 21, CA.
109   (1809) 2 Camp 317.
110   (1791) Peake 102.
111   [1991] 1 QB 1, 21, CA.
112   S. Wilken and K. Ghalys, *The Law of Waiver, Variation and Estoppel* (3rd edn, Oxford, 2012), 2.25 (presenting High Court reception of the *Roffey* case at 2.24); e.g., in *Anangel Atlas Compania Naviera SA* v. *Ishikawajima Harima Heavy Industries Co. Ltd (No. 2)* [1990] 2 Lloyd's Rep 526, Hirst J (noted M. Chen-Wishart in J. Beatson and D. Friedmann (eds.), *Good Faith and Fault in Contract Law* (Oxford, 1995), 130–2) applied the practical benefit analysis; admittedly, Colman J in *South Caribbean Trading* v. *Trafigura Beheer BV* [2004]

Perhaps the Supreme Court might ratify this development. It might even go further, and declare that consideration is no longer required in this context.

> This was the approach adopted in *Antons Trawling Co. Ltd* v. *Smith* (2003), where the New Zealand Court of Appeal said:[113]
>
> > *Stilk* v. *Myrick* can no longer be taken to control [cases involving increasing pacts] where there is no element of duress or other policy factor . . . The importance of consideration is [that it serves] as a valuable signal that the parties intend to be bound by their agreement, rather than an end in itself. Where the parties who have already made such intention clear by entering legal relations have acted upon an agreement to a variation, in the absence of policy reasons to the contrary they should be bound by their agreement.

But an increasing pact would not be binding if it resulted from (1) 'fraud' (no doubt including fraudulent misrepresentations, for example, false statements that the cost of performance has increased significantly), or (2) duress (11.02), or (3) perhaps (as suggested by Coote)[114] some other forms of unacceptable underhand dealing, such as tactical underpricing (for example, where a subcontractor has deliberately underpriced the job to win the deal; this is especially reprehensible if the underpricing occurred during a competitive tender).

10. PART-PAYMENT AT COMMON LAW ('DECREASING PACTS', PART I)

5.30 *The rule in* Pinnel's Case *(1602).*[115] This rule can be formulated as follows: in the absence of a deed (5.03) or fresh consideration, part-payment does not discharge the whole debt, even though the creditor says or promises that he will forgo the unpaid part. Thus, if A owes B £1,000 and B agrees to receive £500 in complete discharge of the debt, *at Common Law* B remains entitled to the unpaid balance, despite this promise (for extinction of A's right to the balance once B 'relies' by making part-payment, see the discussion of *Collier* v. *Wright* at 5.41 ff). The whole debt will be discharged by part-payment only if (1) A provides so-called 'fresh consideration', that is, A, at B's request, does something extra, or A does something not strictly required (such as paying the debt earlier than the due date); or (2) B releases A from the balance by a formal deed.

EWHC 2676 (Comm); [2005] 1 Lloyd's Rep 128, at [107], was unconvinced by the 'practical benefit' reasoning in the *Roffey* case, but Colman J's doubts are rejected by *Chitty on Contracts* (31st edn, London, 2012), 3–069.
113   [2002] NZCA 331; [2003] 2 NZLR 23, at [93]; noted by B. Coote, (2004) 120 LQR 19–23; noting F. M. B. Reynolds and G. H. Treitel, 'Consideration for the Modification of Contracts' (1965) 7 *Malaya Law Review* 1.
114   B. Coote, (2004) 120 LQR 19, 22–3.
115   *Pinnel's Case* (1602) 5 Co Rep 117a (entire Court of Common Pleas); Law Revision Committee, Sixth Interim Report on 'The Statute of Frauds and the Doctrine of Consideration' (1937, Cmd 5449), at [33]; J. Cartwright, *Formation and Variation of Contracts: The Agreement, Formalities, Consideration and Promissory Estoppel* (London, 2014).

5.31　The Common Law rule against decreasing pacts was affirmed by the House of Lords in *Foakes* v. *Beer* (1884),[116] applied by a majority of the Court of Appeal (Danckwerts and Winn LJJ) in *D & C Builders* v. *Rees* (1966)[117] and followed by the Court of Appeal in *Re Selectmove* (1995),[118] admittedly without enthusiasm (see further 5.32). In this last case, the court said that the Common Law rule was intact and could not be subverted by resort to 'practical benefit' reasoning (for such reasoning, in the context of increasing pacts, see 5.27). However, the rule is controversial. Some support it; for example, Janet O'Sullivan in a 1996 article applauds *Foakes* v. *Beer*. She contends that monetary obligations should be treated as sacrosanct.[119] In her opinion, once a debt, always a debt, unless the debt is reduced for good consideration supplied by the debtor. By contrast, the rule's abolition was recommended (so far in vain) by a law reform body in 1937,[120] and Dame Mary Arden, a former Chair of the Law Commission, in an article in 1997, described this rule as 'ridiculous'.[121]

In favour of the rule in Pinnel's Case. There is something to be said in defence of the rule in *Pinnel's Case* (1602) and *Foakes* v. *Beer* (1884).[122]

First, *this is a gift case.* If you owe me money, I have an asset in which I can trade. If I release you from all or part of the debt, I am making you a gift of that part from which you are released. It is axiomatic that a gratuitous promise needs to be supported by a deed. Not only must a gratuitous promise-maker be protected by the formal requirement of a deed from rashness, but it is arguably necessary also to protect a creditor's *inheritance and successors in title.* If enforced, the creditor's promise to accept part-payment as full discharge will reduce the value of his estate (or the creditor company's assets). The creditor might not immediately mind that. But his 'successors' will, especially his trustee in bankruptcy, or liquidator, or those financially interested after the creditor's death.

Secondly, the rule in *Pinnel's Case protects a creditor from pressure* of any type and degree exerted by the debtor in attempting to procure a decreasing pact (we have seen at 5.28 how this factor has been influential in the history of the parallel doctrine concerning 'increasing pacts', and how the decision in *Williams* v. *Roffey & Nicholls* (1991) displaced this factor by placing confidence in the doctrine of duress to provide adequate protection).

Thirdly, the rule in *Pinnel's Case* simplifies adjudication of contractual disputes: an oral promise to release or reduce a debt is not enforceable, and so disputes concerning telephone or face-to-face oral discussion are eliminated. Finally, as we shall see (5.38 ff), this Common Law rule has been *qualified in Equity* by the doctrine of promissory estoppel, enabling the merits of the creditor and debtor's relations to be more flexibly adjusted.

116　(1884) 9 App Cas 605, HL; M. Lobban, in C. Mitchell and P. Mitchell (eds.), *Landmark Cases in the Law of Contract* (Oxford, 2008), 223 ff.
117　[1966] 2 QB 617, 626A, 626D, CA.
118　[1995] 1 WLR 474, CA.
119　J. O'Sullivan, 'In Defence of Foakes v. Beer' [1996] CLJ 219–28.
120　Law Revision Committee, Sixth Interim Report on 'The Statute of Frauds and the Doctrine of Consideration' (1937, Cmd 5449).
121　[1997] CLJ 516, 533.
122　(1602) 5 Co Rep 117a (entire Court of Common Pleas); rule affirmed in *Foakes* v. *Beer* (1884) 9 App Cas 605, HL.

Objection to the Common Law rule. It can be said, against the rule in *Pinnel's Case* (1602),[123] that the Common Law has ignored the creditor's 'practical benefit' in receiving part-payment now (in the hand) rather than having to chase full payment later and eventually failing, perhaps having spent money litigating. In short, the practical objection to this rule is that cash-flow realities should be taken into account. Thus, in *Foakes* v. *Beer* (1884), Lord Blackburn was minded to dissent on the basis that 'a bird in the hand is worth two in the bush'.[124] But he relented and acquiesced in the other Law Lords' decision to affirm the Common Law rule. However, his 'quasi-dissent' convinced a law reform body in 1937[125] to recommend abolition of the rule in *Pinnel's Case*. In *Collier* v. *Wright (Holdings) Ltd* (2007),[126] Arden LJ quoted that 1937 report as follows:

> In *Foakes* v. *Beer* Lord Blackburn was evidently disposed to hold that it was still open to the House of Lords to reconsider the rule based on the *dictum*, but in deference to his colleagues who were of a different opinion he did not press his views. In a few words (at p. 622) he summed up what appears to us to be a powerful argument for the abolition of the rule. He said: 'What principally weighs with me in thinking that Lord Coke made a mistake of fact is my conviction that all men of business, whether merchants or tradesmen, do every day recognise and act on the ground that prompt payment of a part of their demand may be more beneficial to them than it would be to insist on their rights and enforce payment of the whole. Even where the debtor is perfectly solvent, and sure to pay at last, this often is so. Where the credit of the debtor is doubtful it must be more so.' The Law Reform Committee added: 'In our opinion this view is as valid as it was fifty years ago, and we have no hesitation in recommending that legislation should be passed to give effect to it.'

It is instructive to compare UNIDROIT's (non-binding) *Principles of International Commercial Contracts* (2010), Article 5.1.9 of which provides:[127] '(1) [A creditor] may release its right by agreement with the [debtor]. (2) An offer to release a right gratuitously shall be deemed accepted if the [debtor] does not reject the offer without delay after having become aware of it.' In light of this clear provision it can be said that, once again, the bargain theory of contractual modification in English law can be seen to be out of step with the general juristic perception of what is commercially acceptable and reasonable.

5.32 The 'bird in the hand' argument resurfaced before the Court of Appeal in *Re Selectmove*,[128] but the court considered that it lacked the authority to subvert the rule in *Pinnel's Case* by invoking the concept of a 'practical benefit' in receiving immediate partial payment. This would have been too bold a subversion of the ancient rule, and only the Supreme Court can reverse *Foakes* v. *Beer* (1884).[129]

---

123 (1602) 5 Co Rep 117a (entire Court of Common Pleas).

124 (1884) 9 App Cas 605, 622, HL (at 613, 630, the Earl of Selborne LC and Lord Fitzgerald also noted that part-payment is often attractive, rather than the risk of eventual non-payment, if the debtor absconds or his assets are divided on bankruptcy in a derisory share-out).

125 Law Revision Committee, Sixth Interim Report on 'The Statute of Frauds and the Doctrine of Consideration' (1937, Cmd 5449).

126 [2007] EWCA Civ 1329; [2008] 1 WLR 643, at [5].

127 3rd edition, 2010, text and comment, is available at: www.unidroit.org/english/principles/contracts/principles2010/integralversionprinciples2010-e.pdf.

128 [1995] 1 WLR 474, CA; E. Peel, (1994) 110 LQR 353–6.

129 (1884) 9 App Cas 605, HL; cf in Australia, the practical benefit analysis has been applied to uphold landlord's decreasing pact to a tenant: *Musumeci* v. *Winadell Pty Ltd* (1994) 34 NSWLR 723, Sup Ct of NSW.

In *Re Selectmove* (1995), a company alleged that it had agreed with the Inland Revenue to pay its tax liability by instalments. After receipt of some of these, the Revenue applied to wind up the company as a bad debtor. The company argued, among other things, that there was a good contract that the Revenue would not foreclose for full payment so long as the instalments were paid. The Court of Appeal held, first, that no agreement had arisen because the Revenue's employee lacked authority to make any such agreement; secondly, it held that there was no consideration, applying *Foakes* v. *Beer*, for the agreement (nor did the doctrine of promissory estoppel apply (on which see below), not just because of the employee's lack of authority but because the company had failed to pay the instalments on time and so had forfeited any protection in Equity under that doctrine).

5.33 *'Fresh consideration' exonerating the debtor*. The position changes if the debtor supplies fresh consideration and so in a sense *purchases* the entitlement to be discharged fully. In *Pinnel's Case* (1602), Lord Coke put this colourfully, by way of example, as the debtor's gift of a horse, a hawk or a robe. Let us consider some instances of the debtor supplying consideration to support the creditor's promise to accept part-payment as full discharge.[130]

(1) *Accelerated payment in general*. Requested accelerated payment, even by one day or even sooner, is fresh consideration for the creditor's promise to accept half as full payment, provided the parties do a deal: 'You pay part early and I will release you from the unpaid balance.' Early payment involves detriment to the debtor and benefit to the creditor. It might be in the creditor's interest to have £500 paid on 23 March rather than the £1,000 payable on 1 April under the original agreement, if he has a 'cash-flow crisis'. It should be recalled that there is no weighing of the adequacy of consideration (for that aspect of the consideration rule, see 5.11 at (5)).

(2) *Immediate cash payment at creditor's request*. Similarly, there might be consideration if a contract stipulates that payment should be by cheque, but the creditor later requests payment of part in cash, saying that he would then forget about the balance. It is arguable that this confers a real commercial benefit: cheques can take several days to clear and cash payment also guarantees an exchange of value, whereas cheques might be dishonoured.[131] However, the relevant change must have been requested by the creditor, rather than as a variation to suit the debtor alone.[132]

(3) *Compromise of debt when its validity, enforceability, or amount is disputed in good faith*. The rule in *Pinnel's Case* (1602)[133] applies where the debt itself is an ascertained, or ascertainable, sum and it is manifestly enforceable in law for this amount. By contrast, if the debt's existence or validity, or its amount, were genuinely disputed on objectively

---

130 *Pinnel's Case* (1602) 5 Co Rep 117a (entire Court of Common Pleas).
131 Possibility acknowledged by Winn LJ in a dictum in *D & C Builders* v. *Rees* [1966] 2 QB 617, 633, CA.
132 *Vanbergen* v. *St Edmunds Properties* [1934] 2 KB 223, CA (change of place of payment not fresh consideration if variation made to suit the debtor and not the creditor).
133 (1602) 5 Co Rep 117a (entire Court of Common Pleas); rule affirmed in *Foakes* v. *Beer* (1884) 9 App Cas 605, HL.

reasonable grounds, part-payment 'in full and final settlement' would constitute a final discharge, in accordance with the compromise or settlement rule (5.12 at (3)).[134]

5.34 *Part-payment by a third party in full discharge of the debt.* The creditor cannot sue the debtor for the balance if a third party, whether a friend or relative, pays part of the debt to the creditor on the footing that this will discharge the entire contract, and the creditor assents.

> In *Hirachand Punamchand* v. *Temple* (1911), a money-lender received part-payment in this way from the debtor's father.[135] The Court of Appeal held that the money-lender was not entitled to claim the balance from the son. That would be a 'fraud' on the father who had stipulated that his part-payment should discharge the son's entire debt. The decision does not rest on consideration supplied by the debtor. Instead, the Court of Appeal felt determined to uphold the deal struck between the creditor and the third party, the father (the partial payor). The result seems fair and sensible. It should be noted that there is no conflict here with the rule in *Pinnel's Case* (1602) because the partial payor is a third party, the father, and not the debtor, his son. This configuration might now be rationalised as a third party benefit effective under the Contracts (Rights of Third Parties) Act 1999 (7.22), in the sense that the father and creditor agreed that the son, a third party, would be protected against a claim for the unpaid element.
>
> In the *Hirachand* case, it was clear that the payee had assented to the third party's stipulation that the part-payment would preclude any further recourse by the payee against the debtor. But sometimes it is not clear whether receipt or cashing of a cheque given in full and final settlement discloses an accord and satisfaction: see Jacob J's survey in *IRC* v. *Fry* (2001),[136] and *Stour Valley Builders* v. *Stuart* (1992).[137]

5.35 *Absence of fresh consideration: part-payment by cheque.* In *D & C Builders* v. *Rees* (1966), a builder received a cheque from Mrs Rees for part of his genuine claim.[138] The majority judges, Danckwerts and Winn LJJ, held that the payor, Mrs Rees, still owed the balance: payment by cheque, rather than cash, did not constitute fresh consideration.

> In *D & C Builders* v. *Rees* (1966), Mrs Rees, the debtor, unsuccessfully contended that the creditor had received fresh consideration because payment by cheque relieved him of the burden and hazard of carrying lots of coins or notes. Certainly it is inconvenient and perhaps unsafe to carry large amounts of money, but the Court of Appeal rightly held that part-payment by cheque is really the equivalent of part-payment in cash. In making out a

---

134 *Ferguson* v. *Davies* [1997] 1 All ER 315, CA (dicta: because debtor had admitted he was fully liable); *Wigan* v. *Edwards* (1973) 1 ALR 497 (High Court of Australia).
135 [1911] 2 KB 330, CA; *Treitel* (13th edn, London, 2011), 3–108.
136 [2001] STC 1715; [2002] BTC 3.
137 Court of Appeal, 21 December 1992, Lloyd LJ and Connell J, reported [2003] TCLR 8; *The Times*, 22 February 1993; this is a learned judgment, demonstrating that *Day* v. *McLea* (1889) 22 QB 610, CA, has survived and that it supports the statement summarised in the *Stour Valley* case, despite American textbook suggestion to the contrary.
138 [1966] 2 QB 617, CA, overruling *Goddard* v. *O'Brien* (1882) 9 QBD 37, Divisional Court.

cheque rather than paying in cash, the debtor is not doing anything which is financially more onerous. Therefore, part-payment by cheque is not an exception to the rule in *Pinnel's Case* (1602).[139] The balance remains due.

In the *D & C Builders* case Lord Denning MR found his way to the same result by a quite different route (adopting his preferred promissory estoppel analysis, but declaring Mrs Rees to lack 'clean hands'). His approach was for some time considered to be a minority judgment, but the Court of Appeal in *Collier* v. *Wright (Holdings) Ltd* (2007)[140] (5.41) thought that he had been sufficiently supported by Danckwerts LJ.[141] Lord Denning MR in the *D & C Builders* case considered that prima facie the balance had been extinguished in Equity (promissory estoppel) by the creditor's promise to accept part-payment as full discharge. But Lord Denning held that Mrs Rees in fact still owed the balance on these particular facts because she lacked 'clean hands'. Mrs Rees's conduct had been unmeritorious because, in Lord Denning's view, she had exploited the builder's cash-flow crisis: indeed she had coerced him into accepting merely part-payment. For this reason, she could not successfully invoke fastidious Equity's assistance. On this analysis, Mrs Rees had fallen at Equity's last fence.

5.36 *No fresh consideration if joint debtor only pays his arithmetical share.* A joint debtor is liable directly to the creditor to pay the whole of the debt (but the individual debtor who paid can later claim a contribution from the other joint debtors if he pays more than his share). The Court of Appeal in *Collier* v. *Wright (Holdings) Ltd* (2007)[142] (5.41) held that a promise by a creditor to accept payment from a joint debtor of a share of the total debt is subject to the rule in *Pinnel's Case* (1602).[143] And so, although the creditor had agreed to accept this part-payment and to pursue the other joint debtors for the balance, the joint debtor who had paid only in part (as now agreed) nevertheless remained liable to pay the rest. There was no consideration for any release of that joint debtor from the balance of the debt.

5.37 *Other concessions or variations at Common Law: 'waiver' and 'forbearance'.* So far we have been considering promises to accept part-payment as full discharge of the debt. But other types of concessionary pacts might favour a debtor. The creditor might promise:

(1) to give the debtor more time to pay; or

(2) to accept one currency rather than the contractual currency, for example, US dollars rather than Japanese yen, or UK sterling instead of Kenyan shillings (*Alan* v. *El Nasr* (1972),[144] noted later in this paragraph); or

(3) to change the place of payment, for example, London rather than Hong Kong.[145]

---

139 (1602) 5 Co Rep 117a (entire Court of Common Pleas); rule affirmed in *Foakes* v. *Beer* (1884) 9 App Cas 605, HL.
140 [2007] EWCA Civ 1329; [2008] 1 WLR 643.
141 Danckwerts LJ's judgment in the *D & C Builders* case, [1966] 2 QB 617, 625–7, is short: see 5.42 at (5) for comment.
142 [2007] EWCA Civ 1329; [2008] 1 WLR 643, at [5].
143 (1602) 5 Co Rep 117a (entire Court of Common Pleas); rule affirmed in *Foakes* v. *Beer* (1884) 9 App Cas 605, HL.
144 [1972] 2 QB 189, CA.
145 *Vanbergen* v. *St Edmunds Properties* [1934] 2 KB 223, CA (change of place of payment not fresh consideration if change made to suit the debtor and not the creditor).

The Common Law doctrine of 'waiver' (sometimes known as 'forbearance') can give effect to such a concession. For example, in the case of party A's waiver of a time restriction binding upon party B, Denning LJ explained in *Charles Rickards Ltd* v. *Oppenhaim* (1950):[146]

> If [party B leads party A] to believe that he would not insist on the stipulation as to time, and that, if [party B] carried out the work, he would accept it, and [party B] did it [in accordance with the newly agreed time schedule],[147] he could not afterwards set up the stipulation as to the time against them. Whether it be called waiver or forbearance on his part, or an agreed variation or substituted performance, does not matter. It is a kind of estoppel. By his conduct he evinced an intention to affect their legal relations. He made, in effect, a promise not to insist on his strict legal rights. That promise was intended to be acted on, and was in fact acted on. He cannot afterwards go back on it.

The three strands of waiver, estoppel (see 5.49 for a summary of the types of estoppel) and 'binding variations' (contractual changes supported by requested consideration) often become intertwined.[148] *Alan* v. *El Nasr* (1972) illustrates this doctrinal intersection.[149] Despite Lord Denning's attractive suggestion in *Alan* v. *El Nasr*, the doctrine of 'Common Law waiver' continues to be described in the books as distinct from promissory estoppel (on which see the next paragraph). Historically, this is true. But functionally they appear to operate quite similarly and, as *Alan* v. *El Nasr* shows, even identically in some contexts.

In *Alan* v. *El Nasr* (1972), the contract concerned three successive shipments of coffee, for which the price was in Kenyan shillings, payable in three instalments. However, the seller accepted payment in English pounds in respect of the first two shipments. This was a variation of the contract's original terms. The parties found themselves in dispute concerning the appropriate currency for the third payment, because at that point the English pound had been devalued. The Court of Appeal held that the creditor was bound to be consistent. He must accept payment in English pounds for the third payment. This reflected the parties' dealings. 'Waiver' had occurred. The originally stipulated currency of payment could no longer be insisted upon. The various tributaries of 'fair dealing' are explored in the three judgments: (1) Lord Denning MR argued that the basis for this might be a general principle of fair dealing, involving a fusion of 'Common Law waiver' and 'equitable estoppel';[150] (2) Megaw LJ reached the same result by simply applying the notion of 'waiver'; and (3) Stephenson LJ found that a fresh set of terms had arisen: a binding variation.

147   But, on the facts of the case, party B *did not comply with the new time schedule* and this meant that the other party could validly terminate the contract.
148   A. Phipps, 'Resurrecting the Doctrine of Common Law Forbearance' (2007) 123 LQR 286–313.
149   [1972] 2 QB 189, CA.
150   *Charles Rickards Ltd* v. *Oppenhaim* [1950] 1 KB 616, 623, CA.

11. THE EQUITABLE DOCTRINE OF PROMISSORY ESTOPPEL ('DECREASING PACTS', PART II)

5.38 *Main factors.* This form of estoppel[151] (here referred to as 'promissory estoppel', although some commentators prefer the phrase 'equitable forbearance'[152] or 'equitable estoppel')[153] consists of the following elements (see 5.49 for a summary of the types of estoppel):

(1) There must be a clear and unambiguous representation, by words or conduct, regarding the past, present *or future.*

(2) The representee *relies* on this (some form of reliance is necessary, but the court can decide that there is *insufficient* reliance to justify estoppel).[154]

(3) Thereafter, the representor can validly give reasonable notice of his wish to reassert his strict legal rights.[155]

(4) Subject to this last point, the representor is estopped (that is, prevented by law) from acting inconsistently with his representation.

(5) The representee's protection will be adjusted to the extent that justice demands.

(6) But promissory estoppel (being rooted in broad notions of Equity) will not protect a representee if he comes 'with unclean hands' (for example, because he has coerced or cheated the representor into making the statement).[156]

5.39 *The leading nineteenth-century decision.* In *Hughes* v. *Metropolitan Railway* (1877), the House of Lords embraced the doctrine of promissory estoppel, although this decision was not concerned with the variation of a debt.[157] In this case Lord Cairns LC formulated the following general principle of promissory estoppel:[158]

> if parties who have entered into [a contract] afterwards by their own act or with their own consent enter upon a course of negotiation which has the effect of leading one of the parties to suppose that *the strict rights arising under the contract will not be enforced, or will be kept in suspense, or held in abeyance*, the person who otherwise might have enforced those rights will not be allowed to enforce them where it would be inequitable having regard to the dealings which have thus taken place between the parties. [emphasis added]

151 Specialist works: J. Cartwright, *Formation and Variation of Contracts: The Agreement, Formalities, Consideration and Promissory Estoppel* (London, 2014); E. Cooke, *The Modern Law of Estoppel* (Oxford, 2000); K. R. Handley, *Estoppel by Conduct and Election* (2nd edn, London, 2014); G. Spencer Bower and A. K. Turner, *Estoppel by Representation* (4th edn, London, 2004); S. Wilken and K. Ghalys, *The Law of Waiver, Variation and Estoppel* (3rd edn, Oxford, 2012); see also M. Chen-Wishart, 'A Bird in the Hand: Consideration and Promissory Estoppel', in A. Burrows and E. Peel (eds.), *Contract Formation and Parties* (Oxford, 2010); B. McFarlane, 'Contract Formation: Promissory Estoppel', in A. Burrows and E. Peel (eds.), *Contract Formation and Parties* (Oxford, 2010).

152 S. Wilken and K. Ghalys, *The Law of Waiver, Variation and Estoppel* (3rd edn, Oxford, 2012), 8.05 to 8.07.

153 B. McFarlane, 'Understanding Equitable Estoppel: From Metaphors to Better Laws' (2013) 66 CLP 267–305.

154 *'The Post Chaser'* [1982] 1 All ER 19, 25B–27, Goff J (representee's reliance insufficient).

155 *Tool Manufacturing Co. Ltd* v. *Tungsten Electric Co. Ltd* [1955] 1 WLR 761, HL.

156 *D & C Builders* v. *Rees* [1966] 2 QB 617, CA (Lord Denning MR withholding estoppel's protection because Mrs Rees (the debtor) had unfairly coerced the builder (the creditor) into accepting part-payment).

157 (1877) 2 App Cas 439, HL.

158 *Ibid.,* at 448, HL; *Birmingham & District Land Co.* v. *London & NW Railway Co.* (1888) 40 Ch 268, CA.

The facts of *Hughes* v. *Metropolitan Railway* (1877) were as follows. A covenant in his lease obliged the tenant of a property to repair the property on the giving of six months' notice by the landlord. After such a notice had been served by the landlord, the parties negotiated unsuccessfully for the purchase by the tenant of the freehold. The tenant plausibly contended that during these negotiations the landlord had implicitly indicated that the tenant would have more time to repair. When these negotiations petered out, the landlord attempted to forfeit the lease, relying on the lapse of six months from the date of the repair notice. The House of Lords held that the landlord was estopped from acting in this inconsistent, unfair and even oppressive fashion. It was only fair and reasonable that the tenant should be given more time to comply with that obligation. There was no question of extinguishing the duty to repair, merely the granting of a stay on the landlord's self-help right to obtain forfeiture of the lease.

5.40 *The suspension/extinction debate: the* High Trees *dicta (1947).* The doctrine of promissory estoppel shot to greater prominence following a bold dictum of Denning J in the *High Trees* case (1947).[159]

The case concerned a block of flats, High Trees House, in London. The landlord was the parent company. The head tenant held a lease for ninety-nine years. This tenant was the landlord's subsidiary company. The rent was £2,500 a year. The head tenant sublet flats in the block to subtenants. In 1940, enemy bombs began to fall on London. Even before the bombing started, Londoners had been leaving in droves to seek shelter in the less vulnerable counties surrounding London. Such fugitives from the blitz included many of the subtenants of High Trees House. As a result, the head tenant was now in financial difficulty. And so the landlord made a concession: to receive half the rent, £1,250, as long as these wartime difficulties prevailed. This rent reduction operated from 1939 to 1945. In the later stages of the war, the threat of air raids had diminished markedly, although 'V1' flying bombs and 'V2' rockets were still a hazard. Subtenants had gradually resumed occupation of the flats. However, in 1941, the landlord had gone into liquidation. In 1945, the receiver woke up to the fact that the true rent was £2,500, and he asked the head tenant for the arrears, as well as for future rent at £2,500. In the present action, the receiver was seeking a declaration from the court that he could reassert the £2,500 figure for the last two quarters of 1945, and thereafter. Denning J granted the declaration sought. This was the case's *ratio*.

But Denning J, in further remarks unnecessary for the decision, and therefore strictly *obiter dicta*, asserted that Equity's doctrine of promissory estoppel was not confined to giving debtors more time (as noted at 5.39 above, the tenant in the *Hughes* case was given more time to make repairs). In the view of Denning J, promissory estoppel might operate to ensure that a creditor honoured his promise to forgo part of a debt, even though that promise to forgive the debtor the relevant sum was unsupported by fresh consideration. In short, Denning J's suggestion was that estoppel could 'extinguish' and not merely 'suspend' a debt. If so, Equity's doctrine of promissory estoppel would contradict the Common Law rule in *Pinnel's Case*,[160] which preserves the creditor's strict right to payment at Common

---

159 *Central London Property Trust Ltd* v. *High Trees House Ltd* [1947] 1 KB 130, 133–5; Denning later wrote about his theory in 'Recent Developments in the Doctrine of Consideration' (1952) 15 MLR 1.
160 (1602) 5 Co Rep 117a (entire Court of Common Pleas).

Law (in the absence of a deed or fresh consideration, 5.33). Denning J felt bound to turn to Equity's promissory estoppel because Common Law estoppel by representation was not flexible enough. This is because *Jorden* v. *Money* (1854) is regarded as House of Lords authority that Common Law estoppel requires a representation of a past or present fact and does not extend to promises of future conduct or future abstention.[161]

The decision (the *ratio*) in the *High Trees* case was unremarkable (5.40). But the dictum (as Denning J well knew) was a 'bombshell' in the law. The latter aspect of the case provoked two major questions: (1) Was Denning J correct to suggest in his dictum that Equity, outflanking the Common Law rule in *Pinnel's Case*, can legitimately treat a debt (or part of it) as 'extinguished' by the creditor's promise to reduce or release the sum owed? (2) If so, what type of 'reliance' is necessary before the debtor could receive this superior and permanent form of protection? The Court of Appeal in *Collier* v. *P & MJ Wright (Holdings) Ltd* (2007)[162] (5.41) answered 'yes' to question (1). As for question (2), the court adopted Lord Denning's view that 'reliance need only be the debtor's part-payment' (before this, a different form of reliance had seemed to be required, Lord Hodson in *Ajayi* v. *Briscoe* (1964)[163] having suggested that 'the promise only becomes final and irrevocable if the promisee cannot resume his position'). If the *Collier* decision (2007) prevails, and only the Supreme Court can disturb it, this case will have removed sixty years of doctrinal uncertainty, especially concerning question (1) above. Therefore, the *Collier* decision requires scrutiny.

5.41 In *Collier* v. *P & MJ Wright (Holdings) Ltd* (2007)[164] Arden LJ, with the support of her fellow judges, held that the *D & C Builders* case (1966)[165] is binding Court of Appeal authority for these propositions (this passage is a quotation from Arden LJ's judgment in the *Collier* case, 2007): [166]

> [T]hat, if (1) a debtor offers to pay part only of the amount he owes; (2) the creditor voluntarily accepts that offer, and (3) in reliance on the creditor's acceptance the debtor pays that part of the amount he owes in full, the creditor will, by virtue of the doctrine of promissory estoppel, be bound to accept that sum in full and final satisfaction of the whole debt. For him to resile will of itself be inequitable. In addition, in these circumstances, the promissory estoppel has the effect of extinguishing the creditor's right to the balance of the debt. This part of our law originated in the brilliant *obiter dictum* of Denning J, as he then was, in the *High Trees* case. To a significant degree it achieves in practical terms the recommendation of the Law Revision Committee chaired by Lord Wright MR in 1937.[167]

161   (1854) 5 HL Cas 185; 10 ER 868.
162   [2007] EWCA Civ 1329; [2008] 1 WLR 643 (noted by A. Trukhtanov, (2008) 124 LQR 364–8).
163   [1964] 1 WLR 1326, PC; a view favoured by *Treitel* (13th edn, London, 2011), 3–115.
164   [2007] EWCA Civ 1329; [2008] 1 WLR 643 (noted by A. Trukhtanov, (2008) 124 LQR 364–8).
165   [1966] 2 QB 617, CA.
166   [2007] EWCA Civ 1329; [2008] 1 WLR 643, at [42].
167   Referring to Law Revision Committee, Sixth Interim Report on 'The Statute of Frauds and the Doctrine of Consideration' (1937, Cmd 5449).

It appears, therefore, that when a creditor agrees to accept £90m, instead of £100m, of an outstanding debt, part-payment of the £90m (provided that all of £90m is paid) will trigger an extinction of the balance.

The *Collier* case (2007)[168] concerned these facts. Collier was one of three partners liable jointly and severally to the Wrights. This meant that each partner could be sued for the full amount of the debt. Collier alleged that he and the Wrights had reached an agreement that if he paid one-third of the total debt (that is, his notional per capita share), thereupon he would be released from his joint liability for the balance. Collier paid this one-third share. But, after the other two partners became bankrupt, the Wrights sued him for the unpaid two-thirds. The question of Collier's liability arose in insolvency proceedings. Collier was attempting to set aside a 'statutory demand' (a preliminary requirement to making a person bankrupt) made by the Wrights against him. To do so, he needed to show a real prospect of success on the merits at trial. On that question, the Court of Appeal first applied *Pinnel's Case*[169] and held that Collier was still liable at Common Law as a joint debtor for the balance. However, the Court of Appeal held that Collier should be allowed at a final hearing (the case had come before the Court of Appeal as a preliminary question to test the legal merits of Collier's attempted defence) to contend that the doctrine of promissory estoppel might protect him against liability to pay more than his agreed one-third share.

5.42 *Assessment of* Collier v. Wright (2007).[170] There are various problems facing 'the Denning/Arden extinction thesis', and these might be addressed if, in another case, the point arises before the Supreme Court. These problems are as follows:

(1) Suppose an undisputed debt of £100m is owed but the creditor agrees to accept £90m in final settlement, provided it is paid by a specified date. It is not clear what the position would be if the debtor pays the £90m later than the parties had agreed in their decreasing pact. Nor is the position clear if the decreasing pact provides that the £90m is to be paid in tranches of £10m, for each of the next nine months, and the debtor fails to pay, say, the last tranche of £10m. At that point, is the protection of promissory estoppel forfeited so that he now owes £20m (the originally released top slice of £10m now coming back into the reckoning)? This is not discussed in the *Collier* case, although Arden LJ did state (see the quotation above) that the rescheduled part-payment must be paid 'in full'. If so, in the example just given, the answer would be: the debtor's failure to pay the last tranche renders him liable for the *whole* of the original debt (and therefore £20m is now owing, because he has in fact paid only £80m of the original £100m, and promissory estoppel's protection is contingent on the debtor adhering to the terms of the decreasing pact).

(2) As a matter of principle (5.31), it is debatable whether gratuitous debt-releasing concessions should be readily upheld, in the absence of some compelling factor, such as the risk of great hardship to the debtor. Such a gratuitous release would diminish the assets of the creditor, including assets available to his trustee in bankruptcy or to his liquidator.

168 [2007] EWCA Civ 1329; [2008] 1 WLR 643 (noted by A. Trukhtanov, (2008) 124 LQR 364–8).
169 (1602) 5 Co Rep 117a (entire Court of Common Pleas).
170 [2007] EWCA Civ 1329; [2008] 1 WLR 643 (noted by A. Trukhtanov, (2008) 124 LQR 364–8).

(3) 'Extinction' of the creditor's rights in Equity under the *High Trees* doctrine involves a drastic clash between Common Law and Equity. Equitable estoppel is being used to trump the rule in *Pinnel's Case*.

(4) The sequence of nineteenth-century House of Lords precedents was the 'wrong way round' for the purpose of Denning J's dictum in the *High Trees* case: *Foakes* v. *Beer* (1884) (5.31), which ratified the Common Law rule in *Pinnel's Case* (5.30) was decided after *Hughes* v. *Metropolitan Railway* (1877). And yet the House of Lords in *Foakes* v. *Beer* made no reference at all to the equitable doctrine, a remarkable omission.

(5) It is submitted that the judges in the *Collier* case (2007)[171] were too quick, and arguably mistaken, to interpret the *D & C Builders* case[172] as a two-judge affirmation of Lord Denning's 'extinction' thesis (admittedly in the *D & C Builders* case Danckwerts LJ referred to the absence of equitable factors in favour of Mrs Rees;[173] but otherwise he did not specifically address Lord Denning's analysis in that case of promissory estoppel; the third judge, Winn LJ decided the case solely by reference to Common Law principles, the rule in *Pinnel's Case*). However, it appears that only the Supreme Court will be able to reopen this aspect of the *Collier* case. Until that happens, English law is settled.

(6) It is debatable whether the mere fact of part-payment should be sufficient to satisfy the requirement of 'reliance'. Part-payment is not an intrinsically detrimental act, because it is made in pursuance of a subsisting legal obligation. The *Collier* decision on this point adopts, therefore, a very generous approach to the notion of sufficient reliance. The Supreme Court might prefer, in a future case, to revisit this generous approach and require a stronger element of reliance.

(7) Nor is it clear that reliance in this context can only be constituted by part-payment, despite the suggestion in the *Collier* case. Suppose that a creditor states that for the next quarter he will reduce a tenant's rent from £50,000 to £20,000. In reliance on this, the tenant, *ahead of the relevant quarter date*, spends the supposedly released portion of £30,000 on a new training course for its staff. Staff training is an innovation in the tenant company. The *Collier* decision would appear (5.41) not to regard this as reliance effective to extinguish the balance of the next quarter's payment. But pre-*Collier* judicial discussion had indicated that irreversible detrimental reliance (other than part-payment itself) would be capable of extinguishing the relevant part of the debt: Lord Hodson in *Ajayi* v. *Briscoe* (1964)[174] suggested that 'the [creditor's] promise only becomes final and irrevocable if the promisee cannot resume his position.' It is submitted that reliance should not, therefore, be confined to acts of part-payment.

(8) Indeed, reliance, for the purpose of this doctrine, needs to be strong enough, according to earlier case law, to warrant Equity's protection of the representee. This point is related to the next issue (see (9) below). Thus, although the essence of estoppel is that the representee *relies* on the other party's statement, Goff J in 'The Post Chaser' (1982) held that the court can decide that there is *insufficient* reliance to justify estoppel.[175]

---

171 [2007] EWCA Civ 1329; [2008] 1 WLR 643.
172 [1966] 2 QB 617, CA.
173 *Ibid.*, 625–7.
174 [1964] 1 WLR 1326, PC; a view favoured by *Treitel* (13th edn, London, 2011), 3–115.
175 'The Post Chaser' [1982] 1 All ER 19, 25B–27, Goff J (representee's reliance insufficient).

(9) Finally, Longmore LJ's judgment in the *Collier* case states that, in addition to reliance, the court must be convinced that it is equitable, that is, fair in all the circumstances, that estoppel should apply. By contrast, Arden LJ's analysis appears to eliminate this further requirement, by adopting the view that reliance by part-payment is enough and that, thereupon, the creditor cannot resile from his promise to accept part-payment.[176] Arden LJ's approach is mechanistic. By contrast, Longmore LJ suggests that the court has an opportunity to assess whether it would be inequitable for the creditor to resile *even if there has been some reliance* by the debtor. He said:[177]

> There is then a third question, namely whether it would be inequitable for the company to resile from its promise. That cannot be inquired into on this appeal, but I agree that it is arguable that it would be inequitable. There might, however, be much to be said on the other side.

The fact that the creditor has been exposed to duress or fraud would render it not inequitable for him to insist on his strict legal rights. But, even where fraud or duress does not preclude resort to this estoppel, the courts will continue to weigh the suggested reliance to determine whether, or to what extent, the creditor should be estopped from enforcing those strict legal rights.[178]

5.43 *Promissory estoppel not a cause of action.*[179] In *Combe* v. *Combe* (1951), the Court of Appeal, including Denning LJ, held that promissory estoppel operates as a shield and not a sword.[180] It does not establish an independent cause of action. It merely furnishes a defence. Unrequested detrimental reliance on another's promise does not generate a contract: consideration (or a deed) must be shown to support the *initial contract*.[181] And so *promissory* estoppel in England is not a substitute for consideration to support such an initial promise. However, estoppel by representation and promissory estoppel can be used by a claimant in England to overcome *some other impediment* to his claim.

> As Robert Goff J explained in *Amalgamated Investment & Property Co. Ltd* v. *Texas Commerce International Bank Ltd* (1981),[182] estoppel, including estoppel by representation and promissory estoppel, can assist a claimant to make good his claim, but only by *supplementing* a basic cause of action rooted (a) in the provision of consideration or (b) founded perhaps on a deed (as for (b), see *Shah* v. *Shah* (2001),[183] examined in detail at 5.03). It should be noted, however, that proprietary estoppel (5.45) can be used as an independent cause of action (on this type of

---

176 [2007] EWCA Civ 1329; [2008] 1 WLR 643, at [42].
177 *Ibid.*, at [48], *per* Longmore LJ.
178 'The Post Chaser' [1982] 1 All ER 19, 25B–27, Goff J (representee's reliance insufficient).
179 R. Halson, *Contract Law* (2nd edn, London, 2013), 372 ff and R. Halson, [1999] LMCLQ 257; A. Robertson, 'Estoppels and Rights-Creating Events . . . ', in J. W. Neyers, R. Bronaugh and S. G. A. Pitel (eds.), *Exploring Contract Law* (Oxford, 2009), 199 ff; M. Barnes, 'Estoppels as Swords' [2011] LMCLQ 372–92.
180 [1951] 2 KB 215, CA.
181 See nn 8 and 47.
182 [1981] 1 All ER 923, 936–7; and Brandon LJ in the Court of Appeal agreed.
183 [2001] EWCA Civ 527; [2002] QB 35, at [30] to [33], *per* Pill LJ.

estoppel, see *Crabb* v. *Arun District Council*, 1976).[184] But proprietary estoppel is confined to situations where the representee has been induced detrimentally to rely in the belief that *he has, or will shortly acquire, rights in, or in respect of, the representor's land* (or the representor has unconsciously acquiesced in that misunderstanding).

Denning LJ's statement in *Combe* v. *Combe* (1951) is crystal clear:[185]

> Much as I am inclined to favour the principle stated in the *High Trees* case, it is important that it should not be stretched too far, lest it should be endangered. That principle does not create new causes of action where none existed before. It only prevents a party from insisting upon his strict legal rights, when it would be unjust to allow him to enforce them, having regard to the dealings which have taken place between the parties . . .
>
> Seeing that the principle never stands alone as giving a cause of action in itself, it can never do away with the necessity of consideration when that is an essential part of the cause of action. The doctrine of consideration is too firmly fixed to be overthrown by a side-wind. Its ill-effects have been largely mitigated of late, but it still remains a cardinal necessity of the formation of a contract, though not of its modification or discharge.

The English Court of Appeal in *Baird Textile Holdings Ltd* v. *Marks and Spencer plc* (2001)[186] confirmed the *Combe* v. *Combe* restriction (the same limitation applies to the doctrine of estoppel by convention, on which see 5.48 below). Lord Walker in *Cobbe* v. *Yeoman's Row Management Ltd* (2008)[187] cited the *Baird* case without disapproval. He made clear that he was hostile to an expansion of estoppel, fearing that it would produce commercial uncertainty[188] (the *Baird* case is further examined at 6.15).

However, the High Court of Australia in *Walton's Stores (Interstate)* v. *Maher* (1988) has rejected the *Combe* v. *Combe* restriction.[189] And so the Australian court has expanded the principle of protecting detrimental reliance beyond the limits of the English doctrine of proprietary estoppel (on which see 5.45). But, in England, only proprietary estoppel can operate as a cause of action.

The Australian decision in *Walton's Stores (Interstate)* v. *Maher* (1988)[190] concerned negotiations for a property development. The claimant intended to develop its own land by granting a lease of land to the defendant company and then to demolish the existing structures and build to the defendant's specifications. There was extreme urgency, and the claimant jumped the gun and began to demolish before contract terms were agreed. The defendant told its solicitors to 'go slow' in dealing with the legal documentation. The defendant became aware of the demolition work but did nothing for over one month thereafter. The defendant later withdrew from the project when the claimant had completed nearly half the building work. The High Court of Australia held that the claimant had rightly assumed that completion of the formalities of the lease would proceed smoothly. The defendant had acted unconscionably in

---

184   [1976] Ch 179, CA.
185   [1951] 2 KB 215, 219–20, CA.
186   [2001] EWCA Civ 274; [2002] 1 All ER (Comm) 737, CA, at [35] to [39], *per* Morritt LJ, and [54], *per* Judge LJ; similarly, *Newport City Council* v. *Charles* [2008] EWCA Civ 1541; [2009] WLR 1884, at [23], last sentence, *per* Laws LJ.
187   [2008] UKHL 55; [2008] 1 WLR 1752, at [85] (noted by J. Getzler, (2009) 125 LQR 196).
188   *Ibid.*, at [46] and [81], *per* Lord Walker.
189   (1988) 164 CLR 387 (High Court of Australia); *Anson's Law of Contract* (29th edn, Oxford, 2010), 124 ff; R. Halson, *Contract Law* (2nd edn, London, 2013), 377 ff; M. Spence, *Protecting Reliance* (Oxford, 1999), *passim*, advocates an expansive estoppel doctrine, especially in light of the leading Australian cases on estoppel, *Walton's Stores (Interstate) Ltd* v. *Maher* (1988) 164 CLR 387, and *Commonwealth of Australia* v. *Verwayen* (1990) 170 CLR 394; criticised by Peter Jaffey (book review) [2000] *Restitution Law Review* 458–64.
190   (1988) 164 CLR 387 (High Court of Australia).

encouraging an expectation or assumption on the part of the claimant that a contract would come into existence. The claimant had acted to his detriment to the knowledge of the defendant. Basing itself on a broad principle of estoppel, the court awarded the claimant damages in lieu of specific performance.

The English doctrine of proprietary estoppel would not be available on the facts of the *Walton's Stores* case. This is because that doctrine is restricted to the case where expenditure is incurred by a claimant on the defendant's land in the expectation that the claimant will acquire rights over the defendant's land, or on the assumption that the claimant already has such rights over the defendant's land. In the *Walton's Stores* case, the expenditure was incurred by the claimant in respect of his own land in the expectation that he would be developing it for the defendant's eventual use as a prospective tenant of the property.

It would be different if, in order to relocate his premises for the convenience of B, A enters into a matching set of informal agreements (1) to sell his property to B, and to replace this with property (2) to be bought by A from B. On such facts, Woolf J held in the English decision, *Salvation Army Trustee Co. Ltd* v. *West Yorkshire Metropolitan County Council* (1980)[191] that the purchase by A from B at stage (2) precluded B from resiling from the agreement at stage (1). An estoppel will arise in favour of A and broad justice can then be worked out (A was in fact awarded compensation in respect of B's failure to buy the old site).

5.44 *Summary of decreasing pacts*

(1) The rule in *Pinnel's Case* (1602)[192] states that a promise to accept part-payment as full discharge is prima facie ineffective at Common Law. This can be supported on the basis that the creditor's promise is a promissory gift of a valuable asset (the benefit of a binding debt). There are exceptions if the agreement to accept part-payment is clothed as a deed or if 'fresh consideration' is provided, at the creditor's request, such as accelerated payment.

(2) According to the Court of Appeal in the *Collier* case (2007),[193] the equitable doctrine of promissory estoppel can be used to render a debtor, if necessary, immune from liability to pay the balance of a debt. This 'extinctive' aspect of the doctrine will apply if the creditor has received part-payment following his clear promise to reduce or cancel the debt. This victory of Equity over the Common Law rule in *Pinnel's Case* vindicates Denning J's famous dictum in the *High Trees* case.[194] Controversially, however, the *Collier* case (2007) finds solid support for promissory estoppel's suggested 'extinctive' operation in the Court of Appeal's decision in the *D & C Builders* case (1966).[195] However, although the *Collier* decision might have proceeded on a misreading of the authority of the *D & C Builders* case, the law on this point is now settled by the 2007 decision in the *Collier* case, and only the Supreme Court (or the legislature) can change the law.

---

191 *Salvation Army Trustee Co. Ltd* v. *West Yorkshire Metropolitan County Council* (1980) 41 P & CR 179, Woolf J; cf *Western Fish Products Ltd* v. *Penwith District Council* [1981] 2 All ER 204, CA (P spending money on *his own land* in expectation of receiving planning permission from D; no proprietary estoppel since P is not expecting that he has, or will have, any interest in D's land).
192 (1602) 5 Co Rep 117a (entire Court of Common Pleas); rule affirmed in *Foakes* v. *Beer* (1884) 9 App Cas 605, HL.
193 [2007] EWCA Civ 1329; [2008] 1 WLR 643.
194 *Central London Property Trust Ltd* v. *High Trees House Ltd* [1947] 1 KB 130, 133 ff.
195 [1966] 2 QB 617, CA.

(3) A person seeking equitable relief must not have acted unmeritoriously ('she who comes to Equity must come with clean hands'). Lord Denning MR held that this was problematic for the debtor, Mrs Rees, in the *D & C Builders* case. The fact that she had unconscionably coerced the builder-creditor into accepting less than the full amount was enough to bar her from invoking the equitable protection of promissory estoppel.[196]

(4) Although, in England, promissory estoppel or estoppel by representation is not a substitute for consideration (see point (5) below), these doctrines can assist a claimant by overcoming a bar to a cause of action founded on an independent ground, namely, consideration or deed (for example, *Shah* v. *Shah*).[197]

(5) Promissory estoppel in England is not an independent cause of action, and so it has not abolished the requirement of consideration to support the main contract: *Combe* v. *Combe* (1951),[198] affirmed in the *Baird* case (2001).[199] This is in contrast to the willingness in Australia where the courts will recognise a cause of action on the basis of *promissory estoppel* in favour of the representee who has detrimentally relied on a statement, other than a statement that he has or will acquire rights in the representor's land (see 5.43 for a summary of the High Court of Australia's decision in the *Walton's Stores* case).[200] It should be noted that, even in England, *proprietary estoppel* (5.45) is an independent cause of action, but it is confined to these two situations: (i) the representor has made a statement which has led the representee to believe that the latter has, or will acquire, rights in, or in respect of, the representor's land, or (ii) the representor has unconscionably acquiesced in that misunderstanding.

12. PROPRIETARY ESTOPPEL

5.45 As mentioned at 5.02, there are three ways in which a promise can be 'upheld'. We now come to the third: that the other party has detrimentally relied on the defendant's promise or assurance;[201] here, there is no need to show that the detriment *was requested by the defendant*; and so the element of bargained-for detriment is often absent in this context. The factor of induced (albeit unrequested) reliance is crucial if the promise has not been given as a 'deed' (on which see 5.03); nor is there a valid agreement supported by consideration. In the absence of a deed and 'consideration', proprietary estoppel, an equitable doctrine, might rescue a claimant (see 5.49 below for a summary of the types of

---

196 *Ibid.*, at 625.
197 [2001] EWCA Civ 527; [2002] QB 35, at [30] to [33]; distinguished in *Re Gleeds*, see 5.03, n.10.
198 [1951] 2 KB 215, CA.
199 [2001] EWCA Civ 274; [2002] 1 All ER (Comm) 737, at [35] to [39], and [54]; and implicitly affirmed in *Thorner* v. *Major* [2009] UKHL 18; [2009] 1 WLR 776, at [61].
200 (1988) 164 CLR 387 (High Court of Australia).
201 B. McFarlane, *The Law of Proprietary Estoppel* (Oxford, 2014); S. Wilken and K. Ghalys, *The Law of Waiver, Variation and Estoppel* (3rd edn, Oxford, 2012, chapter 11; Lord Neuberger, 'The Stuffing of Minerva's Owl? Taxonomy and Taxidermy in Equity' [2009] CLJ 437–49; M. Dixon, 'Confining and Defining Proprietary Estoppel: The Role of Unconscionability' (2010) 30 LS 408; P. Birks, G. Battersby and P. Critchley, in S. Bright and J. Dewar (eds.), *Land Law: Themes and Perspectives* (Oxford, 1998), chapters 18, 19, 20, especially at 482–5 and 496–505; S. Gardner, (1999) 115 LQR 438 and (2006) 122 LQR 492; A. Robertson, 'Estoppels and Rights-Creating Events … ', in J. W. Neyers, R. Bronaugh and S. G. A. Pitel (eds.), *Exploring Contract Law* (Oxford, 2009), 199 ff.

estoppel). It is an exception to the general unenforceability of gratuitous promises (on which see 5.10). It can give effect to informal promises, to the extent that the case demands, by protecting a person's detrimental reliance concerning his supposed or anticipated rights over the other party's land.[202]

5.46 The House of Lords in *Cobbe* v. *Yeoman's Row Management Ltd* (2008) reviewed the doctrine of proprietary estoppel.[203] This decision supports the following points:

(1) In the context of dealing affecting or concerning land, proprietary estoppel can arise in either of these ways:[204] A spends money improving (or otherwise[205] acts to his detriment vis-à-vis) B's land in the mistaken assumption that A has, or will acquire, rights in that land, and either:

(a) B makes a representation which induces that error; or

(b) B acquiesces (or even if B, at that point, shares A's error, but perhaps B also makes representations which fortify A's belief)[206] in A's error.

(2) If the court finds that the estoppel is engaged on particular facts, the court has a wide discretion to award an appropriate remedy. That remedy is not confined to merely compensating the claimant for his detrimental reliance.

As for 'remedial discretion' in this context,[207] in *Dillwyn* v. *Llewellyn* (1862), the House of Lords used proprietary estoppel to justify an award in favour of a son of his father's property. At great expense, the son had constructed property after the father had informally encouraged the belief that the son would receive title to the property[208] (see also *Cobbe* v. *Yeoman's Row Management Ltd* (2008),[209] and *Thorner* v. *Major* (2009)).[210]

5.47 Proprietary estoppel remains confined to situations relating to land, despite contrary dicta,[211] including Lord Scott's suggestion in *Cobbe* v. *Yeoman's Row Management Ltd* (2008),[212] that 'in principle' this form of estoppel should be 'equally available to chattels or choses in action'. If proprietary estoppel were to expand beyond the present context of dealings with land, this might tend to undermine the whole doctrine of consideration.

---

202   For a summary: *Thorner* v. *Major* [2009] UKHL 18; [2009] 1 WLR 776, at [15], [29] and [72]; *Gillett* v. *Holt* [2001] Ch 210, 225C–D, 232A–F, 235E–F, CA; other leading decisions: *Crabb* v. *Arun District Council* [1976] Ch 179, CA (noted by P. S. Atiyah, (1976) 92 LQR 174; and by P. Millett, (1976) 92 LQR 342); *Taylor Fashions Ltd* v. *Liverpool Victoria Trustee Co. Ltd* [1982] QB 133, 153, Oliver J; the doctrine was applied in *Henry* v. *Henry* [2010] UKPC 3; [2010] 1 All ER 988.

203   [2008] UKHL 55; [2008] 1 WLR 1752 (noted by J. Getzler, (2009) 125 LQR 196; and by B. McFarlane and A. Robertson, 'The Death of Proprietary Estoppel' [2008] LMCLQ 449).

204   *Taylor Fashions Ltd* v. *Liverpool Victoria Trustees Co. Ltd* [1982] QB 133 (note).

205   *Greasley* v. *Cooke* [1980] 1 WLR 1306, CA (domestic services).

206   *Taylor Fashions Ltd* v. *Liverpool Victoria Trustee Co. Ltd* [1982] QB 133, 153.

207   S. Gardner, (1999) 115 LQR 438.

208   (1862) 4 De G F & J 517, HL.

209   [2008] UKHL 55; [2008] 1 WLR 1752 (noted by J. Getzler, (2009) 125 LQR 196; and by B. McFarlane and A. Robertson, 'The Death of Proprietary Estoppel' [2008] LMCLQ 449).

210   [2009] UKHL 18; [2009] 1 WLR 776 (noted by B. McFarlane and A. Robertson (2009) 125 LQR 535–42; B. Sloan, [2009] CLJ 518); applied in *Cook* v. *Thomas* [2010] EWCA Civ 227.

211   *Crabb* v. *Arun District Council* [1976] Ch 179, 193, CA, *per* Scarman LJ; *Taylor Fashions Ltd* v. *Liverpool Victoria Trustee Co. Ltd* [1982] QB 133, 153, *per* Oliver J; *Amalgamated Investment & Property Co. Ltd* v. *Texas Commerce International Bank Ltd* [1982] QB 84, 103–4, 122, *per* Robert Goff J (in the Commercial Court) and Lord Denning MR (in the Court of Appeal).

212   [2008] UKHL 55; [2008] 1 WLR 1752, at [14].

Furthermore, Lord Walker in *Cobbe* v. *Yeoman's Row Management Ltd* (2008) indicated that he was hostile to such an expansion and fearful that it would create commercial uncertainty:[213]

> Equitable estoppel is a flexible doctrine which the Court can use, in appropriate circumstances, to prevent injustice caused by the vagaries and inconstancy of human nature. But it is not a sort of joker or wild card to be used whenever the Court disapproves of the conduct of a litigant who seems to have the law on his side. Flexible though it is, the doctrine must be formulated and applied in a disciplined and principled way. Certainty is important in property transactions.

13. ESTOPPEL BY CONVENTION

5.48 Estoppel by convention[214] differs from the main types of estoppel, 'estoppel by representation', 'promissory estoppel' and 'proprietary estoppel' (each of these has been encountered above at 5.38, 5.45 and 5.03) because it requires *no representation*, nor is it necessary to show that one party has acquiesced in bad faith in the other's error. Instead, its essence is that the *outward course of conduct evidences or varies an agreement*.[215] It requires some *pattern of visible conduct* which indicates a shared assumption.[216] And no such *conduct* can arise merely from a pair of matching assumptions lodged metaphysically in the parties' minds.

> Carnwath LJ in *ING Bank NV* v. *Ros Roca SA* (2011)[217] trawled the authorities.
> And in *Durham* v. *BAI (Run Off) Ltd* (2008), Burton J explained:[218]
>> The three ingredients are succinctly summarised by Bingham LJ in *'The Vistafjord'* (2008),[219] namely that it applies where:
>> '(1) parties have established by their construction of their agreement or their apprehension of its legal effect a conventional basis,
>> (2) on that basis they have regulated their subsequent dealings, to which I would add
>> (3) it would be unjust or unconscionable if one of the parties resiled from that convention.'[220]

213 *Ibid.*, at [46] and [81].
214 Lord Steyn, 'Contract Law: Fulfilling the Reasonable Expectations of Honest Men' (1997) 113 LQR 433, 440; T. Dawson, (1989) 9 LS 16; K. R. Handley, *Estoppel by Conduct and Election* (2nd edn, London, 2014), chapter 8; S. Wilken and K. Ghalys, *The Law of Waiver, Variation and Estoppel* (3rd edn, Oxford, 2012, chapter 10).
215 *Republic of India* v. *India Steamship Co. Ltd* ('*The Indian Endurance*') (No. 2) [1998] AC 878, 914–15, HL, *per* Lord Steyn, clarifying the Court of Appeal's formulation of the doctrine.
216 *Ibid.*, at 914–15; *Bridgewater* v. *Griffiths* [2000] 1 WLR 524, 530, *per* Burton J.
217 [2011] EWCA Civ 353; [2012] 1 WLR 472, at [55] to [73] (Stanley Burnton LJ agreed at [75]); the third judge, Rix LJ, at [85] and [86], preferred to reach the same result by use of promissory estoppel/representation by estoppel.
218 [2008] EWHC 2692 (QB); [2009] 4 All ER 26, at [267] and [268], *per* Burton J.
219 '*The Vistafjord*' [1988] 2 Lloyd's Law Rep 343, 352, CA.
220 The element of unconscionability was absent in the *Durham* case, [2008] EWHC 2692 (QB); [2009] 4 All ER 26, at [284], *per* Burton J.

As Bingham LJ[221] points out ... each party must be 'fully cognizant' of the shared assumption and 'an estoppel by convention requires communications to pass across the line between the parties'.

Estoppel by convention cannot be used to circumvent a statutory prohibition upon contracting out of a protective set of rules.[222]

Estoppel by convention *does not give rise to a cause of action*, but it can clear the way for a contractual, or other, cause of action to be made out.[223] Thus, the defendant bank in the *Amalgamated Investment* case (below) could have used the estoppel to buttress a contractual claim on the guarantee. But the estoppel would not by itself found an action: consideration must exist independently of the estoppel which evidences that agreement. This mirrors the restriction, acknowledged in *Combe* v. *Combe* (1951)[224] (5.43) on the operation of both estoppel by representation and promissory estoppel.

In *Amalgamated Investment & Property Co. Ltd (in liquidation)* v. *Texas Commerce International Bank Ltd* (1982)[225] the claimant had guaranteed in favour of the defendant a loan made by the latter to the claimant's subsidiary. In fact, the defendant made this loan through a subsidiary company called Portsoken, but the wording of the guarantee did not reflect this. Instead, that document declared that the claimant's guarantee was in respect of moneys paid by the defendant rather than by the defendant's subsidiary. The claimant's liquidator sought a declaration that it was not liable on the guarantee for loans made by Portsoken. The Court of Appeal cut through this knot by saying that the claimant guarantor was estopped from denying that in fact it owed money under the guarantee in respect of the true lender, Portsoken. This estoppel reflected the course of dealing between claimant and defendant.

In the Court of Appeal, the first ground of decision was that the guarantee should be interpreted, as a matter of 'construction', as extending to loans made by Portsoken (generally on the process of contractual interpretation see Chapter 14). The estoppel point is perhaps a second *ratio*. (Note that at first instance in that case, Robert Goff J dealt with the case on the basis of estoppel by representation; 5.43 above.)

14. SUMMARY OF TYPES OF ESTOPPEL

5.49   The main types of estoppel[226] are:

(1) *Estoppel by representation.* This normally involves a representation by words, but sometimes it can be by non-verbal conduct, indicating that the representee should be assured that something has happened or is presently the case. *Jorden* v. *Money* (1854) is

---

221   'The Vistafjord' [1988] 2 Lloyd's Law Rep 343, 351, and as he further makes clear in 'The Captain Gregos' *(No. 2)* [1992] Lloyd's Law Rep 395, 405, CA.
222   *Keen* v. *Holland* [1984] 1 WLR 251 (protection under the agricultural holdings legislation).
223   *Amalgamated Investment & Property* case, [1982] 1 QB 84, 132, CA, *per* Brandon LJ.
224   [1951] 2 KB 215, CA.
225   [1982] 1 QB 84, CA.
226   For illuminating discussion (too long to cite here) of the fertile and versatile concept of estoppel, see Lord Denning MR in *McIlkenny* v. *Chief Constable of the West Midlands* [1980] QB 283, 316–7, CA (the case proceeded to the HL as *Hunter* v. *Chief Constable of the West Midlands* [1982] AC 529). For the separate status of estoppel by deed, see *Prime Sight Ltd* v. *Lavarello* [2013] UKPC 22; [2014] AC 436, at [30], *per* Lord Toulson.

regarded as House of Lords authority that Common Law estoppel requires a representation of a past or present fact and does not extend to promises of future conduct or future abstention.[227] For an illustration, see *Shah* v. *Shah* (2001) at 5.03.[228]

(2) *Proprietary estoppel.* This form of estoppel is confined in England to assurances that the representee has or will acquire rights in, or over, the representor's *land*. This type of estoppel can concern the *future* and is not confined to *past or present facts*. The doctrine can also found a cause of action, and so it is not merely a 'shield'. The doctrine is rooted in principles of Equity. Good illustrations are *Crabb* v. *Arun District Council* (1976)[229] and *Thorner* v. *Major* (2009).[230]

(3) *Promissory estoppel.* This form of estoppel has been adopted predominantly in respect of assurances that a debtor (or another person owing a subsisting obligation) will have more time or will be (or has already been) relieved from the remainder of his debt (or other obligation). This type of estoppel can concern the *future* and is not confined to *past or present* facts. However, this form of estoppel does *not* found a cause of action, but is merely a 'shield'. Promissory estoppel is rooted in principles of Equity.[231]

(4) *Estoppel by convention.* This concerns coincident patterns of conduct. Such conduct can indicate that the parties have concurred in treating a subsisting transaction as having a particular effect or application, or that it is valid. This type of estoppel does not require a specific representation. It appears to be regarded as an offshoot of Common Law principle.

(5) *'Contractual Estoppel'.* The Court of Appeal in the *Springwell* case (2010)[232] and the Privy Council in the *Prime Sight* case (2013)[233] confirmed that 'contractual estoppel' enables parties to agree (normally in writing) that specified prior facts or events have not occurred (this topic is considered further at 9.36 ff). A party to such an estoppel is then precluded from acting contrary to that understanding. And so he cannot make assertions or claims inconsistent with the agreed denial of events. Therefore, this operates as an evidential bar: it prevents the contracting parties from making factual allegations which are inconsistent with the contract's terms. This form of estoppel can cover statements expressed as acknowledgments, representations or agreements.

---

227 (1854) 5 HL Cas 185; 10 ER 868; including representations of law, *Re Gleeds, Briggs* v. *Gleeds* [2014] EWHC 1178 (Ch); [2014] 3 WLR 1469, at [26] to [35], *per* Newey J.

228 [2001] EWCA Civ 527; [2002] QB 35, at [30] to [33].

229 [1976] Ch 179, CA (Lord Denning MR, Lawton and Scarman LJJ).

230 [2009] UKHL 18; [2009] 1 WLR 776 (noted by B. McFarlane and A. Robertson, (2009) 125 LQR 535–42).

231 For an intricate attempt to tease out various underlying concepts, see B. McFarlane, 'Understanding Equitable Estoppel: From Metaphors to Better Laws' (2013) 66 CLP 267–305.

232 *Springwell Navigation Corporation* v. *JP Morgan Chase* [2010] EWCA Civ 1221; [2010] 2 CLC 705 (following *Peekay Intermark Ltd* v. *Australia and New Zealand Banking Group Ltd* [2006] EWCA Civ 386; [2006] 2 Lloyd's Rep 511, at [56], [57]); the development has been strongly criticised: G. McMeel, [2011] LMCLQ 185–207; and D. McLauchlan, (2012) 128 LQR 521, 536–9, citing literature.

233 *Prime Sight Ltd* v. *Lavarello* [2013] UKPC 22; [2014] AC 436, at [30], [46] and [47], *per* Lord Toulson.

'Contractual estoppel' is distinct from both estoppel by representation and estoppel by convention because there is no need to show either (a) that there has been reliance on the representation concerning the present or past events (by contrast, reliance must be shown in the case of estoppel by representation), or (b) that it would be unjust or unconscionable for the other party to try to contradict the agreed factual basis (by contrast, this further requirement applies in the case of estoppel by convention).[234] The *Springwell* case (2010) suggests that 'contractual estoppel' would not be effective if it concerned matters which rendered the device contrary to public policy[235] (for example, it is arguable that contractual estoppel could not be used to enable both parties consciously and consensually to circumvent the formal requirements of a deed – on which see 5.03 – although estoppel by representation, which is not a consensual form of estoppel, has been used in that context to protect an innocent representee, *Shah* v. *Shah* noted at 5.03).

(6) *Estoppel by silence or acquiescence.* Rix LJ in *ING Bank NV* v. *Ros Roca SA* (2011) (examined at 3.67 and 9.44) noted the possibility of estoppel by silence or acquiescence where a particular context imports a duty to point out to the other a misapprehension concerning their legal rights.[236]

(7) Res judicata. This concerns the preclusive effect of *judicial decisions between the parties.* Its effect is to bring about 'claim or issue preclusion',[237] thereby preventing claims or issues from being re-litigated between the same parties.[238] This principle also rests on notions of estoppel. *Res judicata* is considered in works on civil procedure. Estoppel by *res judicata* has three elements:

(i) judgments and other relevant decisions (see element (iii) below) will be binding upon both parties (and their privies[239] or successors);[240]

---

234 On this last point, see Aikens LJ in *Springwell Navigation Corporation* v. *JP Morgan Chase* [2010] EWCA Civ 1221; [2010] 2 CLC 705, at [177].

235 *Ibid.,* at [144], *per* Aikens LJ; see also *Prime Sight Ltd* v. *Lavarello* [2013] UKPC 22; [2014] AC 436, at [47], *per* Lord Toulson (noted A. Trukhtanov, (2014) 130 LQR 3–8).

236 [2011] EWCA Civ 353; [2012] 1 WLR 472, at [93], referring to the possibility (citing Bingham J's examination in *Tradax Export SA* v. *Dorada Cia Naviera SA ('The Lutetian')* [1982] 2 Lloyd's Rep 140, 157, of Lord Wilberforce's analysis of estoppel by silence in *Moorgate Mercantile Co Ltd* v. *Twitchings* [1977] AC 890, 903, HL).

237 This terminology, current in the USA and in Canada, has been adopted in ALI/UNIDROIT's *Principles of Transnational Civil Procedure* (Cambridge, 2006), Principles 28.2 and 28.3.

238 The leading decision is *Virgin Atlantic Airways Ltd* v. *Zodiac Seats UK Ltd* [2013] UKSC 46; [2014] AC 160, *per* Lord Sumption, at [17], [20], [22], [26], considering *Arnold* v. *National Westminster Bank plc* [1991] 2 AC 93; for general background (antedating this decision), G. Spencer Bower, A. K. Turner and K. R. Handley, *The Doctrine of Res Judicata* (4th edn, London, 2009); *Andrews on Civil Processes* (Cambridge, 2013), vol. 1, *Court Proceedings*, chapter 16; generally on this topic, N. Andrews, 'Res Judicata and Finality: Estoppel in the Context of Judicial Decisions and Arbitral Awards', in K. Makridou and G. Diamantopoulos (eds.), *Issues of Estoppel and Res Judicata in Anglo-American and Greek Law* (Athens, 2013), 17–39.

239 *McIlkenny* v. *Chief Constable of the West Midlands* [1980] 1 QB 283, CA; *House of Spring Gardens Ltd* v. *Waite* [1991] 1 QB 241, CA; *Black* v. *Yates* [1992] 1 QB 526, 545–9.

240 E.g. *Green* v. *Vickers Defence Systems Ltd* [2002] EWCA Civ 904; *The Times*, 1 July 2002.

(ii) if the judgment was made in a civil matter (a final decision,[241] or consent order);[242] and

(iii) the judgment was made by a competent civil court or tribunal,[243] including courts recognised under English rules of private international law[244] and arbitration proceedings.[245]

QUESTIONS

(1) What is meant by saying that consideration is the 'price' for which the action for breach of promise is 'bought'?

(2) What is the function of consideration if 'nominal consideration' is sufficient to found an enforceable promise?

(3) Explain these statements: (a) in the absence of consideration, a promise will be legally enforceable only if it is a deed or gives rise to a right of action based on proprietary estoppel; (b) an 'executory' contract, involving the exchange of promises, is binding; (c) detriment incurred by the promisee, or a benefit conferred by the promisee, will suffice if requested by the defendant/promisor.

(4) Why is the absence of a 'request' the key to the problem of 'past consideration'?

(5) What must be shown to convert a promise to perform a statutory or public duty into a promise supported by consideration?

(6) What type of 'practical benefit' will generate consideration to support a promise by A to B to pay more for B's performance of a pre-existing contractual duty owed by B to A? Is the law satisfactory?

(7) When will a promise to accept part-payment and release the debtor from the unpaid balance be enforceable (i) at Common Law on the basis of 'fresh consideration' and (ii) in Equity (according to the doctrine of 'promissory estoppel')? Is the law satisfactory?

(8) What is meant by saying that promissory estoppel 'operates as a shield rather than as a sword'? Contrast the position concerning proprietary estoppel.

(9) What are the requirements for a valid deed or covenant?

(10) As noted in Chapter 6, it can be asked: 'Is it satisfactory (in the absence of a deed or covenant) to preserve a two-stage test of legal enforceability, applying both the consideration and intent to create legal relations doctrine?'

---

241 Including a final decision of an interim application: *R* v. *Governor of Brixton Prison, ex parte Osman* [1991] 1 WLR 281; *Possfund* v. *Diamond* [1996] 2 All ER 774, 779; for an example of a non-final decision, see *Buehler AG* v. *Chronos Richardson Ltd* [1998] 2 All ER 960, CA.

242 E.g. *Palmer* v. *Durnford Ford* [1992] 1 QB 483, Simon Tuckey QC sitting as a Deputy High Court Judge; *Green* v. *Vickers Defence Systems Ltd* [2002] EWCA Civ 904; *The Times*, 1 July 2002; *Gairy* v. *Attorney-General of Grenada* [2001] UKPC 30; [2002] 1 AC 167, at [27].

243 *Green* v. *Hampshire County Council* [1979] ICR 861; *Crown Estate Commissioners* v. *Dorset County Council* [1990] Ch 297, Millett J.

244 P. R. Barnett, *Res Judicata, Estoppel and Foreign Judgments: The Preclusive Effects of Foreign Judgments in Private International Law* (Oxford, 2001); P. Rogerson, (1998) CJQ 91.

245 *Andrews on Civil Processes* (Cambridge, 2013), vol. 2, *Arbitration and Mediation*, chapter 17; notably, *Associated Electric & Gas Insurance Services Ltd* v. *European Reinsurance Co of Zurich* [2003] UKPC 11; [2003] 2 CLC 340; [2003] 1 WLR 1041, PC; *R (Coke-Wallis)* v. *Institute of Chartered Accountants in England and Wales* [2011] UKCS 1; [2011] 2 AC 146, at [31], *per* Lord Clarke, citing G. Spencer Bower, A. K. Turner and K. R. Handley, *The Doctrine of Res Judicata* (4th edn, London, 2009), 2.05, and noting *Fidelitas Shipping Co Ltd* v. *V/O Exportchleb* [1966] 1 QB 630, 643 C, CA, *per* Diplock LJ; generally on this topic, N. Andrews, '*Res Judicata* and Finality: Estoppel in the Context of Judicial Decisions and Arbitral Awards', in K. Makridou and G. Diamantopoulos (eds.), *Issues of Estoppel and Res Judicata in Anglo-American and Greek Law* (Athens, 2013), 17–39.

Selected further reading

Analysis and critiques of consideration as a requirement for the formation of agreements not under seal as deeds

P. S. Atiyah, 'Consideration: A Restatement', reprinted in P. S. Atiyah, *Essays on Contract* (Oxford, 1996)

J. Cartwright, *Formation and Variation of Contracts: The Agreement, Formalities, Consideration and Promissory Estoppel* (London, 2014)

A. G. Chloros, 'The Doctrine of Consideration and the Reform of the Law of Contract' (1968) 17 ICLQ 137

G. H. Treitel, 'Consideration: A Critical Analysis of Professor Atiyah's Fundamental Restatement' (1976) 50 *Australian Law Journal* 439

Law Revision Committee, Sixth Interim Report on 'The Statute of Frauds and the Doctrine of Consideration' (1937, Cmd 5449), paras. 17–40 and 50; see also M. Arden, [1997] CLJ 516, 533, citing Harvey McGregor, preface to *Contract Code: Drawn up on Behalf of the English Law Commission* (Milan, 1993), 3

Increasing and decreasing pacts

B. Coote, 'Consideration and Variations: A Different Solution' (2004) 120 LQR 19–23 (noting *Antons Trawling Co. Ltd* v. *Smith* (2003, New Zealand) (5.29))

B. Coote, 'Variations Sans Consideration' (2011) 27 JCL 307

J. O'Sullivan, 'In Defence of Foakes v. Beer' [1996] CLJ 219–28

G. H. Treitel, *Some Landmarks of Twentieth Century Contract Law* (Oxford, 2002), chapter 1

General survey

M. Hogg, 'Competing Theories of Contract: An Emerging Consensus?', in L. DiMatteo, Q. Zhou, S. Saintier, K. Rowley (eds.), *Commercial Contract Law: Transatlantic Perspectives* (Cambridge, 2014), chapter 2

S. Waddams, 'Principle in Contract Law: The Doctrine of Consideration', in J. W. Neyers, R. Bronaugh and S. G. A. Pitel (eds.), *Exploring Contract Law* (Oxford, 2009), 51 ff

S. Waddams, *Principle and Policy in Contract Law: Competing or Complementary Concepts?* (Cambridge, 2011), chapter 3

Chapter contents

6

Intent to create legal relations

1. INTRODUCTION

6.01 Summary of main points

(1) The 'intent to create legal relations' doctrine[1] is additional to the doctrine of consideration (see Chapter 5). Therefore, in the absence of a deed (5.03), if a person wishes to sue on a promise, he must overcome two hurdles: first, he must show that the promise was made in circumstances satisfying the notion of a bargain (the element of 'consideration'). Secondly, he must show that the promise was made and received in circumstances consistent with an 'intent to create legal relations'.

(2) In certain non-commercial contexts, an agreement might not be accompanied by such an 'intent'. The leading case, *Balfour* v. *Balfour* (1919), concerned a maintenance arrangement between spouses who had not formally separated, but who were temporarily living apart, ostensibly still on good terms. In this and similar contexts, the courts presume that promises, even though technically supported by consideration, should remain beyond the pale of legal enforcement.

(3) In applying the doctrine of 'intent to create legal relations' in the non-commercial sphere, the courts can take into account various practical or policy factors, including: the objective triviality of many social or domestic promises; the need to shelter many domestic or social promises from the intrusive civil process and its remedies; and the fear of excessive litigation.

(4) In the commercial sphere, there is a strong presumption that a commercial agreement is intended to create legal relations, although this can be rebutted explicitly or, perhaps, if the context indicates that the parties did not in fact intend to create legally enforceable rights. In particular, parties to a commercial agreement can explicitly exclude legal relations, notably by use of the formula 'subject to contract' (4.17).

---

1   M. Furmston and G. J. Tolhurst, *Contract Formation: Law and Practice* (Oxford, 2010), chapter 10; M. Freeman, in R. Halson (ed.), *Exploring the Boundaries of Contract* (Aldershot, 1996), chapter 4; S. Hedley, 'Keeping Contract in its Place – *Balfour* v. *Balfour* and the Enforceability of Informal Agreements' (1985) 5 OJLS 391; B. Hepple, 'Intent to Create Legal Relations' [1970] CLJ 122; D. Allen, (2000) *Anglo-American Law Review* 204; S. Ball, (1983) 99 LQR 572.

(5) But even a commercial arrangement will be presumed to give rise to a contract only if there is a clear commitment, an 'apparent promise'. A 'letter of comfort' (that is, a parent company's vague indication of its current policy to satisfy its subsidiary's debts) does not disclose such a promise; nor will an open-ended and non-committal pattern of dealings between merchants disclose a hard-edged commitment to maintain legal relations.

(6) At the borderline of commercial and domestic dealings, decisions during the last fifty years indicate a willingness to extend the reach of the law; for example, *Parker* v. *Clark* (1960)[2] (6.11) and *Modahl* v. *British Athletic Federation Ltd* (2002)[3] (6.17). But, curiously, a Methodist minister does not have a contract with her governing church: *Preston (formerly Moore)* v. *President of the Methodist Conference* (2013).[4]

2. FOUNDATIONS OF THE DOCTRINE

6.02 *Genesis of the doctrine. Carlill* v. *Carbolic Smoke Ball Co.* (1893) crystallised the doctrine (for the main discussion of this bizarre case, see 3.43).[5] The Court of Appeal held that the Carbolic Smoke Ball Company's advertisement made plain that prospective customers were intended to believe that the company was making a binding offer to pay £100 if the product did not work. Otherwise, why would the company have declared that £1,000 had been 'deposited in the Alliance Bank' as a token of its serious intent? And so, in this case, a new test of contractual enforcement emerged.

6.03 *Non-commercial and commercial contexts.* It is common to divide this topic into two segments, non-commercial and commercial. Family, domestic or social arrangements are presumed *not* to be intended to have legal force. But in the case of commercial arrangements, the opposite starting point prevails: promises in that context are presumptively intended to be legally binding.[6]

6.04 *Discovering 'intent' or its absence.* Normally, the search for intent to create legal relations is a purely objective process. It takes place without inquiring into the parties' actual beliefs. As Aikens LJ said in *Barbudev* v. *Eurocom Cable Management Bulgaria Eood* (2012):[7] 'On the issue of whether the parties intended to create legal relations . . . [the] court has to consider

---

2 [1960] 1 WLR 286, Devlin J.
3 [2001] EWCA Civ 1447; [2002] 1 WLR 1192, CA, at [50] to [54] and [105].
4 [2013] UKSC 29; [2013] 2 AC 163.
5 [1893] 1 QB 256 CA; A. W. B. Simpson, 'Innovation in Nineteenth Century Contract Law' (1975) 91 LQR 247, at 263–5; and A. W. B. Simpson, 'Quackery and Contract Law: The Case of the Carbolic Smoke Ball' (1985) 14 JLS 345 (the latter is reprinted in A. W. B. Simpson, *Leading Cases in the Common Law* (Oxford, 1995), chapter 10); the *Carbolic Smoke Ball* case was applied in *Bowerman* v. *ABTA Ltd* [1996] CLC 451, noted by G. McMeel, (1997) 113 LQR 47–9.
6 E.g. *Edwards* v. *Skyways Ltd* [1964] 1 WLR 349, 354–5, Megaw J (6.12); *Esso Petroleum Ltd* v. *Commissioners of Customs & Excise* [1976] 1 WLR 1, HL.
7 [2012] EWCA Civ 548; [2012] 2 All ER (Comm) 963, at [30].

the objective conduct of the parties as a whole.' Elias LJ confirmed this in *Attrill* v. *Dresdner Kleinwort Ltd* (2013).[8]

However, in borderline cases, a more nuanced approach is adopted. The court will inquire closely into what the parties actually thought to be the case, no doubt leavening this search for 'intent to create legal relations' by imposing a test of reasonableness. This scrutiny is apparent in Devlin J's decision in *Parker* v. *Clark* (1960, examined at 6.11 below).[9]

6.05 *Rationale of the 'intent to create legal relations' doctrine.* There is a link between this doctrine and the general principle of freedom of contract (1.08). This is because the 'intent' doctrine allows the parties to contract out of the legal regime. For example, the courts will respect an explicit 'gentlemen's agreement': no legal rights are created. The House of Lords held that an explicitly 'honourable pledge' clause excluded legal rights in *Rose & Frank Co.* v. *Crompton Bros* (1925).[10] This case concerned (1) an overarching import arrangement, and (2) a series of specific contracts of sale. As for (1), this was expressed to be 'not entered into ... as a formal or legal agreement, and [it] shall not be subject to legal jurisdiction in the law courts of the United States or England'. The House of Lords held that the clear terms of this overarching import arrangement negatived any legal effect. However, as for (2), *individual* contracts of sale made under its umbrella were legally binding. Both parts of this decision are clearly sound.

6.06 Another exclusionary formula is 'subject to contract' (4.17). This phrase, common in the field of land transactions, but not peculiar to that context, manifests a shared understanding that the relevant consensus is not legally effective as a contract. Although the courts have consistently respected this phrase,[11] the Supreme Court in the *RTS* case (2010) (4.17) held that the parties' conduct can indicate a joint intention to disapply the 'subject to contract' bar, provided (1) all the points of dispute have been resolved during the negotiations, and (2) that the parties have substantially performed under the intended transaction. Another qualification is that estoppel can override the 'subject to contract' formula;[12] and collateral warranties can arise even though the main contract is 'subject to

---

8   [2013] EWCA Civ 394; [2013] 3 All ER 807, at [61], [62], [86], [87], quoting Lord Clarke in *RTS Flexible Systems Ltd* v. *Molkerei Alois Mueller GmbH and Co KG (UK) Productions* [2010] UKSC 14; [2010] 1 WLR 753, at [45], Lord Bingham CJ in *Edmonds* v. *Lawson* [2000] All ER 31, at [21], Megaw J in *Edwards* v. *Skyways* [1964] 1 WLR 349, 355, and Aikens J in *Mamidoil-Jetoil Greek Petroleum SA* v. *Okta Crude Oil Refinery* [2003] 1 Lloyd's Rep 554, and *Lark* v. *Outhwaite* [1991] 2 Lloyd's Rep 132. See also *Gould* v. *Gould* [1970] 1 QB 275, 279, CA, *per* Lord Denning MR.

9   [1960] 1 WLR 286; [1960] 1 All ER 93, Devlin J.

10   [1925] AC 445, HL; *Chitty on Contracts* (31st edn, London, 2012), 2–165 ff; cf the case of a nonexistent supply contract, *Baird Textile Holdings Ltd* v. *Marks and Spencer plc* [2001] EWCA Civ 274; [2002] 1 All ER (Comm) 737 (6.15); an 'honour clause' in a business context is effectively an exclusion clause: *Atiyah's Introduction to the Law of Contract* (6th edn, Oxford, 2005), 99–103.

11   Decisions respecting 'subject to contract' are legion: *Winn* v. *Bull* (1877) 7 Ch D 29; *Chillingworth* v. *Esche* [1924] 1 Ch 97, CA; *Regalian Properties plc* v. *London Dockland Development Corporation* [1995] 1 WLR 212, Rattee J, noted by Key, (1995) 111 LQR 576; E. McKendrick, [1995] *Restitution Law Review* 100. For a rare exception, *Alpenstow Ltd* v. *Regalian Properties Ltd* [1985] 1 WLR 721, Nourse J (noted by C. Harpum, [1985] CLJ 356, emphasising the decision's exceptional features).

12   *Salvation Army Trustee Co. Ltd* v. *West Yorkshire Metropolitan County Council* (1980) 41 P & CR 179, approved but distinguished in *Attorney-General of Hong Kong* v. *Humphreys Estates (Queens Gardens) Ltd* [1987] 1 AC 114, 127, PC; for an Australian decision, see *Walton's Stores (Interstate) Ltd* v. *Maher* (1988) 76 ALJ 513 (High Court of Australia). But note the more restrictive approach displayed by the House of Lords in

contract'.[13] Even if the phrase 'subject to contract' is not explicitly used, the Court of Appeal in *Grant* v. *Bragg* (2009)[14] acknowledged that where the parties have agreed that informal agreements, whether oral or e-mailed, should be finalised in writing (on paper), the effect is to render the parties' dealings impliedly 'subject to contract'. The court distinguished between a binding agreement importing a further obligation to sign a formal written instrument recording the agreement and a non-binding agreement which is capable of becoming binding only if the parties sign or agree written terms. The Court of Appeal rejected the trial judge's view that the parties' e-mail correspondence indicated that they were free to achieve a binding agreement without complying with the formal signing of the draft written agreement.

6.07 A variation on the theme of 'freedom of contract' (1.08) is the position regarding a collective agreement (a consensus between a trade union and an employer). Statute states that such an agreement is presumed to be unenforceable unless the parties explicitly declare otherwise.[15] In that special context, therefore, the law allows the parties to contract *into* the sphere of legal enforceability; otherwise the collective agreement has no legal effect.

6.08 *A filter upon agreements which legally 'count'*. The 'intent to create legal relations' doctrine also affords the courts an opportunity to take into account various practical or policy factors. The result is that the 'intent' doctrine can be used to deny legal effect to technical bargains: such arrangements would be enforceable if consideration alone determined the question of enforceability (see 6.19 ff for discussion of that doctrinal interaction). Three main factors are discernible in the cases (for example, *Balfour* v. *Balfour* (1919), discussed more fully at 6.09).[16]

First, there is the objective triviality of many social or domestic promises. As Warrington LJ said:

> [I]f we were to hold that there was a contract in this case we should have to hold that with regard to all the more or less trivial concerns of life where a wife, at the request of her husband, makes a promise to him, that is a promise which can be enforced in law.[17]

Secondly, it would be inappropriate for domestic or social promises to be subject to the heavy-handed and intrusive process and remedies of the commercial system of contract. As Atkin LJ said:

---

commercial contexts in *Cobbe* v. *Yeoman's Row Management Ltd* [2008] UKHL 55; [2008] 1 WLR 1752, at [14] (noted by J. Getzler, (2009) 125 LQR 196).

13   Collateral warranties can arise even though the main contract is 'subject to contract': *Business Environment Bow Lane Ltd* v. *Deanwater Estates Ltd* [2007] EWCA Civ 622; [2007] L & TR 26 (although such a warranty was not found on the facts: see 9.14). 'Lock out' agreements for a specified period can also be created, even though the main contract is 'subject to contract': *Pitt* v. *PHH Asset Management Ltd* [1994] 1 WLR 327, CA (2.10).

14   [2009] EWCA Civ 1228; [2010] 1 All ER (Comm) 1166, at [28] to [32], *per* Lord Neuberger MR.

15   Section 179 of the Trade Union and Labour Relations (Consolidation) Act 1992.

16   [1919] 2 KB 571, CA.

17   *Ibid.*, at 575, *per* Warrington LJ.

> The Common Law does not regulate the form of agreements between spouses . . .
> The consideration that really obtains for them is that natural love and affection
> which counts for so little in these cold Courts . . . In respect of these promises each
> house is a domain into which the King's writ does not seek to run, and to which his
> officers do not seek to be admitted.[18]

Thirdly, there is the obvious fear of excessive litigation if every technical 'bargain', however
informal or trivial, were capable of being sued upon. As Atkin LJ said (in a passage which is
quoted at greater length in the next paragraph): 'All I can say is that the small Courts of this
country would have to be multiplied one hundredfold if these arrangements were held to
result in legal obligations.'[19]

3. THE 'NON-COMMERCIAL' CONTEXT: LEADING DECISIONS

6.09 *Bargains between spouses while the marriage remains harmonious. Balfour* v. *Balfour*
(1919) contains a famous endorsement by the Court of Appeal of the 'intent to create
legal relations' doctrine in the matrimonial context. Atkin LJ, in a characteristically purple
passage ('high-flown and rhetorical style')[20] (cited above at 6.08), said that the cold courts
are no place for spouses to sue each other for breach of promises if, at the time of the
relevant contract's formation, they were living 'in amity'.[21] The Balfours' marriage had
been intact when they had agreed these maintenance payments. And so, at that stage they
had not been bargaining at arm's length in the manner of estranged spouses or former
partners. It is different if the marriage at the relevant time has already broken down (on this
basis *Balfour* v. *Balfour* (1919) was distinguished by the Court of Appeal in *Merritt* v.
Merritt (1970)).[22]

In *Balfour* v. *Balfour* (1919) the husband and his wife had settled briefly in England. Nine months
later, he returned to his job in Ceylon, but his wife remained in England recuperating from an
illness. Before he had left, the husband had promised to pay her £30 per month during their
enforced but ostensibly amicable separation. At this stage, the marriage was intact. However,
two years later, Mrs Balfour obtained a decree nisi and an order for maintenance. She then sued
for the unpaid payments under the pre-divorce maintenance agreement. The Court of Appeal
held that there was no intent to create legal relations[23] because the Balfours' marriage had still
been intact when they agreed these maintenance payments.

---

18   *Ibid.*, at 579, *per* Atkin LJ; M. Freeman, in R. Halson (ed.), *Exploring the Boundaries of Contract* (Aldershot,
1996), chapter 4, suggests that this is a doubtful point in modern times, although J. O'Sullivan and J. Hilliard,
The Law of Contract (7th edn, Oxford, 2014), 3.8, think that the point is valuable.
19   [1919] 2 KB 571, 577, 579, CA, *per* Duke LJ and Atkin LJ.
20   S. Waddams, *Principle and Policy in Contract Law: Competing or Complementary Concepts?* (Cambridge,
2011), 167.
21   [1919] 2 KB 571, 579, CA; the formula of 'in amity' recurs at 572 and 576.
22   [1970] 1 WLR 1211, 1214, CA.
23   Consideration was also lacking: Warrington and Duke LJJ held that there was no real counter-promise by
the wife, and hence no consideration: *ibid.*, at 575, 577–8, respectively; by contrast, at trial, Sargant J had found
that the wife had made an implicit undertaking not to pledge the husband's credit for more than the £30 per
month which he had promised to pay.

Balfour v. *Balfour* (1919) was distinguished by the Court of Appeal in *Merritt* v. *Merritt* (1970),[24] where a matrimonial agreement was made when the husband was about to leave his wife for another woman. Mrs Merritt had insisted that he should promise in writing that the wife would become solely entitled to the matrimonial home if she paid off the remaining mortgage instalments. The Court of Appeal, upholding her contractual claim, made a declaration that the property should now be transferred into the wife's sole name. Unlike *Balfour* v. *Balfour*, the Merritts' marriage was 'on the rocks' at the time this agreement was made. Widgery LJ concluded:[25] 'The experience of life and human nature which raises this presumption in the case of a husband and wife living together in amity does not support it when the affection which produces that relationship of confidence has gone.'

The *Balfour* case (1919) is often cited for the broad proposition that most types of family financial contracts are legally unenforceable. But this perception of social expectations is open to question. A strong presumption against legal enforcement might no longer be appropriate. Perhaps even agreements between spouses while the marriage is emotionally sound might be accorded enforcement.[26] In any event, a deed will seal matters in favour of enforcement (in the absence of misrepresentation, duress or undue influence).

Baroness Hale acknowledged this last point in *Granatino* v. *Radmacher* (2010):[27]
> There is nothing to stop a husband and wife from making legally binding arrangements ... to regulate their property and affairs while they are still together ... [such as] an agreement to share the ownership or tenancy of the matrimonial home, bank accounts, savings or other assets. Agreements for housekeeping or personal allowances, on the other hand, might run into difficulties [Baroness Hale then summarised *Balfour* v. *Balfour* (1919), discussed already]. But any problems posed by the doctrine of consideration or the need to express contractual intent could be solved by making the agreement by deed.

6.10 *Other family arrangements: mother retracting daughter's 'start up' accommodation. Jones* v. *Padavatton* (1969) is another case often cited as supporting the presumption that family arrangements are unenforceable.[28] However, only Danckwerts LJ invoked the *Balfour* v. *Balfour* presumption concerning 'family relations', the other two Lords Justices reaching the result by different lines of reasoning. On the basis of this decision, it is doubtful whether the presumption applies outside the narrow confines of promises during happy matrimonial relations and manifestly social and informal undertakings.

---

24 [1970] 1 WLR 1211, CA.
25 *Ibid.*, 1214.
26 E. McKendrick, *Contract Law: Text, Cases and Materials* (6th edn, Oxford, 2014), 282, reviews the literature on this.
27 [2010] UKSC 42; [2011] 1 AC 534, at [142]. For developments concerning ante-nuptial agreements, see 20.12.
28 [1969] 1 All ER 328, CA.

Jones v. *Padavatton* (1969) concerned these facts. In 1962, a mother persuaded her daughter, aged 34, to leave her job in Washington DC, go to London, and read for the English Bar, promising to support her during this period of study. In 1964, instead of maintenance, the mother permitted the daughter to reside (without any explicit time-limit) in the mother's second property. In 1967, when the daughter, now aged 39, had yet to pass the Bar exams, the mother successfully sued to regain possession of the property. In reaching this conclusion only Danckwerts LJ adopted the presumption, deduced from the *Balfour* case (1919) (6.09), against enforcement of 'family arrangements'. The other judges (Fenton-Atkinson and Salmon LJJ) instead examined carefully the particular facts, rather than resorting to a mechanical presumption (Fenton-Atkinson LJ finding no intention to create legal relations on the facts and Salmon LJ finding that a valid contract had existed but it had now expired). It is submitted that Salmon LJ's analysis is the most compelling: there had been a contractual licence, but it had ended, following the effluxion of a reasonable period of time during which the daughter was expected to have completed her legal studies.

6.11 *Friends sharing accommodation: a storm in Torquay. Parker* v. *Clark* (1960)[29] is another decision which manifests reluctance to conclude that a non-commercial arrangement is beyond the pale of legal enforceability, especially when the parties have implemented the arrangement over a significant period. In this case Devlin J upheld as legally enforceable a promise between friends to reward a party for 'support services' by a share of the benefited party's estate.

In *Parker* v. *Clark* (1960) the claimants, a couple in their fifties, agreed to sell their house ('The Thimble') and to move in with the defendants, a couple in their late seventies. The claimants and defendants were not related. The claimants also agreed to share many of the outgoings on the property. In return, the defendants promised to accommodate the couple and to leave them a one-third share of the value of their estate when they had both died. The arrangement, only partly recorded in writing, was successful for a year and a half, but then the parties fell out. The defendants evicted the claimants, and the latter sued successfully for damages in respect of 'loss of bargain'. Devlin J awarded damages in favour of the claimants. He dismissed the defence based on the alleged lack of 'intent to create legal relations' because this was not a mere domestic arrangement. Therefore, *Balfour* v. *Balfour* (1919) (6.09) did not preclude legal enforcement.

Other cases of relevance are as follows: in *Lens* v. *Devonshire Club* (1914), Scrutton J refused an action by a golfer for a prize promised by his club. In *Simpkins* v. *Puys* (1955), a tripartite arrangement to participate in a weekly newspaper competition produced winnings for the defendant. Sellers J held that the other two contributors to the entry fee were each entitled to a one-third share of the winnings.[30]

---

29 [1960] 1 All ER 93, Devlin J; see also *Gillett* v. *Holt* [2001] Ch 210, CA (reviewing cases on proprietary estoppel claims concerning promises to leave the claimant property in promisor's will in return for the claimant's future domestic services etc. performed by the promisee in the promisor's lifetime).
30 *The Times*, 4 December 1914 (on which see Scrutton LJ in the *Rose & Crompton* case, [1923] 2 KB 261, 288, CA); [1955] 1 WLR 975.

In *Coward* v. *Motor Insurers Bureau* (1963),[31] the Court of Appeal held that a workman providing a lift on a motorbike to a colleague, the latter making a petrol contribution, had not formed a legal contract for the hire or use of a vehicle. But this last case appears now to be an aberration. The House of Lords in *Albert* v. *Motor Insurers Bureau* (1972)[32] reached a different conclusion. Although in the *Albert* case there was no binding commitment that the driver would be liable for refusing to drive, this did not mean that payment for a completed journey was made wholly *ex gratia* (the background to these decisions was that unless the arrangement was a contract for hire or reward, the Motor Insurers Bureau would not be liable to the injured person if the negligent driver of the vehicle was uninsured).

4. THE 'COMMERCIAL' CONTEXT: LEADING DECISIONS

6.12 *Non-binding commercial language.* Commercial agreements are presumed to be legally binding. Megaw J in *Edwards* v. *Skyways Ltd* (1964) expressed this as the starting point:[33] 'Where the subject matter of the agreement is not domestic or social, but is related to business affairs, the parties may, by using clear words, show that their intention is to make the transaction binding in honour only, and not in law; and the courts will give effect to the expressed intention.' Aikens LJ echoed this in *Barbudev* v. *Eurocom Cable Management Bulgaria Eood* (2012):[34] 'In a commercial context, the onus of demonstrating that there was a lack of intention to create legal relations lies on the party asserting it and it is a heavy one.'

For example, the Court of Appeal in *Attrill* v. *Dresdner Kleinwort Ltd* (2013)[35] (see also on this case 3.44, 4.08, 5.12 and 5.23) held that an investment bank's announcement to its workforce that the bank would be creating a guaranteed minimum €400m bonus chest disclosed an objective intent to create legal relations. The bank's workforce had reasonably concluded that this was a binding commitment.[36] This was not a politician's,[37] comedian's or fair-weather friend's promise.

6.13 But the two Court of Appeal decisions discussed in the next two paragraphs (*Kleinwort Benson* v. *Malaysian Mining* (1989)[38] and *Baird Textile Holdings Ltd* v. *Marks and Spencer plc* (2001)[39] show that the courts will not allow the commercial presumption of an 'intent to create legal relations' to run away with itself. There must be a clear promise, either an

31   [1963] 1 QB 259, CA.
32   [1972] AC 301, 339–40, HL.
33   [1964] 1 WLR 349, 354–5.
34   [2012] EWCA Civ 548; [2012] 2 All ER (Comm) 963, at [30].
35   [2013] EWCA Civ 394; [2013] 3 All ER 807.
36   *Ibid.*, at [61], [62], [86], [87], *per* Elias LJ.
37   S. Waddams, *Principle and Policy in Contract Law: Competing or Complementary Concepts?* (Cambridge, 2011), 168, noting that even a formal contract given by a politician was held by the Canadian Supreme Court not to be legally enforceable: *Canadian Taxpayers Federation* v. *Ontario* (2004) 73 OR (3d) 621 (Sup Ct).
38   [1989] 1 All ER 785, CA.
39   [2001] EWCA Civ 274; [2002] 1 All ER (Comm) 737.

explicit one (which is not stated to be non-binding), or an implicit one which is clearly evidenced by the surrounding facts. Without this, the claim for breach of promise must founder. The 'commercial presumption' only kicks in if there is an express or apparent promise.

6.14 *Letters of comfort.*[40] A so-called letter of comfort does not (unless peculiarly worded so as to contradict their normal import) confer binding assurances as to the availability of future funds. Instead it is a general statement by a parent company regarding its subsidiary's solvency and its general willingness to pay its subsidiary's debts. It is not intended to be a guarantee; indeed its essence is that no binding guarantee is given.[41] Thus a letter of comfort offers lukewarm support and does not supply cast-iron assurance.

Against this background, *Kleinwort Benson* v. *Malaysian Mining* (1989)[42] shows that the 'commercial' presumption should not render a letter of comfort legally binding.

The Court of Appeal held in *Kleinwort Benson* v. *Malaysian Mining Corp. Bhd* (1989)[43] that there was nothing on the facts to rebut the normal construction that a letter of comfort creates no binding assurance. The defendant, a parent company, had given the claimant lender the following written assurance: 'It is our policy to ensure that the business of [X, the subsidiary company] is at all times in a position to meet its liabilities to you under the [loan facility] arrangements.'[44] Comforted by this, the claimant lent a large sum to X, the subsidiary. X defaulted on repayment and became insolvent amid the cacophonous collapse of the world tin market. The lender sued the parent company upon the letter of comfort, but the Court of Appeal (reversing Hirst J) held that the comfort letter had no legal force. The document did not contain a commitment or indeed a promise. The presumption that commercial arrangements are legally enforceable (as recognised in *Edwards* v. *Skyways Ltd* (1964), see above) only applies if one can identify a promise, but the letter in *Kleinwort Benson* v. *Malaysian Mining Corp. Bhd* (1989) was couched in the present tense, that is, it contained the declaration that the present practice was for the parent company's policy to ensure that its subsidiary can meet its liabilities; and this pallid statement did not constitute a promise that it would continue to ensure that this was so.[45] Secondly, the background negotiations revealed that the parent company had refused to give the lender a standard guarantee, and this fortified the view that the comfort letter (like the great majority such letters of comfort) was not intended to create a legal obligation.[46]

---

40 M. Furmston and G. J. Tolhurst, *Contract Formation: Law and Practice* (Oxford, 2010), chapter 7 ('letters of intent'; and including at 7.52 ff 'letters of comfort'); M. Furmston, 'Letters of Intent', in A. Burrows and E. Peel (eds.), *Contract Formation and Parties* (Oxford, 2010).
41 *Per* Maurice Kay LJ in *Associated British Ports* v. *Ferryways NV* [2009] EWCA Civ 189; [2009] 1 Lloyd's Rep 595, at [24] to [27]; *Re Simon Carves Ltd* [2013] EWHC 685 (Ch); [2013] 2 BCLC 100, at [30] to [37] (Sir William Blackburne); and *Re Atlantic Computers Plc (In Administration)* [1995] BCC 696 (Chadwick J).
42 [1989] 1 WLR 379, CA.
43 *Ibid.*
44 *Ibid.*, at 381.
45 *Ibid.*, at 388; M. Furmston and G. J. Tolhurst, *Contract Formation: Law and Practice* (Oxford, 2010), 7.56, noting that the New Zealand Court of Appeal did not adopt this point in *Bank of New Zealand* v. *Ginivan* [1991] 1 NZLR 178.
46 [1989] 1 WLR 379, 392, CA (factual matrix material, on the basis of *Prenn* v. *Simmonds* [1971] 1 WLR 1381, HL), and see the principles of interpretation of written contracts at 14.01.

6.15 *No contractual commitment to support an alleged long-term contract.* The Court of Appeal's decision in *Baird Textile Holdings Ltd* v. *Marks and Spencer plc* (2001)[47] also shows that the *Edwards* v. *Skyways Ltd* (1964: see above) 'commercial' presumption of enforceability will not apply unless the court can first identify an 'explicit' or 'apparent' promise (the latter term concerning a clearly evidenced promise, even though not explicit; in other words, an 'apparent' promise is one which can be clearly inferred from conduct and context). These cases will be further examined in turn.

> In *Baird Textile Holdings Ltd* v. *Marks and Spencer plc* (2001), the claimant, a clothing manufacturer which had dealt solely with Marks and Spencer for over thirty years, was suddenly 'dropped' as a supplier. Its claim for breach of an alleged long-term supply agreement failed because there was no such agreement, merely a long-standing pattern of discrete contracts for particular orders (Marks and Spencer, possessing greater economic power, had all along intended that matters should remain fluid in this way). The claimant could not imply a promise by invoking the *Edwards* v. *Skyways Ltd* (1964: see above) presumption that commercial arrangements are legally enforceable. Mance LJ noted that this would be to put the cart before the horse. Instead, the true logic of the analysis must be: (1) Do the facts disclose any real consensus between the parties that Marks and Spencer were committing themselves to making repeat orders, until they gave reasonable notice to terminate the chain of dealings? (2) If such an 'apparent' consensus emerges, there will be scope for the presumption in favour of legal relations to operate. This presumption would then be appropriate because this was clearly a commercial context. But the present claim foundered at stage (1): no clear implicit consensus could be found on these facts. Therefore, the *Edwards* v. *Skyways* (1964) (see 6.12 above) 'commercial' presumption was a red herring and simply did not apply.

5. BORDERLINE OF 'COMMERCIAL AND NON-COMMERCIAL' RELATIONS

6.16 *Modahl* v. *British Athletic Federation Ltd* (2002)[48] (where an athlete was held to have a contract with her governing athletic board) and *Preston* v. *President of the Methodist Conference* (2013)[49] (where Methodist priest was held not to have a contract with her church) show that there is an uncertain boundary between the 'commercial' and 'non-commercial' spheres of promise-making. In these borderline cases, the courts cannot confidently invoke the presumption of enforceability, nor its converse. Instead, the court must make a value judgment. This can divide experienced judges (there were dissents by Jonathan Parker LJ in *Modahl* v. *British Athletic Federation Ltd* (2002)[50]

---

47 [2001] EWCA Civ 274; [2002] 1 All ER (Comm) 737, at [59] to [70], *per* Mance LJ; on this case, J. Morgan in D. Campbell, L. Mulcahy and S. Wheeler (eds.), *Changing Concepts of Contract* (Basingstoke, 2013), chapter 8.
48 [2001] EWCA Civ 1447; [2002] 1 WLR 1192, CA.
49 [2013] UKSC 29; [2013] 2 AC 163.
50 [2001] EWCA Civ 1447; [2002] 1 WLR 1192, CA (Jonathan Parker LJ at [77] and [80] could discern no intent to create legal relations).

and by Baroness Hale in the *Preston* v. *President of the Methodist Conference* (2013),[51] as noted below).

6.17 In *Modahl* v. *British Athletic Federation Ltd* (2002)[52] an athlete sought damages of c.£1m against the British Athletic Federation (BAF) for an alleged contractual failure to deal fairly with her challenge to the accuracy of a urine test result. The claimant succeeded in establishing a binding contractual relationship (see points (1) and (2) below), but failed to show there had been a breach (see point (3) below).

In *Modahl* v. *British Athletic Federation Ltd* (2002)[53] Diane Modahl, a British international 800 metres runner, failed a laboratory test on a urine sample taken in 1994 during an athletics meeting held in Portugal. This urine test result threatened to destroy her career. She protested her innocence. Eventually, in July 1995 the athletic authorities declared that the test had been a mistake (Portuguese experts were to blame for this error). However, in the meantime, Modahl had suffered turmoil. As mentioned, her contractual claim failed only because there had been no breach. The Court of Appeal decided the following points:

(1) Although there had been no exchange of offer and acceptance, a contract had arisen based on repeated invitations to Modahl to run on behalf of the BAF.

(2) By a majority (Jonathan Parker LJ dissenting), there was an 'intent to create legal relations';[54] the facts concerned an 'arm's length' relationship between a top-class sportswoman and her 'ruling body'; this context is a long way from the matrimonial relationship in *Balfour* v. *Balfour* (1919) (when the parties were still living 'in amity') (on which see 6.09).

(3) Although the contract included an implied term that both parties would be governed by the BAF's rulebook, there had been no breach of that procedure, nor had there been any contractual breach taking the form of 'bias' towards her; and so Modahl's damages claim failed.

6.18 In *Preston* v. *President of the Methodist Conference* (2013)[55] the Supreme Court, by a majority, held[56] that a priest within the Methodist church does not have a contractual relationship with her Church and so was not an employee. It followed that she could not bring a complaint of unfair dismissal.

The *Preston* case (2013) is a surprising result. A line of cases[57] shows that there is no presumption against contractual relations arising in respect of spiritual

---

51 [2013] UKSC 29; [2013] 2 AC 163, at [45] to [49].
52 [2001] EWCA Civ 1447; [2002] 1 WLR 1192, CA.
53 *Ibid.*
54 [2001] EWCA Civ 1447; [2002] 1 WLR 1192, CA, at [51], [52] and [105], *per* Latham and Mance LJJ (but Jonathan Parker LJ at [77] and [80] could discern no intent to create legal relations).
55 [2013] UKSC 29; [2013] 2 AC 163.
56 Notably [2013] UKSC 29; [2013] 2 AC 163, *per* Lord Sumption at [25] and [26] (reversing the Employment Appeal Tribunal and the Court of Appeal).
57 *Percy* v. *Church of Scotland Board of National Mission* [2005] UKHL 73; [2006] 2 AC 28; *Davies* v. *Presbyterian Church of Wales* [1986] 1 WLR 323; HL; *President of the Methodist Conference* v. *Parfitt* [1984] QB 368, CA.

engagements.[58] Instead the courts will adopt a context by context method (religion by religion, sect by sect, dependent on the 'constitution' of the relevant religious organisation).[59] There is a cogent dissent by Baroness Hale in the *Preston* case (2013).[60] She noted that there is no incompatibility between contractual rights and a religious vocation,[61] and she further noted that a person can hold an office and at the same time enjoy contractual relations with the relevant organisation or entity.[62] Baroness Hale concluded that it would be absurd if a Methodist priest could not claim in contract[63] for unpaid stipend, security of accommodation and other promised benefits.

6. THE FUTURE

6.19   The status of 'intent to create legal relations' has become disputed. There are three views: (1) 'intent' is an unnecessary rider to ordinary principles of consensus; (2) 'intent' should be allowed to oust the older doctrine of 'consideration' (see Chapter 5 for that doctrine); (3) 'intent' is here to stay, operating alongside 'consideration'. Of these three views, the third is correct.

6.20   *View (1): 'Intent' doctrine should be subsumed by 'offer and acceptance'.* First, there is a bold and sceptical view: that intent to create legal relations should be excised as a separate doctrine. Instead, 'intent' should be treated as merely an aspect of the 'offer and acceptance' bundle of rules.[64] However, in response to this, it should be noted that the independent nature of the intention to create legal relations doctrine is widely accepted. The doctrine enjoys a secure place both in the practice of the courts and in leading textbooks.

6.21   *View (2): 'Intent' destined to oust consideration?* This is the imperialistic view of the doctrine's prospects: that 'intent to create legal relations' will supplant the doctrine of consideration (see Chapter 5 for that doctrine). According to this view, 'consideration' should be abolished (however, it is likely that this would require legislation because it is too late for this doctrine to be simply abandoned by judicial decision). The present argument is that 'consideration' is an inexact and indirect way of posing the question addressed more precisely by the doctrine of 'intent to create legal relations': is this promise supported by a shared wish to create legally binding rights and duties, or is the promise too casual and informal to have legal force? However, this 'imperialistic' view is open to objection. For

---

58   *Preston* case, [2013] UKSC 29; [2013] 2 AC 163, at [26] *per* Lord Sumption, citing *Percy* v. *Church of Scotland Board of National Mission* [2005] UKHL 73; [2006] 2 AC 28.
59   *Preston* case, [2013] UKSC 29; [2013] 2 AC 163, at [26], *per* Lord Sumption.
60   *Ibid.*, at [45] to [49].
61   *Ibid.*, at [36].
62   *Ibid.*, at [37].
63   *Ibid.*, at [45].
64   M. Furmston (ed.), *Law of Contract* (4th edn, London, 2010), 2.169; J. O'Sullivan and J. Hilliard, *The Law of Contract* (7th edn, Oxford, 2014), 3.12, suggest that 'the doctrine of intent to create legal relations is better viewed as part of the rules on offer and acceptance.' For a rejoinder, see E. McKendrick, *Contract Law: Text, Cases and Materials* (6th edn, Oxford, 2014), 285.

example, McKendrick rightly doubts whether the 'intent' doctrine will or should oust 'consideration':[65] at the core of 'consideration' is the legal system's refusal to give effect to gratuitous promises unless they are (as it were) (i) solemnised in a formal way (by use of a 'deed', 5.03) or (ii) the parties, by use of nominal consideration, signal their intention to create a binding agreement.

6.22 *View (3): Intent to create legal relations is an independent doctrine supplementing consideration.* However, the orthodox approach is that the doctrine of intent to create legal relations has long since taken firm root as a separate test, operating additionally to the bargain test of 'consideration'[66] and the requirement of certainty. The better view is that the consideration or bargain test is not just a roundabout way of discerning an 'intent' to create legal rights (on the basis of a rule-of-thumb inference that a 'bargain' is normally intended to be legally binding, but a promise of pure generosity is not). 'Consideration' encapsulates a paternalistic policy: that the promisor (and those interested in his solvency and prosperity) should be protected against the risk of squandering too liberally his assets (and energies) by making gratuitous promises. And so X's promise to give £1m to Y, or to release T from his debt of £5m, will be given effect only if X makes the effort to clothe his benevolence in the form of a deed (see 5.03 for the requirements of a deed), or the parties, by use of nominal consideration, signal their intention to create a binding agreement.

It is not enough that X in these situations utters the incantation, 'this promise is accompanied by an intention to create legal relations.' Even if the promise were sincerely intended to create legal rights, the purpose of the 'consideration' doctrine is to give the gratuitous promisor the right to change his mind. And so he cannot be sued for the sum not paid nor (in the case of releases) can he, as creditor, be prevented from suing X for the balance not in fact paid (this last point is the Common Law starting point; but Equity, taking the form of promissory estoppel, has qualified the position; see 5.38).

QUESTIONS

(1) Consider the presumption of non-enforceability of agreements made in non-commercial contexts in the light of *Balfour* v. *Balfour* (1919), *Merritt* v. *Merritt* (1970), *Jones* v. *Padavatton* (1969), and *Parker* v. *Clark* (1960).

(2) What must be shown in order to rebut the presumption in a commercial context that the parties intended to create legal relations?

(3) In what sense do *Modahl* v. *British Athletic Federation Ltd* (2002) and *Preston* v. *President of the Methodist Conference* (2013) represent 'borderline' cases, and what are the merits of the dissenting judgments in these cases by Jonathan Parker LJ and Baroness Hale, respectively?

(4) As noted also at Chapter 5, it can be asked: 'Is it satisfactory (in the absence of a deed or covenant) to preserve a two-stage test of legal enforceability, applying both the consideration and intent to create legal relations doctrines?'

---

65 E. McKendrick, *Contract Law* (10th edn, London, 2013), 5.29.
66 McKendrick, *ibid.*, noting that, in Australia, the 'doctrine' has been downgraded to an issue of the burden of proof.

Selected further reading

A. G. Chloros, 'The Doctrine of Consideration and the Reform of the Law of Contract' (1968) 17
    ICLQ 137

S. Hedley, 'Keeping Contract in its Place – *Balfour* v. *Balfour* and the Enforceability of
    Informal Agreements' (1985) 5 OJLS 391, especially 400–4

B. Hepple, 'Intent to Create Legal Relations' [1970] CLJ 122

IV

Third parties and assignment

Chapter contents

7

Third parties

1. INTRODUCTION

7.01 Summary of main points

(1) At Common Law (that is, under the judicial law established prior to the change introduced by the Contracts (Rights of Third Parties) Act 1999) (see the summary at (3) below), a third party cannot enforce a contract intended by the parties to be for her benefit.[1] And so at Common Law, a non-party, T, cannot sue A directly if A promises B that A will pay £1,000 to T, in return for a counter-promise by B to do something. It is different if B assigns this debt to Z, because Z can then sue A. But assignment can only occur after the formation of the contract between A and B. Assignment is examined in Chapter 8.

(2) The Law Commission successfully recommended a legislative system of third party rights:[2] the Contracts (Rights of Third Parties) Act 1999.

(3) The 1999 Act enables a third party to acquire a direct right of action (or the right to benefit from an exclusion clause) either by explicit language (A and B state clearly that 'T can sue A directly') or by implication (A and B agree that A will 'confer a benefit' on T, for example, that A will pay a sum to T); this will normally entitle T to sue A for this amount, even though the right of action was not spelt out by A and B; but A might succeed in countering this inference.

(4) Despite the revolution of the 1999 Act, the Common Law remains relevant, for several reasons:

    (a) To the extent that the Act governs current contracts, the statute overrides the perceived objections to the 'third party contractual rights at Common Law' rule; and an understanding of that background is therefore required.

    (b) Some types of contract are excluded from the legislative scheme; to that extent, the Common Law rule continues to bar a third party from suing.

---

1 R. Merkin (ed.), *Privity of Contract* (London, 2000); for theoretical discussion, see P. Kincaid (ed.), *Privity* (Aldershot, 2001); V. V. Palmer, *The Paths to Privity* (San Francisco, 1992), examines the history of this doctrine; for a review of this book, N. Andrews, (1995) 69 *Tulane Law Review* 1393; for comparative discussion, see V. V. Palmer, 'Contracts in Favour of Third Persons in Europe' (2003) 11 *European Review of Private Law* 8–27; and, on the major English statute, see the literature cited at 7.22 below.
2 Law Commission, 'Privity of Contract: Contracts for the Benefit of Third Parties' (Law Commission Report No. 242, Cm 3329, London, 1996).

(c) It remains possible at Common Law for A to promise to benefit B1 and B2 jointly. This is the doctrine of 'joint promisees': B1 provides consideration jointly on behalf of B1 and B2; A's promise is made to these jointly; B1 and B2 must sue A jointly, but if either B1 or B2 dies, the right of action against A devolves entirely upon the survivor.

(d) The promisee's capacity to obtain remedies in respect of A's breach remains governed by Common Law principles. B's capacity to sue A in respect of non-performance is of great practical importance (see point (7) below).

(5) The greatest challenge to the Common Law privity rule (summarised at (1) above) was Equity's invention in the eighteenth century of 'trusts of promises'. The benefit of A's promise to pay money or to transfer property to T (known as a 'chose in action') can be held by B on trust for T, B thereupon becoming obliged in Equity to sue A for T's benefit. But if B fails to sue A, T (as the 'beneficiary' of the trust) can take the initiative and sue A for default in performance (a plain reversal by Equity of the Common Law privity doctrine). However, the Court of Appeal in *Re Schebsman* (1944)[3] held that the courts would no longer benevolently imply such a trust. This was a tipping point. After 1944, a trust of a promise had to be based on explicit language indicating the contracting parties' shared intention to confer on T an irrevocable entitlement to the benefit of A's promised performance.

(6) The House of Lords in *Midland Silicones* v. *Scruttons* (1962)[4] held that a third party, Z, cannot take the benefit of an exclusion clause (a 'shield' against an action by X) even though parties X and Y have clearly intended that Z should so benefit. This has proved to be an irksome extension of the Common Law privity doctrine. But the *New Zealand Shipping* case (1975)[5] enabled commercial lawyers to circumvent the rule in the *Scruttons* case by finding an express contract between X and Z, the only content of which is that Z performs work in return for X's promise of an exclusion clause; X and Z are then in privity of contract; in this way, the *Scruttons* rule had been sidestepped. Happily, this Common Law contortion is no longer necessary because the Contracts (Rights of Third Parties) Act 1999 enables a third party to acquire the benefit of an exclusion clause.

(7) As mentioned at (4)(d), even after the 1999 Act, it remains important to consider the capacity of the promisee to sue in respect of A's breach of contract, even though the 'target' of A's promise is A and B's agreement that A should benefit T, the third party.

(a) However, B cannot sue A in *debt* if A's promise was to pay money to T.

(b) Furthermore, B cannot sue A for *damages* unless B has suffered *personal* loss (the so-called rule in *Woodar* v. *Wimpey* (1980), although in fact this rule antedates that case) (7.19). Exceptions to the rule in *Woodar* v. *Wimpey* have been introduced, notably in the context (governed by decisions culminating in the *Panatown* case (2001)) where A's promise to B was to build on T's land, or carry out repairs to buildings on that land (whether T at all relevant points owned this site or T acquired it subsequent to the formation of A and B's contract).

(c) If neither a claim in *debt* or for *damages* offers substantial protection of B's interest in A's performance, exceptionally B can obtain an order for *specific performance* (an equitable

3   [1944] Ch 83, CA.
4   [1962] AC 446, 473, HL.
5   [1975] AC 154, PC.

remedy), and thus compel A to execute his promise for T's benefit (on pain of contempt of court if A defaults), as illustrated by *Beswick* v. *Beswick* (1968).

2. THE COMMON LAW DOCTRINE OF PRIVITY

7.02 At Common Law, A and B cannot confer on T, a third party, a direct right of action against A (for the possibility that, after the contract's formation, B might assign his right to X, 'the assignee', see Chapter 8). Nor can parties A and B give T, a third party, the benefit of a 'shield', notably an exclusion clause (generally on exclusion clauses, see Chapter 15). Such a clause might benefit T if A were to sue him in the tort of negligence. Furthermore, freedom of contract (1.08) demands that X and Y cannot impose a burden on a third party, Z, 'behind his back', that is, without Z's consent. And so Z, a third party, cannot be subjected to a duty to pay money to X or Y, nor can X and Y impose on Z the burden of an exclusion clause, preventing Z from being able to sue X or Y, or restricting his capacity to obtain compensation (unless an exceptional context can be found; see 7.56).

7.03 *The third party has not earned the right to sue since he has not provided consideration.* The cases were in a confused state[6] before *Tweddle* v. *Atkinson* (1861).[7] The court in that case held that the third party could not sue for breach of promise by the promisor, party A, because the third party (as distinct from B, the promisee, the other contracting party) had not provided consideration for the promise, that is, the third party had not bought the right to sue.

Tweddle v. *Atkinson* (1861) concerned a written post-nuptial agreement between Tweddle senior (the father of Tweddle junior) and Guy (the father-in-law of Tweddle junior). Tweddle junior was therefore a third party to the contract between Tweddle senior and Guy, who promised each other that they would pay, respectively, £100 and £200 to Tweddle junior, the third party, before 21 August 1855. Guy, the father-in-law, failed to pay and died. Tweddle senior, still alive, had also failed to pay. The son, showing filial respect, sued only Guy's executor for £200. But the claim failed. The court held that the son, as a third party, had not provided consideration for the promise, that is, he had not bought the right to sue.

It can be objected that it should not matter that only B has provided consideration. The function of consideration is to render the contract binding as between A and B (in the absence of a 'deed', for which see 5.03). It is an unconvincing extension of the role of consideration to require a third party to have earned or bought the right to sue given him by the contracting parties. A second weakness of the consideration argument is that one second in time after the contract's formation, B can assign the benefit of the contract to X, an assignee. The fact that X has not given anything to earn this right does not preclude him from acquiring a right by assignment. Thus, if A promises to pay B £1,000, B can assign (make a present of) this debt, a

---

6   See n. 1 above, V. V. Palmer.
7   (1861) 1 B & S 393; 30 LJQB 265; 4 LT 468; cf *Lawrence* v. *Fox*, 20 NY 268 (1859) (the New York Court of Appeals, two years before the *Tweddle* case, decided that a third party beneficiary did have a right of action).

chose in action, to T; T will then have a direct right of action against A; T need not provide consideration to be able to take advantage of the assignment (generally on assignment, see Chapter 8). Frustrated by English law's misguided decision to invoke the doctrine of consideration to deny a third party a right of action, Lord Dunedin (a Scottish Law Lord) said in the *Dunlop* case (1915):[8]

> My Lords, I confess that this case is to my mind apt to nip any budding affection which one might have had for the doctrine of consideration [this judge had been educated in Scotland – a consideration-free zone]. For the effect of that doctrine in the present case is to make it possible for a person to snap his finger at a bargain deliberately made . . . and which the person seeking to enforce it has a legitimate interest to enforce.

7.04   *The pure privity doctrine.* In *Dunlop Pneumatic Tyre Co. Ltd* v. *Selfridge & Co. Ltd* (1915) Lord Haldane LC made an additional point,[9] on which the *Tweddle* case had been silent: that the third party could not sue because he was not an addressee of the promise made by A to B. In other words, *the third party was not a promisee.* Therefore, A was committing himself only to an obligation towards B but not to an obligation towards the third party. Lord Haldane LC said:[10]

> [C]ertain principles[11] are fundamental. One is that only a person who is a party to a contract can sue on it. Our law knows nothing of a *jus quaesitum tertio* [a direct right of action by the third party] arising by way of contract. Such a right may be conferred by way of property, as, for example, under a trust [see 7.48 below], but it cannot be conferred on a stranger to a contract as a right to enforce the contract *in personam* [as a personal obligation].

As Treitel observes,[12] this requirement of 'pure privity' rests on a dogma and is conspicuously circular: a third party cannot sue on a contract; this is because only a party can do so; and a third party is not a party. The Law Commission agreed with this critique.[13]

In *Dunlop Pneumatic Tyre Co. Ltd* v. *Selfridge & Co. Ltd* (1915) Dews had agreed with Dunlop that Dews would not sell Dunlop tyres below a certain price and, further, that retailers buying tyres from Dews would be required to give the same undertaking. Selfridge bought tyres from Dews and gave the undertaking just mentioned. But Selfridge then sold the tyres below the minimum price. Dunlop sued Selfridge for this alleged breach. His claim failed.

The pure privity doctrine includes denying third parties the protection of exclusion clauses. In the *Scruttons* case (1962)[14] (7.48), the House of Lords held that a non-party T cannot 'take advantage' of a contract, even passively, as a 'shield' against A's action, even though A and B

8   [1915] AC 847, 855, HL.
9   *Ibid.*, at 853 (in this same passage he also endorsed the consideration point mentioned in the preceding paragraph).
10   *Ibid.*
11   For reflections on the nature of 'rules' and 'principles' in contract law, S. Waddams, *Principle and Policy in Contract Law: Competing or Complementary Concepts?* (Cambridge, 2011), 17–21.
12   The 'only a party can sue' argument 'begs the question': *Treitel* (13th edn, London, 2011), 14–015.
13   Law Commission, 'Privity of Contract: Contracts for the Benefit of Third Parties' (Law Commission Report No. 242, Cm 3329, London, 1996), 6.13 ff.
14   [1962] AC 446, 473, HL.

have explicitly agreed that A cannot sue T in tort (or that T's liability is restricted). This decision was commercially unattractive because it required greater insurance expenditure, to the ultimate detriment of users of the relevant services (7.48). As we shall see, this problem can now be circumvented at Common Law (7.50) and is directly countered by the 1999 Act (7.49).

7.05 *A vexed issue: the fear that T would acquire irrevocable rights.* A third reason why it had been considered dangerous for T to gain a direct right of action is because even if the consideration and pure privity rationales could be overcome, such a third party direct right of action might be regarded as 'irrevocable', that is, it could not be altered or extinguished by A unilaterally, nor even consensually by A and B.

This reluctance to fetter A and B's powers of 'revocation' or 'variation' is evident in *Re Schebsman* (1944),[15] the leading modern decision concerning the test for finding a 'trust of a promise' in favour of a third party (7.09). More generally, as the Law Commission rightly noted, the present argument links directly with the fact that the third party's right arises gratuitously, without his providing any consideration for it.[16] He should not have initial 'sovereignty' over A and B's agreement, although the position might change once he has acted on it, or assented to it. For this reason, we shall see (7.34) that the Contracts (Rights of Third Parties) Act 1999 provides a balancing of the interests of the three members of the third party triangle.

7.06 *Unsuccessful challenges to the Common Law privity doctrine by Lord Denning.* In various twentieth-century cases, Lord Denning tried unsuccessfully to subvert the Common Law privity doctrine, using a number of arguments and devices, as the author has examined in detail elsewhere.[17] His 'Waterloo' in this campaign was the House of Lords' reversal of his (more precisely, the Court of Appeal's) decision in *Beswick* v. *Beswick* (1968) (7.18).[18]

3. JOINT PROMISEES AT COMMON LAW

7.07 At Common Law, A can direct his promise at more than one person and render them joint promisees. It follows that neither is a third party. Consideration to support A's promise can be validly supplied jointly by B1 and B2, or even de facto by one, provided in this last situation the consideration is given 'jointly on behalf of B1 and B2'. The latter proposition is

---

15   [1944] Ch 83, CA.
16   Law Commission, 'Privity of Contract: Contracts for the Benefit of Third Parties' (Law Commission Report No. 242, Cm 3329, London, 1996), 6.15.
17   N. Andrews, (1995) 69 *Tulane Law Review* 1393.
18   [1968] AC 58, HL (overturning [1966] Ch 538, CA); in the Court of Appeal, Lord Denning MR, with Danckwerts LJ's support, invoked section 56 of the Law of Property Act 1925 to undermine the Common Law authorities; on this difficult provision, see Neuberger J in *Amsprop Trading Ltd* v. *Harris Distribution Ltd* [1997] 1 WLR 1025, 1032, and *Treitel* (13th edn, London, 2011), 14–131 ff.

supported by Australian dicta in *Coulls* v. *Bagot's Executor & Trustee Co. Ltd* (1967)[19] and by many English commentators.[20]

However, Coote, a New Zealand commentator, suggests that B2 should only be treated as having provided consideration if B2 could be sued for its non-provision in the event of B1's failure to provide it.[21] It is submitted that Coote's more restrictive approach is unattractive. It should be enough that B1 has in fact provided consideration jointly on B1 and B2's behalf. The law can then deftly enable B2 to overcome the objection that he has in reality not 'bought the right to sue A' (for the 'consideration problem' where the claimant is a third party, rather than a joint promisee, see the discussion at 7.03 of the rule in *Tweddle* v. *Atkinson* (1861)).[22]

7.08 A further Common Law rule is that a joint promisee can only sue *if he joins his fellow promisee in the relevant claim*.[23]

The dual purpose of this 'joinder rule' is to protect the promisor against the risk of successive actions and to ensure that the court can receive all relevant arguments and information. However, once a joint promisee dies, the doctrine of 'survivorship' causes his right of action to pass to the surviving promisee, rather than to the deceased's estate. If, for example, A promised in 2010 to pay £1,000 to B1 and B2, and B1 died in 2011, thereafter B2 alone can sue A.

4. 'TRUSTS OF PROMISES': A DIRECT RIGHT OF ACTION

7.09 *Genesis.* The 'trust of promises' is the concept that B, as promisee, can assume a second role and become trustee of A's promise to benefit T. The benefit of A's promise to pay money to T, or to transfer property to T (such promises are known as 'choses in action'), can be held by B on trust for T, B thereupon becoming obliged in Equity to sue A for T's benefit. This is based on the notion that the *promise to pay money or to transfer property* is itself a valuable asset, an intangible 'chose in action', even though it is merely a personal relation, a right *in personam*. This equitable concept provided a means of sidestepping the Common Law rule against contractual claims by third parties.[24] This type of trust originated in Lord Hardwicke

---

19 (1967) 119 CLR 460, 478; (1967) 40 ALJR 471, 483 (High Court of Australia), *per* Windeyer J (on the facts, the majority held that there had been no joint promise).
20 E.g. Sir Jack Beatson in Law Commission Consultation Paper, 'Privity of Contract: Contracts for the Benefit of Third Parties' (Law Commission Consultation Paper No. 121, London, 1991), at 3.33; *Chitty on Contracts* (31st edn, London, 2012), 3–042; *Treitel* (13th edn, London, 2011), 13–032.
21 B. Coote, 'Consideration and the Joint Promise' [1978] CLJ 301, 304–5.
22 (1861) 1 B & S 393; 30 LJQB 265; 4 LT 468.
23 CPR 19.3; *Treitel* (13th edn, London, 2011), 13–021; *Chitty on Contracts* (31st edn, London, 2012), 17–09 and 17–010.
24 *Fletcher* v. *Fletcher* (1844) 4 Hare 67 (Wigram V-C); *Lloyd's* v. *Harper* (1880) 16 Ch D 290, CA; *Les Affréteurs Réunis SA* v. *Leopold Walford (London) Ltd* [1919] AC 801, HL; A. L. Corbin, (1930) 46 LQR 12; J. Jaconelli, 'Privity: The Trust Exception Examined' [1998] Conv 99; M. MacIntyre, (1965) 2 *University of*

LC's decision in *Tomlinson* v. *Gill* (1756).[25] This device operated attractively for nearly two centuries. But the Court of Appeal's decision in *Re Schebsman* (1944)[26] (7.12) almost killed it off by insisting that a trust of a promise requires express language. Thereafter, no longer would the courts *imply* such a trust in order to circumvent the Common Law privity doctrine.

7.10 *Who declares the trust?* In the usual case, B will have provided consideration. Then it will be B who declares the trust of a promise, or A and B might jointly agree to its creation. But if (unusually) A's promise is gratuitous, resting on a deed (5.03), Feltham has suggested that it will be A alone who can create the trust and so appoint B to be trustee.[27]

7.11 *Effects of trusts of promises.* The effects of a 'trust of promises' are:
(1) B can sue A on T's behalf; indeed, B is obliged by Equity to sue A on T's behalf.
(2) If B fails to sue A, T can sue A (joining B as co-defendant); this is the elusive *ius quaesitum tertio* (the direct right of action by the third party) which was denied at Common Law under *Tweddle* v. *Atkinson* (1861)[28] and the *Dunlop* case (1915)[29] (7.03 and 7.04).[30]
(3) The claim based on a trust of a promise is not B's personal rights against A, but instead concerns A's direct obligation to T, which B as trustee vindicates vicariously, that is, on behalf of, and for the personal benefit of, T.[31] Accordingly, damages (intended for T's benefit), the agreed sum (payable to T) or property (intended to be transferred to T), will be held by B on trust for T.[32]
(4) A, B and T should each be party to the litigation (or arbitration reference); however, this 'joinder requirement' is intended to protect A against potential double suit by B and T in successive litigation;[33] and so A can 'waive' the need to join B, as the House of Lords acknowledged in *Walford's Case* (1919);[34] if such a waiver occurs, the action will only involve T and A, and B will have dropped out of the picture.
(5) The fact that B assumes a *trust obligation* to protect T's interests means that B cannot agree, or otherwise act, to reduce or extinguish T's rights against A.

7.12 *Test.* Since *Re Schebsman* (1944),[35] there have been two requirements for the creation of a trust of a promise: first, the contracting parties must use express language to create the trust

---

25   (1756) Ambler 330; V. V. Palmer, *The Paths to Privity* (San Francisco, 1992), 130–4.
26   [1944] Ch 83, CA.
27   J. D. Feltham, (1982) 98 LQR 17, approving the approach taken in the USA.
28   (1861) 1 B & S 393; 30 LJQB 265; 4 LT 468.
29   [1915] AC 847, HL.
30   Affirmed by a dictum of Lord Wright in *Vandepitte* v. *Preferred Accident Insurance Corporation of New York* [1933] AC 70, PC; Colman J overlooked this point in *Nisshin Shipping Co. Ltd* v. *Cleaves & Co. Ltd* [2003] EWHC 2602 (Comm); [2004] 1 All ER (Comm) 481; [2004] 1 Lloyd's Rep 38 (see 7.46 on this case).
31   *Lloyd's* v. *Harper* (1880) 16 Ch D 290, CA.
32   *Ibid.*
33   Cf potential double liability and joinder, *Carr-Glynn* v. *Frearson* [1998] 4 All ER 225, 235–6, CA, *per* Chadwick LJ, in the context of *tortious* claims for defective will-making and related testamentary services.
34   *Les Affréteurs Réunis SA* v. *Leopold Walford (London) Ltd* [1919] AC 801, HL.
35   [1944] Ch 83, CA.

(for example, 'this promise is to be held on trust for T' or 'B is to hold A's promise for T's benefit'); secondly, A and B must clearly intend that T should acquire irrevocable rights against A,[36] although this adds little to the notion of an express wish to create a trust.

7.13 It is unfortunate that *Re Schebsman* (1944) ended the courts' use of implied trusts of a promise.[37] Pre-*Schebsman* case law had not insisted on strict proof of an intention to create a trust of a promise (for example, *Fletcher* v. *Fletcher* (1844), where Wigram V-C had held that a promise by A to B to pay a large sum to T imported a trust of a promise in favour of T, without the need for an explicit declaration of a trust).[38] This liberal line of cases had been supported by Corbin at the Yale Law School.[39] Nevertheless, the Court of Appeal in *Re Schebsman* (1944) turned its back on this line of cases.[40]

7.14 However, some 'fossilised relics' from the pre-*Schebsman* era of implied trusts survive. These might be rationalised as based on *mercantile custom*. For example, in *Walford's Case* (1919), the House of Lords gave effect to an implied trust of a promise within a clause between a ship-owner, A, and a charterer, B, for the payment by A of commission to T, a shipbroker, in recognition of fixing the charterparty (a contract for the hire of a ship). That clause was inserted into the contract by B in favour of T.[41] The House of Lords decision that an implied trust of a promise arose in favour of T meant that B was obliged to sue A on T's behalf, failing which T could sue A directly. *Walford's Case* (1919) was followed by Colman J in *Nisshin Shipping Co. Ltd* v. *Cleaves & Co. Ltd* (2004) (for more on this case, see 7.46).[42]

7.15 *Trusts of promises compared with direct rights of action under the 1999 Act.* This comparison is postponed until 7.47 below.

5. ACTIONS BROUGHT BY THE PROMISEE

7.16 Although the Contracts (Rights of Third Parties) Act 1999 will often give T a direct claim against A, this statute does not eliminate the possibility of B suing A at Common Law. And so, *in exercise of his Common Law rights as promisee*, B can sue A for breach of contract, even though the main aim of A's promise was to benefit T. We will examine B's access to the following remedies: debt (not available if the promise were to pay the sum to T), specific performance (exceptionally available to B), damages (a problematic topic) and declarations.

---

36 *Vandepitte* v. *Preferred Accident Insurance Corporation of New York* [1933] AC 70, 80, PC.
37 [1944] Ch 83, CA.
38 (1844) Hare 67, Wigram V-C.
39 A. L. Corbin, (1930) 46 LQR 12; G. H. Treitel, *Some Landmarks of Twentieth Century Contract Law* (Oxford, 2002), 51, notes that Corbin had been asked to write this article by Goodhart, editor of the *Law Quarterly Review*; on Corbin's 1951 treatise, chapter 46, see Treitel, *ibid.*, at 52.
40 Corbin's article, *ibid.*, was cited by the first instance judge ([1943] Ch 366, 370) and so was visible to the Court of Appeal.
41 *Les Affréteurs Réunis SA* v. *Leopold Walford (London) Ltd* [1919] AC 801, HL (applying *Robertson* v. *Wait* (1853) 8 Ex 299); and *UDT* v. *Kirkwood* [1966] 2 QB 431, 454–5, CA.
42 [2004] EWHC 2602 (Comm); [2004] 1 All ER (Comm) 481; [2004] 1 Lloyd's Rep 38.

As for damages, the Act contains a provision designed to counter the risk of A being doubly liable for the same loss (7.42).[43]

7.17 *Debt*. If A promises B, for consideration, to pay a fixed sum to C, B cannot sue and obtain this sum (even on T's behalf). The twofold explanation for this is: first, A promised to pay T and not to pay B (it would be different if B had mandated A to pay T, but B had retained the power to *nominate another payee, including himself*);[44] secondly, even if B were to recover the debt on T's behalf, Common Law lacks the machinery to ensure that B would not keep the money. B would then be unjustly enriched at T's expense.

> It is regrettable that the law has become so rigid. The two points *might be* overcome by permitting B to sue A for debt on condition that *B should be required to hand the money to T*.[45]
> There are two ways of circumventing the current rule: (1) if A promises to pay B, B can immediately assign that debt claim to T and T as assignee can sue A directly (on assignment, see Chapter 8); or (2) under the 1999 Act, T might now have a direct claim against A for payment (7.22 ff).

7.18 *Specific performance*. Exceptionally, as *Beswick v. Beswick* (1968)[46] demonstrates, B might obtain an order of specific performance on T's behalf. The upshot will be that A is compelled to perform precisely as promised and thus T will receive complete satisfaction of A's promise.

> Specific performance is an equitable remedy (18.33). It is an order that the promisor must do exactly what he promised to do, such as convey or purchase land, or transfer shares in a private company. The promisor is compelled to perform on pain of punishment for contempt of court (18.33). An important restriction is that specific performance is only available if other remedies are inadequate on the relevant facts (18.33). Another restriction is that Equity will not compel a person to perform an obligation for the provision of personal services, such as singing or acting in a play (18.33).
> In the present third party context, the leading case concerning specific performance at the suit of B, the promisee, is *Beswick v. Beswick* (1968).[47] In this case, B transferred his coal-merchant's business to A, his nephew, and A promised B to pay £5 per week to T (for the rest of T's life). T was B's wife and A's aunt. After B's death, A paid £5 to T, the widow, and then refused to pay more. T was both a third party *and the promisee's widow and administrator of B's estate* (B had *died intestate*, that is, without having made a valid will). In this (fortuitous) second capacity, B (the administrator) obtained an order of specific performance to compel A to honour the obligation to

---

43 Law Commission, 'Privity of Contract: Contracts for the Benefit of Third Parties' (Law Commission Report No. 242, Cm 3329, London, 1996), 5.12–5.17.
44 *Beswick v. Beswick* [1968] AC 58, 72, 96, HL, *per* Lords Reid and Upjohn (cf the different result in *Cleaver v. Mutual Reserve Fund Life Association* [1892] 1 QB 147, probably turning on the relevant statute, *ibid.*, at 157).
45 N. Andrews, 'Does a Third Party Beneficiary Have a Right in English Law?' (1988) LS 14, 29, for criticism; similarly, A. S. Burrows, *Remedies for Torts and Breach of Contract* (3rd edn, Oxford, 2004), 434–5.
46 [1968] AC 58, HL.
47 [1968] AC 58, HL.

make these periodical payments to T. The House of Lords held that B's 'Common Law' remedies would be inadequate on these facts: B could not sue in debt (7.17); and B's claim for Common Law compensation would be 'nominal' (for example, £5, a token sum to denote technical breach), because B's personal loss was zero on these facts (the estate's claim for substantial compensation would have been successful if B's estate had 'stepped in' and paid the sums to T; then the estate would have (legitimately) suffered loss *in its own name*). But on the facts of the *Beswick* case, 'Common Law remedies would have been inadequate' (on this requirement, see 18.33). It would be quite unjust, therefore, if A, having received and continued to run the coal-merchant business, were left to hide behind the Common Law's inability to provide an adequate remedy on these facts.[48] And so the House of Lords agreed that specific performance was necessary to fill the remedial void. However, T's capacity to intervene in this case was fortuitous: if the aunt had not been B's successor *qua* administrator, she would have remained a simple 'third party beneficiary', unable to obtain direct relief at the suit of B. T, the aunt, would then have been reliant on B's decision whether to sue A on T's behalf (no trust of a promise had arisen in this case: see 7.09). If the facts of *Beswick* v. *Beswick* were to recur after the 1999 Act (7.22), T could obtain specific performance in her own name, whether or not T was also B's administrator.

7.19 *Damages: general rule.* 'The *Woodar* rule'[49] states that B, the promisee, can obtain compensation from A *only for B's personal loss and not for T's loss*. This means that unless B can show personal loss, A is effectively let off the hook. Although criticised,[50] this rule remains the orthodox starting point in this field.[51] However, the rule is hedged around with numerous exceptions.[52] In the next paragraph we will examine the main exception to the *Woodar* rule, where A performs building or repair work under contract with B, but the true victim of the breach is T, who is (or has become) the owner of the relevant property.

Instead of creating a set of exceptions to the basic *Woodar* rule, the Common Law might – and arguably should – have adopted the opposite starting point: that B can obtain compensation on T's behalf, *provided B is furthermore required to hand this money to T* (this might have been easily achieved, for example, by requiring B and T to be joined in the action against A, and the court requiring A to pay damages to T directly).

48 On the underlying factors in this case, see N. Andrews, 'Does a Third Party Beneficiary Have a Right in English Law?' (1988) LS 14, 28–33.

49 Affirmed by dicta in *Woodar Investment Development Ltd* v. *Wimpey Construction UK Ltd* [1980] 1 WLR 227, 283–4, 291, 293, 297, 300, HL.

50 In *Alfred McAlpine Construction Ltd* v. *Panatown* [2001] 1 AC 518, 538, 544D, HL, Lord Goff doubted the proposition, drawing upon G. H. Treitel (1998) 114 LQR 527.

51 A. Burrows, 'No Damages for a Third Party's Loss' (2001) 1 *Oxford University Commonwealth Law Journal* 107, 108, cites *Beswick* v. *Beswick* [1968] AC 58, HL, and *White* v. *Jones* [1995] 2 AC 207, HL, as other instances of the *Woodar* rule.

52 In *Alfred McAlpine Construction Ltd* v. *Panatown* [2001] 1 AC 518, 581–2, HL, Lord Millett examined these exceptional situations.

7.20 *The main exception to the* Woodar *rule: building contracts.*[53] A trilogy of cases (*Linden Gardens Trust Ltd* v. *Lenesta Sludge Disposals Ltd (St Martins Property Corporation Ltd* v. *Sir Robert McAlpine Ltd)* (1994);[54] *Darlington Borough Council* v. *Wiltshier Northern Ltd* (1995);[55] and the *Panatown* case, 2001)[56] concerns either of the following situations: B pays for A's building work (or repair to a building). A's work is defective. A has breached his contract with B. Certainly, B has a contractual claim against A, but T, a non-party, is the true victim either (1) because T acquired title to the relevant site or building *before the breach was discovered*; or (2) because T at all stages owned the property, but B paid for the work, for T's benefit; B would act as paymaster either so that VAT could be (legitimately) avoided (as in the *Panatown* case, below) or so that T, a local authority, could (again legitimately) sidestep local government borrowing restrictions upon T (as in the *Darlington* case, below). The present exception permits B to obtain compensation on T's behalf (normally the cost of cure measure of compensation; see 18.11 on this type of claim), provided T has no direct contractual claim against A. The damages recovered by B are intended to be used to finance repair work contemplated by T or already executed by T.

These building cases extended an early nineteenth-century exception (in *Dunlop* v. *Lambert* (1839))[57] to the (long-standing) *Woodar* rule. The *Dunlop* case (1839) concerned the promisee's capacity to sue on behalf of a *transferee of goods*. The problem examined in *Dunlop* v. *Lambert* (1839) arises when goods are damaged or lost in transit during performance of a contract of carriage between carrier A and owner B. A is liable for breach to B. But B has transferred title to the goods after the contract of carriage was formed between A and B. Thus B owned them at the start of their journey, but T, the third party, by the end. In 'The Albazero' (1977),[58] the House of Lords held that the rule in the *Dunlop* case (1839) allows B to obtain damages on T's behalf only if T has no direct claim against A. Such a direct claim might arise under a bill of lading.

It is convenient to focus on the third in this trilogy, the *Panatown* decision (2001).[59] Here B's action proved unsuccessful because in fact T had a direct contractual claim against A (the A-T link rested on a deed given by A to T). That was fatal to B's attempt to invoke the exception to the *Woodar* rule (that exception remains good law and is supported by *Linden Gardens Trust Ltd* v. *Lenesta Sludge Disposals Ltd* (1994)[60] and *Darlington*

---

53 E. McKendrick, 'The Common Law at Work: The Saga of Alfred McAlpine Construction Ltd v. Panatown' (2003) 3 *Oxford University Commonwealth Law Journal* 145; G. H. Treitel, (1998) 114 LQR 527; I. Duncan Wallace, (1999) 115 LQR 394; H. Unberath, (1999) 155 LQR 535; G. McMeel, [1999] *Restitution Law Review* 21; see discussion at 8.09 of *Offer-Hoar* v. *Larkstore Ltd* [2006] EWCA 1079; [2006] 1 WLR 2926.
54 [1994] 1 AC 85, HL (summarised in the *Panatown* case, [2001] 1 AC 518, 540–2, HL).
55 [1995] 1 WLR 68, CA (summarised in the *Panatown* case, [2001] 1 AC 518, 540–2, HL).
56 [2001] 1 AC 518, HL.
57 (1839) 6 Cl & F 600, HL (Sc); on which see the *Panatown* case, [2001] 1 AC 518, 523 ff, HL.
58 [1977] AC 774, 847–8, HL, *per* Lord Diplock.
59 *Panatown* case, [2001] 1 AC 518, HL; noted by B. Coote, (2001) 117 LQR 81; A. Burrows, (2001) 1 *Oxford University Commonwealth Law Journal* 107.
60 [1994] 1 AC 85, HL (summarised in the *Panatown* case, [2001] 1 AC 518, 540–2, HL).

Borough Council v. *Wiltshier Northern Ltd* (1995).[61] The House of Lords held, by a majority (Lords Clyde,[62] Jauncey[63] and Browne-Wilkinson[64]), that A was not liable to pay B substantial damages. This was because A was liable to T under the deed of due care. According to the '*Albazero*' exception (see '*The Albazero*' (1977))[65] to the rule in *Dunlop* v. *Lambert* (1839),[66] B can obtain damages from A on behalf of T only if T has no direct contractual claim against A.

It is not clear whether the '*Albazero*' exception would be relevant where T has acquired a direct right of action under the Contracts (Rights of Third Parties) Act 1999.

But the better view is that T's right of action under the 1999 Act (under either limb 1 or 2: 7.27 ff) should not be a bar to B's '*Dunlop* v. *Lambert/Linden Gardens Trust*' claim for damages on T's behalf. That conclusion is supported by the double fact (i) that the Act (section 4) preserves the rights of the promisee (suggesting that the promisee's capacity should remain intact and thus B should continue to obtain damages on T's behalf under the '*Dunlop* v. *Lambert/Linden Gardens Trust*' exception to the rule in *Woodar* v. *Wimpey*) and (ii) the reference in section 5 to the recovery by B of damages on T's behalf. These features of the Act point clearly towards the conclusion that B should continue to obtain damages on T's behalf in this building contract context.

'*The Albazaro*' case's restriction is clearly intended to protect A against double liability (successive claims by B and T).

It is submitted that normally the solution to the restriction in '*The Albazero*' is to allow T to be joined as a party to the proceedings and to undertake not to sue A on the deed of care. That would remove the '*Albazero*' obstacle. This would leave the door open for B to obtain damages on T's behalf and thus enable the repair work to be carried out.

But since T is not party to the arbitration agreement between A and B, such an arrangement could not be set up (and neither section 8(1) nor section 8(2) of the Contracts (Rights of Third Parties) Act 1999 will assist T so as to render T party to the arbitration: 7.46). And so the '*Albazero*' objection would continue to prevail.

Query whether it would be enough, if T cannot be joined as party to the arbitration, for T unilaterally to undertake by deed with A or B that T has cancelled, or will not invoke, the deed of due care?

The *Panatown* decision (2001) concerned these facts. In 1989, A, a construction company, agreed with B to build an office block in Cambridge for approximately £10m. At all stages, T owned the site. B was a subsidiary company of T, the true owner. T had (legitimately) used B as a financial conduit to avoid VAT on the construction contract.[67] The result was that T, the site's owner, was a third party to the main building contract. A and B's contract included both an arbitration clause (committing A and B to use only arbitration rather than court proceedings, in the event of a dispute) and a liquidated damages clause, which gave B £35,000 a week for late completion.[68]

---

61 [1995] 1 WLR 68, CA (summarised in the *Panatown* case, [2001] 1 AC 518, 540–2, HL).
62 *Panatown* [2001] 1 AC 518, 531–2, 536, HL.
63 *Ibid.*, at 567–8.
64 *Ibid.*
65 [1977] AC 774, 847–8, HL, *per* Lord Diplock.
66 (1839) 6 Cl & F 600, HL (Sc); on which see the *Panatown* case, [2001] 1 AC 518, 523 ff, HL.
67 *Panatown* [2001] 1 AC 518, 537, HL.
68 *Ibid.*, at 554.

There was also a collateral contract (a 'deed') directly between A and T, the owner, whereby A, the builder, undertook to exercise reasonable care when performing the construction work. This deed was intended to enable T to assign the benefit of the deed to a purchaser in due course (no such sale in fact occurred). T's lawyers had advised that assignment of such a deed would be necessary because T and its successors would have no action in the tort of negligence for pure economic loss.[69]

A's building work was so defective that it was not until 2003 that the offices were fit for use. A had clearly breached the building contract.

In 1992, B brought an arbitration claim against A for breach of contract, seeking (1) substantial damages for the cost of rectifying the work and (2) damages for loss of profit caused by their inability to let the commercial property. There were two reasons why B had sued A (rather than T suing A under the deed). First, the A/B contract contained a set of strict obligations, but the A/T deed merely imposed a duty of care. Secondly, only the A/B contract (and not the A/T deed) was subject to an arbitration clause. Many companies prefer arbitration to High Court litigation. Arbitration offers the twin benefits of confidentiality and the choice of decision-maker(s), whereas court proceedings take place in public and the judge is randomly selected by the court system rather than by the litigants. Arbitration also offers the prospect (sadly, not always realised) of greater efficiency and speed.[70]

The *Panatown* case contains additional discussion of the nature of the damages recoverable by B when the exception is successfully invoked. The better view (the so-called 'narrow view') is that those damages are obtained precisely to fill the remedial gap which would otherwise exist before the advent of the 1999 Act: that T would lack a direct right of action on the contract between A and B, and B would not have suffered personal loss.

In favour of the narrow view: The logic of the *Dunlop* v. *Lambert* (1839)[71] exception (above) is that B is suing *on behalf of T*, and so B *must account to T* for compensation obtained from A. Lords Clyde and Jauncey in the *Panatown* case (2001) were correct to state that when T is both owner of the site and financier of the project, B's damages claim against A must be for *compensation to remedy T's loss*: the so-called 'narrow view' adopted by the House of Lords in the *Linden Gardens* case (1994) as an exception to the *Woodar* rule. This analysis would 'fit' both heads of claim brought by B, but economically suffered by T: *the cost of cure and loss of rental*.

The dissenting judges, Lords Goff[72] and Millett,[73] considered that the '*Albazero*' exception was irrelevant because B should here be treated not as seeking damages on behalf of T but as seeking damages on B's personal behalf.

Against the 'broad view': This approach encounters the following five difficulties.

---

69   *D & F Estates Ltd* v. *Church Commissioners for England and Wales* [1989] AC 177, HL.
70   *Andrews on Civil Processes* (Cambridge, 2013), vol. 2, *Arbitration and Mediation*, chapters 3 and 4, for an outline of arbitration and its attractiveness.
71   (1839) 6 Cl & F 600, HL (Sc).
72   *Panatown* [2001] 1 AC 518, 546–51, HL.
73   *Ibid.*, at 585–92.

(1) The analysis suggested by Lords Goff and Millett, just summarised, can apply only if in fact B has suffered personal loss. That possibility arises only if B has already incurred the expenditure of carrying out repair work or has already hired a new builder to do the repair work and has incurred a liability to pay that builder in due course. In the absence of such upfront loss the most that B can show is that he has an expectation that A should pay for the work to be done. The law should not take the risk of requiring A to pay that sum to B in the hope (the law crossing its fingers) that B will use the money to finance the repair work. And so the law requires that damages recovered by B must be intended for T's benefit. Therefore, those damages in this context must fall within the *Dunlop* v. *Lambert* (1839) exception,[74] and so the '*Albazero*' (1977)[75] obstacle must arise.

(2) Although some commentators suggest that the 'broad view' was also supported by Lord Browne-Wilkinson, his comment was hesitant: 'I will assume that the broader ground is sound in law.'[76]

(3) The 'broad view' approach can be traced to Lord Griffiths' minority speech in the *Linden Gardens* case (1994).[77] That judge's suggestion that B can obtain the cost of cure measure is ambiguous. It might mean (uncontroversially) that the cost of cure will be awarded provided the court is satisfied that this repair is in fact intended. An alternative reading is that B can recover the cost of cure measure of damages *in his own name, no legal strings being attached, so that B can then use that sum howsoever he wishes*. We will call this last approach the 'radical broad view'. The other judges in the *Linden* case (1994) had sensibly refrained from endorsing this last approach.

The 'radical broad view' is not the law. Burrows, a leading authority, says that if B were to retain the cost of cure compensation in his own name, this would be absurd and wrong in principle, for a breach of contract is not necessarily a ground for awarding substantial loss,[78] merely a basis for nominal damages. To gain 'substantial damages', the claimant must prove actual loss.[79] *This must be B's loss, unless an exception to the* Woodar *rule* (above) *applies*.

Burrows' analysis is consistent with remarks by Judge Toulmin QC in *Mirant Asia-Pacific Construction (Hong Kong) Ltd* v. *Ove Arup & Partners International Ltd* (2007): that B cannot receive the cost of cure measure of damages unless he can show that *this money has already been used, or will be used, to effect the necessary repair*.[80]

(4) Even the so-called 'broad view' proponents, Lords Goff and Millett, devised arguments to ensure that B would hold the cost of cure for the benefit of T, who had initially financed the project. Lord Millett suggested that B's substantial damages would 'almost certainly be held on trust to apply them at the direction of the group company [T] which provided the building finance'.[81] Employing a similar technique, Lord Goff contended that B would be obliged under an implied term to hand this money to T.[82] All of this shows that where the repair work is to be financed by T, B should be treated as obtaining damages on T's behalf.

(5) Another problem with the 'radical broad view' is that it would not work at all in situations concerning loss of rental suffered when a commercial property is finished very late. This was the

---

74 (1839) 6 Cl & F 600, HL (Sc); on which see the *Panatown* case, [2001] 1 AC 518, 523 ff, HL.

75 [1977] AC 774, 847–8, HL, *per* Lord Diplock.

76 *Panatown* [2001] 1 AC 518, at 577.

77 [1994] 1 AC 85, 96–7, HL (paragraph numbering added).

78 A. Burrows, 'No Damages for a Third Party's Loss' (2001) 1 *Oxford University Commonwealth Law Journal* 107, 109 ff.

79 *Ibid.*, at 113.

80 [2007] EWHC 918 (TCC); [2008] Bus LR D1, at [630] (referring also, *ibid.*, at [625], to his discussion of the *Panatown* case in *Catlin Estates Ltd* v. *Carter Jonas* [2005] EWHC 2315 (TCC); [2006] PNLR 273).

81 *Panatown* [2001] 1 AC 518, at 592.

82 *Panatown* [2001] 1 AC 518, at 560.

second possible head of claim in the *Panatown* case (2001) (the A/B contract contained a liquidated damages clause quantifying compensation under this head). It would make no sense to attribute this loss to B, who had no power to grant leases of the building.

7.21 *Two more remedies: a declaration and a stay of proceedings.* Finally, if A has promised B that *A will not bring proceedings against T,* B might be able to obtain a declaration or 'stay' of the proceedings (thereby halting those proceedings) to protect the intended third party. *Snelling v. John Snelling Ltd* (1973), noted at 18.39, illustrates this).[83] When seeking such a declaration or stay, B must show that the relief is necessary to protect his own legitimate interest.[84]

However, in this situation, it would now be possible for T, if wrongfully sued by A, to obtain under the 1999 Act (7.22 ff) a declaration or a stay (thereby halting the wrongful proceedings) without T having to rely on B to intervene as a party to the wrongful proceedings to seek a stay on T's behalf.

6. THE CONTRACTS (RIGHTS OF THIRD PARTIES) ACT 1999

7.22 The Act[85] enables T to obtain a direct right of action against A. As we shall see, this direct right of action arises if (1) A and B expressly confer this right on T, or (2) if A and B's contract 'purports to confer a benefit' on T and there is no contrary indication to negative an implied wish that T should have a direct right of action against A. The Act's direct right of action coexists with B's right of action against A at Common Law (on which see the preceding section 5 of this chapter). Commentators refer to (1) as 'limb 1' and to (2) as 'limb 2' (7.27 ff).

7.23 The Act applies to most transactions. But there are five classes of contract where it was felt that the Act might unduly interfere with a settled scheme of rules:[86]

(1) contracts in bills of exchange, promissory notes or other negotiable instruments;[87]

(2) contracts falling within section 14 of the Companies Act 1985;[88]

---

83 [1973] QB 87, Ormrod J.

84 *Gore* v. *Van der Lann* [1967] 2 QB 31, CA.

85 N. Andrews, 'Strangers to Justice No Longer: The Reversal of the Privity Rule under the Contracts (Rights of Third Parties) Act 1999' [2001] CLJ 353–81; H. Beale, 'A Review of the Contracts (Rights of Third Parties) Act 1999', in A. Burrows and E. Peel (eds.), *Contract Formation and Parties* (Oxford, 2010) 225; A. S. Burrows, [2000] LMCLQ 540–54; C. MacMillan, (2000) 63 MLR 721–38; A. Phang, (2002) 18 JCL 32; R. Stevens, (2004) 120 LQR 292–323 (who bemoans its enactment); Law Commission, 'Privity of Contract: Contracts for the Benefit of Third Parties' (Law Commission Report No. 242, Cm 3329, London, 1996), notably Parts VII–XI; V. V. Palmer, 'Contracts in Favour of Third Persons in Europe' (2003) 11 *European Review of Private Law* 8–27.

86 *Treitel* (13th edn, London, 2011), 14–113 to 14–115.

87 Section 6(1) of the 1999 Act.

88 Section 6(2) of the 1999 Act. Section 14 of the Companies Act 1989 ('Effect of memorandum and articles') is now section 33 of the Companies Act 2006.

(3) terms in contracts of employment purporting to enable a third party to sue an employee, or in a worker's contract to sue a 'worker', or in a relevant contract against an agency worker;[89]

(4) terms purporting to enable a third party to sue in the case of carriage of goods by sea;[90]

(5) carriage of goods by rail, road or air, where an international transport convention applies.[91]

Categories (1) to (3) are wholly unaffected by the new legislation. Categories (4) and (5) are unaffected by the 1999 Act as far as active claims by the third party are concerned: but, in the case of categories (4) and (5), terms conferring the benefit of exemption clauses on third parties are covered by the 1999 Act (this 'exception to an exception' is a point of great importance: see 7.49 below).

7.24 *Commencement.* For most contracts, the 1999 Act first operated only from 11 May 2000 (although slightly earlier contracts could expressly incorporate the Act).[92]

7.25 *Naming or other identification of third parties.* Section 1(3) of the Act states:

> *The third party must be expressly identified in the contract by name, as a member of a class or as answering a particular description but need not be in existence when the contract is entered into.*

The provision makes clear that T need not exist when the contract is formed. Therefore, third parties under the Act can include future companies or children not yet born, or indeed not yet conceived.

7.26 Section 1(3) (see above) recognises three modes of identifying T: where T is: (1) 'expressly identified in the contract by name'; or (2) 'as a member of a class'; or (3) 'as answering a particular description', for example, 'employees of B' or 'subcontractors and agents of B'. Modes (2) and (3) were considered by the Court of Appeal in *Avraamides* v. *Colwill* (2006), where it was held that the court will not be prepared to resolve confused or ambiguous references to possible categories of third party beneficiaries.[93]

In greater detail, in *Avraamides* v. *Colwill* (2006), B had earlier contracted to refurbish T's two bathrooms. By a separate transaction, a 'transfer agreement' between A and B, A received B's assets and A assumed B's liabilities. The relevant clause provided: 'The purchaser undertakes to complete outstanding customer orders ... and to pay in the normal course of time any liabilities properly incurred by the company as at 31 March 2003.' T contended that this meant that A had assumed responsibility for B's imperfect performance of B's contract with T.

---

89 Section 6(3) and (4).
90 Section 6(5)(a), (6) and (7); the Carriage of Goods by Sea Act 1992 already deals with third party rights of positive suit in this context.
91 Section 6(5)(b) and (8) of the 1999 Act; Law Commission, 'Privity of Contract: Contracts for the Benefit of Third Parties' (Law Commission Report No. 242, Cm 3329, London, 1996), 12.12 ff.
92 Section 10(2) and (3) of the 1999 Act.
93 [2006] EWCA Civ 1533; [2007] BLR 76.

But the Court of Appeal, applying the present requirement that T has to be expressly identified in the contract by name, class, or by description, regarded A and B's agreement as too vague to satisfy this test. In effect there were non-matching descriptions in this case: (i) customers; and (ii) persons to whom company B had 'properly' incurred 'liability'. Class (ii) was potentially wider than (i); alternatively class (ii) might have been narrower than class (i) if class (ii) were confined to persons to whom it was already apparent at the time of the asset sale that B had 'properly' incurred 'liability'.

Waller LJ (Leveson LJ agreeing) said[94] that 'expressly identified' in section 1(3): 'simply does not allow a process of construction or implication . . . The benefit from the obligation to pay liabilities properly incurred would benefit third parties but of a large number of unidentified classes.'

It is submitted that this statement should be revisited. Although for the purpose of section 1(3) the name, class, or description might be less than pellucid, the court should be prepared to determine whether the third party or parties are identifiable as a matter of commercial certainty. 'Expressly' should not be understood to mean 'immediately and obviously identifiable'. Instead the test should be 'identifiable with confidence, on closer examination'.

Furthermore, there is no reason why more than one class of third party beneficiary should not be included. And a person might qualify under one or under more than one class. On the facts of the *Avraamides* case, where the 1999 Act point was raised late and seems to have been poorly argued, it is submitted that liability for defective bathroom work should have been held to have fallen under either class (i) ('outstanding customer orders') or class (ii) 'liabilities properly incurred . . . as at 31 March 2003'.

This was a limb 2 case (on this limb see 7.29 ff below). The decisive question should have been whether the parties to the transfer agreement, while purporting to confer a benefit on these classes of third party, could counter the presumption that they had an intention to grant third parties a direct right of action. Waller LJ made this comment on this point:[95] 'I am actually doubtful whether it can be said that this agreement, on its true construction, was one under which it was intended that any persons with rights against the company were to be able to enforce them directly against the appellants.'

7.27 *Test for identifying a third party's rights.* Subsections 1(1) and 1(2) of the Act state:

(1) *Subject to the provisions of this Act, a person who is not a party to a contract (a 'third party') may in his own right enforce a term of the contract if –*

    (a) *the contract expressly provides that he may, or*

    (b) *subject to subsection (2), the term purports to confer a benefit on him.*

(2) *Subsection (1)(b) does not apply if on a proper construction of the contract it appears that the parties did not intend the term to be enforceable by the third party.*

Thus, a statutory third party right will arise if *either*:

Limb 1 A and B have expressly stated that T should have a right of action against A (see further the next paragraph);

or

Limb 2 the contract between A and B 'purports to confer a benefit on' the third party and A fails to show any reason to negative T's presumptive direct right of action against A (see further 7.29 and 7.30).

---

94 *Ibid.*, at [19].
95 *Ibid.*, at [20].

7.28 As for limb 1, T might enjoy a right of action even though T is not personally benefited by A's performance, because T is to take as trustee for X.[96] Limb 1 might also be used to confer on a third party the *benefit of an exclusion clause*, section 1(6) providing (see further 7.59 ff):

> *Where a term of a contract excludes or limits liability in relation to any matter references in this Act to the third party enforcing the term shall be construed as references to his availing himself of the exclusion or limitation.*

7.29 As for limb 2, subsections 1(1)(b) and 1(2) involve a two-stage inquiry: (1) where A and B's contract 'purports to confer' on T a 'benefit' (see further 7.30), this promise or clause is deemed furthermore to confer a right of action on T against A (or, in the case of the shield contained within an exclusion clause, T can take advantage of an exemption clause); (2) *unless* on a 'proper construction of the contract it appears that the parties did not intend the term to be enforceable by the third party'. This two-step approach was adopted by Colman J in *Nisshin Shipping Co. Ltd* v. *Cleaves & Co. Ltd* (2004),[97] and approved by the Court of Appeal in the *Laemthong* case (2005).[98]

7.30 According to the Law Commission,[99] application of limb 2 involves a distinction between a direct beneficiary and an 'incidental' one. In *Dolphin Maritime & Aviation Services Ltd* v. *Sveriges Angfartygs Assurans Forening* (2009)[100] Christopher Clarke J said:[101] 'purporting to "confer" a benefit seems to me to connote that the language used by the parties shows that one of the purposes of their bargain (rather than one of its incidental effects if performed) was to benefit the third party.' Christopher Clarke J distinguished[102] between (i) an arrangement whereby A was obliged to pay B, or to make payment to B's agent, and (ii) a situation where A and B agreed that A should pay T. In situation (i), B's agent is not a beneficiary under limb 2 of the 1999 Act, but merely a conduit: the beneficial payee is B, the principal.

In the *Dolphin* case (2009), A's sole obligation was to pay money to B, therefore T (as B's agent) could not complain under the 1999 Act and seek direct payment from A so that T could cream off his commission (T had hoped, as such a conduit, to pass the money to B, its principal, *after deducting T's commission*). That commission had not been paid directly to T by B (B was solvent, but chose not to pay the commission to T).

Clarke J noted (i) that there was no intent that T should be directly benefited under the A and B contract, and instead the primary beneficiary of A's obligation was B, the intended payee.

---

96 P. Kincaid, (1997) 12 JCL 47, 49, 55; Law Commission, 'Privity of Contract: Contracts for the Benefit of Third Parties' (Law Commission Report No. 242, Cm 3329, London, 1996), 7.5 and 7.12–7.16.
97 [2004] EWHC 2602 (Comm); [2004] 1 Lloyd's Rep 38.
98 *Laemthong International Lines Co. Ltd* v. *Abdullah Mohammed Fahem & Co.* [2005] EWCA Civ 519; [2005] 2 All ER (Comm) 167.
99 Law Commission, 'Privity of Contract: Contracts for the Benefit of Third Parties' (Law Commission Report No. 242, Cm 3329, London, 1996), 7.19 ff.
100 [2009] EWHC 716 (Comm); [2010] 1 All ER (Comm) 473; [2009] 2 Lloyd's Rep 123; (2009) 1 CLC 460, at [74] to [84].
101 *Ibid.*, at [74].
102 *Ibid.*, at [76].

The judge also noted (ii) that, at stage two of the limb 2 test, it was not shown that A and B had truly intended that T should have a direct right of action on these facts against A. In effect the decision was that T was not a creditor vis-à-vis A of the portion of the money attributable to T's commission; that A's sole creditor was B; and that from A's perspective, the commission due to T was *res inter alios acta*.

However, the difficulty revealed by the *Dolphin* case is that, for the purpose of limb 2, the imputation of a joint intention by the contracting parties to benefit a third party arises at two stages: (a) there is the threshold issue, under section 1(1)(b), whether the contract purports to confer a benefit on the third party; the word 'purports' invites speculation on the parties' intentions, objectively assessed; and so *resolution of that issue becomes complicated by objective determination whether the parties must be taken to have intended to confer a benefit*; and (b) there is the second-level inquiry under section 1(2) whether the third party was truly intended to receive an enforceable benefit.

The 'incidental benefit' problem, according to the Law Commission (1996),[103] would mean that limb 2 *would not be satisfied* on facts similar to *White v. Jones* (1995) (which antedated the Act).[104] That case concerned a contract between solicitor and client for the amendment of the client's will by codicil. The client wanted to add his two daughters, Pauline and Carole, as legatees, giving them £9,000 each. The solicitor went on holiday. By the time he returned, the testator had died and so it was too late to effect valid legacies by codicil. The prospective legatees sued the solicitor in the tort of negligence. The House of Lords, by a majority of three to two, held that the claim should succeed. The defendant solicitor had been negligent and a duty of care should be recognised in this context. Otherwise, professional negligence would go unremedied. But, in the Law Commission's view, commenting on *White v. Jones* (1995), the intended legatees are not direct third party beneficiaries, but merely 'incidental' beneficiaries. This is because A, the solicitor, agreed to confer the benefit of professional services on B, the testator, who was the *primary* beneficiary. A's performance in carrying out the changes to B's will would only incidentally benefit the intended legatees. And so, such a third party is a merely *incidental beneficiary* lying outside the compass of the 'limb 2' provision (explained above).[105]

7.31 *Third party's remedies.* If T has a right of action under the Act, he can employ (as appropriate) the remedies of debt, specific performance, damages, etc. (for an overview of remedies for breach of contract, see 18.01) in accordance with Common Law and equitable principles (and T can take advantage of any restrictions on his liability towards A contained in the promise made by A to B for T's benefit).[106] Section 1(5) of the Act states:

> *For the purpose of exercising his right to enforce a term of the contract, there shall be available to the third party any remedy that would have been available to him in an action for breach of contract if he had been a party to the contract (and the rules*

---

103 Law Commission, 'Privity of Contract: Contracts for the Benefit of Third Parties' (Law Commission Report No. 242, Cm 3329, London, 1996), 7.19 ff.

104 [1995] 2 AC 207, HL.

105 Law Commission, 'Privity of Contract: Contracts for the Benefit of Third Parties' (Law Commission Report No. 242, Cm 3329, London, 1996), 7.19 ff; cf *Beswick v. Beswick* [1968] AC 58, HL (A promises B to pay T: 7.22).

106 E.g. *Prudential Assurance Co. Ltd* v. *Ayres* [2008] EWCA Civ 52; [2008] 1 All ER 1266, on which see 7.45 (although the Court of Appeal held that T in fact acquired no such immunity on the facts).

> *relating to damages, injunctions, specific performance and other relief shall apply*
> *accordingly).*

7.32 *Specific performance.* In the case of the remedy of specific performance (7.18; more generally see 18.33 ff), the Act creates an exception to the general maxim of Equity that specific performance can only be awarded in favour of someone who has provided consideration ('Equity does not assist a volunteer', that is, a gratuitous promisee or beneficiary). The Act states that T can obtain 'specific performance'. But this must presuppose that B has furnished consideration and that the remedy of specific performance is justified on the facts because debt or damages would be insufficient to protect T. Thus, after the Act, the widow in *Beswick* v. *Beswick* (1968) (see 7.18 above) could now obtain specific performance *in her own name* as a third party.[107]

7.33 *Damages.* As for T's claims for damages, protection under the Act extends not just to his 'reliance loss' (out-of-pocket losses incurred in the belief that the contract would not be breached) but includes his 'expectation interest' (that is, the financial or other material gain that would have been achieved if the promisor had not breached the contract – generally on these types of compensatory measures, see 18.08).[108]

7.34 *Variation or rescission of the contract.*[109] Section 2(1) of the Act provides:

> *Subject to the provisions of this section, where a third party has a right under*
> *section 1 to enforce a term of the contract, the parties to the contract may not, by*
> *agreement, rescind the contract, or vary it in such a way as to extinguish or alter his*
> *entitlement under that right, without his consent if –*

(a) *the third party has communicated his assent to the term to the promisor,*
(b) *the promisor is aware that the third party has relied on the term, or*
(c) *the promisor can reasonably be expected to have foreseen that the third party would*
    rely on the term and the third party has in fact relied on it.

And so, in general, A and B will retain the power to vary or 'rescind' the contract without T's consent. But there are two 'cut-off' points at which the parties will have lost the capacity jointly to vary or extinguish the third party's rights.[110] Thus T will have already gained protection from this unfavourable cancellation or variation if: (1) T has communicated 'assent to the term' to A; or (2) T has relied on A's promise; T's reliance will count if A knew that it had occurred, or at least if it was reasonably foreseeable by A (the Law Commission said that T's reliance need not be 'detrimental').[111] As for (1), it is important to note that the assent must be communicated *not to the promisee but directly to the promisor*

---

107 [1968] AC 58, HL.
108 Law Commission, 'Privity of Contract: Contracts for the Benefit of Third Parties' (Law Commission Report No. 242, Cm 3329, London, 1996), 9.33.
109 N. Andrews, 'Strangers to Justice No Longer: The Reversal of the Privity Rule under the Contracts (Rights of Third Parties) Act 1999' [2001] CLJ 353, 361 ff.
110 *Ibid.,* at 363–6.
111 Law Commission, 'Privity of Contract: Contracts for the Benefit of Third Parties' (Law Commission Report No. 242, Cm 3329, London, 1996), 9.19.

(section 2(1)(a) of the 1999 Act states '*the third party has communicated his assent to the term to the promisor*').

> However, what if (wrongly) the promisee is notified but he then passes on that notification to the promisor? The position is unclear, but it is submitted that it should be enough that the promisor discovers, directly or otherwise, that the third party has communicated his assent. Such discovery should include the situation where the promisee is wrongly notified by the third party but the promisee then volunteers the information to the promisor. Furthermore, suppose the promisee is asked by the third party to pass the information to the promisor. A real conundrum will arise if the promisee then fails to communicate to the promisor, or attempts to do so but the communication misfires.
>
> As just explained, (1) (assent communicated by T to A) and (2) (T's reliance) are the 'cut-off points' at which A and B cease to be able 'by agreement' to 'rescind or vary' the contract so as to diminish or terminate T's interest.
>
> However, T will not have the benefit of either cut-off point if any of the following occurs (situations (i) to (iii) do not constitute examples of a contract, or part of it, being rescinded or varied 'by agreement'; and situation (iv) is also outside the scheme for protecting T):
>
> (i) a decision by A to terminate the contract following B's breach;
>
> (ii) A's decision to rescind the contract following B's misrepresentation, undue influence, non-disclosure (for example, in the case of insurance contracts);
>
> (iii) the contract is terminated by a frustrating event (which occurs automatically and by operation of law; see 16.21);
>
> (iv) furthermore, the third party cannot continue to assert rights against A if the contract, or a part of it, ceases to operate, or is suspended, in accordance with a *force majeure* clause (see 12.06 at (15)); this is because section 1(4) of the Act states: '*This section does not confer a right on a third party to enforce a term of a contract otherwise than subject to and in accordance with other relevant terms of the contract.*'
>
> As noted by the present author in a journal article,[112] the Law Commission (1996) said that A and B cannot create from the outset an irrevocable set of rights for T's benefit, although that view has been subsequently contradicted by Burrows. It is submitted that Burrows is right to suggest that an agreement which explicitly stipulates that a third party will enjoy a right under the Act without needing to consent to it, and that this right will not be revocable by A and B, should take effect as an irrevocable right. Subject to that possibility, A and B will retain the right 'by agreement, [to] rescind the contract, or vary it in such a way as to extinguish or alter [the third party's] entitlement'.

7.35 *Manifestation of assent.* Section 2(2) of the Act specifies how T's 'assent' can be manifested:

> The assent referred to in subsection (1)(a) – (a) may be by words or conduct, and (b) if sent to the promisor by post or other means, shall not be regarded as communicated to the promisor until received by him.

---

112   Andrews, [2001] CLJ 353, 362, noting Law Commission, 'Privity of Contract: Contracts for the Benefit of Third Parties' (Law Commission Report No. 242, Cm 3329, London, 1996), 946; and noting Burrows' contradiction of this in [2000] LMCLQ 540, 547 n. 22, pointing to the wide language of section 2(3)(b) of the 1999 Act, which provides: '[Subsection 2(1)] *is subject to any express term of the contract under which (a) the parties to the contract may by agreement rescind or vary the contract without the consent of the third party, or (b) the consent of the third party is required in circumstances specified in the contract instead of those set out in subsection (1)(a) to (c).*'

'Assent', if successfully communicated by T, need not be accompanied by 'reliance' on T's part. The Act also makes clear that the postal rule (3.21) *will not* apply to T's posted acceptance. And so T's 'assent' must be *received* by A. For example, on Tuesday, A and B agree that A will pay T £5,000 a month; on Wednesday, T posts a letter to A 'assenting' to this proposed payment; on Thursday, A and B agree to terminate the contract and B successfully sends T an e-mail, notifying T of this cancellation; T's letter of 'assent' arrives too late, on Friday.

7.36 *'Master clause' in favour of A and B.* A and B can insert a 'master clause' in the contract for the purpose of retaining the power to vary or extinguish T's putative rights. This clause will prevent T from gaining an irrevocable right against A. The effect is that A and B will have 'contracted out' of the general approach just summarised. Such a master clause (1) must be 'express'; (2) it must form part of the main contract ('term of the contract'); and (3) any exercise of this power should involve A and B acting 'by agreement [to] rescind or vary the contract'. Section 2(3) provides: *Subsection (1) is subject to any express term of the contract under which – (a) the parties to the contract may by agreement rescind or vary the contract without the consent of the third party, or (b) the consent of the third party is required in circumstances specified in the contract instead of those set out in subsection (1)(a) to (c).*

7.37 *Clause permitting variable selection of third party.* Here we will consider two arguments, either of which, if accepted, will have the effect that T will lack the capacity to acquire an irrevocable set of rights by reliance or 'assent'.

(1) *Treitel* (2011) suggests that T's 'assent' or 'reliance' on A and B's promise (in the manner just explained) will make no difference if the terms of A's obligation were expressed to be subject to B's direction: if A promises B to pay £x to (a nomination clause) *T1 or T2, as B decides* or A promises B to pay to *Q1 or, if B later prefers, Q2* (a substitution clause).[113] *Treitel* says: 'in such a case, . . . the contract is not varied. On the contrary, it is performed in accordance with its original terms, under which B has a choice as to the person to whom performance is to be rendered.' In other words, T1 or Q1 could not acquire irrevocable rights by 'assent' to A or reliance on A's promise.

(2) Another way of reaching the same conclusion (a right to alter A's performance without T gaining an irremovable set of rights by reliance or 'assent') is to treat such a nomination or substitution clause as a variation of the contract (contrary to *Treitel*'s argument). On this view, B's power of direction rests on an 'express term' of the contract. But for this argument to work the relevant elective or nomination clause must be an 'express term of the contract under which . . . the parties to the contract may by agreement rescind or vary the contract without the consent of the third party'. It is submitted that such a clause, since initially agreed, must be treated as entitling the relevant party to make such a nomination, even though the act of nomination is placed in the hands of only one party, whether this be the promisor or promise. On this, see the portion of section 2(3) quoted on p. 113 above.

113   *Treitel* (13th edn, London, 2011), 14–105.

7.38 *Common Law rights of promisee preserved.* Section 4 of the Act states: 'Section 1 does not affect any right of the promisee to enforce any term of the contract.' And so T's rights under the Act apply in parallel to B's existing Common Law right to sue A for breach of contract (see 7.16 ff). Thus, the following actions by promisees remain available: (1) claims for damages made by the promisee to protect a third party to receive compensation will continue to have great importance (see the *Panatown*[114] line of cases, 7.20); and (2) claims for specific performance at the suit of B. As for (2), the facts of *Beswick* v. *Beswick* (1968)[115] (7.18) would now involve two alternative routes to justice: B (the uncle's estate) could still sue A and obtain specific performance on those facts, as the House of Lords held in that case; or T, the widow, could sue A directly under limb 2 (7.29) of the Act and obtain *specific performance* without relying on B to take the initiative.

7.39 *Parallel third party rights of action not ousted.* Section 7(1) of the Act preserves 'any right or remedy of a third party that exists or is available apart from the Act'. This refers to any other statutory right or trust-of-a-promise entitlement enabling T to sue A directly. We will return to this overlap in discussion of the *Nisshin* case at 7.46.

7.40 *Right of defence or set-off connecting A and T.* If A is sued by T, A can raise against T any 'defence or set-off' or 'counter-claim' pertaining *as between A and T directly* (unless the contract provides otherwise).[116] If, for example, the A/B contract provides that A should pay T £1m, but in a separate transaction T had incurred a debt to A of £100,000, satisfaction of T's claim against A under the Act will be reduced to take into account (by way of 'set-off') the latter sum. Section 3(4) of the Act states:

> *The promisor shall also have available to him – (a) by way of defence or set-off any matter, and (b) by way of counter-claim any matter not arising from the contract, that would have been available to him by way of defence or set-off or, as the case may be, by way of counter-claim against the third party if the third party had been a party to the contract.*

7.41 *Right of defence or set-off connecting A and B.* T's right of action is *subject to the same rights of defence or set-off that A would enjoy if A had instead been sued by B under the same contract* (unless the contract provides otherwise). Section 3(2) of the Act makes this clear:

> *The promisor shall have available to him by way of defence or set-off any matter that – (a) arises from or in connection with the contract and is relevant to the term, and (b) would have been available to him by way of defence or set-off if the proceedings had been brought by the promisee.*

114 [2001] 1 AC 518, HL.
115 [1968] AC 58, HL.
116 See section 3(5) of the 1999 Act for this last point.

The following situations illustrate how section 3(2) of the Act works:

(1) *Defence (A/B contract voidable).* If B makes a misrepresentation which entitles A to rescind the contract (for the remedy of rescission in this context, see 9.26), and T sues A under the Act, section 3(2) (quoted in the previous paragraph) allows A to raise against T the defence of rescission.

(2) *Defence (condition precedent to A's liability).* Here, A has promised to pay £1,000 to T *if B first pays £5,000 to T*, and B has defaulted; T sues A under the Act; section 3(2) allows A to raise the defence that B's performance is a condition precedent to A's duty to pay.

(3) *Set-off.* Suppose that in clause 99 of a contract, A has promised B to pay £2m to T; but B has incurred a debt to A of £1m under clause 98 of the same contract. Section 3(2) would allow A to set off the £1m owed by B to A when T asks A to pay T the £2m. This is because that right of set-off 'arises from . . . the contract' between A and B in which T is also to be benefited. But *it would be different* if the £1m owed by B to A arose under *a separate contract* having no factual connection with the A/B/T contract. In this last situation, T's action against A would not be subject to A's set-off.

(4) *Defence or set-off: further permutation.* Section 3(2) is the 'default' rule concerning defences and set-off. That default position will not apply if section 3(3) applies. Section 3(3) provides that *if A and B expressly stipulate*, A can enjoy any defence against T's action, *including any right of set-off*, that A would have vis-à-vis B. Section 3(3) will then widen the scope of set-off available to A, so as to cover all sums owed by B to A, even if the relevant liability arose *outside and has no connection with the A/B/T transaction* (see the narrow wording of section 3(2), set out above).

7.42 *Rule excluding 'double compensation' for the same loss.* Section 5 of the Act prevents A being at risk of 'double jeopardy' for the same loss, that is, liability to B at Common Law and liability to T in a claim brought under the Act. Section 5 provides:

> *Where under section 1 a term of a contract is enforceable by a third party, and the promisee has recovered from the promisor a sum[117] in respect of – (a) the third party's loss in respect of the term, or (b) the expense to the promisee of making good to the third party the default of the promisor, then in any proceedings brought in reliance on that section by the third party, the court shall reduce any award to the third party to such extent as it thinks appropriate to take account of the sum recovered by the promisee.*

Three issues arise. First, this provision does not bar a second action by T, but merely instructs the relevant tribunal not to award a double measure of compensation in respect of the same loss.[118] The draftsman seems to have had in mind a 'follow-up' action by T to gain the 'cost of cure' measure of damages, B having already been awarded this sum at Common Law. Here, section 5

---

117 The phrase 'sum recovered' would not include a non-monetary order (specific performance, injunction, declaration, etc.).

118 On this point, see the preceding footnote.

would prevent A from having to pay both B and T the *double* cost of rectifying the defective building on facts similar to the *Panatown* case (7.20).

Secondly, if *B sues first and fails to obtain relief in respect of his loss*, the Act does not prevent T from *successfully suing* A in a second action in respect of the same breach. Successive judgments, by B and T, are possible, although double recovery by B and T is prevented.

Finally, there is the question, 'what if T sues A first and then B sues A?' Here, the Act is silent. The Law Commission thought this a 'non-problem', and commented: 'Nor will there be a problem if the third party first recovered damages because then the promisee would be left with no corresponding loss outstanding.'[119]

7.43 *Limitation of actions.* Section 7(3) applies the contractual limitation periods to claims by the third party founded upon the present Act: six years for ordinary ('simple')[120] contracts and twelve years for deeds (5.03).[121]

7.44 *Exclusion of the Act by the contracting parties.* A and B can insert a clause which excludes the Act, for example:

> The parties to this agreement do not intend that any term of this agreement shall be enforceable by any person who is not a party to this agreement and, accordingly, section 1(1)(b) of the Contracts (Rights of Third Parties) Act 1999 does not apply to any term of this agreement (and any amendments, alterations or supplements to it).

The Act does not spell out this possibility. But the power is implicit and the Law Commission itself discussed this.[122] In fact, many commercial documents contain a clause excluding the Act. This avoids doubt whether non-parties were intended to acquire rights under limb 2 of the Act (7.29).

7.45 *Failure to exclude the Act giving rise to a dispute concerning 'limb 2'.* An example of litigation generated by failure to exclude the 1999 Act is *Prudential Assurance Co. Ltd* v. *Ayres* (2008), where the Court of Appeal reversed Lindsay J's decision that a third party was entitled under limb 2 to a promise granting immunity from liability to pay rent (7.29).[123]

The case concerned a lease which included a special term contained in a clause shielding the tenant partnership from ordinary liability for rent. The judge at first instance (Lindsay J) had upheld a claim based on limb 2 of the 1999 Act. In his view, this clause 'purported' to benefit a

---

119 Law Commission, 'Privity of Contract: Contracts for the Benefit of Third Parties' (Law Commission Report No. 242, Cm 3329, London, 1996), 11.16.
120 Section 5 of the Limitation Act 1980.
121 Section 8 of the Limitation Act 1980 refers to actions on 'specialties', for example, a deed.
122 Law Commission, 'Privity of Contract: Contracts for the Benefit of Third Parties' (Law Commission Report No. 242, Cm 3329, London, 1996), 7.18(iii).
123 [2008] EWCA Civ 52; [2008] 1 All ER 1266 (reversing Lindsay J).

third party Z, an assignee of the relevant lease. Fortunately, on appeal, this curious result was reversed. The Court of Appeal held that the contract's reference to a third party was a drafting error.

7.46 *Arbitration clauses and the 1999 Act.* Section 8 of the Act (introduced at the eleventh hour[124] of the Parliamentary process to deal with arbitration[125] disputes arising under the Act) states:

> *(1) Where – (a) a right under section 1 to enforce a term ('the substantive term') is subject to a term providing for the submission of disputes to arbitration ('the arbitration agreement'), and (b) the arbitration agreement is an agreement in writing for the purposes of Part 1 of the Arbitration Act 1996, the third party shall be treated for the purposes of that Act as a party to the arbitration agreement as regards disputes between himself and the promisor relating to the enforcement of the substantive term by the third party.*
>
> *(2) Where – (a) a third party has a right under section 1 to enforce a term providing for one or more descriptions of dispute between the third party and the promisor to be submitted to arbitration ('the arbitration agreement'), (b) the arbitration agreement is an agreement in writing for the purposes of Part I of the Arbitration Act 1996, and (c) the third party does not fall to be treated under subsection (1) as a party to the arbitration agreement, the third party shall, if he exercises the right, be treated for the purposes of that Act as a party to the arbitration agreement in relation to the matter with respect to which the right is exercised, and be treated as having been so immediately before the exercise of the right.*

Section 8(1) was applied in *Nisshin Shipping Co. Ltd* v. *Cleaves & Co. Ltd* (2003).[126] The subtleties of sections 8(1) and 8(2) were further examined by the Court of Appeal in *Fortress Value Recovery Fund I LCC* v. *Blue Skye Special Opportunities Fund LLP* (2013)[127] and that (somewhat elaborate) discussion is noted in the text below.

Nisshin Shipping Co. Ltd v. *Cleaves & Co. Ltd* (2003)[128] demonstrates two things: (i) that when T, exercising the power conferred by section 8(1) of the 1999 Act, initiates arbitration proceedings against A, T need not join B to those proceedings; (ii) section 8(1) will work with respect to a party's right of action arising under section 1 of the 1999 Act (whether limb 1 or 2), but section 8(1) will not work with respect to a right of action arising under a trust of a promise because section 8(1) is concerned only with third party

---

124 For critical comment on section 8 of the 1999 Act, see V. V. Veeder, 'On Reforming the English Arbitration Act 1996?', in J. Lowry and L. Mistelis, *Commercial Law: Perspectives and Practice* (London, 2006), 243, at 14.12, noting on this point also A. Diamond, 'The Third Man: the 1999 Act Sets Back Separability' (2001) 17 Arb Int 211; and A. Burrows [2000] LMCLQ 540, 551 (as for section 8(2), Veeder, *ibid.*, n. 16 says that it is 'beyond judicial repair').

125 *Andrews on Civil Processes* (Cambridge, 2013), vol. 2, *Arbitration and Mediation*, chapters 3 and 4, for an outline of arbitration and its attractiveness.

126 [2003] EWHC 2602 (Comm); [2004] 1 Lloyd's Rep 38 (criticised, J. Hayton [2011] LMCLQ 565–80).

127 [2013] EWCA Civ 367; [2013] 1 WLR 3466.

128 [2003] EWHC 2602 (Comm); [2004] 1 Lloyd's Rep 38 (criticised, J. Hayton [2011] LMCLQ 565).

rights conferred under section 1 and not third party rights arising in Equity and thus independently of the 1999 Act.

In *Nisshin Shipping Co. Ltd* v. *Cleaves & Co. Ltd* (2003),[129] B chartered A's ship and T brokered this deal. The charterparty stated that T should receive a specified commission payable by A. The charterparty further provided that 'any dispute arising' between A and B should be referred to arbitration (rather than to litigation in the courts). On the facts of this case, and as conceded by counsel on the basis of House of Lords authority directly in point,[130] T also had (in addition to the 1999 Act right of action) a right under a trust of a promise to sue A (B having defaulted in his trustee duty to sue A on T's behalf) (7.11).

Colman J held that T's action under the 1999 Act could (and indeed should) be brought by arbitration, as stated in section 8(1). The arbitration would then be between T and A. There would be no need for T to join B as a party to the arbitration reference.

But section 8(1) would not help T to bring the trust of a promise claim because that subsection is only concerned with claims against A founded on section 1 of the 1999 Act. And so an action by T under the trust of a promise doctrine could not be arbitrated (the arbitration clause only applying as between A and B, and so the arbitrator would lack jurisdiction to hear a claim brought by T).

If T chose to sue A under a trust of a promise in court proceedings, joinder of A, B and T would be required (unless waived by A: 7.11 at (4) above). Would A be entitled to a stay of those proceedings by contending that B would be in breach of the arbitration agreement by participating in those court proceedings? The better view is that B's participation as co-defendant is not enough; the substance of the claim is between T and A, and B's reluctant involvement (the need for which A could in any event waive) should not justify a stay of the proceedings.

The Court of Appeal analysed both sections 8(1) and (2) of the 1999 Act in *Fortress Value Recovery Fund I LCC* v. *Blue Skye Special Opportunities Fund LLP* (2013).[131] In essence a tortious fraud claim had been made against managers (second and third defendants) of an investment company. The claim arose from an underlying agreement which comprised four elements: (a) an investment agreement to which the managers were not party; (b) the contract excluded the managers from liability; (c) the same agreement stated that third parties would be able to assert their rights under the 1999 Act; (d) issues arising under the contract were to be submitted to arbitration. The managers sought a stay (under section 9 of the Arbitration Act 1996), contending that, by a combination of elements (b) to (d), they were entitled to have the dispute heard by arbitration.

At first instance Blair J had refused the stay on the basis that the right of a defence fell outside the scope of section 8(1). The Court of Appeal upheld this denial of a stay, but for different reasons. The Court of Appeal held:

(i) section 8(1) can extend in a very clearly articulated case to the benefit of an exclusion clause;
(ii) but on the present facts Tomlinson[132] and Pill LJJ considered that the parties had not intended that T should have the procedural disadvantage of having to become party to arbitration in order to

129 *Ibid.*
130 *Les Affréteurs Réunis SA* v. *Leopold Walford (London) Ltd* [1919] AC 801, HL (applying *Robertson* v. *Wait* (1853) 8 Ex 299 which had given effect to an implied trust of a promise in this mercantile context).
131 [2013] EWCA Civ 367; [2013] 1 WLR 3466.
132 *Ibid.*, at [29] and [30], and conclusion at [36].

obtain protection of its exclusion from liability (element (d) of their agreement was not explicit enough);

(iii) Another line of reasoning was adopted by Toulson LJ who distinguished between sections 8(1) and 8(2) (although he also agreed with proposition (ii) just set out):[133]

> In summary, section 8(1) allows for [A] to give T an enforceable substantive right, subject to a procedural condition on which [A] may but need not insist. By contrast, section 8(2) allows for [A] to give T an enforceable procedural right, which T may but need not exercise (since the right is unilateral).

Thus Toulson LJ suggested that section 8(1) creates a procedural condition[134] that T must vindicate his right by arbitration *unless A waives that procedural condition*: such a waiver will occur either where T brings court proceedings and A acquiesces in this, or where A brings court proceedings against T; and so T cannot insist on arbitration under section 8(1) if A prefers to use court proceedings.

Toulson LJ noted that, by contrast, the procedural right conferred under section 8(2) confers on T a positive (but unilateral) right to demand that dealings between A and T shall be exclusively adjudicated using arbitration; T would have the right to insist on arbitration only if T had received such a unilateral right under section 8(2) (but this right had not been conferred in the present case).

7.47 *Differences between trusts of promises and direct rights of action under the 1999 Act.* As explained at 7.22 ff, the Contracts (Rights of Third Parties) Act 1999 creates a direct right of action exercisable by T against A, and section 7(1) of the Act preserves any parallel direct rights of action which T might have. Sometimes, T will have both a third party action under the Act and a trust of a promise. If so, various differences arise between these two claims:[135]

(1) Trusts of promises are irrevocable: under a trust of a promise, T acquires at the date of formation an irrevocable right; A and B cannot vary or extinguish it without T's consent. But, under the Act, A and B can agree to vary or extinguish A's rights without his consent until T has notified A or relied on A's promise.

(2) Trusts of promises are confined to money and property transfers: a trust of a promise is applicable only to promises to pay money to T or transfer property to T (and not, for example, a contract to perform services for T's benefit, nor a contract to confer on T the benefit of an exclusion clause).[136] But the Act covers *all* species of contractual obligation in favour of T and the conferring of the protection of exclusion clauses upon T.

(3) Trusts of promises require explicit creation: a trust of a promise can only be created by express language (7.09), whereas rights under the Act under 'limb 2' (7.29) can arise as an offshoot of an intent to confer a benefit on T (without the parties' express stipulation that T shall have a direct right of action).

(4) Trusts of promises litigation normally requires all three parties to participate: in litigation involving a trust of a promise, all three parties must be joined as parties, unless A 'waives'

---

133 *Ibid.*, at [45].
134 Ibid.
135 N. Andrews, 'Strangers to Justice No Longer: Reversal of the Privity Rule under the Contracts (Rights of Third Parties) Act 1999' [2001] CLJ 353, 377–8.
136 *Southern Water* v. *Carey* [1985] 2 All ER 1077, 1083G, *per* Judge David Smout QC, Official Referee.

this requirement (7.11 at (4) above). Under the Act, T can sue A without joining B as a party, whether in arbitration or in litigation.

(5) As for arbitration (7.46), section 8(1) of the Act enables T to accede to A and B's arbitration agreement, if T is suing A under section 1 of the Act. However, section 8(1) does not 'unlock the door to A and B's arbitration agreement' if T's claim is made under a trust of a promise; instead, T can bring a trust claim only by court proceedings.

7. PROTECTION OF EXCLUSION CLAUSES AT COMMON LAW AND UNDER THE 1999 ACT

7.48 *Common Law saga: the privity rule and the benefit of exclusion clauses.* In *Scruttons* v. *Midland Silicones* (1962), the House of Lords held that the privity doctrine prevents T from gaining any rights under a contract to which he is a stranger, even the 'passive' protective rights of an exclusion clause.[137]

The usual context is that A and B have agreed that A will not be free to sue T in tort (or, at least, that T's liability to A will be capped, or subject to a time bar) if T carelessly damages A's goods while they are in transit. The House of Lords in the *Scruttons* case held that the confusing decision in *Elder Dempster & Co. Ltd* v. *Paterson Zochonis & Co.* (1924) had not recognised a doctrine of 'vicarious immunity', that is, a doctrine allowing T to shelter by operation of law behind B's explicit immunity (by exclusion clause) against liability in tort towards A.[138]

The 'no shield to a third party' aspect of the *Scruttons* decision (1962) was widely criticised, and Lord Denning persuasively dissented in the case itself. The majority's decision involved two problems: (1) it was unconvincing in principle; and (2) it did not make commercial sense, because it increased the cost of insurance cover and hence increased the charges made for freight services. As the following discussion will show, the problem created by the *Scruttons* case can now be neatly countered by the 1999 Act (7.48) (a more convoluted evasion was achieved in the 1970s using Common Law devices: the *Himalaya* clause, 7.50).

7.49 *Exclusion clauses and the 1999 Act.* The Act allows the benefit of an exclusion clause to be conferred upon a third party by A and B in each of these important contexts: contracts for carriage of goods by air, sea, rail or road.[139]

7.50 *The 'Himalaya' clause upheld in the* New Zealand Shipping *case.* The Privy Council in *New Zealand Shipping Co. Ltd* v. *AM Satterthwaite & Co. Ltd ('The Eurymedon')* (1975)[140] had found a means of circumventing the rule in the *Scruttons* case (1962).[141] The essence of the

---

137 [1962] AC 446, 473, HL.

138 [1924] AC 522, HL; cf *London Drugs Ltd* v. *Kuehne & Nagel International Ltd* (1992) 97 DLR (4th) 261 (Supreme Court of Canada): third party benefited by exclusion clause; free-standing exception to privity doctrine.

139 On the special position of exclusion clauses, see sections 1(6) and 6(5) ('except that').

140 [1975] AC 154, PC.

141 [1962] AC 446, HL.

reasoning in the *New Zealand Shipping* case is that A and B can validly create a 'side contract' in favour of T, using a so-called '*Himalaya* clause',[142] thus creating *privity of contract between A and T*. Because A and T are now regarded as contracting parties, A being yoked to T, there is no direct conflict with the *Scruttons* case because that decision only prevents a *non-party* from taking the benefit of this 'shield'. Following the *New Zealand Shipping* case (1975),[143] T has lost the problematic status of a 'non-party' and has been 'bumped up' to the superior status of a 'full contractual party'.

In the *New Zealand Shipping* case (1975), A, the owner of goods (the consignor), had paid to have his goods shipped by B, the carrier (if title to the goods passes under a bill of lading, then A1, the consignor, is succeeded by A2, the consignee; A2 then stands in the shoes of A1 and is bound by the A/B and A/T contracts). In the contract of carriage between A and B, there was a cumbersome clause (the so-called '*Himalaya* clause'). This clause purported to create a shield in favour of third parties, such as firms of stevedores (companies responsible for loading and unloading ships). The clause provided:

> [N]o servant or agent of the carrier (including every independent contractor from time to time employed by the carrier) shall in any circumstances whatsoever be under any liability whatsoever to the shipper, consignee or owner and every exception, limitation, condition and liberty herein contained . . . shall also be available and shall extend to protect any such servant or agent . . . and for the purpose of all the foregoing provisions . . . the carrier is or shall be deemed to be acting as agent or trustee on behalf of and for the benefit of all persons who are or might be agents (etc).

T's crane operator negligently dropped goods into the sea and they were damaged. T, the stevedore company, then raised the exemption clause as a defence (or 'shield') against the cargo-owner A's claim in the tort of negligence for damage to A's property. By a three to two majority, the Privy Council upheld this defence in favour of T. The majority's reasoning involved these steps:[144]

(1) B acts as T's agent by inserting a *Himalaya* clause into the A/B contract;[145] that clause is an offer made by A to T, which B, as T's agent, communicates to T.

(2) There is no need for T to communicate to A acceptance of such a unilateral contract; T's performance of the condition is enough.

(3) The contractual relation between A and T is a unilateral contract: that T should have the benefit of the exemption clause in return for his work in unloading B's ship (the exclusion clause will either exclude T's liability in negligence towards A, or cap it, or impose a time limit on A's liability towards T).

(4) It does not matter that T, the stevedores, were already contractually obliged towards B to do this very same work; T provides consideration for A's promise by T's commencement of the job of unloading the ship.[146]

---

142 *Adler* v. *Dickson* ('*The Himalaya*') [1954] 2 Lloyd's Rep 267; [1955] 1 QB 158.
143 [1975] AC 154, PC.
144 For Lord Goff's overview, see '*The Mahkutai*' [1996] AC 650, PC (for details of that case, see 7.52); other overviews are in '*The Starsin*' [2004] 1 AC 715, HL, at [34], [56], [57], [93], [146] to [153], [163] and [197] to [201].
145 '*The Mahkutai*' [1996] AC 650, PC: if B is unauthorised to be T's agent, T can later ratify B's purported agency.
146 Applying *Scotson* v. *Pegg* (1861) 30 LJ Ex 225.

(5) The upshot of this is that the *Himalaya* clause creates privity of contract between A and T, and so T will no longer be a third party; there is no direct conflict with *Scruttons*, which bars only a *non-party* from taking the benefit of this 'shield'.

(6) In *The New York Star* (1981), the sequel to the *New Zealand Shipping* case (1975), the Privy Council took the sensible further step and held that if T has *already unloaded the ship*, and is storing A's goods in a warehouse, awaiting collection, the umbrella of the *Himalaya* clause continues to protect T.[147]

Lord Simon and Viscount Dilhorne dissented in the *New Zealand Shipping* case, objecting that the analysis of offer and acceptance had been quite artificially misapplied on these facts (under general 'offer and acceptance' principles (3.05), T can only accept the offer if T is aware of it).[148] These dissents, however, seem misplaced. On the facts of the *New Zealand Shipping* case, it was not fanciful to impute to T awareness of the offer, since B and T worked closely together. But, in other cases, it must be admitted that it is artificial to impute awareness to T (although in *The New York Star* (1981) the Privy Council dismissed this objection as legal pedantry).[149]

However, there are two important limits upon the operation of the *Himalaya* clause, and these will be examined in the next two paragraphs.

7.51 '*Himalaya' clause ineffective if wrongdoer a maritime 'carrier' of goods*. Does it matter that T is a 'carrier' (although not the primary carrier) of goods by sea? In *'The Starsin'* (2003), the House of Lords answered 'yes',[150] because an international maritime convention (the Hague–Visby Rules) provides that no 'maritime carrier' can exclude his liability.[151]

In *'The Starsin'* (2003), B hired T's ship to transport A's goods from port X to port Y. During the voyage, the cargo was damaged because the hold of T's ship became wet. A, the owner of the goods, did not sue B for breach of contract because B had become insolvent. Instead, A sued T. T attempted to raise an exclusion clause contained in A and B's contract in favour of T.

The House of Lords held that the Hague–Visby Rules invalidate an exclusion clause as between a cargo-owner and any 'carrier', including the ship's owner (note, however, that the Rules apply only where the exclusion clause purports to exclude or restrict the liability of a maritime 'carrier', as distinct from a stevedore or warehouseman).

7.52 '*Himalaya' clause ineffective in case of exclusive jurisdiction clauses*. The Privy Council in *'The Mahkutai'* (1996)[152] reveals another limit upon the operation of *Himalaya* clauses: the analysis used in the *New Zealand Shipping* case (1975)[153] cannot work for exclusive

147 [1981] 1 WLR 138, PC; noted by M. A. Clarke, [1981] CLJ 17; cf *Raymond Burke Motors Ltd* v. *Mersey Docks & Harbour Co.* [1986] 1 Lloyd's Rep 155 (T's negligence occurred *before* the contract of carriage began; cars in a parking 'lot' controlled by T).
148 See 3.08 on *Gibbons* v. *Proctor* and *R* v. *Clarke*.
149 [1981] 1 WLR 138, PC.
150 [2004] 1 AC 715, HL; noted by E. Peel, (2004) 120 LQR 11.
151 [2004] 1 AC 715, HL, at [32], noting Article III, Rule 8, of the Hague–Visby Rules (within Carriage of Goods by Sea Act 1971, Schedule).
152 *'The Mahkutai'* [1996] AC 650, PC.
153 [1975] AC 154, PC.

jurisdiction clauses. Lord Goff in 'The Mahkutai' distinguished between the 'mutual' phenomenon of an exclusive jurisdiction clause (binding *both parties* to a nominated forum) and the unilateral protection conferred by an exclusion clause (limiting or excluding *one party's* liability for breach). Only in the case of an exclusion clause will a *Himalaya* clause confer the benefit of the clause on stevedores, etc.

An exclusive jurisdiction clause stipulates that legal disputes arising from the relevant job or transaction can only be litigated in a nominated jurisdiction (for example, 'in the courts of Singapore'). Such a jurisdiction clause (see the AMT case [2014] EWHC 1085 (Comm) at [36]) creates mutual restrictions and mutual rights, a set of matching shields: both parties are restricted to suing in Singapore. By contrast, an exclusion clause is a single shield protecting only T: A is not intended to have this shield, and so there is no mutuality as between A and T. And so Lord Goff in 'The Mahkutai' (1996) drew a distinction between the 'mutual' phenomenon of an exclusive jurisdiction clause (binding both parties to a nominated forum) and the unilateral protection conferred by an exclusion clause (limiting or excluding one party's liability for breach).

7.53 *Exclusive jurisdiction clauses and the 1999 Act.*[154] The position concerning the 1999 Act is obscure.

Andrews (2001) examined this, and his main points are as follows.[155] Three situations must be distinguished:
(i) Unconditional burden placed on T (invalid under the 1999 Act): A and B's clause states that T can only sue A in a nominated forum. The 1999 Act will not give effect to this. The Act confers benefits: it does not confer pure burdens on third parties. A and B's contract attempts to subject T to a pure burden.
(ii) Conditional burden analysis (valid in all contexts under the 1999 Act): T is given a substantive benefit under the A/B contract, but this is subject to a jurisdictional restriction: this will be a valid restriction. Suppose A promises B that A will pay T £1m money but the A/B contract further provides that any action brought by T can only be brought in a specified forum. It appears that this jurisdiction restriction will be binding on T because it only operates conditionally: T can sue A for £1m but only if T uses the exclusive nominated forum (the analogy is section 8(1) of the 1999 Act concerning conditional benefits, subject to an arbitration clause between A and T).
(iii) Pure benefit analysis (arguably valid under the 1999 Act): The A/B contract does not contain any benefit other than A's 'jurisdictional' promise to B: that if A sues T, A will sue T only in a nominated forum. Arguably the 1999 Act will give effect to this arrangement, although the position is not entirely clear. This issue is likely to arise in the important context of carriage of goods: T will be a stevedore or a craneman. It will then be vital that the jurisdiction clause be classified as an 'exclusion or limitation' clause: only then will there be a key to unlock the 'exception to an

154   R. Merkin (ed.), *Privity of Contract* (London, 2000), 5.123–5.125; A. Burrows, 'The Contracts (Rights of Third Parties) Act 1999 and its Implications for Commercial Contracts' [2000] LMCLQ 540, 552 n. 28; on jurisdiction clauses generally, E. Peel, 'Exclusive Jurisdiction Agreements: Purity and Pragmatism in the Conflict of Laws' [1998] LMCLQ 182.
155   N. Andrews, [2001] CLJ 353, at 375–6.

exception' within categories D and E (the 1999 Act does not normally apply to contracts for carriage of goods; but to this there is an exception if the relevant term is one of exclusion or limitation; this is the result of the interplay of sections 1(6) and 6(5) of the 1999 Act). It is suggested that the jurisdiction clause in context (iii) supplies only a shield and that shield is T's shield alone. The shield protects T from liability to civil suit in any forum other than the specified jurisdiction. That defensive function mirrors the protective operation of ordinary exclusion or limitation clauses. That should lead to the conclusion that the 1999 Act will give effect to such a jurisdictional clause for the protection of T because its essence is an 'exclusion' clause. If that is accepted, such a clause will be upheld under the Act both generally and specifically within the commercial heartland of contracts for the carriage of goods.

7.54 'The Mahkutai' *decision and non-exclusive jurisdiction clauses.* A *non-exclusive* jurisdiction clause (see 12.09) empowers A and/or T to sue each other in a specified jurisdiction *in addition to* any other jurisdictions otherwise available independently of the jurisdiction clause. Such a clause has no restrictive element. Instead, it broadens by consent the available jurisdictions in which litigation can take place.[156] The Privy Council in *'The Mahkutai'* (1996)[157] did not consider this type of jurisdiction clause. If T were to sue A, relying on the combination of a *Himalaya* clause which purports to give T the benefit of a non-exclusive jurisdiction clause (whether a mutual clause or one operating solely in T's favour), it is arguable that the reasoning in *'The Mahkutai'* (1996) would not obstruct T. This is because such a non-exclusive clause contains no restriction: on the contrary, its function is to expand the choice of jurisdictions available to A and T (this is even more obviously the case if the jurisdiction clause is a *non-mutual* non-exclusive jurisdiction clause intended solely to benefit T).

8. PRIVITY OF CONTRACT AND 'BURDENS'

7.55 *General principle.* Contracts cannot be thrust on parties behind their backs. Freedom of contract (1.08), a cornerstone of private law, prevents Z ('Z' denotes the third party) from being burdened without his consent. And so X and Y cannot render Z liable for failure to act for the benefit of X or Y.

7.56 However, there are four exceptions to (perhaps better regarded as qualifications upon) this notion that Z cannot be affected detrimentally by the contractual relations between X and Y. These are: (1) the torts of inducing breach of contract and interference by unlawful means with a contract; (2) restrictive covenants affecting freehold land; (3) injunctions to prevent knowing interference with contractual rights affecting other types of property, especially goods; (4) the doctrine of 'bailment on terms'. For reasons of space, these are not examined in detail in this edition.[158]

---

156 *Deutsche Bank AG* v. *Highland Crusader Offshore Partners LP* [2009] EWCA Civ 725; [2010] 1 WLR 1023, at [50], [64], [105] and [106].
157 [1996] AC 650, PC.
158 See section 8 of Chapter 7 in the first edition, 2011.

QUESTIONS

(1) At Common Law, a third party cannot sue upon a contract (a) to which he is not a party and (b) when he has not supplied consideration. Are these arguments convincing? (For the position concerning Equity and the Contracts (Rights of Third Parties) Act 1999, see questions (2), (6) and (7) below).

(2) The trust of a promise device enabled Equity to intervene to assist third party beneficiaries in respect of promises to pay money or to transfer property. What is the current law governing this equitable device? What is the difference between the third party's position under a trust of a promise and under the Contracts (Rights of Third Parties) Act 1999?

(3) Explain (and reconcile) these propositions: (a) a promisee, party B, cannot successfully sue in debt the promisor, party A, on behalf of a third party; and yet (b) the promisee's action for specific performance in order to enforce periodic debts was successful in *Beswick* v. *Beswick*.

(4) Explain the capacity of the promisee, party B, to obtain damages against the promisor, party A, on behalf of a third party under the *'Dunlop* v. *Lambert/Linden Gardens Trust'* line of cases?

(5) Why did the promisee's, party B's, *'Dunlop* v. *Lambert/Linden Gardens Trust'* claim for damages on the third party's behalf fail in the *Panatown* case?

(6) Distinguish limbs 1 and 2 under the Contracts (Rights of Third Parties) Act 1999. What is the 'incidental benefit' problem under limb 2 of the Contract (Rights of Third Parties) Act 1999?

(7) When does the third party's right of action under the Contracts (Rights of Third Parties) Act 1999 become irrevocable (and hence survive the attempt of A and B consensually to vary or extinguish T's rights)?

(8) Explain why the elaborate '*Himalaya* clause', recognised as effective by the Privy Council in the *New Zealand* case (1975), is no longer necessary after the Contracts (Rights of Third Parties) Act 1999.

(9) 'The impact of the Contract (Rights of Third Parties) Act 1999 in respect of arbitration law and exclusive jurisdiction clauses is obscure.' Discuss.

Selected further reading

On damages at the suit of the promisee

A. Burrows, 'No Damages for a Third Party's Loss' (2001) 1 *Oxford University Commonwealth Law Journal* 107

On the Contract (Rights of Third Parties) Act 1999

N. Andrews, 'Strangers to Justice No Longer: Reversal of the Privity Rule under the Contracts (Rights of Third Parties) Act 1999' [2001] CLJ 353–81

A. S. Burrows, 'The Contracts (Rights of Third Parties) Act 1999 and its Implications for Commercial Contracts' [2000] *Lloyd's Maritime and Commercial Law Quarterly* 540–54

R. Stevens, 'The Contracts (Rights of Third Parties) Act 1999' (2004) 120 LQR 292–323 (who bemoans its enactment)

Law Commission, 'Privity of Contract: Contracts for the Benefit of Third Parties' (Law Commission Report No. 242, London, 1996), notably Parts VII–XI

Chapter contents

8

Assignment

1. INTRODUCTION

8.01 Summary of main points

(1) The holder of certain contractual rights (the promisee and assignor, B) can transfer the right to a third party (the assignee, C) without the promisor's (A's) consent.[1] Thus, where A owes B a debt or other chose in action, the right-holder, B, can assign the benefit of this right to C.

(2) In the case of a statutory assignment,[2] the assignment by B to C must be in writing, and B or C must notify A of the assignment.

(3) Such notice is also desirable in the case of equitable assignments.

(4) Certain rights are intrinsically incapable of being assigned because they are personal to the A/B relationship.

(5) A can preclude an assignment by inserting a prohibitory clause in his contract with B.

2. EFFECTS OF ASSIGNMENT

8.02 Assignment has four effects (here, A is the promisor, B is the promisee, and C is the assignee):

(1) A, once notified, is obliged to pay C.

(2) To enforce the obligation created by the assignment in C's favour, C can sue A directly, without joining B as a party to the claim. This is true of statutory assignment (8.04) and of

---

1 Main sources: A.G. Guest, *Guest on the Law of Assignment* (London, 2012); M. Smith and N. Leslie, *The Law of Assignment* (2nd edn, Oxford, 2013); G. Tolhurst, *The Assignment of Contractual Rights* (Oxford, 2006) (including Australian material); *Anson's Law of Contract* (29th edn, Oxford, 2010), chapter 22; A. P. Bell, *Modern Law of Personal Property* (London, 1989), chapter 15; *Chitty on Contracts* (31st edn, London, 2012), chapter 19; A. M. Tettenborn, 'Assignments, Trusts, Property, and Obligations', in J. W. Neyers, R. Bronaugh and S. G. A. Pitel (eds.), *Exploring Contract Law* (Oxford, 2009), 267 ff; A. M. Tettenborn, 'Problems in Assignment Law', in A. S. Burrows and E. Peel (eds.), *Contract Formation and Parties* (Oxford, 2010); and C. H. Tham, 'The Nature of Equitable Assignment and Anti-Assignment Clauses', in J. W. Neyers, R. Bronaugh and S. G. A. Pitel (eds.), *Exploring Contract Law* (Oxford, 2009), 283 ff.

2 Section 136 of the Law of Property Act 1925.

equitable assignment (8.05) of equitable choses in action. In the case of equitable assignment of a legal chose in action, such as a debt, the assignee must join the assignor as party to the claim (although there might be exceptions, where such joinder becomes unnecessary or it has been waived).[3]

(3) A's obligation to B is discharged if, pursuant to a valid assignment by B to C, A pays C in full.

(4) By contrast, if, after B's assignment of the right to C, A instead pays B, this payment is ineffective to discharge A's newly transferred obligation towards C.

3. NO ASSIGNMENT OF DUTIES

8.03 *Vicarious performance contrasted.* A promisor cannot assign the 'burden' of his obligation to another. Only rights can be assigned, and not duties. Thus, one cannot, without the promisee's consent (that is, the party entitled to contractual performance), transfer the burden of a contract from one promisor to a new party. The explanation for this is that the principle of 'freedom of contract' (1.08) gives the promisee the right to choose 'who the promisor will be', that is, he can decide who will owe him a contractual duty. But there are situations where a party, Z, cannot complain if another, X, in fact performs an outstanding contractual duty owed by Y to Z. This possibility is known as 'vicarious performance' (by X on Y's behalf, for Z's benefit). Technically, vicarious performance is consistent with the principle, stated above, that duties cannot be transferred without the consent of the person who holds the relevant right. The reason why there is no inconsistency is that where vicarious performance occurs, the duty is not transferred. In fact, the original contractual obligation between Y and Z remains intact. A legal change occurs only because Y's obligation to Z is discharged by X's performance. In this situation, X's performance was requested by Y. In effect, Y has subcontracted his task to X, who has then performed satisfactorily.

Thus it might be possible under a contract between Y and Z for Y to subcontract performance to a third party, X. X does not have this burden thrust upon him: he has assented with Y to perform the job. Nor does Z lose his contractual rights against Y. Thus, if X performs satisfactorily, Y's duty to Z is discharged; but, if X performs badly, Y will be in breach of his contract; and X might also be in breach of a tortious duty of care towards Z. Nor can Z legitimately complain that the job has been done by X and not by Y. Such an objection would be valid only if Y's personal identity were crucial to the transaction (contrast the case, for example, where University Z has hired Professor Y to give lectures for a term, but Y, without Z's permission, subcontracts to X, a young scholar of lesser renown; unknown to Z, X gives the lectures instead of Y). However, the assumption for the moment is that Y's identity was not crucial: a reasonable person in Z's position would not object to such subcontracting by Y to X.

---

3 *Chitty on Contracts* (31st edn, London, 2012), 19–038 and 19–039.

4. MODES OF ASSIGNMENT

8.04 *Statutory assignment.*[4] The requirements for assignment of a debt or other chose in action under section 136(1) of the Law of Property Act 1925 are as follows. First, B must assign *in writing* the right to C, that is, B must notify C, and effect the transfer of the contractual right, in written form; B must sign this document; there is no need for C to provide consideration for this transfer. Secondly, there must be written notice to A of the assignment (notice can be given by B or C). The 1925 Act provides that the assignment takes effect 'from the date of such notice'. Thirdly, the assignment must be 'absolute'. This means that A's duty to pay C should not be dependent on A discovering the balance of entitlement between B and C (for example, where B purports to assign so much of A's debt as is necessary to satisfy outstanding obligations owed by B to C; in this situation, the objection is that A cannot readily discover whether he still owes money to C, the assignee, because that question depends on the state of accounts between B and C).[5] Fourthly, there are restrictions on what can be assigned under this statute: (1) one cannot assign part of the debt owed by A to B (but, if B assigns the unpaid balance of A's debt, the assignment can be a valid statutory assignment because B has transferred all that remains of A's debt, and in this sense this is not a partial assignment of A's debt); (2) nor can there be a statutory assignment by way of charge upon a fund or account owed by A to B; finally, (3) the right assigned must either be an existing obligation or a right which will arise under a contract which is already operative; there cannot be a statutory assignment of a wholly prospective right.[6]

8.05 *Equitable assignment.*
(1) *Nature.* If, for some reason, an attempted statutory assignment fails, a valid equitable assignment might nevertheless occur. An equitable assignment is effective even though notice is not given to A, the debtor (contrast statutory assignment where such notice must be given to A). Nevertheless, notice to A in the case of equitable assignment is highly desirable for two reasons: first, because A is then required to pay C directly (A's payment to B, after notice of the assignment, does not discharge A's liability to pay the assignee); secondly, notice determines priority as between successive assignees. If the right assigned is a legal debt or obligation (as opposed to a purely equitable right, for example a right arising by trust or entitlement to a legacy), equitable assignment requires C to join B in any litigation to enforce A's duty. Furthermore, writing is required where the equitable assignment concerns a disposition of a subsisting equitable interest.[7] Subject to that, equitable assignment can be oral (by notification of the transfer to the assignee).

(2) *Equitable assignment can be gratuitous.* There is no need for 'consideration' (on which generally see Chapter 5) in the case of a perfected equitable assignment of an equitable right (although here writing is required: see above). As for gratuitous equitable assignment of a legal chose in action, the better view is that a perfected assignment in

---

4 Section 136(1) of the Law of Property Act 1925 (formerly section 25(6) of the Judicature Act 1873).
5 *Treitel* (13th edn, London, 2011), 15–012, explaining case law on this point.
6 *Ibid.*, at 15–025.
7 Section 53(1)(c) of the Law of Property Act 1925.

Equity can be valid even though there is no consideration and despite non-compliance with the statutory mode of assignment.[8]

(3) *Equitable assignment of a wholly prospective right.* This can take effect as an agreement to assign, but this will require C to have provided consideration to B.

8.06 *Specific statutory contexts.* Assignments of patents and copyright and various other special types of right are subject to specific rules.[9]

5. EXTENT OF THE ASSIGNED RIGHT

8.07 C's claim as assignee can be defeated if A, the main debtor, has a right as against B to rescind the relevant obligation on the basis of B's misrepresentation, non-disclosure or fraud, etc. Thus, C cannot receive as assignee a right or an interest greater than that (purportedly) transferred. For example, if B's 'right' is in fact void for mistake or illegality, C cannot be placed in any superior position vis-à-vis A. This limitation is expressed by saying that C's assigned rights are subject to any 'equities' pertaining as between A and B.[10]

8.08 Furthermore, C's rights against A are also subject to any right of set-off which A has against B arising out of the transaction between A and B. However, if the right of set-off is personal to B, C will not be subject to it, at any rate if the set-off has arisen after notice of assignment to A.[11] If A pays money to C, a valid assignee, but this money was not owing by A to B, so that A has 'overpaid', A cannot recover this payment from C if the contract between A and B provided expressly for adjustment of overpayments directly as between A and B. And A's inability to obtain repayment from the assignee C extends to the situation where B cannot repay A because B has become insolvent.

In *Pan Ocean Shipping Ltd* v. *Creditcorp Ltd ('The Trident Beauty')* (1994),[12] a charterparty between A, the charterer, and B, the owner, entitled B to recover hire from A. B assigned to C these rights to hire. The right assigned was for payment in advance of each period of hire. A paid C, in accordance with this assignment. C's receipt from A of hire covered the period when the vessel was in fact 'off-hire'. A surviving contractual clause between A and B provided that B would repay or make allowance for any over-payment. B had become impecunious. The House of Lords held that A could not recover payment from the assignee.

8.09 *The assignee can recover damages no less extensive than those to which the assignor would have been entitled if the assignment had not taken place. Offer-Hoar* v. *Larkstore Ltd*

---

8   As *Treitel* (13th edn, London, 2011), 15–035, attractively contends.
9   Sections 30 and 32 of the Patents Act 1977, and sections 90 and 94 of the Copyright, Designs and Patents Act 1988; *Chitty on Contracts* (31st edn, London, 2012), 19–003, and *Anson's Law of Contract* (29th edn, Oxford, 2010), 663.
10 *Chitty on Contracts* (31st edn, London, 2012), 19–070 ff.
11 *Anson's Law of Contract* (29th edn, Oxford, 2010), 669–70.
12 [1994] 1 WLR 161, HL.

(2006)[13] acknowledges that, following an assignment of a cause of action by a former landowner to the present owner, the assignee can recover damages no less extensive than those to which B, the assignor, would have been entitled if the assignment had not taken place. However, the assignee cannot augment the liability by bringing to the quantification of the claim factors peculiar to the assignee.[14]

In *Offer-Hoar* v. *Larkstore Ltd* (2006), the facts were as follows. In 1998, A, the promisor, had made a soil report on a site for B, the eventual assignee. The report contained no clause prohibiting assignment. In 1999, B transferred the site to C, a developer. In 2001, damage occurred when there was a landslide on this site. A's failure in A's report to alert B to this danger was a breach of contract. In 2004, B assigned to C the benefit of B's cause of action in respect of A's breach of contract.

The Court of Appeal held that A could not defeat C's claim by saying that the value of C's assignment rights was capped by the amount of loss suffered by B. The rights assigned included the right to compensation in respect of losses as they might unfold from the time the breach of contract had occurred. That liability might emerge after the transfer of the site and either after or before (as on these facts) the assignment. Of course, the decision does not affect any defences A might have as against C based on the rules of limitation of action, causation, remoteness of damage, etc.

Rix LJ[15] linked this aspect of the law concerning assignment with the parallel development of rights by a promisee to sue in respect of loss eventually suffered by a third party transferee of chattels or land, or a third party owner of land who has financed a building contract between A and B affecting that owner's land (on that development, see 7.20). He noted that, in both contexts, the modern law strives to ensure that the party in contractual default is made to pay compensation for the loss which has in fact been suffered. Indeed, had there not been an assignment in this case, a claim by B on behalf of C might have provided a different route to enabling C to receive compensation. But B's assignment to C showed on these facts that B wished to have no part in any such litigation.

---

6. NON-ASSIGNABLE RIGHTS

8.10 The initial agreement between A and B can validly prohibit such a transfer.[16] There are also bars against assignment based on statute or public policy.[17] However, assignments can be valid even though the purpose of the arrangement involved an element of legal evasion, notably: (1) assignment by B to C so that C can bankrupt A, the debtor;[18] or (2) assignment

---

13   [2006] EWCA 1079; [2006] 1 WLR 2926; applied in *Landfast (Anglia) Ltd* v. *Cameron Taylor One Ltd* [2008] EWHC 343 (TCC), Akenhead J.

14   *Dawson* v. *Great Northern and City Railway Co.* [1905] 1 KB 260, CA (considered in the present decision [2006] EWCA 1079; [2006] 1 WLR 2926, at [38], [48], [78] and [87]).

15   [2006] EWCA 1079; [2006] 1 WLR 2926, at [80] to [87].

16   *Linden Gardens Trust Ltd* v. *Lenesta Sludge Disposals Ltd* [1994] 1 AC 85, HL; *Treitel* (13th edn, London, 2011), 15–050; G. J. Tolhurst and J. W. Carter, 'Prohibitions on Assignment: A Choice to be Made' [2014] CLJ 405–34.

17   *Treitel* (13th edn, London, 2011), 15–066 ff.

18   *Fitzroy* v. *Cave* [1905] 2 KB 364, CA.

by B, a company, to C, an individual, so that C (unlike B) will not be vulnerable to an application for security for costs;[19] or (3) assignment by B, a company, to C, an individual, so that C (unlike B) can seek legal aid in respect of the underlying claim.[20]

8.11 Certain rights of action are not assignable:
(1) most tort actions;[21] in particular, in *Simpson* v. *Norfolk and Norwich University Hospital NHS Trust* (2011)[22] the Court of Appeal held that a personal injury claim exercisable by the true victim X cannot be validly assigned to Y so as to enable Y to sue the defendant for damages in the tort of negligence; the doctrine of champerty invalidates such attempted assignments; accordingly, the defendant was entitled to obtain a striking out of the assignee's claim;
(2) unliquidated claims for contractual damages unless C, the purported assignee, has a 'genuine commercial interest' in taking the assignment (for example, C has made a loan to B, the assignor, and is now seeking to recoup some of this by receiving assigned rights as against A);[23] or C, the assignee, has received a proprietary interest and the relevant claim relates to that interest;[24]
(3) a right to rescind a transaction (for example, by reason of undue influence) is not assignable;[25] but one can validly assign a right to seek compensation for breach of contract or a debt;
(4) certain personal undertakings are not transferable. For example, the benefit held by a publisher of an author's agreement to publish a book with that publishing house is not assignable by the publisher to another. Another example is a motor insurance policy, because the identity of the relevant driver is bound, or likely, to involve personal attributes peculiar to that driver. Therefore, the named driver cannot assign the insurance cover to another.[26]

7. ASSIGNMENT DISTINGUISHED FROM OTHER DOCTRINES

8.12 Assignment is the transfer of a contractual right. It can be distinguished from the following:
(1) *Novation*.[27] This involves extinction of one contract (the A/B contract) and replacement by another (the A/C contract): see Lord Selborne's statement in *Scarf* v. *Jardine* (1882),[28] distinguishing novation of A/B contract No. 1 by A/B contract No. 2, and the novation of a contract between A and B by the creation of a contract between A and C, where C is a

---

19 *Norglen Ltd* v. *Reed Rains Provincial Ltd* [1999] 2 AC 1, HL.
20 Consolidated appeal in the *Norglen* case, *ibid.*
21 *Treitel* (13th edn, London, 2011), 15–060, contending that this category should not be applied uncritically.
22 [2011] EWCA Civ 1149; [2012] 1 All ER 1423.
23 *Trendtex Trading Ltd* v. *Crédit Suisse* [1982] AC 679, HL; *Treitel* (13th edn, London, 2011), 15–065.
24 *Ibid.*, at 15–064.
25 *Treitel* (13th edn, London, 2011), at 15–006, noting *Investors Compensation Scheme Ltd* v. *West Bromwich Building Society* [1998] 1 WLR 896, HL.
26 *Treitel* (13th edn, London, 2011), 15–051 ff, citing, notably, *Tolhurst* v. *Associated Portland Cement Manufacturers* [1902] 2 KB 660, 668, CA; see also *Jenkins* v. *Young Bros Transport Ltd* [2006] EWHC 151 (QB); [2006] 1 WLR 3189, at [12].
27 *Treitel* (13th edn, London, 2011), 15–003.
28 (1882) LR 7 App Cas 345, 351, HL.

new party. In the latter case, novation involves A's duty to B being extinguished and a fresh contract arising between A and C. This is not the same mechanism, therefore, as a transfer, by assignment, from B to C of B's right against A.

Where the new party, C, assumes an obligation under the novated contract, the obligation can relate to matters preceding the date of the novation, as *CMA SA* v. *Hyundai MIPO Dockyard Co. Ltd* (2008)[29] shows.

> In *CMA SA* v. *Hyundai MIPO Dockyard Co. Ltd* (2008) Burton J held that a party to a shipbuilding company (that party having joined as a party to this agreement following novation) had breached an arbitration clause requiring that disputes arising from this substantive agreement should be referred only to London arbitrators. That party, in breach of this arbitration clause, continued French court proceedings which had been wrongly commenced before the novation. It was a breach of the arbitration clause for the novated party not to discontinue the French proceedings, once it had become privy to this contractual set of arrangements, including the arbitration clause.[30]

(2) *Third party beneficiary rights.* If A promises B to confer a benefit on T, the latter can acquire a direct right of action under the Contracts (Rights of Third Parties) Act 1999 (7.34 ff). T is then designated a third party beneficiary from the inception of the relevant contract between A and B (those parties might retain powers of variation under the 1999 Act, until C has relied on the A/B undertaking, or C has communicated to A his wish to take advantage of that undertaking). The fact that T acquires a right under the original agreement contrasts with assignment, which is the transfer, subsequent to the contract's formation, of a right from the initial right-holder, B, to a new right-holder, C, the assignee.

(3) *Negotiable instruments.* These are transferable by delivery, or by delivery and endorsement. The new holder acquires a direct right against the debtor without the need for notice to the debtor. The right acquired can be superior to the transferor's.[31]

(4) *Revocable mandate.* B might authorise A to pay C. A's payment (in full) to C will then discharge A's obligation to B. C is normally capable of retaining the money against both A and B. Even while the mandate is operative, C acquires no direct right of action against A.[32] The mandate is revocable by B's notification to A.

29 [2008] EWHC 2791 (Comm); [2009] 1 All ER (Comm) 568; [2009] 1 Lloyd's Rep 213; [2008] 2 CLC 687.

30 In reaching his decision concerning proposition (ii), Burton J said, *ibid.*, at [23]: 'The Novation Agreements are not self-standing, they simply repeople the original contracts.'

31 *Chitty on Contracts* (31st edn, London, 2012), 19–085; *Treitel* (13th edn, London, 2011), 15–046 ff; *Anson's Law of Contract* (29th edn, Oxford, 2010), 677 ff.

32 *Treitel* (13th edn, London, 2011), 15–018.

QUESTIONS

(1) What is the nature of assignment and how is it achieved?
(2) What is the position of the assignee?
(3) Which types of right are non-assignable?
(4) Distinguish (i) assignment, (ii) novation, (iii) third party beneficiary rights of action, (iv) negotiable instruments and (v) revocable mandates.

Selected further reading

A. G. Guest, *Guest on the Law of Assignment* (London, 2012)
M. Smith and N. Leslie, *The Law of Assignment* (2nd edn, Oxford, 2013)

Vitiating elements

Chapter contents

9

Misrepresentation

1. INTRODUCTION

9.01 Summary of main points

(1) A 'misrepresentation' is an inaccurate statement of fact which induces the other party to enter into the contract.[1]

(2) The two remedies which might (depending on the facts) be applicable following a misrepresentation are (i) the mutual dismantling of the parties' benefits received under the contract (known as 'rescission *ab initio*') and/or (ii) damages: thus the relief sought by a party pleading misrepresentation is either or both of (i) and (ii).

(3) Damages are available as of right only if (a) the misrepresentation is fraudulent (the tort of deceit, 9.17), or (b) the misrepresentation is negligent at Common Law (the tort of negligent misstatement, 9.17), or (c) the representor is liable under section 2(1) of the Misrepresentation Act 1967, a statutory tort (9.20). These heads of liability will be explained more fully below.

(4) Currently, the 1967 Act's 'tort', (3)(c) above, is the representee's favoured source of compensation because the damages awarded are equivalent to those available for deceit, under (3)(a) above, and because, once the claimant shows that the statement is false, the burden of proof rests on the representor to show he had reasonable grounds for making the statement.

(5) Even if the misrepresentation is not culpable in any of these ways, the court has a discretion to award damages instead of allowing the contract to be rescinded (section 2(2) of the 1967 Act, cited at 9.29). However, this discretion does not apply if the statement was fraudulent.

(6) Rescission is subject to the following four general equitable 'bars', any of which will be sufficient to preclude rescission: (a) inability to restore the parties in a practical sense to the

---

1   J. Cartwright, *Misrepresentation, Mistake and Non-Disclosure* (3rd edn, London, 2012); D. O'Sullivan, S. Elliott and R. Zakrzewski, *The Law of Rescission* (Oxford, 2008), chapter 4; *Spencer Bower, Turner and Handley's Actionable Misrepresentation* (5th edn, London, 2014); for academic discussion, see S. J. Stoljar, *Mistake and Misrepresentation* (London, 1968), chapters 6 ff; P. S. Atiyah and G. H. Treitel, 'Misrepresentation Act 1967' (1967) 30 MLR 369; D. Capper, 'Remedies for Misrepresentation: An Integrated System', in L. DiMatteo, Q. Zhou, S. Saintier, K. Rowley (eds.), *Commercial Contract Law: Transatlantic Perspectives* (Cambridge, 2014), chapter 16; Law Reform Committee, 'Innocent Misrepresentation' (Tenth Report of the Law Reform Committee, Cmnd 1782, 1962); cf New Zealand, 'Misrepresentations and Breach of Contract' (Report of the Contracts and Commercial Law Reform Committee, Wellington, 1967; reprinted 1978), 9.4.1.

pre-contractual position ('*restitutio in integrum* impossible'); (b) the subject matter of the contract between A and B has been acquired in good faith by a subpurchaser; (c) affirmation of the contract by the representee; or (d) lapse of time rendering it unjust for the contract to be dismantled by rescission.

(7) A misrepresentation can lead a double life: according to section 1(a) of the Misrepresentation Act 1967, even if (as occasionally occurs) a misrepresentation becomes a term of the eventual contract (allowing contractual damages to be awarded), it can simultaneously subsist as a misrepresentation for the purpose of the remedy of rescission.

(8) It should also be noted that misrepresentation cannot be divorced from questions of 'mistake': all instances of misrepresentation involve the inducing of an error or misapprehension in the representee (see Chapter 10 (on mistake) for types of error not attributable to a misrepresentation).

(9) As for duties to disclose, the general proposition is that English law does not require a prospective party to point out to the other an imminent and ordinary bargaining mistake. Nor is there a general positive duty for a prospective party to reveal information which might be relevant to the transaction or to the fixing of its terms. However, a person cannot take unfair advantage of the other's confusion concerning the supposed terms of the agreement; and in specific (but narrowly confined) situations, notably contracts of insurance, the law imposes a positive duty to reveal relevant information.

2. NATURE OF A 'MISREPRESENTATION'

9.02 The essence of a misrepresentation is a false statement made by one person, even if he does not know that it is false, and even if he is not negligent in having made the statement. Unless the statement is fraudulent (when inducement is presumed: see 9.10 at (b) below), the statement must be influential to the extent that the person decides, as a result of being misled, to enter into the contract: that is, his decision to form the agreement is made in reliance on the other's false statement. Rescission can be granted for a wholly innocent misrepresentation, as Sir George Jessel MR explained in *Redgrave* v. *Hurd* (1881)[2] (but some degree of culpability is necessary if damages are sought (see 9.07 and 9.20 below), although liability for breach of contractual assurances is strict (9.12)).

Broken down further, a misrepresentation consists of the following elements (most of which are amplified in text below):

(1) a representation by words or by conduct;

(2) concerning a matter of past or present fact or 'law';[3]

(3) and not a mere matter of opinion;

---

2 (1881) 20 Ch D 1, 12–13, CA (explaining that the representor is culpable for having failed to avoid a misrepresentation, or at least that he should not be allowed to take advantage of his inaccuracy, once it is revealed, even if he was not culpable in making the misrepresentation).

3 Misstatements of law will count: *Brennan* v. *Bolt Burdon* [2004] EWCA Civ 1017; [2005] QB 303 approving Judge Rex Tedd QC in *Pankhania* v. *Hackney London Borough Council* [2002] EWHC 2441 (Ch), at [58]; J. Cartwright, *Misrepresentation, Mistake and Non-Disclosure* (3rd edn, London, 2012), 3.20 ff.

(4) it must be unambiguous, and not a 'mere puff';[4]

(5) it must be 'material', that is, a comment which, objectively, is apt to influence a reasonable person;[5]

(6) and made before the main contract;

(7) the representor must become a party to the contract; and the representation be addressed (normally directly, sometimes indirectly) to the representee who also becomes a party to the contract;

(8) the statement must be false at the time the contract is formed, although not false in a trivial sense;

(9) the statement will be a misrepresentation only if the representee's interpretation was objectively reasonable;

(10) the representee must be (a) aware of the statement, and (b) decisively influenced by it (there is an exception to proposition (b) if the statement was made fraudulently);

(11) the representor will be under a pre-formation duty to correct a statement if it has become false (certainly, if aware of that falsity).

These points, with the exceptions of points (2), (4), (5) and (6), will now be expanded (as for element (5), 'materiality', this is further examined as an aspect of element (10), in the context of inducement and reliance at 9.10 below).

9.03 *Element (1) The misrepresentation must be a statement by words or a representation by conduct.*[6] For example, in *Spice Girls Ltd* v. *Aprilia World Service BV* (2002)[7] the Court of Appeal held conduct suggesting that a pop group was not about to lose one of its members constituted a misrepresentation.

The prospective agreement was for sponsorship of the group (a female pop quintet) on a world tour, in return for the group promoting a motor-scooter. One of the group, namely, Geri Halliwell, 'Ginger Spice', had already told the others that she would be leaving the band quite soon. The famous (but in fact fragile) five preserved an appearance of unity by participating in photo shoots. Such representations by conduct suggested that the band was not about to change its membership in this way. A formal agreement was reached on 6 May 1998. Ginger Spice then left the band on 27 May 1998. Because of Ginger Spice's defection, the scooter promotion ceased to be commercially feasible. The Court of Appeal found the managing company of the band to be liable for damages under section 2(1) of the 1967 Act (cited at 9.20).

In *Gordon* v. *Selico* (1986),[8] the Court of Appeal held that a vendor's decision to cover up dry rot in a property in order to conceal this problem from prospective purchasers and their surveyors was a misrepresentation by conduct that the property did not suffer from dry rot.

---

4   *Dimmock* v. *Hallett* (1866) LR 2 Ch App 21 (sale of land at auction; assurance that land 'fertile and improvable' a mere puff); but not pre-sales talk intended to assist prospective purchasers of real property, *Shaftsbury House (Developments) Limited* v. *Lee* [2010] EWHC 1484 (Ch), at [35], *per* Proudman J (although the claim failed on other grounds).
5   *Chitty on Contracts* (31st edn, London, 2012), 6–039, 6–040; *Museprime Properties Ltd* v. *Adhill Properties Ltd* (1991) 61 P & CR 111, CA; Mance LJ in *MCI Worldcom International Inc.* v. *Primus Telecommunications plc* [2004] EWCA Civ 957; [2004] All ER (Comm) 833, at [30].
6   Cf non-disclosure, 9.44.
7   [2002] EWCA Civ 15; [2002] EMLR 27; *Chitty on Contracts* (31st edn, London, 2012), 6–014, 6–018.
8   (1986) 18 HLR 219; [1986] 1 EGLR 71; (1986) 278 EG 53, CA.

9.04 *Element (3) The statement should not involve the assertion of a mere matter of opinion.* Where the representor fraudulently states that he holds an opinion (and so he lies about his current belief), a misrepresentation of fact occurs with respect to the representor's state of mind or belief. As Bowen LJ said in *Edgington v. Fitzmaurice* (1885): 'the state of a man's mind is as much a fact as the state of his digestion. It is true that it is very difficult to prove what the state of a man's mind at a particular time is, but if it can be ascertained it is as much a fact as anything else.'[9]

As for honest but mistaken statements of opinion, the general rule is that this does not constitute a misrepresentation, but a statement might carry an implication that the person making the statement is not aware of current facts which tend to contradict the favourable literal impression made by that statement. Waller LJ in *IFE Fund SA v. Goldman Sachs* (2007)[10] encapsulated this proposition of law as follows:

> someone may make a statement which is not a representation of fact but which by implication carries with it a representation of fact i.e. in the case where the original representation is one of opinion that the representor is not aware of facts which make the statement of opinion untrue.

For example, in *Smith v. Land and House Property Co.* (1884),[11] a vendor of a property which was subject to a commercial tenancy misleadingly declared that the tenant was 'most desirable' but in fact this tenant had recently been very slow indeed to pay the rent on this property. The Court of Appeal found this to be a statement of fact.

In *Smith v. Land and House Property Co.* (1884)[12] the defendant sold at auction the freehold of 'The Marine Hotel' at Walton-on-the-Naze, after stating in the particulars of sale that the hotel was let for the remaining twenty-seven years at £4,000 a year to 'Mr Fleck', a 'most desirable' tenant. That description suppressed or glossed over the fact that Fleck had been slow in paying the last quarter's rent. The sale was completed in August. Fleck became insolvent in September. The purchaser successfully sought rescission for misrepresentation. Bowen LJ explained:[13]

> if the facts are not equally known to both sides, then a statement of opinion by the one who knows the facts best involves very often a statement of a material fact, for he impliedly states that he knows facts which justify his opinion ... [A] tenant who had paid his last quarter's rent by driblets under pressure must be regarded as an undesirable tenant.

A statement by a professional person, such as a solicitor, tends to be taken to imply that the person is aware of the background and that he has read the relevant documentation.

9   *Edgington v. Fitzmaurice* (1885) 29 Ch D 459, 483, CA, *per* Bowen LJ.
10   [2007] EWCA Civ 811; [2007] 2 Lloyd's Rep 449; [2007] 2 CLC 134, at [32].
11   (1884) 28 Ch D 7, CA (considered in *IFE Fund SA v. Goldman Sachs International* [2007] EWCA Civ 811; [2007] 2 Lloyd's Rep 449, citing also *Hummingbird Motors Ltd v. Hobbs* [1986] RTR 276, CA, and *Sumitomo Bank Ltd v. BBL* [1997] 1 Lloyd's Rep 487, Langley J; and see *Dimmock v. Hallett* (1866) LR 2 Ch App 21).
12   *Ibid.*
13   (1884) 28 Ch D 7, 15–16, CA.

In *Nottingham Patent Brick & Tile Co. Ltd* v. *Butler* (1886),[14] the vendor's solicitor, in the vendor's presence, said that the land to be sold was not known by the solicitor to be subject to any restrictive covenants. The purchaser obtained rescission when he discovered that there was a restrictive covenant, confining the usage of the property to a brickyard. The Court of Appeal held that there had been an implied representation that the lawyer had a reasonable basis for this belief, whereas he had bluffed, not having read the relevant deeds.

It might be different if it is obvious that the representor lacks experience, or knows nothing or very little of the surrounding facts, or where he has made quite clear that he has no intention to make an actionable statement (see discussion below of the *IFE Fund SA* case). As for lack of experience, the clearest example is *Bisset* v. *Wilkinson* (1927).[15]

In *Bisset* v. *Wilkinson* (1927) the vendor, who owned some land in New Zealand (where sheep greatly outnumber the human population), said that the land to be sold would have a capacity to support 2,000 sheep, if the land were converted to a sheep-farm. This was his 'idea'[16] and nothing more: 'as both parties were aware, the [representor] had not and, so far as appears, no other person had at any time carried on sheep-farming upon the unit of land in question. That land as a distinct holding had never constituted a sheep-farm.'[17] The Privy Council held that this was an uneducated 'guesstimate'. It was clear to the representee that the vendor was making a guess and not relying on any knowledge, skill, experience or expert report from a third party source. And so the Privy Council held that the buyer could not rescind. In fact the land's capacity was never ascertained. The buyer's reason for seeking rescission was that the bottom had fallen out of the sheep-farming market: 'Sheep-farming became very unprofitable and they changed their user of the land.'[18]

Furthermore, information can be expressly provided on the basis that there is no accompanying verification, nor an assumption of responsibility to supply updated information.

The Court of Appeal in *IFE Fund SA* v. *Goldman Sachs* (2007)[19] held that no misrepresentation arose when a merchant bank sent information to prospective (and sophisticated) purchasers

---

14 (1886) 16 QBD 778, 787, CA; see also *Brown* v. *Raphael* [1958] Ch 636, 644, 649, CA, *per* Lord Evershed MR and Romer LJ (as explained in *Economides* v. *Commercial Union Assurance Co. plc* [1998] QB 587, 595, 599, CA).
15 [1927] AC 177, PC; similarly, *Economides* v. *Commercial Union Assurance Co. plc* [1998] QB 587, CA (noted M. A. Clarke, [1998] CLJ 24 and H. Bennett, (1998) 61 MLR 886–98); *Royal Bank of Scotland plc* v. *Chandra* [2011] EWCA Civ 192; [2011] NPC 26; [2011] Bus LR D149, notably at [36] and [37].
16 [1927] AC 177, 180, PC.
17 *Ibid.*, 183.
18 *Ibid.*, 179.
19 [2007] EWCA Civ 811; [2007] 2 Lloyd's Rep 449; [2007] 2 CLC 134, the clause is cited at [13]; Waller LJ at [33] to [37], Gage LJ at [74] concluded that no express or implied misrepresentations occurred (upholding Toulson J in [2006] EWHC 2887 (Comm); [2007] 1 Lloyd's Rep 264; [2006] 2 CLC 1043).

of bonds and made clear that it was not assuming liability for inaccuracy. (Further on this case, see 9.40).

In *Avrora Fine Arts Investment Ltd* v. *Christie, Manson & Woods Ltd* (2012) Newey J held that auctioneers had made an implied misrepresentation that they had reasonable grounds to support their opinion that the painting 'Odalisque' was by the Russian early twentieth-century painter, Kustodiev.[20] However, the buyer was confined to an express and 'limited' warranty which enabled him to hand back the painting and to recover the price if the painting was not in fact as thus described (and this was the result in the case). (Further on this case, see 9.39 and 9.40 below).

9.05 *Element (7) The representation must be made by the representor, who becomes a party to the contract.*[21] This is the general requirement. But what if T, not a party to the eventual contract, makes a misrepresentation on which party B relies, and party A is aware of both the misrepresentation's falsity and of B's reliance? Lord Scott in the *Etridge* case (2001) suggested that the law will impute responsibility to A, on the basis that the latter has taken conscious advantage of the third party's supply of misinformation, so that A is aware of B's reliance on false information.[22]

9.06 *Element (7) continued: the representation must have been communicated (directly or otherwise) to the representee who also becomes a party to the contract.*[23] In the case of an action in deceit, the representor must have intended the information to be passed by X to the defendant and acted upon detrimentally.[24] In the case of a negligent misstatement, it is enough that it was reasonably foreseeable that the eventual and indirect representee would rely upon the representation.[25] For a qualification, where another person is substituted for the original representee, see the next paragraph.

9.07 *Element (7) further continued: representee's change of identity.* The Supreme Court in *Cramaso LLP* v. *Ogilvie-Grant* (2014) held that a representation by D to C(1) will continue to operate if, prior to the contract's formation, rather than C(1), C(2), a newly formed partnership or company, etc., becomes party to the contract. C(2) then become the representee and so acquires rights of rescission and/or to damages (this was an appeal from Scotland, but the relevant point is also applicable in English law).[26]

20 [2012] EWHC 2198 (Ch); [2012] PNLR 35, *per* Newey J, at [131], and at [134] (in the earlier passage, citing *Smith* v. *Land and House Property Corp* (1885) LR 28 Ch D 7, 15, CA, *per* Bowen LJ and *Thomson* v. *Christie Manson & Woods Ltd* [2004] EWHC 1101 (QB); [2004] PNLR 42, at [199], *per* Jack J).
21 If the representor is not a party, he might be liable in deceit or negligence at Common Law: *Chitty on Contracts* (31st edn, London, 2012), 6–082.
22 *Royal Bank of Scotland plc* v. *Etridge (No. 2)* [2001] UKHL 44; [2002] 2 AC 773, at [144]; J. Cartwright, *Misrepresentation, Mistake and Non-Disclosure* (3rd edn, London, 2012), 4–75 to 4–78.
23 *Chitty on Contracts* (31st edn, London, 2012), 6–031, 6–032.
24 *Andrews* v. *Mockford* [1896] 1 QB 372, CA.
25 *Smith* v. *Bush* [1990] 1 AC 831, 848, 856, 865, 871–2, HL.
26 *Cramaso LLP* v. *Ogilvie-Grant* [2014] UKSC 9; [2014] AC 1093, at [25] to [31], *per* Lord Reed; and at [56] to [64], *per* Lord Toulson.

9.08 *Element* (8) *Having regard to the whole mass of pre-contractual information supplied by the representor, the allegedly misleading statement must not be false in a trivial sense.* As Rix J said in *Avon Insurance plc* v. *Swire Fraser Ltd* (2000):[27]

> [A] representation may be true without being entirely correct, provided it is substantially correct and the difference between what is represented and what is actually correct would not have been likely to induce a reasonable person in the position of the claimants to enter into the contracts.

9.09 *Element* (9) *If only the representee understood the representation in a sense that would be false, the statement will be a misrepresentation even though the parties placed different interpretations on it.* This is subject to the proviso that the representee's interpretation must have been objectively reasonable.[28]

9.10 *Element* (10) *Reliance and awareness: the representee must be both (i) aware of the statement and (ii) decisively influenced by it.* But there is an exception to proposition (ii) if the statement was made fraudulently.

(a) *Nature of reliance.* The more common form of reliance is for the representee to have been induced to enter the contract.[29] But another possibility is that although the representee had already decided to enter the contract, he was misled by the misrepresentation into accepting a final set of terms less advantageous to him than he might otherwise have achieved.[30]

(b) *Reliance is inferred if the statement was fraudulent.* If the representee was the victim of fraud (provided the representee was aware of the statement and did not choose deliberately to ignore it), the statement is presumed to induce reliance, as the Court of Appeal noted in *County Natwest Bank Ltd* v. *Barton* (1999)[31] and Coulson J confirmed in *Fitzroy Robinson Ltd* v. *Mentmore Towers Ltd* (2009).[32] The rationale for the courts' willingness to lean in favour of the representee is that the other party has been especially heinous.[33]

(c) *In the absence of fraud, reliance must be shown, although it can be inferred from the representation's 'materiality'.* The concept of 'materiality' refers to information which would normally influence a person in the relevant situation to enter the contract. This factor

---

27 [2000] 1 All ER (Comm) 573; [2000] Lloyd's Rep IR 535, at [17]; note Rix J's refusal to engage in 'microscopic' scrutiny of each phrase's accuracy at [200] and [201]; considered in *Raiffeisen Zentralbank Osterreich AG* v. *Royal Bank of Scotland plc* [2010] EWHC 1392 (Comm); [2011] 1 Lloyd's Rep 123, at [139], *per* Christopher Clarke J, and in *Shaftsbury House (Developments) Ltd* v. *Lee* [2010] EWHC 1484 (Ch), at [50], ff, *per* Proudman J.

28 *EA Grimstead & Son Ltd* v. *McGarrigan* [1988–99] Info TLR 384, CA (CA, 27 October 1999; transcript No. 1733 of 1999, pp. 19, 27).

29 The fact that the representee's agent is aware can be decisive: *Strover* v. *Harrington* [1988] Ch 390, Browne-Wilkinson J.

30 E.g. *Clef Aquitaine SARL* v. *Laporte Materials (Barrow) Ltd* [2001] QB 488, CA (9.19: misrepresentation had the effect of depressing the representee's overall level of profit); *Huyton SA* v. *Distribuidora Internacional de Productos Agricolas SA* [2003] EWCA Civ 1104; [2003] 2 Lloyd's Rep 780, at [55] ff.

31 *The Times*, 29 July 1999, CA; *UCB Corporate Services* v. *Williams* [2002] EWCA Civ 555; [2003] 1 P & CR 12, at [86], citing *Downs* v. *Chappell* [1997] 1 WLR 426, 438, CA, *per* Hobhouse LJ; *Barton* v. *Armstrong* [1976] AC 104, 118–19, PC, drawing an analogy between duress as to person and fraud (on that case's significance in the law of duress, see 11.12); generally, *Chitty on Contracts* (31st edn, London, 2012), 6–037.

32 *Fitzroy Robinson Ltd* v. *Mentmore Towers Ltd* [2009] EWHC 1552 (TCC); [2009] EWHC 1552 (TCC); [2009] BLR 505; 125 Con LR 171; [2009] NPC 90, at [111], *per* Coulson J.

33 *Reeves* v. *Commissioner for Metropolitan Police* [2000] 1 AC 360, 394 A, HL, *per* Lord Hobhouse.

can tilt the scales in favour of the representee. This is because in the absence of fraud, reliance must be proved. Reliance requires the statement to have been a decisive reason for the representee entering the contract (except if the statement is fraudulent). But the law infers from a 'material' misrepresentation that there has been reliance.

> More precisely,[34] (a) 'materiality' can be sufficient to establish reliance, provided the representee alleges that he did rely; (b) but 'materiality' is not decisive, because other factors might be adduced by the representor to counter the inference of fact; (c) nor is 'materiality' necessary, because a representee might exceptionally be able to substantiate a plea of reliance without resort to this factor; without the assistance of 'materiality', the representee's task in showing reliance on a non-fraudulent misrepresentation is an uphill struggle because he will need to adduce independent evidence that the statement had the effect of inducing him to enter into the relevant transaction. That will be difficult because, *ex hypothesi*, he is claiming to have relied on something which would not have influenced others in the ordinary course of things.

(d) *Reliance is assessed on a 'but for' or 'decisive influence' basis, but the representation need not be the sole inducement.* These propositions apply in the absence of fraud.

   (i) *Decisive influence*: the representee must have been decisively influenced by it (this is the so-called 'but for' test of causation).[35] This means that the representation must have been operative on the representee's mind so that it made a crucial difference either *in determining that he would enter the contract*, or *that he would do so on a particular basis rather than on another basis.*

   (ii) *The misrepresentation need not be the sole inducement*: the statement (unless fraudulent) must be decisively influential, either because it induced the representee to enter the contract, or at least to assent to the present set of terms (compare the facts of *Clef Aquitaine SARL* v. *Laporte Materials (Barrow) Ltd* (2001),[36] discussed at 9.19 below, where the dispute concerned not the decision to contract, but the level of profit, with or without fraud). But the statement need not be the sole inducement: it is enough that it was one of the factors which induced the representee to enter the contract, or to assent to the present set of terms.[37]

(e) *Representee can omit to check.* The rule in *Redgrave* v. *Hurd* (1881) is that the representation is actionable (giving rise to rescission, for example) even though the representee might have checked the information for himself[38] (although leading

---

34 *Spice Girls Ltd* v. *Aprilia World Service BV* [2002] EWCA Civ 15; [2002] EMLR 27, at [70], *per* Sir Andrew Morritt V-C, citing *Smith* v. *Chadwick* (1884) 9 AC 187, 196, HL, *per* Lord Blackburn (noting that the representee could not, until the mid-nineteenth century, appear as witness in his own cause and could not, therefore, give evidence concerning inducement; hence the need for an inference of law).

35 *Chitty on Contracts* (31st edn, London, 2012), 6–037, for a review of the authorities.

36 [2001] QB 488, CA.

37 *Edgington* v. *Fitzmaurice* (1885) 29 Ch D 459, CA; on which see *Standard Chartered Bank* v. *Pakistan Corporation (Nos. 2 and 4)* [2003] 1 AC 959, HL, at [14] to [19], *per* Lord Hoffmann; *Treitel* (13th edn, London, 2011), 9–021, n. 99, notes Lord Hoffmann's suggestion, *ibid.*, at [17], that this is restricted to fraud.

38 *Redgrave* v. *Hurd* (1881) 20 Ch D 1, CA; *Standard Chartered Bank* v. *Pakistan Corporation (Nos. 2 and 4)* [2003] 1 AC 959, HL, at [14] to [19], *per* Lord Hoffmann.

commentators advocate modification of this approach when the issue is whether the representor *should be liable to compensate for non-fraudulent statements*).[39]

(f) *Representee unaware of the statement.* In all cases (even if the statement is fraudulent), it is possible for the representor to counter the representee's allegation of reliance by showing that in fact the representee was unaware of the statement.

(g) *Representee conducted own inquiries and made own assessment.* In all cases (even if the statement is fraudulent), it is possible for the representor to counter the representee's allegation of reliance by showing that the other party did not act on it, preferring instead to act on his own assessment, including conducting his own inquiries, and so the representee was not influenced by false statement.

> For example, in the *Peekay* case (2006) a non-fraudulent misrepresentation concerning the nature of a proposed investment was made in a 'rough-and-ready' fashion.[40] The representee, a 'sophisticated' and experienced investor, assessed the investment without reliance on this rather casual misrepresentation.[41] In effect the representation was 'white noise'; even if audible, he had chosen not to tune into it.
>
> By contrast, in *Gordon* v. *Selico* (1986),[42] the seller of a ninety-nine year leasehold property made a fraudulent misrepresentation by conduct (having deliberately covered up dry rot). The Court of Appeal held that it was no defence that the representee's surveyor had made an inspection of the premises and had failed to uncover this defect. This was, in short, a successful act of dishonest suppression and the representee had not averted his eyes from a patent defect or elected not to be influenced by surface appearances. Slade LJ said: 'The general principle *caveat emptor* has no application where a purchaser has been induced to enter the contract of purchase by fraud.'[43]

(h) *Representee received and absorbed a correction.* In all cases (even if the statement is fraudulent), the representee might confirm that he has absorbed a correction (normally sent by the representor). But it is necessary that the representor's attempted correction must hit home. It is not enough to attempt to correct a misrepresentation if the attempted correction does not in fact come to the representee's notice.[44] Finally (and clearly a counsel of

---

39 *Chitty on Contracts* (31st edn, London, 2012), 6–042 to 6–043; *Treitel* (13th edn, London, 2011), 9–24 (representee culpably failing to check), considering statements in *Smith* v. *Eric S Bush* [1990] 1 AC 831, 854, 872, HL.

40 *Peekay Intermark Ltd* v. *Australia and New Zealand Banking Group Ltd* [2006] EWCA Civ 386; [2006] 2 Lloyd's Rep 511 (controversially explained by *Treitel* (13th edn, London, 2011), 9–024, as a derogation from the principle in *Redgrave* v. *Hurd* (1881) 20 Ch D 1, CA; *Treitel*'s comment is a misreading of Moore-Bick LJ's discussion in the *Peekay* case at [52]); the *Peekay* case was considered by Gloster J in *JP Morgan Chase Bank* v. *Springwell Navigation Corporation* [2008] EWHC 1186 (Comm), at [482]; affirmed [2010] EWCA Civ 1221; [2010] 2 CLC 705.

41 *Peekay Intermark Ltd* v. *Australia and New Zealand Banking Group Ltd* [2006] EWCA Civ 386; [2006] 2 Lloyd's Rep 511, at [52], *per* Moore-Bick LJ.

42 (1986) 18 HLR 219; [1986] 1 EGLR 71; (1986) 278 EG 53, CA.

43 (1986) 18 HLR 219, 238, distinguishing *Horsfall* v. *Thomas* (1862) 2 F & F 785; 175 ER 1284 on the basis that 'not only was the defect in the gun patent and discoverable on inspection, but the purchaser took no steps to inspect it, so that he did in fact not rely on any misrepresentation as to its condition which might have been made.'

44 *Assicurazioni Generali SpA* v. *Arab Insurance Group* [2002] EWCA Civ 1642; [2003] 1 WLR 577; [2003] 1 All ER (Comm) 140, at [64], *per* Clarke LJ (passage cited in *Peekay* case, [2006] EWCA Civ 386; [2006] 2 Lloyd's Rep 511, at [36]).

prudence), the representor can escape liability by requiring the other party to sign a declaration that he has indeed read a correction.

> In the *Peekay* case, the representee had signed a declaration that he had read and understood the document's accurate description of the subject matter. The Court of Appeal held that this precluded him from asserting that he had not read that correction.[45]

9.11 *Element (11) Statement becoming false after initial affirmation but before formation of contract.* Sometimes an initially accurate statement is rendered inaccurate by a change of circumstances. Does the representor become liable in such circumstances? The current view at the moment is that the representor is responsible for having made a misrepresentation if he had pre-formation knowledge of the falsification but made no correction.

However, the law might not have been finally stated. There is scope for the Court of Appeal, and certainly an opportunity for the Supreme Court of the United Kingdom, to revisit this issue. It is submitted:

(a) as for the right to *rescind*, a strict approach should govern: such a right should arise without the need to show knowledge or fault; but

(b) as for the second remedy, *damages*, it should be necessary to show that the representor was culpable: in the absence of a contractual warranty concerning the continuing accuracy of a statement, liability to pay compensation should require *fault*; but fault might involve *failure to take reasonable steps to monitor the statement's continuing accuracy.*

Thus three levels of responsibility, bad faith, fault, and strict responsibility, can be distinguished.

(1) *Bad faith: need for knowledge.* One view, adopted by Romer LJ and Clauson J (and also supported by Lord Wright MR) in *With v. O'Flanagan* (1936)[46] is that the representor becomes liable if he discovers the change before the contract's formation but fails to correct his earlier statement. Many cases have emphasised the element of bad faith.[47] This can be analysed as breach of a continuing implied representation that the representor honestly continues to believe his statement.[48]

(2) *Fault.* Another view is that the representor becomes liable only if he ought reasonably to have discovered the change of circumstances. Section 2(1) of the Misrepresentation Act

---

45 *Peekay* case, *ibid.*, at [52], *per* Moore-Bick LJ, and at [66] ff, *per* Chadwick LJ; the third judge, Collins J, agreed.

46 [1936] Ch 575, 586, CA, and supported by R. Bigwood, [2005] CLJ 94.

47 In *Banks* v. *Cox* [2002] EWHC (Ch) 2166, at [4], Lawrence Collins J held that this is a case of fraud; see also *Fitzroy Robinson Ltd* v. *Mentmore Towers Ltd* [2009] EWHC 1552 (TCC); [2009] EWHC 1552 (TCC); [2009] BLR 505; 125 Con LR 171; [2009] NPC 90, at [173], *per* Coulson J (knowledge that a vital project manager, despite earlier statement, would no longer be available); *Foodco UK LLP (t/a Muffin Break)* v. *Henry Boot Developments Limited* [2010] EWHC 358 (Ch), at [208] to [215], *per* Lewison J; *Erlson Precision Holdings Ltd* v. *Hampson Industries plc* [2011] EWHC 1137 (Comm), at [43], *per* Field J (sufficient that party A knows that there has been a change; no further requirement that A should know that there is a legal duty for A to correct the false impression).

48 *IFE Fund SA* v. *Goldman Sachs* [2007] EWCA Civ 811; [2007] 2 Lloyd's Rep 449; [2007] 2 CLC 134, at [74], *per* Gage LJ; and at first instance, Toulson J in [2006] EWHC 2887 (Comm); [2007] 1 Lloyd's Rep 264; [2006] 2 CLC 1043, at [60].

1967 (9.20) imposes a duty on the representor to keep under review, at least to a reasonable extent, the veracity of his statements, although that duty ceases to apply once the contract has been formed. In the absence of 'reasonable grounds', the representor would become liable under that provision if a pre-contractual change of events, or perhaps perception, had falsified the earlier statement. Furthermore, Treitel contends that at Common Law a party might have assumed a duty to conduct such a review.[49]

(3) *Strict responsibility.* A third view, adopted by Lord Wright MR in *With* v. *O'Flanagan* (1936),[50] is that the representation is deemed to continue (viz. deemed to be repeated) until the contract is formed; and so it can be automatically falsified by a change of circumstances, whether or not the representor had any control over these events, and irrespective of his awareness of the relevant change (unlike (1), therefore, the representor need not have discovered the falsity of the statement).

Lord Wright MR in *With* v. *O'Flanagan* (1936) supported both approach (1) and approach (3),[51] whereas the majority, Romer LJ and Clauson J, did not discuss approach (3).[52] In the Court of Appeal in *Spice Girls Ltd* v. *Aprilia World Service BV* (2002), Sir Andrew Morritt V-C assumed that approach (1), knowledge, was the test.[53] And knowledge was adopted as the criterion by Lewison J in *Foodco UK LLP (t/a Muffin Break)* v. *Henry Boot Developments Limited* (2010), who said:[54]

> there is no duty to keep the counterparty constantly updated ... The duty is to communicate a change of circumstance which the representor knows has falsified a previous representation where the falsity exists at the date when the contract is concluded.

3. STATEMENTS BECOMING CONTRACTUAL TERMS OR 'COLLATERAL WARRANTIES'

9.12 To obtain 'loss of bargain' damages (18.08), the representee might contend that a pre-contractual misrepresentation has become (1) a 'contractual' term within the main contract or (2) a 'collateral warranty',[55] that is, a side contract subsisting independently of the main contract. The essence of (1) and (2) is that the maker of the statement or assurance is guaranteeing or contractually affirming its accuracy. Loss of bargain damages will place the representee in the position he would have enjoyed if the statement had been true.

49 *Treitel* (13th edn, London, 2011), 9–155. Lord Wright MR in *With* v. *O'Flanagan* [1936] Ch 575, 584, CA, expressed a wider responsibility: 'the failure to disclose, though wrong and a breach of duty, may be due to inadvertence or a failure to realize that the [representor owes a] duty ... not to leave the other party under an error when the representation has become falsified by a change of circumstances.'
50 [1936] Ch 575, 584, CA; in support: J. Cartwright, *Misrepresentation, Mistake and Non-Disclosure* (3rd edn, London, 2012), 4.27 (and seeking to repudiate the requirement of knowledge suggested by R. Bigwood, [2005] CLJ 94).
51 [1936] Ch 575, 583, CA.
52 *Ibid.*, at 586.
53 [2002] EWCA Civ 15; [2002] EMLR 27, at [51].
54 [2010] EWHC 358 (Ch), at [212], *per* Lewison J.
55 K. W. Wedderburn, 'Collateral Contracts' [1959] CLJ 58; *Chitty on Contracts* (31st edn, London, 2012), 12–103; F. A. Paterson, *Collateral Warranties Explained* (London, 1991); D. W. Greig, (1971) 87 LQR 179.

Furthermore, a warranted assurance is a cast-iron commitment. It imposes strict liability, regardless of proof of fraud or carelessness. And the defence of contributory negligence does not apply to breach of strict contractual obligations (18.23), such as breach of a warranty.

9.13 For example, suppose the defendant vendor said: 'This is a genuine "Louis XVI" sideboard.' If that statement had been accurate, the sideboard would have been worth £30,000. In fact, it was a later piece, worth only £1,000. The statement (reinforced by the word 'genuine') is likely to be a term of the contract under section 13(1) of the Sale of Goods Act 1979 (or section 11, Consumer Rights Bill) (correspondence with description).[56] If so, the representee will be entitled to compensation for the difference between these sums. This will be the usual approach unless the purchaser was clearly acting solely on his own superior knowledge.[57]

9.14 *Criteria for finding 'contractual assurances'.* The test governing the finding of a collateral warranty remains strict (despite Lord Denning's suggestion in *Howard Marine* v. *Ogden* (1978) that a more flexible approach be adopted).[58] *Business Environment Bow Lane Ltd* v. *Deanwater Estates Ltd* (2007)[59] (below) exemplifies this strict approach. There the Court of Appeal cited Lord Moulton's seminal comment in the *Heilbut, Symons* case (1913):[60]

> Such collateral contracts, the sole effect of which is to vary or add to the terms of the principal contract, are therefore viewed with suspicion by the law. They must be proved strictly . . . Any laxity on these points would . . . have the effect of lessening the authority of written contracts.

In fact the courts have now watered down Lord Moulton's remarks. The modern tendency is to oppose collateral warranties as a matter of 'caution' (suggesting circumspection) rather than 'suspicion' (suggesting resistance or even hostility).[61]

No collateral warranty arose in the *Business Environment* case (2007).[62] The Court of Appeal gave effect to a clause in a lease which (in accordance with normal commercial expectations) said that the tenant would compensate the landlord for dilapidations. Admittedly the landlord had earlier suggested in writing that this clause would not apply. But the Court of Appeal held

---

56   *Beale* v. *Taylor* [1967] 1 WLR 1193, CA (private seller's description of car as '1961, Herald 1200 convertible'; in fact car made of two halves welded together; only the back half was a '1200' model; statement treated as term of the main contract).

57   *Harlingdon & Leinster Enterprises* v. *Christopher Hull Fine Art* [1991] 1 QB 564, CA (purchaser was an expert and placed no reliance on the seller's attribution of a painting); considered by Buckley J in *Drake* v. *Thos Agnew & Sons Ltd* [2002] EWHC (QB) 294, at [24] to [32].

58   *Howard Marine and Dredging Co. Ltd* v. *A Ogden & Sons (Excavations) Ltd* [1978] QB 574, 590G, CA.

59   [2007] EWCA Civ 622; [2007] L & TR 26, at [23].

60   *Heilbut, Symons & Co.* v. *Buckleton* [1913] AC 30, 47, HL (see also Lord Haldane at 37–9); citing *Chandelor* v. *Lopes* (1603) Cro Jac 4; explained by Denning LJ in the *Oscar Chess* case, [1957] 1 WLR 370, CA; see also *Hopkins* v. *Tanqueray* (1854) 15 CB (NS) 130.

61   Judge Richard Seymour QC in *Wimpole Theatre (a firm)* v. *J J Goodman Ltd* [2012] EWHC 1600 (QB) at [46] and [47], noting Sir Andrew Morritt C in *Business Environment Bow Lane Ltd* v. *Deanwater Estates Ltd* [2007] L & TR 26, at [42].

62   [2007] EWCA Civ 622; [2007] L & TR 26, at [23].

that this surprisingly generous concession had been overtaken by the (written) terms of the lease, which restored normal commercial expectations.[63]

In particular, the courts will consider the following criteria:[64]

(1) *Objective commitment by maker of statement.* The court will conduct an objective assessment of whether the representee was entitled reasonably to assume that the statement was being warranted, that is, guaranteed to be contractually binding.[65] *Yam Seng Pte Ltd* v. *International Trade Corp Ltd* (2013) illustrates this factor.[66]

(2) *Importance to representee emphasised.* The court will consider whether the representee made plain that the matter was crucial to him.[67]

(3) *Obvious importance.* It will also be relevant whether it was obvious from the circumstances that the matter was crucial to the representee. For example, in *City & Westminster Properties (1934) Ltd* v. *Mudd* (1959), the landlord had assured a prospective tenant that he would be free to sleep in the demised business premises at night, despite the prohibition contained in one of the written covenants in the lease. Harman J, noting that inability to sleep on site had been a potential 'deal-breaker', gave effect to this oral assurance by preventing the landlord from terminating the lease for breach of the written non-residential covenant.[68] *Yam Seng Pte Ltd* v. *International Trade Corp Ltd* (2013) also illustrates this factor.[69]

(4) *The court will consider the relative skill, knowledge and expertise of the parties.*[70] In *Dick Bentley Productions* v. *Harold Smith (Motors)* (1965),[71] the Court of Appeal held that a car dealer's statement that a car had covered 20,000 miles since a new engine had been fitted was a contractual warranty. In fact, the car's true mileage since that engine had been fitted was 100,000 (see also *Esso Petroleum Ltd* v. *Mardon* (1976)).[72] By contrast, in *Oscar Chess Ltd* v. *Williams* (1957),[73] no warranty was established when a private vendor, basing himself on a logbook which had been forged by a third party, said in good faith that a car was a 1948 model, when in fact it was a 1939 model; the buyer was an experienced car dealer.

---

63 *Ibid.*, at [47].
64 Cf the farrago of factors successfully enumerated by counsel in the *Howard Marine* case, [1978] QB 574, 583, CA.
65 *Thake* v. *Maurice* [1986] QB 644, CA (3.71); reasonableness is also a factor in the tort of negligent misstatement: *Williams* v. *Natural Life & Health Foods* [1998] 1 WLR 830, 837, HL.
66 [2013] EWHC 111 (QB); [2013] 1 All ER (Comm) 1321; [2013] 1 Lloyd's Rep 526, at [98].
67 E.g. *Bannerman* v. *White* (1861) 10 CB (NS) 844 (prospective buyer asking whether sulphur had been used in cultivation of hops; seller saying 'no'; but it was clear that the purchaser would have walked away if the hops had been sulphurated; therefore the assurance had contractual effect).
68 [1959] Ch 129, 145–6, Harman J.
69 [2013] EWHC 111 (QB); [2013] 1 All ER (Comm) 1321; [2013] 1 Lloyd's Rep 526, at [98].
70 *Harlingdon & Leinster Enterprises* v. *Christopher Hull Fine Art* [1991] 1 QB 564, CA (where the purchaser was an expert and placed no reliance on the seller's attribution of a work of art to a particular painter).
71 [1965] 1 WLR 623, CA.
72 [1976] QB 801, CA.
73 [1957] 1 WLR 370, CA (Morris LJ dissenting).

More difficult are situations where both seller and buyer have expertise. As *Drake* v. *Thos Agnew & Sons Ltd* (2002)[74] demonstrates, there is then scope to determine whether the representee was truly influenced by the other party's statement, especially when the purchaser is aware of uncertainties and risks.

> In *Drake* v. *Thos Agnew & Sons Ltd* (2002) Buckley J held that a seller's statement of opinion, that a painting was by Van Dyck, did not constitute a contractual term (so as to render the contract a sale 'by description' under section 13(1) of the Sale of Goods Act 1979). The buyer's agent was aware that the painting had been recently sold not as a Van Dyck but as a copy ('after Van Dyck'); and the seller had disclosed contrary expert opinion (ultimately decisive at trial) that the painting was not a Van Dyck. In the face of this patent doubt, the seller's statement of opinion was not a warranty or contractual assurance. Overhanging this case was the fact that the buyer's agent, who had real doubts, but 'was financially conflicted' and interested in generating his commission on the deal, decided to push through the purchase.

(5) *Independent verification urged.* The court will consider whether the representor asked the representee to verify the matter for himself.[75]

(6) *Need for independent verification expressly negatived.* Conversely, the court will take into account whether the representor assured the other that such verification was unnecessary.[76]

(7) *A representation of fact is much more likely to have contractual effect than a statement of future fact or future forecast.*[77] However, this is no more than a vague rule of thumb. Certainly, predictions can sometimes involve collateral warranties, especially if made by persons possessing expertise.

For example, in *Esso Petroleum Co. Ltd* v. *Mardon* (1976),[78] a forecast was held to involve a collateral warranty that the maker of it had reasonable grounds for believing the accuracy of his prediction. Esso had made a statement concerning a filling station's likely level of customer demand (a 'throughput' of 200,000 gallons). In fact, as a result of a planning decision, it was already clear that the pumps could only be situated at the rear of the garage. The upshot was that the true figure was 70,000 gallons. The Court of Appeal treated Esso's inaccurate forecast as a collateral warranty, the substance of which was the assurance that they had exercised reasonable care before making this statement

---

74 [2002] EWHC (QB) 294, notably at [24] to [32], considering *Harlingdon & Leinster Enterprises* v. *Christopher Hull Fine Art* [1991] 1 QB 564, CA; cf *Avrora Fine Arts Investment Ltd* v. *Christie, Manson & Woods Ltd* [2012] EWHC 2198 (Ch); [2012] PNLR 35, at [122] and [123], on which 9.04, 9.39, 9.40 (painting subject to an express warranty that the buyer can recover his money if the painting is proved to be other than as described and if the buyer has retained ownership).

75 *Ecay* v. *Godfrey* [1947] Lloyd's Rep 286, Lord Goddard CJ (seller of second-hand boat making clear his belief that the purchaser would be having it surveyed first); cf where the defendant encouraged the plaintiff to rely on his assurance without further inquiry or verification (see next note) in *Schawel* v. *Reade* [1913] 2 IR 64, HL.

76 *Schawel* v. *Reade* [1913] 2 IR 64, HL ('you need not look for anything; the horse is perfectly sound. If there were anything the matter with the horse, I should tell you.').

77 *Business Environment Bow Lane Ltd* v. *Deanwater Estates Ltd* [2007] EWCA Civ 622; [2007] L & TR 26, at [23].

78 [1976] QB 801, CA; distinguished *Shaftsbury House (Developments) Limited* v. *Lee* [2010] EWHC 1484 (Ch), at [45] ff, *per* Proudman J (optimistic statements made in 2007 concerning house or flat prices in London area).

(unusually, therefore, this particular collateral warranty did not operate as a guarantee that there would be 200,000 gallons). A second and alternative basis of decision was that Esso had breached a tortious duty of care and that it was therefore liable to compensate for their negligent misstatement.

(8) *Timing.* The lapse of time between the statement and the making of the formal contract will be taken into account. In general, 'the longer the interval, the greater the presumption must be that the parties did not intend the statement to have contractual effect in relation to a subsequent deal.'[79]

(9) *Subsequent negotiation superseding informal statement.*[80] The court will look at whether the statement is followed by further negotiations and a written contract not containing any term corresponding to the statement. In such a case, it will be harder to infer that the statement was intended to have a contractual effect because the prima facie assumption will be that the written contract includes all the terms the parties wanted to be binding between them.

9.15 *Collateral warranties and the 'parol evidence rule'.* Such 'side-agreements', subsisting independently of the main contract, form an exception to the parol evidence rule (12.02 ff).[81]

This long-standing evidential rule operates to bar parties from adducing 'extrinsic evidence', whether oral or written, for the purpose of supplementing, varying or contradicting the contract's written terms. The rule safeguards the primacy of the agreed text. And so its purpose is to promote certainty, accessibility and finality.

However, a collateral warranty is not a violation of the parol evidence rule because the extrinsic evidence is admitted for the purpose of establishing an independent agreement rather than a variation of the main agreement. It will be seen immediately that use of collateral warranties to evade the parol evidence rule is a 'dodge', a device designed to inject Equity or informality into the context of written contracts.

In fact, businessmen, in the interests of certainty and completeness, often insert into commercial written contracts an 'entire agreement' clause (9.36 and 9.37). Such a clause declares that the final contract contains all relevant contractual terms and assurances or understandings. The result is that collateral agreements are denied any force.

9.16 *Collateral warranties and the (Common Law) privity problem.* Collateral warranties can be used to circumvent problems arising from absence of 'privity of contract' (see 7.02 for the Common Law rule that a third party cannot sue on a contract).

---

79 *Business Environment Bow Lane Ltd* v. *Deanwater Estates Ltd* [2007] EWCA Civ 622; [2007] L & TR 26, at [23] (adopting Lightman J's statement in *Inntrepreneur Pub Company* v. *East Crown Ltd* [2000] 2 Lloyd's Rep 611, 615); the *Business Environment* case also notes: *Henderson* v. *Arthur* [1907] 1 KB 10, CA, *City & Westminster Properties (1934) Ltd* v. *Mudd* [1959] 1 Ch 129 (Harman J) and *Brikom Investments* v. *Carr* [1979] 1 QB 467, CA.

80 *Business Environment Bow Lane Ltd* v. *Deanwater Estates Ltd* [2007] EWCA Civ 622; [2007] L & TR 26, at [23].

81 *Treitel* (13th edn, London, 2011), 6–013 ff; Law Commission, 'The Law of Contract: The Parol Evidence Rule' (Law Commission Report No. 154, Cmnd 9700, London, 1986), 2.32 to 2.36 (noted by G. Marston, [1986] CLJ 192).

Consider these two examples:

(i) In *Shanklin Pier Ltd* v. *Detel Products Ltd* (1951), a supplier of paint (A) was held to have warranted to a pier-owner (B) the fitness of A's paint for painting piers. B relied on this when he stipulated that X, the contractor commissioned to paint the pier, should use A's paint. A collateral warranty was held to subsist between A and B, requiring A to compensate B for the poor quality of the paint used, even though X bought the paint directly from A.[82]

(ii) In *Andrews* v. *Hopkinson* (1957),[83] a car dealer said: 'It's a good little bus [referring to a smaller type of vehicle known as a car]; I'd stake my life on it.' The main contract was between a finance company and the purchaser. McNair J found a collateral warranty between the dealer and the purchaser.

4. TORT CLAIMS FOR CULPABLE MISREPRESENTATIONS

9.17 *The tort of negligent misstatement and the tort of deceit.* The tort of negligent misstatement was established by the House of Lords in *Hedley Byrne* v. *Heller* (1963).[84] A claim for negligent misstatement requires proof of a duty of care (sometimes expressed as a 'special relationship', and in some of the authorities the requirement is known as an 'assumption of responsibility') between the defendant and the claimant, and breach of that duty.[85] The measure of damages is subject to a reasonable foreseeability test of remoteness.[86] This tort was declared available in the pre-contractual context in *Esso Petroleum Ltd* v. *Mardon* (1976).[87]

The tort of deceit requires a representation to be made without an honest belief in its accuracy. Failure to take care to verify is not enough to constitute deceit, provided the representor has the honest belief that what he asserts is true. In *Derry* v. *Peek* (1889), the House of Lords made clear that the *absence of an honest belief* is the essence of a fraudulent misrepresentation. In that case, Lord Herschell summarised the law as follows:[88]

> First, in order to sustain an action of deceit, there must be proof of fraud, and nothing short of that will suffice. Secondly, fraud is proved when it is shewn that a false representation has been made (1) knowingly, or (2) without belief in its truth, or (3) recklessly, careless whether it be true or false . . ..
>
> To prevent a false statement being fraudulent, there must . . . always be an honest belief in its truth . . . [Making] a false statement through want of care falls far short

82 [1951] 2 KB 854, McNair J.
83 [1957] 1 QB 229, McNair J.
84 *Hedley Byrne & Co Ltd* v. *Heller and Partners Ltd* [1964] AC 465, HL; J. Cartwright, *Misrepresentation, Mistake and Non-Disclosure* (3rd edn, London, 2012), chapter 6.
85 Cartwright, for an exhaustive analysis: *ibid.* at 6–16 to 6–25.
86 *The Wagon Mound* [1961] AC 388, PC.
87 [1976] QB 801, CA.
88 *Derry* v. *Peek* (1889) 14 App Cas 337, 374, HL.

of, and is a very different thing from, fraud, and the same may be said of a false representation honestly believed though on insufficient grounds.

A fraudulent statement is presumed to induce reliance (point (10)(b) at 9.10).

As for the measure of damages for deceit,[89] Lord Browne-Wilkinson explained in the leading decision, the *Smith New Court* case (1997):[90]

> [T]he defendant is bound to make reparation for all the damage directly flowing from the transaction; although such damage need not have been foreseeable, it must have been directly caused by the transaction ... In addition, the plaintiff is entitled to recover consequential losses caused by the transaction.[91]

9.18 *Contractual damages vindicate the failure to deliver what was promised.* A promise, warranty, guarantee or contractual assurance creates a right to expect that the subject matter will conform to the promise, etc. By contrast, a tortious misrepresentation yields damages (whether the cause of action is deceit, negligence, or section 2(1) of the Misrepresentation Act 1967, on which 9.20 below) in respect of the money thrown away, including (as 'consequential loss') income-generating opportunities lost, as a result of the actionable misrepresentation.[92]

This difference will now be amplified. Contractual damages give the claimant the difference between the actual value of the subject matter on completion and its warranted value. This is the basic 'loss of bargain' measure (18.08).

For example, suppose V sells a business to P and V has warranted that the volume of business has been and/or will continue to be at level £3m. In fact the volume of business is £1m. P can recover £2m only in contract, not in tort. P's claim is for the difference between the revenue which would have been generated if the warranty had been accurate and the lower level in fact available. That type of 'pure expectation' is created only by a contractual term or a collateral warranty, and the expectation is protected by contractual damages for breach of such an undertaking. Even if the warranty were made fraudulently, the representee's damages *in tort* would not be based on the difference between the subject matter delivered and the subject matter's higher value *as warranted*: only contractual damages protect the warranted value.

By contrast, tort damages (whether the cause of action is deceit, negligence, or section 2(1) of the Misrepresentation Act 1967) will indemnify the representee by placing him in the position in which he would have been if the culpable misrepresentation had not been made. The obvious loss will be the initial 'capital' loss: the difference in value between the price paid and the subject

---

89 For the criticism that damages for deceit are too robustly defined and computed, see J. Devenney, 'Re-Examining Damages for Fraudulent Misrepresentation', in L. DiMatteo, Q. Zhou, S. Saintier, K. Rowley (eds.), *Commercial Contract Law: Transatlantic Perspectives* (Cambridge, 2014), chapter 17.

90 *Smith New Court Securities Ltd* v. *Scrimgeour Vickers (Asset Management) Ltd* [1997] AC 254, 266–7, HL, *per* Lord Browne-Wilkinson (Lord Mustill, *ibid.*, at 269G, said that Lord Browne-Wilkinson's propositions should supersede the statements in *Doyle* v. *Olby* [1969] 2 QB 158, CA, which Lord Mustill regarded as not wholly reliable authority); for a neat illustration of these principles, *Banks* v. *Cox* [2002] EWHC (Ch) 2166, at [13] ff, *per* Lawrence Collins J.

91 E.g. the facts of *Doyle* v. *Olby (Ironmongers) Ltd* [1969] 2 QB 158, CA.

92 *Smith New Court Securities Ltd* v. *Scrimgeour Vickers (Asset Management) Ltd* [1997] AC 254, 281–2, HL, *per* Lord Steyn.

matter's lesser and actual value at the date of completion. Suppose A buys for £500,000 a vessel which B culpably misrepresents as 'sea-going'. Because it is not sea-going this vessel is worth only £200,000. And so A has made a loss of £300,000.

This 'capital' loss can be supplemented by an award of 'consequential' loss, such as money lost in running the defective business or money not gained from pursuing an alternative business (these are 'income losses'; but consequential harm could embrace other forms of loss which flow from a fraudulent or negligent misrepresentation, such as damage to property or even personal injury).

Tort claims are attractive if the transaction was a bad bargain (that is a bargain which 'on day one' was destined to be a loss for the purchaser even if there had been no breach of warranty). Here the purchaser had miscalculated by agreeing to pay too much because the price would have exceeded the subject matter's actual value even if it had corresponded to its warranted quality.

9.19 *Illustrations of 'income losses' and consequential loss receoverable in tort.* As just mentioned, tort damages (whether the cause of action is deceit, negligence or section 2(1) of the Misrepresentation Act 1967) can include compensation for 'lost opportunity for gain'. In essence the claim is for the loss attributable to the fact that the misrepresentation caused the claimant to back (as it were) horse X rather than horse Y. The point is vividly illustrated by *East* v. *Maurer* (1991) (the case of the two Bournemouth hairdressing salons).[93] The claimant bought a hairdressing salon after the defendant had deceitfully tricked her into believing that he would not continue working in his second, nearby, competing salon. In fact, he intended to continue working at his second salon. But the defendant had simply lied about his intentions, telling the claimant that he would be emigrating to Switzerland. The Court of Appeal held that the claimant's damages for deceit included compensation for the notional gain which would have accrued if another horse had been backed: if the claimant had instead invested her capital in a similar but unproblematic salon in the vicinity, that is, a business not blighted by the defendant's decision to continue running a rival salon in the vicinity.

This authority has been developed in the following four cases.

(1) *Clef Aquitaine SARL* v. *Laporte Materials (Barrow) Ltd* (2001) is a variation on this theme because the claim concerned not a hypothetical different deal with someone other than the defendant but the lost chance to strike a better deal with the defendant.[94] The parties had been negotiating terms for the claimant to receive a distributorship to supply the defendant's products in France. The defendant fraudulently gave false figures concerning prices charged by the defendant for those products in the UK. If the claimant had received accurate figures, it would have secured a better bargain with the defendant. The Court of Appeal awarded damages for that loss attributable to a bad set of terms (the extra profit which would have been gained if the defendant had not fraudulently distorted the negotiations concerning the alleged lowest UK supply prices).

---

93   [1991] 1 WLR 461, CA (noted J. Marks, (1992) 108 LQR 386); the decision was approved by Lord Steyn in *Smith New Court Securities Ltd* v. *Scrimgeour Vickers (Asset Management) Ltd* [1997] AC 254, 282, HL.
94   [2001] QB 488, CA.

(2) In *4 Eng Ltd* v. *Harper* (2008),[95] the claimant was unsure whether to buy business E or T, but it chose E as a result of the defendant's fraudulent misrepresentations concerning E's trading performance. The claimant successfully claimed for the loss of the chance (18.12), reckoned by the judge at 80 per cent, to purchase T. This case shows that the *East* v. *Maurer* claim for tortious misrepresentation loss extends to (1) loss of a chance to acquire an alternative particular business (as distinct from the certainty that an alternative, of a generic type, would have been acquired, as in the *East* v. *Maurer* case: see above); and (2) the tortious damages claim extends beyond the income that would have been derived from running the alternative business to include the capital increase that would have accrued if, in due course, the alternative business had been sold by the claimant.

(3) In *Parabola Investments Ltd* v. *Browallia Cal Ltd* (2010)[96] the Court of Appeal held that damages in tort can extend to opportunities for investment which continue to be lost even after the relevant fraud has been discovered. The defendant was vicariously liable for the fraud of one of its traders who had daily misrepresented to the claimant that the relevant trading account was in good health. In fact the overall level of the fund during this period fell by £3.75m – 'capital loss'. The defendant accepted vicarious liability for B's fraud. The claimant successfully sought compensation not only (1) for this capital loss but (2) for the loss of profits which the claimant would have made on alternative trading both during the period of the fraud and (3) during the period from discovery of the fraud until trial.

(4) *Yam Seng Pte Ltd* v. *International Trade Corp Ltd* (2013)[97] examines the defendant's suggestion that tort damages should be reduced, or even reach zero, on the basis that the claimant would have lost some or all of the money even if there had been no tortious misconduct by the defendant. Leggatt J held that sustaining such a defence will be an uphill struggle because the defendant will need to show (i) 'with a reasonable degree of certainty' (ii) 'that the claimant would probably have suffered a loss from entering into an alternative transaction' and (iii) 'the amount of that loss'.[98]

5. DAMAGES UNDER SECTION 2(1) OF THE MISREPRESENTATION ACT 1967

9.20 *A statutory head of tortious damages.* As we shall see, a claimant's preferred potential source of compensation for a pre-contractual misrepresentation (in the absence of a collateral warranty) is section 2(1) of the Misrepresentation Act 1967.[99] This is so for two main reasons: (i) damages are recoverable for all the consequences of the representation,

---

95 [2008] EWHC 915 (Ch); [2009] Ch 91, David Richards J (noted by P. Mitchell, (2009) 125 LQR 12–17).
96 [2010] EWCA Civ 486; [2011] QB 477, at [32] to [60], *per* Toulson LJ, with the agreement of Rimer and Mummery LJJ; *Banks* v. *Cox* [2002] EWHC (Ch) 2166, at [13] ff, *per* Lawrence Collins J, also illustrates a 'loss of income' claim following a fraudulent misrepresentation (in the case itself, a fraudulent failure to correct a falsified statement).
97 [2013] EWHC 111 (QB); [2013] 1 All ER (Comm) 1321; [2013] 1 Lloyd's Rep 526, at [209] to [220].
98 *Ibid.*, at [218] at proposition (6).
99 P. S. Atiyah and G. H. Treitel, (1967) 30 MLR 369; P. Fairest, [1967] CLJ 239; see also R. Taylor, 'Expectation, Reliance and Misrepresentation' (1982) 85 MLR 138; I. Brown and A. Chandler, [1992] LMCLQ 40; R. Hooley, (1991) 107 LQR 547; for the argument that section 2(1) should now be abolished, D. Capper, 'Remedies for Misrepresentation: An Integrated System', in L. DiMatteo, Q. Zhou, S. Saintier, K. Rowley (eds.), *Commercial Contract Law: Transatlantic Perspectives* (Cambridge, 2014), chapter 16.

even if not reasonably foreseeable, subject only to a defence of mitigation; (ii) once the representation is shown to have been inaccurate, the defendant bears the burden of showing reasonable grounds for continuing to believe, until formation, the accuracy of the statement. This provision states:

> Where a person has entered into a contract after a misrepresentation has been made to him by another party thereto and as a result thereof he has suffered loss, then, if the person making the misrepresentation would be liable in respect thereof had the misrepresentation been made fraudulently, that person shall be so liable notwithstanding that the misrepresentation was not made fraudulently, unless he proves that he had reasonable ground to believe and did believe up to the time the contract was made that the facts represented were true.

As Sir Donald Nicholls V-C noted in *Gran Gelato Ltd* v. *Richliff Ltd* (1992),[100] damages under this provision are classified as tortious, adding: 'in short, liability … is essentially founded on negligence, in the sense that the defendant, the representor, did not have reasonable grounds to believe that the facts represented were true.' This means that the representee cannot sue for his expectation interest (9.18, 18.08), that is, on the basis that the statement was a guarantee of accuracy.

In *Yam Seng Pte Ltd* v. *International Trade Corp Ltd* (2013) Leggatt J said:[101]
To establish a right to recover damages under [section 2(1) a claimant must show]:
(1) that it has entered into a contract with the defendant;
(2) that it did so after a representation of fact had been made to it by the defendant (and in reliance on that representation);
(3) that the representation was false; and
(4) that as a result of entering into the contract with the defendant, the claimant has suffered loss.

9.21 *Section 2(1) damages are tortious and patterned on deceit without requiring proof of fraud.* Furthermore, the Court of Appeal in *Royscot* v. *Rogerson* (1991)[102] held that the courts must give effect to the so-called 'fiction of fraud' contained in section 2(1) of the 1967 Act (namely, the parenthetical phrase within section 2(1) which reads: 'if the person making the misrepresentation would be liable in respect thereof had the misrepresentation been made fraudulently'). This curious 'fiction' dispenses with the general remoteness test applicable to negligence claims in tort (the 'reasonable foreseeability' formulation of a remoteness test).[103] And so the representee can recover his loss, however unforeseeable, provided this loss is causally related to the misrepresentation; in other words, provided 'the chain of causation' has not been broken.

---

100 [1992] Ch 560, 573, 575.
101 [2013] EWHC 111 (QB); [2013] 1 All ER (Comm) 1321; [2013] 1 Lloyd's Rep 526, at [200].
102 [1991] 2 QB 297, CA.
103 'The Wagon Mound' [1961] AC 388, PC (summarised by Lord Rodger in *Simmons* v. *British Steel plc* [2004] UKHL 20; [2004] ICR 585, at [67]).

However, this 'Royscot interpretation' might be reversed if section 2(1) were to come before the Supreme Court of the United Kingdom. The door seems ajar, for two members of the House of Lords, Lords Browne-Wilkinson and Steyn in *Smith New Court Securities Ltd* v. *Scrimgeour Vickers (Asset Management) Ltd* (1997)[104] expressed doubt that a statute should be construed so as to distort the reality that the representor has been guilty of negligence or simple fault and not dishonesty. Lord Steyn[105] noted that Richard Hooley[106] has condemned the fraud measure under section 2(1) as 'repugnant' and 'bizarre'. And the same 'fiction of fraud' led Rix J in *Avon Insurance plc* v. *Swire Fraser Ltd* (2000) to describe section 2(1) as a 'mighty weapon'.[107]

In *Yam Seng Pte Ltd* v. *International Trade Corp Ltd* (2013) Leggatt J said that he did not consider that the *Royscot* case's interpretation of section 2(1) was correct, but he acknowledged that it is binding Court of Appeal authority on the need to pattern such damages as though fraud had been established.[108]

How did the fiction of fraud arise? It is an accident of timing. The 1967 Act was a response to the Law Reform Committee's report (July 1962).[109] That report was composed ten months before the tort of negligent misstatement was discovered in the *Hedley Byrne* case, on 28 May 1963.[110] The Committee suggested[111] that statutory compensation should be 'no less extensive' than deceit damages because in 1962 deceit was the only species of tort damages available. This is a case of an insect trapped in amber, because by 1967 it should have been appreciated that the tort of negligent misstatement also supplied a (less generous) measure of damages, being subject to a reasonable foreseeability test of remoteness (this tort was declared available in the pre-contractual context in *Esso Petroleum Ltd* v. *Mardon* (1976)),[112] but the writing had been on the wall since 1963 when *Hedley Byrne* was decided.

9.22 *Defendant's burden of proof under section 2(1)*. Once the claimant has shown that a statement was false, the defendant bears the burden of proof under section 2(1) of showing that he had reasonable grounds for believing the accuracy of his statement. Bridge LJ noted the forensic importance of this point in *Howard Marine* v. *Ogden* (1978).[113]

Howard Marine v. *Ogden* (1978) concerned an inaccurate statement of the capacity of two giant barges. The defendant made the statement on the basis of the capacity figure contained in Lloyd's Register. But Lloyd's had got it wrong. At trial, the defendant admitted that he had hazily

---

104   [1997] AC 254, 267F, 283, HL.
105   *Ibid.*, at 283, HL.
106   (1991) 107 LQR 547.
107   [2000] 1 All ER (Comm) 573; [2000] Lloyd's Rep IR 535, at [14], [200] and [201].
108   [2013] EWHC 111 (QB); [2013] 1 All ER (Comm) 1321; [2013] 1 Lloyd's Rep 526, at [206].
109   Law Reform Committee, 'Innocent Misrepresentation' (Tenth Report of the Law Reform Committee, Cmnd 1782, 1962); D. Capper, 'Remedies for Misrepresentation: An Integrated System', in L. DiMatteo, Q. Zhou, S. Saintier, K. Rowley (eds.), *Commercial Contract Law: Transatlantic Perspectives* (Cambridge, 2014), chapter 16, at 406–7.
110   [1964] AC 465, HL.
111   Law Reform Committee, 'Innocent Misrepresentation' (Law Reform Committee Tenth Report, Cmnd 1782, 1962), at [22].
112   [1976] QB 801, CA.
113   *Howard Marine and Dredging Co. Ltd* v. *A Ogden & Sons (Excavations) Ltd* [1978] QB 574, 590G, CA.

recalled a different figure in the vessel's official specifications, contained in a document kept by his company. But, whether out of over-confidence, laziness or speed, the defendant did not check. The majority (Shaw and Bridge LJJ) held that damages were payable for misrepresentation under section 2(1).

Bridge LJ thought that if it had been necessary to prove that the representor had been negligent at Common Law, the claim would have failed (although he offered no reasoning on this point). In his view, the claim succeeded only because the Act placed the burden on the representor to show 'reasonable grounds' for his belief.

Section 2(1) was not important for Shaw LJ who found the representor guilty of negligence (dissenting Lord Denning MR wholly exonerated the representor).

9.23 Another advantage for claimants under this provision is that they do not need to show a 'special relationship' or satisfy the Common Law requirement of an 'assumption of responsibility' (these are requirements for establishing a duty of care in the tort of negligence; 9.17). In essence, the Common Law entitles a representee to recover damages for economic loss resulting from a negligent misstatement. The Court of Appeal in *Esso Petroleum Ltd* v. *Mardon* (1976)[114] recognised this possibility, acknowledging that tortious liability for negligent misstatements under the principle of *Hedley Byrne & Co.* v. *Heller* (1964)[115] extends to pre-contractual negotiations. But Sir Donald Nicholls V-C in *Gran Gelato Ltd* v. *Richliff Ltd* (1992)[116] held that although in some contexts an agent acting within his authority *might* assume a Common Law duty of care independently of his principal, this is *not so where*, as, on the facts of that case, a vendor's solicitor made a careless statement concerning the relevant property in a conveyancing transaction.

9.24 *Principal liable but not agent.* However, the only person liable under section 2(1) of the 1967 Act is the principal to a transaction, that is, the 'party' to the agreement: section 2(1) does not impose liability on the representor's *agent*.[117] In other words, the person whose culpable 'belief' counts is the principal (the party to the contract and hence defendant) and not his agent (who in fact made the representation).[118]

9.25 *Defences to section 2(1) claims.* There are three defences to a claim under this provision.
(1) The defendant might succeed in showing that he did have reasonable grounds for believing the accuracy of his statement, and that these grounds endured until the contract's formation.
(2) The claimant might have failed to mitigate his loss (generally on the doctrine of mitigation, see 18.22). Here, the representee cannot recover loss to the extent that he

---

114 [1976] QB 801, CA.
115 [1964] AC 465, HL.
116 [1992] Ch 560, 570.
117 *Resolute Maritime Inc.* v. *Nippon Kaiji Kyokai ('The Skopas')* [1983] 1 WLR 857, Mustill J.
118 *MCI WorldCom International Inc.* v. *Primus Telecommunications Inc.* [2004] 1 BCLC 42, Colman J, Commercial Court.

might reasonably have mitigated that loss. The mitigation rule applies to a claim under section 2(1), as well as to a Common Law claim for deceit.[119]

(3) The defendant's liability under section 2(1) can be reduced to take account of the claimant's contributory negligence, because the Law Reform (Contributory Negligence) Act 1945 (18.23) applies to such a claim, provided section 2(1) liability subsists alongside Common Law negligence on the same facts.[120] However, Sir Donald Nicholls noted in the *Gran Gelato* (1992) case that a representee's failure to check the accuracy of a representation is not an example of such contributory negligence.[121] Furthermore, the 1945 Act does *not* apply to the tort action for deceit.[122]

6. RESCISSION AB INITIO

9.26 Misrepresentation normally has the effect of rendering the contract open to rescission rather than a complete nullity. Rescission *ab initio*[123] of a voidable contract (also known as *restitutio in integrum*) involves restoring the parties to their pre-contractual position, that is, a reciprocal giving back and restoration, including, where applicable, indemnification as a substitute for, or to supplement, physical restitution (for financial adjustment to achieve complete restoration of benefits obtained, see 9.27).

> This reflects the distinction between a (supposed) void contract and a valid contract which exists until rescinded or set aside; that is, a voidable agreement.[124] In the case of a void contract (for example, the sale of a car which the purchaser already owns: so-called 'res sua cases', see 10.07), there is no agreement to set aside.

Usually, rescission is normally effected without recourse to court proceedings.

> Such self-help rescission involves the 'rescinding' party's act in notifying the other party (for a qualification in the case of fraudulent misrepresentation by absconding rogues, see the text below on the *Caldwell* case (1965)) that he is setting aside or avoiding the contract, or proposes to do so. Alternatively, rescission can result from an order made by the court, at the innocent party's request: rescission then becomes a formal remedy issued by the court. Of these two modes of rescission, the first type, the extra-judicial 'self-help method', is much more common.

---

119   On the mitigation requirement in deceit, see *Smith New Court* case, [1997] AC 254, 267, HL, at proposition (7), *per* Lord Browne-Wilkinson; and *Downs* v. *Chappell* [1997] 1 WLR 426, CA.
120   *Gran Gelato Ltd* v. *Richliff Group Ltd* [1992] Ch 560, 573–4, *per* Sir Donald Nicholls V-C.
121   *Ibid.*, at 574.
122   *Standard Chartered Bank* v. *Pakistan National Shipping Corporation (Nos. 2 and 4)* [2003] 1 AC 959, HL, at [18], *per* Lord Hoffmann, and [42] to [45], *per* Lord Rodger.
123   D. O'Sullivan, S. Elliott and R. Zakrewski, *The Law of Rescission* (Oxford, 2007), chapters 13 ff; M. A. Clarke, N. Andrews, A. M. Tettenborn, G. Virgo, *Contractual Duties: Performance, Breach, Termination and Remedies* (London, 2012), chapters 3 and 4 (by G. Virgo).
124   This distinction between void and voidable contracts continues to bedevil the contractual doctrine of mistake 'as to person' in English law: 10.24 ff.

This is because it conveniently involves merely private notification to the other party, without judicial intervention.[125]

In the case of a fraudulent misrepresentation, the Court of Appeal in *Car & Universal Finance Co.* v. *Caldwell* (1965) held that the representee can rescind by notifying the world at large (for example, by notifying the police (10.32)).[126] It would be unreasonable to expect the representee to track down the elusive rogue in this situation.

But the court left open the question whether such indirect rescission (rescission, as it were, addressed to the world at large) should be effective where the misrepresentation was non-fraudulent or perhaps in other contexts of vitiated agreements (such as duress or undue influence).

9.27 *Indemnity in event of rescission.* Equity can impose an indemnity in favour of a party who has incurred expense during the currency of the transaction which is now rescinded. That party is entitled to such payment only in respect of expenditure necessarily incurred under the terms of the relevant transaction, as *Whittington* v. *Seale-Hayne* (1900) shows.[127]

In *Whittington* v. *Seale-Hayne* (1900), the defendant, before letting a poultry farm to the plaintiff tenant, had misstated it as in good condition. The plaintiff obtained rescission, and the court held that he could also recover (i) rent paid to the defendant, (ii) rates paid to the rating authority and (iii) the cost of repair work carried out pursuant to an order of the local authority. But the indemnity did not extend to (a) the loss of poultry which had died as a result of the farm's insanitary state, nor (b) to loss of profits from running the business, nor (c) to medical expenses incurred by the manager who had also been rendered ill. Items (a) to (c) were claims in respect of loss without any corresponding ultimate gain to the misrepresentor (recovery in respect of (a) to (c) would require proof of culpability and a successful claim in tort or under section 2(1) of the 1967 Act).

9.28 *Bars to rescission.* There are four general *judicial* bars. There is also a fifth, but *statutory*, bar restricted to non-fraudulent misrepresentation (see section 2(2) of the 1967 Act, 9.29). Any of these bars is sufficient to preclude rescission.

(1) The right of rescission is lost or barred if *restoration is impossible*, that is, the parties can no longer be restored to their original position: *restitutio in integrum* has become impossible.[128]

125 J. O'Sullivan [2000] CLJ 509; a sophisticated critique of the proprietary aspects of rescission is S. Worthington, 'The Proprietary Consequences of Rescission' [2002] *Restitution Law Review* 28–69.
126 [1965] 1 QB 525, CA.
127 (1900) 82 LT 49, Farwell J; J. Cartwright, *Misrepresentation, Mistake and Non-Disclosure* (3rd edn, London, 2012), 4–17.
128 J. Cartwright, *Misrepresentation, Mistake and Non-Disclosure* (3rd edn, London, 2012), 4–52 to 4–58; *Chitty on Contracts* (31st edn, London, 2012), 6–121 ff; M. A. Clarke, N. Andrews, A. M. Tettenborn, G. Virgo, *Contractual Duties: Performance, Breach, Termination and Remedies* (London, 2012), 3–02 to 3–022 (by G. Virgo).

(2) A *third party purchaser for value in good faith without notice* might have bought chattels, shares or land before the innocent party rescinded the contract; if so, rescission is barred.[129]

(3) The innocent party might have *affirmed* the contract and so lost the right to rescind.[130]

(4) There might have been a *substantial lapse of time* since the contract's formation, and, as a result of this lapse of time, rescission might no longer be just.[131]

9.29 *Non-fraudulent misrepresentation: discretion to withhold rescission.* In the case of a *non-fraudulent* misrepresentation, the court has a *statutory* discretion to deny rescission where such a denial would be 'equitable'. If so, the court will award damages in lieu of rescission (either when the court, in its discretion, refuses rescission or, less often, if the court decides to reverse self-help rescission by the representee, *provided the representation was not fraudulent*). Section 2(2) of the Misrepresentation Act 1967 states:

> *Where a person has entered into a contract after a misrepresentation has been made to him otherwise than fraudulently, and he would be entitled, by reason of the misrepresentation, to rescind the contract, then, if it is claimed, in any proceedings arising out of the contract, that the contract ought to be or has been rescinded, the court or arbitrator may declare the contract subsisting and award damages in lieu of rescission, if of opinion that it would be equitable to do so, having regard to the nature of the misrepresentation and the loss that would be caused by it if the contract were upheld, as well as to the loss that rescission would cause to the other party.*

Three points arise concerning this provision.

First, the better view is that section 2(2) presupposes that the right to rescind must subsist at the time the court considers whether to award 'damages in lieu' (this analysis enjoys predominant judicial support,[132] although Jacob J took a different view).[133]

Secondly, liability under section 2(2) does not require proof that the representor was in any way culpable.[134] By contrast, a representor is liable to pay damages *under section 2(1)* (9.20 ff) only if he did not have reasonable grounds for believing the accuracy of his statement.

---

129 J. Cartwright, *ibid.*, 4–59 to 4–60; *Chitty on Contracts*, 6–134; M. A. Clarke et al., *ibid.*, 3–040 to 3–043 (by G. Virgo).

130 J. Cartwright, *ibid.*, 4–39 to 4–47; *Chitty on Contracts*, *ibid.*, 6–129; M. A. Clarke et al., *ibid.*, 3–023 to 3–031 (by G. Virgo).

131 J. Cartwright, *ibid.*, 4–48 to 4–51; *Chitty on Contracts*, *ibid.*, 6–132; M. A. Clarke et al., *ibid.*, 3–033 to 3–039 (by G. Virgo).

132 *Atlantic Lines & Navigation Co. Inc.* v. *Hallam* ('*The Lucy*') [1983] 1 Lloyd's Rep 188, 202, Mustill J; *William Sindall plc* v. *Cambridgeshire County Council* [1994] 1 WLR 1016, 1044E, CA (Evans LJ, dictum); *Floods of Queensferry Ltd* v. *Shand Construction Ltd* [2000] BLR 81 (Judge Humphrey Lloyd QC); *Government of Zanzibar* v. *British Aerospace Ltd* [2000] 1 WLR 2333, 2341B–2344A, Judge Raymond Jack QC; noted by D. Malet, (2001) 117 LQR 524–8; J. O'Sullivan, [2001] CLJ 239; *Pankhania* v. *Hackney London Borough Council* [2002] EWHC 2442 (Ch), at [77], Judge Rex Tedd QC.

133 *Thomas Witter Ltd* v. *TBP Industries Ltd* [1996] 2 All ER 573, 590, Jacob J; noted by H. Beale, (1995) 111 LQR 385–8.

134 *Government of Zanzibar* v. *British Aerospace Ltd* [2000] 1 WLR 2333, 2342C–E, Judge Raymond Jack QC.

Thirdly, the nature of damages under section 2(2) is not clear, but the better view is that such compensation concerns the difference between the price paid and the actual value of the property (as supported by *Chitty*[135] and *Treitel*,[136] who note that this measure is the pecuniary substitute for rescission). This is normally assessed on the basis of the property's value at the time of the property's transfer, rather than including further loss resulting from a subsequent fall in the property's value.[137] However, the court might choose a later date, if it was not practicable for the representee to have rescinded the contract at an earlier point.

Admittedly, some dicta (unattractively) suggest that section 2(2) might provide the 'cost of cure' measure of damages (on this concept, see 18.11),[138] or (again unattractively) that section 2(2) might remedy a claim for 'consequential loss'.[139] But these statements are not authoritative.

7. TERMINATION FOR BREACH AND RESCISSION FOR MISREPRESENTATION CONTRASTED

9.30 'Rescission' is a technical word better applied to *rescission ab initio*, rather than 'termination for breach', and the old-fashioned expression 'rescission for breach' has now been abandoned (the latter now being expressed more precisely as 'termination for breach': see also 17.44 and 17.45). Thus, Lord Wilberforce in *Johnson* v. *Agnew* (1980), emphasising the need to distinguish between termination for breach and rescission for misrepresentation, said:[140] 'In those cases [of rescission *ab initio*], the contract is treated in law as never having come into existence ... [A]cceptance of a repudiatory breach does not bring about "rescission ab initio".' The practical effects of this distinction are:

(1) When a contract is terminated for breach, the innocent party retains the right to sue in respect of breaches of contract[141] or payment obligations[142] which antedate the termination.

---

135 *Chitty on Contracts* (31st edn, London, 2012), 6–104; otherwise, the defendant would be unjustly enriched, as observed by P. Birks, [1997] *Restitution Law Review* 72, 75.

136 *Treitel* (13th edn, London, 2011), 9–071.

137 As on facts of *William Sindall plc* v. *Cambridgeshire County Council* [1994] 1 WLR 1016, CA (where, however, no misrepresentation was established); *Chitty on Contracts* (31st edn, London, 2012), 6–106.

138 *William Sindall plc* v. *Cambridgeshire County Council* [1994] 1 WLR 1016, CA, 1045–6, *per* Evans LJ in a dictum.

139 *Ibid.*; criticised in *Chitty on Contracts* (31st edn, London, 2012), 6–104 ff.

140 [1980] AC 367, 392–3, HL, citing, notably, Lord Porter in *Heyman* v. *Darwins Ltd* [1942] AC 356, 399, HL, and Dixon J in *McDonald* v. *Denny Lascelles Ltd* (1933) 48 CLR 457, 476–7, High Court of Australia; *Johnson* v. *Agnew* was applied in *Howard-Jones* v. *Tate* [2011] EWCA Civ 1330; [2012] 2 All ER 369; [2012] 1 All ER (Comm) 1136.

141 *Photo Production Ltd* v. *Securicor Transport Ltd* [1980] AC 827, 849, HL, *per* Lord Diplock; *Johnson* v. *Agnew* [1980] AC 367, 396, HL, *per* Lord Wilberforce; and see the decisions cited in the next note.

142 *Stocznia Gdanska SA* v. *Latvian SS Co* [1998] 1 WLR 574, HL (liability to pay accrued instalments under contract for construction of a ship); J. Beatson and G. Tolhurst [1998] CLJ 253); *Hurst* v. *Bryk* [2002] 1 AC 185, HL (former partner liable for accrued and accruing rent liability for partnership premises when liability arose before partner accepted other partners' repudiatory breach; although on that context see *Golstein* v. *Bishop* [2014] EWCA Civ 10; [2014] Ch 455 (affirming [2013] EWHC 881 (Ch); [2014] Ch 131, at [116] to [120] (Nugee QC), adopting Neuberger J in *Mullins* v. *Laughton* [2002] EWHC 2761 (Ch); [2003] Ch 250).

(2) The terminating innocent party might himself remain liable in respect of his breaches of contract which antedated termination for the guilty party's breach.[143]

9.31 *Rescission precludes a claim to compensation for breach of contract.* Rescission *ab initio* removes the opportunity to bring a claim for contractual damages based on breach of an obligation contained in the contract. This is because rescission brings the contract to an end with retrospective effect, thus removing the peg on which a claim for breach of contract might otherwise have hung. However, even where the main contract is rescinded, liability can arise under a collateral contract (9.12 to 9.16): disappearance of the main contract will not disturb the side-contract, which has a separate life.

9.32 *Overlapping modes of ending the contract.* Section 1(a) of the Misrepresentation Act 1967 affirms that a representee can have alternative claims for misrepresentation and for breach of contract in respect of a pre-contractual false statement. Section 1 of the Misrepresentation Act 1967 states:

> *Where a person has entered into a contract after a misrepresentation has been made to him, and – (a) the misrepresentation has become a term of the contract; or (b) the contract has been performed; or both, then, if otherwise he would be entitled to rescind the contract without alleging fraud, he shall be so entitled, subject to the provisions of this Act, notwithstanding the matters mentioned in paragraphs (a) and (b) of this section.*

And so the representee is at a fork in the road, and must elect between termination of the contract for breach of an important contractual term incorporated into the contract and rescission for misrepresentation.[144] As just mentioned, the decision to rescind *ab initio* for misrepresentation will preclude an action for damages based upon breach of the term (9.31).

Can a representee have a choice of damages claims for breach of contractual term (warranty, etc.) and compensation for a misrepresentation, where the relevant statement was inaccurate and became a term? Section 1 does not make clear whether a representation which has become a contractual term can also give rise to a damages claim for misrepresentation.[145] It is submitted that, in principle, if the contract is not rescinded, the innocent party should have concurrent

---

143   *Eastwood* v. *Magnox Electric plc* [2004] 1 All ER 991, HL, at [27].
144   M. P. Furmston (ed.), *Cheshire, Fifoot and Furmston's Law of Contract* (Oxford, 16th edn, 2011), 357–9 (on the 'timing' issues for the purpose of section 1, Misrepresentation Act 1967).
145   Conflicting authorities: (1) both damages causes of action arise: *Invertec Ltd* v. *De Mol Holding BV* [2009] EWHC 2471, Arnold J, at [362] to [366]; Waller J in *Naughton* v. *O'Callaghan* [1990] 3 All ER 911; and this analysis was preferred in *Leaf* v. *International Galleries* [1950] 2 KB 86, CA, Denning LJ at 90–91 (noted in *Long* v. *Lloyd* [1958] 1 WLR 753, 761, CA) (2) *per contra*, *Sycamore Bidco Ltd* v. *Breslin* [2012] EWHC 3443 (Ch), at [200] to [210], *per* Mann J; and this approach is supported by *Anson's Law of Contract* (29th edn, Oxford, 2010), 320, citing *Pennsylvania Shipping Co* v. *Compagnie Nationale de Navigation* [1936] 2 All ER 1167, 1173, by Branson J (see also *Compagnie Francaise de Chemins de Fer Paris-Orleans* v. *Leeston Shipping Co Ltd* (1919) 1 Lloyd's Rep 235, 237–8); *Chitty on Contracts* (31st edn, 2012), 6–109, 6–110 does not address the issue; and the point was missed by the Law Reform Committee, 'Innocent Misrepresentation' (Law Reform Committee Tenth Report, Cmnd 1782, 1962) at [16].

claims for compensation for misrepresentation (deceit, section 2(1), or negligent misstatement) and for breach of a term (provided, of course, there is no double recovery for the same loss). For example, Waller J in *Naughton* v. *O'Callaghan* (1990) held that where P bought racehorse 'Y' (possessing a specified pedigree), which had been wrongly described as horse 'X' (having a different pedigree), P was entitled (both on the basis of misrepresentation and breach of contract)[146] to the difference between the price paid and the value of the horse assessed at the time (two years after the sale) when the error was discovered (at that point the horse's value had declined markedly because of a series of poor runs).

8. EXCLUSION CLAUSES AND MISREPRESENTATION: COMMON LAW AND STATUTORY CONTROL

9.33 *Potential liability for fraud.* The Common Law prevents a party from excluding or limiting liability for fraudulent misstatements.[147] The rule operates so as to create a two-stage analysis: (i) a clause which is literally wide enough to include a fraudulent statement will be construed as not extending to fraud, *by virtue of this Common Law rule*; (ii) this will leave intact the non-fraudulent element of the clause (liability for negligent misrepresentation, at Common Law or under section 2(1) of the 1967 Act), and that element can be subjected to the *statutory test of reasonableness* contained in section 3 of the 1967 Act. Gloster J adopted this two-stage approach in the *Six Continents Hotels* (2006) case,[148] and she rejected *Thomas Witter Ltd* v. *TBP Industries Ltd* (1996),[149] where Jacob J had held that if an exclusion clause is literally wide enough to include fraud, then the clause is bound to fail in its entirety under section 3 of the 1967 Act, unless its 'non-fraudulent' element can be severed from its 'fraudulent' element.

9.34 *Statutory control under section 3 of the Misrepresentation Act 1967.* This provision (as substituted by section 8 of the Unfair Contract Terms Act 1977) invalidates a clause if the court concludes that it unreasonably excludes or restricts liability arising from a misrepresentation.[150] This provision is applicable *to all types of contract except contracts for the international supply of goods.*[151] Section 3 of the Misrepresentation Act 1967 states:

146 [1990] 3 All ER 911, 918–9.
147 J. Cartwright, *Misrepresentation, Mistake and Non-Disclosure* (3rd edn, London, 2012), chapter 9; J. Cartwright, in A. Burrows and E. Peel (eds.), *Contract Terms* (Oxford, 2007), chapter 11.
148 *Six Continents Hotels* case, [2006] EWHC 2317 (QB), [53] (consistent with *Government of Zanzibar* v. *British Aerospace Ltd* [2000] 1 WLR 2333, 2344A–2348A (HHJ Jack QC); and implicitly consistent with *Grimstead & Son Ltd* v. *McGarrigan* [1988–99] Info TLR 384, CA (CA, 27 October 1999; transcript No. 1733 of 1999)).
149 [1996] 2 All ER 573, 597–8, Jacob J; noted by H. Beale (1995) 111 LQR 385, 388–9.
150 J. Cartwright, *Misrepresentation, Mistake and Non-Disclosure* (3rd edn, London, 2012), 9.19 ff; J. Cartwright, in A. Burrows and E. Peel (eds.), *Contract Terms* (Oxford, 2007), chapter 11.
151 *Trident Turboprop (Dublin) Ltd* v. *First Flight Couriers* [2009] EWCA Civ 290; [2010] QB 86, at [15] ff *per* Moore-Bick LJ; *Air Transworld Ltd* v. *Bombardier Inc* [2012] EWHC 243 (Comm); [2012] 2 All ER (Comm) 60; [2012] 1 Lloyd's Rep 349, Cooke J.

> *Avoidance of provision excluding liability for misrepresentation: If a contract contains a term which would exclude or restrict – (a) any liability to which a party to a contract may be subject by reason of any misrepresentation made by him before the contract was made; or (b) any remedy available to another party to the contract by reason of such a misrepresentation, that term shall be of no effect except in so far as it satisfies the requirement of reasonableness as stated in section 11(1) of the Unfair Contract Terms Act 1977; and it is for those claiming that the term satisfies that requirement to show that it does.*

9.35 *When is a misrepresentation not a misrepresentation? Fixing the scope of section 3 of the 1967 Act.* For this purpose, the courts have drawn a troublesome distinction between: (a) a contractual provision purporting to preclude any possible 'misrepresentation' and (b) a clause which purports to cut back or exclude liability for a misrepresentation. But the courts have rightly inclined towards placing relevant clauses within category (b), so that section 3 can apply. A line of cases, beginning with *Cremdean Properties Ltd v. Nash* (1977),[152] have emphasised that the courts should have regard to substance rather than form. This requires the courts to determine whether section 3 of the 1967 Act should be engaged because in reality a misrepresentation was made, but its effects are now qualified or negatived by an exclusion clause; or whether section 3 should not catch the relevant clause because the representor has more cleverly precluded a misrepresentation from arising in the first place.

9.36 *Five types of clause.* In English law these types of clause have been considered by the courts: (1) 'entire agreement clause' (see text below at 9.37), that is, an agreement that a party has made no 'warranty' additional, or collateral, to the warranties contained in the relevant written contract; (2) a 'lack of agent's authority clause'; (3) 'no representations made clause', namely, that representations have not been made by a party concerning the relevant transaction; (4) 'mere opinion/non-verification clause', viz., that a party has not assumed any responsibility for any representations made; and (5) 'non-reliance clause', that is, that there has been no reliance on any representation.

It is clear that (1) and (2) are outside the scope of section 3 of the 1967 Act (the position concerning entire agreement clauses, category (1), is noted below at 9.37 and 9.38). The Court of Appeal in the *Springwell* case (see below for details) confirms that (3) to (5) are covered by section 3 of the 1967 Act[153] (although the position concerning (4) is not entirely clear).

---

152 (1977) 244 Estates Gazette 547, CA (see the quotations from Bridge and Scarman LJJ, cited in *Raiffeisen Zentralbank Osterreich AG v. Royal Bank of Scotland plc* [2010] EWHC 1392 (Comm); [2011] 1 Lloyd's Rep 123, at [276] and [277], by Christopher Clarke J) (E. Peel (2001) 117 LQR 545, 549 cites also *South Western General Property Co. Ltd v. Marton* (1982) 263 EG 1090 and *St Marylebone Property Co. Ltd v. Payne* [1994] EGLR 25). And the modern stream: *IFE Fund SA v. Goldman Sachs International* [2007] EWCA Civ 811; [2007] 2 Lloyd's Rep 449; *Raiffeisen Zentralbank Osterreich AG v. Royal Bank of Scotland plc* [2010] EWHC 1392 (Comm); [2011] 1 Lloyd's Rep 123, at [315]; *Springwell Navigation Corporation v. JP Morgan Chase* [2010] EWCA Civ 1221; [2010] 2 CLC 705, at [180].
153 *Springwell Navigation Corporation v. JP Morgan Chase* [2010] EWCA Civ 1221; [2010] 2 CLC 705.

The basis of clauses (3) and (5) is 'contractual estoppel'. The Court of Appeal in the *Springwell* case (2010)[154] confirmed that 'contractual estoppel' enables parties to agree (normally in writing and expressed as acknowledgments, representations or agreements) that specified prior facts or events have not occurred. This creates an evidential bar preventing the contracting parties from making factual allegations inconsistent with that agreed version of events or arrangements.

These five categories will now be considered in detail in turn.

9.37 *Entire agreement clauses generally fall outside section 3 of the 1967 Act.* Such a clause states that the parties' contractual obligations are to be found only within the four corners of the written contract and not in any side or prior agreement.[155] Exclusion of collateral warranties in this manner does not fall within the scope of section 3 of the Misrepresentation Act 1967 because that provision concerns only attempts to exclude or restrict liability for *'misrepresentation'* as distinct from contractual liability arising from breach of warranty.[156]

Lightman J explained in *Inntrepreneur Pub Company* v. *East Crown Ltd* (2000):[157]
> The purpose of an entire agreement clause is to preclude a party to a written agreement from threshing through the undergrowth and finding in the course of negotiations some (chance) remark or statement (often long forgotten or difficult to recall or explain) on which to found a claim such as the present to the existence of a collateral warranty.

But a clause could be hybrid, and be aimed simultaneously (a) to preclude collateral warranties and (b) to exclude or restrict liability for a misrepresentation. Element (b) must be spelt out clearly, as Rix LJ explained in the *AXA* case (2011).[158] The *AXA* case (2011) also decided that even though an entire agreement clause is not subject to section 3 of the Misrepresentation Act 1967, it can be subject to section 3(2)(b)(i) of the Unfair Contract Terms Act 1977 (non-consumer contracts) (modified by the Consumer Rights Bill)[159] if the clause was inserted by A as *part of A's standard written terms of business*, and on the basis that an entire agreement clause

154 *Springwell* case, *ibid.*, following *Peekay Intermark Ltd* v. *Australia and New Zealand Banking Group Ltd* [2006] EWCA Civ 386; [2006] 2 Lloyd's Rep 511, at [56], [57].
155 *Deepak Fertilisers & Petrochemicals Corp* v. *ICI Chemicals and Polymers Ltd* [1999] 1 Lloyd's Rep 387, 395, CA (noted by Gloster J in *Six Continents Hotels Inc* v. *Event Hotels GmbH* [2006] EWHC 2317 (QB), at [49]); D. McLauchlan, 'The Entire Agreement Clause . . . ' (2012) 128 LQR 521–40; M. Barber, 'The Limits of Entire Agreement Clauses' [2012] JBL 486–503.
156 *Inntrepreneur Pub Company* v. *East Crown Ltd* [2000] 2 Lloyd's Rep 611, Lightman J, adopting *McGrath* v. *Shah* (1987) 57 P & CR 452 (Chadwick QC sitting as a Deputy High Court judge); *Six Continents Hotels Inc* v. *Event Hotels GmbH* [2006] EWHC 2317 (QB), at [49], *per* Gloster J, citing *Deepak Fertilisers* v. *ICI Chemicals* [1999] 1 Lloyd's Rep 387, 395, CA, *per* Stuart-Smith LJ; and *Witter* v. *TBP Industries Ltd* [1996] 2 All ER 573, 595, *per* Jacob J.
157 [2000] 2 Lloyd's Rep 611.
158 *AXA Sun Life etc.* v. *Campbell Martin* [2011] EWCA Civ 133; [2011] 2 Lloyd's Rep 1; [2011] 1 CLC 312, at [94]; noted A. Trukhtanov, (2011) 127 LQR 345–50.
159 In respect of business to consumer contracts, the Unfair Contract Terms Act 1977's provisions are to be replaced by the Consumer Rights Bill; and the 1977 Act is to be amended so that it covers business to business and consumer to consumer contracts only.

negatives the legal effect of pre-formation oral or written assurances or undertakings.[160] However, on the facts the court held that the clause was 'reasonable': it did not operate harshly in the relevant commercial context; both parties were commercial companies, capable of understanding the effect of the clause; and the clause had the salutary effect of promoting certainty.[161]

9.38 *'Lack of agent's authority' clause.* As for (2), Brightman J in *Overbrooke Estates v. Glencombe Properties Ltd* (1974) held that section 3 of the 1967 Act does not cover a clause which denies that a party's agent has authority to make statements affecting the principal.[162] (This point should be revisited: the better view is that section 3 should apply because otherwise the salutary statutory control will be too readily evaded.)

9.39 *'No representations made' clause.* As for (3), a 'no representations made' clause, it seems clear that this falls within section 3 of the Misrepresentation Act 1967.

> This was decided in the *Springwell* case (2010),[163] by Aikens LJ; and this last case was noted by Newey J in *Avrora Fine Arts Investment Ltd* v. *Christie, Manson & Woods Ltd* (2012) as clear authority that section 3 of the 1967 Act catches a clause 'stating "no representation or warranty, express or implied, is or will be made . . . in or in relation to such documents or information"'.[164]

9.40 *'Mere opinion given without responsibility' or 'non-verification' clause.* It is unclear whether such a clause falls within section 3 of the 1967 Act, because there is a conflict of judicial views (see text below). It is submitted that the better view is that section 3 of the 1967 Act should apply, otherwise the salutary statutory control will be too readily evaded.

> This issue is on a conceptual or principled knife-edge. As noted by Newey J in the *Avrora* case (2012), the Court of Appeal in the *Springwell* case (2010) approved a lengthy passage (too long to quote here) in Christopher Clarke J's judgment in the *Raiffeisen* case (2010) which captures the dilemma in this context: (a) whether to recognise sophisticated parties' 'open-eyed' denial of responsibility or (b) enable section 3 to be applied to a draftsman's attempt to 'rewrite history' by purporting to deny that representations have been made and/or have had influence.[165]

---

160 [2011] EWCA Civ 133; [2011] 2 Lloyd's Rep 1; [2011] 1 CLC 312, at [50], *per* Stanley Burnton LJ; noted A. Trukhtanov, (2011) 127 LQR 345–50.
161 *Ibid.*, at [59], [64] to [66].
162 [1974] 1 WLR 1335 or [1974] 3 All ER 511, Brightman J; approved in *Museprime Properties Ltd* v. *Adhill Properties Ltd* (1990) 61 P & CR 111, CA.
163 *Springwell Navigation Corporation* v. *JP Morgan Chase* [2010] EWCA Civ 1221; [2010] 2 CLC 705, *per* Aikens LJ, at [182] and [182].
164 [2012] EWHC 2198 (Ch); [2012] PNLR 35, at [143] (case noted L. K. Ho and T. B. Mathias, (2014) 130 LQR 377–82).
165 *Avrora* case [2012] EWHC 2198 (Ch); [2012] PNLR 35, at [142] and [143], *per* Newey J (case noted L. K. Ho and T. B. Mathias, (2014) 130 LQR 377–82), noting both (1) *Raiffeisen Zentralbank Österreich AG* v. *Royal Bank of Scotland plc* [2010] EWHC 1392 (Comm); [2011] 1 Lloyd's Rep 123, at [313] to [315] and (2) Aikens LJ's approval in *Springwell Navigation Corp* v. *JP Morgan Chase Bank* [2010] EWCA Civ 1221; [2010] 2 CLC 705, at [181] of this discussion in *Raiffeisen*.

It is submitted that section 3 of the 1967 Act should apply, otherwise the effect is to immunise such a clause from scrutiny. This proposition is supported by the Court of Appeal in the *Springwell* case (2010),[166] and by Newey J in *Avrora Fine Arts Investment Ltd v. Christie, Manson & Woods Ltd* (2012).[167]

With respect, earlier and opposing opinion is unattractive: Toulson J[168] in the *IFE Fund SA* case (2007) held that a 'no responsibility' or 'no verification clause' would prevent a misrepresentation from arising in the first place and hence such language would not be caught by section 3 of the 1967 Act. The Court of Appeal in *IFE Fund SA* (2007) did not focus on this point.[169]

9.41   *'Non-reliance' clause.* It is clear that such a clause falls within section 3 of the Misrepresentation Act 1967. Aikens LJ in the *Springwell* case (2010) has implicitly swept away doubts on this point[170] (and there is other judicial support, which overcomes earlier doubts).[171]

9.42   *Reasonableness.* When applying the reasonableness test contained in section 3 of the Misrepresentation Act 1967, the court will be strongly influenced by the sophistication, or otherwise, of the (purported) representee (as on the facts of the *Springwell* case, 2010).[172] For example, Lewison J in *Foodco UK LLP (t/a Muffin Break) v. Henry Boot Developments Limited* (2010) said that a non-reliance clause covering negotiations for the grant of commercial leases was not unreasonable for the purpose of section 3 of the 1967 Act, for these reasons.[173] He gave detailed reasons (too long to cite here) for upholding the clause. Essentially, there was no inequality of bargaining power, the parties were both legally

---

166 *Springwell Navigation Corporation* v. *JP Morgan Chase* [2010] EWCA Civ 1221; [2010] 2 CLC 705, at [181] where Aikens LJ (rather tersely) considered these salient phrases: 'neither CMB [nor other Chase entities], will have taken any independent steps to verify the document or information' and 'nor will CMB [or other Chase entities] be responsible or liable … for the fairness, accuracy or completeness of such documents or information.'

167 [2012] EWHC 2198 (Ch); [2012] PNLR 35, at [122] and [123] (case noted L. K. Ho and T. B. Mathias, (2014) 130 LQR 377–82).

168 [2006] EWHC 2887 (Comm); [2007] 1 Lloyd's Rep 264; [2006] 2 CLC 1043, at [68] to [70]; and at [70].

169 [2007] EWCA Civ 811; [2007] 2 Lloyd's Rep 449; [2007] 2 CLC 134 (also on that case see 9.04 above). Gloster J's approval in *Springwell Navigation Corporation* v. *JP Morgan Chase* [2008] EWHC 1186, at [606], of Toulson J's analysis is not in point because Gloster J was noting at this stage only section 2 of the Unfair Contract Terms Act 1977 and not section 3 of the 1967 Act.

170 *Springwell Navigation Corporation* v. *JP Morgan Chase* [2010] EWCA Civ 1221; [2010] 2 CLC 705, at [182], declaring that the following is an exclusion clause: 'the Holder has not relied on and acknowledges that neither CMSCI nor CMIL has made any representations or warranty with respect to the advisability of purchasing this Note.'

171 *Avrora Fine Arts Investment Ltd* v. *Christie, Manson & Woods Ltd* [2012] EWHC 2198 (Ch); [2012] PNLR 35, at [122] and [123], *per* Newey J; *Government of Zanzibar* v. *British Aerospace (Lancaster House) Ltd* [2000] 1 WLR 2333, 2347 H–2348, Judge Raymond Jack QC (E. Peel (2001) 117 LQR 545, 549; J. Cartwright in A. S. Burrows and E. Peel (eds.), *Contract Terms* (Oxford, 2007), 213, at 222–5); for the opposing and unattractive view is *Watford Electronics Ltd* v. *Sanderson CFL Ltd* [2001] EWCA Civ 317; [2001] 1 All ER (Comm) 696, at [40], *per* Chadwick LJ; Hong Kong law, L. Mason [2014] JBL 313–20; on Singapore law, K. C. F. Loi and K. F. K. Low [2014] JBL 155–60.

172 *Springwell Navigation Corporation* v. *JP Morgan Chase* [2010] EWCA Civ 1221; [2010] 2 CLC 705, at [183], upholding Gloster J.

173 [2010] EWHC 358 (Ch), at [177], *per* Lewison J (retail leases situated near junction 11 of the M20 (a motorway); there had been predictions of 88,000 visitors a week; the actual figure turned out to be less than one-tenth of that figure; the decision to uphold the non-reliance clause meant that the claimants needed to establish a fraudulent misrepresentation; but none was proved).

represented during the negotiations, and 'the clause expressly permitted reliance on any [specific] reply given by the [defendant's] solicitors to the [claimants'] solicitors.'

9.43 *Part 2 of the Consumer Rights Bill (replacing the Unfair Terms in Consumer Contracts Regulations 1999).*[174] It might be argued that Part 2 of the Consumer Rights Bill will catch a term or notice which restricts a consumer's rights arising from a misrepresentation made by a trader in respect of the supply of 'goods, digital content or service'[175] (the main discussion of these provisions occurs at 15.28). The four steps necessary to sustain this contention will be: (i) the term or notice operates 'contrary to the requirement of good faith'; (ii) if the term or notice were valid this would cause '*a significant imbalance in the parties' rights and obligations*' either (a) (simply) because the exclusion or restriction will weigh the transaction heavily in favour of the representor 'trader', or (b) because that notice or term will tend to be asymmetrical, operating only to affect the trader; (iii) the phrase '*rights and obligations under the contract*' is to be applied broadly so as to include all rights and obligations arising with respect to the consumer transaction, thus including pre-contractual misrepresentation; (iv) the term or notice will manifestly operate '*to the detriment of the consumer*'.

In *Shaftsbury House (Developments) Limited v. Lee* (2010),[176] Proudman J considered (without deciding) that the 1999 Regulations[177] (antedating the Consumer Rights Bill) would catch an entire agreement clause or a non-reliance clause,[178] although the judge doubted that such a clause would then be invalidated on the present facts.[179]

9. DUTIES TO DISCLOSE

9.44 The starting point in English law[180] (although other systems differ)[181] is the general proposition that a party to pre-contractual negotiations is under no duty to disabuse the other of an error concerning the quality, nature or utility of the transaction's subject matter

---

174   Unfair Terms in Consumer Contracts Regulations 1999 (SI 1999 No. 2083) (which is to be replaced by the Consumer Rights Bill).
175   Matters covered by Part 2 of the Consumer Rights Bill.
176   [2010] EWHC 1484 (Ch).
177   Unfair Terms in Consumer Contracts Regulations 1999 (SI 1999 No. 2083).
178   [2010] EWHC 1484 (Ch), at [61] to [67].
179   *Ibid.*, at [64].
180   J. Cartwright, *Misrepresentation, Mistake and Non-Disclosure* (3rd edn, London, 2012), Part 3; *Chitty on Contracts* (31st edn, London, 2012), 6–150 ff; D. O'Sullivan, S. Elliott, R. Zakrzewski, *The Law of Rescission* (Oxford, 2008), chapter 5; see also H. Beale, *Mistake and Non-Disclosure of Facts* (Oxford, 2012); *Spencer Bower, Turner and Sutton: Actionable Non-Disclosure* (2nd edn, London, 1990); A.-S. Vandenberghe, 'The Role of Information Deficiencies in Contract Enforcement', in A. Ogus and W. H. van Boom (eds.), *Juxtaposing Autonomy and Paternalism in Private Law* (Oxford, 2011), chapter 3.
181   PECL, *Principles of European Contract Law*, Article, 4.107 and UNIDROIT's *Principles of International Commercial Contracts* (3rd edn, 2010), Article 3.2.5 renders a contract voidable if there is *fraudulent* non-disclosure of 'circumstances' and the failure conflicts with 'reasonable commercial standards of fair dealing' (UNIDROIT) or 'good faith and fair dealing' (PECL); PECL Article 4.107(3) specifies various additional factors; on the UNIDROIT principle, M. J. Bonell (ed.), *The UNIDROIT Principles in Practice: Case Law and Bibliography on*

stated (3.64 to 3.67; 10.18 to 10.20). This proposition was stated in *Smith* v. *Hughes* (1871).[182] The same proposition was affirmed, first, by Lord Atkin in *Bell* v. *Lever Bros Ltd* (1932),[183] and, secondly, by Lord Hoffmann in the *BCCI* case (2002),[184] where he commented: '[T]here is obviously room in the dealings of the market for legitimately taking advantage of the known ignorance of the other party.' Blair J held in the *Strydom* case (2009)[185] (the issue was framed as a suggested implied term in fact: 13.09 ff) that a solicitor was not obliged to reveal to his client, who had to pay fees for litigation work, that the same lawyer would be receiving generous payment for the same work under a specific governmental scheme to assist ex-miners who had suffered the relevant industrial disease.

> However, Rix LJ in *ING Bank NV* v. *Ros Roca SA* (2011) suggested that the law might adopt a more nuanced approach (his stimulating discussion is too lengthy to be cited here).[186] Rix LJ distinguished between situations where the parties are engaged in 'commerce in the raw' and situations where there is a strong element of collaboration. However, this distinction is not clear-cut. And the courts might be wary of disturbing the current law which provides a solid starting point. Rix LJ raised the possibility of using estoppel[187] (of which there are various forms; see 5.49) to require collaborative contracting parties not to take advantage of the other party's miscalculation (and indeed estoppel was indeed the solution adopted by the court on the facts of the *ING* case: 3.67).

For the moment, the better view is that each party is entitled to remain silent during the negotiations, permitting the other to make miscalculations, unless one of the following qualifications or exceptions applies:

(1) *Active misrepresentation by a half-truth.* A pre-contractual statement which misleadingly discloses only part of the true position can constitute a misrepresentation (including liability in damages): 'the true import of what was said or written is distorted by what is left unsaid, so that even if the representation is literally true in every particular it is nevertheless misleading.'[188] '[S]ome active misstatement of fact, or, at all events, such a

the *UNIDROIT Principles of International Commercial Contracts* (2nd edn, Ardsley, NY, 2006), 203 ff; S. Vogenauer and J. Kleinheisterkamp (eds.), *Commentary on the UNIDROIT Principles of International Commercial Contracts* (Oxford, 2009), 434 ff (antedating the third edition of the UNIDROIT principles, 2010); for comparative law discussion, B. Nicholas in D. R. Harris and D. Tallon (eds.), *Contract Law Today* (Oxford, 1989), 166–87; on the position in French Law, J. Ghestin in Harris and Tallon, *ibid*; and M. Fabre-Magnan, in J. Beatson and D. Friedmann (eds.), *Good Faith and Fault in Contract Law* (Oxford, 1995), chapter 4.

182 (1871) LR 6 QB 597.
183 [1932] AC 161, 224, HL.
184 *BCCI* v. *Ali* [2002] 1 AC 251, HL, at [70].
185 *Strydom* v. *Vendside Ltd* [2009] EWHC 2130 (QB); [2009] 6 Costs LR 886, at [28] to [33].
186 [2011] EWCA Civ 353; [2012] 1 WLR 472, at [92] to [95].
187 *Ibid.*, at [93], referring to the possibility of estoppel by silence or acquiescence arising in a particular context where the circumstances import a duty to point out to the other a misapprehension concerning their legal rights (citing *Tradax Export SA* v. *Dorada Cia Naviera SA ('The Lutetian')* [1982] 2 Lloyd's Rep 140, 157, where Bingham J considered Lord Wilberforce in *Moorgate Mercantile Co. Ltd* v. *Twitchings* [1977] AC 890, 903, HL).
188 *Atlantic Estates plc* v. *Ezekiel* [1991] 2 EGLR 202, *per* Mustill LJ (cited in *Safehaven Investments Ltd* v. *Springbok Ltd* (1996) 71 P & CR 59 (Ch), at 66, by Jonathan Sumption QC, sitting as a deputy High Court judge).

partial and fragmentary statement of fact, as that the withholding of that which is not stated makes that which is stated absolutely false.'[189]

A half-truth concerning the scope of an exclusion clause occurred in *Curtis* v. *Chemical Cleaning and Dyeing Co.* (1951).[190] The defendant dry-cleaning company told the plaintiff that an exclusion clause which she was about to sign covered loss due only to damage to beads and sequins. In fact this clause covered all forms of damage, including, on the facts, a stain caused during the cleaning process. Because of this misleading statement, the defendant was precluded from relying on the exclusion clause in these circumstances.[191] On a more technical point, it appears that *Curtis* involved non-incorporation of the exclusion clause (so even loss of, for example, beads and sequins would not have been excluded).[192]

---

(2) *Active misrepresentation by misleading conduct.* Deliberate steps taken by B to conceal from A the true state of affairs can constitute misrepresentation by conduct: for examples, see 9.03 at (1), noting *Spice Girls Ltd* v. *Aprilia World Service BV* (2002),[193] and *Gordon* v. *Selico* (1986);[194] as the latter case shows, the active nature of this conduct can produce liability in damages.

(3) *Falsification known to representor before contract formed.* A will have the right to rescind a contract if B has made an initially accurate statement but, before the contract's formation, B discovers (on the controversy whether knowledge is required, see 9.11) a change of situation rendering that statement misleading and B fails to notify this change to A. Furthermore, B's failure to discover the change can sometimes involve an absence of 'reasonable grounds' for maintaining that statement and so expose B to liability to pay compensation under section 2(1) of the 1967 Act (9.20).

(4) *Mistake as to terms of proposed deal: other party acquiescing.* If B knows that A is mistaken regarding B's identity (10.18 to 10.20) or as to the terms of the proposed transaction (*Hartog* v. *Colin & Shields* (1939)[195] (3.63 ff)), the contract cannot be upheld by B. In such a case, either the contract is void and/or (in the case of error as to terms) A might also have the right to insist that the contract proceed on A's supposed version (see the last portion of 3.64).

---

189   *Peek* v. *Gurney* (1873) LR 6 HL 377, 403, *per* Lord Cairns (cited in the *Safehaven* case, *ibid.*).
190   [1951] 1 KB 805, CA.
191   [1951] 1 KB 805, 810, CA, *per* Denning LJ.
192   *Curtis* case, *ibid.*, *per* Somervell and Singleton LJJ (applying the misrepresentation exception to the incorporation-by-signature rule: 15.03) as explained in Rix LJ's dicta in *AXA Sun Life Services plc* v. *Campbell Martin Ltd* [2011] EWCA Civ 133; [2011] 2 Lloyd's Rep 1; [2011] 1 CLC 312 at [99] to [105] (noted A. Trukhtanov, (2011) 127 LQR 345–50); Rix LJ also noting the minority analysis of Denning LJ in the *Curtis* case, that the exclusion clause would still take effect to the extent of the defendant's oral statement).
193   [2002] EWCA Civ 15; [2002] EMLR 27; *Chitty on Contracts* (31st edn, London, 2012), 6–014, 6–018.
194   (1986) 18 HLR 219; [1986] 1 EGLR 71; (1986) 278 EG 53, CA (dry rot; defects deliberately covered up in flat; liability for deceit); similarly, *Schneider* v. *Heath* (1813) 3 Camp 505; 170 ER 1462 (ship kept afloat to conceal defective bottom and broken keel; active misrepresentation).
195   [1939] 3 All ER 566, Singleton J.

Similarly, see 3.67 on the Court of Appeal's decision in *ING Bank NV* v. *Ros Roca SA* (2011),[196] where estoppel by convention (Carnwath LJ's analysis) or promissory estoppel/estoppel by representation (Rix LJ's analysis) was used to prevent a payor resiling from an implicit consensus concerning the level of an investment bank's additional fee.

(5) *Insurance.* Both an insurer and an assured (likewise, a reinsurer and a reassured) are obliged to disclose material facts concerning the proposed transaction,[197] but statute makes an exception in respect of consumers.[198] Court of Appeal[199] and House of Lords[200] authority establish that in this 'insurance' or 'reinsurance' context, failure to disclose does not give the 'victim' a right to compensation but merely a right to rescind the transaction (on rescission, see 9.26).

Similarly, commentators[201] have disapproved the unreasoned attempt, in *Conlon* v. *Simms* (2006), by Lawrence Collins J and, on appeal, by Jonathan Parker LJ,[202] to build a ground of liability for damages from a mere failure to disclose, even if that failure is characterised as fraudulent and even if there is a positive duty to disclose arising from the relationship between the parties, as in the case of prospective partners.

As for the question of inducement and reliance upon non-disclosure in the insurance context, Clarke LJ in *Assicurazioni Generali SpA* v. *Arab Insurance Group (BSC)* (2002) summarised the relevant factors.[203]

(6) *Creditor and guarantees: the creditor fails to disclose unusual matters known to him which affect the risk under the guarantee about to be offered by the guarantor.*[204] A creditor is obliged to reveal circumstances which directly affect the nature of the transaction in respect

196 [2011] EWCA Civ 353; [2012] 1 WLR 472.
197 *Pan Atlantic Insurance Co. Ltd* v. *Pine Top Insurance Co. Ltd* [1995] 1 AC 501, HL applied and considered in *St Paul Fire & Marine Insurance Co. (UK) Ltd* v. *McConnell Dowell Constructors Ltd* [1996] 1 All ER 96, CA; and *Assicurazioni Generali SpA* v. *Arab Insurance Group (BSC)* [2002] EWCA Civ 1642; [2003] 1 All ER (Comm) 140; [2003] 2 CLC 242 (on this doctrine see the literature cited in J. Lowry and P. Rawlings (2012) MLR 1099).
198 Consumer Insurance (Disclosure and Representation) Act 2012; J. Lowry and P. Rawlings (2012) MLR 1099.
199 *Banque Keyser Ullmann SA* v. *Skandia (UK) Insurance Co. Ltd* [1980] 1 QB 665, 774–81, CA, *per* Slade LJ, giving the court's judgment.
200 *Banque Keyser Ullmann SA* v. *Skandia (UK) Insurance Co. Ltd* [1991] 2 AC 249, 280, HL (Lord Templeman, endorsing Slade LJ's judgment, see the previous footnote); and *Manifest Shipping Co.* v. *Uni-Polaris Insurance Co. ('The Star Sea')* [2001] UKHL 1; [2003] 1 AC 469, at [46], *per* Lord Hobhouse.
201 *Anson's Law of Contract* (29th edn, Oxford, 2010), 342–3; J. Cartwright, 'Liability in Tort for Pre-Contractual Non-Disclosure', in A. Burrows and E. Peel (eds.), *Contract Formation and Parties* (Oxford, 2010), 137, at 147–9; J. Cartwright, *Misrepresentation, Mistake and Non-Disclosure* (3rd edn, London, 2012), 17.37; *Chitty on Contracts* (31st edn, London, 2012), 6–151; *Treitel* (13th edn, London, 2011), 9–153 n. 723.
202 [2006] EWHC 401; [2006] 2 All ER 1024, at [202], and supported by Jonathan Parker LJ on appeal, [2006] EWCA Civ 1749; [2008] 1 WLR 484, at [130]. Neither judge cites supporting case law authority, so the point is mere assertion.
203 [2002] EWCA Civ 1642; [2003] 1 All ER (Comm) 140; [2003] 2 CLC 242, at [62].
204 *Hamilton* v. *Watson* (1845) 12 C & F 109, 119, HL, *per* Lord Campbell; considered in *North Shore Ventures Ltd* v. *Anstead Holdings Inc* [2011] EWCA Civ 230; [2012] Ch 31, at [14], [15], [31], [32]; see also *Levett* v.

of which the guarantor is about to act as surety. But this duty of disclosure has been circumscribed in the cases. Furthermore, this limited duty of disclosure applies only to ordinary guarantees and not to 'on demand guarantees'.[205]

(7) *Fiduciaries*. A duty to disclose[206] can arise in negotiations between a principal and his fiduciary, so that the latter is obliged to speak out.[207]

(8) *Relationships of 'trust and confidence' under the rubric of undue influence*. The Court of Appeal in *Hewett* v. *First Plus Financial Group* (2010)[208] (11.29) held that a proven relationship of trust and confidence between husband and wife can import a duty to refrain from deliberate suppression of a material fact, such as non-disclosure of the fact that the husband was having an affair with another person.

(9) *Rectification*. The equitable remedy of rectification can be ordered in A's favour where, during the negotiations, B has perceived that A is mistaken concerning the terms of the proposed transaction but has unconscionably remained silent, allowing the final written terms to be concluded in a manner which contradicts A's assumption (14.31).

QUESTIONS

(1) What are the elements of a misrepresentation?

(2) What is rescission and how does it differ from termination for breach?

(3) When can a contract be rescinded for misrepresentation?

(4) What are the four general bars to rescission and what is the effect of section 2(2) of the Misrepresentation Act 1967?

(5) When will a pre-formation falsification of a statement render the representor liable for a misrepresentation or the contract subject to rescission?

(6) What are the criteria for finding a collateral warranty?

(7) How is section 2(1) of the Misrepresentation Act 1967 advantageous to the representee?

(8) What is the difference between contractual damages for loss of expectation and damages for tort (deceit, negligence or section 2(1) of the Misrepresentation Act 1967)?

(9) What are the main exceptions to the general proposition that there is no pre-contractual duty to disclose?

(10) To which types of clause does section 3 of the Misrepresentation Act 1967 apply?

(11) How might the law applicable to misrepresentations (including collateral warranties) be simplified?

Barclays Bank plc [1995] 1 WLR 1260, Burton QC, Deputy High Court judge; *Crédit Lyonnais Bank Nederland* v. *Export Credit Guarantee Department* [1996] 1 Lloyd's Rep 200, 227, Longmore J.
205   *WS Tankship II BV* v. *The Kwangju Bank Ltd, Seoul Guarantee Insurance Company* [2011] EWHC 3103 (Comm); [2012] CILL 3155, at [149], *per* Blair J (on these different types of guarantee, *ibid.* at [111]).
206   E.g. partners, *Conlon* v. *Simms* [2006] EWCA Civ 1749; [2008] 1 WLR 484; J. Cartwright, *Misrepresentation, Mistake and Non-Disclosure* (3rd edn, London, 2012), 17.33 to 17.36.
207   Generally on fiduciaries, *Calvert* v. *William Hill Credit Ltd* [2008] EWCA Civ 1427; [2009] Ch 330, at [53]; J. Edelman, 'When Do Fiduciary Duties Arise?' (2010) 126 LQR 302.
208   *Hewett* v. *First Plus Financial Group* [2010] EWCA Civ 312; [2010] Fam Law 589.

Selected further reading

D. Capper, 'Remedies for Misrepresentation: An Integrated System', in L. DiMatteo, Q. Zhou, S. Saintier, K. Rowley (eds.), *Commercial Contract Law: Transatlantic Perspectives* (Cambridge, 2014), chapter 16

J. Cartwright, *Misrepresentation, Mistake and Non-Disclosure* (3rd edn, London, 2012) (practitioner work: for reference)

J. Devenney, 'Re-Examining Damages for Fraudulent Misrepresentation', in L. DiMatteo, Q. Zhou, S. Saintier, K. Rowley (eds.), *Commercial Contract Law: Transatlantic Perspectives* (Cambridge, 2014) chapter 17

G. Spark, *Vitiation of Contracts* (Cambridge, 2013), chapter 9, notably pp. 170 to 192

Law Reform, 'Innocent Misrepresentation' (Tenth Report of the Law Reform Committee, Cmnd 1782, 1962) (precursor to the 1967 Act)

Chapter contents

10

Mistake

1. INTRODUCTION

10.01 Summary of main points

(1) The starting point[1] (which is an expression of the objective principle of agreement: 1.10 and 3.55 ff) is that a contract is valid if party A alone is mistaken as to the nature or some aspect of the proposed contract; that is, party B did not induce A's error, nor did B unconscionably acquiesce in that error. This proposition is normally expressed by saying that 'unilateral' error does not vitiate a contract, that is, it does not count (for qualifications, see (2) immediately below).

(2) Unilateral error becomes relevant (the error becomes 'operative', to use the jargon of this topic) only in one of the following three situations:

(a) if B did not speak out to disabuse A of his error when B had been aware of A's error *as to the existence or meaning of an oral or written term*: A's mistake becomes 'operative',[2] enabling A *at Common Law* to be excused from performing the supposed agreement; or

(b) in the case of written contracts, A can *obtain rectification* of the agreement, so that A's 'version' of it is incorporated into the final text (14.25 ff), if B is aware of A's error concerning the terms of the final form of the document but B fails to disabuse A of this error (rectification is separately discussed in Chapter 14); or

(c) a unilateral error can also justify 'refusal of specific performance' (an *equitable* remedy, 18.33)[3] if B is aware of the other's error but fails to disabuse A of this error.

(3) 'Common mistake' applies where the parties to a supposed agreement share a 'fundamental' error which deprives one party (or both) of the benefits which she tried to obtain from the

---

1   Generally on the history of mistake doctrine, see C. MacMillan, *Mistakes in Contract Law* (Oxford, 2010); on the nineteenth century, see M. Lobban, in W. Cornish, J. S. Anderson, R. Cocks, M. Lobban, P. Polden and K. Smith, *The Oxford History of the Laws of England*, vol. XII, *1820–1914: Private Law* (Oxford, 2010), 433 ff; general survey, S. Waddams, *Principle and Policy in Contract Law: Competing or Complementary Concepts?* (Cambridge, 2011), chapter 5.

2   A unilateral error concerning the subject matter is not enough: there is a need for A to be aware of B's error as to terms: *Smith* v. *Hughes* (1871) LR 6 QB 597; A. W. B. Simpson, (1975) 91 LQR 247, 265–9.

3   *Tamplin* v. *James* (1880) 15 Ch D 215, CA.

agreement: see, for example, *Bell* v. *Lever Bros Ltd* (1932)[4] and *'The Great Peace'* (2002).[5] In both cases, this test was not satisfied on the facts. If a contract is void, according to this test, no contractual rights will have arisen.

(4) *The Great Peace'* (2002)[6] formulated this narrow test for shared mistake at Common Law: whether the true circumstances differ radically from the supposed contractual arrangement, to the extent that it is 'impossible' to satisfy that expected performance. However, the 'impossibility' requirement is too strict and will need to be softened;[7] and this requirement is probably inconsistent with the speeches in *Bell* v. *Lever Bros Ltd* (1932), which contemplate a wider test of 'fundamental difference'.

(5) Common mistake will not arise if the relevant matter (for example, pre-contractual destruction or impairment of the subject matter) was subject to an express or implied term, or a risk assumed by one party.

(6) *'The Great Peace'* (2002)[8] repudiates the slender line of cases associated with *Solle* v. *Butcher* (1950), which had espoused an equitable doctrine of shared mistake.[9]

(7) Error as to a party's identity is another category of mistake (10.24 ff). The leading discussion is now *Shogun Finance* v. *Hudson* (2004).[10] 'Identity error' normally concerns a party's fraudulent impersonation. The source of this vexatious 'mistake' problem is that a rogue, X, pretending to be Y, dupes C into selling goods to X, and X then sells the same goods to D, the subpurchaser, who buys them in good faith. X absconds and falls out of the picture. The law has a choice between two analyses: that D has acquired good title from X (the latter having received a 'voidable' title, viz. under a transaction open to rescission, when he dealt with C); or that C remains owner because X had derived no title from C, and so X had no title to transfer to D (under the principle of *nemo dat quod non habet*, D is unprotected if X lacked even a 'voidable' title). Thus, a subpurchaser is unprotected if the main 'contract' between head vendor and rogue was void *ab initio*. However, if the contract is voidable, the subpurchaser can acquire good title if he bought the relevant chattel from the rogue in good faith and before the head vendor had rescinded the contract (on the nature of rescission, see 9.26). *Shogun Finance* v. *Hudson* (2004) supports three propositions: (a) that face-to-face transactions are unlikely to be regarded as void for error as to person, and instead will normally be voidable; this is because one party usually intends to deal with the other who is physically opposite, and the error concerns that person's good faith and creditworthiness, as *Lewis* v. *Averay* (1972) indicates;[11] (b) however, there is a chance that dealings between persons who are not face-to-face might involve a void contract, as in *Cundy* v. *Lindsay* (1878);[12] (c) the identity of parties to a written agreement is established by the names stated in that agreement.[13]

---

4 [1932] AC 161, HL, notably Lord Atkin at 217–27 and Lord Thankerton at 233–6; and see Lord Blanesburgh at 181, middle paragraph.
5 *Great Peace Shipping Ltd* v. *Tsavliris Salvage (International) Ltd* [2002] EWCA Civ 1407; [2003] QB 679; noted by F. M. B. Reynolds, (2003) 119 LQR 177; and by S. Midwinter, (2003) 119 LQR 180.
6 *Ibid.*
7 Cf Sedley LJ in *Brennan* v. *Bolt Burdon* [2004] EWCA Civ 1017; [2005] QB 303, at [60]: 'I think that in cases of mutual mistake of law a different test may be necessary.'
8 *'Great Peace'* case, [2003] QB 679, CA.
9 *Ibid.*, not following *Solle* v. *Butcher* [1950] 1 KB 671, CA.
10 *Shogun Finance Ltd* v. *Hudson* [2004] 1 AC 919, HL, *per* Lords Hobhouse, Phillips and Walker.
11 [1972] 1 QB 198, CA (approved in *Shogun* [2004] 1 AC 919, HL).
12 (1878) 3 App Cas 459, HL (upheld by majority in *Shogun* [2004] 1 AC 919, HL).
13 Upholding Dyson and Brooke LJJ in the Court of Appeal below; and applying *Hector* v. *Lyons* (1988) 58 P & CR 156, CA, at 158–9, 160; e.g., the *Liberty Mercian* case [2013] EWHC 2688 (TCC); [2014] 1 All ER (Comm) 761.

(8) The main survivor of *'The Great Peace'* case's[14] assault on 'mistake' in Equity is the doctrine of *rectification*; that doctrine permits the court to rewrite a documentary agreement to reflect the parties' prior consensus.[15] Rectification is, however, intertwined with the principles of interpreting written contracts, and so it is discussed in Chapter 14, at 14.25 ff.

2. THE NATURE OF MISTAKE

10.02 *Need for apparent agreement.* A 'mistake'[16] only becomes an issue if, first, there is an outward appearance of an agreement, that is, a consensus which is 'objectively discernible' (on this, see Lord Millett in the *Shogun* case).[17] No such outward appearance of accord can be identified if A and B have exchanged offers which relate to manifestly different subject matters, or ambiguously described subject matters.[18] A further step was taken in *Raffles* v. *Wichelhaus* (1864) where an apparent agreement, on closer inspection of the facts, turned out to be no real accord at all (for details of the case, see 4.10).[19]

10.03 *Types of mistake.* 'Mistake' becomes relevant in contract law in three main situations:
   (1) *Induced mistake.* If D makes a material misrepresentation on which P relies, P can claim (a) rescission for misrepresentation and, whether in the alternative or in addition, P can plead (b) that the misrepresentation entitles P to damages at Common Law or under section 2(1) of the Misrepresentation Act 1967 (the damages claim under the 1967 Act is more attractive: see 9.20 ff). Misrepresentation, a major part of contract law, receives detailed discussion in Chapter 9.
   (2) *Shared or common mistake.* D and P are mistaken jointly (they 'share' the mistake) about some essential feature of the subject matter of the contract. Before *'The Great Peace'* (2002), it was considered that, both at Common Law and in Equity, there were doctrines applicable to this situation (see below).[20] But, as will be shown, after *'The Great Peace'* only the Common Law applies to a shared mistake, and Equity no longer applies to that type of mistake.

---

14 [2003] QB 679, CA.

15 *Rose (Frederick E) (London) Ltd* v. *Wm H Pim Jr & Co. Ltd* [1953] 2 QB 450, CA; *Joscelyne* v. *Nissen* [1970] 2 QB 86, CA; *Riverlate Properties* v. *Paul* [1975] Ch 133, CA; *Commission for New Towns* v. *Cooper (GB) Ltd* [1995] Ch 259, CA.

16 D. Friedmann, (2003) 119 LQR 68–85 (thereafter dealing with mistake and restitutionary claims); pre-*Great Peace* literature: J. C. Smith, (1994) 110 LQR 400–19 (radical criticism of common mistake doctrine); earlier criticism along the same lines: C. J. Slade, 'The Myth of Mistake . . .' (1954) 70 LQR 386; J. Cartwright, (1987) 103 LQR 594; A. Phang, (1989) LS 291.

17 *Shogun Finance Ltd* v. *Hudson* [2003] UKHL 62; [2004] 1 AC 919, HL, at [81] (especially second sentence), [82].

18 E.g. *Falck* v. *Williams* [1900] AC 176, PC.

19 (1864) 2 H & C 906; on this 1864 decision, see *'The Great Peace'* [2003] QB 679, CA, at [28] and [29]; G. Gilmore, *The Death of Contract* (Columbus, Ohio, 1974), 35 ff; A. W. B. Simpson, *Leading Cases in the Common Law* (Oxford, 1995), 135 ff; C. MacMillan, *Mistakes in Contract Law* (Oxford, 2010), 186 ff; G. Spark, *Vitiation of Contracts* (Cambridge, 2013), chapter 7.

20 Common Law: e.g. *Smith* v. *Hughes* (1871) LR 6 QBD 597; *Bell* v. *Lever Bros Ltd* [1932] AC 161; *Hartog* v. *Colin and Shields* [1939] 3 All ER 566; *OT Africa* v. *Vickers plc* [1996] 1 Lloyd's Rep 700, Mance J. Equity: *Solle* v. *Butcher* [1950] 1 KB 671, CA (see further 10.13 ff).

(3) *Unilateral mistake known to the other party.*[21] There are two possibilities. First, D is aware[22] of P's error as to terms and fails to disabuse P of this mistake. Secondly, there is an error as to person: P makes an offer to D, P being mistaken as to D's identity (attributes will not do), and D, usually a rogue, purports to accept P's offer.

10.04 *Narrow doctrine.* Mistake in pure form is a residual ground. The tendency in recent decades has been to treat this as a narrow doctrine, subject to the following two main constraining factors:[23] first, the parties' allocation of risks, express or otherwise, will normally prevent a plea of mistake from succeeding; secondly, the courts have adopted a strict approach when applying the concept of 'fundamental mistake' at Common Law. Thus, attempts to invoke the doctrine of mistake in the context of commercial agreements have been largely unsuccessful.[24]

10.05 *Mistake and related doctrines.* Suppose A sells a picture to B for £5m. The picture is believed by both to be a Picasso. This situation gives rise to five possible permutations:
(1) *Breach of contract.* B can return the picture, or sue for damages, if it was a term of the contract that 'it is a Picasso'.[25]
(2) *Misrepresentation.* B can rescind the contract (even if the misrepresentation was not culpable) (and obtain damages if the misrepresentation has been culpable) if A has made a misrepresentation in stating that it is a Picasso.[26]
(3) *Property already owned by purchaser/property destroyed before sale.*[27] The contract is void if the painting sold to B was in fact already B's property.[28] The same is true if the picture is destroyed before the sale through no fault of the vendor.[29]
(4) *Shared error as to 'quality'.* However, mistake in this context is rightly described by *Treitel*[30] as implausible because the contract is likely to contain an express term concerning the painting's authenticity (on which term the purchaser will be able to sue), or the speculative and risk-laden nature of the contract will exclude mistake by allocating the risk or 'gamble' to one of the parties, depending on whether the price was set at a high or a low level.[31] The question arises: what if A and B spontaneously believed that the picture was a

---

21   See previous note.

22   *OT Africa* v. *Vickers* [1996] 1 Lloyd's Rep 700, 703, Mance J ('knowledge' includes imputed knowledge, that is, 'a mistake by one party' 'which the other knew or ought reasonably to have known'; in other words, an obvious error which the non-mistaken party ought to have appreciated: 10.18 to 10.20, 3.63 ff).

23   D. Friedmann, (2003) 119 LQR 68–85 (thereafter dealing with mistake and restitutionary claims).

24   E.g. *Clarion Ltd* v. *National Provident Institution* [2000] 1 WLR 1888, Rimer J.

25   *Harlingdon & Leinster Enterprises Ltd* v. *Christopher Hull Fine Art* [1990] 1 All ER 337, CA; noted by [1990] LMCLQ 455: see 9.06.

26   Under *Derry* v. *Peek* (1889) 14 App Cas 337, HL (on which see 9.17) and section 2(1) of the 1967 Act (on which see 9.20).

27   Categories known, respectively, as *res sua* (I bought or rented my own thing) or *res extincta* (I bought or rented something which has ceased to exist before the sale/lease, or even which never existed).

28   *Cooper* v. *Phibbs* (1867) LR 2 HL 149, 170, *per* Lord Westbury; noted by P. Matthews, (1989) 105 LQR 599; on this case, see 10.14.

29   Section 6 of the Sale of Goods Act 1979.

30   *Treitel* (13th edn, London, 2011), 8–020.

31   On the question of terms in this context, see *Harlingdon & Leinster Enterprises* v. *Christopher Hull Fine Art* [1991] 1 QB 564, CA (purchaser was an expert and placed no reliance on the seller's attribution of a painting); considered by Buckley J in *Drake* v. *Thos Agnew & Sons Ltd* [2002] EWHC (QB) 294, at [24] to [32], on which see 9.14; and *Avrora Fine Arts Investment Ltd* v. *Christie, Manson & Woods Ltd* [2012] EWHC 2198 (Ch); [2012]

Picasso, but it was by someone else? A dictum in Lord Atkin's speech in *Bell* v. *Lever Bros Ltd* (1932), concerning paintings, indicates that the agreement is nevertheless a valid agreement.[32] This is because of the narrow nature of fundamental error at Common Law. Until 2002 a more generous test, enunciated in *Solle* v. *Butcher* (Equity's leading, but controversial, case), potentially enabled B to rescind the contract on the basis of a 'fundamental' error shared by the parties.[33] This rested on an equitable doctrine of common error. As we shall see (10.13 ff), however, the Court of Appeal in *'The Great Peace'* (2002) declared this to be an unsupportable doctrine because it was considered to be inconsistent with a dictum of Lord Atkin in the House of Lords in *Bell* v. *Lever Bros Ltd* (1932).

(5) *Unilateral error as to substance known to the other party.* The contract is not vitiated if B thinks it is a Picasso and A knows of this error. This is regarded as an 'inoperative' and merely 'unilateral' error as to the contract's 'subject matter'. Such an error does not count.[34] But this error does operate if B thinks it is a term of the contract that it is a Picasso, provided A knows that B has this special belief.[35]

3. SHARED MISTAKE AT COMMON LAW

10.06 On this topic[36] the two leading decisions are *Bell* v. *Lever Bros Ltd* (1932), where Lord Atkin's speech is the most important, and *'The Great Peace'* (2002) where the Court of Appeal surveyed the whole topic. In *Bell* v. *Lever Bros Ltd* (1932) (see 10.09), Lord Atkin said:

> [A] mistake will not affect assent unless it is the mistake of both parties, and is as to the existence of some quality which makes the thing without the quality essentially different from the thing as it is believed to be.[37]

The Court of Appeal in *'The Great Peace'* (2002), as we shall see, (unsuccessfully) attempted to render the Common Law doctrine of shared mistake's core element even more restrictive by formulating a test of strict 'impossibility' (this case is examined at 10.10 ff below). In *'The Great Peace'* (2002) Lord Phillips said:[38]

PNLR 35, *per* Newey J, at [131], and at [134]; see also *Thomson* v. *Christie Manson & Woods Ltd* [2004] EWHC 1101 (QB); [2004] PNLR 42, at [199], *per* Jack J.

32   *Bell* v. *Lever Bros Ltd* [1932] AC 161, 224; other restrictive dicta in *Leaf* v. *International Galleries* [1950] 2 KB 86, 89, 94, CA; however, *Treitel* (13th edn, London, 2011), 8–020, thinks this too severe.

33   [1950] 1 KB 671, CA.

34   *Smith* v. *Hughes* (1871) LR 6 QBD 597.

35   On these last two propositions, see *Smith* v. *Hughes* (1871) LR 6 QBD 597 (Common Law); *Solle* v. *Butcher* [1950] 1 KB 671 CA (equitable echo).

36   A. Tettenborn, 'Agreements, Common Mistake and the Purpose of Contract' (2011) 27 JCL 91–118 (contending that the post-*Great Peace* doctrine of common error is too restrictive); G. Spark, *Vitiation of Contracts* (Cambridge, 2013), chapter 4.

37   [1932] AC 161, 218, HL; generally on this decision, see C. MacMillan, *Mistakes in Contract Law* (Oxford, 2010), 259 ff (for a similarly strict Common Law decision, cited in the present decision at 207, 218, 233, Blackburn J in *Kennedy* v. *Panama, New Zealand and Australian Royal Mail Co.* (1867) LR 2 QB 580, 586–8; on which see C. MacMillan, *Mistakes in Contract Law* (Oxford, 2010), 190 ff).

38   [2002] EWCA Civ 1407; [2003] QB 679, at [76].

[T]he following elements must be present if common mistake is to avoid a contract:

(i) there must be a common assumption as to the existence of a state of affairs;

(ii) there must be no warranty by either party that that state of affairs exists;[39]

(iii) the non-existence of the state of affairs must not be attributable to the fault of either party;[40]

(iv) the non-existence of the state of affairs must render performance of the contract impossible;[41]

(v) the state of affairs may be the existence, or a vital attribute, of the consideration to be provided or circumstances which must subsist if performance of the contractual adventure is to be possible.

A rider to (ii), appearing later in the court's judgment, is the proposition that the court must construe the agreement in order to determine whether '[a] party has undertaken the risk that it may not prove possible to perform the contract, and the answer to this question may well be the same as the answer to the question whether the impossibility of performance is attributable to the fault of one or other of the parties'.[42]

Lord Phillips in 'The Great Peace' (2002) also made clear that 'the theory of the implied term is as unrealistic when considering common mistake as when considering frustration', adding: 'avoidance of a contract on the ground of common mistake results from a rule of law.'[43]

10.07 *Instances of contracts void for shared mistake.* There are numerous cases, mostly decided in the nineteenth century, where supposed transactions were held to be void, that is, rendered a complete nullity, on the basis of common mistake: cases within category A (see the text below) are commonly denoted as instances, or extensions, of *res extincta* (that is, a subject matter which no longer exists); and category B (see the text below) concerns so-called *res sua* (that is, the subject matter of the proposed sale or lease is already owned by the 'purchaser'/'tenant').

The following are examples of *res extincta*:

(1) A sale of specific goods where the goods have already perished without the seller being aware, as provided by section 6 of the Sale of Goods Act 1979, a provision reflecting the result in *Couturier* v. *Hastie* (1865).[44]

(2) The same would be true of a sale of specific property which has never existed, unless the contract is conceived as wholly aleatory (if so, the buyer would bear the risk of its

---

39 On element (ii) of this test, see *ibid.*, at [75].

40 On element (iii), see *ibid.*, at [77] to [79], noting the High Court of Australia's decision in *McRae* v. *Commonwealth Disposals Commission* (1951) 84 CLR 377, 408, 410.

41 Cf Lord Radcliffe's radical difference test in *Davis Contractors Ltd* v. *Fareham Urban District Council* [1956] AC 696, 729, HL, quoted at 16.02.

42 [2002] EWCA Civ 1407; [2003] QB 679 at [84]; on the question whether contract distributes the risk, see *William Sindall plc* v. *Cambridgeshire County Council* [1994] 1 WLR 1016, 1034H–1035E, CA; see also *Kalsep Ltd* v. *X-Flow BV, The Times*, 3 May 2001, Pumfrey J, noted by A. Phang, [2002] CLJ 272–3; *Brennan* v. *Bolt Burdon* [2004] EWCA Civ 1017; [2005] QB 303, at [38] to [40].

43 *Great Peace Shipping Ltd* v. *Tsavliris Salvage (International) Ltd* [2003] QB 679, CA, at [73].

44 (1856) 5 HL Cas 673; P. S. Atiyah, (1959) 75 LQR 487; C. MacMillan, *Mistakes in Contract Law* (Oxford, 2010), 181 ff.

non-existence) or the seller has impliedly undertaken to bear responsibility if the subject matter does not exist, as in *McRae* v. *Commonwealth Disposals Commission* (1951).[45]

(3) A guarantee for the payment of rent on machines (or other property) which does not exist: *Associated Japanese Bank Ltd* v. *Crédit du Nord SA* (1989).[46]

(4) The sale of an annuity (creating an income stream for a period) on the name of a person who, unknown to the parties to the supposed sale, is already dead: *Strickland* v. *Turner* (1852).[47]

(5) The transfer of a life assurance policy on the life of a person who is, unknown to either party to the transfer, already dead: *Scott* v. *Coulson* (1903).[48]

(6) The renewal of an insurance policy in ignorance of the fact that the assured has already died: *Pritchard* v. *Merchants' and Tradesman's Mutual Life Assurance Society* (1858).[49]

(7) The sale of a bill of exchange which is in fact invalid for forgery (*Gompertz* v. *Bartlett* (1853))[50] or which is invalid for lack of formality (*Gurney* v. *Womersley* (1854)).[51]

The following is an example of *res sua*:

(1) The purchase of title or the grant of a lease in a property already owned absolutely by the purchaser or the proposed tenant (on the latter situation, see the facts of *Cooper* v. *Phibbs* (1867)[52] at 10.14).

10.08 '*Essential difference*' *test*. These examples of transactions foundering on the basis of initial and profound miscalculations are easily subsumed within the strict criterion of 'impossibility' enunciated in '*The Great Peace*' (2002): see point (iv) of the extract quoted at 10.06 above from the judgment of Lord Phillips in this case: 'the non-existence of the state of affairs must render performance of the contract impossible.' But that criterion cannot prevail and the slightly wider 'essential difference' test is instead appropriate. The latter had been adopted in *Bell* v. *Lever Bros Ltd* (1932) (see below) and remains authoritative.

> This wider test accommodates the nuances of commercial disappointment which must be covered by 'common mistake'.
>
> For example, in 'the Coronation litigation' (16.13), a licence to view the procession was held to be void *ab initio*, neither party being yet aware that the Coronation had just been postponed (one hour earlier) because of the King's ill-health: *Griffith* v. *Brymer* (1903).[53]
>
> And, in the post-*Great Peace* case law, there are already strong hints that 'impossibility' is not the appropriate test. Thus, Sedley LJ in *Brennan* v. *Bolt Burdon* (2004) attractively suggested that the concept of 'impossibility' is too narrow. He suggested that mistake extends to situations

---

45 (1951) 84 CLR 377, High Court of Australia.
46 [1989] 1 WLR 255, Steyn J (where discussion of 'mistake' was technically *obiter*, the case being decided on a question of construction).
47 (1852) 7 Exch 208.
48 [1903] 2 Ch 249, CA.
49 (1858) 3 CB (NS) 622.
50 (1853) 2 E & B 849.
51 (1854) 4 E & B 133.
52 (1867) LR 2 HL 149.
53 (1903) 19 TLR 434, Wright J.

where the parties' shared assumption has proved to be fundamentally unfounded but the contract has not become 'impossible'.[54]

In *Kyle Bay Ltd* v. *Underwriters etc.* (2007), Neuberger LJ suggested that the impossibility test and the 'essential or radical difference' test are broadly similar.[55] In *Champion Investments Ltd* v. *Ahmed* (2004),[56] the judge said that the test was whether the mistake rendered the contract 'essentially different from what the parties believed it to be' (*Bell* v. *Lever Bros Ltd* (1932), on which see 10.09) or 'did it render performance of the contract impossible' (*The Great Peace*', on which see the earlier part of this paragraph, and 10.10 ff).

It seems clear, therefore, that the 'essential difference' test has survived. Furthermore, *Graves* v. *Graves* (2007) (see 10.12 for details)[57] shows that impossibility is too stern a test.

10.09 Bell *v*. Lever Bros Ltd (1932).[58] The facts were as follows:

Two directors, Bell and Snelling, of a company operating in West Africa, were paid large 'severance' payments by a controlling parent company, Lever Brothers Ltd. The latter then discovered that both directors might have been dismissed without compensation because they had committed breaches of their fiduciary[59] duties towards the African company. Lord Blanesburgh, who was a member of the majority, explained that Lever Brothers had arranged for Bell and Snelling to become directors of the Niger Company and its associated companies, but Lever Brothers were not their employers. Therefore, Lever Brothers did not have the power to 'dismiss' Bell or Snelling from employment.[60] Lever Brothers sued to recover these sums. To succeed, the claimant company needed to show that the 'golden handshake' agreements were vitiated by a common mistake. But a bare majority of the House of Lords (overturning the decisions of both the lower courts) held that the error was not serious (or 'fundamental') enough.

Lord Atkin, a member of the majority, after noting that a contract can be void if there is an error as to identity (on which see 10.24 below) or as to the existence of the subject matter at the date of the supposed contract, acknowledged the further possibility of a fundamental error as to the quality of the subject matter. But his test was very narrow:[61]

> Mistake as to quality of the thing contracted for raises more difficult questions. In such a case a mistake will not affect assent unless it is the mistake of both parties, and is as to the existence of some quality which makes the thing without the quality essentially different from the thing as it was believed to be.[62]

54 *Brennan* v. *Bolt Burdon* [2004] EWCA Civ 1017; [2005] QB 303; *Treitel* (13th edn, London, 2011), 8–022 ff; J. Cartwright, *Misrepresentation, Mistake and Non-Disclosure* (3rd edn, London, 2012), 3.34 ff.
55 [2007] EWCA Civ 57; [2007] Lloyd's Rep IR 460, at [23] to [25].
56 [2004] EWHC 1956 (QB), at [32], William Blair QC.
57 [2007] EWCA Civ 660; [2008] HLR 10; [2008] L & TR 15; [2007] 3 FCR 26.
58 [1932] AC 161, HL; on the factual background to this case, see C. MacMillan, (2003) 119 LQR 625; C. MacMillan, *Mistakes in Contract Law* (Oxford, 2010), 259 ff; see also A. Chandler, J. Devenney and J. Poole, 'Common Mistake, Theoretical Justification and Remedial Inflexibility' [2004] JBL 34–58.
59 *Calvert* v. *William Hill Credit Ltd* [2008] EWCA Civ 1427; [2009] Ch 330, at [53]; J. Edelman, 'When Do Fiduciary Duties Arise?' (2010) 126 LQR 302.
60 [1932] AC 161, 172, HL.
61 *Ibid.*, at 218.
62 Compare the more elaborate test in section 6(b) of the New Zealand Contractual Mistakes Act 1977.

Lord Atkin gave various examples of errors not satisfying this 'essentially different quality' test:[63]
> A buys B's horse; he thinks the horse is sound and he pays the price of a sound horse; he would
> certainly not have bought the horse if he had known as the fact is that the horse is unsound. If
> B has made no representation as to soundness and has not contracted that the horse is sound,
> A is bound and cannot recover back the price. A buys a picture from B; both A and B believe it
> to be the work of an old master, and a high price is paid. It turns out to be a modern copy. A has
> no remedy in the absence of representation or warranty . . . [Such] cases . . . can be supported
> on the ground that it is of paramount importance that contracts should be observed, and that
> if parties honestly comply with the essentials of the formation of contracts – i.e., agree in the
> same terms on the same subject matter – they are bound, and must rely on the stipulations of
> the contract for protection from the effect of facts unknown to them.

In *Bell* v. *Lever Bros Ltd* (1932), Lord Blanesburgh, another member of the majority, but whose long
speech is seldom properly considered, explained the commercial considerations which underpin the
majority's decision: first, that the payments under the 'agreements of settlement' were
'sweeteners', intended to secure peace and finality. Thus Lever Bros entered these agreements to
secure the directors' enthusiastic assistance in preparing for the amalgamation of various West
African companies. That corporate restructuring would also entail making them redundant.
Secondly, Lord Blanesburgh noted that the payments were intended to induce them to resign
voluntarily and without controversy. Lever Brothers' interests might have been seriously prejudiced
if the directors had proved recalcitrant, and the entire amalgamation had instead misfired.[64]

Lord Blanesburgh explained that apart from the mistaken assumption that the directors were
still owed money, there were wider factors in play, namely:[65]
> (1) to enlist their support of the amalgamation and to have their assistance in carrying it
> through in all its details to completion: above all, (2) to secure, on May 1 following, the
> voluntary resignation by each appellant of all his offices, results of value, it may have been
> of infinite value, to the prospects of a delicate negotiation in the success of which millions
> of pounds were involved. [numbering added]

Lord Blanesburgh emphasised the fragility and sensitivity of the commercial venture:
> [Results (1) and (2)] could not have been secured if Levers, instead of [making the settlement
> offers], had, with the real offending transactions then disclosed to them, repudiated all
> further obligations under their agreements with the [directors], and as shareholders in Niger
> had sought, in spite of the [directors'] opposition – quite effective for a sufficiently long
> period – to remove them from office.

The case was certainly borderline, but it is submitted that Lord Blanesburgh's explanation
persuasively draws out the wider context and justifies the majority decision allowing the
directors to retain these payments.

However, some commentators have doubted whether the majority's decision is convincing.
For example, JC Smith contended[66] that the case fell squarely within the scope of a notion of *res
sua* or *res extincta*: that Lever Bros had purported to 'buy' something (termination of the
directorships) which they already 'owned' (in the sense that the directorships were already
voidable) or something which has ceased to exist. But Smith's analysis, although ingeniously
presented, fails to reflect the wider factors emphasised by Lord Blanesburgh.

---

63   [1932] AC 161, 218, HL.
64   *Ibid.*, at 200.
65   *Ibid.*, at 181, where these factors are encapsulated.
66   (1994) 110 LQR 400, 414–15.

10.10 'The Great Peace' *(2002).*[67] In this case, the Court of Appeal applied *Bell* v. *Lever Bros Ltd* *(1932)*[68] to these facts:

> The defendant salvage company hired the claimant's ship, *The Great Peace*, for five days to escort a stricken ship, which was in danger of sinking in the Indian Ocean. A third party source had innocently misled the salvage company into believing that the claimant's ship was closest to the stricken vessel. In fact, another ship was closer to the stricken vessel and so better placed to provide 'stand by' assistance. The Court of Appeal (and, earlier, Toulson J) upheld the claimant's action for the agreed five days' hire. Both courts rejected the salvage company's defence of fundamental mistake. The salvage company had delayed cancelling the hire until it was clear that another ship was closer. This strategic delay showed that during the period of hesitation, the claimant's ship might have been of use to the salvage company. The Court of Appeal said:[69] '[T]he fact that the [stricken ship and *The Great Peace*] were considerably further apart than the [defendants] had believed did not mean that the services that *The Great Peace* was in a position to provide were essentially different from those which the parties had envisaged when the contract was concluded.'

> It is suggested that this decision is fair and reasonable. The party requiring urgent assistance should surely bear the risk that hastily gathered information might prove to be inaccurate. The terms of the 'rescue' charter did not explicitly transfer this risk of inaccurate information to the claimant rescue-ship owner, for example, by stating that its ship was believed to be 'the closest ship to the casualty'.[70] And it is arguably in the public interest that contracts for maritime rescue should not be lightly declared void on grounds of mistake.

10.11 *Mistake of law.*[71] The Court of Appeal in *Brennan* v. *Bolt Burdon* (2004) has confirmed that a shared mistake concerning a pure point of law can vitiate a contract.[72]

10.12 *Renaissance of the implied term technique.* The Court of Appeal in *'The Great Peace'* (2002) said that 'the theory of the implied term is as unrealistic when considering common mistake as when considering frustration.'[73] It added: '[A]voidance of a contract on the ground of common mistake results from a rule of law.'[74] However, the later decision in *Graves* v. *Graves* (2007) shows that the 'implied term technique' has not been jettisoned, although on the facts of that case this technique was used to impose an 'implied condition *subsequent*'[75] which terminated an agreement.

---

67 [2002] EWCA Civ 1407; [2003] QB 679; F. M. B. Reynolds, (2003) 119 LQR 177; S. Midwinter, (2003) 119 LQR 180; for other literature considering this decision, see C. MacMillan, in C. Mitchell and P. Mitchell (eds.), *Landmark Cases in the Law of Restitution* (Oxford, 2006), 357 n. 180.
68 [1932] AC 161, HL.
69 [2002] EWCA Civ 1407; [2003] QB 679, at [165].
70 During the parties' discussion, 'closest ship' had been uttered, it seems.
71 On finality and compromises, see N. Andrews, 'Mistaken Settlement of Disputable Claims' [1989] LMCLQ 431.
72 [2004] EWCA Civ 1017; [2005] QB 303; approved in *Meretz Investments NV* v. *ACP Ltd* [2007] EWCA Civ 1303; [2008] Ch 244, at [118].
73 *'The Great Peace'* [2002] EWCA Civ 1407; [2003] QB 679, at [73].
74 *Ibid.*, at [73].
75 [2007] EWCA Civ 660; [2008] HLR 10; [2008] L & TR 15; [2007] 3 FCR 26, at [38] to [41].

The facts of the *Graves* case (2007) were as follows. After Mr and Mrs Graves divorced, the former husband allowed her to become a tenant of his property, provided she paid rent. Both parties had assumed that 90 per cent of her rent would be financed by housing benefit. Later it was discovered that this was an error (benefit could not be validly paid on these facts; the error was a matter of 'law', but such a mistake is now treated as significant, see 10.11). And so the ex-husband applied to evict Mrs Graves because of her non-payment of rent. The claim succeeded, but the court found an implied condition precedent, a term implied so as to terminate the contract. This enabled the court to adjust the parties' relations to achieve broad justice.

4. NO RESCISSION FOR SHARED MISTAKE IN EQUITY: 'THE GREAT PEACE' REPUDIATING SOLLE V. BUTCHER

10.13 The Court of Appeal in *'The Great Peace'* (2002) also held that there is no separate equitable doctrine of rescission for shared mistake.[76] It rejected Denning LJ's decision in *Solle* v. *Butcher* (1950)[77] which had stood – although admittedly not flourished[78] – for fifty years. In *Solle* v. *Butcher*, Denning LJ had said that the equitable remedy of rescission can be awarded in respect of a common or shared mistake concerning a fundamental aspect of the subject matter, provided the party seeking relief was not at fault. Where appropriate, relief would be granted on terms (that is, with strings attached by the court, in order to achieve fairness to both parties).

10.14 In *Solle* v. *Butcher* (1950) Denning LJ had suggested that there were three categories covered by equitable mistake: (1) misrepresentation (on which see Chapter 9); (2) error unconscionably acquiesced in; and (3) shared error.[79]

As for (2), Lord Phillips MR in *'The Great Peace'* indicated that this aspect of equitable relief was not being swept away:[80] '[C]ases of fraud and misrepresentation, and undue influence, are all

---

76 [2002] EWCA Civ 1407; [2003] QB 679; K. F. K. Low, 'Coming to Terms with *The Great Peace* in Common Mistake', in J. W. Neyers, R. Bronaugh and S. G. A. Pitel (eds.), *Exploring Contract Law* (Oxford, 2009), 319 ff.
77 *Solle* v. *Butcher* [1950] 1 KB 671, CA; C. MacMillan, in C. Mitchell and P. Mitchell (eds.), *Landmark Cases in the Law of Restitution* (Oxford, 2006), chapter 12; and she cites (*ibid.*, at 54 n. 166) massive academic literature on the *Solle* case; C. MacMillan, *Mistakes in Contract Law* (Oxford, 2010), 278 ff.
78 Cases applying the *Solle* case had included: *Magee* v. *Pennine Insurance Ltd* [1969] 2 QB 507, 514–15, CA (Lord Denning MR applying his earlier decision); *West Sussex Properties Ltd* v. *Chichester District Council* [2000] All ER (D) 887, CA; *Nutt* v. *Read* (1999) 32 HLR 76, CA; *Laurence* v. *Lexcourt Holdings Ltd* [1978] 1 WLR 1128; *Grist* v. *Bailey* [1967] Ch 532 (Hoffmann LJ, in *William Sindall plc* v. *Cambridgeshire County Council* [1994] 1 WLR 1016, 1035, CA, doubted the validity of both the *Grist* and *Laurence* cases); *Associated Japanese Bank* v. *Crédit du Nord* [1989] 1 WLR 255, 267–8, Steyn J: '[A] narrow doctrine of Common Law mistake (as enunciated in *Bell* v. *Lever Bros Ltd* [1932] AC 161, HL, supplemented by the more flexible doctrine of mistake in Equity (as developed in *Solle* v. *Butcher* [1950] 1 KB 671, CA and later cases), seems to me to be an entirely sensible and satisfactory state of the law.' On this case, see G. H. Treitel, 'Mistake in Contract' (1988) 104 LQR 501; and J. C. Smith, 'Contracts – Mistake, Frustration and Implied Terms' (1994) 110 LQR 400–19; on these decisions, see *'The Great Peace'* [2002] EWCA Civ 1407; [2003] QB 679, CA, at [135] to [151].
79 [1950] 1 KB 671, 692–3, CA.
80 *'The Great Peace'* [2002] EWCA Civ 1407; [2003] QB 679, at [156].

catered for under other existing and uncontentious equitable rules. We are only concerned with the question whether relief might be given for common mistake in circumstances wider than those stipulated in *Bell* v. *Lever Bros Ltd*.'

T. M. Yeo considers a Singaporean decision in which a contract was rescinded in Equity because the purchaser had taken advantage of a manifest error in the price at which computers were advertised by the vendor.[81] As discussed in this book at 3.63, the better view is that there is no need for an equitable doctrine of mistake as to terms, of which the other party is constructively aware. At Common Law, such a transaction will be void. And (in the absence of a misrepresentation by A), B's error as to subject matter cannot give rise to rescission in Equity.[82]

The category which has now been expunged by 'The Great Peace' (2002) is category (3), on which Denning LJ had said this:

> [A] contract is also liable in Equity to be set aside if the parties were under a common misapprehension either as to facts or as to their relative and respective rights, provided that the misapprehension was fundamental and that the party seeking to set it aside was not himself at fault.

This third category has been declared invalid (see the discussion of 'The Great Peace' case below).

Denning LJ in *Solle* v. *Butcher* (1950) had adopted as support for category (3) above the House of Lords decision in *Cooper* v. *Phibbs* (1867)[83] (probably with justification – see ensuing analysis).

In *Cooper* v. *Phibbs* (1867), an uncle had spent money improving an Irish salmon fishery. He then leased it to his nephew. The parties were mistaken as to their legal position. In fact, the nephew was already the owner of it (as tenant for life).[84] The parties were acting, therefore, under a mistake as to their private rights. The nephew's application for rescission was upheld (this was an application to a court of Equity for the setting aside of the contract and consequential relief). But the House of Lords added the condition that allowance should be made in the uncle's favour for the improvements he had made to the fishery. This was worked out by the imposition of a lien in the uncle's favour. Because the uncle had died, the benefit of the lien accrued in favour of the trustee for the uncle's daughters. The basis of this decision has been disputed. *Chitty*[85] cites this 1867 case as a possible example of Equity applying 'general principles of restitution' in the context of a void transaction, but Paul Matthews has contended that the case, properly

---

81   T. M. Yeo, 'Great Peace: A Distant Disturbance' (2005) 121 LQR 393, noting *Chwee Kin Keong* v. *Digilandmall.com Pte Ltd* [2005] 1 SLR 502 (Singapore Court of Appeal).
82   *Statoil ASA* v. *Louis Dreyfus Energy Services LP* ('The Harriette N') [2008] EWHC 2257 (Comm); [2009] 1 All ER (Comm) 1035; [2008] 2 Lloyd's Rep 685, at [98] to [105] (rejecting *Huyton SA* v. *Distribuidora Internacional de Productos Agricolas SA de CV* [2003] 2 Lloyd's Rep 780, at [455]; see also *Harrison* v. *Halliwell Landau* [2004] EWHC 1316 (QB); Andrew Smith J in the *Huyton* case suggested that Equity has a wider power to invalidate a contract where B's error (suspected by A) does not concern a *term*, merely the subject matter; but Aikens J's repudiation of this liberal approach is persuasive).
83   (1867) LR 2 HL 149, 170, *per* Lord Westbury; P. Matthews, (1989) 105 LQR 599; C. MacMillan, *Mistakes in Contract Law* (Oxford, 2010), 62 ff.
84   P. Matthews, (1989) 105 LQR 599, at 606, shows that he was owner under an equitable title.
85   *Chitty on Contracts* (31st edn, London, 2012), 5–062.

scrutinised, did not concern a contract void at Common Law.[86] Instead, it does appear that the contract was regarded by the House of Lords as subsisting until set aside.

Wright J (later Lord Wright, MR, an outstanding judge) assumed in *Robert A Munro & Co.* v. *Meyer* (1930)[87] that there was an equitable doctrine, subsisting in parallel to the narrow Common Law doctrine of common mistake, entitling the court in exercise of its discretion to set aside agreements on the basis of shared error, especially with regard to their 'private legal rights'. However, on the facts of that case he chose not to find that mistake had been operative.

Furthermore, in a learned examination of this aspect of the mistake doctrine, Catherine MacMillan contends that 'prior to *Cooper* v. *Phibbs* there *was* a remedy given by Courts of Equity to rescind a contract for mistake.'[88] And so Denning LJ in the *Solle* case was not creating a new jurisdiction in Equity. It is unfortunate that there was no final appeal to the House of Lords in the *Solle* case; leave for such an appeal had been given, but the parties then decided not to pursue a further appeal.[89]

But, even if Denning LJ had been correct in the *Solle* case to regard *Cooper* v. *Phibbs* (1867) as authority for this equitable doctrine concerning fundamental shared mistake, this is not the end of the story. For, as the Court of Appeal in *'The Great Peace'* (2002) noted, the *Cooper* case (1867) had been reclassified by Lord Atkin in the House of Lords in a dictum in *Bell* v. *Lever Bros Ltd* (1932) as an instance of Common Law mistake, that is, of a *void* rather than a voidable contract.[90] The Court of Appeal in *'The Great Peace'* boldly declared that Lord Atkin's passing remark in *Bell* v. *Lever Bros Ltd* justified, indeed required, abandoning subsequent Court of Appeal decisions in which the courts had applied the doctrine of *Solle* v. *Butcher* (1950), or assumed its validity.[91] The Court of Appeal in *'The Great Peace'* concluded: '[W]e can see no way that *Solle* v. *Butcher* can stand with *Bell* v. *Lever Bros*.'[92]

But Lord Atkin's passing remark in *Bell* v. *Lever Bros Ltd* is a fragile basis on which to conclude that the House of Lords in that 1932 decision had jettisoned the equitable doctrine of rescission for shared mistake. Indeed, before 1966, the House of Lords had been bound by its earlier decisions.[93] Even a dictum by Lord Atkin could not annihilate the House of Lords' statement in *Cooper* v. *Phibbs* (1867) that there is an equitable doctrine to relieve parties from a contract vitiated for shared fundamental error.

---

86 (1989) 105 LQR 599.

87 [1930] 2 KB 312, 334–5 (this case, decided in April 1930) was cited in argument in *'The Great Peace'* [2002] EWCA Civ 1407; [2003] QB 679, 684, but was not cited by Lord Phillips in his judgment in *'The Great Peace'*. Wright J in *Bell* v. *Lever Bros* at first instance (October 1930: reported, with the Court of Appeal judgments, [1931] 1 KB 557, especially at 572) adopted essentially the same analysis as that which he had adopted six months before in the *Robert A Munro* case.

88 C. MacMillan, in C. Mitchell and P. Mitchell (eds.), *Landmark Cases in the Law of Restitution* (Oxford, 2006), at 355 n. 172.

89 *Ibid.*, noting 66 TLR (Pt 1) 448, 468.

90 *'The Great Peace'* case, [2002] EWCA Civ 1407; [2003] QB 679, at [113] to [118], and [126] to [130], especially noting the analysis of Lords Blanesburgh and Atkin, respectively, in *Bell* v. *Lever Bros Ltd* [1932] AC 161, 190, 218, HL.

91 On these later authorities, see *'The Great Peace'* case, [2002] EWCA Civ 1407; [2003] QB 679, at [135] to [152].

92 *Ibid.*, at [160].

93 A practice not relaxed until the House of Lords' Practice Statement [1966] 3 All ER 77, enabling that court, in exceptional situations, to reverse one of its decisions.

10.15 *Is the* Solle *v.* Butcher *approach an extinct legal theory?* How might *'The Great Peace'* (2002) have been assessed on final appeal to the Supreme Court? Denning LJ's suggested equitable doctrine of shared mistake offered three advantages when compared with the Common Law doctrine of shared mistake concerning the supposed agreement's terms or substance. The first alleged advantage would be that Equity might be deployed to widen the ambit of operative shared mistake beyond the narrow limits recognised at Common Law. The objection to this, however, is that the stability of contracts might be seriously threatened by a broader approach to 'shared mistake'. The second alleged advantage is that the equitable technique of rescission can protect the interests of innocent third parties. This is because the contract is merely voidable, and so it subsists until rescinded. Rescission would be 'barred' if a third party, dealing in good faith, without notice and for value, had bought or acquired rights in the subject matter of the purported agreement. The final alleged advantage is that rescission can be ordered 'on terms'.[94] The effect can be to keep the contract alive. But this is controversial because it effectively remakes the bargain for the parties. How should one assess these points? As mentioned, alleged 'advantage one' (a widening of the mistake doctrine) is no real advantage at all because it is arguably unattractive in principle. Advantages 'two' (protection of innocent third parties) and 'three' (flexible readjustment of the contract) are respectable arguments, but they lack sufficient weight to justify a Supreme Court decision to reinstate the *Cooper* v. *Phibbs* and *Solle* v. *Butcher* line of authority.[95]

10.16 *Responses to the* Solle *v.* Butcher *issue in other jurisdictions.* The Singapore Court of Appeal in *Chwee Kin Keong* v. *Digilandmall.com Pte Ltd* (2005) held that it is not possible to rescind a contract in Equity which is void for mistake at Common Law.[96] However, in Canada, the Ontario Court of Appeal in *Miller Paving Ltd* v. *B Gottardo Construction Ltd* (2007) expressed its wish to preserve the equitable doctrine of shared mistake.[97] Rejecting *'The Great Peace'*, Goudge JA said: 'The loss of the flexibility needed to correct unjust results in widely diverse circumstances that would come from eliminating the equitable doctrine of common mistake would, I think, be a step backward.' In Hong Kong, in *Lo Shing Kin* v. *Sy Chin Mong Stephen* (2013) the Hong Kong Court of Appeal left the matter open, having held that the plea of shared error failed on the facts, in this case.[98]

10.17 *Mistake: comparison with the 'soft law' codes.*[99] In English law, the (not entirely uncontroversial) rejection in *'The Great Peace'* (10.13 ff) of a doctrine of equitable shared

---

94 E.g. complicated terms imposed by Stirling J, setting aside an agreement based on common mistake, *Allcard* v. *Walker* [1896] 2 Ch 369, 384–5; for more recent cases, see *'The Great Peace'* [2002] EWCA Civ 1407; [2003] QB 679, at [103] to [106].

95 In New Zealand, the court has received considerable 'remedial flexibility' when deciding whether to uphold or set aside a contract vitiated by mistake: section 7 of the Contractual Mistakes Act 1977.

96 [2005] 1 SLR 502, at [46] and [80].

97 [2007] ONCA 422; (2007) 86 OR (3d) 161; (2007), 285 DLR (4th) 568, at [26], Ontario Court of Appeal; and considering J. McCamus, 'Mistaken Assumptions in Equity: Sound Doctrine or Chimera?' (2004) 40 *Canadian Business Law Journal* 46–86; for references to other Common Law jurisdictions on this topic, see A. Phang, 'Doctrine and Fairness in the Law of Contract' (2009) 29 LS 534, 542 ff.

98 [2013] HKEC 682.

99 G. Spark, *Vitiation of Contracts* (Cambridge, 2013), chapter 8.

mistake concerning the nature of the subject matter has left isolated the Common Law concept of shared mistake rendering the supposed transaction void (10.06 ff). English adoption at Common Law of the concept of voidness can be contrasted with the (non-binding) schemes of both PECL, *Principles of European Contract Law*, and UNIDROIT's *Principles of International Commercial Contracts* (2010), where 'initial impossibility' is expressly stated not to be a ground of invalidity (PECL, Article 4:102; UNIDROIT, Article 3.1.3;[100] contrast on this point English law, where the contract will be void: see 10.07), and shared serious error can only render the contract voidable: (PECL, Articles 4:103, 4:112 to 4:116; UNIDROIT, Articles 3.2.2, 3.2.9 to 3.2.16).

5. UNILATERAL ERROR CONCERNING SUBJECT MATTER

10.18 There is no ground for relief at Common Law if A suffers a mere mistake as to 'the substance' of the subject matter, even if this is known to B. Hence, there is the paradox that it is in A's interest to show that B innocently shared A's error (the situation then becomes one of shared mistake).[101]

10.19 *Smith* v. *Hughes* (1871) established that A's error must not only be known to B, but the error must relate to the supposed *terms of the contract*[102] (for an example of this, see *Hartog* v. *Colin & Shields* (1939),[103] where the buyer took advantage of the seller's obvious error concerning the price of hare skins; and see also the discussion of this topic at 3.63 ff, including (at 3.63) Aikens J in the *Statoil* case (2008)).[104]

10.20 *Knowledge extends to imputed knowledge.* In *OT Africa* v. *Vickers plc* (1996), Mance J said that it is enough that B ought reasonably to have realised that A was mistaken concerning the terms.[105] The point was made as follows in *Wimpole Theatre (a firm)* v. *J J Goodman Ltd* (2012) by Judge Richard Seymour QC who, having cited the *OT Africa* case, commented:[106]

> the court must be satisfied ... with a high degree of assurance both that [party A] was acting under a mistake in agreeing to be bound by that to which, objectively, he agreed, and that [party B] ought reasonably to have been aware of that. It is an improbable scenario.

---

100   3rd edition, 2010, text and comment, is available at: www.unidroit.org/english/principles/contracts/principles2010/integralversionprinciples2010-e.pdf.
101   A. Tettenborn, *An Introduction to the Law of Obligations* (London, 1984), 169.
102   (1871) LR 6 QB 597; J. Phillips, in C. Mitchell and P. Mitchell (eds.), *Landmark Cases in the Law of Contract* (Oxford, 2008), 205 ff; G. Spark, *Vitiation of Contracts* (Cambridge, 2013), chapter 6.
103   [1939] 3 All ER 566, Singleton J.
104   *Statoil ASA* v. *Louis Dreyfus Energy Services LP ('The Harriette N')* [2008] EWHC 2257 (Comm); [2009] 1 All ER (Comm) 1035; [2008] 2 Lloyd's Rep 685, at [95]; J. Cartwright, 'Unilateral Mistake in the English Courts: Reasserting the Traditional Approach' (2009) *Singapore Journal of Legal Studies* 226–34.
105   [1996] 1 Lloyd's Rep 700, 703, Mance J ('knowledge' to include imputed knowledge); *Champion Investments Ltd* v. *Ahmed* [2004] EWHC 1956 (QB), at [34] and [35], William Blair QC.
106   [2012] EWHC 1600 (QB), at [56].

6. DENIAL OF SPECIFIC PERFORMANCE

10.21 Unlike the doctrine of mistake as to terms discussed at 10.19, Equity will refuse specific performance (18.33) even if the error relates merely to the nature of the subject matter of the contract, as opposed to the price or terms regarding that property. But *Tamplin* v. *James* (1880)[107] made clear that Equity will refuse this remedy only if the defendant's error was either induced[108] by the claimant, or the claimant was aware of the other's error and unconscionably failed to disabuse him. Specific performance will also be withheld when the relevant contract is voidable by reason of misrepresentation,[109] undue influence, duress or unconscionable conduct.[110]

> In *Tamplin* v. *James* (1880)[111] the defendant, a purchaser of real property, could not resist specific performance merely because he had misunderstood the precise boundary of an inn when deciding to buy it at auction. This was an instance of *spontaneous* and unilateral error: an error neither *induced* by anything said by the claimant, nor *known* to the claimant.[112]

7. NON EST FACTUM: FUNDAMENTAL ERROR IN SIGNED DOCUMENTS

10.22 *Non est factum*[113] is a very old Common Law doctrine which can invalidate a deed or other written agreement.[114] The doctrine can render that apparent agreement void (rather than merely voidable). The test is whether the document's contents are wholly or radically different from those which the signatory assumed them to be. Normally, this doctrine arises if someone, usually the other party, tricks a person into signing the document. But the doctrine can also operate without the mistaken party having to show that the other party induced this error or was aware of it. It follows that the doctrine is an exception to the objective test of agreement

---

107 (1880) 15 Ch D 215, CA; (repudiating the more lenient approach in *Malins* v. *Freeman* (1837) 2 Keen 25); G. H. Jones and W. Goodhart, *Specific Performance* (2nd edn, London, 1998), 12–13, 104 ff.
108 Cf *Denny* v. *Hancock* (1870) 6 Ch App 1 (buyer's error induced partly by vendor's ambiguous plans; specific performance refused).
109 G. H. Jones and W. Goodhart, *Specific Performance* (2nd edn, London, 1998), 86 ff, also discussing refusal of specific performance on the ground of non-disclosure.
110 *Ibid.*, at 112–16; e.g. *Walters* v. *Morgan* (1861) 3 De G F & J 718 (defendant hurried by claimant into signing contract without knowing property's true value); *Webster* v. *Cecil* (1861) 30 Beav 62 (claimant's offer of £2,000 refused; defendant, by error, offering property for £1,250 rather than £2,250); cf the snapping-up case at Common Law, *Hartog* v. *Colin & Shields* [1939] 3 All ER 566; cf *Centrovincial Estates plc* v. *Merchant Investors Assurance Co. Ltd* [1983] Com LR 158, CA (on the last two decisions see 3.61 and 3.63).
111 (1880) 15 Ch D 215, CA (repudiating the more lenient approach in *Malins* v. *Freeman* (1837) 2 Keen 25.
112 G. H. Jones and W. Goodhart, *Specific Performance* (2nd edn, London, 1998), 106–7; D. Friedmann, (2003) 119 LQR 68.
113 *Gallie* v. *Lee* [1971] AC 1004, HL; *United Dominions Trust Ltd* v. *Western* [1976] QB 513, CA; see also: *Lloyds Bank plc* v. *Waterhouse, The Independent*, 27 February 1990, CA (J. Cartwright, [1990] LMCLQ 338); *Norwich & Peterborough Building Society* v. *Steed (No. 2)* [1993] Ch 116, CA; *Schwartz* v. *Barclays Bank plc* [1995] TLR 452, CA; undue influence (11.23) renders the transaction voidable and not void; an attempt to go further and show, on the facts, that the transaction was a nullity (that is, void *ab initio*), on the basis of *non est factum* was unsuccessful in *Hackett* v. *CPS* [2011] EWHC 1170 (Admin); [2011] Lloyd's Rep FC 371, at [85] to [90], *per* Silber J.
114 G. Spark, *Vitiation of Contracts* (Cambridge, 2013), chapter 3.

(on that topic, see 3.55 ff). In the absence of deception by the other party or a third party, the doctrine will normally require the signatory to lack real understanding of the document by reason of defective education, illness or innate incapacity.

Modern decisions have restricted the scope of the *non est factum* doctrine in three main ways. First, there must be a radical or substantial difference between the document signed and that to which the signatory believed himself to be assenting.[115]

Secondly, 'ordinary principles' of misrepresentation will apply where A signs as a result of B's misrepresentation (rather than because of a third party's misrepresentation) and the validity of the A/B transaction does not affect a third party.[116]

Thirdly, an omission to read a document will nearly always exclude this doctrine.[117]

Failure to read will be irrelevant only if the signatory would have been none the wiser even if he had carefully read the document. That might be so if this particular party lacks the skill or intelligence to discern its true legal sense. However, not reading the relevant contract because one has mislaid one's glasses would not be a valid excuse.[118] (In Australia[119] it has been held that the signatory's carelessness precludes resort to *non est factum* only if that plea might affect a third party.)

8. DEEDS AND 'VOLUNTARY INSTRUMENTS' VOIDABLE IN EQUITY

10.23 In *Pitt* v. *Holt* (2013)[120] the Supreme Court of the United Kingdom noted that a generous test of mistake applies, in accordance with this equitable doctrine, where a party or his successors apply to set aside a voluntary instrument, such as a deed (the transferee not having provided consideration). The test of 'fundamental' shared error does not apply.[121] The transferor's negligence is not a bar.[122] The court will consider the gravity of the causative error.[123] In the *Pitt* case (2013) the Supreme Court set aside a settlement which had created a trust, because it had been made without proper understanding of its tax consequences.

9. MISTAKE CONCERNING A PARTY'S IDENTITY

10.24 *The standard problem.*[124] The source of this vexatious 'mistake' problem is that a rogue, X, pretending to be Y, dupes C into selling goods to X, and X then sells the same goods to D, the

---

115   *Gallie* v. *Lee* [1971] AC 1004, HL.
116   *Lloyd's Bank plc* v. *Waterhouse* 27 February 1990, *The Independent*, CA (J Cartwright [1990] LMCLQ 338), noted by *Chitty* (31st edn, London, 2012), 5–103.
117   *United Dominions Trust Ltd* v. *Western* [1976] QB 513, CA; *Hambros Bank Ltd* v. *British Historic Buildings Trust* [1995] NPC 179.
118   *Gallie* v. *Lee* [1971] AC 1004, HL.
119   *Petelin* v. *Cullen* (1975) 132 CLR 355, High Court of Australia.
120   [2013] UKSC 26; [2013] 2 AC 108.
121   *Ibid.*, at [115].
122   *Ibid.*, at [114].
123   *Ibid.*, at [124] to [128], [142].
124   D. W. McLauchlan, 'Parol Evidence and Contract Formation' (2005) 121 LQR 9; C. MacMillan, 'Mistake as to Identity Clarified?' (2004) 120 LQR 368; A. Phang, P.-W. Lee and P. Koh, 'Mistaken Identity in the House of

subpurchaser, who buys them in good faith. X absconds and falls out of the picture. The law has a choice between two analyses: that D has acquired good title from X (the latter having received a 'voidable' title, viz. under a transaction open to rescission, when he dealt with C); or that C remains owner because X had derived no title from C which he might transfer to D (under the principle of *nemo dat quod non habet*, D is unprotected if X lacked even a 'voidable' title, as just explained).

10.25 As we shall see, in the 'face-to-face' context, *Lewis* v. *Averay* (1972)[125] (10.33) shows that the law inclines strongly (although, even now, perhaps not invariably) towards the former analysis, that the transaction is merely voidable; and this will protect the innocent subpurchaser if the head vendor fails to rescind the main transaction before the moment when the subpurchase took place; whereas, in the other context, when the dealings between C and X do not involve face-to-face contact, the competing analysis persists and the transaction between C and X is void rather than merely voidable: *Cundy* v. *Lindsay* (1878)[126] (10.27).

10.26 The leading decision on error as to identity is *Shogun Finance Ltd* v. *Hudson* (2004)[127] (10.28 ff). It preserves the important precedents in *Cundy* v. *Lindsay* (1878)[128] (10.27) and *Lewis* v. *Averay* (1972)[129] (10.33).

10.27 *Distance dealings: voidness at Common Law*. In *Cundy* v. *Lindsay* (1878),[130] Lindsay, a firm of Belfast linen suppliers, was duped by Blenkarn into sending handkerchiefs to him on credit. The transaction was for a purchase by 'Blenkiron & Co.', a reputable firm known to Lindsay. Accordingly, Lindsay sent the goods to 'Messrs Blenkiron & Co.'. But, having fallen prey to Blenkarn's fraud, Lindsay was misled into sending these goods to the wrong address, where Blenkarn was able to misappropriate them. (Blenkiron & Co.'s premises were at 123 Wood Street, Cheapside, London, but Blenkarn had requested delivery to 37 Wood Street, where he had deviously taken temporary accommodation, in order to take delivery of the fruits of his fraud.) Blenkarn, the 'rogue', then sold the goods to Cundy, who bought in good faith. The House of Lords held that there had been no effective contract between the rogue and the plaintiff Lindsay, that the goods remained the property of Lindsay, and that the action in tort for conversion against the defendant, the subpurchasers, should succeed, therefore. Despite the fact that the defendant was a bona fide purchaser for value, this made no difference because the plaintiff had retained title at Common Law, and the contract between Lindsay and the rogue was void rather than voidable.

Lords' [2004] CLJ 24; G. Spark, *Vitiation of Contracts* (Cambridge, 2013), chapter 5; R. Stevens, 'Objectivity, Mistake and the Parol Evidence Rule', in A. Burrows and E. Peel (eds.), *Contract Terms* (Oxford, 2007), chapter 6, at 110 ff; Law Reform Committee, 'Transfer of Title to Chattels' (Twelfth Report of the Law Reform Committee, Cmnd 2958, 1966).
125 [1972] 1 QB 198, CA.
126 (1878) 3 App Cas 454, HL.
127 [2003] UKHL 62; [2004] 1 AC 919, HL.
128 (1878) 3 App Cas 454, HL.
129 [1972] 1 QB 198, CA.
130 (1878) 3 App Cas 454, HL; C. MacMillan, *Mistakes in Contract Law* (Oxford, 2010), 230 ff.

There were two possible ways of considering the dealings between Blenkarn and Lindsay. First, these dealings might have been considered as an acceptance by Lindsay, the supplier of the goods, of an offer to buy emanating from *the occupier of 37 Wood Street without reference to his name* (if so, a contract between Lindsay and Blenkarn might arise, and it would be voidable because of the latter's fraud). Or this situation could be treated as Lindsay's acceptance of an offer emanating from Blenkiron & Co. (if so, there would be no contract, because there was in fact no true offer made by Blenkiron & Co.; and so, in the absence of any contract between Lindsay and Blenkiron & Co., interception by the rogue Blenkarn would not give him even a 'voidable' title, viz. under a transaction open to rescission). The House of Lords adopted the latter approach, concluding that there had been no effective contract and that the goods remained the property of Lindsay.

At first instance, the first interpretation was adopted. The court emphasised that the goods had been sent to the rogue's address.[131] However, the Court of Appeal and House of Lords reversed this. They held that the true supposition was that Lindsay was dealing with 'Blenkiron & Co.', but there was no substance at all to these dealings, Blenkiron not having made any offer to Lindsay. Instead, the purported transaction between Lindsay and Blenkarn was void. It was further held that no property passed to the rogue under that contract. Hence, no property could be passed to the defendant, Cundy, the subpurchaser.[132] And so Cundy was found liable for the tort of conversion and ordered to pay damages representing the value of the goods. This is a strict tort, which does not require the defendant to have been aware that the goods remained the claimant's property.

In the House of Lords, Lord Cairns LC emphasised that Lindsay had never heard of Blenkarn and had not the slightest intention of dealing with him: 'Their minds never, even for an instant of time rested upon him, and as between him and them there was no consensus of mind which could lead to any agreement or any contract whatever.'[133] This was treated as a clear situation where A intended to contract with B, a real entity, and not with X. This was not a mistake as to X's creditworthiness, but an error concerning X's true identity. None of the dealings involved face-to-face contact between A and X. The decision is generous to the claimant, who might have taken greater care to check that Blenkiron & Co. really did do business at 37 Wood Street.

The Court of Appeal in *King's Norton Metal Co.* v. *Edridge Merritt & Co. Ltd* (1897) distinguished *Cundy* v. *Lindsay*.[134] C delivered on credit a ton of brass rivet wire to X. X was masquerading as a company of substance, 'Hallam & Co.'. But there was no such company. X sold the goods to D. The Court of Appeal held that there was a contract between C and X, namely, a contract with 'the writer of the letters'. *Cundy* v. *Lindsay* was distinguished because in that

---

131 *Lindsay* v. *Cundy* (1876) 1 QBD 348 (Blackburn, Mellor and Lush JJ: valid contract between claimant and the commercial entity at 37 Wood Street; decision preferred, audaciously, by Denning LJ in *Solle* v. *Butcher* [1950] 1 KB 671, 693, CA); for decisions (also examined in the *Cundy* case) concerning goods clearly delivered to A but intercepted or misappropriated by a fraudulent rogue, see *Hardman* v. *Booth* (1863) 1 H & C 803 (noted in *Shogun* [2003] UKHL 62; [2004] 1 AC 919, HL, at [89], [91], [129] to [130] and [186]); *Hollins* v. *Fowler* (1874–5) LR 7 HL 757; on *Boulton* v. *Jones* (1857) 2 H & N 564, Court of Exchequer, see Lord Millett in *Shogun* [2003] UKHL 62; [2004] 1 AC 919, HL, at [94] to [97], and Lord Phillips at [126] (on *Hardman* v. *Booth*, C. MacMillan, *Mistakes in Contract Law* (Oxford, 2010), 224 ff).
132 W. Swadling, 'Rescission, Property, and the Common Law' (2005) 121 LQR 123 (controversially contending that title should not be revested in the vendor until rescission, and that vendor's error as to the (fraudulent) buyer's creditworthiness should result in personal – but not proprietary – protection of vendor).
133 (1878) 3 App Cas 459, 464–5, HL; also *per* Lord Hatherley at 469 and Lord Penzance at 471.
134 (1897) 14 TLR 98, CA; explained in the *Shogun* case, [2003] UKHL 62; [2004] 1 AC 919, HL, at [3], [77], [78], [134] and [135].

earlier case the vendor had intended to deal with Blenkiron & Co., a real entity known to that party.[135] *Cundy* v. *Lindsay* was also distinguished nearly a hundred years later by Waller J in *Citibank NA* v. *Brown Shipley* (1991).[136] But a majority of the House of Lords in *Shogun Finance Ltd* v. *Hudson* (2004) narrowly endorsed the view, supported by *Cundy* v. *Lindsay*, that a supposed contract can be void for error as to identity.[137]

10.28 *The* Shogun *case: upholding* Cundy v. Lindsay. In *Shogun Finance Ltd* v. *Hudson* (2004), a car was ostensibly acquired under a hire-purchase arrangement between the hire-purchase company (Shogun Finance) and 'Patel'. But Patel had no knowledge of this transaction and the rogue, X, had simply perpetrated a fraud by impersonating Patel. The dealings between Shogun Finance and X had not been face-to-face. The majority of the House of Lords (Lords Hobhouse, Phillips and Walker), following the *Cundy* case (10.27 above), concluded that there was no valid contract between Shogun Finance and X. The defendant, who had bought in good faith from X, was liable in the tort of conversion because he was holding a car which continued to be owned by the finance company.

In greater detail, the facts were as follows. X impersonated Patel in order to acquire a Mitsubishi Shogun car under a credit arrangement. The garage-owner, Varieva, sold the car to C, a hire-purchase credit company. X had tricked both C (with which all dealings were by fax or telephone) and Varieva into believing that X was Patel (the latter being a real person). X used Patel's stolen driving licence to bolster the fraud. C checked Patel's credit rating before agreeing to proceed. A written hire-purchase agreement was then concluded in writing between C and Patel. Although X paid part of the deposit of 10 per cent in cash, he gave a bad cheque for the remainder of the deposit.[138] After driving the car away, X soon sold it to D, who bought it in good faith. X then disappeared without trace. The hire-purchase legislation creates an exception to the *nemo dat quod non habet* principle in this hire-purchase context if the ultimate purchaser, D, has bought in good faith from 'the debtor'. Section 27(2) of the Hire Purchase Act 1964 provides:[139]

> Where the disposition ... is to a private purchaser, and he is a purchaser of the motor vehicle in good faith without notice of the hire-purchase ... agreement ... that disposition shall have effect as if the creditor's title to the vehicle has been vested in the debtor immediately before that disposition.

The question was whether the word 'debtor' referred to Patel or to X on the present facts. In other words, was there a hire-purchase agreement between C and X, or between C and Patel, as the document itself declared? If the latter, no obligations would arise between C and Patel. This was because Patel's signature had been forged and he had known nothing of these events.[140]

135 (1897) 14 TLR 98, 99, CA.
136 [1991] 2 All ER 690.
137 [2003] UKHL 62; [2004] 1 AC 919, HL.
138 The cheque was probably made in Patel's name: *ibid.*, at [115], Lord Phillips.
139 Section 27(2) of the Hire Purchase Act 1964 (as substituted by section 192(3)(a) of and Schedule 4, para. 22, to the Consumer Credit Act 1974).
140 *Shogun* [2003] UKHL 62; [2004] 1 AC 919, HL at [56] *per* Lord Millett, and [178] *per* Lord Phillips.

Majority in the Shogun *case.* A bare majority (Lords Hobhouse, Phillips and Walker; Lords Nicholls and Millett dissenting) held that the statutory word 'debtor' (see above) denoted the person named in the document itself, namely, Patel. They held that the dealings for the hire-purchase contract had not taken place face-to-face but by fax and telephone, involving communications from the car dealer's showroom to the credit company's offices.[141] They affirmed that the identity of parties to a written agreement is established by the names stated in that agreement[142] (however, D. W. McLauchlan contends that the parol evidence rule should not be conclusive and that extrinsic evidence should be admissible to determine whether there was consensus or instead a fundamental error as to identity).[143]

Indeed, Lord Hobhouse (a member of the majority in the *Shogun* case) considered the written identification of 'Patel' to be conclusive. Lord Hobhouse was wholly unimpressed by counsel's discussion in this litigation of 'mistake as to person'.[144]

Three things followed from the majority decision: first, no hire-purchase agreement had been entered between C and X; secondly, therefore, in his dealings with X, D was unprotected by the hire-purchase exception to the *nemo dat quod non habet* principle; finally, C had a good claim for conversion against D (as had been held at first instance and by a majority of the Court of Appeal).[145]

Dissenting speeches in the Shogun *case.* Lords Nicholls and Millett said that C had intended to deal with X, the rogue in the showroom, and not with Patel. C had believed X and Patel to be the same person.[146] They proposed that the courts should use the 'voidable' title analysis (already used in face-to-face contexts: see 10.33 below) in this 'distance dealing' situation. Accordingly, they suggested that the House should overrule *Cundy* v. *Lindsay* (1878).[147] Lord Millett attacked the supposed critical distinction between face-to-face and 'distance dealings'.[148] He formulated this principle thus:

> While a person cannot intercept and accept an offer made to some one else, he should normally be treated as intending to contract with the person with whom he is dealing. Provided that the offer is made to him, then whether his acceptance of the offer is obtained by deception or mistake, and whether his mistake is as to the identity of the offer or some material attribute of his, the transaction should result in a contract, albeit one which is voidable.[149]

Lord Millett also suggested that the subpurchaser's interests should be preferred rather than the swindled seller 'who had an opportunity to uncover the fraud'.[150] Lord Nicholls agreed.[151] However, Lord Walker (one of the majority) challenged the dissentients' preference for the subpurchaser rather than the swindled vendor: '[I]t would not be right to make any general

---

141 *Ibid.*, at [51], *per* Lord Hobhouse; *ibid.*, at [167], [176] and [179], *per* Lord Phillips; and *ibid.*, at [191], *per* Lord Walker.

142 Upholding Dyson and Brooke LJJ in the Court of Appeal below; and applying *Hector* v. *Lyons* (1989) 58 P & CR 156, CA, at 158–9, 160.

143 D. W. McLauchlan, 'Parol Evidence and Contract Formation' (2005) 121 LQR 9.

144 *Shogun* [2003] UKHL 62; [2004] 1 AC 919, HL, at [52] to [55], and [45] to [49].

145 *Ibid.*, at [52], *per* Lord Hobhouse: although not pleaded in this case, the garage-owner had also committed conversion by placing the car into the hands of X after the credit company, C, had received title.

146 *Ibid.*, at [38] to [41], *per* Lord Nicholls; and *ibid.*, at [105] to [107], *per* Lord Millett.

147 (1878) 3 App Cas 454, HL.

148 [2003] UKHL 62; [2004] 1 AC 919, HL, at [69] and [70].

149 *Ibid.*

150 *Ibid.*, at [82]; and Law Reform Committee, 'Transfer of Title to Chattels' (Twelfth Report of the Law Reform Committee, Cmnd 2958, 1966) (UK); Uniform Commercial Code (14th edn) (USA), 2–403.

151 [2004] 1 AC 919, HL, at [35]; a point made emphatically by Lord Denning MR in *Lewis* v. *Averay* [1972] 1 QB 198, 207, CA.

assumption as to one innocent party being more deserving than the other.'[152] The dissentients' approach had been supported earlier by Denning LJ's opinion in *Solle* v. *Butcher* (1950)[153] and by the Law Reform Committee (1966).[154]

10.29 *Assessment of the* Shogun *case*. It is submitted that the majority's decision itself in *Shogun Finance Ltd* v. *Hudson* (2004) is sound because the written terms of the hire-purchase agreement made clear that it was Patel's individual credit rating which counted. Secondly, the decision is also attractive as a practical matter. It would be slower and more expensive for the credit company to meet each prospective purchaser before concluding this contract (however, MacMillan takes the opposite view, regarding the credit company's casual 'vetting procedure' as reckless).[155]

10.30 *Apportionment: an unsuccessful judicial suggestion*. Devlin LJ had suggested in the *Ingram* case (1961), that apportionment might be considered as a solution to this problem.[156] This would involve the compromise solution of dividing the loss, perhaps in a discretionary way, between the victims. But the Law Reform Committee (1966) considered this suggestion to be impractical.[157]

10.31 *Face-to-face dealings*. In this situation (a) a fraudulent impostor ('the rogue') tricks the vendor into parting with goods (most cases have concerned cars) on credit; the vendor normally receives a cheque which is not honoured; (b) the rogue's second victim is the innocent final purchaser who acquires a stolen vehicle (or other chattel). The first risk, at (a), can be easily evaded by insisting on clearance of the cheque before the goods are released to the purchaser. This might entail a delay in completion of the sale of several days. The second risk, at (b), is more insidious because there is no system of registration of title to chattels, including cars.

10.32 *Rescission by victim of fraud*. It is important to note that a contract can be rescinded (that is, avoided or set aside *ab initio*) if one party has been the victim of the other's fraudulent misrepresentation. In *Car & Universal Finance Co. Ltd* v. *Caldwell* (1965), the Court of Appeal held that rescission in this context does not require the victim to succeed in tracing the representor and informing him directly of this rescission.[158] That would often be a virtually impossible task. Instead, it is enough if the representee contacts the police and informs them that he has been the victim of such a fraud and wishes to trace the car and repossess it.

---

152 [2004] 1 AC 919, HL, at [182].
153 [1950] 1 KB 671, 691, CA.
154 Law Reform Committee, 'Transfer of Title to Chattels' (Twelfth Report of the Law Reform Committee, Cmnd 2958, 1966).
155 C. MacMillan, 'Mistake as to Identity Clarified?' (2004) 120 LQR 368, 373.
156 [1961] 1 QB 31, CA.
157 Law Reform Committee, 'Transfer of Title to Chattels' (Twelfth Report of the Law Reform Committee, Cmnd 2958, 1966), paras. 9–12 (the Committee considered that the stumbling block would occur where C sells to rogue B, who sells to D1, who sells to D2).
158 [1965] 1 QB 525, CA; if the rogue sub-sells in the ordinary course of business, the subpurchaser can receive good title under section 9 of the Factors Act 1889, or section 25 of the Sale of Goods Act 1979; *Newtons of Wembley Ltd* v. *Williams* [1965] 1 QB 560, CA; *Treitel* (13th edn, London, 2011), 9–088; J. Thornley, [1965] CLJ 24.

Suppose A tells the police at 11.20 am that at 9.00 am that day he had been hoodwinked by B, a rogue, into accepting a cheque and handing over the car keys to B. If B had sold the vehicle at 11.19 am, the innocent subpurchaser would acquire good title to the car; but, if the sub-sale took place later than A's notification to the police, the contract between A and B would have been rescinded already (at 11.20 am) so that it would not be possible for B to pass title to an innocent third party.

10.33 Lewis *v.* Averay: preference for a voidable deal. The Court of Appeal decision in *Lewis* v. *Averay* (1972)[159] was made in favour of the innocent subpurchaser rather than the defrauded head vendor. During a face-to-face meeting, the vendor had been duped into believing that the purchaser, in fact an impostor, was a well-known television actor; and this rogue then left the vendor's premises with the car keys and the car, in return for a worthless cheque. Once the cheque was dishonoured, and the fraud had become apparent, the rogue had already sold the car to an innocent third party. The Court of Appeal unanimously held that the latter acquired good title. This was because the head contract, between the duped vendor and the rogue, had been voidable, and not absolutely void. Title had passed down this chain, therefore, to the innocent subpurchaser.

After *Lewis* v. *Averay* (1972),[160] when might a face-to-face negotiation result in a judicial declaration that the supposed transaction is wholly void?

C the head vendor, would need to show the following: (1) C intended to deal with Y (a real person or company) and not with X, the rogue; (2) X knew of C's intention and error; (3) C's error was crucial to his decision to contract; (4) C took reasonable steps to check X's identity (thinking X to be Y) before contracting with X.

As for element (1), it will be an uphill task for C, the head vendor, to establish that he was really intending only to deal with Y, rather than with X, the flesh-and-blood person standing before him (for this reason, the contract will be merely voidable for fraudulent misrepresentation and, provided the sub-sale precedes any effective rescission of the head-sale by the vendor, an innocent third party will acquire good title and so be protected against liability in the tort of conversion).

C's task is an uphill one, but not impossible. As Lord Walker said in the *Shogun* case (2004), exceptionally C might show that he was proposing to deal with someone other than X, even though C and X stood face-to-face[161] (face-to-face dealings including telephone dealings, but not, of course, e-mail or postal communications).[162]

The *Lewis* case was approved in the *Shogun* case (2004) (10.28 ff), and the contrasting analysis in *Ingram* v. *Little* (1961)[163] was repudiated, echoing rejection of the 1961 case by the Court of Appeal in *Lewis* v. *Averay* (1972).[164] Lords Walker and Millett in the *Shogun* case (2004) thought that the *Ingram* case was wrongly decided because it conflicts with the 'objective

---

159 [1972] 1 QB 198, CA.
160 *Ibid.*
161 [2003] UKHL 62; [2004] 1 AC 919, HL, at [187].
162 *Ibid.*, at [18].
163 [1961] 1 QB 31, CA.
164 [1972] 1 QB 198, 207, 208, CA (Lord Denning regarded the *Ingram* case, [1961] 1 QB 31, CA, as wrong; Phillimore LJ in the *Lewis* case thought that the *Ingram* case was 'special and unusual', and Megaw LJ, [1972] 1 QB 198, 208, found the *Ingram* case difficult to understand).

principle of agreement'.[165] That principle (1.10 and 3.55 ff) requires the law to regard C's offer to sell the goods as directed at the flesh-and-blood person X, unless C can exceptionally show that he has made clear that he is intending only to deal with that person *on the assumption that he is truly the person whom he claims to be.*

In the *Ingram* case (1961),[166] after manifest hesitation, and following a feckless attempt at checking the purchaser's identity, three elderly ladies sold a car to X. X had presented himself as 'P. G. M. Hutchinson' of Caterham, Surrey. Before concluding this deal, one of the ladies went to the Post Office. She verified that there was a Hutchinson at that address. This information mysteriously induced the ladies to believe that the man in their parlour was that very gentleman. Of course, this was a *non sequitur* (unfortunately Miss Marple had not been visiting for tea). They then handed the car keys to X in exchange for a worthless cheque. X soon resold the car to D who bought in good faith. A majority of the Court of Appeal declared that C had a good claim against the innocent subpurchaser D in the tort of conversion because the contract between the elderly ladies and X had been void for error as to X's identity.

10.34 *Identity errors: summary.* It is submitted that the key to this conundrum in the 'identity' cases is whether it is objectively clear that the target of A's dealings was 'Y', the represented identity, as distinct from X (the rogue's true identity).

(1) Usually, in contracts formed by writing (which must include a transaction arising from e-mail or fax), the text of the communications will state that the parties to the intended transaction are to be 'A and Y'. In that situation, only Y, and not X pretending to be Y, can assent to the proposal for a contract with A.

This analysis is clearly adopted by Lord Cairns LC in *Cundy* v. *Lindsay* (1878)[167] and by Lord Hobhouse in the *Shogun* case (2004).[168] The latter rightly founded this approach on the parol evidence rule (12.02). That rule prevents a person from adducing evidence to contradict the written contract's explicit identification of the contractual parties. If the written contract states that the other party is, and must be, 'Y', there can be no valid agreement if in fact Y was unaware of A and X's dealings and so could not have assented to a contract. In this situation, it is clear that the transaction is a nullity because of the complete absence of consent by Y.

If, unusually, the written contract does not identify the parties, it is possible that A might show that the identity of the other side was fundamental to A's wish to deal with the other side. Suppose that A sends or inserts by hand a note to the 'occupier' of a certain premises. Unknown to A, the occupier has changed: it is no longer Y but X. X purports to have accepted A's offer. In that situation, A must show that X knew that A had not intended to deal with X and that Y's identity was crucial to A.[169]

165 *Shogun* case, [2003] UKHL 62; [2004] 1 AC 919, HL, at [185] and [110].
166 [1961] 1 QB 31, CA.
167 (1878) 3 App Cas 454, HL.
168 *Shogun* [2003] UKHL 62; [2004] 1 AC 919, HL, at [52] to [55], and also [45] to [49].
169 *Boulton* v. *Jones* (1857) 27 LJ Ex 117, 119, *per* Bramwell B.

(2) There is an objective presumptive analysis in a face-to-face context (or perhaps when A is in telephone conversation with X) that A and X are dealing with each other. X's flesh-and-blood presence (or his speaking voice, where the phone is used) is all that counts. In the face-to-face context, *Lewis* v. *Averay* (1972)[170] (for the facts of which, see 10.33) demonstrates that the courts are nowadays reluctant to make the finding that A only wished to deal with the prospective purchaser of a car if that purchaser is indeed the very same person he purports to be (namely, 'I will deal with you if and only if you are "Y", as declared'). In this face-to-face context, the objective presumptive analysis just mentioned is open to rebuttal if A has manifested a clear refusal to deal with X unless X is who he claims to be, namely, 'Y'. But this intention to deal solely with Y, rather than with X, must be clearly indicated.

As Lord Walker said in the *Shogun* case (2004), it is not impossible that A might succeed in establishing this.[171] In this regard, (a) witnesses or (b) paper indications will help (as will now be explained); otherwise, it is a question of A convincing the court on the basis of his unsupported oral evidence that he told X, a person who is unlikely to be traced after the fraud, that 'I am banking on you being Y'.

As for (a), it is obviously easier for A to convince the court that he had a special intention only to deal with 'Y', if there are witnesses to the transaction to corroborate A's assertion that he articulated his wish to deal only with Y.

As for (b), another possibility is for a cautious vendor to make his assumption crystal-clear by composing a document, for the purchaser to sign, which states that it is agreed that the proposed deal is between A and 'Y', as X represents himself to be. (Although it will be rare for an ordinary person to be pedantic in this manner, commercial traders will be less reluctant to articulate their assumption, especially if large sums are at stake.)

In situation (b), just explained, if the purchaser is in fact someone other than Y, A can justifiably declare that the contract is ineffective because there has been a failure by 'Y' to agree to the contract. The same result can be conceptualised in another way: by contending that this written contract makes clear that it is a condition precedent to the transaction that Y should be the person actually present at the time of this deal, and thus the true and only party to the proposed deal with party A.

Of course, to avoid these problems, sensible vendors will not part with their property until cash payment has been received in full, or payment by cheque has cleared.

10. RECTIFICATION

10.35 Rectification (a doctrine founded upon common error, or sometimes unilateral mistake known to the other) is intertwined with the principles of interpreting written contracts, and so it is discussed at 14.25.

---

170   [1972] 1 QB 198, CA.
171   [2003] UKHL 62; [2004] 1 AC 919, HL, at [86] and [87].

QUESTIONS

(1) 'When there is an apparent consensus between the parties, a shared error concerning the substance of the agreement must be fundamental.' Explain and illustrate.

(2) Was it both (a) unattractive in principle and (b) bad law for the *Solle* v. *Butcher* (1950) line of cases to have tried to supplement the narrow Common Law doctrine of shared mistake by a less rigid equitable doctrine of shared mistake?

(3) 'In the case of unilateral error, even one party's knowledge or strong suspicion that the other is fundamentally mistaken will make no difference. Instead the mistake must concern a term of the proposed contract.' Explain.

(4) 'It is unlikely that a contract will be held to be void where A and B have conducted face-to-face dealings and B has impersonated X, a third party. But it will be different if the written terms of the contract stipulate that the contract is to be "between A and B" and instead X, impersonating B, purports to have made a valid contract with A.' Explain and illustrate.

Selected further reading

General

H. Beale, *Mistake and Non-Disclosure of Facts* (Oxford, 2012)

J. Cartwright, *Misrepresentation, Mistake and Non-Disclosure* (3rd edn, London, 2012), Part 2 (practitioner work: for reference)

D. Friedmann, 'The Objective Principle and Mistake . . .' (2003) 119 LQR 68, especially 68–84

C. MacMillan, *Mistakes in Contract Law* (Oxford, 2010)

G. Spark, *Vitiation of Contracts* (Cambridge, 2013)

Bell v. Lever Bros Ltd

C. MacMillan, 'How Temptation Led to Mistake: An Explanation of Bell v. Lever Brothers, Limited' (2003) 119 LQR 625 (especially concerning the three stages of this litigation: Wright J at first instance, [1931] 1 KB 557, 567 (MacMillan, 646–9); the Court of Appeal, [1931] 1 KB 588–600 (MacMillan, 649–50); and the House of Lords, [1932] AC 161 (MacMillan, 650–9))

'The Great Peace'

K. F. K. Low, 'Coming to Terms with *The Great Peace* in Common Mistake', in J. W. Neyers, R. Bronaugh and S. G. A. Pitel (eds.), *Exploring Contract Law* (Oxford, 2009), 319 ff

S. Midwinter, (2003) 119 LQR 180

F. M. B. Reynolds, (2003) 119 LQR 177

A. Tettenborn, 'Agreements, Common Mistake and the Purpose of Contract' (2011) 27 JCL 91–118 (contending that the post-*Great Peace* doctrine of common error is too restrictive)

Solle v. Butcher

J. Cartwright, 'Solle v. Butcher and the Doctrine of Mistake in Contract' (1987) 103 LQR 594

C. MacMillan, in C. Mitchell and P. Mitchell (eds.), *Landmark Cases in the Law of Restitution* (Oxford, 2006)

A. Phang (1989) LS 291 (for an argument that Common Law and equitable doctrines of mistake should have been fused)

Pre-'The Great Peace' literature

C. J. Slade, 'The Myth of Mistake in the English Law of Contract' (1954) 70 LQR 386 (for earlier criticism along same lines as Smith, below)

J. C. Smith, 'Contracts – Mistake, Frustration and Implied Terms' (1994) 110 LQR 400 (radical criticism of the doctrine of mistake)

Void contracts and mistake as to identity

C. MacMillan, 'Mistake as to Identity Clarified?' (2004) 120 LQR 368

D. W. McLauchlan, 'Parol Evidence and Contract Formation' (2005) 121 LQR 9

A. Phang, P.-W. Lee and P. Koh, 'Mistaken Identity in the House of Lords' [2004] CLJ 24

R. Stevens, 'Objectivity, Mistake and the Parol Evidence Rule', in A. Burrows and E. Peel (eds.), *Contract Terms* (Oxford, 2007), chapter 6, at 110 ff

Law Reform Committee, 'Transfer of Title to Chattels' (Twelfth Report of the Law Reform Committee, Cmnd 2958, 1966)

Chapter contents

11

Duress, undue influence and unconscionability

1. INTRODUCTION

11.01 Summary of main points

(1) *Duress.* This Common Law doctrine involves the application of (a) unlawful or (b) illegitimate pressure so that the relevant contract or contractual modification is unsafe and should be set aside. As for (a), the pressure will normally take the form of a *threatened* legal wrong (crime, tort, breach of contract, etc.). As for (b), the relevant threat might be regarded as illegitimate even though the act threatened was not unlawful (such as refusing to enter into *future* contracts with the other party). Here a court's decision to regard the threat as 'illegitimate', that is, an unacceptable or morally reprehensible use of pressure involves a value judgement, based on the court's perception of the community's sense of moral and social unacceptability.

(2) *Undue influence.* This is an equitable doctrine. 'Actual undue influence' can involve coercion but it need not. If actual undue influence is shown, there is no need to show that the transaction is objectively 'unfair' and 'unbalanced'. However, the more common situation is that undue influence involves abuse of a relationship by someone occupying a superior or dominant position. Unequal relationships include: (i) solicitor/client, teacher/pupil, spiritual advisor/follower, trustee/beneficiary; (ii) in other situations, the claimant must show that, on the particular facts of the case, he 'looked up to' and so placed 'trust and confidence' in the other. In situations (i) or (ii) the law acknowledges that the danger of abuse exists. If the weaker party can go further and show that the gift or transaction 'calls for explanation', the dominant party must try to save the transaction by demonstrating that the weaker party's consent was free and informed. If the stronger party fails to do so, the transaction or gift is voidable on the basis of 'presumed undue influence', that is, the law's inference, not rebutted by the stronger party, that there has been abuse of a relationship.

(3) *Unconscionability or exploitation.* This is another equitable doctrine. Its essence is that a stronger party has taken unacceptable advantage of the other party's weakness or vulnerability in an exceptionally 'shocking' fashion. As a result, the relevant transaction is severely weighted in favour of the stronger party. Even so, the transaction might be upheld if the decision to

287

contract was made in a free and informed way. Unlike undue influence, there is no need for the exploitation to occur within an established relationship: unconscionability can invalidate contracts which are the result of opportunistic exploitation by a stranger.

(4) *No doctrine of substantive unfairness or inequality of bargaining power.* Substantive unfairness is not a free-standing basis of judicial or statutory intervention (11.42). Such an approach had been suggested by Lord Denning MR in his minority judgment in *Lloyds Bank* v. *Bundy* (1975),[1] but this was rejected in later cases (11.43).[2]

(5) This chapter is concerned with the doctrines of duress, undue influence, and unconscionability (or exploitation). Each doctrine is the product of case law. But these concepts are no longer monopolised by the English courts. Thus the Consumer Protection from Unfair Trading Regulations (2008)[3] lists various 'aggressive' trading practices which impair 'the average consumer's freedom of choice ... through the use of harassment, coercion or undue influence'.[4] It is impossible to stay ahead of the chicanery of vendors. The unworldly will be shocked to discover these examples of 'unfair' trading practices listed in the 2008 Regulations:

'making a materially inaccurate claim concerning the nature and extent of the risk to the personal security of the consumer or his family if the consumer does not purchase the product';[5]

'creating the impression that the consumer cannot leave the premises until a contract is formed';[6]

'making persistent and unwanted solicitations by telephone, fax, e-mail or other remote media except in circumstances and to the extent justified to enforce a contractual obligation';[7]

'including in an advertisement a direct exhortation to children to buy advertised products or persuade their parents or other adults to buy advertised products for them';[8] and

'explicitly informing a consumer that if he does not buy the product or service, the trader's job or livelihood will be in jeopardy'.[9]

For reasons of space, this consumer protective legislation will not be further considered in this chapter.

---

1 [1975] QB 326, 337–40, CA; general survey, S. Waddams, *Principle and Policy in Contract Law: Competing or Complementary Concepts?* (Cambridge, 2011), chapter 4.
2 Notably by Lord Scarman in *National Westminster Bank* v. *Morgan* [1985] AC 686, 708, HL.
3 The Consumer Protection from Unfair Trading Regulations 2008 (SI 2008 No. 1277), especially Reg 7; P. Cartwright, 'Under Pressure: Regulating Aggressive Commercial Practices in the UK' [2011] LMCLQ 123–41, notably at 126–9.
4 Reg 7(3), *ibid.*, provides: 'In this regulation – (a) "coercion" includes the use of physical force; and (b) "undue influence" means exploiting a position of power in relation to the consumer so as to apply pressure, even without using or threatening to use physical force, in a way which significantly limits the consumer's ability to make an informed decision.' These are quite narrow definitions which do not encapsulate (accurately or helpfully) the Common Law or equitable counterparts.
5 *Ibid.*, Schedule 1, para. 12.
6 *Ibid.*, Schedule 1, para. 24.
7 *Ibid.*, Sch 1, para 26.
8 *Ibid.*, Sch 1, para 28.
9 *Ibid.*, Sch 1, para 30.

2. DURESS

11.02 Duress[10] is a Common Law doctrine (Equity's doctrine of coercion is no longer invoked).[11] The essence of 'duress' is improper pressure. This must be sufficiently powerful and influential as to render consent legally unsustainable. Such coercion can involve direct force (violence against a person, or harm to his property or his commercial interests) or a threat of harm (more usual than direct force or other infliction of harm).[12] There is a range of possible threatened harm: (a) personal violence (to injure or kill humans); or (b) property loss or damage (no matter what type of property is involved); or (c) economic harm; or (d) harm to a person's personal or family reputation.[13]

It has become common to classify duress under three categories: duress as to person; duress as to goods; and economic duress.[14] However, this is not exhaustive (see category (d) just mentioned). Indeed categories of coercion are dangerous. The law should not become inflexible. In principle, there is no reason why a threat to damage etc. another's property might not be recognised as contractually coercive; and a threat to harm a public asset (such as a public monument or the seashore, indeed the environment generally) might also be contractually coercive. As Lord Devlin said:

> All that matters to the plaintiff is that, metaphorically speaking, a club has been used. It does not matter to the plaintiff what the club was made of – whether it is a physical club or an economic club or otherwise an illegal club.[15]

11.03 Duress does not extinguish contractual consent but merely vitiates it. Thus, a coerced party is psychologically aware of the transaction: he is neither mistaken about what he is doing, nor is he an automaton. In fact, he is all too 'painfully' aware of what, contrary to

10   R. Bigwood, *Exploitative Contracts* (Oxford, 2003); N. Enonchong, *Duress, Undue Influence and Unconscionable Dealing* (2nd edn, London, 2012); *Goff and Jones on the Law of Unjust Enrichment* (8th edn, London, 2011), chapter 10; A. S. Burrows, *The Law of Restitution* (3rd edn, Oxford, 2012), chapter 10; G. Spark, *Vitiation of Contracts* (Cambridge, 2013), chapter 10; G. Virgo, *Principles of the Law of Restitution* (2nd edn, Oxford, 2006), chapter 9; see also J. Beatson, *Use and Abuse of Unjust Enrichment* (Oxford, 1991), 95–136, and, earlier, [1974] CLJ 94; P. Birks, [1990] LMCLQ 342; J. P. Dawson, (1947) 45 *Michigan Law Review* 253; R. Halson, (1991) 107 LQR 649; E. McKendrick, in A. Burrows and Lord Rodger (eds.), *Mapping the Law: Essays in Memory of Peter Birks* (Oxford, 2006), 181; A. Phang, (1992) 5 JCL 147, and (1990) 53 MLR 107, and [1997] *Restitution Law Review* 53–65; S. A. Smith, [1997] CLJ 342–73; for comparative discussion, see J. du Plessis, in H. MacQueen and R. Zimmermann (eds.), *European Contract Law: Scots and South African Perspectives* (Edinburgh, 2006), chapter 6.
11   Cf the line of cases decided in Equity on the basis of coercion, *as distinct from undue influence*: *Williams* v. *Bayley* (1866) LR 1 HL 200 (classified by Lord Denning MR, in *Lloyds Bank Ltd* v. *Bundy* [1975] QB 326, 338, CA, as a case of 'undue pressure', citing Lord Westbury, (1866) LR 1 HL 200, 218–19); P. Winder (1939) 3 MLR 97, 110 ff and (1962) 82 LQR 165; *Kaufman* v. *Gerson* [1904] 1 KB 591, CA; *Mutual Finance Ltd* v. *Wetton & Sons Ltd* [1939] 2 KB 389, Porter J; *D & C Builders* v. *Rees* [1966] 2 QB 617, 625, CA, *per* Lord Denning MR ('clean hands' concept).
12   For commercial pressure without a threat, *Borrelli* v. *Ting* [2010] UKPC 21; [2010] Bus LR 1718, at [32], [35]; noted C. Comte [2011] LMCLQ 333.
13   Cf *Kaufman* v. *Gerson* [1904] 1 KB 591, CA (threat to prosecute husband, which would produce infamy for his wife's family and children).
14   P. Akman, 'The Relationship between Economic Duress and Abuse of a Dominant Position under Competition Law' [2014] LMCLQ 99–131; for Canadian law on economic duress, M. H. Ogilvie and A. Adodo, [2012] JBL 229–42.
15   *Rookes* v. *Barnard* [1964] AC 1129, 1209, HL, *per* Lord Devlin (spoken in context of tort of intimidation; approving Hamson, [1961] CLJ 191, 192).

his wishes, he is being coerced to do. The coerced person's consent is 'vitiated' because he was not psychologically 'free' when deciding to enter the relevant agreement. The Latin tag for this constrained act of contracting is *coactus volui*: 'I volunteered to act, having been compelled to do so.'

11.04 The four components of duress are:
(1) pressure applied or harm threatened;
(2) improper nature of the direct pressure or threatened harm (unlawful conduct threatened or a threat of an otherwise 'illegitimate' nature);
(3) the objective potency of pressure (not every degree of pressure will suffice); and
(4) the causal impact of the pressure (the pressure must have had the right degree of influence on this party).

These factors will be explained below.

11.05 There are two leading judicial definitions of duress. In *Universe Tankships Inc. of Monrovia v. International Transport Workers Federation ('The Universe Sentinel')* (1983), Lord Scarman said:[16]

> [T]he law regards the threat of unlawful action as illegitimate, whatever the demand. Duress can, of course, exist even if the threat is one of lawful action: whether it does so depends upon the nature of the demand.

And, in *Dimskal Shipping Co. SA v. International Transport Workers Federation ('The Evia Luck No. 2')* (1992), Lord Goff said:

> [E]conomic pressure may be sufficient to amount to duress . . . provided at least that the economic pressure may be characterised as illegitimate and has constituted a significant cause inducing the plaintiff to enter into the relevant contract.[17]

11.06 *Implicit or overt pressure.* A 'threat' is normally explicit, but it might be implicit.[18] Implicit threats should not be found too readily. Thus, a party's statement that he is unwilling to continue performance need not constitute an implicit threat. Instead, it might be merely an honest and non-coercive attempt to explore the chance of a compromise arrangement (11.15).

11.07 *Target of threat and maker of the threat.* The target of the threat is normally the contracting party, who now seeks to set aside the agreement. But it might be directed at third parties towards whom the allegedly coerced party has a special responsibility or attachment.[19]

---

16   [1983] 1 AC 366, 400–1, HL.
17   [1992] 2 AC 152, 165G, HL.
18   In these cases Equity avoided contracts on the basis of coercion when family members had entered transactions to counter implied threats to disclose a relative's serious wrongdoing: *Williams* v. *Bayley* (1866) LR 1 HL 200; *Mutual Finance Ltd* v. *Wetton & Sons Ltd* [1939] 2 KB 389, Porter J.
19   Cases cited in previous note.

Similarly, the threatening party is normally the other contracting party, but where A and B are the prospective parties, and T, a third party, threatens A, the latter should be able to avoid the contract if B knew of this pressure (or perhaps if B should have known).[20]

11.08 *Improper nature of the threat.* The threatened act must be either *unlawful* (a crime, tort or breach of contract or some other legal wrong)[21] or *illegitimate.*

(1) *Unlawful.* The fact that the threatened conduct or pressure is unlawful renders it automatically illegitimate. In *'The Universe Sentinel'* (1983), Lord Scarman said:[22] '[T]he law regards the threat of unlawful action as illegitimate, whatever the demand. Duress can, of course, exist even if the threat is one of lawful action: whether it does so depends upon the nature of the demand.' Any breach of contract is an unlawful act. It follows that a threat of a breach of contract is necessarily the threat of an unlawful act and hence illegitimate. This is the correct and authoritative approach. Admittedly, Dyson J (as he then was) in *DSND Subsea Ltd* v. *Petroleum Geo-Services ASA* (2000) suggested that a threat of a breach of contract is not necessarily illegitimate.[23] But the better view is that every breach of contract is necessarily unlawful and hence necessarily illegitimate. Overarching use of the term 'illegitimacy' should not be used to 'legitimise' such an unlawful threat. This point is further examined at 11.17 ff.

(2) *Illegitimate.* Even if the threatened act is not unlawful, it is possible that it might nevertheless be regarded by the court as illegitimate. This last point is clear in English law, although other Common Law systems have been less enthusiastic.[24] Birks notes: '[I]f … lawful pressures are always exempt, those who devise outrageous but technically lawful means of compulsion must always escape [liability] until the legislature declares the abuse unlawful.'[25]

11.09 *Category (2): lawful threat or pressure: no improper duress in a particular commercial context.* In *CTN Cash & Carry Ltd* v. *Gallaher* (1994) the Court of Appeal held that highly coercive commercial pressure had not been illegitimate.[26] On the facts of that case, the threat was declared not to be illegitimate. Steyn LJ emphasised three points: first, the need for certainty in the commercial sphere; secondly, the importance of maintaining closed transactions; finally, the defendant's good faith in making its demand. He said: 'The aim of our commercial law ought to be to encourage fair dealing between parties. But it is a

---

20 For such an approach, UNIDROIT's *Principles of International Commercial Contracts* (3rd edn, 2010), Article 3.2.8 (3rd edition, 2010, text and comment, is available at: www.unidroit.org/english/principles/contracts/principles2010/integralversionprinciples2010-e.pdf; adding the qualification 'a third party for whose acts the [non-aggrieved] party is responsible'.

21 *Borrelli* v. *Ting* [2010] UKPC 21; [2010] Bus LR 1718, at [32], [35]; noted C. Comte [2011] LMCLQ 333 (forgery and false evidence used in course of stalling strategy to induce liquidator to agree a settlement against extreme time-pressure; unlawful steps rendered conduct as a whole 'unconscionable', *ibid.*, at [32], *per* Lord Saville).

22 *Universe Tankships Inc. of Monrovia* v. *International Transport Workers Federation* [1983] 1 AC 366, 400–1, HL.

23 [2000] BLR 530; noted by R. Bigwood, (2001) 117 LQR 376.

24 See the Commonwealth developments cited at P.-W. Lee, [2012] LMCLQ 478, 481 n. 26.

25 P. B. H. Birks, *An Introduction to the Law of Restitution* (Oxford, 1989), 177.

26 [1994] 4 All ER 714, CA.

mistake for the law to set its sights too highly when the critical enquiry is not whether the conduct is lawful but whether it is morally or socially unacceptable.'[27]

In greater detail, *CTN Cash & Carry Ltd* v. *Gallaher* (1994) concerned these facts. The defendant was a manufacturer of cigarettes. The claimant regularly bought these in bulk for distribution to retailers. The defendant, intending to deliver to the claimant a consignment, left the load at the wrong warehouse (Burnley rather than Preston). A third party stole them. The defendant claimed in good faith (although erroneously, as conceded during the litigation) that the goods had been at the claimant's risk and that the claimant was obliged to pay. The claimant gave in and paid only because of commercial pressure: the defendant threatened a lawful act, namely, to withdraw its 'credit facility' on future sales, that is, to insist on cash payment 'up-front' before making future deliveries. There was no obligation that the defendant should continue supplying goods on this credit basis. The threat was certainly potent, but was it illegitimate? The Court of Appeal held that it was not morally or socially unacceptable. The message of this decision was that the courts should be slow to characterise lawful threats between commercial parties as illegitimate. But the Court of Appeal was not shutting the door on the possibility that other facts might cross the line and a threat might be branded as illegitimate even between commercial parties.

Progress Bulk Carriers Ltd v. *Tube City IMS LLC ('The Cenk Kaptanoglu')* (2012)[28] is borderline: on one view the threat was unlawful; on another view (and the more probable interpretation), it was illegitimate even though not quite unlawful.[29]

In *Progress Bulk Carriers Ltd* v. *Tube City IMS LLC ('The Cenk Kaptanoglu')* (2012) A, a charterer, found itself in a commercial tight spot as a result of (i) B's *earlier* breach of contract (failure to supply the promised ship), (ii) B's subsequent promise to supply a substitute vessel and (iii) B's exploitative decision to renege on the offer at (ii) unless A agreed to waive B's liability arising from the breach at (i). The agreement to waive was voidable for illegitimate pressure applied at stage (iii), the 'root cause'[30] of which was the breach at (i) aggravated by the coercing party's decision to resile from 'replacement' offer at (ii). Even if the threat at stage (iii) was not the breach of a legally binding undertaking so to do (on the basis that the guilty party's only legal obligation[31] was to pay damages for breach, and not to provide substitute performance), this was a wholly unmeritorious and commercially unacceptable attempt to squeeze advantage from a situation created by that party's breach. Cooke J upheld the arbitrators' award to set aside the waiver agreement, noting the second strand of illegitimacy,[32] and quoting Steyn LJ's test in the *CTN Cash and Carry* case (1994): 'the critical enquiry [is] not whether the conduct is lawful but whether it is morally or socially unacceptable.'

27 *Ibid.*, at 719.
28 [2012] EWHC 273 (Comm); [2012] 1 Lloyd's Rep 501; [2012] 1 CLC 365 (appeal heard under section 69 of the Arbitration Act 1996); noted P.-W. Lee, [2012] LMCLQ 478.
29 *Ibid.*, at [30], [42] to [44].
30 *Ibid.*, at [39].
31 *Ibid.*, at [38], noting that the arbitrators' factual decision on this point meant that the High Court did not receive argument that the post-breach promise at stage (ii) was a compromise agreement and itself capable of being breached. Cf without mentioning a compromise agreement, *Chitty on Contracts* (31st edn, London, 2012), 7–047 n. 191 (threat not to compensate or remedy an earlier breach is itself unlawful – this argument requires closer analysis).
32 [2012] EWHC 273 (Comm); [2012] 1 Lloyd's Rep 501; [2012] 1 CLC 365, at [30]; applied at [42] to [44]; at [30], summarising Steyn LJ in the *CTN Cash and Carry* case [1994] 4 All ER 714, 719, CA.

11.10 *No improper pressure suffered by SAS soldier*: in *R* v. *Her Majesty's Attorney-General for England and Wales* (2003),[33] a soldier had signed a confidentiality clause as a condition of remaining with the elite SAS regiment. The Privy Council unanimously rejected his plea that this clause was the result of duress (and by a majority it went on to reject the undue influence plea: 11.30). In short, (a) pressure there had been, but (b) it was neither unlawful nor illegitimate. As for (a), the soldier had been subject to pressure because the threat to require him to leave the SAS was perceived as a severe 'sanction'. But as for (b), Lord Hoffmann explained:[34] (i) the threat was lawful because the Crown was entitled to require a soldier to move between regiments; (ii) and the threat was also legitimate because it was a reasonable response to the justifiable need to maintain confidentiality within the SAS.

11.11 *Objective potency of pressure.* Adopting the objective standard of the reasonably robust person, the threat must be potent enough to give the victim *no effective choice but to give in*[35] (see also 11.20 and 11.21). This is a safety-valve test to prevent transactions being set aside by unusually vulnerable or hyper-sensitive parties. It is submitted that this requirement is sound,[36] otherwise duress would be unacceptably broadened.[37] Thus 'mere'[38] or 'classic'[39] 'commercial pressure' does not count; that is, pressure which is merely part of the 'hurly burly of [ordinary] commercial life'[40] and 'the rough and tumble of the pressures of normal commercial bargaining'.[41]

11.12 *Causal impact of the pressure.* Here the question is: 'Did the threat make all the difference, so that without it the coerced party would not have given consent?' Such a test, the so-called 'but for' or 'decisive influence' test, applies both to economic duress[42] and duress as to goods[43] (see 11.02 for the threefold distinction of 'duress as to person', 'duress as to goods' and 'economic duress'). But, according to the Privy Council in *Barton* v. *Armstrong* (1976),[44] this test does *not* apply to duress as to the person and instead in that category of case the psychological test is weighted in favour of the victim (on the parallel approach in respect of fraudulent misrepresentation, see 9.10 at (b)): it is enough that the coerced party was influenced by the duress and did not choose simply to shrug it off. Furthermore, the burden of proof is on the coercing party to prove that the threat did not have even a

---

33 [2003] UKPC 22; [2003] EMLR 24, at [15] ff.
34 *Ibid.*, at [17] to [20].
35 *B & S Contracts & Design Ltd* v. *Victor Green Publications Ltd* [1984] ICR 419, 428, CA, *per* Kerr LJ; J. O'Sullivan and J. Hilliard, *The Law of Contract* (7th edn, Oxford, 2014), 11.22, call this the 'objective' aspect of coercion.
36 Cf Mance J in the *Huyton* case, [1999] 1 Lloyd's Rep 620, 638.
37 Similarly, UNIDROIT's *Principles of International Commercial Contracts*, Article 3.2.6, referring to a threat 'so imminent and serious as to leave [the threatened person] no reasonable alternative'. (UNIDROIT, 3rd edn, 2010, text and comment, available at: www.unidroit.org/english/principles/contracts/principles2010/integral versionprinciples2010-e.pdf).
38 *'The Siboen and the Sibotre'* [1976] 1 Lloyd's Rep 293, 336, *per* Kerr J, 11.21 of text below.
39 *LCP Holding Ltd* v. *Homburg Holdings BV* [2012] EWHC 3643 (QB), at [42], *per* Judge Mackie QC.
40 *Ibid.*
41 *Ibid.*, at [35], quoting Dyson J in *DSND Subsea Ltd* v. *Petroleum Geo-Services ASA* [2000] BLR 530, at [131].
42 *Huyton SA* v. *Peter Cremer GmbH & Co.* [1999] 1 Lloyd's Rep 620, 636, Mance J.
43 *Dimskal Shipping Co. SA* v. *International Transport Workers Federation ('The Evia Luck No. 2')* [1992] 2 AC 152, 165G, HL.
44 [1976] AC 104, PC; applied in *Antonio* v. *Antonio* [2010] EWHC 1199 (QB).

contributory motivational influence.[45] Since the relevant 'fact' is an *ex post facto* discovery of the coerced party's thought processes and motivation, it will be an uphill task for the guilty party to show that the coerced party was not even partly influenced by the threat of personal harm.

In greater detail, *Barton* v. *Armstrong* (1976) concerned a threat (by Armstrong) to assassinate the claimant (Barton). It was established by the Australian trial judge (Street J), and upheld by the New South Wales Court of Appeal, that the victim of this threat had already made a decision that his own commercial interests would be promoted by entering the relevant transaction. Duress had occurred but it had been water off a duck's back: causally irrelevant. However, the majority of the Privy Council second-guessed these findings of fact, noting that the wrongdoer bore the burden of showing that his threat had simply bounced off the other and had had no motivational impact at all. By contrast, in their joint dissent Lords Wilberforce and Simon of Glaisdale, applying the same 'contributory influence' test, considered that the lower courts' findings of fact had clearly established that the threat to kill had been motivationally irrelevant on these unusual facts.[46]

However, it is submitted that the 'but for' or 'decisive influence' test should be applied uniformly to all three categories of duress. Even if the victim subjected to a violent threat, the transaction should not be invalidated if (no doubt exceptionally) the coercing party has convinced the court that the relevant pressure had no decisive difference upon the other party's decision to enter the contract.

11.13 *Nature of contractual invalidity.* Lord Scarman declared in *Pao On* v. *Lau Yiu Long* (1980) that duress renders the contract voidable in the context of 'economic duress'[47] and the same analysis applies to duress as to goods.[48] The three consequences of treating the transaction as voidable, as distinct from void *ab initio*, are: (1) a subpurchaser, if he receives in good faith and without notice, will acquire good title; (2) the coerced party also has the choice whether to affirm or set aside the relevant coerced transaction (as for (1) and (2), see the parallel points in the context of mistake as to the person, and the *Cundy* v. *Lindsay* and *Shogun* cases, at 10.27 ff); (3) rescission permits the court to make adjustments so that the parties are restored to the position before the contract was formed (9.26 ff).

Although it is probable that the flexible process of rescission (accompanied by the bars to rescission pioneered by Equity) applies also to avoidance of a contract on the basis of Common Law duress,[49] cynical or extreme forms of duress might make a difference. For this reason the

---

45   *Ibid.*, at 120, *per* Lord Cross.
46   *Ibid.*, at 124, *per* Lords Wilberforce and Simon.
47   *Pao On* v. *Lau Yiu Long* [1980] AC 614, PC.
48   *Dimskal Shipping Co. SA* v. *International Transport Workers Federation ('The Evia Luck No. 2')* [1992] 2 AC 152, 165, HL, *per* Lord Goff: 'an English contract which is voidable . . . if . . . induced by duress in the form of blacking or the threat of blacking a vessel'.
49   *Halpern* v. *Halpern (No. 2)* [2007] EWCA Civ 291; [2008] QB 195, at [61] and [76] (rescission for duress: need for claimant to give credit for benefits received: 'counter-restitution').

Privy Council in *Borrelli* v. *Ting* (2012)[50] refused to apply the bar of inability to make restitution (*restitution in integrum* impossible) when the coercing party had been guilty of unlawful and cynical misconduct when applying the relevant pressure.

It is submitted that, in the interest of consistency, the 'voidable' analysis should be applied even where the threat or pressure involves direct personal violence. But there are two loose ends which will require consideration. First, Lord Cross' majority opinion in the Privy Council in *Barton* v. *Armstrong* (1976)[51] contains the unreasoned suggestion that a contract might be wholly *void* if the duress employed involves threatened, or actual, personal violence. Secondly, in the case of written agreements only, the anomalous Common Law doctrine of *non est factum* (10.22) will apply to a case where the signatory has been the victim of direct force (as when the contracting party's act of signature is the result of his hand being moved against his will by a person who is applying direct force, or perhaps a gun is placed to his or her loved one's head), and that doctrine renders the relevant transaction *void*.[52]

11.14 *Defence of affirmation.* If the coerced party affirms the contract after the relevant coercion has ceased to influence him, he will lose the chance to set aside the contract. Mocatta J in 'The Atlantic Baron' (1979) held that an objective approach will be adopted to determine whether the coerced party's overt acts or words indicated that he was affirming the contract, and that party's 'secret mental reservation(s)' will be irrelevant.[53] Affirmation did not apply in *Borrelli* v. *Ting* (2012) even though three years elapsed from the cessation of duress to the coerced party's decision to raise the plea of duress.[54] However, in the case of contracts which are void for coercion (as problematically suggested in respect of duress as to person: 11.13), the defence of affirmation is unavailable: one cannot affirm a nullity.

11.15 *Duress and renegotiation of contracts.*[55] Party A might seek either to increase the remuneration payable by B for A's performance ('increasing pact') or, where A is a debtor, try to procure B's agreement to reduce or cancel the debt ('decreasing pact') (on

50   *Borrelli* v. *Ting* [2010] UKPC 21; [2010] Bus LR 1718, at [39]; in *Halpern* v. *Halpern (No. 2)* [2007] EWCA Civ 291; [2008] QB 195, at [76] this point was deliberately left open (noted, C. Comte [2011] LMCLQ 333).
51   [1976] AC 104, 109, 120, PC; and contrast *Antonio* v. *Antonio* [2010] EWHC 1199 (QB); P Lanham, 'Duress and Void Contracts' (1966) 29 MLR 615.
52   *Goff and Jones, The Law of Unjust Enrichment* (8th edn, London, 2011), 10.006 hints at this; however, *non est factum* (*Gallie* v. *Lee* [1971] AC 1004, HL: 10.22) is in tension with the principle of 'objective consent' (1.10 and 3.55 ff); for an unsuccessful plea of *non est factum* when undue influence had been established, *Hackett* v. *CPS* [2011] EWHC 1170 (Admin); [2011] Lloyd's Rep FC 371, at [85] to [90], *per* Silber J.
53   *North Ocean Shipping* v. *Hyundai Construction Co. Ltd ('The Atlantic Baron')* [1979] QB 705, Mocatta J.
54   *Borrelli* v. *Ting* [2010] UKPC 21; [2010] Bus LR 1718, at [36] and [37]; noted C. Comte [2011] LMCLQ 333.
55   P. Birks, [1990] LMCLQ 342; J. Beatson, *Use and Abuse of Unjust Enrichment* (Oxford, 1991), 95–136; *Goff and Jones, The Law of Unjust Enrichment* (8th edn, London, 2011), chapter 10; A. S. Burrows, *The Law of Restitution* (3rd edn, Oxford, 2012), 224–34; G. Virgo, *Principles of the Law of Restitution* (2nd edn, Oxford, 2006), 203 ff; M. Chen-Wishart, in J. Beatson and D. Friedmann (eds.), *Good Faith and Fault in Contract Law* (Oxford, 1995), 142–3; R. Halson, (1991) 107 LQR 649 and R. Halson, *Contract Law* (2nd edn, London, 2013), 341 ff; E. Macdonald, [1989] JBL 460.

these categories of renegotiation, see 5.25 to 5.44). The more important context concerns 'increasing pacts', that is, a contractual modification under which B promises to pay A more money (5.25 ff). There are various ways in which such a renegotiation can arise:

(1) *The other party initiates renegotiation.* B might take the initiative and invite A to discuss what can be done to improve A's performance or to ensure that A performs on time.

(2) *Non-coercive inquiry.* A might gently and courteously broach the question of revising the terms without making an explicit or veiled threat not to proceed unless better terms are obtained.

(3) *Overt threats.* A might broach the same issue by making a clear threat not to proceed unless the terms are revised to suit A.

(4) *Veiled threats.* A might achieve the same level of coercion without using clear menaces, because it is clear to A and B that the former is implicitly threatening to 'down tools', or the commercial equivalent.

11.16 Economic duress was recognised only as recently as 1976 by Kerr J in 'The Siboen and the Sibotre' (1976).[56] At that time, the doctrine of consideration (the rule in *Stilk* v. *Myrick* (1809): see 5.37)[57] dominated this context: B's promise (*whether or not coerced*) to pay A more for the same job, or otherwise to improve A's terms, would not be supported by consideration because the proposed new deal would not involve A incurring 'detriment'. But extension of duress to encompass economic threats, following Kerr J's pioneering decision in 'The Siboen and the Sibotre' (1976),[58] left the path free for a recrafting of the consideration doctrine in the context of 'increasing pacts'[59] (see 5.26 ff, on *Williams* v. *Roffey & Nicholls* (1991), where no explicit or implicit threat was made).[60] As a result, A (the beneficiary of B's promise to pay more for essentially the same performance as A had already promised) can now invoke the concept of a requested 'practical benefit' (essentially, A's willingness to proceed with the same job, rather than leaving B 'high and dry'), and this will satisfy the consideration requirement. Unless the relevant job has already been completed, so that there is no scope even for this very generous notion of 'practical benefit', a promise to pay more (an 'increasing pact') will be enforceable, in the absence of 'fraud' or 'duress'.

11.17 If the law of duress is to be predictable, it must be grounded in settled and clear principles. One cardinal principle is that a threatened breach of contract is the threat of an intrinsically unlawful act; and thus this type of threat is necessarily 'improper' or 'illegitimate'. It is submitted that Dyson J (as he then was) in *DSND Subsea Ltd* v. *Petroleum Geo-Services ASA* (2000) should not be interpreted to have rejected the proposition that a threatened breach of contract (even one made in good faith) is unlawful and hence necessarily illegitimate:[61]

---

56 [1976] 1 Lloyd's Rep 293, Kerr J; noted, J. Beatson, (1976) 92 LQR 496.
57 (1809) 2 Camp 317, Lord Ellenborough CJ.
58 [1976] 1 Lloyd's Rep 293, Kerr J.
59 Their siblings being 'decreasing pacts', 5.30 ff: the upwards or downwards 'pact' terminology is adopted with gratitude from G. H. Treitel, *Some Landmarks of Twentieth Century Contract Law* (Oxford, 2002), 11.
60 [1991] 1 QB 1, CA.
61 [2000] BLR 530, at [131]; noted by R. Bigwood, (2001) 117 LQR 376; the passage has been adopted without demur in *Huyton SA* v. *Peter Cremer GmbH & Co.* [1999] 1 Lloyd's Rep 620, 637, Mance J; Christopher Clarke J in

In determining whether there has been illegitimate pressure, the court takes into account a range of factors. These include whether there had been an actual or threatened breach of contract; whether the person allegedly exerting the pressure had acted in good or bad faith; whether the victim had any realistic practical alternative but to submit to the pressure; whether the victim protested at the time; and whether he affirmed and sought to rely on the contract.

In this passage, Dyson J used 'illegitimate' as short-hand to express the conclusion: 'yes, the duress in this situation is operative [and hence "illegitimate"].' But that conclusion can only be drawn if each of the following boxes is ticked in the coerced party's favour: (1) the complainant has been subjected to pressure or a threat which is (2) (a) unlawful [the possibility at (a) includes a threatened breach of contract] or (b) illegitimate; (3) if so, was the threat severe enough to leave him no practical choice other than to submit ('objective potency')? (4) did the threat influence the targeted party ('causal impact')?

11.18 However, some commentators have unconvincingly challenged the orthodox view that the threat of a breach of contract is necessarily illegitimate. Thus, Burrows and Halson suggest that the law of duress should not invalidate a renegotiation, even if it was the result of significant pressure, if (1) the new agreement rectifies an imbalance which has occurred since the contract's formation (and without A's fault);[62] or (2), as Burrows contends, if the renegotiation stems from the originally 'unfair' terms of the contract[63] (similar comments are made by S. A. Smith).[64] But neither (1) nor (2) should be accepted. If a contractor runs into trouble, or has failed to do his initial sums correctly, and he forces the other to concede a 'rise' in the remuneration, the coercing party's position is unmeritorious. It is wrong to treat a threatened breach of contract as 'legitimate' because the coercing party has a good faith interest in preserving or enhancing his commercial interests.

11.19 The better (and established – see 11.17) view is that, as Bigwood rightly says, a threatened breach of contract is necessarily illegitimate because it is a threat of an unlawful act.[65] O'Sullivan and Hilliard (2014),[66] Macdonald (1989 and 2010)[67] and Tan (2002) share Bigwood's opinion.[68]

Kolmar Group AG v. Traxpo Enterprises PVT Ltd [2010] EWHC 113 (Comm); [2010] 2 Lloyd's Rep 653, at [92]; *LCP Holding Ltd v. Homburg Holdings BV* [2012] EWHC 3643 (QB), at [35], *per* Judge Mackie QC.
62   A. S. Burrows, *The Law of Restitution* (3rd edn, Oxford, 2011), 275; R. Halson, *Contract Law* (2nd edn, London, 2013), 347–9 (Burrows' argument was doubted by Mance J, in *Huyton SA v. Peter Cremer GmbH & Co.* [1999] 1 Lloyd's Rep 620, 637: 'by no means uncontentious').
63   A. S. Burrows, *ibid.*, 274.
64   *Atiyah's Introduction to the Law of Contract* (6th edn, Oxford, 2006), 268–71.
65   R. Bigwood, (2001) 117 LQR 376, 379.
66   J. O'Sullivan and J. Hilliard, *The Law of Contract* (6th edn, Oxford, 2014), 11.16.
67   E. Macdonald, 'Duress by Threatened Breach of Contract' [1989] JBL 460, at 463, 473; L. Koffman and E. Macdonald, *The Law of Contract* (7th edn, Oxford, 2010), 14.9.
68   D. S. Tan, (2002) 18 Const LJ 86, 91–2.

11.20 *Overwhelming commercial pressure during a renegotiation.* Economic duress has invalidated a renegotiated agreement in many cases.[69] For example, in *Atlas Express Ltd v. Kafco (Importers and Distributors) Ltd* (1989)[70] Tucker J held that a carrier's renegotiation of the carriage rate had been procured by economic duress. The defendant had agreed to make regular deliveries of the claimant's cartons to a third party (Woolworth's). The defendant realised that it had undercharged. It then threatened to stop performance until the claimant agreed to pay more. The claimant caved in, fearing that its contract with Woolworth's would otherwise be lost. Tucker J held that the claimant had been placed 'over a barrel' because commercial exigency demanded that it should keep the Woolworth's contract.[71] And so the claimant could withhold the promised additional payment and recover prior overpayments.

11.21 *Insufficient commercial pressure to vitiate a renegotiated agreement.* In 'The Siboen and the Sibotre' (1976), Kerr J[72] broke new ground (in England) by deciding that economic duress can invalidate a contract or a contractual variation. However, this plea failed on the present facts because the pressure was characterised as 'mere commercial pressure' (it appears that Kerr J had quantified it and regarded it as insufficiently coercive to count).[73]

11.22 *Duress and Equity and tort.* In *D & C Builders* v. *Rees* (1966), Lord Denning MR, applying the doctrine of promissory estoppel (in Equity) (on decreasing pacts, see 5.45 ff; and, on this case, see 5.51), held that a promise to accept a smaller payment, *in discharge of the full debt*, could be binding. But such protection will be withheld if the relevant party (here the debtor, invoking the doctrine as a defence) does not 'come with clean hands'.[74] Coercion is one possible ground for withholding Equity's assistance, although the 'clean hands' principle is not confined to illegitimate threats. And so in the *D & C Builders* case, Lord Denning concluded that Mrs Rees could not take advantage of the doctrine of promissory estoppel because she had coerced the builder's cash-crisis into accepting as full discharge a cheque for part-payment. And the contractual doctrine of duress can involve simultaneous commission of the tort of intimidation.[75]

---

69   Also: 'The Alev' [1989] 1 Lloyd's Rep 138, Hobhouse J; *Huyton SA* v. *Peter Cremer GmbH & Co.* [1999] 1 Lloyd's Rep 620, Mance J (noted, D Nolan, [2000] *Restitution Law Review* 105–14); *Carillion Construction Ltd* v. *Felix UK Ltd* [2001] BLR 1; *Alf Vaughan & Co.* v. *Royscot Trust plc* [1999] 1 All ER (Comm) 856; see also *B & S Contracts & Design Ltd* v. *Victor Green Publications Ltd* [1984] ICR 419, CA; *Adam Opel GmbH* v. *Mitras Automotive UK Ltd* [2008] EWHC 3205 (QB); [2008] Bus LR D55; *Kolmar Group AG* v. *Traxpo Enterprises PVT Ltd* [2010] EWHC 113 (Comm); [2010] 2 Lloyd's Rep 653, at [93] to [96], *per* Christopher Clarke J.
70   [1989] QB 833, Tucker J; noted by D. Fleming, [1989] CLJ 362.
71   [1989] QB 833, 838F.
72   [1976] 1 Lloyd's Rep 293, Kerr J; noted by J. Beatson, (1976) 92 LQR 496.
73   [1976] 1 Lloyd's Rep 293, 336.
74   *D & C Builders* v. *Rees* [1966] 2 QB 617, 625, CA.
75   Christopher Clarke J in *Kolmar Group AG* v. *Traxpo Enterprises PVT Ltd* [2010] EWHC 113 (Comm); [2010] 2 Lloyd's Rep 653, at [119] to [121]; see also *Chitty on Contracts* (31st edn, London, 2012), 7–056; for an unsuccessful claim in the tort of intimidation, *Berezovsky* v. *Abramovich* [2012] EWHC 2463 (Comm), Gloster J (and, earlier, *Berezovsky* v. *Abramovich* [2011] EWCA Civ 153; [2011] 1 WLR 2290).

3. UNDUE INFLUENCE

11.23 *Nature of 'actual undue influence'.*[76] The impact of this equitable doctrine, where it is made out on the facts, is that the relevant contract or lifetime gifts[77] becomes voidable,[78] that is, liable to be set aside (on rescission, see 9.18 ff).[79] When will undue influence be established? The central point is that undue influence, the creature of Equity, is not confined to threats or coercion (although undue influence can take that form). Equity is much more sensitive than the Common Law (the doctrine of duress, already examined) because the latter has only responded to instances of direct force or threatened harm. Undue influence extends to subtle forms of 'persuasion', notably self-regarding conduct by stronger parties within unequal relationships. In fact abuse of relationships, without overt coercion, is the paradigm form of undue influence.[80] As Lord Nicholls said in the *Etridge* case (2002): (i) it 'comprises overt acts of improper pressure or coercion such as unlawful threats'[81] but (ii) it has a broader 'connotation of impropriety',[82] and this can take the form of 'overt acts of persuasion'.[83] Lewison J in *Thompson* v. *Foy* (2009) referred to 'acts of overt persuasion, emotional blackmail or bullying'.[84] Thus actual undue influence can cover a range of improper conduct, including coercion, misleading statements, half-truths, cunning persuasion, artful steps and guile.

Where, quite exceptionally (as noted by Lord Hobhouse in the *Etridge* case, 2002)[85] and outside this paradigm of abuse of pre-existing relationships, there is merely the meeting of

---

76 *Royal Bank of Scotland* v. *Etridge (No. 2)* [2002] 2 AC 773, HL, at [8] (generally on undue influence see Lord Nicholls [6] to [89]; and Lord Scott at [139] to [192]); noted M. Oldham [2002] CLJ 29–32 and D. O'Sullivan (2002) 118 LQR 337–51), summarised by Lewison J in *Thompson* v. *Foy* [2009] EWHC 1076 (Ch); [2010] 1 P & CR 16, at [99], Lewison J (the passage is too long to quote here); and see his supplementary observations at [100], [101]; R. Bigwood, *Exploitative Contracts* (Oxford, 2003); P. Birks and N. Y. Chin, 'On the Nature of Undue Influence', in J. Beatson and D. Friedmann (eds.), *Good Faith and Fault in Contract Law* (Oxford, 1995), 57, especially at 57–60, 63–5, 85–8, 92–7; A. S. Burrows, *The Law of Restitution* (3rd edn, Oxford, 2012), chapter 11; D. Capper, (1998) 114 LQR 479; M. Chen-Wishart, 'Undue Influence: Beyond Impaired Consent and Wrongdoing Towards a Relational Analysis', in A. S. Burrows and A. Rodger (eds.), *Mapping the Law: Essays in Memory of Peter Birks* (Oxford, 2006); M. Chen-Wishart, [2006] CLP 231; N. Enonchong, *Duress, Undue Influence and Unconscionable Dealing* (2nd edn, London, 2012); *Goff and Jones, The Law of Unjust Enrichment* (8th edn, London, 2011), chapter 11; G. Spark, *Vitiation of Contracts* (Cambridge, 2013), chapter 11; G. Virgo, *Principles of the Law of Restitution* (2nd edn, Oxford, 2006), chapter 10; L. McMurtry, [2000] Conv 573; A. Phang and H Tjio, [2002] LMCLQ 231; D. O'Sullivan, (2002) 118 LQR 337–51.
77 On the context where undue influence exerted by X causes C to make a gift to D, and D is required to return the gift, following rescission, P. Ridge, 'Third Party Volunteers and Undue Influence' (2014) 130 LQR 112–30.
78 It is established that undue influence renders the transaction voidable and not void; an attempt to go further and show, on the facts, that the transaction was a nullity (that is, void *ab initio*), on the basis of *non est factum* – this doctrine is considered at 10.22 – was unsuccessful in *Hackett* v. *CPS* [2011] EWHC 1170 (Admin); [2011] Lloyd's Rep FC 371, at [85] to [90], *per* Silber J.
79 Equitable compensation of the victim might be awarded if rescission is no longer possible, for example, because property has been transferred by the victim to third parties who have taken 'for value' in good faith: *Hart* v. *Burbidge* [2013] EWHC 1628 (Ch), at [142], *per* Sir William Blackburne; affirmed [2014] EWCA Civ 992.
80 By contrast, coercion is the historical focus of the *probate* doctrine of undue influence: P. Winder, (1939) 3 MLR 97, 104 ff.
81 *Royal Bank of Scotland* v. *Etridge (No. 2)* [2002] 2 AC 773, HL, at [8] (generally on undue influence see Lord Nicholls [6] to [89]; and Lord Scott at [139] to [192]); noted M. Oldham [2002] CLJ 29–32 and D. O'Sullivan (2002) 118 LQR 337–51.
82 [2002] 2 AC 773, HL, at [32].
83 *Ibid.*, at [7] and [9].
84 [2009] EWHC 1076 (Ch); [2010] 1 P & CR 16, at [112].
85 In *Royal Bank of Scotland plc* v. *Etridge (No. 2)* [2002] 2 AC 773, HL, at [92], *per* Lord Hobhouse: 'Actual undue influence does not depend upon some pre-existing relationship between the two parties though it is most commonly associated with and derives from such a relationship.'

complete strangers, it is difficult to imagine how a stranger, even if charismatic, can lure another into a transaction without (a) duress, (b) misrepresentation or (c) exploiting a person's vulnerability so as justify rescission under the category known as 'unconscionability' (on the last see 11.36 ff below). Suppose that a star-struck fan is overwhelmed on first meeting a 'celebrity'. The fan is induced to enter a contract but without coercive pressure or threats, or misrepresentation, or 'shocking' exploitation of the other's vulnerability. The fan does not appear to have any ground for complaint on the basis of 'actual undue influence'. He is instead the victim of his or her folly. It would be different if the celebrity had, as it were, 'groomed' this particular victim and thus created the opportunity to abuse a relationship which the celebrity had cynically fostered.

The courts have consistently noted the wide and pliable nature of undue influence. For example, Lord Scarman in *National Westminster Bank plc* v. *Morgan* (1985) said that there are no[86] 'precisely defined . . . limits to the equitable jurisdiction of a court to relieve against undue influence'. Lord Clyde said in the *Etridge* case (2002):[87] '[Undue influence] is something which can be more easily recognised when found than exhaustively analysed in the abstract.' And Lindley LJ in *Allcard* v. *Skinner* (1887) said:[88] 'undue influence has . . . been developed by the necessity of grappling with insidious forms of spiritual tyranny and with the infinite varieties of fraud. As no Court has ever attempted to define fraud so no Court has ever attempted to define undue influence.' It should be noted that equitable 'fraud' is not concerned with fraudulent misrepresentation or even dishonesty. Instead it denotes any form of misconduct which is unacceptable to Equity (modern judges have also defined actual undue influence as a species of 'equitable fraud').[89]

Wrongdoing is always a feature. Lord Nicholls said in the *Etridge* case (2002):[90] 'Undue influence has a connotation of impropriety'; the issue is whether:[91] 'the defendant abused the influence he acquired in the parties' relationship [because he] preferred his own interests.' But undue influence does not require wicked, cynical or conscious wrongdoing: it is enough that there has been some self-regarding failure of responsibility within the protected relationship of vulnerability. Responsibility grows out of the relationship, for example, between religious groups and converts, or between banks who have acquired an advisory function and customers who have grown used to relying on the bank's guidance. The dominant party might have acted in some cases in a morally upright and righteous way, but that party will nevertheless be castigated in Equity for not having taken proper steps to ensure that the transaction or gift was the true product of the other party's free consent, and that the latter was insulated from the relevant influence.

In fact undue influence covers a spectrum of objectionable conduct or omissions to act. At one end the misconduct might involve overt arm-twisting or coercion. At the other end of the spectrum, all that can be alleged is that the stronger party has omitted to ensure that the weaker party has been enabled to make a free and informed decision liberated from the

---

86 [1985] AC 686, 709, HL; noted by N. Andrews, [1985] CLJ 192.
87 *Royal Bank of Scotland plc* v. *Etridge (No. 2)* [2002] 2 AC 773, HL, at [92].
88 *Allcard* v. *Skinner* (1887) 36 Ch D 145, 183, CA.
89 Lord Denning MR in *Lloyds Bank Ltd* v. *Bundy* [1975] QB 326, 338A, CA ('some fraud or wrongful act'); Lord Browne-Wilkinson in *CIBC Mortgages plc* v. *Pitt* [1994] 1 AC 200, 209B, HL (a 'species of equitable fraud').
90 *Etridge (No. 2)* [2002] 2 AC 773, HL, at [32].
91 *Ibid.*, at [103].

overshadowing influence of the other.[92] For example, in the seminal case of *Allcard* v. *Skinner* (1887), where a novice in a nunnery had handed over all her property to the convent, Lindley LJ said:[93]

> I believe that in this case there was in fact no unfair or undue influence brought to bear on the plaintiff other than such as inevitably resulted from the training she had received, the promise she had made, the vows she had taken, and the rules to which she submitted herself. But her gifts were in fact made under a pressure which, whilst it lasted, the plaintiff could not resist.

And in the context of a close advisory relationship between a bank's branch manager and his customer, Sir Eric Sachs in *Lloyds Bank* v. *Bundy* (1975) said:

> [O]nce the existence of a special relationship has been established, then any possible use of the relevant influence is, irrespective of the intentions of the persons possessing it, regarded ... as an abuse – unless and until the duty of fiduciary care has been shown to be fulfilled.[94]

The contrast between naked misconduct and relational abuse underlies Ward LJ's comment in *Drew* v. *Daniel* (2005):[95] 'in the case of actual undue influence something has to be done to twist the mind of a [contracting party] whereas in cases of presumed undue influence [where a relationship has been abused] it is more a case of *what has not been done*, namely ensuring that independent advice is available to the donor.' [emphasis added]

There has been some attempt at analysis. Slade LJ in *BCCI* v. *Aboody* (1990) said that actual undue influence comprises these elements: '(a) the other party to the transaction (or someone who induced the transaction for his own benefit) had the capacity to influence the complainant; (b) the influence was exercised; (c) its exercise was undue; (d) its exercise brought about the transaction.'[96] With respect, only (c) seems worthy of special mention. The criterion of 'undue' must be emphasised because the law needs to distinguish between unacceptable ('undue') and ordinary and unexceptionable influences. As Sir William Blackburne said in *Hart* v. *Burbidge* (2013):[97]

> It is not to be suggested that such everyday influences disable a person from freely exercising his or her will. The question only arises when the influences go beyond a point where the freedom of that person to act independently is compromised such that the court concludes that the transaction was not the act of a free agent.

---

92 E.g., in *Abbey National Bank plc* v. *Stringer* [2006] EWCA Civ 338; [2006] 2 P & CR DG15, at [43] to [47], *per* Lloyd LJ, a relationship of trust and confidence between an illiterate mother and her son, exploited by the latter, the transaction 'calling for explanation', but the son having failed to discharge his 'positive duty ... to see that she understands what the transaction is that he is asking her, or indeed telling her, to enter into'; since here 'it is not sufficient for him simply to take her to the document, tell her to sign it and rely upon the fact that she asks no question about it' (quotation at [47]).
93 (1887) 36 Ch D 145, 185, CA.
94 [1975] QB 326, 343, CA.
95 [2005] EWCA Civ 507; [2005] 2 P & CR 14, at [31], [32], [36].
96 [1990] 1 QB 923, 967.
97 [2013] EWHC 1628 (Ch), at [49]; affirmed [2014] EWCA Civ 992.

The tactical advantage of showing actual undue influence is that a victim of actual undue influence is entitled to rescission 'as of right'[98] (although subject to equitable bars) because there is no further need to show that the gift or transaction 'calls for explanation' (the position is different if presumed undue influence is in issue: 11.25 and 11.26).

11.24 *The Birks-Chin theory of undue influence (an unconvincing attempt at academic restructuring).* Birks and Chin (1995)[99] suggested that undue influence is not concerned with wrongdoing or culpable shortcomings. Instead they considered that it is 'claimant-sided': that its essence is 'impairment of the capacity of the plaintiff to make the decision which is impugned'.[100] They said: 'the plaintiff ... has, to a sufficiently extreme degree, a sub-standard judgemental capacity, and the source of the impairment is the character of the relationship in which he finds himself.'[101] This is tantamount to creating a new jurisdiction of 'incapacity', beyond the established situations of mental infirmity and infancy (1.09).

It is submitted that Birks and Chin are wrong to suggest (a) that undue influence should be reconceptualised as a 'claimant-sided' instance of judgemental incapacity (that is, the inability to think straight and make balanced decisions); and (b) that Equity is responsive to improper conduct only within the doctrine of 'unconscionability' (on which 11.36). Instead 'defendant-sided' impropriety is the core of undue influence, and unconscionability is a grievous form of exploitation of acute vulnerability. The Birks-Chin theory is in conflict with the traditional view, restated at the highest level by the Privy Council and House of Lords, that undue influence is Equity's response to improper conduct.[102] And academics have not accepted the Birks analysis.[103] Admittedly, perhaps beguiled by the Birksian analysis, Mummery LJ in *Pesticcio* v. *Huet* (2004) said (approved by first instance cases): '[Undue influence can apply] even though the actions and conduct of the person who benefits from it could not be criticised as wrongful.'[104] But this overlooks the fact that the misconduct underlying a successful plea of undue influence need not be shocking or deliberate.

Birks remained committed to the 'claimant-sided' theory of undue influence. This led him to interpret cases through this unorthodox prism. So for example, Birks[105] presented a highly sanitised version of the donee's conduct in *Hammond* v. *Osborn* (2002),[106] accentuating the

---

98 *CIBC Mortgages plc* v. *Pitt* [1994] 1 AC 200, 209 B–C, HL.
99 P. Birks and N.Y. Chin in J. Beatson and D. Friedmann (eds.), *Good Faith and Fault in Contract Law* (Oxford, 1995), 57–97.
100 *Ibid.*, 59.
101 *Ibid.*, 89.
102 In *R* v. *Her Majesty's Attorney-General for England and Wales* [2003] UKPC 22; [2003] EMLR 24, at [21]; *Royal Bank of Scotland plc* v. *Etridge (No. 2)* [2002] 2 AC 773, HL, at [103].
103 R. Bigwood, *Exploitative Contracts* (Oxford, 2003), 467 ff; and R. Bigwood, (1995) 16 OJLS 503; D. Capper, (2010) 126 LQR 403, 418.
104 [2004] EWCA Civ 372; [2004] NPC 55, at [20]; cited by Christopher Clarke J in *Birmingham City Council* v. *Forde* [2009] EWHC 12 (QB); [2010] 1 All ER 802, at [103], and by Sir William Blackburne in *Hart* v. *Burbidge* [2013] EWHC 1628 (Ch), at [51]; affirmed [2014] EWCA Civ 992.
105 P. Birks, 'Undue Influence as Wrongful Exploitation' (2004) 120 LQR 34–7; see also P. Birks, *Unjust Enrichment* (Oxford, 2005), 176–8.
106 [2002] EWCA Civ 885; [2002] WTLR 1125, at [31].

donor's lack of clear-mindedness. But this is skewed against the evidence: Sir Martin Nourse said that the donee's 'conduct' had a 'sinister appearance', and Ward LJ said that she had not displayed 'fair play'.[107]

11.25 *The three phases of 'presumed undue influence' complaints.* In the absence of proven 'actual undue influence', the complainant must overcome two hurdles:

(1) *hurdle and phase one*: the existence of such a relationship of trust and confidence based on either (a) standard recognition of the parties' roles, for example, the inequality between solicitor and client or doctor and patient, or (b) ad hoc recognition, founded on the parties' particular relationship; for example, one spouse enjoying much greater influence over the other, or a bank's customer developing a special relationship with the bank (see 11.26 for more on this first category);

(2) *hurdle and phase two*: that the transaction 'calls for explanation' (that is, it is substantively one-sided and suspicious) (the 'ace card') (see 11.26 for more on this second category).

For the third phase, *it is incumbent on the superior party to retrieve the position* and demonstrate that the inferior party had entered the transaction 'with her eyes open', exercising a free and informed consent (see 11.27 for more on this third element).

Lord Nicholls enunciated this same triad of phases in the *Etridge* case (2002):[108]

> [*Phase one*] Proof that the complainant placed trust and confidence in the other party in relation to the management of the complainant's financial affairs, coupled with [*Phase two*] a transaction which calls for explanation, will normally be sufficient, failing satisfactory evidence to the contrary, to discharge the burden of proof ... On proof of these two matters the stage is set for the court to infer that, in the absence of a satisfactory explanation, the transaction can only have been procured by undue influence. So [*Phase three*] the evidential burden shifts to [the defendant]. It is for him to produce evidence to counter the inference which otherwise should be drawn.[109] [phase notation added in square brackets]

11.26 *Presumed categories.* The House of Lords in the *Etridge* case (2002)[110] noted that it had become customary to distinguish within the broad category of 'presumed undue influence' cases ('Class 2' situations) between:[111]

(a) those ('Class 2A') which are standard instances of legally recognised protected relationships; and

(b) those ('Class 2B') which are shown on the facts of a particular case to disclose a relationship of trust, confidence, dependence, loyalty, etc.

---

107 *Ibid.*, at [61].
108 *Royal Bank of Scotland plc v. Etridge (No. 2)* [2002] 2 AC 773, HL, at [14].
109 *Ibid.*, per Lord Hobhouse at [107] and Lord Scott at [153].
110 *Royal Bank of Scotland plc v. Etridge (No. 2)* [2002] 2 AC 773, HL, at [8] (generally on undue influence, see Lord Nicholls at [6] to [89], and Lord Scott at [139] to [192]); noted by M. Oldham, [2002] CLJ 29–32 and D. O'Sullivan, (2002) 118 LQR 337–51.
111 See Lord Browne-Wilkinson's exposition in *Barclays Bank plc v. O'Brien* [1994] 1 AC 180, 189–90, HL.

The main examples of relationships within Class 2A, that is, instances of plain inequality between the parties, are: trustee and beneficiary; spiritual advisor (or priest) and devotee;[112] parent and child; guardian and ward; and solicitor and client[113] (even if they are cohabiting).[114] Relationships not falling within class 2A, and requiring, therefore, to be characterised on the facts as one-sided (relationships of 'trust and confidence') include: banker and client (11.30), spouses (case law at 11.29 and 11.32), and grown-up children vis-à-vis vulnerable parents.[115] Once a class 2A or class 2B relationship of 'trust and confidence' applies, or is proved to exist, as Lord Nicholls noted in the *Etridge* case, the irrebuttable presumption is that the 'stronger' party had influence over the other.[116] However, as Lords Nicholls and Hobhouse observed in the same case, within both Class 2A and Class 2B, there is *no presumption* that the dominant party has in fact abused his relationship.[117] Something more must be shown. This is the second hurdle: only if the gift or transaction 'calls for explanation' will the dominant party need to show that in fact the weaker party was not the victim of undue influence. A transaction or gift which appears to 'call for explanation' might in fact be explicable as consistent with ordinary human motives in that context.[118] If so, the second hurdle has not been overcome. And so the third phase in the analysis has not been reached: the stronger party will not be required to retrieve the position by demonstrating the matters mentioned above.

Large gifts will require more cogent explanation. There are no hard-and-fast rules. Context is everything. In *Evans* v. *Lloyd* (2013) the donor had lived with non-relatives for most of his life. He made a gift of farmland to the latter as acts of gratitude and friendship.[119] The gift involved transfer of all his significant assets. Judge Keyser QC in the High Court held that the second hurdle had not been surmounted: the gift was treated as a free act of generosity. But the law should be very slow to draw such a conclusion when the donor has made such a large gift, especially when it amounts to his total patrimony. The decision might be rationalised as the product of the judge's central perception that the donor was actuated by genuine gratitude and that the donees were 'thoroughly decent' people.[120]

The *Etridge* case (2002) discarded the test of 'manifest disadvantage' and substituted the test that the gift or transaction should 'call for explanation' or that it should not be 'readily

---

112 *Allcard* v. *Skinner* (1887) 36 Ch D 145, CA (nun making large gifts to the head of the nunnery; but the nun was too slow in seeking rescission on the facts); and *Morley* v. *Loughman* [1893] 1 Ch 736, 756, Wright J (exertion of ascendancy over a religious convert was proved by clear 'inferences'; no need to rely on any presumption).

113 For parent/child, guardian/ward, and solicitor/client, see the authorities cited in *Chitty on Contracts* (31st edn, London, 2012), 7–078 ff.

114 *Markham* v. *Karsten* [2007] EWHC 1509 (Ch), at [35] and [36], *per* Briggs J.

115 *Abbey National Bank plc* v. *Stringer* [2006] EWCA Civ 338; [2006] 2 P & CR DG 15, at [43]; *Hackett* v. *CPS* [2011] EWHC 1170 (Admin); [2011] Lloyd's Rep FC 371, at [54], *per* Silber J.

116 *Royal Bank of Scotland plc* v. *Etridge (No. 2)* [2002] 2 AC 773, HL, at [18].

117 *Ibid.*, at [14] and [18], *per* Lord Nicholls, and at [104], *per* Lord Hobhouse.

118 *Evans* v. *Lloyd* [2013] EWHC 1725, at [43], [45], noting *Turkey* v. *Awadh* [2005] EWCA Civ 382; [2005] 2 FCR 7; [2005] 2 P & CR 29; [2006] WTLR 553, at [15] *per* Buxton LJ; the transaction in *Abbey National Bank plc* v. *Stringer* [2006] EWCA Civ 338; [2006] 2 P & CR DG15, 'called for explanation' (mortgaging by illiterate mother of her interest in real property; mother's signature given, without explanation of the transaction by financially interested son; proven relationship of trust and confidence); similarly, *Hackett* v. *CPS* [2011] EWHC 1170 (Admin); [2011] Lloyd's Rep FC 371, at [56] ff, *per* Silber J.

119 *Evans* v. *Lloyd* [2013] EWHC 1725.

120 The phrase 'thoroughly decent' and epithet 'decent' recur, almost reaching an apotheosis, at *ibid.*, [56], [60], and [71].

explicable'[121] (the 'calls for explanation' requirement has now been considered in numerous cases).[122] In the same case Lord Nicholls said that ordinarily a spouse's decision to act as surety for the other spouse's debts can be attributed to readily explicable motives.[123] This situation does not, therefore, ordinarily 'call for explanation'.

However, where the guarantor is given at a stage where the lender is merely procuring additional protection without increasing the loan, such a guarantee might 'call for explanation'. This was the context in *Lloyds Bank* v. *Bundy* (1975) when the father provided a second guarantee on behalf of his son's loan in *Lloyds Bank* v. *Bundy* (1975).[124] Where guarantor and borrower are married or emotionally attached, a guarantee for the lender's convenience will 'call for explanation'.

11.27   If the transaction does indeed 'call for explanation', it becomes necessary for the stronger party to satisfy the court that the weaker party's consent was free and informed,[125] and that the consenting party was emancipated from the other's influence.[126] Obtaining independent legal advice is neither necessary nor need it be decisive.[127] As Mummery LJ said in *Pesticcio* v. *Huet* (2004):[128]

> [the court must be] satisfied that the advice and explanation . . . was . . . effective to free the [weaker party] from . . . the influence on his free will and to give him the necessary independence of judgment . . . to make choices with a full appreciation of what he was doing.

Thus the double aim of independent legal advice should be (a) to ensure that the client knows the nature of the proposed transaction and its implications; and (b) that the lawyer's advice should have the effect that the client is also insulated, emancipated[129] and liberated from the relevant noxious influence of the stronger party; in other words, that the lawyer should act as a buffer between client and the stronger party.[130] Consistent with this, the

---

121   *Royal Bank of Scotland plc* v. *Etridge (No. 2)* [2002] 2 AC 773, HL, at [21] to [31], *per* Lord Nicholls.
122   *Evans* v. *Lloyd* [2013] EWHC 1725, at [43], [45], noting *Turkey* v. *Awadh* [2005] EWCA Civ 382; [2005] 2 FCR 7; [2005] 2 P & CR 29; [2006] WTLR 553, at [15] *per* Buxton LJ; and also *Macklin* v. *Dowsett* [2004] EWCA Civ 904; [2005] WTLR 1561, at [30] ff, *per* Auld LJ; *Turkey* v. *Awadh* [2005] EWCA Civ 382; [2005] 2 P & CR 29, at [15], and [20] ff, *per* Buxton LJ; *Thompson* v. *Foy* [2009] EWHC 1076 (Ch); [2010] 1 P & CR 16, at [100] and [108], *per* Lewison J.
123   *Royal Bank of Scotland plc* v. *Etridge (No. 2)* [2002] 2 AC 773, HL, at [30] and [31], *per* Lord Nicholls.
124   [1975] QB 326, CA.
125   *Birmingham City Council* v. *Forde* [2009] EWHC 12 (QB); [2010] 1 All ER 802, at [105], *per* Christopher Clarke J: '[T]he problem is not lack of understanding but lack of independence.'
126   *Hackett* v. *CPS* [2011] EWHC 1170 (Admin); [2011] Lloyd's Rep FC 371, at [63] ff, *per* Silber J.
127   E.g., legal advice scrutinised and not shown to have saved the transaction, in *Hackett* v. *CPS* [2011] EWHC 1170 (Admin); [2011] Lloyd's Rep FC 371, at [73] ff, *per* Silber J.
128   [2004] EWCA Civ 372; [2004] NPC 55, at [23].
129   *Royal Bank of Scotland* v. *Etridge (No. 2)* [2002] 2 AC 773, HL, at [20], *per* Lord Nicholls.
130   *Hart* v. *Burbidge* [2013] EWHC 1628 (Ch), at [42] to [48], [130], *per* Sir William Blackburne (affirmed [2014] EWCA Civ 992); and *Randall* v. *Randall* [2004] EWHC 2258 (Ch); [2005] 1 P & CR DG4, at [38] (a decision of Edward Bartley Jones QC, in the Chancery Division); in the *Hart* case the following cases were cited on this point ([2013] EWHC 1628 (Ch), at [43] ff): *Inche Doria* v. *Shaik Allie Bin Omar* [1929] AC 129, 135, PC, *per* Lord Hailsham LC; *Zamet* v. *Hyman* [1961] 1 WLR 1442, 1446, CA, *per* Evershed MR; *Hammond* v. *Osborn* [2002] EWCA Civ 885; [2002] WTLR 1125, at [25] to [28], *per* Sir Martin Nourse; *Hodson* v. *Hodson* [2006] EWHC 2878 (Ch), at [27], *per* Patten J; *Smith* v. *Cooper* [2010] EWCA Civ 722; [2011] 1 P & CR DG1; [2010] 2 FLR 1521, at [61], *per* Lloyd LJ; and *Etridge (No. 2)* [2001] HL 44; [2002] 2 AC 773, at [20], *per* Lord Nicholls; *Pesticcio* v. *Huet* [2004] EWCA Civ 372; [2004] NPC 55, at [23] *per* Mummery LJ. And see also the *Padden* case in the next note.

Court of Appeal in *Padden* v. *Bevan Ashford* (2011) noted that a legal advisor, faced by a client contemplating a transaction which will 'call for explanation' in due course, has a stringent responsibility to explore carefully the nature of the proposed transaction, to caution against precipitate and imprudent decision-making, and to ensure that there is no undue influence.[131]

11.28 *Relationship of trust and confidence arising during protracted stages of a transaction.* Normally, the relevant relationship will antedate the transaction which is now challenged. But in *Macklin* v. *Dowsett* (2004) the Court of Appeal held that such a relationship had arisen during protracted property dealings between the parties, even though there had been no relationship of trust and confidence between them before those dealings had commenced.[132] Those dealings culminated in the arrangement which was now successfully impugned: Dowsett's grant to Macklin of an option to 'buy out' Dowsett's lifetime rent-free tenancy for a mere £5,000 if Dowsett did not succeed himself in developing the land within the tight 'window' of the terms of a planning permission. The court held that Macklin could not take advantage of that option. It had been obtained as a result of undue influence.

11.29 *Duty not to suppress a material factor arising from a relationship of trust and confidence.* The Court of Appeal in *Hewett* v. *First Plus Financial Group* (2010)[133] held that *once a relationship of trust and confidence is shown to exist* between husband and wife (later cases might extend this to non-marital emotional and long-term relationships), this relationship can import a duty to refrain from deliberate suppression of a material fact. In this case, the husband suppressed the fact that he was having an affair with another woman. Had the wife known this, it is possible – and perhaps likely – that she would not have proceeded with the refinancing of the husband's debts by agreeing to provide security (her share of the matrimonial home) for a loan made by the claimant finance company to her husband. The Court of Appeal held that the lender had constructive notice that the wife had been the victim of a material non-disclosure (the lender had failed to insist that the wife should obtain independent legal advice before assenting to the new financing arrangement, and to her provision of security). For this reason, the lender could not enforce its security against her (although the security provided by the husband in his own name was open to enforcement by the lender, because the husband had defaulted on the loan).

11.30 *Banker and customer.* Because the banker/customer relationship is not in the (hallowed) list of recognised relationships of dependence, *it is a question of fact* whether a particular bank's customer has in fact placed such trust and confidence in a bank's staff or officials. In *National Westminster Bank plc* v. *Morgan* (1985), the House of Lords held that Mrs Morgan's contact 'never went beyond the normal business relationship of banker and customer'.[134] By contrast, in *Lloyds Bank Ltd* v. *Bundy* (1975)[135] the bank had assumed

131 [2011] EWCA Civ 1616; [2012] 1 WLR 1759, at [27] to [54], *per* Lord Neuberger MR.
132 [2004] EWCA Civ 904; [2005] WTLR 1561.
133 *Hewett* v. *First Plus Financial Group* [2010] EWCA Civ 312; [2010] Fam Law 589.
134 [1985] AC 686, 702G, HL; noted, N. Andrews, [1985] CLJ 192.
135 [1975] QB 326, CA.

such a special relationship. In the *Bundy* case a majority of the Court of Appeal, applying orthodox principles of undue influence, held that the bank had 'crossed the line' on the facts of this case. As a result, it had assumed a special relationship of trust and confidence towards their customer, 'old' Mr Bundy, who had guaranteed his only son's business debts with the bank. The court held that the special relationship gave rise to a duty to ensure that the bank's customer did not enter into an especially onerous guarantee of his son's business debts without first having obtained independent legal advice. In the absence of this, the guarantee could be set aside because it was vitiated by undue influence. It will be seen that here undue influence operates to impose a positive duty to act. This is not the same as inferring that there have been 'overt acts of coercion or persuasion'.

In greater detail, *Lloyds Bank Ltd v. Bundy* (1975) involved these facts and legal analysis. Over many years, the Bundys had formed a relatively close relationship with the officials of the bank's Salisbury branch. 'Old' Mr Bundy had already agreed one guarantee of his son's debts. The guarantee was supported by a charge, in favour of the bank, against his property, 'Yew Tree Farm'. Before assenting to this first guarantee, he had obtained independent advice. The fateful transaction concerned a second guarantee: a further secured guarantee for the *son's same debt*. This new transaction gave the bank additional security and reduced the son's borrowing limit. On this occasion, the father signed without obtaining fresh independent legal advice. The bank did not perceive the need to impress upon him the merits of obtaining such advice. The Court of Appeal held by a majority (Cairns and Sachs LJJ) that orthodox principles of undue influence justified rescission of the second guarantee. In short the bank was seriously 'conflicted' on these facts. Sachs LJ explained that:[136]

> The situation was . . . one which to any reasonably sensible person . . . cried aloud for Mr Bundy's need for careful independent advice. The bank's failure on these facts to advise that he should receive such advice was a breach of a fiduciary[137] duty, arising from its position towards Bundy of trust and confidence. [And] . . . it would be contrary to public policy [for the] benefit of the transaction to be retained by the [bank].[138]

The world of banking has changed. There are now, in the modern conditions of faceless, electronic and telephonic banking, many more people in the position of Mrs Morgan in *National Westminster Bank plc v. Morgan* (1985),[139] rather than the one-to-one 'special banking relationship' identified by the Court of Appeal in *Lloyds Bank v. Bundy* (1975).[140]

In *R v. Her Majesty's Attorney-General for England and Wales* (2003),[141] a case concerning a soldier and his employer (the Crown), the Privy Council held that, on the facts, no duty existed to warn a weaker party that he should obtain independent legal advice. Here the soldier had signed

---

136   *Ibid.*, at 345.
137   *Calvert v. William Hill Credit Ltd* [2008] EWCA Civ 1427; [2009] Ch 330, at [53]; J. Edelman, 'When Do Fiduciary Duties Arise?' (2010) 126 LQR 302.
138   [1975] QB 326, 346, CA.
139   [1985] AC 686, HL; noted, N. Andrews, [1985] CLJ 192.
140   [1975] QB 326, CA.
141   [2003] UKPC 22; [2003] EMLR 24.

a confidentiality clause as a condition of remaining within the elite SAS regiment. He later challenged in the New Zealand courts, alleging that the confidentiality agreement should be set aside for duress or undue influence. The Privy Council unanimously rejected the duress (11.10) plea, and, by a majority (Lord Scott dissenting), the undue influence plea. As for the latter, the Privy Council held that, even assuming that the Crown occupied a position of superiority on these facts, there had been no exploitation of its dominant position, nor had there been any objectionable failure to ensure that he should receive independent legal advice.[142] However, Lord Scott dissented on this last point.[143] In his view, this was a 'classic' situation of domination amounting to undue influence, where the Crown should have insisted that a lifetime confidentiality obligation should only be undertaken if an employee has received independent legal advice. Lord Scott's analysis is analogous to the decision of the majority in *Lloyds Bank* v. *Bundy*, examined above.

11.31 *Lenders, guarantors and third parties' wrongdoing.*[144] The House of Lords in the *Etridge* case (2002),[145] now the leading case, reviewed its earlier decisions in *Barclays Bank* v. *O'Brien* (1994)[146] and *CIBC* v. *Pitt* (1994).[147] This line of cases concerns a lender's possible actual or 'constructive' awareness (deemed knowledge) that a guarantor of a loan has been the victim of the borrower's misrepresentation, coercion or undue influence. This tripartite relationship involves the following elements:

(1) A and X are in a non-commercial relationship (whether marital, sexual, emotional, or just friends); X wishes to receive (or in some cases to increase or simply continue) a loan from B, which is normally a bank or other commercial lender; A ultimately agrees to act as surety for X's repayments to B, and so A assumes a direct contractual tie (under a contract of guarantee) with B; the guarantee is normally supported by a charge in favour of B upon A's interest in the matrimonial home or other co-owned property; when lender B calls upon A to honour the guarantee, normally to compel a sale of A's property in accordance with the charge in B's favour, A protests that she has been the victim of some legal wrong or impropriety committed by X; and

(2) B has express or constructive notice of the wrong or impropriety (see further at (3)) committed by X vis-à-vis A, the guarantor (the 'link' between the lender and the guarantor);

(3) this wrong or impropriety might be any of the following:

---

142 *Ibid.*, at [24] to [28].
143 [2003] UKPC 22; [2003] EMLR 24, at [45].
144 N. Enonchong, *Duress, Undue Influence and Unconscionable Dealing* (2nd edn, London, 2012); D. O'Sullivan, S. Elliott and R. Zakrzewski, *The Law of Rescission* (Oxford, 2008), chapter 9.
145 *Royal Bank of Scotland plc* v. *Etridge (No. 2)* [2002] 2 AC 773, HL, at [48], *per* Lord Nicholls: adopted also in both Canada (M. H. Ogilvie, 'The Reception of Etridge (No. 2) in Canada' [2008] JBL 191) and New Zealand (D. Capper, 'The Unconscionable Bargain in the Common Law World' (2010) 126 LQR 403, 413 n. 84); but Australia has adhered to its special Equity for surety wives (*ibid.*, at 411, noting *Garcia* v. *National Australia Bank Ltd* (1998) 194 CLR 395 (High Court of Australia) (applying *Yerkey* v. *Jones* (1939) 63 CLR 649, High Court of Australia)); R. Bigwood, 'From Morgan to Etridge: Tracing the (Dis)Integration of Undue Influence . . .', in J. W. Neyers, R. Bronaugh and S. G. A. Pitel (eds.), *Exploring Contract Law* (Oxford, 2009), 379 ff.
146 [1994] 1 AC 180, HL.
147 [1994] 1 AC 200, HL.

(a) a misrepresentation by the guarantor on which the borrower relied;[148] or

(b) a deliberate and material non-disclosure arising from a relationship of trust and confidence (as in *Hewett* v. *First Plus Financial Group* (2010): see 11.29);[149] or

(c) duress; or

(d) actual undue influence; or

(e) a presumed form of undue influence: if the guarantor wishes to show 'presumed undue influence', it will be necessary to prove both (i) a relationship of trust and confidence (that is, that the guarantor (typically the wife) habitually showed great (but not necessarily complete and unqualified)[150] deference to the other's financial decision-making); and (ii) that the guarantee 'called for explanation' (see the discussion of this requirement at 11.26).

11.32 As for the 'link' between lender and guarantor mentioned above at (2), the House of Lords in *Barclays Bank* v. *O'Brien* (1994)[151] and *CIBC* v. *Pitt* (1994)[152] noted that there are three ways in which a guarantor, A, might show that the contract of surety between her and B is voidable because of X's (the husband, etc.) wrong vis-à-vis A:[153]

(i) B procures A's surety agreement through X where X is used as B's 'agent' and so suffers the consequence of the latter's knowledge being 'imputed' to B; or

(ii) B has actual knowledge of some legal wrong (whether a misrepresentation, undue influence, etc.) committed by X against A, which induced A to stand as X's surety; or

(iii) constructive notice of such a wrong can be imputed to B.

The lender will be 'in the clear' if the surety entered into the guarantee after obtaining independent legal advice. But, if this requirement is not satisfied, the lender becomes vulnerable, on the basis of constructive notice, if the surety was the victim of undue influence or some other legal wrong. Route (iii), constructive notice, will now be explained.

11.33 *Constructive notice.* The House of Lords in the *Etridge* case (2002)[154] made clear that *Barclays Bank* v. *O'Brien* (1994)[155] (see the preceding paragraph) should be reconceptualised as follows. In surety transactions, the lender, normally a bank, is 'put on inquiry' because of its awareness of (a) the emotional nature of the relationship between the borrower and the guarantor and (b) the intrinsically onerous nature of a guarantee of a loan, especially if the loan is supported by a charge upon the Equity within the matrimonial or cohabitants' home. As for (a), marital relations remain the commonest instances of such emotional relationships. But the House of Lords broadened the categories to include all other family, emotional and sexual relationships known to the bank. This will include

---

148 *Royal Bank of Scotland plc* v. *Chandra* [2011] EWCA Civ 192; [2011] NPC 26; [2011] Bus LR D149, notably at [36] and [37] (husband's over-optimistic assessment, made to his wife and the lender, that £700,000 would be enough finance to finish the job; bank forced to spend additional money to complete the development, and made a loss; no misrepresentation).

149 *Hewett* v. *First Plus Financial Group* [2010] EWCA Civ 312; [2010] Fam Law 589.

150 *Ibid.*

151 [1994] 1 AC 180, HL.

152 [1994] 1 AC 200, HL.

153 *Barclays Bank plc* v. *O'Brien* [1994] 1 AC 180, HL; *CIBC Mortgages plc* v. *Pitt* [1994] 1 AC 200, HL.

154 *Royal Bank of Scotland plc* v. *Etridge (No. 2)* [2002] 2 AC 773, HL.

155 *Barclays Bank plc* v. *O'Brien* [1994] 1 AC 180, HL.

the ties between father and daughter,[156] or mother and son. Indeed, *it covers all 'non-commercial' relationships between borrower and guarantor.* However, the House of Lords in the *Etridge* case (2002),[157] following the *Pitt* case (1994),[158] acknowledged that a lender will not be fixed with constructive notice in the case of a joint loan, unless 'the bank is aware that the loan is being made for the husband's purposes, as distinct from their joint purposes', that is, the joint loan will be pocketed solely by the husband.

11.34 *Bank must ensure that the guarantor obtains independent advice.* The bank should require the prospective surety to obtain independent legal advice (or a 'senior' bank official should sufficiently explain the transaction).[159] The *Etridge* case (2002) refines the 'cautionary' steps to be taken by the bank in this situation. The case creates a 'banking protocol' governing the bank's conduct in these matters. If the banking protocol is satisfied, the lender will normally be 'in the clear'[160] even if there has been some impropriety committed by the borrower upon the guarantor (unless the lender has used the borrower as its agent in obtaining the guarantor's consent or the lender has *actual knowledge* of some impropriety or special vulnerability: routes (i) and (ii), respectively, as listed at 11.32 above).[161]

11.35 *The quality of independent legal advice to be received by the guarantor.* The lawyer who advises the prospective guarantor (in many cases this has been a wife) need not be acting solely for that party: the lawyer can be acting jointly for borrower and guarantor. A lawyer instructed by the guarantor, or jointly by borrower and guarantor, for this purpose, would not be an agent for the bank.[162] The lawyer's advice should be thorough, in accordance with clear guidelines given by the House of Lords, effectively a second protocol (the advisory protocol), in the *Etridge* case (2002). This is an exacting duty. The lawyer should refrain from 'rubber-stamping'.[163] The lawyer must explain the nature of the transaction and its effect, including the obvious risks of both the guarantor's bankruptcy and the loss of the matrimonial home; the seriousness of these risks; the prospective guarantor's capacity to walk away from these risks by electing not to sign; and the scope for further negotiation.[164] Thus the solicitor's task is not confined to enabling the prospective surety to understand the transaction; he must go further and act as a buffer between the lender and any source of undue influence (the borrower, probably waiting outside the bank in the car, while the guarantor attends to the paperwork).[165] See 11.27 for analysis of the duty of care owed in this context by lawyers towards their client (as explained in *Padden* v. *Bevan Ashford*, 2011).[166]

---

156   *Royal Bank of Scotland plc* v. *Etridge (No. 2)* [2002] 2 AC 773, HL, at [84].
157   *Ibid.*, at [48], *per* Lord Nicholls.
158   *CIBC Mortgages plc* v. *Pitt* [1994] 1 AC 200, HL.
159   *Royal Bank of Scotland plc* v. *Etridge (No. 2)* [2002] 2 AC 773, HL, at [191] proposition (5).
160   *Ibid.*, at [79] proposition (3) and [191] proposition (4).
161   *Ibid.*, at [191] proposition (6).
162   *Ibid.*, at [77] and [78].
163   *Ibid.*, at [115].
164   *Ibid.*, at [65].
165   *Ibid.*, at [111].
166   [2011] EWCA Civ 1616; [2012] 1 WLR 1759; see also *Hackett* v. *CPS* [2011] EWHC 1170 (Admin); [2011] Lloyd's Rep FC 371, at [73] ff, *per* Silber J.

4. UNCONSCIONABILITY OR EXPLOITATION

11.36 Contracts (and gifts)[167] can be set aside for unconscionability[168] (on rescission, see 9.26 ff). At the core of this equitable doctrine is the notion of conscious and reprehensible exploitation of a position of acute vulnerability: however, there is no need for coercion (compare the doctrine of duress, explained at 11.02); nor is it necessary to show that overt acts of persuasion have been used (compare the doctrine of actual undue influence, explained at 11.02); nor is there need for a relationship of trust and confidence to have antedated the occasion when exploitation occurred (compare the doctrine of presumed undue influence, explained at 11.25, 11.26 and 11.28). In *Alec Lobb (Garages) Ltd* v. *Total Oil GB Ltd* (1983), Peter Millett QC (later Lord Millett) offered this definition of the modern doctrine of unconscionability:[169]

> [T]here must be some impropriety, both in the conduct of the stronger party and in the terms of the transaction itself (though the former may often be inferred from the latter in the absence of an innocent explanation) which in the traditional phrase 'shocks the conscience of the court', and makes it against equity and conscience of the stronger party to retain the benefit of the transaction he has unfairly obtained.

Similarly, Browne-Wilkinson J said in *Multiservice Bookbinding Ltd* v. *Marden* (1979) that Equity intervenes here only if 'one of the parties to [the transaction] has imposed the objectionable terms in a morally reprehensible manner, that is to say, in a way which affects his conscience'.[170]

The modern English doctrine of 'unconscionability' or 'exploitation' is now unified. But in the nineteenth century there were two streams:[171] first, protection of 'expectant' heirs against exploitation;[172] secondly, protection of 'poor, ignorant and necessitous' persons.[173]

---

167 See last sentence of this paragraph on *Evans* v. *Lloyd* [2013] EWHC 1725, at [52].
168 N. Bamforth, [1995] LMCLQ 538; R. Bigwood, *Exploitative Contracts* (Oxford, 2003); P. Birks and N. Y. Chin, 'On the Nature of Undue Influence', in J. Beatson and D. Friedmann (eds.), *Good Faith and Fault in Contract Law* (Oxford, 1995), 57; A. S. Burrows, *The Law of Restitution* (3rd edn, Oxford, 2012), chapter 12; D. Capper, (1998) 114 LQR 479; D. Capper, 'The Unconscionable Bargain in the Common Law World' (2010) 126 LQR 403; M. Conaglen, 'Duress, Undue Influence, and Unconscionable Bargains – The Theoretical Mesh' (1999) 18 NZULR 509; N. Enonchong, *Duress, Undue Influence and Unconscionable Dealing* (2nd edn, London, 2012); *Goff and Jones, The Law of Unjust Enrichment* (8th edn, London, 2011), chapter 11; G. Spark, *Vitiation of Contracts* (Cambridge, 2013), chapter 12; G. Virgo, *Principles of the Law of Restitution* (2nd edn, Oxford, 2006), chapter 10; S. Waddams, (1976) 39 MLR 369; for references to other Common Law jurisdictions on this topic, see A. Phang, 'Doctrine and Fairness in the Law of Contract' (2009) 29 LS 534, 570 ff, and D. Capper, 'The Unconscionable Bargain in the Common Law World' (2010) 126 LQR 403. For the position in the USA, L. DiMatteo, Q. Zhou, S. Saintier, K. Rowley (eds.), *Commercial Contract Law: Transatlantic Perspectives* (Cambridge, 2014), chapter 13 (by C. Knapp).
169 [1983] 1 WLR 87, 94–5 (not disturbed on appeal, [1985] 1 WLR 173, CA); considered by Blair J in *Strydom* v. *Vendside Ltd* [2009] EWHC 2130 (QB); [2009] 6 Costs LR 886, at [34] to [39].
170 [1979] Ch 84, 110.
171 A. S. Burrows, *The Law of Restitution* (3rd edn, Oxford, 2012), 302–3.
172 *Earl of Aylesford* v. *Morris* (1873) LR 8 Ch App 484 (citing Lord Hardwicke in *Earl of Chesterfield* v. *Janssen* (1751) 2 Ves Sen 125, 157); *O'Rorke* v. *Bolinbroke* (1877) LR 2 App Cas 814, 835, HL; cf *Tate* v. *Williamson* (1866) LR 2 Ch App 55 (undue influence between a distant relative and financial manager and a very young man who died at twenty-four from excessive drinking); and see the cases cited in *Fry* v. *Lane* (1888) 40 Ch D 312, 320.
173 *Fry* v. *Lane* (1888) 40 Ch D 312, Kay J: 'poor man with imperfect education' (citing *Evans* v. *Llewellin* (1781) 1 Cox 333; 2 Bro CC 150, two journeymen exploited by their social superior; and *Haygarth* v. *Wearing* (1871) LR 12 Eq 320, Wickens V-C, schoolmistress swindled by brother); *Cresswell* v. *Potter* (note) [1978] 1 WLR 255, Megarry J; on the history, J. L. Barton, (1987) 103 LQR 118.

The better view is that the doctrine of unconscionability, like the doctrine of undue influence, applies not just to contracts but to gifts (*Evans* v. *Lloyd* (2013) convincingly doubting dicta in the *Langton* case (1995) to the contrary).[174]

11.37 In *Strydom* v. *Vendside Ltd* (2009) Blair J summarised the elements of unconscionability as follows:[175]

> (1) one party has to have been disadvantaged in some relevant way as regards the other party, (2) that other party must have exploited that disadvantage in some morally culpable manner, and (3) the resulting transaction must be overreaching and oppressive. No single one of these factors is sufficient – all three elements must be proved, otherwise the enforceability of contracts is undermined ... Where all these requirements are met, (4) the burden then passes to the other party to satisfy the court that the transaction was fair, just and reasonable. [numbering added here]

Thus 'unconscionability' or 'exploitation' consists of four factors:[176]

(a) the vulnerable party's special or serious disadvantage (it appears that the person should be a human being, as distinct from a company, although a person with a controlling interest in a company might be vulnerable);[177]

(b) actual or constructive fraud (the element of conscious and reprehensible exploitation);

(c) highly disadvantageous or 'oppressive'[178] terms (the element of substantive economic harm); and

(d) lack of independent advice.

As for factors (a) to (c), in *Alec Lobb (Garages) Ltd* v. *Total Oil GB Ltd* (1983), Peter Millett QC, the trial judge, had explained:[179]

> First, one party has been at a serious disadvantage to the other, whether through poverty, or ignorance, or lack of advice, or otherwise [almost certainly including alcoholic intoxication[180] but only possibly – although the doubt seems misplaced –

---

174 *Evans* v. *Lloyd* [2013] EWHC 1725, at [52], *per* Judge Keyser QC, doubting dicta in *Langton* v. *Langton* [1995] 3 FCR 521, 538–40; *The Times*, 24 February 1995, Charles QC, sitting in the Chancery Division (quoted without disapproval in a dictum in *Randall* v. *Randall* [2004] EWHC 2258 (Ch); [2005] 1 P & CR DG 4, at [94]); the *Langton* case's dicta were criticised in D. Capper, (2010) 126 LQR 403, 406.

175 [2009] EWHC 2130 (QB); [2009] 6 Costs LR 886, at [36].

176 A. S. Burrows, *The Law of Restitution* (3rd edn, Oxford, 2012), 300; N. Bamforth, [1995] LMCLQ 538, 547 ff; Bamforth cites *Hart* v. *O'Connor* [1985] AC 1000, 1027–8, PC; *Multiservice Bookbinding* v. *Marden* [1979] Ch 84, 105, Browne-Wilkinson J; *Alec Lobb* v. *Total Oil* [1985] 1 WLR 173, CA; and *Boustany* v. *Pigott* (1993) 69 P & CR 298, PC (considered by Arden J in *J A Pye (Oxford) Estates* v. *Ambrose* [1994] NPC 53). As Capper notes, this fourfold analysis has also been articulated in Canada: see D. Capper, (2010) 126 LQR 403, 415, noting Cote J's formulation in *Cain* v. *Clarica Life Insurance* (2005) 263 DLR (4th) 368, at [32] (Alberta Supreme Court) (criteria approved also in Ontario, D. Capper, (2010) 126 LQR 403 at n. 96).

177 *Gustav & Co. Ltd* v. *Macfield Ltd* [2008] 2 NZLR 735, Sup Ct of NZ (however, the cancer on these facts had not impaired judgement, *ibid.*, at [23] and [24]).

178 The terms must be oppressive: *Strydom* v. *Vendside Ltd* [2009] EWHC 2130 (QB); [2009] 6 Costs LR 886, at [39], *per* Blair J.

179 [1983] 1 WLR 87, 94–5 (not disturbed on appeal, [1985] 1 WLR 173, CA); note also the Australian doctrine of 'unconscionability': *Commercial Bank of Australia Ltd* v. *Amadio* (1983) 151 CLR 447; *Louth* v. *Diprose* (1992) 175 CLR 621; *Garcia* v. *National Australia Bank Ltd* (1998) 194 CLR 395 (all three, High Court of Australia; and on the last two cases, A. S. Burrows, *The Law of Restitution* (3rd edn, Oxford, 2012), 305–6); and see *Nichols* v. *Jessup (No. 2)* [1986] NZLR 226.

180 As for drunkenness, the point is cast-iron in Australia: *Blomley* v. *Ryan* (1956) 99 CLR 362.

extending to narcotic addiction,[181] and severe illness causing the party's judgement to be seriously impaired][182] so that circumstances existed of which unfair advantage could be taken … Second, this weakness of the one party has been exploited by the other in some morally culpable manner … And third, the resulting transaction has been not merely hard or improvident but overreaching and oppressive. Where there has been a sale at an undervalue, the undervalue has almost always been substantial, so that it calls for explanation,[183] and is in itself indicative of the presence of some fraud, undue influence, or some other feature.

Factor (a) was condescendingly 'updated' by Megarry J in Cresswell v. Potter (decided in 1968, but reported in 1978)[184] to cover those who are of the 'lower income group' ('poor') and 'less highly educated' ('ignorant'). And, in Canada, factor (a) has been held to embrace these forms of transactional vulnerability: 'an overwhelming imbalance in bargaining power caused by the victim's ignorance of business, illiteracy, ignorance of the language of the bargain, blindness, deafness, illness, senility, or similar disability.'[185]

As for factor (b), the element of exploitation, Lord Templeman in the Privy Council in Boustany v. Pigott (1995)[186] noted that there must be some unconscionable or extortionate abuse of power, some unfair taking advantage of a weaker party's disabling condition or circumstances.[187] It is not enough that there was unequal bargaining power between the parties. More generally, Capper has listed English reported decisions since the 1970s in which unconscionability has been held not to apply to the relevant facts, or, even where this doctrine *was* considered, it was overshadowed by the pleading of another doctrine.[188]

No exploitation or unconscionable abuse was discerned in Evans v. Lloyd (2013) where a farmer, who had lived with non-relatives for most of his life, made a gift of farmland to the latter for reasons of gratitude and friendship.[189] And in the Gustav case (2008) the New Zealand Supreme Court held that the plea of unconscionability must be assessed by reference to the

---

181   As for narcotic addiction, the point was left open (unnecessarily) in *Irvani* v. *Irvani* [2000] 1 Lloyd's Rep 412, 425, CA, *per* Buxton LJ.

182   *Gustav & Co. Ltd* v. *Macfield Ltd* [2008] 2 NZLR 735, Sup Ct of NZ; see n. 177.

183   As noted at 11.26, this phrase is now used, in the context of undue influence, as the better way of expressing the notion of 'manifest disadvantage' (the latter label has now been discarded, except by Lord Millett in *National Commercial Bank (Jamaica) Ltd* v. *Hew* [2003] UKPC 51, at [33]).

184   (1968): (note) [1978] 1 WLR 255, 257–8.

185   D. Capper, (2010) 126 LQR 403, 415, noting Cote J's formulation in *Cain* v. *Clarica Life Insurance* (2005) 263 DLR (4th) 368, at [32] (Alberta Supreme Court) (criteria approved also in Ontario, D. Capper, (2010) 126 LQR 403 at n. 96).

186   (1995) 69 P & CR 298, 303.

187   Citing, among other decisions, *Hart* v. *O'Connor* [1985] AC 1000, PC; *Commercial Bank of Australia* v. *Amadio* (1983) 46 ALR 402, 413, High Court of Australia; *Nichols* v. *Jessup* [1986] NZLR 226; *Louth* v. *Diprose* (1992) 175 CLR 621, High Court of Australia; *Garcia* v. *National Australia Bank Ltd* (1998) 194 CLR 395, High Court of Australia (on the last two cases, see A. S. Burrows, *The Law of Restitution* (3rd edn, Oxford, 2012), at 305–6).

188   D. Capper, (2010) 126 LQR 403, 406–7, noting these cases: *Burmah Oil Co.* v. *Bank of England, The Times*, 4 July 1981, Ch; *Watkin* v. *Watson-Smith, The Times*, 3 July 1986; *Irvani* v. *Irvani* [2000] 1 Lloyd's Rep 412, CA; *Portman Building Society* v. *Dusangh* [2000] 2 All ER (Comm) 221, CA (noted, L. McMurtry, [2000] Conv 573); *Jones* v. *Morgan* [2001] Lloyd's Rep Bank 323 (noted, J. Devenney, [2002] JBL 539); *Kalsep Ltd* v. *X-Flow BV, The Times*, 3 May 2001, Ch; *Humphreys* v. *Humphreys* [2004] EWHC 2201 (Ch); [2005] 1 FCR 712 (and see now, *Strydom* v. *Vendside Ltd* [2009] EWHC 2130 (QB); [2009] 6 Costs LR 886). See also *Evans* v. *Lloyd* (2013), in text immediately below.

189   *Evans* v. *Lloyd* [2013] EWHC 1725, at [76], *per* Judge Keyser QC.

contract's formation, rather than some later date, except where the impugned consent concerns a variation of the pre-existing contract.[190]

11.38 *Relationship between unconscionability and undue influence.*[191] There are two points of contrast. First, unconscionability requires a high level of conscious exploitation and hence unacceptable conduct, whereas undue influence need only involve a technical abuse of a vulnerable relationship (11.23 and 11.30 above). The second point of contrast is that in general undue influence is rooted in abuse of relationships (11.23 above), whereas unconscionability can involve opportunistic exploitation by a stranger of another's vulnerability. This second point was emphasised by Buxton LJ in *Irvani* v. *Irvani* (2000).[192]

11.39 So-called 'gross disparity', a principle rather similar to the English equitable doctrine of unconscionability, has been adopted in Article 3.2.7(1) of UNIDROIT's *Principles of International Commercial Contracts* (2010):[193]

> A party may avoid the contract or an individual term of it if, at the time of the conclusion of the contract, the contract or term unjustifiably gave the other party an excessive advantage. Regard is to be had, among other factors, to (a) the fact that the other party has taken unfair advantage of the first party's dependence, economic distress or urgent needs, or of its improvidence, ignorance, inexperience or lack of bargaining skill, and (b) the nature and purpose of the contract.

But, as Comment 2(a) to this principle adds: 'superior bargaining power due to market conditions alone is not sufficient.'

---

190   *Gustav & Co. Ltd* v. *Macfield Ltd* [2008] 2 NZLR 735, at [21], Sup Ct of NZ.
191   P. Birks and N. Y. Chin, 'On the Nature of Undue Influence', in J. Beatson and D. Friedmann (eds.), *Good Faith and Fault in Contract Law* (Oxford, 1995), 57, especially at 57–60, 63–5, 85–8, 92–7; Bigwood's discussion of Birks and Chin: R. Bigwood, 'Contract and the Liberal Conception of Contract: Observing Basic Distinctions Part II' (2000) 16 JCL 191, 200; R. Bigwood, *Exploitative Contracts* (Oxford, 2003), 467 ff; R. Bigwood, 'Contracts by Unfair Advantage: From Exploitation to Transactional Neglect' (1995) 16 OJLS 503; P. Birks, [1997] *Restitution Law Review* 72, 76 n. 20; P. Birks, 'Undue Influence as Wrongful Exploitation' (2004) 120 LQR 34–7; D. Capper, 'Undue Influence and Unconscionability: A Rationalisation' (1998) 114 LQR 479; D. Capper, 'The Unconscionable Bargain in the Common Law World' (2010) 126 LQR 403, 416–19; M. Chen-Wishart, 'Undue Influence: Beyond Impaired Consent and Wrongdoing towards a Relational Analysis', in A. S. Burrows and A. Rodger (eds.), *Mapping the Law: Essays in Memory of Peter Birks* (Oxford, 2006); M. Chen-Wishart, 'Undue Influence: Vindicating Relationships of Influence' [2006] CLP 231; M. Conaglen, 'Duress, Undue Influence, and Unconscionable Bargains – The Theoretical Mesh' (1999) 18 NZULR 509; J. P. Devenney and A. Chandler, 'Unconscionability and the Taxonomy of Undue Influence' [2007] JBL 541, at 560–1; N. Enonchong, *Duress, Undue Influence and Unconscionable Dealing* (2nd edn, London, 2012); A. Mason, 'The Place of Equity and Equitable Doctrines in the Contemporary Common Law World – An Australian Perspective', in D. Waters (ed.), *Equity, Fiduciaries and Trusts* (Toronto, 1993); L. McMurtry, 'Unconscionability and Undue Influence: An Interaction?' [2000] Conv 573; A. Phang and H. Tjio, 'The Uncertain Boundaries of Undue Influence' [2002] LMCLQ 231; G. Spark, *Vitiation of Contracts* (Cambridge, 2013), chapters 11 and 12.
192   [2000] 1 Lloyd's Rep 412, 424, CA.
193   3rd edition, 2010, text and comment, is available at: www.unidroit.org/english/principles/contracts/principles2010/integralversionprinciples2010-e.pdf.

5. SUBSTANTIVELY UNFAIR BARGAINS

11.40 In *Hart* v. *O'Connor* (1985),[194] Lord Brightman distinguished 'procedural' and 'substantive' unfairness:[195]

> [A contract] may be unfair by reason of the unfair manner in which it was brought into existence . . . It will be convenient to call this 'procedural unfairness'. [Or it may] be described (accurately or inaccurately) as 'unfair' by reason of the fact that the terms of the contract are more favourable to one party than to the other . . . 'contractual imbalance' . . . Equity will not relieve a party from a contract on the ground only that there is contractual imbalance not amounting to unconscionable dealing.

Duress and undue influence involve 'procedural unfairness' because they both involve defective consent. This is to be contrasted with a complaint based on the extreme one-sidedness of the bargain, or based on the fact that a particular obligation is draconian. As Lord Brightman acknowledged, the mere fact that a contract is economically disadvantageous towards one party does not justify setting aside or readjusting that transaction.

11.41 Indeed, it is fundamental (5.11 at (5)) that the English courts 'do not weigh the adequacy of consideration'. In England there is no judicial doctrine of *laesio enormis* (*lésion*, in French) nor a concept of fair exchange.[196] There are, however, exceptional situations where, according to English law, an agreement can be upset or revised because the transaction or relevant term is perceived as intrinsically too harsh, unfair or mischievous, for example: (1) the equitable penalty rule (19.02); (2) control of excessive deposits (see 19.32 (statute) and 19.35 (Common Law)); (3) the rule against unreasonable restraints of trade (20.20);[197] (4) the Admiralty jurisdiction to relieve against extortionate maritime salvage agreements;[198] (5) statutory protection against over-severe clauses exempting a party from liability (the Unfair Contract Terms Act 1977 (15.08)); (6) the statutory power to control overreaching consumer credit contracts;[199] and (7) Part 2 of the Consumer Rights Bill (formerly the Unfair Terms in Consumer Contracts Regulations 1999) (15.28).

194   [1985] AC 1000, 1024, PC.
195   S. Smith, (1996) 112 LQR 138; M. Trebilcock, 'The Doctrine of Inequality of Bargaining Power: Post-Benthamite Economics in the House of Lords' (1976) 26 *University of Toronto Law Journal* 359; and see also materials on the penalty jurisdiction, 19.02, and the deposit doctrine, 19.25; on the history of harsh bargains, see J. L. Barton, (1987) 103 LQR 118.
196   Cf French law of this doctrine: Code Civil, Articles 1674 ff; B. Nicholas, *French Law of Contract* (2nd edn, Oxford, 1992), 137 ff; such a doctrine also applies in Jersey, *Snell* v. *Beadle* [2001] UKPC 5; [2001] 2 AC 304.
197   E.g. *Schroeder* v. *MacCaulay* [1974] 1 WLR 1308, HL (young songwriter's improvident bargain).
198   *Akerblom* v. *Price* (1881) 7 QBD 129, 133, CA; *'The Port Caledonia'* and *'The Anna'* [1903] P 184 (topic now regulated by section 224 of and Schedule 11 to the Merchant Shipping Act 1995; this allows a proper reward to be granted if the agreement is unfair); on the admiralty jurisdiction, Lord Denning MR in *Lloyds Bank Ltd* v. *Bundy* [1975] QB 326, 339, CA; the jurisdiction does not extend to non-tidal waters: *'The Goring'* [1988] AC 831, HL.
199   Sections 140A and 140B of the Consumer Credit Act 1974 (inserted by section 19 of the Consumer Credit Act 2006), imposing a criterion of unfairness in favour of the debtor.

6. NO DOCTRINE OF 'INEQUALITY OF BARGAINING POWER'

11.42 *Lord Denning's lead balloon.* In *Lloyds Bank Ltd* v. *Bundy* (1975), Lord Denning MR attempted to fashion a theory of 'inequality of bargaining power'[200] by interweaving three strands: (1) procedural and (2) substantive unfairness, and (3) the concept of 'inequality of bargaining power':

> through all these instances there runs a single thread. They rest on 'inequality of bargaining power'. By virtue of it, the English law gives relief to one who, without independent advice, enters into a contract upon terms which are very unfair or transfers property for a consideration which is grossly inadequate, when his bargaining power is grievously impaired by reason of his own needs or desires, or by his own ignorance or infirmity, coupled with undue influences or pressures brought to bear on him by or for the benefit of the other.

11.43 But Lord Denning's 'inequality of bargaining power' doctrine was the minority approach in the *Bundy* case (for the majority's approach, see 11.30). And his bold proposal was rejected in later case law.[201] This rejection is sound, for three reasons. First, the proposal would introduce great uncertainty, as Dillon LJ commented in the *Alec Lobb* case (1985):[202] 'inequality of bargaining power must . . . be a relative concept. It is seldom in any negotiation that the bargaining powers of the parties are absolutely equal.'[203] Secondly, legislation is the preferred method of countering the problems of inequality of bargaining power or substantive unfairness. Whether an 'unfair' imbalance subsists in consumer contracts is now extensively determined by Part 2 of the Consumer Rights Bill (formerly, the Unfair Terms in Consumer Contracts Regulations 1999) (15.28) and the Unfair Contract Terms Act 1977 (the latter in the context of exclusion clauses, 15.08). As noted by Lord Scarman in *National Westminster Bank plc* v. *Morgan* (1985)[204] and Steyn LJ in *CTN Cash & Carry Ltd* v. *Gallahers* (1994),[205] the courts regard the possibility of regulating contracts by reference to market imbalance and substantive harshness as a delicate task, even a quasi-political one. For this reason, and in the interest of precision, such regulation[206] is better undertaken by legislation. Parliament (including the European legislative authorities) is better placed than the courts to implement such social and economic regulation. In fact some legislation is clearly a response to acute inequality of bargaining power in particular contexts, notably the Consumer Rights Bill (15.28)

---

200 [1975] QB 326, 337–40, CA.
201 Notably, by Lord Scarman in *National Westminster Bank* v. *Morgan* [1985] AC 686, 708, HL; see also the discussion in the current paragraph of the text.
202 Cf in another context (relief against forfeiture of proprietary interests) Lord Hoffmann's convincing warning against introducing uncertainty into commercial law through an over-extension of equitable discretion: *Union Eagle Ltd* v. *Golden Achievement Ltd* [1997] AC 514, 519D, 523, PC: 17.24.
203 *Alec Lobb Garages Ltd* v. *Total Oil Great Britain Ltd* [1985] 1 WLR 173, 183, CA, *per* Dillon LJ.
204 [1985] AC 686, 708, HL.
205 [1994] 4 All ER 714, 718–19, CA.
206 H. G. Collins, *Regulating Contracts* (Oxford, 1999).

and the Consumer Credit legislation.[207] Good examples are the power to reopen extortionate credit transactions under the Consumer Credit Act 1974[208] and the complex UK and European Union schemes for countering anti-competitive practices and for controlling monopolies.[209] Thirdly, Lord Denning's suggestion involved a mongrel doctrine, mixing up (1) coercion, improper influence and exploitation, (2) substantive unfairness and (3) inequality of bargaining power.

QUESTIONS

(1) What are the four main elements of duress?

(2) What are the differences between duress as to person and other types of duress? Are these differences justified?

(3) Is a threatened breach of contract an illegitimate threat?

(4) When will pressure be illegitimate even though the threatened act is lawful?

(5) What is the essence of undue influence?

(6) Is there any overlap between duress and undue influence?

(7) What is the Birks-Chin theory of undue influence? Is this theory convincing?

(8) What is the distinction between actual undue influence and presumed undue influence?

(9) When is a lender put on inquiry concerning wrongdoing committed by the borrower and affecting the guarantor? What must the lender do if he is to prevent the guarantee agreement being rendered voidable as a result of the borrower's conduct vis-à-vis the guarantor?

(10) What are the three main elements of the doctrine of unconscionability?

(11) What are the differences between undue influence and unconscionability?

(12) Why was Lord Denning MR's 'inequality of bargaining power' theory in *Lloyds Bank* v. *Bundy* (1975) rejected?

Selected further reading

The topics in this chapter have stimulated much academic literature (see also the bibliography in G. Spark, *Vitiation of Contracts* (Cambridge, 2013), 322 ff). These are some of the more interesting.

General

R. Bigwood, *Exploitative Contracts* (Oxford, 2003) (a long and detailed examination)

N. Enonchong, *Duress, Undue Influence and Unconscionable Dealing* (2nd edn, London, 2012)

---

207 On this last context, sections 140A and 140B of the Consumer Credit Act 1974 (inserted by section 19 of the Consumer Credit Act 2006), imposing a criterion of unfairness in favour of the debtor; Consumer Credit (EU Directive) Regulations 2010/1010.

208 Sections 137–40 of the Consumer Credit Act 1974; applied in *Paragon Finance plc* v. *Nash* [2002] 1 WLR 685, CA, at [49] to [68] (note the lacuna identified at [67]); see now new sections 140A and 140B of the Consumer Credit Act 1974, inserted by section 19 of the Consumer Credit Act 2006 (imposing a broad criterion of unfairness in favour of the debtor); on section 140A, *Plevin* v. *Paragon Personal Finance Ltd* [2014] UKSC 61; [2014] 1 WLR 4222, at [10], [17] to [20], [24], [26], [29] to [34].

209 *Chitty on Contracts* (31st edn, London, 2012), chapter 42; and *Bellamy and Child's European Community Law of Competition* (7th edn, Oxford, 2013).

G. Spark, *Vitiation of Contracts* (Cambridge, 2013), chapters 10 (Duress), 11 (Undue Influence), 12 (Unconscionability)

S. Waddams, 'Autonomy and Paternalism from a Common Law Perspective: Setting Aside Disadvantageous Transactions', in A. Ogus and W. H. van Boom (eds.), *Juxtaposing Autonomy and Paternalism in Private Law* (Oxford, 2011), chapter 7

S. Waddams, *Principle and Policy in Contract Law: Competing or Complementary Concepts?* (Cambridge, 2011), chapter 4 (Unequal Transactions)

Coercion

P. Birks, 'The Travails of Duress' [1990] LMCLQ 342

A. S. Burrows, *The Law of Restitution* (3rd edn, Oxford, 2010), chapter 10

J. P. Dawson, 'Economic Duress: An Essay in Perspective' (1947) 45 *Michigan Law Review* 253

J. Morgan, *Great Debates in Contract Law* (London, 2012), chapter 7

G. Spark, *Vitiation of Contracts* (Cambridge, 2013), chapter 10, notably pp. 212–29

P. Winder, 'The Equitable Doctrine of Pressure' (1962) 82 LQR 165

Undue influence and unconscionability

N. Bamforth, 'Unconscionability as a Vitiating Factor' [1995] LMCLQ 538

P. Birks, 'Undue Influence as Wrongful Exploitation' (2004) 120 LQR 34–7 (reiteration of his 'claimant-sided theory' stated in the article by Birks and Chin listed below)

P. Birks and N. Y. Chin, 'On the Nature of Undue Influence', in J. Beatson and D. Friedmann (eds.), *Good Faith and Fault in Contract Law* (Oxford, 1995), 57, especially at 57–60, 63–5, 85–8, 92–7; for a reply to Birks and Chin, see R. Bigwood, *Exploitative Contracts* (Oxford, 2003), 467 ff; for a rejoinder, see P. Birks [1997] *Restitution Law Review* 72, 76 n. 20; Birks and Chin's argument has not been adopted: for further criticism, see the 1998 article by Capper listed below

A. S. Burrows, *The Law of Restitution* (3rd edn, Oxford, 2010), chapters 11 and 12

D. Capper, 'Undue Influence and Unconscionability: A Rationalisation' (1998) 114 LQR 479, especially 492–504

D. Capper, 'The Unconscionable Bargain in the Common Law World' (2010) 126 LQR 403

M. Chen-Wishart, 'Undue Influence: Beyond Impaired Consent and Wrongdoing Towards a Relational Analysis', in A. S. Burrows and A. Rodger (eds.), *Mapping the Law: Essays in Memory of Peter Birks* (Oxford, 2006)

M. Chen-Wishart, 'Undue Influence: Vindicating Relationships of Influence' [2006] CLP 231

J. Morgan, *Great Debates in Contract Law* (London, 2012), chapter 7

G. Spark, *Vitiation of Contracts* (Cambridge, 2013), chapter 11, notably pp. 251–72; chapter 12, notably pp. 279–95 (and see chapter 13)

S. Waddams, 'Unconscionability in Contracts' (1976) 39 MLR 369

Substantive unfairness

S. Smith, 'In Defence of Substantive Unfairness' (1996) 112 LQR 138

Inequality of bargaining power

J. Morgan, *Great Debates in Contract Law* (London, 2012), chapter 7

M. Trebilcock, 'The Doctrine of Inequality of Bargaining Power: Post-Benthamite Economics in the House of Lords' (1976) 26 *University of Toronto Law Journal* 359

History

J. L. Barton, 'The Enforcement of Hard Bargains' (1987) 103 LQR 118

VI

Terms and interpretation

Chapter contents

12

Terms in general

1. INCORPORATION OF TERMS

12.01 The topic of *incorporation of terms* is examined in detail at 15.02 ff. The leading decisions are: *Parker v. South Eastern Railway Co.* (1877),[1] *Interfoto v. Stiletto* (1989),[2] *O'Brien v. MGN Ltd* (2001),[3] *L'Estrange v. F Graucob Ltd* (1934),[4] *Olley v. Marlborough Court Ltd* (1949),[5] *Thornton v. Shoe Lane Parking* (1971),[6] *Chapelton v. Barry Urban District Council* (1940),[7] *British Crane Hire Corporation Ltd v. Ipswich Plant Hire Ltd* (1975);[8] and see 3.34 ff on *Tekdata Intercommunications v. Amphenol Ltd* (2009)[9] and 'the battle of the forms'.

The restrictive (and hence protective) Common Law rules concerning incorporation have evolved with respect to exclusion clauses and other onerous clauses. (*Interfoto v. Stiletto* (1989)[10] noted that the Common Law incorporation doctrine applies not just to exclusion clauses but to all 'onerous or unusual' clauses; but it has been suggested that the category might be confined to 'particularly onerous or unusual' clauses[11] secreted in the fine mesh of the other party's standard terms.) A similar analysis applies, as noted at 15.02, in some contexts under the Consumer Rights Bill, Part 2. A 'trader', as against a consumer, can successfully insert a term defining the subject matter of the contract or affecting the price of goods or services (including contracts for the supply of 'digital content') only if the term is '*prominent*', that is, the proposed term will be operative only 'if it is brought to the consumer's attention in such a way that the average consumer would be aware of the

---

1   (1877) 2 CPD 416, 423, CA.
2   [1989] QB 433, CA.
3   [2001] EWCA Civ 1279; *The Times*, 8 August 2001; [2002] CLC 33.
4   [1934] 2 KB 394, Divisional Court; J. R. Spencer, 'Signature, Consent and the Rule in *L'Estrange* v. *Graucob*' [1973] CLJ 104; D. McLauchlan, 'The Entire Agreement Clause . . . ' (2012) 128 LQR 521, 531–3.
5   [1949] 1 KB 532, CA.
6   [1971] 2 QB 163, CA.
7   [1940] 1 KB 532, CA.
8   [1975] QB 303, CA ('course of dealing', on this legal approach, E. Macdonald, (1988) 8 LS 48).
9   [2009] EWCA Civ 1209; [2010] 1 Lloyd's Rep 357.
10   [1989] QB 433, CA.
11   *HIH Casualty & General Insurance Ltd* v. *New Hampshire Insurance Co* [2001] EWCA Civ 735; [2001] 2 All ER (Comm) 39, at [211], *per* Rix LJ; and Gloster J in *JP Morgan Chase Bank* v. *Springwell Navigation Corp.* [2008] EWHC 1186, at [578] ff (affirmed [2010] EWCA Civ 1221; [2010] 2 CLC 705).

term'; and here an average consumer means one 'who is reasonably well-informed, observant and circumspect'.[12]

2. THE PAROL EVIDENCE RULE

12.02 *Scope of rule.*[13] The rule prevents a party resorting to outside oral or written evidence *to add to, subtract from, vary, or contradict* the written terms; and so a party cannot for this purpose give oral evidence of what he or even both parties intended, nor refer to drafts or other aspects of negotiation. This rule applies if a contract is wholly contained in writing. It does not apply if the contract is only partly written and partly oral.[14] It should be noted that:

(i) the parol evidence rule is different from the now abrogated 'best evidence' rule (the need to produce an original document; a rule now excised from English civil law)[15] and

(ii) the parol evidence rule is also distinct from the exclusionary rule barring reference to pre-formation communications for the purpose of interpreting contractual written language (on which see 14.15).

12.03 *Qualifications upon operation of the rule.* There are four qualifications upon (or circumventions of) the parol evidence rule. First, there is the doctrine of *rectification*: 14.25 ff. Secondly, *collateral warranties*, normally based on oral assurances, are treated as free-standing agreements (9.12 ff). Formally, therefore, collateral warranties do not violate the parol evidence rule, which is concerned only with the integrity of the written agreement. That rule does not prohibit proof of additional and free-standing contracts. It is common for commercial agreements to contain an 'entire agreement' clause to exclude such side-agreements (9.36 and 9.37).[16] Thirdly, there are questions of *contractual invalidity* etc. Extrinsic evidence is admissible to show that the supposed written contract is invalid, void, vitiated or otherwise inoperative for any of these reasons: (i) mistake; (ii) lack of consideration; (iii) statutory non-compliance; (iv) illegality; (v) fraud; (vi) misrepresentation; (vii) duress; (viii) the agreement is subject to a condition precedent; (ix) the agreement has been subsequently varied or discharged by consensus. Fourthly, extrinsic evidence is admissible to show that it is one type of agreement (for example, a mortgage rather than a conveyance), or to reveal the identity of the parties, or to discover the subject matter of the agreement.[17]

---

12   Consumer Rights Bill.
13   *Chitty on Contracts* (31st edn, London, 2012), 12–096 ff; *Treitel* (13th edn, London, 2011), 6–013 ff; Law Commission 'The Parol Evidence Rule' (Law Commission No. 154, Cmnd 9700, 1986) (noted G. Marston [1986] CLJ 192); D. McLauchlan, *The Parol Evidence Rule* (Wellington, 1976), D. W. McLauchlan, 'Parol Evidence and Contract Formation' (2005) 121 LQR 9, and D. McLauchlan, 'The Entire Agreement Clause ...' (2012) 128 LQR 521, at 526–30; R. Stevens, 'Objectivity, Mistake and the Parol Evidence Rule', in A. Burrows and E. Peel (eds.), *Contract Terms* (Oxford, 2007), chapter 6, at 107 ff. For a highly sceptical discussion of this rule (besides McLauchlan (2012) above), see G. McMeel, *The Construction of Contracts: Interpretation, Implication and Rectification* (2nd edn, Oxford, 2011), 15–08 ff.
14   Law Commission, 'The Parol Evidence Rule' (Law Commission No. 154, Cmnd 9700, 1986), 2.10, 2.11.
15   Rule now excised from English law following the *Springsteen* case [2001] EWCA Civ 513; [2001] CPLR 369; [2001] EMLR 654, CA.
16   *Chitty on Contracts* (31st edn, London, 2012), 12–104.
17   Law Commission, 'The Parol Evidence Rule' (Law Commission No. 154, Cmnd 9700, 1986), 12–106 to 12–113, 12–122, 12–123.

12.04 *Rationale of the rule.* There are five reasons supporting the parol evidence rule: (i) reference to outside material or oral statements would complicate and unsettle the process of discovering the agreement's meaning and effect; (ii) it is notorious that some negotiations involve rapid and not always transparent shifts of position;[18] (iii) the rule acknowledges that only the final written version of the contract counts; the parties should be expected to check and double-check the final document; (iv) third parties might have innocently relied upon the document, but they are unlikely to have been privy to the parties' prior negotiations;[19] and (v) if the rule did not exist, parties might be tempted to manufacture 'self-serving' declarations of their preferred interpretation during the negotiations.

12.05 *Assessment of the rule.* On the one hand the rule seems to stand for certainty, the integrity of an agreed text and avoidance of side disputes. On the other hand, the rule yields to proof that the text is not in fact the exclusive source of contractual arrangements between the parties. Some might even regard this 'rule' as largely a mirage[20] because it is easily displaced by adducing evidence that the ostensible written contract is not a free-standing agreement but an amalgam of written and oral undertakings (14.03), or that there is a separate 'collateral warranty' subsisting in parallel to the main written agreement (9.12 ff). However, in Treitel's opinion (2011), the 'parol evidence rule' creates a presumption that a contract in writing which *looks* like an agreement fixed in writing is indeed a complete agreement unless the party resisting that shows that the parties did not intend the agreement to be an exclusive statement of their relations.[21] Robert Stevens suggests that:[22]

> Once it is shown that the parties have agreed to be bound to the terms of a contract wholly embodied in a written instrument, each is bound by its terms although one or other might not know what they are, and even though the content of previous negotiations might be inconsistent with the terms contained in the contract … Giving effect to different terms from those contained in the written agreement would be contrary to the agreement the parties have reached.

It is submitted that the parol evidence rule remains an important starting point in English contractual analysis. Lord Hobhouse 'saluted' this rule in the *Shogun* case (2003), describing it as 'one of the main reasons for the international success of English law',[23] and he added:

> The relevant principle is well summarised in Phipson on Evidence: 'When the parties have deliberately put their agreement into writing, it is conclusively presumed between themselves and their privies that they intend the writing to form

18 *Prenn* v. *Simmonds* [1971] 1 WLR 1381, 1384, HL, *per* Lord Wilberforce.
19 Law Commission, 'The Parol Evidence Rule' (Law Commission No. 154, Cmnd 9700, 1986), 2–43, on the position of assignees.
20 G. McMeel, *The Construction of Contracts: Interpretation, Implication and Rectification* (2nd edn, Oxford, 2011), 15–08 ff; Law Commission, 'The Parol Evidence Rule' (Law Commission No. 154, Cmnd 9700, 1986); *Chitty on Contracts* (31st edn, London, 2012), 12–096 ff; K. Wedderburn, 'Collateral Contracts' [1959] CLJ 58.
21 Treitel (13th edn, London, 2011), 6–014.
22 R. Stevens in A. Burrows and E. Peel (eds.), *Contract Terms* (Oxford, 2007), 102, 107.
23 *Shogun Finance Ltd* v. *Hudson* [2003] UKHL 62; [2003] UKHL 62; [2004] 1 AC 919, HL, at [49], *per* Lord Hobhouse (10.28 ff for detailed examination of this case); see also *Bank of Australasia* v. *Palmer* [1897] AC 540, 545, PC, *per* Lord Morris.

a full and final statement of their intentions, and one which should be placed beyond the reach of future controversy, bad faith or treacherous memory.'

And in the context of interpretation of written contracts, and the closely related exclusionary rule concerning pre-contractual negotiations (14.15 ff), Lord Hoffmann in *Chartbrook Ltd* v. *Persimmon Homes Ltd* (2009) said:[24]

> There is certainly a view in the profession that the less one has to resort to any form of background in aid of interpretation, the better. The document should so far as possible speak for itself. As Popham CJ said in the *Countess of Rutland's Case* (1604) 5 Co. Rep 25 b, 26a:
>
> 'it would be inconvenient, that matters in writing made by advice and on consideration, and which finally import the certain truth of the agreement of the parties should be controlled by averment of the parties to be proved by the uncertain testimony of slippery memory.'

3. OVERVIEW OF SUBSTANTIVE TERMS

12.06 Terms are promissory or non-promissory, express or implied. On these and related points, the reader is referred to other parts of this work, as indicated:

(1) classification of promissory obligations: conditions; innominate (or 'intermediate') terms, and warranties: 17.19 ff;

(2) non-promissory terms: these are terms which prevent the contract from operating (so-called 'conditions precedent'):[25] 2.07, 7.41, 10.34, 12.03; or which cause the contract to terminate ('conditions subsequent': 10.12); as well as termination clauses:[26] 16.29, 17.25 ff;

(3) the distinction between a misrepresentation and a promissory term: 9.12 and 9.30 ff;

(4) the possibility that a statement might be treated as both a misrepresentation and a contractual term: 9.30 ff;

(5) criteria for determining whether a pre-contractual assurance has effect as a contractual term: 9.14;

(6) collateral warranties: 9.12 ff;

(7) implied terms: 13.01 ff;

(8) incorporation of terms: 15.02;

(9) entire agreement clauses: 9.36 and 9.37;

(10) non-reliance clauses: 9.36 and 9.41;

(11) exclusion clauses in general: 15.01 ff; and for exclusion clauses and misrepresentation: 9.33 ff;

(12) unfair terms in general: 15.28 ff;

(13) interpretation of written contracts: 14.01 ff;

---

24 [2009] UKHL 38; [2009] 1 AC 1101, at [36].

25 G. H. Treitel, '"Conditions" and "Conditions Precedent"' (1990) 106 LQR 185.

26 S. Whittaker, 'Termination Clauses', in A. Burrows and E. Peel (eds.), *Contract Terms* (Oxford, 2007), chapter 13; J. Randall, 'Express Termination Clauses' [2014] CLJ 113–41.

(14) agreements to negotiate: English law does not recognise an agreement to bargain or negotiate in good faith the terms of the proposed main contract (see 2.07 on *Walford* v. *Miles* (1992));[27] but the following (2.10 ff) are valid, provided the promise is supported by consideration: (i) a 'lockout' or 'exclusivity' agreement *for a specified period*[28] not to deal or negotiate with outsiders, but only to negotiate with the other party; (ii) an agreement to procure a third party's permission (for example, planning permission or an export licence), by taking 'reasonable' or 'best endeavours';[29]

(15) *force majeure* clauses: such a clause declares when a party will be released from his obligations, or excused from liability for default, by reason of freak and excusable supervening events[30] (4.24, 16.09, considering *Thames Valley Power Ltd* v. *Total Gas & Power Ltd* (2005);[31] and 16.19, for reference to the clause in *'The Super Servant Two'* (1990));

(16) retention of title clauses: these operate to confer security on vendors;[32]

(17) express repayment clauses: 14.07 at (5).

4. CHOICE OF LAW AND DISPUTE-RESOLUTION CLAUSES

12.07 *Choice of law clauses.*[33] Such a clause specifies which national system of contract law will apply to the transaction. The parties can thus exclude an undesirable national system of contract law, or specify a neutral contractual system (neutral, that is, by reference to the parties' nationality, domicile or place of business).

12.08 *Mediation agreements.*[34] Parties will often agree that they will mediate in good faith before formal litigation or arbitration. Colman J in *Cable & Wireless plc* v. *IBM UK* (2002)[35] (4.22) upheld such a mediation clause. He held that, in the face of such an undertaking, a party's

---

27 [1992] 2 AC 128, HL; P. Neill, (1992) 108 LQR 405; A. Berg, (2003) 110 LQR 357; also invalid is an agreement to use best or reasonable endeavours to reach agreement on the subject matter or the price: *Little* v. *Courage* (1995) 70 P & CR 469, 476, CA, *per* Millett LJ.

28 *Walford* v. *Miles* [1992] 2 AC 128, HL, applied in *Pitt* v. *PHH Asset Management Ltd* [1994] 1 WLR 327, CA.

29 *Walford* v. *Miles* [1992] 2 AC 128, HL, and *Little* v. *Courage* (1995) 70 P & CR 469, 476, CA, both acknowledge this.

30 E. McKendrick (ed.), *Force Majeure and Frustration of Contract* (2nd edn, London, 1995), especially at 34; E. McKendrick, 'The Regulation of Long-Term Contracts in English Law', in J. Beatson and D. Friedmann (eds.), *Good Faith and Fault in Contract Law* (Oxford, 1995), 305, 323 ff; E. McKendrick, 'Force Majeure Clauses: The Gap between Doctrine and Practice', in A. Burrows and E. Peel (eds.), *Contract Terms* (Oxford, 2007), chapter 12; *Chitty on Contracts* (31st edn, London, 2012), 14–140 ff.

31 [2005] EWHC 2208 (Comm); [2006] 1 Lloyd's Rep 441.

32 L. Gulliver, 'Retention of Title Clauses: A Question of Balance', in A. Burrows and E. Peel (eds.), *Contract Terms* (Oxford, 2007), chapter 14; for a convenient summary, see *Atiyah's Sale of Goods* (12th edn, London, 2010), 12–13; see also K. C. F. Loi, (2012) 128 LQR 412–42.

33 A. Briggs, *Agreements on Jurisdiction and Choice of Law* (Oxford, 2008), chapters 10 and 11; A. Briggs, in A. Burrows and E. Peel (eds.), *Contract Terms* (Oxford, 2007), chapter 15; on the Rome I Regulation, *Dicey, Morris and Collins on the Conflicts of Laws* (15th edn, London, 2012), chapters 32 and 33 (on Regulation (EC) No. 593/2008, effective in the UK on 17 December 2009).

34 *Sulamerica Cia Nacional de Seguros SA* v. *Enesa Engenharia SA* [2012] EWCA Civ 638; [2013] 1 WLR 102; for criticism, N. Andrews, 'Mediation Agreements: Time for a More Creative Approach by the English Courts' (2013) 18 Revue de Droit Uniforme 6–16 (also known as *Uniform Law Review*); K. P. Berger, 'Law and Practice of Escalation Clauses' (2006) 22 Arbitration Int 1–17.

35 *Cable & Wireless plc* v. *IBM United Kingdom Ltd* [2002] 2 All ER (Comm) 1041, Colman J.

decision to bypass mediation is a breach of the dispute-resolution agreement. He granted a stay upon premature court litigation, thus requiring the parties to reconsider mediation. However, *Sulamerica Cia Nacional de Seguros SA* v. *Enesa Engenharia SA* (2012)[36] (4.22) established that a mediation agreement will be valid in English law only if (i) the mediation clause is final and thus does not require any further negotiation over its own terms; (ii) the clause nominates a mediation provider or indicates how one is to be appointed; and (iii) the mediation process should be either already finalised under the rules of the agreed mediation provider or the parties must themselves supply minimum details.

12.09 *Jurisdiction clauses.*[37] (See also 7.52 to 7.54 and 12.11.) An exclusive jurisdiction clause stipulates that legal disputes arising from the relevant transaction can only be litigated in the nominated jurisdiction, for example the courts of London or Hong Kong.[38] A non-exclusive jurisdiction clause confers jurisdiction on the relevant nominated courts even though in the absence of such a clause, that jurisdiction would not have been available to the parties.[39]

12.10 *Arbitration clauses.*[40] (See also 4.15 and 4.16.) The Arbitration Act 1996 requires an arbitration agreement to be in writing.[41] Arbitration agreements concern agreements 'to submit to arbitration present or future disputes'.[42] In *Premium Nafta Products Ltd* v. *Fili Shipping Co. Ltd* (2007), the House of Lords held that, in accordance with the principle of 'separability' (acknowledged by section 7 of the Arbitration Act 1996), the invalidity of the main contract does not necessarily entail the invalidity of the arbitration agreement.[43] The arbitration clause will be invalid only if both the main contract and the arbitration clause are the product of forgery, or 'if a party alleges that someone who purported to sign [the main contract and arbitration clause] as agent on his behalf had no authority whatever to conclude any agreement on his behalf'.[44]

12.11 *Anti-suit relief to uphold arbitration clauses.* The Supreme Court of the United Kingdom in *AES Ust-Kamenogorsk Hydropower Plant LLP* v. *Ust-Kamenogorsk Hydropower Plant*

---

36   [2012] EWCA Civ 638; [2013] 1 WLR 102; for criticism, N. Andrews, n. 34 above.
37   A. Briggs, *Agreements on Jurisdiction and Choice of Law* (Oxford, 2008); D. Joseph, *Jurisdiction and Arbitration Agreements and Their Enforcement* (2nd edn, London, 2010); A. Briggs, 'The Subtle Variety of Jurisdiction Agreements' [2012] LMCLQ 364–81; T. Hartley, *Choice-of-Court Agreements under the European and International Instruments* (Oxford, 2013); Dicey, Morris and Collins on the Conflicts of Laws (15th edn, London, 2012), 12–099 ff.
38   E.g. *Nomura International plc* v. *Banca Monte dei Paschi Di Siena Spa* [2013] EWHC 3187 (Comm); [2014] 1 WLR 1584 at [16], [17], [80] to [83], Eder J.
39   *Deutsche Bank AG* v. *Highland Crusader Offshore Partners LP* [2009] EWCA Civ 725; [2010] 1 WLR 1023, at [50], [64], [105] and [106].
40   D. Joseph, *Jurisdiction and Arbitration Agreements and Their Enforcement* (2nd edn, London, 2010); Dicey, Morris and Collins on the Conflicts of Laws (15th edn, London, 2012), 16–68 ff; *Andrews on Civil Processes* (Cambridge, 2013), vol. 2, Arbitration and Mediation, chapters 9 and 10; N. Andrews, 'Courts Ensuring Compliance with Arbitration Clauses' (2014) 26 (41) *European Business LR* 587–604.
41   Section 3 of the Arbitration Act 1996; M. Mustill and S. Boyd, *Commercial Arbitration: Companion Volume* (London, 2001), 16, and at 258 ff.
42   Sections 6(1) and 82(1) of the Arbitration Act 1996.
43   *Premium Nafta Products Ltd* v. *Fili Shipping Co. Ltd* [2007] UKHL 40; [2007] 4 All ER 951.
44   *Ibid.*, at [17] to [19].

$(2013)^{45}$ confirmed that anti-suit injunctions can be awarded *by the English courts* under section 37 of the Senior Courts Act 1981 (the general power to issue injunctions). The court confirmed also that the injunction gives effect to an implicit negative undertaking in any arbitration agreement that both parties will exclusively pursue arbitration for the purpose of obtaining a determination on the subject matter of the dispute covered by the contemplated arbitration. This power is, however, restricted to improper proceedings outside 'Europe' (that is, those EU Member States subscribing to the Jurisdiction Regulation 2012^{46} or any non-EU jurisdictions party to the Lugano Convention on Jurisdiction and the Recognition and Enforcement of Judgments in Civil and Commercial Matters).

(1) *Jurisdiction clauses within the EU or for Lugano Convention countries.* The European Court of Justice's decision in *Turner* v. *Grovit* $(2005)^{47}$ prevents the English courts from issuing anti-suit injunctions to enforce exclusive English jurisdiction clauses where the offending court proceedings have been commenced within the European jurisdictional zone.

(2) *Arbitration clauses within the EU or for Lugano Convention countries.* The European Court of Justice's decision in *Allianz SpA* v. *West Tankers* $(2009)^{48}$ prevents the Common Law anti-suit injunction from being issued to counter breach of arbitration clauses by the commencement of inconsistent *court* litigation within the *same* European jurisdictional zone. But recital 12 of the Jurisdiction Regulation (2012) (effective from 10 January 2015) makes clear that a judgment by a Member State court on the substance of a civil or commercial case is binding even though that decision involved an incidental decision that the dispute was not subject to a valid arbitration clause.

(3) *Anti-suit relief in the non-European context.* An English anti-suit injunction can still be granted to prevent a person from bringing, or continuing to pursue, *non-European* (see the text above) proceedings (in court or otherwise) brought in breach of an exclusive jurisdiction clause^{49} or arbitration clause; for example, a clause nominating English High Court litigation, or arbitration in London, in breach of which a party to the clause commences proceedings (whether court litigation or arbitration) in, say, Buenos Aires. If the nominated forum is outside England (say, Tokyo or Sydney), but a party to the relevant clause commences English court proceedings in breach of this, the 'English litigation' defendant can seek a stay of those improper proceedings. Both the injunction and stay are subject to exceptions, notably if the relevant proceedings include parties or issues lying beyond the scope of the clause.^{50}

12.12 *Arbitration: finality clauses.* Care and precision are required to exclude under English law the qualified right of appeal on a point of law from an arbitration award to the English

---

45 [2013] UKSC 35; [2013] 1 WLR 1889; on this topic, *Dicey, Morris and Collins on the Conflicts of Laws* (15th edn, London, 2012), 16–088, but antedating the *AES* case.

46 The revised Regulation (EU Regulation 1215/2012) came into force on 9 January 2013, but most changes take effect as of 10 January 2015 (superseding Council Regulation (EC) No. 44/2001 of 22 December 2001 on 'jurisdiction and the recognition and enforcement of judgments in civil and commercial matters').

47 *Turner* v. *Grovit* (Case C-159/02) [2005] 1 AC 101, ECJ; for comment, see N. Andrews, 'Abuse of Process and Obstructive Tactics under the Brussels Jurisdictional System . . .' (2005) *European Community Private Law Review* 8–15 (this journal is also entitled *Zeitschrift für Gemeinschaftsprivatrecht* and *Revue de droit privé international*).

48 Case C-185/07 [2009] 1 AC 1138; [2009] 1 Lloyd's Rep 413 (noted by E. Peel, (2009) 125 LQR 365).

49 *Deutsche Bank AG* v. *Highland Crusader Offshore Partners LP* [2009] EWCA Civ 725; [2010] 1 WLR 1023, at [50] ff, contains an eight-point distillation of principles concerning jurisdiction clauses and anti-suit relief.

50 *Donohue* v. *Armco Inc.* [2001] UKHL 64; [2002] 1 All ER 749, HL.

Commercial Court. In *Shell Egypt West Manzala GmbH* v. *Dana Gas Egypt Ltd* (2009),[51] Gloster J held that a clause stating that an arbitration award is 'final, conclusive and binding' is not an effective exclusion of a High Court appeal. By contrast, in *Sheffield United Football Club Ltd* v. *West Ham United Football Club plc* (2008),[52] Teare J held that an arbitration clause had explicitly excluded further review or appeal by a court of law; and he further held that the same clause did not by implication create a right to seek review by recourse to a higher level of arbitration.

12.13 *Asymmetrical or hybrid arbitration and jurisdiction clauses.* These enable one party to opt out of court proceedings in England by taking the case to arbitration or, conversely, enable a party to opt out of arbitration and instead bring proceedings before an English court. The English High Court has upheld so-called 'hybrid' dispute-resolution clauses.[53]

QUESTIONS

(1) Summarise the (a) Common Law and (b) statutory rules concerning incorporation of terms.
(2) What is the parol evidence rule, and what are the main qualifications upon its operation?
(3) Explain the distinction between promissory and non-promissory terms.
(4) What is the principle of 'separability' of arbitration agreements?

Selected further reading

Terms in general

A. Burrows and E. Peel (eds.), *Contract Terms* (Oxford, 2007)
K. Wedderburn, 'Collateral Contracts' [1959] CLJ 58
     See also Chapter 13 on implied terms and Chapter 15 on exclusion clauses.

Specific clauses

Andrews on Civil Processes (Cambridge, 2013), vol. 2, *Arbitration and Mediation*, chapter 9
     (arbitration agreements), and 1.34 ff (mediation agreements)
A. Briggs, *Agreements on Jurisdiction and Choice of Law* (Oxford, 2008)
D. Joseph, *Jurisdiction and Arbitration Agreements and Their Enforcement* (2nd edn, London, 2010)
J. Randall, 'Express Termination Clauses' [2014] CLJ 113–41
S. Rowan, 'For the Recognition of Remedial Terms Agreed Inter Partes' (2010) 126 LQR 448
S. Whittaker, 'Termination Clauses', in A. Burrows and E. Peel (eds.), *Contract Terms* (Oxford, 2007), chapter 13

---

51 [2009] EWHC 2097 (Comm).
52 [2008] EWHC 2855 (Comm); [2009] 1 Lloyd's Rep 167.
53 *NB Three Shipping Ltd* v. *Harebell Shipping Ltd* [2004] EWHC 2001 (Comm); [2005] 1 Lloyd's Rep 509, Morison J; *Law Debenture Trust Corporation plc* v. *Elektrim Finance BV* [2005] EWHC 1412 (Ch); [2005] 2 Lloyd's Rep 755, Mann J; S. Nesbitt and H. Quinlan, (2006) 22 *Arbitration International* 133; D. Joseph, *Jurisdiction and Arbitration Agreements and their Enforcement* (2nd edn, London, 2010), 4–31.

Chapter contents

13

Implied terms

1. INTRODUCTION

13.01 Summary of main points

(1) There are three types of implied term:[1] (i) those implied by law (that is, by statute or by judicial decision); (ii) those implied in fact; and (iii) those implied on the basis of custom or trade usage (see 13.03, 13.09, 13.17 below, respectively).[2]

(2) A term implied in law can arise under statute, for example, certain provisions of the Sale of Goods Act 1979.

(3) Judicial precedent is another source of terms implied in law: the High Court or higher courts, in exercise of their Common Law power to pronounce binding decisions, can find such an implied term. It is now admitted (13.03) that judicially prescribed terms implied *in law* will reflect policy considerations and matters of general exigency. A term implied in law by the courts is designed to reflect the essential incidents of well-established transactions.

(4) The courts are more circumspect in finding a term to be *implied in fact*. This category of implication involves imputing to the parties a readily acknowledged tacit understanding. For this purpose, the so-called 'officious bystander' or 'no need to mention' test is the favoured divining rod (MacKinnon LJ formulated the 'officious bystander' test in *Shirlaw* v. *Southern Foundries (1926) Ltd* (1939): see 13.11).[3] An older and more vague criterion is the 'business efficacy' test, the so-called '*Moorcock* test' (1889) (13.10):[4] without the suggested term, the

---

1 *Luxor (Eastbourne) Ltd* v. *Cooper* [1941] AC 108, 137–8, HL, *per* Lord Wright; see also *Bank of Nova Scotia* v. *Hellenic Mutual War Risks ('The Good Luck')* [1989] 3 All ER 628, 665–8, CA, and in *Philips Electronique Grand Publique SA* v. *British Sky Broadcasting Ltd* [1995] EMLR 472, CA: on the latter case, see 13.15.
2 Generally on this topic, R. Austen-Baker, *Implied Terms in English Contract Law* (Cheltenham, 2011); R. Austen-Baker, 'Implied Terms in English Contract Law', in L. DiMatteo, Q. Zhou, S. Saintier, K. Rowley (eds.), *Commercial Contract Law: Transatlantic Perspectives* (Cambridge, 2014), chapter 10; see also the literature on the *Belize* case cited at 13.16; older discussion: A. Phang, [1990] JBL 394, [1993] JBL 242, [1994] JBL 255, [1998] JBL 1; 'The Challenge of Principled Gap-Filling: a Study of Implied Terms in a Comparative Context' [2014] JBL 263–312; E. Peden, (2001) 117 LQR 459–76; T. Rakoff, in J. Beatson and D. Friedmann (eds.), *Good Faith and Fault in Contract Law* (Oxford, 1995), 191 (mostly from a US perspective); C. A. Riley, (2000) 20 OJLS 367–90; R. Goode, 'Usage and its Reception in Transnational Commercial Law' (1997) 46 ICLQ 1.
3 [1939] 2 KB 206, 227–8, CA (affirmed [1940] AC 701, HL).
4 (1889) 14 PD 64, 68, CA; A. Phang, [1998] JBL 1.

contract would not make any real business sense. But this approach can become unruly, for it might be misapplied as a pretext or licence to create a term to which the parties had not implicitly agreed, and to which they would never jointly have assented.

(5) For a term to be implied on the basis of custom or trade usage, the suggested term must be very clearly supported by settled practice.

(6) The technique of implying terms on any of the three bases mentioned at (1) above – law, fact or custom – allows the courts (and the legislature in the case of terms *implied in law*) to do justice in either a generous or circumspect fashion, depending on the context. The English method of 'implying terms' under these various rubrics largely explains the absence of an express general principle of commercial good faith in the performance of contracts (generally on the good faith issue, see 21.01).

(7) Under English law, there will often be overlapping liability in the tort of negligence and in contract, based on an implied term that the defendant must exercise reasonable care or display customary skill (13.20).

13.02 Implied terms (especially those implied by law; see 13.03) are more common than express terms. Every day, millions of transactions are entered into without writing, and without a single spoken word, for English shopkeepers and consumers respect each other's human right to remain mute. Against this silent background, the law fleshes out these transactions by implying terms, notably terms implied in law.

2. TERMS IMPLIED IN LAW

13.03 As Lord Steyn in *Equitable Life Assurance Co. Ltd* v. *Hyman* (2002) explained, terms implied in law are 'incidents impliedly annexed to particular forms of contracts … Such standardised implied terms operate as general default rules.'[5] Implied terms in law are often the product of legislation governing particular standard contracts. The legislation concerning sales of goods is the best example.[6] As for judicially recognised implied terms in law, the House of Lords admitted that general considerations of policy underpin decisions whether to add to this canon of terms implied in law.[7] Elizabeth Peden has identified a wide array of factors in the modern cases.[8] And Lord Steyn has suggested that when implying a term in law, the overall consideration is the court's perception of what is 'reasonable' in transactions of a common type.[9] Indeed the Court of Appeal in the *Crossley* case (2004)

---

5 [2002] 1 AC 408, 458–9 HL; comments of Lord Somervell in *Lister* v. *Romford Ice & Cold Storage Co.* [1957] AC 555, 598, HL; for overt gap-filling and explicit reference to fairness, in the context of credit card payments, see *Re Charge Card Services Ltd* [1989] Ch 497, 513, CA.

6 Sections 13–15 of the Sale of Goods Act 1979.

7 Lord Wright in *Luxor (Eastbourne) Ltd* v. *Cooper* [1941] AC 108, 137, HL; Viscount Simonds and Lord Tucker in *Lister* v. *Romford Ice & Cold Storage Co.* [1957] AC 555, 576, 594, HL.

8 E. Peden, 'Policy Concerns Behind Implication of Terms in Law' (2001) LQR 459–76.

9 Lord Steyn, 'Contract Law: Fulfilling the Reasonable Expectations of Honest Men' (1997) 113 LQR 433, 442.

admitted that the concept of 'necessity' is 'somewhat protean'[10] and that the 'existence and scope of standardised implied terms [that is, those implied in law] raise questions of reasonableness, fairness and the balancing of competing policy considerations'.[11] This analysis was approved in *Geys* v. *Société Générale* (2012) by Baroness Hale (see also on that case 13.08 at (6) below).[12]

13.04 *Local authority duty to 'high-rise' flats tenants.* In *Liverpool City Council* v. *Irwin* (1977), the issue was whether an implied term in law should be recognised to govern the so-called 'common parts' of local authority 'high-rise' flats (an important but often unsatisfactory type of housing in modern Britain).[13] The House of Lords regarded themselves as finding, as a matter of law, an *implied obligation essential to the relations between a landlord and tenants inhabiting a block of flats.*

> In *Liverpool City Council* v. *Irwin* (1977) tenants had complained that the local authority had failed to maintain the stairways and lifts. Many of the tenants were either elderly or parents of young children. The House of Lords held that the landlord should exercise reasonable care to keep the common parts in reasonable repair. Such a term should be implied as a matter of law (although, on the facts, it was held that the obligation had not been breached). Although the speeches contain various formulations of the general test for finding an implied term in law, the gist is that the court here found *an obligation essential to the relations between a landlord and tenants inhabiting a block of flats.* This is encapsulated in Lord Salmon's statement that 'the whole transaction would become futile, inefficacious and absurd' unless 'in a 15 storey block of flats or maisonettes ... the landlords were under [a] legal duty to take reasonable care to keep the lifts in working order and the staircases lit'.[14]

13.05 *Arbitration.*[15] In *Michael Wilson & Partners Ltd* v. *Emmott* (2008), the Court of Appeal acknowledged that an obligation of confidentiality arises as a matter of law in arbitration references conducted in accordance with English law[16] (for earlier recognition of this implied term of law, see *Ali Shipping Corporation* v. *Shipyard Trogir* (1999)).[17] This implied term governs all documents 'prepared for', 'used' and 'disclosed during' such arbitration. In the *Michael Wilson* case (2008), Lawrence Collins LJ commented:[18] 'This is in reality a substantive rule of arbitration law reached through the device of an implied term.'

---

10 *Crossley* v. *Faithful & Gould Holdings Ltd* [2004] ICR 1615, CA, at [34], *per* Dyson LJ.
11 *Ibid.,* at [36]; and see the quotation at [30], from *Anson's Law of Contract.* (See now *Anson* (29th edn, Oxford, 2010), 155.)
12 [2012] UKSC 63; [2013] 1 AC 523, at [55] to [60].
13 [1977] AC 239, HL.
14 [1977] AC 239, 263, HL; cited by Lord Scarman in *Tai Hing Cotton Mill Ltd* v. *Liu Chong Hing Bank Ltd* [1986] AC 80, 105, PC and by Peter Coulson QC (sitting as a judge of the High Court) in *Jani-King (GB) Ltd* v. *Pula Enterprises Ltd* [2007] EWHC 2433 (QBD); [2008] 1 Lloyd's Rep 305, at [47].
15 On confidentiality in arbitration, N. Andrews, *Andrews on Civil Processes* (Cambridge, 2013), vol. 2, *Arbitration and Mediation,* chapter 8, and literature cited therein.
16 [2008] EWCA Civ 184; [2008] 1 Lloyd's Rep 616.
17 [1999] 1 WLR 314, CA.
18 [2008] EWCA Civ 184; [2008] 1 Lloyd's Rep 616, at [105] and [106].

13.06 *Holiday injury: tour operator's contractual duty of care.* Both at Common Law and under a statutory provision,[19] a tour operator is contractually required to take reasonable steps to guard against personal injury.

> However, in *Evans* v. *Kosmar Villa Operators* (2008),[20] the Court of Appeal held that this duty did not require the operator to protect a 17-year-old against the danger of injury caused by diving into the shallow end of a swimming pool. The court took the view that the claimant had spent enough time at the hotel to have appreciated this risk; but he had momentarily forgotten it, or decided to run this risk. The decision does not, however, convincingly address the fact that the defendant had not taken active steps to stamp out the practice of 'copycat diving'. A more exacting duty, as found by the trial judge, seems appropriate.

13.07 *Consumer credit.* In *Durkin* v. *DSG Retail Ltd* (2014)[21] the claimant bought a laptop, having been assured by the vendor that it had a special feature ('the assurance'). Part of the price was financed by a consumer credit payment made by the defendant. The next day the sale was terminated because the claimant returned the item, having discovered that it did not comply with the assurance. But the claimant suffered a credit blacklisting for failure to pay on an underlying transaction which had been cancelled. The Supreme Court held that there is an implied term in such a credit contract that the transaction is conditional on survival of the underlying purchase.[22] The defendant was liable in damages for tort for failure to have accepted and investigated these events (the sum awarded was £8,000 for damage to the claimant's credit).[23] Although this was an appeal from Scotland, this decision also states English law.

13.08 *Employment cases.* This has been a fertile context for the implication of terms in law. In the *ASLEF* case (1972), the Court of Appeal implied a term that employees will not act so as to prevent effective performance of their duties and of their employers' enterprise.[24]

> In this case railway employees had disruptively stuck to the very letter of their contract in order to produce industrial chaos (so-called 'working to rule'). With feigned zeal, they had carefully checked each carriage door before allowing passenger trains to leave the platform. This had caused chaotic delay. Buckley and Roskill LJJ implied a term that employees would not wreck their employer's commercial venture.

---

19 Package Travel, Package Holidays and Package Tours Regulations 1992 (SI 1992 No. 3288), Reg 15; *Titshall* v. *Querty Travel Ltd* [2011] EWCA Civ 1569; [2012] 2 All ER 627.
20 [2007] EWCA Civ 1003; [2008] 1 WLR 297.
21 [2014] UKSC 21; [2014] 1 WLR 1148.
22 *Ibid.*, at [26].
23 *Ibid.*, at [32] to [39].
24 *Secretary of State for Employment* v. *ASLEF (No. 2)* [1972] 2 QB 455, CA.

But, as the following decisions show, the courts have been willing to mould the employment contract, using the implied term device, to impose various additional obligations upon employers.[25]

(1) *Overworking the young. Johnstone* v. *Bloomsbury Health Authority* (1992) (see also 13.20) concerned junior doctors' working hours within the National Health Service.[26] The Court of Appeal affirmed that there is an implied term that a health employer will not overwork its staff so that their health is harmed. This tortious duty of care overlaps with an identical contractual implied term (in law): 'the two duties run side by side'.[27] The Court of Appeal wrestled with the problem of reconciling this implied duty with an express term which allowed the employer to extend the working week (by forty-eight hours on top of the basic forty hours). A majority of the court held that this power was subject to the implied term requiring the employer to safeguard the employee against injury or illness.[28]

(2) *Crooked management damaging the future prospects of innocent employees.* The House of Lords in *Malik (and Mahmud)* v. *Bank of Credit and Commerce International SA* (1998) recognised a general implied term that the employer should not behave in a way which will destroy or threaten the relationship of confidence and trust between him and his employees.[29]

In *Malik (and Mahmud)* v. *Bank of Credit and Commerce International SA* (1998) the employer was a bank run by crooked officials (but only its senior officers had been dealing dishonestly). The bank became insolvent. The liquidator terminated the plaintiffs' employment contracts. The House of Lords recognised that there is an implied term in law that an employer will not act dishonestly, because such misconduct will taint innocent employees. Because of the 'stigma' of their association with the dishonest bank, they might find it hard to gain new and equivalent employment. Although the House of Lords created this new employee's right to seek compensation, in the next stage of the litigation the claim for 'stigma' damages failed on the facts, because the employees could not show that they had in fact suffered loss through the stigma of this association.[30]

---

(3) *No power to resile from a bank's promise to fund a bonus pool for its staff.* The trust and confidence implied term recognised in the *Malik* case (above) is a potent source of protection. This implied term was held to have been breached in *Attrill* v. *Dresdner*

---

25   See the statements of high authority on the general background to this judicial activism: *Crossley* v. *Faithful & Gould Holdings Ltd* [2004] ICR 1615, CA, at [36] to [42]; for a study of implied terms in this context, see R. Rideout, in R. Halson (ed.), *Exploring the Boundaries of Contract* (Aldershot, 1996), chapter 7.
26   [1992] 1 QB 333, CA; noted by A. Weir, [1991] CLJ 397.
27   [1992] 1 QB 333, 343D, CA, *per* Stuart-Smith LJ.
28   *Ibid.*, at 344F, *per* Stuart-Smith LJ; 350–1, *per* Sir Nicolas Browne-Wilkinson (express power to require up to forty-eight extra hours, to be construed as subject to the implied term not to injure the claimant); Leggatt LJ dissented at 348.
29   [1998] 1 AC 20, 45–6, HL, *per* Lord Steyn.
30   The 'factual sequel': *Bank of Credit & Commerce International SA (in liquidation)* v. *Ali (No. 2)* [2002] EWCA Civ 82; [2002] 3 All ER 750; [2002] ICR 1258.

Kleinwort Ltd (2013)[31] when the bank sought to 'move the goal-posts', having already promised to provide a generous bonus fund. In August 2008 the defendant investment bank's management had promised high-earning employees a bonus pool of €400m for the January 2009 'season'. But in late December 2008 and early 2009, under pressure from the new management (a German bank which had acquired the business) management sought to resile from this (by purporting to introduce a 'material adverse change' clause).[32] That was held to violate the present implied term.

(4) *Assistance in avoiding a pensions snare.* In *Scally* v. *Southern Health Board* (1992),[33] the House of Lords held that an employer was obliged to bring to an employee's attention certain pension technicalities. Such information would enable the employee to 'buy' extra pensionable 'years' and so enhance his eventual pension. The basis was not an implied term in fact,[34] but a term implied in law 'based on wider considerations' and in recognition of a 'necessary incident of a definable category of contractual relationship'.[35] Lord Bridge formulated this implied term with considerable precision as follows:[36]

> [The implied term found on the present facts will apply only where]: (1) the terms of the contract of employment have not been negotiated with the individual employee but result from negotiation with a representative body or are otherwise incorporated by reference; (2) a particular term of the contract makes available to the employee a valuable right contingent upon action being taken by him to avail himself of its benefit; (3) the employee cannot, in all the circumstances, reasonably be expected to be aware of the term unless it is drawn to his attention.

The *Scally* case was described at first instance in the *Crossley* case (see below) as 'a bridgehead from which there has been no advance'.[37] It would appear that the striking features of the *Scally* case's facts was that employees could not 'reasonably be expected to be aware' of this valuable benefit, which was the product of higher level industry-wide negotiation, unless the employer brought it to their attention. Finally on this case, some commentators have suggested that the *Scally* case renders the 'implied in law or in fact' distinction 'fragile'.[38] This criticism is unconvincing. Lord Bridge's very precise formulation – just set out – seems apt when one considers the multiplicity of employment relationships and the variety of possible issues.

31 [2013] EWCA Civ 394; [2013] 3 All ER 807.
32 *Ibid.*, at [28]; see [101] for formulation of the trust and confidence implied term; and at [143] it was concluded that the implied term had been breached.
33 [1992] 1 AC 294, 306G–307E, HL (noted by M. Freedland, (1992) 21 ILJ 135); distinguished in *University of Nottingham* v. *Eyett* [1999] 2 All ER 437, 443G–4; [1999] ICR 721, Hart J; *National Home Loans Corporation* v. *Giffen & Archer* [1997] 3 All ER 808, 814–16, CA; *Oughtram* v. *Academy Plastics* [2001] ICR 367, CA; *Hagen* v. *ICI Chemicals & Polymers Ltd* [2002] IRLR 31, Elias J; cases reviewed in *Crossley* v. *Faithful & Gould Holdings Ltd* [2004] ICR 1615, CA; cf also, no duty upon bank to inform customer of new type of account: *Suriya & Douglas* v. *Midland Bank, The Times,* 29 March 1999, CA.
34 [1992] 1 AC 294, 306G.
35 *Ibid.*, at 307.
36 *Ibid.*
37 [2004] ICR 1615, CA, at [20], *per* Judge Peter Langan QC, cited by Dyson LJ.
38 *Anson's Law of Contract* (29th edn, Oxford, 2010), 156–7; A. Phang, [1993] JBL 242, and [1994] JBL 255.

(5) *No duty to provide more detailed pensions advice.* The Court of Appeal in *Crossley* v. *Faithful & Gould Holdings Ltd* (2004)[39] noted that cases subsequent[40] to the *Scally* case had refused to recognise a general implied term in law that employers should exercise care to protect their employees' financial well-being. In the *Crossley* case, the claimant was a senior employee who had taken retirement without proper regard for his pension rights. But the Court of Appeal held it would be 'unfair and unreasonable' to impose upon employers a general or demanding duty to provide financial advice.[41] The employee can seek his own advice, and the employer might have a conflict of interests.[42]

(6) *Exercise of termination power.* In *Geys* v. *Société Générale* (2012) Baroness Hale held that there is an implied term that an employer will make clear to an employee that a payment made to that person is an exercise of the employer's power (this termination power having been expressly stipulated within the contract of employment) to terminate the contract straightaway by paying salary in lieu of notice.[43]

3. TERMS IMPLIED IN FACT

13.09 *A stricter approach.* We have seen in the preceding section that the criteria for finding a term implied *in law* are relatively free-ranging because that type of regulation requires the courts, in the absence of statutory intervention, to fashion minimal rules for the operation of standard legal relationships. The courts are not then tied to a single criterion of the parties' tacit joint intention. By contrast, the courts will not find an implied term *in fact* merely because it would be 'reasonable' or 'fair'. Instead, here the courts are endeavouring to tease out the parties' unexpressed common intention. As Lord Wright said in the *Luxor* case (1941) of this type of implied term: '[The courts will not] embark on a reconstruction of the agreement on equitable principles, or on a view of what the parties should, in the opinion of the Court, reasonably have contemplated . . . Judges . . . have no right to make contracts for the parties.'[44]

13.10 *'Business efficacy' test: genesis.* This test emerged in Bowen LJ's judgment in *'The Moorcock'* (1889):[45]

> In business transactions such as this, what the law desires to effect by the implication is to give such business efficacy to the transaction as must have been intended at all events by both parties who are businessmen; not to impose on one side all the perils of the transaction, or to emancipate one side from all the chances

39 [2004] ICR 1615, CA.

40 *University of Nottingham* v. *Eyett* [1999] 2 All ER 437, 443G–4; [1999] ICR 721, Hart J; *Oughtram* v. *Academy Plastics* [2001] ICR 367, CA; *Hagen* v. *ICI Chemicals & Polymers Ltd* [2002] IRLR 31, Elias J.

41 [2004] ICR 1615, CA, at [43].

42 *Ibid.,* at [44].

43 [2012] UKSC 63; [2013] 1 AC 523, at [55] to [60].

44 *Luxor (Eastbourne) Ltd* v. *Cooper* [1941] AC 108, 137, HL.

45 (1889) 14 PD 64, 68, CA; A. Phang, [1998] JBL 1; for the observation that this decision is as much about terms implied in law as those implied in fact, R. Austen-Baker, 'Implied Terms in English Contract Law', in L. DiMatteo, Q. Zhou, S. Saintier, K. Rowley (eds.), *Commercial Contract Law: Transatlantic Perspectives* (Cambridge, 2014), chapter 10, at 234.

of failure, but to make each party promise in law as much, at all events, as it must have been in the contemplation of both parties that he should be responsible for in respect of those perils or chances.

> In 'The Moorcock' (1889), the claimant moored their boat at the defendant's wharf on the River Thames, not realising that at low tide the vessel would rest on a mound in the river (which did not evenly support the whole vessel). This rendered the berth unsafe. The claimant's vessel was damaged when it came to rest on that mound. The Court of Appeal held that the contract (under which the claimant would pay for use of the defendant's cranes, but not for the mooring itself) imported an implied term that the defendant would take reasonable steps to guard against or point out physical hazards not known to the claimant. The defendant's commercial gain from crane charges could only be 'honestly' (the word used by Lord Esher MR) earned if the defendant took minimal legal responsibility to point out the hazard lurking beneath the water.

The problem with the 'business efficacy' test is its pliability: at one extreme it could be used too liberally to reflect a broader range of factors supporting inclusion of a particular term. In the *Strydom* case (2009),[46] Blair J explained that the 'business efficacy' test is not a licence for the court to exercise a benevolent discretion, or 'to introduce terms to make the contract fairer or more reasonable'.

> Bowen LJ's *ex tempore* judgment in 1889, read as a whole, is less than crystal clear, and ranges quite broadly.[47] MacKinnon LJ in the *Shirlaw* case (1939)[48] was critical of this test: 'a Court is too often invited to [find an implied term of fact] upon vague and uncertain grounds ... backed by ... citation ... from ... Bowen LJ in 'The Moorcock'. They are sentences from an *extempore* judgment ... I fancy that he would have been rather surprised ... that these general remarks ... would come to be a favourite citation of a supposed principle of law.'

The 'business efficacy' test was successfully invoked by claimants in *Silverman v. Imperial London Hotels Ltd* (1927),[49] who, with the hotel management's permission, had slept on couches within a Turkish bath. These couches were infested with bugs and these had bitten the claimants. Swift J used the 'business efficacy' test to impose strict liability on these facts. He said:

> Applying [the '*Moorcock* test'] ... the parties in this case contemplated that the cubicle and ... couch ... should be free from bugs or other insects which might inflict harm upon the plaintiff ... It avails the defendants nothing although they have taken every possible step in an endeavour to make them fit.

46 *Strydom v. Vendside Ltd* [2009] EWHC 2130 (QB); [2009] 6 Costs LR 886, at [33].
47 As observed by MacKinnon LJ in *Shirlaw v. Southern Foundries (1926) Ltd* [1939] 2 KB 206, 227, CA (affirmed [1940] AC 701, HL).
48 *Ibid.*
49 [1927] All ER 712, 714; 137 LT 57; 43 TLR 260.

By contrast, the *'Moorcock'* (1889) 'business efficacy' test did not avail the claimant in *Easton* v. *Hitchcock* (1912),[50] where the Divisional Court (unconvincingly) considered that it would be excessive to impose responsibility on the claimant, a 'female private detective or inquiry agent', for breach of confidentiality committed by one of her former employees (after he had left the defendant's employment). The breach had involved tipping off the defendant's husband that the claimant's private detectives were clandestinely following him. This rendered the claimant's work 'useless'[51] and the defendant refused to pay, but she was held liable in debt for the agency's agreed fee. Hamilton J said:[52]

> I think it impossible to hold that the plaintiff [had impliedly] warranted that [the agency's] servants would not make improper disclosures after they had ceased to be in her employment . . . If the [implied] warranty is . . . to continue for a week it must equally hold good during the whole of the departed servant's life.

Another borderline case is Blair J's decision in the *Strydom* case (2009),[53] where he refused to find an implied term (proposed by the claimant on the basis of business efficacy) within a conditional fee agreement.[54] It was unsuccessfully contended that the solicitor should have disclosed to his client that the solicitor would receive a fee for conducting the relevant claim not just from the claimant but from a government agency (in connection with industrial injury claims arising from 'White Finger' syndrome).

13.11 *'Officious bystander test'*. The main criterion adopted by the courts for the finding of a term implied *in fact* is the 'officious bystander' test. The test amounts to this: whether, following the intervention of a kindly and imaginary pedant habitually given to stalking negotiating parties, the prospective contractual parties would have readily assented to the proposed term at the time of formation. The test emphasises the need for 'obviousness': and this demanding criterion prevents an implied term from being recognised if one party would never, or only doubtfully, have assented to it. This test establishes a very high threshold: a term will not be recognised if one of the parties can plausibly protest that if the matter had been explicitly raised during negotiation, he would not have assented to it. The attraction of this approach is that it does not conflict with the principle of freedom of contract (1.08), that is, respect for the parties' general liberty to fix their own terms. MacKinnon LJ formulated the 'officious bystander' test in *Shirlaw* v. *Southern Foundries (1926) Ltd* (1939) as follows:[55]

> If I may quote from an essay which I wrote some years ago, I then said: 'Prima facie that which in any contract is left to be implied and need not be expressed is

---

50 [1912] 1 KB 535, Divisional Court.
51 *Ibid.*, at 538, *per* Lush J.
52 *Ibid.*, at 537–8.
53 *Strydom* v. *Vendside Ltd* [2009] EWHC 2130 (QB); [2009] 6 Costs LR 886, at [28] to [33].
54 On conditional fee agreements, *Andrews on Civil Processes* (Cambridge, 2013), vol. 1, *Court Proceedings*, chapter 20.
55 *Ibid.* In fact, as noted by A. Phang [1998] JBL 1 and D. Foxton, *The Life of Thomas E. Scrutton* (Cambridge, 2013), 250, this test clearly echoes Scrutton LJ's statement in *Reigate* v. *Union Manufacturing Co. (Ramsbottom) Ltd* [1918] 1 KB 592, 605, CA (Scrutton had been MacKinnon's pupil-master at the Bar), where Scrutton LJ, attempting to explain the 'business efficacy' test, hit on this objective criterion: 'if it is such a term that it can confidently be said that if at the time the contract was being negotiated someone had said to the parties, 'What will happen in such a case', they would both have replied, 'Of course, so and so will happen; we did not trouble to say that; it is too clear.'

something so obvious that it goes without saying; so that, if, while the parties were making their bargain, an officious bystander were to suggest some express provision for it in their agreement, they would testily suppress him with a common "Oh, of course!"' At least it is true, I think, that, if a term were never implied by a judge unless it could pass that test, he could not be held to be wrong.

MacKinnon LJ's statement has become the leading decision on terms *implied in fact*, much cited in modern cases. Indeed, as *Philips Electronique Grand Publique SA v. British Sky Broadcasting Ltd* (1995)[56] illustrates (see 13.15 below), the officious bystander test trumps the test in 'The Moorcock' (1889) (13.10): if a putative term which is supported by the 'business efficacy' test does not also satisfy the 'officious bystander' test, the courts will refuse to recognise it as a term to be implied in fact.

Sometimes, the concept of 'business efficacy' has been merged, even in the same passage or sentence, with the 'officious bystander' test.[57]

For example, Lord Wright in the House of Lords in *Luxor (Eastbourne) Ltd* v. *Cooper* (1941) said:[58]

there may be cases where obviously some term must be implied if the intention of the parties is not to be defeated, some term of which it can be predicated that 'it goes without saying', some term not expressed but necessary to give to the transaction such business efficacy as the parties must have intended . . . The implication must arise inevitably to give effect to the intention of the parties.

And Lord Pearson said in *Trollope & Colls Ltd.* v. *North West Metropolitan Regional Hospital Board* (1973):[59]

it is not enough for the court to find that such a term would have been adopted by the parties as reasonable men if it had been suggested to them: it must have been a term that went without saying, a term necessary to give business efficacy to the contract.

An even wider amalgam of factors was assembled by Lord Simon in *BP Refinery (Westernport) Pty Ltd* v. *Shire of Hastings* (1978), giving the Privy Council's judgment, noting that the 'business efficacy' test is not a sufficient criterion, and identifying this range of factors ('which may overlap'):[60]

(1) it must be reasonable and equitable; (2) it must be necessary to give business efficacy to the contract, so that no term will be implied if the contract is effective without it; (3) it must be so obvious that 'it goes without saying'; (4) it must be capable of clear expression;[61] (5) it must not contradict any express term of the contract.[62]

56 [1995] EMLR 472, CA.
57 *Owen Pell Ltd* v. *Bindi (London) Ltd* [2008] EWHC 1420 (TCC); [2008] BLR 436, at [10] (Frances Kirkham, sitting as a Deputy High Court Judge).
58 [1941] AC 108, 137, HL.
59 [1973] 1 WLR 601, 609, HL.
60 (1978) 52 ALJR 20, 26, PC; these factors were applied in *Jim Ennis Construction Ltd* v. *Premier Asphalt Ltd* [2009] EWHC 1906 (TCC); 125 Con LR 141, at [22] to [25], *per* HHJ Stephen Davies.
61 A vague and uncertain term is unlikely to be accepted: *Shell* v. *Lostock* [1977] 1 All ER 481, 491G, CA, *per* Ormrod LJ; cf Bridge LJ's dissent, *ibid.*, at 494. For an example of a suggested implied term which could not be satisfactorily formulated, but admitted of several possible variants, see *Luxor (Eastbourne) Ltd* v. *Cooper* [1941] AC 108, 115–18, HL, Viscount Simon LC concluding at 117: 'I find it impossible to formulate with adequate precision the tests which should determine whether or not a "just excuse" exists for disregarding the alleged implied term, and this leads me to consider whether there really is any such implied term at all.'
62 *County Homesearch Co. (Thames & Chilterns) Ltd* v. *Cowham* [2008] EWCA Civ 26, at [19]; [2008] 1 WLR 909. As for factor (5), an express power to award or deny performance points was held not to be regulated by an

Commenting on the 'officious bystander' and 'business efficacy' criteria, Lord Hoffmann said in *Attorney-General for Belize* v. *Belize Telecom Ltd* (2009) (problematic aspects of his discussion are noted at 13.16):[63]

> [T]his list is best regarded, not as a series of independent tests which must each be surmounted, but rather as a collection of different ways in which judges have tried to express the central idea that the proposed implied term must spell out what the contract actually involves.

The following two cases illustrate the uphill struggle faced by a party seeking to invoke the 'officious bystander' test (the proposed implied term was found only in the third of these cases).

On the facts of *Spring* v. *National Amalgamated Stevedores and Dockers Society* (1956)[64] the objective bystander would not have elicited immediate consensus on the proposed term. The Transport and General Workers' Union (TGWU) dismissed Spring, a Liverpool docker, from their union because he had joined another trade union. The Bridlington Agreement, applicable between trades unions, prohibited each trade union from soliciting membership from each other. The TGWU alleged that in his contract of membership with the TGWU, the need for a member of the TGWU to comply with the Bridlington Agreement had been incorporated as an implied term in fact. Sir Leonard Stone V-C rejected this:[65] 'If the [officious bystander] . . . had asked the plaintiff, "Won't you put into it some reference to the Bridlington Agreement?", I think (indeed, I have no doubt) the plaintiff would have answered "What's that?".'

Similarly, in *R Griggs Group* v. *Evans (No. 1)* (2005), Evans was commissioned to produce a logo for the owners of 'Doc Martens' footwear. Evans contended that he retained world-wide copyright in the logo. Jacob LJ (the trial judge) dismissed the contention that Evans should have that right on the basis of the 'objective bystander' test. Indeed Jacob LJ suggested that this analysis was nothing short of 'fantastic' because 'the answer would surely have been "of course not"'.[66]

But in *Weldon* v. *GRE Linked Life Assurance Ltd* (2002), Nelson J held that an implied term should be found to prevent a company cancelling a life insurance policy after it had itself inefficiently failed to collect payment under a direct debit arrangement.[67]

And in *Yam Seng Pte Ltd* v. *International Trade Corp Ltd* (2013) Leggatt J implied as a matter of necessity an implied term in a distributorship agreement that the supplier 'would not authorise the sale of any product in the domestic market of any territory covered by the

implied term in *Mid Essex Hospital Services NHS Trust* v. *Compass Group UK and Ireland Ltd (t/a Medirest)* [2013] EWCA Civ 200; [2013] BLR 265, at [92].
63   [2009] UKPC 10; [2009] 2 All ER 1127; [2009] BCC 433, at [27].
64   [1956] 1 WLR 585.
65   *Ibid.*, 599.
66   [2005] EWCA Civ 11; [2005] FSR 31, at [19].
67   [2000] 2 All ER (Comm) 914, at [19] to [21], Nelson J.

Agreement at a lower retail price than the duty free retail price for the product which had been specified in the Agreement'.[68]

13.12 *Contamination of 'policy factors' when finding terms implied in fact.* Unfortunately, some modern decisions have hinted that the quest for implied terms in fact might become policy-orientated.[69] This would unacceptably conflate the settled[70] distinction between terms implied in fact and terms implied in law. The courts should not loosen the criteria for discovering an implied term in fact by referring to the objective standard of hypothetical parties' 'reasonable expectations'.

> As Lord Wright said in the *Luxor* case (1941) of this type of implied term: '[The courts will not] embark on a reconstruction of the agreement on equitable principles, or on a view of what the parties should, in the opinion of the Court, reasonably have contemplated . . . Judges . . . have no right to make contracts for the parties.'[71] Lord Hoffmann in *Attorney-General for Belize* v. *Belize Telecom Ltd* (2009) conceded that terms implied in fact are not found by reference to the test of reasonableness, but by reference to a more demanding criterion of necessity.[72]

13.13 *Financial services cases: a disastrously implied term in fact.* However, the House of Lords erred by inserting an implied term in fact into a complex relationship in *Equitable Life Assurance Co. Ltd* v. *Hyman* (2002).[73] With respect, the result was to tie the hands of the pension company unacceptably. This was a highly debatable restructuring of policyholders' rights, and the decision caused havoc.

> The House of Lords considered the predicament of a financially overstretched life insurance and pension company which had proposed to reduce 'final bonus' payments, to the prejudice of one category of policyholders (a group consisting of 90,000 persons). These contracts contained a clause giving the company an ostensibly absolute discretion both whether to grant final bonuses and, if so, how to fix the level of these bonuses. The company had run into difficulty because it had been offering guaranteed annuity rates without making an extra charge. After May 1995, the guaranteed rate had outstripped the current annuity rate. To compensate, the company adopted the new practice of requiring members who were close to retirement to elect whether to opt for the lower current rate, calculating the final bonus accordingly, or to take a lower final bonus if they instead opted to receive the guaranteed rate.

---

68 [2013] EWHC 111 (QB); [2013] 1 All ER (Comm) 1321; [2013] 1 Lloyd's Rep 526; [2013] BLR 147, at [164]: see more generally on this case, 21.16.
69 *Paragon Finance plc* v. *Nash* [2001] EWCA Civ 1466; [2002] 1 WLR 685, at [36] (third sentence), and [42] (second sentence), *per* Dyson LJ; *Equitable Life Assurance Co. Ltd* v. *Hyman* [2002] 1 AC 408, 459, HL, *per* Lord Steyn.
70 Lord Steyn, (1997) 113 LQR 432, 442.
71 *Luxor (Eastbourne) Ltd* v. *Cooper* [1941] AC 108, 137, HL.
72 [2009] UKPC 10; [2009] 2 All ER 1127; [2009] BCC 433, at [19].
73 [2002] 1 AC 408, HL; noted by A. Berg, [2002] JBL 570; for observations on this case, Lord Grabiner, 'The Iterative Process of Contractual Interpretation' (2012) 128 LQR 41, 56 ff; on the subsequent litigation against the company's auditors, see L. Roach, (2006) 17 *International Company and Commercial Law Review* 117.

Scott V-C at first instance (and Morritt LJ in his dissent in the Court of Appeal) had persuasively decided that the contract did not create an express right to a final bonus, and that there was no implied term which would create such a right (by radically fettering the company's discretion as to the grant or quantification of these bonuses).

But Lord Woolf MR and Waller LJ in the Court of Appeal, and all five members of the House of Lords, recognised an implied term of fact which prevented the company from making a reduced final bonus to the 90,000 disaffected policyholders (members who, unlike the other members, had contracted – without extra payment – to receive guaranteed annuity rates). In the House of Lords, Lord Steyn said that this 'individualised' implied term arose after construction of the entire policy and its context, and that it was founded upon the 'stringent' test of 'strict necessity'.[74] This was in fact a highly debatable finding of an implied term.[75]

The result of the House of Lords decision was that the company almost became insolvent and needed to be commercially rescued. This decision came as a commercial surprise because it ran counter to the emerging practice recognised by the Treasury and other companies (as Morritt LJ, in his dissenting judgment in the Court of Appeal, had noted).[76] Certainly the contractual term 'implied in fact' on complicated commercial facts in this case was a long way removed from the commercially transparent context in which MacKinnon LJ in the *Shirlaw* case (1939) (13.11) applied the 'officious bystander' test. It is also ironic that the Equitable Life company had financed the litigation, in the interest of achieving 'closure', as a representative claim for a declaration.[77] The House of Lords' decision was binding on all the company's policyholders.

13.14 *Lender's implied term in fact.*[78] In *Paragon Finance plc* v. *Nash* (2002)[79] the Court of Appeal held that there is an implied term that the lender must exercise an express power to vary the rate of interest payable by its customer *without dishonesty, capriciousness or for an improper purpose.*[80] This would prevent the lender from increasing interest to an extent, or in a manner, which no other lender could reasonably make.[81] The court drew back from stating that the implied term further outlawed any allegedly 'unreasonable' exercise of this power.[82]

However, the *Paragon* implied term (that a party will not exercise a discretion in 'an arbitrary, irrational or capricious manner') was not applied in *Mid Essex Hospital Services NHS Trust* v. *Compass Group UK and Ireland Ltd (t/a Medirest)* (2013) in order to regulate a

---

74   [2002] 1 AC 408, 459H, *per* Lord Steyn.

75   The decision is persuasively criticised by Lord Grabiner, 'The Iterative Process of Contractual Interpretation' (2012) 128 LQR 41, 56 ff (who had been counsel in the lower stages of this litigation).

76   [2002] 1 AC 408, 438–9, at [110], CA, *per* Morritt LJ.

77   Generally on 'representative proceedings', *Andrews on Civil Processes* (Cambridge, 2013), vol. 1, *Court Processes*, 22.09 ff.

78   R. Hooley, 'Controlling Contractual Discretion' [2013] CLJ 65–90.

79   *Paragon Finance plc* v. *Nash* [2001] EWCA Civ 1466; [2002] 1 WLR 685, at [36] to [42], *per* Dyson LJ, reviewing earlier case law, notably *Gan Insurance Co. Ltd* v. *Tai Ping Insurance Co. Ltd (No. 2)* [2001] 2 All ER (Comm) 299, CA (noted by V. Sims and R. Goddard, [2002] CLJ 269–71).

80   *Paragon Finance plc* v. *Nash* [2001] EWCA Civ 1466; [2002] 1 WLR 685, at [32] and [36].

81   *Ibid.*, drawing upon *Gan Insurance Co. Ltd* v. *Tai Ping Insurance Co. Ltd (No. 2)* [2001] 2 All ER (Comm) 299, CA, at [64] to [73], *per* Mance LJ (implied term that reinsurer's discretion to approve proposed settlement must not be absurdly unreasonable or based on extraneous and non-commercial considerations).

82   *Paragon* case, [2001] EWCA Civ 1466; [2002] 1 WLR 685, at [37] to [42].

NHS Trust's express power to award or deny performance points concerning the other party's catering services.[83]

The Court of Appeal's decision in *Paragon* v. *Nash* (2002) involved a transplant into private law of the famous *Wednesbury* principles, well known to students of public law.[84] These public law principles are used in judicial review proceedings to regulate decisions made by government or other 'public' authorities. It is established that a public authority's decision cannot be judicially impugned unless it was *wholly unreasonable*, that is, a decision that no person could possibly have made; in other words, a perverse or 'mad-hat' decision.

Later decisions in the *private law* field indicate that the courts have maintained this narrow criterion of extreme unreasonableness.[85] This narrow approach is attractive: it satisfies the need for the courts to provide minimal protection of a disadvantaged party, but it shields the courts from the charge that they have constructed an entirely new contract for the parties, which would be contrary to the principle of freedom of contract (1.08). Lord Wright in *Luxor (Eastbourne) Ltd* v. *Cooper* (1941) noted:[86] 'Judges ... have no right to make contracts for the parties.' The restrictive approach in *Paragon* v. *Nash* just considered is not confined to discretions concerning financial charges, as Brooke LJ's general remarks in *Ludgate Insurance Co. Ltd* v. *Citibank NA* (1998) make clear.[87]

Hooley has made a careful study of related expressed and implied contractual duties.[88] He notes, in particular, the restrictive comments of Cooke J in *SNCB Holding* v. *UBS AG* (2012),[89] and of Rix LJ in *Socimer International Bank Ltd* v. *Standard Bank London Ltd* (2008).[90]

13.15 *Implied terms and complex commercial agreements: the need to tread gingerly.* The Court of Appeal's important decision in *Philips Electronique Grand Publique SA* v. *British Sky Broadcasting Ltd* (1995)[91] shows that the courts are wary of implying a term of fact into a

---

83 [2013] EWCA Civ 200; [2013] BLR 265, at [92].

84 *Associated Provincial Picture Houses* v. *Wednesbury Corporation* [1948] 1 KB 223, CA.

85 *Paragon Finance plc* v. *Plender* [2005] EWCA Civ 760; [2005] 1 WLR 3412, especially at [118] (lender could adopt a policy in pursuit of a genuine commercial reason of tracking similar commercial rates of interest); *Lymington Marina Ltd* v. *MacNamara* [2007] EWCA Civ 151; [2007] Bus LR D29 (right to withhold permission for sub-licence not to be exercised on wholly unreasonable, capricious, arbitrary or bad faith reasons). *Barclays Bank plc* v. *Unicredit Bank AG* [2012] EWHC 3655 (Comm); [2012] EWHC 3655 (Comm); [2013] 2 Lloyd's Rep 1; [2014] 1 BCLC 342, at [56] to [67], *per* Popplewell J (for a careful review of authorities; in the *Barclays* case the clause required 'commercial reasonableness' and this imported objective elements, although the decision-maker could give priority to its commercial interests).

86 [1941] AC 108, 137–8, HL.

87 [1998] Lloyds LR 221, CA, at [35]; followed in *Jani-King (GB) Ltd* v. *Pula Enterprises Ltd* [2007] EWHC 2433 (QBD); [2008] 1 Lloyd's Rep 305, at [34]. And see the general survey in *Barclays Bank plc* v. *Unicredit Bank AG* [2012] EWHC 3655 (Comm); [2013] 2 Lloyd's Rep 1, at [56] to [67], *per* Popplewell J.

88 R. Hooley, 'Controlling Contractual Discretion' [2013] CLJ 65–90.

89 [2012] EWHC 2044 (Comm), at [72] and [112] (avoidance of dishonesty); Hooley, n. 88 above, at 75.

90 [2008] EWCA Civ 116; [2008] 1 Lloyd's Rep 558, at [66] (contractual discretion to be exercised honestly ('honesty, good faith and genuineness') and without objective 'arbitrariness, capriciousness, perversity and irrationality'), on which Hooley, n. 88 above, at 68–9, 73, 76. See also *Marex* case [2013] EWHC 2155 (Comm); [2014] 1 All ER (Comm) 122.

91 [1995] EMLR 472, CA; Sir Bernard Rix, 'Lord Bingham's Contributions to Commercial Law', in M. Andenas and D. Fairgrieve (eds.), *Tom Bingham and the Transformation of the Law: A Liber Amicorum* (Oxford, 2009), 675; cited with approval by Rix LJ in *Socimer International Bank Ltd (in liquidation)* v. *Standard Bank London Ltd (No. 2)* [2008] EWCA Civ 116; [2008] 1 Lloyd's Rep 558, at [105]; and by Sir Anthony Clarke MR in *Mediterranean Salvage & Towage Ltd* v. *Seamar Trading & Commerce Inc. ('The Reborn')* [2009] EWCA Civ 531; [2009] 2 Lloyd's Rep 639, at [16] and [17] (quoted in 13.16 below).

detailed contract which represents a 'closely negotiated compromise between … conflicting objectives'[92] because it would be perilous to impute a common intention in this context.[93] The claimant was a manufacturer of satellite television receivers. This company had been left high-and-dry when the defendant, which had contracted for the claimant to *manufacture* such receivers, proposed to merge with its rival and so kill off all UK demand for the claimant's equipment. The agreement did not commit the defendant to purchase such equipment. The risk of the product ceasing to be relevant in this competitive market had been clearly allocated under the carefully constructed written contract. An implied term in favour of the claimant would be a judicial wrecking-ball.

Philips had agreed with BSB, a satellite television company, to *manufacture* satellite television receivers. At the time there was considerable competition to establish market leadership in the UK. One year after the contract had been formed, BSB, realising that its rival, Sky, had emerged victorious, announced that it would merge with Sky. This rendered Philips' equipment useless. The Court of Appeal denied that Philips was entitled to this proposed implied term: 'that BSB would not commit any act which would tend to impede or render impossible the marketing of the receivers and/or to render the receivers useless or unmarketable'. Applying the 'officious bystander' test, there was no basis for finding such a term; nor, applying the slightly vaguer 'business efficacy' test, should the term be recognised.

The decision is commercially sound. As the Court of Appeal noted: (1) BSB had not agreed to purchase Philips' equipment; (2) BSB had not assumed the risk that the market in products designed by Philips would collapse; (3) all the indications were that the parties would have engaged in tough negotiation if Philips had sought such contractual protection; (4) the supposed implied term would have completely fettered BSB's commercial decision-making (including its economic decision to merge with a more successful rival).

The decision is also doctrinally interesting because it demonstrates that the 'objective bystander' test is the dominant criterion. Even if (as the first instance judge evidently thought when he had wrongly decided in favour of BSB) Philips had an arguable case that the proposed implied term might be consistent with 'business efficacy' (in the sense that there would be no point in manufacturing receivers for a company which had decided to merge with a rival which used a different type of receiver), it would fly in the face of the 'officious bystander' test to impute to the parties a tacit assent to the proposed term. And so the 'officious bystander' test trumped the vaguer notion of 'business efficacy'.

13.16 *Much ado about written contracts.* Lord Hoffmann, in *Attorney-General for Belize* v. *Belize Telecom Ltd* (2009),[94] one of his final judicial contributions to contract law, attempted to subsume the implication of terms in fact (in the context of written contracts) into his more general theory of objective construction of such contract (see Chapter 14). Lord Hoffmann

---

92 *Ali* v. *Christian Salvesen* [1997] 1 All ER 721, 726, CA (in the context of a collective agreement governing employment relations).
93 *Ibid.*, at 726–7.
94 [2009] UKPC 10; [2009] 2 All ER 1127; [2009] BCC 433, at [21] (see also [16] to [27]) (n. 96 for literature on this case).

in *Attorney-General for Belize* v. *Belize Telecom Ltd* (2009) criticised both the 'officious bystander' and 'business efficacy' tests. He suggested that the true test is how a *written contract* should be construed by its reasonable addressee, so as to give effect to the overall purpose of the document (viz., a 'teleological interpretation') but eschewing the criterion of implication on the basis of reasonableness. He said (numbering added):[95]

(1) '[I]n every case in which it is said that some provision ought to be implied in an instrument, the question for the court is whether such a provision would spell out in express words what the instrument, read against the relevant background, would reasonably be understood to mean.'

(2) '[This] question can be reformulated in various ways which a court may find helpful in providing an answer – the implied term must "go without saying", it must be "necessary to give business efficacy to the contract" and so on – but these are not in the Board's opinion to be treated as different or additional tests.'

(3) 'There is only one question: is that what the instrument, read as a whole against the relevant background, would reasonably be understood to mean?'

This discussion must be treated with caution for many reasons[96] (although McLauchlan is supportive).[97] First, it should not engender an injudiciously liberal discovery of implied terms. Secondly, Lord Hoffmann at passage (2), just cited, should not be construed as challenging the established doctrine that terms in fact can be found within written contracts.[98] Thirdly, the dismissive remarks, at passage (2), fail to acknowledge the long-standing success of the 'officious bystander' test.[99] Fourthly, Lord Hoffmann's emphasis upon the perspective of the reasonable addressee of the relevant document can hardly supply the answer for implication of terms in unwritten contracts. Finally, Lord Hoffmann's invitation to imply a term, based on what the relevant text 'would reasonably be understood to mean'[100] makes no reference to the need for a strict approach to the implication of terms into written contracts. But such a circumspect approach had been earlier endorsed by (i) Bingham LJ in *Philips Electronique Grand Public SA* v. *British Sky Broadcasting Ltd*

---

95   [2009] UKPC 10; [2009] 2 All ER 1127; [2009] BCC 433, at [21].

96   R. Ahdar, 'Contract Doctrine, Predictability and the Nebulous Exception' [2014] CLJ 39, 43, noting Singaporean rejection of the *Belize* suggestion, in *Foo Jong Peng* [2012] SGCA 55; [2012] 4 SLR 1267, at [36] (on this case, D. McLauchlan, [2014] LMCLQ 203, 221–2; and G. Yihan, [2013] JBL 237), and *Sembcorp Marine Ltd* v. *PPL Holdings Ltd* [2013] SGCA 43; [2013] 4 SLR 193, at [76] to [101] (on this case, D. McLauchlan, [2014] LMCLQ 203, 226, 232–4; and at 234 ff noting other Commonwealth discussion of the *Belize* case, noting the positive reception in the Sup Ct of NZ in *Dysart Timbers Ltd* v. *Nielsen* [2009] NZSC 43; [2009] 3 NZLR 160, at [25], [62], [64]); W. Courtney and J. W. Carter (2014) 31 JCL 151; P. S. Davies, 'Recent Developments in the Law of Implied Terms' [2010] LMCLQ 140 and in 'Construing Commercial Contracts: No Need for Violence', in M. Freeman and F. Smith (eds.), *Law and Language: Current Legal Issues 2011*, vol. 15 (Oxford, 2013), 434; Lord Grabiner, 'The Iterative Process of Contractual Interpretation' (2012) 128 LQR 41, 59–60; J. McCaughran, 'Implied Terms: The Journey of the Man on the Clapham Omnibus' [2011] CLJ 607–22; E. Macdonald, 'Casting Aside "Officious Bystanders" and "Business Efficacy"' (2000) 26 JCL 97; for a positive reception, R. Hooley, 'Implied Terms after *Belize*' [2014] CLJ 315–49; also on the *Belize* case, notes by K. F. K. Low, (2009) 125 LQR 561; C. Peters, [2009] CLJ 513; earlier, A. Kramer, 'Implication in Fact as an Instance of Contractual Interpretation' [2004] CLJ 384.

97   D. McLauchlan, 'Construction and Implication: in Defence of *Belize Telecom*' [2014] LMCLQ 203–40.

98   *Luxor (Eastbourne) Ltd* v. *Cooper* [1941] AC 108, 137, HL; similarly, *Owen Pell Ltd* v. *Bindi (London) Ltd* [2008] EWHC 1420 (TCC); [2008] BLR 436, at [10] (Frances Kirkham, sitting as a Deputy High Court Judge).

99   [2009] UKPC 10; [2009] 2 All ER 1127; [2009] BCC 433, at [25].

100   *Attorney-General for Belize* v. *Belize Telecom Ltd* [2009] UKPC 10; [2009] 2 All ER 1127; [2009] BCC 433, at [21].

(1995) and (ii) the Court of Appeal in *Ali* v. *Christian Salvesen* (1997).[101] Those earlier authorities rightly emphasise the need for a very cautious process when implying terms into written contracts. As Bingham LJ said in the *Philips* case (1995): 'it is tempting for the court then to fashion a term which will reflect the merits of the situation as they then appear. Tempting, but wrong.'[102]

In *Yam Seng Pte Ltd* v. *International Trade Corp Ltd* (2013) Leggatt J noted that implied terms will be more readily discovered if the written contract is 'skeletal'.[103]

The full text of Bingham LJ's statement in the *Philips* case is as follows:[104]

The courts' usual role in contractual interpretation [of written contracts] is . . . to attribute the true meaning to the language in which the parties themselves have expressed their contract. The implication of contract terms involves a different and altogether more ambitious undertaking: the interpolation of terms to deal with matters for which, *ex hypothesi*, the parties themselves have made no provision.

Bingham LJ added:

It is because the implication of terms is so potentially intrusive that the law imposes strict constraints on the exercise of this extraordinary power . . . The question of whether a term should be implied, and if so what, almost inevitably arises after a crisis has been reached in the performance of the contract. So the court comes to the task of implication with the benefit of hindsight, and it is tempting for the court then to fashion a term which will reflect the merits of the situation as they then appear. Tempting, but wrong.'[105]

In fact, in the wake of *Attorney-General for Belize* v. *Belize Telecom Ltd* (2009), English courts were quick to reaffirm that terms implied in fact are found only where they are obviously appropriate or necessary. Sir Anthony Clarke MR said in *Mediterranean Salvage & Towage Ltd* v. *Seamar Trading & Commerce Inc. ('The Reborn')* (2009):[106]

---

101   [1997] 1 All ER 721, 726, CA.
102   [1995] EMLR 472, 481, CA, *per* Bingham LJ (adopted by Jacob LJ in *R Griggs* v. *Evans (No. 1)* [2005] EWCA Civ 11; [2005] FSR 31, at [13], and by Lightman J in *Ray* v. *Classic FM plc* [1998] FSR 622, 641); for other cases concerning the reluctance to find an implied term when the express terms already cover the relevant topic, and for similar judicial statements, see *Jackson* v. *Dear* [2013] EWCA Civ 89; [2014] 1 BCLC 186, at [31], quoting *Aspdin* v. *Austin* (1844) 5 QB 671 at 684, *per* Lord Denman CJ; and quoting MacKinnon LJ in *Broome* v. *Parkless Co-Operative Society etc.* [1940] 1 All ER 603, 612. Similarly, *Luxor (Eastbourne) Ltd* v. *Cooper* [1941] AC 108, 137, HL, *per* Lord Wright; *Mid Essex Hospital Services NHS Trust* v. *Compass Group UK and Ireland Ltd (t/a Medirest)* [2013] EWCA Civ 200; [2013] BLR 265, at [92]; *ServicePower Asia Pacific Pty Ltd* v. *ServicePower Business Solutions Ltd* [2009] EWHC 179 (Ch); [2010] 1 All ER (Comm) 238, at [25] ff, William Trower QC; *Ali* v. *Christian Salvesen* [1997] 1 All ER 721, 726, CA.
103   [2013] EWHC 111 (QB); [2013] 1 All ER (Comm) 1321; [2013] 1 Lloyd's Rep 526, at [161]: 'the Agreement is a skeletal document which does not attempt to specify the parties' obligations in any detail. In relation to such a document it is easier than in the case of a detailed and professionally drafted contract to suppose that a part of the bargain has not been expressly stated.'
104   *Philips* case, [1995] EMLR 472, 481, CA, *per* Bingham LJ.
105   For endorsement, Lord Grabiner, 'The Iterative Process of Contractual Interpretation' (2012) 128 LQR 41, 60–1.
106   [2009] EWCA Civ 531; [2009] 2 Lloyd's Rep 639, at [18]. Endorsed in: *Proton Energy Group SA* v. *Orlen Liuteva* [2013] EWHC 2872 (Comm); [2014] 1 All ER (Comm) 972; [2014] 1 Lloyd's Rep 100, at [43] and [44], Judge Mackie QC; *Groveholt Ltd* v. *Hughes* [2010] EWCA Civ 538, at [45], *per* Arden LJ; see also *Re Coroin Ltd* [2013] EWCA Civ 781; [2014] BCC 14; [2013] 2 BCLC 583, at [84] (and *Stena Line Ltd* v. *Merchant Navy Ratings Pension Fund Trustees Ltd* [2011] EWCA Civ 543; [2011] Pensions LR 223, at [36] to [41]), on which see text below; R. Hooley, 'Implied Terms after *Belize*' [2014] CLJ 315, 316 notes the plethora of cases in which the *Belize* case has been cited, but the jury is still out on the case's importance.

The significance of both *Liverpool City Council* v. *Irwin*[107] and the *Philips Electronique* case[108] is that they both stress the importance of the test of necessity. Is the proposed implied term necessary to make the contract work? That seems to me to be an entirely appropriate question to ask in considering whether a term should be implied on the assumed facts in this case.

(Admittedly, that comment involves an elision of terms implied in law and in fact, and the touchstone of necessity is applicable only to terms implied in fact, whereas wider factors regulate implied terms of law.)

However, in *Re Coroin Ltd* (2013) Arden LJ was more positive concerning Lord Hoffmann's remarks in the *Belize* case, preferring to see the process of implying terms in fact as rooted in the holistic task of placing the written contract in context and effectuating the parties' reasonable expectations:[109]

the meaning and effect of the process of testing necessity for the purposes of an implied term is not an exercise to be carried out in a manner detached from the reasonable expectations of the parties to the particular agreement being interpreted. In that way, the Common Law continues to insist in this field on party autonomy as a key principle of contract law.

There is a thin line between giving meaning to explicit words and implying a missing term by way of reasonable construction.[110] Lord Grabiner QC, a highly experienced English commercial advocate, offers a sensible compromise in this passage:[111]

the court should not fill a perceived gap in the contract unless, without doing so, the contract will not work. The law of implication is properly within the superstructure of interpretation, but it is an intrusive process. The starting point should be an assumption that no term will be implied if the express terms of the contract produce a result that is workable.

4. IMPLIED TERMS: CUSTOM OR TRADE USAGE

13.17 A term can be implied to reflect the custom of a locality or the usage of a particular trade[112] and, as Parke B's decision in *Hutton* v. *Warren* (1836) shows,[113] this is possible even though

107 [1977] AC 239, HL.
108 [1995] EMLR 472, CA; Sir Bernard Rix, 'Lord Bingham's Contributions to Commercial Law', in M. Andenas and D. Fairgrieve (eds.), *Tom Bingham and the Transformation of the Law: A Liber Amicorum* (Oxford, 2009), 675.
109 [2013] EWCA Civ 781; [2014] BCC 14; [2013] 2 BCLC 583, at [84]; and citing her longer discussion of the *Belize* case in *Stena Line Ltd* v. *Merchant Navy Ratings Pension Fund Trustees Ltd* [2011] EWCA Civ 543; [2011] Pensions LR 223, at [36] to [41], where she had said at [41]: 'the process of interpretation is an objective one; the court does not ask what the parties intended any more that it asks what it would have been reasonable for them to agree. [And there is no scope for interpretation] by reference to the views of a reasonable bystander or of one of the parties to the document.'
110 *Aspect Contracts (Asbestos) Ltd* v. *Higgins Construction plc* [2013] EWCA 1541; [2014] 1 WLR 1220, at [11] to [13], *per* Longmore LJ (relevant right held to be 'as close being explicit as it is possible to be', at [12]).
111 Lord Grabiner, 'The Iterative Process of Contractual Interpretation' (2012) 128 LQR 41.
112 R. Goode, 'Usage and its Reception in Transnational Commercial Law' (1997) 46 ICLQ 1–36. *Liverpool City Council* v. *Irwin* [1977] AC 239, 253, HL, *per* Lord Wilberforce; *Baker* v. *Black Sea & Baltic General Insurance Co. Ltd* [1998] 1 WLR 974, 983–4, HL, 979–80, 982–4, HL; *Turner* v. *Royal Bank of Scotland plc* [1999] 2 All ER (Comm) 664, CA.
113 (1836) 1 M & W 466; 150 ER 517.

the contract is in writing or it is a formal deed (5.03). This is because implied terms are an exception to the 'parol evidence rule'[114] (that rule operates in general to exclude evidence aimed at varying or supplementing written terms: see 12.02).

13.18 The relevant market usage must be 'universal and acknowledged' (as the House of Lords said in *Baker* v. *Black Sea & Baltic General Insurance Co. Ltd* (1998)).[115] Ungoed-Thomas J, in the *Cunliffe-Owen* case (1967),[116] set out five criteria to govern recognition of an implied term based on custom:

(1) The custom must be 'notorious'. In other words, the custom must be so readily ascertainable that the parties can be taken to have assented to it. For example, in *Turner* v. *Royal Bank of Scotland plc* (1999), a banking practice was held not to be notorious:[117] the relevant practice entailed banks divulging confidential information concerning their clients' accounts to third parties regarding creditworthiness.

(2) The custom must be 'certain', that is, clearly established.

(3) The custom must be 'reasonable'.[118]

(4) The custom must not be inconsistent with the contract's written terms: as the maxim states, *expressum facit cessare tacitum* ('what is spelt out overrides what is implicit').[119] This point was acknowledged by the House of Lords in the *Leopold Walford* case (1919).[120]

(5) The custom must be perceived as binding in law. As the Court of Appeal held in the *General Reinsurance Corporation* case (1983), mere regularity of conduct is not enough, because it might be an expression of courtesy or concession.[121]

13.19 Establishing a custom is a mixed question of fact and law.[122] Resort will often be had to experts to establish the requisite 'continuity of acts'.[123] A pattern of conduct can be difficult to prove if (as can often occur) expert opinion is sharply divided.[124] Questions might also arise not on whether a custom exists but on its precise ambit.[125] Finally, the concept of 'trade usage' can be employed to justify incorporation of terms into a transaction between businessmen. On this basis, the Court of Appeal in *British Crane Hire Corporation Ltd* v. *Ipswich Plant Hire Ltd* (1975)[126] held that the claimant's standard written term, which

114 M & W report, *ibid.*, at 475.
115 [1998] 1 WLR 974, 983–4, HL, *per* Lord Lloyd.
116 *Cunliffe-Owen* v. *Teather & Greenwood* [1967] 1 WLR 1421, 1438–9, Ungoed-Thomas J (concerning customs of the London Stock Exchange).
117 [1999] 2 All ER (Comm) 664, CA.
118 *Robinson* v. *Mollett* (1875) LR 7 HL 802, 836–8, HL.
119 *Johnstone* v. *Bloomsbury Health Authority* [1992] 1 QB 333, CA (13.07, 13.20), noted by A. Weir, [1991] CLJ 397; adopted in *McLory* v. *Post Office* [1993] 1 All ER 457, 462D, David Neuberger QC, sitting as a Deputy High Court Judge.
120 *Les Affréteurs Réunis SA* v. *Leopold Walford (London) Ltd* [1919] AC 801, HL (cf *ibid.*, 808, for Lord Birkenhead's doubt concerning this custom).
121 *General Reinsurance Corporation* v. *Forsakringsaktiebologet Fennia Patria* [1983] QB 856, 874, CA, *per* Slade LJ (custom in insurance market merely matter of 'grace' and so non-binding).
122 *Cunliffe-Owen* v. *Teather & Greenwood* [1967] 1 WLR 1421, 1438B, Ungoed-Thomas J.
123 *Ibid.*, at 1438D–E.
124 E.g. *Libyan Arab Foreign Bank* v. *Bankers Trust Co.* [1989] QB 728, 755–60, *per* Staughton J (foreign bond market); R. Goode, (1997) 46 ICLQ 1, 8–9.
125 *Cunliffe-Owen* case, [1967] 1 WLR 1421, 1456E.
126 [1975] QB 303, CA.

was widespread in the industry, had been impliedly incorporated into an urgently concluded oral contract of hire (provided the relevant term is 'reasonable'):[127] '[B]oth parties knew quite well that conditions were habitually imposed by the supplier of these machines: and both parties knew the substance of those conditions.'[128]

5. IMPLIED TERMS AND THE TORT OF NEGLIGENCE

13.20 In many situations governed by contract, the tort of negligence will also impose liability for personal injury, physical damage or even economic loss arising from careless performance of a duty assumed by the defendant. This tort and contractual implied terms often provide the same or a very similar regime of rights and duties in many standard relationships. For example, the Court of Appeal's decision in *Johnstone* v. *Bloomsbury Health Authority* (1992)[129] (13.08) concerned the position of junior doctors required to work very long hours within the National Health Service when qualifying to practise. Leggatt LJ and Browne-Wilkinson V-C noted the following principle contained in the *Tai Hing* case (1979) (13.21): '[The parties' mutual obligations in tort] cannot be any greater than those to be found expressly or by necessary implication in their contract.'[130]

13.21 But, at any rate in commercial disputes concerning economic loss, the courts are wary of permitting the law of negligence to outflank the settled regime of responsibility prescribed by implied terms. The courts do not permit tortious liability to operate inconsistently with the relevant contractual matrix of implied terms, as the Privy Council's decision in *Tai Hing Ltd* v. *Liu Chong Hing Bank* (1979) shows.[131] The law of contract requires a bank's customer (1) to exercise care in drawing cheques so as not to facilitate fraud or forgery, and (2) to inform the bank at once of any unauthorised cheques of which he becomes aware. These two propositions were long ago fixed as implied terms.[132] Against this background, Lord Scarman protested in the *Tai Hing* case that it would be undesirable for the tort of negligence to muddy these clear contractual waters by imposing a wider duty of care upon a customer.[133]

13.22 Similarly, Lord Bridge in the *Scally* case (1992)[134] (13.08 at (4)) said that it would be 'positively misleading' to use the tort of negligence to determine whether an employer owed a responsibility to point out to an employee the financial benefit in taking advantage of a recently agreed collective agreement relating to pension entitlement. Instead, this issue fell under the rubric of contractual 'implied terms'.

---

127   *Ibid.*, at 314.
128   *Ibid.*, at 311B.
129   [1992] 1 QB 333, 340G, CA; noted by A. Weir, [1991] CLJ 397.
130   *Ibid.*, at 347E, 350A, CA.
131   [1979] AC 91, PC.
132   *Ibid.*, at 108.
133   *Ibid.*, at 107.
134   *Scally* v. *Southern Health Board* [1992] 1 AC 294, 303–4, HL.

6. IMPLIED TERMS AND GOOD FAITH

13.23 This topic is examined at 21.15 ff.[135]

7. IMPLIED TERMS AND THE DOCTRINES OF MISTAKE AND FRUSTRATION

13.24 The interplay between these doctrines and the concept of an 'implied term' has a long judicial and scholarly history. As for the doctrine of frustration (on which see Chapter 16), Blackburn J in the first modern decision, *Taylor* v. *Caldwell* (1863),[136] based the doctrine's operation upon an implied term. But this theory was decisively rejected by Lord Radcliffe in *Davis Contractors Ltd* v. *Fareham Urban District Council* (1956)[137] and by Lord Denning MR in *'The Eugenia'* (1964)[138] as stretching reality and introducing a fictitious 'tacit consent' (both passages quoted at 16.03). As for 'mistake', the implied term approach to cases of *initial impossibility* and other pre-formation errors took longer to dislodge. However, Lord Phillips in *'The Great Peace'* emphatically rejected the implied theory of mistake (as noted at 10.06). He said that 'the theory of the implied term is as unrealistic when considering common mistake as when considering frustration', and added: 'Avoidance of a contract on the ground of common mistake results from a rule of law.'[139]

QUESTIONS

(1) What are the three types of implied term?

(2) In what sense do policy factors influence recognition of terms implied in law?

(3) What are the two tests for terms implied in fact, and which is dominant?

(4) Consider the merits of the terms implied in the following cases: *Equitable Life Assurance Co. Ltd* v. *Hyman* (2002) and *Paragon Finance plc* v. *Nash* (2002).

(5) What is the significance of Lord Hoffmann's remarks concerning implied terms and written contracts in the Privy Council in *Attorney-General for Belize* v. *Belize Telecom Ltd* (2009)?

Selected further reading

General

R. Austen-Baker, *Implied Terms in English Contract Law* (Cheltenham, 2011)

R. Austen-Baker, 'Implied Terms in English Contract Law', in L. DiMatteo, Q. Zhou, S. Saintier, K. Rowley (eds.), *Commercial Contract Law: Transatlantic Perspectives* (Cambridge, 2014), chapter 10

---

135   See, notably, H. G. Collins, 'Implied Terms: the Foundation in Good Faith and Fair Dealing' (2014) 67 CLP 297–331.

136   (1863) 3 B & S 826; 122 ER 309.

137   [1956] AC 696, HL.

138   *Ocean Tramp Tankers Corporation* v. *V/O Sovfracht ('The Eugenia')* [1964] 2 QB 226, 238, CA.

139   *Great Peace Shipping Ltd* v. *Tsavliris Salvage (International) Ltd* [2003] QB 679, CA, at [73].

Terms judicially implied in law

E. Peden, 'Policy Concerns Behind Implication of Terms in Law' (2001) 117 LQR 459–76, especially
467 ff

Terms implied in fact

R. Hooley, 'Implied Terms after *Belize*' [2014] CLJ 315–49

J. McCaughran, 'Implied Terms: The Journey of the Man on the Clapham Omnibus' [2011] CLJ
607–22

A. Phang, 'The Challenge of Principled Gap-Filling: a Study of Implied Terms in a Comparative
Context' [2014] JBL 263–312

Wider perspective of commercial reasonableness

R. Hooley, 'Controlling Contractual Discretion' [2013] CLJ 65–90

Lord Steyn, 'Contract Law: Fulfilling the Reasonable Expectations of Honest Men' (1997) 113 LQR
433, 442

Chapter contents

14

Interpretation and rectification of written contracts

1. INTRODUCTION

14.01 Summary of main points

(1) *Modern foundations.*[1] 'Interpretation [of written contracts] is the ascertainment of meaning which the document would convey to a reasonable person having all the background knowledge which would reasonably have been available to the parties in the situation in which they were at

---

1 *Main textbooks*: R. Calnan, *Principles of Contractual Interpretation* (Oxford, 2014); K. Lewison, *Interpretation of Contracts* (5th edn, London, 2011); G. McMeel, *The Construction of Contracts: Interpretation, Implication and Rectification* (2nd edn, Oxford, 2011) (see also McMeel's article in (2011) *European Business Law Review* 437–49; and McMeel, 'The Principles and Policies of Contractual Construction', in A. Burrows and E. Peel (eds.), *Contract Terms* (Oxford, 2007), chapter 3); C. Mitchell, *Interpretation of Contracts* (London, 2007); from an Australian perspective, J. W. Carter, *The Construction of Commercial Contracts* (Oxford, 2013) (and see J. W. Carter, 'Context and Literalism in Construction' (2014) 31 JCL 100–19 (surveying English, Australian, Singaporean and USA law).

Other discussion: Lord Bingham, 'A New Thing Under the Sun: The Interpretation of Contract and the ICS Decision' (2008) 12 ELR 374; R. Buxton, '"Construction" and Rectification After *Chartbrook*' [2010] CLJ 253; J. Cartwright, 'Interpretation of English Law in Light of the Common Frame of Reference' in H. Snijders and S. Vogenauer (eds.), *Content and Meaning of National Law in the Context of Transnational Law* (Munich, 2009); Lord Grabiner, 'The Iterative Process of Contractual Interpretation' (2012) 128 LQR 41; P. Hellwege, 'Objectivity and Subjectivity in Contract Interpretation', in A. Burrows, D. Johnston, R. Zimmermann (eds.), *Judge and Jurist: Essays in Memory of Lord Rodger of Earlsferry* (Oxford, 2013), 455–72; Lord Hoffmann, 'The Intolerable Wrestle with Words and Meanings' (1997) *South Africa Law Journal* 656; J. Kostritsky, in L. DiMatteo, Q. Zhou, S. Saintier, K. Rowley (eds.), *Commercial Contract Law: Transatlantic Perspectives* (Cambridge, 2014), chapter 11; E. McKendrick, in S. Worthington (ed.), *Commercial Law and Commercial Practice* (Oxford, 2003); D. McLauchlan, 'Contract Interpretation: What is it About?' (2009) 31 *Sydney Law Review* 5; D. McLauchlan, 'Common Intention and Contract Interpretation' [2011] LMCLQ 30–50; D. McLauchlan, 'Construction and Implication: in Defence of *Belize Telecom*' [2014] LMCLQ 203–40; C. Mitchell, 'Obligations in Commercial Contracts: A Matter of Law or Interpretation?' (2012) 65 CLP 455–88; Lord Nicholls, 'My Kingdom for a Horse: the Meaning of Words' (2005) 121 LQR 577; Lord Phillips, 'The Interpretation of Contracts and Statutes' (2002) 68 *Arbitration* 17; Spigelmann CJ, 'From Text to Contract: Contemporary Contractual Interpretation' (2007) 81 ALJ 322; Sir Christopher Staughton, 'How Do The Courts Interpret Commercial Contracts?' [1999] CLJ 303; C. Valcke, 'On Comparing French and English Contract Law: Insights from Social Contract Theory' (2009) JCL 69–95 (cited as 'illuminating' by Lord Hoffmann in the *Chartbrook* case [2009] UKHL 38; [2009] 1 AC 1001, at [39]); C. Valcke, 'Contractual Interpretation at Common Law and Civil Law: An Exercise in Comparative Legal Rhetoric', in J. W. Neyers, R. Bronaugh, S. G. A. Pitel, *Exploring Contract Law* (Oxford, 2009), 77 ff; S. Vogenauer, 'Interpretation of Contracts: Concluding Comparative Observations', in A. Burrows and E. Peel (eds.), *Contract Terms* (Oxford, 2007), chapter 7.

the time of the contract' (Lord Hoffmann in the *Investors Compensation Scheme* case (1998): see the full quotation at 14.02).

In *Marley* v. *Rawlings* (2014) Lord Neuberger summarised the position concerning interpretation of written contracts.[2]

> When interpreting a contract, the court is concerned to find the intention of the party or parties, and it does this by identifying the meaning of the relevant words, (a) in the light of (i) the natural and ordinary meaning of those words, (ii) the overall purpose of the document, (iii) any other provisions of the document, (iv) the facts known or assumed by the parties at the time that the document was executed, and (v) common sense, but (b) ignoring subjective evidence of any party's intentions.

(2) *Criteria.* The criteria are 'objectivity' and 'commercial common sense', but the latter is not to be abused in order to rewrite contracts in the interests of abstract fairness.

(3) *Sources:*

    (a) *Factual matrix and background information.* The courts are not tied to the literal wording of the written contract, but can consider the parties' common intention against the background of the transaction. However, in making this extended search, Lord Hoffmann in the *BCCI* case (2001)[3] (14.12) said that courts and arbitrators should not allow parties to adduce excessive quantities of background information.

    (b) *Background information must be accessible.* In the *Sigma* case (2009, 14.13) Lord Collins (with the support of Lords Mance and Hope) disapproved[4] too broad a search for background information (see (a) above) when, as in the *Sigma* case itself, the parties to the relevant transaction might not have been present at its birth, and had instead become second-hand or more remote recipients of others' contractual text which had been in circulation in the relevant financial market.

    (c) *Bar on reference to negotiation evidence.* When seeking to interpret written contracts, a party cannot adduce, without his opponent's permission, the parties' prior negotiations. Five reasons have been suggested as supports for this bar (14.16): (i) avoidance of 'uncertainty and unpredictability', (ii) the fact that interested third parties cannot be guaranteed access to such negotiation history, (iii) such dealings are notoriously shifting and so such evidence would be unhelpful, (iv) one-sided impressions might contaminate the inquiry so that the objective approach to interpretation (see (1) above) would be undermined; (v) 'sophisticated and knowledgeable negotiators would be tempted to lay a paper trail of self-serving documents'.

    (d) *But negotiation evidence admissible to support a plea of rectification.* This evidential bar does not apply to the equitable remedy of rectification (14.27). And so claims for rectification are often brought in conjunction with a pleading based on ordinary 'interpretation' (as in the *Chartbrook* case itself).[5]

(4) *'Corrective construction'.*[6] The House of Lords in *Chartbrook Ltd* v. *Persimmon Homes Ltd* (2009) held that a court can 'construe' by wholly recasting a relevant phrase or portion of a

---

2   [2014] UKSC 2; [2014] 2 WLR 213.
3   [2001] 1 AC 251, at [39], HL.
4   *Sigma* case, [2009] UKSC 2; [2010] 1 All ER 571; [2010] BCC 40, at [35] to [37].
5   [2009] UKHL 38; [2009] 1 AC 1101.
6   The phrase adopted by Lewison LJ in *Cherry Tree Investments Ltd* v. *Landmain Ltd* [2012] EWCA Civ 736; [2013] Ch 305, at [97] and also used in Arden LJ's judgment.

written contract when it is obvious that the drafting has gone awry and the parties' true pre-formation shared meaning can be ascertained by consideration of the commercial purpose of the agreement and internal hints in the text: 14.22 ff. Such 'corrective construction' has a similar function to the more formal equitable doctrine of 'rectification' (see (5) below), because both doctrines have the effect of revising a document. The safer course is to plead both 'construction' and 'rectification'.

(5) *Limits upon judicial construction of written terms.* Lord Mustill in *Charter Reinsurance Co. Ltd v. Fagan* (1997) (14.21) said that it is illegitimate for courts or arbitrators to 'force upon the words a meaning which they cannot fairly bear', since this would be 'to substitute for the bargain actually made one which the court believes could better have been made'.

(6) *Rectification: an equitable remedy.* This remedy allows the court to declare that a written contract should be reconstituted because by joint mistake it fails to reflect the parties' pre-formation 'common continuing intention'. The elements are: 'the parties had a common continuing intention . . . at the time of execution . . . [and that intention is] to be established objectively, that is to say by reference to what an objective observer would have thought the intentions of the parties to be; and by mistake, the instrument did not reflect that common intention' (the *Daventry* case (2011) *per* Etherton LJ cited at 14.28). However, a mere unilateral error does *not* support a claim for rectification, unless the other party's position is wholly unmeritorious, in particular, because he has dishonestly acquiesced in the other's mistake (14.31 ff).

2. INTERPRETATION: MODERN FOUNDATIONS

14.02 *The* Investors Compensation Scheme *(1998) principles.* The following passage in Lord Hoffmann's leading speech in *Investors Compensation Scheme* (1998) is seminal.[7]

(i) Interpretation is the ascertainment of meaning which the document would convey to a reasonable person having all the background knowledge which would reasonably have been available to the parties in the situation in which they were at the time of the contract.

(ii) The background [has been described] as the 'matrix of fact', but this phrase is, if anything, an understated description of what the background may include, subject to the requirement that it should have been reasonably available to the parties and to the exception to be mentioned next, it includes absolutely anything which would have affected the way in which the language of the document would have been understood by a reasonable man.

(iii) The law excludes from the admissible background the previous negotiations of the parties and the declarations of subjective intent.[8] The law makes this distinction for reasons of practical policy and, in this respect only, legal interpretation differs from the way

---

7 [1998] 1 WLR 896, 912–13, HL; and this statement was treated by the UK Supreme Court as canonical in *Re Sigma Finance Corporation (in administrative receivership)* [2009] UKSC 2; [2010] 1 All ER 571; [2010] BCC 40, at [10].

8 *Prenn v. Simmonds* [1971] 1 WLR 1381, 1383 G, HL.

we would interpret utterances in ordinary life. The boundaries of this exception are unclear. But this is not the occasion on which to explore them.

(iv) The meaning which a document (or any other utterance) would convey to a reasonable man is not the same thing as the meaning of words. The meaning of words is a matter of dictionaries and grammars; the meaning of the document is what the parties using those words against the relevant background would reasonably have been understood to mean. The background may not merely enable the reasonable man to choose between the possible meanings of words which are ambiguous but even (as occasionally happens in ordinary life) to conclude that the parties must, for whatever reason, have used the wrong words or syntax.

(v) (a) The 'rule' that words should be given their 'natural and ordinary meaning' reflects the common sense proposition that we do not easily accept that people have made linguistic mistakes, particularly in formal documents. (b) On the other hand, if one would nevertheless conclude from the background that something must have gone wrong with the language, the law does not require judges to attribute to the parties an intention which they plainly could not have had. [Letters (a) and (b) added here]

As for (i) to (iv), the seeds for this contextual approach had been sown by Lord Wilberforce in the 1970s, as Lord Hoffmann acknowledged.[9]

Judicial restatements of the ICS principles. These have been restated by several judges (with counsel's assistance): (1) Longmore LJ in *Absalon* v. *TRCU Ltd* (2005) (approving the four-fold summary adopted by Aikens J at first instance);[10] (2) Simon J in *HHR Pascal BV* v. *W2005 Puppet II BV* (2009);[11] (3) Walker J in *British American Insurance (Kenya) Ltd* v. *Matelec SAL* (2013);[12] (4) Peter Prescott QC (sitting as a Deputy High Court judge) in the *Oxonica* case (2008)[13] (attractively surveying this topic's development); and (5) Aikens LJ in the *Barbudev* case (2012).[14]

14.03 *Judicial law.* All the rules governing interpretation of written contracts, as well as the equitable doctrine of rectification, are the creature of judicial decision-making resulting mostly from appellate[15] review of first instance judgments or arbitral awards in which

---

9   Lord Hoffmann in *Kirin-Amgen Inc* v. *Hoechst Marion Roussel Ltd* [2004] UKHL 46; [2005] 1 All ER 667; [2005] RPC 9 (for a magisterial overview at [27] to [35]), noting at [30]: 'The speeches of Lord Wilberforce in *Prenn* v. *Simmonds* [1971] 1 WLR 1381 and *Reardon Smith Line Ltd* v. *Yngvar Hansen-Tangen* [1976] 1 WLR 989 are milestones along this road.'
10   *Absalon* v. *TRCU Ltd* [2005] EWCA Civ 1586; [2006] 1 All ER (Comm) 375; [2006] 2 Lloyd's Rep 129 approving Aikens J in *Absalon* v. *TRCU Ltd* [2005] EWHC 1090 (Comm); [2005] 2 Lloyd's Rep 735, at [24] and [25].
11   [2009] EWHC 2771 (Comm); [2010] 1 All ER (Comm) 399, at [35].
12   [2013] EWHC 3278 (Comm), at [46].
13   [2008] EWHC 2127 (Patents Court); not disturbed on appeal, [2009] EWCA Civ 668.
14   *Barbudev* v. *Eurocom Cable Management Bulgaria Eood* [2012] EWCA Civ 548; [2012] 2 All ER (Comm) 963, at [31], noting *Rainy Sky* v. *Kookmin Bank* [2011] 1 WLR 2900 at [21] *per* Lord Clarke of Stone-cum-Ebony JSC.
15   On the system of appeal in English court proceedings, *Andrews on Civil Processes* (Cambridge, 2013), vol. 1, *Court Proceedings*, at chapter 15; on appeals from arbitral awards on points of English law, *ibid.*, vol. 2, *Arbitration and Mediation*, paras. 18.67 ff.

English contract law has been applied.[16] This is the most important and dynamic topic in English contract law.

> If English law governs the relevant agreement, interpretation of (wholly) 'written contracts' (including electronic documents)[17] is a question of law,[18] whereas interpretation of contracts not wholly contained in writing (whether oral, or part written and part oral) is a 'matter of fact'. Appeal courts have power to review first instance errors of law, but in general defer to findings of fact.[19]
>
> As for the equitable remedy of rectification (see 14.25 below), a leading textbook notes:[20]
>
> > although the applicable principles underpinning rectification are a question of law, whether or not a particular instrument should be rectified is a question of fact; [whereas] the correct construction of a particular written contract is a question of law. Thus appeals concerning interpretation are much more common than appeals on the issue of rectification.

14.04 *Interpretation and other contractual doctrines.*

(1) *The parol evidence rule.*[21] This rule (12.02) concerns attempts to make textual changes by reference to information external to the written contract. It thus functionally overlaps with the exclusionary rule barring reference to pre-formation communications for the purpose of interpreting contractual written language.[22]

(2) *Interpretation and implied terms.* As explained at 13.16, the courts can imply a term into a written contract, but they will be slow to do so if the contract is closely drafted and made between parties of roughly equal bargaining power.

(3) *Overlapping legal submissions.* It is quite common (on the principle that pleaders will throw everything, including the kitchen sink, at a case) for the court to be required to consider a miscellany of doctrines, including interpretation, rectification, implied terms, collateral warranties and principles of mistake (for example, Judge Richard Seymour QC in *Wimpole Theatre (a firm)* v. *JJ Goodman Ltd* (2012) summarises a mass of connected doctrines).[23]

---

16   In the case of arbitration references where the 'seat' is within England and Wales, the High Court in London must first give permission for an appeal on a point of English law to proceed to the High Court: sections 69(2) and 69(3) of the Arbitration Act 1996 (England and Wales).

17   *Chitty on Contracts* (31st edn, London, 2012), 12–048.

18   *Ibid.,* 12–046.

19   *Andrews on Civil Processes* (Cambridge, 2013), vol. 1, *Court Proceedings,* at 15.12 and 15.72 ff.

20   *Snell's Principles of Equity* (32nd edn, London, 2010), 16.11.

21   *Chitty on Contracts* (31st edn, London, 2012), 12–096 ff; *Treitel* (13th edn, London, 2011), 6–013 ff; Law Commission, 'The Parol Evidence Rule' (Law Commission No. 154, Cmnd 9700, 1986) (noted G. Marston [1986] CLJ 192); D. W. McLauchlan, *The Parol Evidence Rule* (1976); R Stevens, 'Objectivity, Mistake and the Parol Evidence Rule', in A. Burrows and E. Peel (eds.), *Contract Terms* (Oxford, 2007), chapter 6, at 107 ff. For a highly sceptical discussion of this rule, G. McMeel, *The Construction of Contracts: Interpretation, Implication and Rectification* (2nd edn, Oxford, 2011), 15–08 ff.

22   Cf the undifferentiated presentation of rules (i) to (iii) in G. McMeel, *ibid.,* 5.30.

23   [2012] EWHC 1600 (QB) at [35] to [56].

3. INTERPRETATION: CRITERIA

14.05 *Two criteria.* The criteria are 'objectivity' and 'commercial common sense', but the latter is not to be abused as a licence to rewrite contracts in the interests of abstract fairness. In England the 'objective principle of agreement' precludes reference to a party's undisclosed and personal understanding of the written terms' meaning and effect. The courts should always construe written contracts with sensitivity to business 'common sense', and not just in cases of emergency when seeking to avoid an absurd or wholly unreasonable construction. However, commercial common sense is not a warrant for rewriting a contract to achieve a 'fairer result' (even assuming that this can be perceived): where there is no ambiguity, the court should give effect to the contract's clear meaning.

14.06 *Objectivity.* In England the 'objective principle of agreement' precludes reference to a party's undisclosed and personal understanding of the written terms' meaning and effect.[24] Lord Hoffmann, in the *Investors Compensation Scheme* case (1998), said: 'Interpretation [of written contracts] is the ascertainment of meaning which the document would convey to a reasonable person having all the background knowledge which would reasonably have been available to the parties in the situation in which they were at the time of the contract.'[25]

On this fundamental topic the English approach is in vivid contrast with that adopted within other jurisdictions where the search is for the parties' actual, as distinct from imputed, intention.[26]

In *Kirin-Amgen Inc* v. *Hoechst Marion Roussel Ltd* (2004) Lord Hoffmann elaborated upon objective ascertainment of meaning:[27]

Construction, whether of a patent[28] or any other document, is of course not directly concerned with what the author meant to say. There is no window into the mind of the

---

24 *Reardon Smith Line Limited* v. *Hansen Tangen* [1976] 1 WLR 989, 996, HL, *per* Lord Wilberforce.
25 [1998] 1 WLR 896, 912–3, HL.
26 For comparative observations on interpretation of contracts, M. J. Bonell, 'The UNIDROIT Principles and CISG – Sources of Inspiration for English Courts?' [2006] 11 *Uniform Law Review* 305; M. J. Bonell (ed.), *The UNIDROIT Principles in Practice: Case Law and Bibliography on the UNIDROIT Principles of International Commercial Contracts* (2nd edn, Ardsley, NY, 2006), 144; E. Clive in H. MacQueen and R. Zimmermann (eds.), *European Contract Law: Scots and South African Perspectives* (Edinburgh, 2006), chapter 7 at 183; E. A. Farnsworth, 'Comparative Contract Law' in M. Reimann and R. Zimmermann (eds.), *The Oxford Handbook of Comparative Law* (Oxford, 2006), chapter 28, at 920 ff.; C Valcke, 'On Comparing French and English Contract Law: Insights from Social Contract Theory' (2009) JCL 69–95; 'Contractual Interpretation: at Common Law and Civil Law: An Exercise in Comparative Legal Rhetoric' in J. W. Neyers, R. Bronaugh, S. G. A. Pitel (eds.), *Exploring Contract Law* (Oxford, 2009), 77–114; S. Vogenauer, 'Interpretation of Contracts: Concluding Comparative Observations', in A. Burrows and E. Peel (eds.), *Contract Terms* (Oxford, 2007), chapter 7; S. Vogenauer and J. Kleinheisterkamp (eds.), *Commentary on the UNIDROIT Principles of International Commercial Contracts* (Oxford, 2009), 311; K. Zweigert and H. Kötz, *An Introduction to Comparative Law* (trans. A. Weir, 3rd edn, Oxford, 1998), chapter 30 (although their discussion of English law is now out of date because of the developments in the present text).
27 In *Kirin-Amgen Inc* v. *Hoechst Marion Roussel Ltd* [2004] UKHL 46; [2005] 1 All ER 667; [2005] RPC 9, at [32], noting that: 'I have discussed these questions at some length in *Mannai Investment Co Ltd v. Eagle Star Life Assurance Co Ltd* [1997] A.C. 749 and *Investors Compensation Scheme Ltd v. West Bromwich Building Society* [1998] 1 W.L.R. 896.'
28 That case concerned a patent dispute, but this does not undermine the generality of this passage.

patentee or the author of any other document. Construction is objective in the sense that it is concerned with what a reasonable person to whom the utterance was addressed would have understood the author to be using the words to mean. Notice, however, that it is not, as is sometimes said, 'the meaning of the words the author used', but rather what the notional addressee would have understood the author to mean by using those words.

Lord Hoffmann continued in *Kirin-Amgen Inc* v. *Hoechst Marion Roussel Ltd* (2004):

> The meaning of words is a matter of convention, governed by rules, which can be found in dictionaries and grammars. What the author would have been understood to mean by using those words is not simply a matter of rules. It is highly sensitive to the context of, and background to, the particular utterance. It depends not only upon the words the author has chosen but also upon the identity of the audience he is taken to have been addressing and the knowledge and assumptions which one attributes to that audience.

It is normally impermissible for a party to produce evidence of the pre-contractual dealings – the negotiations – in order to elucidate the finally agreed terms.

To this last proposition there is a large exception when a party seeks the equitable remedy of rectification (14.25). In essence, rectification is an equitable remedy enabling the court to insert new words to reflect the pre-formation true consensus, objectively ascertained. Thus rectification enables the court to declare that the written terms must be altered if it is shown that in their final formulation of the contract's written terms, the parties have failed to reproduce accurately their prior and uninterrupted consensus. This consensus will be determined objectively. And it must have an outwardly discernible subsistence.

14.07 *Commercial common sense.* The courts should construe written instruments, including contracts, in a 'commercial' way, with sensitivity to business 'common sense'.[29] The courts need not wait until confronted by an extremely unreasonable or absurd documentary provision before adopting this perspective.[30] There are many statements supporting this need to consider business common sense.

(1) Lord Diplock said in *Antaios Cia Naviera SA* v. *Salen Rederierna AB* (1985):[31] 'if detailed semantic and syntactical analysis of words in a commercial contract is going to lead to a conclusion that flouts business common sense, it must be made to yield to business common sense.'

(2) Lord Steyn said in *Mannai Investment Co.* v. *Eagle Star Life Assurance* (1997):[32] 'Words are ... interpreted in the way in which a reasonable commercial person would construe them. And the standard of the reasonable commercial person is hostile to technical interpretations and undue emphasis on niceties of language.'

(3) Lord Bingham said in *'The Starsin'* (2003):[33]

> The court must of course construe the whole instrument before it in its factual context, and cannot ignore the terms of the contract. But it must seek to give effect to the contract as intended, so as not to frustrate the reasonable expectations of

29 *Antaios Cia Naviera SA* v. *Salen Rederierna AB* [1985] AC 191, 201, HL, *per* Lord Diplock.
30 *Rainy Sky* case [2011] UKSC 50; [2011] 1 WLR 2900, at [20].
31 [1985] AC 191, 201, HL.
32 [1997] AC 749, HL (a majority decision concerning a rent notice); P. V. Baker (1998) 114 LQR 55–62.
33 [2003] UKHL 12; [2004] 1 AC 715, at [12]; and see similar remarks at [10] (Lord Bingham noted *'The Okehampton'* [1913] P 173, 180, *per* Hamilton LJ (later Lord Sumner)).

businessmen. If an obviously inappropriate form is used, its language must be adapted to apply to the particular case.

(4) Lord Hope endorsed this approach in the Supreme Court in *Multi-Link Leisure* v. *North Lanarkshire* (2010),[34] noting that this was consistent with Lord Hoffmann's principles in *Investors' Compensation Scheme Ltd* v. *West Bromwich Building Society* (1998).[35]

(5) The Supreme Court has confirmed this approach in the *Rainy Sky* case (2011),[36] where Lord Clarke said:[37]

> It is not in my judgment necessary to conclude that, unless the most natural meaning of the words produces a result so extreme as to suggest that it was unintended, the court must give effect to that meaning ...
>
> If there are two possible constructions, the court is entitled to prefer the construction which is consistent with business common sense and to reject the other.

In the *Rainy Sky* case (2011)[38] the dispute involved interpretation of bonds. Those bonds, issued by a bank, concerned repayment by a shipyard of prepayments for the purchase of ships under construction. The bank contended that the relevant clause in these bonds did not cover the case where the payee could not make repayment to the purchaser because of the payee's insolvency. If so, the bonds would only cover a less obvious commercial failure to repay: the payee's *refusal*, although solvent, to repay when the payor has justifiably terminated the contract and is entitled to recover the payment, as specified in clause 2, quoted below.

The clauses stated:

[2] ... you [the payor/purchasers] are entitled, upon your ... termination, cancellation or rescission of the Contract or upon a Total Loss of the Vessel, to repayment of the pre-delivery instalments of the Contract Price paid by you prior to such termination or a Total Loss of the Vessel ...

[3] In consideration of your agreement to make the pre-delivery instalments under the Contract ... we [the bank] hereby, as primary obligor, irrevocably and unconditionally undertake to pay to you ... on your first written demand, all such sums due to you under the Contract.

The Supreme Court (reversing the Court of Appeal) held that the words 'all such sums' in clause 3 were not dependent upon clause 2. Instead clause 3 could be construed in favour of the purchaser: 'all such sums' would thus catch money which the payee did not repay because of the payee's insolvency.

Lord Clarke said:[39]

34 [2010] UKSC 47; [2011] 1 All ER 175, at [21]; decision criticised by D. McLauchlan, 'A Construction Conundrum?' [2011] LMCLQ 428–48.

35 [1998] 1 WLR 896, 913, HL.

36 *Rainy Sky SA* v. *Kookmin Bank* [2011] UKSC 50; [2011] 1 WLR 2900.

37 *Ibid.*, respectively at [20], [21], [40]; cited in *L Batley Pet Products Ltd* v. *North Lanarkshire Council* [2014] UKSC 27; [2014] 3 All ER 64, at [18].

38 *Rainy Sky SA* v. *Kookmin Bank* [2011] UKSC 50; [2011] 1 WLR 2900; noted P. S. Davies [2012] LMCLQ 26–9.

39 *Ibid.*, at [40].

> Since the language of paragraph [3] is capable of two meanings it is appropriate for the court to have regard to considerations of commercial common sense in resolving the question what a reasonable person would have understood the parties to have meant.

14.08 *Commercial common sense: not a licence to rewrite the contract in the interests of abstract fairness.* The Court of Appeal in *Procter and Gamble Co.* v. *Svenska Cellulosa Aktiebolaget SCA* (2012) emphasised that the *Rainy Sky* case is not a warrant for rewriting a contract to achieve a 'fairer result' (even assuming that this can be perceived): where there is no ambiguity, the court should give effect to the contract's clear meaning.[40]

> On the facts of the *Procter & Gamble* case, the court held that the parties had agreed that the price for an expensive industrial plant would be in Euros, but the payment of such sums would be in pounds. The parties had not agreed a fixed rate of conversion of Euros to pounds. After formation, the Euro/pound exchange rate moved disadvantageously for the buyer. But the buyer could not show, whether by a process of interpretation, implication of terms, or rectification, that there was a consensus that Euros were to be converted to pounds at the rate (favourable to the buyer) prevailing at the date of the contract, as distinct from the subsequent dates of delivery.
>
> One of the commercial documents exchanged by the parties bore an annotation giving a rate of exchange applicable at that date. But this was not intended to impose a fixed exchange rate. It merely recorded a process of calculation made on the spot at that juncture of the parties' dealings. In the absence of a fixed currency provision, the adverse currency movement was to be borne by the buyer, and it was not the court's task to save that party from this economic result.
>
> For another illustration of the court refusing to rewrite a contract in order to 'substitute a new and fairer bargain', see *Bashir* v. *Ali* (2011) (see the quotation at 14.24 below).[41]

4. INTERPRETATION: SOURCES

14.09 *Whole contract to be considered.* The principle that the whole contract must be considered when interpreting a particular clause, phrase or word is a cardinal feature of interpretation under English law: see, notably, the *Sigma* (2009: on which 14.13)[42] and the *Charter Reinsurance* (1997)[43] cases (see text immediately below). The same approach is recognised in the (non-binding) codes: PECL, *Principles of European Contract Law*, Article 5:105; and UNIDROIT's *Principles of International Commercial Contracts* (2010), Article 4.4.[44]

---

40 [2012] EWCA Civ 1413, at [22] and at [38], *per* Moore-Bick and Rix LJJ; see also *Ardagh* case [2013] EWCA Civ 900; [2014] STC 26, at [66].
41 [2011] EWCA Civ 707; [2011] 2 P & CR 12, at [39] and [40], *per* Etherton LJ.
42 *In Re Sigma Finance Corporation (in administrative receivership)* [2009] UKSC 2; [2010] 1 All ER 571; [2010] BCC 40.
43 Lord Mustill in *Charter Reinsurance Co. Ltd* v. *Fagan* [1997] AC 313, 384, HL, quoted in the *Sigma* case, *ibid.*, at [9].
44 3rd edition, 2010, text and comment, is available at: www.unidroit.org/english/principles/contracts/prin ciples2010/integralversionprinciples2010-e.pdf.

The House of Lords' decision in *Charter Reinsurance Co. Ltd* v. *Fagan* (1997)[45] demonstrates the pitfall of becoming attached to one's 'first blush' and seemingly 'common sense' reading of commercial words, without pausing more carefully to consider the entire contractual document (and its factual matrix: see 14.11) (and Lord Mustill's speech is magisterial).

The question was whether a reinsurer had agreed to indemnify the reinsured only if the latter's liability had accrued and been quantified and discharged by payment (the so-called 'actual disbursement' interpretation) or whether it was enough that the liability to indemnify had arisen and been quantified, without actual discharge of that liability (the liability to pay or finalised quantification interpretation). The semantic battle was fought over the words 'actually paid'.

The House of Lords held that a commercially sensitive reading of that phrase in this particular reinsurance agreement led to this conclusion (admittedly surprising, because it appears to be the very opposite of one's first understanding): the contract did not create a condition precedent to the reinsurer's liability that the reinsured should actually have discharged the relevant liability.

14.10 *Original assumptions.* Objectively determined, the original assumptions, including the parties' 'purposes and values', are relevant when seeking to give effect to the contract. Mance LJ said in *Debenhams Retail plc* v. *Sun Alliance and London Assurance Co. Ltd* (2005)[46] that the court must 'promote the purposes and values which are expressed or implicit in the wording and reach an interpretation which applies the ... wording to the changed circumstances in a manner consistent with them'. But the Supreme Court's decision in *Lloyds TSB Foundation for Scotland* v. *Lloyds Group plc* (2013)[47] shows that it will be different if, at the time of the original agreement, the parties could not possibly have contemplated a novel and drastic development (Lord Mance in *Lloyds TSB Foundation for Scotland* v. *Lloyds Group plc* (2013) referring to 'the radically different legal and accounting context which existed by 2009').[48]

In *Lloyds TSB Foundation for Scotland* v. *Lloyds Group plc* (2013) a deed of covenant, dated 1997, stated that the Lloyds Banking Group would pay to a charitable foundation, the appellants ('the Foundation'), (a) £38,920 or (b) (if higher) a specified percentage of the group's pre-tax profits, as defined in the deed.

Eight years later, in 2005, listed companies were required to include in their audited accounts unrealised gains, known as 'negative goodwill' or 'gains on acquisition'. In 2009 Lloyds Banking Group acquired and 'rescued' HBOS (a stricken bank) for half its book price. This newly accounted item (worth £11billion – the amount of the 'negative goodwill') would generate an apparent 'profit' (but in fact quite illusory, because the acquired company was financially stricken) of £1billion.

45   [1997] AC 313, HL.
46   [2005] EWCA Civ 868; [2005] STC 1443; [2006] 1 P & CR 8; [2005] 3 EGLR 34; [2005] 38 EG 142; [2005] BTC 5464; [2005] NPC 9 (cited in the *Lloyds* case by Lord Mance, [2013] UKSC 3; [2013] 1 WLR 366, at [23], and considered in detail by Lord Clarke, *ibid.*, at [51]); K. Lewison, *Interpretation of Contracts* (5th edn, 2011), 261–2.
47   [2013] UKSC 3; [2013] 1 WLR 366.
48   *Ibid.*, at [31].

The Supreme Court held that an item creating the mirage of an enhanced or actual profit, based on this accountancy change, could be safely disregarded. The parties could not reasonably have contemplated the radical change in accountancy practice implemented eight years after the 1997 deed.[49]

14.11 *Context and the background 'factual matrix'.* The English courts will adopt a contextual approach to interpretation rather than a narrow 'dictionary meaning' approach: see Lord Hoffmann's seminal statement in *Investors Compensation Scheme Ltd* v. *West Bromwich Building Society* (1998)[50] (which he traced to decisions in the 1970s).[51] The courts permit the parties to refer to the contractual setting, expressed variously as the transaction's 'commercial purpose', 'genesis', 'background', 'context', its location in the relevant 'market',[52] or its 'landscape'.[53] But it must be emphasised that 'background' *does not extend to pre-contractual negotiations* (on that, see below; however, in the case of applications for rectification, there is an exception to the bar on evidence of pre-contractual negotiations: see further below).

The courts are alert to the need for a contextual approach: 'No one has ever made an "acontextual" statement. There is always some context to any utterance, however meagre.'[54] And 'courts will never construe words in a vacuum'.[55]

In his synopsis in *Marley* v. *Rawlings* (2014) Lord Neuberger indicated that 'context' concerns the state of affairs at the time of the contract ('the facts known or assumed by the parties at the time that the document was executed') and 'the overall purpose of the document' (whole passage cited at 14.01 above).[56]

14.12 *Rationing 'factual matrix' evidence.* Lord Hoffmann in the *BCCI* case (2001) said that the courts and arbitral tribunals, rather than encouraging an uncontrolled 'trawl' through all background material, should curb attempts by parties to adduce excessive quantities of background information.[57]

49   [2013] UKSC 3; [2013] 1 WLR 366, at [19], *per* Lord Mance, citing the first instance judge; similarly, *ibid.*, at [22] and [25].
50   [1998] 1 WLR 896, 912–3, HL; E. McKendrick, in S. Worthington (ed.), *Commercial Law and Commercial Practice* (London, 2003) 139–62.
51   *Prenn* v. *Simmonds* [1971] 1 WLR 1381, 1384–6, HL and *Reardon Smith Line Limited* v. *Hansen Tangen* [1976] 1 WLR 989, HL; in the *Prenn* case, at 1384, Lord Wilberforce traced the 'anti-literal' approach to mid-nineteenth century case law.
52   The leading comment is by Lord Wilberforce in *Reardon Smith Line Limited* v. *Hansen Tangen* [1976] 1 WLR 989, 995–6, HL; see Sir Christopher Staughton [1999] CLJ 303 on the problem of the 'factual matrix'.
53   *Charter Reinsurance Co. Ltd* v. *Fagan* [1997] AC 313, 384, HL, *per* Lord Mustill: 'The words must be set in the landscape of the instrument as a whole.'
54   *Marley* v. *Rawlings* [2014] UKSC 2; [2014] 2 WLR 213, at [20], Lord Neuberger citing Lord Hoffmann in *Kirin-Amgen Inc* v. *Hoechst Marion Roussel Ltd* [2004] UKHL 46; [2005] 1 All ER 667; [2005] RPC 9, at [64].
55   *Marley* v. *Rawlings* [2014] UKSC 2; [2014] 2 WLR 213, at [20], Lord Neuberger citing Sir Thomas Bingham MR in *Arbuthnott* v. *Fagan* [1995] CLC 1396, 1400.
56   [2014] UKSC 2; [2014] 2 WLR 213, at [19].
57   [2001] 1 AC 251, at [39], HL.

Rix LJ *Procter and Gamble Co.* v. *Svenska Cellulosa Aktiebolaget SCA* (2012)[58] noted that the Common Law tool of pre-trial disclosure of documents[59] is an important procedural support for the construction of documents.

However, some judges, notably, Sir Christopher Staughton (a former Lord Justice of Appeal),[60] and Lightman J (a former Chancery judge),[61] suggested that permitting the parties to refer to background material might induce parties to deluge the court with masses of material adduced to provide details of the document's background or 'factual matrix'.

Lightman J suggested that the parties should be required to offer a detailed pleading of that 'matrix'.[62] Berg suggests that 'admissible background [material] should be limited to the sort of facts likely to be readily available to a lawyer asked to advise in circumstances in which a decision has to be taken without delay as to the course of action to be taken under the contract.'[63]

Berg has warned that reconstruction of the 'background' can be expensive, painstaking and even impossible, when the 'parties' are complex organisations, represented by legal and other professions 'teams', and the parties' successors are now required retrospectively and minutely to examine the transaction's pre-formation landscape in order to capture its tacit nuances.[64]

Berg notes the Chief Justice of New South Wales' condemnation of Lord Hoffmann's 'background' principle: 'it is not a schema that can be applied to a substantial range of commercial contractual relationships'.[65]

14.13 *Accessibility of background material.* The relevant 'background' must have been accessible to the present parties: in the *Sigma* case (2009) Lord Collins emphasised this point.[66] It should not be buried in the archaeological remains of an original transaction formed between different persons or entities – as where a standard document was created by parties X and Y, long ago, but the current dispute concerns A and B, who are strangers to the original document, but have adopted it, along with many hundreds or even thousands of other contracting parties in the relevant 'market'.

---

58   [2012] EWCA Civ 1413, at [38].

59   The leading rules are codified at CPR Part 31: for comment on these procedural rules, *Andrews on Civil Processes* (Cambridge, 2013), vol. 1, *Court Proceedings*, at chapter 11.

60   *New Hampshire Insurance Co.* v. *MGN Ltd, The Times*, 25 July 1995, CA; *Scottish Power plc* v. *Britoil (Exploration) plc, The Times*, 2 December 1997, CA; Staughton [1999] CLJ 303.

61   *Wire TV Ltd* v. *CableTel (UK) Ltd* [1988] CLC 244, 257; Sir Gavin Lightman in 'Civil Litigation in the Twenty-First Century' (1998) 17 CJQ 373; similarly, E. McKendrick in S. Worthington (ed.), *Commercial Law and Commercial Practice* (Oxford, 2003) 139, 147.

62   E. McKendrick, *ibid.*

63   A. Berg (2006) 122 LQR 354, 362.

64   A. Berg (2008) 124 LQR 6, 12–14.

65   *Ibid.*, at 14, citing an address given by this Australian judge in March 2007.

66   But in the *Sigma* case, [2009] UKSC 2; [2010] 1 All ER 571; [2010] BCC 40, at [35] to [37], Lord Collins (with the support of Lords Mance and Hope) disapproved too broad a search for background information when, as in the *Sigma* case itself, the parties to the relevant transaction might not have been present at its birth, and had instead become second-hand or remoter recipients of others' contractual text which had been in circulation in the relevant financial market; and for the problem of rectification of public documents, *Cherry Tree Investments Ltd* v. *Landmain Ltd* [2012] EWCA Civ 736; [2013] Ch 305, noted P. S. Davies, (2013) 129 LQR 24–7; M. Barber and R. Thomas, (2014) 77 MLR 597–618.

14.14 *Factual matrix and 'objective facts'.* The Supreme Court in *Oceanbulk Shipping and Trading SA* v. *TMT Asia Ltd* (2010)[67] held (i) that 'objective facts communicated by one party to the other in the course of the negotiations' can be taken into account as background factual matrix evidence; and (ii) that 'without prejudice' negotiations, which result in a settlement agreement, can be admitted for this purpose; (iii) the combination of (i) and (ii) would enable the court to determine the scope of the settlement agreement. As for point (ii), to decide otherwise would be to create an unprincipled distinction between interpretation of all other commercial contracts and interpretation of settlement agreements.[68]

14.15 *Pre-contractual negotiation bar.* The English rule (confirmed by the House of Lords in *Chartbrook Ltd* v. *Persimmon Homes Ltd*, 2009)[69] is that when seeking to interpret written contracts (as distinct from oral or partly written contracts), a party cannot adduce, without his opponent's permission, evidence of the *parties' prior negotiations*. (This rule is not followed in most other jurisdictions of the world: 14.16.) This is rather like trying to assess the personality and characteristics of sixth-form interview candidates without having met their parents (and in turn the grandparents); but, in the interests of economy, only the most recent generation is interviewed.

> In *Chartbrook Ltd* v. *Persimmon Homes Ltd* (2009)[70] Lord Hoffmann said:[71]
>> The rule may well mean ... that parties are sometimes held bound by a contract in terms which, upon a full investigation of the course of negotiations, a reasonable observer would not have taken them to have intended. But a system which sometimes allows this to happen may be justified in the more general interest of economy and predictability in obtaining advice and adjudicating disputes. It is, after all, usually possible to avoid surprises by carefully reading the documents before signing them and there are the safety nets of rectification and estoppel by convention.
>
> Lord Hoffmann noted Lord Blackburn's adoption in 1878 of the following statement by Lord Gifford, a Scottish judge, in 1877:[72]
>> The very purpose of a formal contract is to put an end to the disputes which would inevitably arise if the matter were left upon verbal negotiations or upon mixed communings partly consisting of letters and partly of conversations. The written contract is that which is to be appealed to by both parties, however different it may be from their previous demands or stipulations, whether contained in letters or in verbal conversation.

---

67 [2010] UKSC 44; [2011] 1 AC 662; noted P. S. Davies [2011] CLJ 24–7, highlighting the artificial distinction between resort to negotiation evidence for discovery of background facts (allowed) and of the trend of negotiations (not allowed).

68 *Ibid.*, at [40].

69 *Chartbrook Ltd* v. *Persimmon Homes Ltd* [2009] UKHL 38; [2009] 1 AC 1101; noted D. McLauchlan (2010) 126 LQR 8–14.

70 *Chartbrook Ltd* v. *Persimmon Homes Ltd* [2009] UKHL 38; [2009] 1 AC 1101; noted D. McLauchlan (2010) 126 LQR 8–14; noted J. O'Sullivan [2009] CLJ 510.

71 *Ibid.*, at [41].

72 *Ibid.*, at [29], citing Lord Blackburn, *Inglis* v. *John Buttery & Co.* (1878) 3 App Cas 552, 577, HL, adopting Lord Gifford (1877) 4 R 58, 69–70, in the *Inglis* case.

In the *Chartbrook* case (2009) Lord Rodger added:[73]

> [T]here are no particular pressing circumstances which call for a change. The House is simply being asked to make a fresh policy decision and, in effect, to legislate to provide for a different rule. The wisdom of the proposed change is, however, debatable. So, if there is to be a change, it should be on the basis of a fully informed debate in a forum where the competing policies can be properly investigated and evaluated.

14.16 The five rationales for this bar are:[74] (i) avoidance of 'uncertainty and unpredictability'; (ii) the fact that interested third parties cannot be guaranteed access to such negotiation history; (iii) such dealings are notoriously shifting and so such evidence would be unhelpful; (iv) one-sided impressions might contaminate the inquiry so that the objective approach to interpretation would be undermined; and (v) 'sophisticated and knowledgeable negotiators would be tempted to lay a paper trail of self-serving documents'.[75]

As for argument (v), Lord Hoffmann gave reasons for supporting Collins LJ's scepticism.[76]
But Lord Hoffmann placed emphasis on arguments (i) to (iv), especially (i), concerning uncertainty and unpredictability:[77]

> [The bar on admission of pre-contractual negotiations] reflects what may be a sound practical intuition that the law of contract is an institution designed to enforce promises with a high degree of predictability and that the more one allows conventional meanings or syntax to be displaced by inferences drawn from background, the less predictable the outcome is likely to be ... [The] imprecision of the line between negotiation and provisional agreement is the very reason why in every case of dispute over interpretation, one or other of the parties is likely to require a court or arbitrator to take the course of negotiations into account.

McKendrick draws attention to the contrast between the English exclusionary rules of interpretation (barring reference to negotiations and post-formation conduct) and the liberal styles of interpretation espoused by the 'Principles of European Contract Law'. That 'soft law code' is heavily influenced by civilian methods. It permits the court to have regard to a wide range of factors, including good faith and the Janus-like perspectives of pre- and post-formation dealings.[78] UNIDROIT's *Principles of International Commercial Contracts*

---

73 [2009] UKHL 38; [2009] 1 AC 1101, at [70].

74 As collected by Briggs J at first instance in *Chartbrook Ltd* v. *Persimmon Homes Ltd* [2007] EWHC 409 (Ch), at [23], drawing upon Lord Nicholls' famous lecture, 'My Kingdom for a Horse: the Meaning of Words' (2005) 121 LQR 577; in his note on the House of Lords' decision in the *Chartbrook* case, D. McLauchlan (2010) 126 LQR 8, 9–11 rejects these various suggested justifications; see also G. Yihan, 'A Wrong Turn in History: Re-Understanding the Exclusionary Rule Against Prior Negotiations in Contractual Interpretation' [2014] JBL 360–87.

75 *Chartbrook* v. *Persimmons* [2008] EWCA Civ 183; [2008] 2 All ER (Comm) 387, at [111], *per* Collins LJ; this argument is described as unconvincing by D. McLauchlan (2010) 126 LQR 8, 11.

76 [2009] UKHL 38; [2009] 1 AC 1101, at [40]. For a survey of UK and NZ lawyers, J. Bayley, 'Prior Negotiations and Subsequent Conduct in Contract Interpretation: Principles and Practical Concerns' (2012) 28 JCL 179.

77 *Ibid.*, at [37], *per* Lord Hoffmann.

78 E. McKendrick in S. Worthington (ed.), *Commercial Law and Commercial Practice* (Oxford, 2003), 139, 161–2, noting *Principles of European Contract Law*, Article 5.102 (a), (b) and (g).

(2010), Article 4.3[79] permits a similarly wide range of matters to be taken into account. In the *Chartbrook* case (2009),[80] Lord Hoffmann (in passages too long to quote here) considered the different approaches of English law and 'soft law' codes influenced by civilian ideas.[81]

Furthermore, the Dubai International Financial Centre's codification of commercial contract law permits such pre-formation and post-formation references (Article 51).[82]

Lawrence Collins LJ in the Court of Appeal in *Chartbrook Ltd* v. *Persimmon Homes Ltd* (2008) noted that in the USA there is some support (although not unanimous) for courts referring to negotiations when construing written agreement if they conspicuously lack clarity.[83]

However, parties tend to plead rectification as well as presenting arguments based on ordinary interpretation. And so the court gains access to pre-contractual negotiations (14.27) for the purpose of that *equitable doctrine*. It follows that the trial judge will not be blind to the pre-contractual negotiations. To this extent, the doctrinal contrast between English law and civilian systems is a matter of no great practical significance.[84]

14.17 *Three exceptions to the bar on negotiation evidence*. However, in the *Chartbrook* case (2009) Lord Hoffmann noted that it is acceptable to adduce extrinsic evidence of negotiations in the following three situations:[85] (1) the contract contains words or phrases that have been used in *a quite unusual sense* by the parties in a course of dealing, or the relevant wording is used in a special sense by, for example, members of a particular trade, etc.; (2) estoppel by convention; and (3) rectification (14.27). And so claims for rectification are often brought in conjunction with a pleading based on ordinary 'interpretation'.[86] Each exception will continue to be troublesome, for they are in truth three large holes in the general doctrine which purports to exclude reference to pre-contractual negotiations.

14.18 *'Special meaning' exception*. As for exception (1), Lord Hoffmann said in the *Chartbrook* case (2009):[87]

> [E]vidence may always be adduced that the parties habitually used words in an unconventional sense in order to support an argument that words in a contract should bear a similar unconventional meaning. This ... is akin to the principle by which a linguistic usage in a trade or among a religious sect may be proved: compare *Shore v. Wilson* (1842) 9 Cl & F 355. For this purpose it does not matter whether the evidence of usage by the parties was in the course of negotiations or on

---

79   3rd edition, 2010, text and comment, is available at: www.unidroit.org/english/principles/contracts/principles2010/integralversionprinciples2010-e.pdf.

80   [2009] UKHL 38; [2009] 1 AC 1101; noted D. McLauchlan (2010) 126 LQR 8–14.

81   *Ibid.*, at [39].

82   www.difc.ae/laws_regulations/laws/files/Contract_Law.pdf.

83   [2008] EWCA Civ 183; [2008] 2 All ER (Comm) 387, at [108] to [113], *per* Lawrence Collins LJ.

84   E. Clive, in H. MacQueen and R. Zimmermann (eds.), *European Contract Law: Scots and South African Perspectives* (Edinburgh, 2006), chapter 7 at 183.

85   For acute analysis of each of these exceptions, D. McLauchlan, 'Common Intention and Contract Interpretation' [2011] LMCLQ 30–50.

86   On this two-pronged approach, G. McMeel (2011) *European Business Law Review* 437–49, and R. Buxton, '"Construction" and Rectification After *Chartbrook*' [2010] CLJ 253 and A. Burrows, 'Construction and Rectification', in A. Burrows and E. Peel (eds.), *Contract Terms* (Oxford, 2007), 88 ff.

87   [2009] UKHL 38; [2009] 1 AC 1101, at [45].

any other occasion. It is simply evidence of the linguistic usage which they had in common.

However, McLauchlan (2010)[88] has rightly suggested that this qualification is troublesome because there is no workable distinction between an 'unusual' meaning and a choice between more than one 'ordinary' meaning.

14.19 *'Estoppel by convention' exception.* This second exception arises where the parties have outwardly reached an agreement concerning words in the written contract so that each is estopped from denying the non-literal construction which they wish to place on those words. This is 'estoppel by convention'. To establish estoppel by convention (5.48), an implicit agreement must be manifested in the parties' pattern of behaviour and interaction, namely, proof that, *subsequent to formation, the parties had implicitly agreed on how the written terms should be interpreted or modified.*[89] Unless restricted to post-formation dealings, this exception might tend to eat up the main rule.

> However, Lord Hoffmann's discussion of this exception to the bar on negotiation evidence does not appear to restrict the focus to post-formation dealings, because he said in the *Chartbrook* case (2009):[90] 'if the parties have negotiated an agreement upon some common assumption, which may include an assumption that certain words will bear a certain meaning, they may be estopped from contending that the words should be given a different meaning'.[91]
> And for an application of estoppel by convention, see *ING Bank NV* v. *Ros Roca SA* (2011).[92]

14.20 *Post-formation conduct.* A written contract should not be construed by reference to the parties' conduct subsequent to the contract's formation.[93] However, there are two exceptions: (1) if it can be shown that the parties had specifically *agreed to vary or discharge the agreement;*[94] or (2) if the doctrine of *estoppel by convention* applies (see preceding paragraph).

5. INTERPRETATION: 'CORRECTIVE CONSTRUCTION'

14.21 *Court not to overstretch its powers of interpretation.* Before examining the modern fashion to second-guess and correct manifestly defective text (see 14.22) it is important to

---

88 D. McLauchlan (2010) 126 LQR 8, 12 (case note).

89 *Amalgamated Investment & Property Co. Ltd* v. *Texas Commerce International Bank Ltd* [1982] QB 84, 120, CA, *per* Lord Denning MR: 'So here we have . . . evidence of subsequent conduct to come to our aid. It is available – not so as to construe the contract – but to see how they themselves acted on it. Under the guise of estoppel [by convention] we can prevent either party from going back on the interpretation they themselves gave to it.'

90 [2009] UKHL 38; [2009] 1 AC 1101, at [47].

91 [2009] UKHL 38; [2009] 1 AC 1101, at [47].

92 [2011] EWCA Civ 353; [2012] 1 WLR 472 Carnwath LJ's analysis, *ibid.*, [55] to [73], Stanley Burnton LJ agreeing at [75]; but the third judge applied promissory estoppel/representation by estoppel (Rix LJ's analysis, at [85], [86]).

93 *Whitworth Street Estates (Manchester) Ltd* v. *James Miller & Partners Ltd* [1970] AC 583, 603, HL, *per* Lord Reid.

94 *Chitty on Contracts* (31st edn, London, 2012), 12–111.

emphasise that the court (and arbitral tribunals) applying English law are bound to give effect to a contractual text: they must not illegitimately rewrite the contract if its meaning is clear and does not lead to commercial absurdity. Lord Mustill in *Charter Reinsurance Co. Ltd v. Fagan* (1997) warned that it is illegitimate for courts or arbitrators to 'force upon the words a meaning which they cannot fairly bear', since this would be 'to substitute for the bargain actually made one which the court believes could better have been made'.[95] Similarly, Rix LJ said in *ING Bank NV v. Ros Roca SA* (2011):[96] 'Judges should not see in *Chartbrook Ltd v. Persimmon Homes Ltd* [2009] AC 1101 an open sesame for reconstructing the parties' contract, but an opportunity to remedy by construction a clear error of language which could not have been intended.'

> A fundamental tenet of English contract law is that the courts will respect the terms of a contract entered into by two consenting parties. Lord Radcliffe in *Bridge v. Campbell Discount Co. Ltd* (1962) noted that an English judge is not empowered 'to serve as a general adjuster of men's bargains'.[97]
>
> As it was put in a US case: 'Every man is master of the contract which he chooses to make, and it is of vast importance that contracts should be enforced according to the words and intention of the parties.'[98]

14.22 *Nature of 'corrective construction'*.[99] The House of Lords in *Chartbrook Ltd v. Persimmon Homes Ltd* (2009)[100] held that a judge can 'construe' a contract by wholly recasting a relevant phrase or portion of a written contract when (i) it is obvious that the drafting has gone awry and (ii) the parties' true meaning is also obvious, as a matter of objective interpretation.[101] Thus both ordinary interpretation principles and the doctrine of rectification can have the effect of revising a document. The safer course is for a party who is seeking a favourable judicial decision on a disputed written contract to plead both 'construction' (in the 'corrective' style just explained) and 'rectification' (summarised below).

---

95 [1997] AC 313, 388, HL.
96 [2011] EWCA Civ 353; [2012] 1 WLR 472.
97 [1962] AC 600, 626, HL.
98 *Clarke and others* v. *Watson and others* (1865) 18 CBR, US 278; [1861–73] All ER Rep 482 *per* Erie CJ at 483.
99 *Investors Compensation Scheme* case [1998] 1 WLR 896, 912–3, HL (propositions (iv) and (v)). A. Burrows, 'Construction and Rectification' in A. Burrows and E. Peel (eds.), *Contract Terms* (Oxford, 2007), 77; R. Buxton, '"Construction" and Rectification After *Chartbrook*' [2010] CLJ 253; D. Hodge, *Rectification: The Modern Law and Practice Governing Claims of Rectification* (London, 2010), 10.13 ff (see also, *ibid.*, 1–13, citing Lord Hoffmann in *Jumbo King Ltd* v. *Faithful Properties Ltd* [1999] HKFCA 80; [1999] 2 HKCFAR 279); G. McMeel, *The Construction of Contracts: Interpretation, Implication and Rectification* (2nd edn, Oxford, 2011), chapter 17; G. McMeel (2011) *European Business Law Review* 437–49.
100 [2009] UKHL 38; [2009] 1 AC 1101; noted D. McLauchlan (2010) 126 LQR 8–14.
101 Arden LJ in *Cherry Tree Investments Ltd* v. *Landmain Ltd* [2012] EWCA Civ 736; [2013] Ch 305, at [63], identified a three-fold set of criteria: 'In particular: (i) it must be clear from the admissible background that the parties have made a mistake and what that mistake is; (ii) it must be clear, from the rest of the agreement interpreted with the admissible background, what the parties intended to agree; and (iii) *the mistake must be one of language or syntax.*' [emphasis added]

'Corrective construction' is mentioned last in Lord Hoffmann's statement of principle in *Investors Compensation Scheme* (1998):[102]

> (v) (a) The 'rule' that words should be given their 'natural and ordinary meaning' reflects the common sense proposition that we do not easily accept that people have made linguistic mistakes, particularly in formal documents. (b) *On the other hand, if one would nevertheless conclude from the background that something must have gone wrong with the language, the law does not require judges to attribute to the parties an intention which they plainly could not have had.* [emphasis and letters (a) and (b) added]

In the *Chartbrook* case (2009), Lord Hoffmann summarised the governing principles as follows:[103]

> In *East v. Pantiles* (Plant Hire) (1981), Brightman J stated the conditions for what he called 'correction of mistakes by construction: . . . first, there must be a clear mistake on the face of the instrument; secondly, it must be clear what correction ought to be made in order to cure the mistake. If those conditions are satisfied, then the correction is made as a matter of construction.'

Lord Hoffmann continued (also in the *Chartbrook* case, 2009):[104]

> [In] deciding whether there is a clear mistake, the court is not confined to reading the document without regard to its background or context. As the exercise is part of the single task of interpretation, the background and context must always be taken into consideration.

Lord Hoffmann added in the *Chartbrook* case:[105]

> [T]here is not, so to speak, a limit to the amount of red ink or verbal rearrangement or correction which the court is allowed. All that is required is that it should be clear that something has gone wrong with the language and that it should be clear what a reasonable person would have understood the parties to have meant.

However, in *Marley v. Rawlings* (2014), in dicta (the case concerned rectification of wills under statutory powers), Lord Neuberger noted that the second sentence of this principle (see (v)(b) above) is 'controversial' (see further 14.42 below on the controversy concerning the appropriate relationship between corrective construction and rectification).[106] And he noted[107] the criticism of Sir Richard Buxton (2010) in the *Cambridge Law Journal* (2010)[108] (see below), which was approved by *Lewison on the Interpretation of Contracts* (2011).[109]

Burrows notes[110] that 'corrective construction' has eroded the distinction between (a) textual emendation (changing words, or moving them around) and (b) exegesis (that is, elucidation, or making sense, of a 'stable' text, without changing words or shifting their place). This is a widely expressed invitation to potential litigants to contest matters of interpretation. It will continue to stimulate much litigation.[111]

---

102 [1998] 1 WLR 896, 912–13, HL.
103 [2009] UKHL 38; [2009] 1 AC 1101, at [22] to [25].
104 *Ibid.*, at [24].
105 *Chartbrook Ltd* v. *Persimmon Homes Ltd* [2009] AC 1101, at [25].
106 [2014] UKSC 2; [2014] 2 WLR 213, at [37].
107 *Ibid.*, at [39].
108 '"Construction" and Rectification after *Chartbrook*' [2010] CLJ 253.
109 *Lewison on The Interpretation of Contracts* (5th edn, 2011), at 9.03 n. 67.
110 A. Burrows, 'Construction and Rectification' in A. Burrows and E. Peel (eds.), *Contract Terms* (Oxford, 2007), 77, 79 n. 9.
111 E.g., *Bishops Wholesale Newsagency Ltd* v. *Surridge Dawson Ltd* [2009] EWHC 2578 (Ch); [2010] 2 BCLC 546, Judge Mackie QC; *CDV Software Entertainment AG* v. *Gamecock Media Europe Ltd* [2009] EWHC 2965 (Ch), Gloster J; *Deutsche Bank AG* v. *Sebastian Holdings Inc* [2009] EWHC 2132 (Comm); [2009] 2 CLC 908,

Sir Richard Buxton, a former Lord Justice of Appeal, has suggested:[112] (i) that 'corrective construction' is an ill-conceived innovation of the *Investors Compensation Scheme* 'restatement', and (ii) that rectification should be the sole legal technique available to recast the text of the written contract.

Buxton's 2010 article was cited by the Supreme Court in *Oceanbulk Shipping and Trading SA* v. *TMT Asia Ltd* (2010),[113] but Lord Clarke distanced himself from proposition (ii), just summarised.

The matter has been left unresolved by Lewison LJ in *Cherry Tree Investments Ltd* v. *Landmain Ltd* (2012),[114] who also referred neutrally to discussion by Buxton, Burrows and McMeel.[115] And Lord Grabiner QC has suggested that when it is clear that the written terms fail to reflect the parties' true consensus, the appropriate legal technique is rectification or estoppel by convention[116] (for example, in *ING Bank NV* v. *Ros Roca SA* (2011)).[117]

14.23 *Illustrations of 'corrective construction'.* There are many examples of the courts invoking this style of interpretation: *Holding & Barnes plc* v. *Hill House Hammond Ltd (No. 1)* (2001);[118] *Littman* v. *Aspen Oil (Broking) Ltd* (2005);[119] *KPMG LLP* v. *Network Rail Infrastructure Ltd* (2007);[120] *Chartbrook Ltd* v. *Persimmon Homes Ltd* (2009);[121] *Multi-Link Leisure* v. *North Lanarkshire* (2010);[122] *Springwell Navigation Corporation* v. *JP Morgan Chase* (2010);[123] *Pink Floyd Music Ltd* v. *EMI Records Ltd* (2010);[124] *Chartbrook Ltd* v. *Persimmon Homes Ltd* (2009).[125] (And now see the *Caresse Navigation* case [2014] EWCA Civ 1366; [2015] 2 WLR 43.) Here are two illustrations.

(1) In *Littman* v. *Aspen Oil (Broking) Ltd* (2005)[126] a lease contained a mutual break clause exercisable by either party upon giving six months' written notice. The landlord had intended that the contract should permit the tenant to exercise this break clause only if the tenant had complied with its covenants at the relevant time. But the botched text (see the words in italic below; emphasis added) stated: 'that up to the Termination Date in the case of

Walker J; *HHR Pascal BV* v. *W2005 Puppet II BV* [2009] EWHC 2771 (Comm); [2010] 1 All ER (Comm) 399; *NHS Business Services Authority* v. *Ingram* [2009] EWHC 2486 (Ch).
112   R. Buxton, '"Construction" and Rectification After *Chartbrook*' [2010] CLJ 253.
113   [2010] UKSC 44; [2010] 3 WLR 1424, at [45], first sentence.
114   [2012] EWCA Civ 736; [2013] Ch 305.
115   [2012] EWCA Civ 736; [2013] Ch 305, at [90] and [91], citing A. Burrows, 'Construction and Rectification', in A. Burrows and E. Peel (eds.), *Contract Terms* (Oxford, 2007) (at 9: 'the new contextual approach means that construction has swallowed up much of what only rectification could have previously achieved'); G. McMeel, *The Construction of Contracts* (2nd edn, Oxford, 2011), 17.63 (rectification is 'on the point of being rendered largely superfluous'); and R. Buxton, '"Construction" and Rectification after *Chartbrook*' [2010] CLJ 253.
116   Lord Grabiner, 'The Iterative Process of Contractual Interpretation' (2012) 128 LQR 41, 50.
117   [2011] EWCA Civ 353; [2012] 1 WLR 472.
118   [2001] EWCA Civ 1334; [2002] L & TR 103.
119   [2005] EWCA Civ 1579; [2006] 2 P & CR 2; [2006] L & TR 9; [2005] NPC 150.
120   [2007] EWCA Civ 363; [2007] Bus LR 1336.
121   [2009] UKHL 38; [2009] 1 AC 1101; noted D. McLauchlan (2010) 126 LQR 8–14.
122   [2010] UKSC 47; [2011] 1 All ER 175; for observations on this case, Lord Grabiner, 'The Iterative Process of Contractual Interpretation' (2012) 128 LQR 41, 52–3.
123   [2010] EWCA Civ 1221; [2010] 2 CLC 705, at [132] to [140].
124   [2010] EWCA Civ 1429; [2011] 1 WLR 770. Lord Neuberger MR and Laws LJ held that an agreement for exploitation of the 'records' of Pink Floyd could be construed as embracing digital recordings by the same band. To decide otherwise would run counter to the obvious commercial purpose of the transaction. However, Carnwath LJ dissented, finding there was no such obvious mistake.
125   [2009] UKHL 38; [2009] 1 AC 1101; noted D. McLauchlan (2010) 126 LQR 8–14.
126   [2005] EWCA Civ 1579; [2006] 2 P & CR 2; [2006] L & TR 9; [2005] NPC 150.

a notice *given by the Landlord* the Tenant shall have paid the rents . . . and shall have duly observed and performed the Tenant's covenants . . . and the conditions herein contained'. The Court of Appeal upheld Hart J's decision that the words highlighted above should be construed to read: 'given by the Tenant'. There is no need for the corrupted text to be grammatically or syntactically wrong. Such 'construction' could cure a manifest slip, otherwise the final text would be commercial nonsense.

(2) Another illustration is *Pink Floyd Music Ltd* v. *EMI Records Ltd* (2010)[127] where Lord Neuberger MR and Laws LJ held that an agreement for exploitation of the 'records' of Pink Floyd could be construed as embracing digital recordings by the same band. To decide otherwise would run counter to the obvious commercial purpose of the transaction. However, Carnwath LJ dissented on the facts in finding there was no such obvious mistake.

14.24 *Situations where 'corrective construction' is unavailable.* Such a reconstruction will not be possible in any of the following situations:

(1) *The only real complaint is that both parties have misunderstood the extent of the subject matter. Bashir* v. *Ali* (2011), where Etherton LJ said:[128]

> The wording of the documentation in the present case is clear . . . It may have resulted in a good bargain for one of the parties, but, as Lord Hoffmann pointed out in *Chartbrook* at [20], that is not itself a sufficient reason for supposing that the contract does not mean what it says.

Etherton LJ added:[129] 'There may be a case in which the commercial advantage would be so great that it moves the case into the sphere of irrationality and arbitrariness. That, however, is not the present case.'

(2) *A clause is flawed but does not contain an inner solution.* The Court of Appeal in *ING Bank NV* v. *Ros Roca SA* (2011)[130] held that it was not possible, on the facts, to apply the technique of 'constructive interpretation' to rewrite a clause concerning an investment bank's 'additional fee'.

(3) *The contract is beyond verbal redemption.* This was the position in *Fairstate Ltd* v. *General Enterprise & Management Ltd* (2010),[131] where the judge said:[132] 'the defects in the agreement recorded in the Guarantee Form are so fundamental and extensive that they cannot sufficiently be cured, either by purposive construction, or by rectification, or by any combination of those approaches.' (In the same case the plea of rectification failed because there had been no clear prior consensus concerning the effect and scope of the guarantee.)

(4) *Public registers.* The Court of Appeal in *Cherry Tree Investments Ltd* v. *Landmain Ltd* (2012)[133] held that corrective interpretation could not be used to change a public document

127 [2010] EWCA Civ 1429; [2011] 1 WLR 770.
128 [2011] EWCA Civ 707; [2011] 2 P & CR 12, at [39].
129 *Ibid.*, at [40].
130 [2011] EWCA Civ 353; [2012] 1 WLR 472 (but the court was able to achieve a favourable outcome for the bank by employing the doctrine of estoppel by convention to take account of post-formation dealings).
131 [2010] EWHC 3072 (QB); [2011] 2 All ER (Comm) 497; 133 Con LR 112 (Richard Salter QC, Deputy).
132 *Ibid.*, at [94].
133 [2012] EWCA Civ 736; [2013] Ch 305, at [121].

(a land registration) to reflect a special clause concerning the operation of the relevant registered interest. The majority (Lewison and Longmore LJJ) were persuaded that it was necessary to insulate such public registers from corrective interpretation by reference to collateral information which might not be accessible to third parties. The attraction of the majority's decision is that it gives priority to the statutory process of rectification which has been introduced in that particular context under the land registration legislation.[134] No such application for statutory rectification had been made in this case. In her dissent, Arden LJ agreed that in other situations the position of third parties might be important but, since the present case did not involve prejudice to any third parties, corrective interpretation should be permitted.[135]

6. RECTIFICATION

14.25 *The two grounds.*[136] There are two separate grounds for rectifying written contracts:[137] (1) common intention rectification based on a mismatch between (a) the objectively agreed version of the transaction subsisting immediately prior to the written form, and (b) the parties' final instrument which purports to give unaltered effect to that agreed version; or (2) unilateral mistake, where party D has reprehensibly failed to point out to party C that the written terms of their imminent transaction will not accord with C's mistaken understanding concerning the contents of that written agreement. These two heads will now be taken in turn.

134 *Ibid.*, at [117] ff (notably at [121]), noting Schedule 4 to the Land Registration Act 2002.
135 *Ibid.*, at [54] to [60]; here argument was rejected by Lewison LJ at [122].
136 D. Hodge, *Rectification: The Modern Law and Practice Governing Claims for Rectification for Mistake* (London, 2010); *Snell's Principles of Equity* (32nd edn, London, 2010), chapter 16; *Chitty on Contracts* (31st edn, London, 2012), 5–110 ff; *Treitel* (13th edn, London, 2011), 8–059 ff; comment: P. S. Davies, 'Rectifying the Course of Rectification', (2012) MLR 412–26; D. McLauchlan, 'The "Drastic" Remedy of Rectification for Unilateral Mistake' (2008) 124 LQR 608, especially 608–10, 639–40; K. Lewison, lecture reprinted as Appendix to the first supplement to K. Lewison, *The Interpretation of Contracts* (London, 2007); D. McLauchlan, 'Refining Rectification' (2014) 130 LQR 83; J. Ruddell, 'Common Intention and Rectification for Common Mistake' [2014] LMCLQ 48–75, notably at 64–6, and 70–5; M. Smith, 'Rectification of Contracts for Common Mistake' (2007) 123 LQR 116, especially 130 to end; Lord Toulson, 'Does Rectification Require Rectifying' (October 2013 speech) (http://supremecourt.uk/docs/speech-131031.pdf); and on the connection with interpretation in general, G. McMeel (2011) *European Business Law Review* 437–49, R. Buxton, '"Construction" and Rectification After *Chartbrook*' [2010] CLJ 253 and A. Burrows, 'Construction and Rectification', in A. Burrows and E. Peel (eds.), *Contract Terms* (Oxford, 2007), 88 ff.
137 Rectification applies generally to (written) 'instruments' and thus includes, e.g., nominations of pensions beneficiaries: *Collins v. Jones and Jones*, The Times, 3 February 2000 (Stanley Burnton QC); and for other unilateral instruments (such as leasehold notices or patents), see *Marley v. Rawlings* [2014] UKSC 2; [2014] 2 WLR 213, at [21], [22], [27], [77] (case noted B Hacker (2014) 130 LQR 360–5) (in *Marley* at [21], noting *Mannai Investment Co. Ltd* v. *Eagle Star Life Assurance Co. Ltd* [1997] AC 749, HL, *per* Lord Steyn at 770C–771D, and Lord Hoffmann at 779H–780F – landlord and tenancy notices; and, on patents, [2014] UKSC 2; [2014] 2 WLR 213, at [20] and [22], noting Lord Hoffmann's speech in *Kirin-Amgen Inc* v. *Hoechst Marion Roussel Ltd* [2004] UKHL 46; [2005] 1 All ER 667; [2005] RPC 9 (at [27] to [35]), and Lord Diplock's in *Catnic Components Ltd* v. *Hill & Smith Ltd* [1982] RPC 183, 243, HL); but testamentary wills are subject to the special statutory regime of section 20 of the Administration of Justice Act 1982; on such statutory rectification of wills, *Marley* case, *ibid.* (testator X executing his spouse's will, because of solicitor's error; rectification of whole document available); *per* Lord Neuberger at [53]: 'I can see no reason in principle why a wholesale correction should be ruled out as a permissible exercise of the court's power to rectify, as a matter of principle. On the contrary: to impose such a restriction on the power of rectification would be unprincipled – and it would also lead to uncertainty.'

14.26 *Residual status of rectification.* Rectification is a doctrine of last resort.[138] It applies only if other techniques, such as Common Law interpretation, or even the implication (13.01 ff) of terms at Common Law,[139] do not yield a solution. In particular, rectification need not be invoked if the court can as a matter of 'corrective interpretation' revise the relevant document; and this is possible if (a) it is clear that the present wording makes no commercial sense, and (b) it is apparent how the document should be reconstructed (as explained at 14.22 above). As McLauchlan observes,[140] rectification will be the only route to cure the defective document (and 'corrective interpretation' will not avail) if (i) the plea of rectification is that a term was left out or (ii) wrongly included or (iii) the factual matrix material does not indicate that something has gone wrong and that there is an obvious solution supplied using the technique of 'corrective interpretation'.

14.27 *Rectification and evidence.* The party seeking rectification must satisfy a high standard of proof, especially where both parties have been professionally advised.[141] Rectification admits much greater light into the process of illuminating the dark corners of the written text than the process of Common Law interpretation. When considering a claim for rectification, the court can admit extrinsic evidence, that is, evidence of discussion or documentary material outside the text of the written agreement (and see 14.42). Thus rectification is an exception to the 'parol evidence rule' (12.02) (this is the special English rule governing written contracts – that evidence outside the written contract cannot be used by a party to vary, supplement or contradict that document's contents). And so the parol evidence rule does not restrict the process of discerning the parties' pre-contractual intentions and negotiations for the purpose of rectification.

Nor does an 'entire agreement' clause bar external evidence if that evidence is adduced during an application for rectification of a written contract. (An 'entire agreement' clause is a stipulation in the main contract stating that the parties agree to exclude from their agreement any prior and external assurances or warranties or promises: 9.36 and 9.37.) It has been suggested at first instance that it would be inappropriate for the 'entire agreement' clause to exclude such evidence in this context because the function of such a clause is to bar resort to oral undertakings or satellite written assurances independently of

---

138 *Snell's Principles of Equity* (32nd edn, London, 2010), 16–002: 'Rectification will not be decreed if the desired result can conveniently be achieved by other means: by reliance upon Common Law rights, or by agreement between the parties.' *Snell*, at 16–009, also notes that the 'touchstone' for implied terms, including in the context of written contracts, remains a demanding matter of 'necessity', as noted by Sir Anthony Clarke MR, in *Mediterranean Salvage & Towage Ltd* v. *Seamar Trading & Commerce Inc*, 'The Reborn' [2009] EWCA Civ 53; [2009] 2 Lloyd's Rep 639, at [18]; 13.16 on this case and its attractively sceptical reception of Lord Hoffmann's discussion in *Attorney-General for Belize* v. *Belize Telecom Ltd* [2009] UKPC 10; [2009] 2 All ER 1127, at [16] to [27], especially [21]; and see G. McMeel, *The Construction of Contracts: Interpretation, Implication and Rectification* (2nd edn, Oxford, 2011), chapters 10 and 11.
139 *Holaw (470) Ltd* v. *Stockton Estates Ltd* (2000) 81 P & CR 404, at [41], *per* Neuberger J, at [44] (if a point is so obvious that it goes without saying, the judge said that the appropriate doctrine is implied terms, rather than equitable rectification).
140 D. McLauchlan, 'Refining Rectification' (2014) 130 LQR 83 (83 at n. 1).
141 *James Hay Pension Trustees Ltd* v. *Hird* [2005] EWHC 1093 (Ch), at [81]; *Surgicraft Ltd* v. *Paradigm Biodevices Inc* [2010] EWHC 1291 (Ch), at [69], *per* Christopher Pycroft QC (Deputy High Court Judge); *Traditional Structures Ltd* v. *HW Construction Ltd* [2010] EWHC 1530 (TCC), at [34].

the main written contract (prior or collateral promises). By contrast, rectification is invoked to show that the main contract does not record accurately the parties' true consensus.[142]

14.28 *Common intention rectification.* In the *Daventry* case (2011) Etherton LJ summarised the law of common intention rectification (a statement approved by Lord Neuberger MR in the same case)[143] as follows:[144]

(1) the parties had a common continuing intention, whether or not amounting to an agreement, in respect of a particular matter in the instrument to be rectified;

(2) which existed at the time of execution of the instrument sought to be rectified;

(3) such common continuing intention to be established objectively, that is to say by reference to what an objective observer would have thought the intentions of the parties to be; and

(4) by mistake, the instrument did not reflect that common intention.

The following comments by Etherton LJ in the Daventry case are helpful:

> [80] the requirements for rectification for mutual mistake can be re-phrased as: (1) the parties had a common continuing intention, whether or not amounting to an agreement, in respect of a particular matter in the instrument to be rectified; (2) which existed at the time of execution of the instrument sought to be rectified; (3) such common continuing intention to be established objectively, that is to say by reference to what an objective observer would have thought the intentions of the parties to be; and (4) by mistake, the instrument did not reflect that common intention.

> [88] where there was objectively a prior accord ... and one of the parties ... changed their mind, that is to say objectively made apparent to the other party that they intended to enter into the transaction on different terms ... [Here] it is right that, if the documentation as executed gives effect to the objectively indicated change of mind, a claim for rectification to give effect to the earlier prior accord should be refused. Once again, to do otherwise would force on the defendant a contract which they never intended to make on the basis of the claimant's uncommunicated subjective intention to enter into a contract on the basis of the original accord notwithstanding the defendant's objectively communicated change of mind.

As for elements (1) and (3), the relevant 'common continuing intention' must be established on the balance of probabilities as subsisting as an objective matter, but an articulated agreement (although usual) is not strictly necessary. This point will now be elaborated.

The better view (supported, for example, by McLauchlan)[145] is that the court is entitled to order rectification if, as a result of objective inquiry, it is satisfied that (i) (*actual agreement*)

---

142 *Surgicraft Ltd v. Paradigm Biodevices Inc* [2010] EWHC 1291 (Ch), at [73], *per* Christopher Pycroft QC (Deputy High Court Judge); *Snell's Principles of Equity* (32nd edn, London, 2010), 16–008; *Chitty on Contracts* (31st edn, London, 2012), 5–112; D. McLauchlan, 'The Entire Agreement Clause ...' (2012) 128 LQR 521, 533–6, criticising the more restrictive approach of Hildyard J in *Procter & Gamble Co. v. Svenska Cellulosa Aktiebolaget SCA* [2012] EHC 498 (Ch), at [102] (denying rectification to add a term, as distinct from amending an incorporated term, when the document is subject to an entire agreement clause).

143 *Daventry District Council v. Daventry & District Housing Ltd* [2011] EWCA Civ 1153; [2012] 1 WLR 1333, at [227]; noted Paul S. Davies, 'Rectifying the Course of Rectification', (2012) MLR 412–426.

144 *Ibid.*, at [80].

145 D. McLauchlan, 'Refining Rectification' (2014) 130 LQR 83.

parties C and D in fact agreed[146] that the contract should refer to matters X, Y and Z but in fact the written agreement mistakenly refers to P, Q and R; or (ii) (*objective agreement*) parties C and D were not united in wishing the agreement to comprise matters X, Y and Z, but the objective assessment of the parties' pre-formation dealings is that the agreement concerned X, Y and Z. It should be enough that the court can establish (i) or, where appropriate, (ii). The law should no longer[147] insist that the parties have articulated the agreement so that (prior to formation) it has been outwardly formulated in a particular manner (although such articulation will be the usual situation).

However, if (this point is more fully explained in the next paragraph) the parties have hit upon a particular pre-formation formula (not having appreciated the confusion that might lurk beneath that formula), and the written contract mirrors that formula, rectification is unavailable. This is because there is no mismatch between their outward prior consensus and the eventual written terms.[148]

14.29 *Pre-formation articulated formula decisive unless formula itself failed to reflect parties' clear and joint understanding.* The Court of Appeal in *Rose* v. *Pim* (1953) decided that rectification cannot be used to go behind the parties' articulated formula in order to unpick the parties' underlying confusion or ignorance concerning their transaction's subject matter or purpose.[149] But it can be different if the formula was preceded by an objectively apparent consensus, as in *Grand Metropolitan plc* v. *William Hill Group* (1997).[150]

> In greater detail, in *Rose* v. *Pim* (1953) the buyer received an order from a customer for 'Moroccan horsebeans known here as feveroles'. The seller innocently assured the buyer that 'horsebeans' and 'feveroles' were interchangeable words to describe the same type of bean. In fact horsebeans

146   No agreement is necessary if the instrument is not a contract but a voluntary settlement: *Day* v. *Day* [2013] EWCA Civ 280; [2014] Ch 114 (noted F. Dawson, (2014) 130 LQR 356–359) (enough that the settlor's unilateral and subjective intention was not successfully achieved by the terms of the relevant settlement, provided, of course, that intention can be accurately and convincingly identified); similarly, *per* Lawrence Collins J in *AMP (UK) plc* v. *Booker* [2000] EWHC 42 (Ch); [2000] PLR 77, at [62]; *Drake Insurance plc* v. *McDonald* [2005] EWHC 3287 (Ch); [2005] PLR 401, at [26] and [27], Warren J (distinguishing powers contained in pension schemes and rectification of bilateral contracts); see also remarks by *Allnutt* v. *Wilding* [2007] EWCA Civ 412; [2007] WTLR 941; [2007] BTC 8003, at [13] ff, *per* Mummery LJ.
147   D. Hodge, *Rectification: The Modern Law and Practice Governing Claims for Rectification for Mistake* (London, 2010), 3–10 ff. See also n. 148.
148   *Frederick E Rose (London) Ltd* v. *William H Pim Jnr & Co. Ltd* [1953] 2 QB 450, CA; *Holaw (470) Ltd* v. *Stockton Estates Ltd* (2000) 81 P & CR 404, at [41], *per* Neuberger J, especially at [41]; *AMP (UK) plc* v. *Booker* [2000] EWHC 42 (Ch); [2000] PLR 77, at [61], *per* Lawrence Collins J; *T & N Ltd* v. *Royal & Sun Alliance plc* [2003] EWHC 1016 (Ch); [2003] 2 All ER (Comm) 939, at [133] ff, *per* Lawrence Collins J; *James Hay Pension Trustees Ltd* v. *Hird* [2005] EWHC 1093 (Ch), at [113] (a recapitulation by reference to his earlier judgments), *per* Lawrence Collins J; *Platinum Investment Trust* case [2006] EWHC 1893 (Ch), at [26], *per* Pumfrey J (who in the last sentence of [26] inclines to the heterodox view that a common intention, if proved, is enough; the true view is that there must be a consensus, objectively manifested, not a mere coincidence of subjective intentions; consistent with this, in *Drake Insurance plc* v. *McDonald* [2005] EWHC 3287 (Ch); [2005] PLR 401, at [26] and [27], Warren J distinguished powers contained in pension schemes and rectification of bilateral contracts; and on the latter context, *Allnutt* v. *Wilding* [2007] EWCA Civ 412; [2007] WTLR 941; [2007] BTC 8003, at [13] ff, *per* Mummery LJ); D. Hodge, *Rectification: The Modern Law and Practice Governing Claims for Rectification for Mistake* (London, 2010), 3–10 ff.
149   *Frederick E Rose (London) Ltd* v. *William H Pim Jnr & Co. Ltd* [1953] 2 QB 450, CA; D. Hodge, *Rectification: The Modern Law and Practice Governing Claims for Rectification for Mistake* (London, 2010), 3–10 ff. See also materials cited in the preceding note.
150   [1997] 1 BCLC 390, 394–5, 420.

is a generic term embracing feves, fevettes and feveroles. The parties settled upon the label 'horsebeans'. The agreement recorded accurately the parties' prior understanding that their contract was for 'horsebeans'. The buyer's customer really wanted 'feveroles'. But the buyer was instead supplied with feves, an inferior bean, or at least one not to the liking of the buyer's customer. The buyer was forced to sell the unwanted feves to a third party. The buyer sought rectification of the written contract to substitute 'feveroles' for 'horsebeans', which would then entitle the buyer to obtain damages for non-performance (feves, the goods supplied, and then sub-sold, not being in fact the same as feveroles). The Court of Appeal refused rectification: the written terms accurately reflected the outward accord (the word 'horsebeans').

As Morris LJ put it, this was a contract for 'horsebeans simpliciter' and not for 'horsebeans of the type feveroles'. The remedy of rescission was not available to the buyer because he had sold the unwanted consignment of 'feves' to a third party.

Denning LJ considered that the plaintiff had thrown away their best plea by abandoning at trial a claim for damages based on breach of a collateral warranty (9.12 ff), namely the contention that the seller had orally warranted that 'feveroles' were equivalent to 'horsebeans'. Treitel notes that the purchaser in *Rose* v. *Pim* might now have a remedy for damages under section 2(1) of the Misrepresentation Act 1967, if he can show that the seller had had no reasonable grounds for believing the accuracy of its pre-contractual statement (9.20).[151]

Arden J's decision in *Grand Metropolitan plc* v. *William Hill Group* (1997)[152] qualifies the principle, just explained, in *Rose* v. *Pim* (1953).[153] Rectification can be granted if the following steps can be discerned: the parties have enjoyed a *clear understanding of the relevant matter or issue during their negotiations and there is objective evidence of that common understanding* (unlike on the facts of *Rose* v. *Pim* where they were 'all at sea' on the relevant subject matter). The parties have then *attempted to formulate this*; but *their chosen language fails to capture their true understanding*; this clumsy formulation has been inserted into the final agreement.[154] According to Arden J, substance can prevail over form because the formula used fails to give proper effect to the underlying and clear consensus at which they were verbally aiming.

In *Grand Metropolitan plc* v. *William Hill Group* (1997)[155] the contract did not reflect the parties' common intention concerning the basis upon which the relevant company's accounts would be drawn up. Arden J was able to identify such a common intention. However, the parties' pre-contractual attempt to clothe that intention in words had been misconceived. That unfortunate wording was carried forward into the eventual written agreement. The learned judge held that Equity could give effect to the underlying shared intention. This was not a case where the parties had settled upon an inappropriate label without understanding what the true purpose or underlying basis of their transaction was or might be.

It is submitted that Arden J's decision in *Grand Metropolitan plc* v. *William Hill Group* (1997)[156] is sound and that there is a true ground of distinction between that case and *Rose* v. *Pim* (1953).[157] This is also consistent with the following passage in the *Chartbrook* case

---

151   (12th edn, London, 2007, by E Peel), 8–066, n. 373.
152   [1997] 1 BCLC 390, 394–5, 420.
153   [1953] 2 QB 450, CA.
154   See Glanville Williams' subtle comment, (1954) 17 MLR 154–5, cited by D McLauchlan (2008) 124 LQR 608, 615 n. 29.
155   [1997] 1 BCLC 390.
156   *Ibid.*
157   [1953] 2 QB 450, CA.

(2009),[158] which suggests that rectification can penetrate agreed but inapt formulae and give effect to clearly evidenced outward agreement concerning the relevant aspect of the transaction: 'it is generally accepted that Brightman J was right in *Re Butlin* [1976] Ch 251 in holding that rectification is available not only when the parties intended to use different words but also when they mistakenly thought their words bore a different meaning' (*per* Lord Hoffmann).

The horsebean case (*Rose* v. *Pim* (1953))[159] and company accounting basis case (*Grand Metropolitan plc* (1997))[160] might be contrasted as follows. Suppose X and Y, who are ignorant of the language of board games and the niceties of chess and draughts, agree to play 'a board game with black and white pieces'. Y is disappointed when X, in purported compliance with this agreement, wants to play draughts rather than chess because Y has since discovered that the latter is intellectually more challenging. Y cannot obtain an order to rectify this agreement to substitute 'chess' for the wording in fact adopted. The parties were all at sea: they did not have a clue what they intended to agree upon. Contrast the situation where other parties have a shared and more concrete understanding of what they want to play: they want to play chess (which they have just witnessed being played), although they do not know the name for that particular game. Instead they orally agree to play 'draughts'. This misnomer is inserted into their written contract. Rectification is possible because the agreed label 'draughts' can be shown to be inconsistent with an unaltered common intention to play chess (the game they both in fact aspired to play).

14.30 *Need for an unbroken continuing intention.* If the earlier stage of the negotiations involves the parties agreeing a set of terms 'A, B and C', but the final version is a set of terms 'X, Y and Z', it might be clear that the parties have substituted for elements 'A, B and C' new elements 'X, Y and Z'. If that is the case, there should be no scope for rectifying the contract to restore the terms 'A, B and C'. The simple reason for rectification being denied is that the parties have freely substituted new terms and agreed on those terms. It follows that rectification will be appropriate only if there has been a *continuing and unbroken intention to enter into a contract based on terms 'A, B and C'*. On the facts just mentioned no such unbroken consensus exists and thus the final terms should stand: 'X, Y and Z'.

A troublesome development is the Court of Appeal's majority decision in the *Daventry* case (2011).[161] In the *Daventry* case the District Council ('DDC') successfully obtained rectification against a housing association ('DDH'). During the negotiations, the original version of the document had allocated the financial burden for a pension shortfall to DDH. DDH's negotiator had spotted this snag but had tactically chosen not to focus on this point. Later DDH clearly introduced into the second phase of the negotiations a competing clause which placed the burden on DDC. The latter appeared, on legal advice, to have accepted this change.

158   [2009] UKHL 38; [2009] 1 AC 1101, at [46].
159   [1953] 2 QB 450, CA.
160   [1997] 1 BCLC 390.
161   *Daventry District Council* v. *Daventry & District Housing Ltd* [2011] EWCA Civ 1153; [2012] 1 WLR 1333 (Toulson LJ and Lord Neuberger MR; but Etherton LJ dissenting; and overturning Vos J); noted P. S. Davies, 'Rectifying the Course of Rectification', (2012) MLR 412–26.

But Toulson LJ[162] and Lord Neuberger MR[163] (the latter 'not without hesitation')[164] held that the subsequent change had not been clearly enough signalled to DDC, even though (i) this final wording clearly contradicted the earlier version and (ii) this final version was available to be read by DDC's officials and their lawyers.

With respect, where there has been a clear break in the pattern of the relevant contractual language, and a new version has been presented by party A and adopted by party B (applying ordinary principles governing sequential negotiations, B having failed to raise objection to this clearly contradictory new clause or new set of terms), and A has not accepted unconscionably, the contract should proceed on these finally settled terms.

14.31 *Unilateral mistake rectification.* The general rule is that the court will not grant rectification simply to reflect one party's mistaken understanding.[165] However, the exception to this arises if party B is aware that party A is mistaken concerning the contents or meaning of the written terms. Where that exception applies, rectification is therefore available. For this purpose, B will be 'aware' of the other's error in any of three situations: (1) if he had actual knowledge; or (2) was wilfully blind to an obvious fact; or (3) he wilfully or recklessly failed, contrary to the notion of reasonableness and honesty, to inquire whether there had in fact been a mistake.[166] Although it has been said that the law does not require proof of 'sharp practice',[167] all three situations necessarily import a lack of good faith, or want of probity, on B's part.[168] Equity takes the view that in situations (1) to (3), if B stays silent B cannot take advantage of A's mistake, and that the contract can be rectified in A's favour.[169] This is justified on the basis of B's unconscionable bad faith, or reprehensible acquiescence in A's error. This is a strong equitable intervention because the mistaken party achieves 'total victory': a contract is

---

162 *Ibid.*, at [178].

163 *Ibid.*, at [213] to [225].

164 *Ibid.*, at [227].

165 *Riverlate Properties* v. *Paul* [1975] Ch 133, CA.

166 *Commission for New Towns* v. *Cooper (GB) Limited* [1995] Ch 259, 281 D, 292 F, CA; *George Wimpey UK Ltd* v. *VI Construction Ltd* [2005] EWCA Civ 77; [2005] BLR 135; 103 Con LR 67; [2005] 2 P & CR DG5, at [79]; *Traditional Structures Ltd* v. *HW Construction Ltd* [2010] EWHC 1530 (TCC).

167 *Thomas Bates Ltd* v. *Wyndham's (Lingerie) Ltd* [1981] 1 WLR 505, 515 H, CA, *per* Buckley LJ: 'Undoubtedly I think in any such case the conduct of the defendant must be such as to make it inequitable that he should be allowed to object to the rectification of the document. If this necessarily implies some measure of "sharp practice", so be it; but for my part I think that the doctrine is one which depends more upon the equity of the position.'

168 *George Wimpey UK Ltd* v. *VI Construction Ltd* [2005] EWCA Civ 77; [2005] BLR 135; 103 Con LR 67; [2005] 2 P & CR DG5, at [79].

169 *A Roberts & Co. Ltd* v. *Leicestershire CC* [1961] Ch 555, 570, Pennycuick J (noted R. E. Megarry (1961) 77 LQR 313–6); *'The Olympic Pride'* [1980] 2 Lloyd's Rep 67, Mustill J; *Thomas Bates Ltd* v. *Wyndham's (Lingerie) Ltd* [1981] 1 WLR 505, CA; *Agip SpA* v. *Navigazione Alta Italia SpA*, *'The Nai Genova and the Nai Superba'* [1984] 1 Lloyd's Rep 353, 365, CA; *Commission for New Towns* v. *Cooper (GB) Limited* [1995] Ch 259, CA (noted D. Mossop (1996) 10 JCL 259–63); *George Wimpey UK Ltd* v. *VI Components Ltd* [2005] EWCA Civ 77; [2005] BLR 135; 103 Con LR 67; [2005] 2 P & CR DG5; *Traditional Structures Ltd* v. *HW Construction Ltd* [2010] EWHC 1530 (TCC), at [25] to [31]; D. McLauchlan, 'The "Drastic" Remedy of Rectification for Unilateral Mistake' (2008) 124 LQR 608–40 (who thinks this category of rectification has been misunderstood; although a first instance judge is not at liberty to reconsider this category of rectification because he is bound by Court of Appeal authority: *Traditional Structures* case, *ibid.*, at [32] and [33]).

recast to reflect his unilateral understanding, even though there was no shared understanding supporting this version of the contract.[170]

In *George Wimpey UK Ltd* v. *VI Components Ltd* (2005) both (i) the requirement of error on A's part and (ii) some form of knowledge on B's part were absent. As for (i), the Court of Appeal held that there was no evidence that A's board of directors (the 'decision-making' entity) had made an error.[171] As for (ii), even if, contrary to (i), A had been mistaken, it had not been shown that B, a relatively inexperienced party, knew of any such error. Therefore, B had not taken unfair advantage of A.

Chartbrook Ltd v. *Persimmon Homes Ltd* (2008) is another case illustrating the uphill task in proving that A suffered the requisite error and that B knew of it.[172] At first instance (on the House of Lords' decision, which dispensed with the need to invoke rectification, 14.22), Briggs J had said:[173]

> In unilateral mistake cases the reason why convincing proof is needed of the [defendant's] knowledge of the claimant's mistake is because of the inherent improbability that the [defendant] would behave so inequitably as to keep silent, once he knows about it.
>
> The effect of a successful rectification claim based on unilateral mistake is always that it imposes a contract upon the defendant which he did not intend to make. It is the unconscionable conduct involved in staying silent when aware of the claimant's mistake that makes it just to impose a different contract upon him from that by which he intended to be bound. For that reason as well, convincing proof is needed that the defendant's conduct, taken as a whole, fell short of the requirements of good conscience.

The law concerning unilateral mistake rectification was summarised by Judge Richard Seymour QC in *Wimpole Theatre (a firm)* v. *J J Goodman Ltd* (2012):[174]

> [T]he court [must] be satisfied: (1) that the party alleged to have entered into the written contract by mistake did actually have, at the moment of entering into the contract, a specific intention that the contract should contain a provision which it does not in fact contain, or should not contain a provision which it does contain; (2) that the other party actually knew of that specific intention, or turned a blind eye to such knowledge; (3) that the evidence of both of these elements is demonstrated on the material put before the court on the balance of probabilities, but with a high degree of assurance.

As Burrows observes, the relevant 'unilateral error' might concern a point of confusion which arose in one party's mind before, and independently of, the settling of the final written terms in binding contractual form.[175] But the more usual situation is a last-minute problem: in reducing the terms into a final draft for the parties to clothe as their agreement, one of the parties, normally A, erroneously omits, adds or 'botches' one or more of the terms; B is alive to this error, but he fails to point it out to A. It will be usual for the error to be detrimental to A, and

170   *Rowallan Group Ltd* v. *Edgehill Portfolio No. 1 Ltd* [2007] EWHC 32 (Ch); [2007] NPC 9, at [14], *per* Lightman J: 'the remedy of rectification for unilateral mistake is a drastic remedy, for it has the result of imposing on the defendant ... a contract that he did not, and did not intend, to make.' D. Hodge, *Rectification: The Modern Law and Practice Governing Claims of Rectification* (London, 2010), 4–90 to 4–93.

171   *George Wimpey* case, [2005] EWCA Civ 77; [2005] BLR 135; 103 Con LR 67; [2005] 2 P & CR DG5.

172   [2008] EWCA Civ 183; [2008] 2 All ER (Comm) 387.

173   *Chartbrook Ltd* v. *Persimmon Homes Ltd* [2007] EWHC 409 (Ch), *per* Briggs J, at [136].

174   [2012] EWHC 1600 (QB) at [54].

175   Analysis of *A Roberts & Co. Ltd* v. *Leicestershire CC* [1961] Ch 555, 570, Pennycuick J (on which R. E. Megarry (1961) 77 LQR 313–6 and A. Burrows in A. Burrows and E. Peel (eds.), *Contract Terms* (Oxford, 2007), 88 ff).

correspondingly beneficial to B. But it seems that detriment to A is enough. Although the usual situation is that A's unilateral error is *known to B*, the jurisdiction to provide rectification is not confined to that situation, and instead extends to wilful blindness.[176]

McLauchlan (2008) has argued that the category of rectification for unilateral error known to the other party should be reconceptualised.[177] In his view, A is entitled to rectification in this context not because B has been aware of A's mistake and because B's silence injects into the equation an inequitable or unconscionable factor. Instead McLauchlan suggests that rectification gives effect to a *shared intention* in this context because A is 'led reasonably to believe that [B] assented to [A]'s understanding of the terms, so that rectification will give effect to the parties' agreement as objectively ascertained'.[178] This is an interesting suggestion, but two counter-remarks seem necessary. First, McLauchlan's notion can be explored by the English courts only at the highest level,[179] because there is Court of Appeal authority that the test requires proof that B knew of A's error, or was wilfully blind, or wilfully or recklessly failed to inquire. Secondly, McLauchlan's proposal would yield rectification if the parties' pre-contractual dealings disclose (i) a clearly articulated consensus ('common intention' rectification) or (ii) a set of terms to which B has positively or implicitly inclined (McLauchlan's reconstitution of the 'second head'). The objection is that limb (ii) might open the door too widely to disputes concerning rectification and so weaken the primacy of final written terms.

14.32 *Unilateral error and underhand negotiations.* This paragraph concerns a straw in the wind. The law is not settled on this point. In the *Commission for New Towns* case (1995), Stuart-Smith LJ[180] (unattractively) suggested that unilateral mistake can give rise to rectification where party B has deliberately lulled the other party into agreeing a document on terms which benefit B and harm A's interests. This involves B tactically creating a 'smokescreen' during negotiations.

It is submitted that this suggested further route to rectification will carry little traffic because the main route to 'non-consensual' rectification is bad faith acquiescence (14.31). Indeed a future Court of Appeal should sceptically revisit Stuart-Smith LJ's dicta, and at the very least provide a clearer and more satisfactory rationale (these dicta present a curious hybrid of bad faith without proof of knowledge at the moment of contracting, and of misrepresentation without proof of inducement).

Unfortunately, the Court of Appeal in *Hurst Stores & Interiors* v. *ML Europe Projects Ltd* (2004) expressed general approval of this dictum.[181] However, this appears to have rested on a concession by counsel, and the point was not material to the decision in this 2004 case.

176   *Commission for New Towns* v. *Cooper (GB) Limited* [1995] Ch 259, 281 D, 292 F, CA; *George Wimpey UK Ltd* v. *VI Construction Ltd* [2005] EWCA Civ 77; [2005] BLR 135; 103 Con LR 67; [2005] 2 P & CR DG5, at [79]; *Traditional Structures Ltd* v. *HW Construction Ltd* [2010] EWHC 1530 (TCC).
177   D. McLauchlan, 'The "Drastic" Remedy of Rectification for Unilateral Mistake' (2008) 124 LQR 608, 610, 640.
178   *Ibid.*
179   *Traditional Structures Ltd* v. *HW Construction Ltd* [2010] EWHC 1530 (TCC), at [32] and [33], where it was said that a first instance judge, since bound by authority, cannot adopt McLauchlan's view.
180   *Commission for New Towns* v. *Cooper (GB) Limited* [1995] Ch 259, 280, CA; this is a dictum.
181   [2004] EWCA Civ 490; (2004) 24 BLR 249; (2004) 94 Con LR 66, at [19] and [20], *per* Buxton LJ.

> Therefore, the dictum in the *Commission for New Towns* case (1995) remains alive for reconsideration by the Court of Appeal.

14.33 *Error of law.* Rectification should be available where the relevant drafting error arises from an error of law.[182]

14.34 *Formal transactions.* Rectification can be granted to establish a written valid contract where the parties had clearly shared the intention that a contract for the conveyance of land would be effective.[183] Here the remedy is effective to constitute an agreement which would otherwise be invalid for failure to satisfy formalities. A variation on this is a more recent English decision, where rectification was granted to revise a guarantee (the document had been signed by the guarantor, but its terms had not been properly recorded).[184]

14.35 *'Explosion' of rectification claims.* Although rectification is a doctrine of last resort (14.26), there has been an 'explosion' of claims for rectification. This is attributable to these three factors: first, to the increasing complexity of commercial and other written contracts; secondly, to the tendency for successive drafts to be composed using the 'cut and paste' style of word-processing; finally, to the richness of accessible electronic records of negotiations.[185]

14.36 *Third party rights.* Rectification will not be awarded if this would harm a third party who has, in good faith and for consideration, acquired rights in the relevant subject matter.[186] But there must be good faith.[187] Consider the case where the document which is to be rectified was between A and B, but the present dispute is between A and D. In this situation, rectification in favour of A, and to D's disadvantage, is available provided D is not a bona fide purchaser (as where it is shown that a portion of land was not intended to be included in the A/B transaction, and D knew that, following a blunder in the drafting of the A/B document, the literal terms of the A/D transaction purported to give D the same portion of land; rectification can be ordered of the A/B and A/D transactions; and D is in fact the trustee of the wrongly conveyed portion for the benefit of A, the original vendor).[188]

---

182   Applying the analogy of *Brennan* v. *Bolt Burdon* [2004] EWCA Civ 1017; [2005] QB 303; this development approved by Arden LJ in *Meretz Investments NV* v. *ACP Ltd* [2007] EWCA Civ 1303; [2008] Ch 244, at [118].
183   *Domb* v. *Isoz* [1980] 1 Ch 548, 559, CA, *per* Buckley LJ (followed in *Sindel* v. *Georgiou* (1984) 154 CLR 661, 667–8; 55 ALR 1, 4–5, High Court of Australia).
184   *GMAC Commercial Credit Development Ltd* v. *Sandhu* [2004] EWHC 716 (Comm), Richard Siberry QC, at [50] to [58].
185   D. Hodge, *Rectification: The Modern Law and Practice Governing Claims of Rectification* (London, 2010), foreword by Lord Neuberger MR, at p. vii.
186   *Smith* v. *Jones* [1954] 1 WLR 1089, 1091–3, *per* Upjohn J; *Chitty on Contracts* (31st edn, London, 2012), 5–139; *Meagher, Gummow, Lehane's Equity: Doctrines and Remedies* (4th edn, Sydney, 2002), 899, n. 31; A. Berg (2008) 124 LQR 6, 12.
187   *Craddock Bros* v. *Hunt* [1923] 2 Ch 136, 151, 154–5, 158–9, CA, *per* Lord Sterndale MR and Warrington LJ (Younger LJ dissenting).
188   *Ibid.*

14.37 *Rectification barred by prejudicial delay ('laches'), acquiescence or affirmation.* Rectification is also denied if a party 'sleeps on his rights'. Instead he must take prompt action by applying to the court for rectification (the equitable defences of 'laches' – a defence rooted in protection against prejudice caused by delay[189] (and which was encapsulated by Lawrence Collins J, as he then was, in the *T & N* case (2003))[190] – and 'acquiescence'; affirmation, with knowledge of the right to rectification, is another bar).

14.38 *Arbitrator's power to order rectification.* An arbitration clause might be widely drawn so as to permit such an order.[191] The Arbitration Act 1996 also permits the arbitrator or panel to order rectification.[192]

7. CONCLUDING REMARKS

14.39 *Pressure-points in the law of interpretation.* The three main issues are: over-confident interpretation crossing the line and becoming judicial revision; the invisibility of pre-contractual negotiations (the negotiation evidence bar); the relevance of pre-contractual negotiations for the purpose of the equitable remedy of rectification and the tactical importance of combining claims for 'corrective interpretation' (14.22) and rectification.

14.40 *Over-confident interpretation.* Some consider that English law has moved too drastically away from giving primacy to contractual language and has veered towards a liberal interpretation of that language to give effect to 'business common sense' and to cure 'obvious errors'.

14.41 *The negotiation evidence bar and 'ordinary interpretation'.* The courts remain committed to exclusion of pre-contractual negotiations when construing contracts; it is different if the parties have settled on a quite unusual meaning during their negotiations or if the courts are required to consider a rectification plea. This insistence on the 'negotiation evidence bar' can be rationalised on various bases, notably that it would slow down, complicate and even obfuscate the task of giving objective meaning to the contractual

189 *Spry's Equitable Remedies* (6th edn, 2001), 617–9; *Meagher, Gummow, Lehane's Equity: Doctrines and Remedies*, ibid., p. 899 text at nn. 32, 33; *Treitel* (13th edn, London, 2011), 8–071 appears to be alone in regarding 'lapse of time' as enough.
190 *T & N Ltd* v. *Royal & Sun Alliance plc* [2003] EWHC 1016 (Ch); [2003] 2 All ER (Comm) 939, at [140], *per* Lawrence Collins J: 'If the party seeking equitable relief has not been reasonably diligent in seeking it, and in consequence the position of the other party has been prejudiced or it would now be unjust or unreasonable to grant the relief, it will be debarred from pursuing his remedy on the ground of laches. What amounts to reasonable diligence and what circumstances will render it inequitable to grant the relief will vary with the type of relief sought and the facts of the particular case: *Lindsay Petroleum Co.* v. *Hurd* [1874] LR 5 PC 221, 239, *per* Lord Selborne; *Erlanger* v. *New Sombrero Phosphate Co* (1878) 3 App Cas 1218, 1279, *per* Lord Blackburn; *Chitty, Contracts*, 28th ed. 1999, vol 1, para 29–140. But for the purposes of laches time runs only from notice of the error: *Beal v. Kyte* [1907] 1 Ch 564, 566; *Snell's Equity*, 13th ed, 2000, para 3–19.'
191 *Ashville Investments Ltd* v. *Elmer Contractors Ltd* [1989] QB 488, CA (wide review of the authorities).
192 Section 48(5) of the Arbitration Act 1996.

text; and that having lifted this 'bar', parties would opportunistically try to bolster their chances of gaining a favourable interpretation by laying a 'paper trail' supporting their preferred interpretation.

14.42 *Tactical importance of raising simultaneous interpretation and rectification issues.* The left hand does not know what the right hand is doing: when hearing a rectification plea, the courts will admit evidence of pre-contractual negotiations (14.27) but, as just noted, such evidence is not admitted for the purpose of Common Law interpretation (14.41). And yet these doctrines overlap functionally. Thus 'corrective interpretation' (14.22 to 14.24) and rectification enable the court to revise a document. Furthermore, there is no difference in the 'timing' of both interpretation and rectification. Once the court has declared (i) a 'corrective construction'[193]: or (ii) it orders rectification[194] (unless, perhaps, special terms[195] are added to the order), the relevant text is construed or rectified, and hence operative on that basis, from the contract's commencement date. Not surprisingly, parties seek to maximise the chances of gaining a favourable outcome on a disputed written contract by pleading both 'corrective construction' (14.22 above) and rectification. However, there is this procedural difference. A rectification claim will often require oral evidence from factual witnesses at trial (directed at the history of the negotiations), whereas documentary evidence will normally suffice for the purpose of issues of Common Law interpretation. Thus the latter is susceptible of being adjudicated by (pre-trial) summary judgment under CPR Part 24,[196] whereas many rectification claims must await disposal at trial.

QUESTIONS

(1) What is meant when the courts say that they are attempting to find the 'objective' interpretation of written contracts?

(2) What is the basis of the bar on receiving evidence concerning the parties' pre-contractual negotiations? And how does this bar relate to the parol evidence rule (12.02)?

(3) Illustrate this proposition: 'the courts interpret written contracts in accordance with commercial common sense.'

---

193   Lewison LJ said in *Cherry Tree Investments Ltd* v. *Landmain Ltd* [2012] EWCA Civ 736; [2013] Ch 305, at [99]: 'A contract cannot mean one thing when it is made and another thing following court proceedings. Nor, in my judgment, can it mean one thing to some people (e.g. the parties to it) and another thing to others who might be affected by it.'

194   Lewison LJ added in the *Cherry Tree* case, *ibid.*, at [121: 'the effect of the court's [rectification] order is retrospective, and the document will be read as if it had always been in its rectified form: *Craddock Bros Ltd* v. *Hunt* [1923] 2 Ch 136, 151.'

195   Rectification (an order made from outside the document) can be withheld or imposed on terms, as Lord Neuberger observed in *Marley* v. *Rawlings* [2014] UKSC 2; [2014] 2 WLR 213, at [40].

196   CPR Part 24 can be used for a 'short point of law or construction' provided 'the court is satisfied that it has before it all the evidence necessary for the proper determination of the question and that the parties have had an adequate opportunity to address it in argument', *per* Lewison J, in *EasyAir Ltd* v. *Opal Telecom Ltd* [2009] EWHC 339 (Ch) at [15], approved in *AC Ward Ltd* v. *Catlin (Five) Ltd* [2009] EWCA Civ 1098; [2010] Lloyd's Rep IR 301, at [24]; and cited by Floyd J in *Joint Stock Co. Aeroflot – Russian Airlines* v. *Berezovsky* [2012] EWHC 3017 (Ch), at [56]. On summary judgment in English court proceedings, *Andrews on Civil Processes* (Cambridge, 2013), vol. 1, *Court Proceedings*, at 10.79 ff.

(4) To what extent will the courts permit the parties to produce evidence of background circumstances ('factual matrix')?
(5) What is 'corrective construction', and what are its limits?
(6) What are the two heads of rectification?
(7) What is the functional overlap between 'corrective construction' and rectification?
(8) Taking into account both the principles of interpretation and the remedy of rectification, is the law in this field unsatisfactory in any respect(s)?

Selected further reading

Interpretation is the 'hottest' topic in English contract law. It has recently produced a massive amount of literature. These are some of the leading discussions of the inter-related topics appearing in this chapter:

I. Investors Compensation Scheme (1998) principles of interpretation for written contracts

A. Berg, 'Thrashing Through the Undergrowth' (2006) 122 LQR 354, especially 358–62
Lord Grabiner, 'The Iterative Process of Contractual Interpretation' (2012) 128 LQR 41
Lord Nicholls, 'My Kingdom for a Horse: the Meaning of Words' (2005) 121 LQR 577, especially 585–8 (although Lord Hoffmann in *Chartbrook Ltd* v. *Persimmon Homes Ltd* [2009] UKHL 38; [2009] 1 AC 1101, at [41] (see 14.15) did not find persuasive Lord Nicholls's plea in that article for abolition of the rule barring evidence of negotiations as an aid to interpretation of written contracts)
G. Yihan, 'A Wrong Turn in History: Re-Understanding the Exclusionary Rule Against Prior Negotiations in Contractual Interpretation' [2014] JBL 360–87

II. Other systems' approach to pre-contractual negotiations as aid to interpretation

M. J. Bonell (ed.), *The UNIDROIT Principles in Practice: Case Law and Bibliography on the UNIDROIT Principles of International Commercial Contracts* (2nd edn, Ardsley, NY, 2006), 234 ff
E. Clive, in H. MacQueen and R. Zimmermann (eds.), *European Contract Law: Scots and South African Perspectives* (Edinburgh, 2006), chapter 7 at 183
S. Vogenauer and J. Kleinheisterkamp (eds.), *Commentary on the UNIDROIT Principles of International Commercial Contracts* (Oxford, 2009), 510 ff (antedating the third edition of UNIDROIT'S *Principles of International Commercial Contracts* (3rd edition, 2010), text and comment. However, the provisions (Articles 4.1 to 4.8) concerning interpretation are unchanged from the second edition (2004); third edition available at: www.unidroit.org/eng lish/principles/contracts/principles2010/integralversionprinciples2010-e.pdf

III. Equitable doctrine of rectification

D. Hodge, *Rectification: The Modern Law and Practice Governing Claims of Rectification* (London, 2010)
D. McLauchlan, 'The "Drastic" Remedy of Rectification for Unilateral Mistake' (2008) 124 LQR 608–40, especially 608–10, 639–40
D. McLauchlan, 'Refining Rectification' (2014) 130 LQR 83

J. Ruddell, 'Common Intention and Rectification for Common Mistake' [2014] LMCLQ 48–75, notably at 64–6 and 70–5

R. (Lord) Toulson, 'Does Rectification Require Rectifying' (October 2013 speech) (http://supreme court.uk/docs/speech-131031.pdf)

IV. Connection between interpretation to iron out drafting snags and rectification in Equity

A. Burrows, 'Construction and Rectification', in A. Burrows and E. Peel (eds.), *Contract Terms* (Oxford, 2007), 77, especially 90 to end

R. Buxton, '"Construction" and Rectification After *Chartbrook*' [2010] CLJ 253

V. Comparative discussion

J. W. Carter, 'Context and Literalism in Construction' (2014) 31 JCL 100–19 (surveying English, Australian, Singaporean and USA law)

C. Valcke, 'On Comparing French and English Contract Law: Insights from Social Contract Theory' (2009) JCL 69–95 (cited as 'illuminating' by Lord Hoffmann in the *Chartbrook* case [2009] UKHL 38; [2009] 1 AC 1001, at [39])

C. Valcke, 'Contractual Interpretation at Common Law and Civil Law: An Exercise in Comparative Legal Rhetoric', in J. W. Neyers, R. Bronaugh, S. G. A. Pitel, *Exploring Contract Law* (Oxford, 2009), 77 ff

Chapter contents

15

Exclusion clauses and 'unfair terms'

1. INTRODUCTION

15.01 Summary of main points

(1) *Types of exclusion clause.*[1] There are three main types of exclusion clause:
   (a) total exclusion: 'X Co. will not be liable to you at all for breach of any of these obligations', sometimes known as an 'exemption clause';
   (b) time restriction: 'If you want to claim compensation you must notify your claim within [a specified period] of the alleged harm';
   (c) a financial cap: 'Liability to pay compensation shall not exceed £x'.

(2) *Common Law responses to exclusion clauses.* The Common Law has tried to deal with the problem of exclusion clauses by employing three main techniques or rules: first, incorporation and 'notice'; secondly, 'construction' (that is, restrictive interpretation of written agreement *contra proferentem*, so as to lean against interpretation which might favour the person relying on the clause, and see 15.05 for broader adoption of this technique in the consumer context as a result of legislation); thirdly, at Common Law, there is a rule invalidating attempts to exclude or restrict liability for fraud (15.04). Thus, before proceeding to consider the second stage of legal control, namely, statutory restrictions (on which see 15.08 and 15.28), at Common Law the three questions to be posed when considering an exclusion clause's effect are:
   (a) Has the proposed exclusion clause become part of the contract (the question of 'incorporation' and of 'notice': 15.02 and 15.03)?
   (b) If so, does the exclusion clause's wording cover the relevant head of loss (15.05 and 15.06)?
   (c) Does the exclusion clause purport to exclude or restrict liability for fraud (15.04)?
   At Common Law, a clause can fail for *any* of the three reasons mentioned at (a) to (c) above.

(3) *Issues arising under statute.* Here, the questions are:

---

1 The Consumer Rights Bill will need to be taken into account when using this literature: R. Lawson, *Exclusion Clauses and Unfair Contract Terms* (10th edn, London, 2011); *Chitty on Contracts* (31st edn, London, 2012), chapters 14 and 15; *Treitel* (13th edn, London, 2011), chapter 7.

(a) Does the clause become automatically invalid under the statutory systems of control; or

(b) Is the clause at least vulnerable to a statutory test of reasonableness (for example, under sections 2(1) or 3 of the Unfair Contract Terms Act 1977 (non-consumer contracts) (again, this is to be modified by the Consumer Rights Bill, or section 3 of the Misrepresentation Act 1967 (generally on section 3 of the 1967 Act, see 9.33), or the Consumer Rights Bill (15.28); each of these statutory schemes contains 'reasonableness' tests)?

2. INCORPORATION OF EXCLUSION CLAUSES

15.02   *The test.* A line of Common Law decisions requires a party seeking protection from an exclusion clause to take reasonable steps to bring it to the other's attention. And so a clause becomes *incorporated* within the contract (although it might, at the next stage of inquiry, be invalidated as intrinsically unacceptable or 'unreasonable' in accordance with a statutory rule: see 15.08 ff) if either (1) the party purportedly subject to the exclusion clause knew that there was a contractual document containing terms, or that same party at least knew that the document referred to such terms; or (2) the other party (now seeking to raise the exclusion clause as a defence) took reasonably sufficient steps to give the other side notice of the conditions. If so, the customer need not know that the relevant document consisted of, or referred to, contractual conditions; provided he was aware that the document contained writing.

The seminal decision on the 'ticket' issue is *Parker* v. *South Eastern Railway Co.* (1877).[2] Here a passenger had deposited a bag with contents exceeding the value of £10, but the receipt stated that it was a condition that the defendant company would not be liable for loss exceeding £10. The bag was lost. The Court of Appeal held that it would be enough that the passenger knew there was writing on the receipt. Mellish LJ formulated this series of tests:[3]

> [I]f the person receiving the ticket did not see or know that there was any writing on the ticket, he is not bound by the conditions; that if he knew there was writing, and knew or believed that the writing contained conditions, then he is bound by the conditions; that if he knew there was writing on the ticket, but did not know or believe that the writing contained conditions, nevertheless he would be bound, if the delivering of the ticket to him in such a manner that he could see there was writing upon it, was, in the opinion of the jury, reasonable notice that the writing contained conditions.

As noted by Megaw LJ in *Thornton* v. *Shoe Lane Parking* (1971):[4]

> *Parker* v. *South Eastern Railway Co.* (1877) . . . established that the appropriate questions . . . in a ticket case were: (1) Did the passenger know that there was printing on the railway

---

2   (1877) 2 CPD 416, CA.
3   *Ibid.,* 423, CA.
4   [1971] 2 QB 163, 171–2, CA.

ticket? (2) Did he know that the ticket contained or referred to conditions? and (3) Did the railway company do what was reasonable in the way of notifying prospective passengers of the existence of conditions and where their terms might be considered?

Over a century later, Bingham LJ in *Interfoto* v. *Stiletto* (1989)[5] noted that this 'reasonable steps' test applies not just to exclusion clauses but to all 'onerous or unusual' clauses (perhaps only if 'particularly', or 'extremely' 'onerous or unusual')[6] lurking in the undergrowth of the other party's standard terms (the clause in question in the *Interfoto* case concerned a special payment in the event of delayed return of hired material: see the text below).

In *Interfoto* v. *Stiletto* (1989),[7] a commercial party, Stiletto, had hired transparencies from Interfoto, a photographic library. Stiletto was later invoiced for an exorbitant sum. Stiletto disputed liability to pay this amount. Interfoto's small-print terms imposed a large daily fee for each transparency if they were retained for longer than fourteen days, namely, £5 for each item for each extra day (it was thus a liquidated damages clause (19.01 ff) which smacked of a penalty). Interfoto's charges were about ten times higher than those charged by competitors. The eventual bill for late return was a massive amount, £4,000. The initial delivery note had been headed 'Conditions'. However, nothing more had been done to impress upon the customer the importance of these proposed terms. Nor had Stiletto signed to acknowledge notice of these terms.

Although this term was not an exclusion clause, the Court of Appeal in *Interfoto* v. *Stiletto* (1989) held that the nineteenth-century 'ticket' case law (concerning exclusion clauses) also applies to 'onerous or unusual' terms, even if the relevant clause is not an exclusion clause (the clause in the *Interfoto* case was described by Bingham LJ in that very decision and later by Hobhouse LJ and Rix LJ as 'extortionate').[8] The adequate notice test stated in the *Parker* case (1877) (see above) was not satisfied in the *Interfoto* case because the Court of Appeal held that Interfoto had not done enough to alert its customer to the especially onerous nature of the clause. And so the £4,000 contract claim failed.

5 [1989] QB 433, CA; noted by H. McLean, [1988] CLJ 172; P. A. Chandler and J. A. Holland, (1988) 104 LQR 359; Sir Bernard Rix, 'Lord Bingham's Contributions to Commercial Law', in M. Andenas and D. Fairgrieve (eds.), *Tom Bingham and the Transformation of the Law: A Liber Amicorum* (Oxford, 2009), 668–71; the 'ticket' cases and the *Interfoto* decision were considered in *AEG (UK) Ltd* v. *Logic Resource Ltd* [1996] CLC 265, CA (clause restricting non-consumer purchaser's rights 'extremely onerous and unusual', *per* Hirst and Waite LJJ; Hobhouse LJ adopting a more nuanced approach on the issue of incorporation, at 276–8) and in dicta in *Shepherd Homes Ltd* v. *Encia Remediation Ltd* [2007] EWHC 70 (TCC); [2007] BLR 135; 110 Con LR 90, at [57] to [69], *per* Christopher Clarke J.
6 The adverbs 'particularly' and 'extremely' (qualifying the adjectives 'onerous and unusual') recur in all three judgments in *AEG (UK) Ltd* v. *Logic Resource Ltd* [1996] CLC 265, 269–5, 277, CA; see also *HIH Casualty & General Insurance Ltd* v. *New Hampshire Insurance Co.* [2001] EWCA Civ 735; [2001] 2 All ER (Comm) 39, at [211], *per* Rix LJ; Gloster J in *JP Morgan Chase Bank* v. *Springwell Navigation Corp.* [2008] EWHC 1186, at [578] ff (affirmed [2010] EWCA Civ 1221; [2010] 2 CLC 705).
7 [1989] QB 433, CA; E. Macdonald, (1988) JBL 375.
8 *AEG (UK) Ltd* v. *Logic Resource Ltd* [1996] CLC 265, 276, 277, CA, *per* Hobhouse LJ (noting the *Interfoto* case [1989] QB 433, 445, CA, *per* Bingham LJ); *HIH Casualty & General Insurance Ltd* v. *New Hampshire Insurance Co.* [2001] EWCA Civ 735; [2001] 2 All ER (Comm) 39, at [211], *per* Rix LJ, characterising the term in *Interfoto* as 'not merely unusual, but very onerous, unreasonable and extortionate'.

For a case where the adequate notice test was satisfied, and where in any event the clause was neither 'onerous' nor 'unusual', see *O'Brien* v. *MGN Ltd* (2001).[9]

The *Interfoto* case overlaps with the (non-binding) UNIDROIT *Principles of International Commercial Contracts* (2010), Article 2.1.20,[10] which refers to a 'term contained in standard terms which is of such a character that the other party could not reasonably have expected it', and requires such a clause to be 'expressly accepted' by the other party. However, as noted, the *Interfoto* case is not confined to 'standard terms' and the concept, adopted in that case, of 'onerous or unusual' clauses is wider than the approach employed in the 'soft law' codes, which refer to 'surprising terms'.

Statute prescribes a similar requirement for the protection of consumers[11] (see summary of this aspect of the Consumer Rights Bill, at 15.30).

15.03 There is extensive case law on other aspects of the issue whether an exclusion clause has been successfully incorporated into a contract. These matters can be categorised as follows.

(1) *Signatures.* A signature is effective to incorporate an exclusion clause. The Common Law rule is straightforward: if the innocent party has signed a document, he is taken objectively to have assented to the exclusion clause, even if in fact he had not read it, or at least did not understand its effect. This was affirmed in *L'Estrange* v. *F Graucob Ltd* (1934), where the claimant had bought a defective cigarette slot machine for her Llandudno café.[12]

In *L'Estrange* v. *F Graucob Ltd* (1934), Miss Harriett Mary L'Estrange, a café proprietor, bought an automatic slot machine (selling cigarettes) from the defendant company. The machine proved to be defective, soon becoming jammed and quite useless. But she had imprudently signed away nearly all her protection in a document containing small print. This included an exclusion clause: 'any express or implied condition, statement, or warranty, statutory or otherwise not stated herein is hereby excluded.' The Divisional Court held that her decision to sign this document and to conclude this agreement had the effect of incorporating the exclusion clause, whether or not she had in fact read or understood the clause. The court added that there are various exceptions to this, although none of these was satisfied on the present facts: duress; fraud; misrepresentation (see the *Curtis* case, summarised at 9.44); or the *non est factum* doctrine (10.22).[13]

The English decision in *L'Estrange* v. *Graucob* (1934) has been distinguished in Canada in *Tilden Rent-A-Car* v. *Clendenning* (1978), where it was held that a party's signature is ineffective to incorporate a term if the other party, the *proferens*, was aware that the signatory had not read

9 [2001] EWCA Civ 1279; *The Times*, 8 August 2001; [2002] CLC 33; noted by J. Elvin, [2002] CLJ 19 ('scratch-card' winner; printed rules restricting winners to two in one week; neither 'onerous' nor 'unusual', *ibid.*, at [21] and [24]); similarly, *Photolibrary Group Ltd* v. *Burda Senator Verlag GmbH* [2008] EWHC 1343 (QB); [2008] 2 All ER (Comm) 881, at [12] and [60], *per* Jack J.

10 3rd edition, 2010, text and comment, is available at: www.unidroit.org/english/principles/contracts/principles2010/integralversionprinciples2010-e.pdf.

11 For this problem from the perspective of 'online' contracts, see L. DiMatteo, Q. Zhou, S. Saintier, K. Rowley (eds.), *Commercial Contract Law: Transatlantic Perspectives* (Cambridge, 2014), chapter 8 (by N. Kim); see also, in the same work, T. Joo, chapter 3, on USA case law concerning consumer arbitration clauses.

12 [1934] 2 KB 394, Divisional Court; J. R. Spencer, 'Signature, Consent and the Rule in *L'Estrange* v. *Graucob*' [1973] CLJ 104; D. McLauchlan, 'The Entire Agreement Clause . . . ' (2012) 128 LQR 521, 532–3.

13 *Gallie* v. *Lee* [1971] AC 1004, HL.

an onerous clause, such as an exclusion clause (on the facts of the *Tilden* case, the relevant clause contained a strict limitation of the insurer's liability in a car-hire insurance policy).[14] The Ontario Court of Appeal held that the defendant customer's signature on this contractual document was not decisive. The rental company obviously knew that the customer had not read the relevant clause in this document and that he was therefore unaware of this harsh and unusual term. For this reason, there was no justice in applying the blanket rule that signature incorporated all clauses, however surprising or unusual, and even if, to the other party's knowledge, the signatory had not bothered to read the document's relevant small print. This point is cogently made by John Spencer in his seminal treatment of this topic,[15] and his argument was approved by the Ontario Court of Appeal in this case. The *Tilden* case's gloss upon the *L'Estrange* case seems sound: it is a modest additional requirement to require the signatory to sign, or at least to add his initials, to indicate assent to especially onerous clauses within such hire documents. Users of car hire will be familiar with this sensible practice.

(2) *Notice coming too late.* An exclusion clause will have no effect if it comes to a party's notice only after the contract has been formed.

In *Olley v. Marlborough Court Ltd* (1949), the claimant booked a room in a hotel.[16] Later, some valuables were stolen from the room. The hotelier was guilty of negligence in allowing a thief access to the room. However, the defendant hotelier tried to escape liability for this negligence by relying on an exclusion clause placed in the hotel room. But this exclusion clause had not come to the claimant's notice until she had gone upstairs to her room. The court held that this clause had no effect because it had come to the claimant's notice too late.

Similarly, in *Thornton v. Shoe Lane Parking* (1971), the Court of Appeal held that notice of an exclusion clause came too late because the contract had already been formed once the driver of a car had entered the defendant's automated car park.[17]

(3) *Contractual intent.* There is also the issue of whether the clause was contained in a document which appeared to have contractual force.

In *Chapelton v. Barry Urban District Council* (1940), the claimant paid 2d (two old pence) for the hire of two deckchairs from the municipal authority (one for him, the other for his girlfriend, Miss Andrews). He fell through the canvas of one (not deliberately) and injured his back. He sued for breach of contract. The Court of Appeal held that the defendant's written exclusion clause – contained on the back of his receipt for the chairs – had not been incorporated. This document was not objectively intended to affect contractual rights. Slesser LJ said that the receipt was not a document which could reasonably be expected to contain terms. And MacKinnon LJ said that

---

14 (1978) 83 DLR (3d) 400; 18 OR (2d) 601.
15 J. R. Spencer, 'Signature, Consent and the Rule in *L'Estrange* v. *Graucob*' [1973] CLJ 103, 114–16; for Singaporean discussion, S. A. Booysen, [2013] LMCLQ 21–6.
16 [1949] 1 KB 532, CA.
17 [1971] 2 QB 163, CA.

the defendant had not done enough to bring to the claimant's attention the condition on the back of the receipt.[18]

(4) *Course of dealing.* A term might be incorporated by a consistent course of dealing between the parties.[19] As for the 'battle of the forms' (on which see 3.34), the Court of Appeal in *Tekdata Intercommunications* v. *Amphenol Ltd* (2009)[20] acknowledged the authority of *Butler Machine Tool Co. Ltd* v. *Ex-Cell-O Corporation (England) Ltd* (1979), where the majority of the Court of Appeal (Lawton and Bridge LJJ) adopted the 'last shot' approach.[21]

(5) *Incorporation is possible on the basis of trade usage.*[22]

3. FRAUD AND EXCLUSION CLAUSES

15.04 There is a Common Law principle invalidating as contrary to public policy attempts to exclude or restrict liability for fraud (see also 9.33 for examination of this rule).[23] The Court of Appeal in *Regus (UK) Ltd* v. *Epcot Solutions Ltd* (2008)[24] held that this Common Law bar encompasses 'fraud or wilful, reckless or malicious damage' but not an ordinary 'intentional' breach of contract (for the *presumption* that an exclusion clause does not cover deliberate breach, see 15.06).

4. STRICT INTERPRETATION AT COMMON LAW

15.05 The courts will adopt a strict interpretation of wide or unclear language contained in an exclusion clause (this is known as interpretation *contra proferentem;*[25] the identity of the *proferens* might not always be obvious, if the document has been bandied around, as Peter Prescott QC noted in the *Oxonica* case, 2008).[26] This restrictive style of interpretation works to the disadvantage of the so-called *proferens*, that is, the party seeking to put forward an exclusion clause (and some other analogous clauses). In particular, there is a Common Law rule that clear language must be used to exclude contractual liability for negligence.

---

18 [1940] 1 KB 532, CA.
19 *Chitty on Contracts* (31st edn, London, 2012), 12–011, citing extensive case law; E. Macdonald, (1988) 8 LS 48.
20 [2009] EWCA Civ 1209; [2010] 1 Lloyd's Rep 357.
21 [1979] 1 WLR 401, 405H, 406D, 407E, CA.
22 *British Crane Hire Corporation Ltd* v. *Ipswich Plant Hire Ltd* [1975] QB 303, CA; see 13.19.
23 *S Pearson & Son Ltd* v. *Dublin Corporation* [1907] AC 351, 353, 362, HL; considered in *HIH Casualty and General Insurance Ltd* v. *Chase Manhattan Bank* [2003] 2 Lloyd's Rep 61, HL, at [16] *per* Lord Bingham, [98] *per* Lord Hobhouse, *per* Lord Hoffmann at [76] and [81], and *per* Lord Scott at [122]); noted by K. R. Handley, (2003) 119 LQR 537–41; *Granville Oils & Chemicals Ltd* v. *Davis Turner & Co. Ltd* [2003] EWCA Civ 570; [2003] 1 All ER (Comm) 819; [2003] 2 Lloyd's Rep 356, at [13] ff.
24 [2008] EWCA Civ 361; [2009] 1 All ER (Comm) 586, at [33] ff.
25 *Chitty on Contracts* (31st edn, London, 2012), chapter 14.
26 See discussion under the heading '*contra proferentem*' in [2008] EWHC 2127 (Patents Court); not disturbed on appeal, [2009] EWCA Civ 668.

The House of Lords in the *HIH Casualty* case (2003) noted the continuing relevance of the so-called *Canada Steamship* case's (1952) principles of construction.[27] These are:

(1) Effect will be given to an *express exclusion of liability for negligence at Common Law* (although statute might nullify or modify this exclusion: see 15.08).

(2) A clause will not be effective to exclude negligence if the relevant wording does not explicitly refer to negligence and if the language is wide enough to cover a 'head of damage ... other than that of negligence ... which is not so fanciful or remote that the proferens cannot be supposed to have desired protection against it'.

The *Canada Steamship* principles were applied by Lord Hope in *Geys* v. *Société Générale* (2012) in respect of an employer's attempt to restrict liability for wrongful termination.[28]

Furthermore, European consumer protection legislation (implemented as Part 2 of the Consumer Rights Bill, generally 15.28 ff), extends this style of interpretation in favour of consumers who are subject to written terms contained in consumer contracts for the supply of goods or services.[29]

15.06 *Clear wording will be respected in exclusion clauses in a commercial context.* In *Photo Production Ltd* v. *Securicor Transport Ltd* (1980),[30] the House of Lords held that exclusion clauses can validly operate at Common Law, even if they concern major or core forms of breach, provided clear and unambiguous language is used. Lord Wilberforce said:[31]

> After [the Unfair Contract Terms Act 1977, as amended by the Consumer Rights Bill], in commercial matters generally when the parties are not of unequal bargaining power, and when risks are normally borne by insurance, ... there is everything to be said ... for leaving the parties free to apportion the risks as they think fit and for respecting their decisions.

And, in the same case, Lord Diplock said:[32]

> In commercial contracts negotiated between businessmen capable of looking after their own interests and of deciding how risks inherent in the performance of various kinds of contract can be most economically borne (generally by insurance), it is ... wrong to place a strained construction upon words in an exclusion clause which are clear and susceptible of one meaning only.

The House of Lords in the *Photo Production* case (1980) also rejected the so-called 'fundamental breach' doctrine. Lord Denning had been the main proponent of this doctrine, in the Court of Appeal in that case, and in several earlier cases. According to

---

27   *HIH Casualty and General Insurance Ltd* v. *Chase Manhattan Bank* [2003] 2 Lloyd's Rep 61, HL, at [11], [59] to [63] and [95], citing *Canada Steamship Lines Ltd* v. *R* [1952] AC 192, 208, PC, *per* Lord Morton.

28   [2012] UKSC 63; [2013] 1 AC 523, at [37] to [40]; see also *Greenwich Millennium* case [2014] EWCA Civ 960; [2014] 1 WLR 3517, at [68] and [94].

29   The Consumer Rights Bill contains a statutory version of the *contra proferentem* rule in favour of consumers; relatedly, the same Bill emphasises the need for a term's presentation by traders to be 'transparent' and 'prominent'.

30   [1980] AC 827, HL.

31   *Ibid.*, at 843.

32   *Ibid.*, at 850–1 (passage cited in *Deepak Fertilisers & Petrochemicals Corporation* v. *ICI Chemicals and Polymers Ltd* [1999] 1 Lloyd's Rep 387, CA, at [20]).

that now discredited view, exclusion clauses, even if clearly worded, could not validly exclude or restrict liability for serious breach of core contractual obligations. However:

(i) *Internet Broadcasting Corporation Ltd* v. *MAR LLC* (2009; also noted at 17.03)[33] confirms that there is a presumption that an exclusion clause, although literally wide enough, will not be construed to exclude liability for loss of profit flowing from a personal and deliberate repudiation of the relevant contractual undertaking.

(ii) The Court of Appeal held in *William Hare Ltd* v. *Shepherd Construction Ltd* (2010) that a clause purporting to exclude B's liability to pay subcontractors, X, Y and Z, if the employer, A, has not paid the main contractor, B, will not be construed favourably to B, even though such a construction might be commercially obvious. The reason for this strict approach is that such a 'pay only if paid' clause is an exclusion of liability. Thus the *contra proferentem* principle is dominant. It 'trumps' the process of 'corrective construction' established in the *Investors Compensation Scheme* line of cases (14.22).[34]

(iii) *Markerstudy Insurance Co. Ltd* v. *Endsleigh Insurance Services Ltd* (2010)[35] notes a line of cases[36] concerning attempts to exclude liability for 'indirect and consequential losses', when the clause also purports to extend the exclusion of liability to species of named losses which might not also be 'indirect or consequential'. These decisions state that the exclusion is confined to indirect and consequential loss, and that the specified examples of loss are treated as exemplification of that category, rather than additions to the zone of exclusion. This pattern of restrictive construction is consistent with the view (a) that ambiguous language is to be construed *contra proferentem*, and (b) that the words 'indirect or consequential' have acquired a settled meaning, namely matters falling within the second limbo of *Hadley* v. *Baxendale* (1854).[37]

(iv) In the context of misrepresentation, and noting the inability of simple entire agreement clauses (9.36 and 9.37) to exclude liability for 'representations', Rix LJ said in the *AXA* case (2011):[38]

> the exclusion of liability for misrepresentation has to be clearly stated. It can be done by clauses which state the parties' agreement that there have been no representations made; or that there has been no reliance on any representations; or by an express exclusion of liability for misrepresentation. However, save in such contexts, and particularly where the word 'representations' takes its place alongside other words expressive of contractual obligation, talk of the parties'

33 [2009] EWHC 844 (Ch); [2010] 1 All ER (Comm) 112; [2009] 2 Lloyd's Rep 295 (Gabriel Moss QC) (distillation of principles at [33]).

34 [2010] EWCA Civ 283; [2010] BLR 358, at [18].

35 [2010] EWHC 281 (Comm), at [9] ff, per David Steel J.

36 *Ferryways NV* v. *Associated British Ports (The Humber Way)* [2008] EWHC 225 (Comm); [2008] 1 Lloyd's Rep 639; [2008] 1 CLC 117, at [78] ff, per Teare J; *BHP Petroleum Ltd* v. *British Steel plc* [1999] 2 All ER (Comm) 544; [1999] 2 Lloyd's Rep 583, where Rix J cited these cases: *Millar's Machinery Company Limited* v. *David Way and Son* [1935] 40 Com Cas 204; *Saint Line Ltd* v. *Richardsons, Westgarth & Co. Ltd* [1940] 2 KB 99; *Croudace Construction Ltd* v. *Cawoods Concrete Products Ltd* [1978] 2 Lloyd's Rep 55; *British Sugar plc* v. *NEI Power Projects Ltd* (1999) 87 BLR 42, and *Deepak Fertilisers and Petrochemical Corpn* v. *ICI* [1999] 1 Lloyd's Rep 387.

37 (1854) 9 Exch 341.

38 *AXA Sun Life Services plc* v. *Campbell Martin Ltd* [2011] EWCA Civ 133; [2011] 2 Lloyd's Rep 1; [2011] 1 CLC 312, at [94] (noted A. Trukhtanov, (2011) 127 LQR 345–50).

contract superseding such prior agreement will not by itself absolve a party of misrepresentation where its ingredients can be proved.

5. EXCLUSION CLAUSES AND THE MISREPRESENTATION ACT 1967

15.07 This topic[39] is examined in detail at 9.33. Here, it is enough to note that section 3 of the Misrepresentation Act 1967, applicable to (nearly)[40] all types of contract, authorises the court to invalidate a clause if it unreasonably excludes or restricts liability arising from a misrepresentation. The Court of Appeal in *Cremdean Properties Ltd* v. *Nash* (1977) said that if the reality is that a misrepresentation was made, section 3 of the 1967 Act cannot be evaded by clauses which purport to deny that fact.[41]

6. STATUTORY CONTROL OF EXCLUSION CLAUSES IN GENERAL

15.08 *Sources.* The Unfair Contract Terms Act 1977 ('UCTA 1977') is to be modified by the Consumer Rights Bill. A clean dichotomy is achieved: the scope of UCTA 1977 is narrowed so that it is now only applicable to non-consumer contracts, whereas business ('trader') to consumer contracts are subject to the Consumer Rights Bill; that is, contractual terms or notices purporting to protect a 'trader' and to prejudice a 'consumer'.[42] There is a list in the 'Explanatory Notes' of reports conducted in preparation for the Bill.[43]

39   J. Cartwright, *Misrepresentation, Mistake and Non-Disclosure* (3rd edn, London, 2012), 9.19.
40   *Trident Turboprop (Dublin) Ltd* v. *First Flight Couriers* [2009] EWCA Civ 290; [2010] QB 86, at [15] ff *per* Moore-Bick LJ; *Air Transworld Ltd* v. *Bombadier Inc* [2012] EWHC 243 (Comm); [2012] 2 All ER (Comm) 60; [2012] 1 Lloyd's Rep 349, Cooke J (section 26, UCTA 1977, disapplies section 3 of the Misrepresentation Act 1967).
41   (1977) 244 EG 547, CA (see the quotations from Bridge and Scarman LJJ, cited in *Raiffeisen Zentralbank Osterreich AG* v. *Royal Bank of Scotland plc* [2010] EWHC 1392 (Comm); [2011] 1 Lloyd's Rep 123, at [276] and [277], by Christopher Clarke J); E. Peel, (2001) 117 LQR 545, 549, also noting *South Western General Property Co. Ltd* v. *Marton* (1982) 263 EG 1090 and *St Marylebone Property Co. Ltd* v. *Payne* [1994] EGLR 25.
42   Sections 2(2), 76(2), CRA 2014.
43   (www.publications.parliament.uk/pa/bills/cbill/2013–2014/0161/en/14161en.htm), at paras. 15 to 18 (most recent first):
  (i) 'Unfair Terms in Consumer Contracts – Advice to BIS', The Law Commission and The Scottish Law Commission (2013);
  (ii) 'Enhancing Consumer Confidence by Clarifying Consumer Law', Department for Business, Innovation, and Skills (BIS) (2012);
  (iii) 'Consumer Law Review: Summary of Responses', (BIS, 2009);
  (iv) 'Consumer Remedies for Faulty Goods', The Law Commission No. 317/The Scottish Law Commission No. 216 (Cmnd 7725, 2009);
  (v) 'Benchmarking the Performance of the UK Framework Supporting Consumer Empowerment Through Comparison Against Relevant International Comparator Countries' (study for BERR by University of East Anglia, 2008);
  (vi) R. Bradgate, 'Consumer Rights in Digital Products' (BIS, 2010);
  (vii) G. Howells and C. Twigg-Flesner, 'Consolidation and Simplification of UK Consumer Law' (BIS, 2010);
  (viii) 'Implementation of EU Legislation', Davidson Report (Lord Davidson QC) (HM Treasury, HMSO, 2006);
  (ix) 'Unfair Terms in Contracts', The Law Commission Report No. 292/The Scottish Law Commission No. 199 (Cmnd 6464, 2005).

15.09 *Exclusion clauses concerning negligence under non-consumer and consumer contracts.* Sections 2(1) and 2(2) of UCTA 1977 (in the case of non-consumer contracts)[44] and the Consumer Rights Bill (in the case of consumer contracts) control exclusion clauses intended to exclude or restrict liability for breach of a contractual obligation if that express or implied term requires the exercise of reasonable care.[45] Section 2(1) of UCTA 1977 and the Consumer Rights Bill provide that an exclusion clause (or notice) cannot exclude or restrict liability for death or personal injury.[46] Section 2(2) of UCTA 1977 (in the case of non-consumer contracts)[47] provides that where the relevant contractual negligence has caused other types of loss or harm, the relevant exclusion clause is subject to a reasonableness test.

15.10 *Standard written terms in non-consumer contracts.* Section 3 of UCTA 1977 (as mentioned, this statute is now only applicable to non-consumer contracts)[48] extends (unlike section 2(1) and (2), just mentioned) to exclusion clauses seeking to affect liability arising from breach of *strict obligations* (although section 3 is not confined to strict obligations). Section 3 covers exclusion clauses inserted within the defendant's *standard written terms of business.*[49] But here the courts are not bound to invalidate such an exclusion clause and instead they possess a statutory discretion whether to uphold the clause or to find that it is invalid because it is 'unreasonable'. This discretion permits the courts to consider a wide range of considerations.

15.11 *Statutory implied terms within non-consumer and consumer contracts.* Such implied terms, inserted as a matter of law by statute, appear in contracts for the sale of goods,[50] or for the supply of goods and services,[51] or for the supply of 'digital content'[52] (that is 'data which are produced and supplied in digital form').[53]

15.12 In the case of *non-consumer contracts*, UCTA 1977 provides that liability arising from breach of the implied term that the seller (or party supplying goods under hire-purchase) has good title[54] cannot be excluded.[55] As for other relevant implied terms, a party can exclude or restrict liability 'in so far as the term satisfies the requirement of

---

44 See the amendment in the Consumer Rights Bill, adding a new section 2(3), UCTA 1977.
45 Section 1(1), UCTA; section 1(4) renders it immaterial whether breach is inadvertent or intentional, or whether liability is personal or vicarious; similarly, see the Consumer Rights Bill for the definition of 'negligence'.
46 Section 14, UCTA 1977.
47 Consumer Rights Bill adds a new section 2(3), UCTA 1977.
48 Consumer Rights Bill restricts the scope of section 3, UCTA 1977.
49 E.g., *St Albans City & DC* v. *International Computers Ltd* [1996] 4 All ER 481, 491, CA (terms 'standard' despite negotiations resulting in slight modification).
50 E.g., sections 13 to 15 of the Sale of Goods Act 1979; sections 9 to 30, CRA 2014 (applicable to consumer contracts).
51 Sections 2 to 10, Supply of Goods and Services Act 1982 (the effect of the Consumer Rights Bill is that the 1982 Act now applies only to covers business to business contracts and consumer to consumer contracts).
52 Consumer Rights Bill.
53 *Ibid.*
54 E.g., section 12 of the Sale of Goods Act 1979.
55 Sections 6(1), 7(1), UCTA 1977.

reasonableness'.[56] Attempts wholly to exclude liability in commercial contracts for supply of defective goods have been struck down as unreasonable.[57] This would be the likely outcome if the facts of *L'Estrange* v. *F Graucob Ltd* (1934) were to recur (where the purchaser was not a consumer: on this case, see 15.03).[58]

15.13 In the case of *consumer contracts*, legislation invalidates a term which purports to exclude liability for breach of a statutory implied term.[59]

15.14 *The test of 'reasonableness' in respect of non-consumer contracts under UCTA 1977.* UCTA 1977 places the burden of proof of satisfying the requirement of reasonableness on the party who seeks protection from the relevant clause.[60] Various provisions of UCTA 1977 require the courts to apply a test of 'reasonableness' to determine whether a particular clause is valid.[61] Section 11(2) of and Schedule 2 to UCTA 1977 provide five guidelines when determining whether the exclusion clause is reasonable. The guidelines within section 11(2) are expressed to apply to questions of reasonableness arising under sections 6 and 7 of the 1977 Act (concerning the sale, hire-purchase and supply of goods). However, the courts have consistently held that these guidelines should extend to all questions of reasonableness falling within UCTA 1977, notably under section 3 of the 1977 Act.[62] But non-statutory guidelines have also emerged: Potter LJ in *Overseas Medical Supplies Ltd* v. *Orient Transport Services Ltd* (1999) identified eight judicially recognised factors relevant to this question of 'reasonableness' (the full text of Potter LJ's exposition is quoted here):[63]

(i) the way in which the relevant conditions came into being and are used generally;

(ii) the five guidelines as to reasonableness set out in Schedule 2 [to UCTA 1977];

(iii) [as for] equality of bargaining position the court will have regard not only to the question whether the customer was obliged to use the services of the supplier, but also the question how far it would have been practicable and convenient to go elsewhere;

(iv) the question of reasonableness must be assessed having regard to the relevant clause viewed as a whole; it is not right to take any particular part of the clause in isolation, although it must be viewed against a breach of contract which is the subject of the case;

---

56 Sections 6(1A), 7(1A) UCTA 1977 (to be inserted by the Consumer Rights Bill).

57 *Britvic Soft Drinks Ltd* v. *Messer Ltd* [2002] 1 Lloyd's Rep 20; [2002] 3 All ER (Comm) 321, CA (clause wholly excluding liability for failure to supply satisfactory goods was unreasonable); similarly, *Bacardi-Martini Beverages Ltd* v. *Thomas Hardy Packaging Ltd* [2002] EWCA Civ 549, CA.

58 [1934] 2 KB 394, Div. Ct.

59 Consumer Rights Bill.

60 Section 11(5), UCTA 1977; this point was emphasised in *AEG (UK) Ltd* v. *Logic Resource Ltd* [1996] CLC 265, 278, CA, by Hobhouse LJ.

61 Notably sections 2(2), 3, 6(1A), 11, Schedule 2, UCTA 1977; for similar control, section 3 of the Misrepresentation Act 1967 (9.33).

62 *Chitty on Contracts* (31st edn, London, 2012), 14–092 to 14–099; *Stewart Gill Ltd* v. *Horatio Myer & Co. Ltd* [1992] QB 600, 608, CA; *Monarch Airlines Ltd* v. *London Luton Airport Ltd* [1998] 1 Lloyd's Rep 403, 412, col 1, Clarke J; *Schenkers Ltd* v. *Overland Shoes Ltd* [1998] 1 Lloyd's Rep 498, 505, CA; *Overseas Medical Supplies Ltd* v. *Orient Transport Services Ltd* [1999] 2 Lloyd's Rep 272, at [10], *per* Potter LJ; *Balmoral Group Ltd* v. *Borealis UK Ltd* [2001] 1 Lloyd's Rep 93; *Granville Oil and Chemicals Ltd* v. *Davis Turner and Co. Ltd* [2003] CLC 418, 423, CA; *Sterling Hydraulics Ltd* v. *Dichtomatik Ltd* [2006] EWHC 2004 (QB); [2007] 1 Lloyd's Rep 8, Judge Havelock-Allan QC; *Shepherd Homes Ltd* v. *Encia Remediation Ltd* [2007] EWHC 70 (TCC); [2007] BLR 135; 110 Con LR 90, at [93], Christopher Clarke J; *Lobster Group Ltd* v. *Heidelberg Graphic Equipment Ltd* [2009] EWHC 1919 (TCC), Ramsey J, at [115].

63 [1999] 2 Lloyd's Rep 273, 276, CA.

(v) the reality of the consent of the customer to the supplier's clause will be a significant consideration;

(vi) in cases of limitation rather than exclusion of liability, the size of the limit compared with other limits in widely used standard terms may also be relevant;

(vii) while the availability of insurance to the supplier is relevant, it is by no means a decisive factor;

(viii) the presence of a term allowing for an option to contract without the limitation clause but with a price increase in lieu is important; however, if the condition works in such a way as to leave little time to put such option into effect, this may effectively eliminate the option as a factor indicating reasonableness.

15.15 In *Watford Electronics Ltd* v. *Sanderson CFL Ltd* (2001)[64] Chadwick LJ said that the courts should be 'very cautious' before deciding to invalidate (under UCTA 1977) an exclusion clause made between 'experienced businessmen' of equal bargaining strength unless 'one party has, in effect, taken unfair advantage of the other or [the court is satisfied] that a term is so unreasonable that it cannot properly have been understood or considered'. This attractive approach has been endorsed in later cases: for example, Gloster J in *JP Morgan Chase* v. *Springwell Navigation Corp* (2008),[65] collecting such endorsements in various cases; and see also the Court of Appeal in the *Regus* case (2008).[66]

15.16 First instance decisions concerning the statutory test of reasonableness are unlikely to be rejected on appeal: 'the appellate court should treat the original decision with the utmost respect and refrain from interference with it unless satisfied that it proceeded upon some erroneous principle or was plainly and obviously wrong.'[67]

15.17 There are many reported cases illustrating how the courts apply the test of reasonableness under UCTA 1977, and the following discussion will examine some of these.[68]

Cases upholding clauses

15.18 *Entire agreement clause upheld.* As discussed at 9.37 the Court of Appeal in the *AXA Sun Life* case (2011)[69] held that such a clause, the effect of which is to invalidate collateral warranties, was consistent with the statutory reasonableness test. Section 3 of UCTA 1977

---

64 [2001] 1 All ER (Comm) 696; [2001] BLR 143, CA; noted E. Peel (2001) 117 LQR 545.

65 [2008] EWHC 1186, Gloster J, at [603] ff.

66 *Regus (UK) Ltd* v. *Epcot Solutions Ltd* [2008] EWCA Civ 361; [2009] 1 All ER (Comm) 586, at [40].

67 *George Mitchell (Chesterhall) Ltd* v. *Finney Lock Seeds Ltd* [1983] 2 AC 803, 810, HL, *per* Lord Bridge.

68 See also: *Lobster Group Ltd* v. *Heidelberg Graphic Equipment Ltd* [2009] EWHC 1919 (TCC), Ramsey J, collecting the following cases at [121]: *Charlotte Thirty and Bison* v. *Croker* (1990) 24 Con LR 46 (QBD); *Edmund Murray* v. *BSP International Foundations* (1993) 33 Con LR 1, CA; *Lease Management Services* v. *Purnell Secretarial Services* [1994] CCLR 127; *The Times*, 1 April 1994, CA; *Rees Hough Ltd* v. *Redland Reinforced Plastics Ltd* (1984) 27 BLR 136; (1984) 1 Const LJ 67 (QBD); *Salvage Association* v. *CAP Financial Services Ltd* [1995] FSR 654 (QBD); *Sovereign Finance* v. *Silver Crest* [1999] GCCR 2187, Longmore J; *Watford Electronics Ltd* v. *Sanderson CFL Ltd* [2001] 1 All ER (Comm) 696; [2001] BLR 143, CA; noted E. Peel (2001) 117 LQR 545; and *Regus (UK) Ltd* v. *Epcot Solutions Ltd* [2008] EWCA Civ 361; [2009] 1 All ER (Comm) 586 (on which see the *Lobster* case, [2009] EWHC 1919 (TCC), at [121]).

69 *AXA Sun Life Services plc* v. *Campbell Martin Ltd* [2011] EWCA Civ 133; [2011] 2 Lloyd's Rep 1; [2011] 1 CLC 312 (noted A. Trukhtanov, (2011) 127 LQR 345–50).

applied to such a clause. But 'reasonableness' was satisfied: both parties were commercial entities; the party challenging the clause's operation had had ample chance to read and understand it; such a clause conduces to commercial certainty; and so there was no good reason to refuse to give the clause effect in this case.

15.19 *Defective software: supplier limiting liability to price paid to commercial customer.* In *Watford Electronics Ltd* v. *Sanderson CFL Ltd* (2001), the supplier of defective software to a commercial customer succeeded in restricting its liability for loss to the contract price.[70] A further exclusion of liability for indirect or consequential loss was also upheld as reasonable. Chadwick LJ gave weight to the following factors which tended to support a decision to uphold this exclusion clause:[71] (1) the significant risk that a non-standard or 'customised' software product might not perform satisfactorily; and the consequential risk that the commercial customer's operation might not be as profitable as it had expected; (2) the supplier is better placed to assess the risk of malfunction; but the customer is better placed to assess the potential loss; (3) the risks were insurable (a factor given weight in the *Regus* case, 2008);[72] (4) the parties had the opportunity, and indeed this was taken on the present facts,[73] to negotiate the price, taking into account these risks; and (5) experienced businessmen should be assumed to be the best judges of the commercial fairness of their agreements. Chadwick LJ said that the courts should be 'very cautious' in invalidating as unreasonable (under the statute) an exclusion clause made between 'experienced businessmen' of equal bargaining strength unless 'one party has, in effect, taken unfair advantage of the other or [the court is satisfied] that a term is so unreasonable that it cannot properly have been understood or considered'.

15.20 *Limitation clauses or completely protective clauses in contracts between businesses.* Applying UCTA 1977's test of reasonableness, the courts have upheld *limitation* clauses: (1) imposing a restriction on an architect's liability;[74] and (2) concerning liability for damage to other property (and associated loss) arising from the sale of bulk carbon dioxide.[75] However, clauses *wholly excluding* liability are less likely to be upheld as reasonable. Such a clause was in fact declared unreasonable in two cases concerning benzene traces in carbon dioxide supplied to manufacturers of soft drinks.[76]

15.21 *Airport excluding liability to aircraft owner for negligence. Monarch Airlines Ltd* v. *London Luton Airport Ltd* (1998)[77] concerned damage to a commercial aircraft as a result of loose paving slabs on the defendant's runway. The aircraft was insured for US$30m. Liability for simple negligence was excluded. The judge held that the exclusion clause was fair: the

---

70   [2001] 1 All ER (Comm) 696; [2001] BLR 143, CA; noted by E. Peel, (2001) 117 LQR 545.
71   [2001] 1 All ER (Comm) 696; [2001] BLR 143, CA, at [54] to [56].
72   *Regus (UK) Ltd* v. *Epcot Solutions Ltd* [2008] EWCA Civ 361; [2009] 1 All ER (Comm) 586, at [41] ff.
73   *Watford Electronics Ltd* v. *Sanderson CFL Ltd* [2001] 1 All ER (Comm) 696; [2001] BLR 143, CA, at [56].
74   *Moores* v. *Yakely Associates Ltd* (1999) 62 Constr LR 76 (standard RIBA form, £250,000 limit).
75   *Britvic Soft Drinks Ltd* v. *Messer Ltd* [2002] 1 Lloyd's Rep 20; [2002] 3 All ER (Comm) 321, CA: limitation clause point decided by Tomlinson J, not disturbed on appeal (and see next note).
76   *Britvic* case, *ibid.* (total exclusion clause for failure to supply satisfactory goods was unreasonable); similarly, *Bacardi-Martini Beverages Ltd* v. *Thomas Hardy Packaging Ltd* [2002] EWCA Civ 549, CA.
77   [1998] 1 Lloyd's Rep 403.

exclusion was generally accepted in this market, and insurance within the market was arranged on this basis.[78]

15.22 *Restriction upon consequential financial loss: defective software: restriction upheld.* In *Watford Electronics Ltd* v. *Sanderson CFL Ltd* (2001), the supplier of defective software to a commercial customer succeeded in capping its liability for loss by reference to the contract price.[79] A further exclusion of liability for indirect or consequential loss was also upheld as reasonable.

Cases invalidating clauses

15.23 *Unreasonable limitation clause: commercial supply to farmer of defective seeds.* In *George Mitchell* v. *Finney Lock Seeds Ltd* (1983), the House of Lords invalidated a limitation clause in a sale between merchants.[80] The case concerned defective cabbage seed supplied to the claimant, a farmer, by a seed-merchant, the defendant. The farmer had lost a 60-acre crop of cabbage, and his claim for lost revenue was over £60,000. But the limitation clause in the contract of sale limited liability to the purchase price, roughly £200. The House of Lords held that this clause was unreasonable and so invalid. In reaching this decision, the court considered these factors:

it was usual in that business for a seed dealer to pay higher compensation as an *ex gratia* payment;

this demonstrated that the defendant regarded the clause as unreasonable;[81]

seed merchants could obtain insurance without materially increasing their costs;

the defendant should have realised that the variety of cabbage supplied by the defendant could not be grown commercially in the plaintiff's locality (East Lothian).

15.24 *Limitation clause: commercial supply of software to local authority.* In *St Albans City & District Council* v. *International Computers Ltd* (1996),[82] the defendant computer company, a big player in this market, supplied software to a local authority, and this would be used to enable the latter to compile a community charge (the poll tax) database. But the software contained an error. This caused the local authority to overestimate its population by 3 per cent. As a result, the authority did not recover as much money as it might have done. It claimed loss of over £1m (which the Court of Appeal later reduced). The computer company's exclusion clause limited liability to £100,000. The Court of Appeal upheld Scott Baker J's decision that this exclusion clause was invalid. The relevant factors (which were held to outweigh various competing factors: see the text below for these) were:[83]

---

78   *Ibid.*, at 414.
79   [2001] 1 All ER (Comm) 696; [2001] BLR 143, CA; noted by E. Peel, (2001) 117 LQR 545.
80   [1983] 2 AC 803, HL (decided pre-UCTA 1977, but still useful for the articulation of factors).
81   A factor regarded by Lord Bridge as 'decisive' in [1983] 2 AC 803, HL (cf *Schenkers* case, [1998] 1 Lloyd's Rep 498, 508, CA, disregarding the fact that the clauses had not been rigorously applied during the parties' long-standing relationship).
82   [1995] FSR 686, 704–11, Scott Baker J (affirmed, [1996] 4 All ER 481, CA), noted by S. Hedley, [1997] CLJ 21 (but damages reduced because, in the following year, the local authority partially recouped this shortfall).
83   Sections 3, 6 and 7, UCTA 1977.

the defendant company's economic size;

the fact that the defendant had product liability insurance of £50m;

there were few companies from which the plaintiff might have bought its software, and all dealt on a standard basis;

the authority's financial shortfall would otherwise be borne by the local population (reduced services or higher local taxes).

The competing factors, outweighed by the factors just recited, were:

the general consideration that agreements should be given effect;

the presumption that a contracting party agrees to the terms of a deal 'with his eyes open';

such limitation of liability was standard in the software industry;

software for sophisticated commercial or business use was a 'developing' area of technology.

15.25 In *Pegler Ltd* v. *Wang (UK) Ltd* (2000), another software case, Judge Bowsher QC declared unreasonable a clause which excluded liability for indirect, special and consequential loss, and which imposed a two-year contractual limit for claims.[84] But this case seems to have turned on a special feature: that the supplier had made a misrepresentation concerning the equipment.

15.26 *Unreasonable restriction of liability: supplier of defective equipment attempting to confine liability to supply of replacement parts.* In *Edmund Murray* v. *BSP International Foundations Ltd* (1993), the claimant ordered a drilling rig from the defendant, who constructed it to the claimant's specification.[85] The rig was defective. The claimant sued for breach of contract. It was held that it was unreasonable for the defendant to exclude liability for breach of both express and implied terms for failure to satisfy these specifications and instead to restrict liability to the supply of spare parts. The court applied sections 3 and 7 of UCTA 1977.

15.27 *Non-consumer contracts: effect of UCTA 1977 unreasonableness on offending clause.* Stewart Gill Ltd v. Horatio Myer & Co. Ltd (1992)[86] establishes that if part of an exclusion clause fails to satisfy the test of reasonableness, or it is otherwise invalid under UCTA 1977, the courts will not rewrite the clause in order to preserve any 'reasonable' part. However, there is some scope for rescue. An apparently composite clause might be severable, and then at least part might survive.[87] In the *Watford Electronics* case (2001), the Court of Appeal held that the following composite clause was severable, and that each sentence should be considered as a separate exclusion clause:

---

84 [2000] BLR 218.
85 (1993) 33 Const LR 1, CA.
86 [1992] QB 600, CA; *Thomas Witter Ltd* v. *TBP Industries Ltd* [1996] 2 All ER 573, 597–8, Jacob J; generally see *Chitty on Contracts* (31st edn, London, 2012), 14–100 to 14–102.
87 *Edmund Murray* v. *BSP International Foundations Ltd* (1993) 33 Const LR 1, CA (remitting the severance issue to the trial judge).

Clause 7.3 Neither the Company nor the Customer shall be liable for any claims for indirect or consequential losses whether arising from negligence or otherwise. In no event shall the Company's liability under the Contract exceed the price paid by the Customer to the Company for the [software] connected with any claim.[88]

7. UNFAIR TERMS IN CONSUMER CONTRACTS

15.28 *Scope.*[89] Part 2 of the Consumer Rights Bill ('the Bill')[90] (replacing a set of Regulations)[91] covers many types of 'unfair' terms and not just exclusion clauses. The protection is, however, confined to consumers. Under the Bill, a consumer can only be an 'individual'[92] (as distinct from a company, public authority or other non-human legal entity). The other party must be a 'trader'[93] supplying goods,[94] 'digital content'[95] (that is 'data which are produced and supplied in digital form')[96] or services.

15.29 *The Consumer Rights Bill's test of unfairness.* A term (section 62(4) of the CRA 2014) or consumer notice[97] (section 64(6)) will be invalid as against the consumer[98] if the term or notice is '*unfair*'. This will be so '*if, contrary to the requirement of good faith,* [the term or notice] *causes a significant imbalance in the parties' rights and obligations under the contract to the detriment of the consumer.*'[99] There is some further guidance:[100]

> *Whether a term is fair is to be determined – (a) taking into account the nature of the subject matter of the contract, and (b) by reference to all the circumstances existing when the term was agreed and to all of the other terms of the contract or of any other contract on which it depends.*

Part 1 of Schedule 2 'contains an indicative and non-exhaustive list of terms of consumer contracts that may be regarded as unfair'.[101]

---

88 This case was applied in *Regus (UK) Ltd* v. *Epcot Solutions Ltd* [2008] EWCA Civ 361; [2009] 1 All ER (Comm) 586, at [44] ff.

89 See 15.08 for citation of reports preceding the Bill.

90 See the Explanatory Notes (www.publications.parliament.uk/pa/bills/cbill/2013-2014/0161/en/1416 1en.htm); see also the summary available within the following document: (www.parliament.uk/business/publications/research/briefing-papers/LLN-2014-023/consumer-rights-bill-hl-bill-29-of-201415).

91 Unfair Terms in Consumer Contracts Regulations 1999 (SI 1999/2083) (replaced by the CRA 2014, Part 2).

92 Consumer Rights Bill.

93 *Ibid.*

94 *Ibid.*

95 *Ibid.*

96 *Ibid.*

97 A notice 'includes an announcement, whether or not in writing, and any communication or purported communication': the Bill.

98 *Ibid.*

99 *Ibid.* (for the suggestion, dicta not necessary for decision, that a consumer might succeed in showing that an English jurisdiction clause is 'unfair' on this basis, see *Standard Bank London Ltd* v. *Apostolakis (No. 2)* [2002] CLC 939, at [42] to [51], *per* David Steel J).

100 Consumer Rights Bill

101 *Ibid.*

15.30 *The need for clear language ('transparency').* The Consumer Rights Bill provides that a trader (i) can rely on an oral or written term or a (oral or written) notice[102] in a consumer contract only if the term or notice is *'transparent'*, that is, *'if it is expressed in plain and intelligible language and (in the case of a written term) is legible'.*[103] In the case of a term there is the further requirement (ii) that the term should be *'prominent'*, that is, it will be operative (or incorporated) only *'if it is brought to the consumer's attention in such a way that the average consumer would be aware of the term'*; and here an average consumer means one *'who is reasonably well-informed, observant and circumspect'.*[104]

15.31 The requirement of transparency[105] is a free-standing feature of the Consumer Rights Bill. Therefore, this requirement governs all consumer contracts and any type of oral or written term or notice. The requirement applies, therefore, even to those terms which are otherwise exempted from the test of 'unfairness' (a term which *'specifies the main subject matter of the contract'*; or a term where *'the assessment is of the appropriateness of the price payable under the contract by comparison with the goods, digital content or services supplied under it').*[106]

15.32 The overriding and free-standing nature of the transparency requirement is not new. This point was noted in *Bankers Insurance Co. Ltd* v. *South* (2003)[107] in the context of the (now superseded) 1999 Regulations.[108] In that case South had hired a jet ski and had injured Gardner. A clause in South's insurance policy stated: 'For each person insured we will NOT pay . . . compensation or other costs arising from accidents involving your ownership or possession of any . . . motorized waterborne craft.' Although the transparency test applied, the clause was held to be sufficiently clear and so it was upheld.

15.33 As mentioned at 15.05, one of the Common Law techniques for countering exclusion clauses is the *contra proferentem* style of interpretation. In addition, but extending to all types of term in consumer contracts, the Consumer Rights Bill extends this style of interpretation in favour of consumers who are subject to terms (written or unwritten) (or to consumer notices, again whether or not written) contained in consumer contracts,[109] that is, contracts where a 'trader'[110] supplies goods,[111] 'digital content'[112] – that is 'data which

---

102   A notice 'includes an announcement, whether or not in writing, and any communication or purported communication': section 61(8), *ibid.*
103   *Ibid.*
104   *Ibid.*
105   *Ibid.*
106   *Ibid.*
107   [2003] EWHC 380 (QB).
108   Unfair Terms in Consumer Contracts Regulations 1999 (SI 1999/2083), Reg 6(2) (the 1999 Regulations are replaced by the CRA 2014 (Part 2)).
109   The Consumer Rights Bill contains a statutory version of the *contra proferentem* rule in favour of consumers; relatedly, the Bill will emphasise the need for a term's presentation by traders to be 'transparent' and 'prominent'.
110   *Ibid.*
111   *Ibid.*
112   *Ibid.*

are produced and supplied in digital form')[113] or services. Thus the Consumer Rights Bill states: '*If a term in a consumer contract, or a consumer notice, could have different meanings, the meaning that is most favourable to the consumer is to prevail.*'

15.34 *Terms not subject to the 'unfairness' test.* For the purpose of the Consumer Rights Bill, terms which define or fix the nature of the contractual 'subject matter' or the 'price' applicable to the transaction are not judicially reviewable and hence are 'off-limits', that is, not capable of being invalidated on the ground that they fail the statutory test of fairness. Such terms are:

   (i) a term which 'specifies the main subject matter of the contract'; or
   (ii) a term where 'the assessment is of the appropriateness of the price payable under the contract by comparison with the goods, digital content or services supplied under it'.[114] However, these two 'unfairness exemptions' do not apply to terms within the list contained in Part 1 of Schedule 2 of the Bill.[115] And even if a term falls within categories (i) and (ii), the term must be 'transparent and prominent'.[116]

15.35 *Earlier cases concerning the 'unfairness' exemption.* There are two English decisions to consider, even though both concerned statutory predecessors to the Consumer Rights Bill.[117]

15.36 *Unsuccessful bank charges challenge.* First, it will be interesting to see whether there is any attempt to reopen the bank charges issue. The Supreme Court of the United Kingdom in *The Office of Fair Trading* v. *Abbey National plc* (2009)[118] held that bank charges for unauthorised overdrafts on current accounts fell within the exemption corresponding to element (ii), just set out. However, the Bill has slightly altered the wording of that element. Under the old wording (contained in the 1999 Regulations)[119] the 'price' exemption was formulated as follows: the '*adequacy of the price or remuneration, as against the goods or services supplied in exchange*'. By (slight) contrast, the Bill's formulation is: '*the assessment is of the appropriateness of the price payable under the contract by comparison with the goods, digital content or services supplied under it*'.[120] The concept of 'adequacy' has been replaced by that of 'appropriateness'. But the topic declared off-limits has not changed: the target of the prohibited 'unfairness' inquiry is the same, namely 'price'. For this reason, it is unlikely that the courts would regard the Bill's formulation of exemption (ii) ('price') as sufficient to justify reopening the Supreme Court's decision that bank charges on unauthorised current account overdrafts constitute (part of) the 'price' payable under the consumer contract and thus fall within this exemption. It is useful to note some of the statements made in that decision.

---

113   *Ibid.*
114   *Ibid.*
115   *Ibid.*
116   *Ibid.*
117   On these decisions, C. Willett, 'General Clauses and the Competing Ethics of European Consumer Law in the UK' [2012] CLJ 412–40.
118   The *Office of Fair Trading* v. *Abbey National plc* [2009] UKSC 6; [2010] 1 AC 696; noted S. Whittaker (2011) 74 MLR 106–22; A. Arora [2012] JBL 44; see also C. Willett, n. 117 above.
119   Unfair Terms in Consumer Contracts Regulations 1999 (SI 1999/2083), Reg 6(2) (the 1999 Regulations are replaced by the Bill).
120   Consumer Rights Bill.

Lord Walker said:[121]

> Bank charges levied on personal current account customers in respect of unauthorised overdrafts (including unpaid item charges and other related charges) constitute part of the price or remuneration for the banking services provided and, in so far as the terms giving rise to the charges are in plain intelligible language, no assessment under the [1999 Regulations] of the fairness of those terms may relate to their adequacy as against the services supplied.

Lord Phillips said:[122]

> [T]he Banks now rely on the Relevant Charges as an important part of the revenue that they generate from the current account services. If they did not receive the Relevant Charges they would not be able profitably to provide current account services to their customers in credit without making a charge to augment the value of the use of their funds.

Lord Mance said:[123]

> [T]here is no reason why the price or remuneration payable for a package of services should not consist of a contingent liability. The uneconomic nature of the Relevant Charges from the customers' viewpoint constitutes the importance of the charges from the banks' viewpoint, and the plain intelligible language of the banking contracts made evident that there must be a considerable element of cross-subsidy in respect of customers while they remained in credit.

15.37 *A second pre-Consumer Rights Bill decision.* In *Director General of Fair Trading* v. *First National Bank plc* (2002)[124] the House of Lords held that these 'no go' contractual terms (see 15.34 above), falling beyond the controls of the statutory test of unfairness, must be narrowly construed, otherwise the protective function of this legislation would be defeated. This decision was made under the 1994 Regulations[125] (which, along with the intermediate 1999 Regulations,[126] contained provisions similar to the 'unfairness exemptions' (i) and (ii) just mentioned).

No violation was found on the facts of *Director General of Fair Trading* v. *First National Bank plc* (2002). This was a test case concerning a loan company. This company's standard terms provided that debtors should continue to pay the contractual rate of interest even after court judgments entered against the debtor and in favour of the creditor. Statutory rules provided that, after a

---

121 *The Office of Fair Trading* v. *Abbey National plc* [2009] UKSC 6; [2010] 1 AC 696, at [51].
122 *Ibid.*, at [88].
123 *Ibid.*, at [117].
124 [2002] 1 AC 481, HL; C. MacMillan [2002] CLJ 22; C. Willett, 'General Clauses and the Competing Ethics of European Consumer Law in the UK' [2012] CLJ 412–40.
125 Unfair Terms in Consumer Contracts Regulations 1994/3159, Reg 3(2) (the 1994 Regulations were replaced by the Unfair Terms in Consumer Contracts Regulations 1999 (SI 1999/2083), which will be superseded by the Consumer Rights Bill).
126 Unfair Terms in Consumer Contracts Regulations 1999 (SI 1999/2083), Reg 6(2) (the 1999 Regulations are to be replaced by the Consumer Rights Bill).

judgment, the debt should become payable in instalments but at rates of interest lower than those provided in the current contract. The contract stated that these higher rates of interest would remain payable until the debt was fully discharged (and the statutory default rules were thus contractually excluded). The House of Lords held that this demanding contractual rate of interest was subject to the unfairness test of the (1994) Regulations.[127] However, the House of Lords concluded that the arrangement was not unfair.[128]

15.38 *Agreed penalties.* The Consumer Rights Bill ('the Bill) presumptively invalidates a stipulation requiring a consumer to pay 'a disproportionately high sum in compensation', and this therefore overlaps with the Common Law's penalty jurisdiction (19.01 ff).[129]

15.39 *Enforcement proceedings.* The Bill will assist individual consumers in civil proceedings, to which the consumer is a party as a claimant or defendant. But a regime of effective rights requires that substantive rights should be supported by effective access to justice.[130] Accordingly, Parliament has recognised that additional procedural teeth are required.[131] To this end, the Bill introduces a three-level supplementary system of 'enforcement':

(i) investigation;

(ii) injunctive litigation initiated by regulators;

(iii) collective redress (civil litigation involving multi-party claims or class actions).

As for (i), the Bill provides for investigation by various authorities.[132] For (ii), the Act seeks to strengthen the capacity of regulators (listed in Schedule 3(8)) to consider a 'relevant complaint' and to seek injunctions to prevent use of certain types of invalidated terms (amending the Enterprise Act 2002).[133] As for (iii), the Bill creates the framework for collective redress, by civil proceedings, under the Competition Act 1998. Such collective redress can involve opt-in civil claims (multi-party claims in which all claimants must be individually included) or opt-out class actions (representative proceedings in which the represented persons can be defined as a class but need not be individually joined as active parties).[134] These complicated procedural mechanisms lie beyond the compass of this work.[135]

127 [2002] 1 AC 481, HL at [12], *per* Lord Bingham.

128 *Ibid.*, at [24].

129 The Bill, Schedule 2, Part 1, paras. 5 and 6, *ibid.*

130 See *Andrews on Civil Processes*, (Cambridge, 2013) vol. 1, *Court Proceedings*, 25.15 to 25.35 for access to justice issues, and chapter 20 for 'no win, no fee' systems of costs.

131 Generally on strategies for ensuring protection in this sphere, J. Braucher, 'Unfair Terms in Comparative Perspective', in L. DiMatteo, Q. Zhou, S. Saintier, K. Rowley (eds.), *Commercial Contract Law: Transatlantic Perspectives* (Cambridge, 2014), chapter 14; see also M. Kenny, in same work, chapter 15, at 379–81.

132 The Bill, Schedules 5 and 6.

133 Schedules 3, 4 and 7, *ibid.*

134 Schedule 8, *ibid.*

135 On 'opt-in' multi-party (including Group Litigation Orders) and 'opt-out' representative proceedings, *Andrews on Civil Processes* (Cambridge 2013), vol. 1, *Court Proceedings*, chapter 22 (composed before the Bill).

QUESTIONS

(1) What are the main types of exclusion clause?

(2) What are the Common Law techniques employed in respect of exclusion clauses?

(3) What is the scope of sections 2(2) and 3 of the Unfair Contract Terms Act 1977?

(4) What factors are relevant when determining whether an exclusion clause is 'reasonable' for the purpose of the Unfair Contract Terms Act 1977?

(5) Collect four reported decisions in which the test of 'reasonableness' (Unfair Contract Terms Act 1977) has been applied.

(6) What is the position concerning attempts to exclude or restrict statutory implied terms protecting consumers?

(7) Summarise the 'unfairness' test and the scope of Part 2 of the Consumer Rights Bill (formerly the Unfair Terms in Consumer Regulations 1999).

(8) Is there any significant English case law illustrating the operation of the matters mentioned at (7)?

Selected further reading

J. Braucher, 'Unfair Terms in Comparative Perspective', in L. DiMatteo, Q. Zhou, S. Saintier, K. Rowley (eds.), *Commercial Contract Law: Transatlantic Perspectives* (Cambridge, 2014), chapter 14

E. Peel, 'Whither Contra Proferentem?', in A. Burrows and E. Peel (eds.), *Contract Terms* (Oxford, 2007), chapter 4

J. R. Spencer, 'Signature, Consent and the Rule in *L'Estrange v. Graucob*' [1973] CLJ 104

VII

Breakdown and liability

Chapter contents

16

Frustration

1. INTRODUCTION

16.01 Summary of main points

(1) Frustration concerns drastic changes subsequent to formation.[1] The doctrine terminates the contract by operation of law, releasing the parties from their future obligations under the contract. The Law Reform (Frustrated Contracts) Act 1943 provides for some (limited) adjustment of the parties' position once the contract has been terminated.

(2) The frustration doctrine has been kept very narrow. It is not enough that a contract becomes unexpectedly difficult or more expensive to perform. The doctrine is not an occasion for compassionate relief, but is reserved for extreme or overwhelming instances of supervening illegality, impossibility or annihilation of the obvious purpose of the contract (see next paragraph).

(3) There are three categories of situation: (a) supervening illegality, that is, performance of the contract becomes illegal because of a legal change subsequent to the contract's formation;[2] (b) supervening physical impossibility; or (c) 'frustration of the venture' where there is either catastrophic delay in executing a venture or where the abstract basis of the contract disappears, rendering the contract pointless when compared with its original central purpose; this third category, also known as 'frustration of the purpose', is very seldom successfully pleaded.

(4) Frustration operates only if the contract contains neither an express nor an implied allocation of the relevant risk to one of the parties (for the parallel approach within the doctrine of mistake,

---

1 G. H. Treitel, *Frustration and Force Majeure* (3rd edn, London, 2014); E. McKendrick (ed.), *Force Majeure and Frustration of Contract* (2nd edn, London, 1995); Clarke in M.A. Clarke, N. Andrews, A. M. Tettenborn, G. Virgo, *Contractual Duties: Performance, Breach, Termination and Remedies* (London, 2012), Part III, chapters 16 to 18; a comparative study is B. Nicholas (1974) 48 *Tulane Law Review* 946; for other approaches, see the Vienna Convention on Contracts for the International Sale of Goods, the *Principles of European Contract Law* and the UNIDROIT Principles; W. Lorenz, 'Contract Modification as a Result of Change of Circumstances', in J. Beatson and D. Friedmann (eds.), *Good Faith and Fault in Contract Law* (Oxford, 1995), 357.
2 Section 1(1) of the Law Reform (Frustrated Contracts) Act 1943 refers to contracts which have become 'impossible of performance or been otherwise frustrated'.

see 16.03). In particular, *force majeure* clauses can excuse a party from liability in respect of defined supervening events.

(5) Even if an event is foreseen or foreseeable, or a matter is discussed inconclusively, it is not impossible that frustration might still arise.

(6) Various types of 'default' (not confined to breach, but extending to self-interested 'choice') preclude frustration: so-called 'self-induced frustration'.

(7) Indefinite contracts, that is, agreements which are not of fixed duration, are subject to an implied term enabling either party to give reasonable notice to the other that the contract will be terminated.

2. MAIN THREADS OF THE DOCTRINE

16.02 *Definition and genesis.*[3] Lord Radcliffe gave the leading definition of the doctrine in *Davis Contractors Ltd* v. *Fareham Urban District Council* (1956) (for the facts of this case, see 16.09):[4]

> Frustration occurs whenever the law recognises that without default of either party a contractual obligation has become incapable of being performed because the circumstances in which performance is called for would render it a thing radically different from that which was undertaken by the contract. *Non haec in foedera veni.* It was not this which I promised to do.

Blackburn J in *Taylor* v. *Caldwell* (1863) first acknowledged a general doctrine of frustration (for the facts, see 16.08).[5] His innovation in that case was to fashion a general doctrine, based on these pre-existing instances where a party is excused from performance: (1) a contracting party's death in a contract of personal services (his spiritual survival not being enough, as where the piano recitalist dies halfway through the concert); (2) destruction of specific goods after property has passed to the buyer; (3) bailment where goods are destroyed without the bailee's fault. In effect Blackburn J joined up the dots, creating a new general doctrine which extended to physical annihilation of the contract's subject matter (on the facts of this case, destruction of the music hall), and which was capable of further expansion over the ensuing decades.

And so 'frustration' is a 'latecomer' within the Common Law system of contract. Before 1863, the general approach was very strict (although not quite absolute).

---

3 G. H. Treitel, *Frustration and Force Majeure* (3rd edn, London, 2014), chapters 1 and 2.
4 *Davis Contractors Ltd* v. *Fareham Urban District Council* [1956] AC 696, 729, HL, *per* Lord Radcliffe; considered in *Pioneer Shipping Ltd* v. *BTP Tioxide Ltd* ('The Nema') [1982] AC 724, 744, 751–2, HL; 'The Great Peace' [2002] EWCA Civ 1407; [2003] QB 679, at [70]; Mustill LJ in *FC Shepherd* v. *Jerrom* [1987] QB 301, 321–2, CA, attractively chronicled the evolution of the frustration doctrine; there is a careful analysis of the leading authorities in *Islamic Republic of Iran Shipping Lines* v. *Steamship Mutual Underwriting Association (Bermuda) Ltd* [2010] EWHC 2661 (Comm); [2011] 1 Lloyd's Rep 195; [2011] 2 All ER (Comm) 609, at [101] to [107], *per* Beatson J.
5 (1863) 3 B & S 826; 122 ER 309; A. W. B. Simpson, (1975) 91 LQR 247, 269–73; C. MacMillan, in C. Mitchell and P. Mitchell (eds.), *Landmark Cases in the Law of Contract* (Oxford, 2008), 167 ff.

The pre-1863 very strict approach is evident from *Paradine* v. *Jayne* (1647),[6] which concerned the turmoil caused by the English Civil War. Paradine sued Jayne for three years' rent arrears in respect of seventeen acres of land leased to him in 1637 for twenty-one years at a rent of £21 per year, in Bedminster, Bristol. The tenant was held liable to pay, even though irresistible third party force had prevented him from occupying the demised premises during this period (the Royalist army, led by Prince Rupert, had seized and occupied the land during the English Civil War).[7] The lease contained no *force majeure* clause. And so the obligation to pay rent applied strictly ('strict' but not absolute: for the exceptional possibility, only recognised in the late twentieth century, that a lease might become frustrated, see 16.14 below; for example, the relevant land might fall into the sea, or perhaps a new canyon might swallow it up, or a new and permanent mass of water might permanently submerge it, or a nuclear accident might render it unusable).

16.03 *Frustration does not rest on an implied term.*[8] *Taylor* v. *Caldwell* (1863)[9] was based on the theory that frustration involves an implied term, causing the contract to be terminated. But that theory was long ago abandoned because the implied term (at any rate if regarded as a real tacit consensus rather than a legal construct) is a fiction, it being highly implausible to suppose that the parties had implicitly agreed to such detailed risk allocation;[10] instead it is better and more candid to rationalise the doctrine of frustration as an exceptional release of both parties, based on a rule of law.

Abandonment of the implied term theory occurred in *Davis Contractors Ltd* v. *Fareham Urban District Council* (1956) where Lord Radcliffe noted:[11]

> [T]here is something of a logical difficulty in seeing how the parties could even impliedly have provided for something which *ex hypothesi* they neither expected nor foresaw; and the . . . implied term [theory disguises] . . . the true action of the court which consists in applying an objective rule of the law of contract to the contractual obligations that the parties have imposed upon themselves.

Similarly, Lord Denning MR said in *'The Eugenia'* (1964):[12]

> [T]he theory of an implied term has now been discarded . . . for the simple reason that it does not represent the truth. The parties would not have said: 'It is all over between us.' They would have differed about what was to happen. Each would have sought to insert reservations or qualifications of one kind or another.

6 (1647) Aleyn 26; 82 ER 897 (Court of King's Bench); D. Ibbetson, in F. D. Rose (ed.), *Consensus ad Idem: Essays on the Law of Contract in Honour of Guenter Treitel* (London, 1996), chapter 1.
7   D. Ibbetson, *ibid*.
8   G. H. Treitel, *Frustration and Force Majeure* (3rd edn, London, 2014), chapter 16.
9   (1863) 3 B & S 826; 122 ER 309; D. J. Ibbetson, *A Historical Introduction to the Law of Obligations* (Oxford, 1999), 224.
10   Consider the wry comment in a Scottish case, *James Scott & Sons Ltd* v. *Del Sel* 1922 SC 592, 597: 'A tiger has escaped from a travelling menagerie. The milkgirl fails to deliver the milk. [If the milkman is exonerated from failure to deliver] it would hardly seem reasonable to base that exoneration on the ground that "tiger days excepted" must be held as if written into the contract.'
11   [1956] AC 696, HL.
12   [1964] 2 QB 226, 238, CA; see, further, 16.06 on this case.

16.04 *Mistake or frustration? A question of timing.* Here there is a doctrinal meridian: the date of the relevant event will determine whether it is the doctrine of mistake (on which see Chapter 10) or frustration which must be considered.

In *Griffith* v. *Brymer* (1903), a 'room with a view' had been booked after the Coronation of Edward VII had already been postponed.[13] Neither party realised that this postponement had already been announced. The contract was held to be void for mistake. The converse situation (where the contract was formed before the Coronation's postponement, and so gave rise to frustration) is examined at 16.13 below in the discussion of *Krell* v. *Henry* (1903).

In *Amalgamated Investment & Property Co. Ltd* v. *John Walker & Sons Ltd* (1977)[14] a commercial development was concluded just before that site was listed as a building of special architectural or historical interest. The point concerning this timing is that relevant doctrine was not mistake, but frustration. However, the Court of Appeal held that the purchaser remained bound: the planning decision was not drastic enough to constitute frustration because it did not fundamentally affect the purchaser's acquisition of title (see further on this case 16.05, concerning allocation of risk).

16.05 *Risk allocated to one party.*[15] Frustration operates only if the relevant risk is not allocated to a party[16] in accordance with (i) an express[17] term, or (ii) a pre-existing rule,[18] or (iii) an implied allocation based on the court's assessment of the particular context.

As for (ii): an example of the courts imputing a risk to a party is *Amalgamated Investment & Property Co. Ltd* v. *John Walker & Sons Ltd* (1977).[19] The Court of Appeal held that a purchaser of land takes the risk that, subsequent to the contract's formation, the property might become listed as a building of special architectural or historical interest. And so no frustration occurred, even though the planning restriction prevented the purchaser from developing the site as he had intended.

As for (iii), Rix LJ noted in '*The Sea Angel*' (2007) that this requires close examination of the relevant commercial context, always bearing in mind that contractual excuses on the basis of frustration are not to be handed out like confetti:[20]

> [A]llocation . . . of risk is not simply a matter of express or implied provision but may also depend on less easily defined matters such as 'the contemplation of the parties' . . . [The *Davis Contractors* (1956)] test of 'radically different' is important: it tells us that the doctrine is not to be lightly invoked; that mere incidence of expense or delay or onerousness

---

13 (1903) TLR 434, Wright J.
14 [1977] 1 WLR 164, CA.
15 G. H. Treitel, *Frustration and Force Majeure* (3rd edn, London, 2014), chapter 12.
16 *National Carriers Ltd* v. *Panalpina (Northern) Ltd* [1981] AC 675, 712, HL, *per* Lord Simon.
17 For cases where express terms were construed not to preclude frustration, see *Metropolitan Water Board* v. *Dick, Kerr & Co.* [1918] AC 119, HL; and *Bank Line Ltd* v. *Arthur Capel & Co.* [1919] AC 435, HL.
18 '*The Great Peace*' [2002] EWCA Civ 1407; [2003] QB 679, at [74], *per* Lord Phillips CJ.
19 [1977] 1 WLR 164, CA.
20 *Edwinton Commercial Corporation* v. *Tsavliris Russ Ltd* ('*The Sea Angel*') [2007] EWCA Civ 547; [2007] 2 Lloyd's Rep 517, at [111].

is not sufficient; and that there has to be, as it were, a break in identity between the contract as provided for and contemplated and its performance in the new circumstances.

Rix LJ's 'multi-factorial' approach in *'The Sea Angel'* (2007)[21] concerning (a) allocation of risk and (b) the gravity of the supervening events was summarised by Beatson J in *Islamic Republic of Iran Shipping Lines* v. *Steamship Mutual Underwriting Association (Bermuda) Ltd* (2010) as follows:[22]

> Some of these factors exist at the time of the contract . . . [namely] the terms of the contract, its matrix or context, and the parties' knowledge, expectations, assumptions and contemplations, in particular as to risk, as at that time so far as these can be ascribed mutually objectively. The other factors are post-contractual . . . [namely] the nature of the supervening event and the parties' reasonable and objectively ascertainable calculations as to the possibility of future performance in the new circumstances.

16.06 *Foreseeability, foresight and inconclusive negotiation.*[23] The better view is that even though the relevant supervening event is foreseen or foreseeable, or a matter is discussed but terms are not settled, frustration might still arise because these are not absolute impediments to frustration. Instead, they are merely factors concerning the issue whether one party has impliedly assumed the risk of the relevant event's occurrence.[24] All that can be said is that a foreseen event is less likely to give rise to frustration, but it *might*: and that an unforeseen event is more likely to give rise to frustration (provided, of course, the *Davis Contractors* case's test is satisfied). The true position can be summarised as follows:

(1) supervening illegality, even if foreseen, counts as frustration; trading with the enemy is one such type of illegality; so parties contracting against the imminent outbreak of war will find their contract frustrated if that rule of illegality applies to their contract.

(2) A foreseeable event does not necessarily preclude frustration; the real issue is whether that risk is expressly or implicitly allocated to one party; if not, frustration is a possibility.

(3) Foreseen events might well involve risks borne by a party; but this is not necessarily so; and so even a foreseen event might give rise to frustration.

(4) If the parties unsuccessfully discuss what to do about a possible event (other than illegality: see above), the court can determine which party, if any, bears the relevant risk; and if neither party bears the risk, this leaves open the possibility that frustration might arise.

> These propositions are consistent with Rix LJ's comments in *'The Sea Angel'* (2007):[25]
> Even events which are not merely foreseen but made the subject of express contractual provision may lead to frustration: as occurs when an event such as a strike, or a restraint of prices, lasts for so long as to go beyond the risk assumed under the contract and to render performance radically different from that contracted for. However . . . the less that an event,

---

21 *Ibid.*
22 [2010] EWHC 2661 (Comm); [2011] 1 Lloyd's Rep 195; [2011] 2 All ER (Comm) 609, at [105].
23 G. H. Treitel, *Frustration and Force Majeure* (3rd edn, London, 2014), chapter 13.
24 *Maritime National Fish Ltd* v. *Ocean Trawlers Ltd* [1935] AC 524, 526, PC, *per* Lord Wright.
25 *Edwinton Commercial Corporation* v. *Tsavliris Russ Ltd* (*'The Sea Angel'*) [2007] EWCA Civ 547; [2007] 2 Lloyd's Rep 517, at [127].

in its type and its impact, is foreseeable, the more likely it is to be a factor which, depending on other factors in the case, may lead on to frustration.

Earlier Lord Denning MR said in 'The Eugenia' (1964):[26]

> It has frequently been said that the doctrine of frustration only applies when the new situation is 'unforeseen' or 'unexpected' or 'uncontemplated', as if that were an essential feature. But it is not so. . . . The only relevance of it being 'unforeseen' is this: If the parties did not foresee anything of the kind happening, you can readily infer they have made no provision for it: whereas, if they did foresee it, you would expect them to make provision for it.

3. THE SCOPE OF FRUSTRATION

16.07 The contract will be frustrated if, subsequent to the contract's formation, performance of the contract becomes illegal[27] (for the situation where the contract is illegal from its inception, or one or more party chooses to perform it in an illegal fashion, see Chapter 20). It is not possible to contract out of supervening illegality if to do so would be contrary to public policy.[28]

(1) In the *Fibrosa* (1943) case,[29] a contract for the supply of machinery by a British company of machinery to a port in Poland was frustrated when the German forces took control of Poland. Performance would entail the supplier trading with the enemy, a clear-cut instance of illegality. This case is further examined at 16.21.

Other examples of supervening illegality are:

(2) In *Metropolitan Water Board* v. *Dick, Kerr & Co.* (1918) (also at 16.12), a contract, formed in 1914, required the builder to construct a reservoir within six years.[30] However, in 1916, an order was made under the Defence of the Realm legislation requiring the contractors to stop work. The House of Lords held that the extent of interruption here was so great that the contract had become frustrated by reason of supervening illegality.

(3) In *Gamerco SA* v. *ICM/Fair Warning (Agency) Ltd* (1995),[31] a contract for the promotion of a rock concert in Madrid was frustrated when the Spanish authorities issued a prohibition on use of the chosen venue because of crumbling masonry (on the consequence of this, see the discussion of the case at 16.23).

By contrast, Beatson J held in the *Islamic Republic of Iran Shipping* case (2010) that partial supervening illegality had not frustrated a contract of marine insurance.[32]

26 'The Eugenia' [1964] 2 QB 226, CA; cf C. Hall, (1984) 4 LS 300 (proposing a recklessness basis).
27 G. H. Treitel, *Frustration and Force Majeure* (3rd edn, London, 2014), chapter 8.
28 *Ertel Bieber & Co.* v. *Rio Tinto Co. Ltd* [1918] AC 260, 273, HL.
29 [1943] AC 32, 39–40, HL.
30 *Metropolitan Water Board* v. *Dick, Kerr & Co.* [1918] AC 119, HL.
31 [1995] 1 WLR 1226, Garland J.
32 *Islamic Republic of Iran Shipping Lines* v. *Steamship Mutual Underwriting Association (Bermuda) Ltd* [2010] EWHC 2661 (Comm); [2011] 1 Lloyd's Rep 195; [2011] 2 All ER (Comm) 609, notably at [115], [116], [121], [126] to [128].

16.08 *Physical impossibility.*[33] Contracts for the performance of personal services are frustrated if, before completion of the relevant task, (a) the performer is incapacitated (without his fault) by illness, or becomes mentally incapable of acting,[34] or dies; or (b) the physical subject matter of the proposed performance has been destroyed or it has disappeared without any default by the parties. As for (b), this is illustrated by *Taylor* v. *Caldwell* (1863)[35] (the decision which established the modern doctrine) where a fire had destroyed the venue which was at the centre of the contract; neither party had been at fault, and the risk of such a major problem had not been impliedly allocated to either party.

> The defendant in *Taylor* v. *Caldwell* (1863) had agreed to make available to the claimant a music hall and gardens for four days. The claimant agreed on these days to provide artistes who would entertain. It was a kind of joint venture. Performance of the contract was frustrated by a fire which gutted the music hall. This fire was not attributable to the fault, or breach, of either party. The claimant claimed £58 as expenses, mostly advertising costs. But the court rejected the claim. It declared the contract had ended once the music hall was consumed by the flames. Therefore, if the defendant had counter-claimed for unpaid hire, that claim would also have failed.

16.09 *Difficulty and 'impracticability': no frustration.*[36] The fact that a contract becomes more difficult to perform is not enough to constitute frustration. The leading discussion is *Davis Contractors Ltd* v. *Fareham Urban District Council* (1956)[37] (in fact this case is a leading authority for four reasons: first, it made clear that the implied term theory must be abandoned; secondly, it established the 'radical difference' general criterion of frustration; thirdly, it demonstrated that commercial hardship does not constitute frustration; finally, in the context of construction contracts, it decided that a builder bears the risk of building materials becoming scarce, with consequent delay).

> *Davis Contractors Ltd* v. *Fareham Urban District Council* (1956) concerned a contract to build seventy-eight houses for a price of approximately £94,000, and the work to be completed within eight months. However, there were two snags. First, labour shortages slowed down the work so that it took twenty-two months. Such shortages were not unforeseeable in the chaotic post-war period. Secondly, the cost of doing the work rose to approximately £115,000. The builder soldiered on and finished the job. He then audaciously claimed more than the contract price. His strategy was to contend that the contract had become frustrated by operation of law. If the arbitrator were to accept this argument, the result would be that

---

33 G. H. Treitel, *Frustration and Force Majeure* (3rd edn, London, 2014), chapters 3 to 5.
34 But no frustration arose when a client ceased to have capacity to instruct solicitors: *Blankley* v. *Central Manchester and Manchester Children's University Hospitals NHS Trust* [2014] EWHC 168; [2014] 1 WLR 2683, at [37] ff, *per* Phillips J.
35 (1863) 3 B & S 826; 122 ER 309.
36 G. H. Treitel, *Frustration and Force Majeure* (3rd edn, London, 2014), chapter 6.
37 [1956] AC 696, HL.

from the date of discharge (the moment at which 'frustration' ended the contract), his post-frustration work should be remunerated at the higher market rate. This would be in accordance with a *quantum meruit*, an extra-contractual and restitutionary claim. The arbitrator upheld this strategy. But the House of Lords, rejecting this award as wrong in law, held that there was no scope on these facts for finding frustration because these changes were not drastic enough to satisfy that doctrine. And so the builder remained bound by the original price.

The decision in *Davis Contractors Ltd* v. *Fareham Urban District Council* (1956) is tough but commercially sound. The cost of the work had increased by less than 25 per cent. This increase in cost unfortunately eliminated the builder's profit margin: the actual cost of building exceeded the agreed price for the job. But this made no difference. This risk is borne by the builder. The contract cannot be dissolved just because 'the going gets tough'. It is not enough that a party's profit margin is reduced or that the deal becomes an economic disaster for this party.

It might even be the law that no increase in expense can ever amount to frustration, no matter how severe the hardship to the affected party.

Although Beatson (1996)[38] suggested that a safety valve should be created for really extreme situations of increased difficulty, there is abundant judicial authority against this.

For example, in *British Movietonews Ltd* v. *London District Cinemas* (1952),[39] Lord Simon said:

[Contractual parties] are often faced, in the course of carrying it out, with a turn of events which they did not at all anticipate – a wholly abnormal rise or fall in prices, a sudden depreciation of currency, an unexpected obstacle to execution or the like. Yet this does not of itself affect the bargain they have made.

Lord Radcliffe said in the *Davis* case (1956): 'it is not hardship or inconvenience or material loss itself which calls the principle of frustration into play.'[40]

Lord Denning MR said in 'The Eugenia' (1964):[41]

[T]he fact that it has become more onerous or more expensive for one party than he thought is not sufficient to bring about a frustration. It must be more than merely more onerous or more expensive. It must be positively unjust to hold the parties bound.

The strict approach of English law sends a clear message to negotiating parties that they cannot escape their bargains except in extreme circumstances where the contract becomes impossible or illegal, or its very foundation has been annihilated by a change of circumstance (on that unusual possibility, see 16.13).

---

38 J. Beatson, 'Increased Expense and Frustration', in F. D. Rose (ed.), *Consensus ad Idem: Essays on the Law of Contract in Honour of Guenter Treitel* (London, 1996), 121; on 1920s German hyper-inflation, see W. Lorenz, in J. Beatson and D. Friedmann (eds.), *Good Faith and Fault in Contract Law* (Oxford, 1995), 357, 365 ff.
39 [1952] AC 166, 185, HL.
40 *Davis Contractors Ltd* v. *Fareham Urban District Council* [1956] AC 696, 729, HL, *per* Lord Radcliffe; considered in 'The Great Peace' [2002] EWCA Civ 1407; [2003] QB 679, at [70]; *Pioneer Shipping Ltd* v. *BTP Tioxide Ltd ('The Nema')* [1982] AC 724, 744, 751–2, HL.
41 [1964] 2 QB 226, 239, CA.

Provision can be made in the contract, by insertion of *force majeure*[42] or hardship clauses, to achieve a consensual modification of this strict regime. A *force majeure* clause declares when a party will be released from his obligations, or excused from liability for default, by reason of freak and excusable supervening events (see also 16. 19, for reference to the clause in 'The Super Servant Two' (1990)).

But, in *Thames Valley Power Ltd* v. *Total Gas & Power Ltd* (2005),[43] Clarke J held that even a *force majeure* clause will not exonerate an energy supplier, who has agreed to supply energy under a fifteen-year contract, despite the fact that there has been a very significant increase in the wholesale price. The supply of energy remained possible, even though increases in the costs of supply had rendered the contract very unattractive to the energy company.

16.10 *Supply of generic goods: an uphill struggle to excuse non-supply.* A wholesale seller owes a strict (although not quite an absolute) duty to procure goods from sources 'further up the chain': he will seldom succeed in showing that the stated source has dried up so entirely that it was impossible to obtain a supply.[44]

16.11 *Successful plea of frustration: supply unavoidably blocked from nominated foreign source.* Frustration might occur if the sole foreign supplier has placed an embargo on all supplies of the relevant commodity *from the stipulated foreign source*, as noted in *Société Cooperative Suisse des Céréales et Matières Fourragères* v. *La Plata Cereal Company SA* (1946).[45]

16.12 *Frustrating delay: 'it all depends'.* Whether delay operates to frustrate the relevant contract will depend on the context. The potential impact of delay is that the contract, although in due course capable of performance, has suffered a drastic restructuring. And so the original assumptions have radically altered. Delay, where it has this drastic venture, causes the 'venture' to be frustrated (see the *Jackson* case (1874) later in this paragraph). Thus, the House of Lords in 'The Nema' restored the arbitrator's decision that strikes had caused delay sufficient to frustrate a charterparty for the year 1979. As Lord Roskill explained in that case, it is a question of 'degree'.[46]

---

42 E. McKendrick (ed.), *Force Majeure and Frustration of Contract* (2nd edn, London, 1995), especially at 34; E. McKendrick, 'The Regulation of Long-Term Contracts in English Law', in J. Beatson and D. Friedmann (eds.), *Good Faith and Fault in Contract Law* (Oxford, 1995), 305, 323 ff; E. McKendrick, 'Force Majeure Clauses: The Gap between Doctrine and Practice', in A. Burrows and E. Peel (eds.), *Contract Terms* (Oxford, 2007), chapter 12; *Chitty on Contracts* (31st edn, London, 2012), 14–140 ff.
43 [2005] EWHC 2208 (Comm); [2006] 1 Lloyd's Rep 441.
44 *Blackburn Bobbin* v. *TW Allen* [1918] 2 KB 467, CA; *CTI Group Inc.* v. *Transclear SA* [2008] EWCA Civ 856, at [14] and [23], *per* Moore-Bick LJ.
45 (1946) 80 Lloyd's Rep 530, Morris J.
46 *Pioneer Shipping Ltd* v. *BTP Tioxide Ltd* ('The Nema') [1982] AC 724, 752, HL, *per* Lord Roskill.

Delay was found to be *sufficient* in *Metropolitan Water Board* v. *Dick, Kerr & Co.* (1918) (16.07).[47] This was an agreement for construction of a reservoir within six years. The work was then affected by a wartime government order which required the contractor to stop work and sell their construction plant. The House of Lords concluded that the contract had been frustrated even though the contract provided for an extension of time in the event of delays 'howsoever occasioned'. Those words, although literally wide enough, were held not to cover the drastic 'event' in question. But in many commercial cases the courts have found delay to be insufficient to constitute frustration on the facts.

Similarly, in *Jackson* v. *Union Marine Insurance Co. Ltd* (1874),[48] P's ship had been chartered to carry rails from Newport in Wales to San Francisco. The ship ran aground on its way from Liverpool to Newport, where loading was to take place. Repairs took nine months. And so X, the charterer, hired another vessel, and decided not to pay P. P successfully claimed against his insurer for this loss of payment. The court held that if P had sued X for payment of the freight, X could have pleaded that the venture had been radically changed in view of the delay, and that the contract for carriage had been frustrated.

Delay was found to be *insufficient* in the following three cases:

In the *Davis Contractors* case (1956)[49] (16.09), a building contract expected to last eight months in fact took twenty-two months.

In 'The Eugenia' (1964), a voyage expected to last 108 days (the originally intended route from the Black Sea to India was to go via the Suez Canal) in fact lasted 138 days (it was necessary to go the long way round, via the Cape of Good Hope).[50]

In 'The Sea Angel' (2007), a vessel, hired for up to twenty days to assist in a salvage operation, was prevented from leaving its port by the Pakistani port authority until payment had been made for the loss caused by pollution (oil leaking from a tanker which the salvage vessel had been hired to rescue).[51] Extricating the salvage vessel from this situation prolonged the transaction by over three months (as mentioned, the anticipated length of the salvage hire was merely twenty days). The Court of Appeal held that this delay and duration fell within the scope of the risk borne by the charterer. That party was, therefore, liable to pay hire at the agreed daily rate.

16.13 *Frustration of the venture or purpose: exceptional source of frustration.*[52] We have already noted instances where delay is so severe that it is held to have wrecked a particular commercial venture (see, for example, 16.12 on *Metropolitan Water Board* v. *Dick, Kerr & Co.* (1918)[53] and *Jackson* v. *Union Marine Insurance Co. Ltd*, 1874).[54] Beyond those

---

47 [1918] AC 119, H; also on the facts of *Jackson* v. *Union Marine Insurance Co. Ltd* (1874) LR 10 CP 125.
48 (1874) LR 10 CP 125, Exchequer Chamber.
49 [1956] AC 696, HL.
50 [1964] 2 QB 226, CA.
51 *Edwinton Commercial Corporation* v. *Tsavliris Russ Ltd* ('*The Sea Angel*') [2007] EWCA Civ 547; [2007] 2 Lloyd's Rep 517, at [132] and [133].
52 G. H. Treitel, *Frustration and Force Majeure* (3rd edn, London, 2014), chapter 7.
53 [1918] AC 119, H; also on the facts of *Jackson* v. *Union Marine Insurance Co. Ltd* (1874) LR 10 CP 125.
54 (1874) LR 10 CP 125, Exchequer Chamber.

situations, however, frustration of the venture is seldom satisfied in practice (Mustill LJ in *FC Shepherd* v. *Jerrom* (1987) noted[55] that this concept seems to have appeared first in *Jackson* v. *Union Marine Insurance Co. Ltd* (1874)).[56] An unusual instance is *Krell* v. *Henry* (1903), in which the hire of a room for one day overlooking the ceremonial Coronation procession of King Edward VII was frustrated because the event had to be postponed when the King fell ill.[57] It was clear that the hire was for the specific purpose of witnessing a one-off event on a special occasion: the licensee could not sensibly be expected to languish in this room if the procession did not take place that day. The risk that the Coronation would be postponed could not fairly be allocated to the licensee. Explaining this result, Vaughan-Williams LJ made two main points, but arguably failed to make clear a third point: (i) that frustration includes a third category (in addition to supervening impossibility or physical impossibility) known as 'frustration of the venture', that is, the doctrine might extend to inability to realise the substance or foundation of the contract, and (ii) for this purpose the court is not tied to express definitions within the contract of this 'substance' or 'foundation'. However, we can see in retrospect that Vaughan-Williams LJ omitted to note (iii) that the category of 'frustration of the venture' is extremely narrow and hence rare.[58]

Krell v. *Henry* (1903) was distinguished by the Court of Appeal in *Herne Bay Steam Boat Co.* v. *Hutton* (1903). In the latter case, the 'foundation' of the contract had not wholly disappeared. Indeed, a large part of it remained.[59]

The *Herne Bay Steam Boat* case (1903) concerned the commercial hire of a craft to be offered to members of the public so that, on payment, they could inspect the great naval review at Spithead. These events were to take place after the Coronation of Edward VII. The Court of Appeal held that his illness, and the postponement of the Coronation, did not render the contract of hire a 'complete waste of time' (to use modern parlance). And so there was no frustration. The King's absence at the review did not destroy the public's opportunity to see the magnificent array of warships at anchor.

This decision is sound. The King's presence would have enhanced the sense of occasion (because he would have been recently crowned). But his absence did not turn the naval review into a 'non-event'. It would perhaps have been different if the purpose of the hire had been specifically advertised in these terms: 'Vessel available for hire during King's review of the Fleet'. However, objectively, this was not the sole or predominant purpose of the hire on the facts of the case. The risk of slight public disappointment (and consequently a reduction in the public's interest in trips to view the fleet) was rightly allocated to the party who hired the craft.

It is submitted that *Krell* v. *Henry* and the *Herne Bay Steam Boat* case, although divergent in their results, are both soundly decided. *Krell* v. *Henry* shows that a contract can be

---

55 [1987] QB 301, 322, CA.
56 (1874) LR 10 CP 125, 145.
57 [1903] 2 KB 740, CA (Lord Wright in the *Maritime National Fish* case, [1935] AC 524, 529, PC, noting the exceptional nature of *Krell* v. *Henry*).
58 [1903] 2 KB 740, 749, CA.
59 [1903] 2 KB 683, CA.

frustrated even though it has not become illegal to perform[60] and even though the contracting parties and the physical subject matter of the contract remain intact. Exceptionally, the *abstract platform* of the contract can disappear, rendering physical performance a hollow and futile activity. But it is also necessary to show that the risk of this disappointment cannot be reasonably imputed to the disappointed party (the licensee in *Krell* v. *Henry*; compare the hapless spectator at Lord's cricket ground who enjoys only ten overs and one ball[61] of 'live action', whereupon the rest of the day is rained off or play stops for 'bad light'). By contrast, the *Herne Bay Steam Boat* case shows that such abstract 'frustration of the venture' will not occur if only *part* of the anticipated contractual satisfaction has been removed by the relevant supervening change of circumstance, as opposed to all or most of it.

Furthermore, the disappointed party in the *Herne Bay Steam Boat* case was intending to use this vessel for commercial profit and was not, therefore, a consumer (unlike the parallel party, the licensee, in the *Krell* case). Although not articulated in the cases as a factor, arguably the status of the respective parties in these cases and the fact that the charterer in the *Herne Bay Steam Boat* case was taking a business risk are relevant factors. For it was appropriate for the consumer in *Krell* v. *Henry* to be released from payment for a performance which had become totally pointless, but it would have been inappropriate to have released the commercial charterer in the *Herne Bay Steam Boat* case from a bargain which had become less attractive but not a hopeless venture. Interesting problems would have arisen if the licensee in the *Krell* case had been a Coronation view tout (buying assignable licences for gain) or if, conversely, the party hiring the vessel in the *Herne Bay Steam Boat* case had been acting for reasons of personal pleasure, especially if he had expressed keen interest in seeing the Royal visit to Spithead.

16.14 *Leases:*[62] The House of Lords in *National Carriers Ltd* v. *Panalpina (Northern) Ltd* (1981) held that leases (of interests in land) could be frustrated (although this will be quite exceptional).[63] For example, a lease would be terminated if it were for ninety-nine years and after only a couple of years the demised premises, situated on a cliff-top, fell into the sea as a result of coastal erosion.

National Carriers Ltd v. *Panalpina (Northern) Ltd* (1981) concerned a ten-year lease of a warehouse to the defendant. The only access to the warehouse was by a street. After five years of the term had elapsed, the local authority closed that street, for roughly eighteen months. This closure was necessary because a building opposite had been discovered to be in a dangerously

---

60   The 'venture' concept was also in play in *Islamic Republic of Iran Shipping Lines* v. *Steamship Mutual Underwriting Association (Bermuda) Ltd* [2010] EWHC 2661 (Comm); [2011] 1 Lloyd's Rep 195; [2011] 2 All ER (Comm) 609, where Beatson J held that partial supervening illegality did not have the effect of frustrating a contract of marine insurance, because its essence had not been radically altered: notably at [115], [116], [121], [126] to [128].
61   At Test cricket matches, ticket-money is not refunded if a specified number of overs are played on the relevant day.
62   G. H. Treitel, *Frustration and Force Majeure* (3rd edn, London, 2014), chapter 11.
63   [1981] AC 675, HL.

derelict state. The landlord sought to recover unpaid rent. The defendants claimed that the lease had been frustrated. The House of Lords noted that frustration is a possibility in the case of leases, but not on these facts: the period of sterilised use in this case was too short to constitute a radical deprivation of the tenant's enjoyment of the lease, considering the overall length of the lease and the fact that normality would resume for the final three years of the lease. Lord Wilberforce said:[64] 'this does not approach the gravity of a frustrating event. Out of 10 years it will have lost less than two years of use: there will be nearly three years left after the interruption has ceased.'

4. DEFAULT AND SELF-INDUCED FRUSTRATION

16.15 The party pleading frustration must not have brought the incapacitating event upon himself.[65] The 'outside event or extraneous change of situation' must not be something which the party 'seeking to rely on it had the means and opportunity to prevent'.[66]

More precisely, the doctrine of 'self-induced frustration' can arise where the alleged frustrating event is in fact attributable to: (1) a party's breach of contract;[67] or (2) perhaps other forms of blameworthy conduct (although this situation might be treated as turning on breach of an implied term) (see the text below for more on this category); or (3) his criminal wrongdoing;[68] or (4) his 'choice' or 'election' to prefer his own interests or those of another customer.[69]

As for (2), 'other forms of blameworthy conduct', Bingham LJ said in *The Super Servant Two'* (1990) that the concept of breach of a duty by the defendant should not be placed into a legal 'straitjacket' and that a party's fault will normally preclude frustration: 'A fine test of legal duty is inappropriate; what is needed is a pragmatic judgment whether a party seeking to rely on an event as discharging him from a contractual promise was himself responsible for the occurrence of that event.'[70]

There are dicta in the House of Lords decision in the *Joseph Constantine* case (1942) concerning the hypothetical prima donna who catches a cold through neglect of her health, but this discussion was inconclusive.[71] It is submitted that the law should recognise an implied term that a person will take reasonable steps, and avoid obvious risks, to keep open the possibility that he will be physically able to perform his contract. Breach of such an implied term will involve 'self-induced frustration' and render him liable to pay damages.

---

64 *Ibid.*, at 697–8.

65 G. H. Treitel, *Frustration and Force Majeure* (3rd edn, London, 2014), chapter 14.

66 *J Lauritzen* v. *Wijsmuller BV ('The Super Servant Two')* [1990] 1 Lloyd's Rep 1, 8, CA (hereafter 'The Super Servant Two').

67 *Paal Wilson* v. *Blumenthal ('The Hannah Blumenthal')* [1983] 1 AC 854, HL; see also *The Monarch SS* case, [1949] AC 196, HL.

68 *FC Shepherd* v. *Jerrom* [1987] QB 301, CA.

69 *Maritime National Fish* v. *Ocean Trawlers* [1935] AC 524, PC; *'The Super Servant Two'* [1990] 1 Lloyd's Rep 1, CA.

70 [1990] 1 Lloyd's Rep 1, at 10.

71 *Joseph Constantine SS Co.* v. *Imperial Smelting Corporation Ltd* [1942] AC 154, 166–7, 179, 195, 202, HL; see also *'The Super Servant Two'* [1990] 1 Lloyd's Rep 1, 8, CA ('fault' is inconsistent with frustration).

16.16 Nor can a party invoke his own default when it tactically suits him, in order to escape the conclusion that the contract has been terminated by frustration operating automatically on the relevant facts. This unsurprising proposition emerges from *FC Shepherd* v. *Jerrom* (1986).[72]

In *FC Shepherd* v. *Jerrom* (1986) an employee had been convicted of a crime committed out of work and sentenced to a period of Borstal training, which lasted thirty-nine weeks. He later brought a claim for unfair dismissal under the employment protection legislation (a complaint which is heard by an employment tribunal). The question was whether (1) the employer had dismissed the employee (as the latter contended), or (2) whether the contract had been terminated by operation of law, in accordance with the doctrine of frustration. The Court of Appeal concluded that it was a case of (2), and so the employee's complaint should fail *in limine*. The Court of Appeal held that it would be inappropriate for a party to plead his own self-induced frustration in this counter-intuitively self-serving fashion. Accordingly, there had been a frustration by operation of law and thus no active 'dismissal' by the employer.

16.17 *Choice precludes frustration.* 'The Super Servant Two' (1990)[73] decides that frustration does not apply if it remained physically possible for a party to have performed his contract, but he chose not to do so, either (1) because he preferred to advance his own interests, or (2) because (again without prioritising the other party's interests) he had committed himself to use the available resources for a contract with a third party (taking the risk of a clear, or at least potential, 'double-booking'). It is not enough, therefore, that in either of these situations the crisis has arisen from a supervening event without that party's default. However much sympathy one might have for his plight, the fact that this party has made this choice destroys any chance of frustration applying. Situation (1) is illustrated by the *Maritime National* case (1935)[74] and (2) by 'The Super Servant Two' (1990).[75] These cases will be considered in turn.

16.18 In the *Maritime National* case (1935), the Privy Council held that a charterer could not invoke frustration because the facts disclosed an example of self-induced incapacity.[76] The defendant ('the charterer') hired a trawler, the 'St Cuthbert', from the claimant ('the owner'). The charterer already had four other trawlers. As the parties foresaw, the trawlers could only operate under government licence. The charterer received only three licences, although he had applied for five. He then chose to use these licences against three of his vessels, electing not to license the 'St Cuthbert'. When the owner sued him for the hire charges, the charterer unsuccessfully argued that the contract of hire had been frustrated

---

72 [1987] QB 301, CA; on which see M. Mustill, 'Anticipatory Breach', in *Butterworths Lectures 1989–90* (London, 1990), 3, 75–6.
73 'The Super Servant Two' [1990] 1 Lloyd's Rep 1, 10, CA.
74 *Maritime National Fish Ltd* v. *Ocean Trawlers Ltd* [1935] AC 524, PC.
75 'The Super Servant Two' [1990] 1 Lloyd's Rep 1, 10, CA.
76 *Maritime National Fish Ltd* v. *Ocean Trawlers Ltd* [1935] AC 524, PC.

by his inability to obtain sufficient licences. The Privy Council held that the charterer's decision to allocate the three licences to ships other than the present chartered vessel was an act of self-induced frustration.

16.19 The second, and now the leading, decision on this topic is 'The Super Servant Two' (1990).[77] The decision boils down to this: if Y hires out to X either vessel The Super Servant One or vessel The Super Servant Two, the allocation being postponed to suit Y, supervening and excused unavailability of The Super Servant Two does not also excuse Y from his duty to provide The Super Servant One, which is the back-up vessel. It is of no relevance to X that Y has double-booked The Super Servant One, the back-up vessel, having decided to use it to make money in a contract with a different customer.

> In 'The Super Servant Two' (1990), the defendant contracted to carry the claimant's drilling rig from Japan to Rotterdam on either of his two giant barges, The Super Servant One or The Super Servant Two. After the contract's formation, the defendant decided to allocate The Super Servant Two for this job, using The Super Servant One for another job with a third party (these giant barges seem to have been commercially interchangeable, possessing the same dimensions, etc.). But, before the The Super Servant Two could be moved to work on the claimant's job, that vessel sank in the Zaire River. The terms of the contract stated that the contract could be performed by use of either of two named vessels: the contract did not restrict performance to the vessel which, on these facts, later became unavailable through no fault of the owner. The fact that the contract could be performed using alternative vessels could work to the rig-owner's advantage (increasing the chances of a barge remaining available) and to the barge-owner's advantage (enabling him to avoid the other party's potentially problematic objection that only a single nominated vessel could be used for the job).
>
> The Court of Appeal held that the sinking of The Super Servant Two did not exonerate the defendant. The contract with the claimant had stipulated that either The Super Servant One or Two would be used. The defendant could not hide behind its own commercial decision to use The Super Servant One for the parallel contract with the third party. There was no reason why the claimant should suffer as a result of the defendant's commercial deployment of his remaining vessel. That deployment had been made to suit the defendant, and he had earned extra revenue from it.

The decision is sound. As Bingham LJ observed, the defendant's option to use The Super Servant One or Two had been inserted by the defendant *for its commercial convenience*.[78] Similarly, Dillon LJ noted that the defendant had extracted *extra revenue* from its The Super Servant One customers before finally allocating The Super Servant Two to the contract with the claimant.[79] It would have been different if the contract had exclusively nominated The Super Servant Two[80] (assuming, of course, that its subsequent sinking was not attributable

---

77 'The Super Servant Two' [1990] 1 Lloyd's Rep 1, CA.
78 Ibid., at 10.
79 Ibid., at 13 col. 2.
80 Ibid., at 9 col. 2, per Bingham LJ.

to the defendant's default). That would have sent the clear message: 'everything depends on the physical availability of *The Super Servant Two*; if it sinks etc., without my fault, you cannot sue me for non-supply.'

A final aspect of this case is that the contract in *'The Super Servant Two'* (1990) contained a *force majeure* clause (16.09) which literally would be effective to exclude the defendant's liability arising from the sinking of *Two*. But the Court of Appeal held that this clause would not exonerate the defendant if there had been negligence on its part. Since the litigation was being conducted at this stage on preliminary points, the eventual result is not reported.

16.20 *The conundrum of short supply and too many customers.* Suppose that a Lincolnshire pea farmer, D, agrees to supply in the 2010 season 100 tonnes to each of X, Y and Z at a specified rate of payment. This is a reasonable contract since last year D achieved a yield of 500 tonnes in all. But, because of natural events outside his control, the risk of which was not impliedly allocated to the farmer, the 2010 yield is only 100 tonnes. What can D do? The following discussion assumes that D has failed to contract on the basis that his commitment to supply is 'subject to availability, including adverse growing conditions'. English law is clear: none of the contracts is frustrated; and so Y and Z have good claims for breach of contract against D if he delivers the 100 tonnes to X. This approach is supported by *'The Super Servant Two'* decision (see 16.19 above). Some might regard this as harsh. The better view, however, is that the English rule is commercially realistic and the result is clear. Of course, different approaches might have been adopted: to allow D a defence if his decision to supply X was based on the fact that D's contract with X was concluded before the other contracts (first come, first served) or if he split his 100 tonnes equally between X, Y and Z, regardless of the contract date.[81]

Of course, on different facts, if a farmer without fault finds that he has insufficient goods to supply a single buyer, and it was apparent that the farmer was agreeing to supply peas produced from his land, the contract will be partially frustrated to the extent of the shortfall: X agrees to supply 100 tonnes of peas to Y. There are no other buyers. Due to unprecedented hailstorms, X's yield is only 50 tonnes. X is excused from failure to supply more than 50 tonnes.

5. THE AFTERMATH OF FRUSTRATION

16.21 Frustration[82] 'brings the contract to an end forthwith, without more and automatically' (that is, without any need for the parties to be aware that it has

---

81 For this approach in the USA, see Uniform Commercial Code, 2–615; cases adopting such an approach are distinguished in *'The Super Servant Two'* [1990] 1 Lloyd's Rep 1, 9 col. 1, as applicable to construction of *force majeure* clauses; Dillon LJ in particular [1990] 1 Lloyd's Rep 1, 13–14, rejected a 'reasonableness' approach.
82 G. H. Treitel, *Frustration and Force Majeure* (3rd edn, London, 2014), chapter 15; E. McKendrick (ed.), *Force Majeure and Frustration of Contract* (2nd edn, London, 1995); *Goff and Jones, The Law of Unjust Enrichment* (8th edn, London, 2011), chapter 15; E. McKendrick, 'Frustration, Restitution and Loss Adjustment', in

occurred).[83] It releases the parties from their unperformed obligations. For most (but not all)[84] types of contract, the Law Reform (Frustrated Contracts) Act 1943 has ameliorated the following three Common Law consequences of frustration:

(1) At Common Law, money paid before the contract is frustrated can be recovered only if there is a total failure of consideration (section 1(2) of the 1943 Act now changes this, in the context of frustration). In the *Fibrosa* case (1943),[85] the House of Lords reversed the Court of Appeal's fallacious decision in *Chandler* v. *Webster* (1904),[86] which had held that there can be no total failure of consideration unless a contract is rescinded *ab initio*. Instead, as the House of Lords clarified, money is repayable if the payor has received not one jot of performance by the payee under the contract.

(2) At Common Law, accrued obligations to pay remained enforceable (section 1(2) of the 1943 Act now changes this, in the context of frustration).

(3) At Common Law, there was no scope to award recompense for partially completed work (this is because of the doctrine of entire obligations: payment is owed for contractual performance only if that performance, or a severable part of it, is completed or substantially performed before the contract's frustration; generally on the Common Law doctrine of entire obligations and substantial performance, see 17.46) (section 1(3) of the 1943 Act now changes this in the context of frustration).

16.22 In *BP Exploration Co. (Libya) Ltd* v. *Hunt (No. 2)* (1979), Robert Goff J summarised the effect of sections 1(2) and (3) of the 1943 Act:[87]

> The [Act] is not designed to do certain things: (i) It is not designed to apportion the loss between the parties . . . (ii) It is not concerned to put the parties in the position in which they would have been if the contract had been performed. (iii) It is not concerned to restore the parties to the position they were in before the contract was made.

Section 1(2) of the 1943 Act states:

> *All sums paid or payable to any party in pursuance of the contract before the time when the parties were so discharged (in this Act referred to as 'the time of discharge') shall, in the case of sums so paid, be recoverable from him as money received by him for the use of the party by whom the sums were paid, and, in the case of sums so payable, cease to be so payable: Provided that, if the party to whom the*

A. Burrows (ed.), *Essays on Restitution* (Oxford, 1991), 147; G. L. Williams, *Law Reform (Frustrated Contracts) Act 1943* (London, 1944).

83   *Hirji Mulji* v. *Cheong Yue Steamship Co. Ltd* [1926] AC 497, 505, PC, *per* Lord Sumner.

84   Section 5(2) of the Law Reform (Frustrated Contracts) Act 1943 creates exceptions in the case of voyage charterparties, contracts for the carriage of goods by sea, insurance agreements and contracts for the sale of specific goods; cf *Islamic Republic of Iran Shipping Lines* v. *Steamship Mutual Underwriting Association (Bermuda) Ltd* [2010] EWHC 2661 (Comm); [2011] 1 Lloyd's Rep 195; [2011] 2 All ER (Comm) 609 (the insurance contract had not been frustrated; if it had been, the premium would not be recoverable unless there had been total failure of consideration – on this see next note).

85   *Fibrosa Spolka Akcyjna* v. *Fairbairn Lawson Combe Barbour Ltd* [1943] AC 32, 45–8, HL.

86   [1904] 1 KB 493, 499–501, CA, *per* Lord Collins MR.

87   The main discussion by Robert Goff J is at [1979] 1 WLR 783, 799; subsidiary aspects are examined in successive appeals, [1981] 1 WLR 232, CA; [1982] 2 AC 352, HL.

> *sums were so paid or payable incurred expenses before the time of discharge in, or*
> *for the purpose of, the performance of the contract, the court may, if it considers it*
> *just to do so having regard to all the circumstances of the case, allow him to retain*
> *or, as the case may be, recover the whole or any part of the sums so paid or payable,*
> *not being an amount in excess of the expenses so incurred.*

The effect of section 1(2) is that a party can reclaim money paid before the frustrating event, even if there has been some partial performance by the recipient. This reverses the *Fibrosa* case (1943) in this context.[88] But this refund is subject to the recipient's counter-claim for an allowance for his expenditure: see the second part of section 1(2), after the words 'Provided that' above. The allowance referred to therein is at the court's discretion (16.23).

Another aspect of section 1(2) is that it reverses the Common Law by prima facie cancelling an outstanding liability to pay if this duty has arisen (liability has 'accrued') before the contract was frustrated. But this provisional cancellation can be reversed, in whole or in part, if, in exercise of the court's discretion (16.23), it is decided that the intended payee should be paid such unpaid sums to cover the payee's expenditure.

16.23 The upshot of section 1(2) is that in general the payee must repay money paid and forget money payable but not yet paid unless he can persuade the court that (a) the paid and (b) payable but unpaid sums should be used as a 'kitty' out of which it would be fair to reimburse his expenses, in full or at least in part. The 'kitty' (comprising (a) and (b)) is the maximum fund available under section 1(2) for this purpose.

Thus, under section 1(2) of the 1943 Act, the court receives a twofold discretion: to order repayment; and to reverse cancellation of debts already accrued. In *Gamerco SA v. ICM/ Fair Warning (Agency) Ltd* (1995), Garland J held that the court has a free hand when exercising these discretions.[89] He rejected two rigid approaches: to split the payee's reliance on an equal basis between him and the payor; or to allow the payee always to retain the money to the extent of his reliance.

> In the *Gamerco* case (1995), the claimant company had hired the defendant rock band to perform at a concert in a Madrid stadium. The contract was subject to English law. After the contract's formation, the Spanish authorities condemned the proposed venue as unsafe. This prohibition was, therefore, a supervening event. As a result, the contract had been frustrated. The claimant had made a large prepayment to the band. Garland J held (i) that the payee has the onus of establishing that there should be some 'discretionary retention',[90] but in this case the defendant had not adduced clear evidence of its expenditure in preparation for the concert;[91] and (ii) the court's discretion is wholly unfettered; there are thus no fixed rules, nor even rules of thumb, such as a presumption of 'total retention' of sums paid or payable, or a presumption that the losses suffered by both parties should be cumulated and then split equally, by adjustment of the

---

88 [1943] AC 32, HL.
89 [1995] 1 WLR 1226.
90 *Ibid.*, at 1235G.
91 *Ibid.*, at 1237F.

award under this sub-section.[92] On the facts of this case Garland J held (iii) that the claimant should recover the whole prepayment, and he noted that the payor's wasted expenditure certainly exceeded the amount of that recovery.

16.24 What of performance other than by payment of money (use of goods or performance of services)? Section 1(3) of the 1943 Act provides:

> Where any party to the contract has, by reason of anything done by any other party thereto in, or for the purpose of, the performance of the contract, obtained a valuable benefit (other than a payment of money to which the last foregoing subsection applies) before the time of discharge, there shall be recoverable from him by the said other party such sum (if any), not exceeding the value of the said benefit to the party obtaining it, as the court considers just, having regard to all the circumstances of the case and, in particular –
>
> (a) the amount of any expenses incurred before the time of discharge by the benefited party in, or for the purpose of, the performance of the contract, including any sums paid or payable by him to any other party in pursuance of the contract and retained or recoverable by that party under the last foregoing subsection, and
> (b) the effect, in relation to the said benefit, of the circumstances giving rise to the frustration of the contract.

There are two stages in the application of section 1(3): (1) quantifying the valuable benefit obtained prior to the date of frustration; (2) assessing the just sum payable to the performing party, that sum not to exceed the amount established at stage (1). At stage (2) the court will take into account the impact of the frustrating event upon the relevant benefit.

16.25 The only reported English case on section 1(3) of the 1943 Act is *BP Exploration Co. (Libya) Ltd v. Hunt (No. 2)* (1979).[93] It is unfortunate that the only reported English decision on section 1(3) is a factual nightmare for students and advisors.

The claimant, British Petroleum, had entered into a complicated joint venture with the defendant, Hunt. The parties had agreed to develop and exploit an oil field in Libya. Hunt owned the oil concession. The terms of this contract gave BP a right to 'reimbursement oil'. Once reimbursed for its expenditure in developing the oil field, the oil revenue would be divided equally between the two parties. BP expended large sums on the project. As a result, the parties succeeded in extracting oil. The contract had operated successfully for almost five years, when the Libyan government decided to expropriate the oil field.

Robert Goff J held that, in principle, the valuable benefit obtained by Hunt on these facts was not the oil but the enhancement of the value of the oil rights. So the judge assessed the benefit by reference to the amount of oil received by Hunt and the amount of the Libyan government's compensation for the expropriation. The total was approximately US$85m. He then awarded a

---

92   *Ibid.*, at 1236–7.
93   The main discussion by Robert Goff J is at [1979] 1 WLR 783; subsidiary aspects are examined in successive appeals, [1981] 1 WLR 232, CA; [1982] 2 AC 352, HL.

'just sum' of approximately US$11m, which took account of: (1) the fact that the field had been expropriated; (2) the parties' pre-existing receipts under the contract; and (3) Hunt's recovery of modest compensation from the Libyan government.

16.26 Perhaps a more illuminating approach to section 1(3) is to take the following hypothetical case. Suppose A agrees with B to build a factory for £2m. Halfway through the job, the factory is destroyed in a fire caused by vandals. At that point, A had spent £1.25m. No money was yet owed by B to A. Goff J suggested in the following dictum in *BP* v. *Hunt (No. 2)* that the valuable benefit under section 1(3) in this context would be the scrap value of A's ruined work.[94] However, this dictum involves a misconstruction of this provision, as Treitel contends[95] (Treitel noting that section 1(3) requires the court to identify a 'valuable benefit' obtained 'before' the contract's termination; the relevant 'valuable benefit', therefore, would be the value of the building *before* the conflagration). Instead, as Treitel observes, the structure of section 1(3) requires the court to assess a 'just sum'; and in making this assessment it must take into account all the factors, including, as directed by section 1(3)(b), the impact on the valuable benefit of the events giving rise to the frustration. On the present imaginary[96] facts, the fire destroyed the building. On this basis, it seems likely that the court would fix the valuable benefit at either £1m or £1.25m. It might then split this loss between A and B. But the court has a complete discretion whether to give A full protection, zero protection or a partial award. The court cannot award more than the valuable benefit.

This discussion of the building which burns down concerns a situation where Goff J's analysis requires identification of an 'end product', a term not in fact used in section 1(3). However, Goff J added that the end-product analysis will not apply to services consisting of the surveying of land or the transport of goods:[97]

> [I]n some cases the services will have no end product; for example, where the services consist of doing such work as surveying, or transporting goods. In each case, it is necessary to ask the question: what benefit has the defendant obtained by reason of the plaintiff's contractual performance?

16.27 Section 1(5) of the 1943 Act provides that if an express term of the contract *required* B (or A) to insure against a risk, that term must be taken into account for the purpose of determining whether any sum should be recovered or retained under section 1(2) and section 1(3). But, if either A or B had in fact decided to take out insurance, *even though he had not been expressly bound to do so under the A/B contract*, the court *cannot* take the fact of insurance into account. The rationale of this distinction is that a contractual allocation of risk can be inferred (and then taken into account under the Act) only if one party was contractually obliged to take out insurance.

---

94 [1979] 1 WLR 783, 801–2.
95 *Treitel* (13th edn, London, 2011), 19–103 (discussing the facts of *Appleby* v. *Myers* (1867) LR 2 CP 651).
96 The nineteenth-century case, *Appleby* v. *Myers* (1867) LR 2 CP 651, involved very similar facts (a factory consumed by fire, causing destruction of, among other things, machinery installed by one of the parties), although, of course, this case antedated the 1943 Act.
97 [1979] 1 WLR 783, 801–2.

16.28 *Summary of sub-sections 1(2) and 1(3).*

(1) Section 1(2) of the 1943 Act permits the court or arbitrator to engage in *qualified loss adjustment*. The device used is that of a 'kitty' consisting of sums paid or payable before the time of contractual termination:

(a) prima facie that sum is repayable or the sum payable need not be paid; but

(b) this is qualified by the court's discretion to allow the 'kitty' holder to keep or recover in respect of his expenses.

As for (b), *Gamerco SA* v. *ICM/Fair Warning (Agency) Ltd* (1995)[98] emphasises the absence of rules or even a presumption governing how that kitty is to be distributed under the Act.

(2) Section 1(3) can be rationalised as the award of a *restitutionary* valuation of the benefit of non-monetary contractual performance, subject to discretionary loss adjustment (award of a just sum not to exceed the valuable benefit received).

(3) Although section 1(2) can be loosely explained as reflecting the commercial implication that money paid or payable is available to protect the payee, section 1(3) rests on no such parallel implication. The truth is, therefore, that section 1(3) is *a hybrid device, allowing qualified restitution for non-monetary benefits.*

6. TERMINATION OF CONTRACTS OF INDEFINITE DURATION

16.29 Long-term contracts, *unless of fixed duration*, are subject to an implied term enabling one party to give reasonable notice to the other that the contract will be terminated.[99]

For example, in *Staffordshire Area Health Authority* v. *South Staffordshire Waterworks Co.* (1978), a majority of the Court of Appeal held that a 1929 agreement to supply 5,000 gallons of water a day free of charge, thereafter at seven old pence per 1,000 gallons 'at all times hereafter', was neither a perpetual contract nor (as was evident) a contract of fixed duration. Since the contract was of indefinite duration, the Court of Appeal held that it was terminable by the giving of reasonable notice.[100] The water company was prepared to continue the supply, charging, for daily usage in excess of 5,000 gallons, the 1970s price for commercial supply (see further 17.29).

BMS Computer Solutions Ltd v. *AB Agri Ltd* (2010)[101] shows that a clause purporting to confer on a licensee a 'perpetual' entitlement might be construed as merely creating an entitlement of no fixed duration; if so, the licensor can give reasonable notice to terminate the entitlement.[102] By contrast, where the contract is of a *fixed duration*, there will be no implied term that a party can terminate it by giving reasonable notice, as *Jani-King (GB) Ltd*

---

98 [1995] 1 WLR 1226, Garland J.

99 E. McKendrick, 'The Regulation of Long-Term Contracts in English Law', in J. Beatson and D. Friedmann (eds.), *Good Faith and Fault in Contract Law* (Oxford, 1995), 305.

100 [1978] 1 WLR 1387, CA, *per* (Reginald) Goff and Cumming-Bruce LJJ; at *ibid.*, 1397–8, Lord Denning MR, in a minority opinion, reached the same conclusion by the heterodox route of finding frustration to be satisfied by inflation; T. A. Downes, (1985) 101 LQR 98, 104–8.

101 [2010] EWHC 464 Ch, Sales J.

102 See his cogent articulation of supporting reasons, *ibid.*, at [18].

v. *Pula Enterprises Ltd* (2007) shows.[103] Finally, it was held in *ServicePower Asia Pacific Pty Ltd* v. *ServicePower Business Solutions Ltd* (2009) that the court will not construe a contract as being subject to an implied termination clause if an express term already covers the giving of notice.[104]

In *Geys* v. *Société Général* (2012) Baroness Hale noted that a party needs to act in an unequivocal manner when purporting to exercise a termination clause or other unilateral notice clause.[105]

7. POST-FORMATION HARDSHIP: EXCEPTIONAL DENIAL OF SPECIFIC PERFORMANCE

16.30 Exceptionally, the court can withhold specific performance (on this *equitable* remedy, see 18.33) if events subsequent to the contract's formation have rendered it wholly unjust to compel the relevant party to perform. This is not because the contract has been frustrated but because exceptional circumstances justify confining the party in breach to liability to pay Common Law compensation.

> Such extreme facts occurred in *Patel* v. *Ali* (1984). Goulding J refused to order specific performance against the vendor of domestic premises. Since the contract's formation she had lost a leg, *and* this physical disability now made it necessary for her to remain close to people capable of assisting her.[106] The courts should be slow to broaden this category.

QUESTIONS

(1) What was the significance of *Taylor* v. *Caldwell* (1863), and what was the law before that decision?

(2) Why was the implied term theory of frustration abandoned?

(3) Why is *Davis Contractors Ltd* v. *Fareham Urban District Council* (1956) a landmark decision?

(4) In which categories of situation can frustration occur?

(5) '*Griffith* v. *Brymer* (1903) and *Amalgamated Investment & Property Co. Ltd* v. *John Walker & Sons Ltd* (1977) show that timing is crucial.' Explain this comment.

(6) On what basis can *Herne Bay Steam Boat Co.* v. *Hutton* (1903) be distinguished from *Krell* v. *Henry* (1903)? What if the licence granted in *Krell* v. *Henry* had been commercial and the licensee had originally intended to assign its benefit?

(7) What is Rix LJ's 'multi-factorial' approach in *'The Sea Angel'* (2007) to risk-allocation and frustration?

---

103 [2007] EWHC 2433 (QBD); [2008] 1 Lloyd's Rep 305, at [60] to [66], *per* Coulson J; also, on this case, see 21.06.

104 [2009] EWHC 179 (Ch); [2010] 1 All ER (Comm) 238, at [25] ff (William Trower QC).

105 [2012] UKSC 63; [2013] 1 AC 523, at [52].

106 [1984] Ch 283.

(8) In the light of Lord Denning MR's remarks in *'The Eugenia'* (1964), what is the connection between frustration and foreseeability?

(9) In the light of *FC Shepherd* v. *Jerrom* (1986) and *'The Super Servant Two'* (1990), what is 'self-induced' frustration?

(10) Putting aside the 1943 Act, what is the effect of frustration on the contract at Common Law?

(11) What is the effect of section 1(2) of the 1943 Act, taking into account *Gamerco SA* v. *ICM/Fair Warning (Agency) Ltd* (1995)? Contrast the position at Common Law, as established in the *Fibrosa* case (1943).

(12) What is the effect of section 1(3) of the 1943 Act, taking into account *BP Exploration Co. (Libya) Ltd* v. *Hunt (No. 2)* (1979, Robert Goff J)?

(13) What did *Staffordshire Area Health Authority* v. *South Staffordshire Waterworks Co.* (1978) decide?

(14) What did *Patel* v. *Ali* (1984) decide?

Selected further reading

History

D. Ibbetson, in F. D. Rose (ed.), *Consensus ad Idem: Essays in the Law of Contract in Honour of Guenter Treitel* (London, 1996), chapter 1 (for an earlier history)

A. W. B. Simpson, 'Innovation in Nineteenth Century Contract Law' (1975) 91 LQR 247, at 269–73

Exceptional increases in expense

J. Beatson, 'Increased Expense and Frustration', in F. D. Rose (ed.), *Consensus ad Idem: Essays in the Law of Contract in Honour of Guenter Treitel* (London, 1996), 121

Adjustment of frustrated contracts: the Law Reform (Frustrated Contracts) Act 1943

E. McKendrick, 'Frustration, Restitution and Loss Adjustment', in A. Burrows (ed.), *Essays on Restitution* (Oxford, 1991), 147

Risk allocation and force majeure clauses

E. McKendrick (ed.), *Force Majeure and Frustration of Contract* (2nd edn, London, 1995), especially at 34

E. McKendrick, 'The Regulation of Long-Term Contracts in English Law', in J. Beatson and D. Friedmann (eds.), *Good Faith and Fault in Contract Law* (Oxford, 1995), 305, 323 ff

E. McKendrick, 'Force Majeure Clauses: The Gap between Doctrine and Practice', in A. Burrows and E. Peel (eds.), *Contract Terms* (Oxford, 2007), chapter 12

J. Morgan, *Great Debates in Contract Law* (London, 2012), chapter 5

Chapter contents

17

Breach and performance

1. INTRODUCTION

17.01 Summary of main points

(1) Breach involves contractual default which is *unexcused*.[1] The source of the possible excuse might be: (i) an exclusion clause (15.01); or (ii) an exculpatory clause, such as a *force majeure* clause (stipulating that a party will be released from his obligation by reason of freak and excusable supervening events: 16.09); or (iii) the law of frustration (16.01); (iv) the fact that the other party's default excuses the current party from performing (17.46); or (v) the innocent party has waived his rights to complain about the relevant breach.

(2) *Main forms of breach.* Breach can occur by declaration (see category (i) below) or misconduct (or omission) (see categories (ii) and (iii) below).

   (i) *Explicit or implicit renunciation.* If, whether before or at the time of performance, a party declares or indicates by conduct that he does not intend to perform, the other party can 'elect' to end the contract straightaway and sue for compensation.

   (ii) *Culpably rendering future performance impossible.* Before the performance is due, B might have culpably (that is, without lawful excuse) prevented the contract from being performed.

   (iii) *Defective performance.* Performance in general might be defective in a myriad ways: total non-performance; the tender or supply of wrong or shoddy subject matter or useless or unsatisfactory services; performance might be delayed or too slow; or the guilty party might do that which he promised not to do, for example, by working for a rival company in breach of an obligation to perform exclusively for the claimant's benefit.

Of these three forms of breach, the most common is (iii) ('defective performance'); mode (i) is the next most common ('renunciation'); mode (ii) (self-induced culpable impossibility) is quite uncommon because the innocent party will here need to take the risk that he has misjudged the situation and that instead the other party might yet have retrieved the situation.

---

1 M. A. Clarke, N. Andrews, A. M. Tettenborn, G. Virgo, *Contractual Duties: Performance, Breach, Termination and Remedies* (London, 2012) (breach and performance section by N. Andrews); Q. Liu, *Anticipatory Breach* (Oxford, 2011); J. E. Stannard and D. Capper, *Termination for Breach of Contract* (Oxford, 2014). From an Australian perspective, J. W. Carter, *Carter's Breach of Contract* (Oxford, 2012), reviewed by N. Andrews [2013] CLJ 214–7.

(3) Every breach entitles the innocent party to recover at least 'nominal damages' (a token sum signifying the fact that there has been a technical legal wrong, for example, sums of £5 or £10).[2] Breach (if unexcused – for sources of excuse see above) might expose the guilty party to a claim for substantial damages, or debt, or specific performance, or an injunction, or at least a declaration that breach has occurred (on these remedies: 18.01). The innocent party can recover substantial damages if recognised loss is shown (for the various tests applicable to such damages claims, see 18.14 ff).

(4) The innocent party is entitled to terminate a contract for breach only if there has been a serious breach. That will be so only if (17.04):

   (a) the other party has shown a clear unwillingness to satisfy his contract ('renunciation'); or

   (b) performance has been rendered impossible by the unexcused default; or

   (c) there has been a serious breach: a repudiatory breach (an actual breach by conduct, or sometimes by omission, which is grave enough that it 'goes to the root of the contract'), or breach of an important term (a 'condition': see next paragraph) or of another term which can give rise to termination, depending on the seriousness of the breach (an 'innominate term').

(5) A 'condition' (17.19) will arise in one of five situations: when (a) statute so provides, or (b) a binding decision has classified the relevant term in this way or (c) if the relevant obligation is expressed to be a 'condition' (see, however, below) or (d) the obligation is subject to a clause entitling the innocent party to terminate the contract for failure to satisfy the obligation, or (e) if, on the facts of the present case, and in the absence of criteria (a) to (d), the court decides that it is appropriate to classify a neutral term as a condition.

(6) Even a serious breach (as defined at (4)) does not automatically cause the contract to be terminated. Instead the innocent party has a choice (17.37 and 18.03): he can (i) 'accept the repudiation' and thus terminate the contract and sue for damages, or (ii) he can affirm the contract and sue for damages.[3]

(7) Termination for breach (as distinct from rescission for misrepresentation, etc., see next paragraph) operates to end the contract from that point in time, but only prospectively; it does not annihilate the contract retrospectively (17.45 and 17.45). The main result of this analysis is that the innocent party retains the right to sue in respect of preceding breaches.

(8) By contrast, 'rescission' (for example, for misrepresentation: 9.26) is the avoidance, that is, the setting aside, of voidable contracts, and such avoidance involves returning the parties to the original position as though the contract never existed. That analysis precludes actions for breach of contract: the contract is dead.

(9) The question of breach is technically distinct from the right to refuse performance if the other side has failed to complete performance of an obligation, where the parties' obligations are 'dependent' (17.46). Where B's obligation is dependent on A's performance, B can withhold performance if A fails to perform *for whatever reason* (including supervening illegality or impossibility or other instances of 'frustration': 16.01).

---

2   Putting aside failure to pay money, for which the action is one for debt: see 18.02 ff.
3   *Fercometal SARL* v. *Mediterranean Shipping Co. SA ('The Simona')* [1989] AC 788, HL; *Vitol SA* v. *Norelf Ltd ('The Santa Clara')* [1996] AC 800, HL.

17.02 *Strict or non-strict obligations.* Breach of contract can involve failure to satisfy a strict obligation (for example, a seller's statutory obligations to deliver goods which (1) correspond to their contractual description, (2) are of satisfactory quality, and (3) are reasonably fit for their intended purpose).[4] However, some contractual obligations require only the exercise of reasonable care, or the meeting of the relevant professional level of diligence.[5] The law is highly pragmatic in this respect.

The Court of Appeal in *Platform Funding Ltd* v. *Bank of Scotland plc* (2009)[6] acknowledged that in a contract for professional services (doctors, lawyers, surveyors, vets, etc.), the professional will normally merely owe a duty to exercise due care, but there can be exceptional instances of strict liability: (1) in accordance with the specific terms of the agreement or on assurances given by the professional in the course of his performance, or (2) based on the relevant context.[7] However, there was no binding oral guarantee in the 'unsuccessful vasectomy' case, *Thake* v. *Maurice* (1986) (3.68).[8]

It was held in *Evans* v. *Kosmar Villa Operators* (2008)[9] (13.06) that a tour operator owes a duty to take reasonable steps to guard its customers and guests against personal injury,[10] but this duty did not extend to liability for injury suffered by a 17-year-old who dived into the shallow end of a swimming pool, because he was aware of the danger and the defendant had taken adequate precautions.

Atkinson J in *Aerial Advertising Co* v. *Batchelors Peas Ltd (Manchester)* (1938) held that performance of an aerial advertising campaign on behalf of a dried peas company[11] imported an implied term to use reasonable skill and care not to harm the company's interests, and certainly not to fly advertising planes on occasions which will bring its customer into hatred and contempt. In breach of that term the advertiser flew over a town during the Armistice service just before 11 am on 11 November. This provoked public outrage and the advertising was a commercial disaster.

As the Court of Appeal noted in *Urban 1 (Blonk Street) Ltd* v. *Ayres* (2013), contractual obligations to perform within a reasonable time are particularly troublesome because the issue whether there has been breach will raise a range of imponderable factors.[12]

Strict liability was imposed for bug bites suffered by a visitor to the Turkish baths in *Silverman* v. *Imperial London Hotels Ltd* (1927)[13] (13.10).

The House of Lords affirmed in *Henderson* v. *Merrett Syndicates Ltd* (1995)[14] (1.23) that when a contractual duty of care overlaps with an essentially similar duty of care imposed by

---

4   Sections 13–15 of the Sale of Goods Act 1979.
5   Generally, section 13 of the Supply of Goods and Services Act 1982.
6   [2008] EWCA Civ 930; [2009] QB 426; J. W. Carter, *Carter's Breach of Contract* (Oxford, 2012), 2.33 to 2.67.
7   *Ibid.*, at [48], *per* Rix LJ.
8   [1986] QB 644, CA.
9   [2007] EWCA Civ 1003; [2008] 1 WLR 297.
10   Package Travel, Package Holidays and Package Tours Regulations 1992 (SI 1992 No. 3288), Reg 15.
11   [1938] 2 All ER 788, 792.
12   *Urban 1 (Blonk Street) Ltd* v. *Ayres* [2013] EWCA Civ 816 [2014] 1 WLR 756, at [49], *per* Sir Terence Etherton C (citing *Hick* v. *Raymond & Reid* [1893] AC 22, 32–3, HL, *per* Lord Watson, and the fuller discussion by Maurice Kay LJ in *Peregrine Systems Ltd* v. *Steria Ltd* [2005] EWCA Civ 239; [2005] Info TLR 294, at [15], noting Judge Richard Seymour QC in *Astea (UK) Ltd* v. *Time Group Ltd* [2003] EWHC 725 (TCC), at [144]).
13   [1927] All ER 712, 714; 137 LT 57; 43 TLR 260.
14   [1995] 2 AC 145, HL.

the tort of negligence (a case of 'concurrent' obligations), a claimant can select whichever cause of action he prefers, or indeed plead both (see also the discussion of contributory negligence at 18.23).

17.03 *No special category of deliberate breach.* The fact that breach is deliberate makes no difference, except, as noted by the House of Lords in the *Suisse Atlantique* case (1966): (1) an exclusion clause *might not* be construed to extend this far;[15] and (2) the fact that a breach is deliberate might be relevant in determining whether the guilty party has evinced an intention no longer to be bound by the contract.[16] Furthermore, deliberate breach does not give rise to liability for exemplary damages in English contract law: indeed, exemplary damages are not available at all for breach of contract (18.07 at (5)).

2. ENTITLEMENT TO TERMINATE FOR BREACH

17.04 The innocent party is entitled to terminate a contract for breach in any of these five situations:

(a) the other party has shown a clear unwillingness to satisfy his contract ('renunciation': 17.06); or

(b) performance has been rendered impossible by the default of the guilty party; or

(c) the contract has been breached in a serious manner going to the root of the innocent party's contractual expectations ('repudiation'); or

(d) there has been a breach of an important term (a 'condition'); or

(e) the facts disclose a serious breach of an innominate term (17.32).

As for (d), a 'condition' here refers to a promissory obligation. A promissory condition will arise when statute so provides, or if the contract itself uses the word 'condition' or a phrase with equivalent effect, or if the court construes a neutral term as a condition. Where the contract contains an *express right to terminate for breach*, the innocent party can exercise simultaneously an express power *to terminate for breach* and the Common Law right to terminate a contract because of the other party's repudiatory breach.[17] If the breach (as just explained) gives rise to the right to terminate, the innocent party has a choice: he can accept the repudiation and thus terminate the contract and sue for damages, or he can affirm the contract and sue for damages.[18] This is known as 'the right to elect'.[19]

---

15 *Internet Broadcasting Corporation Ltd* v. *MAR LLC* [2009] EWHC 844 (Ch); [2009] 2 Lloyd's Rep 295 (see especially at [33]).

16 *Suisse Atlantique Société d'Armement Maritime SA* v. *NV Rotterdamsche* [1967] 1 AC 361, 435, HL (on 'deliberateness', see *ibid.*, at 394E, *per* Viscount Dilhorne, 397–8, *per* Lord Reid, 414, *per* Lord Hodson, and 429, *per* Lord Upjohn); R. Brownsword, in C. Mitchell and P. Mitchell (eds.), *Landmark Cases in the Law of Contract* (Oxford, 2008), 299 ff.

17 *Stocznia Gdynia SA* v. *Gearbulk Holdings Ltd* [2009] EWCA Civ 75; [2010] QB 27 (noted E. Peel (2009) 125 LQR 378–84).

18 *Fermometal SARL* v. *Mediterranean Shipping Co. SA, 'The Simona'* [1989] AC 788, HL; *Vitol SA* v. *Norelf Ltd, 'The Santa Clara'* [1996] AC 800, HL.

19 On the subtleties of this analysis, J. W. Carter, 'Discharge as the Basis for Termination for Breach of Contract' (2012) 128 LQR 283–302.

The situations listed as (a) to (e) earlier in this paragraph can be reduced to a three-fold classification (see text below) if categories (c) to (e) are combined. Such a trichotomy has the disadvantage of elision, for most breaches occur during or at the time of performance, and the law has drawn important distinctions in this respect (situation (c) to (e), above).

Lord Porter said in *Heyman* v. *Darwins Ltd* (1942):[20] 'The three sets of circumstances giving rise to a discharge contract [for breach] are tabulated by Anson [in the 1937 edition] as: (1) renunciation by a party of his liabilities . . . (2) impossibility created by his own act; (3) total or partial failure of performance.'

17.05 *Date for assessment of the strength of the case in favour of termination.* The Court of Appeal in *Ampurius Nu Homes Holdings Ltd* v. *Telford Homes (Creekside) Ltd* (2013) made clear that the relevant date is the time when the innocent party purports justifiably to terminate for repudiation, and not the earlier date of actual breach.[21] This is because matters might have changed in the interval (however short it might be) between breach and the decision to terminate. For example, as in the *Ampurius* case, the guilty party might have taken steps towards curing or mitigating his earlier default.[22]

3. RENUNCIATION AND REPUDIATORY BREACH

17.06 *Terminology.* In *Heyman* v. *Darwins Ltd* (1942), Lord Wright said: 'The word "repudiation" . . . is an ambiguous word constantly used without precise definition.'[23] The source of this confusion is that the expression 'repudiation' (or 'repudiatory breach') is sometimes used in a generic sense to embrace this triad of types of serious breach: (a) an anticipatory breach by renunciation, or renunciation at the time of expected performance; or (b) anticipatory breach by self-created impossibility; or (c) substantial breach justifying termination (a repudiatory breach, or breach of a condition or serious breach of an intermediate term, or a serious pattern of default (17.26 on *Rice* v. *Great Yarmouth BC* (2000)).[24] It is suggested that 'renunciation' is a clearer way of expressing the forms of breach in (a) because this involves verbal notification of unwillingness or inability to perform; and 'repudiation' (and 'repudiatory breach') might be usefully confined to categories (b) and (c), because both concern non-verbal and actual default.

17.07 *Nature of renunciation.* Renunciation – whether by (i) words or (ii) implication from conduct – is the communication of an intention that the renouncing party no longer

---

20 [1942] AC 356, 397, HL; noted by Devlin J in *Universal Cargo Carriers Corporation* v. *Citati* [1957] 2 QB 401, 436–8; J. E. Stannard and D. Capper, *Termination for Breach of Contract* (Oxford, 2014), Part III.
21 [2013] EWCA Civ 577; [2013] 4 All ER 377, at [43], citing Diplock LJ in *Hongkong Fir Shipping Co. Ltd* v. *Kawasaki Kisen Kaisha Ltd* [1962] 2 QB 26, 72, CA.
22 [2013] EWCA Civ 577; [2013] 4 All ER 377, at [44] and [63], *per* Lewison LJ (approved by Longmore LJ at [79]).
23 [1942] AC 356, 378, HL; *cf* J. W. Carter, *Carter's Breach of Contract* (Oxford, 2012), 7.03 and 7.07, preferring not to use 'renunciation' and instead 'repudiation'.
24 *The Times*, 26 July 2000; (2001) 3 LGLR 4, CA, at [38].

wishes to be bound at all by the contract, or at least that he wishes to break free, in a material way, from the fetters of the contract. The other party must be notified, or at least receive clear evidence, of that renunciation.

As for (ii) the circumstances will indicate whether a party's breach discloses a wider intimation that he is walking away from the contract or intending to perform it on his own (deviating) terms. As Bowen LJ said in *Mersey Steel and Iron Co. Ltd v. Naylor, Benzon & Co.* (1882):[25] 'the test [is] whether the conduct of one party to the contract was really inconsistent with an intention to be bound any longer by the contract.'

In *Federal Commerce & Navigation Co. v. Molena Alpha Inc, 'The Nanfri'* (1979)[26] Lord Wilberforce cited Lord Cockburn CJ in *Freeth v. Burr* (1874): 'an intimation of an intention to abandon and altogether to refuse performance of the contract' or 'to evince an intention no longer to be bound by the contract'.[27]

More generally on the two species of renunciation, the Court of Appeal in *Ampurius Nu Homes Holdings Ltd v. Telford Homes (Creekside) Ltd* (2013) adopted these textbook formulations:[28]

Explicit renunciation:

> A renunciation of a contract occurs when one party by words or conduct evinces an intention not to perform, or expressly declares that he is or will be unable to perform, his obligations under the contract in some essential respect. The renunciation may occur before or at the time fixed for performance. An absolute refusal [will count] . . . as will also a clear and unambiguous assertion by one party that he will be unable to perform when the time for performance should arrive.

Implicit renunciation:

> This arises where 'actions of the party in default are such as to lead a reasonable person to conclude that he no longer intends to be bound by its provisions. The renunciation is then evidenced by conduct.'
>
> Also the party in default: ' . . . may intend in fact to fulfil (the contract) but may be determined to do so only in a manner substantially inconsistent with his obligations'[29] . . . . [This depends on] . . . whether the non-performance of those obligations will amount to a breach of a condition of the contract or deprive him of substantially the whole [promised] benefit.

Flaux J in *'The Pro Victor'* (2009)[30] noted Donaldson LJ's remarks on the nature of renunciation in *'The Hermosa'* (1982):[31]

25 *Mersey Steel and Iron Co. Ltd v. Naylor, Benzon & Co.* (1881–2) LR 9 QBD 648, 670, CA. (Not disturbed on appeal: *Mersey Steel and Iron Co. Ltd v. Naylor, Benzon & Co.* (1883–4) LR 9 App Cas 434, HL.)

26 [1979] AC 757, 778–9, HL.

27 (1874) LR 9 CP 208, 213, *per* Lord Coleridge CJ (Court of Common Pleas); cited by Earl of Selborne LC in *Mersey Steel and Iron Co. (Limited)* v. *Naylor, Benzon & Co.* (1883–4) LR 9 App Cas 434, 438–9, HL; Lord Salmon collected various formulations of the test in *Woodar Investment Development Ltd* v. *Wimpey Construction UK Ltd* [1980] 1 WLR 277, 287–8, HL.

28 [2013] EWCA Civ 577; [2013] 4 All ER 377, at [70], citing *Chitty on Contracts* (31st edn, London, 2012), 24–018.

29 This internal quotation is from *Ross T Smyth & Co.* v. *TD Bailey Son & Co.* [1940] 3 All ER 60, 72, HL, *per* Lord Wright.

30 *SK Shipping (S) PTE Ltd* v. *Petroexport Ltd* ('*The Pro Victor'*) [2009] EWHC 2974; [2010] 2 Lloyd's Rep 158, Flaux J at [86] to [87].

31 '*The Hermosa'* [1982] 1 Lloyd's Rep 570, 572–3, CA, *per* Donaldson LJ (noting (a) to (c) can be 'gleaned' from *Woodar* v. *Wimpey* [1980] 1 WLR 277, HL; but proposition (d) was enunciated afresh in '*The Hermosa'*).

(a) . . . renunciation is a drastic conclusion which should only be held to arise in clear cases of a refusal to perform contractual obligations . . . going to the root of the contract.

(b) The refusal must not only be clear, but must be absolute . . . [T]he declaration gives rise to a right of dissolution only if . . . it is clear that it is not conditional upon his present appreciation of his obligations proving correct when the time for performance arrives.

(c) What does or does not amount to a sufficient refusal is to be judged in the light of whether a reasonable person in the position of the party claiming to be freed from the contract would regard the refusal as being clear and absolute.

(d) . . . the conduct relied upon is to be considered as at the time of when it is treated as terminating the contract, in the light of the then existing circumstances.

Element (c), just cited, was endorsed by Etherton LJ in *Eminence Property Developments Ltd* v. *Heaney* (2010).[32] In *'The Pro Victor'* (2009) Flaux J suggested, in dicta, that if party Y knows that X did not intend a renunciation, the objective approach will not be applied.[33] Liu has criticised this suggestion.[34] However, it is submitted that Flaux J's suggestion is attractive: Y should not be able to snap up a literal renunciation if Y realises that X had no such intention.

17.08 *Repudiation.* This involves an actual breach of contract by conduct (or sometimes by omission) which is grave enough that it 'goes to the root of the contract';[35] that is, the breach is really serious.

The same idea is conveyed by the test suggested by Lord Wright in *Ross T Smyth & Co. Ltd* v. *TD Bailey, Son & Co.* (1940):[36] whether the guilty party has conducted himself in a way which is 'substantially inconsistent with his contractual obligations'.

The 'going to the root' test was also used in *Poussard* v. *Spiers* (1876)[37] to justify an impresario's decision to find a non-temporary replacement, in order to keep a new opera from becoming an immediate commercial disaster. Atkinson J in *Aerial Advertising Co.* v. *Batchelors Peas Ltd (Manchester)* (1938) (on the facts see 17.02 above) employed the concept of 'commercially wholly unreasonable to carry on'.[38]

The facts supporting the plea that there has been implicit renunciation (see further 17.07 above) can involve actual repudiation. And so there can be overlapping analysis. *Yam Seng Pte Ltd* v. *International Trade Corp Ltd* (2013) illustrates this overlap.[39] Furthermore, there is a line of cases, each concerning late payment under contracts requiring successive payments. The issue is whether

---

32   [2010] EWCA Civ 1168; [2011] 2 All ER (Comm) 223 at [61] to [64].

33   *SK Shipping (S) PTE Ltd* v. *Petroexport Ltd ('The Pro Victor')* [2009] EWHC 2974; [2010] 2 Lloyd's Rep 158, Flaux J at [89] to [98].

34   Q. Liu, *Anticipatory Breach* (Oxford, 2011), 76.

35   *Federal Commerce & Navigation Co.* v. *Molena Alpha Inc, 'The Nanfri'* [1979] AC 757, 778–9, 783, 784, 785, 786, HL; *Woodar Investment Development Ltd* v. *Wimpey Construction UK Ltd* [1980] 1 WLR 277, 286–7, 298, HL; *Decro-Wall International SA* v. *Practitioners in Marketing Ltd* [1971] 1 WLR 361, 374, 380, CA (where Sachs LJ traces the phrase to Lord Ellenborough CJ, in *Davidson* v. *Wynne* (1810) 12 East 381, 389; 104 ER 149, 153); Blackburn J used this criterion in *Bettini* v. *Gye* (1876) 1 QBD 183, 189; generally, J. W. Carter, *Carter's Breach of Contract* (Oxford, 2012), chapters 8 and 9; cf Lewison LJ's sceptical comments (*Urban 1 (Blonk Street) Ltd* v. *Ayres* [2013] EWCA Civ 816 [2014] 1 WLR 756, at [50]) concerning this metaphor.

36   [1940] 3 All ER 60, 72, HL.

37   (1876) 1 QBD 410, 415, *per* Blackburn J.

38   [1938] 2 All ER 788, 794.

39   [2013] EWHC 111 (QB); [2013] 1 All ER (Comm) 1321; [2013] 1 Lloyd's Rep 526, at [114] and [115].

there has been an implicit renunciation or a manifested repudiation. That determination will hinge on whether:[40]

(i) the payor has evinced an intention no longer to be bound by the contract; conversely, it might be evident that despite late payment, the payor wishes the contract to proceed (*Freeth* case (1874) and *Mersey Steel* case (1884));

(ii) the payor has made a unilateral attempt at radically recasting the payment obligation (*Withers* case (1831));

(iii) late payment has been used as an instrument to try to procure a wider renegotiation (*Dymocks* case (2002); and compare the borderline *Valilas* case (2014));

(iv) the payee was entitled to infer that the payor would be unable to pay (not found in the *Decro-Wall* case (1971) or the *Shyam Jewellers* case (2001)).

17.09 *Good faith does not prima facie exculpate a party whose words or conduct involve default.* In general (for qualifications, see end of this paragraph) breach can arise despite the guilty party's belief that he is not acting wrongly: prima facie X's serious non-compliance (proposed or actual), although presented in good faith, will constitute a renunciation or repudiation if X was not in fact justified under the contract in resiling in this way. The fundamental decision is *Federal Commerce & Navigation Co.* v. *Molena Alpha Inc*, 'The *Nanfri*' (1979).[41] A shipowner, acting on incorrect legal advice, refused to issue pre-paid bills of lading. The House of Lords unanimously held that the breach justified termination and that the owner's good faith was irrelevant: such good faith does not 'cleanse' a renunciation or repudiation. There were three salient factors: (i) *clarity* – the repudiation was clear and emphatic; (ii) *danger* – the innocent charterer was placed in a very tight corner because the charterer's clientele, namely third party cargo dealers in the relevant trade, as noted by later decisions;[42] (iii) *lack of time* – there was no time to spare, no commercial 'window' within which to sort out this difference.

17.10 *Safety-valve exceptions to prevent exploitation of the other's good faith false steps.* However, X's serious non-compliance (proposed or actual), although presented in good faith,[43] will

---

40   Payee's termination justified: *Withers* v. *Reynolds* (1831) 2 B & Ad 882; 109 ER 1370; *Dymocks Franchise Systems (NSW) Pty Ltd.* v. *Todd* [2002] UKPC 50; [2002] 2 All ER (Comm) 849, 870, *per* Lord Browne-Wilkinson; Payee's termination not justified: *Freeth* v. *Burr* (1874) LR 9 CP 208 (Court of Common Pleas); *Mersey Steel and Iron Co. Ltd* v. *Naylor, Benzon & Co.* (1883–4) LR 9 App Cas 434, HL; *Decro-Wall International SA* v. *Practitioners in Marketing Ltd* [1971] 1 WLR 361, 379–80, CA; *Shyam Jewellers Ltd* v. *Cheeseman* [2001] EWCA Civ 1818; official transcript on Westlaw; *Valilas* v. *Januzaj* [2014] EWCA Civ 436 (Arden and Floyd LJJ, Underhill LJ dissenting).
41   [1979] AC 757, HL.
42   *Dalkia Utilities Services plc* v. *Celtech International Ltd* [2006] EWHC 63 (Comm); [2006] 1 Lloyd's Rep 599, at [148], *per* Christopher Clarke J; *Gulf Agri Trade FZCO* v. *Aston Agro Industrial AG* [2008] EWHC 1252 (Comm); [2009] 1 All ER (Comm) 991; [2008] 2 Lloyd's Rep 376, at [43], *per* Aikens J.
43   A similar tendency is discernible in New Zealand and Australian cases: *Starlight Enterprises Ltd* v. *Lapco Enterprises Ltd* [1979] 2 NZLR 744, NZCA, especially Richardson J at 747–8; applied in *Oxborough* v. *North Harbour Builders Ltd* [2002] 1 NZLR 145, NZCA, at [13]; similarly, *The Edge Buying Group (Queenstown 2010)* v. *Coca-Cola Amatil Ltd* (2002) NZCA 145/02, noted M Chetwin (2003) NZLJ 117; High Court of Australia in *DTR Nominees Pty Ltd* v. *Mona Homes Pty Ltd* (1978) 138 CLR 423, 432 (bona fide dispute as to the construction of a land transaction did not justify inferring that the mistaken party had evinced an intention not to perform the contract).

not justify Y in terminating the contract if (a) it was reasonable for Y to have had the matter referred to a neutral third party (*Woodar Investment Development Ltd* v. *Wimpey Construction UK Ltd* (1980);[44] or (b) Y could have checked the position with X (*Vaswani* v. *Italian Motors (Sales & Services) Ltd* (1996));[45] or (c) Y should have corrected X's obvious error (*Eminence Property Developments Ltd* v. *Heaney* (2010)).[46]

In the *Woodar* case (1980)[47] the claimant had agreed to sell land to the defendant, completion to occur after gaining planning permission. The defendant purchaser resiled from the deal, invoking in good faith, but mistakenly, a purported contractual right, contained in an obscure clause, to withdraw. A majority of the House of Lords (Lords Wilberforce, Keith and Scarman; dissenting, Lords Salmon and Russell) held that no repudiation had occurred on these facts, and that the defendant had not absolutely refused to perform. The majority considered that the parties understood that the defendant had not adopted a 'take it or leave it stand': and the point had arisen in advance of the crucial date for completion. There was, it appears, time to have sorted out this problem. In this light, the *Woodar* case is an exception to the general proposition. The law should not be inverted so as to render a good faith infringement of a contract a non-breach.[48]

In the *Vaswani* case (1996),[49] the sellers, Hong Kong luxury car-dealers, had purported to increase the price payable for purchase of a Ferrari Testarossa sports car (from £179,500 to £218,800). In fact they had no contractual right to do this. But the Privy Council held that this did not amount to repudiation. The new figure had not been presented on a 'take it or leave it' basis. The buyer could, and indeed should, have challenged the increase. And so the buyer had been snatching at an 'exit sign'. It did not exist. The buyer had wrongly terminated on this basis and run away from the deal. This meant that the seller was entitled to retain the deposit (£44,875).

In *Eminence Property Developments Ltd* v. *Heaney* (2010)[50] the purchaser mistakenly gave premature notice to terminate a contract for the purchase of flats. The Court of Appeal held that the innocent party had concocted in effect a storm in a teacup because it was obvious (i) that the purchaser had made a clerical error; (ii) that it was not in the purchaser's commercial economic interest to pull out; and (iii) if alerted to this error, the purchaser would have readily put right the error and stayed faithful to the contract.

---

44 [1980] 1 WLR 277, HL (but time seldom permits this to occur: *James Shaffer Ltd.* v. *Findlay Durham & Brodie* [1953] 1 WLR 106, 118, CA, *per* Singleton LJ).
45 [1996] 1 WLR 270, 277, PC (Lord Woolf).
46 [2010] EWCA Civ 1168; [2011] 2 All ER (Comm) 223, generally at [61] to [65], notably, at [65] sub-para. (4); approved in *Oates* v. *Hooper* [2010] EWCA Civ 1346, [2010] NPC 119 and *Samarenko* v. *Dawn Hill House Ltd* [2011] EWCA Civ 1445; [2013] Ch 36.
47 *Woodar* case [1980] 1 WLR 277, HL.
48 Cf, for such an inversion, *Golstein* v. *Bishop* [2013] EWHC 881 Ch; [2014] Ch 131 (Nugee QC), at [161], treating the *Woodar* case as dominant and not citing the *Federal Commerce* case [1979] AC 757, HL.
49 [1996] 1 WLR 270, 276–7, PC (Lord Woolf); noted E. Peel [1996] LMCLQ 309.
50 [2010] EWCA Civ 1168; [2011] 2 All ER (Comm) 223 at [61] to [64], having considered (among other decisions) *Federal Commerce & Navigation Co.* v. *Molena Alpha Inc, 'The Nanfri'* [1979] AC 757, HL; *Woodar* v. *Wimpey* [1980] 1 WLR 277, HL; *Vaswani* v. *Italian Motors (Sales & Services) Ltd* [1996] 1 WLR 270, 277, PC; and *Dalkia Utilities Services plc* v. *Celtech International Ltd* [2006] EWHC 63 (Comm); [2006] 1 Lloyd's Rep 599, Christopher Clarke J.

17.11 *Good reason exists for termination but the wrong reason was invoked at the time.* What if the innocent party in effect pulls the wrong lever, but could have pulled another lever justifying his decision to terminate the contract by reason of the other's breach? The law is here on the side of the confused innocent party. Thus the Court of Appeal noted in *Force India Formula One Team Ltd* v. *Etihad Airways PJSC* (2010): 'where one party to a contract has repudiated it, the other may validly accept that repudiation by bringing the contract to an end, even if he gives the wrong reason for doing so or no reason at all.'[51]

In *Force India Formula One Team Ltd* v. *Etihad Airways PJSC* (2010) racing car sponsors had purported to terminate the contract by invoking termination clauses. In fact these did not cover the relevant events. Nevertheless, the sponsors had made clear that they wished to terminate the contract by reason of the other party's serious non-compliance with the transaction. Termination for repudiatory breach at Common Law remained available, even though the innocent party had chased down an inappropriate alley in trying to end the contract.

But the Court of Appeal in *Glencore Grain Rotterdam BV* v. *Lebanese Organisation for International Commerce* (1997)[52] held that party A's failure to take the correct point is fatal if party B could have put right this default within the contractual deadline if B had been notified by A of the relevant default.[53] Secondly, estoppel by conduct or representation might render it unjust for party A, the innocent party, to invoke the true ground if party B has altered his position in a harmful fashion.[54] Thirdly, the Court of Appeal in *Cavanagh* v. *William Evans Ltd* (2012)[55] held that an employer is bound to pay a sum promised as pay in lieu of notice when it has chosen to exercise a contractual right to terminate a contract of employment on that basis; even though the employer subsequently discovers that the employee has committed breaches which would justify termination for repudiation.

17.12 *Repetitive breach in continuing contracts.* In continuing contracts (that is, where a party's performance occurs in stages or over a significant period), a party's *repeated breaches* might justify the other party in terminating the contract even though there has been neither a breach of a 'condition', nor a clear renunciation (communication of unwillingness to honour the contract) nor repudiatory breach (conduct striking at the root of the contract). The court will assess whether the other side's repeated default is grave enough, presently and prospectively, to strike at the root of the other party's contractual expectations. In *Alan Auld Associates Ltd* v. *Rick Pollard Associates* (2008) the Court of Appeal concluded that a spate of breaches of payment obligations justified termination because they had been 'substantial, persistent, and cynical'.[56]

---

51   [2010] EWCA Civ 1051; [2011] ETLR 10, at [116]; *Tele2 International Card Company SA* v. *Post Office Ltd* [2009] EWCA Civ 9, at [30] n. 17, *per* Aikens J (noting *Boston Deep Sea and Ice Co.* v. *Ansell* (1888) 39 Ch D 339, 364, CA, *per* Bowen LJ; *British and Benningtons Ltd* v. *NorthWestern Cahar Tea Co. Ltd* [1923] AC 48, 71–2, HL, *per* Lord Sumner; and see *'The Mihalis Angelos'* [1971] 1 QB 164, 193, 195, CA).
52   [1997] 4 All ER 514, CA.
53   *Ibid.*, at 526 (noting *Heisler* v. *Anglo-Dal Ltd* [1954] 1 WLR 1273, 1278, CA).
54   [1997] 4 All ER 514, 530–1, CA, noting *Panchaud Frères SA* v. *Etablissements General Grain Co.* [1970] 1 Lloyd's Rep 53, CA (the latter case contains loose dicta, especially by Winn LJ at 59).
55   [2012] EWCA Civ 697; [2013] 1 WLR 238.
56   [2008] EWCA Civ 655; [2008] BLR 419, at [20], *per* Tuckey LJ.

In *Rice* v. *Great Yarmouth Borough Council* (2000),[57] Hale LJ said that the test (not satisfied on the facts of that case, 17.26) is whether the innocent party: 'would thereby be deprived of a substantial part of that which it had contracted for' or failure to supply (adequately) 'aspects of the contract' which are 'so important' that failure is 'sufficient in itself' to justify termination.

4. ANTICIPATORY BREACH

17.13 Such breach[58] can take one of two forms:[59] (i) advance renunciation (for example, an airline notifies passengers that it has cancelled a flight several weeks in advance) and (ii) prevention of future performance, again when the date for performance has not arrived. It is clearly convenient for the promisee to be able to respond immediately by both terminating the contract and claiming compensation. This will prevent waste. It will also release the promise from a futile period of 'let's wait and see whether he changes his mind and decides to perform after all'.[60] As Lord Campbell CJ said in *Hochster* v. *De La Tour* (1853):[61] 'Instead of remaining idle and laying out money in preparations which must be useless, [the claimant] is at liberty to seek service under another employer, which would go in mitigation of the damages to which he would otherwise be entitled for a breach of the contract.'

See 18.21 on the controversial majority decision of the House of Lords in *Golden Strait Corporation* v. *Nippon Yusen Kubishika Kaisha ('The Golden Victory')* (2007),[62] where it was held that damages for anticipatory breach should reflect post-breach events if they reduce or eliminate the claimant's loss. However, Lords Bingham and Walker dissented, the latter saying:[63] 'In this case an objective and well-informed observer, looking at the matter [at the time of the renunciation] would have thought . . . that the prospect of the war clause option being exercised . . . was a mere possibility carrying little or no weight in commercial terms.' Lord Mustill in the *Law Quarterly Review* supports the dissentients, suggesting that the cause

---

57   *The Times*, 26 July 2000; (2001) 3 LGLR 4, CA, at [38] (distinguished in the *Alan Auld* case, preceding note, [2008] EWCA Civ 655; [2008] BLR 419, at [17] and [20] as a case where there was a 'raft of obligation' of different significance).

58   Q. Liu, *Anticipatory Breach* (Oxford, 2011) (drawing on Q. Liu, 'The *White & Carter* Principle: A Restatement' (2011) MLR 171; Q. Liu, 'Inferring Future Breach: Towards a Unifying Test of Anticipatory Breach of Contract' [2007] CLJ 574; Q. Liu, 'The Test of Fundamentality in Anticipatory Breach Cases: *Spirent v. Quake*' (2008) 46 *Canadian Business Law Journal* 7; Q. Liu, 'Accepted Anticipatory Breach: Duty of Mitigation and Damages Assessment' [2006] LMCLQ 17; Q. Liu, 'The Date for Assessing Damages for Loss of Prospective Performance Under a Contract' [2007] LMCLQ 273; see also, Q. Liu, 'Claiming Damages Upon an Anticipatory Breach: Why Should an Acceptance Be Necessary?' (2005) LS 559.

59   E.g., *Berkeley Community Villages Ltd* v. *Pullen* [2007] EWHC 1330 Ch; [2007] 3 EGLR 101; [2007] 24 EG 169 (CS); [2007] NPC 71, at [79], *per* Morgan J.

60   E.g., Q. Liu, *Anticipatory Breach* (Oxford, 2010), 163–4.

61   (1853) 2 E & B 678, 690; 22 LJ (QB) 455.

62   [2007] UKHL 12, [2007] 2 AC 353; noted Lord Mustill (2008) 124 LQR 569; J. Morgan [2007] CLJ 263; C. Nicholls (2008) JBL 91; B. Coote (2007) 123 LQR 503; Sir Bernard Rix, in M. Andenas and D. Fairgrieve (eds.), *Tom Bingham and the Transformation of the Law: A Liber Amicorum* (Oxford, 2009), 679–83.

63   [2007] UKHL 12, [2007] 2 AC 353, at [46].

of action based on anticipatory breach should be conceptualised as loss of the value of contractual rights, assessed as the market value of those rights at the time of discharge, with appropriate adjustment to reflect contingencies *then also affecting* the value of those rights.[64] It is submitted that the majority's decision in *'The Golden Victory'* (2007) is unsound.

17.14 *Anticipatory breach by stating one's unwillingness to perform.*[65] This type of anticipatory breach was first recognised only in the mid-nineteenth century (see *'The Simona'* (1989) for Lord Ackner's survey of the doctrine's development,[66] noting, in particular, the seminal nineteenth-century cases of *Hochster* v. *De La Tour* (1853)[67] and *Frost* v. *Knight* (1872), examined below).[68] However, Y commits an anticipatory breach by renunciation only if he has expressed unwillingness to perform or by his conduct Y has brought about a situation where it can be inferred that he did not intend to proceed with the contract (Popplewell J quotes an illuminating passage, too long to be cited here, in *Geden Operations Ltd* v. *Dry Bulk Handy Holdings Inc ('The Bulk Uruguay')* (2014)).[69] By contrast, the court will not find anticipatory breach if the cause of X's anxiety regarding Y's future performance is a contingency for which Y is not responsible. Popplewell J so held in the *Geden* case. Here Y had chartered a ship to X, but the ultimate owner of the ship was Z, a third party. There was a chance that Z might in future decline to grant permission for the vessel to enter waters subject to the risk of piracy.[70] It was held (not disturbing an arbitral award) that Y had not committed an anticipatory breach by renunciation simply because Y, when performing in the future, would be subject to Z's discretion.

In *Hochster* v. *De La Tour* (1853), the defendant engaged the claimant to act as courier on a projected foreign tour, starting on 1 June.[71] On 11 May, just over two weeks before the tour was to begin, the defendant renounced the engagement. It was held that the innocent party had a choice whether to accept the repudiation, or to keep the contract alive pending the date for due performance. There would be no 'breach' if the innocent party decided not to accept the repudiation. In the present case, the claimant was entitled to seek damages immediately, once he had accepted this renunciation. It was not necessary for him to wait to see whether the defendant might change his mind.

---

64   Lord Mustill (2008) 124 LQR 569.
65   M. Mustill, *Anticipatory Breach: Butterworths Lectures 1989–90* (London, 1990) (and (2008) 124 LQR 569, at 576 ff); J. C. Smith in E. Lomnicka and C. J. G. Morse (eds.), *Contemporary Issues in Commercial Law: Essays in Honour of AG Guest* (London, 1994), 175.
66   *Fercometal SARL* v. *Mediterranean Shipping Co. SA ('The Simona')* [1989] AC 788, 797–805, HL.
67   (1853) 2 E & B 678; 22 LJ (QB) 455.
68   (1872) LR 7 Ex 111.
69   [2014] EWHC 885 (Comm), at [19], *per* Popplewell J, citing *Smith's Leading Cases* (13th edn, 1929), 38 to 41; noting that this passage had been cited with approval in *Universal Cargo Carriers Corporation* v. *Citati (No. 1)* [1957] 2 QB 401, 441, *per* Devlin J.
70   *Geden* case [2014] EWHC 885 (Comm), at [20] to [22].
71   (1853) 2 E & B 678; 22 LJ (QB) 455; P. Mitchell, in C. Mitchell and P. Mitchell (eds.), *Landmark Cases in the Law of Contract* (Oxford, 2008), 135.

In *Frost* v. *Knight* (1872),[72] the defendant had agreed to marry the claimant, once the defendant's father had died (engagement agreements are no longer actionable).[73] The defendant broke off the engagement before his father's death. Cockburn CJ said that this renunciation became a breach once the innocent party 'treated the undertaking as broken'. The guilty party's announcement only becomes wrongful if the other party decides that he will respond by calling off the contract. The innocent party can then demand compensation.

17.15 *Disablement at the 'anticipatory' stage: impossibility by culpable self-inducement.* Another form of anticipatory breach is where the guilty party incapacitates himself or prevents performance before the scheduled date.[74] This need not involve deliberate sabotaging of the contract. It is enough that the default involves breach of an express or implied term. Devlin J noted in *Universal Cargo Carriers Corporation* v. *Citati* (1957)[75] that termination on this basis involves the 'serious risk' that the court might find that in fact the other party's inability to perform had not been shown to be inexorable or sufficiently probable.

And so, to avoid this danger, the prudent course is to contend instead that the other party has *expressly renounced* the contract. The onus of proof is on the party alleging that the other was guilty of self-disablement; the standard of proof is the balance of probabilities; and what has to be shown is that there is a clear case of disablement (whether this requires complete impossibility or practical or very near impossibility is not made clear by the cases, but the better view is that there must be no realistic chance of successful performance). Thus Popplewell J in *Geden Operations Ltd* v. *Dry Bulk Handy Holdings Inc ('The Bulk Uruguay')* (2014) referred to the need for inevitable default:[76]

> [S]elf induced impossibility is narrowly confined to those cases where breach is rendered inevitable. Save for possibilities which are so remote that in practice they can be ignored, what is required is inevitability. It is not sufficient if something is done which makes future performance unlikely, even very unlikely, still less that it renders performance uncertain . . . That is why renunciation is often a more favoured basis for invoking the doctrine of anticipatory breach.

In *Alfred Toepfer International GmbH* v. *Itex Itagrani Export SA* (1993)[77] the seller prematurely calculated that the buyer would be unable to load a cargo in full. In fact it

---

72 (1872) LR 7 Ex 111; M. J. Mustill (2008) 124 LQR 569, 577, noting G. Frost, *Promises Broken* (Charlottesville, VA, 1995).
73 Since 31 December 1970: section 1(1) of the Law Reform (Miscellaneous Provisions) Act 1970.
74 *Heyman* v. *Darwins Ltd* [1942] AC 356, 397, HL, *per* Lord Porter.
75 [1957] 2 QB 401, 436–8 (not disturbed on appeal on this point: [1957] 1 WLR 979, CA and [1958] 2 QB 254, CA); M. J. Mustill, *Anticipatory Breach: Butterworths Lectures 1989–90* (1990), 69 ff; M. J. Mustill (2008) 124 LQR 569, 580 n. 23 notes the galaxy of commercial talent employed in arguing this case.
76 [2014] EWHC 885 (Comm), at [18] (see also [17]).
77 [1993] 1 Lloyd's Rep 360, Saville J; similarly *Continental Contractors Ltd and Ernest Beck & Co. Ltd* v. *Medway Oil & Storage Co. Ltd* (1926) 25 Lloyd's Rep 288 – suppliers of kerosene had not 'wholly and finally disabled' themselves, even though they had encountered difficulties in procuring a supply (the *Toepfer* case and other authorities were considered by Proudman J in *Ridgewood Properties Group Ltd* v. *Valero Energy Ltd* [2013] EWHC 98 (Ch); [2013] Ch 525, at [30], [31], [107], considering *Synge* v. *Synge* [1894] 1 QB 466; *Ogdens Ltd* v. *Nelson* [1905] AC 109; *Fratelli Sorrentino* v. *Buerger* [1915] 1 KB 307; *Omnium d'Enterprises* v. *Sutherland* [1919] 1 KB 618, CA).

was not at all certain that the buyer would have failed to do so. And so the seller was held to have repudiated. Saville J commented:[78] '[In] the present case there was only a chance that the buyers would be unable to perform.'

17.16 *Can we just check that you are on track to perform?* Under English law, a party has no *right* to demand an assurance from the other side that it is still able and willing to carry on.[79]

> By contrast, Article 8:105 of the *Principles of European Contract Law* ('soft' law, not binding on the English courts)[80] enables a party to seek 'adequate assurance of due performance' and in the meantime 'withhold performance of its own obligations'; and the party seeking reassurance will acquire the right to terminate if 'this assurance is not provided within a reasonable time' and 'if [that party] still reasonably believes that there will be a fundamental non-performance by the other party and gives notice of termination without delay'. UNIDROIT's *Principles of International Commercial Contracts* (2010), Article 7.3.4,[81] and US Uniform Commercial Code, 2–609(1), contain similar provisions. However, such a 'reassurance' mechanism might well stir up a hornet's nest of accusation and counter-accusation.

17.17 *Innocent party's decision to maintain the contract and sue for agreed remuneration.* A majority of the House of Lords in *White & Carter* v. *McGregor* (1962)[82] held that the innocent party might sometimes have the capacity to keep open the contract (the right to 'affirm the contract'), and complete his side of the bargain. He can then sue for the agreed price. Later cases have qualified this and prevented the innocent party from saddling the other party with unwanted performance (for details, see 18.03 ff).

17.18 *Injunction to restrain an anticipated breach?* In *Berkeley Community Villages Ltd* v. *Pullen* (2007)[83] (also on this case, see 2.13) P, a landowner, proposed to sell part of the land to a third party. That would deprive B, with whom P had entered into a development contract, of its right to commission. The proposed sale would involve a breach. P had conceded[84] that an injunction would be available if Morgan J found that the proposed sale would involve breach. The judge added dicta[85] (not necessary for his decision in view of this concession) that an injunction would have been available for anticipatory breach of an obligation (here, clause 10).[86] The injunction would prevent a party taking a step which would preclude him from complying in due course with that obligation even where that party's capacity to

---

78   [1993] 1 Lloyd's Rep 360, Saville J.
79   J. Carter, 'Suspending Contract Performance for Breach', in J. Beatson and D. Friedmann (eds.), *Good Faith and Fault in Contract Law* (Oxford, 1995), 485, 487–8, citing authorities.
80   T. Naudé, in H. MacQueen and R. Zimmermann (eds.), *European Contract Law: Scots and South African Perspectives* (Edinburgh, 2006), chapter 11.
81   3rd edition, 2010, text and comment, is available at: www.unidroit.org/english/principles/contracts/prin ciples2010/integralversionprinciples2010-e.pdf.
82   [1962] AC 413, HL.
83   [2007] EWHC 1330 (Ch); [2007] 3 EGLR 101; [2007] 24 EG 169 (CS); [2007] NPC 71.
84   *Ibid.*, at [142].
85   *Ibid.*, at [79] to [83].
86   Clause 10.

execute fully the relevant obligation is contingent on a third party's permission (such as planning permission).

5. BREACH OF CONDITION

17.19 *Classification of promissory terms.* There are three types of promissory obligation: conditions; intermediate or innominate terms; and warranties. There is no fourth category of 'fundamental term'.[87]

Breach of a condition entitles the other party to obtain damages and to terminate for breach of contract. Breach of an intermediate term also entitles the innocent party to claim damages; whether it also justifies termination of the contract depends on an assessment of the breach's gravity on the particular facts. But breach of a warranty (now a backwater category) gives rise only to a duty to pay damages. It becomes crucial, therefore, to determine whether a particular contractual obligation should be classified as a condition, an intermediate term or a warranty. Often the categorisation, established by reference to the factors discussed at 17.20, is clear and works satisfactorily. However, sometimes the matter is perplexing (for example, note the division of opinion in *Schuler (L) AG* v. *Wickman Machine Tool Sales Ltd* (1974) (17.21)).

17.20 *When is a term a 'condition'?* Classification occurs by reference to statute, judicial decision, or express or implied designation by the parties. A term is a condition, rather than one of the other two kinds of promissory term, in any of the following five situations (this classification was declared as 'neat' by Waller LJ in *'The Seaflower'* (2001),[88] who adopted the statement by *Chitty on Contracts* (although it should be noted that *Chitty* does not separate items (3) and (4) in this list):[89]

(1) statute explicitly classifies the term in this way;[90]

(2) there is a binding judicial decision supporting classification of a particular term as a 'condition'; examples abound;[91]

---

87 *Suisse Atlantique Société d'Armement Maritime SA* v. *NV Rotterdamsche* [1967] 1 AC 361, HL; *Photo Production Ltd* v. *Securicor Transport Ltd* [1980] AC 827, HL.

88 *BS & N Ltd (BVI)* v. *Micado Shipping Ltd (Malta)* ('*The Seaflower*') [2001] 1 Lloyd's Rep 341, at [42].

89 *Chitty on Contracts* (31st edn, London, 2012), 12–040; J. E. Stannard and D. Capper, *Termination for Breach of Contract* (Oxford, 2014), chapter 5.

90 E.g. sections 12(5A), 13(1A), 14(6) and 15(3) of the Sale of Goods Act 1979 (as amended); sections 13–15 must be read subject to section 15A (as amended by the Consumer Rights Bill).

91 '*The Mihalis Angelos*' [1971] 1 QB 164, CA (owner's statement in a charterparty that the vessel was 'expected ready to load under this charter about [a specified date]'); *Bunge Corporation* v. *Tradax Export SA* [1981] 1 WLR 711, HL (clause requiring the buyer to give at least fifteen days' notice to the seller of the buyer's intention to ship the goods, whereupon the seller could decide which port to use for the shipment); *Compagnie Commerciale Sucre et Denrees* v. *C Czarnikow* ('*The Naxos*') [1990] 1 WLR 1337, HL; noted by M. Clarke, [1991] CLJ 29 (clause requiring the sellers to have goods ready for delivery on the arrival of the vessel at port); *BS & N Ltd (BVI)* v. *Micado Shipping Ltd (Malta)* ('*The Seaflower*') [2001] 1 Lloyd's Rep 341, CA (clause requiring the owners to obtain approval, within sixty days, from a specified oil company, Exxon, that the latter consented to use of the relevant vessel); *Barber* v. *NWS Bank plc* [1996] 1 WLR 641, 646, CA (hire-purchase dealer had breached a condition that he would have title to a car which was sold (conditionally) to the claimant on hire-purchase); *Samarenko* v. *Dawn Hill House Ltd* [2011] EWCA Civ 1445; [2013] Ch 36, at [24] to [27], [52] to [54], [60] and [64] (contract for the sale of land; buyer's failure to pay a 10 per cent deposit on the stipulated day and on the revised deadline for payment) (case noted J. W. Carter (2013)

(3) a term is described in the contract as a 'condition' and upon construction it has that technical meaning; the leading case is *Schuler (L) AG* v. *Wickman Machine Tool Sales Ltd* (1974);[92]

(4) the parties have explicitly agreed that breach of that term, no matter what the factual consequences, or perhaps breach of any term (again irrespective of the consequences), will entitle the innocent party to terminate the contract for breach (for case law, noted *Rice* v. *Great Yarmouth Borough Council* (2000),[93] see 17.26 below);[94] or

(5) as a matter of general construction of the contract, even though the contract has not explicitly stipulated this.[95] A clause is to be understood to be intended to operate as a condition; the courts must then consider whether 'the parties must, by necessary implication, have intended that the innocent party would be discharged from further performance of his obligations in the event that the term was not fully and precisely complied with.'[96]

> As for category (5), an instructive decision is *PT Berlian Laju Tanker TBK* v. *Nuse Shipping Ltd* ('*The Aktor*') (2008).[97] The seller of a ship had agreed to receive a 10 per cent deposit at a Singapore bank. But the full price, 100 per cent payment, had to be paid at a Greek bank. The buyer had paid the 10 per cent deposit into a joint account held at a Singaporean bank. Christopher Clarke J held that it was a condition that a 100 per cent payment should be made in Greece.

17.21 '*Condition' not always used in a technical sense.* By a majority, the House of Lords in *Schuler (L) AG* v. *Wickman Machine Tool Sales Ltd* (1974) held that on proper construction of the contract, the word 'condition' (contained in clause 7(b)) might not have been intended to operate in a technical sense; therefore, breach of the relevant obligation does not necessarily justify termination.[98] The majority's decision turns on the need to harmonise different clauses within the contract. There was tension between those clauses. But it was held that the innocent party could not invoke clause 7(b) (containing the word 'condition') in order to bypass clause 11(a)(1) which provided that the innocent party must first serve notice on the other party, requiring the latter to take remedial steps. But Lord Wilberforce dissented.

129 LQR 149–52); *Kuwait Rocks Co.* v. *AMN Bulkcarriers Inc* ('*The Astra'*) [2013] EWHC 865 (Comm); [2013] 2 Lloyd's Rep 69, Flaux J; noted J. Shirley (2013) 130 LQR 185–8 (charterer's duty to pay hire punctually a condition; so expressed in relevant clause).

92   [1974] AC 235, HL; noted by J. H. Baker, [1973] CLJ 196, R. Brownsword, (1974) 37 MLR 104, and F. A. Mann, (1973) 89 LQR 464.

93   *The Times*, 26 July 2000; (2001) 3 LGLR 4, CA; S. Whittaker, 'Termination Clauses', in A. Burrows and E. Peel (eds.), *Contract Terms* (Oxford, 2007), chapter 13, at 273–83.

94   *Lombard North Central plc* v. *Butterworth* [1987] QB 527, CA.

95   *Bunge Corporation New York* v. *Tradax SA* [1981] 1 WLR 711, 715–16, HL.

96   *Ibid.*, at 715–16, 726, HL (also citing Lord Diplock in *Photo Production* v. *Securicor Transport Ltd* [1980] AC 822, 840, HL).

97   [2008] EWHC 1330 (Comm); [2008] 2 All ER (Comm) 784; [2008] 2 Lloyd's Rep 246.

98   [1974] AC 235, HL; noted by J. H. Baker, [1973] CLJ 196, R. Brownsword, (1974) 37 MLR 104, and F. A. Mann, (1973) 89 LQR 464.

In greater detail, *Schuler (L) AG* v. *Wickman Machine Tool Sales Ltd* (1974) concerned these facts and analysis.

W agreed to act as a distribution agent for S, a German manufacturer. Clause 7(b) required W to send a representative at least once a week to six specified motor manufacturers. W had committed itself to making roughly 1,400 visits over a four-and-a-half-year period to solicit orders for 'panel pressers' (equipment used in the manufacture of vehicles). This clause was labelled a 'condition'. Another clause, 11(a)(1), allowed a party to terminate the contract in the event of a 'material breach', provided the relevant breach had not been remedied within sixty days after the aggrieved party had given written notice. S sought to bypass this clause, and instead purported to terminate the contract on the basis of breaches of clause 7(b). S had waived earlier defaults. But W consistently failed to make significant percentages of the stipulated visits.

The House of Lords held that 'condition' had not been used in a technical sense, and agreed with the other aspects of the Court of Appeal's decision. But Lord Wilberforce dissented.

The House of Lords held that 'condition' in clause 7 should be linked (somewhat clumsily) with the reference elsewhere in the agreement (clause 11) to 'material' breach. Lord Reid hesitatingly concluded[99] that a spate of failed visits could be (partly) 'remedied' in the sense that the agent could 'put his house in order' and reform its 'system' of future visits (similarly, Lord Kilbrandon).[100] And so the sixty-day notice period to remedy had to be complied with. The German company had not been justified in terminating the contract on these facts.

Another (but not sufficient)[101] strand of reasoning in the *Schuler* case concerned the hypothetical case of a 'one-off'[102] unexcused missed visit. Lord Reid said: 'The more unreasonable the result the more unlikely it is that the parties can have intended it.'[103] But it is submitted that such a construction is justified only quite exceptionally, when it would lead to a *very or wholly* unreasonable result and the relevant word or phrase admits of more than one meaning.

Finally, Whittaker has noted that facts similar to the *Schuler* case would now fall within the Commercial Agents (Council Directive) Regulations 1993.[104]

17.22 *Statutory control in sales of goods transactions upon 'over-technical' resort to termination.* The Consumer Rights Bill (Schedule 1 para. 15) will extend section 15A of the Sale of Goods Act 1979 to consumer contracts – that section was previously confined to contracts where

---

99   *Ibid.*, at 252: 'The contract is so obscure that I can have no confidence that this is its true meaning.'
100 *Ibid.*, at 271.
101 Lord Reid, *ibid.*, at 251, would have construed the word 'condition' in clause 7 in its technical sense if clause 11 had not existed, creating a conflict between clauses 7 and 11.
102 In fact the amount of default was scarcely negligible (between 13 January and 27 October 1964, 18 out of 240 visits were missed for no good reason; the degree of default had influenced Lord Wilberforce, who dissented: he said that the contract demanded 'aggressive, insistent punctuality and efficiency': [1974] AC 235, 263, HL).
103 *Ibid.*, at 251, *per* Lord Reid (a useful 'rule of thumb', *per* Lord Mustill in *Charter Reinsurance Co. Ltd* v. *Fagan* [1997] AC 313, 387–8, HL; e.g., applied in *Trafigura Beheer BV* v. *Navigazione Montanari SpA* [2014] EWHC 129; [2014] 1 Lloyd's Rep 550, at [9], *per* Andrew Smith J).
104 S. Whittaker, 'Termination Clauses', in A. Burrows and E. Peel (eds.), *Contract Terms* (Oxford, 2007), chapter 13, at 267–73.

the buyer was not a consumer. Under section 15A[105] of the 1979 Act, a buyer is confined to damages, and cannot reject the goods, if (i) the breach is so 'slight' that it would be 'unreasonable' to reject the goods; (ii) the contract neither expressly nor impliedly precludes this conclusion.[106] This result is expressed as follows: '[T]he breach is not to be treated as a breach of condition but may be treated as a breach of warranty.' The seller bears the burden of proving (i).[107] The test stated at (i) is an objective inquiry: there is no need to prove subjective bad faith on the buyer's part. The same provision states that it will not apply if 'a contrary intention appears in, or is to be implied from, the contract'.[108] Section 15A will not, therefore, apply where the parties have *expressly categorised the relevant term as a condition*, thereby permitting termination, no matter how slight the breach, or where the parties have expressly stated that termination is justified no matter how slight the defective performance might be. Section 15A does not render the seller's obligation an intermediate term in the Common Law sense. Instead, this provision permits the buyer to terminate unless the breach is 'slight'. If the breach is not slight, the *second* issue of reasonableness does not arise. By contrast, breach of an intermediate term justifies termination only if the innocent party is substantially deprived of the expected benefit (17.33).

Section 15A and two older cases. In *Re Moore & Co. and Landauer & Co.* (1921),[109] the commercial buyer was held to be entitled to reject goods (some of which were) sent in boxes of twenty-four rather than in boxes of thirty, the contract having required boxing in quantities of thirty (such boxing would form a binding feature of a sale by description under section 13(1) of the Sale of Goods Act 1979). Scrutton LJ said that the boxing stipulation might matter if the buyer had agreed to a sub-sale on the same terms.[110] This discrepancy looks 'slight' and it seems unlikely that the commercial buyer would remain entitled to reject under the section 15A.

However, deviations in 'packaging' are one thing. What of deviations from the agreed substance of the goods? Treitel[111] wonders whether section 15A would change the result in *Arcos* v. *Ronaasen* (1933) where the supply of timber of 9/16ths of an inch was held not to be equivalent to the contractually stipulated dimension of half an inch (8/16ths).[112] If, as Treitel suggests, a 1/16th discrepancy is not necessarily 'slight', the commercial buyer would remain entitled to reject the goods.

---

105   Section 30(2A) of the 1979 Act adopts a similar approach where goods delivered are less than, or greater than, the quantity contracted for, but this quantitative deviation is 'so slight that it would be unreasonable' for the buyer to reject the goods; for comparative analysis (comparing the UN 'Vienna' Convention on the International Sale of Goods, 'CISG'), D. Saidov, in L. DiMatteo, Q. Zhou, S. Saintier, K. Rowley (eds.), *Commercial Contract Law: Transatlantic Perspectives* (Cambridge, 2014), chapter 18.
106   On this last factor, see section 15A(2) of the Sale of Goods Act 1979.
107   *Ibid.*, section 15A(3).
108   *Ibid.*, section 15A(2).
109   [1921] 2 KB 519, CA.
110   *Ibid.*, at 524.
111   *Treitel* (13th edn, London, 2011), 18–054.
112   [1933] AC 470, HL; on this case, D. Campbell in D. Campbell, L. Mulcahy and S. Wheeler (eds.), *Changing Concepts of Contract* (Basingstoke, 2013), chapter 7.

17.23 'Time of the essence'.[113] In Lombard North Central plc v. Butterworth (1987), Mustill LJ said:[114]

> A stipulation [contained in the original terms of the relevant transaction] that time is of the essence ... denotes that timely performance is a condition of the contract. The consequence is that delay in performance is treated as going to the root of the contract, without regard to the magnitude of the breach.

This becomes a vexed issue in, notably, conveyancing transactions,[115] contracts of hire,[116] and contractual investment instruments (BNP Paribas v. Wockhardt EU Operations (Swiss) AG (2009)).[117] An ex facie neutral time stipulation might be construed by the court as neither a mere warranty nor an intermediate or innominate term but instead as a condition.[118] However, in commercial arrangements, the modern tendency is to give effect to strict time stipulations (whether or not couched expressly as 'conditions'), if the courts perceive that commercial certainty is important in that context.[119]

  If the time stipulation is neither expressly or on construction a condition (as explained above), but B has already been guilty of delay, A may give notice[120] requiring the contract to be performed within a reasonable[121] time. Such a notice does not elevate the obligation to the level of a condition;[122] instead the notice operates as evidence of the date by which the promisee considers it reasonable to require the contract to be performed;[123] and thus the innocent party will need to show that the post-notification delay involves an element of serious default justifying termination, namely: (i) the failure to comply with the notice is held to be repudiatory[124] in the sense that it goes

---

113   Sir Terence Etherton C restated the leading principles in Urban 1 (Blonk Street) Ltd v. Ayres [2013] EWCA Civ 816 [2014] 1 WLR 756 at [44]; J. Stannard, 'In the Contractual Last Chance Saloon: Notices Making Time of the Essence' (2004) 120 LQR 137; J. E. Stannard, Delay in the Performance of Contractual Obligations (Oxford, 2007), especially chapters 1–3.

114   [1987] QB 527, 535–6, CA.

115   The case law is extensive: see the authorities collected in Urban 1 (Blonk Street) Ltd v. Ayres [2013] EWCA Civ 816 [2014] 1 WLR 756 at [44] (see also Ampurius Nu Homes Holdings Ltd v. Telford Homes (Creekside) Ltd [2013] EWCA Civ 577; [2013] 4 All ER 377).

116   E.g., the Lombard case, [1987] QB 527, 535–6, CA and including ships, Mardorf Peach & Co. Ltd v. Attica Sea Carriers Corp of Liberia, 'The Laconia' [1977] AC 850, HL; see now Kuwait Rocks Co. v. AMN Bulkcarriers Inc ('The Astra') [2013] EWHC 865 (Comm); [2013] 2 Lloyd's Rep 69, Flaux J; noted J. Shirley (2013) 130 LQR 185–8 (charterer's duty to pay hire punctually a condition; so expressed in relevant clause).

117   [2009] EWHC 3116 (Comm), at [32].

118   United Scientific Holdings Ltd v. Burnley BC [1978] AC 904, 944, HL, approving a passage in Halsbury's Laws of England.

119   E.g., Bunge Corporation New York v. Tradax SA [1981] 1 WLR 711, 715–6, 726, HL (also citing Lord Diplock in the Photo Production case [1980] AC 822, 840, HL).

120   BNP Paribas v. Wockhardt EU Operations (Swiss) AG [2009] EWHC 3116 (Comm), at [40], per Christopher Clarke J noting Re Olympia & York Canary Wharf Ltd (No. 2) [1993] BCC 159, Morritt J; and Clarke J's own decision in Dalkia Utilities Services plc v. Celtech International Ltd [2006] EWHC 63 (Comm); [2006] 1 Lloyd's Rep 599; [2006] 2 P & CR 9, at [131]; see also in Samarenko v. Dawn Hill House Ltd [2011] EWCA Civ 1445; [2013] Ch 36, at [37] ff, per Lewison LJ (case noted J. W. Carter (2013) 129 LQR 149–52).

121   Behzadi v. Shaftesbury Hotels Ltd [1992] Ch 1, CA.

122   Urban 1 (Blonk Street) Ltd v. Ayres [2013] EWCA Civ 816 [2014] 1 WLR 756, at [44] (proposition (6)), per Sir Terence Etherton C; Behzadi v. Shaftesbury Hotels Ltd [1992] Ch 1, 24, CA, per Purchas LJ.

123   Lord Simon of Glaisdale in United Scientific Holdings Ltd v. Burnley BC [1978] AC 904, 946E–47A; Behzadi v. Shaftesbury Hotels Ltd [1992] Ch 1, 24, CA, per Purchas LJ: Re Olympia & York Canary Wharf Ltd (No. 2) [1993] BCC 159 173, Morritt J; Astea (UK) Ltd v. Time Group Ltd [2003] EWHC 725, TCC, at [147] ff.

124   Dominion Corporate Trustees Ltd v. Debenhams Properties Ltd [2010] EWHC 1193 (Ch); [2010] NPC 63, at [55], per Kitchin J, for a payment default which was not repudiatory, etc.

to the 'root' of the contract;[125] or (ii) breach of an intermediate term which has gone to the root of the expected consideration;[126] or (iii) the dilatory party's default discloses a renunciation, that is, an implicit 'intimation' (see 17.07) to abandon the contract.

No such serious delay was shown in *Urban 1 (Blonk Street) Ltd* v. *Ayres* (2013).[127] The defendants had agreed to buy a lease of a flat from the claimant vendor. The accommodation was still under construction. The parties did not make clear what was to happen if there were delay in finishing the work, which was set for December 2008. The Court of Appeal held that there was an implied innominate term that the flat would be finished within a reasonable time. On the facts, the delay was about four weeks, and hence 'trivial' (a lease of 125 years was to be granted),[128] and so there had been no serious delay and no implied renunciation.[129] The purchasers had acted, therefore, precipitately in calling off this contract. Damages were available; the deposit had been validly forfeited; specific performance was no longer sought.

17.24 *Relief against forfeiture of proprietary or possessory interests (the Equitable relief doctrine).*[130] This doctrine protects borrowers or tenants suffering forfeiture following non-payment of mortgage debts or of rent. It covers all forms of property; but not money[131] unless held under trust;[132] and the doctrine (therefore) does not extend to mere *in personam* rights (rights under licences;[133] or a 'time charterparty').[134] Sometimes it is too late to seek relief because the relevant subject matter has already been sold to an innocent third party.[135] However, the doctrine does not operate in favour of a purchaser of land who pays late: see discussion of *Union Eagle Ltd* v. *Golden Achievement Ltd* (1997)[136] below.

---

125   E.g., failure to pay a deposit in a real property contract by the agreed date, that date having been notified as crucial: *Samarenko* v. *Dawn Hill House Ltd* [2011] EWCA Civ 1445; [2013] Ch 36, at [37] ff, concluding at [47], *per* Lewison LJ (case noted J. W. Carter (2013) 129 LQR 149–52).

126   *Re Olympia & York Canary Wharf Ltd (No. 2)* [1993] BCC 159, 165–73, especially at 173; *Ocular Sciences Ltd* v. *Aspect Vision Care Ltd* [1997] RPC 289, 433, *per* Laddie J; *Astea (UK) Ltd* v. *Time Group Ltd* [2003] EWHC 725, TCC, at [151].

127   [2013] EWCA Civ 816 [2014] 1 WLR 756 (see, notably, the statement of general principle at [44], *per* Etherton C).

128   *Ibid.*, at [60], *per* Etherton C, and 'trivial' at [69], *per* Floyd LJ.

129   *Ibid.*, at [48].

130   Robert Walker LJ in *On Demand plc* v. *Gerson plc* [2001] 1 WLR 155, 163G–72, CA (reversed on another basis at [2003] 1 AC 368, HL); L. Gullifer, in A. Burrows and E. Peel (eds.), *Commercial Remedies: Current Issues and Problems* (Oxford, 2003), 191, at 212 ff.

131   *UK Housing Alliance (North West) Ltd* v. *Francis* [2010] EWCA Civ 117; [2010] 3 All ER 519, at [14], *per* Longmore LJ (loss of contingent right to a payment; noted by C. Conte, (2010) 126 LQR 529–34).

132   *Nutting* v. *Baldwin* [1995] 1 WLR 201, 209, *per* Rattee J.

133   *Sport Internationals Bussum BV* v. *Inter-Footwear Ltd* [1984] 1 WLR 776, HL (considered in *Celestial Aviation 1 Ltd* v. *Paramount Airways Private Ltd* [2010] EWHC 185 (Comm); [2010] 1 CLC 15, Hamblen J; noted by L. Aitken, (2010) 126 LQR 505–7; see also *UK Housing Alliance (North West) Ltd* v. *Francis* [2010] EWCA Civ 117; [2010] 3 All ER 519, at [14]; noted by C. Conte, (2010) 126 LQR 529–34).

134   'The Scaptrade' [1983] 2 AC 694, HL.

135   *Ibid.*

136   [1997] AC 514, PC.

The Union Eagle *case (1997).* This case concerned the purchase of a flat in Hong Kong. The buyer's tender of the price was ten minutes late. The vendor decided to terminate the contract and forfeit the deposit (the market price was rising). The buyer unsuccessfully contended that even before attempting to pay, he had acquired an inchoate equitable title to the property and that Equity would relieve against such forfeiture in the interests of fairness. But the Privy Council held that this doctrine does not apply here. Lord Hoffmann held that Equity would not intervene; vendors deserved 'bright line' protection; they should be free to walk away from the deal if the purchase money is paid late when punctual performance 'is of the essence'. The decision is admirably robust. It contrasts with the pro-guilty party case law concerning intermediate terms (17.32) and the decisions in the *Schuler* (17.21) and *Rice* (17.26) cases.

17.25 *Termination rights in general.*[137] There are three possible types of termination right but only the third of these is exercisable in consequence of breach: (1) an express right to cancel without showing the other party's breach; (2) an implied right to serve notice to cancel without showing the other party's breach;[138] (3) an express right to terminate in respect of the other party's breach (see further 17.28 below). In *Geys* v. *Société Générale* (2012) Baroness Hale noted that a party needs to act in an unequivocal manner when purporting to exercise a termination clause or other unilateral notice clause.[139]

17.26 *Termination clauses consequent on breach: spelling out the possibility of termination for breach.* The *Schuler* (1974) decision (17.21) shows that the word 'condition' might sometimes be construed as a 'term'. The safer course is *to spell out the innocent party's unqualified right to terminate for any breach of the relevant obligation.* However, *Rice* v. *Great Yarmouth Borough Council* (2000) reveals that very careful drafting indeed is required if the innocent party is to achieve an unobstructed right to terminate.[140]

The *Rice* case (2000) was a four-year contract for the claimant to maintain the defendant's sports and parks facilities. The written contract gave the defendant the right to terminate for 'breach of any of [Rice's] obligations under the Contract'. The defendant terminated the contract because of shortcomings in performance. The Court of Appeal held that 'any' should not be taken to mean 'any at all', otherwise the parties would have created a 'draconian' contractual regime,[141] and that extreme interpretation would 'fly in the face of commercial sense'. Instead

137   J. E. Stannard and D. Capper, *Termination for Breach of Contract* (Oxford, 2014), chapter 8; E. Peel, 'The Termination Paradox' [2013] LMCLQ 519–43; J. Randall, 'Express Termination Clauses' [2014] CLJ 113–41; S. Whittaker, 'Termination Clauses', in A. Burrows and E. Peel (eds.), *Contract Terms* (Oxford, 2007), chapter 13.
138   Whittaker, *ibid.*; J. Randall, 'Express Termination Clauses' [2014] CLJ 113–41.
139   [2012] UKSC 63; [2013] 1 AC 523, at [52].
140   *The Times,* 26 July 2000; (2001) 3 LGLR 4, CA; S. Whittaker, 'Termination Clauses', in A. Burrows and E. Peel (eds.), *Contract Terms* (Oxford, 2007), chapter 13, at 273–83; for Australian case law, J. W. Carter, *Carter's Breach of Contract* (Oxford, 2012), 5.04 ff.
141   *The Times,* 26 July 2000; (2001) 3 LGLR 4, CA, at [22], *per* Hale LJ.

'any' meant 'any repudiatory' breach.[142] And so termination would be justified only if there had been 'repudiation' of the overall contract by a pattern of breaches.[143] But the breaches had not been cumulatively serious enough.

Burrows has queried whether a clause would be upheld if it states that termination would be justified for 'any breach, however trivial'.[144] The answer must be: 'yes' because, if the parties are commercial parties, the principle of freedom of contract (1.08 ff) requires the courts not to override such wording.

It is submitted that, as noted by Kitchin J in *Dominion Corporate Trustees Ltd* v. *Debenhams Properties Ltd* (2010),[145] the *Rice* case (2000) (and its precursor, the *Antaios* case, 1985) should be understood to turn on the extremely varied range of possible breaches capable of being committed by the service provider on the facts of each case. But where the scope of the obligation is narrow and the wording is watertight, effect must be given to the termination provision.

The Court of Appeal's rather cavalier redrafting of the termination clause in the *Rice* case (2000) can be contrasted with the admirably robust application in *BNP Paribas* v. *Wockhardt EU Operations (Swiss) AG* (2009)[146] of a termination clause. In the latter case Christopher Clarke J was required to examine a sophisticated financial instrument. He concluded that the parties had intended that breach would necessarily entitle the innocent party to terminate the contract. Christopher Clarke J said:[147] 'the parties have ... spelt out the consequences which result from a breach of condition. It is unrealistic to suppose that, having done so, they are to be taken to have intended that a failure to pay should be regarded as a warranty or an innominate term.'

In *Kuwait Rocks Co.* v. *AMN Bulkcarriers Inc ('The Astra')* (2013) Flaux J held that the following clause gave the owner a right to terminate the contract and to recover damages for breach: 'failing the punctual and regular payment of the hire, or bank guarantee ... the Owners shall be at liberty to withdraw the vessel from the service of the Charterers, without prejudice to any claim they (the Owners) may otherwise have.'[148]

17.27 *Coexistence of a termination clause (consequent on breach) and Common Law termination rights.* Where the contract contains an *express right to terminate for breach*, the innocent party can exercise simultaneously an express power *to terminate for breach* and the

---

142   Adopting *Antaios Compania Naviera SA* v. *Salen Rederierna AB* [1985] AC 191, 200–1, HL (clause entitling owner to terminate the charterparty for 'any' breach did not cover minor breach, but only a repudiatory breach); on which *Multi-Link Leisure* v. *North Lanarkshire* [2010] UKSC 47; [2011] 1 All ER 175, at [21], *per* Lord Hope.

143   *The Times*, 26 July 2000; (2001) 3 LGLR 4, CA, at [17], *per* Hale LJ.

144   A. S. Burrows, *A Casebook on Contract* (4th edn, Oxford, 2013), 347.

145   *Dominion Corporate Trustees Ltd* v. *Debenhams Properties Ltd* [2010] EWHC 1193 (Ch); [2010] NPC 63, at [32], *per* Kitchin J ('a multitude of obligations, many of which are of minor importance and which can be broken in many different ways').

146   [2009] EWHC 3116 (Comm); 132 Con LR 177.

147   *Ibid.*, at [33].

148   *Kuwait Rocks Co.* v. *AMN Bulkcarriers Inc ('The Astra')* [2013] EWHC 865 (Comm); [2013] 2 Lloyd's Rep 69, Flaux J; noted J. Shirley (2013) 130 LQR 185–8 (charterer's duty to pay hire punctually a condition; so expressed in relevant clause).

Common Law right to terminate a contract because of the other party's repudiatory breach.[149] However, the case law on this topic has become convoluted and treacherous, as both Peel and Liu have noted.[150]

17.28 *Express right to cancel without demonstrating the other party's serious breach.* As for cancellation rights of type (1), a contract might expressly permit a party to terminate a contract in specified circumstances, even in the absence of a Common Law right to terminate for breach. Where this occurs, the party who terminates might be entitled to obtain damages in respect of past breaches, but he will not be able to obtain damages for loss of the remaining period of the contract *unless the facts disclose that there has been a repudiatory breach in respect of which the innocent party has terminated the contract*[151] (as the Court of Appeal explained in the *Lombard* case (1987), there had been no such repudiatory breach on the facts of the *Financings* case (1963)).[152]

17.29 *Implied rights to give notice to cancel without demonstrating the other party's serious breach.* In contracts of indefinite duration, the courts will find an *implied term* that either party can terminate the contract, without breach of contract, by giving the other reasonable notice.

> For example in *Staffordshire Area Health Authority* v. *South Staffordshire Waterworks Co.* (1978)[153] a 1929 water supply agreement was expressed to apply 'at all times hereafter' and it imposed a charge to the hospital of seven old pence for each 1,000 gallons so supplied, exceeding the first 5,000 gallons. By 1978, that was an uneconomic rate of payment. At the Court of Appeal, (Reginald) Goff and Cumming-Bruce LJJ held that this was a contract of indefinite duration and hence it was capable of being terminated by either party on giving reasonable notice. As for future supply, the Court of Appeal contemplated that the parties would reach a compromise on the question of the new price for supply. The third judge, Lord Denning MR, suggested a novel theory permitting release from contracts which have become economically very disadvantageous because of inflation; but this radical approach was not accepted by the other judges in the case.

17.30 *Express terms concerning 'material' breach.*[154] The courts do not use the concept of 'material breach', but contractual draftsmen often use this phrase. Such a breach is not

---

149   *Stocznia Gdynia SA* v. *Gearbulk Holdings Ltd* [2009] EWCA Civ 75; [2010] QB 27 (noted E. Peel (2009) 125 LQR 378–84).

150   Q. Liu, 'The Puzzle of Unintended Acceptance of Repudiation' [2011] LMCLQ 4–11, noting Tomlinson J's decision in *Shell Egypt Manzala GmbH* v. *Dana Gas Egypt Ltd* [2010] EWHC 465 (Comm), at [31], [32], where A's reliance on a termination clause was held not to have been a simultaneous acceptance of B's repudiatory breach.

151   *Financings Ltd* v. *Baldock* [1963] 2 QB 104, 110–11, 121, CA; Nicholls LJ in *Lombard North Central plc* v. *Butterworth* [1987] QB 527, 541–3, 546, CA; noted by G. H. Treitel, [1987] LMCLQ 143; W. Bojczuk, [1987] JBL 353; B. Opeskin, (1990) 106 LQR 293.

152   Nicholls LJ in the *Lombard* case, [1987] QB 527, 541–2, noting Diplock LJ in the *Financings* case, [1963] 2 QB 104, 121, CA.

153   [1978] 1 WLR 1387, CA.

154   See further M. A. Clarke, N. Andrews, A. M. Tettenborn, G. Virgo, *Contractual Duties: Performance, Breach, Termination and Remedies* (London, 2012) (breach and performance section by N. Andrews), 9–018 ff.

trivial, nor need it be so serious as to justify breach, applying the criterion of Common Law termination for breach; the breach will be material if it is 'substantial' or 'a serious matter'.[155] It is then common for the express language of the relevant contract to entitle an innocent party to terminate but to allow the guilty party to have a chance to remedy the matter (for example, in the leading case, *Schuler* v. *Wickman* (1974)).[156]

17.31 *Express terms concerning 'remediable' breach.*[157] The Court of Appeal in *Force India Formula One Team Ltd* v. *Etihad Airways PJSC* (2010),[158] applying the concept of 'remediable' breaches, considered that the harm could not be undone in that case.[159]

> In *Force India Formula One Team Ltd* v. *Etihad Airways PJSC* (2010) a 'formula one' racing team had breached their sponsorship agreement (i) by restyling the team so as to excise reference to their Abu Dhabi sponsors, and (ii) by changing the livery logo of the team. A clause allowed the sponsors to terminate for breach if there had been 'material' breaches which had not been remedied within a specified period. Rix LJ held that the breaches committed by the racing team were not 'remediable' because, as he said, the genie could not be put back into the bottle, nor could the clock be put back.[160]

But in other situations (Lord Reid in *Schuler* v. *Wickman* (1974)[161] suggested that this is the more usual usage) it might be enough that the default could be stopped, as for the future (as noted by Lords Reid, Simon, and Kilbrandon in the *Schuler* case).[162]

6. BREACH OF INTERMEDIATE OR INNOMINATE TERMS

17.32 *Intermediate (or innominate) terms – nature.* This category of promissory term is fact-sensitive: the question whether breach of an intermediate term justifies termination requires assessment of the consequences of breach on the particular facts of the case. If those consequences are really severe (17.33), the innocent party can justifiably terminate.

---

155   *Mid Essex Hospital Services NHS Trust* v. *Compass Group UK and Ireland Ltd* [2013] EWCA Civ 200; [2013] BLR 265 at [126], *per* Jackson LJ (having considered, at [124] and [125]; *Dalkia Utilities Services plc* v. *Celltech International Ltd* [2006] EWHC 63 (Comm); [2006] 1 Lloyd's Rep 599, at [102], *per* Christopher Clarke J ('neither trivial nor minimal' and 'serious'); and *Fitzroy House Epsworth Street (No. 1) Ltd* v. *Financial Times Ltd* [2006] EWCA Civ 329; [2006] 1 WLR 2207, at [35] (Sir Andrew Morritt C, '"substantial" and "material", depending on the context, are interchangeable. The word "reasonable" connotes a different test').
156   [1974] AC 235, 248–9, HL (clause 11(a)(i)).
157   See further M. A. Clarke, N. Andrews, A. M. Tettenborn, G. Virgo, *Contractual Duties: Performance, Breach, Termination and Remedies* (London, 2012) (breach and performance section by N. Andrews), 9–029 ff.
158   [2010] EWCA Civ 1051; [2011] ETLR 10, at [100] to [109].
159   *Ibid.*, at [108]: where, *per* Rix LJ, 'the breach or breaches are repeated, cumulative, continuing and repudiatory'.
160   [2010] EWCA Civ 1051; [2011] ETLR 10, at [108].
161   [1974] AC 235, 249–50, HL.
162   [1974] AC 235, 249–50, 265, 271, HL (as noted in the *Force India* case, [2010] EWCA Civ 1051; [2011] ETLR 10, at [104] to [107]).

The category was resuscitated from obscurity by the Court of Appeal in *Hongkong Fir Shipping Co. Ltd* v. *Kawasaki Kisen Kaisha Ltd* (1962).[163]

In the *Hongkong Fir* case (1962), Diplock LJ rejected the contention that the law recognises only a simple dichotomy of promissory term consisting of 'conditions' and 'warranties', the latter producing only liability in damages, and the former entitling the innocent party additionally to terminate the contract.[164] He accepted that some obligations can be breached only in a way which will necessarily have very serious consequences. Conversely, other contractual obligations might never have serious consequences, and so they should be regarded as 'warranties'.[165] But, as he emphasised, this leaves a large category of obligations 'of a more complex nature' where it will depend on the actual events following breach whether the innocent party can justify termination.

Lord Wilberforce in the *Schuler* case (1974)[166] and Lord Denning in 'The Hansa Nord' (1976)[167] suggested that the broad notion of an intermediate term antedated the *Hongkong Fir* decision. As for the simple dichotomy of conditions and warranties within the phraseology of the sale of goods legislation, it has been suggested that this is attributable to the influence of Sir Frederick Pollock, the textbook writer (as suggested by Robert Goff QC and Brian Davenport during argument before the Court of Appeal in 'The Mihalis Angelos',[168] and noted by Lord Denning MR in that case).[169] The view that there were only two types of term explains the structure of the Sale of Goods Act 1893 (and its successor, the 1979 Act), which refers only to conditions and warranties, and makes no reference to intermediate terms. But Lewison LJ suggests that the late nineteenth-century case law had adopted a 'binary' (condition/warranty) classification independently of the sale of goods context.[170]

The intermediate term category has been recognised in Australia,[171] New Zealand[172] and elsewhere.[173]

17.33 *Intermediate terms – circumstances justifying termination.* Diplock LJ[174] (but not Upjohn LJ)[175] in the *Hongkong Fir* case (1962) suggested that the true test is to consider whether the breach's effect has been to 'deprive the [innocent party] of substantially the whole benefit

---

163   [1962] 2 QB 1, CA; J. E. Stannard and D. Capper, *Termination for Breach of Contract* (Oxford, 2014), chapter 6; D. Nolan, in C. Mitchell and P. Mitchell (eds.), *Landmark Cases in the Law of Contract* (Oxford, 2008), 269 ff; and, for Lord Diplock's own account of this decision, see 'The Law of Contract in the Eighties' (1981) 15 *University of British Columbia Law Review* 371.
164   [1962] 2 QB 1, 69–70, CA.
165   *Ibid.*, at 70.
166   [1974] AC 235, 262F, HL: 'I do not think this was anything new.'
167   'The Hansa Nord' [1976] 1 QB 44, 60, CA.
168   'The Mihalis Angelos' [1971] 1 QB 164, 187 (counsel).
169   *Ibid.*, at 193, *per* Lord Denning MR.
170   *Samarenko* v. *Dawn Hill House Ltd* [2011] EWCA Civ 1445; [2013] Ch 36, at [28] and [29], *per* Lewison LJ, citing *Bentsen* v. *Taylor, Sons & Co. (No. 2)* [1893] 2 QB 274, 281, CA, *per* Bowen LJ (a charterparty case).
171   *Koompahtoo Local Aboriginal Land Council* v. *Sanpine Pty Ltd* [2007] HCA 61; (2007) 82 ALJR 345 (Kirby J dissenting, who would prefer to eliminate warranties and adopt an essential/inessential term dichotomy: for criticism, N. Andrews [2013] CLJ 214, 216–17; K. Dharmanda and A. Papamatheos, (2008) 124 LQR 373.
172   *Holmes* v. *Burgess* [1975] 2 NZLR 311, 318–20.
173   A. Phang, 'Doctrine and Fairness in the Law of Contract' (2009) 29 LS 534, 546 ff.
174   [1962] 2 QB 1, at 69–70, CA.
175   [1962] 2 QB 1, 64.

which it was the intention of the parties that he should obtain'. That is a very high threshold. Should it be enough that the breach is serious and 'goes to the root'? There has been inconclusive re-examination of this issue.[176]

> An attractive lowering of the bar for termination for breach of an innominate term is discernible in the leading Australian decision. The High Court of Australia in *Koompahtoo Local Aboriginal Land Council* v. *Sanpine Pty Ltd* (2007)[177] said that the innominate term doctrine permits termination for 'serious and substantial breaches of contract'. The same court appeared to treat the phrase 'breach going to the root of the contract' and breach depriving the innocent party of 'a substantial part of the contract' as synonymous.[178]

It is submitted that the better formulation (which would achieve uniformity across the various heads of breach of contractual terms) is that the relevant breach must go to the root of the contemplated performance;[179] it should be enough that breach produces serious or substantially adverse consequences for the innocent party so that termination is a proportionate and reasonable response. (As for the date for assessing the scale of detriment consequent on breach, *Ampurius Nu Homes Holdings Ltd* v. *Telford Homes (Creekside) Ltd* (2013: on which 17.05) makes clear that the relevant date is that of termination rather than the earlier date of breach.)[180]

17.34 *Intermediate terms – no termination justified on facts of the* Hongkong Fir case. In the *Hongkong Fir* case (1962),[181] the Court of Appeal held that express terms as to seaworthiness should not be treated as conditions; and the court further held, agreeing with Salmon J at first instance, that termination was not justified for breach of intermediate terms on these facts.

> The *Hongkong Fir* case concerned a two-year charterparty which required the ship to be 'in every way fitted for ordinary cargo service' and maintained in a 'thoroughly efficient state in hull and machinery during service'. The ship seems to have been well short of 'shipshape and Bristol fashion': the chief engineer was addicted to drink, the crew was insufficient and there were

176 *Ampurius Nu Homes Holdings Ltd* v. *Telford Homes (Creekside) Ltd* [2013] EWCA Civ 577; [2013] 4 All ER 377, at [38] to [50], *per* Lewison LJ; *Urban 1 (Blonk Street) Ltd* v. *Ayres* [2013] EWCA Civ 816; [2014] 1 WLR 756, at [57], *per* Etherton C.
177 [2007] HCA 61; (2007) 82 ALJR 345; (2008) 241 ALR 88, High Court of Australia (Gleeson CJ, Gummow, Heydon, Crennan JJ), at [52].
178 *Ibid.*, at [54] and [71].
179 E.g, *Dominion Corporate Trustees Ltd* v. *Debenhams Properties Ltd* [2010] EWHC 1193 (Ch); [2010] NPC 63, at [52], *per* Kitchin J; Lord Denning MR referred only to Upjohn LJ's 'breach going to the root' formulation, and he ignored Diplock LJ's formulation: *'The Hansa Nord'* [1976] QB 44, at 60–1 (citing Upjohn LJ in the *Hongkong Fir* case at [1962] 2 QB 1, 64). *Koompahtoo Local Aboriginal Land Council* v. *Sanpine Pty Ltd* [2007] HCA 61; (2007) 82 ALJR 345; (2008) 241 ALR 88, at [52], [54] and [71]. Despite Lewison LJ's sceptical comments (*Urban 1 (Blonk Street) Ltd* v. *Ayres* [2013] EWCA Civ 816; [2014] 1 WLR 756, at [50]), this metaphorical expression is helpful.
180 [2013] EWCA Civ 577; [2013] 4 All ER 377, at [43], citing Diplock LJ in *Hongkong Fir Shipping Co. Ltd* v. *Kawasaki Kisen Kaisha Ltd* [1962] 2 QB 26, 72, CA.
181 [1962] 2 QB 1, CA.

several serious breakdowns in the machinery.[182] The charterers repudiated the agreement before the two-year period had elapsed, because there had been a significant fall in the market rate for hire of such vessels, and they were now locked into an uneconomic contract.[183] The termination was held to be unjustified. First, the obligations were 'intermediate' or 'innominate' obligations (Diplock[184] and Upjohn LJJ;[185] Sellers LJ even classified the term as a 'warranty').[186] On this point the majority noted that the 'seaworthiness' obligations could be breached in a variety of ways, some of them serious, others relatively minor. The court concluded that the breaches did not deprive the charterer of substantially the whole of benefit expected under the contract.

17.35 *Intermediate terms – sale of goods.* In *'The Hansa Nord'* (1976), the Court of Appeal held that an express term in a sale of goods contract might be classified as an intermediate term even though the statute (then the 1893 Sale of Goods Act, now the 1979 Act) does not include that expression and instead refers (in its classification of terms) to the dichotomy of conditions and warranties.[187]

The contract in *'The Hansa Nord'* (1976) concerned the supply to Rotterdam of citrus pulp pellets for use in making cattle-feed. It was an express term that they should be delivered in good condition. The buyer rejected them when he discovered that some of the cargo was less than perfect (the market price had fallen so that this had become a bad bargain for the buyer). The seller then resold the goods at auction to an importer, X. The buyer (who had just pulled out from the original deal) later bought these goods from X, but for a much smaller sum than he had originally agreed to pay the original vendor (£33,720 rather than £100,000). The product was still fit for use in making cattle-feed. The Court of Appeal:

(i) rejected the contention that there is no room within the Sale of Goods legislation for the 'intermediate' term; instead section 62(2) of the 1979 Act requires the 'rules of the Common Law' to apply to sale-of-goods transactions;[188] 'rules of the Common Law' include the classificatory rule stated (or perhaps 'rediscovered') in the *Hongkong Fir* case (1962) (17.34);

(ii) there had been no breach of the (then applicable) statutory implied term that the goods must be of 'merchantable quality' on the present facts;[189]

(iii) the court remitted the case for assessment of damages, based on the difference in the value of the goods supplied and of sound goods.

---

182   See the clear analysis of this fundamental authority in *Ampurius Nu Homes Holdings Ltd* v. *Telford Homes (Creekside) Ltd* [2013] EWCA Civ 577; [2013] 4 All ER 377, at [38] to [52], and [61], [63].

183   [1962] 2 QB 1, at 39 (Salmon J).

184   *Ibid.*, at 62, CA.

185   *Ibid.*, at 64, CA.

186   *Ibid.*, at 60, CA.

187   *'The Hansa Nord'* [1976] QB 44, CA, noted by A. Weir, [1976] CLJ 33.

188   *Ibid.*, at 72, 83, CA.

189   *Ibid.*, at 61–3, 77, 79, CA, considering section 14(2) of the Sale of Goods Act 1893; now section 14(2) of the 1979 Act, which is concerned with the implied term that goods be of 'satisfactory quality', as amplified by section 14(2A) to (2F).

17.36 *Intermediate terms – assessment.* The intermediate term doctrine is pro-guilty party, shielding him from the innocent party's over-zealous or punctilious demand for precise performance. The intermediate term device is certainly an antidote to a ('draconian') regime of 'zero tolerance', where the innocent party can terminate a contract for technical and trivial breach, snapping at the slightest opportunity to end the contract. But this antidote comes at a price. First, it can induce sloppiness in performance in commercial contexts. Secondly, it introduces considerable uncertainty in the application of contractual terms: assessment whether breach of an intermediate term justifies termination can divide both arbitral panels and judges. Obtaining a final answer might require protracted and expensive litigation, and the decision might be taken on more than one appeal.

7. THE PROCESS OF TERMINATION FOR BREACH

17.37 *Innocent party's choice.*[190] Faced by the other party's repudiation (anticipatory breach, or renunciation at time of due performance, or other breach which justifies termination), the innocent party has a choice: he can accept the repudiation and thus terminate the contract and sue for damages, or he can affirm the contract and sue for damages.[191] This is known as 'the right to elect'. The same 'elective', as distinct from 'automatic', analysis applies to employment contracts.[192] There is an exception to this 'elective' or non-automatic termination analysis in the context of insurance contracts.[193]

17.38 *Binding nature of the election.* The law requires firm adherence to the innocent party's decision to terminate or to affirm the contract. Once this decision has been communicated, it is too late to try to resurrect the contract:[194] 'What is dead is dead.'[195] Therefore, it is too late once the contract has been terminated for breach for the innocent party to revive the contract by a unilateral decision. Instead the contract can only be resurrected by the parties' joint decision.[196] Similarly, once the innocent party decides to affirm the contract, he cannot change his mind, at least where he has full knowledge[197] of the relevant facts and of his right to terminate. A party can waive a breach of condition, or, in the case of sales of goods, a buyer can be treated under statutory rules as having 'accepted' the goods.[198]

190   J. E. Stannard and D. Capper, *Termination for Breach of Contract* (Oxford, 2014), chapter 4; J. W. Carter, 'Discharge as the Basis for Termination for Breach of Contract' (2012) 128 LQR 283–302.
191   *Fercometal SARL* v. *Mediterranean Shipping Co. SA ('The Simona')* [1989] AC 788, HL; *Vitol SA* v. *Norelf Ltd ('The Santa Clara')* [1996] AC 800, HL.
192   *Geys* v. *Société Générale, London Branch* [2012] UKSC 63; [2013] 1 AC 523 (noted D. Cabrelli and R. Zahn, (2013) 76 MLR 1106–19; and L. Aitken, (2013) 129 LQR 335–7).
193   *Bank of Nova Scotia* v. *Hellenic Mutual War Risk Association (Bermuda) Ltd ('The Good Luck')* [1992] 1 AC 233, HL; G. H. Treitel, *Some Landmarks of Twentieth Century Contract Law* (Oxford, 2002), 127.
194   *Yukong Line of Korea* v. *Rendsburg Investments Corporation of Liberia* [1996] 2 Lloyd's Rep 604, 607, Moore-Bick J, proposition (4).
195   Lord Wilberforce in *Johnson* v. *Agnew* [1980] AC 367, 398, HL.
196   Q. Liu, *Anticipatory Breach* (Oxford, 2011), 127, at n. 637, citing J Ewart, *Waiver Distributed* (Cambridge, MA, 1917), 83–4.
197   *Peyman* v. *Lanjani* [1985] Ch 457, CA; for an example of affirmation and waiver of the right to terminate, *Peregrine Systems Ltd* v. *Steria Ltd* [2005] EWCA Civ 239; [2005] Info TLR 294, at [16] to [23].
198   For 'acceptance' in the context of sales of goods, see sections 11(4), 35, 35A and 36 of the Sale of Goods Act 1979.

Furthermore, Lord Goff in *'The Kanchenjunga'* (1990) said that the innocent party might be estopped from terminating because his conduct has caused the other party to change his position.[199]

> Lord Goff's idea was explained by Aikens LJ in *Tele2 International Card Company SA* v. *Post Office Ltd* (2009) as follows:[200]
>> Where, with knowledge of the relevant facts, the party that has the right to terminate the contract acts in a manner which is consistent only with it having chosen one or other of two alternative and inconsistent courses of action open to it (i.e., to terminate or affirm the contract), then it will be held to have made its election accordingly.

17.39 *No third choice.* The innocent party has no 'third' choice. He cannot 'affirm the contract and yet be absolved from tendering further performance unless and until [the repudiating party] gives reasonable notice that he is once again able and willing to perform'.[201] In other words, once the innocent party decides to continue with the contract, he too is 'back on track' and must comply with his contractual obligations as they remain or arise (in fact, in the absence of termination for breach, the contract has not ceased to 'tick').

> As Lord Ackner explained in *'The Simona'* (1989):[202] 'such a [third] choice would negate the contract being kept alive for the benefit of both parties and would deny the party who [attempted to repudiate], the right to take advantage of any supervening circumstance which would justify him in declining to complete.'[203]

17.40 *Innocent party's pause for thought.* However, *'The Simona'* case does not prevent the courts from recognising the innocent party's need to pause for thought. According to Rix LJ in the *Stocznia* case (2003), the innocent party must have a reasonable opportunity to assess briefly his option whether to affirm or to terminate, just as in international rugby the fourth official can be given a reasonable time to study camera footage to determine whether a disputed try should be awarded. But the time for assessment is short:[204] 'If [the innocent

---

199 [1990] 1 Lloyd's Rep 391, 399, HL, *per* Lord Goff; for other Common Law discussion, see G. H. Jones (with P. Schlechtriem), 'Breach of Contract', in *International Encyclopaedia of Comparative Law*, vol. VII, *Contracts in General* (Tübingen, 1999), 15–134, 15–135.
200 [2009] EWCA Civ 9, at [53]; Aikens LJ's exegesis was noted by Rix LJ in *Force India Formula One Team Ltd* v. *Etihad Airways PJSC* [2010] EWCA Civ 1051; [2011] ETLR 10, at [112].
201 *Fercometal SARL* v. *Mediterranean Shipping Co. SA* (*'The Simona'*) [1989] AC 788, 805E, HL, *per* Lord Ackner (criticised by G. H. Jones and W. Goodhart, *Specific Performance* (2nd edn, London, 1996), 69–72, considering the Australian cases of *Foran* v. *Wight* (1989) 168 CLR 385 (High Court of Australia), and *Peter Turnbull & Co.* v. *Mundus Trading Co. (Australasia)* (1954) 90 CLR 235 (High Court of Australia); M. Mustill, *Anticipatory Breach: Butterworths Lectures 1989–90* (London, 1990), 65–8 and J. Carter, in J. Beatson and D. Friedmann (eds.), *Good Faith and Fault in Contract Law* (Oxford, 1995), 485, 498, 502–4.
202 *Fercometal SARL* v. *Mediterranean Shipping Co. SA* (*'The Simona'*) [1989] AC 788, 805E–F, HL.
203 *Ibid.*
204 *Stocznia Gdanska SA* v. *Latvian Shipping Co. (No. 3)* [2002] EWCA Civ 889; [2002] 2 All ER (Comm) 768, at [87].

party] does nothing for too long, there may come a time when the law will treat him as having affirmed.'

Rix LJ returned to this idea in *Force India Formula One Team Ltd v. Etihad Airways PJSC* (2010).[205] He held that under this 'middle ground' sponsors should be accorded a decent interval within which to assess whether to terminate the sponsorship agreement in response to the racing team's repudiation of some of its leading requirements. This 'make your mind up' period was quite generous because it fell within the fallow period between racing seasons.

This notion of a period for reflection is commercially attractive. However, Liu finds this idea wholly unattractive and pours icy water on this development.[206]

17.41 *New opportunity to terminate.* A party might gain a fresh right to elect to terminate the contract because the other party commits a fresh repudiation,[207] or because the guilty party's breach is continuous, such as a failure to pay money.[208] As Rix LJ said, also in the *Stocznia* case (2003):[209] 'If [the innocent party] maintains the contract in being for the moment, while reserving his right to treat it as repudiated if his contractual party persists in his repudiation, then he has not yet elected.'

17.42 *The decision to terminate for breach.* Lord Hope in *Geys v. Société Générale, London Branch* (2012) said that 'the requirement is for a real acceptance – a conscious intention to bring the contract to an end, or the doing of something that is inconsistent with its continuation'.[210] The innocent party's decision whether to affirm or terminate the contract requires no particular form. It can be manifested expressly or impliedly (see also 17.07).[211]

17.43 *A decision to terminate effected by conduct or silence.* But can such a decision be inferred from conduct or silence? The answers are: from conduct, certainly; from silence, occasionally, but only if the inference can be safely drawn from the relevant context.

Lord Steyn in the House of Lords in *Vitol SA v. Norelf Ltd* (1996) explained that *conduct* can be effective to communicate a decision to terminate the contract:

---

205 [2010] EWCA Civ 1051; [2011] ETLR 10, at [122].

206 Q. Liu, *Anticipatory Breach* (Oxford, 2011), 132 ff; *ibid.*, at 135 commenting: 'this "third option" has a dubious status in law. It is in fact an ephemeral, undefined and thus unreal option.'

207 *Yukong Line of Korea v. Rendsburg Investments Corporation of Liberia* [1996] 2 Lloyd's Rep 604, Moore-Bick J, proposition (5).

208 *Stocznia* case, [2002] EWCA Civ 889; [2002] 2 All ER (Comm) 768, at [96] to [100].

209 *Ibid.*, at [87].

210 [2012] UKSC 63; [2013] 1 AC 523, at [17].

211 *Vitol SA v. Norelf Ltd* ('The Santa Clara') [1996] AC 800, 810–11, HL, *per* Lord Steyn; *Yukong Line of Korea v. Rendsburg Investments Corporation of Liberia* [1996] 2 Lloyd's Rep 604, Moore-Bick J, proposition (7).

> An act of acceptance of a repudiation requires no particular form . . . It is sufficient that the communication or conduct clearly and unequivocally conveys to the repudiating party that that aggrieved party is treating the contract as at an end.[212]

Lord Steyn added that context might support an inference that a repudiatory breach or renunciation *has been accepted by the innocent party*, as where an employer wrongfully dismissed an employee, and the latter fails to reappear for work on the following day or indeed thereafter.[213] Lord Steyn's statement is concerned not with the innocent party's mental decision to 'call off the contract' but with the 'conveying' of that decision to the other party.

In *Ridgewood Properties Group Ltd* v. *Valero Energy Ltd* (2013)[214] Proudman J held that the innocent party had not (i) elected to terminate the contract but had decided to pursue the contract;[215] and (ii) in any event that party had not communicated acceptance of a repudiatory breach, nor could the guilty party be said to have inferred such acceptance on the basis of the innocent party's conduct.[216] The breach consisted of transfers of filling stations to third parties without reserving rights in favour of the claimant. The claimant held options to develop the sites. But the claimant's post-breach conduct did not disclose an intention to terminate for breach, no clear decision to terminate was established, and in fact the pointers were instead that the claimant had been still interested in pursuing the agreements.

Questions concerning the timing of an innocent party's acceptance of the other repudiation can arise (some light is shed on these issues in *Gisda Cyf* v. *Barratt* (2010),[217] although that decision is concerned directly with the statutory context of employment protection).[218]

17.44 *Termination for breach and rescission for misrepresentation etc. contrasted.* In essence a contract can be ended either because there is some initial defect in the consensus (it is 'vitiated') or because something occurs subsequent to formation which causes or justifies termination. In *Hurst* v. *Bryk* (2002), Lord Millett said that 'failure to distinguish between discharge for breach and rescission *ab initio* has led many courts astray and continues to do so'.[219] As noted by Lord Wilberforce in *Johnson* v. *Agnew* (1980), the word 'rescission' must be used only to describe the process of setting aside retrospectively a contract which is vitiated by reason of misrepresentation, or other grounds of initial invalidity:[220] '[I]t is now quite clear, under the general law of contract, that acceptance of a repudiatory breach does not bring about "rescission *ab initio*".'

(1) Initial vitiation produces rescission; but (2) subsequent events, whether frustration (16.01) or breach, give rise to termination. 'Rescission' (9.26 ff) involves the contract being dismantled with

---

212 *Vitol SA* v. *Norelf Ltd ('The Santa Clara')* [1996] AC 800, 810–11, *per* Lord Steyn, noted by S. Hedley, [1996] CLJ 430–2.
213 *Ibid.*, at 811, *per* Lord Steyn; similarly, *Force India Formula One Team Ltd* v. *Etihad Airways PJSC* [2010] EWCA Civ 1051; [2011] ETLR 10, at [112], *per* Rix LJ.
214 [2013] EWHC 98 (Ch); [2013] Ch 525.
215 *Ibid.*, at [84].
216 *Ibid.*, at [99] to [101].
217 [2010] UKSC 41; [2010] ICR 1475; [2010] 4 All ER 851.
218 Section 111 of the Employment Rights Act 1996.
219 [2002] 1 AC 185, 194, HL.
220 [1980] AC 367, 392–3, HL; applied in *Howard-Jones* v. *Tate* [2011] EWCA Civ 1330; [2012] 2 All ER 369; [2012] 1 All ER (Comm) 1136.

retroactive effect, with a mutual restoration of benefits. As for (2), such termination brings the contract to an end from that point in time, but only prospectively. It does not annihilate the contract retrospectively. This is, therefore, prospective termination or termination *in futuro* (see also 9.30 to 9.32).[221]

The 'prospective' operation of termination for breach accords with the (non-binding) *Principles of European Contract Law*, Article 9:305(1), and with UNIDROIT's *Principles of International Commercial Contracts* (2010), Article 7.3.5.[222]

17.45 Four things follow from the fact that termination for breach operates only to terminate the contract in a prospective manner.

(1) The innocent party retains the right to sue in respect of preceding breaches (in so far as these have not become statute-barred)[223] as well as holding the guilty party liable in damages for the harmful consequences of that termination.

(2) The guilty party remains liable for any unpaid sums which have 'accrued' before that date of termination, for example, a partner's liability to make contributions to partnership expenses[224] or liability to pay accrued instalments under contract for construction of a ship.[225]

(3) The innocent party's unpaid accrued sums (that is, debts or other liabilities which have become payable prior to the date of termination, but which were not paid by that date) will be set-off against the guilty party's total liabilities to pay damages, etc. If the innocent party's liabilities exceed the guilty party's liabilities, the latter can recover this balance.

(4) Furthermore, various ancillary obligations will continue to apply, notably: exclusion clauses (generally on these, 15.01);[226] liquidated damages clauses (generally on these, 19.01); choice of law clauses,[227] jurisdiction clauses,[228] mediation clauses,[229] arbitration

---

221 J. W. Carter, *Carter's Breach of Contract* (Oxford, 2012), 3.41, offers a convincing analysis of termination for breach: 'The contract is never terminated by a promisee's election to terminate. What is terminated is the duty of the parties to perform, and to be ready and willing to perform.' As modern case law makes clear (see next paragraph), various incidents of the contract survive 'termination', although not the primary duties to perform.

222 3rd edition, 2010, text and comment, is available at: www.unidroit.org/english/principles/contracts/principles2010/integralversionprinciples2010-e.pdf.

223 Principally, *Photo Production Ltd* v. *Securicor Transport Ltd* [1980] AC 827, 849, HL, *per* Lord Diplock; *Johnson* v. *Agnew* [1980] AC 367, 396, HL, Lord Wilberforce; *Bank of Boston Connecticut* v. *European Grain and Shipping Ltd* [1989] AC 1056, 1098–9, HL, *per* Lord Brandon; *Hurst* v. *Bryk* [2002] 1 AC 185, HL. On *Johnson* v. *Agnew* [1980] AC 367, HL, see the study by C. Mitchell, in C. Mitchell and P. Mitchell (eds.), *Landmark Cases in the Law of Contract* (Oxford, 2008), 351 ff.

224 *Hurst* v. *Bryk* [2002] 1 AC 185, HL, but the actual decision, that partnerships can be dissolved under Common Law principles of repudiatory breach, has been held to be unsound: Neuberger J in *Mullins* v. *Laughton* [2002] EWHC 2761 (Ch); [2003] Ch 250.

225 *Stocznia Gdanska SA* v. *Latvian SS Co.* [1998] 1 WLR 574, HL, noted J. Beatson and G.Tolhurst [1998] CLJ 253.

226 *Photo Production* case [1980] AC 827, HL.

227 This follows *a fortiori* from *Mackender* v. *Feldia AG* [1967] 2 QB 590, CA (rescission for non-disclosure under an insurance contract does not wipe out (i) a jurisdiction and (ii) a choice of law clause: especially, Diplock LJ at 603–4).

228 See *Mackender* case, preceding note; generally, *Port Jackson Stevedoring Pty* v. *Salmond & Spraggon (Australia) Pty* ('The New York Star') [1981] 1 WLR 138, 145, PC.

229 *Cable & Wireless plc* v. *IBM United Kingdom Ltd* [2002] 2 All ER (Comm) 1041, Colman J; *Sulamerica Cia Nacional de Seguros SA* v. *Enesa Engenharia SA* [2012] EWCA Civ 638; [2013] 1 WLR 102.

clauses;[230] (generally on the last four categories, see 12.07 ff); a consensual time bar;[231] a stipulation for a retainer in an agency contract;[232] and, finally, a clause allowing inspection of documents.[233]

> However, restrictive covenants (inserted into partnership or employment contracts) do not survive in favour of the guilty party[234] (this remains[235] the law although one judge had criticised this analysis).[236] Lord Wilson noted that this point is the subject of 'debate' in *Geys* v. *Société Générale* (2012).[237]
>
> The position concerning confidentiality clauses has been left open.[238]
>
> It should also be noted that, in an instalment contract, party A might repudiate only vis-à-vis a severable part of the contract, justifying termination by B of that part, but not justifying termination of the whole contract.[239]

8. THE ENTIRE OBLIGATION RULE

17.46 In contracts for services, or for goods and services, payment might be expressly or impliedly postponed until the job is completed. The entire obligation rule[240] will then prevent the contractor from becoming entitled to payment until conclusion of the job. For example, in contracts between householders and jobbing builders, the consumer normally postpones payment until the whole job is done (only a fool, although they exist, would pay a builder or decorator by the hour or by the day: but nearly all litigants are fools, because their lawyers are usually paid by the six-minute 'unit'). The entire obligation rule also reduces litigation, because it confers a self-help defensive remedy (a shield) upon the innocent party. The latter is spared the inconvenience, delay, expense and anxiety of seeking damages for the cost of curing a defective job in the courts.

---

230 *Heyman* v. *Darwins Ltd* [1942] AC 356, 374, HL.
231 *Port Jackson Stevedoring Pty* v. *Salmond & Spraggon (Australia) Pty*, 'The New York Star' [1981] 1 WLR 138, 145, PC, *per* Lord Wilberforce.
232 *Duffen* v. *FRA BO Spa (No. 2)* [2000] 1 Lloyd's Rep 180 (Judge Hallgarten QC, Central County Court, London).
233 *Yasuda Fire & Marine Insurance Co. of Europe Ltd* v. *Orion Marine Insurance Underwriting Agency Ltd* [1995] QB 174, Colman J.
234 *General Billposting Co. Ltd* v. *Atkinson* [1909] AC 118, HL (for Commonwealth cases, F. Dawson, (2013) 129 LQR 508–13).
235 *Group Lotus plc* v. *1Malaysia Racing Team SDN BHD* [2011] EWHC 1366 (Ch), at [364] to [371], *per* Peter Smith J.
236 *Campbell* v. *Frisbee* [2002] EWCA Civ 1374; [2003] ICR 141, at [22], *per* Lord Phillips.
237 [2012] UKSC 63; [2013] 1 AC 523, at [68].
238 [2002] EWCA Civ 1374; [2003] ICR 141, at [22].
239 *Friends Provident Life & Pensions Ltd* v. *Sirius International Insurance Corp.* [2005] EWCA Civ 601; [2005] 2 Lloyd's Rep 517, at [31].
240 B. McFarlane and R. Stevens, (2002) 118 LQR 569; J. W. Carter, *Carter's Breach of Contract* (Oxford, 2012), 6.84 to 6.93; G. H. Jones (with P. Schlechtriem), 'Breach of Contract', in *International Encyclopaedia of Comparative Law*, vol. VII, *Contracts in General* (Tübingen, 1999), 15–16 to 15–19 and 15–124 to 15–128.

17.47 *Mixed sets of contractual obligations.* Treitel[241] notes that the correct terminology is 'entire obligations' rather than 'entire contracts', giving this neat example:[242] 'A building contract may provide for payments as the work progresses, subject to a "retention fund" to be paid over on completion. There is then a series of severable obligations to complete each stage as well as an entire obligation to complete the whole.' In other words, the bonus payment (the retention fund) is dependent on complete performance of the whole, whereas the segmented payments[243] are triggered by completion of each phase. Once a particular obligation is characterised as 'entire', there is no scope for allowing substantial satisfaction of *that* obligation. But not all the obligations expressly or impliedly undertaken by a party may be entire. Thus the agreement might be 'entire' in requiring the job to be 'finished' but not entire as to the quality of the work or the time. However, the courts – no doubt reflecting the layman's need for more rough-and-ready language – approach the issue in terms of 'substantial performance' of the relevant obligation (or, 'substantial performance of the contract'), and do not characterise or 'split' a duty to perform into particular obligations of 'completion', 'quality' and 'timely execution'.[244]

17.48 In the typical case of a contract for work and materials, it will often be necessary for the job to be completed before payment is due. The notion of 'completion' is pliable. If the job is to replace a floor with new tiling, then even 95 per cent of the job will not constitute 'completion'. But if the contractor fits all the tiles, and a day later, some of these have 'lifted' because the job was done carelessly, the courts would probably regard this as 'completion', but subject to a reduction for the cost of cure. There are borderline instances where it can be disputed whether the failure is in the quantity or quality of performance:[245]

> Take a contract for a lump sum to decorate a house; the contract provides that there shall be three coats of oil paint, but in one of the rooms only two coats of paint are put on. Can anybody seriously say that ... the [innocent party] could ... take the benefit of all the [work] without paying a penny?

However, there will come a point at which unsatisfactory performance of an ostensibly 'completed' job will be regarded as 'no real job at all', so that the price will not be due (for example, see the facts of *Bolton* v. *Mahadeva* (1972): a heating system was installed but proved so defective, and indeed dangerous, that the Court of Appeal regarded it as an entirely bad job).[246]

241   *Treitel* (13th edn, London, 2011), at 17–037.
242   Ibid.
243   This is how the additional payments for each completed flat were structured in *Williams* v. *Roffey & Nicholls (Contractors) Ltd* [1991] 1 QB 1, CA; the Court of Appeal upheld Rupert Jackson QC's decision that there had been substantial performance of various flats under this renegotiated rate of payment before the subcontractor finally relinquished the overall job: ibid., at 9–10 and 19, *per* Glidewell LJ, and at 19, *per* Russell LJ.
244   E.g., *Bolton* v. *Mahadeva* [1972] 1 WLR 1010, 1013, CA, *per* Cairns LJ, 'substantial performance of the contract'; for similar usage, see the references in B. McFarlane and R. Stevens, 'In Defence of *Sumpter* v. *Hedges*' (2002) 118 LQR 569, 571 n. 12.
245   *H Dakin & Co. Ltd* v. *Lee* [1916] 1 KB 566, 579, CA, *per* Lord Cozens-Hardy MR.
246   [1972] 1 WLR 1010, CA.

17.49 At Common Law, it made no difference whether the failure to complete the contractual obligation involved breach or frustration.

> In *Cutter* v. *Powell* (1795),[247] P hired C as a second mate for a voyage from Jamaica to Liverpool at a rate significantly higher than the local rate. Before the ship had reached Liverpool, C died and his widow sued for wages. The claim failed because payment required completion of the trip, and it did not matter whether C had jumped ship, been killed on board or died of natural causes (see now the Law Reform (Frustrated Contracts) Act 1943 (16.21): 'just sum' in respect of the 'valuable benefit' conferred on the other party).

17.50 Sometimes, the contract creates divisible obligations, that is, where 'different parts of the consideration may be assigned to severable parts of the performance, for example, an agreement for payment *pro rata*'.[248]

17.51 The so-called 'substantial performance' doctrine might enable the performer to claim the agreed sum even if performance has not been perfect. Then the innocent party's protection is confined to a cross-claim or deduction in respect of defective performance.[249] But the doctrine of substantial performance will not apply if the failure to perform is significant:[250] this depends on questions of proportionality, reasonableness and fairness.[251] The doctrine is traceable to the eighteenth century.[252] The three leading[253] modern decisions are *Sumpter* v. *Hedges* (1898),[254] *Bolton* v. *Mahadeva* (1972)[255] and *Hoenig* v. *Isaacs* (1952)[256] (these cases will be examined in that order because substantial performance occurred only in the third of these cases).

17.52 In *Sumpter* v. *Hedges* (1898) a builder agreed to construct two houses for the defendant at a price of £565.[257] He performed £333 worth of this, but was forced to abandon the job because of lack of funds. The innocent party had already paid £219 (made up of £119 cash and two horses worth £100). The Court of Appeal held that the innocent party was not liable to pay the rest of the lump sum, because this obligation arose only on completion of the work. A claim for a *quantum meruit* (a restitutionary claim for the value of the services and goods used) also failed because the builder's partial work (the partly finished building) had

---

247 *Cutter* v. *Powell* (1795) 6 Term Rep 320; 101 ER 573; M. Dockray, (2001) 117 LQR 664.
248 *Chitty on Contracts* (31st edn, London, 2012), 21–028.
249 *Hoenig* v. *Isaacs* [1952] 2 All ER 176, CA (discussed 17.56).
250 *Sumpter* v. *Hedges* [1898] 1 QB 673 (17.54).
251 As mentioned in *Bolton* v. *Mahadeva* [1972] 1 WLR 1010, CA (17.55).
252 *Boone* v. *Eyre* (1779) 1 Hy Bl 273n (summarised in the notes to *Cutter* v. *Powell* (1795) 6 Term Rep 320; *Smith's Leading Cases* (13th edn, 1929); Lord Denning MR in '*The Hansa Nord*' [1976] 1 QB 44, 60, CA).
253 Other modern decisions: *Vigers* v. *Cook* [1919] 2 KB 475, 482, CA; *Williams* v. *Roffey & Nicholls (Contractors) Ltd* [1991] 1 QB 1, 17, CA; *Pilbrow* v. *Pearless de Rougemont & Co.* [1993] 3 All ER 355, 361B, 360, CA; *Systech International Ltd* v. *PC Harrington Contractors Ltd* [2012] EWCA Civ 1371; [2013] 2 All ER 69, at [17], [31], [32] (adjudicator in construction dispute not entitled to fee if his decision is unenforceable).
254 [1898] 1 QB 673, CA.
255 [1972] 1 WLR 1010, CA.
256 [1952] 2 All ER 176, CA.
257 [1898] 1 QB 673, CA.

acceded to the defendant's land (as where bricks and mortar now form a wall), and so the latter had not impliedly assumed a liability to pay a reasonable value for this partial performance (or become, to use the modern analysis, liable under restitutionary principles). However, the defendant was liable to pay for loose materials left on site because these materials had not acceded to his land, but had been knowingly appropriated by the defendant.

17.53 In *Bolton* v. *Mahadeva* (1972), the claimant had agreed to fit a heating and domestic hot-water system for £560.[258] After the job was 'done', the defendant refused to pay, because the heating system produced 10 per cent less warmth than required, and it also emitted fumes.[259] The Court of Appeal held that the defendant's duty to pay the lump sum had not arisen on these facts. The level of defective performance was high. Sachs LJ considered that the work had not merely been 'shoddy': it had failed to achieve 'its primary purpose' because the level of heating was inadequate and the appliance emitted fumes.[260] In short, the issue is whether A's degree of inadequate performance or non-performance has deprived B of substantially the whole of the benefit for which B had stipulated and on which B's duty to pay is dependent.[261]

17.54 On the other side of the line, in *Hoenig* v. *Isaacs* (1952), the claimant agreed to redecorate and furnish the defendant's flat for £750.[262] The breach consisted of minor defects in the furniture provided by the claimant. But these could be rectified for £55. The Court of Appeal held that the claimant had a good claim for the price, subject to a deduction under a cross-claim of £55 in respect of the defective performance. In short, the job had been done in *Hoenig* and the defects were relatively minor imperfections.

17.55 The courts during the twentieth century showed a disinclination to find that there has been a failure to satisfy an entire obligation in a contract involving materials and services or work: *H Dakin & Co. Ltd* v. *Lee* (1916),[263] *Hoenig* v. *Isaacs* (1952),[264] and *Williams* v. *Roffey & Nicholls (Contractors) Ltd* (1991).[265] And Denning LJ in the *Hoenig* case went further,[266] expressing a disinclination to construe a contract as entire just because the contract is structured so that the price is withheld until the 'end' of the job. Of the cases going the other way, *Bolton* v. *Mahadeva* (1972)[267] might be explained as a salutary exception to this trend, for there the work was quite seriously bad, indeed dangerous, and the contractor had shrugged his shoulders when asked to come and fix the defective work; there was a

---

258 [1972] 1 WLR 1009, CA.
259 *Ibid.*, at 1013F.
260 *Ibid.*, at 1015F.
261 G. H. Jones (with P. Schlechtriem), 'Breach of Contract', in *International Encyclopaedia of Comparative Law*, vol. VII, *Contracts in General* (Tübingen, 1999), 15–19, noting Australian criticism.
262 [1952] 2 All ER 176, CA.
263 [1916] 1 KB 566, CA (upholding Ridley and Sankey JJ, Divisional Court, but reversing the Official Referee).
264 [1952] 2 All ER 176, 182, CA.
265 [1991] 1 QB 1, CA (at 9–10 and 19, Glidewell and Russell LJJ applied the *Hoenig* case; Purchas LJ did not address this point).
266 [1952] 2 All ER 176, at 180–1, CA.
267 [1972] 1 WLR 1009, CA.

suggestion of a law firm 'trying to pull a fast one' in *Pilbrow* v. *Pearless de Rougemont & Co.* (1993);[268] and the especially ghoulish failure by the undertaker in the *Vigers* case (1919) to satisfy a crucial element of the contemplated performance (the capacity to take the coffin into the church for the funeral service) justifiably disentitled that party from claiming its fee.[269] *Wiluszynski* v. *Tower Hamlets LBC* (1989)[270] shows that an employee cannot claim wages or salary if his employer has made clear that his proposed or continuing partial or defective performance, if intentionally persisted in, will not qualify the employee for payment.

17.56 Some commentators consider that the entire obligation rule can operate harshly where a party is indubitably in breach (the 1943 Act now deals with the problem of frustration) and he has conferred a large non-returnable benefit on the innocent party,[271] and the latter has not voluntarily accepted the benefit. For this reason, the Law Commission had proposed that supposed victims of the present doctrine should be given a statutory claim for the benefit of the work conferred in this situation.[272] However Brian Davenport QC, as Law Commissioner, added a timely note of dissent:

> Experience has shown that it is all too common for . . . builders not to complete one job . . . before moving on to the next . . . [The recommendations for 'reform' would] remove from the householder almost the only effective sanction he has . . . [because it would prevent him] from saying 'unless you come back I shan't pay you a penny'.

These cogent remarks induced Lord Hailsham LC to withhold legislative support for the proposal,[273] a position attractively supported by McFarlane and Stevens.[274]

QUESTIONS

(1) What is a breach of contract?
(2) What are the two types of anticipatory breach?
(3) What is 'renunciation', and what is a 'repudiatory breach'?
(4) What are the three types of promissory term?
(5) When is an innocent party entitled to terminate the contract for breach?
(6) Does it matter if a party fails to perform, or states that performance will be withheld, believing in good faith but mistakenly that the contract is consistent with this?
(7) How does one determine whether a term is a 'condition'?
(8) What is the effect of a clause providing that a party can terminate for 'any breach' committed by the other party?

---

268 [1993] 3 All ER 355; [1999] 2 Costs LR 109, CA.
269 *Vigers* v. *Cook* [1919] 2 KB 475, Divisional Court and CA.
270 [1989] ICR 493, 503, CA; G. Mead (1991) 11 LS 172; B. McFarlane and R. Stevens, 'In Defence of *Sumpter* v. *Hedges*' (2002) 118 LQR 569, 590–1.
271 This opinion is 'almost uniform' among 'leading unjust enrichment scholars', according to B. McFarlane and R. Stevens, 'In Defence of *Sumpter* v. *Hedges*' (2002) 118 LQR 569 at n. 6 listing the extensive literature.
272 Law Commission, 'Law of Contract; Pecuniary Restitution on Breach of Contract' (Law Commission No. 121, 1983); considered in detail by A. Burrows (1984) 47 MLR 76.
273 Law Commission, *ibid.* at 36–7, Brian Davenport QC; for the final rejection Law Commission, 19th Annual Report (1983–4), see 2.11.
274 B. McFarlane and R. Stevens, 'In Defence of *Sumpter* v. *Hedges*' (2002) 118 LQR 569, 572–82.

(9) When does breach of an intermediate or innominate term entitle the innocent party to terminate the contract?

(10) Why was it arguable that intermediate or innominate terms do not apply to sale of goods transactions?

(11) To what extent is a buyer's right to reject goods on the basis of technical breach controlled by section 15A of the Sale of Goods Act 1979?

(12) Faced by an opportunity to terminate for breach, what are the innocent party's choices?

(13) How is termination for breach carried out by the innocent party?

(14) Distinguish termination for breach and rescission for misrepresentation, duress, undue influence, etc.

(15) Distinguish breach and a party's capacity to withhold performance if the other party has not satisfied his counter-obligation.

Selected further reading

Breach

Specialist works

J. Birds, R. Bradgate, C. Villiers, *Termination of Contracts* (Chichester, 1995), chapters 1, 2, 10

J. W. Carter, *Carter's Breach of Contract* (Oxford, 2012) (reviewed N. Andrews [2013] CLJ 214–17)

M. A. Clarke, N. Andrews, A. M. Tettenborn, G. Virgo, *Contractual Duties: Performance, Breach, Termination and Remedies* (London, 2012) (breach and performance section by N. Andrews)

Q. Liu, *Anticipatory Breach* (Oxford, 2011)

M. J. Mustill, 'Anticipatory Breach: The Common Law at Work', *Butterworths Lectures 1989–90* (1990)

J. E. Stannard, *Delay in the Performance of Contractual Obligations* (Oxford, 2007)

J. E. Stannard and D. Capper, *Termination for Breach of Contract* (Oxford, 2014)

Journal discussion

R. Brownsword, 'Retrieving Reasons, Retrieving Rationality: a New Look at the Right to Withdraw for Breach of Contract' (1992) 5 JCL 83

J. W. Carter, 'Discharge as the Basis for Termination for Breach of Contract' (2012) 128 LQR 283–302

J. Randall, 'Express Termination Clauses' [2014] CLJ 113–41

S. Whittaker, 'Termination Clauses', in A. S. Burrows and E. Peel (eds.), *Contract Terms* (Oxford, 2007), chapter 13 (discussion of many related decisions concerning 'material breach' and similar contract drafting)

Entire obligation rule

M. Dockray, '*Cutter* v. *Powell*: A Trip Outside the Text' (2001) 117 LQR 664

B. McFarlane and R. Stevens, 'In Defence of *Sumpter* v. *Hedges*' (2002) 118 LQR 569, 572–86, 594 to end

Law Commission: 'Pecuniary Restitution on Breach of Contract' (Law Commission No. 121, 1983), 36–7

VIII

Remedies for breach

Chapter contents

18

Judicial remedies for breach of contract

1. INTRODUCTION

18.01 Summary of main points

Judicial remedies for breach. The main[1] judicial (on agreed remedies, see Chapter 19) remedies for breach of contract are listed in this paragraph and examined in detail in the remainder of the chapter. Of these remedies, debt is the main workhorse; damages is the next most important. Equity (1.25) can provide coercive orders of specific performance or injunctions, but in English law these heavily sanctioned remedies (see 18.33 on contempt of court sanctions where the order is disobeyed) are relatively minor instruments. Instead of these 'specific' remedies, therefore, the main work in remedying breach of contract is shared by the money remedies, debt and damages. Of course, it is more efficient, cheaper and quicker if the innocent party can invoke a self-help remedy or at least refer to an agreed remedial provision: see Chapter 19 for discussion of 'consensual' and hence non-judicial remedies of deposits, a form of self-help, and liquidated damages (damages having been fixed in advance by the parties).

(1) *The action for debt.* This is the most common remedy of all. The main controversy (18.03) is whether a party who has yet to complete performance can legitimately complete that task and earn the right to sue the other party for debt (the so-called 'agreed sum'), when the latter has attempted to call off the job (an unaccepted repudiation, also known as an attempted anticipatory breach: see the section on breach at 17.37).

(2) *Compensatory damages.* This is the claim to make good loss. The cumulative requirements are:[2] (a) the loss should be causally connected to the breach (18.15); (b) the loss must not be too remote (18.16); (c) the claimant must not have failed to mitigate loss (18.22) (contributory negligence, allowing damages to be reduced on a percentage basis, is not a general defence, but applies only if there has been on the facts both a breach of contract and a concurrent failure in tort to exercise due care: 18.23). The main aim of compensatory damages for breach of contract is

---

1 The minor remedies of declarations or 'stays upon legal proceedings' are noted at 18.32 and 18.39. For a general survey, S. Waddams, *Principle and Policy in Contract Law: Competing or Complementary Concepts?* (Cambridge, 2011), chapter 7.

2 A. Burrows, 'Limitations on Compensation', in A. S. Burrows and E. Peel (eds.), *Commercial Remedies: Current Issues and Problems* (Oxford, 2003), 27.

to place the innocent party in the position she would have been in if the contract had been properly performed; the so-called 'expectation' or 'loss of bargain' measure (18.08). But if loss of profit is too hard to prove, a 'fall-back' type of damages is to restore the claimant monetarily to the position she enjoyed before the contract was breached; the so-called 'reliance loss' measure (18.08 and 18.09).

(3) *Restitutionary claims: money awards to reverse the defendant's unjust enrichment.* Such claims (18.26) comprise:

(a) recompense for goods supplied or services rendered;

(b) recovery of payments based on failure of consideration;

(c) profit-stripping claim based on equitable remedy of account.

Only (c) requires proof of a breach of contract. By contrast (a) and (b) arise without the need to show any breach of contract. Indeed, it is often necessary to invoke categories (a) and (b) precisely because no contract has arisen, or it was invalid at its inception. And categories (a) and (b) are available only if no valid contract governs the parties' relations.

(4) *Interest on money claims.* The court has these powers to award interest:

(i) 'when giving judgment on the principal sum' (for damages or debt), the court can award *simple* interest under section 35A of the Senior Courts Act 1981;

(ii) *simple* interest can also be awarded where the principal sum was (fully) paid only after commencement of formal proceedings but before judgment was obtained (section 35A of the Senior Courts Act 1981); and

(iii) *Sempra Metals Ltd* v. *Inland Revenue Commissioners* (2007)[3] decides that *simple and compound*[4] interest can be awarded at Common Law for breaches of contract,[5] provided the contractual remoteness test is satisfied;[6]

(iv) even where no proceedings were commenced with respect to the principal sum, the Late Payment of Commercial Debts (Interest) Act 1998 (as amended)[7] confers a right to simple interest (at a specified level) on the unpaid price of goods or services if the supplier and recipient are both acting in the course of business (section 2).[8]

(5) *Specific performance.* This remedy is narrow in scope in England. It is an 'equitable remedy' (on Equity, see 1.25). Specific performance is seldom encountered outside its heartland – contracts for the sale or exchange of interests in land (18.33). There can be no specific performance of contracts for personal services (18.33), nor against a company to require it to 'run a business'

---

3 [2007] UKHL 34; [2008] 1 AC 561, at [94] to [100], *per* Lord Nicholls; at [16], *per* Lord Hope; at [164] and [165], *per* Lord Walker; at [226], *per* Lord Mance; at [140], *per* Lord Scott; noted by G. Virgo, [2007] CLJ 510; C. Nicholls, (2008) 124 LQR 199; *McGregor on Damages* (19th edn, London, 2014), chapter 18; and, for fuller discussion, see P. Ridge, 'Pre-Judgment Compound Interest' (2010) 126 LQR 279–301; the *Sempra* case was considered in *Parabola Investments Ltd* v. *Browallia Cal Ltd* [2010] EWCA Civ 486 at [51] ff: also on that case see 9.13. The *Sempra* decision renders otiose recommendations made by Law Commission, 'Pre-Judgment Interest on Debts and Damages' (Law Commission Report No. 287, London, 2004); earlier, Law Commission, 'Compound Interest' (Law Commission Consultation Paper No. 167, London, 2002).

4 Also available in arbitral proceedings: section 49(3) of the Arbitration Act 1996.

5 [2007] UKHL 34; [2008] 1 AC 561, at [216], *per* Lord Mance, on the relevance of remoteness.

6 *Ibid.*, at [216], *per* Lord Mance, on the relevance of remoteness.

7 Late Payment of Commercial Debts Regulations 2002 (SI 2002 No. 1674); Late Payment of Commercial Debts Regulations 2013 (SI 2013 No. 395); Late Payment of Commercial Debts (No. 2) Regulations 2013 (SI 2013 No. 908); *Martrade Shipping & Transport GmbH* v. *United Enterprises Corpn* [2014] EWHC 1884 (Comm); [2015] 1 WLR 1 (section 12(1) of 1998 Act renders that statute inapplicable where main transaction has no 'significant connection' with the UK).

8 As for the dates when interest becomes payable, sections 4(3) and (4) of the Late Payment of Commercial Debts (Interest) Act 1998.

(18.34). Contracts to transfer movable property are remedied by damages awards, unless the subject matter is 'unique' or very nearly so (18.35). Specific performance ensures compliance with promises. But this remedy is heavy-handed and coercive, requiring the defendant positively to act. It has the further disadvantage of running counter to the concern that the innocent party should take steps to mitigate his loss by quickly entering the market for satisfaction from an alternative source.

(6) *Injunction.* As just mentioned, specific performance is a mandatory injunction requiring performance of a positive obligation; other injunctions can be awarded to stop a party from breaching a negative obligation (a promise not to do something); but no such injunction will be granted if its indirect effect will be to coerce a person into performing a contract for personal services (18.38).

2. DEBT CLAIMS

18.02 Debt[9] is the most important remedy because most claims for contractual default are attempts to obtain payment of specified sums (price, hire charges, insurance premium, rent, etc.).

> Debt claims are Common Law actions. Judgment in favour of the creditor leads to enforcement against the defendant's assets.[10] Exceptionally, however, in *Beswick v. Beswick* (1968),[11] a 'money remedy' was supported by an injunctive order, and hence ultimately sanctioned by contempt of court. In this case, the debtor had agreed to pay periodic sums to the promisee's wife, a third party. The promisee's estate successfully claimed that the debtor should be compelled, by order of specific performance, to continue paying periodical sums to this third party.

One of the rules within the so-called 'penalty doctrine' (19.16) is that a debtor cannot be required to pay a sum exceeding the principal and interest owed (on recovery of interest, see 18.01 at (4) above).

18.03 A problematic aspect of contract law concerns the remedy for 'debt' and the principles of repudiatory breach. An innocent party has an 'election'[12] – a choice – whether to 'accept' the repudiation or to 'affirm' the contract, as noted by the Supreme Court in *Geys v. Société Générale, London Branch* (2012).[13]

---

9 A. M. Tettenborn, in M. A. Clarke, N. Andrews, A. M. Tettenborn, G. Virgo, *Contractual Duties: Performance, Breach, Termination and Remedies* (London, 2012), chapter 19.
10 On the methods of enforcing money judgments, *Andrews on Civil Processes* (Cambridge, 2013), vol. 1, *Court Proceedings*, 17.05.
11 [1968] AC 58, HL.
12 On the subtleties of this analysis, J. W. Carter, 'Discharge as the Basis for Termination for Breach of Contract' (2012) 128 LQR 283–302.
13 [2012] UKSC 63; [2013] 1 AC 523.

The exercise of this choice was examined by the House of Lords in *White & Carter v. McGregor* (1962).[14] The majority decision (Lords Reid, Hodson and Tucker) was that, in general, the party interested in performing can do so even though the other party had declared that he no longer wanted or needed the relevant performance. On the facts of this case the 'pursuer' (a claimant in Scots legal terminology) sought payment of the price agreed for its advertising services. The 'defender' (a Scots defendant) had ordered these services but immediately tried to cancel the contract. It was held that the pursuer was not bound to 'accept', that is, acquiesce in, this proposed cancellation. Instead, the pursuer could legitimately complete performance and claim in debt for the agreed payment.[15] An unusual feature of this situation was that the innocent party could complete his performance without any cooperation from the other party.

It is now clear that there are two restrictions upon the innocent party's opportunity to take advantage of the 'debt rule':[16] (1) the claimant cannot succeed in suing for debt if his performance requires the other party's cooperation; and (2) the claimant must show a 'legitimate interest' in pursuing his unwanted performance. The second requirement will be applied quite generously in favour of the innocent party (but this approach is criticised at 18.06).

However, the two dissentients in *White & Carter* v. *McGregor* (1962) (Lords Morton and Keith) considered this claim for debt to be highly inefficient, unmeritorious and in conflict with the economic goal of encouraging innocent parties to restrict their losses by 'mitigating' (generally on this doctrine, see 18.22). But the technical response to this dissenting argument is that the mitigation doctrine is confined to claims for damages, and that the claimant is here asserting a right to a debt. Debt and damages are subject to different regimes:[17] the mitigation doctrine does not apply to debt claims.

Reichman v. *Beveridge* (2006)[18] confirms that a landlord is under no obligation to mitigate by accepting a business tenant's attempted renunciation (furthermore, the landlord lacks a right to compensation in respect of future loss of rent).[19]

---

14 [1962] AC 413, HL; A. S. Burrows, *Remedies for Torts and Breach of Contract* (3rd edn, Oxford, 2004), 435–44 (citing US material at 437); J. W. Carter, A. Phang and S. Phang, (1999) 15 JCL 97; A. Tettenborn and D. Wilby, *The Law of Damages* (2nd edn, London, 2010), 5.65 ff.; K. Scott, [1962] CLJ 12; P. M. Nienaber, [1962] CLJ 213; A. L. Goodhart, (1962) 78 LQR 263; M. Furmston, (1962) 25 MLR 364; Tabachnik, [1972] CLP 149; Priestley J, (1991) 3 JCL 218; for references to US and Canadian materials or case law, see *Anson's Law of Contract* (29th edn, Oxford, 2010), 575 n. 21 (US law, which differs from English law on this topic, was cited in *Clea Shipping Corporation* v. *Bulk Oil International ('The Alaskan Trader')* [1984] 1 All ER 129, 137, *per* Lloyd J); see also Q. Liu, *Anticipatory Breach* (Oxford, 2011) (drawing on Q. Liu, 'The *White & Carter* Principle: A Restatement' (2011) MLR 171; and see other literature by Liu cited at 17.13 of this book).
15 In fact, the pursuer part-performed and the defender failed to pay the relevant instalment. An acceleration clause (19.18) rendered the defendant liable for all the instalments in the event of non-payment of one instalment.
16 A. S. Burrows, *Remedies for Torts and Breach of Contract* (3rd edn, Oxford, 2004), 433–40.
17 On the differences between debt and damages, Millett LJ in *Jervis* v. *Harris* [1996] Ch 195, 202–3, CA.
18 [2006] EWCA Civ 1659; [2007] 1 P & CR 20; [2007] L & TR 18 (critically noted by M. Pawlowski, (2010) 126 MLR 361–5 on the proposition that a landlord cannot recover damages for loss of future rent).
19 *Ibid.*, at [18].

18.04 *The 'cooperation' qualification.* The leading discussion of this topic is Cooke J's survey in *Isabella Shipowner SA* v. *Shagang Shipping Co. Ltd ('The Aquafaith')* (2012)[20] Cooke J, drawing upon *Ministry of Sound (Ireland)* v. *World Online Ltd* (2003)[21] (see text below).

In *Hounslow London Borough Council* v. *Twickenham Garden Developments Ltd* (1971), Megarry J held that a builder could not perform once the owner of the site had ordered him to stop work. It would be going too far to require the owner to allow the builder access to the site.[22]

In *Ministry of Sound (Ireland)* v. *World Online Ltd* (2003)[23] Nicholas Strauss QC (Deputy High Court judge) held that a packaging company had a prima facie valid claim for the last instalment under a two-year contract requiring it to give publicity to the defendant's CDs because the defendant could not factually obstruct the substance of the claimant's performance. He also found a 'legitimate interest' (18.05 case (3), below).

In *Isabella Shipowner SA* v. *Shagang Shipping Co. Ltd ('The Aquafaith')* (2012)[24] Cooke J made clear that the owner's provision of a vessel under a time charterparty does not involve the charterer's cooperation. If the vessel is made available for the charterer's use, but the latter chooses not to issue orders to the ship's master, the owner is entitled to claim hire: 'In order to complete their side of the bargain, the owners do not need the charterers to do anything in order for them to earn the hire in question.'[25] Hire is payable in advance and so the owner 'can hold the ship available to the charterer without any need for the charterer to do anything in order to maintain [the owner's] claim for hire'. It is different if the hire takes the form of a demise charterparty: 'The very essence of the demise charter is that possession of the vessel is given to the demise charterer so that, as soon as possession is retaken by the owner, the latter can no longer be entitled to hire under the demise charter.'[26]

Lord Sumption in *Geys* v. *Société Générale* (2012)[27] acknowledged the cooperation restriction upon the innocent party's capacity to keep open the contract. However, the majority in that case did not accept Lord Sumption's suggestion[28] that the innocent party has no right of election unless the guilty party's obligations are specifically enforceable.[29]

---

20 [2012] EWHC 1077 (Comm); [2012] 2 All ER (Comm) 461; [2012] 2 Lloyd's Rep 61, at [37]; see also *Barclays Bank plc* v. *Unicredit Bank AG* [2012] EWHC 3655 (Comm); [2012] EWHC 3655 (Comm); [2013] 2 Lloyd's Rep 1; [2014] 1 BCLC 342, at [105].

21 [2003] EWHC 2178; [2003] 2 All ER (Comm) 823; on this decision, Q. Liu, *Anticipatory Breach* (Oxford, 2011), 204 ff.

22 [1971] Ch 233, 253–4.

23 [2003] EWHC 2178; [2003] 2 All ER (Comm) 823; on this decision, Q. Liu, *Anticipatory Breach* (Oxford, 2011), 204 ff.

24 [2012] EWHC 1077 (Comm); [2012] 2 All ER (Comm) 461; [2012] 2 Lloyd's Rep 61, at [37]; see also *Barclays Bank plc* v. *Unicredit Bank AG* [2012] EWHC 3655 (Comm); [2012] EWHC 3655 (Comm); [2013] 2 Lloyd's Rep 1; [2014] 1 BCLC 342, at [105].

25 *Ibid.*

26 *Ibid.*, at [40].

27 [2012] UKSC 63; [2013] 1 AC 523, at [115] and [116] (Lord Sumption dissenting on a narrower issue, but not on this point of principle); case noted D. Cabrelli and R. Zahn, (2013) 76 MLR 1106–19; and L. Aitken, (2013) 129 LQR 335–7).

28 *Ibid.*, at [116].

29 *Ibid.*, at [89], *per* Lord Wilson, adopting K. Ewing's article, 'Remedies for Breach of the Contract of Employment' [1993] CLJ 405, 410–11: '[Why should it be that] the contract is automatically terminated by the unilateral repudiation of either party, simply because it is not capable of specific performance. As such the argument is hopelessly circular.'

18.05 *Innocent party lacking a 'legitimate interest'*. As the Court of Appeal in *Reichman* v. *Beveridge* (2006) noted,[30] explaining the genesis of this second requirement, only Lord Reid in *White & Carter* v. *McGregor* (1962)[31] had ventured this idea, 'neither Lord Hodson nor Lord Tucker [the other members of the majority] alluded to such a possibility'. For this reason, the Supreme Court could yet decide that the law should be wholly remoulded (18.06). In the *White & Carter* case (1962), Lord Reid said:

> It may well be that, if it can be shown that a person has no legitimate interest, financial or otherwise, in performing the contract rather than claiming damages, he ought not to be allowed to saddle the other party with an additional burden with no benefit to himself ... And just as a party is not allowed to enforce a penalty, so he ought not to be allowed to penalise the other party by taking one course when another is equally advantageous to him.

But (echoing Kerr J in 1974)[32] Simon J in *'The Dynamic'* (2003) said that this restriction applies only (i) in extreme cases, 'where damages would be an adequate remedy and where an election to keep the contract alive would be unreasonable'; (ii) that the 'burden is on the contract-breaker to show that the innocent party has no legitimate interest'; and (iii) it is not enough to show 'that the benefit to the [innocent party] is small in comparison to the loss to the contract breaker'.[33] And Cooke J in *Isabella Shipowner SA* v. *Shagang Shipping Co. Ltd* *('The Aquafaith')* (2012)[34] formulated element (i) as follows: 'an innocent party will have no legitimate interest in maintaining the contract if damages are an adequate remedy and his insistence on maintaining the contract can be described as "wholly unreasonable", "extremely unreasonable" or, perhaps, in my words, "perverse".' In short, the innocent party's attempt to keep the contract alive must be a decision which is 'beyond the pale'.[35]

As we shall see, only one reported case has turned on proof that the creditor lacked a 'legitimate interest' (case (6) below).

'Performer enjoying a legitimate interest'

(1) In *'The Odenfeld'* (1978),[36] Kerr J held that a shipowner did have a 'legitimate interest' in maintaining the vessel on hire to the charterer until September 1976.[37] Simon J in *'The Dynamic'* (2003) decided a similar charterparty case in the same way.[38] Similarly, *Isabella Shipowner SA* v. *Shagang Shipping Co. Ltd ('The Aquafaith')* (2012) Cooke J held[39]

---

30 [2006] EWCA Civ 1659; [2007] 1 P & CR 20; [2007] L & TR 18, at [14] (and at [15] summarising the case law).
31 [1962] AC 413, 431, HL.
32 *Gator Shipping Corporation* v. *Trans-Asiatic Oil Ltd SA and Occidental Shipping Establishment ('The Odenfeld')* [1978] 2 Lloyd's Rep 357, 374, Kerr J.
33 *Ocean Marine Navigation Ltd* v. *Koch Carbon Inc. ('The Dynamic')* [2003] EWHC 1936; [2003] 2 Lloyd's Rep 693, at [23], *per* Simon J.
34 [2012] EWHC 1077 (Comm); [2012] 2 All ER (Comm) 461; [2012] 2 Lloyd's Rep 61, at [44].
35 *Ibid.,* at [49].
36 *Gator Shipping Corporation* v. *Trans-Asiatic Oil Ltd SA and Occidental Shipping Establishment ('The Odenfeld')* [1978] 2 Lloyd's Rep 357, 373, Kerr J.
37 *Ibid.,* at 374.
38 *Ocean Marine Navigation Ltd* v. *Koch Carbon Inc. ('The Dynamic')* [2003] EWHC 1936; [2003] 2 Lloyd's Rep 693, at [23], *per* Simon J.
39 [2012] EWHC 1077 (Comm); [2012] 2 All ER (Comm) 461; [2012] 2 Lloyd's Rep 61, at [56].

(reversing the arbitrator)[40] that there was nothing exceptional or wholly unreasonable in an owner maintaining a time-chartered vessel at the other party's expense when the latter had tried to return it 94 days early. (But contrast case (6) below for a time charterparty kept alive by an owner, but where no legitimate interest was identified.)

(2) In *Barclays Bank plc* v. *Unicredit Bank AG* (2012) Popplewell J held that a bank was entitled to claim charges for providing a facility even when the commercial party had sought to cancel the arrangement.[41]

(3) In *Ministry of Sound (Ireland)* v. *World Online Ltd* (2003),[42] Nicholas Strauss QC, sitting as a Deputy High Court Judge, held that the claimant had a legitimate interest in continuing to provide publicity for the defendant[43] (the facts are analogous to the unwanted advertising in the *White & Carter* case, 18.03).

(4) In *Reichman* v. *Beveridge* (2006)[44] the Court of Appeal confirmed that a landlord is entitled to make periodic demands (an action in debt) in respect of rent accruing during the residue of a business tenancy (the case is analogous to the cases at (1) and (2) concerning hire from charterparties). Most business tenancies will involve 'quarterly' rent obligations (payment every three months).

The 'no legitimate interest' cases

There is hardly anything on the other side of the 'legitimate interest' ledger.

(5) Dicta (but no binding decision) in *Attica Sea Carriers Corporation* v. *Ferrostaal Poseidon Bulk Reederei GmbH ('The Puerto Buitrago')* (1976)[45] suggest that it would be illegitimate, because disproportionate, for a shipowner to have insisted on charging for repairs (US$2m) at the end of a charter exceeding the ship's value (US$1m).[46] This discussion was defended by Cooke J in *Isabella Shipowner SA* v. *Shagang Shipping Co. Ltd ('The Aquafaith')* (2012) on the basis that it was a demise charterparty (requiring the charterer's cooperation)[47] and that the owner's proposed repairs would be 'an exercise in futility'.[48]

(6) Lloyd J in *Clea Shipping Corporation* v. *Bulk Oil International ('The Alaskan Trader')* (1984),[49] upheld, but without enthusiasm, the arbitrator's decision that a shipowner was not entitled to keep a two year time-chartered vessel on hire, with full crew, for eight months and to charge this to the charterer (contrast cases (1) and (2) above). *'The Alaskan Trader'* was rationalised by Cooke J in *Isabella Shipowner SA* v. *Shagang Shipping Co. Ltd ('The Aquafaith')* (2012) as resting on Lloyd J's recognition that an experienced arbitrator had

---

40 *Ibid.*, at [51] and [52]: 'a finding of no legitimate interest [on the present facts] is not simply a finding of fact with which this court cannot interfere. It is a conclusion based upon a misunderstanding of the test, a failure to take into account relevant factors and the taking into account of irrelevant matters.'
41 *Barclays Bank plc* v. *Unicredit Bank AG* [2012] EWHC 3655 (Comm); [2012] EWHC 3655 (Comm); [2013] 2 Lloyd's Rep 1; [2014] 1 BCLC 342, at [110] and [111].
42 [2003] EWHC 2178; [2003] 2 All ER (Comm) 823.
43 *Ibid.*, at [64] to [66].
44 [2006] EWCA Civ 1659; [2007] 1 P & CR 20; [2007] L & TR 18.
45 [1976] 1 Lloyd's Rep 250, CA.
46 *Ibid.*, at 255.
47 [2012] EWHC 1077 (Comm); [2012] 2 All ER (Comm) 461; [2012] 2 Lloyd's Rep 61, at [40].
48 *Ibid.*, at [44].
49 [1984] 1 All ER 129, 136–7, Lloyd J.

applied the correct test and that the owner's bold claim in *'The Alaskan Trader'* to be entitled to keep a vessel on hire for eight dormant months was a 'commercial absurdity'.[50]

18.06 *Assessment of the 'legitimate interest' criterion.* Other systems have refused to follow the lead of English (and Scots) law in making this distinction in the reach of mitigation between debt and damages claims[51] (see, notably, Carter's examination of the position adopted in the USA).[52] Furthermore, the Scottish Law Commission has recommended reform.[53]

It is submitted that the starting point should be reversed: that the normal rule should be that once a party has announced that it is no longer interested in remaining party to the contract, the other party should be confined to damages (assuming these are available and adequate). More precisely, the innocent party should only be allowed to maintain the contract and sue eventually in debt, despite the other party's attempted cancellation, if:

(i) damages would be (a) inadequate or (b) unavailable (for example, as in commercial leases, the *Reichman* case (2006), noted above); factor (a) ('inadequacy') should include consideration whether the remedy of damages would be commercially hazardous because of the risk[54] of insolvency during a prolonged wait for compensation;[55] however, mere difficulty in assessing damages should not be sufficient: damages can be awarded despite difficulty in assessment;[56]

(ii) the 'interest' which the innocent party is seeking to promote by keeping the contract alive is (a) important (a convincing commercial or other significant interest), (b) obvious (known to the guilty party, or otherwise obvious) and (c) proportionate (having regard to any disproportion between the innocent party's interest in upholding the contract and the consequent hardship to the other party in not being able to end the relationship);

(iii) however, the burden of proof should be on the party who has attempted to end the contract to show that the innocent party should be confined to damages in the light of factors mentioned at (i) and (ii).

Applying the criteria of this proposed new regime, it would be highly unlikely that fees would be owed[57] if: (a) a management consultant went ahead with a trip to Hong Kong in order to make a report after the other party has tried to cancel the contract (the example given by Lord Reid in the *White & Carter* case, 1962);[58] or if (b) a surveyor proceeded with a report on a property which the client is no longer interested in buying; or if (c) an

---

50 [2012] EWHC 1077 (Comm); [2012] 2 All ER (Comm) 461; [2012] 2 Lloyd's Rep 61, at [44].
51 *Anson's Law of Contract* (29th edn, Oxford, 2010), 575 n. 21, citing US and Canadian materials or case law.
52 J. W. Carter, *Breach of Contract* (2nd edn, Sydney, 1991), [1127] ff.
53 L. McGregor, in J. Smits, D. Haas and G. Hesen (eds.), *Specific Performance in Contract Law: National and Other Perspectives* (Antwerp, 2008), 67, 89, noting *Report on Remedies for Breach of Contract* (Scottish Law Commission Report No. 174, Edinburgh, 1999), Part II.
54 J. W. Carter (2012) 128 LQR 490, 492 suggests that there is an 'ever-present risk of insolvency in the commercial world'; but this should not be a knock-down argument against reconsideration of the current law.
55 For Cooke J's pragmatic discussion of this issue, *Isabella Shipowner SA v. Shagang Shipping Co. Ltd ('The Aquafaith')* [2012] EWHC 1077 (Comm); [2012] 2 All ER (Comm) 461; [2012] 2 Lloyd's Rep 61, at [47] (noted J. W. Carter (2012) 128 LQR 490–93).
56 Unless quantification of damages is intractably complicated: *Barclays Bank plc v. Unicredit Bank AG* [2012] EWHC 3655 (Comm); [2012] EWHC 3655 (Comm); [2013] 2 Lloyd's Rep 1; [2014] 1 BCLC 342, at [111].
57 These examples are given on the assumption that the innocent party can perform without the other's cooperation.
58 [1962] AC 413, 428–9, 442, HL, *per* Lord Reid (Lord Keith also quoting this example).

advertising or publicity firm continued to provide services no longer wanted (again, as in the *White & Carter* case or as in the *Ministry of Sound* case (2003)); or if (d) a freelance writer or lecturer were to continue to send written reports or other material, or research work, even after the requesting party has cancelled the arrangement; or (e) an architect continued to draw up plans even after the project has been cancelled.

3. DAMAGES

18.07 *Outline of main points.*[59] The main points of this topic are as follows:

(1) *Nominal damages.* For any breach of contract, a claimant is entitled to nominal damages. This is a token sum signifying the fact that there has been a technical legal wrong (sums of £5 or £10, for example).[60]

(2) *Substantial damages.* Such damages can be awarded only if the claimant shows a recognised[61] type of loss, such as economic loss, personal injury or damage to property,[62] otherwise the claimant can recover merely a token amount as nominal damages. There is also a restriction against making damages awards for wholly 'speculative loss' (18.12).

(3) *Protection of expectations and indemnification of reliance loss.*[63] The main aim of compensatory damages is to place the promisee in the position he would have been in if the contract had been properly performed. This is the so-called 'expectation' or 'loss of bargain' measure (18.08).[64] As Parke B said in *Robinson* v. *Harman* (1848), the main aim of contractual damages is to place the claimant (the promisee) in the position he would have been in if the promise had been performed or the warranty had been accurate.[65] The idea of 'expectation' is linked to the idea of a 'performance interest'. (A special form of damages

---

59   A. Kramer, *The Law of Contract Damages* (Oxford, 2014); *McGregor on Damages* (19th edn, London, 2014), notably, chapter 2, 6, 8, 9; A. S. Burrows, *Remedies for Torts and Breach of Contract* (3rd edn, Oxford, 2004); A. Tettenborn and D. Wilby, *The Law of Damages* (2nd edn, London, 2010), 6.03 ff, and chapter 19; A. Kramer, *The Law of Contract Damages* (Oxford, 2014).

60   A. Kramer, *ibid.*, section 23.1; *McGregor on Damages* (19th edn, London, 2014), chapter 12.

61   *Bank of Credit & Commerce International SA (in liquidation)* v. *Ali (No. 2)* [2002] EWCA Civ 82; [2002] 3 All ER 750; [2002] ICR 1258; [2002] IRLR 460, at [14], *per* Pill LJ.

62   E.g. limits upon damages for disappointment (*Farley* v. *Skinner* [2001] UKHL 49; [2002] 2 AC 732, HL, noted at 18.13 below); contractual damages are unavailable for damage to reputation except in special situations: A. Burrows, in A. Burrows (ed.), *English Private Law* (3rd edn, Oxford, 2013), 21.56 ff, for exceptions.

63   A. M. Tettenborn, in M. A. Clarke, N. Andrews, A. M. Tettenborn, G. Virgo, *Contractual Duties: Performance, Breach, Termination and Remedies* (London, 2012), 21.034 ff.

64   For comment, in the context of specific performance (18.33 to 18.35), on the absence in all contexts of a positive right to receive complete and full performance, D. Campbell and R. Halson, in L. DiMatteo, Q. Zhou, S. Saintier, K. Rowley (eds.), *Commercial Contract Law: Transatlantic Perspectives* (Cambridge, 2014), chapter 12.

65   (1848) 1 Exch 850, 855; on the claimant's expectation or performance interest, L. L. Fuller and W. R. Perdue, 'The Reliance Interest in Contract Damages' (1936) 46 *Yale Law Journal* 52 and 373 (in two parts); D. Friedmann, 'The Performance Interest in Contract Damages' (1995) 111 LQR 628; D. Friedmann, 'A Comment on Fuller and Perdue' (2001) 1 *Issues in Legal Scholarship* 11; P. Jaffey, 'Damages and the Protection of Contractual Reliance', in D. Saidov and R. Cunnington (eds.), *Contract Damages: Domestic and International Perspectives* (Oxford, 2008), chapter 6; R. Stevens, 'Damages and the Right to Performance . . . ', in J. W. Neyers, R. Bronaugh and S. G. A. Pitel (eds.), *Exploring Contract Law* (Oxford, 2009), 171 ff; C. Webb, 'Justifying Damages', in J. W. Neyers, R. Bronaugh and S. G. A. Pitel (eds.), *Exploring Contract Law* (Oxford, 2009), 139 ff; D. Pearce and R. Halson, 'Damages for Breach of Contract: Compensation, Restitution, and Vindication' (2008) 28 OJLS 73–98.

aimed at achieving for the claimant that which the defendant failed to provide is known as the 'cost of cure' or reinstatement measure of damages: 18.11.)[66] A subsidiary type of damages is to restore the claimant monetarily to the position he enjoyed before the contract was breached, the so-called 'reliance loss' measure (18.08 and 18.09).

(4) *Damages are to compensate for loss rather than to disgorge the defendant's gain.* The general function of damages is to compensate rather than to prevent the defendant's unjust enrichment. However, the House of Lords in *Attorney-General* v. *Blake* (2001)[67] recognised that the courts can make an exceptional and discretionary award, known as an equitable account, to strip a defendant of a gain made following breach of contract (18.30).

(5) *Compensation is not punishment.* Contractual damages are intended to compensate the claimant, rather than to punish the defendant.[68]

(6) *Main limiting factors.*[69] Damages are subject to three general restrictions (causation, remoteness and mitigation), and (in the case of overlapping duties to exercise reasonable care, in contract and tort law) to the defence of contributory negligence. These doctrines are examined in detail at 18.14 ff below.

(7) *True compensation.*[70] The compensatory aim necessarily precludes double compensation or over-compensation for the same loss (and thus damages should reflect the fact that the claimant would have paid tax on the sums which the compensation is intended to replace).[71]

(8) *Damages are generally assessed at the date of breach.* In general,[72] damages are assessed with regard to the facts as they subsisted at the time of breach,[73] notably in the cases of failure to accept or to deliver goods in contracts of sale.[74] However, a large exception to this proposition was introduced by the House of Lords in *'The Golden Victory'*

---

66   D. Harris, A. Ogus and J. Phillips, 'Contract Remedies and the Consumer Surplus' (1979) 95 LQR 581; D. Pearce and R. Halson, 'Damages for Breach of Contract: Compensation, Restitution, and Vindication' (2008) 28 OJLS 73, 82, 91–3.

67   [2001] 1 AC 268, HL.

68   *Ruxley Electronics and Construction Ltd* v. *Forsyth* [1996] 1 AC 344, 365, HL; *Addis* v. *Gramophone Co. Ltd* [1909] AC 488, HL (considered in *Edwards* v. *Chesterfield Royal Hospital NHS Foundation Trust* [2011] UKSC 58; [2012] 2 AC 22; on which C. Barnard and L. Merrett (2013) CLJ 313); A. Kramer, *The Law of Contract Damages* (Oxford, 2014), section 23.3; R. Cunnington, 'Should Punitive Damages be Part of the Judicial Arsenal in Contract Cases?' (2006) 26 LS 369; J. Morgan, *Contract Law* (Basingstoke, 2012), 252–7; S. Rowan, (2010) 30 *Oxford University Commonwealth Law Journal* 495; otherwise in Canada, *Royal Bank of Canada* v. *Got* (2000) 17 DLR (4th) 385 (Supreme Court of Canada), noted by J. Edelman, (2001) 117 LQR 539; *Whiten* v. *Pilot Insurance Co.* [2002] SCC 18; [2002] 1 SCR 595 (Supreme Court of Canada); *Honda Canada Inc.* v. *Keays* [2008] SCC 39; (2008) 294 DLR (4th) 371 (Supreme Court of Canada), noted by M. McInnes, (2009) 125 LQR 16, at 19–20; as for punitive damages in English tort law, see *Kuddus* v. *Chief Constable of Leicestershire* [2002] 2 AC 122, HL, and *A* v. *Bottrill* [2003] 1 AC 449, PC.

69   *McGregor on Damages* (19th edn, London, 2014), chapter 6.

70   A. M. Tettenborn, in M. A. Clarke, N. Andrews, A. M. Tettenborn, G. Virgo, *Contractual Duties: Performance, Breach, Termination and Remedies* (London, 2012), 21.07 to 21.33; A. Burrows, 'Limitations on Compensation', in A. S. Burrows and E. Peel (eds.), *Commercial Remedies: Current Issues and Problems* (Oxford, 2003), 27 (although this antedates the *Transfield* case, on which see 18.20 below).

71   A. S. Burrows, *Remedies for Torts and Breach of Contract* (3rd edn, Oxford, 2004), 199 ff (noting *British Transport Commission* v. *Gourley* [1956] AC 185, HL, and associated cases).

72   Cf Lord Wilberforce in *Johnson* v. *Agnew* [1980] 367, 401, HL: 'not an absolute rule . . . the court has power to fix such other date as may be appropriate'.

73   S. Waddams, 'The Date for the Assessment of Damages' (1981) 97 LQR 445–61; A. Kramer, *The Law of Contract Damages* (Oxford, 2014), chapter 17; against the existence of this approach, A. Dyson and A. Kramer, 'There is No "Breach Date Rule" . . . ' (2014) 130 LQR 259–81.

74   Respectively, sections 50(3) and 51(3) of the Sale of Goods Act 1979.

(2007),[75] where facts subsequent to the breach were shown to have inevitably reduced the value of the damages claim (see also 18.21). Furthermore, the Court of Appeal in *Hooper* v. *Oates* (2013) held[76] that the breach date is unlikely to apply in respect of land transactions. In that case the purchaser had defaulted in 2008 when the property was worth £605,000, and the vendor had then endeavoured to sell it, but without success. The vendor eventually despaired and decided to retain the property. But at that stage the value had fallen to £495,000. The court held that there had been no failure to take reasonable steps to mitigate its loss. And so the vendor was entitled to damages (£110,000) measured by the difference between the price and the property's value at the date when the vendor had decided to retain the property.

(9) *Finality.* A claimant cannot obtain damages in successive actions in respect of the same cause of action: 'Damages resulting from one and the same cause of action must be assessed and recovered once and for all.'[77]

(10) *Other restrictions on damages.*

(a) *'Impecuniosity'.* As Burrows notes, a claimant cannot be prevented from recovering loss merely because that loss stems from his lack of funds or 'impecuniosity'; although the *Liesbosch* case (1933), which enunciated this principle, has not been formally overruled, the case is now largely treated as bad law.[78]

(b) *Litigation costs and damages.*[79] Costs incurred in bringing or defending a claim against the other party are recoverable only under the costs regime of the procedural rules,[80] unless (i) B's breach led to A incurring litigation expenses vis-à-vis a third party;[81] or (ii) B's breach led A to incur litigation costs in a *foreign jurisdiction*.[82]

(c) *Defendant's choice or discretion in performing contract: assessment of damages when defendant in breach. Durham Tees Valley Airport Ltd* v. *bmibaby Ltd* (2010)[83] (for this case's facts, see 4.08) has confirmed the following propositions.

---

75 'The Golden Victory' [2007] UKHL 12; [2007] 2 AC 353; M. Furmston, 'Actual Damages, etc', in D. Saidov and R. Cunnington (eds), *Contract Damages: Domestic and International Perspectives* (Oxford, 2008), 419, at 424 ff; D. McLauchlan, 'Expectation Damages, etc', in D. Saidov and R. Cunnington (eds.), *ibid.*, chapter 15; J. Morgan [2007] CLJ 263; G. H. Treitel (2007) 123 LQR 9; B. Coote (2007) 123 LQR 503; C. Nicholls (2008) JBL 91; M. Mustill (2008) 124 LQR 569–85; Sir Bernard Rix, 'Lord Bingham's Contributions to Commercial Law', in M. Andenas and D. Fairgrieve (eds.), *Tom Bingham and the Transformation of the Law: A Liber Amicorum* (Oxford, 2009), at 679–83; earlier, S. Waddams, 'The Date for the Assessment of Damages' (1981) 97 LQR 445.
76 [2013] EWCA Civ 91; [2014] Ch 287, notably at [34] to [40], *per* Lloyd LJ (noted, A. Dyson and A. Kramer, 'There is No "Breach Date Rule" ... ' (2014) 130 LQR 259–81).
77 *Brunsden* v. *Humphrey* (1884) 14 QBD 141, 147, CA, *per* Bowen LJ; *Republic of India* v. *India Steamship Co. Ltd* ('The Indian Grace') [1993] AC 410, 420–1, HL; L. A. Collins, (1992) 108 LQR 393, 394; *Jaggard* v. *Sawyer* [1995] 1 WLR 269, 284, CA; *Deeny* v. *Gooda Walker Ltd* [1995] 1 WLR 1206, 1214; A. Kramer, *The Law of Contract Damages* (Oxford, 2014), section 1.2C; G. Spencer Bower, A. K. Turner and K. R. Handley, *The Doctrine of Res Judicata* (4th edn, London, 2009), chapter 21; N. Andrews, *Andrews on Civil Processes* (Cambridge, 2013), vol. 1, *Court Proceedings*, 16.84; A. S. Burrows, *Remedies for Torts and Breach of Contract* (3rd edn, Oxford, 2004), 174 ff.
78 *Lagden* v. *O'Connor* [2004] 1 AC 1067, at [62], rejecting *Liesbosch* v. *Owners of the Steamship Edison* ('The Edison') [1933] AC 449, HL.
79 L. Merrett, 'Costs as Damages' (2009) 125 LQR 468; A. Kramer, *The Law of Contract Damages* (Oxford, 2014), sections 20.2 to 20.4.
80 Notably, CPR Part 44; *Andrews on Civil Processes* (Cambridge, 2013), vol. 1, *Court Proceedings*, chapters 18 to 20.
81 E.g. *British Racing Drivers Club* v. *Hextall Erskine & Co.* [1996] BCC 727, Carnwath J.
82 E.g. *Union Discount Co. Ltd* v. *Zoller* [2001] EWCA Civ 1755; [2002] 1 WLR 1517.
83 [2010] EWCA Civ 485; [2011] 1 All ER (Comm) 731; [2011] 1 Lloyd's Rep 68, at [79], *per* Patten LJ (Toulson and Mummery LJJ agreed, [147], [150]), considering, notably, *Abrahams* v. *Herbert Reiach Ltd* [1922] 1 KB 477,

(i)   Damages will only be awarded if the claimant is entitled to recover compensation in respect of benefits which the defendant was legally obliged to confer.

(ii) However, where it is clear that the claimant has suffered loss in respect of a legally protected right, but the defendant had a choice between two or more ways to perform, the claimant will be awarded damages on the less or least onerous basis, tilting matters in favour of the defendant.

(iii) Where, however, the defendant's performance involves a single obligation, within which he enjoys elements of discretion, the courts are prepared to regulate this by reference to standards of reasonableness, where necessary and appropriate.

(11) *Agreed compensation.* In advance of breach, the parties can agree (provided the sum is not punitive) upon the measure of damages which the innocent party will receive in the event of breach: see 19.01.

Types of damages claims

18.08 *Expectation and reliance loss claims.* The law distinguishes 'expectation' and 'reliance' damages for breach of contract. The former measure of damages aims to place the claimant in the economic position which he would have enjoyed had the defendant not breached the contract. This forward-looking measure of compensation protects the promisee's interest in making a gain under a profitable contract. Otherwise, where the claimant cannot prove lost profits, or such a claim is too difficult to quantify, in the absence of a successful claim for loss of profit or expectation damages, the claimant is reduced to seeking his 'out-of-pocket' expenditure incurred when attempting to perform his side of the contract.

> This was the position in *Anglia Television Ltd* v. *Reed* (1972), where the defendant actor failed to participate in filming, but the claimant company could not show that its intended film would have been profitable.[84] The Court of Appeal awarded compensation for the expenses wasted when the project had to be scrapped, and the award also covered pre-contractual expenditure made in contemplation of the filming.

To avoid over-compensation, a claim for gross profits must be reduced to account for the claimant's expenditure in realising those profits. In short, only net profits are recoverable.

18.09 There are two restrictions on the reliance loss claim. The defendant might show (the burden being upon that party)[85] that the claimant had no chance of 'covering his expenses' even if

CA (preferring the approach of Atkin LJ to Scrutton LJ's); *Lavarack* v. *Woods of Colchester* [1967] 1 QB 278, CA; *Paula Lee Ltd* v. *Zehil & Co. Ltd* [1983] 2 All ER 390, Mustill J; *Kurt A Becher GmbH & Co. KG* v. *Roplak Enterprises SA ('The World Navigator')* [1991] 2 Lloyd's Rep 23, CA; *Cantor Fitzgerald International* v. *Horkulak* [2004] EWCA Civ 1287; [2005] ICR 402. See also A. M. Tettenborn, in M. A. Clarke, N. Andrews, A. M. Tettenborn, G. Virgo, *Contractual Duties: Performance, Breach, Termination and Remedies* (London, 2012), 21.76 to 21.84.

84   [1972] 1 QB 60, CA.

85   *CCC Films* v. *Impact Quadrant Ltd* [1985] QB 16, Hutchison J; that decision was followed in *Grange* v. *Quinn* [2013] EWCA Civ 24; [2013] 1 P & CR 18 (tenant of commercial premises entitled to recover as damages

the contract had not been breached; in other words, that the contract was inherently loss-making for the innocent party.[86] In such a case, the defendant need only pay non-compensatory 'nominal damages', signifying his bare and technical breach. This restriction can be justified for two reasons: first, as a matter of causation, the claimant would have been impoverished by the contract even if everything had been performed perfectly, and so he suffered no loss as a result of the breach; and, secondly, otherwise an award of substantial damages would be punitive.

For the second restriction, reliance loss might be eliminated because the claimant has successfully mitigated its loss (18.22). In *Omak Maritime Ltd* v. *Mamola Challenger Shipping Co. Ltd, 'The Mamola Challenger'* (2010)[87] the owner had incurred nearly US$ 90,000 fitting out a vessel to suit the charterer, under a long-term time charterparty. The charterer later repudiated the contract. However, the owner was quickly able to recoup the $90,000 loss because the market rate had risen well above the level of the contract rate. Teare J held that the claimant's mitigation had been successful and there had been no resulting reliance loss.

18.10 *Comparison of contractual and tort damages (actions for deceit[88] or negligence)*. As noted at 9.19, the torts of deceit and negligence (and the statutory tort of section 2(1) of the Misrepresentation Act 1967) enable claimants to recover in respect of lost economic opportunities, on the basis of 'consequential damages'. Since tort law and contract both protect economic expectations, what is the difference between the compensatory scheme within tort law and contractual damages? The difference is that contractual obligations, based on promises and assurances (including 'warranties') give rise to the *source of the relevant protected expectations*. It then becomes necessary for contractual damages to be awarded to vindicate those expectations, which – in the absence of the relevant undertaking or warranty – would not have arisen.

Warranted expectations are, therefore, contractually supported hopes *which would not exist if the party had not received a promise or assurance under the relevant contract*. For example, if D warrants that the subject matter of the contract will have a certain quality, but it lacks it, P can obtain contractual damages for the gain which would have accrued if the subject matter had possessed that quality. That type of pure expectation is protected only by a contractual term or collateral warranty. But *when the chance of gain exists independently of a contractual promise made by the party now in breach*, tort damages can reflect the claimant's economic loss. This is the basis of the successful tort

the premium paid on agreeing a six-year lease; lease terminated by landlord in breach of contract; *per* Gloster J (sitting in the Court of Appeal), the defendant landlord had not shown that the claimant would have inevitably suffered a loss under the contract; *per* Jackson LJ a special rule applies here in favour of the recovery of the premium as damages; *per* Arden LJ (dissenting) the lower court's decision in favour of the landlord should not be factually challenged by revisiting the relevant expert evidence; a restitutionary claim for total or partial failure was not pleaded).

86   The seminal case is *C & P Haulage* v. *Middleton* [1983] 1 WLR 1461, CA.
87   [2010] EWHC 2026 (Comm); [2011] Bus LR 212; [2011] 1 Lloyd's Rep 47; [2010] 2 CLC 194, at [59]; noted D. McLauchlan (2011) 127 LQR 23–7; A. Tettenborn [2011] LMCLQ 1–4.
88   *Derry* v. *Peek* (1889) 14 App Cas 337, HL; *Smith New Court* case, [1997] AC 254, HL.

claims (both based on deceit) upheld in the *East* v. *Maurer* (1991)[89] line of cases, and examined at 9.18.

To make this more concrete, the following example assumes that Y bought X's car for £5,000 after X had warranted that it had done '50,000 miles only', and the car has in fact done 100,000 miles. The car's actual value in that state is £4,000. If it had done only 50,000 miles, it would have been worth £12,000. Consider the following claims:

(1) In contract, Y can obtain as damages the difference between the market value of the goods at the time of delivery, £4,000 (not the price paid), and the value the car would have had if the car had complied with its warranty, £12,000;[90] and so Y's loss of bargain measure is worth £8,000; that is, the difference between the value of goods received and their warranted value: section 53(3) of the Sale of Goods Act 1979.

(2) In tort, Y can obtain as damages the difference between the price paid, £5,000, and the product's actual value, £4,000 (the representee's immediate out-of-pocket loss); and so £1,000 would be awarded if Y's claim were successful in tort on the basis of deceit or breach of a Common Law duty to avoid negligent misstatement. Therefore, Y will seek the contractual measure in (1) rather than the tortious measure in (2).

(3) Where the warranted value is less than the agreed price for the product ('bad bargain'), Y's contractual entitlement will be zero (no 'loss of expectation') (although nominal damages will be available to reflect the technical nature of the breach). Instead, only tortious (non-nominal) damages will assist the claimant: tort law will give Y the difference between the sum paid and the (lower) value of the car delivered – the claimant's out-of-pocket harm. If the car would have been worth only £4,000 even if it had only done 50,000 miles, that is, even if the warranty had been accurate, but Y had paid more than that true value (here, £5,000, an excess of £1,000), Y will have made a 'bad bargain'; Y's contractual damages claim will result in nominal damages. But, on these same facts, Y can still recover £1,000 in the torts of deceit or negligence, the difference between the sum paid and the value of the car delivered; that is the amount which Y has wasted as a result of X's fraud or misrepresentation. These torts are wrongs committed independently of the seller's breach of contract.

18.11   *'Cost of cure' (or 'reinstatement') damages.*[91] This is the measure which funds substitute performance by a third party or indemnifies the claimant for the cost, already incurred, of putting right the defendant's breach. The cost of cure measure is normally prospective, a source of funding for work which is contemplated, although sometimes the work has already been funded by the claimant so that this party is out of pocket. At the core of the court's decision is an assessment of the proportionality or reasonableness of making this award ('problems of proportionality and reasonableness'). Such prospective cost of cure

---

89   [1991] 1 WLR 461 CA, noted J. Marks (1992) 108 LQR 386; *East* v. *Maurer* approved by Lord Steyn in *Smith New Court* case, [1997] AC 254, HL.

90   It is the buyer's loss on an immediate notional resale which counts: the 'difference between what he can get for the car and what he might have got for the car'.

91   A. M. Tettenborn, in M. A. Clarke, N. Andrews, A. M. Tettenborn, G. Virgo, *Contractual Duties: Performance, Breach, Termination and Remedies* (London, 2012), 21.65 to 21.75; D. Winterton, 'Money Awards Substituting for Performance' [2012] LMCLQ 446–70.

damages often exceed the diminution in value of the relevant subject matter (for example, see the *Radford* v. *De Froberville* case (1997) below).

Courts have been reluctant to award cost of cure damages which appear pointless or excessive.[92] In *Tito* v. *Waddell (No. 2)* (1977), a mining company had breached an undertaking to reconstruct a Pacific island after extracting minerals.[93] The claimant islanders had lived for many years on another island 1,500 miles away. The cost of complete refurbishment was 'disproportionate'. The claimants had no real interest in spending the money on refurbishing the island. Instead, ordinary loss of value damages were awarded (diminution in the land's value as a result of the default; a modest amount which would enable them, if they wished, to make a 'cosmetic' rehabilitation of the island).[94]

It is different if the cost of cure will yield satisfaction of an important and manifestly reasonable interest, and the claimant has a clear intention to use the money for the relevant purpose. And so Oliver J awarded the cost of cure measure in *Radford* v. *De Froberville* (1977), where the defendant's failure to construct a wall could be remedied by the claimant paying a third party to construct the wall on the claimant's side of the relevant boundary.[95]

Conversely, if the cost of cure measure will rectify the breach more cheaply than an award of damages measured by the subject matter's diminution in market value, the courts will award the cost of cure measure, because this is consistent with the defendant's duty to mitigate (18.22).[96]

Here are the main points concerning cost of cure damages.

Will the innocent party use the money to finance the 'cure'? Here the problem is over-compensation: the innocent party will receive a windfall if a large sum is awarded for the purpose of a 'cure', but the money is not used for that purpose and the loss occasioned by the breach is much less than the cost of cure award. If the substitute performance or remedial work has already been done, this problem does not arise[97] and instead the question is whether the expenditure was consistent with the duty to mitigate (18.22). But if no remedial work has been undertaken, the court should not make a cost of cure award if the claimant has no real intention to use the cost of cure damages to carry out remedial works.[98] Conversely, the court should not be induced to make such an award just because the claimant convincingly expresses a desire to effect the relevant 'cure'. Such a genuine and fixed intention[99] (fortified, perhaps, as in the *Ruxley* case (1996), by offering

---

92   E.g., *Sunrock Aircraft Corp.* v. *Scandinavian Airlines Systems* [2007] EWCA Civ 882; [2007] 2 Lloyd's Rep 612 (no justification to finance removal of 'scabs' on an aircraft; imperfections made no difference to aircraft's value, reliability, etc.).

93   [1977] Ch 106, 328, *per* Megarry V-C.

94   *Ibid.*, at 341–342A; American authorities cited by G. H. Jones, (1983) 99 LQR 443, 448–9.

95   [1977] 1 WLR 1262, 1268–88, 1284 letter E, Oliver J; D. Harris, A. Ogus and J. Phillips, (1979) 95 LQR 581, at 581–2, 590; G. H. Jones, (1983) 99 LQR 443, 450; H. Beale, in P. B. H. Birks (ed.), *Wrongs and Remedies in the Twenty-First Century* (Oxford, 1996), 231; for Australian discussion, see *Tabcorp Holdings Ltd* v. *Bowen Investments Pty Ltd* [2009] HCA 8; (2009) ALJR 390 (cost of cure damages for tenant's breach of a no-alteration clause).

96   *Ruxley Electronics and Construction Ltd* v. *Forsyth* [1996] 1 AC 344, 366D, HL, *per* Lord Lloyd.

97   *Tito* v. *Waddell (No. 2)* [1977] Ch 106, 333A, citing *Jones* v. *Herxheimer* [1950] 2 KB 106.

98   *Radford* v. *De Froberville* [1977] 1 WLR 1262, 1270E, *per* Oliver J (claimant's wish to spend the money was clear: see *ibid.*, at 1282); *Wigsell* v. *School for the Indigent Blind* (1882) 8 QBD 357 (Cave and Field JJ, Divisional Court); in *Tito* v. *Waddell (No. 2)* [1977] 106, 333, *per* Megarry V-C.

99   *Tito* v. *Waddell (No. 2)* [1977] Ch 106, 333–4, 336, discussing the so-called 'indicia of serious intent'; *Wigsell* v. *School for the Indigent Blind* (1882) 8 QBD 357, 363–4; *Radford* v. *De Froberville* [1977] 1 WLR 1262, 1282, *per* Oliver J.

a formal undertaking to spend the money on repairs) is a relevant factor but not decisive[100] because (as in the *Ruxley* case) this measure of damages might be inappropriate on the facts.

Proportionality and reasonableness. Such issues loomed large on the facts of *Ruxley Electronics and Construction Ltd* v. *Forsyth* (1996).[101] A wealthy homeowner had commissioned a swimming pool company to install a pool to agreed specifications. At one end, however, the pool was 18 inches less deep than specified. Putting it right would cost £21,560. There had been no market diminution in the owner's property value. The House of Lords held that the cost of cure measure would here be 'unreasonable' (according to Lord Jauncey)[102] and 'disproportionate' (as noted by Lord Lloyd of Berwick).[103] The House noted that the trial judge had (1) found that the customer had no real intention of reconstructing the pool; (2) found that 'flat' diving was still safe, even taking account of the fact that X was quite tall; (3) found that there was no market diminution of value; (4) and had instead awarded £2,500 for loss of amenity (a claim for intangible loss, including overall disappointment). Lords Jauncey and Lloyd said that the customer's (tactical) willingness to give an undertaking to spend the cost of cure damages on repairs made no difference,[104] because the trial judge had found that the customer had no real intention of rebuilding the pool.[105] The customer's proffered undertaking was transparently an attempt to obtain a substantial award of damages for vindictive purposes. However, this runs counter to the compensatory aim: for the innocent party 'cannot be allowed to create a loss, which does not exist, in order to punish the defendants for breach of contract'.[106]

Five other points on this topic are:

(i) The *Ruxley* litigation began as a debt claim by the swimming pool builder, who was still owed some money for the job, and the wealthy customer counter-claimed for cost of cure damages (even though the contractor had already reconstructed the pool once, after it had developed a crack).[107]

(ii) As for the final award in the *Ruxley* case of £2,500 in favour of the pool owner, Lord Mustill said that this vindicated the innocent party's 'consumer surplus', that is, damages aimed at reflecting legitimate consumer dissatisfaction in the absence of objective market-price diminution in value.[108] Lord Lloyd preferred to treat this award as an instance of disappointment damages.[109]

---

100   [1996] 1 AC 344, 373 HL, *per* Lord Lloyd.
101   *Ibid.*
102   *Ibid.*, at 357, HL.
103   *Ibid.*, at 366, HL (noting Cardozo J in the Court of Appeals of New York in *Jacob & Youngs* v. *Kent* 129 NE 889 (1921)).
104   *Ibid.*, at 359C, 373E.
105   *Ibid.*, at 372H.
106   *Ibid.*, at 373E.
107   [1994] 1 WLR 650, 652, CA.
108   E.g. the 'bad holiday' cases: *Jarvis* v. *Swan Tours Ltd* [1973] QB 233, CA, *Jackson* v. *Horizon Holidays Ltd* [1975] 1 WLR 1468, CA.
109   *Ruxley Electronics and Construction Ltd* v. *Forsyth* [1996] 1 AC 344, 374, HL.

(iii) The House of Lords in the *Ruxley* case acknowledged that the general measure in building cases is nevertheless the cost of cure[110] (as *Iggleden* v. *Fairview New Homes (Shooters Hill) Ltd* (2007) illustrates).[111]

(iv) The cost of cure measure should not be confused with harm *already suffered*. In *Dean* v. *Ainley* (1987)[112] the vendor's failure to damp-proof a cellar had *already* rendered that room unusable for a long period. Kerr LJ's discussion conflated loss of use (already suffered) and the prospective cost of preventing such damp.

(v) Solène Rowan has contended that the courts should be prepared to uphold a clause stipulating that the cost of cure measure should be available to the innocent party.[113]

18.12 *Loss of chance claims and the problem of speculative loss.* This is the problem of 'speculative loss'. In *Allied Maples Group* v. *Simmons & Simmons* (1995)[114] the test laid down was that loss of chance damages are available only if the relevance chance was 'real' or 'substantial'.

In *Allied Maples Group* v. *Simmons & Simmons* (1995), the defendant firm of City solicitors (acting for a purchaser) negligently failed to try to reinsert a protective 'warranty', in favour of the buyer, into a prospective agreement. The case raised the problem of calibrating the level of chance that the defendant lawyers had of inducing the vendor's advisors to reinsert this warranty. The test laid down is that damages can be awarded for such a lost chance only if what has been lost is a 'real' or 'substantial' chance. On these facts the majority[115] held that the chance was strong enough (Millett LJ dissented on this question of assessment, although not on the applicable test).[116]

A similar problem arises concerning claims for lost future business. In *Jackson* v. *Royal Bank of Scotland* (2005), the House of Lords upheld a trial judge's award of four years of lost *future* business between the claimant and X. The claimant had been selling imported 'doggie chews' to X.[117] Disaster struck when the defendant bank let slip to X, in breach of contract, details of the claimant's 'mark-up' (the difference between the purchase price in the Far East and the much higher on-sale price in the UK). After this disclosure, X bought directly from the Far East, cutting out the middle-man (the claimant). The four-year award of damages reflected the chance that transactions between the claimant and the wholesaler might well have petered out in due course, even if the defendant bank had not committed its breach of contract.

110 *East Ham Corporation* v. *Bernard Sunley & Sons Ltd* [1966] AC 406, HL, and *Linden Gardens Trust Ltd* v. *Lenesta Sludge Disposals Ltd* [1994] 1 AC 85, 110G, HL, *per* Lord Browne-Wilkinson (generally on that case, see 7.26).
111 [2007] EWHC 1573 (TCC), Coulson J.
112 [1987] 3 All ER 748, 755, CA.
113 S. Rowan, 'For the Recognition of Remedial Terms Agreed Inter Partes' (2010) 126 LQR 448, 455–7.
114 [1995] 1 WLR 1602, CA, noted by T. Church, [1996] CLJ 187; considered in *4 Eng Ltd* v. *Harper* [2008] EWHC 915 (Ch); [2009] Ch 91 (noted by P. Mitchell, (2009) 125 LQR 12–17) (on which see 9.18); *McGregor on Damages* (19th edn, London, 2014), chapter 10.
115 Stuart-Smith and Hobhouse LJJ.
116 Millett LJ, dissenting, would instead have ordered that the matter be reopened for further evidence.
117 [2005] UKHL 3; [2005] 1 WLR 377, at [43].

18.13 *Compensation for aggravation or consumer disappointment.*[118] The starting point is that, in general, a defendant is not liable for mental distress caused by breach of contract, even though the distress is not too remote a consequence of the breach.[119] The House of Lords' discussion in *Farley* v. *Skinner* (2002), the leading case, reveals three main exceptions to this proposition:[120]

(1) Proof of 'physical' discomfort (including noise), which engenders such negative feelings.[121]

(2) The contract has as one of its main[122] purposes (a) the avoidance of aggravation (such as liability of surveyors commissioned to inspect property or the liability of lawyers retained to obtain injunctive relief against violent or threatening persons); or (b) conferment of pleasure (holiday companies[123] or photographers at 'one-off' special occasions).[124]

(3) The 'consumer surplus' measure of compensation;[125] the phrase 'consumer surplus' denotes a non-pecuniary type of non-performance. It is vindicated by a contractual 'solatium', or loss of amenity award; such a claim is for 'loss' which, although palpable to consumers, is not reflected concretely in the 'market'. The leading discussion of the 'consumer surplus' concept is the *Ruxley* case (1996)[126] (18.11), where a 'consumer' recovered a modest sum of £2,500 for the disappointment he suffered because the other party had failed to construct a swimming pool of specified depth.

---

118   A. Kramer, *The Law of Contract Damages* (Oxford, 2014), chapter 19; A. M. Tettenborn, in M. A. Clarke, N. Andrews, A. M. Tettenborn, G. Virgo, *Contractual Duties: Performance, Breach, Termination and Remedies* (London, 2012), chapter 22.

119   *Addis* v. *Gramophone Co. Ltd* [1909] AC 488, HL; *Watts* v. *Morrow* [1991] 1 WLR 1421, 1445, CA, *per* Bingham LJ; *Johnson* v. *Gore, Wood & Co.* [2002] 2 AC 1, 37–8, HL; *Hamilton Jones* v. *David and Snape* [2003] EWHC 3147 (Ch); [2004] 1 All ER 657, at [52] ff, Neuberger J.

120   [2001] UKHL 49; [2002] 2 AC 732, HL, noted D. Capper, (2002) 118 LQR 193 and E. McKendrick and M. Graham, [2002] LMCLQ 161; cf Canada: *Fidler* v. *Sun Life Assurance Co. of Canada Ltd* [2006] SCC 30; [2006] 2 SCR 3 (Supreme Court of Canada), noted by M. Clapton and M. McInnes, (2007) 123 LQR 26–9; and *Honda Canada Inc.* v. *Keays* [2008] SCC 39; (2008) 294 DLR (4th) 371 (Supreme Court of Canada), noted by M. McInnes, (2009) 125 LQR 16.

121   E.g. *Farley* v. *Skinner* [2001] UKHL 49; [2002] 2 AC 732, HL, and *Hobbs* v. *London and South Western Railway Co.* (1875) LR 10 QB 111, CA (physical inconvenience of late-night walk in the rain; considered in *Milner* v. *Carnival plc (trading as Cunard)* [2010] EWCA Civ 389; [2010] 3 All ER 701, at [31] ff); breach of landlord's repairing obligation, *English Churches Housing Group* v. *Shine* [2004] EWCA Civ 434.

122   *Farley* v. *Skinner* [2001] UKHL 49; [2002] 2 AC 732, at [24], *per* Lord Steyn: 'a major or important object of the contract is to give pleasure, relaxation or peace of mind.'

123   *Milner* v. *Carnival plc (trading as Cunard)* [2010] EWCA Civ 389; [2010] 3 All ER 701, at [32] ff (noting parsimonious awards for bad holiday – perhaps because many lawyers are too busy to take holidays – at [54] ff; and disappointment damages for a most unhappy 'luxury cruise' were pegged at £4,500 for the wife and £4,000 for the husband.

124   *Farley* v. *Skinner* [2001] UKHL 49; [2002] 2 AC 732, at [52] to [69]; solicitors have been liable under this heading: *Heywood* v. *Wellers* [1976] QB 446, CA, and *Hamilton Jones* v. *David & Snape* [2003] EWHC 3147 (Ch); [2004] 1 WLR 921, Neuberger J.

125   *Ruxley Electronics and Construction Ltd* v. *Forsyth* [1996] AC 344, HL; D. Harris, A. Ogus and J. Phillips, (1979) 95 LQR 581, cited by Lord Mustill in the *Ruxley* case.

126   *Ruxley Electronics and Construction Ltd* v. *Forsyth* [1996] AC 344, HL; literature on the *Ruxley* case includes H. Beale in P. B. H. Birks (ed.), *Wrongs & Remedies in the Twenty-First Century* (Oxford, 1996), 227–9; J. O'Sullivan, in F. D. Rose (ed.), *Failure of Contract* (Oxford, 1997), chapter 1; E. Peel, in *ibid.*, at chapter 2; B. Coote, [1997] CLJ 537, especially on facts (538–9) and proposals for reform (566, 569–70); J. Cartwright, in A. Burrows and E. Peel (eds.), *Commercial Remedies: Current Issues and Problems* (Oxford, 2003), 9–13.

As Lord Scott said in the *Farley* case, the difference between (2) and (3) is that (2) involves consequential loss, whereas (3) involves denying the claimant the benefit of a promised performance.

There is a regime for non-tangible harm in the field of employment disputes.[127] In particular, actions for bullying at work can produce extensive liability, and such claims for breach of duty can straddle contractual and tortious obligations.[128]

Limits on contractual damages claims

18.14　These limits are: (1) causation; (2) remoteness and the satellite concept of 'scope of duty'; (3) mitigation of loss; and (4) contributory negligence.[129] Limits (1) to (3) apply to all contractual damages claims, but (4) is confined to breach of contractual duties of care where the obligation overlaps with a tortious duty of care.

18.15　*Causation.*[130] The defendant's breach must have been the 'effective cause' of the claimant's loss, and it is not enough in contract law that the connection between breach and loss satisfied a 'but for' inquiry. The two leading modern cases are *Galoo* v. *Bright Grahame Murray* (1994)[131] and *Supershield Ltd* v. *Siemens Building Technologies FE Ltd* (2010).[132] In the *Galoo* case (which concerned financial loss) Glidewell LJ said, applying common sense, that the court must determine whether the contractual breach was the 'effective' or 'dominant' cause of the loss;[133] it will not be this if the breach merely provided the occasion or opportunity for the claimant to sustain loss. In the *Supershield* case (2010), a case involving property damage, the defendant's contractual breach involved failure to tighten a valve, which led to a flood; but the defendant could not exonerate itself by pointing the causal finger at subsequent failures in the back-up systems, further down the chain of events.

In *Galoo* v. *Bright Grahame Murray* (1994),[134] the defendant accountancy firm breached its contract by negligently failing to carry out an audit of two companies. Those companies later

---

127　On the interaction of the statutory system of compensation for unfair dismissal and Common Law duties of 'trust and confidence', see *Johnson* v. *Unisys Ltd* [2001] UKHL 13; [2003] 1 AC 518; *Dunnachie* v. *Kingston-upon-Hull City Council* [2004] UKHL 36; [2005] 1 AC 226; *Eastwood* v. *Magnox Electric plc* [2004] UKHL 35; [2005] 1 AC 503.
128　*Helen Green* v. *DB Group (UK) Ltd* [2006] EWHC 1898 (QB), Owen J.
129　*McGregor on Damages* (19th edn, London, 2014), chapters 6 to 9.
130　A. M. Tettenborn, in M. A. Clarke, N. Andrews, A. M. Tettenborn, G. Virgo, *Contractual Duties: Performance, Breach, Termination and Remedies* (London, 2012), 24.02 to 24.26.
131　[1994] 1 WLR 1360, CA.
132　[2010] EWCA Civ 7; [2010] NPC 5.
133　*Ibid.*, at 1374–5 Glidewell LJ (Evans and Waite LJJ agreed); citing *Monarch Steamship Co. Ltd.* v. *Karlshamns Oljefabriker A/B* [1949] AC 196, HL; *Quinn* v. *Burch Bros. (Builders) Ltd.* [1966] 2 QB 370, CA. The Australian authorities considered were: *Alexander* v. *Cambridge Credit Corporation Ltd* (1987) 9 NSWLR 310 (NSWCA), especially Mahoney JA at 333–5 and McHugh JA at 359 (on similar facts); and High Court of Australia in *March* v. *E & MH Stramare Pty Ltd* [1991] 171 CLR 506, 515, Mason CJ (action in tort of negligence – 'but for' test not the sole criterion of causation).
134　[1994] 1 WLR 1360, CA; A. S. Burrows, *Remedies for Torts and Breach of Contract* (3rd edn, Oxford, 2004), 107.

became insolvent, whereupon their shareholders and liquidators sought compensation against the defendants. The claim foundered on the question of causation because the Court of Appeal held that the defendant's breach had not been a sufficient factor in the companies' subsequent commercial activity. Instead, the loss involved an independent set of decisions by the companies' directors to continue to trade.

In the *Supershield* case[135] the owners (Deka) and occupiers (Slaughter and May) of One Bunhill Row, a law office in the City of London, suffered loss when the basement of a new building became flooded as a result of overflow from a tank feeding a sprinkler system. The chronologically prior cause of the flood was a subcontractor's failure to tighten sufficiently a nut on the water valve within the building's sprinkler tanks. Siemens had already indemnified the owners and tenants of the building. Siemens then sued Supershield, the contractor to which Siemens had delegated the task of installing the sprinkler tank and its valve. Supershield unsuccessfully tried to defend itself by suggesting that its breach had been causally overtaken and so was irrelevant (referring to an overflow tank which had become blocked, a warning system which had failed and routine maintenance during which the loose nut had not been spotted). Dismissing this causation defence, Toulson LJ said[136] that the defective valve 'was an effective cause of the flood' and 'the blockage of the drains did not take away the potency of the overflow to cause damage, but rather failed to reduce it'. (A 'remoteness' defence also failed: 18.16.)

18.16 *Remoteness.* This concerns the line of cases stemming from *Hadley* v. *Baxendale* (1854).[137] A contractual claim for compensation will fail if the relevant loss is too 'remote', having regard to the parties' field of 'contemplation' at the time the contract was formed. The remoteness doctrine is an additional constraint upon recoverable damages, operating alongside causation (18.15) and mitigation (18.22). For the most part remoteness involves a predictive or crystal-ball gazing criterion: was the loss sufficiently in view at the time of the contract's formation as a 'serious possibility', taking into account normal occurrences and any special knowledge acquired by the defendant at that stage? However, a double-check is occasionally required: the predictability criterion will need to be supplemented by a

---

135 [2010] EWCA Civ 7; [2010] NPC 5.
136 *Ibid.*, at [32] and [33].
137 (1854) 9 Exch 341 (see also literature cited at 18.20. arising from the *Transfield* case); A. Kramer, *The Law of Contract Damages* (Oxford, 2014), chapter 14; *McGregor on Damages* (19th edn, London, 2014), chapter 8; on this doctrine's history, see R. Danzig, (1975) 4 *Journal of Legal Studies* 249; F. Faust, (1994) 15 *Journal of Legal History* 41; D. J. Ibbetson, *A Historical Introduction to the Law of Obligations* (Oxford, 1999), 229–31; M. Lobban, in W. Cornish, J. S. Anderson, R. Cocks, M. Lobban, P. Polden and K. Smith, *The Oxford History of the Laws of England*, vol. XII, *1820–1914: Private Law* (Oxford, 2010), 541 ff; A. W. B. Simpson, (1975) 91 LQR 247, 273–7; W. Swain, 'The Classical Model of Contract: The Product of a Revolution in Legal Thought' (2010) 30 LS 513, 531; and G. T. Washington, (1932) 48 LQR 90, 97 ff; on its modern application, see A. S. Burrows, *Remedies for Torts and Breach of Contract* (3rd edn, Oxford, 2004), 83 ff; A. M. Tettenborn, in M. A. Clarke, N. Andrews, A. M. Tettenborn, G. Virgo, *Contractual Duties: Performance, Breach, Termination and Remedies* (London, 2012), chapter 23; A. Tettenborn and D. Wilby, *The Law of Damages* (2nd edn, London, 2010), 6.03 ff; A. Kramer, in N. Cohen and E. McKendrick (eds.), *Comparative Remedies for Breach of Contract* (Oxford, 2005), 249; A. M. Tettenborn, (2007) 23 JCL 120; A. Robertson, (2008) 28 LS 172; J. Gordley, 'The Foreseeability Limitation on Liability in Contract', in A. Hartkamp and C. Joustra (eds.), *Towards a European Civil Code* (3rd edn, Nijmegen, 2004), chapter 11. On the *Transfield* case, [2008] UKHL 48; [2009] 1 AC 61, see literature cited at 18.20.

wider consideration of the commercial context and of the contract's nature and object (18.20), as explained by Lord Walker[138] in the *Transfield* case, and as ratified by leading first instance judges (18.20).

The contractual 'remoteness of damage' doctrine can be formulated as follows:

(1) The defendant in breach of contract is only liable to pay damages if the relevant *type of loss* (see (3) below for a qualification concerning *unusually high levels of profit*) was reasonably contemplated by both parties at the time of the contract's formation as a serious possibility,[139] taking into account (a) ('limb 1') the ordinary course of things and (b) ('limb 2')[140] any special knowledge which caused the defendant to have assumed a wider responsibility than in (a).[141]

(2) However, objective appreciation of the contractual context might justify cutting down the scope of the defendant's liability.

(3) There is no need to have contemplated the scale of the loss,[142] unless the claim is for unusually high levels of profit.

There was an audacious but unsuccessful attempt to use limb 2 (see (1)(b) of the preceding formulation: special knowledge) to reduce or even exclude the defendant's liability in *Supershield Ltd* v. *Siemens Building Technologies FE Ltd* (2010)[143] (see 18.15 for the facts). The Court of Appeal held that it should make no difference that the parties, as technicians on a complex construction job, had special knowledge that ordinarily a loose nut would not lead to a building flooding, because back-up systems would avert such a calamity.[144] In the same way it would be unacceptable if brakes were ill-fitted to a car but the mechanic attempted to escape liability for the claimant's severe injury caused by the car careering down a bank by the side of a road, after the brakes failed, by pleading that ordinarily no injury would be suffered if the claimant had been wearing a seat-belt, if the air-bag within the car had not malfunctioned and if road barriers had been constructed to customary standards of strength.

18.17 *Contrasting remoteness tests in contract law and in the tort of negligence.* The (relatively pro-defendant) contractual principle of remoteness is to be contrasted with the test

---

138 [2008] UKHL 48; [2009] 1 AC 61, at [78], *per* Lord Walker.

139 Lord Walker in the *Transfield* case, [2008] UKHL 48; [2009] 1 AC 61, at [76], noting 'The Heron II' [1969] 1 AC 350, 400, 415, 425, HL, *per* Lords Morris, Pearce and Upjohn, who 'approved the expressions "real danger" and "serious possibility"', although Lord Reid in 'The Heron II' at 390 disapproved the latter formulation; A. S. Burrows, *Remedies for Torts and Breach of Contract* (3rd edn, Oxford, 2004), 88, 94.

140 The two limbs are parts of a composite rule or 'principle': *per* Lord Mance in *Sempra Metals Ltd* v. *Inland Revenue Commissioners* [2007] UKHL 34; [2008] 1 AC 561, at [215]; and *per* Lord Walker in *Jackson* v. *Royal Bank of Scotland plc* [2005] 1 WLR 377, HL, at [46] to [48].

141 *Mulvenna* v. *Royal Bank of Scotland plc* [2003] EWCA Civ 1112, at [24] and [25], *per* Waller LJ.

142 *Parsons* v. *Uttley Ingham* [1978] QB 791, CA; *Brown* v. *KMR Services Ltd* [1995] 4 All ER 598, CA.

143 [2010] EWCA Civ 7; [2010] NPC 5, on this point at [35] to [45].

144 *Ibid.*, at [44].

applicable to negligence claims in tort, the so-called 'reasonable foreseeability' test in *'The Wagon Mound'* case (1961).[145] There are three[146] points of contrast.

(1) *Tort test more generous to claimants.* The criterion of 'reasonable foreseeability' in the tort of negligence is less exacting than the contractual remoteness test concerning contemplation as a 'serious possibility'.

(2) *Different dates for assessment.* The tort test is not restricted to contemplated events assessed at the time of the contract, and indeed, in many tort cases, there will be no contract, merely an accident between strangers. Instead, the tort test operates with respect to facts and circumstances subsisting at the time of the defendant's breach of his duty of care.

(3) *Special knowledge second limb*: the 'second limb' of the contract test (limb 2 of the test stated at 18.16 above) does not appear as part of the tort test.

Finally, Burrows contends that the Court of Appeal's decision in *Brown* v. *KMR Services Ltd* (1995) (18.19, case (6))[147] might be interpreted as deciding that the contract test should apply to both a contractual and a tortious claim when there is a business relationship between the parties giving rise to overlapping obligations in contract and tort.[148]

18.18 *Leading cases concerning remoteness.* There are seven leading cases, of which the most fundamental (containing the fullest conceptual discussion) on remoteness in contract law is *Transfield Shipping Inc.* v. *Mercator ('The Achilleas')* (2008)[149] (for the six other leading pre-*Transfield* cases, see below at 18.19, examining *Hadley* v. *Baxendale* (1854);[150] the *Victoria Laundry* case (1949);[151] *C Czarnikow Ltd* v. *Koufos ('The Heron II')* (1969);[152] *H Parsons (Livestock) Ltd* v. *Uttley Ingham & Co. Ltd* (1978);[153] *Balfour Beatty Construction Ltd* v. *Scottish Power* (1994);[154] and *Brown* v. *KMR Services Ltd* (1995).[155]

18.19 *Pre-*Transfield *case law on contractual remoteness.* It is important to consider the elaboration of the remoteness doctrine within the case law since 1854.

(1) *Hadley* v. *Baxendale* (1854)[156] concerned a contract for carriage of a broken crank shaft, in fact the claimant's only crank shaft, from the claimant's mill at Gloucester to and then

---

145   For the tort test, see *'The Wagon Mound'* [1961] AC 388, PC (summarised by Lord Rodger in *Simmons* v. *British Steel plc* [2004] UKHL 20; [2004] ICR 585, at [67]); on aspects of the remoteness tests in contract and tort, see A. Kramer, in D. Saidov and R. Cunnington (eds.), *Contract Damages: Domestic and International Perspectives* (Oxford, 2008), chapter 12.

146   *Quaere* whether the *Victoria Laundry* case's differentiation in *contractual damages* between ordinary and extraordinary loss of profits (case (2) above) would ever be necessary in the context of *tort* claims (in deceit or negligence) for income loss (on this line of cases, commencing with *East* v. *Maurer* (1991), see 9.19).

147   [1995] 4 All ER 598, CA.

148   A. S. Burrows, *Remedies for Torts and Breach of Contract* (3rd edn, Oxford, 2004), 93–4; cf Sir Thomas Bingham MR in the *Banque Bruxelles Lambert* case, [1995] QB 375, 405E, CA (a terse elision of tort and contract tests but without citation of authorities).

149   [2008] UKHL 48; [2009] 1 AC 61: see literature cited at 18.20.

150   (1854) 9 Exch 341.

151   [1949] 2 KB 528, CA.

152   [1969] 1 AC 350, HL.

153   [1978] QB 791, CA.

154   1994 SLT 807; *The Times*, 23 March 1994 (a Scots case taken on final appeal to the House of Lords).

155   [1995] 4 All ER 598, CA.

156   (1854) 9 Exch 341.

back from a third party engineer at Greenwich. The defendant carrier was not liable for the customer's five days of production losses attributable to delayed delivery of equipment because that loss was a special vulnerability not brought home to the carrier at the time of the contract's formation.

> Contrary to the headnote in the law report, this special vulnerability had not in fact been communicated by the miller.[157] Alderson B said that the ordinary assumption would be that the claimant had a replacement crank, or that there were other reasons why the mill was not capable of being used at this time.
> This seminal case established the two-limb test formulated in the text above at 18.16 and which was expressed by Baron Alderson as follows:
>> [Contractual damages] should be such as may fairly and reasonably be considered, either arising naturally, i.e. according to the usual course of things from such breach of contract itself, or such as may reasonably be supposed to have been in the contemplation of both parties, at the time they made the contract as the probable result of the breach of it ... [The plaintiff's] loss would neither have flowed naturally from the breach of this contract in the great multitude of such cases occurring under ordinary circumstances, nor were the special circumstances, which, perhaps, would have made it a reasonable and natural consequence of such breach, communicated to or known by the defendants.[158]

(2) In the *Victoria Laundry* case (1949),[159] the defendant supplier of an industrial boiler was not liable to pay compensation for loss of profits arising from an 'exceptionally lucrative' deal between the claimant and a third party; the defendant would be liable only for 'ordinary' levels of lost profits.

> The defendant vendor agreed to supply an industrial boiler to the defendant. This was a major purchase. It must have been obvious that the claimant would not have a spare boiler and indeed the defendant knew that the boiler was required for immediate use in the claimant's business. In breach of contract, the defendant supplied the item five months late. The claimant was held to be entitled to recover ordinary profits on contracts with customers (dyeing contracts). The Court of Appeal held that the defendant's liability did not extend to exceptionally lucrative profits to be obtained under a deal with the Ministry of Supply, because that level of revenue was not to be contemplated in the ordinary course of things and the defendant had received no notification of the claimant's intention to expand his business in this fashion.[160] In the *Transfield* case (2008: 18.20), Lord Hoffmann approved the *Victoria Laundry* decision:[161]
>> the Court of Appeal [in the *Victoria Laundry* case] did not regard 'loss of profits from the laundry business' as a single type of loss. They distinguished losses from 'particularly

---

157 As clarified by Asquith LJ, *Victoria Laundry* case [1949] 2 KB 528, 537, CA.
158 *Ibid.*, 354.
159 [1949] 2 KB 528, CA.
160 *Ibid.*, 543.
161 [2008] UKHL 48; [2009] 1 AC 61, at [22], *per* Lord Hoffmann.

> lucrative dyeing contracts' as a different type of loss ... The vendor of the boilers would have regarded the profits on these contracts as a different and higher form of risk than the general risk of loss of profits by the laundry.

(3) *C Czarnikow Ltd v. Koufos ('The Heron II')* (1969)[162] is House of Lords authority (according to later interpretation) that the remoteness test in contract law requires that the loss should be contemplated as a 'serious possibility'.[163] The House of Lords rejected the test of a mere likelihood or an 'on the cards' possibility.[164] The defendant carrier deviated, in breach of contract, en route to Basra (in Iraq), where the defendant was to unload the claimant's consignment of sugar. The cargo arrived at Basra nine days later, as a result of this deviation. The defendant did not know that the claimant intended to sell the sugar in Basra. But the defendant did know that there was a market for this commodity at the port of destination. During the period of delayed arrival, the Basra sugar price had fallen. The House of Lords upheld the arbitrator's award of damages for this difference in value.[165]

(4) In *H Parsons (Livestock) Ltd v. Uttley Ingham & Co. Ltd* (1978)[166] the defendant supplied and installed at the claimant's pig farm a hopper for the storage of pig nuts. The defendant failed to adjust the top of the hopper so that it would provide ventilation to its contents, and so the nuts became mouldy. The claimant fed them to his pigs, who fell very ill, 254 fatally, with intestinal poisoning (*E coli*). The Court of Appeal unanimously held that the property loss sustained on these facts was not too remote. The majority, Scarman and Orr LJJ, held that the farmer's loss should be characterised as 'illness' suffered by his livestock. The parties should be taken to have contemplated this as 'a serious possibility'.[167] There was no need for the parties to have foreseen the fatal nature of that illness.[168]

> Lord Denning MR, in a minority judgment which has not become accepted, said that although this was a claim for breach of contract, the complaint did not concern loss of profits, and so the appropriate test was the tort of negligence test established in the *Wagon Mound* (1961) line of cases, namely, reasonable foreseeability.[169] In his view, the more demanding *Hadley* v. *Baxendale* (1854) remoteness test should be confined to contractual claims for loss of profits.[170] However, to repeat: Lord Denning's analysis is not the law.

162 [1969] 1 AC 350, HL.
163 E.g., Lord Hoffmann, (2010) 14 *Edinburgh Law Review* 47, 51.
164 [1969] 1 AC 350, 424–5, *per* Lord Upjohn.
165 Rejecting the contrary decision in '*The Parana*' (1877) 2 PD 118, CA.
166 [1978] QB 791, CA.
167 *Ibid.*, at 805–6.
168 *Ibid.*, at 813.
169 [1978] QB 791, 801–4, CA, citing '*The Wagon Mound*' *(No. 1)* [1961] AC 388, PC, and '*The Wagon Mound*' *(No. 2)* [1967] 1 AC 617, PC.
170 Adopting H. L. A. Hart and A. Honoré, *Causation in the Law* (Oxford, 1959), 281–7; now (2nd edn, Oxford, 1985), 320–1.

(5) In *Balfour Beatty Construction Ltd* v. *Scottish Power* (1994)[171] the defendant supplier of electricity was not liable for losses caused by an interruption in the flow of electricity to a building site, where cement was being used to construct pillars supporting a roadway. As a result of the power shutdown, the pursuer had had to redo some of the construction work, at considerable expense. The pursuer's loss was not contemplated as a 'serious possibility', applying limb 1 of the contractual remoteness test, and no special knowledge had been present or imparted so as to trigger wider liability under limb 2.

(6) In *Brown* v. *KMR Services Ltd* (1995)[172] Lloyd's names (who had been rendered liable on the insurance market for vast amounts) sued their members' agents for breach of contract and negligence. The defendants unsuccessfully contended that the losses in the relevant years were so catastrophic that they were both unforeseeable in tort and too remote in contract.[173] The upshot of the *Brown* case is that a contractual claim for economic loss – viz. liabilities incurred and money paid out – (as distinct from loss of *profits*, that is money which might otherwise have been earned or gained) requires merely contemplation (as a 'serious possibility') of the relevant head of loss; and contemplation of the extent of that economic loss is necessary *only in claims for loss of profits* (the latter point being covered by the *Victoria Laundry* case (1949) (case (2) in this paragraph)).

18.20 *Leading decision on contractual remoteness:* Transfield Shipping Inc. *v.* Mercator ('The Achilleas') *2008).*[174] The law of contractual remoteness has become slightly more complicated as a result of the lack of unison within the judgments in this case. But we will see that reports of the demise of *Hadley* v. *Baxendale* (1854) are greatly exaggerated. That line of cases lives on, but subject to a gloss (see sub-paragraph C below).

The House of Lords unanimously held (reversing the arbitral award, the award had been upheld by both Christopher Clarke J and the Court of Appeal) that the defendant charterer was not liable for loss of an attractive rate of hire arranged by the ship-owner in a 'follow-on' 191-day charterparty with a third party. The defendant's nine-day delay in returning the vessel had forced the owner to agree to accept a lower rate of hire from the third party, especially because the market rate had recently fallen (the reduction was US$8,000 a day and the new charter with Z was to last for many months). Instead the owners could only

---

171   1994 SLT 807; *The Times*, 23 March 1994 (a Scots case taken on final appeal to the House of Lords); H. MacQueen, [1996] *Juridical Review* 295; A. Burrows, *Understanding the Law of Obligations* (Oxford, 1998), 160 ff.
172   [1995] 4 All ER 598, CA; A. S. Burrows, in A. S. Burrows and E. Peel (eds.), *Commercial Remedies: Current Issues and Problems* (Oxford, 2003), 34–6; for a successful claim against engineers in respect of loss consequent on a fall in real property prices following delayed supply of development drawings, *James Grimes Partnership Ltd* v. *Gubbins* [2013] EWCA Civ 37; [2013] PNLR 17; [2013] BLR 126, at [20] and [24], *per* Keane LJ; noted J. Goodwin, (2013) 129 LQR 486–8 (Tomlinson LJ, *ibid.*, at [34], resiling from his view in *Pindell* v. *AirAsia Bhd* [2010] EWHC 2516 (Comm); [2011] 2 All ER (Comm) 396; [2012] 2 CLC 1, at [88], that fluctuations in a 'volatile' market are 'axiomatically' not recoverable.
173   [1995] 4 All ER 598, 620–1, 642–3, CA.
174   [2008] UKHL 48; [2009] 1 AC 61; B. Coote, (2010) 26 JCL 211; D. Foxton, [2009] LMCLQ 461–87; V.P. Goldberg (2013) 66 CLP 107–130; G. Gordon, (2009) 13 *Edinburgh Law Review* 125–30; Lord Hoffmann, (2010) 14 *Edinburgh Law Review* 47–61; H. Hunter, (2014) 31 JCL 120–130; A. Kramer, (2009) 125 LQR 408–15; D. McLauchlan, (2009) 9 *Oxford University Commonwealth Law Journal* 109–39; S. S. Naravane, [2012] JBL 404–18; J. O'Sullivan, [2009] CLJ 34–7; E. Peel, (2009) 125 LQR 6–12; M. Stiggelbout, [2012] LMCLQ 97–121; P. C. K. Wee, [2010] LMCLQ 150–76.

recover damages for the nine-day delay, assessed as the difference between the agreed rate and the (higher) market rate for that short period.

On one view, the claim failed for remoteness (Lords Rodger and Walker and Baroness Hale). According to this traditional approach, one might explain the absence of liability as consistent with the established rule (see the *Victoria Laundry* case (1949: 18.19 case (2))[175] that the law differentiates between different segments of lost profits, withholding liability for a specially lucrative dependent contract unless this aggravated risk has been notified to the defendant and he has assumed responsibility for it at the time of formation.

Traditional contemplation reasoning. In the *Transfield* case the market rate for hiring ships had fluctuated in an extreme way during the currency of the relevant contract: the claimant had at first been able to demand a high level of hire in the 'follow-on' contract; but then the claimant had been induced by Z, the third party, to reduce that price to reflect the subsequent market fall. This seesaw effect was quite out of the ordinary, in Lord Rodger's opinion, who noted that the loss occurred only[176] 'because of the extremely volatile market conditions which produced both the owners' initial (particularly lucrative) transaction, with a third party, and the subsequent pressure on the owners to accept a lower rate for that fixture'.

Applying the simple calculus of *Hadley* v. *Baxendale* 'contemplation', Lord Rodger concluded that the claimant owner's loss of profit was too remote under limb 1 of that test; and limb 2 of the *Hadley* v. *Baxendale* test could not rescue the claim because the owner had not communicated that the owner would be exposed to special financial vulnerability.[177] Such traditional remoteness analysis was sufficient to support the majority's conclusion (Lords Rodger and Walker and Baroness Hale adopting this simple *ratio* – although Lord Walker added a gloss – see below).

A. *The bigger picture in the* Transfield *case.* Apart from pure unpredictability, four other factors supported the decision that the charterer should not bear responsibility for this very large amount of lost profit:[178] (i) the market assumptions were that the charterer was not liable (the decisions in favour of the owner made by the majority of the arbitrators, of the High Court and Court of Appeal had surprised the market);[179] (ii) the owner would not normally suffer this loss because it would be able to mitigate for having missed the lucrative fixture by going into the market and finding a no less lucrative fixture;[180] (iii) the owner's claim was the result of a renegotiation of the lucrative rate of the new fixture, and that

---

175 [1949] 2 KB 528, CA.
176 [2008] UKHL 48; [2009] 1 AC 61, at [60], *per* Lord Rodger (with Lord Walker's and Baroness Hale's concurrence). But generalisation from this case is dangerous, cf in *James Grimes Partnership Ltd* v. *Gubbins* [2013] EWCA Civ 37; [2013] PNLR 17; [2013] BLR 126 (noted J. Goodwin, (2013) 129 LQR 486–8) Tomlinson LJ revised his view in *Pindell* v. *AirAsia Bhd* [2010] EWHC 2516 (Comm); [2011] 2 All ER (Comm) 396; [2012] 2 CLC 1, at [88], that fluctuations in a 'volatile' market are 'axiomatically' not recoverable.
177 [2008] UKHL 48; [2009] 1 AC 61, at [59], *per* Lord Rodger.
178 *Ibid.,* at [36], *per* Lord Hope.
179 Christopher Clarke J [2007] 1 Lloyd's Rep 19 and the Court of Appeal (Ward, Tuckey and Rix LJJ) [2007] 2 Lloyd's Rep 555 upheld the arbitrator's majority decision.
180 As Lord Rodger said, [2008] UKHL 48; [2009] 1 AC 61, at [54]: 'the parties would reasonably contemplate that, for the most part, the availability of the market would protect the owners if they lost a fixture.' The point is repeated at [57].

renegotiation was in effect a 'decreasing pact' between the owner and the third party over which the defendant charterer had no control; (iv) shipping claims would become fraught with uncertainty if charterers' liability for late delivery extended to loss of profits consequent on failure to keep, or (as in the *Transfield* case) adverse renegotiation of the rate payable under, lucrative follow-on fixtures because litigation would ensue on the issue of 'where to draw the line' on such recovery.

B. *A suggested additional test of scope of duty.* In fact Lords Hoffmann and Hope in the *Transfield* case attempted to introduce a radical new strand into contractual damages claims. Lord Hoffmann, in particular, preferred to address these background points directly by invoking his 'scope of duty' theory as the basis for denying the extended damages claim in the *Transfield* case (he had given the leading speech in the case, *Banque Bruxelles Lambert SA* v. *Eagle Star Insurance Co. Ltd* (the *SAAMCO* case, 1997),[181] which engendered this development in the law of tort).

C. Hadley v. Baxendale *subject to an occasional caveat or gloss.* It is in fact clear that the *Transfield* case has not introduced a second and parallel scope of duty test into contractual damages law, nor has this decision ousted the *Hadley* v. *Baxendale* line of cases on remoteness. Instead the *Transfield* case has added a gloss to that test: that predictability is not always sufficient so as to render the defendant liable for a particular category of loss or for the full loss within that category. Instead, but 'exceptionally'[182] and in 'relatively rare'[183] instances, it might be necessary to conduct a wider examination of the commercial context, and the contract's nature and object will justify reducing (the more usual case) or perhaps expanding (this is likely to be very rare, however) the traditional remoteness test. This outcome is pleasing because in the *Transfield* case Baroness Hale had rightly expressed concern that the scope of duty approach might introduce uncertainty into disputes concerning commercial damages claims.[184]

D. *Scope of duty test.* This test (see text below) applies only to tort law and to contract claims where there is overlapping liability in contract and in tort by the same defendant based on the same standard of care. By contrast, if there is no concurrent tort liability, 'scope of duty' should not apply as an independent doctrine and instead, as explained above, the issue whether relevant loss is recoverable, or recoverable in full, can be satisfactorily addressed using the contractual test of remoteness, supplemented by the gloss noted in the cases examined earlier (notably in Hamblen J's summary in 'The Sylvia' (2010)[185] of the post-*Transfield* approach).

---

181 Lord Hoffmann had given the leading speech in the case, *Banque Bruxelles Lambert SA* v. *Eagle Star Insurance Co. Ltd* (the *SAAMCO* case) [1997] AC 191, HL which engendered this development in the law of tort: see further in the text below.
182 A. M. Tettenborn, in M. A. Clarke, N. Andrews, A. M. Tettenborn, G. Virgo, *Contractual Duties: Performance, Breach, Termination and Remedies* (London, 2012), 23.28.
183 Hamblen J in 'The Sylvia' [2010] EWHC 542 (Comm); [2010] 2 Lloyd's Rep 81; [2010] 1 CLC 470, at [40], [41].
184 [2008] UKHL 48; [2009] 1 AC 61, at [93], *per* Baroness Hale.
185 Hamblen J in 'The Sylvia' [2010] EWHC 542 (Comm); [2010] 2 Lloyd's Rep 81; [2010] 1 CLC 470, at [40], [41].

Background to the debate on *Transfield*:

(1) In addition to Lord Walker's remarks in the *Transfield case* (2008),[186] there is ample post-*Transfield* authority[187] confirming that the remoteness test in contract law continues to apply, based on the *Hadley v. Baxendale* line of cases (see the pre-*Transfield* case law set out below). Consistent with this, Lord Walker said in the *Transfield case* (2008)[188] that the *Hadley v. Baxendale* line of 'remoteness' case addresses 'not simply a question of probability' but also 'the question of *what the contracting parties must be taken to have had in mind, having regard to the nature and object of their business transaction*'. [emphasis added]

(2) Normally, such a 'second-level check on the extent of liability' might operate to reduce liability (so-called 'exclusionary' instances), as in the tort cases where damages have been restricted by overt reference to a scope of duty test: *Banque Bruxelles Lambert SA v. Eagle Star Insurance Co. Ltd* (the *SAAMCO* case) (1997)[189] and the *Haugesund Kommune (No. 2)* case (2011).[190]

(3) But, as Lord Walker noted in the *Transfield* case (2008), occasionally the extent of liability might be expanded (so-called 'inclusionary' instances):[191]

> If a manufacturer of lightning conductors sells a defective conductor and the customer's house burns down as a result, the manufacturer will not escape liability by proving that only one in a hundred of his customers' buildings had actually been struck by lightning ... [What] is most important is the common expectation, objectively assessed, on the basis of which the parties are entering into their contract.

(4) Similarly, Toulson LJ said in the *Supershield* case (2010) (a post-*Transfield* case):[192] 'the question is not simply one of probability, but of what the contracting parties must be taken to have had in mind, having regard to the nature and object of their business transaction.'

(5) There is a helpful summary of the post-*Transfield* approach by Hamblen J in 'The Sylvia' (2010),[193] where he makes these points: (a) The *Transfield* case 'results in an amalgam of the orthodox and the broader approach. The orthodox approach remains the general test of remoteness applicable in the great majority of cases.' (b) 'However, there may be "unusual" cases, such as [the *Transfield* case] itself, in which the context, surrounding circumstances or general understanding in the relevant market make it necessary specifically to consider whether there has been an assumption of responsibility [viz. scope of duty reasoning].' But, (c) the need to resort to (b) will be confined to 'those relatively rare cases where the application of the general test leads or may lead to an unquantifiable, unpredictable, uncontrollable or disproportionate liability or

---

186 *Ibid.*, at [78], *per* Lord Walker, noting support for this approach in the literature: A. Kramer, in N. Cohen and E. McKendrick (eds.), *Comparative Remedies for Breach of Contract* (Oxford, 2005), 249; A. M. Tettenborn (2007) 23 JCL 120; A. Robertson (2008) 28 LS 172.

187 *Supershield Ltd v. Siemens Building Technologies FE Ltd* [2010] EWCA Civ 7; [2010] NPC 5, at [37], *per* Toulson LJ; Hamblen J in 'The Sylvia' [2010] EWHC 542 (Comm); [2010] 2 Lloyd's Rep 81; [2010] 1 CLC 470, at [40], [41]; Flaux J in *ASM Shipping Ltd of India v. TTMI Ltd of England ('The Amer Energy')* [2009] 1 Lloyd's Rep 293, at [17] to [19]; *Ispat Industries Ltd. v. Western Bulk Pte. Ltd* [2011] EWHC 93 (Comm) at [52], *per* Teare J; and *per* Supperstone J in *Shah v. HSBC Private Bank (UK) Ltd* [2012] EWHC 1283 (QB); *The Times*, 11 July 2012 at [227], and [232]. See also *James Grimes Partnership Ltd v. Gubbins* [2013] EWCA Civ 37; [2013] BLR 126, at [20] and [24], *per* Keane LJ (noted J. Goodwin, (2013) 129 LQR 486–8).

188 [2008] UKHL 48; [2009] 1 AC 61, at [78] and [79], *per* Lord Walker, noting support for this approach in the literature: A. Kramer, in N. Cohen and E. McKendrick (eds.), *Comparative Remedies for Breach of Contract* (Oxford, 2005), 249; A. M. Tettenborn (2007) 23 JCL 120; A. Robertson (2008) 28 LS 172.

189 [1997] AC 191, HL.

190 *Haugesund Kommune v. Depfa ACS Bank (No. 2)* [2011] EWCA Civ 33; [2011] 1 CLC 166; [2011] PNLR 14.

191 [2008] UKHL 48; [2009] 1 AC 61, at [78], *per* Lord Walker.

192 [2010] EWCA Civ 7; [2010] NPC 5, at [42].

193 Hamblen J in 'The Sylvia' [2010] EWHC 542 (Comm); [2010] 2 Lloyd's Rep 81; [2010] 1 CLC 470, at [40], [41].

where . . . liability would be contrary to market understanding and expectations'; in other words, 'In the great majority of cases . . . [traditional issues of reasonable contemplation, namely] the fact that the type of loss arises in the ordinary course of things or out of special known circumstances will carry with it the necessary assumption of responsibility.'[194]

(6) Nor, after retiring from the Bench, does Lord Hoffmann seem to dissent from this gloss on the *Hadley* v. *Baxendale* test. In the *Edinburgh Law Review* (2010), Lord Hoffmann wrote:[195]

> what obligation to make compensation for breach of contract would a reasonable observer understand the contracting party to have undertaken? In the ordinary way, that will be compensation for any loss which the parties would reasonably have regarded as likely to flow from the breach. But there may be cases in which a reasonable man would consider that a *greater or lesser obligation* was being accepted. [emphasis added]

(7) *Background concerning the scope of duty test.*[196]

(a) *Nature.* The scope of duty test is a general test in the law of tort and extends beyond professional negligence cases (see the next paragraph), to (i) liability in respect of a suicidal employee;[197] and (ii) the voluntary undertaking by a bookmaker to deny the claimant a telephone betting account.[198]

(b) *Genesis.* The House of Lords in *Banque Bruxelles Lambert SA* v. *Eagle Star Insurance Co. Ltd* (the *SAAMCO* case, 1997)[199] applied this test in the context of a surveyor's negligent valuation of property, when (a) the basic head of claim is directly attributable to his breach and is recoverable but (b) that loss has become aggravated by a fall in the market price of the relevant subject matter. Only the loss at (a) is recoverable, according to the House of Lords in the *Banque Bruxelles/SAAMCO* case.

(c) *Illustration of test.* In the *Haugesund Kommune (No. 2)* case (2011) negligent solicitors[200] had failed to identify that certain loan agreements made to Norwegian public authorities would be void under Norwegian law.[201] But the scope of duty criterion excluded liability attributable to the borrowers' 'lack of creditworthiness' or deliberate refusal to repay. In short there was no link between the defendant's negligence and the lenders' failure to recoup the loans from the borrowers.

18.21 *Damages to reflect post-breach events.* The House of Lords decision in *Golden Strait Corporation* v. *Nippon Yusen Kubishika Kaisha ('The Golden Victory')* (2007) makes clear that assessment of damages should reflect post-breach facts *if they are already known and they would have had the effect of diminishing the claimant's loss.*[202]

---

194 *Ibid.*, at [41].
195 (2010) 14 *Edinburgh Law Review* 47, 55.
196 The doctrine is already deep-rooted in the tort of negligence, including overlapping contractual and tortious duties of care: see the cases noted by Rix LJ in *Haugesund Kommune* v. *Depfa ACS Bank (No. 2)* [2011] EWCA Civ 33; [2011] 1 CLC 166; [2011] PNLR 14, at [42] to [68].
197 E.g. *Corr* v. *IBC Vehicles Ltd* [2008] UKHL 13; [2008] 2 All ER 943, at [9] and [10].
198 *Calvert* v. *William Hill Credit Ltd* [2008] EWCA Civ 1427; [2009] Ch 330, at [46] and [47]: citing at [43] ff Lord Hoffmann's discussion of 'Causation' in (2005) LQR 592.
199 *Banque Bruxelles Lambert SA* v. *Eagle Star Insurance Co. Ltd* (the '*SAAMCO*' case) [1997] AC 191, HL.
200 *Haugesund Kommune* v. *Depfa ACS Bank (No. 2)* [2011] EWCA Civ 33; [2011] 1 CLC 166; [2011] PNLR 14, at [77], [80], [87], *per* Rix LJ.
201 The same legal calamity befell lenders to British local authorities: *Hazell* v. *Hammersmith & Fulham LBC* [1992] 2 AC 1, HL.
202 [2007] UKHL 12; [2007] 2 AC 353.

In December 2001, a charterer had repudiated the contract by returning the ship early (contract to run for seven years from 1998). The question was whether damages (which fell to be assessed as from 2001) should reflect the fact that the contract would have been terminated, without breach, by the charterer subsequently invoking a war clause. It was clear (as found by the arbitrator) that the charterer would have so cancelled the contract once war was declared between the USA and Iraq in March 2003.

A majority of the House of Lords,[203] upholding the Court of Appeal, held that it would be unjust not to take account of these supervening events when assessing the damages. They rejected the concept that the innocent party's right to compensation is to be worked out without regard to these subsequent events. The outbreak of war would have entitled the charterer to invoke the war clause. From that point, the charterer would have been absolved from contractual liability to pay hire. In the majority's opinion, damages must reflect this hindsight; to fail to do so would involve 'over-compensation'.

It is submitted that the decision is unsound. Lord Bingham's dissent is persuasive.[204]

> The House of Lords decision in 'The Golden Victory' (2007) has provoked debate among commentators, the majority finding the decision unconvincing. Thus Reynolds,[205] Morgan[206] and Coote[207] say that this decision is unattractive, first, because it introduces 'unwelcome uncertainty'; secondly, because it discourages settlement of the claim at the time of the breach; thirdly, as noted by Lord Mustill (writing in a journal), because it overrides the established view that termination occurs following an anticipatory breach, damages should be worked out at that date of termination.[208]
>
> However, Burrows approves the majority's decision, suggesting that the chronological starting point for assessment of damages should be, and in his opinion has become, the date of judgment at trial.[209] Liu also supports the majority's decision.[210]

18.22 *Mitigation of damage principle.*[211] The claimant must take reasonable steps to mitigate his loss, either by reducing or even by eliminating that loss. If mitigation efforts are

---

203   Lords Scott, Carswell and Brown (dissents by Lords Bingham and Walker).
204   [2007] UKHL 12; [2007] 2 AC 353, notably at [22] and [23] (too long to cite here); in essence on the basis that the innocent party had lost a four-year charterparty which was marketable at the date of breach.
205   F. M. B. Reynolds, (2008) HKLJ 333.
206   C. J. Morgan, [2007] CLJ 263, 264–5.
207   B. Coote, (2007) 123 LQR 503, 510.
208   M. Mustill, (2008) 124 LQR 569, 584.
209   A. S. Burrows, in M. Andenas and D. Fairgrieve (eds.), *Tom Bingham and the Transformation of the Law: A Liber Amicorum* (Oxford, 2009), 598–601; A. S. Burrows, *Remedies for Torts and Breach of Contract* (3rd edn, Oxford, 2004), 188 ff, and opposing S. Waddams, 'The Date for the Assessment of Damages' (1981) 97 LQR 445.
210   [2007] LMCLQ 273; see also A. Dyson and A. Kramer, 'There is No "Breach Date Rule" . . . ' (2014) 130 LQR 259–81.
211   A. S. Burrows, *Remedies for Torts and Breach of Contract* (3rd edn, Oxford, 2004), 122–8; M. Bridge, 'Mitigation of Damages in Contract and the Meaning of Avoidable Loss' (1989) 105 LQR 398; M. Bridge, 'The Market Rule of Damages Assessment', in D. Saidov and R. Cunnington (eds.), *Contract Damages: Domestic and International Perspectives* (Oxford, 2008), chapter 18; A. Dyson and A. Kramer, 'There is No "Breach Date Rule" . . . ' (2014) 130 LQR 259–81; A. Kramer, *The Law of Contract Damages* (Oxford, 2014), chapter 15; *McGregor on Damages* (19th edn, London, 2014), chapter 9; H. McGregor, 'The Role of Mitigation in the Assessment of Damages', in D. Saidov and R. Cunnington (eds.), *Contract Damages: Domestic and*

successful, the defendant's liability is adjusted accordingly; and, if there is a failure to mitigate, to that extent damages will also be reduced. Thus, in the *British Westinghouse* case (1912), Viscount Haldane LC said: '[This principle] imposes on a plaintiff the duty of taking all reasonable steps to mitigate the loss consequent on the breach and debars him from claiming any part of the damage which is due to his neglect to take such steps.'[212]

The mitigation principle will now be elaborated.

Duty to endeavour to reduce or eliminate loss

The main mitigation rule is that an innocent party is expected to take reasonable steps to reduce or eliminate the loss caused by, or likely to ensue from, the other party's breach of contract (or tortious misconduct).

The defendant bears the burden of proving that there has been a failure to mitigate.[213] The question whether a party has satisfied the mitigation principle is treated as an issue of fact, which appellate courts are highly unlikely to disturb.[214] Both propositions are illustrated by *Lombard North Central plc* v. *Automobile World (UK) Ltd* (2010)[215] where the Court of Appeal upheld a trial judge's decision that the innocent party, having repossessed a luxury car after the purchaser defaulted in paying instalments, had taken reasonable steps to get the best second-hand price within the market. Rix LJ added:

> the duty to mitigate is not a demanding one. *Ex hypothesi*, it is the party in breach which has placed the other party in a difficult situation. The burden of proof is therefore on the party in breach to demonstrate a failure to mitigate. The other party only has to do what is reasonable in the circumstances.

Normally, 'reasonable steps' do not require a claimant to engage in litigation,[216] unless that course is exceptionally predictable and risk-free.[217] Certainly, the claimant is not required to sue third parties if this will injure its commercial reputation.[218]

International Perspectives (Oxford, 2008), chapter 14; A. M. Tettenborn, in M. A. Clarke, N. Andrews, A. M. Tettenborn, G. Virgo, *Contractual Duties: Performance, Breach, Termination and Remedies* (London, 2012), 24.38 to 24.69; for comparative sources, see G. H. Treitel, *Remedies for Breach of Contract* (Oxford, 1988), [145] ff; *Principles of European Contract Law*, Article 9:505, and UNIDROIT's *Principles of International Commercial Contracts*, Article 7.4.8; and the (abortive) *Contract Code: Drawn up on Behalf of the English Law Commission* (Milan, 1993), section 439.

212   [1912] AC 673, 689, HL; e.g. houseowner had not acted unreasonably in refusing to allow the builder to effect repairs: *Iggleden* v. *Fairview New Homes (Shooters Hill) Ltd* [2007] EWHC 1573 (TCC), Coulson J.
213   *Geest plc* v. *Lansiquot* [2002] UKPC 48; [2002] 1 WLR 3111, PC; *Roper* v. *Johnson* (1873) LR 8 CP 167, 178, 181–2.
214   E.g. *'The Solholt'* [1983] 1 Lloyd's Rep 605, CA.
215   [2010] EWCA Civ 20, at [72], *per* Rix LJ.
216   *Pilkington* v. *Wood* [1953] Ch 770, Harman J.
217   *Horsfall* v. *Haywards* [1999] PNLR 583, 588, CA, considering *Western Trust & Savings Ltd* v. *Travers & Co.* [1997] PNLR 295, CA and *Walker* v. *Geo. H Medlicott* [1999] 1 All ER 685, CA (application for rectification of a will under section 20 of the Administration of Justice Act 1982).
218   *James Finlay & Co.* v. *Kwik Hoo Tong* [1929] 1 KB 400, CA; *London and South of England Building Society* v. *Stone* [1983] 3 All ER 105, CA.

Examples

(1) *Wrongful dismissal.* An employee who is wrongfully dismissed must try to re-enter the job market. However, if the defendant offers an alternative position, there will be no failure by the employee to mitigate his loss if the new offer involves a demotion, as in *Shindler* v. *Northern Raincoat Co. Ltd* (1960), where a senior manager did not have to suffer the indignity of appointment at a lower rank.[219] Subject to that, sometimes the responsibility to attempt a reasonable mitigation of loss requires the innocent party to accept an offer of re-employment with the defendant, as stated in *Brace* v. *Calder* (1895).[220]

(2) *Sale of goods: failure to supply or purchase.* The assumption is that the innocent party can resell to a third party or repurchase from a third party, thereby mitigating his loss, provided there is an 'available market' for such goods. Thus, a seller or buyer (respectively), when suing for damages for non-acceptance of goods or non-delivery, should recover prima facie the difference between the price agreed and the (higher) market value of substitute goods, these differences in amounts to be calculated at the date of agreed delivery or, if no such date was agreed, the date of breach.[221]

(3) *Sale of goods: no obligation to mitigate by accepting shoddy or inferior goods.* In *Heaven & Kesterton Ltd* v. *Etablissements Francois Albiac et Cie* (1956), the seller had tendered timber of inferior quality.[222] The buyer rejected it. Devlin J held that the mitigation principle did not require the buyer to accept these shoddy goods.

(4) *Problematic case.*[223] In *'The Solholt'* (1983), the buyer justifiably terminated a contract for the purchase of a vessel for US$5m by 31 August.[224] The Court of Appeal, however, unconvincingly denied the buyer its normal compensatory measure (at the date of termination, the vessel's value had already increased 10 per cent to US$5.5m). Michael Bridge contends that the buyer should have been entitled to the initial 10 per cent increase in the ship's value (US$500,000)[225] as a 'loss of bargain' which had already arisen. That claim should not have been nullified by the buyer's alleged 'mitigation' failure. Resort to mitigation here involves an overreaching or misapplication of that concept. The effect is *ex post facto* to deny the innocent party his crystallised right to contractual compensation.[226]

---

219 [1960] 1 WLR 1038, Diplock J; *Yetton* v. *Eastwoods Froy Ltd* [1967] 1 WLR 104, 118C–D, 119D (no default in mitigation), Blain J, reviewing the case law.

220 [1895] 2 KB 253, CA.

221 Sections 50(3) and 51(3) of the Sale of Goods Act 1979.

222 [1956] 2 Lloyd's Rep 316, Devlin J (appropriateness of such a rejection now subject to section 15A of the Sale of Goods Act 1979 (17.35) if the basis of the termination were a breach of an implied statutory term concerning quality).

223 H. McGregor, 'The Role of Mitigation in the Assessment of Damages', in D. Saidov and R. Cunnington (eds.), *Contract Damages: Domestic and International Perspectives* (Oxford, 2008), chapter 14, at 335.

224 [1983] 1 Lloyd's Rep 605, CA, noted by E. Lomnicka, (1983) LQR 495–7; cf *Sealace Shipping Co. Ltd* v. *Ocean Voice Ltd* [1996] 1 Lloyd's Rep 120, 125 CA (on which see *Ruxley Electronics and Construction Ltd* v. *Forsyth* [1996] 1 AC 344, 371H, HL; the latter case itself is also an example of a damages claim disproportionate to the innocent party's true loss).

225 M. Bridge, (1989) 105 LQR 398, 417.

226 A similar criticism can be made of the *Payzu* case, [1919] 2 KB 581, CA (buyer expected, in name of mitigation, to have succumbed to seller's repudiatory breach, requiring cash payment, rather than payment within agreed one month period); cf vendor in breach of contract; no vacant possession; property occupied by a sitting tenant; no duty to accept vendor's offer of repurchase of real property: *Strutt* v. *Whitnell* [1975] 1 WLR 870, CA; approved by Bridge (1989) 105 LQR 398, 422–3; MacKenna J, the third appeal judge, distinguished the

Mitigation in face of hazardous breach

Schering Agrochemicals Ltd v. *Resibel NVSA* (1992)[227] demonstrates that the mitigation principle applies if a claimant fails to take appropriate precautions after he has become aware of a probable breach of contract which creates a serious hazard. Conversely, *County Ltd* v. *Girozentrale Securities* (1996)[228] shows that no duty to mitigate arises if the claimant was ignorant of the breach.

In *Schering Agrochemicals Ltd* v. *Resibel NVSA* (1992), the defendant had supplied defective bottle-sealing machinery to the claimant, together with a safety alarm system.[229] If the bottles, containing dangerous chemicals, were not kept moving on the processing belt, an explosion would occur. After the claimant's management turned a blind eye to this problem, an explosion and fire destroyed the factory. The claimant lost the action for compensation because its recklessness constituted a failure to mitigate the defendant's breach.

The claimant will not lose, however, if he was unaware of the defendant's breach. Thus in *County Ltd* v. *Girozentrale Securities* (1996)[230] the defendant stockbrokers had arranged to approach potential investors to buy shares in R plc, this sale being underwritten by the claimant. The defendants, in breach of contract, had not prepared the ground properly and had made over-sanguine predictions that the shares would sell like hot cakes. In fact proposed investors melted away. The claimant lost £7m. The defendant brokers tried to deflect liability onto the claimant, implausibly contending that the claimant should have checked the strength of market interest. But the Court of Appeal rejected this: the defendant was in breach; the claimant did not know this at first;[231] the claimant acted reasonably once it did discover the defendant's contractual shortcomings;[232] overall, therefore, the mitigation defence did not shield the defendant on these facts.

Recovery of extra loss for successful or unsuccessful attempts to mitigate

The innocent party is entitled to recover from the defendant any expense or additional loss incurred when taking reasonable steps to mitigate the loss.[233] Such loss is recoverable even if the attempt at mitigation was unsuccessful, provided this attempt was reasonable.[234]

Payzu case as one where the buyer was not being forced to undo a transaction where property had already passed.

227   Court of Appeal, 26 November 1992, unreported, Court of Appeal transcript No. 1298 of 1992, noted by A. S. Burrows, (1993) 109 LQR 175.
228   *County Ltd* v. *Girozentrale Securities* [1996] 3 All ER 834, CA.
229   Court of Appeal, 26 November 1992, unreported, Court of Appeal transcript No. 1298 of 1992 (the *ratio* summarised here is that of Nolan and Purchas LJJ; Scott LJ's concurring reasoning is based on a different and doubtful analysis).
230   *Ibid.*
231   *Ibid.*, at 859A–B, *per* Hobhouse LJ.
232   *Ibid.*, at 858F.
233   H. McGregor, 'The Role of Mitigation in the Assessment of Damages', in D. Saidov and R. Cunnington (eds.), *Contract Damages: Domestic and International Perspectives* (Oxford, 2008), chapter 14, at 336.
234   *Esso Petroleum Co. Ltd* v. *Mardon* [1976] QB 801, CA.

In *Banco de Portugal* v. *Waterlow & Sons Ltd* (1932),[235] the defendant was commissioned by the claimant bank to print bank notes in a new issue of Portuguese currency. The defendant breached its contract by allowing thousands of these new notes to fall into the hands of an international criminal who fraudulently put them into circulation. The House of Lords held that the claimant bank had acted reasonably in buying up these notes and cancelling this issue because these measures were commensurate with the perilous situation created by the breach. Such loss was recoverable even though it was not foreseeable at the contract's commencement.

In *Holden Ltd* v. *Bostock & Co. Ltd* (1902),[236] the defendant sold sugar to the claimant for brewing purposes. But the sugar was contaminated with arsenic. The claimant incurred advertising expenditure to reassure customers that the danger of arsenic poisoning had been countered. This expense had been reasonably incurred in mitigation, and so it could be recovered.

But in *'The Borag'* (1981),[237] the Court of Appeal refused to allow a claim for excessive interest charges incurred on a loan taken out by the claimant in order to finance the release of a ship detained in breach of contract. These high charges were not a reasonable act of mitigation.

Mitigation in fact achieved

The House of Lords in *British Westinghouse Electric Co. Ltd* v. *Underground Electric Railways* (1912) made clear that the innocent party must offset against his damages any benefits which in fact accrue to him as a result of steps taken by him in response to the relevant breach.[238]

In *British Westinghouse Electric Co. Ltd* v. *Underground Electric Railways* (1912), the seller supplied defective turbines. The buyer enterprisingly decided to use alternative and superior turbines, which it bought from a third party supplier. As a result, the buyer's business operated much more profitably than it would have done even if the seller had supplied non-defective turbines. The buyer claimed two heads of loss: (1) the loss attributable to running the deficient machines before they were replaced; and (2) the cost of installing the new machines. Head (1) was unproblematic. But head (2) was, in the House of Lords' opinion, subject to the mitigation principle: the buyer's expenses in buying and installing the replacement machines had been recouped by the extra profitability of the new machines.[239] Viscount Haldane LC said that the decision to buy superior turbines was 'a natural and prudent course followed by those whose

235 [1932] AC 452, HL.
236 (1902) 18 TLR 317.
237 [1981] 1 All ER 856, CA.
238 *British Westinghouse Electric Co. Ltd* v. *Underground Electric Railways* [1912] AC 673, 691, HL (For close re-examination of the case, A. Dyson, [2012] LMCLQ 412–25, preferring to explain the case as concerned with benefits accruing in course of steps taken in pursuance of a duty to mitigate); subsequent cases reviewed in *Primavera* v. *Allied Dunbar Assurance plc* [2002] EWCA Civ 1327; [2003] PNLR 276, CA; see also the sale of defective goods case law, where the purchaser succeeds in reselling without suffering pecuniary loss, K. E. Barnett, (2014) 130 LQR 387, examining the English and Australian authorities).
239 [1912] AC 673, HL.

> object was to avoid further loss, and . . . it formed part of a continuous dealing with the situation in which they found themselves, and was not an independent or disconnected transaction'.[240] With this guidance, the case was remitted to the arbitrator.

It will be different if it is held that the claimant's gain or saving has no sufficient connection with the defendant's breach other than an 'historical connection'.[241] The courts have regard to: (1) the interval between the initial wrong and the claimant's subsequent benefit (the *Hussey* (1990)[242] and *Gardner* (1997)[243] cases); (2) inconvenience or disruption to the claimant occurring during that interval; (3) the claimant's effort (including complex negotiations with third parties), determination, and ingenuity in achieving that benefit; (4) whether the achievement of that benefit involved a deviation from the intended use of the subject matter of the relevant contract (real estate redeveloped, rather than use as a residence, as in the *Hussey* case); and (5) whether, as a matter of commercial prudence, it was appropriate for the innocent party to use a different product in the interest of achieving an economy (as in the *British Westinghouse* case).[244]

Replacement following breach

In *Harbutt's 'Plasticine' Ltd* v. *Wayne Tank & Pump Co. Ltd* (1970),[245] the Court of Appeal held that there should be no reduction in the claimant's damages (based on the 'cost of cure' measure), enabling the claimant to reconstruct its factory which had been destroyed as a result of the defendant's breach of contract (equipment supplied by the defendant had caused a catastrophic fire in the claimant's factory). There was no justification for reducing those damages to reflect the 'betterment' value of the new factory.

Similarly, in *Bacon* v. *Cooper (Metals) Ltd* (1982),[246] the claimant received an award of damages enabling it to replace defective machinery. As a result, the claimant would obtain equipment having a longer life than the original machinery. Cantley J held, however, that no allowance should be made to reflect this improvement.

But where it is cheaper to repair rather than to replace, the mitigation principle will confine the innocent party to recovering the cost of cure measure of compensation rather than suing for the larger sum necessary to purchase a complete replacement.[247]

---

240 *Ibid.*, at 691–2.
241 *Primavera* v. *Allied Dunbar Assurance plc* [2002] EWCA Civ 1327; [2003] PNLR 276, CA, at [52], *per* Latham LJ; H. McGregor, 'The Role of Mitigation in the Assessment of Damages', in D. Saidov and R. Cunnington (eds.), *Contract Damages: Domestic and International Perspectives* (Oxford, 2008), chapter 14, at 336 ff.
242 *Hussey* v. *Eels* [1990] 2 QB 227, 241 CA, *per* Mustill LJ, noted by A. J. Oakley, [1990] CLJ 394; *Primavera* v. *Allied Dunbar Assurance plc* [2002] EWCA Civ 1327; [2003] PNLR 276, CA.
243 *Gardner* v. *Marsh & Parsons (a firm)* [1997] 1 WLR 489, CA.
244 *British Westinghouse Electric Co. Ltd* v. *Underground Electric Railways* [1912] AC 673, 691, HL.
245 [1970] QB 447, CA.
246 [1982] 1 All ER 397, 400–2, Cantley J.
247 *Ruxley Electronics and Construction Ltd* v. *Forsyth* [1996] 1 AC 344, 366 D, HL, Lord Lloyd.

Mitigation principle does not apply to claim for debt

The mitigation principle concerns only claims for damages, and so it does not apply to a claim for debt; see 18.02 on the *White & Carter* case (1962), (although the Supreme Court might usefully revisit this topic).

18.23 *Claimant's 'contributory negligence' and the Law Reform (Contributory Negligence) Act 1945.*[248] Section 1(1) of the Act states:

> *Where any person suffers damage as the result partly of his own fault and partly of the fault of any other person or persons, a claim in respect of that damage shall not be defeated by reason of the fault of the person suffering the damage, but the damages recoverable in respect thereof shall be reduced to such extent as the court thinks just and equitable having regard to the claimant's share in the responsibility for the damage.*

Fault is defined in section 4 as: 'negligence, breach of statutory duty or other act or omission which gives rise to a liability in tort or would, apart from this Act, give rise to the defence of contributory negligence'.

The defence of contributory negligence has little impact upon contractual claims for damages and instead applies only where (a) the relevant contractual obligation was to exercise reasonable care (and many contractual obligations are *strict*), and (b) the relevant breach of contract has occurred within a relationship where the defendant *is also liable in the tort of negligence for the same default* (or, in other words, where there is 'concurrent' liability in contract and tort: see 1.23 and 17.02). Proposition (a) reflects the wording of the 1945 Act. Proposition (b) was established in *Forsikringsaktieselskapet Vesta* v. *Butcher* (1989) (the *Vesta* case), where the Court of Appeal approved the following trichotomy which had been formulated by Hobhouse J, at first instance, in this case:[249]

> The question whether the [Law Reform (Contributory Negligence) Act 1945] applies to claims brought in contract can arise in a number of classes of case.

(1) Where the defendant's liability arises from some contractual provision which does not depend on negligence on the part of the defendant.

(2) Where the defendant's liability arises from a contractual obligation which is expressed in terms of taking care (or its equivalent) but does not correspond to a Common Law duty to take care which would exist in the given case independently of contract (but this restriction is ripe for reform).[250]

---

248 *McGregor on Damages* (19th edn, London, 2014), chapter 7; A. M. Tettenborn, in M. A. Clarke, N. Andrews, A. M. Tettenborn, G. Virgo, *Contractual Duties: Performance, Breach, Termination and Remedies* (London, 2012), 24.70 to 24.76.
249 *Forsikringsaktieselskapet Vesta* v. *Butcher* (affirmed on other points by the House of Lords, [1989] AC 852, 860, where the Court of Appeal's decision is also reported); Court of Appeal approving Hobhouse J at [1986] 2 All ER 488, 508 (by contrast, the High Court of Australia has held that contributory negligence does not apply to the contractual claim in this context: *Astley* v. *Austrust Ltd* (1999) 161 ALR 144, G. Davis and J. Knowler (1999) 23 *MUL Rev* 795).
250 A. S. Burrows, *Remedies for Torts and Breach of Contract* (3rd edn, Oxford, 2004), 142–3, noting Law Commission, 'Contributory Negligence as a Defence in Contract' (Law Commission Report No. 219, London, 1993).

(3) Where the defendant's liability in contract is the same as his liability in the tort of negligence independently of the existence of any contract.

In the *Vesta* case, the Court of Appeal declared itself bound by earlier authority to confine the 1945 Act to category (3).[251] It will be rare for a situation to fall within category (2) (stand-alone contractual duty of care) rather than category (3) (concurrent contractual and tortious duties of care).[252] In *Barclays Bank plc* v. *Fairclough Building* (1995), the Court of Appeal affirmed that the 1945 Act does not apply to a category (1) case (contractual strict liability).[253]

Two more points should be noted. First, the 1945 Act does not apply to the action for deceit (see also 9.23).[254] Secondly, the 1945 Act does apply to a claim for damages under section 2(1) of the Misrepresentation Act 1967 (9.20), provided the claimant enjoys a parallel Common Law action for negligence against the representor.[255]

> *Should category (1) be subject to the contributory negligence defence?* Burrows[256] answers 'yes' to this question (even though the Law Commission in 1993 concluded that no such change should be made).[257] The first objection to Burrows' suggestion is that the claimant's fault and the defendant's strict liability breach are not *in pari materia*: like is not compared with like. The second objection is that extension of contributory negligence to all contractual breaches would create uncertainty and even injustice. For example, the buyer of defective goods, confronted by an expanded defence of contributory negligence, might hesitate 'to hold out' until trial for full compensation, preferring to accept 25, 50 or 75 per cent, rather than the whole amount.

18.24 *Damages for loss of an opportunity to bargain: the 'user principle'.*

(1) The essential idea is that the court can award the victim a sum designed to simulate a notional release or relaxation fee which might have been paid by the defendant if he had courteously sought permission to make 'use' of the claimant's protected interest.

---

251 [1989] AC 852, 860, at 867F, CA, following *Sayers* v. *Harlow Urban District Council* [1958] 1 WLR 623, CA; *UCB Bank plc* v. *Hebherd Winstanley & Pugh, The Times*, 25 August 1999, CA.

252 *Raflatac Ltd* v. *Eade* [1999] 1 Lloyd's Rep 506, Colman J; on the extensive incidence of overlapping contractual and tortious duties of care, see *Henderson* v. *Merrett Syndicates Ltd* [1995] 2 AC 145, HL (see 1.23).

253 [1995] QB 214, CA, noted by C. Hopkins, [1995] CLJ 20–3; A. S. Burrows, *Remedies for Torts and Breach of Contract* (3rd edn, Oxford, 2004), 136–44.

254 *Standard Chartered Bank* v. *Pakistan Corporation (Nos. 2 and 4)* [2003] 1 AC 959, HL, at [18], *per* Lord Hoffmann, and [42] to [45], *per* Lord Rodger.

255 *Gran Gelato Ltd* v. *Richliff Ltd* [1992] Ch 560, Nicholls V-C.

256 A. S. Burrows, *Remedies for Torts and Breach of Contract* (3rd edn, Oxford, 2004), 141 ff; A. Porat, (1995) 111 LQR 228–34; A. Porat, 'A Comparative Fault Defence in Contract Law' (2009) 107 *Michigan Law Review* 1397–1412 (part of the symposium on 'Fault in American Contract Law').

257 Law Commission, 'Contributory Negligence as a Defence in Contract' (Law Commission Report No. 219, London, 1993) (rejecting its view in 'Contributory Negligence as a Defence in Contract', Working Paper No. 114, London, 1990); on the reasons for the Law Commission's change of mind, see C. Hopkins, [1995] CLJ 20, 22. Criticised A. S. Burrows, *Remedies for Torts and Breach of Contract* (3rd edn, Oxford, 2004), 142–3.

Brightman J's decision in *Wrotham Park Estate Co.* v. *Parkside Homes* (1974) is the modern starting point for 'user principle' damages.[258] In breach of a restrictive covenant, the defendant had built some houses on its land. In an action for damages in lieu of an injunction (which would have required demolition of these dwellings), Brightman J chose not to award the innocent party the whole of the gain made from this breach. Instead, he awarded the claimant a rather modest percentage (5 per cent) of the defendant's profit. Commenting on the *Wrotham Park* case (1974), Lord Nicholls said in the *Blake* case (2001):[259]

> For social and economic reasons the court refused to . . . order . . . demolition of houses built on land burdened with a restrictive covenant. Instead, Brightman J . . . assessed the damages at 5 *per cent* of the developer's anticipated profit, this being the amount of money which could reasonably have been demanded for a relaxation of the covenant.

Obviously, the *Wrotham Park* award fell 95 per cent short of being a full-blown 'account' of profits.[260]

(2) It appears that such an award is available in a wide range of situations where there is no other identifiable financial loss,[261] the main criterion being that 'it would be manifestly unjust to leave the claimants with an award for no or nominal damages'.[262]

(3) Stadlen J in the *Giedo* case (2010) examined the issue of quantifying user principle damages, noting that relevant criteria for assessing such compensation are: either (a) a portion of the defendant's gain or (b) (less usually, but as on the facts of the *Giedo* case) the cost saved by the defendant in not performing his contractual obligation.[263]

(4) The better view is that the award of a 'user principle' sum is compensatory: it is designed to remedy loss of a bargaining opportunity. This is so whether the claim is focused on (a) or (b), as just mentioned. In each situation the court is trying to hit on a fair figure representing the 'buy-out' value of the claimant's rights. And so the courts try to mimic possible negotiation for a fee to be paid in return for relaxing the claimant's restrictive covenant.[264] The remedy and its quantification involve the attempt to rewrite history because the claimant was denied the opportunity to carry out such a negotiation with the defendant, the latter having instead gone behind the claimant's back and breached the contract.

---

258 [1974] 1 WLR 798, Brightman J; A. Kramer, *The Law of Contract Damages* (Oxford, 2014), chapter 22; and section 23.2; *McGregor on Damages* (19th edn, London, 2014), chapter 14.

259 [2001] 1 AC 268, 282–3, HL.

260 On the reasons for this ungenerous award, *Giedo* case [2010] EWHC 2373 (QB), at [554], *per* Stadlen J.

261 *Giedo Van Der Garde BV* v. *Force India Formula One Team Limited* [2010] EWHC 2373 (QB), at [499] to [559] (noted D. Winterton and F. Wilmot-Smith (2012) 128 LQR 23); where Stadlen J reviewed the scope for awarding 'Wrotham Park' damages; at [533] Stadlen J concluded that such an award is available even though 'the claimants advanced no claim for an injunction or specific performance, or the fact that there would have been no prospect of such an order being granted; . . . damages are not claimed under Lord Cairns' Act in lieu of an injunction; . . . the claim is not based on a breach of a restrictive covenant; and . . . the claim is based on breach of contract rather than invasion of property rights.' Noting also, at [525] ff, notably at [535], *Pell Frischmann Engineering Ltd* v. *Bow Valley Iran Ltd* [2009] UKPC 45; [2011] 1 WLR 2370.

262 *Giedo* case [2010] EWHC 2373 (QB), at [538], *per* Stadlen J.

263 *Ibid.*, at [549]: 'where there is no evidence of the amount of anticipated profits . . . the court may . . . have regard to the amount of anticipated costs which the defendant would save in the event of being released from its contractual obligations.'

264 This is a problematic hypothetical exercise: P. Devonshire, 'The Hypothetical Negotiation Measure: An Untenable Fiction?' [2012] LMCLQ 393–411.

As for point (4), Stadlen J in the *Giedo* case (2010) has demonstrated that there is clear judicial support for the compensatory analysis in a line of cases.[265] For example, not only Lord Nicholls[266] but Lord Hobhouse in the *Blake* case (2001) explained, with characteristic trenchancy, that the *Wrotham Park* case (1974), summarised above, involves compensation for denial of the chance to levy payment as a condition of releasing or modifying valuable rights: 'there has [been] either actually or in effect . . . a compulsory purchase of the plaintiff's right of refusal . . . What the plaintiff has lost is the sum which he could have exacted from the defendant as the price of his consent to the development.' And he added: 'This is an example of compensatory damages. They are damages for breach. They do not involve any concept of restitution and so to describe them is an error.'[267] Similarly, in the *WWF (No. 2)* case (2007) Chadwick LJ said 'that damages on the *Wrotham Park* basis' are 'a compensatory remedy'.[268]

18.25 *Further illustration of user principle damages.* In *Experience Hendrix LLC* v. *PPX Enterprises Inc.* (2005),[269] which was decided after the *Blake* case (18.30 below), the Court of Appeal awarded the claimant a less generous sum designed to reflect 'loss of opportunity to bargain for release or relaxation of the relevant rights', rather than an award of a full-blown account of profits.

In *Experience Hendrix LLC* v. *PPX Enterprises Inc.* (2005) the estate of Jimi Hendrix (a rock guitarist) sued in respect of a settlement agreement which it had agreed with PPX. In breach of that settlement, PPX had used master tapes. The Court of Appeal held that damages representing a reasonable price for their use should be awarded rather than *a full account of the defendant's profits gained as a result of this breach*. Mance LJ noted that there was nothing 'akin to a fiduciary relationship'[270] in the *Hendrix* case, contrasting the *Blake* case, where the former employee had signed a life-time undertaking not to reveal official secrets (18.30).

---

265 *Giedo* case [2010] EWHC 2373 (QB), at [540] to [548]; however, a 'schools dispute' has arisen in the academic literature: the view that *Wrotham Park* damages are compensatory is opposed by Burrows, who contends that the notional bargain is a mere fiction (A. S. Burrows, in M. Andenas and D. Fairgrieve (eds.), *Tom Bingham and the Transformation of the Law: A Liber Amicorum* (Oxford, 2009), 594–8; and A. S. Burrows, 'Are "Damages on the *Wrotham Park* Basis" Compensatory, Restitutionary or Neither?', in D. Saidov and R. Cunnington (eds.), *Contract Damages: Domestic and International Perspectives* (Oxford, 2008), chapter 7); but this allegation of fiction is flatly denied by Waddams: S. Waddams, 'Gains Derived from Breach of Contract: Historical and Conceptual Perspectives', in *ibid.*, 200 ff (earlier R. J. Sharpe and S. Waddams, (1982) 2 OJLS 290; cf his remark at S. Waddams, *Dimensions of Private Law* (Cambridge, 2003), 109); other discussion and dicta on this vexed issue are conveniently collected at R. Cunnington, (2007) 123 LQR 48, including *Jaggard* v. *Sawyer* [1995] 1 WLR 269, 281–2, 291, CA, *per* Bingham MR, and Millett LJ, the latter rejecting Steyn LJ's comment in *Surrey County Council* v. *Bredero Homes Ltd* [1983] 1 WLR 1361, 1369, CA, that the 'compensatory' theory involves a 'fiction'; *Gafford* v. *Graham* (1998) 76 P & CR 18; see also R. Cunnington, 'The Assessment of Gains-Based Damages for Breach of Contract' (2008) 71 MLR 559–86.
266 [2001] 1 AC 268, 281 letter G, HL, as noted by Stadlen J in the *Giedo* case [2010] EWHC 2373 (QB), at [540].
267 [2001] 1 AC 268, 298, HL.
268 *WWF (No. 2)* case [2007] EWCA Civ 286; [2008] 1 WLR 445, at [59]. Numbering added.
269 [2003] EWCA Civ 323; [2003] 1 All ER (Comm) 830, CA.
270 *Calvert* v. *William Hill Credit Ltd* [2008] EWCA Civ 1427; [2009] Ch 330, at [53]; J. Edelman, 'When do Fiduciary Duties Arise?' (2010) 126 LQR 302.

User principle damages for loss of opportunity to bargain were also awarded in *Lane* v. *O'Brien Homes Ltd* (2004). In this case, an extra house had been built, in breach of an agreement. The builder's profit from this breach was £280,000. But the judge merely awarded damages of £150,000 for loss of opportunity to bargain.[271]

4. RESTITUTIONARY CLAIMS

18.26 Restitutionary claims[272] are based on the defendant's unjust enrichment. The claim is not for the claimant's loss, but for the defendant's enrichment at the claimant's expense. There are three main forms of restitutionary relief relevant to contract law: (1) money recovered for a total failure of consideration (on express recovery of payment clauses, see 14.07 at (5)); (2) recovery in respect of goods or services; and (3) disgorgement of gains made in breach of contract. These will be explained in turn in the succeeding paragraphs.

Most restitutionary remedies arise independently of breach. However, breach of contract is an essential element in one restitutionary remedy, namely, the remedy of 'equitable account' (*Attorney-General* v. *Blake* (2001), noted at 18.30). The relevant enrichment can be money or services or goods. This cause of action can take various forms: it might be that the benefit was conferred as a result of the claimant's mistake of fact or law; or that there was a (total) failure of consideration, or duress, or undue influence, or abuse of fiduciary relationship[273] or an unjustified tax demand.

18.27 *Money recovered for a total failure of consideration.* A payor is entitled to recover money where there has been a 'total failure of consideration'.[274] The *Fibrosa* case (1942)[275] provides an example (which must suffice, for reasons of space).[276]

---

271 [2004] EWHC 303 (QB).

272 T. Baloch, *Unjust Enrichment and Contract* (Oxford, 2009); A. S. Burrows, *The Law of Restitution* (3rd edn, Oxford, 2011); *Goff and Jones on the Law of Unjust Enrichment* (8th edn, London, 2011); G. Virgo, *The Principles of the Law of Restitution* (2nd edn, Oxford, 2006); G. Virgo, in *Chitty on Contracts* (31st edn, London, 2012), chapter 29; A. S. Burrows, E. McKendrick and J. Edelman, *Cases and Materials on the Law of Restitution* (2nd edn, Oxford, 2007).

273 *Calvert* v. *William Hill Credit Ltd* [2008] EWCA Civ 1427; [2009] Ch 330, at [53]; J. Edelman, 'When Do Fiduciary Duties Arise?' (2010) 126 LQR 302.

274 For comment or criticism, F. Wilmot-Smith. 'Reconsidering "total" failure' [2013] CLJ 414; P. B. H. Birks, in F. D. Rose (ed.), *Consensus ad Idem: Essays on the Law of Contract in Honour of Guenter Treitel* (London, 1996), chapter 9.

275 [1943] AC 32, HL.

276 An important survey is *Giedo Van Der Garde BV* v. *Force India Formula One Team Limited* [2010] EWHC 2373 (QB), at [233] ff, notably at [323], [354], [359] to [361], [366], [377] (noted D. Winterton and F. Wilmot-Smith (2012) 128 LQR 23); other leading cases include *Rowland* v. *Divall* [1923] 2 KB 500, CA; *Rover International Ltd* v. *Cannon Films Sales Ltd* [1989] 1 WLR 912; *Barber* v. *NWS Bank* [1996] 1 WLR 641, CA; *Pan Ocean Shipping* v. *Creditcorp* ('*The Trident Beauty*') [1994] 1 WLR 161, 164–5, HL; *Stocznia Gdanska SA* v. *Latvian Shipping Co.* [1998] 1 WLR 574, HL; for restitution of money under a void contract, see *Westdeutsche Landesbank Girozentrale* v. *Islington London Borough Council* [1996] AC 669, 683, HL; *Guinness Mahon & Co. Ltd* v. *Kensington & Chelsea Royal London Borough Council* [1999] QB 215, 234–40, CA, Robert Walker LJ (considered in *Haugesund Kommune* v. *Depfa ACS Bank (No. 1)* [2010] EWCA Civ 579; [2012] QB 549, at [62] and [85]; noted by A. Briggs and J. Edelman, (2010) 126 LQR 501, 503); decisions allowing partial failure in special situations: *Goss* v. *Chilcott* [1996] AC 788, PC (approving the High Court of Australia's decision in *David Securities Pty Ltd* v. *Commonwealth of Australia* (1992) 109 ALR 57, High Court of Australia); *Baltic Shipping Co.* v. *Dillon* ('*The Mikhail Lermontov*') (1993) 176 CLR 344, High Court of Australia; *DO Ferguson & Associates* v. *Sohl* (1992) 62 BLR 95, CA.

The *Fibrosa* case (1942) concerned an agreement (subject to English law) for an English supplier to sell machinery to be delivered to a Polish port. The foreign buyer paid £1,000 in advance. The contract was frustrated (16.07 case (1)) because the (supervening) German occupation of Poland in 1939 rendered performance illegal (the contract then terminated by operation of law in accordance with the rule that there can be no trading with the enemy: it had become, as a result of supervening events, illegal to perform).

The House of Lords held that the prepayment should be repaid because the payor had not received any of the promised 'consideration', that is, none of the machinery had been delivered. The House of Lords overruled the decision in *Chandler* v. *Webster* (1904),[277] where the Court of Appeal had fallaciously barred recovery of payments whenever the payee had made to the payor a promise of performance. As the House of Lords noted in *Fibrosa*, although 'consideration' relevant to the formation of contracts (5.10 ff) can consist in the making of a promise, what counts in the context of the restitutionary claim for 'failure of consideration' is not the promise but actual performance of that promise. Furthermore, the House of Lords in the *Fibrosa* case held that in this transaction the relevant performance was delivery of machinery, and that preparation for its delivery did not count. For this reason, non-delivery involved total failure of performance.

18.28   In the context of frustrated contracts, however, recovery of money is now subject to the Law Reform (Frustrated Contracts) Act 1943 (16.21). The 1943 Act is confined to frustrated contracts. In that (narrow) category, section 1(2) of the Act allows money to be recovered even in the absence of a 'total failure'. But such recovery under the 1943 Act is subject to adjustment between the parties.[278] Apart from frustrated contracts, where this Act applies, the Common Law claim for repayment based on 'total failure' (see the preceding paragraph) still applies to various other contexts.

18.29   *Recovery in respect of goods or services.* This is illustrated by the *British Steel* case (1984) (2.04)[279] and the *Whittle* case (2009)[280] (4.17). In the *British Steel* case (1984), Goff J held that there had been no true agreement because negotiations had not resolved the issue of potential liability for late delivery of building materials to the defendant's order. The question of restitutionary relief arose because British Steel had supplied steel to the defendant company, which had used it in its building project. It was plainly just that the building company should pay a fair market sum to the claimant. This award was based on restitutionary or unjust enrichment principles. The *British Steel* case concerned goods, but a similar award is available in the case of services performed to the order of the defendant, even though there is no agreement or no valid contract.[281] Here, a restitutionary sum of

---

277   [1904] 1 KB 493, CA.
278   Section 1(2) of the Law Reform (Frustrated Contracts) Act 1943.
279   *British Steel Corporation* v. *Cleveland Bridge* [1984] 1 All ER 504, Goff J.
280   *Whittle Movers Ltd* v. *Hollywood Express Ltd* [2009] EWCA Civ 1189; [2009] CLC 771, Waller, Dyson and Lloyd LJJ; noted by P. S. Davies, (2010) 126 LQR 175–9.
281   *Goff and Jones on the Law of Unjust Enrichment* (8th edn, London, 2011), chapter 16; *MSM Consulting Ltd* v. *United Republic of Tanzania* [2009] EWHC 121 (QB), at [171], *per* Clarke J (distilling principles, with the assistance of Nicholas Strauss QC's decision in *Countrywide Communications Ltd* v. *ICL Pathway Ltd* [2000] CLC 324, 349: noted by P. Jaffey, [2000] *Restitution Law Review* 270–5).

recompense, conferring a reasonable sum, can be awarded (known as a *quantum meruit*) for the performing party's benefit, as in *Planché* v. *Colburn* (1831) (recompense for work done in composing material no longer required by the defendant publisher),[282] *Craven-Ellis* v. *Canons Ltd* (1936) (services performed under void contract),[283] *William Lacey* v. *Davis* (1957) (work carried out in anticipation of contract; risk of abortive negotiations with defendant)[284] and *Benedetti* v. *Sawiris* (2013) (*quantum meruit* should be calculated on the basis of the objective value of services, reflecting the normal 'market value'; this mode of quantification does not permit the figure to be augmented to reflect figures used in negotiations concerning performance of the work; there are also dicta that the valuation might be below the objective level in some circumstances).[285]

18.30 *Disgorgement of gains made in breach of contract.* The House of Lords in *Attorney-General* v. *Blake* (2001)[286] introduced the remedy of an account of profits for a simple breach of contract, without the need to satisfy either breach of fiduciary duty (for example, breaches of contract by agents[287] or solicitors);[288] or infringement of a proprietary right.[289] The pre-*Blake* case law had thrown up at least one example of injustice.[290] Lord Nicholls (who gave the main speech)[291] said that this remedy of an account should be treated as quite exceptional, and that it should be granted only if all four of the following (mostly opaque) criteria are satisfied: first, the claimant can show a legitimate interest; secondly, all other remedies are inadequate; thirdly, the court in its discretion regards this as an appropriate response to the breach; and, fourthly, the gain is attributable to that breach.[292]

---

282   (1831) 8 Bing 14.
283   [1936] 2 KB 403, CA.
284   [1957] 1 WLR 932, Barry J (see 12.04).
285   [2013] UKSC 50; [2014] AC 938 (noted M. McInnes (2014) 130 LQR 8–13; G. Virgo [2013] CLJ 508–11; C. Mitchell [2013] LMCLQ 436); see also *Littlewoods Retail Ltd* v. *Revenue and Customs Commissioners* [2014] EWHC 868 (Ch) and *Harrison* v. *Madejski* [2014] EWCA Civ 361.
286   [2001] 1 AC 268 HL; K. Barnett, *Accounting for Profit for Breach of Contract* (Oxford, 2012); J. Edelman, *Gain-Based Damages* (Oxford, 2002), chapter 5; E. McKendrick in A. S. Burrows and E. Peel (eds.), *Commercial Remedies: Current Issues and Problems* (Oxford, 2003), 93–119; A. S. Burrows, *Remedies for Torts and Breach of Contract* (3rd edn, Oxford, 2004), 395–407; J. Beatson, (2002) 118 LQR 377; A. S. Burrows, 'Are "Damages on the *Wrotham Park* Basis" Compensatory, Restitutionary or Neither?'; A. M. Tettenborn, in M. A. Clarke, N. Andrews, A. M. Tettenborn, G. Virgo, *Contractual Duties: Performance, Breach, Termination and Remedies* (London, 2012), chapter 26; S. Waddams, 'Gains Derived from Breach of Contract: Historical and Conceptual Perspectives', and R. Cunnington, 'The Measure and Availability of Gains-Based Damages for Breach of Contract', both in D. Saidov and R. Cunnington (eds.), *Contract Damages: Domestic and International Perspectives* (Oxford, 2008); R. Cunnington, 'The Assessment of Gains-Based Damages for Breach of Contract' (2008) 71 MLR 559–86. On clauses stipulating that profit-disgorgement should be available to the innocent party, S. Rowan, 'For the Recognition of Remedial Terms Agreed Inter Partes' (2010) 126 LQR 448, 457–60. From a Scottish perspective, A. Gray, 'Disgorgement Damages' [2013] JBL 657–78.
287   Cf *Walsh* v. *Shanahan* [2013] EWCA Civ 411; [2013] 2 P & CR DG7 (agency ended; misuse of confidential information; account would be disproportionate).
288   *Calvert* v. *William Hill Credit Ltd* [2008] EWCA Civ 1427; [2009] Ch 330, at [53]; J. Edelman, 'When Do Fiduciary Duties Arise?' (2010) 126 LQR 302.
289   As in the case of restrictive covenants agreed between freeholders (that is, an undertaking by A, a landowner, to B, another landowner, that A will refrain from certain activities, such as using the property for business purposes rather than as a residence).
290   *Surrey County Council* v. *Bredero Homes* [1993] 1 WLR 1361, CA (contractual restraint on density of development site; agreement not a proprietary interest; and so no account of profits); P. B. H. Birks, (1993) 109 LQR 518, 520–1.
291   [2001] 1 AC 268, HL.
292   *Ibid.*, at 285.

In *Attorney-General* v. *Blake* (2001), Blake, having been convicted in the 1960s of espionage,[293] had been imprisoned in England. But he escaped to Moscow where he eventually published his memoirs. The UK government wanted to prevent the spy's London publisher from sending a second royalty cheque to the author in Russia. The House of Lords held that an 'equitable account' can be awarded against a party in breach in order to 'strip' him of a profit made at the claimant's expense, that is, as a result of a breach of contract. An injunction was granted to compel the publisher to pay the royalty sum to the Crown, Blake's employer before he had been dismissed for treachery. (In fact Brian Simpson[294] contends that there was no contractual provision; and Sir Richard Buxton,[295] in a journal article, has shown that the 'equitable account' argument, a point only considered by the House of Lords, in fact rendered this decision highly problematic.)

18.31 *Post-Blake case law.*[296] The *Blake* case has produced no deluge, indeed hardly a drop of consequence. An isolated application is Morritt V-C's pre-trial decision in *Esso Petroleum Ltd* v. *Niad Ltd* (2001) not to strike out a claim for an account of profits made by a petrol retailer in breach of the supplier's contractual requirement that retailers should reduce pump prices to match local competitors' prices. The decision to allow this claim to proceed in this commercial context is unconvincing. However, because this was not a final decision on the merits at trial,[297] the decision has little, if any, binding effect.

Sales J in the *Vercoe* case (2010) emphasised the non-negotiable nature of the contractual rights in the *Blake* case, and the non-commercial context of that case, contrasting the post-*Blake* judicial preference for awarding (the less generous measure of) 'loss of bargaining opportunity' (so-called 'user principle') damages (on which see 18.24 above):[298]

> [I]t may be more appropriate to award an account of profits [viz. a complete disgorgement of gain] where the right in question is of a kind where it would never be reasonable to expect that it could be bought out for some reasonable fee, so that it is accordingly deserving of a particularly high level of protection (such as the promise to keep state secrets which was in issue in Blake's case, which was classified as an exceptional case meriting such an award, and rights to protection under established fiduciary relationships, where trust between the parties rather than a purely commercial relationship is regarded as central to the obligations in question).

Sales J added:[299]

293 For details on the background, A. W. B. Simpson, 'A Decision Per Incuriam' (2009) 125 LQR 433.
294 *Ibid.*, at 436–887, suggests that Blake did not have a contract of employment and had not 'signed' the Official Secrets Act in any contractual sense.
295 R. Buxton, 'How the Common Law Gets Made . . . ' (2009) 125 LQR 60, 73 ff.
296 Summarised by Arden LJ in *Devenish Nutrition Ltd* v. *Sanofi-Anetis SA* [2008] EWCA Civ 1086; [2009] Ch 390, at [40] and [62] to [70]; noted by D. Sheehan, (2009) 125 LQR 222; C. Rotherham, 'Gains-Based Relief after AG v. Blake' (2010) 126 LQR 102–30; see also *Vercoe* v. *Rutland Fund Management* [2010] EWHC 424 (Ch); [2010] Bus LR D141, Sales J; noted by P. Devonshire, (2010) 126 LQR 526; and see the authorities collected by R. Ahdar, 'Contract Doctrine, Predictability and the Nebulous Exception' [2014] CLJ 39, at 48, n. 56.
297 *The Times*, 19 April 2003, Morritt V-C.
298 *Vercoe* v. *Rutland Fund Management* [2010] EWHC 424 (Ch); [2010] Bus LR D141, at [340]; more generally, [339] to [346] (noted by P. Devonshire, (2010) 126 LQR 526).
299 *Ibid.*, at [341].

[W]here one is not dealing with infringement of a right which is clearly proprietary in nature (such as intellectual property in the form of a patent . . .) and there is nothing exceptional to indicate that the defendant should never have been entitled to adopt a commercial approach in deciding how to behave in relation to that right, the appropriate remedy is likely to be an award of damages assessed by reference to a reasonable buy out fee rather than an account of profits.

5. DECLARATIONS

18.32 A declaration is a non-monetary and non-coercive remedy. It merely involves the court stating definitively the facts and legal result in an action. Sometimes, that is enough. Indeed, a declaration might be the only relief sought.[300] For example, in *Lock v. Bell* (1931), a vendor obtained a declaration that the deposit of £120 on the sale of a public house had been forfeited validly.[301] And, in *Patten v. Burke Publishing Co. Ltd* (1991), a writer, now proposing to deal with publisher B, sought a declaration that he could safely do so because he was no longer contractually committed to write for publisher A.[302] So-called 'negative declarations' (applications to gain a binding declaration that the claimant *is not legally liable to the other party*) are often sought in English civil proceedings as a tactic to preclude proceedings by a defendant against a claimant in another jurisdiction.[303] Finally, it should be noted that where no substantial loss has resulted, or substantial damages have not been claimed, an award of 'nominal damages' (on which see 18.07 at (1) above) is functionally equivalent to a declaration that 'there has been a bare breach'.

6. SPECIFIC PERFORMANCE

18.33 *Nature and criteria.*[304] This is a coercive remedy fashioned by Equity (1.25) and non-compliance is severely sanctioned. Specific performance is a form of injunction. A person

---

300   J. Woolf, *Zamir and Woolf: The Declaratory Judgment* (4th edn, London, 2011).
301   [1931] 1 Ch 35, Maugham J.
302   [1991] 1 WLR 541.
303   *Dicey, Morris and Collins on the Conflicts of Laws* (15th edn, London, 2012), 12–048 ff.
304   G. H. Jones and W. Goodhart, *Specific Performance* (2nd edn, London, 1996); A. S. Burrows, *Remedies for Torts and Breach of Contract* (3rd edn, Oxford, 2004), chapter 20; A. M. Tettenborn, in M. A. Clarke, N. Andrews, A. M. Tettenborn, G. Virgo, *Contractual Duties: Performance, Breach, Termination and Remedies* (London, 2012), chapter 27; D. Friedmann, 'Economic Aspects of Damages and Specific Performance Compared', in D. Saidov and R. Cunnington (eds.), *Contract Damages: Domestic and International Perspectives* (Oxford, 2008), chapter 2; comparative account: J. Smits, D. Haas and G. Hesen (eds.), *Specific Performance in Contract Law: National and Other Perspectives* (Antwerp, 2008); G. H. Treitel, *Remedies for Breach of Contract: A Comparative Account* (Oxford, 1988) (see also *ibid.*, at 63 ff for a comparative discussion concerning the Common Law); E. Yorio, *Contract Enforcement: Specific Performance and Injunctions* (New York, 1989); on the nineteenth-century history of this topic, see M. Lobban, in W. Cornish, J. S. Anderson, R. Cocks, M. Lobban, P. Polden and K. Smith, *The Oxford History of the Laws of England*, vol. XII, *1820–1914: Private Law* (Oxford, 2010), 548 ff; on the unavailability in England (see discussion at 18.34) (by contrast with Scotland) of specific performance to enforce tenants' 'keep open' clauses in commercial leases, D. Campbell and R. Halson, in L. DiMatteo, Q. Zhou, S. Saintier, K. Rowley (eds.), *Commercial Contract Law: Transatlantic Perspectives* (Cambridge, 2014), chapter 12.

will be guilty of contempt of court[305] (and become a 'contemnor') if he breaches an injunction or an order of specific performance addressed to him. As Lord Hoffmann said in *Co-operative Insurance Services* v. *Argyll Stores Ltd* (1998): 'the ... procedure of punishment for contempt ... is a powerful weapon.'[306] A 'contemnor' can be committed for contempt of court,[307] a quasi-criminal wrong for which the standard of proof is 'beyond reasonable doubt' rather than the lower civil standard of proof 'on the balance of probabilities'.[308] The civil court, when hearing proceedings for committal of a contemnor, can apply the following sanctions to the contemnor: imprisonment for up to two years;[309] a fine; or, in the case of both individuals[310] and companies, 'sequestration' of assets[311] ('sequestrators', officers of the court, appointed specially, can then seize the contemnor's property and sell it).[312]

Specific performance in England[313] is the primary remedy only in the context of agreements for (i) the transfer of land or of (ii) shares in *private* companies,[314] or (iii) to uphold contractual obligations to disclose information or make materials available for inspection. In situations (i) and (ii) the relevant subject matter is regarded as 'unique'. In situation (iii), damages are manifestly not an adequate remedy: *Yasuda Fire & Marine Insurance Co. of Europe Ltd* v. *Orion Marine Insurance Underwriting Agency Ltd* (1995).[315] Specific performance is normally sought after a breach has occurred, but it can be granted in anticipation of a breach.[316]

Furthermore, the remedy is residual: that is, it is available only if the remedies of damages or debt would provide inadequate relief (see also 18.37). But specific performance cannot be ordered unless the contract is supported by consideration.

If A promises (a gratuitous promise) by deed (5.03) and without consideration that A will pay B (or T, a third party) £1,000 each Monday for the next 50 weeks, specific performance is not available to compel A to perform and so B (or T, suing under the Contracts (Rights of Third

---

305 *Arlidge, Eady and Smith on Contempt* (4th edn, London, 2011).
306 [1998] AC 1, 15.
307 RSC Order 52 in Schedule 1 to the CPR; and CCR Order 29 in Schedule 2 to the CPR.
308 *Z Bank* v. *D1* [1974] 1 Lloyd's Rep 656, 660, Colman J.
309 *Harris* v. *Harris* [2001] EWCA Civ 1645; [2002] Fam 253, CA, at [12] to [14], noting section 14(1) of the Contempt of Court Act 1981, restricting the period to a maximum of two years' imprisonment.
310 *Raja* v. *Van Hoogstraten* [2004] EWCA Civ 968; [2004] 4 All ER 793, at [71] ff.
311 RSC Order 45, rules 3(1)(c), 4(2)(c) and 5(1)(b)(i)(ii); RSC Order 46, rule 5; on the court's inherent power, see *Webster* v. *Southwark London Borough Council* [1983] QB 698.
312 *IRC* v. *Hoogstraten* [1985] QB 1077, CA; *Raja* v. *Van Hoogstraten* [2007] EWHC 1743 (Ch).
313 Contrast Canada, where, even in respect of land purchases, priority is given to damages and the duty to mitigate: M. McInnes, (2013) 129 LQR 165–9, noting *Southcott Estate Inc* v. *Toronto District School Board* [2012] SCC 51; (2012) 351 DLR (4th) 541.
314 For specific performance to compel the transfer of shares in a *private* company, see *Harvela* v. *Royal Trust Bank of Canada* [1986] AC 207, HL.
315 [1995] QB 174, 191–2, Colman J (Commercial Court).
316 *Zucker* v. *Tyndall Holdings plc* [1992] 1 WLR 1127, 1133–4, CA *per* Neill LJ, considering *Hasham* v. *Zenab* [1960] AC 316, 329–30, PC, *per* Lord Tucker who referred to a two-stage procedure: a declaratory stage and consequential directions for performance; noted R. E. Megarry (1960) 76 LQR 200; *Johnson* v. *Agnew* [1980] 367, HL; and authorities considered by G. H. Jones and W. Goodhart, *Specific Performance* (2nd edn, London, 1996) 236–7, and Q. Liu, *Anticipatory Breach* (Oxford, 2011), 217–19.

Parties) Act 1999) would have to sue in debt for each default in payment. If B supplies consideration the position would change and B could obtain specific performance on the authority of *Beswick* v. *Beswick* (1968) (7.18) or T could bring a direct action seeking specific performance under limb 2 of the 1999 Act, as explained at 7.29.

As mentioned, the party who fails to comply with such an order will be in contempt of court (and, as a 'contemnor', be liable to fines, imprisonment or seizure of assets).[317]

Specific performance is certainly unavailable to compel an individual to perform personal services, for example to work for an employer (and see the discussion of injunctions below).[318]

In the case of contracts of employment, this restriction is enshrined in the Trade Union and Labour Relations (Consolidation) Act 1992 (section 236):

> No court shall, whether by way of – (a) an order for specific performance . . . of a contract of employment, or (b) an injunction . . . restraining a breach or threatened breach of such a contract, compel an employee to do any work or attend at any place for the doing of any work.

Nor will it make a difference if a party has stipulated that the other's obligation(s) will be specifically enforceable, because the courts will resist attempts to bind their hands or to reduce them to rubber-stamping functionaries[319] (for a contrary suggestion, see Solène Rowan's discussion, noting American case law).[320]

Even if the relevant type of contract is one where specific performance is available in principle, the court will be guided by various subsidiary factors when deciding whether to exercise its 'discretion' to order specific performance:[321] whether the claimant's conduct has been unmeritorious ('lack of clean hands'); delay; acquiescence; 'mutuality' (that is, when the claimant, who is seeking specific performance, has yet to satisfy his side of the bargain, and the court must consider whether the defendant is protected against the risk of default by the claimant);[322] vagueness; problems of continuing supervision; and hardship (see 16.31 on *Patel* v. *Ali*, 1984).[323]

---

317 *Arlidge, Eady and Smith on Contempt* (4th edn, London, 2011).
318 G. H. Jones and W. Goodhart, *Specific Performance* (2nd edn, London, 1996), 169–83; P. Saprai, 'The Principle against Self-Enslavement in Contract Law' (2009) 26 JCL 25–44.
319 *Quadrant Visual Communications Ltd* v. *Hutchison Telephone (UK) Ltd* [1993] BCLC 442, 451, CA; cf., *Warner Bros Pictures Inc.* v. *Nelson* [1937] 1 KB 209, 220–1.
320 S. Rowan, 'For the Recognition of Remedial Terms Agreed Inter Partes' (2010) 126 LQR 448, 449–55, 470–5.
321 *Co-operative Insurance Society* v. *Argyll Stores (Holdings) Ltd* [1998] AC 1, HL, noted by G. H. Jones, [1997] CLJ 488; *Rainbow Estates Ltd* v. *Tokenhold Ltd* [1999] Ch 64, 68G–74; *Beswick* v. *Beswick* [1968] AC 58, HL; *Price* v. *Strange* [1978] Ch 337, CA; *Tito* v. *Waddell (No. 2)* [1977] Ch 106, 321–8, Megarry V-C; *Verrall* v. *Great Yarmouth District Council* [1980] 1 All ER 839, CA; *Posner* v. *Scott-Lewis* [1987] Ch 25, Mervyn-Davies J, noted by G. H. Jones, [1987] CLJ 21–3.
322 *Price* v. *Strange* [1978] Ch 337, CA.
323 [1984] Ch 283, Goulding J.

On these grounds for denial of the remedy, Lord Hoffmann commented in *Co-operative Insurance Services* v. *Argyll Stores Ltd* (1998):[324]

> Of course the grant or refusal of specific performance remains a matter for the judge's discretion. There are no binding rules, but this does not mean that there cannot be settled principles, founded upon practical considerations of the kind which I have discussed, which do not have to be re-examined in every case, but which the courts will apply in all but exceptional circumstances.

Claims for injunctive relief or specific performance are subject to the equitable bars of laches and acquiescence, and the statutory periods of limitation do not apply.[325]

18.34 *Leading examination of the remedy's scope:* Co-operative Insurance Services *v.* Argyll Stores Ltd *(1998).* In this important case, the House of Lords held that specific performance is not available to compel a tenant to honour a long-running covenant to 'keep open' a business. More generally, the case contains important observations on the need to retain a modest and residual function for specific performance. This seems quite justified (some[326] had wrongly predicted that *Beswick* v. *Beswick* (1968) might have heralded a major expansion of specific performance). Apart from agreements to transfer land (where specific performance is the primary remedy), English law is right to confine this remedy to a residual role, for three main reasons.[327]

First, specific performance is a heavy-handed remedy, sanctioned by contempt of court powers. It should be narrowly confined, otherwise it threatens to become a remedial sledgehammer.

Secondly, the mitigation principle requires that, in general, an innocent party should be required to act straightaway in order to reduce or even eliminate his loss, and he should not be at liberty to wait for the court to order the guilty party to perform.[328] Lord Hoffmann noted on order to compel someone to carry on a business at a loss 'cannot be in the public interest' because 'it is not only a waste of resources but yokes the parties together in a continuing hostile relationship', whereas damages would allow the parties to 'go their separate ways and the wounds of conflict can heal'.[329]

Thirdly, the parties can insert liquidated damages clauses or require payment of a deposit to apply leverage to induce performance (on agreed protection of this type, see 19.02 and 19.27).

---

324 [1998] AC 1, 16, HL.

325 *P&O Nedlloyd BV* v. *Arab Metals Co.* [2006] EWCA Civ 1717; [2007] 1 WLR 2288; *Andrews on Civil Processes* (Cambridge, 2013), vol. 1, *Court Proceedings,* chapter 8; A. McGee, *Limitation Periods* (7th edn, 2014); N. Andrews, 'Reform of Limitation of Actions: The Quest for Sound Policy' [1998] CLJ 588–610; for comparative discussion, R. Zimmermann, *Comparative Foundations of a European Law of Set-off and Prescription* (Cambridge, 2002; UNIDROIT's *Principles of International Commercial Contracts* (3rd edn, International Institute for the Unification of Private Law, Rome, 2010), chapter 10.

326 E.g. F. H. Lawson, *Remedies of English Law* (2nd edn, London, 1980), 223.

327 S. M. Waddams, 'The Choice of Remedy for Breach of Contract', in J. Beatson and D. Friedmann (eds.), *Good Faith and Fault in Contract Law* (Oxford, 1995), 471 ff, provides a compelling defence of the residual role of coercive specific relief.

328 D. Friedmann, 'Economic Aspects of Damages and Specific Performance Compared', in D. Saidov and R. Cunnington (eds.), *Contract Damages: Domestic and International Perspectives* (Oxford, 2008), chapter 2, at 86 ff.

329 *Co-operative Insurance Society Ltd* v. *Argyll Stores (Holdings) Ltd* [1998] AC 1, 15–16, HL, *per* Lord Hoffmann.

The *Co-operative Insurance* case (1998) concerned a lease for a supermarket site in a Sheffield shopping mall. The thirty-five-year lease, granted in 1979, included a clause that the tenant would continue trading for the same period (a so-called 'keep open' clause). The relevant clause stated: '[The tenant will] keep the demised premises open for retail trade during the usual hours of business in the locality [and it will keep] the display windows properly dressed in a suitable manner in keeping with a good class parade of shops.' Another clause required the tenant to offer a 'full range of grocery provisions'.

In 1994, when the tenancy still had more than nineteen years to run, the defendant supermarket chain handed back the keys to the landlord (the defendant had made a loss of £70,000 in the previous year).[330] The claimant landlord sought specific performance to force the defendant to trade at this site until 2014, or until it sublet or assigned to another supermarket company.

The House of Lords held that the relevant clause was insufficiently precise.[331] And, in any event, specific performance could not[332] be granted to compel a party to run a business, otherwise, the courts will become embroiled in a litany of minor complaints and counter-arguments.

Lord Hoffmann also noted (1) the residual status of the equitable remedy of specific performance, (2) the nature of the 'constant supervision' problem and (3) the danger of oppression.

As for (1): 'Specific performance is traditionally regarded in English law as an exceptional remedy, as opposed to the Common Law damages to which a successful plaintiff is entitled as of right.'[333]

As for (2), Lord Hoffmann said: '[One must] distinguish between orders which require a defendant to carry on an activity, such as running a business over a more or less extended period of time, and orders which require him to achieve a result [such as, building contracts and repairing covenants].'[334]

As for (3), Lord Hoffmann said: '[The court should not] deliver over the defendants to the plaintiff bound hand and foot, in order to be made subject to any extortionate demand that he may possibly make.'[335]

18.35 *Scarce goods.*[336] Specific performance is not awarded to compel transfers of chattels unless they are special, indeed 'unique' (for example, 'Princess Diana's wedding dress' or Bobby Moore's World Cup winner's medal).[337] Reported cases have produced an eclectic collection: unusual china jars;[338] stones from old Westminster Bridge;[339] an Adam-style

---

330 [1998] AC 1, 10, HL

331 [1998] AC 1, 17, HL.

332 Such 'keep open' clauses are specifically enforced in Scotland: but D. Campbell and R. Halson, in L. DiMatteo, Q. Zhou, S. Saintier, K. Rowley (eds.), *Commercial Contract Law: Transatlantic Perspectives* (Cambridge, 2014), chapter 12, contend that the English position is preferable; examining, notably at 471–9, among many Scottish decisions, *Retail Parks Investments Ltd* v. *The Royal Bank of Scotland (No. 2)* [1996] SC 227 (IH Ex Div); *Highland & Universal Properties Ltd* v. *Safeway Properties Ltd*, 2000 SLT 297 (IH); *Co-operative Insurance Society Ltd* v. *Halfords Ltd (No. 2)*, 1999 SLT 697 (OH); see further literature cited by Campbell and Halson, including D. Pearce, 'Remedies for Breach of a Keep-Open Covenant' (2008) 24 JCL 199.

333 [1998] AC 1, 11.

334 *Ibid.*, at 40; however, Burrows is deeply sceptical of this suggested distinction: A. S. Burrows, *Remedies for Torts and Breach of Contract* (3rd edn, Oxford, 2004), 475–81.

335 *Ibid.* (quoting Lord Westbury LC in *Isenberg* v. *East India House Estate Co. Ltd* (1863) 3 De GJ & S 263, 273).

336 G. H. Jones and W. Goodhart, *Specific Performance* (2nd edn, London, 1996), 143–54.

337 The history of English performances since 1966 underlines the continuing 'uniqueness' of that medal.

338 *Falcke* v. *Gray* (1859) 4 Drew 651.

339 *Thorn* v. *Public Works Commissioners* (1863) 32 Beav 490.

door;[340] and a 'practically unique' ship.[341] But, in general, the duty to mitigate (18.22) requires the disappointed party to re-enter the market and find a substitute supplier. Unless the subject matter is 'unique', the disappointed buyer is confined to his remedy in damages, and this is so even if he can show a convincing 'sentimental attachment' to the relevant chattel. However, Burrows finds this too rigid.[342]

The general refusal to order specific performance of agreements for the transfer of movable property is reasonable. This is because the subject matter is generic or fungible, and hence easily substituted. However, sometimes even fungibles can become alarmingly scarce. This can justify exceptional relief. Thus, in *Sky Petroleum Ltd* v. *VIP Petroleum Ltd* (1974), Goulding J recognised that exceptional market conditions can render damages an inadequate remedy for default even in the supply of a commodity (wholesale petrol).[343] As a result of steps taken by the OPEC cartel during the 1970s 'oil crisis', wholesale petrol supplies had become scarce. Unless it gained the present remedy, the claimant would have been forced out of business.[344] Goulding J awarded an interim injunction, equivalent to specific performance, to compel an oil supplier to deliver petrol to a retailer.[345]

But even that extreme case is open to doubt, in light of the later (but now rather dated) Court of Appeal decision in *Société des Industries Metallurgiques SA* v. *Bronx Engineering Co. Ltd* (1975).[346] The court held that damages would be adequate when a seller refused to supply machinery, even though it would take almost a year for an alternative manufacturer to supply the claimant. However, Burrows attractively contends that 'commercial uniqueness' should lead to specific performance if 'an accurate assessment of the claimant's losses is so difficult that [he] is likely to be incorrectly compensated'.[347]

In fact there is a modern line of first instance decisions in which the courts have granted orders (before, or even at,[348] trial) to compel delivery of goods in contexts where supply is crucial to a commercial party's economic interest and the parties are (at least for a time)[349] locked into a relationship.[350]

---

340 *Phillips* v. *Lamdin* [1949] 2 KB 33, 41, Croom-Johnson J.
341 *Behnke* v. *Bede Shipping Co. Ltd* [1927] 1 KB 649, Wright J; this test was not satisfied in 'The Stena Nautica' (No. 2) [1982] 2 Lloyd's Rep 336, Parker J; cf the wide dictum of Browne-Wilkinson V-C in *Bristol Airport plc* v. *Powdrill* [1990] Ch 744, 759 CA (lease of an aircraft is specifically enforceable; every aircraft is unique; but ship cases not cited).
342 A. S. Burrows, *Remedies for Torts and Breach of Contract* (3rd edn, Oxford, 2004), 464, suggesting that the 'consumer surplus' factor might be borne in mind here: on which see 18.34.
343 [1974] 1 WLR 576, Goulding J, where the goods were not even 'specific or ascertained' for the purpose of section 52 of the Sale of Goods Act 1979; *Re Wait* [1927] 1 Ch 606, CA (specific performance unavailable outside the limits of that provision); generally, see Treitel, [1966] JBL 211, A. S. Burrows, *Remedies for Torts and Breach of Contract* (3rd edn, Oxford, 2004), 462 ff.
344 [1974] 1 WLR 576, 578–9, Goulding J.
345 *Ibid.*
346 [1975] 1 Lloyd's Rep 465, CA.
347 A. S. Burrows, *Remedies for Torts and Breach of Contract* (3rd edn, Oxford, 2004), 463.
348 See *Thames Valley Power Ltd* v. *Total Gas & Power Ltd* [2005] EWHC 2208 (Comm); [2006] 1 Lloyd's Rep 441, at [63], *per* Christopher Clarke J (supply of gas under long-term contract), where the order was named as specific performance.
349 But that period was potentially for many years in the case just cited.
350 R. Halson, *Contract Law* (2nd edn, London, 2013), 444–5, noting *Land Rover Group Ltd* v. *UPF (UK) Ltd* [2002] EWHC 3183; [2003] BCLC 222 (mandatory injunction against insolvent company to compel supply until trial of Land Rover parts); similar order made in *Aston Martin Lagonda Ltd* v. *Automobile Industrial Partnerships Ltd* (Birmingham, High Court, 2009, unreported); and in *SSL International plc* v. *TTK LIG Ltd* [2011] EWHC 1695 (Ch); (2011) 108(28) LSG 21, Mann J (supply of condoms); *Thames Valley Power Ltd* v. *Total*

7. INJUNCTIONS

18.36 The general rule is that injunctions are readily awarded to prevent a defendant from breaching a 'negative' promise, that is, an undertaking not to do something;[351] for example, to enforce restrictive covenants requiring landowners to desist from using the premises for specified purposes (such as, 'the owner will not use these premises, or allow them to be used, for the purpose of selling intoxicating liquor'). In such a case, an injunction is not subject to the restriction (which governs specific performance) that damages would be an inadequate remedy (18.33). Burrows suggests that the courts have gone too far in awarding injunctions without inquiring whether damages would be sufficient protection,[352] but he acknowledges that the constant supervision problem and the mitigation issue do not complicate this context.[353] (As for clauses stipulating that injunctions should be available, Solène Rowan has challenged the view that the courts will not countenance a usurpation of their discretionary control of this award.)[354]

18.37 An injunction can be awarded either to prevent the anticipated wrong ('prohibitory' relief) or to reverse the relevant wrong (a 'mandatory' injunction), but there is a discretion to award damages 'in lieu' of an injunction.[355] Furthermore, the principle of supplementary relief – that injunctions (including specific performance) are unavailable 'unless damages are inadequate' – is not be applied mechanically: clauses limiting or excluding damages for breach do not oust the court's capacity to award interim or final injunctive relief.[356]

18.38 *Personal services and close relations.* Equity will refuse to use its coercive machinery if the indirect effect will be to apply such compulsion to require a person to perform personal relations or remain in a close relationship between mutual confidence (just as specific performance will not be granted to compel direct performance of such an obligation, 18.33). For example, if a defendant actor, manager, employee or sportsman has agreed not to work for anyone other than the claimant for a specified period, an injunction to enforce this negative undertaking might indirectly impose compulsion on the defendant to work for, or

Gas & Power Ltd [2005] EWHC 2208 (Comm); [2006] 1 Lloyd's Rep 441, at [63], *per* Christopher Clarke J (supply of gas under long-term contract).
351 *Doherty* v. *Allman* (1878) 3 App Cas 709, 720, HL, *per* Lord Cairns LC; considered in *Insurance Company* v. *Lloyd's Syndicate* [1994] CLC 1303, 1309–10, by Colman J; generally, A. M. Tettenborn, in M. A. Clarke, N. Andrews, A. M. Tettenborn, G. Virgo, *Contractual Duties: Performance, Breach, Termination and Remedies* (London, 2012), chapter 28.
352 However, Akenhead J in *Simon Carves Ltd* v. *Ensus UK Ltd* [2011] EWHC 657 (TCC); [2011] BLR 340; 135 Con LR 96, at [36], did examine closely the applicant's exposure to extensive and unquantifiable loss if the injunction were not granted; but it is unclear why, if proof of loss is not a condition precedent to the injunction in this context, the capacity to measure loss and thus award damages, should be a bar on the grant of the injunction.
353 A. S. Burrows, *Remedies for Torts and Breach of Contract* (3rd edn, Oxford, 2004), 527–9.
354 S. Rowan, 'For the Recognition of Remedial Terms Agreed Inter Partes' (2010) 126 LQR 448, 449–55, 470–5.
355 E.g. *Oxy-Electric Ltd* v. *Zaiduddin* [1991] 1 WLR 115, Hoffmann J (application for striking out refused; case to proceed to trial); *Jaggard* v. *Sawyer* [1995] 1 WLR 269, CA (injunction refused; damages in lieu awarded under section 50 of the Senior Courts Act 1981).
356 *AB* v. *CD* [2014] EWCA Civ 229; [2014] 3 All ER 667, *per* Underhill LJ at [25] to [30]; noted P. G. Turner [2014] CLJ 493–6 (applying Mance LJ in *Bath & NE Somerset DC* v. *Mowlem plc* [2004] EWCA 722; [2004] BLR 153, CA, at [15]).

with, the claimant.[357] The leading modern re-examination of this restriction on injunctive relief is *Warren* v. *Mendy* (1989) (see below).[358] But, as the Court of Appeal in the *LauritzenCool* case (2006)[359] acknowledged, the liberal principle that *individuals* should not be compelled (directly or indirectly) to work for others does not apply if the defendant is a company (nor, relatedly be yoked within relationships of trust and confidence when the relationship has fallen down or is in a precarious state). And so in that case it was legitimate to issue an injunction to prevent a company from removing its two ships from the charterer.

Similarly, in *Regent International Hotels (UK) Ltd* v. *Pageguide Ltd* (1985)[360] Ackner LJ contrasted a personal relationship between a pop group and a manager (where an injunction would be inappropriate)[361] and the commercial context of a company's undertaking to manage a hotel (where an injunction would be appropriate, as in the *Regent International Hotel* case itself).

In *Warren* v. *Mendy* (1989),[362] the claimant, a boxing manager, sought an injunction to restrain the defendant from interfering[363] with a management contract between him and Benn, a talented young boxer. The Court of Appeal held that an injunction should not be granted against the third party otherwise Benn, the *contracting* party, would be indirectly compelled to continue to serve under the claimant's management. Nourse LJ noted:[364] 'the human necessity of maintaining the skill or talent may practically bind the servant to the contract, compelling him to perform it.' Therefore, the court must have:[365] 'a realistic regard for . . . the psychological and material, and sometimes the physical, need of the servant to maintain the skill or talent. The longer the term for which an injunction is sought, the more readily will compulsion be inferred.' This was because Benn, as a highly paid boxer in a notoriously short sporting career, did not have the practical choice of 'stacking supermarket shelves' as an alternative source of income.

Warren v. *Mendy* (1989)[366] examined these cases (see also Lord Wilson's remarks in *Geys* v. *Société Générale*, 2012):[367]

Lumley v. *Wagner* (1852):[368] Lord St Leonards, LC, granted an injunction against an opera singer. Although she could not be compelled to sing, she could be restrained, for three months – a relatively short engagement – from singing for a rival impresario, in breach of her express negative undertaking not to sing for a rival during this period.

---

357 *Warren* v. *Mendy* [1989] 1 WLR 853, CA, noted by H. McLean, [1990] CLJ 28, noting *Lumley* v. *Wagner* (1852) 1 De GM & G 604, and *Warner Bros Pictures Inc.* v. *Nelson* [1937] 1 KB 209, and *Page One Records Ltd* v. *Britton* [1968] 1 WLR 157 ('The Troggs' case); Mance LJ in *LauritzenCool AB* v. *Lady Navigation Inc.* [2005] EWCA Civ 579; [2006] All ER 866, CA (18.22); P. Saprai, 'The Principle against Self-Enslavement in Contract Law' (2009) 25 JCL 26.
358 [1989] 1 WLR 853, CA.
359 *LauritzenCool AB* v. *Lady Navigation Inc.* [2005] EWCA Civ 579; [2006] All ER 866, CA, at [30].
360 *The Times*, 13 May 1985, CA.
361 *Page One Records Ltd* v. *Britton* [1968] 1 WLR 157.
362 [1989] 1 WLR 853, CA.
363 The so-called 'economic torts' protect the claimant's interest in restraining a third party from inducing breach of a contract, or from interfering with its performance: see 17.56.
364 [1989] 1 WLR 853, at 857.
365 *Ibid.*, at 867.
366 [1989] 1 WLR 853, 860–8, CA, *per* Nourse LJ.
367 [2012] UKSC 63; [2013] 1 AC 523, at [70] ff.
368 (1852) 1 De GM & G 604.

In *Whitwood Chemical Co.* v. *Hardman* (1891)[369] the Court of Appeal held that no injunction should be granted to enforce the defendant's express negative undertaking, and so require the defendant to concentrate all his employment energies and time on the plaintiff company, as he had agreed. There were still over four years of employment still to run.[370]

In *Warner Bros Pictures Inc* v. *Nelson* (1937)[371] Branson J enforced an exclusivity clause by issuing an injunction against the actress, Bette Davis, for three years from 1936 *within England and Wales*. Although Nourse LJ in *Warren* v. *Mendy* (1989)[372] doubted this decision, the territorial restriction just mentioned makes the result palatable: she might still have worked for a rival outside the UK and USA (the contract would have enabled the claimant to obtain an injunction within the USA).

In *Page One Records Ltd* v. *Britton* (1968),[373] Stamp J refused an injunction to require a pop group, 'The Troggs', to stay loyal to their manager, with whom they had fallen out. The contract was for five years. Stamp J noted the need for mutual confidence in such a close working relationship.[374]

8. 'STAYS' UPON LEGAL PROCEEDINGS

18.39 This is a decision by the court to place proceedings in suspense, until the 'stay' is lifted.[375] A 'stay' is sometimes a contractual remedy, in the sense that it can be a judicial response to a breach of contract.[376]

For example, in *Cable & Wireless plc* v. *IBM United Kingdom Ltd* (2002) (4.22), Colman J upheld an agreement by two commercial parties whereby: (1) they agreed to negotiate disputes (see also 2.10 on the *Emirates* case); (2) they further agreed thereafter, if necessary, to conduct a mediated negotiation; and (3) an aggrieved party could, if necessary, finally resort to formal litigation. One party had jumped straight from stage (1) to stage (3). The judge held that failure by one party to proceed to stage (2) involved a breach. The 'remedy' was to issue a stay of the High Court proceedings brought at stage (3), prematurely on these facts, in breach of the dispute-resolution agreement.[377]

369   [1891] 2 Ch 416, CA.
370   Lindley LJ at 427–8 said that an express negative clause is essential; similarly, Kay LJ at 431.
371   [1937] I KB 209.
372   [1989] 1 WLR 853, 865, CA.
373   [1968] 1 WLR 157.
374   *Ibid.*, at 165, *per* Stamp J.
375   Section 49(3) of the Senior Court Act 1981 acknowledges the court's inherent power to issue a stay; the technique is used in a range of situations; for example, to suspend English court proceedings in order to give effect to an arbitration agreement nominating a foreign seat, as required by section 9 of the Arbitration Act 1996 (on this topic, *Dicey, Morris and Collins on the Conflicts of Laws* (15th edn, London, 2012), 16–066 ff; *Andrews on Civil Processes* (Cambridge, 2013), vol. 2, Arbitration and Mediation, 10.03 ff; and noting at 10.14 the availability of the court's inherent jurisdiction, e.g., in *Reichhold Norway ASA* v. *Goldman Sachs International* [2000] 1 WLR 173, CA, see also *Dicey*, cited above, at 16–082); or in accordance with the *forum non conveniens* doctrine (on which, *Dicey*, cited above, at 12–007 ff; *Andrews on Civil Processes* (Cambridge, 2013), vol. 1, *Court Proceedings*, 5.28).
376   Conversely, when an exclusive jurisdiction clause nominates England, but related proceedings are on foot in another jurisdiction, the court might even so stay the English proceedings: *Nomura International plc* v. *Banca Monte dei Paschi Di Siena Spa* [2013] EWHC 3187 (Comm); [2014] 1 WLR 1584 at [16], [17], [80] to [83], Eder J.
377   [2002] 2 All ER (Comm) 1041.

But the court can go further and, rather than stay proceedings, dismiss a claim, where such a final disposal of the matter is appropriate. That was Ormrod J's conclusion in *Snelling* v. *John Snelling Ltd* (1973).[378] Here three brothers (C, X and Y) had agreed ('the promise') that they would not sue their family company to recover sums to which they were otherwise entitled. C, the claimant, broke rank and sued the company. The other two brothers, X and Y, were joined as parties to the proceedings. Although the old Common Law privity doctrine at the date of this case (7.03, 7.04, but note nowadays the third party could be protected under the 1999 Act, 7.22) did not permit the company to take advantage of a contract to which it was not party, Ormrod J held that X and Y could, as promisees, invoke the promise for the defendant company's protection. And rather than grant a mere stay, the appropriate final relief was to dismiss outright the claim.

QUESTIONS

The main topics

(1) What are the *White & Carter* case's restrictions upon the claim for debt?
(2) When does specific performance apply, and is the law too restrictive?
(3) When, in the interest of personal liberty, will an injunction not be granted to restrain a party from breaching a negative undertaking (a promise not to do something)?
(4) Define contractual remoteness. How does it differ from *Wagon Mound* reasonable foreseeability in the tort of negligence?
(5) The contractual test of remoteness is pliable enough to include scope of duty reasoning. Do you agree?

Specific issues

(6) When will damages be available for non-pecuniary loss, such as disappointment and hurt feelings, etc.?
(7) When are damages available for loss of a chance?
(8) Distinguish reliance damages and 'expectation interest' (or loss of bargain, or 'performance interest') damages. What are the restrictions on the former?
(9) 'Contractual damages for loss of bargain compensate for failure to satisfy an expectation created by the relevant promise, whereas tort damages can, at best, merely compensate for loss of opportunities existing independently of the tort cause of action.' Explain.
(10) Which factors regulate the award of cost of cure or reinstatement damages?
(11) Illustrate the notion of an 'effective cause'.
(12) 'The mitigation principle prevents the claimant from recovering damages for avoidable loss.' Explain.
(13) 'From the perspective of contractual damages, contributory negligence is a defence concerned only with avoiding a mismatch between tortious and contractual analysis.' Explain.
(14) At what date should contractual damages be assessed?
(15) 'The restitutionary remedy of an account for breach of contract is scarcely worth mentioning and in practice is overshadowed by the award of "user principle" damages.' Explain.

---

378   [1973] QB 87, 99, Ormrod J.

(16) 'Restitutionary or unjust enrichment claims normally apply without the need to show breach of contract, and indeed often arise precisely because a contract has not materialised or the relevant agreement is invalid, etc.' Explain this comment.

Selected further reading

General (detailed analysis)

A. S. Burrows (ed.), *English Private Law* (3rd edn, Oxford, 2013), chapter 21

A. M. Tettenborn, in M. A. Clarke, N. Andrews, A. M. Tettenborn, G. Virgo, *Contractual Duties: Performance, Breach, Termination and Remedies* (London, 2012), Part IV, Remedies

General (theory)

N. Cohen and E. McKendrick (eds.), *Comparative Remedies for Breach of Contract* (Oxford, 2005)

C. Rickett (ed.), *Justifying Private Law Remedies* (Oxford, 2008)

D. Saidov and R. Cunnington (eds.), *Contract Damages: Domestic and International Perspectives* (Oxford, 2008)

Debt

J. W. Carter (2012) 128 LQR 490 (on the *White & Carter* issue)

A. M. Tettenborn, in M. A. Clarke, N. Andrews, A. M. Tettenborn, G. Virgo, *Contractual Duties: Performance, Breach, Termination and Remedies* (London, 2012), chapter 19

Expectation or performance interest damages for breach of contract

D. Friedmann, 'The Performance Interest in Contract Damages' (1995) 111 LQR 628 (considering also the 'classic' article by L. L. Fuller and W. R. Perdue, 'The Reliance Interest in Contract Damages' (1936) 46 *Yale Law Journal* 52 and 373 (in two parts))

A. M. Tettenborn, in M. A. Clarke, N. Andrews, A. M. Tettenborn, G. Virgo, *Contractual Duties: Performance, Breach, Termination and Remedies* (London, 2012), 21.034 ff

Cost of cure damages

A. M. Tettenborn, in M. A. Clarke, N. Andrews, A. M. Tettenborn, G. Virgo, *Contractual Duties: Performance, Breach, Termination and Remedies* (London, 2012), 21.65 to 21.75

D. Winterton, 'Money Awards Substituting for Performance' [2012] LMCLQ 446–70

Date of assessment of damages

B. Coote, (2007) 123 LQR 503

A. Dyson and A. Kramer, 'There is No "Breach Date Rule" ...' (2014) 130 LQR 259–81

M. Furmston, 'Actual Damages, Notional Damages and Loss of a Chance', in D. Saidov and R. Cunnington (eds.), *Contract Damages: Domestic and International Perspectives* (Oxford, 2008), 419, at 424 ff

D. McLauchlan, 'Expectation Damages: Avoided Loss, Offsetting Gains and Subsequent Events', in D. Saidov and R. Cunnington (eds.), *Contract Damages: Domestic and International Perspectives* (Oxford, 2008), chapter 15

J. Morgan, [2007] CLJ 263

M. Mustill, (2008) 124 LQR 569

C. Nicholls, [2008] JBL 91

Sir Bernard Rix, 'Lord Bingham's Contributions to Commercial Law', in M. Andenas and D. Fairgrieve (eds.), *Tom Bingham and the Transformation of the Law: A Liber Amicorum* (Oxford, 2009), 679–83

G. H. Treitel, (2007) 123 LQR 9

'Consumer surplus' damages

D. Harris, A. Ogus and J. Phillips, 'Contract Remedies and the Consumer Surplus' (1979) 95 LQR 581, especially 580–6, 595–6, 604–10 (cited by Lord Millett in the *Panatown* case [2001] 1 AC 518, 589)

Disappointment damages in general

D. Capper, (2002) 118 LQR 193–6

E. McKendrick and M. Graham, 'The Sky's the Limit: Contractual Damages for Non-Pecuniary Loss' [2002] LMCLQ 161

A. M. Tettenborn, in M. A. Clarke, N. Andrews, A. M. Tettenborn, G. Virgo, *Contractual Duties: Performance, Breach, Termination and Remedies* (London, 2012), chapter 22

Causation

A. M. Tettenborn, in M. A. Clarke, N. Andrews, A. M. Tettenborn, G. Virgo, *Contractual Duties: Performance, Breach, Termination and Remedies* (London, 2012), 24.02 to 24.26

Remoteness

D. Foxton, [2009] LMCLQ 461–87

G. Gordon, (2009) *Edinburgh Law Review* 125–30

Lord Hoffmann, (2010) 14 *Edinburgh Law Review* 47–61

A. Kramer, (2009) 125 LQR 408–15

D. McLauchlan, (2009) 9 *Oxford University Commonwealth Law Journal* 109–39

J. O'Sullivan, [2009] CLJ 34–7

E. Peel, (2009) 125 LQR 6–12

M. Stiggelbout, [2012] LMCLQ 97–121 (cogent summary and criticism of the scope of duty emphasis within the *Transfield* case)

A. M. Tettenborn, in M. A. Clarke, N. Andrews, A. M. Tettenborn, G. Virgo, *Contractual Duties: Performance, Breach, Termination and Remedies* (London, 2012), chapter 23

P. C. K. Wee, [2010] LMCLQ 150–76

Mitigation of loss

M. Bridge, 'Mitigation of Damages in Contract and the Meaning of Avoidable Loss' (1989) 105 LQR 398

M. Bridge, 'The Market Rule of Damages Assessment', in D. Saidov and R. Cunnington (eds.), *Contract Damages: Domestic and International Perspectives* (Oxford, 2008), chapter 18

H. McGregor, 'The Role of Mitigation in the Assessment of Damages', in D. Saidov and R. Cunnington (eds.), *Contract Damages: Domestic and International Perspectives* (Oxford, 2008), chapter 14

A. M. Tettenborn, in M. A. Clarke, N. Andrews, A. M. Tettenborn, G. Virgo, *Contractual Duties: Performance, Breach, Termination and Remedies* (London, 2012), 24.38 to 24.69

Contributory negligence

C. Hopkins, [1995] CLJ 20–3

A. M. Tettenborn, in M. A. Clarke, N. Andrews, A. M. Tettenborn, G. Virgo, *Contractual Duties: Performance, Breach, Termination and Remedies* (London, 2012), 24.38 to 24.70 ff

Account of profits and gains–based claims

K. Barnett, *Accounting for Profit for Breach of Contract* (Oxford, 2012)

A. Burrows, 'Are "Damages on the Wrotham Park Basis" Compensatory, Restitutionary or Neither?', in D. Saidov and R. Cunnington (eds.), *Contract Damages: Domestic and International Perspectives* (Oxford, 2008), chapter 7

R. Cunnington, 'The Measure and Availability of Gains-Based Damages for Breach of Contract', in D. Saidov and R. Cunnington (eds.), *Contract Damages: Domestic and International Perspectives* (Oxford, 2008), chapter 9

J. Edelman, *Gain-Based Damages* (Oxford, 2002), chapter 5

A. M. Tettenborn, in M. A. Clarke, N. Andrews, A. M. Tettenborn, G. Virgo, *Contractual Duties: Performance, Breach, Termination and Remedies* (London, 2012), chapter 26

S. Waddams, 'Gains Derived from Breach of Contract: Historical and Conceptual Perspectives', in D. Saidov and R. Cunnington (eds.), *Contract Damages: Domestic and International Perspectives* (Oxford, 2008), chapter 8

Recovery of payment after failure of consideration

Goff and Jones on the Law of Unjust Enrichment (8th edn, London, 2011), chapters 12 and 13

A. Burrows, E. McKendrick and J. Edelman, *Cases and Materials on the Law of Restitution* (2nd edn, Oxford, 2007), 362–86

G. Virgo, in *Chitty on Contracts* (31st edn, London, 2012), 29–056 ff

Specific performance and injunctions

A. Burrows (ed.), *English Private Law* (3rd edn, Oxford, 2013), 21.182 to 21.199 (specific performance); 21.200 ff (injunctions)

D. Friedmann, 'Economic Aspects of Damages and Specific Performance Compared', in D. Saidov and R. Cunnington (eds.), *Contract Damages: Domestic and International Perspectives* (Oxford, 2008), chapter 2

Chapter contents

19

Consensual remedies for breach of contract: liquidated damages and deposits

1. INTRODUCTION

19.01 Summary of main points

(1) The parties can agree upon 'liquidated damages', that is, an amount of compensation payable in the event of breach of the contract, or one of its terms; or they can agree that a sum should be paid in advance as a deposit to induce a party to perform (see (5) below). These are the two main topics discussed in this chapter.

(2) The 'penalty doctrine' invalidates a liquidated damages clause which stipulates that the party in breach shall pay a sum that is 'extravagant and unconscionable' in comparison with the greatest loss that could be contemplated at the time the contract was formed, as likely to be suffered by breach of the relevant substantive term.

(3) But the penalty doctrine only applies to sums payable upon breach and not where the sum is payable in other circumstances.

(4) The courts can invalidate (but are reluctant to do so) liquidated clauses contained in commercial agreements. Some commentators suggest that the court should go further and abandon their penalty jurisdiction, and that the law would be confined to the Consumer Rights Bill, Part 2 (previously, the Unfair Terms in Consumer Contracts Regulations 1999) (applicable only where the disadvantaged party is a consumer: 15.28). However, this contention is not the law and, as submitted here, should not be adopted.

(5) Deposits are sums paid to secure completion of the anticipated performance. A deposit is validly forfeited if the payor has defaulted in performance of the contract (unless the controls mentioned at (7) below invalidate the deposit).

(6) The amount of the deposit does not have to correspond with the likely loss: in other words, the 'penalty jurisdiction' (see above) does not govern deposits. The innocent party is entitled to seek Common Law compensation in excess of the deposit, if such additional loss can be shown.

(7) A deposit of 10 per cent for completion of a contract for the purchase of land, or the conclusion of a contract for the grant of a lease of real property, is now standard. Such a deposit will survive

539

challenge under both (a) the statutory regime applicable to 'relief' against forfeiture of deposits, and (b) the Common Law doctrine for relief against deposits 'unreasonable' in amount.

2. LIQUIDATED DAMAGES AND THE PENALTY DOCTRINE

19.02 *Attractions of the liquidated damages clause.* Liquidated damages clauses[1] are attractive for many reasons: first, such a clause enables the parties at the moment of contractual formation to know the extent of their prospective liability; secondly, once breach has occurred, the clause relieves the claimant of the expense and uncertainty of proving loss;[2] thirdly, it maintains fidelity to promises by acting as an incentive to performance; and, finally, it enables a party to stipulate for (non-punitive) protection beyond the technical limits of Common Law damages (see below). However, the 'penalty doctrine' prevents the innocent party stipulating for a flagrantly punitive, and hence non-compensatory, sum. The same doctrine also protects the guilty party from being coerced into soldiering on and avoiding the monetary sanction. Without this rule, well-advised parties could use money sanctions to induce individuals to perform personal services even if they no longer wished to do so. As mentioned at 18.33 and 18.38, specific performance or injunctions will not be granted where their *direct or indirect* effect would be to compel performance of such contracts.

19.03 *Fundamental statement of the penalty doctrine.* Dillon LJ noted in 1989: 'There is no doubt that the [English penalty doctrine] originated in Equity [1.25], and is of long standing.'[3] As for this doctrine's detailed rules, Lord Dunedin gave the seminal analysis in *Dunlop Pneumatic Tyre Co. Ltd* v. *New Garage and Motor Co. Ltd* (1915) (the numbering was added by the judge):[4]

1. Though the parties to a contract who use the words 'penalty' or 'liquidated damages' may prima facie be supposed to mean what they say, yet the expression used is not conclusive. The Court must find out whether the payment stipulated is in truth a penalty or liquidated damages . . .

1 A. S. Burrows, *Remedies for Torts and Breach of Contract* (3rd edn, Oxford, 2004), 440–55, especially 449–51; M. Chen-Wishart, in P. B. H. Birks (ed.), *Wrongs and Remedies in the Twenty-First Century* (Oxford, 1996); T. Downes, in P. B. H. Birks (ed.), *Wrongs and Remedies in the Twenty-First Century* (Oxford, 1996); L. Gullifer, in A. S. Burrows and E. Peel (eds.), *Commercial Remedies: Current Issues and Problems* (Oxford, 2003), 191; R. Halson, *Contract Law* (2nd edn, London, 2012), 504–17; *McGregor on Damages* (19th edn, London, 2014), chapter 15; R. Halson, 'Neglected Insights into Agreed Remedies', in D. Campbell, L. Mulcahy and S. Wheeler (eds.), *Changing Concepts of Contract: Essays in Honour of Ian Macneil* (Basingstoke, 2013), chapter 5; S. Rowan, 'For the Recognition of Remedial Terms Agreed Inter Partes' (2010) 126 LQR 448, 460 ff; Scottish Law Commission, 'Penalty Clauses' (Scottish Law Commission Report No. 171, Edinburgh, 1999); G. H. Treitel, *Remedies for Breach of Contract: A Comparative Account* (Oxford, 1988), 208–34; on the nineteenth-century history of this topic, see M. Lobban, in W. Cornish, J. S. Anderson, R. Cocks, M. Lobban, P. Polden and K. Smith, *The Oxford History of the Laws of England*, vol. XII, *1820–1914: Private Law* (Oxford, 2010), 523 ff.
2 *Robophone Facilities Ltd* v. *Blank* [1966] 1 WLR 1428, 1447F, CA, *per* Diplock LJ.
3 *Jobson* v. *Johnson* [1989] 1 WLR 1026, 1032, CA, *per* Dillon LJ.
4 *Dunlop Pneumatic Tyre Co. Ltd* v. *New Garage and Motor Co. Ltd* [1915] AC 70, 86–8, HL, *per* Lord Dunedin; for a careful exegesis, *El Makdessi* v. *Cavendish Square Holdings BV* [2013] EWCA Civ 1539; [2014] BLR 246, at [55], *per* Christopher Clarke LJ (an appeal is outstanding) (noted E. Peel, (2014) 130 LQR 365–70).

2. The essence of a penalty is a payment of money stipulated as in terrorem of the offending party; the essence of liquidated damages is a genuine covenanted pre-estimate of damage . . .

3. The question whether a sum stipulated is a penalty or liquidated damages is a question of construction to be decided upon the terms and inherent circumstances of each particular contract, judged of as at the time of the making of the contract, not as at the time of the breach . . .

4. To assist this task of construction various tests have been suggested, which if applicable to the case under consideration may prove helpful, or even conclusive. Such are:

    (a) It will be held to be a penalty if the sum stipulated for is extravagant and unconscionable in amount in comparison with the greatest loss that could conceivably be proved to have followed from the breach.

    (b) It will be held to be a penalty if the breach consists only in not paying a sum of money, and the sum stipulated is a sum greater than the sum which ought to have been paid . . . This though one of the most ancient instances is truly a corollary to the last test . . .

    (c) There is a presumption (but no more) that it is a penalty when 'a single lump sum is made payable by way of compensation, on the occurrence of one or more or all of several events, some of which may occasion serious and others but trifling damage'. On the other hand:

    (d) It is no obstacle to the sum stipulated being a genuine pre-estimate of damage, that the consequences of the breach are such as to make precise pre-estimation almost an impossibility. On the contrary, that is just the situation when it is probable that pre-estimated damage was the true bargain between the parties.

    Point (d) is important: the courts must be alive to the difficulties faced when trying to make a precise prediction of the losses likely to flow from breach.[5]

19.04 In the *Alfred McAlpine* case (2005),[6] Jackson J glossed the words in (b) above in *Dunlop Pneumatic Tyre Co. Ltd* v. *New Garage and Motor Co. Ltd* (1915) (19.03). In his view, those words require 'a substantial discrepancy between the level of damages stipulated in the contract and the level of damages which is likely to be suffered'. And in the *BNP Paribas* case (2009) Christopher Clarke J said: 'the court may look to see whether or not the sum is disproportionate to the least important of the contractual undertakings to which it applies and thus whether it represents an extravagant or unconscionable sum in relation to such a breach.'[7] There is another valuable review of this topic by Christopher Clarke LJ in *El Makdessi* v. *Cavendish Square Holdings BV* (2013).[8]

---

5 *Ibid.*, at 87–8.
6 *Alfred McAlpine Capital Projects Ltd* v. *Tilebox Ltd* [2005] EWHC (TCC) 281; [2005] BLR 271, 280, at [48], *per* Jackson J.
7 *BNP Paribas* v. *Wockhardt EU Operations (Swiss) AG* [2009] EWHC 3116 (Comm), 132 Con LR 177, 132 Con LR 177, at [26], *per* Christopher Clarke J.
8 [2013] EWCA Civ 1539; [2014] BLR 246, at [55] ff, *per* Christopher Clarke LJ (an appeal is outstanding) (noted E. Peel, (2014) 130 LQR 365–70).

For example, in *CMC Group plc* v. *Michael Zhang* (2006),[9] a settlement agreement between the parties provided that if Z continued to make complaints of ill-treatment against CMC's employees, Z would have to pay a sum equivalent to the amount of the settlement (US$40,000). The Court of Appeal held that this clause was a penalty because it bore no relation to the loss likely to flow from breach, and it had been inserted to deter breach of the settlement agreement rather than to quantify loss.

19.05 A liquidated damages clause can validly provide more generous compensation than that awarded by the courts. This laissez-faire approach to agreed 'compensation' seems sound, unless the clause aims to confer an 'extravagant and unconscionable' right to payment.[10] For example, the parties can displace the rules governing remoteness (18.16),[11] or mitigation (18.22)[12] (but it is unclear whether the general rule denying recovery for 'profits gained from breach' can be displaced?).[13] In *Makdessi* v. *Cavendish Square Holdings BV* (2013)[14] the Court of Appeal also emphasised that even where it is 'extravagant and unconscionable', the relevant clause will not be condemned as a penalty if there is some further 'commercial justification', but this is unhelpfully open-ended.[15]

19.06 *Objective test.* In the *Alfred McAlpine* case (2005),[16] Jackson J also noted that the test is objective. It 'does not turn upon the genuineness or honesty of the party or parties who made the pre-estimate' (furthermore, the parties' own description of the relevant damages clause as 'liquidated' or 'penalty' is not decisive).[17] The party arguing for invalidity of the damages clause has the burden of proof of showing that it is a penalty.[18]

19.07 *Assessment at date of formation and not of breach.* The penalty test is applied retrospectively by the court, with regard to the situation 'as at the time of the making of the contract, not as

9 [2006] EWCA Civ 408.
10 *Murray* v. *Leisureplay plc* [2005] EWCA 963; [2005] IRLR 946, CA; noting also the result in the *Dunlop Pneumatic* case, [1915] AC 70, HL.
11 *Robophone* case, [1966] 1 WLR 1428, 1447–9, CA, *per* Diplock LJ: clause proving enhanced recovery in respect of loss not covered by 'limb 2' of *Hadley* v. *Baxendale* (1854) 9 Exch 341 (18.16); but, surprisingly, the Law Commission thought this unpersuasive: Law Commission, 'Penalty Clauses and Forfeiture of Monies Paid' (Law Commission Consultation Paper No. 61, London, 1975), at [44].
12 *Murray* v. *Leisureplay plc* [2005] EWCA 963; [2005] IRLR 946, CA (upholding a clause requiring the guilty party to pay a wrongfully dismissed party a year's salary in the event of breach, without adjustment requiring the employee to mitigate his loss).
13 A. S. Burrows, *Remedies for Torts and Breach of Contract* (3rd edn, Oxford, 2004), 444–5 (considering development in *Attorney-General* v. *Blake* [2001] 1 AC 268, HL, 18.30).
14 [2013] EWCA Civ 1539; [2014] BLR 246, at [117] to [121], *per* Christopher Clarke LJ (an appeal is outstanding) (noted E. Peel, (2014) 130 LQR 365–70).
15 Cf *ibid.*, at [121] for this list of justifiable circumstances; 'a modest extra interest in respect of a defaulting loan; a provision for the payment of the costs of earlier litigation; a generous measure of damages for wrongful dismissal; an allocation of credit risk; or the provision of capital which would be needed if a promised guarantee of a loan was not forthcoming'.
16 *Alfred McAlpine Capital Projects Ltd* v. *Tilebox Ltd* [2005] EWHC (TCC) 281; [2005] BLR 271, 280, at [48], *per* Jackson J.
17 *Elphinstone* v. *Monkland Iron and Coal Co.* (1886) 11 App Cas 32; *Cellulose Acetate Silk Co. Ltd* v. *Widnes Foundry (1925) Ltd* [1933] AC 20, 25 HL; see also the *Duffen* case, at 19.15.
18 *Murray* v. *Leisureplay plc* [2005] EWCA 963; [2005] IRLR 946, CA, at [106], *per* Clarke LJ.

at the time of the breach'[19] (although the actual loss is a clue to 'what could reasonably be expected to be the loss at the time the contract was made').[20]

19.08 *Breach triggering liability.* The House of Lords affirmed in the *Export Credits Guarantee Department* case (1983) (19.09),[21] and the Court of Appeal in the *Euro London Appointments* case (2006)[22] confirmed, that a clause challenged on the basis that it was in fact a penalty must concern a payment which is triggered by *breach*, that is, *a culpable failure to satisfy a contractual obligation.* If there is a different trigger, the relevant clause will not be a penalty.

> In *Office of Fair Trading* v. *Abbey National plc* (2008)[23] Andrew Smith J held[24] that the penalty doctrine cannot apply to the banking practice (supported by written terms) of charging a fee for unauthorised loans granted by the bank when a customer exceeds his credit limit on his current account. In that situation, the customer does not commit a breach of his contract towards the bank. And so the fee cannot be regarded as a penalty at Common Law (also on the bank charges litigation, see 15.36). (The 'penalty' point under consideration here was not taken to the Court of Appeal[25] nor to the Supreme Court.)
>
> Peel notes that the High Court of Australia has not accepted the 'breach' restriction on the operation of the penalty jurisdiction.[26]

19.09 *Need for breach as between payor and payee.* As the House of Lords further stated in the *Export Credits* case (1983),[27] the penalty doctrine can be invoked by the proposed *payor* only where the clause is triggered by *breach of an obligation owed by the payor to the payee.*

---

19   *Dunlop Pneumatic Tyre Co. Ltd* v. *New Garage and Motor Co. Ltd* [1915] AC 70, 87, HL, citing *Commissioner for Public Works* v. *Hills* [1906] AC 368, PC, and *Webster* v. *Bosanquet* [1912] AC 394, PC; Law Commission, 'Penalty Clauses and Forfeiture of Monies Paid' (Law Commission Consultation Paper No. 61, London, 1975), at [30] and [41] (noting that the converse approach has gained favour in several other jurisdictions).
20   *Philips Hong Kong Ltd* v. *Attorney-General for Hong Kong* (1993) 61 BLR 41, 59, PC, *per* Lord Woolf; 'date of formation' principle not adopted in the USA, P. R. Kaplan, (1977) 50 *Southern California Law Review* 1055, 1072.
21   *Export Credits Guarantee Department* v. *Universal Oil Products Co.* [1983] 1 WLR 399, HL (applied in *Jervis* v. *Harris* [1996] Ch 195, CA, and in the *Euro London* case: see 19.08); for earlier criticism, see *Bridge* v. *Campbell Discount* [1962] AC 600, 631, HL, *per* Lord Denning; Law Commission, 'Penalty Clauses and Forfeiture of Monies Paid' (Law Commission Consultation Paper No. 61, London, 1975), Part III.
22   *Euro London Appointments Ltd* v. *Claessens International Ltd* [2006] EWCA Civ 385; [2006] 2 Lloyd's Rep 436, at [29]; also supported by *Export Credits Guarantee Department* v. *Universal Oil Products Co.* [1983] 1 WLR 399, HL (19.09) (applied in *Jervis* v. *Harris* [1996] Ch 195, CA), both cited by Andrew Smith J in *Office of Fair Trading* v. *Abbey National plc* [2008] EWHC 875 (Comm), at [295] ff.
23   [2008] EWHC 875 (Comm); M. Chen-Wishart, (2008) 124 LQR 501–8; P. S. Davies, [2008] CLJ 466–9.
24   [2008] EWHC 875 (Comm), at [295] to [323].
25   [2009] EWCA Civ 116, at [11]; M. Chen-Wishart, (2009) 125 LQR 389–93; but note Lord Phillips' dictum at [2009] UKSC 6; [2010] 1 AC 696, at [83], on which see C. Conte, (2010) 126 LQR 529, 531, also noting the (orthodox) decision on this point in *UK Housing Alliance (North West) Ltd* v. *Francis* [2010] EWCA Civ 117; [2010] 3 All ER 51.
26   *Andrews* v. *Australia and New Zealand Banking Group Ltd* [2012] HCA 30; (2012) 290 ALR 595; noted E. Peel, (2013) 129 LQR 152–7; B. Mason, [2013] LMCLQ 233–59; the decision is strongly criticised in J. W. Carter, W. Courtney, E. Peden, A. Stewart, and G. J. Tolhurst, 'Contractual Penalties: Resurrecting the Equitable Jurisdiction' (2013) 30 JCL 99–132.
27   [1983] 1 WLR 399, HL (applied in *Jervis* v. *Harris* [1996] Ch 195, CA and in the *Euro London* case: see 19.08); for earlier criticism, see *Bridge* v. *Campbell Discount* [1962] AC 600, 631, HL, *per* Lord Denning; Law

In *Export Credits Guarantee Department* v. *Universal Oil Products Co.* (1983), the Export Credits Guarantee Department (ECGD) agreed to guarantee payments by Universal Oil Products (UOP) to Kleinwort Benson, a bank. In the event of the ECGD becoming liable on those contracts of guarantee, UOP agreed to indemnify the ECGD. UOP argued that its liability to the ECGD was triggered by UOP's breach vis-à-vis Kleinwort Benson, and so the ECGD/UOP obligation might be vulnerable to attack as a penalty. But the defect in this argument was that English law required the breach to have been a primary obligation owed by the payor to the payee, that is, by UOP to the ECGD. In this case, there was no such primary obligation; instead, that primary obligation was owed by UOP to Kleinwort Benson.[28]

19.10 *Types of clause covered by the penalty jurisdiction.* The penalty doctrine is not confined to clauses ('liquidated damages clauses') quantifying[29] the amount of damages to be paid in the event of breach (although that will be the most common type of clause). In fact, four other types of clause are subject to this jurisdiction:

(1) loss of a right to a refund, or loss of a right to a payment;[30]

(2) loss of a right to a discount;[31]

(3) clauses requiring the re-transfer of property in the event of the payor's default, where the value of the property to be handed back exceeds the amount of the monetary default;[32]

(4) a 'debt' payable in the event of breach, for example, liability to pay a price if – in contravention of another obligation in the same contract – the buyer does not purchase a minimum quantity from the other party.

As for (4), Burton J said in the *M & J Polymers* case (2008): 'It is clear that, for example, a minimum payment clause in a hire-purchase agreement can be held to be a penalty, even though expressed as a claim in debt.'[33] However, on the facts of that case, Burton J could discern no objectionable penalty:[34] 'The negotiations took place between extremely well qualified, able and savvy commercial men against a very significant commercial background, including a background of previous dealings.'

Commission, 'Penalty Clauses and Forfeiture of Monies Paid' (Law Commission Consultation Paper No. 61, London, 1975), Part III.
28 [1983] 1 WLR 399, 401, 403, HL; considered in *Euro London* case, [2006] EWCA Civ 385; [2006] 2 Lloyd's Rep 436, at [28], *per* Clarke LJ.
29 *BNP Paribas* v. *Wockhardt EU Operations (Swiss) AG* [2009] EWHC 3116 (Comm), 132 Con LR 177, at [26], *per* Christopher Clarke J.
30 *General Trading Company (Holdings) Ltd* v. *Richmond Corporation Ltd* [2008] EWHC 1479 (Comm); [2008] 2 Lloyd's Rep 475, at [113], *per* Beatson J (this point was *obiter*, see [109]; but the review of modern developments at [109] to [131] is helpful). On this issue [2013] EWCA Civ 1539; [2014] BLR 246, at [53], *per* Christopher Clarke LJ (an appeal is outstanding) (noted E. Peel, (2014) 130 LQR 365–70).
31 On (2) and (3), see the *Euro London* case, [2006] EWCA Civ 385; [2006] 2 Lloyd's Rep 436 (considered in the *M & J Polymers Ltd* case, [2008] EWHC 344 (Comm), at [42]).
32 *Jobson* v. *Johnson* [1989] 1 WLR 1026, CA.
33 *M & J Polymers Ltd* v. *Imerys Minerals Ltd* [2008] EWHC 344 (Comm); [2008] 1 Lloyd's Rep 541, at [41], *per* Burton J.
34 *Ibid.,* at [40] to [48], especially at [46].

19.11 *Commercial parties.* Lord Woolf said in the *Philips Hong Kong* case (1993):[35] '[T]he court has to be careful not to set too stringent a standard and to bear in mind that what the parties have agreed should normally be upheld. Any other approach will lead to undesirable uncertainty, especially in commercial contract.'[36]

> Jackson J in the *Alfred McAlpine* case (2005) also noted that the courts are reluctant to upset liquidated damages clauses if they have been agreed between non-consumers.[37] He found only a handful of 'cases where the relevant clause has been struck down as a penalty',[38] and these were, in his word, situations where 'there was a very wide gulf between (a) the level of damages likely to be suffered, and (b) the level of damages stipulated in the contract'.
>
> In the *BNP Paribas* case (2009) Christopher Clarke J emphasised that English courts are reluctant to find a penalty when the parties have entered a contract of a sophisticated nature, based on a standard form widely used in international commerce, and it is evident that both parties have entered the transaction with their eyes open, enjoying access to legal advice.[39] He added: 'The policy of the law is to encourage the use of liquidated damages clauses especially in commercial contracts.'[40]

19.12 *Equality of bargaining power.* Nevertheless, as the Court of Appeal's decision in the *Jeancharm* case (2003) shows, even between commercial parties of roughly equal bargaining strength, an intrinsically 'extravagant and unconscionable' clause (on the facts, one which required payment of interest on a commercial debt of 260 per cent a year) will be struck down.[41] However, Jacob LJ said in the *Jeancharm* case: '[O]ne should be careful before deciding whether or not a clause is a penalty when the parties are of equal bargaining power.'[42] The opening proposition in this paragraph is confirmed in *Makdessi* v. *Cavendish Square Holdings BV* (2013) by the Court of Appeal.[43]

---

35 *Philips Hong Kong Ltd* v. *Attorney-General for Hong Kong* (1993) 61 BLR 41, 54–5, 59, PC; *Robophone Facilities Ltd* v. *Blank* [1966] 1 WLR 1428, 1447, CA, *per* Diplock LJ.

36 *Philips Hong Kong Ltd* v. *Attorney-General for Hong Kong* (1993) 61 BLR 41, 61.

37 *Alfred McAlpine Capital Projects Ltd* v. *Tilebox Ltd* [2005] EWHC (TCC) 281; [2005] BLR 271, 280, at [48], *per* Jackson J.

38 Citing *Commissioner of Public Works* v. *Hills* [1906] AC 368, PC, *Bridge* v. *Campbell Discount Co. Ltd* [1962] AC 600, HL, *Workers Trust and Merchant Bank Ltd* v. *Dojap Investments Ltd* [1993] AC 573, PC (arguably a case on Common Law relief against excessive deposits: see 19.35) and *Ariston SRL* v. *Charly Records* (Court of Appeal, 13 March 1990); see also *CMC Group plc* v. *Michael Zhang* [2006] EWCA Civ 408 (unreported); *Jobson* v. *Johnson* [1989] 1 WLR 1026, CA; *Duffen* v. *FRA BO SpA*, *The Times*, 15 June 1998, CA; *Jeancharm Ltd* v. *Barnet Football Club Ltd* [2003] EWCA Civ 58, 92 Con LR 26.

39 *BNP Paribas* v. *Wockhardt EU Operations (Swiss) AG* [2009] EWHC 3116 (Comm), 132 Con LR 177, at [23] ff, *per* Christopher Clarke J.

40 *Ibid.*, at [25], citing *Murray* v. *Leisureplay plc* [2005] EWCA Civ 963, at [114] and Diplock, LJ in *Robophone* v. *Blank* [1966] 1 WLR 1428, 1447.

41 *Jeancharm Ltd* v. *Barnet Football Club Ltd* [2003] EWCA Civ 58; 92 Con LR 26.

42 *Ibid.*, at [15].

43 [2013] EWCA Civ 1539; [2014] BLR 246, at [75], *per* Christopher Clarke LJ (an appeal is outstanding): 'the fact that the clause has been agreed between parties of equal bargaining power who have competent advice cannot be determinative. The question whether a clause is penal habitually arises in commercial contracts, which enjoy no immunity from the doctrine.'

19.13 *Muddying the waters: the suggested test of 'no deterrent purpose'.* The Court of Appeal in the *Murray* case (2007) said that the real issue is whether the innocent party's main *purpose* was to insert a payment clause containing a sum *so large that it would deter the other from breaching*, rather than to provide compensation.[44] The court said that there should be no automatic conclusion that a non-compensatory element renders the clause 'deterrent' in aim and hence invalidates the clause. Otherwise, Buxton LJ said, the approach would become unacceptably 'rigid and inflexible'.[45] Burton J followed this approach in the *M & J Polymers* case (2008).[46]

19.14 The criterion of a 'deterrent purpose' is a controversial change of emphasis, although it was repeated in the Court of Appeal in *Makdessi* v. *Cavendish Square Holdings BV* (2013).[47] The test in the seminal *Dunlop* case (19.03) refers to an 'extravagant and oppressive' difference between 'the greatest possible loss' and the amount stipulated for. This is an objective test, pitched in favour of the payee, and, it is submitted, this approach is sound. It is submitted that there is no need to obscure matters by referring to the payee's intention in procuring the relevant clause: after all, no real monetary threat can be made unless the stipulated sum greatly exceeds the ordinary Common Law measure of compensation (so that emphasis on the clause's function or intent becomes rather jejune).[48] For this reason, the search for a *deterrent purpose* is unhelpful, as Lord Radcliffe noted in *Bridge* v. *Campbell Discount* (1962).[49] Furthermore, the quest for a *deterrent purpose* would complicate matters because it would require the court to determine what the common intention of the parties was, who inserted the relevant clause, and what the purpose of its insertion was. To avoid these difficulties, it is submitted that the law should be kept simple and that the objective approach should remain: whether the stipulated sum is 'extravagant and unconscionable'.

19.15 *Single sum payable in a range of situations.* The claimant must take some care not to apply a single liquidated damages clause to deal with: (1) a contract containing a number of obligations which can be breached in a number of ways; or (2) a single obligation which might be breached in different ways and at different times so as to cause widely differing amounts of loss.[50] However, these two sub-rules are presumptions, as *Dunlop Pneumatic Tyre Co. Ltd* v. *New Garage and Motor Co. Ltd* (1915) makes clear. They are not rigid rules.

---

44 *Murray* v. *Leisureplay plc* [2005] EWCA 963; [2005] IRLR 946, at [110] to [118], especially at [106], *per* Clarke and Buxton LJJ (noting *Cines Bes Filmclik ve Yapincilik AS* v. *United International Pictures* [2003] EWCA Civ 1669, at [13], *per* Mance LJ, and *Lordsvale Finance plc* v. *Bank of Zambia* [1996] QB 752, 762G, Colman J).
45 *Murray* v. *Leisureplay plc* [2005] EWCA 963; [2005] IRLR 946, at [42].
46 [2008] EWHC 344 (Comm); [2008] 1 Lloyd's Rep 541, at [40] to [48], especially at [46]; and *General Trading Company (Holdings) Ltd* v. *Richmond Corporation Ltd* [2008] EWHC 1479 (Comm); [2008] 2 Lloyd's Rep 475, at [109] ff, *per* Beatson J (an *obiter* discussion, but a helpful review of modern developments).
47 [2013] EWCA Civ 1539; [2014] BLR 246, at [120], [121], [124], *per* Christopher Clarke LJ (an appeal is outstanding).
48 *Ibid.*, at [120], *per* Christopher Clarke LJ (an appeal is outstanding): 'where the amount to be paid or lost is out of all proportion to the loss attributable to the breach ... the provisions are likely to be regarded as penal because their function is to act as a deterrent.'
49 [1962] AC 600, 621–2, HL.
50 *Dunlop Pneumatic Tyre Company* v. *New Garage* [1915] AC 79, 97–9, HL.

For example, in the *Dunlop* case, the relevant clause survived attack on this basis.[51] But, in *Duffen* v. *FRA BO SpA* (1998), a clause was invalidated:[52]

> The clause in *Duffen* v. *FRA BO SpA* (1998) stipulated that in the event of X being wrongly dismissed from his agency by Y, Y would pay X '£100,000 by way of liquidated damages which sum is agreed by the parties to be a reasonable pre-estimate of the loss and damage which the agent will suffer on termination of this agreement'. The Court of Appeal held that this was a penalty. It was not graduated to reflect the length of the unexpired term of the agency contract. The range of possible loss was £180,000 to £6,000, depending on the date of breach. Otton LJ described the stipulated sum as 'extravagant and unconscionable' and, on the facts, liable to confer a 'substantial windfall' upon X.

19.16 *Penalty in the context of money obligations.* A clause stipulating that non-payment of £x will require payment of £x and £y is a penalty (unless £y is a sum by way of interest set at a commercially acceptable level: see the *Jeancharm* case (2003) at 19.17). As Lord Dunedin said in the *Dunlop* case (1915):[53] 'It will be held to be a penalty if the breach consists only in not paying a sum of money, and the sum stipulated is a sum greater than the sum which ought to have been paid.'

But, in the modern cases, some flexibility has been shown. Thus, Colman J in the *Lordsvale* case (1996) upheld a clause in a loan agreement which stipulated that the borrower's default in making repayments would trigger a *prospective* and 'modest' increase of 1 per cent in the level of interest.[54]

> Colman J in the *Lordsvale* case (1996) admitted that this prospective increase was not a genuine pre-estimate of the loss. But he considered that the increase was justified and proportionate. This was because the borrower's default rendered that party a greater credit risk. It would have been different if the clause had provided that default would lead to a retrospective increase in the level of interest for the loan. In that situation, an increase in interest would apply to the whole period from the date of the loan. Such an increase would not be tailored to apply only from the date of default, which might occur at any stage in the currency of the loan.

19.17 The Court of Appeal in *Jeancharm Ltd* v. *Barnet Football Club Ltd* (2003) struck down as a penalty a clause stipulating that late payment of a commercial debt (the defendant club's liability for football shirts) would attract interest at the rate of 5 per cent per week.[55] This amounted to an annual rate of 260 per cent. This exorbitant rate of interest was intrinsically

---

51 *Ibid.*, at 87.
52 *The Times*, 15 June 1998, CA.
53 *Dunlop* case, [1915] AC 70, 87, HL, *per* Lord Dunedin; similarly, *Jobson* v. *Johnson* [1989] 1 WLR 1026, 1041, CA, *per* Nicholls LJ.
54 *Lordsvale Finance plc* v. *Bank of Zambia* [1996] QB 752, 763–7, Colman J (consistent with Canadian, Australian and New York banking law).
55 [2003] EWCA Civ 58; 92 Con LR 26.

punitive. It could not be regarded as a genuine pre-estimate of loss (despite a desperate attempt by the payee's counsel to argue that the sum was intended to cover his client's 'administrative costs'). The court held that there was no need to show that the payee had oppressively exploited a commercially dominant position.

19.18 *Acceleration clauses.* Such a clause works in this way. B's obligations consist of a series of payments by instalment. The clause states that, upon default, *all of these become payable in a lump sum.* And so B's overall liability is accelerated. It is clear, as confirmed by Christopher Clarke J in the *BNP Paribas* case (2009), that 'there is nothing penal in a provision which requires the acceleration in the event of breach of an amount which, without breach, would become due later.'[56] The courts take the view that the correct analysis is that the debtor *can postpone performance of the lump sum obligation by making punctual instalment payments.* This approach to acceleration clauses can obviously produce hardship. However, as Woolf J observed in *Wadham Stringer Finance Ltd* v. *Meaney* (1981), Parliament has acknowledged the validity of acceleration clauses, referring to section 30(1) of the Hire-Purchase Act 1965.[57]

19.19 *Consequence of finding a penalty.* A penalty clause is invalid beyond the amount of loss actually suffered. Thus, the party in breach is nevertheless liable to pay Common Law compensation if the innocent party can prove substantial loss. Furthermore, the penalty clause is not wholly void: instead, the clause cannot be enforced beyond the level of true compensation. An action on a 'scaled down' penalty clause (its penal element having been excised) is technically a debt claim, rather than one for damages.[58] But, in practice, the penalty is regarded as a dead letter and the claim will instead be framed as one for Common Law damages based on general compensatory principles.[59]

19.20 *Valid liquidated damages clause acts as a cap.* If the amount payable under a valid liquidated damages clause turns out to be less than the loss suffered, the innocent party is bound by this figure. He cannot obtain greater compensation by suing for Common Law damages.

For example, in the *Cellulose Acetate Silk* case (1933),[60] the contract concerned the construction of a factory. A clause stipulated that compensation for delay in completion would be at the rate of £20 per week. In fact, there was a delay of thirty weeks, and the actual loss suffered was £5,850, whereas the liquidated damages clause would yield only £600. The House of Lords held

---

56 *BNP Paribas* v. *Wockhardt EU Operations (Swiss) AG* [2009] EWHC 3116 (Comm), 132 Con LR 177, at [38], *per* Christopher Clarke J, citing *Protector Endowment Loan and Annuity Co.* v. *Grice* (1880) 5 QBD 121, and 'The Angelic Star' [1988] I Lloyd's Rep 122, 125–7; see also: *Wallingford* v. *Mutual Society* (1880) 5 App Cas 685, HL; *Wadham Stringer Finance Ltd* v. *Meaney* [1981] 1 WLR 39; *White and Carter (Councils) Ltd* v. *McGregor* [1962] AC 413, 426–7, HL.
57 [1981] 1 WLR 39, 48.
58 *Jobson* v. *Johnson* [1989] 1 WLR 1026, 1039–41, CA, Nicholls LJ.
59 *Jobson* case, *ibid.*; R. Halson, *Contract Law* (2nd edn, London, 2012), 514.
60 *Cellulose Acetate Silk Co. Ltd* v. *Widnes Foundry (1925) Ltd* [1933] AC 20, HL.

that the claimant was confined to £600, since the clause was not a penalty. Lord Atkin said that the parties had deliberately agreed to a clause which 'under-compensated' the innocent party. But it was not a pure limitation clause (that is, merely a financial cap on damages, but not imposing a minimum level of recovery: 15.01). Instead, the clause could have benefited the owners even if the loss suffered had been less than £20 per week.

As Burrows comments,[61] the more natural interpretation will be that the under-compensating clause was intended to be a cap. As such it will be open to challenge under the Unfair Contract Terms Act 1977 (in the case of non-consumer transactions) (15.08) or the Consumer Rights Bill, Part 2 (consumer purchases; replacing the Unfair Terms in Consumer Contracts Regulations 1999) (15.28).

19.21 *Invalid liquidated damages clause not a cap.* If the *under-compensating clause* (see preceding paragraph) is technically a *penalty* (for example, it fails to differentiate between different types of obligations which might be breached), the innocent party can sue at Common Law for damages to cover his greater loss. In this situation, the penalty provision has no effect,[62] even if the innocent party had inserted it into the contract.

In *Wall* v. *Rederiaktiebolaget Luggude* (1915),[63] Bailhache J invalidated a clause contained in a charterparty. The clause fixed the owner's liability under a charterparty to the amount of freight payable (on the facts, £1,125). In the event, the loss suffered by the charterer was £3,000. The judge held that the clause had not been intended to operate as a limitation clause. Instead, it was a penalty. And so the innocent party could ignore it and sue for his damages under Common Law principles.

This decision was approved by three members of the House of Lords in *Watts, Watts & Co. Ltd* v. *Mitsui & Co. Ltd* (1917)[64] (although this proposition's soundness was doubted by Lord Atkin in the *Cellulose* case (1933),[65] and by Diplock LJ in the *Robophone* case (1966)).[66]

However, it is odd that a party can invoke the penalty doctrine when it was he who inserted it.

The Supreme Court of Canada has held that the party stipulating for the penalty should not have the benefit of the limitation.[67] Burrows and Halson favour that approach.[68]

But the counter-arguments are: (1) a clause is a penalty 'at birth' (the date of the contract's formation) irrespective of the amount of loss in fact suffered; and (2) the court should not be required to discover which party demanded that the clause be inserted.

61   A. S. Burrows, *Remedies for Torts and Breach of Contract* (3rd edn, Oxford, 2004), 448–9.
62   *Jobson* v. *Johnson* [1989] 1 WLR 1026, 1039–41, CA, *per* Nicholls LJ.
63   [1915] 3 KB 66, Bailhache J.
64   [1917] AC 227, 235, 245, 246, HL.
65   [1933] AC 20, 26, HL.
66   [1966] 1 WLR 1428, 1446, CA.
67   *Elsley* v. *JG Collins Insurance Agencies Ltd* (1978) 83 DLR (3d) 1, 14–15 (Supreme Court of Canada).
68   A. S. Burrows, *Remedies for Torts and Breach of Contract* (3rd edn, Oxford, 2004), 447–8; R. Halson, *Contract Law* (2nd edn, London, 2012), 514; A. H. Hudson, (1974) 90 LQR 31, (1975) 91 LQR 25, and (1985) 101 LQR 480; Gordon, (1974) 90 LQR 296; J. L. Barton, (1976) 92 LQR 20; W. F. Fritz, (1954) 33 *Texas Law Review* 196.

19.22 *Critique of the penalty doctrine (1): fetter on freedom of contract.* Some commentators have criticised the penalty doctrine, suggesting that it is an unjustified fetter on the principle of freedom of contract (1.08).[69] Admittedly, the law must protect *consumers* against liability to pay penalties.[70] But here the Consumer Rights Bill, Part 2 (formerly the Unfair Terms in Consumer Contracts Regulations 1999) (15.28) provides an adequate tool (the Regulations state that if a term requires a consumer – confined to a 'natural person' – in breach of a contract to pay a 'disproportionately high sum in compensation' to a supplier of goods or services, this term will probably be regarded as unfair and so invalid).[71] 'Common Law penalty critics' recognise the need for *statutory protection of consumers*. But these critics would prefer that business parties should be free to fashion 'private sanctions'. If these critics were allowed to remould the law, therefore, the *judicial* penalty doctrine would be abolished. This would leave the statutory consumer protection as the only source of protection, and thus confined to contracts affecting consumers. Is this suggested remoulding of the law attractive?

19.23 *Rejoinder to the critics.* It is submitted that the Common Law penalty doctrine has a legitimate role. It should continue to apply both to consumer transactions and to *business-to-business transactions*. In general, monetary *punishment* is not an acceptable feature of contractual remedies. Such punishment will be appropriate only where the guilty party has seriously defied an injunction or order for specific performance, exposing himself to committal for contempt of court (18.33).

> Even the Court of Appeal has expressed surprise that the doctrine appears to conflict with the freedom of contract principle. In *Makdessi* v. *Cavendish Square Holdings BV* (2013) Christopher Clarke LJ said:[72]
>
> > The law of penalties is a blatant interference with freedom of contract. In *Robophone Facilities Ltd* v. *Blank* [1966] 1 WLR 1428 Diplock LJ said that he made 'no attempt where so many others have failed to rationalise this common law rule'. The rule is traceable to the preparedness of a court of equity to restrain the enforcement at common law of penal bonds i.e. bonds providing for the payment of a sum of money upon the non-payment of principal and interest due under another instrument. The common law courts adopted the doctrine and applied it to situations other than penal bonds.
>
> But the truth is that the principle of freedom of contract is subject to legitimate exceptions and qualifications based on protection of parties from overreaching, draconian and excessive provisions which exceed what is commercially tough, but tolerable, and demand relief on the basis of substantive fairness.

69 T. Downes, in P. B. H. Birks (ed.), *Wrongs and Remedies in the Twenty-First Century* (Oxford, 1996), 249, 265–6; M. Chen-Wishart, *ibid.*, at 279 ff; *Elsey* v. *JG Collins Insurance Agencies Ltd* (1978) 83 DLR 1, 15, Dickson J (Supreme Court of Canada); and see E. Peel, (2013) 129 LQR 152, 156 (noting *Andrews* v. *Australia and New Zealand Banking Group Ltd* [2012] HCA 30; (2012) 290 ALR 595; and E. Peel's further comments at (2014) 130 LQR 365, 369–70).
70 T. Downes, in P. B. H. Birks (ed.), *Wrongs and Remedies in the Twenty-First Century* (Oxford, 1996), 249.
71 Schedule 2, para. 1(e) (an 'indicative' provision).
72 [2013] EWCA Civ 1539; [2014] BLR 246, at [120], [121], [124], *per* Christopher Clarke LJ (an appeal is outstanding).

19.24 *Critique of the penalty doctrine (2): over-complicated rules.* The real criticism, it is submitted, is not that the judicial penalty doctrine survives, but that it has become so complex. In Victorian times, the rule could be stated relatively simply. But, nowadays, the case law has greatly complicated this doctrine. This can be contrasted with clear statements contained in foreign codes and 'soft law' transnational documents (although some English commercial lawyers might contend that these foreign statements are rather too brief).

> The Principles of European Contract Law, Article 9:509(2), states:
>> However, despite any agreement to the contrary the specified sum may be reduced to a reasonable amount where it is grossly excessive in relation to the loss resulting from the non-performance and the other circumstances.
>
> UNIDROIT's *Principles of International Commercial Contracts* (2010), Article 7.4.13(2), provides:[73]
>> However, notwithstanding any agreement to the contrary the specified sum may be reduced to a reasonable amount where it is grossly excessive in relation to the harm resulting from the non-performance and to the other circumstances.
>
> The French *Code Civil*, Article 1152(2), provides:[74]
>> The judge can, of his own motion or otherwise, diminish or increase the agreed penalty if it is manifestly excessive or derisory. Any provision in the contract to the contrary shall be deemed not to have been made.

3. RELIEF AGAINST FORFEITURE OF MONEY INSTALMENTS

19.25 Equity can relieve a party in breach against forfeiture of instalments already paid if the sum retained by the innocent party would be wholly disproportionate to the loss suffered by him as a result of the breach (see next paragraph for details).

19.26 The English authority supporting this is *Stockloser* v. *Johnson* (1954),[75] although the point was not directly decided in that case.

> Denning LJ enunciated two criteria: the sum to be forfeited must be penal; and, secondly, its retention would be unconscionable.[76] These tests should be applied at the time of the claim, not

---

73   3rd edition, 2010, text and comment, is available at:http://www.unidroit.org/english/principles/contracts/principles2010/integralversionprinciples2010-e.pdf.
74   B. Nicholas, *The French Law of Contract* (2nd edn, Oxford, 1992), 235–6; Scottish Law Commission, 'Penalty Clauses' (Scottish Law Commission Report No. 171, Edinburgh, 1999) proposed a 'manifestly excessive' reformulation of the present doctrine.
75   [1954] 1 QB 476, 483–5, 490, CA; considered in *Cadogan Petroleum Holdings Ltd* v. *Global Process Systems LLC* [2013] EWHC 214 (Comm); [2013] 2 Lloyd's Rep 26; [2013] 1 CLC 721, Eder J (noted L. Aitken (2013) 129 LQR 489–91); *Goff and Jones on the Law of Unjust Enrichment* (8th edn, London, 2011), 14.20 ff; see also *Stern* v. *McArthur* (1988) 165 CLJ 489, High Court of Australia (on which see *Union Eagle Ltd* v. *Golden Achievement Ltd* [1997] AC 514, 522, PC: 17.40); L. Gullifer, in A. S. Burrows and E. Peel (eds.), *Commercial Remedies: Current Issues and Problems* (Oxford, 2003), 191, 205–12.
76   *Ibid.*, at 490.

at the earlier date of the transaction's formation.[77] It is submitted that Denning and Somervell LJJ's suggestion is attractive. The sums to be forfeited are not deposits in the strict sense (on deposits, see 19.27). The courts should be willing to discover whether the innocent party's retention of the sums would operate punitively and unfairly (on the analogy of the penalty jurisdiction, see 19.02).

4. DEPOSITS

19.27 A deposit[78] is a valuable means of exerting pressure on the payor to comply with his contract. It is an 'earnest' payment. The penalty doctrine (19.02) does not apply to deposits, and so it makes no difference that a deposit is not a genuine pre-estimate of the vendor's likely loss.[79] This means that the entire deposit can be validly forfeited even though that innocent party's actual loss is less than the amount of the deposit (provided the deposit is not vulnerable to Common Law or statutory challenge: see 19.31 ff).[80]

19.28 Forfeiture of the deposit is justified if the payor fails without lawful excuse to fulfil the relevant transaction. The deposit will be lost when the purchaser manifestly abandons the contract, or clearly defaults, or if he delays in completing the sale to such a degree that the court can conclude that he has repudiated his contract.[81] Conversely, if the transaction goes smoothly, without the payor defaulting, the deposit will be put towards the purchase money. Of course, the payee must hand back the deposit if the contract came to an end as a result of his own default.[82] Finally, a prepayment cannot be forfeited if it was not paid as a deposit.

In *Mayson* v. *Clouet* (1924), the Privy Council held that forfeiture was restricted to a deposit of 10 per cent. The purchaser had made two further instalments, each of a further 10 per cent. He had then defaulted. The court held that only the first 10 per cent was a deposit, and that the further payments should be returned.[83]

---

77 *Ibid.*, at 492.
78 *Goff and Jones on the Law of Unjust Enrichment* (8th edn, London, 2011), chapter 14; L. Gullifer, in A. S. Burrows and E. Peel (eds.), *Commercial Remedies: Current Issues and Problems* (Oxford, 2003), 191, 205 ff; R. Halson, *Contract Law* (2nd edn, London, 2012), 517–21; Law Commission, 'Penalty Clauses and Forfeiture of Monies Paid' (Law Commission Consultation Paper No. 61, London, 1975); *Meagher, Gummow and Lehane's Equity: Doctrines and Remedies* (4th edn, Sydney, 2003), 18–080 to 18–125; G. H. Treitel, *Remedies for Breach of Contract: A Comparative Account* (Oxford, 1988), 234 ff.
79 *Workers Trust & Merchant Bank Ltd* v. *Dojap Investments Ltd* [1993] AC 573, 579, PC, *per* Lord Browne-Wilkinson; followed in *Polyset Ltd* v. *Panhandat Ltd* [2003] 3 HKLRD 319 (35 per cent deposit on commercial property held to be penal; compensation award substituted); L. Ho, (2003) 119 LQR 34.
80 *Workers Trust & Merchant Bank Ltd* v. *Dojap Investments Ltd* [1993] AC 573, 578F, PC.
81 *Howe* v. *Smith* (1884) 27 Ch D 89, CA (delay justified forfeiture); cf the facts of *Cole* v. *Rose* [1978] 3 All ER 1121, 1129, at letter 'H'.
82 *Cole* v. *Rose* [1978] 3 All ER 1121; C. Harpum, [1984] CLJ 134, 170.
83 [1924] AC 980, PC.

19.29 In principle, there should be no objection to the payee seeking compensation over and above[84] the amount of the deposit, unless the deposit is intended to place a cap on the payor's liability for breach. It is submitted that the normal construction should be that the deposit is an earnest payment and not a pre-estimate of the payor's total potential liability. It is also clear that when calculating the amount of compensation for a breach, the fact that the innocent party has forfeited a deposit in relation to that breach must be taken into account when fixing the amount of compensation, otherwise the imposition of the deposit would be wholly penal and the award of compensation would be excessive because it would not accurately reflect the true extent of the loss.[85]

Forfeiture of a deposit given before the main agreement is reached, a 'pre-contract deposit', is subject to slightly different rules:[86] prima facie, the money can be reclaimed at any point from the payee or stakeholder;[87] but there can be an independent contract supported by consideration,[88] or perhaps even a non-contractual stipulation, rendering the pre-contract deposit irrecoverable if the payor does not enter the main contract, for reasons other than the payee's default.[89] Ultimately, however, what counts is whether the payor has received what he bargained for and thus whether it would be just for the payee to retain the deposit. For example, in *Sharma* v. *Simposh Ltd* (2011) the Court of Appeal held that a pre-transaction deposit was not recoverable because the payor had received the benefit of contemplated performance:[90]

> [T]he claimants got what they paid for; as agreed, the defendant took the property off the market pending its completion and kept open its offer to sell it to the claimants at a fixed price. The claimants' expectations were therefore fulfilled and there is no injustice in the defendant retaining the sums paid to it. The agreement did not amount to a legally binding contract, but is nevertheless highly relevant as a matter of fact to the question whether there was a failure in the fulfilment of the parties' expectations such that denial of repayment would leave the defendant unjustly enriched.

Sharma v. *Simposh Ltd* (2011) involved an oral option and an oral lock out agreement (generally on lock out arrangements, see 2.10). There had been a substantial payment, by way of deposit, to secure these benefits and notional rights. The defendant payee had undertaken not to offer the development property to anyone else and instead to offer it to the payor once the construction was completed. The payee had done its part[91] but the payor had then decided not to invest. The Court of Appeal concluded that the deposit was not recoverable because the payor had received the benefit of contemplated performance. Although the oral agreement was void for failure to satisfy formalities,[92] property in the payment had passed to the payee.

---

84 *Lock* v. *Bell* [1931] 1 Ch 35, Maugham J; *Shuttleworth* v. *Clews* [1910] 1 Ch 176.
85 *Ng* v. *Ashley King (Developments) Ltd* [2010] EWHC 456 (Ch); [2011] Ch 115, at [17] ff, especially at [51], *per* Lewison J.
86 *Gribbon* v. *Lutton* [2001] EWCA Civ 1956; [2002] QB 902; considered in *Goff and Jones on the Law of Unjust Enrichment* (8th edn, London, 2011), 14.02, 14.07, 14.11.
87 *Gribbon* case, *ibid.*, at [14], approving Pennycuick V-C in *Potters* v. *Loppert* [1973] Ch 399, 405, 413.
88 *Gribbon* case, *ibid.*, where all the judges accepted this possibility.
89 *Ibid.*, at [64], *per* Robert Walker LJ (attractive in principle, but not the basis of a clear and unanimous decision).
90 [2011] EWCA Civ 1383; [2013] Ch 23.
91 *Ibid.*, at [26].
92 *Ibid.*, at [24], noting section 2(1) of the Law of Property (Miscellaneous Provisions) Act 1989 (on which see 5.07).

> Toulson LJ explained:[93] '[The claimant depositor must] establish a recognised ground of restitution. In this case the only suggested ground is failure of consideration. Since the claimants [the payor] obtained the benefit for which the payment was made ... [the] justice of the matter is entirely on the defendant's side.'

19.30 What if a deposit is owed (the duty to pay having 'accrued'), but not paid? Can it be claimed by the party who (upon receipt) is entitled to 'forfeit' this sum? The answer is 'yes, provided the contract has in fact ended through the payor's default'.[94] Furthermore, failure to pay a deposit can constitute a repudiatory breach of the contract, itself justifying termination of the contract,[95] including the situation where the vendor has renotified the purchaser of the need to make this agreed payment.[96] Upon termination for breach in the situation just mentioned, the innocent party can obtain damages, and these can include the amount of the deposit.[97]

19.31 *Sources of relief: introduction.* There are two possibilities for relief, although these will not necessarily apply to all contexts (for details of each, see the remainder of this chapter): (1) in contracts for the *sale or exchange of land* there is a *statutory* discretion to relieve against forfeiture of deposits;[98] and (2) there is a *Common Law* power to regulate excessive deposits; deposits of more than 10 per cent of the purchase price in contracts for the sale of land (or of a leasehold[99] interest) are normally[100] invalid (exceptionally, a larger deposit in a land transaction might be justified if there are 'special circumstances'). If a deposit is excessive at Common Law, the deposit must be repaid, 'less any damage actually proved to have been suffered as a result of non-completion'.[101]

19.32 *Statutory relief to order repayment of deposits in the context of land transactions.*[102] Section 49 of the Law of Property Act 1925 allows a court, 'if it thinks fit', to 'order the repayment of

---

93 *Ibid.*, at [55] (reversing the first instance judge, who had concluded that the money was recoverable because the contract was void: a *non sequitur*, as the Court of Appeal demonstrated).

94 *Damon Cia Naviera SA* v. *Hapag-Lloyd International SA* [1985] 1 WLR 435, 449G, 456F, CA; followed in *Ng* v. *Ashley King (Developments) Ltd* [2010] EWHC 456 (Ch); [2011] Ch 115, at [36], [37], [51] and [52], *per* Lewison J; see also *Griffon Shipping LLC* v. *Firodi Shipping Ltd* ('The MV *Griffon*') [2013] EWCA Civ 1567; [2014] 1 All ER (Comm) 593 and *Cadogan Petroleum Holdings Ltd* v. *Global Process Systems LLC* [2013] EWHC 214 (Comm); [2013] 2 Lloyd's Rep 26; [2013] 1 CLC 721, Eder J (noted L. Aitken (2013) 129 LQR 489–91).

95 *Damon* case, [1985] 1 WLR 435, 446 E, 456; *Samarenko* v. *Dawn Hill House Ltd* [2011] EWCA Civ 1445; [2013] Ch 36, at [24] to [27], [52] to [54], [60] and [64] (contract for the sale of land; buyer's failure to pay a 10 per cent deposit on the stipulated day and on the revised deadline for payment) (case noted J.W. Carter (2013) 129 LQR 149–52).

96 A. J. Oakley [1994] Conv 41, 44, citing *Millichamp* v. *Jones* [1982] 1 WLR 1422, and *John Willmott Homes* v. *Read* [1985] 51 P & CR 90.

97 *Damon* case, [1985] 1 WLR 435, 449, 457, CA (Robert Goff LJ dissented); or as an accrued debt, *Griffon* case above.

98 Section 49(2) of the Law of Property Act 1925: see 19.32 ff.

99 E.g. *Maktoum* v. *South Lodge Flats Ltd*, The Times, 21 April 1980.

100 *Omar* v. *El-Wakil* [2001] EWCA Civ 1090; [2002] 2 P & CR 3 (at pp. 36 ff), CA (upholding a deposit of over 30 per cent in a conveyance of a business, both at Common Law and under section 49(2) of the 1925 Act; no citation of the *Workers Trust* case, see the next note).

101 *Workers Trust & Merchant Bank Ltd* v. *Dojap Investments Ltd* [1993] AC 573, 582, PC (citing *Commissioner of Public Works* v. *Hills* [1906] AC 368, PC).

102 *Goff and Jones on the Law of Unjust Enrichment* (8th edn, London, 2011), 14.29 ff.

any deposit'. But this provision applies only to contracts for the 'sale or exchange of any interest of land'.[103]

19.33 In the *Aribisala* case (2007),[104] Alan Steinfield QC, sitting as a Deputy High Court Judge, held that this provision cannot be excluded by the parties' agreement (for the sequel to this litigation, see 19.34) because such an arrangement would be an attempt to oust the jurisdiction of the court and hence contrary to public policy (on this aspect of public policy, see 20.19).

19.34 The Court of Appeal in *Midill (97PL) Ltd* v. *Park Lane Estates Ltd and Gomba International* (2008) conducted a thorough review of the case law concerning section 49(2) of the 1925 Act. The following points emerge from Carnwath LJ's discussion.[105]

A deposit is an earnest payment, and it follows that the court should be slow to offer relief to a defaulting party under this provision. Something exceptional is required. It will not be enough that the loss suffered by the vendor is less than the amount of the deposit. Nor, as on the facts of the *Midill* case, is it enough that the vendor has subsequently been successful in selling the property to a third party for a profit, because the market has risen during this time.

> However, the court acknowledged the soundness of Neuberger J's decision in the *Tennaro* case (2003)[106] to relieve the defaulting purchaser from forfeiture of his deposit on those facts (on this case, see below).
>
> Carnwath LJ in the *Midill* case summarised the decision in the *Tennaro* case as follows:[107]
>
>> Three related contracts to grant long leases of three flats in the same block (Nos. 37, 32 and 31) were entered into between the vendor (Majorarch Ltd) and the purchaser (Tennaro Ltd). Deposits were paid in each case. The vendor served notices to complete in respect of the three contracts and, on the purchaser's failure to comply, purported to rescind each of the agreements and to forfeit the deposits.
>>
>> Neuberger J rejected the [section 49(2)] claim for return of the deposit in respect of flat 37 (whose value had dropped by some £400,000), but allowed it for the other two flats. In respect of flat 32, the benefit of the agreement had been assigned to a third party, who had himself (at 'about the time that the contract with the buyer would have been completed') made an offer to purchase it for a price substantially higher than the contract price, which had been rejected by the vendor without explanation . . .
>>
>> In respect of flat 31, the buyer had been willing to purchase that flat alone at the purchase price, but the seller required it to be bought along with flat 37. Neuberger J concluded 'on

103 Section 49(2)(3) of the 1925 Act.
104 *Aribisala* v. *St James Homes (Grosvenor Dock) Ltd (No. 1)* [2007] EWHC 1694 (Ch) (Alan Steinfield QC, sitting as a Deputy High Court Judge).
105 [2008] EWCA Civ 1227; [2009] 1 WLR 2460 (considering, especially, *Omar* v. *El-Wakil* [2001] EWCA Civ 1090; [2002] 2 P & CR 3 (at pp. 36 ff), CA; *Tennaro Ltd* v. *Majorarch* [2003] EWHC 2601; [2004] 1 P & CR 13, Neuberger J; and *Bidaisee* v. *Sampath* (1995) 46 WIR 461, PC, a case which had languished in obscurity).
106 *Tennaro Ltd* v. *Majorarch* [2003] EWHC 2601; [2004] 1 P & CR 13, Neuberger J.
107 [2008] EWCA Civ 1227; [2009] 1 WLR 2460, at [47] to [49]; *Goff and Jones on the Law of Unjust Enrichment* (8th edn, London, 2011), 14.35.

balance' that in this case also the deposit should be repaid. He noted, in particular, that the seller had had the opportunity to complete at the contract price, and had not come forward with any explanation of this refusal; and . . . that, on the basis of its then market value, the flat could have been resold at 15 per cent above the contract price.

Carnwath LJ then distinguished the present case as follows:[108]

> [The judge in the *Midill* case] was entitled to find that it was not enough that the vendor sold at a higher price some months after the date for completion. That delay distinguishes the case from the *Tennaro Ltd* case. There is nothing to suggest that the price rise [in the *Midill* case] was exceptional, in relation to movements in the market generally. There is no obvious reason why the purchaser should have the benefit of any such price rise. It was the vendor who had borne the risk and cost of holding the property during the intervening period. I also agree with the judge that to decide otherwise would add undesirable uncertainty to the well established contractual understanding.

19.35 *Common Law jurisdiction to control excessive deposits.* In *Workers Trust & Merchant Bank Ltd* v. *Dojap Investments Ltd* (1993), the Privy Council affirmed that a deposit exceeding a 'reasonable' percentage is invalid at Common Law.[109]

> The *Workers Trust* case (1993) concerned a 25 per cent deposit relating to real property in Jamaica. Deposits of 15–30 per cent were quite common in modern Jamaican land deals. Nevertheless, the Privy Council regarded these sums as unreasonably high. They were unacceptable deviations from the customary level of 10 per cent, which had long since been accepted within the UK and indeed in Jamaica.[110] Prima facie, the vendor should return the entire 25 per cent deposit. But the Privy Council held back a significant amount of the deposit as a 'fund' out of which any compensation due to the vendor should be paid.

19.36 The *Workers Trust* decision (1993) does not preclude the possibility that a payee might establish 'special circumstances' justifying a deposit in excess of 10 per cent[111] (that is, the vendor might be exposed to high loss). But no such special case had been shown on the facts of that case.[112]

19.37 Finally, the *Workers Trust* decision (1993) is easy to apply where a customary amount has emerged as the reasonable level (10 per cent in land transactions according to the Privy Council). But what if there is no such settled understanding, as in the case of deposits for the sale of chattels?[113] In *Vaswani* v. *Italian Motors* (1996), the Privy Council upheld a car seller's deposit of 25 per cent for a sports car to be built to the purchaser's special order.[114]

108   *Ibid.*, at [54].
109   [1993] AC 573, PC (G. H. Jones and W. Goodhart, *Specific Performance* (2nd edn, London, 1996), 303–4; C. Harpum, [1993] CLJ 389; H. Beale, (1993) 109 LQR 524; M. Thompson, [1994] Conv 58).
110   [1993] AC 573, 579, PC.
111   *Ibid.*, at 580.
112   *Ibid.*, at 581D–F.
113   Beale, (1993) 109 LQR 524, 529.
114   [1996] 1 WLR 270, PC.

The court did not suggest that the deposit might be attacked as unreasonable at Common Law. But in a future case it might be held that the Common Law jurisdiction to invalidate excessive deposits is applicable *even if* the transaction does not concern land. Where a transaction concerns a *consumer*, the Consumer Rights Bill, Part 2 (replacing the Unfair Terms in Consumer Contracts Regulations 1999) will also apply (15.28).

QUESTIONS

(1) At Common Law, what is the test for determining whether a clause is a penalty? What is the consequence of such a finding?

(2) Since the courts are reluctant to strike down a liquidated damages clause agreed between commercial parties, and because there is a statutory regime protecting consumers against penalties, is there a strong case for retaining the Common Law doctrine concerning penalties?

(3) What is the legal effect of a valid deposit?

(4) What are the controls upon the forfeiture of excessive deposits?

Selected further reading

M. Chen-Wishart, in P. B. H. Birks (ed.), *Wrongs and Remedies in the Twenty-First Century* (Oxford, 1996), chapter 12

T. Downes, in P. B. H. Birks (ed.), *Wrongs and Remedies in the Twenty-First Century* (Oxford, 1996), chapter 11

L. Gullifer, in A. Burrows and E. Peel (eds.), *Commercial Remedies: Current Issues and Problems* (Oxford, 2003), 191

S. Rowan, 'For the Recognition of Remedial Terms Agreed Inter Partes' (2010) 126 LQR 448, 460 ff

Scottish Law Commission, 'Penalty Clauses' (Scottish Law Commission Report No. 171, Edinburgh, 1999)

IX

Illegality and public policy

Chapter contents

20

The illegality doctrine

1. INTRODUCTION

20.01 Summary of main points

(1) 'The doctrine of illegality in the law of contract is knotty. That is a mild way to describe it. It is one of the least satisfactory parts of the law of contract' (*per* Toulson LJ in *ParkingEye Ltd* v. *Somerfield Stores Ltd* (2012).[1] The long-standing illegality doctrine[2] (the defence known as *ex turpi causa non actio oritur*: 20.03) has been applied to prevent a wrongdoer or wholly unmeritorious party from obtaining relief in the civil law. Modern courts have abandoned an over-fastidious, over-reactive, mechanistic or myopic approach to this defence. Instead they now consider whether denial of civil relief will be consistent with the policy underlying the relevant head of illegality or public policy (20.02 to 20.04). A vivid example is *Hounga* v. *Allen* (2014) (20.03) (enslavement of an illegal immigrant as a household help). This case concerned a claim for the statutory 'tort' of racial discrimination. The claim was allowed to proceed even though the claimant had been aware of her illegal entry into the United Kingdom. This decision shows that the illegality defence will only bar a claim if there is a sufficient connection between that wrongdoing and the claim; furthermore, the court should be sensitive to the legal system's potential embarrassment if the defendant is seen to triumph in circumstances where there is a clear public policy that the defendant has himself infringed (on these facts, taking advantage of the claimant's fear of being deported as an illegal immigrant).

(2) Agreements are illegal, and hence unenforceable, if they involve an undertaking to commit a crime (20.05). An agreement is also illegal if the parties jointly and deliberately undertake to commit a legal wrong, such as a tort or breach of trust (20.06).

(3) Prima facie, if statute (a) expressly or (b) by 'necessary implication' prohibits a transaction, neither party can enforce it, not even a party who is unaware of the relevant prohibition (*Re Mahmoud and Ispahani* (1921): 20.07). However, as for (a), a party intended to be protected by

---

1 [2012] EWCA Civ 1338; [2013] QB 840, at [43], [44], [46] and [47].
2 *Chitty on Contracts* (31st edn, London, 2012), chapter 16; R. A. Buckley, *Illegality and Public Policy* (3rd edn, London, 2013); N. Enonchong, *Illegal Transactions* (London, 1998); for a wider perspective, see M. J. Trebilcock, *The Limits of Freedom of Contract* (Cambridge, MA, 1997); general survey, S. Waddams, *Principle and Policy in Contract Law: Competing or Complementary Concepts?* (Cambridge, 2011), chapter 6; and for a notable recent case, 20.03, n.18.

the statutory invalidity might be able to sue on the transaction (*Nash* v. *Halifax Building Society* (1979): 20.08); and, as for (b), in the absence of an express prohibition, the court will be reluctant to find an implied prohibition of a type of transaction if contractual invalidity within that context will operate harshly on a category of innocent parties (*Hughes* v. *Asset Managers plc* (1995): 20.08). Nor will the court find an implied prohibition of a type of transaction if the contract does not directly fall within the scope of the relevant statutory prohibition (*St John Shipping Corporation* v. *Joseph Rank Ltd* (1957): 20.09).

(4) Following the Gambling Act 2005, gambling contracts are no longer illegal as such (although particular gambling offences can arise, and so affect gambling contracts, for example, where there is unlicensed commercial gambling or unlicensed use of premises for gambling purposes; and the Gambling Commission can declare particular bets to be void: 20.10).

(5) In the absence of the invalidity summarised at (2) and (3) above, a contract can be invalidated because it is contrary to public policy. The effect is to deprive a party of the right to sue on the contract, and to entitle the other party to raise illegality as a defence to the contractual claim (20.11).

(6) If the contract is not expressly prohibited by statute, nor is it prohibited by necessary implication, and provided performance of the agreement will not necessarily entail illegality, a claimant is not disabled from suing on a contract if he has no knowledge of the defendant's illegal performance (*Archbolds (Freightage) Ltd* v. *S Spanglett Ltd* (1961): 20.22). But the claimant cannot sue on the contract if he became consciously implicated in illegal performance (*Ashmore, Benson, Pease & Co. Ltd* v. *AV Dawson Ltd* (1973): 20.23). What counts as 'implication', for this purpose, will depend on a range of factors (*Hall* v. *Woolston Hall Leisure* (2001) and *Anglo Petroleum Ltd* v. *TFB (Mortgages) Ltd* (2007): 20.24).

(7) The consequences of illegality are summarised at 20.25 and 20.26. The main points are as follows:

   (a) Neither party can sue on a contract in situations of invalidity summarised at (2), (3) and (5) above.

   (b) But a claim upon a contract might not fail if the claimant was not consciously implicated in the defendant's decision to perform it in an illegal fashion, as summarised at (6) above.

   (c) The claimant might have a separate action in tort for the defendant's deceit, or a valid claim for breach of a collateral contract.

   (d) The fact that possession in property has been acquired under an illegal contract does not preclude an action by the claimant owner to recover that property (or to obtain damages for conversion, in the case of chattels). Property can pass under an illegal contract by which title was intended to be transferred.

   (e) Sometimes, the court can sever an illegal portion of an overall transaction, and so give contractual effect to the lawful and uncontaminated part.

   (f) The court is entitled, indeed required, to refuse to give contractual effect to an illegal transaction even if its illegal nature only emerges incidentally during the conduct of the case.

   (g) Restitutionary consequences are summarised at 20.26.

20.02 The Law Commission acknowledged (with understatement) that the law of illegality in contract law is 'an intricate web of tangled rules that are difficult to ascertain and distinguish'. As the Law Commission stated in its 1999 Consultation Paper,[3] legislation has not been recommended, other than in the context of illegality affecting proprietary interests under trusts law.[4]

And so, in the field of contract law, the Law Commission, in 2009, expressed the hope that the courts will develop a clearer statement of 'the policies that underlie the illegality defence' and allow that defence 'to succeed only ... where it has some merit'.[5] Case law in contract law (20.04, 20.05) and in tort (20.03) has followed the lead suggested by the Law Commission. Unless the relevant contract is expressly or by necessary implication invalidated by statute, the courts are prepared to make a sensitive inquiry whether underlying policy considerations justify barring a contractual claim (see, notably, 20.06 on the Court of Appeal in *ParkingEye Ltd* v. *Somerfield Stores Ltd* (2012) where the Law Commission's discussion was extensively cited).[6] This is not a collapse of settled law into a loose discretion (as had been proposed in 1999),[7] but rather elucidation of policies supporting the inherited body of law to ensure that those policies are properly applied, but not overplayed.

As Toulson LJ noted in *ParkingEye Ltd* v. *Somerfield Stores Ltd* (2012):[8]

> After much study and consultation, [the English Law Commission] concluded that a statutory scheme was not the best solution ... [and] that the courts [should] apply the law in a manner which was principled but moved away from the indiscriminate application of inflexible rules capable of producing injustice.

Toulson LJ also commented:

> [I]t is better and more honest that the court should look openly at the underlying policy factors and reach a balanced judgment in each case for reasons articulated by it ... [In] the area of illegality, experience has shown that ... there may be conflicting considerations and that the rules need to be developed and applied in a way which enables the court to balance them fairly.[9]

What are the relevant policies? The Law Commission's 2009 Consultation Paper suggests this list:[10]

---

3   Law Commission, 'The Illegality Defence' (Law Commission Consultation Paper No. 189, London, 2009), 1.14, 3.122.

4   On which see the recommendations in Law Commission, 'The Illegality Defence' (Law Commission Report No. 320, London, 2010).

5   Law Commission, 'The Illegality Defence' (Law Commission Consultation Paper No. 189, London, 2009), 1.14.

6   [2012] EWCA Civ 1338; [2013] QB 840, at [30], [31], *per* Jacob LJ, and at [48] to [52], *per* Toulson LJ.

7   Law Commission, 'Illegal Transactions; the Effect of Illegality on Contracts and Trusts' (Law Commission Consultation Paper No. 154, London, 1999).

8   [2012] EWCA Civ 1338; [2013] QB 840, at [48].

9   *Ibid.*, at [54].

10   Law Commission, 'The Illegality Defence' (Law Commission Consultation Paper No. 189, London, 2009), 2.05 to 2.29.

(1) whether barring the claim will further the purpose underlying the offence or head of public policy;

(2) whether allowing the claim will create unacceptable inconsistency between actionable civil rights and the relevant offence or head of public policy;

(3) that the claimant should not be allowed to benefit, or perhaps make positive claims, in respect of his criminal or perhaps other serious wrongdoing;

(4) whether the barring of the claim will send a salutary and appropriate deterrent message to others, similarly placed, that they should not commit the relevant offence or infringe the item of public policy;

(5) whether barring the claim is appropriate or necessary in order to protect the civil process against abuse of its mechanisms;

(6) possibly (this policy being the subject of intense dispute) whether the barring of the claim is appropriate in order to punish the claimant for his wrongdoing or moral turpitude.

Building on this list of policies, the Law Commission in 2009[11] articulated various 'factors'[12] that the court might consider when applying the existing law to particular contexts:

(a) 'whether the claim would undermine the purpose of the prohibiting rule';

(b) 'the seriousness of the offence';

(c) 'the causal connection between the claim and the illegal conduct';

(d) 'the comparative guilt of the parties'; and

(e) 'the proportionality of denying the claim'.

The Law Commission concluded, first, that 'ultimately a balancing exercise is called for which weighs up the application of the various policies at stake'; and, secondly, the defence of illegality to a contractual claim should succeed 'only when depriving the claimant of his or her contractual rights is a proportionate response based on the relevant illegality policies'.[13] In its 2010 report, 'The Illegality Defence', the Law Commission suggested that the courts are now moving away from a 'mechanistic' application of the illegality bar.[14]

20.03 *The* ex turpi causa *defence.* The illegality defence (*ex turpi causa non actio oritur* or 'no civil claim can be founded on an unlawful or wicked ground') has a long history. The defence is not confined to contract law.[15] In *Hounga* v. *Allen* (2014) Lord Hughes noted that a claimant who is party to an unlawful arrangement (the claimant had knowingly entered the country as an illegal immigrant) is prima facie prevented from taking advantage of the wrongdoing:[16]

---

11 *Ibid.*, at 3.126 ff.

12 Cf *Hounga* v. *Allen* [2014] UKSC 47; [2014] 1 WLR 2889 (on which see 20.03).

13 Law Commission, 'The Illegality Defence' (Law Commission Consultation Paper No. 189, London, 2009), at 3.142.

14 Law Commission, 'The Illegality Defence' (Law Commission Report No. 320, London, 2010), 1.11 ff, especially 3.10 ff.

15 E.g. in *Safeway Stores* v. *Twigger* [2010] EWHC 11 (Comm); [2010] 3 All ER 577 the defence was considered in the context of claims pleaded as breach of contract, breach of fiduciary duty and negligence.

16 [2014] UKSC 47; [2014] 1 WLR 2889, at [56].

When a court is considering whether illegality bars a civil claim, it is essentially focusing on the position of the claimant vis-à-vis the court from which she seeks relief. It is not primarily focusing on the relative merits of the claimant and the defendant. It is in the nature of illegality that, when it succeeds as a bar to a claim, the defendant is the unworthy beneficiary of an undeserved windfall. But this is not because the defendant has the merits on his side; it is because the law cannot support the claimant's claim to relief.

Lord Hughes also noted[17] that the *ex turpi causa* principle had been classicially expressed by Lord Mansfield in *Holman* v. *Johnson* (1775):[18]

The objection, that a contract is immoral or illegal as between plaintiff and defendant, sounds at all times very ill in the mouth of the defendant. It is not for his sake, however, that the objection is ever allowed; but it is founded in general principles of policy, which the defendant has advantage of, contrary to the real justice, as between him and the plaintiff, by accident, if I may so say. The principle of public policy is this; *ex dolo malo non oritur actio*. No court will lend its aid to a man who founds his cause of action upon an immoral or an illegal act . . . [U]pon that ground the court goes; not for the sake of the defendant, but because they will not lend their aid to such a plaintiff. So if the plaintiff and defendant were to change sides, and the defendant was to bring his action against the plaintiff, the latter would then have the advantage of it; for where both are equally in fault, *potior est conditio defendentis*.

However, modern law has abandoned an over-fastidious, over-reactive, mechanistic or myopic approach to this defence. In *Gray* v. *Thames Trains Ltd* (2009)[19] (see next paragraph for details), Lord Hoffmann suggested that the *ex turpi causa* principle cannot be reduced to a single criterion:[20] 'The maxim *ex turpi causa* expresses not so much a principle as a policy. Furthermore, that policy is not based upon a single justification but on a group of reasons, which vary in different situations.'

The result in *Hounga* v. *Allen* (2014) (see below) shows that the courts will not guillotine an action (procedurally this occurs by giving effect to the *ex turpi causa* defence) just because the claimant is implicated in a form of unlawfulness. There must be a sufficient connection between the claimant's wrongdoing and the claim which that party makes; and the court should be sensitive to the wider ramification if the defendant is seen to triumph in circumstances where there is a clear public policy that the defendant has himself infringed (taking advantage of the claimant's fear of being arrested and deported as an illegal immigrant). In this way the *ex turpi causa* preclusive principle must yield to a wider

---

17 *Ibid.*
18 (1775) 1 Cowp 341, 343 (1775) 1 Cowp 341, 343; the doctrine is reviewed by Lord Sumption in *Les Laboratoires Servier* v. *Apotex Inc* [2014] UKSC 55; [2014] 3 WLR 1257, at [13] ff, notably at [22], [25], [28], [29], [30].
19 [2009] UKHL 33; [2009] 1 AC 1339 (noted by Paul S. Davies (2009) 125 LQR 557).
20 *Ibid.*, at [30]; cited by the Court of Appeal in *ParkingEye Ltd* v. *Somerfield Stores Ltd* [2012] EWCA Civ 1338; [2013] QB 840, at [30], [31], *per* Jacob LJ, and at [55], *per* Toulson LJ; and in the tort context, *Joyce* v. *O'Brien* [2013] EWCA Civ 546; [2014] 1 WLR 70, especially at [22], [27] to [29], [47], [52], *per* Elias LJ.

examination of the context of the claim and even recognition of the extreme unevenness between the merits of the parties' respective cases.

In *Hounga* v. *Allen* (2014) the Supreme Court of the United Kingdom held that an illegal immigrant, who had been unlawfully brought into England from Nigeria when she was a young teenager, should be permitted to claim for racial discriminatory dismissal against her employer.[21] The claim (which was remitted to the first instance tribunal for further investigation) arose out of a contractual relationship but the cause of action was not based on breach of contract. She had served unpaid as an au pair in the employer's household, in effect been coerced into acting as the latter's household slave for a period of eighteen months, and then been shown the door and dumped on the (British) streets. The Supreme Court's unanimous decision is a convincing application of public policy. For it would be quite unconvincing to allow this young person's complicity in illegal trafficking to preclude her from claiming compensation in respect of her discriminatory treatment. Lord Hughes said:[22] 'the claim of statutory tort in the present case was set in the context of the claimant's unlawful immigration, but that there was not a sufficiently close connection between the illegality and the tort to bar her claim.'

Thus the Supreme Court made clear that this decision to permit her claim for this statutory tort did not necessarily open the door to a (purely) contractual claim.[23] Lord Hughes said:[24] 'Contrast her claim [no longer active during this appeal] to recover for breach of contract of employment (or, by statutory extension, for unfair dismissal), when such claims depend on a lawfully enforceable contract of employment but her whole employment was forbidden and illegal.' But this comment is not conclusive because contractual claims (for unfair dismissal and for unpaid wages) had been dismissed in the lower courts. This aspect of the case remains open for further examination.

By contrast the connection between the claimant's wrongdoing and the cause(s) of action was held to be too strong to permit the claim in *Stone & Rolls Ltd* v. *Moore Stephens* (2009).[25] Here a majority of the House of Lords (Lords Phillips, Brown and Walker) held that the *ex turpi causa* principle prevented the liquidator of a company from successfully bringing contractual or tortious claims against auditors who had failed to identify that the company was being run fraudulently as a 'one man company'. The liquidator was the extension of the company and the company was in turn inextricably represented by the fraudster. The result was that both a contract and concurrent tort claim for damages failed.

20.04 **Public policy and tort claims.** *Gray* v. *Thames Trains Ltd* (2009) concerned a claim for lost earnings and other damages, stemming from the claimant's imprisonment for homicide. He had killed a pedestrian, with whom he had had an argument, by running to a relative's

---

21 [2014] UKSC 47; [2014] 1 WLR 2889.
22 *Ibid.*, at [59].
23 *Ibid.*, at [24] and [59].
24 *Ibid.*, at [59].
25 [2009] UKHL 39; [2009] 1 AC 1391 (noted by P. Watts, (2010) 126 LQR 14–20; and D. Halpern, (2010) 73 MLR 487; considered in *Safeway Stores* v. *Twigger* [2010] EWHC 11 (Comm); [2010] 3 All ER 577 on the issue of corporate liability).

nearby flat, grabbing a kitchen knife, chasing the pedestrian, and stabbing him. This willingness to kill in response to trivial provocation had been triggered by the trauma of a train crash, two years before (the Ladbroke Grove rail disaster), in which the claimant had been injured. That injury was the result of the defendant train company's negligence.[26] The House of Lords held that the *ex turpi causa* principle precluded Gray's claim for damages. The claimant's act of criminal homicide was voluntary conduct. The law could not offer compensation for loss consequent upon the claimant's conviction for that criminal wrong.

2. AGREEMENTS TO COMMIT A LEGAL WRONG

20.05 Agreements are illegal, and hence unenforceable, if they involve an undertaking to commit a crime[27] (certainly if both are conspiring to commit a deliberate wrong,[28] but perhaps also even if neither party is aware of the criminality,[29] although this aspect of the law is not clear).[30] Indeed, an agreement to commit a crime is invalid, and the agreement itself constitutes the criminal wrong of conspiracy. If the parties had not at first committed themselves to an unlawful purpose, the courts will be prepared to examine whether there was a possibility of the contract being performed in a lawful fashion.[31] An agreement is also illegal if the parties jointly and deliberately undertake to commit a legal wrong, such as a tort or breach of trust. But if one party was unaware that contractual performance would involve a *civil wrong*, the better view is that he is entitled to recover the relevant fee, etc., for the whole of his performance, and not just for that part which was not unlawful. This is Treitel's[32] attractive suggestion concerning a loose end within *Clay* v. *Yates* (1856),[33] where a publisher was entitled to payment for the work he had done before he realised that the remaining part of the job would involve a libel upon a third party. Furthermore, payment cannot be obtained if it was made conditional on performance of an unlawful act. At the time of *Beresford* v. *Royal Insurance Co. Ltd* (1938),[34] suicide was a crime. The life insurance policy in that case covered suicide.

---

26 *Ibid.*, at [20] to [23].
27 For discussion of the *ex turpi causa* principle in the context of injury sustained during performance of a joint enterprise to steal, *Joyce* v. *O'Brien* [2013] EWCA Civ 546; [2014] 1 WLR 70, especially at [22], [27] to [29], [47], [52], *per* Elias LJ.
28 E.g. *Taylor* v. *Bhail* [1996] CLC 377, CA (headmaster of school and builder agreeing to inflate apparent price of repair work by £1,000; in return, builder awarded the job; builder's action for unpaid part of price failed both in contract law, because of illegal arrangement to defraud insurance company, and in restitution law, because he was party to the scam).
29 *J. M. Allan (Merchandising)* v. *Cloke* [1963] 2 QB 340, 348, CA, *per* Lord Denning MR (roulette wheel hired by defendant initially for an unlawful purpose, although neither party was aware of this; owner of wheel unable to claim for hire; wheel had been returned by defendant); noted by Law Commission, 'Illegal Transactions: The Effect of Illegality on Contracts and Trusts' (Law Commission Consultation Paper No. 154, London, 1999), 2.20.
30 Law Commission, *ibid.*, at 2.22, noting the contrary suggestion by Pearce LJ in *Archbolds (Freightage) Ltd* v. *S Spanglett Ltd* [1961] 1 QB 374, 387, CA.
31 *Waugh* v. *Morris* (1873) LR 8 QB 202.
32 *Treitel* (13th edn, London, 2011), 11–016.
33 (1856) 1 H & N 73.
34 [1938] AC 586, HL.

It was held that the successful suicide's estate could not claim insurance on this policy.[35] However, an agreement to indemnify a person for his legal costs in civil proceedings is not unlawful, even though the misconduct involved criminal and civil wrongdoing, provided the agreement to indemnify is made after the criminal and civil wrongdoing has already taken place[36] (the facts concerned a newspaper's agreement to indemnify its employees for legal costs arising from the phone hacking scandal).

3. INCIDENTAL ILLEGALITY DURING PERFORMANCE: A FLEXIBLE APPROACH

20.06 Here the problem is as follows. During the course of performance, a party commits (as he was aware from the contract's commencement that he might) an unlawful act, or perhaps a series of unlawful acts. The other party is not implicated. The contract was capable of lawful performance. The illegality is not part of the main performance of the contract. Later the innocent party snatches at this in order to terminate and to escape liability to pay or to do its part. In such a situation, the Court of Appeal in *ParkingEye Ltd* v. *Somerfield Stores Ltd* (2012)[37] emphasised the need to avoid a mechanical, 'unduly sanctimonious'[38] and disproportionate[39] application of principles of public policy and illegality. Toulson LJ refused to recognise 'a fixed rule that any intention from the outset to do something in the performance of the contract which would in fact be illegal must vitiate any claim by the party' because such an approach would be 'too crude and capable of giving rise to injustice'.[40]

> The claimant in *ParkingEye Ltd* v. *Somerfield Stores Ltd* (2012)[41] agreed for fifteen months to provide the defendant supermarket chain with an automated car-park monitoring and control system. This system enabled the claimant to collect charges from any customer whose vehicle remained parked beyond the free parking period (these charges would be debts owed by customers to the supermarket;[42] these sums were held not to be penalties (19.02), but were instead recoverable liquidated sums; but higher charges imposed for very late payments would be penalties). The claimant would pocket these charges and would thus have an incentive to pursue these claims aggressively.

---

35 The Suicide Act 1961 decriminalised suicide; however, on suicide pacts and the crime of aiding and assisting suicide, see *Dunbar* v. *Plant* [1998] Ch 412, CA (limited scope for statutory relief against forfeiture of benefits obtained from the successful suicide's estate by the unsuccessful attempted suicide); applied in *Glover* v. *Staffordshire Police Authority* [2006] EWHC 2414 (Admin); [2007] ICR 661.
36 *Mulcaire* v. *News Group Newspapers Ltd* [2011] EWHC 3469 (Ch); [2012] Ch 435, at [45], *per* Sir Andrew Morritt C.
37 [2012] EWCA Civ 1338; [2013] QB 840.
38 *Ibid.*, at [38], *per* Jacob LJ.
39 *Ibid.*, at [38] and [39], *per* Jacob LJ; and at [79], *per* Toulson LJ.
40 *Ibid.*, at [63].
41 [2012] EWCA Civ 1338; [2013] QB 840.
42 *Ibid.*, at [22].

After several months, the defendant terminated the contract on the basis that the claimant had made illegal representations in demand letters (the third demand letter in the escalating sequence) sent to customers, thereby committing the civil wrong of deceit vis-à-vis those customers. The main falsehood[43] was that the claimant had authority to bring civil proceedings against the over-staying parties who failed to pay the relevant charges.

The Court of Appeal held that the defendant supermarket's termination of the contract had not been justified. And so the supermarket had to pay substantial damages for breach.[44] The illegality here did not provide the defendant with a basis for not performing its obligations and for purporting to terminate for good cause.[45] This was because the claimant's unlawful intention (its offending standard letters had been drafted before formation of the contract)[46] had formed a minor part of the overall performance. The court also considered: (i) the object and intent of the party (the claimant) seeking to enforce the contract; (ii) whether the illegality was a major and ineluctable performance part of the contract or conversely whether the illegality was incidental or even peripheral;[47] and (iii) the nature of the illegality.

It was not here necessary to focus on (iii) because (i) and (ii) supplied sufficient guidance on these facts. Here relieving the defendant from its duty to pay would be disproportionate (£300,000 was still owed). The illegality was incidental to only part of the performance of the contract and was far from central to it.[48] And the defendant should have reacted more quickly. Once aware of the objectionable nature of the third letter, it should have drawn the matter to the claimant's attention. It was likely that the claimant would have stepped into line and eliminated the element of deceit.[49] To decide otherwise would confer a windfall reward for the defendant.

4. AGREEMENTS EXPRESSLY OR IMPLIEDLY PROHIBITED BY STATUTE

20.07 An agreement might sometimes be prohibited, whether expressly or by 'necessary implication',[50] by statute. If so, the result is that neither party can enforce it, not even a party who is unaware of the relevant prohibition (for possible escape from this, see 20.08). In *Re Mahmoud and Ispahani* (1921),[51] statute required licences for the sale and purchase of linseed oil. The defendant falsely told the plaintiff that he had a licence. In fact, only the plaintiff had a licence. When the defendant refused to accept delivery, the plaintiff sued for damages. The defendant successfully pleaded the defence of illegality. The Court of Appeal held that the defence, however unmeritorious on these facts (Bankes LJ described the

---

43 *Ibid.*, [59], *per* Toulson LJ; at [11], *per* Jacob LJ, for details of other false information contained in the claimant's 'third' standard letter.
44 *Ibid.*, at [23] ff.
45 *Ibid.*, notably at [30] to [32], [35], [37] to [40], [63] to [65], [69], 72], [75], [77] to [79].
46 *Ibid.*, at [19].
47 *Ibid.*, at [32] ('minor and incidental transgressions').
48 *Ibid.*, at [71].
49 *Ibid.*, at [68] and [78].
50 R. A. Buckley, 'Implied Statutory Prohibition of Contracts' (1975) 38 MLR 535.
51 [1921] 2 KB 716, CA (Atkin, Scrutton and Bankes LJJ); similarly, the innocent claimant in *Chai Sau Yin* v. *Liew Kwee Sam* [1962] AC 304, PC, noted by Law Commission, 'Illegal Transactions: The Effect of Illegality on Contracts and Trusts' (Law Commission Consultation Paper No. 154, London, 1999), 2.18.

defendant's stance as 'shabby'),[52] should prevail because the contract was expressly prohibited by the statute, unless both parties were licensed.

20.08 By contrast, Browne-Wilkinson J in *Nash* v. *Halifax Building Society* (1979)[53] held that a building society could recover money advanced under a contract of loan supported by a mortgage (the 'second' mortgage on the relevant property) even though statute[54] prohibited building societies from making loans on the security of property already subject to a mortgage or charge in favour of a third party. The judge said: '[T]he section is designed to protect the building society as a whole and, accordingly, although the transaction was illegal, the society is entitled to recover moneys advanced under such an advance and enforce the security given for its repayment.' Similarly, the Court of Appeal in *Hughes* v. *Asset Managers plc* (1995) drew back from construing a statute, requiring investment contracts to be drawn up only by licensed investment agents, as an implied prohibition upon formation of the relevant contracts. Otherwise, as Saville LJ observed,[55] the invalidity of all such contracts would have catastrophic consequences not only for investment companies (who might be expected in general to be capable of being diligent to avoid this hazard, and who are normally cash recipients) but, on the other side of this transaction, for investors (that is, institutions and ordinary members of the public). The same risk of total invalidity having an unmerited and harsh impact upon innocent non-professionals explains why the Financial Services and Markets Act 2000 enables insured persons (but not insurance companies) to sue on insurance contracts, where the relevant insurance business is transacted in breach of the regulatory system.[56]

20.09 In other cases, the court has been asked to determine whether the relevant statutory offence impliedly prohibits a type of contract. In *St John Shipping Corporation* v. *Joseph Rank Ltd* (1957),[57] Devlin J held that a statutory offence did not entail implied prohibition of the relevant contract. Here, the plaintiff shipper had been fined by magistrates for the statutory offence of overloading a ship, but the fine had not kept up with inflation. The defendant charterer, ostensibly *pour encourager les autres*, withheld some of the freight payable under the contract of carriage, pleading as a defence that the plaintiff's performance of the contract had been illegal. Devlin J declined to find that the contract had been impliedly prohibited. He said:[58]

> [A] court ought to be very slow to hold that a statute intends to interfere with the rights and remedies given by the ordinary law of contract. Caution in this respect is,

---

52 [1921] 2 KB 716, 724, CA.
53 [1979] Ch 584, 591.
54 Section 32 of the Building Societies Act 1962.
55 [1995] 3 All ER 669, 674, CA.
56 Section 28 of the Financial Services and Markets Act 2000; for the unfortunate case law background, notably, *Phoenix General Insurance Co. of Greece SA* v. *Halvanon* [1988] QB 216, 273, CA, which necessitated this change, see Law Commission, 'The Illegality Defence' (Law Commission Consultation Paper No. 189, London, 2009), 3.101.
57 [1957] 1 QB 267.
58 *Ibid.*, at 289; for similar remarks on the proliferation of statutory offences of varying heinousness and technicality, *Shaw* v. *Groom* [1970] 2 QB 504, 523, CA, *per* Sachs LJ.

I think, especially necessary in these times when so much of commercial life is governed by regulations of one sort or another, which may easily be broken without wicked intent.

(This case was considered in *ParkingEye Ltd* v. *Somerfield Stores Ltd*, 2012.)[59]

5. GAMBLING CONTRACTS NO LONGER NECESSARILY INVALID

20.10 Part 17 ('Legality and Enforceability of Gambling Contracts') of the Gambling Act 2005 took effect on 1 September 2007.[60] Section 335 of the Act, and associated provisions, repeal the numerous statutes which had invalidated such transactions. The new provision states:[61]

(1) *The fact that a contract relates to gambling shall not prevent its enforcement.*

(2) *Subsection (1) is without prejudice to any rule of law preventing the enforcement of a contract on the grounds of unlawfulness (other than a rule relating specifically to gambling).* 'Gambling'[62] embraces 'gaming' (a 'game of chance for a prize'),[63] 'betting'[64] and participation in a 'lottery'.[65] The position can be summarised as follows. Gambling contracts are no longer illegal as such. But a gambling transaction might contain some other element which renders the transaction unlawful. That illegal element might arise (1) under the Gambling Act 2005 itself, which creates offences for unlicensed commercial gambling and unlicensed use of premises for gambling purposes;[66] or (2) outside the statute, for example, where gambling is linked sufficiently with arrangements for the provision of prostitution (on that context, see 20.12). In addition, the 2005 Act empowers the Gambling Commission to declare particular bets to be void,[67] in which case any stake or winnings can be recovered as a debt from the payee.[68]

6. PUBLIC POLICY

20.11 Other contracts can be invalidated because the agreement is contrary to public policy (regarded by some as an 'unruly horse', but by others as a horse that can be mastered by a skilled rider).[69] Lord Denning was not slow to proclaim his equestrian skills, for this purpose:[70]

59 [2012] EWCA Civ 1338; [2013] QB 840, at [60] to [64], *per* Toulson LJ.
60 *Smith & Monkcom: The Law of Gambling* (3rd edn, Haywards Heath, 2009); J. Davey, 'Gambling Contract Law ...' [2013] JBL 614–41.
61 Section 335 of the Gambling Act 2005.
62 Section 3, *ibid.*
63 Section 6, *ibid.*
64 Section 9, *ibid.*
65 Sections 14 and 15, *ibid.*
66 Sections 33 and 37, *ibid.*
67 Section 336(1), *ibid.*
68 Section 336(2), *ibid.*
69 For wider perspectives, A. Chong, 'Transnational Public Policy in Civil and Commercial Matters' (2012) 128 LQR 88–113.
70 *Enderby Town FC Ltd* v. *Football Association* [1971] Ch 591, 606–7, CA, *per* Lord Denning MR.

I know that over 300 years ago Hobart CJ said that 'Public policy is an unruly horse'. It has often been repeated since. So unruly is the horse, it is said [*per* Burrough J in *Richardson* v. *Mellish* (1824) 2 Bing 229, 252], that no judge should ever try to mount it lest it run away with him. I disagree. With a good man in the saddle, the unruly horse can be kept in control. It can jump over obstacles. It can leap the fences put up by fictions and come down on the side of justice.

Where public policy invalidates a transaction, the effect, once again, is to deprive a party of the right to sue on the contract, and to entitle the other to raise illegality as a defence to the contractual claim. The main heads of public policy are set out in 20.12 to 20.20. A variation on this is that the courts might expose the agreement as a sham transaction.[71]

20.12 *Contracting involving, or tending to promote, sexual immorality.* In *Pearce* v. *Brooks* (1866),[72] the plaintiff coachbuilders could not recover hire charges in respect of its horse-drawn carriage, nor claim compensation for damage caused to this carriage. It had been let in a state which was 'curiously constructed' to enable the defendant, a prostitute, to attract clients. It was enough that the plaintiff knew that the contract involved assistance in her 'immoral calling'. There was no need for the parties to have agreed that the hire would be paid directly from the prostitute's illicit earnings.

> In *Pearce* v. *Brooks* (1866) Martin B explained:[73]
>> The [defence] states first the fact that the defendant was to the plaintiffs' knowledge a prostitute; second, that the brougham was furnished to enable her to exercise her immoral calling; third, that the plaintiffs expected to be paid out of the earnings of her prostitution. In my opinion the plea is good if the third averment be struck out; and if, therefore, there is evidence that the brougham was, to the knowledge of the plaintiffs, hired for the purpose of such display as would assist the defendant in her immoral occupation, the substance of the plea is proved, and the contract was illegal.
>
> In *Coral Leisure Group Ltd* v. *Barnett* (1981),[74] Barnett brought a claim for unfair dismissal against a casino company. In his written claim, Barnett had alleged (*potentially* self-defeatingly, but see below) that part of his duties was to pay for prostitutes to be used by the casino's rich clientele. But the Employment Appeal Tribunal held that he had not thereby defeated his claim for unfair dismissal: the illegal element in the performance of this contract did not render the entire contract invalid for illegality. It would be different if: (1) the contract had been prohibited by statute, or (2) the parties to the contract had formed, from the beginning, the intention of pursuing this illegal purpose. In the absence of (1) or (2), Browne-Wilkinson J held that the contract could be asserted by the employee.

---

71   E.g. the cases noted by K. R. Handley, (2011) 127 LQR 171–3.
72   (1866) LR 1 Exch 213, Court of Exchequer, Pollock CB, Martin, Pigott and Bramwell BB.
73   *Ibid.*, at 219.
74   [1981] ICR 503, 509, EAT, and later cases; on this troublesome line of cases, see Law Commission, 'The Illegality Defence' (Law Commission Consultation Paper No. 189, London, 2009), 3.37 to 3.42, and S. Forshaw and M. Pigerstorfer, (2005) 34 ILJ 158.

20.13 *Unacceptable agreements concerning matrimony.* There are two types of agreement concerning matrimony which historically have been unenforceable on the ground of public policy, namely, a marriage brokerage agreement, and an ante-nuptial agreement. The former remains unenforceable; the latter is no longer so.

Hermann v. Charlesworth (1905)[75] recognises that a marriage brokerage agreement (that is, an agreement to find a potential spouse for a fee) is contrary to public policy. This remains law, although it appears to be archaic. But mere 'dating agency' services are outside the scope of this rule and hence not unlawful.

Ante-nuptial and post-nuptial agreements concerning future property arrangements between spouses or prospective spouses, in the event of future separation, are no longer contrary to public policy. The Supreme Court in *Granatino v. Radmacher* (2010)[76] declared that such an agreement is no longer contrary to public policy. However, the most common context will concern the impact of such an agreement on the matrimonial jurisdiction to make property orders consequent on divorce. In that context, the agreement will inform exercise by the court of the discretion concerning property distribution, although the court will not be mechanically bound by the agreement when making this decision. This is so for the following reasons.

First, the court has the ultimate statutory discretion as to how property should be distributed upon divorce, in accordance with sections 23–25 of the Matrimonial Causes Act 1973.[77] Secondly, the court might decide that an ante-nuptial (or indeed a post-nuptial) agreement was the product of improper influence (widely defined).[78] Thirdly, the court might decide that there has been a significant change of circumstances since the agreement was made.[79] Finally, there is the overriding need to ensure that the agreement does not operate to the prejudice of children of the marriage.[80] Baroness Hale dissented in some respects (see below). But she also supplied a valuable (non-dissenting) exposition of the current law (too long to be cited here).[81]

20.14 *Servitude.* An agreement to become enslaved to the other party (or another person) will be contrary to public policy (for a gruesome instance of exploitation of a young illegal immigrant in circumstances akin to, if not involving absolute, enslavement, *Hounga v. Allen* (2014) noted at 20.03 above).[82]

---

75 [1905] 2 KB 123, CA.
76 [2010] UKSC 42; [2011] 1 AC 534; noted J. Miles (2011) 74 MLR 430–44 and by J. Herring, P. G. Harris, and R. H. George, (2011) 127 LQR 335–9; generally on this topic, J. Scherpe (ed.), *Marital Agreements and Private Autonomy in Comparative Perspective* (Oxford, 2012).
77 *Ibid.,* at [52] and [74].
78 *Ibid.,* at [71] and [72].
79 *Ibid.,* at [81] and [82].
80 *Ibid.,* at [77].
81 *Ibid.,* at [154].
82 [2014] UKSC 47; [2014] 1 WLR 2889, at [56].

In *Horwood* v. *Millar's Timber and Trading Co. Ltd* (1916),[83] a borrower, Bunyan, agreed that until the loan was repaid, he would pay *all* his earnings towards repayment, and furthermore that he would not take another job, and finally that he would not move house without the lender's permission. One can see how, from the lender's perspective, these were attractive precautions. But Lush and Sankey JJ held that these severe restrictions offended the Common Law protection of the liberty to earn a living and the related freedom to move residence for that purpose. Therefore, the loan was illegal. At the time of the action, Bunyan had already enlisted for the Great War in 1914. The action was against his employer. It was for an account of all earnings and bonuses accruing in favour of the borrower, Bunyan, and payable by his employer (the loan agreement contained an assignment by Bunyan to the plaintiff lender of his earnings payable to him by the defendant). It would appear that the loan would also have been unenforceable against Bunyan (but, as mentioned, he was away at the front).

20.15 *Contracts affecting foreign policy.* Both at Common Law and by statute,[84] contracts involving trading with the enemy are contrary to public policy. The Trading with the Enemy Act 1939 (as amended) now defines 'enemy'.[85]

20.16 *Agreements to deceive or cheat public authorities.*[86] In *Miller* v. *Karlinski* (1945),[87] the Court of Appeal invalidated an 'income tax scam'. Here the employee was to be paid a specified weekly sum as salary and to recover from his employer the amount payable out of that sum in respect of income tax by including it in an account for travelling expenses. The court held that this was not severable and that the whole contract was illegal as being contrary to public policy. And so no action was possible to recover arrears of salary.

The Court of Appeal in *Skilton* v. *Sullivan* (1994)[88] noted that an agreement is illegal if the parties have shared the purpose of avoiding or postponing VAT. But no such shared purpose existed on the facts. And so the claimant vendor was entitled to sue for the balance in respect of a supply of Koi carp.

20.17 *Bribery offences and corruption.* The topic of bribery is now dominated by the Bribery Act 2010[89] (although there have been transitional prosecutions under the preceding

---

83   [1916] 2 KB 44, Divisional Court; P. Saprai, 'The Principle against Self-Enslavement in Contract Law' (2009) 25 JCL 26.
84   Trading with the Enemy Act 1939 (as amended).
85   Section 2 of the Trading with the Enemy Act 1939 (as amended).
86   See also the Bribery Act 2010.
87   (1945) 62 TLR 85, CA; cf *Hall* v. *Woolston Hall Leisure* [2001] 1 WLR 225, CA (tax fraud; but employee aware although not a participant in the employer's fraudulent avoidance of tax and national insurance payments; employee not precluded from seeking compensation for sex discrimination); similarly, *Alexander* v. *Rayson* [1936] 1 KB 169, CA (fraud on rating authority); cf *Hounga* v. *Allen* [2014] UKSC 47; [2014] 1 WLR 2889 (on which see 20.03).
88   *The Times*, 25 March 1994.
89   Bribery Act 2010; E. O'Shea, *The Bribery Act 2010: A Practical Guide* (Bristol, 2011); N. Cropp [2011] CLR 122–41; S. Gentle [2011] CLR 101–10; J. Horder (2011) 74 MLR 911–31 and (2011) 127 LQR 37–54; C. Monteith [2011] CLR 111–21; G. Sullivan [2011] CLR 87–100; A. Wells (2011) *Business Law Review* 186; C. Wells [2012] JBL 420–31.

legislation).[90] This creates offences[91] concerning the offer, giving, requesting or receipt of a bribe, contrary to reasonable expectations,[92] for the purpose of causing a function (not confined to public functions)[93] to be exercised 'improperly'.[94] The 2010 Act also addresses the problem of bribery of foreign public officials,[95] and makes provision for the problem of foreign customs and expectations.[96]

> In addition to the statutory precedessors[97] to the Bribery Act 2010, the Common Law had invalidated certain forms of agreements involving corruption. In *Amalgamated Society of Railway Servants* v. *Osborne* (1910), the House of Lords held that an MP cannot contract with a third party that he will cast his vote in Parliament in a particular way.[98] And in *Parkinson* v. *College of Ambulance Ltd* (1925),[99] an agreement foundered under this head because it involved payment for a knighthood. This type of sordid practice is now an offence.[100]

20.18 *Contracts tending to pervert the course of justice.* An agreement to procure false testimony,[101] suppress evidence[102] or influence a juror or adjudicator will infringe this head of policy (see also the Bribery Act 2010, 20.17 above). Agreements to take a financial stake in the outcome of the proceedings or to share the fruits of a civil action (damages, etc.) remain contrary to Common Law (so-called 'maintenance and champerty').[103] However, the Courts and Legal Services Act 1990 (as amended) allows lawyers to agree to conduct a case on a no-win-no-fee basis. This has been the foundation for the introduction of (a) conditional fee agreements ('CFAs'), since 1995, and (b) damages-based agreements

---

90   *R* v. *J* [2013] EWCA Crim 2287; [2014] 1 WLR 1857; [2014] 1 Cr App R 21, on the Prevention of Corruption Act 1906 (see Lord Thomas CJ's judgment at [9] ff concerning the Public Bodies Corrupt Practices Act 1889, the 1906 Act just mentioned, and the Prevention of Corruption Act 1916).

91   Sections 1 and 2 of the Bribery Act 2010; *Hansard*, HL vol. 715, col. 1086 (9 December 2009) states: '[The Act] creates two general offences of bribery, a third specific offence of bribing a foreign public official and finally a new corporate offence of failing to prevent bribery ... The general offences, in [sections 1 and 2], cover on one side of the coin the offer, promise and giving of a financial or other advantage, and on the flip side the request, agreeing to receive or acceptance of such an advantage. These offences focus on the conduct of the payer or the recipient of a bribe and describe six scenarios, each involving the improper performance of a function, where one or other offence would be committed. These new offences will apply to functions of a public nature as well as in a business, professional or employment context.'

92   Section 5, Bribery Act 2010.

93   Section 3, *ibid.*

94   Section 4, *ibid.*

95   Section 6, *ibid.*

96   Section 5(2), *ibid.* (Phillips J had grappled with this problem in *Lemenda Trading Co. Ltd* v. *African Middle East Petroleum Co. Ltd* [1988] QB 448).

97   For these statutes, see note above concerning *R* v. *J* [2013] EWCA Crim 2287; [2014] 1 WLR 1857; [2014] 1 Cr App R 21, at [9] ff.

98   [1910] AC 87, HL.

99   [1925] 2 KB 1, Lush J.

100   Honours (Prevention of Abuse) Act 1925.

101   *R* v. *Andrews* [1973] QB 422, CA, *per* Lord Widgery CJ.

102   *R* v. *Ali* [1993] CLR 396, CA (offence extends to agreement that potential witness should not give evidence); *R* v. *Panayiotou* [1973] 3 All ER 112, CA (attempt to procure dropping of charge).

103   J. Sorabji and R. Musgrove, 'Litigation, Costs, Funding, and the Future', in D. Dwyer (ed.), *The Civil Procedure Rules Ten Years On* (Oxford, 2009), 229, at 235, examining *Arkin* v. *Borchard Lines Ltd* [2005] EWCA Civ 655; [2005] 1 WLR 3055, at [40].

('DBAs') since April 2013.[104] Both permit a client to enter into a contract for legal services concerning civil litigation or arbitration where the lawyer's remuneration is dependent on his client's success in obtaining a favourable judgment or settlement. A CFA permits a solicitor or barrister in England and Wales to undertake to perform litigation services on the understanding that his normal legal fee will not be payable if the client is unsuccessful in the relevant proceedings; but if he achieves success for his client, the lawyer will receive an enhanced fee, consisting of his ordinary fee (normally, in the case of solicitors, this will be based on hourly charges) and a percentage of that fee (the percentage 'uplift' cannot exceed 100 per cent). In practice, the victorious lawyer's fee will be paid by the losing party (in accordance with the 'loser must pay' costs rule in English civil proceedings). The Legal Aid, Sentencing, and Punishment of Offenders Act 2012 ('LASPO') amended the CFA system by preventing the successful party from recovering his lawyer's success fee and an 'after-the-event' legal expenses premium (known as 'the ATE premium') from the defeated party.[105] But many pre-LASPO cases are in the (long) 'costs pipe-line'. The dicta of Lord Neuberger in *Coventry v. Lawrence* (2014)[106] have cast a cloud over the legality of the statutory system for the recovery by the victorious party of success fees and ATE premia incurred in respect of pre-LASPO CFA fee arrangements.[107]

A DBA is permitted in all fields of civil proceedings.[108] The parent legislation has been supplemented by the Damages-Based Agreements Regulations 2013.[109] In essence, a DBA operates as follows.[110] A legal representative (lawyer) can agree with the client[111] that professional remuneration will be waived unless the case is won. In the event of victory, the lawyer's payment will be expressed by reference to the money recovered by the client from the opponent.[112] The amount of this contingent payment is, however, capped as a percentage of the 'sums ultimately recovered' by the client from the opponent.

That percentage cap is 35 per cent in the case of employment disputes,[113] 25 per cent in the case of personal injury disputes[114] and 50 per cent in all other cases.[115]

---

104   *Andrews on Civil Processes* (Cambridge, 2013), vol. 1, *Court Proceedings*, chapter 20.
105   Sections 44(4) and 46(1) of the Legal Aid, Sentencing, and Punishment of Offenders Act 2012, adding a new section 58A(6), and a new section 58C to the Courts and Legal Services Act 1990. *Andrews on Civil Processes* (Cambridge, 2013), vol. 1, *Court Proceedings*, 20.29 to 20.34.
106   [2014] UKSC 46; [2014] 3 WLR 555, at [32] to [47].
107   This rather convoluted aspect of the costs-shifting regime is summarised in *Andrews on Civil Processes* (Cambridge, 2013), vol. 1, *Court Proceedings*, 20.35 to 20.66.
108   Section 58AA(3)(a) of the Courts and Legal Services Act 1990 (amended by section 45 of the Legal Aid, Sentencing, and Punishment of Offenders Act 2012); Damages-Based Agreements Regulations 2013/609; CPR 44.18.
109   See preceding note.
110   The new system is an expansion of the DBA arrangements formerly confined to employment matters.
111   Reg 1(2), Damages-Based Agreements Regulations 2013/609.
112   Section 58AA(3)(a) of the Courts and Legal Services Act 1990 (amended by section 45 of the Legal Aid, Sentencing, and Punishment of Offenders Act 2012).
113   Reg 7, Damages-Based Agreements Regulations 2013/609.
114   Reg 4(2), *ibid.*
115   Reg 4(3), *ibid.*

However, both CFAs and DBAs remain invalid, under the Common Law public policy prohibition, if the relevant statutory scheme has not been satisfied.[116]

> More generally, in *Sibthorpe* v. *Southwark LBC* (2011)[117] the Court of Appeal held that there is no public policy objection, based on the doctrines of champerty and maintenance, in a solicitor providing his client with an indemnity if the case is lost to cover that client's costs liability to the victorious opponent. Lord Neuberger MR (as he then was) said:[118]
>
>> [T]he cases on champerty . . . all involve arrangements whereby there is a gain if the action in question succeed . . . [What] is different about the indemnity [in the present case] is that there is just a loss if the action fails.
>
> The decision reflects the modern tendency not to expand the doctrine of champerty; it promotes access to justice; and it involves a pragmatic appreciation of the lawyer's capacity to maintain professional standards of probity even when conducting a case in which he personally has a real financial interest (in the sense that defeat will involve an aggravated form of loss for his firm).

20.19 *Agreements to oust the court's jurisdiction.* Such a contract is illegal. But, in the case of arbitration agreements, the Arbitration Act 1996 upholds a written arbitration agreement[119] and allows a party to seek a stay of English legal proceedings brought 'in respect of a matter which under the [arbitration] agreement is to be referred to arbitration'.[120] The court will grant a stay unless the arbitration agreement is 'null and void, inoperative, or incapable of being performed'.[121] As for points of English law determined by the arbitrator, the parties can agree that the arbitrator, in making his award, can 'dispense with reasons'. And so the parties can exclude the court's power to hear an appeal.[122] Subject to that, an appeal on a point of English law can be referred to the High Court, but only if the parties agree or if the court itself grants 'leave to appeal'. For this purpose, the High Court applies a restrictive set of 'filtering' criteria.[123] The Act's definition of matters of 'law' is confined to English law. This places findings of foreign law beyond the scope of High Court appeal.[124]

20.20 *Agreements involving a restraint of trade.*[125] The courts eschew any general power to invalidate terms or contracts on the ground of reasonableness. But, where an

---

116   E.g. in the case of CFAs which fail to comply with the scheme: *Awwad* v. *Geraghty* [2001] QB 570, 596, CA, noted by N. Andrews, [2000] CLJ 265–7, and A. Walters, (2000) 116 LQR 371–7 (and not following *Thai Trading Co.* v. *Taylor* [1998] QB 781, CA, noted by N. Andrews [1998] CLJ 469).
117   [2011] EWCA Civ 25; [2011] 1 WLR 2111; noted A. Sedgwick (2011) 30 CJQ 261.
118   *Ibid.*, at [42].
119   Section 5 of the Arbitration Act 1996.
120   Section 9(1), *ibid.*
121   Section 9(5), *ibid.*
122   Section 69(1), *ibid.*
123   Section 69(3), *ibid.*
124   Section 82(1), *ibid.*
125   J. D. Heydon, *The Restraint of Trade Doctrine* (3rd edn, Chatswood, 2009); M. J. Trebilcock, *The Common Law of Restraint of Trade – A Legal and Economic Analysis* (Toronto, 1986); S. Smith, 'Reconstructing Restraint of Trade' (1995) 15 OJLS 565.

arrangement unreasonably stultifies a person's legitimate interest in pursuing a trade or profession, or otherwise engaging in useful economic activity, the doctrine of 'restraint of trade' can invalidate the offending provision (which might be an entire agreement, a free-standing clause or at least part of a clause which can be excised using the process of 'severance',[126] leaving the remaining portion of the clause operative). The law on this topic is highly detailed, and only a sketch can be provided here. Employment contracts (the doctrine can extend to other forms of association) might provide that upon ceasing to be an employee, the former employee will not exploit his ex-employer's trade secrets or confidential information, or solicit custom from the contacts acquired by the employee during his employment with the covenantee (the employee is only released from such a restrictive covenant if he is wrongly dismissed by the employer). Thus restrictive covenants do not survive in favour of the guilty party.[127] Lord Wilson noted that this point is the subject of 'debate' in *Geys* v. *Société Générale* (2012).[128] However, this remains[129] the law, despite some judicial criticism.[130]

Another well-established form of restraint of trade arises when the seller of a business, transferred along with its goodwill (the benefit of its established client base), agrees with the purchaser not to carry on a business which will compete with the buyer's newly acquired business.

Furthermore, in various contexts an agreement might unacceptably preclude a party from exercising a freedom that he might otherwise have.

For example, in *Esso Petroleum Co. Ltd* v. *Harper's Garage (Stourport) Ltd* (1968),[131] the House of Lords struck down a twenty-one-year solus agreement which required the petrol retailer, the owner of the site, not to buy fuel from anyone other than Esso. In return, the retailer received a reduction in the wholesale price. But, in the same litigation, it was held that a four-year solus agreement was acceptable: the petrol company was justified, for that period, in protecting its interest by securing a reasonable degree of continuity in its supply to retailers. The reader is referred to a long passage in Lord Reid's speech where these matters are explained.[132]

In *A Schroeder Music Publishing Co. Ltd* v. *Macaulay* (1974),[133] the House of Lords invalidated a music agency agreement under which a 21-year-old songwriter agreed to assign copyright in all his songs composed during the next five years. The agreement could be extended to ten years if his royalties exceeded £5,000 in the first period. The publisher was not obliged to publish his works. Although the songwriter was committed to the contract for five, or even ten years, the publisher could terminate the contract on one month's notice. The songwriter, Macaulay, proved to be a success. He then obtained a declaration that the contract was void as contrary to public policy, because it was an unreasonable restraint of

---

126   *Treitel* (13th edn, London, 2011), 11–152 ff.
127   *General Billposting Co. Ltd* v. *Atkinson* [1909] AC 118, HL.
128   [2012] UKSC 63; [2013] 1 AC 523, at [68].
129   *Group Lotus plc* v. *1Malaysia Racing Team SDN BHD* [2011] EWHC 1366 (Ch), at [364] to [371], *per* Peter Smith J.
130   *Campbell* v. *Frisbee* [2002] EWCA Civ 1374; [2003] ICR 141, at [22], *per* Lord Phillips.
131   [1968] AC 269, HL.
132   *Ibid.*, at 301–3.
133   [1974] 1 WLR 1308, HL.

trade (no relief beyond this bare declaration is mentioned in the law report). The publisher failed to show that this restraint of trade could be justified as reasonable. Lord Reid found the following arrangement to be unenforceable:[134]

> [T]he respondent assigned to the appellants 'the full copyright for the whole world' in every musical composition 'composed created or conceived' by him alone or in collaboration with any other person during a period of five or it might be ten years. He received no payment (apart from an initial £50) unless his work was published and the appellants need not publish unless they chose to do so. And if they did not publish he had no right to terminate the agreement or to have copyrights re-assigned to him.

20.21 All covenants in restraint of trade must be justified as reasonable having regard to both (a) the interests of the contracting party and (b) the interests of the public. The covenant must be aimed at protecting the legitimate interests of the covenantee. In the case of the sale of a business, the buyer has a legitimate interest in protecting the integrity of the established client base – which it has bought – from being undermined by rival competition by the seller. But an employer has no legitimate interest in stopping its former employee from setting up a rival business. Instead, its protection is confined to its interests in protecting its trade secrets, or other confidential information, and in preventing the employee from filching his custom by taking advantage of customer details and contacts acquired during the period of employment. The employee's covenant cannot catch types of business which differ from the covenantee's. Furthermore, the covenant must not contain a restriction which is excessive in geographical scope.

In *Mason v. Provident Clothing & Supply Co.* (1913), the restriction concerned work as a commercial canvasser within twenty-five miles of London (an area over 1,000 times larger than the employee's usual field of work), and this was held to be too broad.[135]

Nor should the restriction endure too long.[136]

Similarly, in cases concerning the sale of a business with goodwill, the length of the period of restraint and its area of operation must be reasonable.

However, in one famous case, *Nordenfelt v. Maxim Nordenfelt Guns and Ammunition Co. Ltd* (1894), the sale of an armaments business contained a restrictive covenant preventing the vendor from engaging in rival trade for twenty-five years anywhere else in the world. The House of Lords held that this was not excessive, because the vendor, a Swedish millionaire arms manufacturer, had already achieved a worldwide sales base.[137]

---

134 *Ibid.*, at 1313–15, HL.
135 [1913] AC 724, HL.
136 A five-year period was held to be unreasonable in *M & S Drapers v. Reynolds* [1957] 1 WLR 9, CA.
137 [1894] AC 535, HL.

7. IS THE CLAIMANT SUFFICIENTLY ASSOCIATED WITH THE DEFENDANT'S UNLAWFUL PERFORMANCE?

20.22 *Innocent party can sue if contract is not prohibited by statute and its performance does not necessarily involve unlawful conduct.* If the contract is not expressly prohibited by statute, nor by necessary implication, and provided performance of the agreement will not necessarily entail illegality, a claimant is not disabled from suing on a contract if he has no knowledge of the defendant's illegal performance. In *Archbolds (Freightage) Ltd v. S. Spanglett Ltd* (1961),[138] the plaintiff had contracted for the defendant to transport goods by van, not knowing that the defendant's particular van was unlicensed for this purpose and that its use in this way would involve an offence. The plaintiff's goods were lost in transit (they were stolen as a result of the defendant's negligence), and the plaintiff sued for loss on the basis of contractual breach. The Court of Appeal rejected the defence based on illegality: this was not a case of a contract expressly or implied prohibited; nor had the parties jointly agreed to commit an offence or infringe public policy; nor, finally, had the plaintiff been aware that use of this particular van in this transaction would involve a criminal wrong.[139]

20.23 *Inability to sue if claimant participates in an unlawful performance.*[140] Although the contract is not prohibited by statute, nor does its performance necessarily involve unlawful conduct, the claimant will be unable to sue on it if he became aware that the contract will in fact be performed in an illegal fashion and he becomes implicated in that wrongdoing. He is then precluded by the defence of illegality from being able to enforce the contract. This was decided by the Court of Appeal in *Ashmore, Benson, Pease & Co. Ltd* v. *A.V. Dawson Ltd* (1973).[141] In that case, the defendant agreed to transport the plaintiff's goods, but the defendant overloaded its lorry, contrary to statute. The defendant knew this was an offence. The plaintiff's goods were damaged when the lorry toppled over. The plaintiff's contractual claim for this loss failed. The plaintiff's manager had been implicated in the defendant's illegal performance: he knew that the loading involved breach of the relevant statute; indeed this had happened before; and, furthermore, the plaintiff company's connivance in this criminal activity enabled it to make a saving in its transport costs.

20.24 In *Hall* v. *Woolston Hall Leisure* (2001),[142] Mance LJ suggested that the *ratio* of the *Ashmore* case involved not merely the claimant's knowledge of the criminal activity but participation in that wrongdoing, in the sense that the claimant was not merely turning a blind eye to the wrong, but collusively making a gain from this acquiescence. Similarly, in *Anglo Petroleum*

---

138   [1961] 1 QB 374, CA.
139   [1961] 1 QB 374, 387–8, *per* Pearce LJ.
140   J. Goudkamp, 'The Defence of Joint Illegal Enterprise' (2010) 34 Melbourne University LR 425; cf *Hounga* v. *Allen* [2014] UKSC 47; [2014] 1 WLR 2889 (on which see 20.03). A. F. H. Loke, 'Tainting Illegality' (2014) 34 LS 560–81.
141   [1973] 1 WLR 828, CA.
142   [2001] 1 WLR 225, at [80].

Ltd v. *TFB (Mortgages) Ltd* (2007),[143] Mummery LJ noted that participation does not arise solely from knowledge of the other's criminal or unlawful use of the relevant object or service. If that were so, no one could sue on a contract to supply basic living items (food and ordinary clothing) to a prostitute.

The courts will have regard to:

the special nature of the goods or services supplied (the 'ornamental carriage' in *Pearce* v. *Brooks*: 20.12);

whether the supplier is directly profiting from the defendant's illegal activity (as in the *Ashmore* case: 20.23);

the heinousness of the claimant's activity (repeated dealings, as in the *Ashmore* case); and

the gravity of defendant's wrongdoing (for example, the liquidator of a former quarrying business sells detonators to suspicious laymen, and it turns out that they are terrorists).

But the law has not been fully worked out, as Mummery LJ's judgment in the *Anglo Petroleum* case (2007) shows.[144]

8. CONSEQUENCES OF ILLEGALITY

20.25 There are nine main propositions.

(1) Where the contract is expressly or by necessary implication prohibited by contract, neither party can sue on it (20.07 to 20.09).

(2) The same applies where the contract is invalid because the common purpose of the transaction was to commit a crime or other (serious) legal wrong (20.06).

(3) We have seen that the claim upon a contract might not fail if the claimant was not consciously implicated in the defendant's decision to perform it in an illegal fashion (20.22); compare the situation where the claimant knowingly participates in unlawful performance (20.23); but the claimant can sue if he has been guilty of only incidental illegality during performance (20.06).

(4) Sometimes, the courts have found that despite the invalidity of the principal contract, the claimant has a separate action for the tort of deceit[145] committed by the defendant, or that there is a valid claim for breach of a collateral contract.[146]

---

143 *Anglo Petroleum Ltd* v. *TFB (Mortgages) Ltd* [2007] EWCA Civ 456; [2007] BCC 407 (acknowledging, however, that the law remains malleable: *ibid.*, at [73] to [82]).

144 [2007] EWCA Civ 456; [2007] BCC 407, at [73] to [82]. A. F. H. Loke, 'Tainting Illegality' (2014) 34 LS 560–81.

145 *Shelley* v. *Paddock* [1980] QB 384, 357, CA (defendant swindled the claimant into paying for property not in fact owned by defendant; but claimant had breached exchange-control rules; action based on defendant's fraudulent misrepresentation that he was owner permitted): for an argument that sometimes the defendant might be held to have assumed a tortious duty to save the claimant from the trap (known to, or reasonably ascertainable by, a more knowledgeable defendant), see N. Enonchong, [2000] *Restitution Law Review* 241, 250 ff.

146 *Strongman (1945) Ltd* v. *Sincock* [1955] 2 QB 525, CA (defendant refusing to pay for claimant's building work because licence not obtained for such work; defendant, an architect, had undertaken to obtain such a licence; main building contract invalid because unlicensed work; but defendant's collateral assurance, that licence would be obtained, enforceable and claimant able to recover payment for his work as damages for breach of that collateral warranty).

(5) The claimant might be entitled to a claim for recovery of money paid or for a *quantum meruit* in respect of services or a *quantum valebat* for goods delivered. The Law Commission has recently provided a detailed study of opportunities for restitution to avoid the defendant's unjust enrichment,[147] and a summary is provided at 20.26.

(6) The fact that possession in property has been acquired under an illegal contract does not preclude an action by the claimant owner to recover that property (or to obtain damages for conversion, in the case of chattels).[148]

(7) Property can pass under an illegal contract by which title was intended to be transferred.[149] The Law Commission has examined these last two topics.[150]

(8) In some situations, the court can sever an illegal portion of a transaction, and thus give effect to the lawful and uncontaminated part of the transaction:[151]

   (a) *Taylor v. Bhail* (1996)[152] demonstrates that the court will not sever parts of an undertaking if it perceives that they are in substance inextricably linked, and that severance would emit the 'wrong message' to the commercial community by condoning an unacceptable practice.

   (b) As for textual severance of an illegal part of a written contract which is otherwise lawful, Treitel notes:[153] (i) it is unclear whether this type of severance is possible outside the contexts of contracts in restraint of trade or agreements to exclude the court's jurisdiction; (ii) severance requires the possibility of clean[154] textual excision; that is, the offending part can be removed allowing the lawful remainder to stand intact; textual rearrangement is not possible; (iii) severance must not alter the whole nature of the contract;[155] furthermore (iv) '[i]t can hardly be imagined that a Court would enforce a promise, however inherently valid and however severable, if contained in a contract one of the terms of which provided for assassination.'[156] And it follows that the proposed severance must be assessed by considering the heinousness of the relevant transaction.

(9) The court is entitled, indeed required, to refuse to give contractual effect to an illegal transaction even if its illegal nature only emerges incidentally during the conduct of the case.

---

147 Law Commission, 'The Illegality Defence' (Law Commission Consultation Paper No. 189, London, 2009), Part 4, at 65–85.
148 *Bowmakers Ltd v. Barnet Instruments Ltd* [1945] KB 65, CA.
149 *Singh v. Ali* [1960] AC 167, 176, PC; *Belvoir Finance Co. v. Stapleton* [1971] 1 QB 210, CA.
150 Law Commission, 'The Illegality Defence' (Law Commission Consultation Paper No. 189, London, 2009), Part 5, at 86–93.
151 *Chitty on Contracts* (31st edn, London, 2012), 16–197 ff.
152 [1996] CLC 377.
153 *Treitel* (13th edn, London, 2011), 11–159 to 11–164.
154 Illustrated by *Goldsoll v. Goldman* [1915] 1 Ch 292, CA (deleting geographical references without distorting overall grammatical sense of relevant sentence); for a slightly more flexible approach, see *T. Lucas & Co. v. Mitchell* [1874] Ch 129, CA.
155 E.g. *Attwood v. Lamont* [1920] 3 KB 571, 577–8, CA, where Lord Sterndale MR made clear that this test arises in addition to the court's capacity to effect a 'blue-pencil' excision of an offending part of the text.
156 *McFarlane v. Daniell* (1938) 38 SR (NSW) 337, *per* Jordan CJ.

The Court of Appeal in *Birkett* v. *Acorn Business Machines Ltd* (1999) explained the matter as follows:[157]

> If a transaction is on its face, that is to say merely by looking at its terms and without additional evidence, manifestly illegal, the Court will refuse to enforce it, whether or not either party alleges illegality. If a transaction is not on its face manifestly illegal but there is before the Court persuasive and comprehensive evidence of illegality, the court may refuse to enforce it even if illegality has not been pleaded or alleged. The principle behind the court's intervention of its own motion in such a case is to ensure that its process is not being abused by inviting it to enforce *sub silentio* a contract whose enforcement is contrary to public policy. Thus, in Re Mahmoud and Ispahani, Scrutton LJ observed:[158] 'In my view the court is bound, once it knows that the contract is illegal, to take the objection and to refuse to enforce the contract, whether its knowledge comes from the statement of the party who was guilty of the illegality, or whether its knowledge comes from outside sources. The court does not sit to enforce illegal contracts. There is no question of estoppel; it is for the protection of the public that the court refuses to enforce such a contract.'

Furthermore, in *Skilton* v. *Sullivan* (1994) (20.16), the Court of Appeal said that if the VAT authorities had not already been informed, the court would have been obliged to report to those authorities the fact that one of the parties had dishonestly violated the VAT rules.[159]

20.26 If the contract is illegal, the starting point is that prima facie the defendant can raise the defence of illegality to the claimant's action for restitution.

Examples where this rule operates satisfactorily are *Parkinson* v. *College of Ambulance Ltd* (1925),[160] where the plaintiff had made a large donation to charity, following the charity's suggestion that it could reciprocate by procuring him a knighthood. His claim to recover on the basis of total failure of consideration was met by the defence of illegality. And, in *Berg* v. *Sadler & Moore* (1937), the plaintiff used false pretences to buy cigarettes from a tobacco association. He was unable to recover his money from the intended seller.[161]

However, there are exceptions to the claimant's inability to obtain restitution under a contract which is invalid for illegality. A party can recover money paid, or obtain recompense in respect of goods or services, where:

(1) he was ignorant of a fact which caused the transaction to be illegal;[162] it is not clear whether there is a more general possibility of restitution based on the claimant's innocence;

---

157 [1999] 2 All ER 429, 433, *per* Colman J, sitting with Sedley LJ; applied in *Pickering* v. *Deacon* [2003] EWCA Civ 554; *The Times*, 19 April 2003.
158 [1921] 2 KB 716, 729, CA.
159 *The Times*, 25 March 1994 (end of Beldam LJ's judgment).
160 [1925] 2 KB 1, Lush J.
161 [1937] 2 KB 158, CA.
162 *Oom* v. *Bruce* (1810) 12 East 225, 226; 104 ER 87, 88 (insurance for cargo on ship proceeding to England from Russia; at time of contract, plaintiff insured had been unaware that war had recently arisen between these nations; on trading with the enemy, see 20.15).

thus, it is uncertain[163] whether a mere mistake of law (that is, a mistake not induced by the defendant) might now suffice; it has been contended that the Court of Appeal's decision in *Mohamed* v. *Alaga & Co.* (2000)[164] might support this, at least where the defendant, a solicitor, is blameworthy in not appreciating that the contract was illegal, and the claimant cannot be expected to have known of a recondite point of illegality; this possibility requires clarification by the courts, but it appears that the law is inclining in this direction; or

(2) the party seeking restitution belongs to a class of persons intended to be protected by the relevant illegality rule;[165] or

(3) the claimant was induced to enter the contract by the defendant's misrepresentation of fact, or fraudulent misrepresentation of law[166] (which might now extend to misrepresentations of law even if the misrepresentation was innocent);[167] or

(4) the claimant has been induced to enter the contract by the defendant's duress;[168] or

(5) a final opportunity for restitution arises in the case of certain decisions to resile from an unlawful transaction; the claimant (even though at first conscious of the illegality, and perhaps a main player in it) can obtain restitution if:

(a) the illegal scheme was voluntarily abandoned by him (that is, he did not abandon it only because he took fright or because he decided to mitigate his position once the illegality had been discovered by authorities or third parties)[169] and

(b) its purpose has not already been fully achieved.[170]

---

163 *Hughes* v. *Liverpool Victoria Friendly Society* [1916] 2 KB 482, CA (fraudulent misrepresentation of law; claimant able to recover premiums on illegal life insurance contract); cf *Harse* v. *Pearl Life Assurance Co.* [1904] 1 KB 558, CA (innocent misrepresentation of law not entitling claimant to recover premiums on illegal life insurance contract); cf now *Kleinwort Benson Ltd* v. *Lincoln City Council* [1999] 1 AC 153, HL, abolishing the mistake of law bar to recovery of money paid by error; on the possible impact of this in the context of illegal contracts, see Law Commission, 'The Illegality Defence' (Law Commission Consultation Paper No. 189, London, 2009), 2.42.

164 [2000] 1 WLR 190, CA: claimant performing (a) translation and (b) client introduction services for defendant solicitor; element (b) unlawful; whole contract for (a) and (b) invalid for illegality; but claimant awarded a *quantum meruit* in respect of (a); N. Enonchong, [2000] *Restitution Law Review* 241, criticises this decision's reasoning; other decisions have distinguished the *Mohamed* case: see Law Commission, 'The Illegality Defence' (Law Commission Consultation Paper No. 189, London, 2009), 4.26 ff, on *Awwad* v. *Geraghty* [2001] QB 570, 596, CA; and dicta in *Dal-Sterling Group* v. *WSP South West Ltd* [2002] TCLR 20, TCC.

165 *Kiriri Cotton Co. Ltd* v. *Dewani* [1960] AC 192, 204, PC, *per* Lord Denning (payment of premium by tenant contrary to Ugandan regulations; but statute held to be intended to protect tenants); *Green* v. *Portsmouth Stadium* [1953] 2 QB 190, CA (bookmaker, at defendant stadium's request, making unlawful payments to stadium; although denied access to stadium, unable to recover payments; statutory invalidity not aimed at protection of bookmakers but of the public at large).

166 *Brennan* v. *Bolt Burdon* [2004] EWCA Civ 1017; [2005] QB 303; *Treitel* (13th edn, London, 2011), 8–022 ff; this decision allows rescission, etc., for misrepresentations of law; on the possible impact of this in the context of illegal contracts, see Law Commission, 'The Illegality Defence' (Law Commission Consultation Paper No. 189, London, 2009), 4.15.

167 *Kleinwort Benson Ltd* v. *Lincoln City Council* [1999] 1 AC 153, HL, abolished the mistake of law bar to recovery of money paid in error.

168 *Smith* v. *Cuff* (1817) 6 M & S 160, 165; 105 ER 1203, 1205, Lord Ellenborough; *Davies* v. *London and Provincial Marine Insurance Co.* (1878) 8 Ch D 469, Fry J.

169 *Tribe* v. *Tribe* [1996] Ch 107, 135, CA, *per* Millett LJ; Law Commission, 'The Illegality Defence' (Law Commission Consultation Paper No. 189, London, 2009), 4.52.

170 Law Commission, 'The Illegality Defence' (Law Commission Consultation Paper No. 189, London, 2009), 4.45 ff, considering, notably, *Taylor* v. *Bowers* (1876) 1 QBD 291, CA; *Kearley* v. *Thomson* (1890) 24 QBD 291, CA; *Bigos* v. *Boustead* [1951] 1 All ER 92, 97, Pritchard J; *Tribe* v. *Tribe* [1996] Ch 107, CA.

QUESTIONS

(1) Distinguish (a) contracts which are expressly or by necessary implication illegal; (b) agreements to perform contracts in an unlawful manner; (c) contracts performed illegally by party A and in which party B becomes consciously implicated.

(2) Illustrate the proposition that a party's incidental illegality during performance will not necessarily preclude him from suing on the relevant contract.

(3) Summarise the impact of public policy in the following contexts:

(a) contracts involving allocation of assets after divorce;

(b) contracts concerning remuneration of lawyers in respect of litigation services;

(c) contracts allegedly tainted by bribery or corruption.

(4) What are the contractual and restitutionary consequences of illegality?

Selected further reading

Chitty on Contracts (31st edn, London, 2012), chapter 16

R. A. Buckley, *Illegality and Public Policy* (3rd edn, London, 2013)

N. Enonchong, *Illegal Transactions* (London, 1998) (2nd edn forthcoming)

A. F. H. Loke, 'Tainting Illegality' (2014) 34 LS 560–81

S. Waddams, *Principle and Policy in Contract Law: Competing or Complementary Concepts?* (Cambridge, 2011), chapter 6 (for a historical overview)

Law Commission, 'Illegal Transactions: The Effect of Illegality on Contracts and Trusts' (Law Commission Consultation Paper No. 154, London, 1999) (for an earlier discussion of the topic)

Law Commission, 'The Illegality Defence' (Law Commission Consultation Paper No. 189, London, 2009), Parts 3–5 (Part 3 contains a good overview of this topic, including reference to foreign legal systems and to the EU dimension)

Law Commission, 'The Illegality Defence' (Law Commission Report No. 320, London, 2010), Part 3

X

The future

Chapter contents

21

The good faith debate

1. INTRODUCTION

21.01 Summary of main points

(1) English law does not recognise as valid an agreement to negotiate in good faith or reasonably the terms of the main contract. Nor should English law adopt a general principle of good faith in the pre-contractual context.

(2) What of good faith during performance? When one considers the range and pliability of English doctrines already embodying a notion of good faith or fair dealing, it seems unlikely that many cases will be differently decided if good faith were explicitly introduced as a general principle.

(3) However, it would be a different matter if the English law of contract were to be placed in the hands of a supra-national court. Outsiders would not be attuned to the tradition of the Common Law, its peculiar methods and its values.

(4) Furthermore, the inevitable anxiety and uncertainty experienced within the legal profession when advising their clients would outweigh the speculative and marginal benefits of such a change.

2. ENGLISH LAW'S DISTINCTIVENESS

21.02 This topic has produced new literature,[1] adding to a large store of discussion.[2] The author's argument will be that (1) in English law the principle of good faith is not at all required in the context of *pre-contractual negotiations* because of the highly developed and fertile array of existing doctrines; and (2) as for articulating in English law the concept of good faith as a general principle governing *performance of contracts*, the case is more evenly balanced; however, there would be only a slight benefit in making such a change; there would be a problem for practitioners adjusting to the new concept but the courts would be unlikely to use the concept dynamically. In short, good faith as a general norm regulating performance of contracts might become an empty affirmation of the pervasive sensitivity of Common Law and Equity to problems of fair dealing; and it would add little, if anything. And so, at 21.20, the author concludes that the inevitable anxiety and uncertainty experienced within the legal profession when advising their clients might in fact outweigh the possible and marginal benefits of such a change.

21.03 Good faith can apply both in the performance of contracts and, at the pre-contractual phase, to control the parties' capacity to withdraw from pre-contractual negotiations. The concept might refer simply to the avoidance of dishonesty or bad faith; or it might be held to import

1 *New discussion* (concerning, as noted below at 21.16, *Yam Seng Pte Ltd* v. *International Trade Corp Ltd* [2013] EWHC 111 (QB); [2013] 1 All ER (Comm) 1321; [2013] BLR 147 (notably at [141], [144], [147], and [154]; considered by Beatson LJ, in *Mid Essex Hospital Services NHS Trust* v. *Compass Group UK and Ireland Ltd (Trading As Medirest)* [2013] EWCA Civ 200; [2013] BLR 265; [2013] CILL 3342, at [150]): S. Bogle, 'Disclosing Good Faith in English Contract Law' (2014) 18 *Edinburgh Law Review* 141–5; D. Campbell, 'Good faith and the ubiquity of the "relational" contract' (2014) 77 MLR 475–492; E. Granger [2013] LMCLQ 418; S. Whittaker, 'Good Faith, Implied Terms and Commercial Contracts' (2013) 129 LQR 463; more generally, H. Hoskins, 'Contractual obligations to negotiate in good faith: faithfulness to the agreed common purpose' (2014) 130 LQR 131–159; M. Arden, 'Coming to Terms with Good Faith' (2013) 30 JCL 199; L. DiMatteo, Q. Zhou, S. Saintier, K. Rowley (eds.), *Commercial Contract Law: Transatlantic Perspectives* (Cambridge, 2014), chapter 9 (by Z. Ollerenshaw).
2 *Earlier discussion*: J. Beatson and D. Friedmann (eds.), *Good Faith and Fault in Contract Law* (Oxford, 1995), chapter 2 (N. Cohen, Israel), chapter 6 (E. A. Farnsworth, USA) and chapter 7 (W. Ebke and B. M. Steinhauer, Germany); A. Berg, (2003) 119 LQR 357; R. Brownsword, *Contract Law: Themes for the Twenty-First Century* (2nd edn, Oxford, 2006), chapter 5 (also in R. Brownsword, in M. Furmston (ed.), *The Law of Contract* (4th edn, London, 2010), chapter 1); S. G. Burton and E. G. Andersen, *Contractual Good Faith* (Boston, 1995); M. Clarke, (1993) 23 HKLJ 318; H. G. Collins, (1994) 14 OJLS 229; H. G. Collins, *The Law of Contract* (4th edn, Cambridge, 2003), chapters 10 and 15; A. Forte (ed.), *Good Faith in Contract and Property Law* (Oxford, 1999); M. Furmston and G. J. Tolhurst, *Contract Formation: Law and Practice* (Oxford, 2010), chapters 12 and 13 (pre-contractual dealings); R. Harrison, *Good Faith in Sales* (London, 1997); O. Lando, 'Is Good Faith an Overarching General Clause in the Principles of European Contract Law?', in *Liber Amicorum Guido Alpa: National Private Law Systems* (London, 2007), 601; E. McKendrick, 'The Meaning of Good Faith', in *Liber Amicorum Guido Alpa: National Private Law Systems* (London, 2007), 687; E. McKendrick, *Contract Law: Text, Cases and Materials* (4th edn, Oxford, 2010), chapter 15; H. MacQueen, 'Good Faith, Mixed Legal Systems and the Principles of European Contract Law', in *Liber Amicorum Guido Alpa: National Private Law Systems* (London, 2007), 614; J. O'Connor, *Good Faith in English Law* (Aldershot, 1990), chapter 3; R. Summers, 'The General Duty of Good Faith – Its Recognition and Conceptualization' (1982) 67 Cornell LR 810; J. Stapleton, 'Good Faith in Private Law' (1999) 52 CLP 1; Lord Steyn, 'Contract Law: Fulfilling the Reasonable Expectations of Honest Men' (1997) 113 LQR 433; G. Teubner, (1998) 61 MLR 11; R. Zimmermann and S. Whittaker (eds.), *Good Faith in European Contract Law* (Cambridge, 2000) (reviewed, N. Andrews (2001) *Civil Justice Quarterly* 197); H. MacQueen and R. Zimmermann (eds.), *European Contract Law: Scots and South African Perspectives* (Edinburgh, 2006), 17–18 (Zimmermann), and chapter 2 (MacQueen) (and see also references at R. Hooley, 'Controlling Contractual Discretion' [2013] CLJ 65, 74 n. 54).

more extensive responsibilities to avoid reprehensible or unacceptable misconduct; or even a positive duty in some contexts to point out potential snags and dangers to the other side.

> As McKendrick notes:[3] 'There is a spectrum of possible meanings ... At the one end of the spectrum good faith means no more than honesty ... At the other end of the spectrum good faith may require [a party] ... to give priority to the best interests of the other party', as in the manner of a fiduciary.
> As noted below at 21.16, Leggatt J, in dicta in *Yam Seng Pte Ltd* v. *International Trade Corp Ltd* (2013), has proposed a more energetic use of an implied term of good faith, going further than avoidance of lying.[4]

21.04 Certainly good faith is not an explicitly recognised general doctrine in English contract law (however, see 21.06 to 21.09 for specific judicial and statutory contexts where good faith is recognised or immanent).

> As Bingham LJ said in *Interfoto Picture Library Ltd* v. *Stiletto Visual Programmes Ltd* (1989):[5]
> In many civil law systems ... the law of obligations recognises and enforces an overriding principle that in making and carrying out contracts parties should act in good faith ... [Its] effect is perhaps most aptly conveyed by such metaphorical colloquialisms as 'playing fair', 'coming clean'. It is in essence a principle of fair and open dealing ... English law has, characteristically, committed itself to no such overriding principle but has developed piecemeal solutions in response to demonstrated problems of unfairness.

21.05 There is little doubt that England stands almost isolated in this respect.

> Good faith in the performance of contracts is a prominent feature of civil law systems of contract law (section 242 of the German *Bürgerliches Gesetzbuch* (BGB); Article 1134 of the French Civil Code; Articles 1337, 1366 and 1375 of the Italian Civil Code); and the same concept has been adopted in the USA, both in the *Restatement of the Law Second, Contracts* (1981, section 205) and the Uniform Commercial Code (1–203); furthermore, UNIDROIT's *Principles of International Commercial Contracts* (2010), Article 1.7,[6] the Principles of European Contract Law, Article 2:201, and the Common Frame of Reference, Article III–1:103,[7] adopt this principle.

---

3   E. McKendrick, 'The Meaning of Good Faith', in *Liber Amicorum Guido Alpa: National Private Law Systems* (London, 2007), 687, 692, 696.

4   [2013] EWHC 111 (QB); [2013] 1 All ER (Comm) 1321; [2013] 1 Lloyd's Rep 526; [2013] BLR 147 (notably at [141], [144], [147], and [154]).

5   [1989] QB 433, 439, CA.

6   3rd edition, 2010, text and comment, is available at: www.unidroit.org/english/principles/contracts/principles2010/integralversionprinciples2010-e.pdf.

7   *Principles, Definitions and Model Rules of European Private Law Draft Common Frame of Reference*, C. von Bar and E. Clive (eds.) (6 vols., Oxford, 2010), prepared by the 'Study Group on a European Civil Code' and the 'Research Group on EC Private Law (Acquis Group)'.

21.06 However, some English judges have perhaps gone too far in proclaiming the capacity of contracting parties to act without regard to notions of fair dealing. These remarks no longer chime with modern approaches. In particular, Lord Reid in *White & Carter* v. *McGregor* (1962) (on appeal from Scotland) said that in English law a contractual right or power need not be exercised reasonably, 'equitably' or in good faith:[8]

> It might be, but it never has been, the law that a person is only entitled to enforce his contractual rights in a reasonable way, and that a court will not support an attempt to enforce them in an unreasonable way. One reason why that is not the law is, no doubt, because it would create too much uncertainty to require the court to decide whether it is reasonable or equitable to allow a party to enforce his full rights under a contract.

Lord Reid's statement needs to be qualified, for he suggests that there is no attempt at all by the courts to control the exercise of contractual powers.

The first reason for qualifying his statement is that authorities, including *Paragon Finance plc* v. *Nash* (2002),[9] cited at 13.14 above, adopt an (admittedly) restrictive approach to judicial regulation of a party's exercise of contractual discretion.

A second noteworthy development is that the House of Lords in *Malik (and Mahmud)* v. *Bank of Credit and Commerce International SA* (1998) (13.08 case (2)) recognised a general implied term that the employer should not behave in a way which will destroy or threaten the relationship of confidence and trust between him and his employees.[10] But that special relationship has been distinguished from other contexts. In *Jani-King (GB) Ltd* v. *Pula Enterprises Ltd* (2007), Coulson J noted that, in accordance with a settled line of cases, in ordinary commercial contracts there is no implied term that the parties will refrain 'from acting in such a way as to destroy or seriously damage the relationship of trust and confidence between them'.[11]

3. THE ETHICAL SENSITIVITY OF ENGLISH CONTRACT LAW

21.07 In fact, there are many English *judicial* doctrines which impose ethical restraints on contractual conduct (see 21.08 for statutory examples):

(1) *Estoppel doctrines (promissory estoppel, and other species of estoppel)* (5.38 to 5.49).
(2) *Unconscionable advantage.* Nullification of agreements where one party has unconscionably acquiesced in the other's mistake, the 'snapping-up' cases decided at Common Law (3.63) and rectification where one party has unconscionably acquiesced in the other's misapprehension concerning a prospective written contract's contents (14.31).

---

8 [1962] AC 413, 430, HL, *per* Lord Reid; similarly, *Chapman* v. *Honig* [1963] 2 QB 502, 520–1, CA; cf *McLory* v. *Post Office* [1993] 1 All ER 457, 462–5, *per* David Neuberger QC, sitting as a Deputy High Court Judge; A. Weir, in P. Cane and J. Stapleton (eds.), *The Law of Obligations: Essays in Celebration of John Fleming* (Oxford, 1998), 123–4, citing *Balfour Beatty* v. *Docklands Light Railway* (1996) 78 BLR 49, CA.
9 *Paragon Finance plc* v. *Nash* [2001] EWCA Civ 1466; [2002] 1 WLR 685.
10 [1998] 1 AC 20, 45–6, HL, *per* Lord Steyn (recognition of new cause of action for 'stigma damages': loss to former employees of fraudulent employer when those former employees find it impossible to re-enter the same job market because of their association with their fraudulent former employer).
11 [2007] EWHC 2433 (QBD); [2008] 1 Lloyd's Rep 305, at [48] ff.

(3) *Vitiating factors.* Grounds of vitiation based upon coercion, undue influence or exploitation (Chapter 11).

(4) *Specific duties to disclose* (9.44).

(5) *Fiduciary duties.* The duties of fair dealing imposed on agents and other fiduciaries when they contract with their principals, beneficiaries or other protected persons.[12]

(6) *Implied terms.* Notably, recognition of the duty to avoid wholly unreasonable unilateral revision of terms in finance agreements (*Paragon Finance plc* v. *Nash* (2002): 13.14) and the Privy Council in *Pratt Contractors Ltd* v. *Transit New Zealand* (2003) (3.49) has acknowledged that there is an implied duty on the part of the invitor to conduct the tender process in good faith.[13] As noted below at 21.16, Leggatt J, in dicta in *Yam Seng Pte Ltd* v. *International Trade Corp Ltd* (2013), has proposed a more energetic use of an implied term of good faith to regulate long-term or cooperative agreements, although this suggestion has yet to be precisely examined.[14]

(7) *The penalty jurisdiction* (19.02).

(8) *Equitable relief against forfeiture of proprietary or possessory interests* (17.24).

(9) *Disproportionate or over-severe termination of contracts following breach.* The courts have developed the notion that unless the contractual obligation clearly requires very strict compliance, a party should be denied the right to terminate a contract where this would be a wholly disproportionate or over-severe response to the relevant breach. '*The Hansa Nord*' (1976) (building on the *Hongkong Fir* category of intermediate terms, 17.32 ff) and *Rice* v. *Great Yarmouth Borough Council* (2000) (17.26) exemplify this.

21.08 There are also statutory examples.

(1) Part 2 of the Consumer Rights Bill (formerly the Unfair Terms in Consumer Contracts Regulations 1999, see 15.28) refers explicitly to '*the requirement*' of '*good faith*' as the foundation of a statutory test of '*unfairness*' enabling the courts to regulate certain types of clause within contracts for the supply of goods or services affecting a consumer.

> In the House of Lords' decision in *Director-General of Fair Trading* v. *First National Bank* (2002),[15] Lord Bingham said[16] that this imported a requirement of fair and open dealing, and that openness required clarity and 'no pitfalls'.
>
> He added that fair dealing requires that the supplier should not, deliberately or otherwise, take advantage of the consumer's necessity, indigence, lack of experience, unfamiliarity or weak bargaining position. Lord Bingham recalled that the great eighteenth-century judge, Lord Mansfield, had been a champion of good faith in the insurance context.[17]

---

12   *Calvert* v. *William Hill Credit Ltd* [2008] EWCA Civ 1427; [2009] Ch 330, at [53]; J. Edelman, 'When Do Fiduciary Duties Arise?' (2010) 126 LQR 302.
13   [2003] UKPC 83; [2004] BLR 143; 100 Con LR 29.
14   [2013] EWHC 111 (QB); [2013] 1 All ER (Comm) 1321; [2013] 1 Lloyd's Rep 526; [2013] BLR 147 (notably at [141], [144], [147], and [154]).
15   [2002] 1 AC 481; [2001] UKHL 52.
16   *Ibid.*, at [17].
17   An allusion to, notably, *Carter* v. *Boehm* (1766) 3 Burr 1905.

Lord Steyn in *Director-General of Fair Trading* v. *First National Bank* (2002)[18] rejected the view that good faith in this consumer context should be limited to 'procedural' shortcomings, as distinct from broader notions of unfairness and overreaching.

(2) Section 15A of the Sale of Goods Act 1979 (17.22) prevents termination by a buyer for breach of implied terms if the relevant breach is trivial. It is designed to temper the perceived harshness of the Common Law's approach to the rejection of goods on technical (and bad faith) grounds, when the relevant defect does not cause the buyer any real loss or problem.

4. LACK OF GOOD FAITH: BLOTS ON THE LAW?

21.09 Admittedly, there are some decisions which might *appear* to be an affront to any notion of good faith: *Arcos* v. *Ronaasen* (1933) (17.22), *Union Eagle Ltd* v. *Golden Achievement Ltd* (1997) (17.24) and *White & Carter* v. *McGregor* (1962) (18.03). But, and this is the better view, each of these decisions can in fact be justified.

First, the *Arcos* case (1933)[19] (17.22) is not as outlandish as might at first appear: the discrepancy in the width of the timber supplied was not microscopic (although this made no difference to the buyer, it seems; but he might have changed his mind and either wished to use the wood for a new purpose where the difference might matter, or he might have decided to try to sell the timber, when its exact specification might again have mattered).

Secondly, the buyer's ten-minute delay in paying for the real property in the *Union Eagle* case (1997) (17.24) might have made a difference if there were dependent transactions. However, as Lord Hoffmann persuasively suggested in this case, there is a need for a very bright line indeed in commercial conveyancing transactions.

Finally, the *White & Carter* (1962) problem (see further 18.03) is a classic dilemma which divided the House of Lords three to two, and all but one of the subsequent decisions (18.05) have favoured the innocent party's right to maintain the contract.

5. THE PRE-FORMATION CONTEXT

21.10 *Express agreements to negotiate in good faith.* The law is summarised at 2.07. The main proposition is that English law does not recognise as valid an agreement to negotiate in good faith or reasonably the terms of the main contract. In the leading case, *Walford* v. *Miles* (1992)[20] (2.07), the House of Lords held that an agreement to negotiate in good faith or reasonably is uncertain and void. The rationale for this is that a purported obligation to

---

18 [2001] UKHL 52; [2002] 1 AC 481, at [36].
19 [1933] AC 470, HL; on this case, D. Campbell in D. Campbell, L. Mulcahy and S. Wheeler (eds.), *Changing Concepts of Contract* (Palgrave, Basingstoke, 2013), chapter 7.
20 [1992] 2 AC 128, HL.

bargain in good faith (or reasonably) is too vague, and that 'policing' such an obligation would embroil the courts in complicated inquiries into the reasons for the breakdown of negotiations. It is submitted that *Walford* v. *Miles* (1992) is sound: an express agreement to negotiate *towards the main contract* should remain void for uncertainty.

21.11 *Good faith as a general pre-contractual source of regulation?* Here the question arises: should English law adopt an extra-contractual and general principle of good faith in the pre-contractual context? It is suggested that the better view is that such a concept would add nothing, and even subtract from the current law's broad range of protection during the pre-formation phase. The context is complex and varied. Different contexts receive different legal treatments. The existing miscellany of doctrines is quite adequate (proprietary estoppel, restitution, tortious liability for certain types of misrepresentation, implied collateral warranties, as in *Blackpool and Fylde Aero Club* v. *Blackpool Borough Council* (1990) (3.48)). As Hugh Collins has noted, English law is exacting in this sphere, requiring even a positive obligation to respect certain expectations engendered by the parties' pre-contractual dealings.[21]

21.12 By contrast, Berg's list of 'good faith obligations' (2.09), which he offers as a rejoinder to *Walford* v. *Miles* (1992) (2.07), would provide much material for litigation where large deals break down. Berg proposes Utopian standards of fair dealing: that each negotiating party should 'have an open mind' and 'a willingness to consider' the other side's proposals; there should be 'an obligation not to take advantage' of the other side's ignorance; and there should be a duty 'not to withdraw giving as the cause something which … is extremely unreasonable'.[22] It is not clear that even a convocation of bishops would wish to subject themselves to this demanding set of criteria.

6. GOOD FAITH TO TAKE CENTRAL STAGE AS A CENTRAL PRINCIPLE?

21.13 This leaves the question whether the English courts should introduce good faith as a central, even dominant, principle applicable across the whole range of contractual issues: the validity of agreement, variation of obligations, matters of contractual interpretation, process of termination for breach and on other grounds, grant of remedies. Brownsword has set out the arguments for and against introducing such a duty:[23]

Arguments in favour: (1) good faith can be dealt with by the courts in a 'clean and direct fashion', 'coherently and effectively'; (2) such recognition would ensure that the law reflects 'reasonable expectations'; and (3) its recognition as an explicit and general doctrine will foster a 'culture of trust and co-operation'.

Counter-arguments: (a) 'English contract law is premised on adversarial self-interested dealing'; (b) good faith is too vague an idea; its implementation would require 'difficult

21 H. G. Collins, *The Law of Contract* (4th edn, Cambridge, 2003), chapter 10.
22 A. Berg, (2003) 119 LQR 357, 363.
23 R. Brownsword, in M. Furmston (ed.), *The Law of Contract* (4th edn, London, 2010), 1.81 ff.

inquiries into contracting parties' reasons'; and (c) it would be inappropriate in contexts where the parties' dealings 'openly tolerate opportunism'.

21.14 Lord Steyn (the retired Law Lord, but who was educated within the Roman–Dutch tradition) has famously used the formula 'Fulfilling the Reasonable Expectations of Honest Men' as a means of persuading common lawyers to embrace good faith (his phrase is intended to encapsulate sound commercial practice or the values of the marketplace).[24] And, as he commented judicially in *First Energy (UK) Ltd* v. *Hungarian International Bank Ltd* (1993):[25]

> [T]he reasonable expectations of honest men must be protected . . . It is the objective which has been and still is the principal moulding force of our law of contract . . . [If] the *prima facie* solution to a problem runs counter to [this], this criterion requires a rigorous re-examination of the problem to ascertain whether the law does indeed compel demonstrable unfairness.

21.15 It is submitted that the selective and fact-sensitive technique of implying terms enables the English courts to do justice in a free and generous fashion guided by the criteria of commercial necessity and basic understanding of minimum levels of fair dealing.[26] As we saw in Chapter 13, the implied term technique is also precise (prescribing rules for specific types of transactions, 'terms implied in law', or even recognising one-off 'terms implied in fact').

21.16 Consistent with this is the suggestion made by Leggatt J, in dicta in *Yam Seng Pte Ltd* v. *International Trade Corp Ltd* (2013), that the courts should adopt a more energetic use of an implied term of good faith, going further than avoidance of lying[27] and importing a duty of 'fair dealing', notably within so-called 'relational'[28] contracts requiring mutual trust between parties (see below). The present case concerned a distributorship agreement of almost three years' duration.

Leggatt J's judgment notes the factors which have impeded recognition of a general implied term of good faith.[29] But he comments that the English 'jurisdiction would appear to be swimming against the tide', citing the wider contexts of European law, American[30] and Commonwealth tendencies. He also notes the process of construing written contract by

---

24 Lord Steyn, 'Contract Law: Fulfilling the Reasonable Expectations of Honest Men' (1997) 113 LQR 433.
25 [1993] 2 Lloyd's Rep 194, 196, CA.
26 H. G. Collins, 'Implied Terms: the Foundation in Good Faith and Fair Dealing' (2014) 67 CLP 297–331.
27 [2013] EWHC 111 (QB); [2013] 1 All ER (Comm) 1321; [2013] 1 Lloyd's Rep 526; [2013] BLR 147 (notably at [141], [144], [147], and [154]); noted by S. Bogle, 'Disclosing Good Faith in English Contract Law' (2014) 18 *Edinburgh Law Review* 141–5; D. Campbell, 'Good Faith and the Ubiquity of the "Relational" Contract' (2014) 77 MLR 475–92; S. Whittaker, 'Good Faith, Implied Terms and Commercial Contracts' (2013) 129 LQR 463; E. Granger [2013] LMCLQ 418; more generally, H. Hoskins, 'Contractual Obligations to Negotiate in Good Faith: Faithfulness to the Agreed Common Purpose' (2014) 130 LQR 131–59. See also the dicta in *Berkeley Community Villages Ltd* v. *Pullen* [2007] EWHC 1330; [2007] NPC 71, at [141], *per* Morgan J (on this case, 2.13).
28 On 'relational contracts' see the essays in D. Campbell, L. Mulcahy and S. Wheeler (eds.), *Changing Concepts of Contract* (Basingstoke, 2013) (for example, H. Beale, chapter 6); D. Campbell, 'Good Faith and the Ubiquity of the "Relational" Contract' (2014) 77 MLR 475.
29 [2013] EWHC 111 (QB); [2013] 1 All ER (Comm) 1321; [2013] 1 Lloyd's Rep 526; [2013] BLR 147, at [123], referring to the incremental technique, the tradition of individualism and uncertainty.
30 D. Campbell, 'Good Faith and the Ubiquity of the "Relational" Contract' (2014) 77 MLR 475, 490 n. 91 for extensive US references; and see L. DiMatteo, Q. Zhou, S. Saintier, K. Rowley (eds.), *Commercial Contract Law: Transatlantic Perspectives* (Cambridge, 2014), chapter 13 (by C. Knapp).

having regard to 'shared values and norms of behaviour',[31] notably the duty to avoid dishonesty,[32] but (at least in some contexts and in a restricted sense) the duty to avoid conduct which would stultify the contract.[33] In particular, he referred to 'relational' contracts which 'require a high degree of communication, cooperation and predictable performance based on mutual trust and confidence and involve expectations of loyalty which are … implicit … and necessary to give business efficacy to the arrangements'.[34] And he said: 'examples of such relational contracts might include some joint venture agreements, franchise agreements and long term distributorship agreements.'[35] Implied terms can be found on a case-by-case basis: 'the content of the duty is heavily dependent on context and is established through a process of construction of the contract, its recognition is entirely consistent with the case by case approach favoured by the common law.'[36] And he suggested that the nomenclature of 'fair dealing' should be preferred to the 'red flag' of good faith:[37]

> I see no objection, and some advantage, in describing the duty as one of good faith 'and fair dealing'. I see no objection, as the duty does not involve the court in imposing its view of what is substantively fair on the parties. What constitutes fair dealing is defined by the contract and by those standards of conduct to which, objectively, the parties must reasonably have assumed compliance without the need to state them. The advantage of including reference to fair dealing is that it draws attention to the fact that the standard is objective and distinguishes the relevant concept of good faith from other senses in which the expression 'good faith' is used.

And he concluded this stimulating analysis by suggesting that 'there is nothing unduly vague or unworkable about the concept … [because it] involves no more uncertainty than is inherent in the process of contractual interpretation.'[38]

To dispel any fear of a runaway new concept, in *Mid Essex Hospital Services NHS Trust* v. *Compass Group UK and Ireland Ltd (Trading As Medirest)* (2013) Beatson LJ (an authority on contract law, former Law Commissioner and former Professor of law in Cambridge) has attractively emphasised the incremental, objective and commercial character of the implied term of fair dealing:[39]

---

31 *Ibid.*, at [134].
32 *Ibid.*, at [135] and [136], citing, in particular, Lord Hoffmann's statement in *HIH Casualty and General Insurance Ltd* v. *Chase Manhattan Bank* [2003] 2 Lloyd's Rep 61, HL, at [68]: 'in the absence of words which expressly refer to dishonesty, it goes without saying that underlying the contractual arrangements of the parties there will be a common assumption that the persons involved will behave honestly.'
33 [2013] EWHC 111 (QB); [2013] 1 All ER (Comm) 1321; [2013] 1 Lloyd's Rep 526; [2013] BLR 147, at [139], citing 'the body of cases in which terms requiring cooperation in the performance of the contract have been implied: see *Mackay* v. *Dick* (1881) 6 App Cas 251, 263, HL.'
34 *Yam Seng* case [2013] EWHC 111 (QB); [2013] 1 All ER (Comm) 1321; [2013] 1 Lloyd's Rep 526; [2013] BLR 147, at [142].
35 *Ibid.*, at [142].
36 *Ibid.*, at [147].
37 *Ibid.*, at [151].
38 *Ibid.*, at [152].
39 [2013] EWCA Civ 200; [2013] BLR 265; [2013] CILL 3342, at [150].

[Leggatt J's] discussion [in *Yam Seng Pte Ltd* v. *International Trade Corp Ltd* (2013)] emphasised that 'what good faith requires is sensitive to context', that the test of good faith is objective in the sense that it depends on whether, in the particular context, the conduct would be regarded as commercially unacceptable by reasonable and honest people, and that its content 'is established through a process of construction of the contract'.

21.17 *Good faith as the obverse of dishonesty.* Even if good faith were introduced ('implied' or 'imposed') as a general requirement of contractual performance, this might be restricted to the *avoidance of dishonest conduct*. There is some support (besides the discussion in *Yam Seng Pte Ltd* v. *International Trade Corp Ltd* (2013) of the duty to avoid dishonesty; see preceding paragraph)[40] for the implied term that a party will refrain from dishonest conduct. In *Philips Electronique Grand Publique SA* v. *British Sky Broadcasting Ltd* (1995), Sir Thomas Bingham MR hinted that he would be prepared to find an implied term of that restricted nature (the case is considered more fully at 13.16),[41] although on the facts there had been no breach of good faith in this sense. As for express terms, as noted at 2.13, duties of 'utmost good faith' have been considered in the *Berkeley Community Villages* (2007)[42] and *CPC Group Ltd* (2010) cases[43] (and see 13.14 on Hooley's study of related expressed and implied contractual duties).[44] Lady Justice Arden, in a lecture, has suggested that the courts can give effect to clauses expressly requiring good faith. She notes that such a clause can be used as an overarching interpretative tool, a source of obligation and a means of filling gaps.[45]

7. CONCLUDING REMARKS

21.18 *The need for a measure and circumspect approach.* The brave new law of fair dealing should proceed cautiously by little steps and not in wild leaps and bounds. As suggested at 21.11 above, the case for a pre-formation general doctrine of good faith is not compelling. As for the post-formation context, the better view (see 21.15) is that a general duty of good faith would be unsettling and unhelpful.

21.19 *The implied term technique.* It should be enough that English law continues to employ the selective and fact-sensitive technique of implying terms. This approach is precise, enabling the courts to prescribe rules for specific types of transactions, 'terms implied in law', or at least recognising one-off 'terms implied in fact'. And it seems consistent with Leggatt J's dicta in

---

40   [2013] EWHC 111 (QB); [2013] 1 All ER (Comm) 1321; [2013] 1 Lloyd's Rep 526; [2013] BLR 147.
41   [1995] EMLR 472, CA.
42   [2007] EWHC 1330 (Ch); [2007] NPC 71, Morgan J.
43   *CPC Group Ltd* v. *Qatari Diar Real Estate Investment Company* [2010] EWHC 1535; [2010] NPC 74, at [237] ff, Vos J.
44   R. Hooley, 'Controlling Contractual Discretion' [2013] CLJ 65–90.
45   M. Arden, 'Coming to Terms with Good Faith' (2013) 30 JCL 199, 213, noting *McKillen* v. *Misland (Cyprus) Investments Ltd* [2013] EWCA Civ 781; and also noting H. O. Hunter, 'The Growing Uncertainty about Good Faith in American Contract Law' (2004) 20 JCL 50.

Yam Seng Pte Ltd v. *International Trade Corp Ltd* (2013) (21.16)[46] that an implied term in law of 'fair dealing' (a phrase which might be preferred to the 'red flag' of good faith)[47] should be incorporated into 'relational contracts' such as 'joint venture agreements, franchise agreements and long term distributorship agreements'.[48] As Leggatt J suggests:[49] 'What constitutes fair dealing is defined by the contract and by those standards of conduct to which, objectively, the parties must reasonably have assumed compliance without the need to state them.' A close analogy (perhaps even an example, dressed up in different language) is the decision of the House of Lords in *Malik (and Mahmud)* v. *Bank of Credit and Commerce International SA* (1998) (13.08 case (2) and 21.06) (term implied in law that employers will not destroy the relationship of confidence and trust between themselves and their employees).[50] But, as *Jani-King (GB) Ltd* v. *Pula Enterprises Ltd* (2007) shows (21.06), in ordinary commercial contracts there is no implied term that the parties will refrain 'from acting in such a way as to destroy or seriously damage the relationship of trust and confidence between them'.[51]

21.20 *The unsettling effect of a broader notion of good faith.* Adoption of good faith as a general standard or norm, applicable to all aspects of contractual performance across the gamut of contracts, would place settled rules and principles in a state of systemic uncertainty. Such a good faith 'big-bang' would provoke a spate of litigation in which established doctrine would need to be re-examined through the new prism. A long period of uncertainty would be unwelcome. New generations of judges might be seduced to 'make their mark' by experimenting with the new concept.

21.21 Cui bono? What would be the point of introducing such a contractual *grundnorm*? Litigants would expensively have to discover whether the law has been rendered more pliable. However, it is unlikely that the new concept would produce any significant change: the English courts are unlikely to change their spots. The values of commercial certainty and predictability, and the need to keep the law rooted in the ordinary or reasonable expectations of businesses and consumers, would have a salutary restraining effect upon the good faith principle. For example, English courts would surely not use the explicit concept of good faith to reverse the settled doctrine that a prospective party is not obliged to point out the other side's misapprehension concerning the nature of the proposed subject matter.[52] More generally, when one considers the range and pliability of English doctrines already embodying a notion of good faith or fair dealing, it seems

---

46 [2013] EWHC 111 (QB); [2013] 1 All ER (Comm) 1321; [2013] 1 Lloyd's Rep 526; [2013] BLR 147 (notably at [141], [144], [147], and [154]).
47 *Ibid.,* at [150].
48 *Ibid.,* at [142].
49 *Ibid.,* at [150].
50 [1998] 1 AC 20, 45–6, HL, *per* Lord Steyn.
51 [2007] EWHC 2433 (QBD); [2008] 1 Lloyd's Rep 305, at [48] ff.
52 *Smith* v. *Hughes* (1871) LR 6 QB 597; *Bell* v. *Lever Bros Ltd* [1932] AC 161, 224, HL; *BCCI* v. *Ali* [2002] 1 AC 251, HL, at [72], on which see 3.64 to 3.67.

unlikely that many cases will be differently decided if good faith were explicitly introduced as a general principle.

21.22 *English judges in the 'good faith saddle'.*[53] If good faith were introduced as a pervasive contractual requirement, but the application of this dynamic concept were entrusted solely to English judges, the new 'meta-principle' would be unlikely to cause the array of Common Law doctrines and rules, developed over centuries, to unravel. The inevitable anxiety and uncertainty experienced within the legal profession when advising their clients would outweigh the speculative benefits of such a change. Common Law doctrines and techniques, and equitable concepts already embedded in the English case law, have not proved to be petrified or infertile.

21.23 *What if the English courts were to lose control of the Common Law?* This is the real source of anxiety for the future of the Common Law system of general contract law. If English law of contract were to be placed in the hands of a supra-national court, the English system would then have lost control. Within the European judicial and law-making systems, the Common Law voice is always going to be drowned out by a civilian chorus. And the Common Law vote will often become a mere dissent. It would follow that the concept of good faith would be applied and developed, perhaps aggressively, by outsiders not attuned to the tradition of the Common Law, its peculiar methods and its values. This would lead to sustained doctrinal meltdown.

21.24 It is, therefore, to be hoped that whatever might be the fate of English law, the legal systems of Australia, Canada, Hong Kong, India, New Zealand, Pakistan, Singapore, and the other members of the Common Law 'family', will continue to develop the law of contract without the distraction of the meta-principle of good faith. Instead the technique of implied terms should be adopted (21.18 and 21.19).

QUESTIONS

(1) What does good faith mean?

(2) Should English law adopt a principle of good faith to regulate pre-formation dealings, including the conduct of negotiations?

(3) What is the significance of the English technique of implied terms as far as the good faith debate is concerned?

(4) Assess the arguments for and against adoption of a general principle of good faith to govern the operation of contracts.

(5) Should English contract lawyers be encouraged to learn new tricks? Who will pay while they are learning these tricks?

---

53   Cf *Enderby Town FC Ltd* v. *Football Association* [1971] Ch 591, 606–7, CA, *per* Lord Denning MR (referring to 'public policy', on which see 20.11).

Selected further reading

Recent case law has stimulated fresh discussion (see the works cited at n. 1 in this chapter; and for earlier discussion, see n. 2).

R. Brownsword, *Contract Law: Themes for the Twenty-First Century* (2nd edn, Oxford, 2006), chapter 5 (also R. Brownsword, in M. Furmston (ed.), *The Law of Contract* (4th edn, London, 2010), chapter 1)

H. G. Collins, 'Implied Terms: the Foundation in Good Faith and Fair Dealing' (2014) 67 CLP 297–331

M. Furmston and G. J. Tolhurst, *Contract Formation: Law and Practice* (Oxford, 2010), chapters 12 and 13 (pre-contractual dealings)

H. MacQueen, 'Good Faith', in H. MacQueen and R. Zimmermann (eds.), *European Contract Law: Scots and South African Perspectives* (Edinburgh, 2006), chapter 2

E. McKendrick, *Contract Law: Text, Cases and Materials* (6th edn, Oxford, 2014), chapter 15

Lord Steyn, 'Contract Law: Fulfilling the Reasonable Expectations of Honest Men' (1997) 113 LQR 433

S. Whittaker, 'Good Faith, Implied Terms and Commercial Contracts' (2013) 129 LQR 463

R. Zimmermann and S. Whittaker (eds.), *Good Faith in European Contract Law* (Cambridge, 2000)

Chapter contents

22

Codification

1. INTRODUCTION

22.01 Summary of main points

(1) Most English contractual doctrines are dominated by case law.

(2) Case law is a mixed blessing: judicial decision-making is flexible, whereas legislation is fixed; but English decisions are often long and difficult to unravel; the non-abstract and pragmatic strength of English contract law derives from its having been developed in response to real cases.

(3) Compiling a code would be an occasion for spring-cleaning and innovation. However, a new code does not remain free from judicial glosses for long.

(4) Perhaps the best option would be an English contract code which is non-mandatory, but capable of being chosen as the applicable law by parties. This would be especially attractive for 'cross-border' transactions to which at least one party is foreign (neither resident, registered as a company, present, nor carrying on business within England).

2. THE CONTROVERSY CONCERNING A CODE

22.02 *Dominance of case law in English contract law.* Students of English contract law are expected to learn many leading cases, and indeed casebooks bulging with minor ones. They soon learn the characteristic 'string' effect of cases: that a leading case has a number of smaller decisions, which establish a line of cases. Most English contractual doctrines are dominated by case law, notably offer and acceptance, consideration, intent to create legal relations, mistake, misrepresentation, duress, undue influence, unconscionability or exploitation, certainty, breach, frustration, interpretation, remedies and illegality.

22.03 *The fine texture of the Common Law.* The long tradition of English case law has produced a finely meshed set of decisions covering most of the obvious points, many of the less obvious ones, and even some of the really bizarre ones (such as the contractual liability of those who supply defective remedies for influenza,[1] or who fail to ensure that pig-nut hoppers are properly ventilated, resulting in the death of 254 pigs[2]).

22.04 *Gaps often capable of being filled by predicting judicial responses.* There are lacunae and loose ends within this body of case law. But most of these are quite trifling. Or, if the gap initially looks quite large, in practice one can often predict quite confidently how, say, an experienced adjudicator, such as a Commercial Court judge, would decide the matter.[3]

22.05 *Contexts where statute predominates.* Admittedly, statute rather than case law is the dominant source in some areas of English contract law.[4] Examples are: the conferring of rights upon third parties by the Contracts (Rights of Third Parties) Act 1999 (7.22), the control of unfair or unreasonable exclusion clauses by the Unfair Contract Terms Act 1977 (15.07 and 15.08) and the control of unfair clauses in consumer contracts by Part 2 of the Consumer Rights Bill (formerly, the Unfair Terms in Consumer Contracts Regulations 1999) (15.28).

22.06 *Contexts where statute and Common Law are intertwined.* There have been several incursions of statute into fields which nevertheless remain dominated by judicial law, notably, the Law Reform (Frustrated Contracts) Act 1943 (16.21), the Law Reform (Contributory Negligence) Act 1945 (18.23) and the Misrepresentation Act 1967 (9.20). These statutes are relatively minor. But they have become problematic.[5] They have not been successfully implanted within the flesh of the Common Law. These provisions have reminded us that judicial decision-making is flexible but legislation is fixed, and Parliament's aims are not always obvious. The result is a tension between pliable (judicial) and inflexible (legislative) law.

22.07 *A fresh start.* A code is composed of a set of legislative provisions.[6] It is normally quite systematic and relatively succinct (although the text might be amplified by comments and

---

1   *Carlill* v. *Carbolic Smoke Ball Co.* [1893] 1 QB 256, CA.

2   *Parsons Ltd* v. *Uttley Ingham & Co.* [1978] QB 791, CA; the Common Law has been described by Tony Allen, of the Centre for Effective Dispute Resolution (CEDR) in London, as 'a coral reef made up of the dead bodies of litigants (and their bankrupted estates)'.

3   On the quality of Commercial Court judges, see N. Andrews, *English Civil Justice: Progress and Remedies: Nagoya Lectures* (Tokyo, 2007), 3–03.

4   On the Victorian flurry of codification of particular transactions (Bills of Exchange Act 1882, the Factors Act 1889, the Partnership Act 1890, the Sale of Goods Act 1893 and later the Marine Insurance Act 1906), A. Rodger, 'The Codification of Commercial Law in Victorian England' (1992) 108 LQR 570.

5   Generally, A. Burrows, 'The Relationship between Common Law and Statute in the Law of Obligations' (2012) 128 LQR 232–59.

6   M. Arden, [1997] CLJ 516; H. G. Collins, 'Why Europe Needs a Civil Code', in *Liber Amicorum Guido Alpa: National Private Law Systems* (London, 2007), 259; H. G. Collins, *The European Civil Code: The Way Forward* (Cambridge, 2008); R. Goode, 'Removing the Obstacles to Commercial Law Reform' (2007) 123 LQR 602–17 (and earlier 'The Codification of Commercial Law' (1988) 14 *Monash University Law Review* 135); Lord Falconer, speech, www.dca.gov.uk/speeches/2005/lc150905.htm; A. Hartkamp and C. Joustra (eds.), *Towards a European Civil Code* (3rd edn, Nijmegen, 2004); H. Kronke, (2005) *Loyola of Los Angeles Law Review* 287–99; O. Lando, *Principles of European Contract Law and UNIDROIT Principles: Similarities, Differences and Perspectives* (Rome, 2002); Lord Mance, 'Is Europe Aiming to Civilise the Common Law?' (Chancery Bar Lecture, Lincoln's Inn, 27 March 2006); W. Swain, 'Contract codification in Australia ... ' (2014) 36 Sydney LR 131–49 (www.austlii.edu.au/au/journals/SydLRev/2014/5.pdf); A. Tettenborn,

illustrations, as in the case of the American Law Institute's Restatements). Code drafters can start with clean sheets of paper and produce a pleasingly coherent set of provisions, delineating categories, subcategories, rules and subrules, and identifying overarching principles. The author has participated in this process, in Rome, in the field of civil procedure (the American Law Institute/UNIDROIT's *Principles of Transnational Civil Procedure*, 2000 to 2004,[7] on which the author has commented in 2009,[8] and extensions of this project jointly sponsored by UNIDROIT and the European Law Institute, begun in 2014). There is no doubt that compiling a code would be an occasion for spring-cleaning, perhaps even for major innovation. Lumber could be jettisoned. A code would be up to date (however fleetingly) and portable.[9] Of course, in the age of the Internet and memory sticks, physical weight has become no real problem. Instead, the problem is the 'tsunami' of electronic information.

22.08   However, the portents are not favourable. One of the aims of the 1998 English civil procedure code (the Civil Procedure Rules 1998) was to achieve 'simplicity'.[10] In fact, it has quickly evolved into a lush and complex code, longer than its predecessor.[11] Furthermore, a clean new code does not remain free from judicial glosses for long. Experience in codified systems has shown that judicial decisions by higher courts soon become an important appendage to the legislative text. In some instances, notably the French law of tort, the giant edifice of the law rests on the support of a handful of rather vacuous provisions in the code. And so even if England and Wales were to adopt a code for contract law, it would not be long before practitioners were rummaging in the case law to find out 'what the code really means'.

22.09   *Reluctance to abandon the case law tradition.* Some influential English judges and jurists are hostile to the notion of codifying contract law. This attitude cannot be dismissed as mere complacency, conservatism or sentimental attachment to hard law painfully absorbed over decades of study and practice. Instead, the underpinning considerations are as follows.

First, the current law works tolerably well, so why try to fix it? England and Wales is a unified jurisdiction. One can contrast the USA, where there are many State jurisdictions

'Codifying Contracts –An Idea Whose Time Has Come?' (2014) 67 CLP 273–95; S. Vogenauer (ed.), *The Harmonisation of European Contract Law* (Oxford, 2005); *Clifford Chance Survey on European Contract Law* (London, April 2005); N. Andrews, 'Le Droit Anglais: a-t-il besoin d'un Code?', in *Essays in Honour of Konstantinos D. Kerameus* (Athens and Brussels, 2009), 19–26. A recent codification of contract law (the 'contract law' code promulgated by the Dubai International Financial Centre), drawing on English law, but interspersed with material copied from UNIDROIT's *Principles of International Commercial Contracts (2010)* (see the examples collected at 22.18), is available at www.unidroit.org/english/princi ples/contracts/principles2010/integralversionprinciples2010-e.pdf.

7   Accessible   at   www.unidroit.org/english/principles/civilprocedure/ali-unidroitprinciples-e.pdf.   Also published as *ALI/UNIDROIT: Principles of Transnational Civil Procedure* (Cambridge, 2006).

8   N. Andrews, 'The Modern Procedural Synthesis: The American Law Institute and UNIDROIT's "Principles and Rules of Transnational Civil Procedure"' (2008) 164 *Revista de Processo* 109 (Brazil), also published in (2009) *Tijdschrift voor Civiele Rechtspleging* 52 (Netherlands).

9   Cf this practical problem in nineteenth-century colonial administration: Indian Contract Act 1872: text at 22.14.

10   N. Andrews, *English Civil Justice: Progress and Remedies: Nagoya Lectures* (Shinzan Sha Publishers, Tokyo, 2007), chapter 2.

11   See www.justice.gov.uk/courts/procedure-rules/civil.

within a federal entity. Americans receive nationwide guidance from the 'Restatement of Contracts' and from the 'Uniform Commercial Code'.

Secondly, the pragmatic strength of English contract law derives from its having been laid down and refined in response to real cases. It is not abstract and over-intellectual doctrine, the lucubration of law professors. Instead, the Common Law consists of propositions 'hammered out on the anvil' of adversarial debate in the courtroom.[12] Forensic debate can be intense. In the highest courts, debates between counsel can occupy days, involving meticulous reference to dozens of precedent decisions, both English and foreign. Furthermore, English judges are not snatched from the lecture halls and placed in the highest judicial chamber, as happens in some jurisdictions (although some English judges were briefly academics before entering practice and acting for clients).[13] All English judges have had experience, often over several decades, as practitioners, mostly as barristers.

Thirdly, the courts, especially the appellate courts, have been slow to permit doctrines to emerge or develop in ways which would render English law uncertain[14] or substantively out of step with the reasonable expectations of business people. Proof of the law's attractiveness is that English contract law is often chosen by 'transnational' contracting parties as the applicable law.[15] Negotiation of commercial contracts and resolution of disputes arising from them are big international business. London lawyers take a good slice of that business. Finally, it is not unreasonable for English lawyers to be resistant to academically inspired pan-European projects. One might tolerate, even admire, British loyalty to the political and socio-economic programme of the European Union. But this continental commitment is to be weighed against the benefits of preserving the precious and remarkable legacy of the Common Law. More generally, is it not preferable that competition between legal systems should continue, rather than be stifled by adherence to worldwide or European uniformity?

3. ENGLISH PRECEDENTS – AN UNGODLY JUMBLE?

22.10 *The accidents of litigation.* The system of Common Law decision-making is haphazard. It depends on the adventitious selection by claimants and appellants of disputes and issues to be litigated and taken on appeal. Indeed, this led Lord Radcliffe to observe that the House of Lords (now the Supreme Court) has little real opportunity to keep lower court decisions under review.[16] Furthermore, the true rule can remain uncertain – at least at its edges – for

---

12   Cf Lord Steyn in *Attorney-General* v. *Blake* [2001] 1 AC 268, 291, HL: 'Exceptions to the general principle that there is no remedy for disgorgement of profits against a contract breaker are best hammered out on the anvil of concrete cases.' Generally on that decision, see 18.30 ff.

13   Modern judges who have held academic positions for more than four years in British universities include: Lord Goff (Lincoln College, Oxford), Baroness Hale (University of Manchester), Lord Hoffmann (University College, Oxford), Lord Rodger (New College, Oxford), Sir Patrick Elias (Pembroke College, Cambridge) and Sir Jack Beatson (Oxford and Cambridge); with the exception of Beatson, appointment to the High Court occurred after they had already ceased to hold academic positions; some judges have held visiting professorships, notably Lord (Lawrence) Collins and the former Lord Justice, Sir Robin Jacob.

14   A possible exception is *Attorney-General* v. *Blake* [2001] 1 AC 268, 291, HL: see 18.30 ff.

15   N. Andrews, *English Civil Justice: Progress and Remedies: Nagoya Lectures* (Tokyo, 2007), 3–06.

16   Lord Radcliffe (1973) 36 MLR 559, reviewing L. Blom-Cooper and G. Drewry, *Final Appeal: A Study of the House of Lords in its Judicial Capacity* (Oxford, 1972).

many years, even for decades. A good example is the eventual 'cleansing of the Common Law' concerning compensation for late payment of debts (see the *Sempra* case (2007)[17] at 18.01 at (4)); but a counter-example is the baroque mix of Common Law and Equity encrusting the rule in *Pinnel's Case* (1602),[18] a rule reluctantly followed by the House of Lords in *Foakes* v. *Beer* (1884)[19] (5.30 ff), exposition of which requires careful analysis of an intricate network of rules and exceptions.

22.11 *The flow of precedents.* But the problem just mentioned should not be exaggerated. There is enough litigation before the English High Court and Court of Appeal to keep the Common Law system revolving and refreshed (although Cartwright has noted the relative paucity of contract cases proceeding to the Supreme Court).[20] The arbitration system has yet to stifle this flow.[21]

22.12 *Judicial prolixity.* The main problem is over-supply of information. A balance must be struck between judgments which are inadequately reasoned and too terse, cryptic and formulaic, and decisions (especially when multiple judgments are given by an appellate court)[22] which are too long and difficult to unravel.[23] The law of contract in England fails to satisfy any reasonable criteria of accessibility and transparency. The process of working out the substance of the rule can occupy people in hours of reading. Discovering the law is a time-consuming, skilled and specialist craft, and the answers are not always rock-solid. In the nineteenth century appellate judgments were quite short. They became longer during the twentieth century. And, as every modern author knows, cut-and-paste word processing promotes prolixity. Even when the modern Court of Appeal or Supreme Court gives a single judgment, that decision is often very lengthy.

---

17   [2007] UKHL 34; [2008] 1 AC 561.

18   (1602) 5 Co Rep 117a (entire Court of Common Pleas).

19   (1884) 9 App Cas 605, HL.

20   J. Cartwright, 'The English Law of Contract: Time for Review?' (2009) 17 *European Review of Private Law* 155, 162 n. 29, noting that, in 2007, only seven House of Lords decisions concerned substantive contract law.

21   The conduit is section 69 of the Arbitration Act 1996, empowering the High Court to grant permission for appeals relating to points of English substantive law, unless section 69 has been excluded by the parties; on section 69, *Andrews on Civil Processes* (Cambridge, 2013), vol. 2, *Arbitration and Mediation*, 18.67 ff.

22   On that issue, *ibid.*, vol. 1, *Court Proceedings*, 29.46 ff.

23   M. Arden, 'Judgment Writing: Are Shorter Judgments Achievable?' (2012) 128 LQR 515–20; P. Bull, 'Judgment Writing: an Antipodean Response' (2013) 129 LQR 7–10; *Wuhan Guoyu etc.* v. *Emporiki Bank of Greece SA* [2012] EWCA Civ 1629; [2013] 1 All ER (Comm) 1191; [2012] 2 CLC 986; [2013] BLR 74; [2013] CILL 3300, at [22] *per* Longmore LJ: 'The judge decided that the document was a traditional guarantee and not an "on-demand" bond. I mean no disrespect to the judge whatever when I say that the judgment is an exhausting document. Entirely understandably he found it necessary, in order to resolve this question of construction, to cite no less than 20 authorities and deliver a judgment of 93 paragraphs. Beatson J needed to cite a similar number of authorities in *Meritz* v. *Jan de Nul* [2011] 2 CLC 842. But something has surely gone wrong if this comparatively simple question of construction requires such lengthy consideration. It is a problem of our system of precedent, that as more and more cases get decided, it seems to be necessary for judges at first instance to consider each case and determine how near or how far the document in question differs from the document construed in each past case. The commercial community deserves better than this, if better can be done.'

The sources of prolixity are:

detailed narration of facts and evidence;

minute and exhaustive analysis of earlier decisions, with copious citation of earlier judicial formulations, so that each new judgment becomes an anthology of decades or decisions rather than a crisp and accessible distillation of rule, principle, exception, qualification, trends and leading factors (but as every author knows, crispness takes longer);

unwillingness to encapsulate, perhaps out of fear of over-simplification, perhaps because of lack of time (the pressures on judges, notably in the busy parts of the High Court and in the Court of Appeal, have become very considerable);

it is also a judicial convention to address in detail all the submissions on points of law made by counsel, even if some (sometimes all) of these are very weak.

On appeal, much of this factual exposition legal analysis is repeated by other judges within the majority.

For example, in *Alfred McAlpine Construction Ltd* v. *Panatown Ltd* (2001)[24] (7.20) concerning procedural steps arising from breach of a building contract, the House of Lords' judgments run to 46,000 words. In the *Etridge* case (2002),[25] the leading case on the equitable doctrine of undue influence (11.23 ff), the speeches run to 53,000 words, and 374 paragraphs.

Even if the applicable law is statute, English decisions tend to consider other leading judicial discussion of the relevant provision, or its predecessors. Furthermore, even first instance decisions in commercial or public law are often quite lengthy. A trial judge has to ascertain the facts and explain how conflicting points of evidence have been assessed and resolved. The judge must also address each of the arguments presented on the law. These professional responsibilities are reinforced by the desire not to reduce one's chances of promotion by acquiring a reputation for 'cutting corners' in the analysis of precedent decisions.

This explains, for example, the lengthy first instance decisions, containing detailed examinations of precedent decisions in, for example, *Tito* v. *Waddell (No. 2)* (1977: 18.11),[26] *JP Morgan Chase* v. *Springwell Navigation Corp* (2008: 15.15),[27] the 'Bank Charges litigation' (2008–9: 15.36 and 19.08),[28] and the 'Chelsea Barracks' case (2010) (2.11 and 2.13).[29] Electronic and paper reported decisions of the superior court now contain paragraph numbering. This change occurred during the last decade or so. This simple device has enabled textbook writers to identify the salient portions of important Common Law authorities, and it has broken the tradition of relying on the authoritative pagination of the Law Reports.

24 [2001] 1 AC 518, HL; on this litigious 'saga', E. McKendrick, 'The Common Law at Work: The Saga of *Alfred McAlpine Construction Ltd* v. *Panatown Ltd*' (2003) 3(2) *Oxford University Commonwealth Law Journal* 145–80.

25 *Royal Bank of Scotland* v. *Etridge (No. 2)* [2002] 2 AC 773, HL.

26 [1977] Ch 106, Sir Robert Megarry V-C (852 paragraphs and 131,000 words).

27 [2008] EWHC 1186, Gloster J (742 paragraphs); Gloster J had the misfortune to hear more than one monster case at first instance (for a cause célèbre involving Russian 'oligarchs', an unsuccessful claim in the tort of intimidation, *Berezovsky* v. *Abramovich* [2012] EWHC 2463 (Comm), Gloster J, and, earlier in this litigation, *Berezovsky* v. *Abramovich* [2011] EWCA Civ 153; [2011] 1 WLR 2290).

28 *Abbey National plc* v. *Office of Fair Trading* [2008] EWHC 875 (Comm); [2008] 2 All ER (Comm) 625, Andrew Smith J (450 paragraphs); (final appeal: [2009] UKSC 6; [2010] 1 AC 696).

29 *CPC Group Ltd* v. *Qatari Diar Real Estate Investment Company* [2010] EWHC 1535; [2010] NPC 74 (320 paragraphs).

22.13 *The Common Law is rescued by leading textbooks.* Although judges have perhaps despaired of restating the law crisply in their judgments, textbook writers have risen to this challenge. Thus, *Chitty*,[30] a highly detailed work, bridges the communication gap between the law reports and those seeking a quick answer. After all, most practitioners have less than a day to find the legal answer (or even an approximate one) to a commercial client's demand for rapid advice.

4. ATTEMPTS AT CODIFYING ENGLISH CONTRACT LAW

22.14 The Indian Contract Act 1872,[31] a codification of the Common Law's general principles of contract law, continues to apply in the Indian subcontinent. It has been supplemented by the local courts and parallel case law development in London (and elsewhere in the Common Law world). It is interesting that this legislation crossed the Indian Ocean and was adopted in some of the former British colonies in East Africa (for example, in Kenya).

22.15 The Scottish and English Law Commissions combined to produce a draft Contract Code (the project ran from 1965 to 1973).[32] Treitel, the greatest living contract scholar in the UK, was heavily involved.[33] The Scots pulled out in 1973.[34] The project was eventually 'suspended'. The draft (not yet cast into statutory form) was published much later, but in Italy. The foreign place of publication is significant: the modern codification project was sent into exile, like Ovid or Napoleon (but see the Dubai International Financial Centre's codification which is based substantially, although not exclusively, on English contract law).[35]

Writing nearly thirty years after the collapse of this project, Treitel expressed no regret that the English Law Commission's project had not come to fruition:[36]

> In retrospect, [the decision to suspend the project indefinitely] seems to have been a sound one. Codification of contract law faces a dilemma. In Common Law countries that have codes of . . . contract law (such as India and the Field Code States in the United States) the vague language of the relevant codes has done little, if anything, to improve the 'clarity and accessibility' of contract law which were the Law Commission's declared aims in launching the project. A more precise and detailed Code along the lines envisaged in the Law Commission's Seventh Annual Report in 1972 might have helped to promote these objectives, but only . . . at the expense of an unacceptable degree of rigidity.

---

30   *Chitty on Contracts* (31st edn, London, 2012).
31   On William Macpherson, the main architect, see C. MacMillan, *Mistakes in Contract Law* (Oxford, 2010), 108 ff.
32   Harvey McGregor QC, *Contract Code: Drawn up on Behalf of the English Law Commission* (Milan, 1993); J. Cartwright, 'The English Law of Contract: Time for Review?' (2009) 17 *European Review of Private Law* 155, 168 ff.
33   G. H. Treitel, *Some Landmarks of Twentieth Century Contract Law* (Oxford, 2002), 4–9.
34   *Ibid.*, at 8.
35   This codification of the Common Law rules of contract is available at www.difc.ae/laws-regulations/ (Dubai International Financial Centre).
36   G. H. Treitel, *Some Landmarks of Twentieth Century Contract Law* (Oxford, 2002), 8.

And he concluded:

> On balance ... the decision to 'suspend' the process was indeed a fortunate one; development by judicial activity, and, where appropriate, by legislation reforming specific parts of the subject, has proved to be the preferable option.

22.16 Distinct from general contract codes, there are the mini-codes on specific English contracts: the Bills of Exchange Act 1882, the Partnership Act 1890, the Sale of Goods Act 1893 (now 1979), the Marine Insurance Act 1906 and the Arbitration Act 1996 (the 1882, 1893 and 1906 Acts were drafted by Chalmers). For the most part, the legislature has here codified parts of the Common Law: before their enactment, the law consisted of a mosaic of judicial decisions. Thus, Lord Mustill has commented on how the English law of arbitration, before the 1996 enactment, could only be deduced by reading a mountain of cases.[37]

22.17 *Uniform law projects.* There is a great deal of formal written law in the field of transnational carriage of goods.[38] These are examples of internationally agreed 'uniform' law which have been incorporated into English law.

22.18 *Sincerest form of flattery.* The Dubai International Financial Centre ('DIFC') has produced a codification of commercial contract law which is based substantially, although not exclusively, on English contract law, and which is intended to be applied in arbitration or other litigation conducted in Dubai.[39] This is not 'English law', but rather English law as refined, modified and codified by the advisors to the Dubai authorities (the advisors and draftsmen were English experts). However, both in form and in content, the DIFC code might portend the future in England. Some of this code's provisions are adopted verbatim from UNIDROIT's *Principles of International Commercial Contracts* (2010);[40] for example, the provisions concerning points left open by the parties (DIFC, Article 27; UNIDROIT, Article 2.1.14), price determination (DIFC, Article 62; UNIDROIT, Article 5.1.7), implied terms (DIFC, Article 57; UNIDROIT, Article 5.1.2) and interpretation (DIFC, Articles 49 to 55; UNIDROIT, Article 4.1 to 4.7).

5. AN OPT-IN CONTRACT CODE

22.19 *Enhancing the law's accessibility within the foreign market.* Perhaps pressure to produce a blending of Common Law and various civil law traditions might one day prove irresistible. The present signs, however, are that within England and Wales there is no imminent wish to abandon the contract rules of the Common Law in favour of a code. But what if the position were to change? In what way might a contract code be introduced? I would suggest that there are five possibilities, but only the fifth is attractive and feasible:

37 M. Mustill and S. Boyd, *Commercial Arbitration* (London, 2001) (and earlier editions).
38 For English legislation incorporating such international shipping conventions, see *Treitel* (13th edn, London, 2011), 7–093 n. 496.
39 Available at www.difc.ae/laws-regulations/ (Dubai International Financial Centre).
40 3rd edition, 2010, text and comment, is available at: www.unidroit.org/english/principles/contracts/principles2010/integralversionprinciples2010-e.pdf.

(1) A *global contract code*, perhaps influenced by UNIDROIT's *Principles of International Commercial Contracts* (2010).[41] But it is highly unlikely that English lawyers will favour renunciation of the Common Law inheritance in the name of global harmonisation.

(2) A *European code*, perhaps based on either of the non-binding European codes already drafted (see 23.01 for references). Such a code might become mandatory for commercial or consumer contracts. There are well-organised juristic movements which have been promoting the concept of European harmonisation, especially in the field of private law (see material cited at 23.01). The Common Law has become besieged. Again, it is highly unlikely that English lawyers will support renunciation of the Common Law system of contract law in the name of harmonisation.

(3) An *international Common Law code*, representing the synthesis of English, Australian, Canadian, New Zealand, US and other Common Law jurisdictions (such a code might be mandatory in the relevant jurisdictions). But the USA is legally autonomous; the Commonwealth nations have become independent-minded members of a Common Law diaspora; final appeal to the Privy Council in London, the umbilical cord, has been severed in nearly all instances (no such appeals now take place from Australia, Canada, Hong Kong or New Zealand). In short, the historical ties of Common Law kinship are much weaker than the competing forces of nationalism and geographical distance. It is quite unlikely that such a project would capture the Common Law imagination. The Common Law jurisdictions are now disparate and scarcely connected.[42]

(4) A purely *English* contract code which is *mandatory* (although perhaps restricted either to consumer or non-consumer matters). But this idea was rejected by the Law Commission (22.15) in 1973 because there appeared to be no overall advantage in freezing judicial development of contractual doctrine at Common Law.

(5) A purely *English* contract code, which is *(initially) non-mandatory*, and thus not binding on anyone unless both parties to the relevant transaction have opted to adopt it; such a code, therefore, would be capable of being chosen as the applicable law by parties, notably by those engaged in commerce. It seems likely that this facility would be especially attractive for cross-border transactions to which at least one party is 'foreign' (neither resident, registered as a company, present, nor carrying on business within England). It will be common for the same transaction to stipulate that the English courts will have jurisdiction or that disputes will be arbitrated before a tribunal having its seat in England. (If successful, such a code, although initially optional, could be made mandatory and such a decision might be made in order to prime the adjudication system, if there are insufficient examples of the code being adopted by parties).

22.20 It would be interesting (not least for the drafting team involved) for England to experiment with the last possibility (point (5) in the previous paragraph). English lawyers should keep an open mind to the possibility of: improving substantive law; rendering it still more up to date and predictable; jettisoning some of its doctrinal baggage; re-examining some of its rigidities; refining some of its rules; and taking advantage of other legal systems' good ideas.

---

41 *Ibid.*
42 M. Furmston, 'A Study of Contract Law in the Major Commonwealth Jurisdictions' (2014) 31 JCL 61, 67ff, but advocating greater communication.

22.21 The author has commented elsewhere on the importance of maintaining resort to the Commercial Court in London.[43] The contract code could be frequently updated. Commentaries would follow. These would link the contract code with both case law developments and pre-existing case law.[44] In this way, the foreign litigant would receive the benefit of being able readily 'to look up a point of English contract law'. This might enhance English law's position in the global marketplace.

QUESTIONS

(1) What is a code, and what are its advantages? Compare the advantages (if any) and disadvantages of the English precedent system.
(2) How important has legislation been within the general part of English contract law?
(3) Has English contract law been codified in any part of the world? Why not in England?
(4) What are the options for an English contract code?

Selected further reading

M. Arden, 'Time for an English Commercial Code?' [1997] CLJ 516

J. Cartwright, 'The English Law of Contract: Time for Review?' (2009) 17 *European Review of Private Law* 155, 168 ff

R. Goode, 'Removing the Obstacles to Commercial Law Reform' (2007) 122 LQR 602–17

H. McGregor, *Contract Code: Drawn up on Behalf of the English Law Commission* (Milan, 1993)

A. Rodger, 'The Codification of Commercial Law in Victorian England' (1992) 108 LQR 570

A. Tettenborn, 'Codifying Contracts – An Idea Whose Time Has Come?' (2014) 67 CLP 273–95

G. H. Treitel, *Some Landmarks of Twentieth Century Contract Law* (Oxford, 2002), 4–9

A non-English codification of the English rules of contract is available at www.difc.ae/laws-regulations/ (Dubai International Financial Centre).

---

43 N. Andrews, *English Civil Justice: Progress and Remedies: Nagoya Lectures* (Tokyo, 2007), chapter 3; on the question of 'proof of foreign law in English civil proceedings', *ibid.*, at chapter 5, and referring to other literature.

44 Lord Diplock, however, considered that the English do not understand that a code requires abandonment of all that precedes: remarks in his Green Lecture, 'The Law of Contract in the Eighties' (1981) 15 *University of British Columbia Law Review* 371; however, compare Lord Halsbury LC's remark, in *Vagliano Bros* v. *Bank of England* [1891] AC 107, HL, concerning the need to treat codification as a fresh start.

Chapter contents

23

International and European 'soft law' codes: lessons for English law?

1. INTRODUCTION

23.01 Summary of main points

There are various 'soft law codes' (completed, subject to periodical revision, in draft, or merely contemplated), of which these are the most visible:[1]

(1) the global 'commercial' contract code, UNIDROIT's *Principles of International Commercial Contracts* (2010);[2]

(2) 'PECL', *'Principles of European Contract Law'*, composed by the (Lando) Commission for European Contract Law;[3]

(3) the 'ECC', the draft 'European Code of Contracts', composed by the Academy of European private law specialists, under the direction of Giuseppe Gandolfi;

(4) 'DCFR', *Draft Common Frame of Reference*, prepared by the 'Study Group on a European Civil Code' and the 'Research Group on EC Private Law (Acquis Group)';

---

1   Generally on the European soft-law and EU law initiatives, C. Twigg-Flesner, *The Europeanisation of Contract Law* (2nd edn, Abingdon, 2013); and for a global perspective, M. Faure and André Van der Walt (eds.), *Globalization and Private Law: The Way Forward* (Cheltenham, 2010).

2   3rd edition, 2010, text and comment, is available at: www.unidroit.org/english/principles/contracts/prin ciples2010/integralversionprinciples2010-e.pdf. M. J. Bonell has for many years been a leading force within the UNIDROIT organisation and has had a remarkable influence upon this influential work; see also M. J. Bonell, 'Do We Need a Global Commercial Code?' (2000–2003) vol. V, *Revue de droit uniforme (Uniform Law Review)* 469–81; M. J. Bonell (ed.), *The UNIDROIT Principles in Practice: Case Law and Bibliography on the UNIDROIT Principles of International Commercial Contracts* (2nd edn, 2006); S. Vogenauer and J. Kleinheisterkamp (eds.), *Commentary on the UNIDROIT Principles of International Commercial Contracts* (Oxford, 2009) (antedating the third edition of the UNIDROIT principles, 2010). See also observations by M. Furmston, (2014) 31 JCL 61, 65–6.

3   O. Lando and H. Beale (eds.), *Principles of European Contract Law* (The Hague, 2000); H. G. Collins, *The European Civil Code: The Way Forward* (Cambridge, 2008).

(5) 'CESL', *Common European Sales Law*, a proposal for an 'optional instrument'.[4] The ECC, soft-law code (3), is in part a revision of code (2).[5]

23.02 As listed above, there are various 'soft law codes'. Each code contains rules differing from the Common Law. None is binding in any State. However, the intellectual and 'transnational' weight of these remarkable projects cannot be ignored. On this, the French scholar Bénédicte Fauvarque-Cosson comments:[6] 'In carrying out its mission, European scholarship does not have the pretention of replacing the legislator. At best, it will act as a guide, sometimes to be followed, sometimes disregarded. This form of contribution is one of a series of initiatives which aim to develop a true common legal culture in Europe.'

Hector MacQueen (2014) has succinctly chronicled these developments;[7] and there are other summaries of these projects in the essay by Bénédicte Fauvarque-Cosson, 'The Contribution of European Jurists in the Field of European Contract Law' (all four projects),[8] of projects (1) and (4) in Stefan Vogenauer's study (2010);[9] and on all these developments in Mel Kenny's study (2014).[10] Another source of harmonised law is the Vienna Convention on the International Sale of Goods ('CISG'),[11] which has not been ratified by the United Kingdom.

As for (1), the UNIDROIT principles are international, as distinct from (merely) European; and their emphasis is upon commercial contracts, and not consumer relations.

4   H. MacQueen, 'Europeanisation of Contract Law and the Proposed Common European Sales Law', in L. DiMatteo, Q. Zhou, S. Saintier, K. Rowley (eds.), *Commercial Contract Law: Transatlantic Perspectives* (Cambridge, 2014), chapter 21; S. Whittaker, 'The Proposed "Common European Sales Law": Legal Framework and the Agreement of the Parties' (2012) 75 MLR 578; English Law Commission and Scottish Law Commission, 'An Optional Common European Sales Law … Advice to the UK Government' (2011) (http://law commission.justice.gov.uk/docs/Common_European_Sales_Law_Summary.pdf).

5   *Principles, Definitions and Model Rules of European Private Law Draft Common Frame of Reference*, C. von Bar and E. Clive (eds.) (6 vols., Oxford, 2010); H. Eidenmüller, F. Faust, H. C. Grigoleit, N. Jansen, G. Wagner and R. Zimmermann, 'The Common Frame of Reference for European Private Law – Policy Choices and Codification Problems' (2008) 28 OJLS 659–708.

6   B. Fauvarque-Cosson, 'The Contribution of European Jurists in the Field of European Contract Law', in *Liber Amicorum Guido Alpa: National Private Law Systems* (London, 2007), 363, 368–9.

7   H. MacQueen, 'Europeanisation of Contract Law and the Proposed Common European Sales Law' in L. DiMatteo, Q. Zhou, S. Saintier, K. Rowley (eds.), *Commercial Contract Law: Transatlantic Perspectives* (Cambridge, 2014), chapter 21, at 530–1.

8   B. Fauvarque-Cosson, 'The Contribution of European Jurists in the Field of European Contract Law', in *Liber Amicorum Guido Alpa: National Private Law Systems* (London, 2007), 363, 365; J. Cartwright, 'The English Law of Contract: Time for Review?' (2009) *European Review of Private Law* 155, 17–32.

9   S. Vogenauer, 'Common Frame of Reference and UNIDROIT Principles of International Commercial Contracts: Coexistence, Competition, or Overkill of Soft Law?' (2010) 6 *European Review of Contract Law* issue 6; and http://ssrn.com/abstract=1581352

10   M. Kenny, 'The (D)CFR Initiative and Consumer Unfair Terms', in L. DiMatteo, Q. Zhou, S. Saintier, K. Rowley (eds.), *Commercial Contract Law: Transatlantic Perspectives* (Cambridge, 2014), chapter 15.

11   Generally on that instrument (which has been adopted by nearly 80 nations), L. DiMatteo, 'Harmonization of International Sales Law', in L. DiMatteo, Q. Zhou, S. Saintier, K. Rowley (eds.), *Commercial Contract Law: Transatlantic Perspectives* (Cambridge, 2014), chapter 22 (for details of ratifying nations, *ibid.*, at n. 46); and in the same volume, D. Saidov, chapter 18.

As for (2) Fauvarque-Cosson notes that the ECC code 'purports less to promote the single market . . . It remains faithful to the civil law tradition, in particular to the humanist ideals found in the French tradition.'

As for (3), 'PECL', Fauvarque-Cosson comments: 'The "principles", largely inspired by the laws of different Member States, were elaborated by comparing national laws. They are drafted using terms . . . so precise and structured that they are more akin to a set of rules ready to be introduced into a Civil Code.'

As for (4), the DCFR, H. Eidenmüller and colleagues comment: 'Notwithstanding its unwieldy name, the text is nothing less than the draft of the central components [not confined to contract law] of a European Civil Code.'[12]

As for (5), 'CESL', Hector MacQueen explains: 'it takes the form of an "optional instrument", meaning that it is a set of rules applying to sale of goods and supply of digital content contracts that the parties can choose to govern their particular transaction.'[13] The proposed Regulation will be 'directly applicable to Member States and become part of their domestic laws, operating alongside those laws insofar as it does not supplant them'.[14] But it will be confined to cross-border transactions in which the vendor is a trader, although the other party need not be a consumer.[15]

In the face of this renaissance of European and global private law scholarship, it would be insular for English lawyers simply to dismiss these projects. But many English lawyers are wary of the legal system succumbing to harmonisation, and – much worse – having its law modified and distorted by a supra-national court having powers to issue final interpretation (the model, of course, for the European Court of Justice, especially its interpretation of the Jurisdiction Regulation). For example, Lord Hobhouse, a former House of Lords judge, wrote in 1990:[16]

> [I]nternational commerce is best served not by imposing deficient legal schemes upon it but by encouraging the development of the best schemes in a climate of free competition and choice . . . What should no longer be tolerated is the unthinking acceptance of a goal of uniformity and its doctrinaire imposition on the commercial community.

An example of the independence of the Common Law is seen in CISG[17] which has been adopted by nearly eighty[18] nations.

---

12 H. Eidenmüller, 'The Common Frame of Reference for European Private Law – Policy Choices and Codification Problems', (2008) OJLS 659.
13 H. MacQueen, 'Europeanisation of Contract Law and the Proposed Common European Sales Law' in L. DiMatteo, Q. Zhou, S. Saintier, K. Rowley (eds.), *Commercial Contract Law: Transatlantic Perspectives* (Cambridge, 2014), chapter 21, at 532.
14 *Ibid.*, at 533.
15 *Ibid.*, at 533–4.
16 (1990) 106 LQR 530.
17 L. DiMatteo, 'Harmonization of International Sales Law', in L. DiMatteo, Q. Zhou, S. Saintier, K. Rowley (eds.), *Commercial Contract Law: Transatlantic Perspectives* (Cambridge, 2014), chapter 22; and see D. Saidov, chapter 18.
18 DiMatteo, *ibid.*, at 570, n. 46.

23.03 At the other end of the harmonisation spectrum, Hugh Collins has suggested that the eventual achievement of a private law code, including contract law, within Europe will foster a sense of community and citizenship:[19]

> If Europe is to progress further in its aims of securing peace and prosperity for its citizens, for the time being it should concentrate not on building controversial supranational sovereign institutions, but rather on helping to support and sustain transnational networks of civil society ... Common rules and principles of private law will provide a superior basis for constructing a transnational civil society ... Development of a civil code, perhaps commencing with contract law, would serve as the next institutional step in creating a system of governance that reinforces the complex aims ... of ever-closer unity whilst respecting the sovereignty of nation States.

Collins adds:[20]

> My reasons for believing in the need for a European civil code have little to do with the completion of the internal market, the removal of barriers to cross-border trade, the reduction of transaction costs, or a solution to the perils encountered by frontier workers.

23.04 A variation on the transnational theme is extensive use of standard form contracts within transnational commerce, for example, in the context of financial instruments and derivatives. As Braithwaite notes, in the absence of arbitration clauses, such transactions can come before national courts, especially at times of financial crisis within the relevant markets.[21] The same author notes that English courts tend to emphasise the need for 'commercial clarity, certainty, and predictability'.[22]

23.05 Furthermore, there is the widely debated issue whether transnational commerce can draw upon a body of settled contractual principles, a new-age *ius gentium*, known as *lex mercatoria*. The literature is extensive.[23] Naturally, there are sceptics and enthusiasts, romantics and pragmatists.

---

19   H. G. Collins, 'Why Europe Needs a Civil Code: European Identity and the Social Model', in *Liber Amicorum Guido Alpa: National Private Law Systems* (London, 2007), 259, 268.

20   *Ibid.*, at 259.

21   J. Braithwaite, 'Standard Form Contracts as Transnational Law: Evidence from the Derivatives Markets' (2012) 75 MLR 779.

22   J. Braithwaite, *ibid.*, at 801, citing *Lomas* v. *JFB Firth Rixson Inc* [2010] EWHC 3372 (Ch); [2011] 2 BCLC 120, at [53] 'The ISDA Master Agreement ... is probably the most important standard market agreement used in the financial world ... It is axiomatic that it should, as far as possible, be interpreted in a way that serves the objectives of clarity, certainty and predictability, so that the very large number of parties using it should know where they stand.' (Briggs J's decision was reversed, although not in respect of these remarks: [2012] EWCA Civ 419; [2012] 2 All ER (Comm) 1076).

23   For a convenient array of citations, J. Braithwaite, *ibid.*, nn 1–33, citing, notably, Lord Mustill, 'The new Lex Mercatoria: the First Twenty-five Years' (1988) 4 *Arbitration International* 86 (a sceptic); K. Berger, *The Creeping Codification of the New Lex Mercatoria* (2nd edn, The Hague, 2010); see also B. Goldman, 'The Applicable Law: General Principles of Law – The *Lex Mercatoria*', in J. D. M. Lew (ed.), *Contemporary Problems in International Arbitration* (London, 1986) 113.

2. MAIN DIFFERENCES BETWEEN THE 'SOFT LAW' CODES AND ENGLISH CONTRACT LAW

23.06 If we confine attention to UNIDROIT's *Principles of International Commercial Contracts* (2010)[24] and to PECL, the *Principles of European Contract Law*,[25] the following topics are obvious points of contrast between the approaches adopted in the 'soft law' codes and in English law. For reasons of space, it is not possible here to do more than list these points of contrast:

23.07 *General requirement of good faith.* (On the position in English law, see 21.01 ff.) PECL, Article 2:101, UNIDROIT's *Principles of International Commercial Contracts* (2010), Article 1.7, and DCFR, Article III-1:103[26] all adopt this principle as a requirement which operates post-formation. The duty of good faith applies also to pre-contractual negotiations. Thus, PECL, Article 2:301 ('Negotiations Contrary to Good Faith'), states:

(1) *A party is free to negotiate and is not liable for failure to reach an agreement.*

(2) *However, a party who has negotiated or broken off negotiations contrary to good faith and fair dealing is liable for the losses caused to the other party.*

(3) *It is contrary to good faith and fair dealing, in particular, for a party to enter into or continue negotiations with no real intention of reaching an agreement with the other party.* UNIDROIT's *Principles of International Commercial Contracts* (2010), Article 2.1.15, contains a similar provision.

23.08 *Firm offers.* PECL, Article 2:210(3), and UNIDROIT's *Principles of International Commercial Contracts* (2010), Article 2.1.4(2) both provide for irrevocability. On the contrasting position in English law, see 3.36 to 3.38.

23.09 *Acceptance rules.* PECL, Article 2:210(3),[27] and UNIDROIT's *Principles of International Commercial Contracts* (2010), Article 2.1.6(2) both provide for acceptance on receipt. On the English postal exception to this approach, see 3.21ff; and for partial adoption of that rule, protecting the offeree against revocation if posting of the acceptance precedes notification of revocation, see PECL, Article 2:202(1), and UNIDROIT, Article 2.1.4(1).

Battle of the forms. PECL, Article 2:209, states that 'general conditions form part of the contract to the extent that they are common in substance';[28] and UNIDROIT's *Principles of International Commercial Contracts* (2010), Article 2.1.22, states that 'a contract is concluded on the basis of the agreed terms and of any standard terms which are common

---

24   3rd edition, 2010, text and comment, is available at: www.unidroit.org/english/principles/contracts/principles2010/integralversionprinciples2010-e.pdf.
25   O. Lando and H. Beale (eds.), *Principles of European Contract Law* (The Hague, 2000).
26   *Principles, Definitions and Model Rules of European Private Law Draft Common Frame of Reference*, C. von Bar and E. Clive (eds.) (6 vols., Oxford, 2010), prepared by the 'Study Group on a European Civil Code' and the 'Research Group on EC Private Law (Acquis Group)'.
27   G. Quinot, in H. MacQueen and R. Zimmermann (eds.), *European Contract Law: Scots and South African Perspectives* (Edinburgh, 2006), chapter 3.
28   A. D. M. Forte, in H. MacQueen and R. Zimmermann (eds.), *European Contract Law: Scots and South African Perspectives* (Edinburgh, 2006), chapter 4.

in substance unless one party clearly indicates in advance, or later and without undue delay informs the other party, that it does not intend to be bound by such a contract'. On the contrasting position in English law, adopting instead the 'last shot' or 'mirror image' analysis, see 3.34 and 3.35.

23.10 *Absence of a doctrine of consideration for the formation or modification of contracts.* Neither PECL, Article 2:101(1), nor UNIDROIT (see below) requires such an element: it is enough that the contract or agreed modification was intended to create legal relations, that the agreement is otherwise not vitiated by reason of coercion, etc., and that it is not unlawful. Thus PECL, Article 2:101(1) ('Conditions for the Conclusion of a Contract') states: '*A contract is concluded if: the parties intend to be legally bound, and they reach a sufficient agreement without any further requirement.*'

UNIDROIT's *Principles of International Commercial Contracts* (2010), Article 1.3[29] makes no reference to the Common Law requirement of a deed or consideration.

> On the English general requirement of consideration for both the formation and the modification of a contract, see Chapter 5; but for comment on the loosening of this 'consideration' requirement for both increasing pacts (more money for the same task) and decreasing pacts (reduction in the price payable or in the level of performance owed) in the context of contractual modification, see 5.25 to 5.44. On the English rules governing deeds (or 'covenants'), see 5.03.

23.11 *Mistake.* In '*The Great Peace*' (2002) (10.13), the Court of Appeal rejected a doctrine of equitable shared mistake concerning the nature of the subject matter. That boldly negative decision has left isolated the Common Law concept of shared mistake rendering the supposed transaction *void* (10.06 ff). This can be contrasted with the schemes of both PECL and UNIDROIT, where:

(1) 'initial impossibility' is expressly stated not to be a ground of invalidity (PECL, Article 4:102; UNIDROIT's *Principles of International Commercial Contracts* (2010), Article 3.1.3) (contrast on this point English law, where the contract will be void: 10.06 ff); and

(2) shared serious error can only render the contract *voidable*: (PECL, Articles 4:103, 4:112 to 4:116; UNIDROIT, Articles 3.2.2, 3.2.9 to 3.2.16).

23.12 *Supervening difficulty.* PECL, Article 6:111, states:

> *(2) If . . . performance of the contract becomes excessively onerous because of a change of circumstances, the parties are bound to enter into negotiations with a view to adapting the contract or terminating it*

In default of such agreement, there is provision for judicial termination or revision. UNIDROIT's *Principles of International Commercial Contracts* (2010), Articles 6.2.2 and 6.2.3, permit renegotiation or, in default of agreement, judicial termination or revision, in

---

29 3rd edition, 2010, text and comment, is available at: www.unidroit.org/english/principles/contracts/principles2010/integralversionprinciples2010-e.pdf.

respect of 'the occurrence of events fundamentally [altering] the equilibrium of the contract', provided the matter is not covered by the risk of the contract. On the contrasting position in English law, adopting a restrictive approach to pleas of 'frustration', see 16.01 ff.

23.13 *Interpretation.* For the English rules restricting evidence concerning the parties' negotiations or subsequent conduct, see 14.15 to 14.19; and on the functional overlap of the English interpretation and rectification doctrines, see 14.42. PECL, Article 5:101 ('General Rules of Interpretation') states:[30]

(1) *A contract is to be interpreted according to the common intention of the parties even if this differs from the literal meaning of the words.*

(2) *If it is established that one party intended the contract to have a particular meaning, and at the time of the conclusion of the contract the other party could not have been unaware of the first party's intention, the contract is to be interpreted in the way intended by the first party.*

(3) *If an intention cannot be established according to (1) or (2), the contract is to be interpreted according to the meaning that reasonable persons of the same kind as the parties would give to it in the same circumstances.*

And PECL, Article 5:102 ('Relevant Circumstances'), states:

> *In interpreting the contract, regard shall be had, in particular, to:*
> *(a) the circumstances in which it was concluded, including the preliminary negotiations; (b) the conduct of the parties, even subsequent to the conclusion of the contract; (c) the nature and purpose of the contract; (d) the interpretation which has already been given to similar clauses by the parties and the practices they have established between themselves; (e) the meaning commonly given to terms and expressions in the branch of activity concerned and the interpretation similar clauses may already have received; (f) usages; and (g) good faith and fair dealing.*

UNIDROIT's *Principles of International Commercial Contracts* (2010), Article 4.3,[31] permits a similarly wide range of matters to be taken into account.

23.14 *Assurance of performance.* See PECL, Article 8:105 (17.14);[32] UNIDROIT's *Principles of International Commercial Contracts* (2010), Article 7.3.4, contains a similar provision. Contrast the position in English law: 17.16.

23.15 *Specific performance.* For the English approach, confining this remedy in practice to agreements for the transfer of interests in land or shares in *private* companies or 'unique' chattels, and to precise and easily supervised tasks not involving 'personal services' by

---

30 E. Clive, in H. MacQueen and R. Zimmermann (eds.), *European Contract Law: Scots and South African Perspectives* (Edinburgh, 2006), chapter 7.

31 3rd edition, 2010, text and comment, is available at: www.unidroit.org/english/principles/contracts/principles2010/integralversionprinciples2010-e.pdf.

32 T. Naudé, in H. MacQueen and R. Zimmermann (eds.), *European Contract Law: Scots and South African Perspectives* (Edinburgh, 2006), chapter 11.

individuals (as distinct from companies), see 18.33 ff. PECL, Article 9:102 ('Non-Monetary Obligations'), states:[33]

(1) *The aggrieved party is entitled to specific performance of an obligation other than one to pay money, including the remedying of a defective performance.*

(2) *Specific performance cannot, however, be obtained where:*
    (a) performance would be unlawful or impossible; or (b) performance would cause the debtor unreasonable effort or expense; or (c) the performance consists in the provision of services or work of a personal character or depends upon a personal relationship, or (d) the aggrieved party may reasonably obtain performance from another source.

(3) *The aggrieved party will lose the right to specific performance if it fails to seek it within a reasonable time after it has or ought to have become aware of the non-performance.*

UNIDROIT's *Principles of International Commercial Contracts* (2010), Article 7.2.2, contains a similar provision.

23.16 *Damages and the defence of contributory negligence.* Contributory negligence is contemplated even in respect of the primary wrongdoer's breach of a strict obligation in PECL, Article 9:504 and UNIDROIT's *Principles of International Commercial Contracts* (2010), Article 7.4.7. This contrasts with the position in English law, as explained at 18.23.

23.17 *Remoteness of damage.* The English test is considered in detail at 18.16 ff. It is instructive to compare the formulations of the remoteness test contained in PECL, Article 9:503,[34] UNIDROIT's *Principles of International Commercial Contracts* (2010), Article 7.4.4,[35] and CISG[36] (not ratified by the UK). PECL, Article 9:503 ('Foreseeability') states:

> *The non-performing party is liable only for loss which it foresaw or could reasonably have foreseen at the time of conclusion of the contract as a likely result of its non-performance, unless the non-performance was intentional or grossly negligent.*

UNIDROIT, Article 7.4.4 ('Foreseeability of Harm'), states:

> *The non-performing party is liable only for harm which it foresaw or could reasonably have foreseen at the time of the conclusion [viz. formation] of the contract as being likely to result from its non-performance.*

And CISG, Article 74, states:

> *Such damages may not exceed the loss which the party in breach foresaw or ought to have foreseen at the time of the conclusion of the contract, in the light of the facts and matters of which he then knew or ought to have known, as a possible consequence of the breach of contract.*

---

33   S. Eiselen, in *ibid.*, chapter 10.

34   *Ibid.*, at 270 ff.

35   3rd edition, 2010, text and comment, is available at: www.unidroit.org/english/principles/contracts/principles2010/integralversionprinciples2010-e.pdf.

36   Generally on that instrument, L. DiMatteo, 'Harmonization of International Sales Law', in L. DiMatteo, Q. Zhou, S. Saintier, K. Rowley (eds.), *Commercial Contract Law: Transatlantic Perspectives* (Cambridge, 2014), chapter 22; and see D. Saidov, in the same volume, chapter 18.

The following comparative remarks on these three provisions may be made:

(1) *Lower level of foresight than in England.* All three non-English tests cited above seem to be calibrated slightly more generously than English law in favour of the innocent party: the UNIDROIT and PECL tests refer to harm which is 'likely' to result; the CISG test refers to harm which is a 'possible' consequence: as noted at 18.16, in English law the '*serious possibility*' test is the preferred formulation,[37] and is approved by Burrows.[38]

(2) *Assessed at time of formation.* However, the three non-English tests also unite in applying the test of foreseeability at the time of the contract's formation, rather than its breach; and this is also the English approach (18.16).

(3) *Foresight rather than contemplation.* Furthermore, the three non-English tests use the language of 'foresight' rather than 'contemplation'. The latter term seems preferable in England because 'foresight' or 'foreseeability' invites confusion between the contractual test and the more claimant-friendly remoteness test for negligence (18.17): a local problem, perhaps.

(4) *Defendant's foresight rather than joint contemplation.* All three non-English tests adopt the perspective of the party in breach, finding it unnecessary to refer to the other party's contemplation or foresight.[39] This contrasts with the bilateral focus of the English approach, considering both parties' contemplation (although not much seems to turn on this point in practice: see 18.19 case (1), *Hadley* v. *Baxendale*, (1854)[40] where Baron Alderson referred to the 'contemplation of both parties', at least for the purpose of limb 2 (special information).

(5) *Ordinary course of things and special circumstances.* Only the Vienna Convention echoes Baron Alderson's distinction in *Hadley* v. *Baxendale* (see above) between contemplation of harm occurring in the ordinary course of things and special contemplation in light of particular information.

(6) *Type and extent of losses.* In the case of contractual claims for *lost profits*, a distinction has been made, and remains important, between ordinary loss of profits and loss of exceptional profits, that is, a distinction between *degrees* of loss under the same broad head of lost profits: see the *Victoria Laundry* case (1949) (18.16 at (3) and 18.19 case (2)) (extent of profits matters). The official Comment on UNIDROIT Article 7.4.4 acknowledges[41] the distinction drawn in English law between the type or head of loss and its extent, but adds: 'unless the extent is such as to transform the harm into one of a different kind'. The same point has been made in England (see the ensuing quotation).

> In the *Transfield* case (2008: 18.20), Lord Hoffmann approved the *Victoria Laundry* decision:[42] the Court of Appeal [in the *Victoria Laundry* case] did not regard 'loss of profits from the laundry business' as a single type of loss. They distinguished losses from 'particularly

---

37   Lord Walker in the *Transfield* case, [2008] UKHL 48; [2009] 1 AC 61, at [76] noting '*The Heron II*' [1969] 1 AC 350, 400, 415 and 425.

38   A. S. Burrows, *Remedies for Torts and Breach of Contract* (3rd edn, Oxford, 2004), 88, 94.

39   S. Eiselen, in H. MacQueen and R. Zimmermann (eds.), *European Contract Law: Scots and South African Perspectives* (Edinburgh, 2006), chapter 10, at 277, commending this one-sided inquiry.

40   (1854) 9 Exch 341.

41   3rd edition, 2010, text and comment, is available at: www.unidroit.org/english/principles/contracts/principles2010/integralversionprinciples2010-e.pdf.

42   [2008] UKHL 48; [2009] 1 AC 61, at [22], *per* Lord Hoffmann.

> lucrative dyeing contracts' as a different type of loss … The vendor of the boilers would have regarded the profits on these contracts as a different and higher form of risk than the general risk of loss of profits by the laundry.

(7) *Remoteness and scope of duty.* The three soft law texts cited here are (mercifully) free from the tangle now besetting English law, following the introduction of an overlapping test of 'scope of duty': see the discussion of the *Transfield* case (2008) at 18.20, notably at sub-paragraphs D and (7).

(8) *Heinous breach.* Only PECL adopts an 'all the consequences of breach' sub-rule for a breach which is grossly negligent or intentional (this feature is not incorporated into either UNIDROIT's *Principles of International Commercial Contracts* (2010) or CISG). English law does not make this distinction for the purpose of *breach of contract*, although the 'all the consequences' test is applicable to actions in tort for deceit: on the *Smith New Court* test, see 9.17.

QUESTIONS

1 What are the differences between the 'soft law codes' and English contract law on the following topics:
 (a) the battle of the forms;
 (b) the English 'consideration' requirement;
 (c) interpretation of written contracts;
 (d) contributory negligence;
 (e) remoteness of damages.

2 In your opinion, which approach is preferable?

Selected further reading

M. J. Bonell, 'Do We Need a Global Commercial Code?' (2000–3) 5 *Uniform Law Review/Revue de droit uniforme* 469–81

R. Goode, *Commercial Law in the Next Millennium* (London, 1998) 88–105

Lord Mance, 'Is Europe Aiming to Civilise the Common Law?' (Chancery Bar Lecture, Lincoln's Inn, 27 March 2006)

S. Vogenauer, 'Common Frame of Reference and UNIDROIT Principles of International Commercial Contracts: Coexistence, Competition, or Overkill of Soft Law?' (2010) 6 *European Review of Contract Law*, issue 6; and http://ssrn.com/abstract=1581352

S. Whittaker, 'A Framework of Principle for European Contract Law' (2009) 125 LQR 617

R. Zimmermann, 'Ius Commune and the Principles of European Contract Law: Contemporary Renewal of an Old Idea', in H. MacQueen and R. Zimmermann (eds.), *European Contract Law: Scots and South African Perspectives* (Edinburgh, 2006), chapter 1

Bibliography

For a detailed bibliography: A. Kramer, *Contract Law: An Index and Digest of Published Writings* (Oxford, 2010).

Literature on topics within contract law are noted in individual chapters, normally in the opening footnotes.

Main general works

Texts

Anson's Law of Contract, J. Beatson, A. S. Burrows, J. Cartwright (eds.) (29th edn, Oxford, 2010)

M. Chen-Wishart, *Contract Law* (4th edn, Oxford, 2012)

Cheshire, Fifoot and Furmston, The Law of Contract, M. Furmston (ed.) (16th edn, Oxford, 2012)

Chitty on Contracts (31st edn, London, 2012)

M. Furmston (ed.), *The Law of Contract* (4th edn, London, 2010)

R. Halson, *Contract Law* (2nd edn, London, 2013)

Koffman and Macdonald's Law of Contract (8th edn, Oxford, 2014)

E. McKendrick, *Contract Law* (10th edn, London, 2013)

J. O'Sullivan and J. Hilliard, *The Law of Contract* (6th edn, Oxford, 2014)

J. Poole, *Textbook on Contract Law* (12th edn, Oxford, 2014)

G. H. Treitel, *The Law of Contract*, E. Peel (ed.) (13th edn, London, 2011)

Casebooks

H. G. Beale, W. D. Bishop, M. P. Furmston, *Contract: Cases and Materials* (5th edn, Oxford, 2008)

A. S. Burrows, *A Casebook on Contract* (4th edn, Oxford, 2013)

E. McKendrick, *Text, Cases and Materials* (6th edn, Oxford, 2014)

J. Poole, *Casebook on Contract* (12th edn, Oxford, 2014)

Smith and Thomas, A Casebook on Contract, R. Brownsword (ed.) (12th edn, London, by R. Brownsword, 2009)

R. Stone, J. Devenney, R. Cunnington, *Text, Cases and Materials on Contract Law* (3rd edn, London, 2014)

Other general works

J. Adams and R. Brownsword, *Key Issues in Contract* (London, 1995)

Atiyah's Introduction to the Law of Contract, S. Smith (ed.) (6th edn, Oxford, 2006)

R. Brownsword, *Contract Law: Themes for the Twenty-first Century* (2nd edn, Oxford, 2006)

A. S. Burrows, *Understanding the Law of Obligations* (Oxford, 1998)

D. Campbell, H. G. Collins, J. Wightman (eds.), *Implicit Dimensions of Contract* (Oxford, 2003)

D. Campbell, L. Mulcahy, S. Wheeler (eds.), *Changing Concepts of Contract: Essays in Honour of Ian Macneil* (Basingstoke, 2013)

H. G. Collins, *The Law of Contract* (4th edn, Cambridge, 2003)

K. Dharmananga and L. Firios (eds.), *Long-term Contracts* (Annandale, Australia, 2013)

L. DiMatteo, Q. Zhou, S. Saintier, K. Rowley (eds.), *Commercial Contract Law: Transatlantic Perspectives* (Cambridge, 2014)

M. Hogg, *Promises and Contract Law: Comparative Perspectives* (Cambridge, 2011)

I. R. Macneil, *The Relational Theory of Contract* (London, 2001)

C. Mitchell, *Contract Law and Contract Practice* (Oxford, 2013)

J. Morgan, *Contract Law* (Palgrave's 'Great Debates' series) (London, 2012)

J. Morgan, *Contract Law Minimalism* (Cambridge, 2013)

J. W. Neyers, R. Bronaugh, S. G. A. Pitel, *Exploring Contract Law* (Oxford, 2009)

A. Ogus and W. H. van Boom (eds.), *Juxtaposing Autonomy and Paternalism in Private Law* (Oxford, 2011)

S. Smith, *Contract Theory* (Oxford, 2004)

S. Waddams, *Principle and Policy in Contract Law: Competing or Complementary Concepts?* (Cambridge, 2011)

S. Worthington (ed.), *Commercial Law and Commercial Practice* (Oxford, 2003)

Index